Grants generously given by the
University of Colorado, Richard Adloff,
Virginia Thompson Adloff, and Charles S. Gardner
have made possible the publication of this monograph

CHINA'S MANAGEMENT
of the
AMERICAN BARBARIANS

A Study of Sino-American Relations,
1841-1861, with Documents

by

Earl Swisher

1972
OCTAGON BOOKS
New York

Reprinted 1972

by special arrangement with The Association for Asian Studies

OCTAGON BOOKS

A Division of Farrar, Straus & Giroux, Inc.

19 Union Square West

New York, N. Y. 10003

Library of Congress Catalog Card Number: 70-38817

ISBN 0-374-97686-4

Manufactured by Braun-Brumfield, Inc.
Ann Arbor, Michigan

Printed in the United States of America

TABLE OF CONTENTS

FOREWORD

In his Introduction Professor Swisher has set forth clearly and incisively the background, objectives, and general significance of the 546 Chinese documents forming the heart of this book. He has also made explicit his approach to the mechanics of selecting, editing, and interpreting the material. We have here inestimably valuable material hitherto unavailable for correcting and supplementing accepted knowledge about the diplomatic relations of China and the United States from 1841 to 1861. So much has now been said and written about the importance of the multiple archival study of foreign relations that it is hardly necessary to emphasize the great debt of all scholars in the field of Chinese-American relations to Professor Swisher for this contribution − a labor of fifteen years. To it he has brought, as every one of his expositions, comments, and notes testifies, not only linguistic and semantic skill, but extensive knowledge based on a long study of Western as well as Chinese sources and on China itself and the Chinese. We may hope that either Professor Swisher or some other well equipped scholar may someday present us with as careful and intelligent a translation and exposition of Chinese documents relating to America in the period between 1861 and 1875 and thereafter. Meantime the publication of this material will be quickly and generally recognized as a major event in Far Eastern studies.

It would be unfortunate, however, if this rich body of documents should be regarded solely or even chiefly as an important contribution to our knowledge of American diplomatic history in the narrower sense. For it should be clear that it is not enough for Americans to study the diplomatic relations alone or the economy and culture of the major areas of the world from our own angle of vision. It is immensely important for us to study the impacts of America on the rest of the world, the images of America that other peoples have held and now hold. This is indispensable if we are to understand our own history and civilization in terms of more than one dimension. It is equally indispensable if we are to make wise decisions today and tomorrow in our relations with other peoples.

For some years a body of scholars, French, German, Swiss, Norwegian, and American, have concerned themselves with the historical reputation and "influence" of the United States in Western Europe. To this group must be added a very few Latin Americans who have been interested in the intercultural relations of their countries with the United States. Those of us who have been interested in this chapter of international intercultural relations have been increasingly aware of both the difficulties and the importance of the field. These difficulties are enhanced in the case of efforts to approach an understanding of the influence and reputation of the United States in the last hundred years in China. Few students of American intellectual and cultural history have had any appreciable knowledge of Chinese history and culture, let alone the language. In the documents that Professor Swisher now presents we have for the first time something that reaches far beyond the secondhand accounts of the presumed Chinese reactions to Americans available in the Chinese Repository and other missionary publications, in the reports of American merchants in China, and in dispatches of members of our foreign service. Here, in short, is an important body of new material for the student of the American character and of the reactions of other peoples to it.

Fortunately, Professor Swisher has provided both the student of diplomatic history and of international cultural relations with helpful aids in the informed and lucid expositions of the nature and development of the Chinese official apparatus for dealing with foreigners. He has also indicated, specifically, the meaning of terms which otherwise would lead to misunderstanding by anyone unfamiliar with the Chinese language and culture. Nor has he failed to relate the Chinese materials dealing with America to collateral American sources. In addition, his sensitiveness to chronology and to the complications resulting from the role of America in association with other western powers, make the use of the documents to both the student of American diplomatic and of American intellectual history far more valuable than might have been the case. Throughout the work the evidence of Professor Swisher's erudition, imagination, and sound judgment is sustained.

It would be impossible and unfair in a foreword to try to indicate what either the student of American diplomatic history or of the American image in China will find in these meaty pages. But one may say that the material clearly shows the importance of the particular background, personality, and attitudes of the Chinese officials dealing with the "barbarians." One may further add that we see here the importance of the time element. For there were many Chinese reactions to the Americans, and these varied with the officials and with the situation and point in time. Also here and there one has glimpses of the reactions to America of Chinese merchants and even of the masses, though in general the material reveals primarily official Chinese views of American policies, interests, and characteristics. The "inscrutable" Chinese attitude toward the foreigner, including the American, becomes, for the scholar limited to Western languages, far more understandable than it has ever appeared. And in the mixture of shrewd, naive, distorted, and realistic reactions to America of Chinese imperial officials, the student of America's relations with China, and of American life, will find much to invite close study. Here, in fact, a world we have only glimpsed is now opened to us.

Merle Curti

University of Wisconsin

INTRODUCTION

China's Management of the American Barbarians is a variation to suit the specific situation, of the Chinese title of the collection of documents which is the original of this book. The Ch'ing Tai Ch'ou Pan I Wu Shih Mo,[1] literally translated, means "The Management of Barbarian Affairs of the Ch'ing Dynasty from Beginning to End." Consequently, in setting out to present an English translation of those sections of this important work which deal with the United States, with introductory chapters and notes, it seemed obvious to paraphrase the Chinese title and call it China's Management of the American Barbarians. However, this is not just a quaint or provocative phraseology. It typifies a period of Sino-American relations when China regarded all Westerners as irritating intruders at her ocean frontiers. The confidence born of the long history of a highly civilized and economically self-sufficient great nation convinced China that she could so "manage" these Western "barbarians" as to preserve intact her national integrity. More specifically, the Manchu dynasty in power in China in the nineteenth century hoped to manage the United States, as the principal of the minor trading states, first, in order to bolster its alien dynastic rule over China and, second, to thwart the Manchus' principal antagonist, Great Britain. The Manchu rule had already been weakened by a decline in the ability and forcefulness of its emperors since the end of the eighteenth century. It was to suffer still more, during the course of the nineteenth century, from major internal rebellions. The great Taiping Rebellion which all but swept the Manchus from the throne after 1850, was followed by other disastrous uprisings of the Nien Fei and the Mohammedan rebels. Consequently, the foreign threats, centered from the Chinese point of view in the Opium Question and international trade, were of crucial importance. It is not surprising that the harassed Manchus should occasionally look to the United States and France as a desperate but forlorn hope of escape from their many trials. Hence, China's Management of the

---

1 *Ch'ing Tai Ch'ou Pan I Wu Shih Mo* (The Management of Barbarian Affairs of the Ch'ing Dynasty from Beginning to End), Peiping, Palace Museum, 1930. Reign of Tao-kuang, 40 v.; reign of Hsien-feng, 40 v.; reign of T'ung-chih, 50 v.; cited hereafter by the initial letters of the last four words of the Chinese title: IWSM. Following the Chinese book style, the citations will give series, book or *chüan* number, page number obverse or reverse, and line or column. E.g. a citation occurring in the first to the tenth lines or columns (1-10) of the reverse side (b) of page seventeen (17) of the fifty-sixth book or *chüan* (56), of the Tao-kuang (1836-1849) series (TK) of the *Ch'ing Tai Ch'ou Pan I Wu Shih Mo* (IWSM), will be cited: IWSM. TK 56; 17b, 1-10.

American Barbarians, which is a Chinese documentary history of relations with the United States from 1841 to 1861, is set in the larger
frame of China's struggle with Great Britain and of the Manchu emperors' attempt to withstand internal rebellion.

The Chinese collection entitled Ch'ou Pan I Wu Shih Mo, or "The
Management of Barbarian Affairs from Beginning to End," had its inception sometime in the last decade of the Tao-kuang reign period
(1820-1850), probably about 1845. China's official concern with the
Opium Question from 1836, the war with England from 1838-1841, the
resultant Treaty of Nanking in 1842, with its supplements the following year, the Treaty of Wang-hsia with the United States in 1844, and
the Treaty of Whampoa with France later the same year, cumulatively
forced upon the attention of the emperor and court the importance of
"barbarian affairs." The memorials presented to the throne by the
governors, governors general, and imperial commissioners first at
Canton, then at Shanghai and the other treaty ports, and ultimately at
Tientsin at the very threshold of the Forbidden City in Peking,
seductively suggested that the solution of the whole problem on the
ocean frontier lay in the adroit, or as we should say, diplomatic
"management" of foreign traders and foreign officials.

As a result of this pressure and suggestion, the Tao-kuang
emperor set up a special "Barbarian Affairs Bureau" (I Wu Chu),
within the State Historiographer's Office (Kuo Shih Kuan), with the
function of compiling from official records all the edicts, rescripts,
memorials, diplomatic correspondence, and miscellaneous papers
relating to foreign countries and foreign affairs.[2] This was distinct
from the routine function of the state historiographers of compiling
materials and writing biographies for ultimate inclusion in the
standard history of the reign and of the dynasty. The Barbarian Affairs Bureau was to collect all pertinent data, whether included in the
Shih Lu or "Veritable Records" of the reign or not, copy it out and
present it for imperial scrutiny and for the guidance of the Grand
Council in handling China's foreign affairs and formulating China's

---

2 The data that follow are drawn from the context of IWSM itself, from the intro-
   ductions and forewords of each of the Tao-kuang, Hsien-feng, and T'ung-chih series
   of the IWSM, and from the following reviews and articles: T.F. Tsiang, "China after
   the Victory of Taku, June 25, 1859," American Historical Review, v. 35 (1929),
   p. 79-84; review by Ping Chia Kuo, ibid., v. 36 (1930), p. 870-871; T.F. Tsiang,
   "New Light on Chinese Diplomatic History," Journal of Modern History, v. 3 (1931),
   p. 578-591; Walter Fuchs, "Neues Material zur Mandjurischen Literatur aus Pekinger
   Bibliotheken," Asia Major, v. 8 (1931), p. 469-482; Alfred K'ai-ming Ch'iu, "Chinese Historical Documents of the Ch'ing Dynasty, 1644-1911," Pacific Historical
   Review, v. 1 (1932), p. 324-336; Cyrus H. Peake, "Documents Available for Research
   on the Modern History of China," American Historical Review, v. 38 (1932), p. 61-
   70; and Knight Biggerstaff, "Some Notes on the Tung-hua Lu and the Shih-lu,"
   Harvard Journal of Asiatic Studies, v. 4 (1939), p. 101-115.

foreign policy.

This Barbarian Affairs Bureau, despite the fundamentalist tone of its title, was an indication that the court in Peking was aware of the fact that these relations with European countries and the United States constituted something new in China's history. At the head of the Bureau and personally charged with the compilation of the documents was Tu Shou-t'ien (1787-1852), a native of Shantung province.[3] Grand Preceptor and Grand Secretary Tu Shou-t'ien, to use his honorific posthumous titles, was a chin-shih (Ph.D.) with high honors of 1823, and Hanlin academician. He was tutor and intimate of the Tao-kuang emperor when the latter was crown prince, and after his emperor's death, Tu Shou-t'ien was entrusted with editing his literary works. He was thus a scholar and bibliophile but there is nothing in his official biography to indicate that he had any special interest in foreign affairs His connection with the Ch'ou Pan I Wu Shih Mo was probably little more than titular.

Nevertheless, the compilation of documents for the last fifteen years of the Tao-kuang reign period was carried on to the end of the reign. In 1856, the Historiographical Commission, now headed by Wen-ch'ing (1796-1856), who was concurrently Grand Secretary,[4] presented the Tao-kuang series of the Ch'ou Pan I Wu Shih Mo to the emperor. The Historiographical Commission at that time comprised ten members including Director General Wen-ch'ing. There were five Manchus on the Commission, including the director general and Hua-sha-na,[5] who was one of the negotiators of the Treaties of Tientsin in 1858. In addition there were four Chinese and one Mongol. All the members held concurrent posts in the Peking government.

The preface to the Tao-kuang series explains that the broad purpose of the original Commission was to gather all materials pertinent to an understanding of China's foreign relations. It particularly notes that the compilers have included all memorials and papers whether included in the Shih Lu or not, pointing out that documents which did not require imperial action were not recorded in the Shih Lu but were preserved in this collection. Moreover, where the Shih Lu incorporates only brief summaries of memorials and often abstracts edicts and rescripts, the editors of the Ch'ou Pan I Wu Shih Mo reproduced all documents in their full text. In addition, the preface points out many of the technical details of the compilation. It obviously irked the scholarly Chinese officials to preserve the crude colloquialisms of treaty port Chinese, especially the jargon of Canton and Fukien, as well as the literary barbarities of the correspondence (in their best Chinese) of British, American, and French representa-

---

3 Hummel, A. W. (Ed.), *Eminent Chinese of the Ch'ing Period*, Washington, 1943-44, v. 2, p. 779-780.

4 Hummel, *op. cit.*, v. 2, p. 852-853.

5 See context *infra*; also Hummel, *op. cit.*, v. 1, p. 428.

tives or rather their missionary secretaries, "all imperfectly expressed and hard to decipher;" but in the interest of historical accuracy they are incorporated intact. Needless to say, in this period, 1841-
1861, no papers in any Western language are included. The traditional
Chinese respect for archival integrity, if not always for historicity, is
evidenced by the editorial statement: "This compilation is not so much
to show that past actions were right or wrong, as to serve as a reference for future generations."[6]

The Hsien-feng series of the Ch'ou Pan I Wu Shih Mo, covering
the twelve-year period, 1850-1861, was compiled in accordance with
an imperial edict of 1861. It was completed and presented in a memorial to the throne dated May, 1867, under the signature of Chia Chen,
then Director General of the Historiographical Commission. Chia
Chen (1798-1874) was a Chinese and was concurrently Grand Secretary, having first been appointed to this high post in 1855; he held it
for one year and then, after a lapse of three years, was reappointed in
1859, and remained in office until 1867.[7] The Historiographical
Commission at this time was made up of nine members, four Chinese
including the director general, four Manchus including Imperial
Clansman Ling-kuei, and one Mongol, specifically designated as
Mongol Assistant Director. The only outstanding name in the list is
that of Grand Secretary Wen-hsiang (1818-1876), Manchu scholar-
official who became chancellor of the Hanlin Academy and was
prominently identified with Prince Kung in the Tsungli Yamen.[8]

The T'ung-chih series, covering the period from 1861 to 1875, is
not included in this study, but it was likewise compiled by an imperial
commission under the Historiographical Office and was presented to
the emperor in September, 1880, by Director General Pao-yün (1807-
1891), who was concurrently Grand Secretary.[9] Pao-yün, a Manchu,
had been a director under Chia Chen in 1867, when the Hsien-feng
series was completed.

The year 1875 marked the end of the Barbarian Affairs Bureau
and of the official compilation of documents relating to China's foreign
affairs. The three separate series, Tao-kuang, Hsien-feng, and T'ung-
chih, covered the period from 1836 to 1875. A manuscript copy, in the
neat and precise calligraphy of the professional court clerk, was made
for presentation to the emperor and for permanent record in the imperial archives. This copy on folded sheets of red-ruled paper of
about folio size was sewed into fascicules and bound in covers, where
it remained intact until discovered by republican library officials in
1925. Another copy was also made, possibly a draft of the official
manuscript, possibly an informal and unofficial copy made subse-

6   IWSM. TK. Intro. 1a, 7-8.

7   Hummel, op. cit., v. 1, p. 376.

8   See context infra and Hummel, op. cit., v. 2, p. 853-855.

9   Hummel, op. cit., v. 2, p. 854.

quently.[10]

This second and inferior copy fell into the hands of one Wang Tao-fu (styled Nien-wei), who was for twenty years, 1884-1904, chief of the secretariat of the Grand Council. Chief Clerk Wang immediately recognized the value of this documentary history of China's foreign relations and set out to continue the good work as a personal project. He was in an excellent position to do this and methodically copied out in extenso every document relating to foreign affairs which passed through his office. He continued this worthy practice until his death in 1905.

Wang Tao-fu's manuscript, as well as the second copy of the Ch'ou Pan I Wu Shih Mo, remained in his family's possession, unnoticed until after the Manchu emperors had been swept from the throne by the Revolution of 1911-1912.

After the Revolution had "declassified" the formerly secret documents, Mr. Wang Hsi-yün (styled Liang), son of the original compiler, made his private collection, housed in the family library in Peking, available to his personal friends. Among the most interested of the users was a young historian, just returned from Oberlin and Columbia, named T.F. Tsiang.[11] Here at last was someone fully prepared to appreciate this Chinese counterpart of Die Grosse Politik der Europaischen Kabinette. Dr. Tsiang, first at Nankai University and later at Tsing Hua, made full use of these materials for his research, copied out a large excerpt folio, which was still in Tsing Hua University Library in 1948, and made plans with Mr. Wang Hsi-yün to edit and publish the entire collection. The unique character of the Wang manuscript is attested by the fact that the Chinese National Historical Commission engaged in compiling the standard history of the Manchu dynasty, the Ch'ing Shih Kao, made use of it for want of any more official or complete version.

In the meantime and before Dr. Tsiang had completed the edit-

---

10 Dr. Hu Shih of the Gest Library, now at Princeton University, writes of these copies: "My own checking seems to show that the Hsien-feng and T'ung-chih Series were undoubtedly copies which Wang Yen-wei had ordered made of the Official Copy. The Tao-kuang Series, however, seems to be a later copy made in the Republican period. This is evidenced by a complete absence of all usual formalities in dealing with the Emperor or an Imperial Decree. There was even an attempt to 'edit' this copy (1) by changing the title to 'Ch'ou Pan Yang Wu Shih Mo' (instead of I Wu), and (2) by changing the forms of such words as Ying-chili (England) and I-sheng (barbarian merchant) into Yang-sheng (foreign merchant), etc." Letter to the author dated October 17, 1951.

11 Dr. T.F. Tsiang (Chiang T'ing-fu), b. 1891, is one of China's foremost living scholars and is now heading the Chinese delegation to the United Nations. He has published, from the Wang collection, Select Documents Illustrating the History of Chinese Diplomacy (in Chinese), Shanghai, 2 v., 1929-1931, and was for many years managing editor of the Chinese Social and Political Science Review. His numerous scholarly articles are noted in the text below and in the bibliography.

ing and publication job which he had undertaken for Mr. Wang Hsi-yün, something happened within the walls of the Forbidden City, now the Palace Museum, in Peking. After the Revolution had destroyed both the Manchus and the monarchy, the Republic appointed a committee of scholars to investigate and preserve the uncounted tons of manuscripts in the archives, as well as the books, paintings, jades, bronzes, silk, procelains, and clocks making up the treasures of the Manchu imperial palace.

Among other finds of the historical committee was the original official manuscript of the Ch'ou Pan I Wu Shih Mo. The one hundred books (chüan) bound in fifty volumes of the T'ung-chih series (1861-1875) were discovered first, in 1925. The eighty volumes of the Tao-kuang and Hsien-feng series were found soon after and the committee set about to find means of publishing the documents.

It was not until the Nationalist expeditionary armies reached Peking in 1928, and shortly afterward established the National Government in Nanking, that funds became available through pre-publication subscriptions and post-publication sales. In the interest of integrity of the collection and in view of the almost perfect condition of the manuscript, the committee determined on the photo-lithographic method of printing. Photographic plates were prepared, resulting in the exact reproduction of the original manuscript, reduced to one-quarter size, which we now have in the handsome palace edition. This decision preserved the original sequence according to the arbitrary chronological order of the receipt of the documents at the palace, at the expense of subject arrangement, accurate dating of the origin of the documents, and indexing, such as modern Western-trained scholarship would have supplied.

Mr. Wang Hsi-yün and Dr. T. F. Tsiang recognized the superiority of the palace manuscript and abandoned their plans for the publication of the private text of the Ch'ou Pan I Wu Shih Mo. The palace publication of 1930 provided the official documentary material from 1836 down to 1875.

The Palace Museum then proceeded to publish the continuation record made available through the foresight and paintstaking efforts of Wang Tao-fu and the generosity of his son. [12] The result was the publication in 1932 of the Ch'ing Chi Wai Chiao Shih Liao (Foreign Relations Documents for the Latter Part of the Ch'ing Dynasty) in two series. The Kuang-hsü series, covering the period from 1875 to 1904, comprises 218 chüan in 109 volumes. The Hsüan-t'ung series, carrying

---

12 The Wang family manuscript was used for this publication. According to Dr. T.F. Tsiang in a letter to the author dated September 11, 1951, "the original manuscript has never been found in the Palace Museum, in spite of diligent search." The Wang collection was subsequently sold to the Gest Library, deposited first in McGill University and now at Princeton.

the record up to 1912, and supplied through the efforts of Mr. Wang Hsi-yün,[13] comprises 24 chüan in 12 volumes. Unlike the Ch'ou Pan I Wu Shih Mo series, this later set is supplied with a valuable index extending to 12 chüan in 6 volumes, and is supplemented with photographs and maps reproduced from the palace collection. It also differs in that the materials have been edited and arranged by modern scholars and the publication is set in moveable type instead of being reproduced photographically.

In addition to these official and semi-official compilations, Dr. T. F. Tsiang compiled a supplement to the three series of the Ch'ou Pan I Wu Shih Mo from the archives of the Grand Council while they were housed in the Ta Kao Tien in Peking. His manuscript was carried by Tsing Hua University officials, ahead of the Japanese invasion of Peking in 1937, to a small town twenty-five miles outside of Chungking. The Japanese dropped a bomb on the very building where the manuscript was housed and it, along with other Tsing Hua library materials, was completely destroyed. Fortunately, however, Professor John K. Fairbank had hired clerks to make a copy of Dr. Tsiang's supplement and this copy is now at Harvard University.[14]

For the comparatively scanty materials dealing with China's foreign relations prior to 1836, a publication entitled Ch'ing Tai Wai Chiao Shih Liao has appeared in two series. The Chia-ch'ing series, 1796-1821, was published in 1932 and is in 6 volumes; the Tao-kuang series, covering the first fifteen years of the Tao-kuang reign, 1821-1836, is in 4 volumes and appeared in 1933. The documents in these series are casual and scattered and do not form a continuous record of China's diplomatic history comparable to that for the period after 1836.

In addition to these specialized publications in the field of Chinese diplomatic history during the Manchu period, there are several other publications of documents which occasionally contain materials pertinent to China's foreign relations. The Palace Museum between the years 1928 and 1930 published ten volumes of documents selected from its voluminous archives under the title of Chang Ku Ts'ung Pien.

---

13 Dr. Tsiang states that Mr. Wang "compiled the material from newspapers, gazettes, and such published, collected writings as he could find" to bring the record up to 1912. *Ibid.*

14 *Ibid.* Professor Fairbank has confirmed this statement of Dr. Tsiang, adding that "it is now here at Harvard in the original Chinese written form of the copyists. However. . .the greater part of what I had them take referred to the Customs which was my particular subject and interest so that there are gaps in the number sequence which Dr. Tsiang originally set up, and the thing is not as complete as it might be." The author has not examined this manuscript but Dr. Fairbank is of the opinion that it would not affect this study. Letter to the author dated October 5, 1951.

Beginning in March, 1930, this was followed by a monthly publication entitled <u>Wen</u> <u>Hsien</u> <u>Ts'ung</u> <u>Pien</u>. A series dealing especially with historical, although not necessarily diplomatic, materials, published every ten days, was inaugurated by the Palace Museum in June, 1930, under the title of <u>Shih</u> <u>Liao</u> <u>Hsün</u> <u>K'an</u>. These publications have suf-fered many irregularities due to international war and internal disorders in China. In addition, there are ten volumes of selected documents edited and published by the renowned Chinese antiquarian Lo Chen-yü during the period, beginning in 1924, when he had many of the documents from the National Archives in his private possession and before they were recovered by the Palace Museum. His publication is entitled <u>Shih</u> <u>Liao</u> <u>Ts'ung</u> <u>K'an</u>. These again are not directly concerned with diplomatic history.

So much for China's documentary record of her dealings with foreign countries during the Ch'ing dynasty, 1644 to 1912. Obviously, here is a storehouse of source material in China to supplement the archives and published materials of Great Britain, the United States, France, Russia, and, for the latter part of the period, Japan. Modern Chinese scholars have already pointed out that some previously accepted concepts of Chinese diplomatic history will have to be changed in the light of these new materials. The Chinese point of view and China's foreign policy can now for the first time be studied directly and authoritatively from the record of Chinese officials themselves. A picture of the rivalries and intrigues in the court at Peking, what went on within the moat and behind the high walls surrounding the Forbidden City, will gradually emerge as these materials are analyzed by trained modern scholars. From the western point of view particularly, the heretofore shadowy figures of Chinese officials, courtiers, and emperors can be brought into full focus and be made to assume their distinctive, personalized forms. Even the scattered and often erroneously assigned and dated Chinese documents which were already available to us in private Chinese publications, in the pages of the <u>Chinese</u> <u>Repository</u>, the writings of English and American contemporaries, and incorporated in state papers in London, Paris, and Washington, can now be placed in their proper setting and the often faulty translations checked against the Chinese originals. This will be the work of generations of scholars and will produce many detailed articles, monographs, and surveys.

The purpose of the present study is both limited and exploratory. If it provides materials and impetus for new studies in the field, its objective will have been accomplished. In the first place it is limited chronologically. In going through the documents of the <u>Ch'ou</u> <u>Pan</u> <u>I</u> <u>Wu</u> <u>Shih</u> <u>Mo</u> soon after they appeared in 1930, the writer was struck by the peculiar significance of the period prior to 1861. This was the era of violent conflict between England and China at the time of the First Opium War, and again between the Anglo-French allies and

China in 1858 to 1860. It terminated with the establishment in Peking of the Tsungli Yamen for the handling of China's foreign relations at the capital, instead of at the ocean frontier and in the treaty ports. The intitial date for this study was easily established by the first document in the collection dealing with the United States, which is dated February 6, 1841. Thus a convenient twenty-year period, 1841-1861, was logically if somewhat arbitrarily defined.

The peculiar significance of this period lies in the fact that it was one not only of violence but also of indirect contact. After 1861 Sino-Western diplomacy was at least formally comparable to the international relations of other countries. The Tsungli Yamen thereafter functioned as the Foreign Office or State Department in the Peking government, and ministers and eventually ambassadors from the countries of the world were accredited to China. Diplomatic correspondence was exchanged between China and the West on at least a semblance of equality, although it was many years before the Chinese court and Chinese conservative and traditional officials were willing to accept this, to them, humiliating situation in good faith.

The documents before 1861, on the other hand, have the peculiar flavor of family correspondence between the provinces and the court, a correspondence carried on in terms and with an intimacy never intended for the "barbarian eyes" of Western officials and governments. During this period very few direct communications were exchanged. Most of the documents are in the form of memorials written by provincial officials or specially commissioned Peking agents located on the ocean frontiers and at the commercial ports. They, or more often their local subordinates, met the foreign representatives, and local Chinese merchants dealt with European and American traders. From these personal or second-hand contacts the memorialists reported their versions of foreign affairs to the emperor and court in Peking and asked for instruction and advice in carrying out their duties. The second largest group of documents consists of edicts issued by or in the name of the emperor to the Grand Council or the Grand Secretariat for relay to the provincial officials or imperial commissioners. A third group comprises philosophical and academic observations on foreign policy and the conduct of foreign relations by metropolitan censors and other officials not in direct contact with foreigners. A fourth type, small in extent but extremely interesting in content, contains the personal, often interlinear, comments of the emperor himself, scrawled on the original documents in the best manner of Kaiser Wilhelm in the Grosse Politik collection, and meticulously preserved by the compilers of the Ch'ou Pan I Wu Shih Mo. The fifth and final type of documents is that of the actual diplomatic correspondence itself, translated into Chinese in the case of the European and American notes, and incorporated in the Chinese record. This last group also includes précis and treaties proposed or agreed to between the

Western countries and China. For the period up to 1861, this conventional type of document is comparatively insignificant.

Consequently, it is apparent that this period provides an almost completely off-the-record insight into Chinese official mentality and Chinese official policy in the newly important field of international relations. This accounts for the rather shocking terminology of the documents of this period, in which both provincial and court officials consistently use the terms "English barbarians," "American barbarians," "French barbarians"; consuls and ministers alike are "barbarian chieftains"; occasionally even the extremely colloquial term "foreign devil" creeps in; and the whole conduct of foreign affairs is a matter of the "management" of troublesome, obstructive, inferiors. This should not be regarded as anti-foreignism or even conservatism, because even the most progressive Chinese statesmen of the day used this accepted terminology to propound policies which were sympathetic toward the West, or to advocate extension of international relations. Rather, these offensive terms should be regarded as expressions of China's traditional world view, in which China had always been in fact the center or "Middle Kingdom," surrounded by admiring if sometimes jealous and ambitious barbarian states. Nor should this terminology obscure the real value of the revealing documents of this period.

This situation in its full scope never existed again after 1861, so that the period does have a distinctive character deserving separate treatment and study, such as can only be made by direct access to the documents in extenso. Consequently, it has been felt that the presentation of the source material of this period in literal translation will serve a purpose which no amount of analysis and comment could possibly achieve.

The reasons for dealing with Sino-American relations, aside from the obvious ones of a natural interest in our own Far Eastern policy and in China's policy vis-a-vis us, and the fact that a considerable amount of work in Sino-British relations has already been done, perhaps deserve a little explanation. The principal reason is that the United States was the most important neutral state during this period and therefore presented a problem and an opportunity--or at least an occasional temptation--to China. The court at Peking was dealing with Great Britain as its principal antagonist, and most of its decisions regarding England were decided for it by force majeure. The United States, on the other hand, played a very minor role, did not engage in hostilities against China, and Americans in China gave the impression at least of being tractable and subservient to Chinese laws and regulations. There were the further facts that the United States had twice fought against England, that she had broken away from the British Empire, and that Americans appeared to like the Chinese people and to admire, through a glass darkly, Chinese culture. These naturally led a few Chinese officials, as early as

1840, to play with the idea of "utilizing the American barbarians" or at
least of keeping them interested in China so as to prevent their joining
up with England, and in general of keeping them in mind in a possible
policy of "using barbarians to curb barbarians." This is not a major
theme in Chinese diplomacy, but a constantly recurring minor one, and
the United States, more than any other country during this period, is
brought up by Chinese officials in this connection. Americans are invariably regarded as more available for Chinese "management" than
are French or Russians.

Another interesting feature of Sino-American relations during
this period is the early foreshadowing of constructive American cooperation with China and assistance to her in the still vaguely comprehended problem of Westernization. Hong merchants in Canton looked
to Americans, not exclusively of course, to help them build steamers.
Chinese officials took advantage of the invitations of American naval
officers to examine Western warships and armaments. Americans
were employed to train Chinese artisans to make submarine mines and
torpedoes. By the end of the period, 1861, a major Chinese statesman
was prepared to ask for, and receive, American assistance in building
a modern arsenal and in training a modern Chinese army.

For these reasons, it has appeared to the writer that a translation
of the Chinese documents dealing with the United States, under the
title of China's Management of the American Barbarians, might blaze
a trail for other more analytical studies of Sino-American relations
by qualified scholars who might otherwise be unable to use the Chinese
documents. At any rate, that is the justification for this project, which
has occupied the research and translation efforts of some fifteen years.

In carrying it out, it was first necessary to scan the entire eighty
unindexed volumes of the Tao-kuang and Hsien-feng series of the Ch'ou
Pan I Wu Shih Mo for the segregation of materials dealing with the
United States. In part this was an easy task, as it was no great strain
to determine that a memorial dealing with the Ili frontier or an edict
giving instructions to Chinese officials for carrying on negotiations with
Ignatieff were not relevant. On the other hand, papers concerned
primarily with England or France had to be read carefully to determine
if there were references or even insinuations of a Chinese attitude
toward the United States. By this process, 546 documents were selected for translation, almost all of them in extenso, although a few,
on closer examination, were excerpted. A beginning of the translation
was made at Harvard in 1933 and 1934, but the major part was done in
1937-1938, when a Rockefeller Foundation grant made it possible to
spend a year in Peking. There a draft translation, with the assistance
of a non-English-speaking Chinese hsien-sheng (private teacher)--
actually a tenth generation Peking Mongol--was completed. This work
was utilized in the completion of a doctoral dissertation at Harvard.

The experience derived from this translation and research seemed to indicate that the greatest contribution would be in the form of translation rather than in a monographic study. Another Rockefeller grant after World War II made a second year of residence in Peking possible in 1947-1948, during which the entire draft translation was revised with the view of making it as literal and documentary as possible, again with the assistance of a Chinese hsien-sheng.

To complete this process, the entire manuscript has been twice checked. Many valuable suggestions and corrections were made by Professor John K. Fairbank of Harvard. In addition, at Professor Fairbank's suggestion, the services of Dr. E-tu Zen-Sun of Johns Hopkins and Goucher were secured to make a careful check of the translations against the original Chinese text. Dr. Zen-Sun is not only completely bi-lingual but is also a mature and discriminating scholar in her own right, and her valuable assistance is gratefully acknowledged. All these suggestions and corrections have been incorporated into the final text. Although the result is not guaranteed to be perfect, there can be a reasonable confidence in its essential accuracy. The effort has been entirely in the direction of securing a strictly accurate translation, with as close adherence to the Chinese original as the fundamental differences of the two languages allow, rather than a paraphrase such as so many nineteenth century sinologues produced. It is hoped that the resulting texts are accurate enough to stand as documents rather than as commentaries. If the phraseology is not always as felictous as it might be, this is at least partly because of the effort to be literal and to retain more of the original word order and phraseology than would ordinarily be justified by the canons of good English style.

The original documents are headed by dates corresponding to the time of recording in the imperial archives. These dates are in duplicate, one in the cyclical form, the other in political form, i. e., by reign, lunar month, and day. With the aid of modern standard concordances, all these dates have been converted to their equivalents in the Christian calendar. When specific dates are mentioned in the text these have also been converted. In the numerous cases where events are reported as occuring in a certain (lunar) month of the Chinese calendar, the text is translated literally and the corresponding period according to our calendar is added in parenthesis. For example, "in the ninth month of last year (October 4-November 3, 1842), an American appeared . . ." This is an obvious necessity because the lunar month does not coincide with any single month in our calendar. For the convenience of the reader, the documents have also been numbered, classified as to form, and given descriptive titles.

There remains the consideration of the value and uniqueness of the materials contained in the Ch'ou Pan I Wu Shih Mo and of the selections from it embodied in this book. Alfred K'ai-ming Ch'iu has pointed out that the contents of this collection are not limited to any strict "diplomatic" classification, but record also China's early "attempts at internal and social reforms."[14] Professor T. F. Tsiang has made a count of the contents of the Tao-kuang series (1836-1849) and finds that there are 1,244 edicts, 1,380 memorials, 24 treaties and diplomatic notes, and 3 miscellaneous papers, making a total of 2,651 documents in the forty volumes. Of the miscellaneous papers, he says, "two are popular manifestoes to foreigners, and the third is a a plan to defeat them in war, drafted by a low official." He then goes on to say:[15]

A small percentage of the decrees had been published before, either in *extenso* or in abstract, in *Tung Hua Lu* or *Shen Suen (Sheng-hsün)*. Take, for example, the year 1841. The present publication for the year includes 438 decrees, of which 23 *in extenso* and 19 in abstract are found in *Tung Hua Lu,* and 136 *in extenso* are found in *Shen Suen.* Although 1841 cannot be called representative, the figures here given do indicate the large number of decrees published for the first time in this work. The same holds true for the memorials to the throne, which are really more important than the decrees. The papers of Lin Tse-su had been published by his family, but one very important paper, unfavorable to Lin's memory, had been suppressed. The memorials of Hsu Kuang-tsin had also been published, but the book is very rare. Yukien's papers had been the common property of scholars; and the joint memorial of Kiying, Ilipu, and Niu Kien on the treaty of Nanking, and the reports of Kiying on the treaties of the Bogue, Wanghia, and Whampoa had been published by the Waichiaopu. That is all. Undoubtedly the *Peking Gazette* published many of the memorials as they were presented to the throne, but no library, I believe, has a complete file for the thirties and forties of the last century. The overwhelming majority of the memorials in the Palace collection are therefore new material. Similarly, the papers of Kishen, most of the papers of Kiying and Ilipu, the papers of Teng Ting-cheng, of Niu Kien, of Liu Yun-ko, of Yishan, of Iliang, and of many others, provincial governors and metropolitan censors, are here for the first time rendered accessible. Many of the memorials have marginal notes from the hand of the Emperor. . . and these are entirely new to the scholarly world. . . .

Strange to say, some of these papers, now accessible in the original, have existed on the pages of the *Chinese Repository,* or in such books as those of Sir Francis Davis and W. D. Bernard in English translation, but the number of such papers is not large. On the other hand, the quantity of papers hitherto accessible to Chinese-reading scholars and not to others is far larger. Furthermore, the translation, wherever it existed, was in many cases inaccurate; in other cases, papers were inaccurately dated or attributed to the wrong person. If the present collection should be translated into English or French, the value to Western scholars would be even greater than the original has been to Chinese scholars.

---

14 *Op. cit.* (note 2 above), p. 324-325.
15 Tsiang, "New Light. . .," *op. cit.,* p. 580-581.

The spot check of Professor Tsiang is borne out in the experience of the present study. Of the 546 documents selected and translated, 19 were found to exist in partial or complete translation in the Chinese Repository, in American state papers, and in the works of two modern Chinese scholars, P. C. Kuo and T. F. Tsiang himself, and appropriate reference to these has been made in the text. In all cases, with the exception of the two documents translated by Professor Tsiang, the existing translations were found to be rather free renditions with numerous omissions and errors. Hence, although these earlier translations have invariably been consulted, the translations in this work have all been done independently.

An exhaustive check of the documents in this study was made against the Ta Ch'ing Shih Lu[16] or "Veritable Record" of the Manchu dynasty. It was found that of the 546 documents we have selected from the Ch'ou Pan I Wu Shih Mo, less than 200 appeared in the Shih Lu, and these were limited to edicts and very brief summaries of memorials. Usually, the only indication of the subject matter of even the long and important memorials was a digest of a line or two incorporated in the resultant edict. Some of the dates in the Shih Lu were found to be one or two days later than those given in the Ch'ou Pan I Wu Shih Mo, indicating that the latter used the date when the document was received while the Shih Lu used the date when the action was taken. This discrepancy, however, occurs only occasionally. Most of the dates coincide. In general it can be said that only a small amount of the useful information provided by the documents in the Ch'ou Pan I Wu Shih Mo — especially that contained in the memorials — is to be found in the Shih Lu, which limits itself to the edicts and other action papers of the court. On the other hand, no new material was found to exist independently in the Shih Lu. Nothing in the Shih Lu was found to be in disagreement with the material in the Ch'ou Pan I Wu Shih Mo, although the incidents are often over-simplified in the former.

The most interesting observation in comparing the Shih Lu and Ch'ou Pan I Wu Shih Mo is the fact that in the "Veritable Record" of the emperor and court, all the offensive and colloquial language in reference to foreigners and foreign countries is translated into polite forms. "Barbarians" become foreigners ("ocean men," yang jen), "barbarian chiefs" become foreign officials (yang yüan or yang kuan), and the opprobrious "mouth" radicals are omitted from Chinese characters used in transliterating foreign proper names. This indicates a degree of editing by the official historiographers who compiled the Shih Lu not usually suspected, because the original edicts, as well as the memorials and personal comments of the emperor, invariably used the "barbarian" terminology.

---

16 See review by Biggerstaff, *op. cit.* (note 2 above).

On the positive side, it is clear from a comparison of the two records that it would be impossible to reconstruct any coherent picture
of Chinese attitudes or policy from the Shih Lu alone, which is only
useful to check against the Ch'ou Pan I Wu Shih Mo for specific edicts
and court action, and to be sure the dates correspond. The reason for
this is obvious, since the purpose of the Shih Lu is to record the activities of the emperor in his official political capacity, while the purpose of the Ch'ou Pan I Wu Shih Mo is to provide in their fullest extent
all the official materials pertinent to "China's Management of Barbarian Affairs from Beginning to End."

Before closing this introduction, the author wishes to add a few
personal acknowledgments: to his wife, Lois Chapin, for twice typing
and correcting the draft; to a succession of long suffering Chinese
hsien-sheng, who toiled long hours explaining the Chinese texts; to the
officials of the Palace Museum at Peking for their cooperation in the
use of the archives; to Professor Derk Bodde, whose assiduous editing
has brought the manuscript to the point of printability; and finally to
Professor John K. Fairbank and Miss Elizabeth McLeod of Harvard
and Dr. Eugene H. Wilson of Colorado, who have read successive
parts of the manuscript in its final preparation for the press.

                                        Earl Swisher

University of Colorado

PART I. CHINA AND THE UNITED STATES, 1841-1861

Chapter 1

The Handling of Chinese Foreign Affairs, 1841-1861

The years 1841 to 1861 constitute a special period in the handling of foreign affairs by the Chinese government. The old regime of the Co-hong and Factories at Canton broke down with the outbreak of Anglo-Chinese hostilities and the system was officially abolished by the treaties signed with China, 1842-1844. Prior to 1841, foreigners in China dealt with China only through the medium of the Chinese merchants guild or Co-hong in Canton and had no official contact with Chinese officials. During this period, to be sure, foreign consuls and trade superintendents did actually have occasional and limited access to certain local officials such as the "Hoppo" or customs superintendent and the district magistrate (chih-hsien) These contacts, however, were rare and were confined to matters dealing with trade and to the occasional homicide in which a foreigner was involved at Canton or Whampoa. Strictly speaking, then, there were no foreign relations with China before 1841 and the insistence of Great Britain on the establishment of machinery for the conduct of foreign affairs was one cause of the so-called Opium War.

Beginning with the establishment of the Tsungli Yamen in 1861, China for the first time in her history had the machinery for dealing with other powers of the world on a basis of equality. This concession was wrested from China by force, including the capture and occupation of the imperial capital, Peking, and was embodied in the treaties negotiated in 1858 and ratified in Peking in 1860. From this time forward, then, China's foreign affairs were handled in a comparatively orthodox, Western fashion, and the governmental machinery was somewhat less of a mystery to foreign diplomats and presents no peculiar problem to Western students.

The twenty-year period between the ending of China's diplomatic seclusion and the inauguration of semi-orthodox foreign relations, which is the subject of this study, is both a transitional and a formative period. Hence some knowledge of the official machinery, official policy, and official mentality of the time is essential to a full understanding of subsequent periods in Chinese history.

In this chapter the attempt will be made to outline the organization and workings of Chinese foreign relations from 1841, and particularly from 1842 to 1861. No attempt will be made to present the entire structure of Chinese government; only those offices and officials who were important in the management of foreign affairs will be considered.

During this period China was only partially opened to foreigners. At the outset, the only point of contact was Canton, as had already been the case from the beginning of American trade to China in 1784. With the British treaty of 1842 and the American treaty of 1844, four additional ports were opened: Amoy and Foochow in Fukien province, Ningpo in Chekiang province, and Shanghai in Kiangsu province. Toward the end of the period, Tientsin and the nearby ports of Pei-t'ang and Ta-ku, in Chihli (now Hopei) province, became points of foreign pressure on China; in 1859, the first American minister reached Peking. It was a year and a war later, however, before Peking, the capital, was to become a permanent place of residence of foreign representatives to China.

In each of the treaty ports, the Chinese official with whom the foreign commissioners and ministers had the most frequent contact was the tao-t'ai or Intendant of Circuit. The tao-t'ai was a key official in the Chinese official hierarchy, in which he ranked 4a, in a scale of nine. He was just high enough to be called ta-jen, corresponding possibly to "Excellency, " but still low enough to be in contact with real people and real problems. He maintained a large yamen or official compound, wore the azure button on his cap, and the wild goose embroidered on his plaque or "Mandarin Square. " The tao-t'ai was a man of importance, and paid and received calls with a great deal of pomp and ceremony.

As indicated by the translation of his title, the tao-t'ai or Intendant of Circuit had jurisdiction over two or more prefectures, independent sub-prefectures, or departments, the names of which were prefixed to his title. The particular importance of the tao-t'ai in the foreign relations of China during this period, however, is due to two special functions which he performed. First, the tao-t'ai in whose circuit lay a treaty port often performed diplomatic functions and served as intermediary in intercourse with foreigners. Second, in the five ports open to foreign trade during this period, the tao-t'ai often served as superintendent of customs. In this capacity, he succeeded to the duties formerly performed by the "Hoppo" or customs superintendent at Canton.

Although there were tao-t'ai at each of the treaty ports, that of Shanghai was by far the most prominent. His official title was Su-Sung-T'ai tao-t'ai, and his jurisdiction, which included Shanghai, covered the two prefectures of Soochow Fu and Sung-chiang-fu, together with the sub-prefecture of T'ai-ts'ang Chih-li Chou. The importance of the Shanghai tao-t'ai derived not only from the volume of the Shanghai trade and the rapid growth of the city, but also from the fact that Shanghai, unlike Canton, was not a provincial capital. Consequently, the Shanghai tao-t'ai was the highest official resident at the

port. At times during the latter part of this period, the Shanghai tao-
t'ai was virtual, albeit entirely unofficial, foreign minister of China
and exercised tremendous responsibility.

The next local official with whom the foreigners dealt was the
provincial governor or hsün-fu. He ranked two grades above the tao-
t'ai, or 2b in the nine official grades. He wore the red coral button on
his cap, and had a golden pheasant embroidered on his official plaque
or "Mandarin Square." His place in foreign affairs is a minor one.
There were four governors who, owing to the existence within their
provinces of one or more treaty ports, had potential contact with
foreigners, namely, those of Kwangtung, Fukien, Chekiang, and Kiangsu. With the exceptions of Canton and Foochow, however, the port city
itself was not the provincial capital, and consequently the governor
seldom had occasion to deal with foreigners. In Canton, and occasionally in other provinces, the governor did meet a foreign commissioner,
but more frequently he memorialized the results of negotiations between
the local tao-t'ai and the foreigner. On the whole, the provincial governors
avoided questions of diplomacy and tried to relegate them either down to
the tao-t'ai or up to the governor general.

The governor general or tsung-tu was, again, a key official in the
machinery of foreign relations during this period. Having the grade of
1b, he wore the top-ranking ruby button on his cap, and had the white
crane embroidered on his "Mandarin Square." He was ex officio a
president of the Board of War and also carried the title of associate
president of the Court of Censors. In Western accounts of the nineteenth
century, the governor general is usually referred to as "viceroy" and
several famous or notorious viceroys figure very prominently in this
period.

There were two specific reasons for the prominence of governors
general in foreign affairs. First, the American treaty negotiated by
Caleb Cushing for the United States at Wang-hsia (Wang Hiya), outside
Macao, in 1844, provided, as an alternate procedure, that "communications from the government of the United States to the court of China
shall be transmitted ... through the Governor-general of the Liang
Kwang, that of Min and Cheh, or that of Liang Kiang."[1]

This placed in the hands of three governors general of China some
responsibilities of handling foreign affairs. The three involved were,
first the governor general of Liang-kuang, commonly called the
"Canton viceroy." The governor general of Liang-kuang had jurisdiction over the two provinces of Kwangtung and Kwangsi and had his
official residence at Canton. The second was the governor general
of Min-Che, whose jurisdiction also comprised two provinces, Fukien
and Chekiang, in which were three treaty ports, Amoy, Foochow, and
Ningpo. The third was the governor general of Liang-chiang, whose

---

1 Miller, Hunter, *Treaties and other International Acts of the United States of
   America,* 8 v., Washington, v. 4. p. 569.

jurisdiction comprised three provinces, Kiangsu, Kiangsi, and Anhui, and whose official yamen was in Chiang-ning-fu or Nanking. The treaty port of Shanghai fell within his jurisdiction.

Besides these three governors general specified by treaty, a fourth became involved when the Western powers pushed their negotiations from the treaty ports to Tientsin and Peking. This was the governor general of Chihli (now Hopei) province. He was unique in that his jurisdiction covered only the one, the metropolitan, province, and in that he had no provincial governors under him. The governor general of Chihli was compelled to deal with the foreigners whenever they came north to the mouth of the Pei-ho, or forced their way up that river to Tientsin, where he was obliged by circumstances to transfer his official yamen. Up to 1870, the legal capital continued at Pao-ting.

Finally, the list of Chinese officials, outside the court of Peking, who dealt with foreign affairs is topped by the imperial commissioner or ch'in-ch'ai. This high functionary, who bore a special commission direct from the emperor, has been called "imperial envoy, " "ambassador extraordinary, " or "imperial high commissioner. " These extraordinary appointments had been reserved before 1842 for occasions when provincial affairs got out of hand or rebellions broke out. When an imperial commissioner arrived on the scene, his authority superceded that of both governor general and governor, and he was restricted only by the limits of his commission. When his special task was completed, he would ordinarily return to Peking, but on occasion he remained on the scene along with the provincial officials, taking full charge of the task covered by his commission, but leaving all other matters to the regular officials. [2]

Imperial commissioners appear in the foreign relations of this period in two ways. First, as special agents of the emperor, imperial commissioners were sent to handle new and unorthodox matters which were too much for the ordinary provincial authorities. This practice began with the famous imperial commissioner, Lin Tse-hsü, who was sent to settle the opium question in 1839, and continued through a long and distinguished line of imperial commissioners, headed by Ch'i-ying (Kiying), sent to negotiate treaties with foreigners at Nanking, at the Bogue Forts (below Whampoa), at Wang-hsia, and, ineffectively, at Tientsin. These imperial commissioners carried a tremendous amount of prestige and were accepted by the foreigners as the equivalent of envoy extraordinary and minister plenipotentiary. Actually, they did not have full powers but had to refer everything to the emperor. Furthermore, their appointment did not introduce any new element in the administrative machinery of China, nor did it represent any new relationship between China and

---

2 Morse, Hosea Ballou, *The International Relations of the Chinese Empire*, 2 v., London, 1910, v.1, p. 15.

the West. The imperial commissioner was simply sent to deal with a crisis which might just as well have been a rebellion or a flood.

The second role of the imperial commissioner, in relation to foreign affairs, did, on the contrary, introduce a new element in Chinese administrative machinery, and did represent a new element in the relations between China and the West. With the abolition of the Canton Co-hong as the medium through which all foreign affairs were handled, accomplished by Article V of the Treaty of Nanking, August 29, 1842, [3] some new agency had to be created. This was accomplished by adding to the duties of the governor general of Liang-kuang or Canton the role of "Imperial Commissioner charged with the superintendence of the concerns of foreign nations with China, " to use the terminology of the American Treaty of Wang-hsia.[4] This title was incorporated into the Chinese treaty as the Pan-li wai-kuo shih-wu chih ch'in-ch'ai ta-ch'en, [5] although, throughout the period, Chinese official documents referred to him as the "Imperial Commissioner incharge-of Barbarian Affairs. "[6] This represented an innovation in two respects; first, because it was a continuing delegation of imperial authority, and, second, because it created a special agency for the handling of foreign affairs, completely independent of both the Court of Dependencies (Li Fan Yüan)[7] and the Board of Rites (Li Pu).[8]

Thus the Canton governor general, in this additional capacity, became virtually the first Chinese minister of foreign affairs, although in practice he proved to be a poor substitute. This was brought to the attention of the West when British and French warships bombarded Canton and allied troops scaled the eastern wall of Canton, December 29, 1857. [9] When the troops entered the yamen of the imperial commissioner and governor general of Liang-kuang, Yeh Ming-ch'en, they found the originals of the treaties with Great Britain, France, and the United States, as well as the memorials and edicts pertinent to foreign affairs of the period, 1854-1856. Included in the files were the original of the Cushing Treaty of 1844, and the original powers of Commodore Biddle to exchange ratifications. United States

---

3 Hertslet, Sir Edward, *Treaties, etc., between Great Britain and China; and between China and Foreign Powers; and Orders in Council, Rules, Regulations, Acts of Parliament, Decrees, and Notifications affecting British Interests in China*, London, 1896, 2 v., v. 1, p. 7.

4 Miller, *op. cit.*, v. 4, p. 569.

5 *Ibid.*, v. 4, p. 596.

6 IWSM. HF 25, 19a, 1.

7 Brunnert, H.S. and V.V. Hagelstrom, *Present Day Political Organization of China*, Shanghai, 1912, p. 160.

8 *Ibid.*, p. 124.

9 U. S. Cong. 36:1, S. *Ex. Doc.* 30 (1032). 86.

Minister William B. Reed was informed by the British, who turned the
American documents over to him, that these had been found "confused-
ly packed in trunks in the house where Yeh was captured and whither
they seemed to have been removed from his yamen or official residence. The other papers consisted of diplomatic correspondence,
though not of recent date, and imperial rescripts relating to foreign affairs, confirming the idea that practically the foreign office of China
had for many years been at Canton. "[10]

This discovery by the British was regarded as evidence of China's
bad faith in carrying out the terms of the treaties. Probably, however,
the institution of a sort of Chinese foreign office at Canton and the
creation of a quasi Chinese foreign minister in the person of the governor general of Liang-kuang represented a progressive step in the re-
orientation of China.

The above offices account for the official functionaries with whom
foreign representatives dealt at the ports and in the provinces. They
represent, of course, only a small segment of the vast hierarchy of
Chinese officialdom, since foreign affairs, during this period, were
still regarded as border troubles and their importance treated as
peripheral. Besides these officials, there was another group on the
local level who occupied an indeterminable but probably important place
in foreign relations. These were the chai-shih, unofficial officials
usually falling into the class known as "expectant" magistrate or "expectant" tao-t'ai. These persons were qualified to serve in the posts
for which they were "expectant" and had their names entered on the
register of the Board of Civil Office at Peking, but had not been, and
in many cases never would be, appointed to a substantive post. Admission to this state of "expectancy" was in theory the result of passing
the regular civil service examinations, [11] but, at least in the nineteenth
century, "expectancy" was purchased by wealthy merchants for the
prestige it afforded, without any desire or intention of becoming an
active official.

The importance of this class to the conduct of foreign relations to
1861, lay in the fact that wealthy merchants at Canton and Shanghai,
often the successors to the old hong merchants, frequently bought such
"expectancies." Because of their contact with foreigners, their
knowledge of the new type of commerce and tariff, and their vital
interest in foreign affairs, these local "expectant" officials were often
called in to advise provincial officials and particularly to assist imperial commissioners sent from the court. These and a swarm of
more humble folk, recruited from the old "linguist" or interpreter
class, from domestic servants who had worked for foreigners, and an
occasional Chinese who had gone abroad or worked aboard a foreign

---

10 U. S. Cong. 36: 1, S. Ex. Doc. 30 (1032). 89.

11 Morse, op. cit., v. 1, p. 16.

ship, constituted a new class of "experts" in foreign affairs. [12] They were commonly called "barbarian experts, " and were held in official contempt, but probably exercised considerable influence on negotiators and negotiations during this period. Quite different from the situation which prevailed later in the nineteenth century, these early experts on foreign affairs had very slight knowledge of English and their knowledge of Western institutions was certainly limited.

If we turn now from the handling of foreign affairs by Chinese local officials and by specially commissioned persons sent out from the court, the other matter for consideration is that of the machinery of the central government at Peking. Popular ideas prevalent at the time held that the emperor of China relegated foreign affairs to the Board of Rites or the Court of Dependencies, but some contemporary British officials had a clearer idea of the workings of the Chinese government. The British had gone to Peking (and Jehol) on two occasions, the Macartney mission in 1793 and the Amherst mission in 1816, so China was not so much a mystery to them as it was to the Americans. The first American official to go to Peking was our minister Ward, in 1859, and he did not add much to the knowledge of the West.

The Chinese secretary of the British mission in 1858, Thomas Wade, gave a clear, though incomplete, picture of the way the government in Peking worked, in the handling of foreign affairs The key organ, he said with complete accuracy, was the Grand Council. In a memorandum to William. B. Reed, dated April 10, 1858, he wrote:

The members of the great council, literally the council of war, which is composed of the secretaries of state, presidents and vice-presidents of boards, and other metropolitan officials, are selected specially by the Emperor, irrespectively of nationality, Manchu, Mongolian, or Chinese. Its functions are the preparation and trans-mission or promulgation of the Emperor's decisions, and the advis-ing of his Majesty in all important matters of peace or war. . . . Their relation to the head of the state must be regarded as more intimate than in the case of any other court, confidential in-structions occasionally passing through their hands without being communicated even to the *nui-kok* ⌊*Nei-ko,* Grand Secretariat⌋, or cabinet. . . . They have a separate hall of assembly, but. . .a certain number attend daily within the forbidden precinct of the palace, waiting to be called before the Emperor. This may happen once in the day, or more than once. A mat or cushion is placed for them to sit upon in the imperial presence--I believe their ex-clusive privilege--and they either submit drafts of decrees to be issued in the name of the Emperor, or, on occasion, receive his opinion in the autograph vermilion pencil upon the face of the documents already before him. In the case of extra-metropolitan correspondence, at least, the original memorial appears always, to

---

12 *Cf.* Teng Ssǔ-yü, *Chang Hsi and the Treaty of Nanking,* Chicago, 1944.

be returned to the high officer from whom it came. It bears some
notice in the vermilion pencil, for which some folds of blank paper
are left at the close. When the copy is to be what we term a decree,
it is drafted and copied on a separate sheet by the council, and
then apparently submitted to the Emperor. . . .. This is transmitted
with the original memorial returned in a cover bearing the seal of
the ⌊Grand⌋ Council, none of whose names appear in the note advising
the officer addressed of their instructions to write to him. [13]

The extremely simple administrative procedure which Thomas
Wade described in 1858 is essentially correct, although access to
Chinese materials of the Ch'ing dynasty has added much detail to his
picture. Foreign diplomats, prior to 1861, may have felt that they
were treated with scant respect and that foreign affairs were lost in a
maze of oriental chicanery, but, administratively at least, all matters
relating to foreigners, even the most trivial, went straight to the
emperor and to the highest organ of state, the Grand Council. The
other organ mentioned by Wade, the Nei-ko or Grand Secretariat, had
even less to do with the management of foreign affairs than he imagined.
Actually, all matters concerning the United States and Europe, with the
exception of Russia, were handled exclusively by the emperor and the
grand councillors. This fact was not clear to nineteenth century historians, who of necessity relied for much of their information upon
Jesuit reports of the Ming dynasty or of the earliest reigns of the Manchu dynasty, when the Nei-ko or Grand Secretariat (Cabinet) was the
most powerful organ in the central administration.

The establishment of the Grand Council or Chün Chi Ch'u[14] is
placed by some historians at 1729, by others at 1730, but 1729 appears
to be correct. It was first called the Office of Military Supplies (Chün
Hsü Chü) and was intended "to deal secretly with imperial military
strategy."[15] Originally designed as the emperor's personal staff to
expedite military affairs, it was perpetuated as an administrative
organ, but only in 1732 was it issued an official seal and the official
title of Chün Chi Ch'u or Grand Council.[16]

---

13 U. S. Cong. 36 : 1; Sen. Ex. Doc. 30 (1032). 446-447.

14 Most of the material for this brief summary of the Grand Council is based on the
    Ta Ch'ing Hui Tien, section on the Grand Council; the Ch'ing Shih Kao, section
    on the Grand Council; and an unpublished master's thesis (in Chinese) by Teng
    Ssŭ-yü entitled "A Study of the Central Government During the T'ang, Sung, Yuan,
    Ming, and Ch'ing Dynasties," MS in Yenching University Library, Peiping, sum-
    marized by Mr. Kuo Wan-yu.

15 Fairbank, J. K., and Teng Ssŭ-yü, "On the Types and Uses of Ch'ing Documents,"
    Harvard Journal of Asiatic Studies (HJAS) 5 (1940). 23.

16 For a general account of the central government under the Manchus, see Pao Chao
    Hsieh, The Government of China (1644-1911), Baltimore, 1925; on the Emperor,
    p. 24-44; on the Grand Secretariat, p. 68-77; on the Grand Council, p. 77-87;
    on the new Foreign Office, p. 235-254.

The occasion for the establishment of the Grand Council, in 1732, was the urgent logistical problem created by the Ch'ing-hai or Kokonor uprising. Teng Ssŭ-yü, however, finds three good reasons for setting up this new organ. First, it was to secure secrecy in dealing with military affairs. During the Yung-cheng period (1723-1735), there were military operations in both the western and northern sectors. As the Grand Secretariat (Nei-ko), which the Manchus had inherited from the Ming dynasty, was located outside T'ai-ho Men, the south gate of the main palace leading to Wu Men, at a considerable distance from the audience hall, and since the number employed in the Grand Secretariat was very large, it was feared that secrets would leak out. Consequently, the new Office of Military Supplies was set up inside Lung-tsung Men, immediately adjoining the audience hall, and its numbers rigidly restricted. Second, the Grand Council was intended to circumvent the power of the emperor's own Manchu advisers (I-cheng ta-ch'en). According to Chao Lien: "At the beginning of the dynasty, military and political affairs were entirely handled by the I-cheng ta-ch'en, but a majority of them were hereditary nobles and did not understand politics. The Yung-cheng Emperor realized their weakness and set up the Grand Council. Thereafter affairs of state were closely guarded and the shortcomings of the I-cheng finally overcome. "[17] The third reason for the establishment of the Grand Council was to achieve a maximum concentration of power. All able emperors of China struggled constantly with their own ministers and under such efficient emperors as Han Wu Ti (140-86 B.C.) a prime minister was powerless. The Yung-cheng emperor was suspicious and cruel and established the Grand Council to frustrate the grand secretaries. Of these three reasons, the modern Chinese critic observes, "the first is immediate, the second is remote, while the third is the real reason. " According to this interpretation, the Grand Council was a Manchu instrument of tyranny devised to nullify the traditional Chinese restrictions placed on imperial authority

It is clear that the Grand Council was originally established for the expedition of military affairs, a special organ for a special occasion rather than a permanent administrative body. But thereafter wars continued year after year and the Grand Council could not be dissolved. Gradually its powers extended beyond military affairs, until no political matter, large or small, was free from its interference. It stood above the Six Boards. It came, as a body, to occupy much the same position as the prime minister (ch'eng-hsiang) of the Ming dynasty, and the Privy Council (Shu Mi Yüan) of the Sung dynasty. During the Ch'ien-lung period (1735-1795), it was officially called the Supreme Political Council (Tsung Li Cheng Wu Ch'u), which indicates more ac-

---

17 *Hsiao T'ing Tsa Lu* (Miscellaneous Notes on Ch'ing History), quoted by Teng Ssŭ-yü; *cf.* Hummel, *Eminent Chinese of The Ch'ing Period*, v. 1, p. 78-80.

curately its power.   The <u>Draft</u> <u>Ch'ing</u> <u>History</u> states: "From the Yung-cheng period on, for one hundred and eighty years, authority rested not in the Grand Secretariat but in the Grand Council, which appears to be the organ of virtual sovereignty. "[18]

The functions of the Grand Council are described in the <u>Institutes</u> <u>of</u> <u>the</u> <u>Ch'ing</u> <u>Dynasty</u>: "The Grand Councillors are responsible for drafting edicts, take charge of all important military and state matters, and advise the Emperor on all affairs of state.   They are constantly in the Forbidden City awaiting summons for audience and accompany the Emperor to the Summer Palace and the Western Park (Jehol).   Routine edicts issued by the Emperor go to the Grand Secretariat; edicts to the Grand Council are issued sealed.   On receipt of Imperial Edicts, the Grand Council discusses major policies and decides important judicial cases. "[19]

Obviously, the Grand Councillors personally reflected the imperial will and were in a position to receive from above and transmit below. "In short, the Grand Council was in many respects a sort of imperial private secretariat. . ."[20]

The grand councillors paid heavily, in exactions upon them, for this unlimited imperial confidence.   The usual time for audience was from three to five o'clock in the morning, but they could be summoned at any time and were frequently called in several times in one day.   In audience, as Thomas Wade observed in 1858, they were allowed to sit on mats in the imperial presence.

The actual division between the work done personally by the emperor and that done by the grand councillors is indeterminable. They were anonymous and everything they did was in the name of the emperor.   The form of edicts on important, as distinguished from routine matters, consisted of orders from the emperor to the grand councillors. [21] Actually the grand councillors drafted the edicts on the basis of imperial autograph directions scrawled in vermilion on the original memorial, or on the basis of oral instruction from the emperor delivered during the audience.   This formula was fairly well defined: for memorials which were endorsed by the emperor, they drafted the appropriate edicts; in the case of memorials which had not received vermilion endorsement, they were held until the emperor's will became known.

In this procedure, two things stand out clearly.   First, the

---

18   *Ch'ing Shih Kao*,"Chün-chi ta-ch'en nien-piao" (Chronological Table of Grand Councillors), ch. 182, p. 1a.

19   *Ta Ch'ing Hui Tien*, section on "Civil Officials" (*Chih-kuan*), quoted by Teng Ssŭ-yü.

20   Fairbank and Teng, *op. cit.*, p. 24.

21   Fairbank and Teng, *op. cit.*, p. 25.

emperor's prerogative was carefully preserved. At least in theory and probably in practice, the emperor saw all important memorials before they were seen by the grand councillors. [22] Second, the old cabinet or Grand Secretariat was completely by-passed. In the documents examined in this study, the only edicts addressed to the Grand Secretariat are routine orders regarding appointments. There is no instance of a matter of foreign policy being taken up with the Grand Secretariat.

The importance of this administrative procedure is obvious. The fact that all foreign affairs were considered personally by the emperor and/or discussed by the Grand Council, who drafted and issued the necessary edicts, indicates that relations with Europe and the United States were not considered lightly. Foreign relations, although scornfully called "barbarian affairs," were never regarded as routine but were treated as primary problems of state.

It should be kept in mind, however, that the Grand Council was no foreign office. Its concern with "barbarian affairs" was only one of its multifarious functions. The original military functions of the Grand Council were never relinquished and it was supposed to be fully informed on the geography of the empire, troops, finances, and supplies, whenever the emperor required these data for military purposes. It also recommended all important civil and military appointments, was a final court of review, provided lists of subjects for palace examinations, and provided the emperor with notes when he felt like composing poetry. Under the supervision of the Grand Council were the Office of Military Archives and the Manchu-Chinese Translation Office.

Although the duties of the Grand Council were onerous, the original intent of keeping it small and personally responsible to the emperor was retained. The number was indefinite but was usually five or six. Its members were chosen from the Grand Secretariat or from the roster of presidents and vice presidents of the various boards, and were divided into grand councillors and probationers. From 1735 to 1875, the number of grand councillors totaled 107, of whom 62 were Manchus and 45 were Chinese. Traditionally the emperors of the Ch'ing dynasty did not allow their own hereditary nobility to hold important offices, so there were seldom Manchu princes in the Council. Notable exceptions to this general rule were Yung-hsing Prince Ch'eng who was appointed grand councillor during the Chia-ch'ing period (1796-1821), but was soon dismissed by edict, and the well-known I-hsin Prince Kung, who became a grand councillor during the Hsien-feng period (1850-1861).

Besides the grand councillors themselves, there were necessarily a considerable number of lesser functionaries to carry out the inevitable drafting, copying, and general housework involved in every administrative office. To perform this, there were thirty-two secre-

---

22 Fairbank and Teng, *op. cit.*, p. 26.

taries attached to the Council, divided into four sections: first and
second Manchu secretaries, and first and second Chinese secretaries.
These were all chosen from the clerks of the Six Boards. The Chinese
secretaries were usually either metropolitan graduates (chin-shih) or
provincial graduates (chü-jen). Manchu secretaries were usually required to have passed the examinations in their own language with the
so-called "translation" degree (fan-i chin-shih). The duties of the
secretaries were to draft edicts, register incoming memorials, and
to try judicial cases--always under the direction of the grand councillors themselves. In the nineteenth century, the powers of the secretaries increased as they were allowed to be received by the emperor
personally and discuss state affairs. When vacancies occurred in the
Grand Council, secretaries could be promoted directly to the Council
itself, so they were sometimes called "little grard councillors."

For the period from 1840 to 1861, with which we are concerned,
the chronological tables for the Grand Council have been examined in
the Draft Ch'ing History (Ch'ing Shih Kao). This compilation shows
that the total number of grand councillors during the twenty years was
twenty-three, of whom eleven were Manchus and twelve were Chinese.
This indicates a marked difference from the ratio of 62:45 cited above
for the entire period from 1735 to 1875, showing that the general pre-
ponderance of Manchus on the Grand Council did not hold for the latter
part of that period. Considering the twenty-year period (1840-1861)
separately, two Chinese and one Manchu served for twelve years each,
another Manchu served for eleven years, and two other Chinese
served ten years each. Other periods of service on the Council ranged
from one to nine years.

In general the size of the Grand Council from 1840 to 1861 was in
conformity with the general pattern for the dynasty. For the seven
years from 1840 through 1846, there were consistently five members,
consisting of two Manchus and three Chinese. For the nine years from
1847 through 1855, the membership of the Council was six, but the
Manchu-Chinese ratio was not uniform. In 1847 and 1848, the ratio
was 3:3; for the next three years, there were two Manchus and four
Chinese; for the next five years, through 1855, the ratio was again 3:3.
In the two years, 1856 and 1857, the membership of the Grand Council
dropped to four and the ratio was two Manchus to two Chinese. During
the last three years, 1858-1860, the membership was again five and the
ratio was again two Manchus to three Chinese. In 1861, however,
which was not included in the above compilation, the membership of
the Grand Council was suddenly increased to ten, of which at least two
members were specially delegated to serve in the newly established
Office of Foreign Affairs or Tsungli Yamen. The enlarged Council was
evenly divided, five Manchus and five Chinese. [23] The implication

23 This is still within the range stated by Fairbank and Teng: "The number of Grand

appears to be that the Grand Council was expanded in order to accommodate the new administrative organ forced upon China by the treaties of 1861. At any rate it is clear that in the reorganization of the central government, the transition was smoothed by the fact that the Tsungli Yamen was created by the simple process of expanding and dividing the Grand Council. [24]

As to the character of the Grand Council for this particular period, as compared with its general character for the entire period of its existence, only the most general observations can be made. Modern Chinese students of institutional history regard the status of the Grand Council as decadent during the nineteenth century. During the Tao-kuang period (1821-1850), it functioned mechanically but exercised no real initiative; hence it has been said of the Grand Council that "these thirty years were as one day." In the Hsien-feng period (1851-1861), the powers of the Grand Council continued to decline and everything was done by imperial order. During the latter half of the reign, however, the vigorous Prince Kung seems to have restored some life to the senile body. After 1861, with the ablest men serving in the Tsungli Yamen, the grand councillors degenerated into robots, signing their names mechanically without any real powers.

A modern writer has caricatured the Grand Council in its final dotage as follows: "When the Grand Councillors were received in audience, they knelt in a fixed order. The leading one, who confronted the emperor, was called 'the Face' of the Grand Council; the second, who spoke only when he was spoken to, was called 'the Mouth'; the third, who drafted the Edicts without knowing what they meant, was called 'the Hand'; and the last, who ran errands, was called 'the Legs.' The secretaries of the Grand Council were divided into two classes: 'walking corpses' and 'day dreamers who died in their sleep.'"[25] By this time the Grand Council had become entirely useless and was replaced by a responsible cabinet just on the eve of the Revolution.

From the above description of that portion of the Chinese official hierarchy directly concerned with foreign affairs, the general picture of the period 1841-1861 becomes clear. On the local level, in the ports and at Tientsin, foreign representatives dealt with the tao-t'ai, the governor, and with the governor general or viceroy. Local dealings were climaxed by the appearance of the imperial commissioner,

---

Councillors was never fixed. Usually there were five or six, but the number ranged between the extremes of three and twelve." *Op. cit.;* p. 22.

24 *Cf.* statement by Fairbank and Teng that "... during the existence of the Tsungli Yamen (for the management of foreign affairs) from 1860 to 1901, there were eighteen men who held office both in that body and the Council." *Op. cit.,* p. 23.

25 *Kuang Hsüan Hsiao Chi* (Notes on the Kuang-hsü and Hsüan-t'ung Periods, 1875-1912), quoted by Teng Ssŭ-yü, *op. cit.*

either in the person of the emperor's delegate specially appointed for a
particular occasion, or in the person of the governor general at Canton
with the additional duty of imperial commissioner for "barbarian affairs." At the court at Peking the picture is equally clear and even
more simple. The emperor and his personal secretariat, the Grand
Council, handled all problems involving the foreigners with a maximum
of efficiency and a minimum of red tape. The only obscurity involves
the degree of personal initiative taken by the emperor and the amount of
judgment and decision exercised by the grand councillors. This obscurity can hardly be resolved, but whichever was the case, the
responsibility was clearly that of the emperor. In the case of the two
emperors involved in this period, Tao-kuang and Hsien-feng, it appears
probable that they were their own foreign ministers.

It remains, finally, to reconstruct exactly how this machinery
worked, insofar as the affairs of the various foreign powers are concerned. For example, an American commissioner or minister came
to China during the period, 1844-1860. He presented his credentials
to the governor general and imperial commissioner at Canton. This
was his first step, but should it fail because the Canton official was
absent on other affairs, was indisposed, or, being hide-bound by
tradition, refused to see foreigners, the American envoy had several
other alternatives. He might go to Shanghai and try to make contact
with the governor general of Liang-kiang. He might go to Amoy or
Foochow or Ningpo and try to get in touch with the govenor general of
Min-Che. On the other hand, he might aim at a lower level and deal
with one of the provincial governors or even with the local tao-t'ai.

At whatever point the American made contact with a Chinese official, and whatever business he transacted with him--presentation of
credentials, making of a complaint on behalf of American merchants
or missionaries, proposing treaty revision, adjusting tariff claims--
the end result was a memorial (tsou). This means that the governor,
governor general, imperial commissioner, or a combination of all
three, memorialized the emperor on behalf of the American commissioner. This memorial might incorporate the American's credentials, incorporate other papers which the American envoy wished
to have presented to the emperor, might report the Chinese officials'
version of conversations and negotiations with the American envoy,
or merely describe the activities of the foreigners in Chinese waters.
In other words, the instrument linking the provinces and ports with
the central government was the memorial and, since the American
representative dealt with officials in the provinces and the ports,
his contact was one stage removed--he had to depend on their
memorials in his behalf.

The memorial was prepared in the local office, sealed, placed
between boards and delivered to the local post station. [26] This

---

26 The following data on the physical handling of official mail are taken from the

station, whether it be in Canton, Soochow (the nearest provincial ya-men to Shanghai), or Tientsin, was a part of the official postal system maintained by the Peking government under the supervision of the Board of War.   Horses for this elaborate network, which reached to the remotest parts of the empire, were supplied by the Remount Department.   Once committed to this agency, the memorial was carried by express post at the rate of three hundred li, approximately one hundred miles, per day.   If, however, the memorial was urgent, the governor general or imperial commissioner might specify a special express rate of 400 li, 500 li, or up to a maximum of 600 li (200 miles) per day.   According to a careful check by Fairbank and Teng, the memorial might require anywhere from 15 to 49 days to reach Peking from Canton.   On the average, however, the record was good, and about twenty days usually saw a Canton memorial in Peking. From Shanghai, the time ranged from 7 to 14 days, with an average of ten.   When negotiations took place in Tientsin, memorials required only a little more than twenty-four hours to reach the capital.

Once the memorial had arrived in Peking, it was carried directly to the Couriers' Office, outside the main gate of the Forbidden City. From the Couriers' Office it was taken to the Chancery of Memorials. The Chancery secretaries handed it to palace eunuchs, who were able to deliver it to the emperor's private apartments. [27]

The emperor then examined the memorial.   If he "endorsed it in vermilion," it simply went to the grand councillors, who drafted the appropriate edict.   If the emperor was not certain, he might discuss the memorial with the grand councillors in audience the following morning and orally instruct them to draft an edict.   Finally, the emperor might turn down one corner of the memorial, indicating that further consideration was required.

When, by one of the three processes indicated above, the will of the emperor was expressed, the memorial was sent to the Grand Council.   Copies of the memorial were made for the various files, and the original returned to the memorialist.   The grand councillors then drafted an edict expressing the imperial will.   This edict was published and incorporated in a court letter addressed to the provincial officials involved.   The court letter was then sent direct to the Couriers' Office, and started on its way back to Tientsin, Shanghai, or Canton.   The courier services, riding night and day, carried the court letter back and delivered it to the imperial commissioner or

article by John K. Fairbank and Teng Ssŭ-yü, "On the Transmission of Ch'ing Documents," HJAS 4(1939).12-46.

27   Procedural handling of provincial memorials, Tsou-pen, is taken from Fairbank and Teng, op. cit., HJAS 5(1940).25-33;   the same authors in their previous article state that memorials went to the Grand Council before reaching the emperor (HJAS 4 [1939].39).   This appears to be in error.

governor, who then conveyed it, either orally or in writing, to the American envoy. The whole process required, on the average, some 43 days if the American representative was in Canton, 23 days if he were in Shanghai, or 5 days if he were in Tientsin.

The whole procedure was remarkably simple and direct and actual examination of documents dealing with foreign affairs shows that there was seldom any inefficiency or delay in their handling. The entire process at the palace took normally two to five days, but in emergencies a decision could be secured and an order started on its way within a few hours. One of the features of this procedural pattern is the essential part played by the emperor. Modern scholars have observed after careful study of the whole administrative machinery as affecting foreign affairs that ". . . for an understanding of Manchu policy attention must be centered upon the personality of the Emperor and the influences affecting him . . . The Emperor was required to play a part, passive though it might be, in the making of every important decision. This fact of personal rule has been commented upon for generations past, yet its implications, from an administrative point of view, have seldom been explored. "[28]

---

28   Fairbank and Teng, *op. cit.*, HJAS 5(1940). 33.

Chapter 2

Chinese Personnel Involved in Dealing
with the United States, 1841-1861

Official relations between the United States and China begin with
the arrival at Macao of Commodore Lawrence Kearney, April, 1842,
in command of the East India Squadron of the United States Fleet. [1]
Prior to this, America had been represented in China by a series of
merchant consuls, beginning with Samuel Shaw, who was "elected"
by the Confederation Congress in 1785, and concluding with Paul S.
Forbes, who was consul at Canton in 1844. Commodore Kearney was
followed by Caleb Cushing, sent out to China by President Tyler to
negotiate our first treaty with China, in 1844. Alexander H. Everett,
John W. Davis, Humphrey Marshall, and Robert M. McLane served
successively as commissioners to China from 1845 to 1854. Then Dr.
Peter Parker, missionary doctor, who had served variously as interpreter, advisor, and charge' ad interim since 1844, was made
commissioner and served until August, 1857. William B. Reed was
the first to serve in the newly elevated rank of envoy extraordinary
and minister plenipotentiary, 1857-1858, and finally John E. Ward,
the first American official to enter Peking, closed the period ending
in December, 1860.

The Chinese personnel who dealt with this succession of American
commissioners and ministers has always been shadowy and unreal. Due
to the fact that there was no foreign office or department of state in the
government at Peking, it has been assumed that China had neither
foreign minister nor foreign policy. True as this was prior to 1841,
it does not represent the actual picture from that date to 1861, when
China formally instituted the Tsungli Yamen or Foreign Office at the
capital. Access to the voluminous Chinese documents dealing with
"barbarian affairs" for this important interim period makes it clear
that a kind of foreign minister, in one form or another, did exist in
China. In other words, there was, during this period, a succession
of Chinese officials who gave serious concern to, or even devoted a
large portion of their time and energy to, the problem of foreign affairs. It also transpires that, stumbling and tentative though they
were, steps were taken toward the formulation of a Chinese foreign
policy or, at least, certain attitudes toward "foreign devils" were
formed on the part of a small group of Chinese officials.

The question of attitudes is dealt with in the following chapter.

---

1 The American official record of this period is well summarized by Tyler Dennett,
Americans in Eastern Asia, New York, 1922, p. 91-241, 279-345.

The present purpose is to examine the personnel factor on the Chinese side of the picture. Only those persons with whom the Americans dealt will be considered, although most of these will be the same individuals with whom Britain, France, and Russia also dealt in their relations with China. In fact, it should be kept in mind that the United States was playing a minor and, at times, ignominious role on the Chinese stage. The principal role was played throughout by Great Britain.

The first high Chinese official to make an issue of foreign affairs was, of course, the famous Lin Tse-hsü (1785-1850), the dynamic imperial commissioner who was sent to Canton in 1838, to settle once and for all the opium question. [2] He was a major figure in Sino-British relations and might be regarded as China's first foreign minister from 1838 to his dismissal, September 28, 1840. Americans, however, had no direct dealings with Commissioner Lin and there are only passing references to him in the Sino-American documents.

Both Commodore Kearney and Caleb Cushing, however, dealt with Ch'i-yung or Kiying, who was virtually Chinese foreign minister from 1842 to 1848. Ch'i-ying, who died in 1858, was an imperial clansman, which meant that he was able to trace his descent back direct to the founder of the dynasty, Hsien-tsu or Nurhachi (1583-1615), and that he was entitled to wear the yellow girdle. As a Manchu he belonged to the Plain Blue Banner, which was next to the last of the eight banners. He had grown up as companion of Emperor Hsüan-tsung (of the Tao-kuang period) and became his trusted personal minister after the latter ascended the throne in 1820. Prior to 1842, he held various posts of responsibility and profit in the Peking government, but had done nothing to point to a career in foreign affairs. If there was any trend in his career before this time, it was one indicative of financial and military abilities. Toward the end of the first Opium War, Ch'i-ying was appointed Tartar General of Canton with the idea of taking aggressive measures against the British. Before he reached his new post, the British were moving up the Yangtze River. Ch'i-ying tarried in Central China, where first-hand observation of British arms convinced him of the necessity of concluding peace. He had already been made an imperial commissioner and in this capacity he headed the Chinese delegation which accepted British terms on board a British warship under the walls of Nanking, August 29, 1842.

Captain Granville G. Loch, with the British party at Nanking, described Ch'i-ying as follows:

---

2 Formal biographical notices with appropriate references are listed alphabetically
   in the appendix of this volume. For biographies of all important persons, see
   also Arthur W. Hummel (ed.), *Eminent Chinese of the Ch'ing Period*, 2 v., Washington,
   1943-1944.

His age may be between sixty and seventy: he is a stout, hale, good-
humored-looking old gentleman with a firm step and upright carriage. At
first we were prejudiced against his intellectual endowments, but when
business commenced, he threw off his apparent dullness, and became all
animation, and evinced considerable shrewdness and observation. He wore
a dark silk dress without embroidery, girded by a yellow belt, the indication of his high birth, and a summer cap with a red opaque ball and
peacock's feather.[3]

This graphic picture of Ch'i-ying is footnoted by the handsome
portrait which was specially made for and presented to Caleb Cushing
in 1844.[4] A contemporary estimate of Ch'i-ying's policy is made by
Sir John Francis Davis, who was also present on board H. M. S.
Cornwallis in 1842:

To Keying the case was comparatively new, for until lately he had been
occupied at a distance in Manchouria. But he was thoroughly acquainted
with the true interests of the Tartar dynasty. Taught by recent events,
he proceeded on the conviction that this war could not go on without
endangering the throne. He acted on private instructions, to consider
no sacrifice too great to prevent such a crisis, and that whatever was
done with that view would be approved, if not by the cabinet (of whom
some are always Chinese), yet by the emperor and the high Manchow
officers. With him it was a question of facts and figures. He showed
that so much would be lost by protracting the struggle, and so much
gained by immediately bringing it to a conclusion. When difficulties
occurred, he dispelled them by a short and cogent argument. "If we do
not make peace, all is lost."[5]

Cushing described Ch'i-ying more formally as "a Manchu of high
qualities of head and heart, and of perfect accomplishment."[6] Like
the British, the American delegation found him conciliatory, cooperative, intelligent, and, particularly when stimulated by a little liquor,
affable and even maudlin.

The importance of Ch'i-ying, however, lies in the fact that he became, in 1844, the first Chinese official formally commissioned by the
emperor to handle foreign affairs, in addition to his ordinary duties as
governor general of Liang-kuang.[7] With this act he became China's
first foreign minister, and in this capacity he served for four years,
1844-1848. As long as he remained at Canton, China's foreign policy
was one of conciliation, adjustment, and realism. This was de-

---

3 Quoted by Harley Farnsworth MacNair, *Modern Chinese History: Selected Readings*,
   Shanghai, 1923, p. 168-169.

4 Now in the Boston Museum of Fine Arts.

5 Quoted by MacNair, *op. cit.*, 173-174.

6 Fuess, Claude M., *The Life of Caleb Cushing*, 2 v., New York, 1923, v.1, p. 441.

7 Edict, April 22, 1844, IWSM.TK 71; 18b-19a.

nounced by the "war party" at Peking as pusillanimous. Despite the
emperor's loyal support of Ch'i-ying, he was recalled in 1848, denounced on November 30, 1850, for having "oppressed the people to
please the foreigners, " and degraded.

The Chinese "foreign office" continued to be in Canton until 1858,
with the powers of imperial commissioner attached to the governor
general. Both the personality and the policy which marked the Ch'i-ying
period were lacking, however, and the next three commissioners drove
the foreigners to Shanghai for redress of their grievances. Ch'i-ying
was succeeded by Hsü Kuang-chin (native of Lu-i, Honan; chin-shih of
1820; died 1858), a Chinese who had been governor of Kwangtung since
1846. When he became acting governor general and imperial commissioner in 1848, he quickly terminated the "era of good feeling"
which Ch'i-ying had inaugurated, pursued a policy of non-intercourse
with foreigners, encouraged the Cantonese gentry and rabble to resist
the British in their attempts to secure entrance to the "city" of Canton,
and generally paved the way for the breakdown of foreign relations
which came after him.

The third Canton "foreign minister" was the notorious Yeh Ming-
ch'en (1807-1859). Well known in Western annals as Viceroy Yeh, he
was a native of Han-yang, Hupeh, a chin-shih of 1835, and Hanlin
academician. Both Britons and Americans regarded him as obstinate,
uncommunicative, and committed to a policy of virtual repudiation of
the treaties of 1842-1844. Most of his dealings were with the British,
whose prisoner he eventually became. Americans were only slightly
involved in the developments in Canton which led to the second Anglo-
Chinese War in 1858. Despite the obstructive tactics Imperial Commissioner Yeh used at Canton, his numerous and detailed memorials
reveal him as a serious and intelligent student of Chinese foreign
relations. His policy was the opposite of that of Ch'i-ying. He hoped
to hold the treaties to the absolute minimum in interpretation, to
separate the other powers from China's principal foe, Great Britain,
and to build up a military force which would ultimately make it possible to repel the foreigners. His two specific objectives were first,
to prevent the British from access to the city of Canton, and second,
to block treaty revision at the end of twelve years, which was provided
in the American treaty. Yeh Ming-ch'en had a thorough knowledge of
the treaties and made serious attempts to utilize English materials.
It is perhaps as good a comment on his intellectual curiosity as any to
note that when he was finally captured by the British and carried to
India as a prisoner, he spent his time reading the London Times and
studying the parliamentary debates.

After the recall of Ch'i-ying in 1848, the actual handling of China's
foreign relations shifted more and more from Canton to Shanghai. There
were several reasons for this, the first being the rapid development of
Shanghai as the major port of China. Trade and money were rapidly

gravitating to Shanghai, which by 1850 had already equalled and was soon to outstrip Canton as a commercial port. Besides this main fact, other minor ones contributed to the foreign gravitation to Shanghai. It had no background of the Co-hong and trade regulations which lay heavy on Canton. The Shanghai populace was generally friendly and free from the violent anti-foreignism which swept over Canton from time to time. Finally, in Shanghai a new type of Chinese merchant and official was arising, tied to foreign trade and the treaties, personally intimate with foreigners, and rapidly acquiring an entirely new outlook on the world and on China's place in it.

This new development in Chinese foreign relations is well represented by Wu Chien-chang. Known to foreigners generally as "Samqua" and to his Chinese contemporaries, even in Peking, as an "expert on barbarian affairs," Wu was a Cantonese, native of Hsiang-shan (now called Chung-shan), on the delta below Canton and contiguous to the Portuguese colony of Macao. "Samqua" was probably never the head of the T'ung-shun Hong, founded in Canton in 1832, but he was certainly a member of the family that controlled it, and both his money and his background were from the Canton Co-hong or Chinese Merchants' Guild, which had a monopoly of foreign trade until 1842. Wu became collegian of the Imperial Academy, obtaining his degree by purchase. He served as acting tao-t'ai of Shanghai in 1843, and continued as "expectant" until 1851, when he again became acting tao-t'ai in virtual charge of Shanghai's foreign relations. He was concurrently superintendent of customs. Moreover, he was closely identified, possibly as partner, with the American firm of Russell and Company, and had many American friends. When the Triad Rebels captured Shanghai in 1853, Wu took refuge with Americans, and when Chinese customs collections broke down, he sanctioned the first Foreign Inspectorate. He later organized China's first modern navy--a fleet of foreign ships hired by him to assist in the recapture of Shanghai by imperialist forces. July 11, 1854, he was impeached for embezzlement-of funds and collusion with foreigners (specifically, Russell and Company) and was sentenced to deportation the following April. Appeals of friends and generous donations to the imperial war chest secured his pardon and, as late as 1858, he is still mentioned as expectant tao-t'ai at Shanghai.

Wu Chien-chang's career is significant, for this is a transitional period of China's foreign relations. His wealth came from foreign trade and his usefulness from his knowledge and understanding of foreigners. High Chinese officials respected him because of his proficiency in English, which made it impossible for interpreters to take advantage of him. Actually, his English was the broken pidgin of Canton godowns, but it was probably as good as his outlandish Cantonese Mandarin. The British laughed at his presumptuousness and were inclined to regard him with derision and suspicion, but Americans, both merchants and officials, seem to have had a high respect for him. A modern scholar concludes that "there can be no doubt that Samqua was a shrewd man gifted with persistence and relatively sophisticated as to barbarian ways."[8]

While Wu Chien-chang was dominating the scene at Shanghai, his superior and memorialist was Hsü Nai-chao, governor of Kiangsu. Governor Hsü avoided foreign contacts, refused to meet American Commissioner McLane, and relied wholly upon Tao-t'ai Wu. When Hsü Nai-chao was removed from office, July 7, 1854, one of the charges against him was his blind confidence in Wu Chien-chang and his support of the latter's pro-foreign commercial policy.

The next real foreign minister of China was Ho Kuei-ch'ing (1816-1862), a Yunnanese, chin-shih of 1835, and Hanlin academician. Appointed governor general of Liang-chiang in 1857, his primary concern was the Taiping Rebellion, but in the course of his official duties he became more and more involved in the foreign affairs of Shanghai, which fell within his jurisdiction. After the negotiation of the treaties at Tientsin in 1858, he was made a member of the imperial commission set up at Shanghai to revise the tariff schedule and commercial regulations, supplementary to the treaties. He emerged as one of the statesmen of the period.

Ho Kuei-ch'ing has had no particular recognition by Western writers, but his memorials from 1857 to 1860 show a realistic understanding of "barbarian affairs." His foreign policy involved (1) rejection of the "Secret Plan" concocted at court to secure abrogation of the treaties in exchange for free trade; (2) recognition of the fallacy of trying to play one Western power off against another; (3) advocacy of the purchase of Western arms and ships, the adoption of Western military training and organization, and the employment of Western aid in suppressing the Taipings. He argued this broad, liberal policy with an intelligence and courage which placed him ahead of his colleagues of this period. He was opposed by the court party and in the end was officially proved to be a physical coward. He was tried and executed in Peking in 1862, despite the efforts of many friends, including foreigners, to save him.

The last official figure in the Shanghai scene for this period was Hsüeh Huan (1815-1880). A native of Szechwan and chü-jen of the Tao-kuang period, Hsüeh is the one "liberal" of this period who survived the opposition of the court party and continued in power into the post-1860 period.

Hsüeh Huan became Shanghai tao-t'ai in 1857, and in connection with his duties in organizing volunteers to expel the Triad Rebels from the city, he made many contacts with Chinese and foreign merchants

---

8   Fairbank, J.K.,"The Provisional System at Shanghai in 1853-54," *Chinese Social and Political Science Review*, v. 18 (January, 1935), p. 475.

and with the foreign consuls. Enjoying the powerful and understanding support of Ho Kuei-ch'ing, he was virtually in charge of foreign affairs in Shanghai from 1857 to 1862. In October, 1858, he was made judicial commissioner (vice-governor) of Kiangsu province and assisted in negotiating the tariff schedule with England and France. Like his superior, Ho Kuei-ch'ing, he opposed the "Secret Plan" of the court to cancel the Tientsin treaties, and, when the imperial commission arrived from Peking committed to this plan, persuaded them not to present it to the foreign envoys. Despite the emperor's exasperation with the commissioners for listening to this advice, he recognized Hsüeh Huan's grasp of foreign affairs. The documents carry the emperor's autograph Vermilion Comment that if the foreigners insisted on residence in Peking, "Hsüeh Huan must be kept in the capital as permanent director."[9] This is probably the first imperial suggestion of the possibility of having a Chinese foreign minister reside in Peking.

Hsüeh was later called to Tientsin and to Peking to assist in foreign affairs. In 1860, he was made Imperial Commissioner in-charge-of Commercial Affairs of the Five Ports, with the rank of governor and the temporary authority of governor general. This appointment indicates the intention of the court to keep foreign affairs out of Peking as long as possible, despite the reluctant establishment of the Tsungli Yamen, and would have resulted in Shanghai replacing Canton as the location of China's foreign office. Hsüeh continued to serve in Shanghai, where his memorials reveal a solid business sense, statesmanship, and diplomacy, such as few Chinese officials possessed during this period. He had Ch'i-ying's knack of reporting to the throne in terms that made a complete reversal of traditional policy palatable to the emperor and court. He advocated and passed on to Ho Kuei-ch'ing, and to the Peking government, adoption of foreign arms, industry, trade methods, and even urged the reform of China's documentary style in dealing with foreigners. He was proud of his ability to get along with the merchants and consuls at Shanghai, and saw no loss to China in the process.

Hsüeh was appointed to the Tsungli Yamen in 1862, and continued an active participation in China's foreign affairs until his retirement in 1877.

When the handling of China's foreign relations was shifted from Shanghai to Tientsin, the principal figure on the Chinese side was a Manchu named Kuei-liang (1785-1862), who was seventy years old before he ever saw a foreigner. His first assignment was to deal with Bowring and McLane at Tientsin in 1854, and for the next eight years, Kuei-liang played a prominent part in diplomacy. A Manchu plain red bannerman, father-in-law of Prince Kung, and with a distinguished

---

9 IWSM.HF 38; 3a,3.

official career, Kuei-liang was a suitable person to form the link
between the period of the "provincial foreign office, " located successively in Canton, Shanghai, and Tientsin, and the Peking headquarters,
the Tsungli Yamen, set up in 1861.

An American observer, Dr. S. Wells Williams, described Kuei-
liang in 1858 as "a well-preserved man of seventy-four, tall and not
too large for his height, placid in speech and countenance, having a
stoop of the shoulders and a quavering tone of voice, which more than
anything else indicates his age. " Another American noted his "kindly
aspect and gentle demeanor. "[10]

In 1858, Kuei-liang was co-negotiator and signer of the treaties of
Tientsin, including that of the United States (William B. Reed). He
was later sent to Shanghai to negotiate the tariff schedule, secretly
instructed to offer the foreigners "free trade" at the ports if they
would forego the four most obnoxious provisions of the treaties, including residence at Peking. Kuei-liang was persuaded by Ho Kuei-
ch'ing and Hsüeh Huan to abandon this "Secret Plan, " but did secure a
promise that the powers would not insist on permanent residence in
the capital. He was prepared to fulfil the residual treaty provisions,
including exchange of ratifications in Peking, in good faith. In 1859,
it was Kuei-liang who met United States Commissioner Ward and
arranged for his visit to Peking and exchange of ratifications at Pei-
t'ang. The following year, when the British and French returned
north, Kuei-liang was again sent to negotiate. After the hostilities
and occupation of Peking by the Allies, Kuei-liang was a member of
the commission, headed by his son-in-law, Prince Kung, which signed
the treaties. When the Tsungli Yamen was set up in January, 1861,
Kuei-liang was a member of the new foreign office and later became
grand councillor. Thus, he continued active in foreign affairs until
his death in 1862.

As for the personnel directing foreign affairs in Peking, only the
most general comment can be made on the basis of the Chinese documents. The Grand Council, on the whole, acted anonymously, either
in the name of the emperor or as a body. The names of individual
grand councillors rarely occur either in the memorials or the edicts.
There are references, particularly in contemporary Western documents, to a "war party" at court and to a cleavage between Manchus,
who were regarded as conciliatory and pro-foreign, and Chinese, who
were regarded as vindictive haters of the foreign devils. There is no
way of substantiating or refuting these theories from the Chinese
documents themselves. However, certain generalizations can be
made about the personalities which dominated foreign policy in the
Peking government. [11]

---

10 Both quotations cited by Fang Chao-ying in Hummel, *op. cit.*, v. 1, p. 430.

11 This does not preclude the possibility of further research, utilizing new

It seems probable that the friendly policy which prevailed through most of the Tao-kuang period, to 1848, was based on a triumvirate of prominent Manchus: Ch'i-ying, Mu-chang-a, and the Tao-kuang emperor himself. Both Ch'i-ying and Mu-chang-a were childhood companions of the emperor, who consistently favored them with responsible and lucrative positions and remained loyal to them until his death. It is this happy combination of Ch'i-ying in the field, Mu-chang-a in the Grand Council, and Hsüan-tsung (Tao-kuang) on the throne, which was the basis for the "era of good feeling" lauded by foreign observers.

Mu-chang-a (1782-1856) was born in the same year as his emperor. He was a member of the Bordered Blue Banner, received his chin-shih degree in 1805, and was admitted to the Hanlin Academy. After holding routine positions during the Chia-ch'ing period, he began his real official career when Hsüan-tsung came to the throne in 1820, and gradually acquired great power in the court, serving in such capacities as minister of the imperial household, president of the Censorate, and minister of the Court of Colonial Affairs. In 1828, he was made grand councillor and by 1837 had become the most powerful member of that body. From 1837 to 1848, the first crucial period of China's foreign relations, Mu-chang-a was virtual premier of China.

Mu-chang-a's policy appears to have been one of building up political power by means of a strong court faction supported by loyal followers in key positions in the provinces. There is little indication of real statesmanship or understanding of the new issues of foreign relations. He supported Ch'i-ying in a policy of conciliation and appeasement of the foreign powers and secured the approval of the Treaty of Nanking. This friendly combination was still in power when Cushing arrived in China and the Treaty of Wang-hsia (1844) received Mu-chang-a's approval. He was opposed by another grand councillor, Wang Ting (1768-1842), who is supposed to have committed suicide as a protest to the humiliating Treaty of Nanking.

Mu-chang-a also incurred the enmity of the heir apparent, and when Wen-tsung (Hsien-feng) came to the throne, an edict of December 1, 1850 denounced Mu-chang-a and deprived him of all official duties. His eminent service saved him from exile or execution, but his official career ended and he never served again under the new emperor.

During this period of Mu-chang-a's domination of the Grand Council, there were at all times two Manchus (or Mongols) and three Chinese councillors. The other non-Chinese were first Lung-wen, a Manchu, until January 1841, and then Sai-shang-a, a Mongol (died 1875), who was dismissed in the autumn of 1852, ten months after Mu-chang-a's

---

materials, revealing a full and fascinating story of the inner workings of the Grand Council. Such study will have to be based on private papers of the individuals involved.

dismissal. Both Lung-wen and Sai-shang-a were military men; although foreigners regarded Lung-wen as friendly, little is known of the foreign policy of either. Of the Chinese grand councillors, Wang Ting has already been mentioned as opposing Ch'i-ying's appeasement policy in 1842 and, reportedly, committing suicide in protest. P'an Shih-en (1770-1854) was a scholar without any interest in foreign affairs, while as to Ho Ju-lin, nothing is known of his foreign policy, if any. Foreign affairs were still a minor concern of the Chinese government as a whole, and it is probable that Mu-chang-a's opinion predominated as long as he was head of the Grand Council.

The only other grand councillor known to be a war-monger and opponent of Mu-chang-a, was another Chinese, Ch'i Chü-tsao (1793-1866). He succeeded Wang Ting in 1843, and kept the loyal opposition alive after Wang's suicide. It is probable that Ch'i continued the war-party tradition in the court and that he was in the favor of Emperor Wen-tsung. At any rate, he rose in power and, on the dismissal of Sai-shang-a, became chief of the grand councillors, which lofty post he held for two years from the autumn of 1852. Finally, in October, 1854, he retired on sick leave and died in 1866. Ch'i Chün-tsao was a distinguished scholar, poet, and calligrapher, and his bitterly anti-foreign feelings were apparently academic and patriotic.

Before Ch'i Chün-tsao's retirement, Emperor Wen-tsung had already made an exception to the general rule and appointed an imperial prince to the Grand Council. I-hsin Prince Kung (1833-1898), sixth son of the Tao-kuang emperor, was a half-brother and boyhood companion of the heir apparent who became Emperor Wen-tsung (Hsien-feng). Prince Kung was summoned by imperial command, November 7, 1853, to assume office in the Grand Council; within three months he became the chief councillor. He shared the emperor's hostility to foreigners and probably headed the war-party in the court at Peking. He continued to lead the Grand Council until the autumn of 1856, when he was excused to prepare the texts for the Empress Dowager's funeral rites. He remained in obscurity for two or three years, suffering the emperor's displeasure, but gradually resumed power in the government. He continued to be anti-foreign and to advocate war against the barbarians. In 1858, he severely criticized the Tientsin treaties signed by his father-in-law, Kuei-liang, and in 1859 headed the commission which tried and punished Ch'i-ying.

Prince Kung's transformation from virulent barbarian-baiter to the enlightened minister and elder statesman of the last forty years of the nineteenth century came about through bitter humiliation. When the British and French occupied Peking and sacked the Summer Palace in 1860, the emperor fled to Jehol, never to return. It was Prince Kung's thankless duty to return to the capital in October, 1860, and sign the convention and treaties acknowledging China's final surrender to the West. It was at his suggestion, January 20, 1861, that the

Tsungli Yamen was established to handle China's foreign relations.

After Prince Kung's retirement from the Grand Council in 1855, he was replaced by another Manchu, Wen-ch'ing (1796-1856), who had already served in the Grand Council twice, once in 1837-1840, and again for a year (1847-1848) toward the end of the Tao-kuang era. Wen-ch'ing died in December, 1856, having served as head of the Council for sixteen months. There is no indication of his policy with regard to foreign affairs.

The last incumbent of the post of chief of the Grand Council was a Chinese, P'eng Yün-chang (1792-1862), who had served in the Grand Council since June, 1851. P'eng was a liberal, or at least a cautious moderate, in regard to foreign policy and opposed the war-party in the government. When he succeeded Wen-ch'ing in 1857, he supported Ho Kuei-ch'ing, who was recommending a constructive foreign policy in Shanghai. The possibility thus arose of another era of good feeling based on a combination such as had existed with Ch'i-ying and Mu-chang-a in the Tao-kuang era. This, however, would have been a Chinese, rather than a Manchu diplomatic team, and the focus would have been at Shanghai rather than at Canton. That no such happy denouement of the Chinese foreign policy drama came about is probably due to two factors. First, the opposition to P'eng Yün-chang was no longer that of a frustrated Chinese, such as Wang Ting who had committed suicide in 1842. Rather, he was opposed by the rabid anti-foreign Manchu grand councillor, Mu-yin, who precipitated the hostilities in 1860. Second, P'eng Yün-chang's imperial master was not "Reason's Glory, " Tao-kuang, but Emperor Wen-tsung (Hsien-feng), who consistently favored the war-party throughout the eleven years of his reign.

Consequently this interim period of China's foreign relations, during which she experimented with administrative machinery and policies, and when Manchu and Chinese officials variously tried their skills at diplomacy, ended with a tragic victory for those councillors who would defy the barbarians and drive them from China. The result was foreign violence within the walls of the Forbidden City and the Imperial gardens of Peking. This violence, beginning at Canton, spread to Nanking, battered down the Ta-ku forts, pushed up the Pei-ho to Tientsin, and finally, in 1860, breached the walls of Peking and drove emperor and court in flight out of China itself to Jehol.

Finally, in presenting the dramatis personae of China's foreign relations from 1841 to 1861, the principal characters must needs be the emperors themselves. Despite the vast hierarchy of Chinese officials, Manchu bannermen, imperial clansmen, grand secretaries and grand councillors, the modern scholar, like the nineteenth century observer, is confronted with the reality of personal rule. The emperor still had to play the ultimate role in every state act. This was particularly true in an unorthodox field like that of the new type

of foreign relations with which China was now confronted. The emper-
or not only determined the principles and formulated the policies,
selected the officials and expelled those who failed to carry out his
wishes; he also read the memorials reporting to him the details of
negotiations with foreigners, made marginal and inter-linear comments
on these memorials, indicated in autograph endorsements the action
that should be taken, and even on occasion wrote out an edict in vermilion ink. Thus, particularly in the new field of foreign affairs, the
emperor was no mere figurehead. He could be and in some instances
probably was actually the foreign minister of China.

     This period covers parts of two reigns: first, the Tao-kuang reign
(1820-1850), when the monarch was Emperor Hsüan-tsung; and second,
the Hsien-feng reign (1851-1861), when the ruler was Emperor Wen-
tsung. No attempt will be made to describe or evaluate these two
emperors or to characterize their reigns. However, a few general
statements will be ventured, which may contribute to an understanding
of the foreign relations of this period. Also some specific data will be
presented from the Chinese documents concerning the United States.

     Emperor Hsüan-tsung (1782-1850), whose personal name was Min-
ning, displayed the martial qualities of his Manchu race by his skill at
archery, his fondness for hunting, and his predilection for military
activities. At the age of thirty-eight he came to the throne as the
sixth emperor of the Ch'ing or Manchu dynasty. His reign (1820-1850)
was designated Tao-kuang, which his only English biographer has
translated as "Reason's Glory."[12] Emperor Hsüan-tsung was plagued
with problems of overpopulation and a reduced standard of living, with
floods and famines and rebellions. Most of these difficulties he
interpreted as economic and undertook government economies and
special levies to meet them.

     Emperor Hsüan-tsung was also faced with the opium question,
which combined official corruption, drainage of silver from the country,
and demoralization of the people, and ended in foreign attack and invasion of Chinese territory. The emperor supported Lin Tse-hsü's
opium suppression policy but, when this failed, supported Ch'i-ying's
conciliation program. Although Emperor Hsüan-tsung's actions
during the first Opium War (1839-1842) showed "indecision, ignorance, and miserliness,"[13] he did have enough realism to accept
the inevitable and to overrule the war-party in his court. He continued his support of Ch'i-ying and Mu-chang-a's policy until 1848,
and his personal support of these two ministers until his death.

     The best indication of Emperor Hsüan-tsung's personal concern
with foreign affairs is the record of the period. In the present study,

---

12 Gutzlaff, Charles, *Life of Taou-Kwang*, London, 1852.

13 Fang Chao-ying in Hummel, *op. cit.*, v. 1, p. 575.

seventy-two memorials dealing with or affecting the United States have
been translated. Thirty-three or nearly half bear chu-p'i, "vermilion
endorsements, " written by the emperor's own hand. [14] These endorsements or comments were written on the original memorial by the emper-
or, in vermilion ink which was reserved for his exclusive use. The
endorsed memorials were then returned to the memorialists. Copies
of them made for the archives preserved these imperial endorsements
in red ink, and were classified as hung-pen or "red memorials. " [15]

The comments made by Emperor Hsüan-tsung on memorials dealing with the United States are not uniform. Of the thirty-three vermilion
endorsements, twelve are limited to three characters each, the laconic
chih-tao-la. This stock phrase means literally, "We know it" or "Noted, "
and is scrawled in vermilion ink at the end of memorials which the
emperor has perused. Perhaps the nearest equivalent in modern official routine is the next to meaningless "OK. " At most this endorsement means that the emperor has read the memorial. It indicates no
approval or criticism of the memorial and gives no clue to the form
the edict in reply is to take. On the other hand, this meagre endorsement does not necessarily mean that the emperor has given any serious
attention to the matter at all. It may merely mean that the memorial
has passed through his hands.

Nine of the thirty-three endorsements made by Emperor Hsüan-
tsung, however, are specific comments and recommendations. These
remarks are often caustic and incisive and indicate strong opinions on
the matters raised in the memorial. This type of vermilion endorsement may run to several lines or a page or more. The phraseology is
not stereotyped; rather it is often colorful and colloquial, leaving no
doubt of the imperial praise or blame directed at the memorialist.
This type of endorsement not only shows keen imperial interest in the
subject matter, but constitutes a specific directive for action. The
purport and often the phraseology of the endorsement is incorporated
into an edict which executes the imperial will.

In addition to the foregoing twelve formal and nine specific endorsements on the Tao-kuang memorials, there are twelve vermilion endorsements in the form of interlinear or marginal comments. These are
dashed onto the memorial as immediate reactions of the emperor to the
report of the memorialist. They express his strong revulsion to the
opium traffic, his disgust with official weakness and corruption (particularly when any attempt to deceive the emperor is detected), his
deep concern for money matters, and his conventional attitude toward
barbarians. At the same time, however, they reveal a realistic acceptance of the facts of foreign trade, of the ineffectiveness of his own

---

14 Fairbank and Teng, *op. cit.*, HJAS, 5(1949).49.

15 *Ibid.*, p. 52.

military forces, and of the overwhelming force of foreign, particularly British, arms. These interlinear endorsements are indicative
of the personal rule of Emperor Hsüan-tsung and also of the personality
of the ruler.

The second reign comprising this interim period is that of Emper-
or Wen-tsung, whose reign period is designated Hsien-feng, "All
Prosperous" — a title more hopeful than descriptive, as his reign was
even more disastrous than that of his father. I-chu, who ruled China
from 1850 to 1861 as Emperor Wen-tsung, was the fourth son of
Hsüan-tsung, and grew up with his half brother, I-hsin Prince Kung,
whose mother educated both of them. The Hsien-feng era saw two
major crises for China and the Manchu dynasty: the Taiping Rebellion
and a second international war, this time with the allied fleets of
England and France hammering at Ta-ku and Tientsin and allied
armies occupying Peking.

Unlike Hsüan-tsung, Emperor Wen-tsung appears to have been
definitely hostile to foreigners. Instead of restraining and over-ruling
the war-party at court, he either supported it or acquiesced in its
provocative, anti-foreign program.

If the documents of the Hsien-feng period dealing with the United
States are at all indicative of the energy of Emperor Wen-tsung and of
his interest in foreign affairs, he was no less of a personal ruler than
his predecessor. The ratios of memorials to imperial endorsements
of the two reign periods are almost the same.

For the Hsien-feng period, two hundred and twenty memorials
dealing with the United States have been translated. Ninety-four of
these, or again nearly one-half, bear vermilion endorsements. Like
the imperial comments of the Tao-kuang period, Emperor Wen-tsung's
endorsements show varying degrees of interest in and understanding of
foreign relations. Forty of the ninety-four endorsements are formal,
chih-tao-la ("Noted") scrawls at the end of as many memorials. Fifteen
others are only slightly more indicative of imperial concern. This
second group varies in terminology but all the notations are general,
e. g., "Read and comprehended, " "Thoroughly understood, " etc., without any specific opinion or reaction being expressed. Thus fifty-five of
the endorsements are formal or general.

Thirty, however, or nearly one third of the total, are specific
comments in which the emperor often expressed himself at length and
forcefully. As would be expected from the foregoing generalizations
about the Hsien-feng reign, his views are inclined to be vindictive and
chauvinistic. He supported the non-cooperative and provocative policy
of Yeh Ming-ch'en and condemned the weakness and conciliation of Ho
Kuei-ch'ing and Wu Chien-chang. Perhaps Wen-tsung's position is
best indicated in his bitter condemnation and punishment of Ch'i-ying
(1858) and his high praise for the Mongol hero of 1859, Prince General
Seng-ko-lin-ch'in.

Besides the thirty vermilion endorsements involving specific comments, there are two other indices of Emperor Wen-tsung's personal interest in affairs of state. There are seven instances of interlinear or marginal comments and two vermilion edicts, that is, edicts drafted and copied out by the emperor personally. The first vermilion edict is dated June 29, 1858, and orders the death, by suicide, of Ch'i-ying, following his condemnation by the Imperial Clan Court. The second vermilion edict, dated June 6, 1859, authorizes the exchange of ratifications at Peking after all attempts to have the exchange effected at Shanghai had failed.

When the Allied armies entered Peking, the emperor fled to Jehol. The failure of China's arms, particularly the inability of Prince Seng-ko-lin-ch'in to stop the alien tide, completely unnerved him. He entrusted peace negotiations and, subsequently, foreign affairs to Prince Kung, while the remainder of the administration fell largely to the Manchu imperial clansman, Su-shun. [16] Meanwhile, at Jehol, from which place he never returned, the emperor "gave himself to excesses, probably with a view to self-destruction." [17] He died August 11, 1861, but the era of which he was the latter exponent had ended a year before with his flight from Peking.

Finally, there remain for recognition in this period those official, semi-official, and unofficial underlings who point the way to a new era in China's foreign relations and international status.

Some of these trail-blazers were local gentry, merchants, or even servants whose knowledge of barbarian affairs and smattering of pidgin English made them indispensable to the local governors, governors general, and imperial commissioners who found themselves unable to cope with barbarian affairs. Others were expectant local officials, often wealthy hong merchants who had bought official rank, and whose knowledge of foreign trade, customs, administration, finance, or banking offered skills which had suddenly become necessary but were hardly to be found in the classically trained Chinese official or in the aristocratic military-minded Manchus of the nineteenth century. Some of this new class of experts made their contribution through personal contact and familiarity with foreigners; some were charlatans, servants or coolies who capitalized on a smattering of English; some acquired foreign mannerisms to pose as authorities on the Western world. Finally, a special category of pioneers arose. These latter were gentry and officials who became interested in Western knowledge, machinery, armament, munitions, and ship-building, and who hoped to introduce these novelties into China.

On the whole, this new group of Chinese, who anticipate the

---

16 See Hummel, *op. cit.*, v. 2, p. 666-669.

17 Fang Chao-ying in Hummel, *op. cit.*, v. 1, p. 380.

returned student, liberal reformer, and revolutionary by a couple of generations, must always remain anonymous. Undoubtedly hundreds of Chinese in Canton and Shanghai were getting new ideas and forming new attachments during this period to 1861, and their names will never be known.

However, in the documents dealing with the United States, about forty-five "barbarian experts" and pioneers are mentioned at least by name, and some of their activities are described in enough detail to warrant mention. Naturally, almost none of these humble people has a biography in a standard collection or receives mention in Chinese history. Whatever is known of them has to be gleaned from the context of the memorials of the period. It should be kept in mind, moreover, that the ones hereinafter cited are only those whose names appear in the documents concerning the United States. The same persons and many others would undoubtedly be found in the documents dealing with other countries for the same period.

The first group centers around Ch'i-ying. From the time Ch'i-ying began dealing with the British at Nanking and later at Canton and the Bogue, he was keenly aware of the need for specialists in dealing with foreigners, and much of his success was undoubtedly due to the fact that he relied heavily on them. Once he discovered this kind of competence in a man, he sought him out whenever special need arose. For instance, one Ch'en Pai-ling[18] was a garrison officer at Canton in 1842, who assisted Ch'i-ying in his negotiations with the British at the Bogue. In 1843 when Ch'i-ying was governor general of Liang-chiang, he recalled that Ch'en Pai-ling was "thoroughly familiar with the barbarian temper," found him serving as chiliarch of the Hung-hu (Hunan) regiment, and drafted him to investigate the foreign situation on the Kiangsu seaboard and on the island of Chusan. At the same time he recognized in Ch'iu Yung-an, serving as a sergeant in the Nanking city garrison, another "barbarian expert," and sent him on the mission with Ch'en Pai-ling. There is no way of knowing wherein the competence of these men lay, but it is significant that Ch'i-ying sought them out and utilized them.

As soon as Ch'i-ying was ordered to return to Canton to meet Caleb Cushing and negotiate the American treaty, he began to look around for experts who had helped him during the negotiations with England in 1842 and 1843. At Nan-hsiung, Kwangtung, en route to Canton, he met Chao Ch'ang-ling, a Cantonese, one-time prefect of of Chao-ch'ing, Kwangtung, and expectant ministerial secretary.

---

18 The Chinese characters and all the biographical material available for the persons mentioned in this section will be found listed alphabetically in the glossary of biographical references at the end of the book.

Chao had worked closely with Ch'i-ying at Canton in 1843, and was regarded as an expert on barbarian affairs. Ch'i-ying was delighted to meet him at Nan-hsiung and promptly drafted him to assist in negotiating the American treaty. Ch'en Chih-kang had been an officer in the Canton garrison in 1843, had assisted in the negotiations, and Ch'i-ying was disappointed to find that he was not available in 1844. He did secure the assistance of Wu T'ing-hsien, a Cantonese, probably a member of the famous hong-merchant family. Wu was a degraded official on probation, but Ch'i-ying regarded him as "thoroughly conversant with the barbarian conditions" and was glad to utilize his talents. At least one Manchu was regarded by Ch'i-ying as a barbarian expert. Consequently, T'ung-lin, expectant sub-prefect, was also enlisted to advise him in the negotiations.

Another whose aid Ch'i-ying sought in 1844 was not an anonymous underling. Wen-feng (died 1860) was a Chinese plain yellow bannerman, whose original Chinese surname was T'ung. He was Canton Customs Superintendent (Hoppo) and as early as 1842 became interested in a project to build or purchase Western type warships. He assisted Ch'i-ying in the negotiation of the supplementary Treaty of the Bogue in 1843. This was not his last appearance in the foreign relations field, however. In 1860, when the emperor fled before the British and French armies, Wen-feng was left behind to defend the Summer Palace. When the Allies sacked and burned the palace, Wen-feng drowned himself in the artificial lake in the imperial garden and thus achieved immortality as a loyal, though ineffective, minister.

In the later Canton period, 1856-1858, other specialists in barbarian affairs were sought out and utilized. In 1856, after the breakdown of negotiations following the Arrow incident and the bombardment of Canton by British naval units, two Cantonese were employed by Imperial Commissioner Yeh Ming-ch'en to treat with the British Consul, Harry Parkes. One of these was a member of the Canton gentry named Su T'ing-k'uei, of whom nothing further is known. The other was Wu Ch'ung-yüeh (1810-1863), fifth son of Wu Ping-chien, and, like his father, a hong merchant known to foreigners as Houqua, and head of the I-ho Company (known in contemporary literature as Ewo Hong). Wu Ch'ung-yüeh was the wealthiest member of the Co-hong and the particular friend and patron of American merchants. His career is indicative of the rise of the Canton bourgeoisie and the dependence of Chinese officialdom upon this new class. He obtained, by purchase, his hsiu-ts'ai degree at the age of thirteen (sui), and his chü-jen degree in 1831, as a result of his father's contribution of 30,000 taels for flood control. During the next sixteen years he competed four times for his chin-shih degree, but failed every time. In 1833 he entered the Co-hong, and in 1843 inherited his father's immense fortune. His policy in dealing with the British was literally "peace at any price" and he was willing to pay the price

out of his own pocket. For his diplomatic efforts and his generous
contributions, Houqua was awarded the red coral button of a second
class official and the brevet rank of financial commissioner.

Imperial Commissioner Yeh Ming-ch'en employed a man named
Hsü Wen-shen as a kind of major domo for his meeting with British
and French military officers representing Lord Elgin and Baron Gros
aboard ship at White Goose Tything, opposite the Canton Bund,
December 12, 1857. Hsü was expectant assistant sub-prefect of Nan-
hai (Canton) and for years had handled the Canton government's
communications with barbarians. He had previously been deputy
magistrate of Kowloon, opposite Hong Kong. Yeh Ming-ch'en regarded him as invaluable because he was generally recognized and
trusted by Hong Kong officials and merchants. Although no specific
mention is made of it, he probably knew at least pidgin English.

Another type of extra-official function was performed by Lo Tun-
yen. Because of the practice of the Chinese government never to employ an official in his native province, regular magistrates and prefects were always aliens and had little personal influence with the
people. Consequently, when a native local leader was needed to stir
up the people, an expectant, degraded, or retired official was called
for. Lo Tun-yen was a native Cantonese, had served as board vice-
president in Peking, but was on leave. In 1858, he was ordered by
edict to enlist local militia and trainbands to drive the British from
Canton. Such a person, who both knew the barbarians and had the
respect of his fellow countrymen, was regarded as particularly suitable for this important service.

In Shanghai, where no tradition of foreign trade existed, experts
on barbarian affairs were particularly in demand. Cantonese, especially, capitalized on their long experience in dealing with foreigners, their
knowledge of English, and their business connections. When Shanghai
officials wanted to charter foreign warships to use against the Taiping
rebels in 1853, they employed Lieutenant Colonel Chang P'an-lung. He
was regarded as an expert because as a petty officer he had acted as
deputy for Commissioner Niu Chien at Nanking in 1842. Two Ningpo
merchants were employed by the Shanghai tao-t'ai to negotiate with
the foreign consuls in 1854 to secure their cooperation in defense
against the rebels. Chang T'ing-hsüeh, Hanlin bachelor and expectant
magistrate, was operating a foreign goods store. He was regarded as
a specialist on foreign affairs, and with his relative, Yang Fang, was
deputized to carry out negotiations for the charter and purchase of
foreign ships. Similarly, one Liang Chih, Cantonese expert, was
sought out by Shanghai officials to "manage" the foreigners in 1858.
Shanghai Tao-t'ai Wu Hsü, in 1859, made use of a merchant named
Hsi K'uan in an attempt to persuade the foreign envoys to exchange
ratifications in Shanghai and possibly to agree to some modification of
the Tientsin treaties. Ts'ai Chen-wu, Cantonese resident of Shanghai,

who had purchased the brevet rank of <u>tao-t'ai</u>, was reported by memorial to be "thoroughly familiar with barbarian affairs. " He was ordered by edict, September 24, 1858, to report to the Board of Civil Office at Peking for appointment to assist in the negotiations at Shanghai following the Tientsin treaties.

The profession of barbarian expert invited fraud. One Huang Chung-yü, Cantonese specialist in foreign affairs, was sought in 1859 to assist the imperial commissioners at Shanghai. He could not be located but was reported to be in Canton "wearing the button and sash of the fifth rank and conducting separate negotiations. " Actually he was a brevet first-class sub-prefect and district magistrate. He arrived in Shanghai, January 1, 1859, and enjoyed the full confidence of Kuei-liang. When the foreign envoys became difficult, he was ordered to talk them out of going to Peking--with what effect, is a matter of history. The use of these mountebanks was indicative of the contempt in which foreigners were held. They were supposed to meet the barbarian on his own level, to which the scholar-official could not stoop. It was a part of the classical axiom to "rule barbarians with misrule."

When negotiations shifted to Tientsin, Cantonese proficiency in barbarian affairs was even more in demand. Ch'en Chao-lin, native of Kwangtung, was local magistrate and director of the Fukien-Kwangtung Guildhall in Tientsin in 1858. He was recognized by Governor General T'an T'ing-hsiang as an expert on barbarian affairs and charged with the responsibility of raising trainbands to resist foreign invasion. Ch'en was also expected to check on his Cantonese and Fukienese compatriots in Tientsin, whose loyalty was somewhat suspect. To check on Ch'en and to assist in training local militia, the governor general appointed three natives of Chihli (Hopei), who were either expectants or officials on leave: Chen-lin, Ch'un-pao, and Fei Yin-chang.

Two officials who had participated in the negotiations with the British in 1850, Chang Ch'i-yüan and Chang Tien-yüan, were both regarded as "old barbarian hands" but were excused in 1854, when Bowring and McLane arrived, because of military responsibilities. Any contact with foreigners marked an official for further diplomatic duty, as well as for official suspicion. Ch'ing-ming, a Manchu, was director of the Board of Punishments in 1859. Because he had been associated with the imperial commission at Shanghai in 1858, he was delegated to assist in the exchange of ratifications with Ward at Peit'ang, August 16, 1859. Similarly, Ch'un Hsin-ho was one of the local officials who met the British in Tientsin in 1850. When Bowring and McLane came in 1854, he carried on the preliminary negotiations with Medhurst and Parker. By this time he was a veteran of foreign affairs and in 1858, now financial commissioner of Chihli (Hopei), he was summoned to assist in the negotiations before and after hostilities. His name appears on all the memorials up to the arrival of Kuei-liang and Hua-sha-na. Although he did not continue as a memorialist, his name is mentioned later so it is apparent that his advice was still sought by the imperial commissioners. Huang Hui-lien, a Cantonese who came to Tientsin with the British in 1858 and remained after the hostilities, spoke "fluent" English and was regarded as an authority on the West. He advised Prince Seng-ko-lin-ch'in on the Western practice of requiring indemnity of the party which asked for terms. In 1859, Huang was ordered to fraternize with the two British prisoners taken by Prince Seng, one of whom was thought to be an American but was actually a Canadian, in the hope of utilizing them to get terms from the British and French.

Incidentally, there is one expert on Russian affairs mentioned in the documents. Te-hsiang, a Manchu, assistant department director, apparently spoke Russian and was used as officer messenger and major domo in negotiations with the Russians in 1860. He became suspect, however, because he was too "intimate" with the Russians and was dismissed.

A final and quite different category of barbarian experts is represented by Chinese officials and merchants who recognized the weakness of China and the strength of Europe and consciously set out to do something about it. Some of these were academicians who advocated the acquisition of knowledge of the West; others were practical people who bought Western ships and guns, experimented in shipbuilding and munitions making, and emulated Western military and naval tactics. These were the pioneers who were to assume great prominence after 1860. During this earlier period, however, these men were ahead of their times and were going against, but trying to change, the tide. Only those pioneers who are mentioned in the documents dealing with the United States will be discussed here.

It is interesting to note, in this connection, that the two Chinese officials whom the foreigners regarded as the most virulent barbarian haters, Lin Tse-hsü and Yeh Ming-ch'en, were both intelligent students of the West and pioneers in the utilization of Western knowledge in China.

Imperial Commissioner Lin Tse-hsü (1785-1850) is best known for his vigorous enforcement of opium prohibition from 1838 to 1840, which provoked the first Anglo-Chinese war. During his Canton administration, however, he was impressed by Western knowledge and weapons. He employed a staff at his yamen to collect and translate such Western materials as were available, mostly periodicals. His principal interests were geography and science; in the latter field he concentrated on weapons and maritime defense.

The results of his researches were published under the title Ssu-Chou Chih or "World Gazeteer," which was a pioneer work in the field. Lin's work stimulated Wei Yüan (1794-1856), China's first scholar-geographer of the West, to compile his famous Hai Kuo T'u Chih,

"Atlas and Gazeteer of Foreign Countries, " which appeared in 1844. The practical importance of these studies is indicated in Wei Yüan's statement in his preface that "he compiled the Hai Kuo T'u Chih in the hope that it would be of service to his country in dealing with foreign nations. "[19]

Wei acknowledges Lin's Ssu Chou Chih as one of his sources. The real significance of Wei's work was only gradually realized by the Chinese. In 1858, when Peking was threatened by Allied forces, Wang Mao-yin, senior vice president of the Board of War, memorialized, July 9th, recommending that the Hai Kuo T'u Chih be made required reading for all officials entrusted with foreign affairs. He urged that the atlas and gazeteer be republished by the government and distributed to all officials.

The notorious Viceroy Yeh was less of a scholar than Lin Tse-hsü, but he did employ translators to extract and make available materials from Hong Kong newspapers and other English materials available in China. He showed a keen, if scornful, interest in British affairs and during his lonely exile in India, studied the London Times and the Parliamentary Debates.

Another pioneer geographer was Hsü Chi-yü (1795-1873), who was appointed financial commissioner of Fukien province. Here he met the American missionary, David Abeel, who gave him a world atlas. After five years study of this and other sources, Hsü published, in 1850, his Ying Huan Chih Lüeh or "World Geography. " He was denounced in 1851 for being too friendly with foreigners, and spent several years in retirement. He was eventually vindicated, however, and called to Peking, where he was appointed to the Tsungli Yamen in 1865, while his "World Geography" was reprinted the following year by the Chinese foreign office. His work was twice reprinted in Japan, 1859 and 1861. He served in the Tsungli Yamen until 1869.

Another academic pioneer was Lo Ping-chang (1793-1867), Cantonese authority on foreign affairs. Chin-shih of 1832 and Hanlin academician, Lo Ping-chang came to be regarded as an expert on Western naval warfare and armament. More scholastic was Chin Ying-lin, sub-director of the Grand Court of Revision, who memorialized on the strength of Western fleets and the necessity of building up a strong Chinese navy. Chin's knowledge, however, was strictly from the book. After reading descriptions of Western ships, he decided that they were no improvement over Chinese models. He recommended building up a strong navy composed of ships of various types drawn from Chinese history. Nevertheless, he was a forerunner of the later nineteenth century reformers, and his published writings, Ch'ih Hua T'ang and Shih Wen Chi, are important contributions.

---

19 Tu Lien-che in Hummel, *op. cit.*, v. 2, p. 851.

In Canton, however, more practical pioneers were at work. Fang Hsiung-fei, undergraduate at Canton in 1842, advised General I-shan on the corruption involved in the building of Chinese war junks, and urged the use of foreign ships. The real promoters were a group of wealthy and patiotic hong merchants. P'an Shih-ch'eng, well known to Americans in Canton as Puan Kei-qua, a member of the T'ung-wen Hong and descendant of the famous hong merchant, P'an Chen-ch'eng, was a recognized authority on foreign affairs and a trusted advisor of Ch'i-ying. In 1841-1842, P'an Shih-ch'eng built a Western-type war-ship, at his own expense, at a cost of 19,000 taels. He also bought foreign cannon and hired foreign artisans to build torpedoes in a plant near Canton. He later undertook to build a squadron to patrol the South China Sea, but after the hostilities of 1839-1842 were concluded, China lost interest in his project. He did succeed in interesting, temporarily, the Manchu general, Na-erh-ching-e, in building ships on Western models. Another of the Canton merchants, P'an Shih-jung, built a small steamer near Canton and launched it in 1842, in inland waters. He was convinced, however, that the machinery was too complicated for native workmen. Hence he recommended, if further steam navigation were to be attempted, that foreign artisans be recruited in Macao. Another hong merchant of the same firm, P'an Cheng-wei, who was the third Puan Kei-qua, collaborated with Wu Ping-chien (Houqua) of Ewo Hong, in the purchase of one American and one Spanish ship in 1843, and turned them over to the Canton authorities. Official interest had already waned, however, and the two foreign ships were reported as being good but too small and rather old. Monarchies as well as democracies are ungrateful.

All of this pioneering work before 1861 was tentative and in-effective. No real reform or even material progress was made until later in the century. Nevertheless the seeds were planted during this interim period and the work of these obscure "experts on barbarian affairs" and stumbling pioneers cannot be completely ignored.

Chapter 3

Attitudes of Chinese Officials toward the United States,
1841-1861

The enigma of Chinese psychology and of the mental attitudes of
Chinese toward Europeans and Americans has long intrigued Westerners.
Every tourist and businessman in China has wondered in his occasional
reflective moments, what the rickshaw coolie or the domestic servant
"really thinks" of him. Diplomats have been at a loss to understand
the point of view of.their Chinese and Manchu colleagues and, failing of
any solution, have either attributed to them their own feelings or attitudes or have dismissed them as "inscrutable Orientals." Nevertheless,
an understanding of Sino-Western relations on any level must discover
some basic Chinese point of view on which to function.
Superficial and somewhat farcical explanations of China's attitude
toward the West have long been current in Western literature. Perhaps
the best known is derived from the "mandates" and letters of the
emperor of the Ch'ien-lung period to George III of England on the occasion of Earl MacCartney's mission to China in 1793.
The preamble to one of these "mandates" is often cited to show
the haughty presumptuousness and supercilious condescension of the
Chinese Emperor toward the upstart king of a small and distant isle.
The text is familiar:[1]

> You, O King, live beyond the confines of many seas, nevertheless, im-
> pelled by your humble desire to partake of the benefits of civiliza-
> tion, you have dispatched a mission respectfully bearing your memorial.
> Your Envoy has crossed the seas and paid his respects at my Court on
> the anniversary of my birthday. To show your devotion, you have also
> sent offerings of your country's produce.

Somewhat less familiar is the letter of the Tao-kuang emperor
addressed to President Tyler on the occasion of Caleb Cushing's
mission to China in 1843-1844. This letter is much shorter and therefore less condescending than the earlier one to George III. The Emper-
or "hopes the President is well," commends Cushing for the long
distance he has traversed to come to China, and is considerably relieved that the American envoy has agreed to negotiate at Canton with
Ch'i-ying (Kiying). "We could not bear to order him to submit to the
hardships of further travel (and thus) he was prevented from coming

---

1 Translation by J.O.P. Bland, *Annals and Memoirs of the Court of Peking,* London,
   1914; quoted by MacNair, *op. cit.,* p. 2.

to Peking and being received in audience."[2]

Numerous similar examples of Chinese official attitudes toward
the West, during the period before 1861, could be cited. These are
interesting and important but they all bear the stamp of diplomatic
language. Condescending as these Chinese documents appear to the
nationalistically minded Westerner of the nineteenth century, they were
still couched in the polite forms reserved for strangers from afar and
guests of the empire. To the Chinese officials of the day, these imperial mandates appeared magnanimous and probably better than the
foreigners deserved. [3] Formal letters from emperor to king or president can hardly represent fully the real attitudes of Chinese officialdom toward the West.

As a small contribution to the larger topic of China's reaction to
the Western impact, the present chapter presents certain attitudes
toward European states, but concentrates on the attitudes of Chinese
officials toward one Western state, namely the United States, over a
limited period, 1841-1861. The materials used differ in type from
those cited above in that they are limited to opinions and evaluations
current within the Chinese official family circle. The materials used
herein are exclusively those in circulation between province and court,
between governor general and emperor, or between provincial official
and Grand Council in Peking. They represent quite a different category from the formal exchange between states, even those between
kings of lowly "tributary" states and the Son of Heaven.

The purpose of this chapter is to present some two hundred examples of Chinese official expressions of attitudes toward Western
states and individuals. These examples have been culled from several
thousands which occur in the one hundred and sixty <u>chüan</u> or chapters
of Chinese documents covering her foreign relations of this period
(1841-1861), all of which have been examined with some care. The
examples cited range from the meaningless <u>cliche'</u> to shrewd observations gleaned from first-hand experience in dealing with Europeans
and Americans. An attempt has been made to classify these opinions
according to type and subject matter and also to show some early
evolutionary tendency in the direction of the formulation of a Chinese
foreign policy.

Before passing judgment on the Chinese officials and statesmen
of this period, it should be borne in mind that very few of them had any
extensive contact with foreigners. As stated earlier, the trading
contact at Canton was restricted to the hong merchant and the Hoppo

---

2 Translation by Raymond Parker Tenney, MS in National Archives, Washington, D.C.,
   cited by Chu Shih-chia, "Tao-kuang to President Tyler," *Harvard Journal of
   Asiatic Studies*, v. 7 (1942-1943), p. 172.

3 See, for example, the criticisms by Yüan Fu-hsün of England's over-generous
   treatment by the Chinese court, cited in MacNair, *op. cit.*, p. 12-13.

(customs commissioner) and it was but rarely that the local magistrate, the governor, or the governor general, even at Canton, had any personal relations with foreigners. After 1842, the contacts between Western commissioners and local officials became more common but the relationship was still outside the bounds of routine officialdom and no specialized department of foreign affairs existed.

During this period, Chinese officials were faced with a baffling and unwanted situation and were forced to deal with it as best they could. The first tendency, naturally, was to force the new wine into old casks. When this did not succeed, a few Chinese officials began to experiment with new casks which could contain the strong and cor- rosive element introduced from the West. This procedure required a kind of experimentation and curiosity for which the tradition-bound Confucian official was ill suited.

The clues to a new foreign policy for China came from outside the official circle. Hong merchants in Canton and newly rich gentry in Shanghai were probably the first to recognize the possibilities of deal- ing advantageously with foreigners, but their ideas gradually permeated the lower ranks of officialdom. Before the end of the period, however, the beginnings of a new realism are apparent in the opinions of a few top-ranking Chinese officials. By the end of the Hsien-feng period, it is possible to detect a new kind of statesmanship in the ranks of Chinese officialdom.

At the outset, the reader must be reminded again that the Chinese government, down to the enforced establishment in 1861 of a foreign office, at first called the Tsungli\Yamen, dealt with European countries and the United States in a special category called "barbarian affairs" (i-wu). This category was distinguished from China's relations and correspondence with Mongolia and other Asiatic states, including Russia, through the Court of Dependencies (Li Fan Yüan), [4] and with numerous tributary states, through the Board of Rites (Li Pu)[5] This special category is attested in various official sources. For example, the collection of documents which is the basis for the major portion of this book is called "The Management of Barbarian Affairs from Begin- ning to End" (Ch'ou Pan I Wu Shih Mo). As another example, when the British forces captured Canton in 1857-1858, they found in the governor general's yamen a file of British, American, and French treaties and correspondence labeled the "Management of Barbarian Affairs Yellow Chest" (Pan Li I Wu Huang Hsiang). [6] Again, when the British and French looted and burned the Summer Palace near Peking, in 1860,

4 Brunnert, H.S., and V.V. Hagelstrom, *Present Day Political Organization of China*, Shanghai, 1912, p. 160.

5 *Ibid.*, p. 124.

6 IWSM. HF 25;19a, 1.

they destroyed one copy of the foreign office file labeled "Records of
the Four Barbarians" (Ssu I Ko Tang).[7] The Grand Secretariat, in an
official edict as late as 1858, referred to Yeh Ming-ch'en at Canton as
"Imperial Commissioner in-charge-of Barbarian Affairs" (Ch'inch'ai ta-ch'en, pan-li i-wu).[8] Thus the official use of the term "barbarian affairs" is well established.

Not only was the term "barbarian affairs" used officially throughout the period to 1861, but it clearly carried overtones of contempt for
foreigners and this attitude was, on occasion, utilized to arouse the
populace against Westerners in China. When Lo Tun-yen was engaged
in recruiting local militia in Kwangtung in 1858, he wrote:[9]

> As to Your official's previous statements regarding the cutting of a
> great seal to furnish a recruiting caption, because popular indig-
> nation against barbarians was great, ever since the barbarians entered
> the city the local officials have forbidden any use of the term
> "barbarian affairs," even going to the length of referring in writ-
> ings and public documents to "barbarian affairs" as "ocean affairs"
> and as the "affairs of foreign countries," not daring to revile
> them with the term "barbarian." Your officials, after repeated
> deliberation, insisted on the cutting on the seal of the in-
> scription "Management of Barbarian Affairs" to enable us to arouse
> popular feeling.

Another Chinese official, Ho Kuei-ch'ing, governor of Liang-
chiang in 1858, made a clear statement of terminology:[10]

> Those barbarians who trade back and forth are called barbarian
> merchants; those who superintend the trading affairs of the vari-
> ous ports and take the surplus for their country's use, were first
> called public envoys. Now they presumptuously call themselves
> ministers, while we regard them as "barbarian chiefs". . .

At the same time that Chinese officialdom used this derogatory
terminology to apply to foreigners, it frowned upon American presumptuousness in using the imperial pronoun Chen for the President
of the United States,[11] was scornful of the use of an equalitarian
expression like "Chinese and foreigners are one family,"[12] and was
indignant when the British (1858) "did not allow the use of the two

---

7   IWSM. HF 69;17b, 3-5.

8   IWSM. HF 17;4b, 9.

9   IWSM. HF 22;39b, 3-8.

10 IWSM. HF 31;18a, 9-18b, 2.

11 IWSM. HF 13;16b, 7.

12 IWSM. HF 22;41a, 3-7.

words 'foreign devil' (fan-kuei), and when proclamations of the Imperial Commissioners of 'Great England' (Ta-ying-kuo) and 'Great
France' (Ta-fa-kuo) were put up everywhere in Canton."[13]

There is thus no question that the term "barbarian" was commonly
and officially used in nineteenth century China. Nor is its use new in
Chinese literature. The term i is used in classical Chinese to denote
"rude and barbarous tribes," especially "those on the east of China, of
whom there were nine tribes."[14] These tribes, said Confucius, "even
with their princes were still not equal to China with her anarchy."[15]
Mencius said, "I have heard of men using the doctrines of our great
land to change barbarians, but I have never yet heard of any being
changed by barbarians."[16] These barbarian tribes surrounding the
Middle Kingdom are represented throughout the classics as peoples un-
schooled in the writings and philosophies of China, but eager to be
"transformed by the virtue" of China. "When (T'ang) pursued his work
(of civilization) in the east, the rude tribes of the west murmured...
Their cry was--why does he make us last?"[17] In the Book of History
(Shu Ching), the term i is modified by various place names, such as
the Huai-i, Lai-i, Ho-i, and K'un-i, as well as the "island barbarians"
and the "southern barbarians," just as in the Manchu dynasty it was
qualified as the "English barbarians," the "French barbarians," and the
"American barbarians."

The colloquial equivalent of the classical "barbarian" is "foreign
devil," and in some districts "foreign dog."[18] The British bitterly resented the use of i or "barbarian" applied to them, and consistently refused official communications in which the term was used.[19] As soon
as they were in a position to dictate to the Chinese, as in Canton in
1858, they sternly forbade the use of "opprobrious language," either
spoken or written.[20] Americans were less sensitive about what the
Chinese called them and the most distinguished American sinologist
of the nineteenth century, S. Wells Williams, maintained that while
"foreign devil" was disrespectful, i or barbarian merely meant that
the person so designated could not read Chinese. He said that "used as
a general term, without opprobrious addition, I is as well adapted as

---

13 IWSM. HF 18; 14b, 4-6.

14 Legge, Chinese Classics, v. 1, p. 328.

15 Analects, III, 5; Legge, op. cit., v. 1, p. 20.

16 Mencius, IIIa, 4, 12; Legge, op. cit., v. 2, p. 129-130.

17 Mencius, Ib, 11, 2; Legge, op. cit., v. 2, p. 47.

18 Lane-Poole, Stanley, Life of Sir Harry Parkes, London, 1894, v. 1, p. 105.

19 Ibid., v. 1, p. 77 and 134.

20 Ibid., v. 1, p. 280.

any other to denote all foreigners."[21]

Having established the fact of general official use of the term i or barbarian, our main interest is to ascertain how it was used in official papers and what it connoted. The Chinese documents dealing with foreign countries, prior to 1861, consist on the one hand mainly of memorials from the governors general, governors, other provincial officials, occasional censors, and imperial princes, all addressed to the court of Peking, and, on the other hand, of edicts, issued in the name of the emperor by the Grand Council and the Grand Secretariat. These documents circulated only within the circle of Chinese official-dom and so are completely unguarded. They are entirely free from polite phrases or diplomatic embroidery.

Many of the characterizations of Britons, Frenchmen, and Americans as "barbarians" appear to be conventional and, as official clichés, occur over and over in the texts with apparently little meaning. One of the most persistent official expressions is that "Barbarians are by nature inscrutable,"[22] which neatly counters Bret Harte and Kipling. Other common expressions are: "Barbarians are inherently cunning and malicious";[23] "Barbarians are by nature impatient and without understanding of values";[24] "Inconstancy is a fundamental trait of barbarians."[25] Barbarians were also insatiable,[26] avaricious,[27] and they "cunningly devised many plans."[28] Some of the expressions used are more derogatory. "Although barbarians have the feelings of dogs and sheep, they still have regard for their own interests."[29] "Their dog-sheep nature is fundamentally hard to subdue."[30]

Beyond these generalizations were observations which appear to be first hand, and to represent actual evaluations of "barbarian" character as distinguished from Chinese and Manchu traits. For instance, such statements as "It is the nature of barbarians to be impatient,"[31] and "Barbarians think only of profit,"[32] are easily identifiable. The harassed Chinese official on the frontier also saw an element of weakness in the Western temperament: "Barbarians are most resentful of annoyances and if these accumulate perhaps eventu-

21 *Middle Kingdom* (1883 ed.), v. 2, p. 461-462.
22 IWSM. HF 7;32a, 8.
23 IWSM. HF 8;28a, 8.
24 IWSM. TK 71;9a, 6-7.
25 IWSM. HF 23;17a, 2.
26 IWSM. HF 21;11a, 7.
27 IWSM. HF 72;6a, 8.
28 IWSM. TK 26;19a, 2.
29 IWSM. HF 32;23a, 1.
30 IWSM. HF 23;7a, 6.
31 IWSM. HF 36;38b, 5.
32 IWSM. HF 9;52b, 8.

ally they will be discouraged."[33] On the other hand the barbarians were "fickle and inconstant, perverse in feelings and words, not by any means to be managed by mere words."[34] Reasoning with them was futile because they "respected strength and ridiculed weakness."[35]

Repeated contact with Western fleets and landing forces convinced the Chinese officials that "barbarian nature is inscrutable and our defense must be rigorous,"[36] but they reassured themselves that while barbarians "... are naturally arrogant and anxious to excel, crafty and greedy for gain, ... once badly beaten, they will refrain from opposition."[37] Military force was the only argument they could understand because they were "suspicious and liked action."[38] The combination of the subjective and traditional Chinese official attitude with an enforced realism is well expressed in the statement, "Although these barbarians have all the characteristics of human beings, they are unusually cruel and cunning and depend on the strength of their ships and the superiority of their cannon."[39] The Chinese officials were no longer dealing in generalities, but were giving expression to the hard fact of Western material strength.

Adding to the consternation of the Chinese official was the discovery that there were different kinds of barbarians. When a British ship was wrecked on Formosa in 1842, the local official reported "that the eighteen white barbarians captured include the leader.. and two accomplices, who are all red barbarians. Besides, there are four persons... (who are) also red barbarians. Because their hair is slightly yellow, they are called red barbarians. Along with the eleven white barbarians, they are all natives of the English mother country ... In addition, there are thirty black barbarians, all natives of Bombay." The Formosan official professed horror at the violent attitude of the British and reminded the emperor that "these island barbarians from ancient times onward have known only love of gain and fundamentally are not different from dogs and sheep."[40]

Another early memorialist lapsed into the colloquial in distinguishing the different kinds of barbarians: "White Devils are fond of women, Red Devils are fond of money, Black Devils are fond of wine."[41] According to still current Cantonese terminology, these three categories would refer to Portuguese, British (or Dutch), and Sikhs (or Parsees)

---

33 IWSM. HF 32; 17a, 2.
34 IWSM. HF 36; 14a, 8.
35 IWSM. HF 9; 4a, 3.
36 IWSM. HF 20; 16a, 8-9.
37 IWSM. HF 18; 10b, 6-7.
38 IWSM. TK 65; 32b, 7.
39 IWSM. HF 31; 34b, 7-8.
40 IWSM. TK 59; 16a, 5-16b, 2.
41 IWSM. TK 41; 23b, 8-9.

respectively. Even as late as 1859, Prince Seng-ko-lin-ch'in was
confused by S. Wells Williams' refusal to acknowledge as an American
a captured Canadian soldier, and was not particularly helped by
Williams' explanation "that the soldiers of the three countries are inter-
changeable, that America contained Englishmen and Frenchmen, and
when there was fighting, the flag was the only criterion."[42]

By the middle of the century, however, the principal Western
countries represented in China were well known and the Chinese official
began to make comparisons. "While all barbarians are insatiably
avaricious by nature, Russian barbarians are inscrutable and French
barbarians are crafty."[43] "The barbarians' attitude is not uniform.
The English and French defy reason and, while the Russians and Americans are affable, they too want to satisfy their demands, so there is no
distinction between them. ... Thus, while Russia and America realize
English and French tyranny and presumptuousness, they do not prevent
it; on the contrary they both condone their acts, sitting by to get the
fisherman's share."[44] The allusion is to the Chinese fable of a kingfisher that seized a clam, which in turn closed on the kingfisher's bill.
Neither was willing to let go until a fisherman came along and took
them both. According to another observation, "the English barbarians'
craftiness is manifold, their proud tyranny is uncontrollable; Americans do nothing but follow their direction."[45]

The British, of course, were the prototype of all barbarians. The
Chinese found them "overbearing and tyrannical,"[46] "unusually cunning,"[47] "by nature and appearance treacherous and unusually faithless,"[48] "devoted to trade,"[49] and "fundamentally not different from
dogs and sheep."[50] Besides these generalizations, there was an occasional specific example of the Englishman's actions in China, such
as the report from Canton during British-French occupation, 1858, of
"...having their chair bearers... wear red buttons and peacock
feathers [Chinese official insignia], intentionally insulting China,
[which] was even more obnoxious. We hear that this is all Harry
Parkes' doing."[51] Which, we might add, it was.[52]

The French were identified in the Chinese mind with mercenary

42 IWSM. HF 39;40b, 8-10.
43 IWSM. HF 72;4a, 3.
44 IWSM. HF 21;38a, 10-39a, 10.
45 IWSM. HF 9;39b, 5-6.
46 IWSM. TK 21;38b, 5; 28, 4a, 10.
47 IWSM. HF 42;20a, 1.
48 IWSM. TK 26;38b, 8.
49 1WSM. TK 26;37b, 7.
50 IWSM. TK 58;47a, 2; 59;16b, 2.
51 IWSM. HF 19;19b, 10-20a, 1.
52 Lane-Poole, op. cit., v. 1, p. 264-289.

soldiers and Catholicism.   When de Bourboulon came to China in 1854, his position was analyzed as follows: "Although the French barbarians' trade is not large, their military strength is very great.   Whenever the other barbarians need soldiers they all make use of their strength. Their nationals in China are engaged only in the propagation of Catholicism and they have long since asked permission to establish a Catholic Church at the capital, to preach in the North, and to travel throughout the interior."[53]   The Chinese were convinced that the other Western countries were absolutely dependent on France for troops: "So these barbarians, using this to their own advantage, sit back and get rich like so many merchants."[54]   It was the good fortune of the Canton Imperial Commissioner Yeh Ming-ch'en to discover why French trade with China was slight.   "In the one item of tea, the barbarian traders of this country [France] do not trade much with our Chinese merchants. After persistent inquiry it has been learned that this country's everyday hot drink is called coffee, which is produced in barbarian lands. This takes the place of Chinese tea, while England and America cannot get along without Chinese tea."[55]

Russia comes into the picture only at the very end of the period and Chinese officials were generally distrustful of her.   Even when, in 1860, Russia offered to train and equip a modern Chinese army, Prince Kung shied off.   "As these barbarians are naturally crafty with rich promises and honeyed words, Your officials could hardly be sure they were not harboring other purposes."[56]

The United States presented a confusing and conflicting problem to the Chinese officials.   They were inclined to think that Americans "compared with the Russian barbarians are trustworthy and their speech reasonable, but they are very suspicious and obstinate."[57]   They were, hopefully, thought to "resent the English barbarians and revere China."[58]   Geographically, the United States was regarded as being even further to the west than Europe, just as we regarded China as the "Far East."   Pacific Ocean consciousness was very late in developing and there was no Commodore Perry to explain to China, as he did to Japan, that both Japan and China were just "off the coast of California."   The Chinese had a hazy picture of the United States as "an isolated place outside the pale, solitary and ignorant."[59]   One can imagine Peter Parker trying diligently to get across a picture of the New England trade, of the great open spaces, and of the hardy virtues

53 IWSM. HF 10;2b, 7-10.
54 IWSM. HF 41;7a, 2-3.
55 IWSM. HF 11;19a, 8-10.
56 IWSM. HF 69;30a, 2-3.
57 IWSM. HF 22;1b, 10-2a, 1.
58 IWSM. TK 23;33b, 2.
59 IWSM. TK 73;29a, 6.

of the frontiersman, but all China understood was that America was "maritime, uncultivated, and primitive."[60]

When Caleb Cushing arrived to negotiate the first treaty in 1844, his bearing and language were regarded as respectful and obedient, and he was given credit for sincerity in conforming with Chinese customs and admiring Chinese principles, but the court was concerned about a medium of communication. To the Americans, "living outside the pale, (our) language is unintelligible." How, in Heaven's name, could a letter be addressed to them? Ch'i-ying replied:[61]

> Your slave begs to note that the location of the United States is in the Far West. Of all the countries it is the most uncivilized and remote. Now they hope for the Imperial Favor of granting a special Imperial Mandate which can be kept forever. We have both commended the sincerity of their love of justice and strengthened their determination of turning toward culture. The different races of the world are all grateful for Imperial charity. It is only that the said country is in an isolated place outside the pale, solitary and ignorant. Not only in the forms of edicts and laws are they entirely unversed, but if the meaning be rather deep, they would probably not even be able to comprehend. It would seem that we must be somewhat simple and use words that will express our meaning.

Ch'i-ying goes on to recommend a Manchu text, although he himself (a Manchu closely related to the imperial family) was unable to write the formal Manchu script required in official correspondence, because "the people of the said country have occasionally been to Russia and place the greatest value on Manchu letters."[62] Incidentally, Caleb Cushing, in preparation for his diplomatic mission to China, had studied Manchu in preference to Chinese.

After the Treaty of Wang-hsia was signed, Ch'i-ying, possibly from materials furnished him by Cushing, presented the court a thumbnail sketch of American history:[63]

> ...America was originally a large continent in the extreme west, as different from China as night from day, a vast country with a sparse population. Before the Ming (1388-1644), no one knew the country... Although she established her country not more than a few decades ago, her territory is broad, her people diligent, and her products abundant. Hence of all the barbarians of the west, which along with England and France are regarded as great powers, only the United States is noteworthy, while Holland and Spain, although established previously, on the contrary do not come up to the recent status of the said country.

---

60 IWSM. TK 74;2b, 10.
61 IWSM. TK 73;28b, 2-29a, 1.
62 IWSM. TK 73;29a, 1-29b,4; the letter to President Tyler was actually presented in both Manchu and Chinese texts. See Chu Shih-chia, *op. cit.*
63 IWSM. TK 74;17b, 2-18b, 4.

Ch'i-ying felt that the United States should be rewarded for her peaceful and respectful attitude, but could hardly be allowed to go to Peking as "the said country has never come to court or paid tribute. With the laws of the Heavenly Dynasty they are not fully acquainted."[64]

The United States was regarded as a particularly difficult problem. From time to time Chinese officials saw the advantage of favoring her with an imperial audience as a means of getting American support against England and France, but they could never see just how it could be facilitated. The Americans were friendly, but they seemed to have no sense of dignity or understanding of ceremony. 1-liang, governor general of Liang-chiang in 1853, expressed this contradiction:[65]

> It is noted that the outside dependencies conquered by our Dynasty all have annual presentations, and the liege officials of the various countries paying tribute, after they arrive at the capital, must first practice the ritual of bowing and kneeling. Thereafter they are ordered to be presented according to rank. Besides never having been in the class admitted to audience, the United States ordinarily has no official costumes, and still they claim equal rank for themselves and ignorantly puff themselves up. They are not worthy of consideration. How can we treat them like the various dependent states and cause the development of other difficulties? Yet it is impolitic to treat them with unusual courtesy and cause the gradual budding of covetous desires.

The problem of dealing with the United States was made more difficult by her lack of sinologists. Ch'i-ying complained in 1844:[66]

> ...The Americans' difficulty of understanding is much greater than the English barbarians' because the English barbarians had Morrison and others. Although they were artful and cunning they were somewhat conversant with Chinese written and spoken language and when there was business one could discuss it with them. The American barbarians have only Parker and Bridgman who do not know many Chinese characters. They are versed only in the Cantonese local dialect, with the result that it is hard to understand each other's point of view, and a great deal of energy is consumed.

The Chinese officials gradually became convinced that they could expect nothing but good intentions from the United States and that no assistance, either against the British or against the Taipings, was forthcoming. Even the most hopeful complained "that the Americans ordinarily speak respectfully but are taking advantage of the present situation to make demands; while they speak of 'helping to put down rebellion,' absolutely no faith can be placed in them."[67]

---

64 IWSM. TK 71;24a, 3-5.
65 IWSM. HF 6;25b, 2-9.
66 IWSM. TK 72;3b, 8-4a, 1.
67 IWSM. HF 8;21a, 1-3.

The personalities of individual Americans made no great impression upon Chinese officialdom during this period, probably because of the language difficulty. A gifted linguist like the English Sir Harry Parkes made a much greater impression, adverse though it was, upon them. It was observed that the American "Chief McLane's language and actions, compared to the English chief, Bowring, were fairly respectful and obedient," but "his attitude was still inscrutable."[68] He did receive, however, one of the few specific credits conceded by Chinese officials to foreigners during this period. Ho Kuei-ch'ing said that "it was the American Chief McLane who decided that as the Hung [i.e., the Taiping] rebels had none of the five relationships [wu-lun or moral obligations] nor even a criminal law they were not worth consideration, and so he shifted [American] policy in our direction."[69] Humphrey Marshall is given the dubious honor of weakening the white man's solidarity in China. One official observed "that of the various countries trading at Shanghai, only Consul Alcock and Vice Consul Thomas Wade are most crafty. Last year American Commissioner Marshall told Wu Chien-chang confidentially that their attitude was inscrutable."[70]

The only American commissioner, to 1861, who knew any Chinese was Dr. Peter Parker, and he, like Sir Harry Parkes, was singled out by the Chinese officials for attack. They said that "his mentality was inscrutable,"[71] and offered an elaborate explanation for his warped mind:[72]

> ...After the American envoy, McLane, went home, last winter Parker re-
> placed him and came to Canton. This chief was originally an American
> physician, had been in Canton for twenty years, and was generally re-
> garded as crafty. In 1854, when the Cantonese rebels were making trouble,
> this chief had secret relations with various rebel leaders and besides
> he boasted to various barbarian merchants that the rebels were sure to
> succeed. Then when the government troops reduced the rebels to complete
> submission, the chief lost so much face that in the summer of last year
> he went home of his own accord. Unexpectedly, after McLane went home due
> to illness, the king of that country, as he [Parker] had been in Canton
> for many years, sent him back to Canton to take over the duties as envoy.
> Chief Parker still cherished resentment in his heart and was determined
> to find other expressions for his personal views and to silence people's
> ridicule.

It was one thing for the Chinese official to identify and attempt to understand the barbarian on the border; it was another thing to know how to handle him. One basic principle was that "the laws of the

---

68   IWSM. HF 8; 34b, 8-9.
69   IWSM. HF 32; 5b, 10-6a, 2.
70   IWSM. HF 7; 30b, 8-10.
71   IWSM. HF 13; 14b, 4.
72   IWSM. HF 13; 11a, 8-11b, 4.

Heavenly Court being established cannot suffer the least change."[73]
The barbarian must be dealt with within the frame of the Chinese
constitution. The emperor "regards Chinese and outsiders with the
same benevolence; those who obey, he soothes; those who rebel, he
chastises."[74] When the Americans sought the advantages that Britain
had gained in 1842-1843, this traditional formula was applied. "Naturally (we) should treat them equally and not give rise to occasions for
disappointment, encouraging admiration and gratitude in them, and
further strengthen their sincerity in turning toward civilization."[75]

    Another classical principle, and the one most often cited and
hopefully clung to throughout the nineteenth century, was to "use
barbarians to curb barbarians."[76] This might be applied negatively,
to prevent the powers from getting together: "Divide and rule";[77] or
positively: "Play them off and encourage them until they destroy one
another."[78] It was reasoned that "as dogs and sheep are naturally inconstant, it should not be hard to separate them and, by using barbarians to curb barbarians, to sow mutual disaffection and gradually
weaken them."[79]

    It was regarded as hopeless to apply to Europeans and Americans
even the forms used in dealing with Annam or Liu-ch'iu. "These
people outside the pale, in regard to the designations and forms are
in utter darkness. If we use our documentary forms to determine
authoritatively their rank, even if we wore out our tongues and parched
our lips we could not avoid the smiling response of a deaf man."[80]
Consequently it was better to rule barbarians with misrule and not
try to rationalize. Ch'i-ying expressed this point of view in 1844, in
reporting his negotiations with Cushing:[81]

> As the barbarians were born and bred in outer wilderness, there is much
> in the institutes of the Heavenly Court that they do not understand but
> as they always pretend to understand, it is hard to explain reasonably.
> For instance, the Emperor's transmitted words are all passed on by the
> Grand Councillors but the barbarians regard them as *Vermilion Endorse-
> ments.* If shown not to be Imperial writings at all, then there would be
> no means of maintaining their trust. This, then, is something that
> should not be made clear.

    In spite of the discouraging and thankless task of trying to deal

---

73 IWSM. TK 63;30a, 4
74 IWSM. TK 24;36b, 8.
75 IWSM. TK 72;34b, 2-3.
76 IWSM. HF 19; 2a, 8.
77 IWSM. HF 19; 2a, 8.
78 IWSM. TK 24;37a, 3-4.
79 IWSM. HF 20;7b, 3-5.
80 IWSM. TK 73;20a, 3-8.
81 IWSM. TK 73;18b, 6-19a, 1.

rationally with Englishmen, Frenchmen, and Americans, the Chinese official's deep-rooted faith in human nature never quite failed him. "Although they are wolf cubs with wild natures and we dare not trust that they will not turn on us, still sincerity can accomplish wonders and it would seem that we should be able to bring them under our sway."[82] The means, however, would have to be on a fairly low level because "after all, the natures of scorpions and wolves can never be treated with human reason."[83]

With more personal contacts established between Chinese officials and foreigners in the ports, a more realistic attitude toward foreign relations gradually developed. Before the end of the period (1861), a Shanghai official memorialized that the only method of handling barbarians was that suggested by the emperor, namely: "Holding firmly to the treaties, to exemplify them with good faith, humble them with reason, and mollify them with favor--these three, and besides them there is no good plan."[84] When more and greater concessions were wrung from China, officials rationalized this as a policy of "giving leash as a means of control."[85] Some argued that "the method of controlling barbarians consists entirely in conforming to their nature and taming them,"[86] although the emperor and the court were inclined to take a dim view of this. Ultimately, the heretical view came to be expressed that China must "use their methods and adapt them to her own uses."[87] Chinese officials were beginning to realize that the West might have something of value to China and that the darkness outside the pale might not be as dense as they had imagined. One high court official urged that Wei Yüan's Hai Kuo T'u Chih, an atlas of Western countries based on foreign sources, be made available to all government officials in order to bring about a better understanding of the world outside of China. "Now today," argued this proto-reformer, "the countries beyond the seas are daily striving for mastery. Although as man sees things, there are differences between China and the outside, as Heaven sees them there may be no difference between them. The Book of History says, 'Great Heaven has no affections; It helps only the virtuous.'"[88]

A Shanghai official expressed the same revolutionary idea in more practical terms and even suggested that China herself might be at fault: "When we negotiate with these barbarians it is essential to have someone thoroughly familiar with the barbarian temperament

82   IWSM. TK 65; 33a, 3-4.
83   IWSM. HF 39; 14a, 7.
84   IWSM. HF 9; 47b, 9-10.
85   IWSM. TK 25; 42a, 10.
86   IWSM. HF 53; 43a, 2.
87   IWSM. HF 58; 43b, 4.
88   IWSM. HF 28; 48b, 8-10; Legge, op. cit., v. 3(II), p. 490.

in the hope that in the exchange of civilities, everything will be in order. Besides, the wording of our state papers is full of meaningless conventions. It is always from these trivialities that calamities develop. So we should consider everything carefully."[89]

Freed from the conventions and prejudices of Canton, Shanghai officials became convinced that it was not impossible to get along with foreigners and actually boasted that they had found the secret: "Shanghai's management of barbarians has consisted of taming them by catering to their moods. If the barbarian mood was avaricious, we feigned indifference to money; if the barbarian mood was proud, we treated them with deference; if the barbarian mood was crafty but had a false front of sincerity, then we showed trust in them. Therefore, for more than ten years there has been mutual accord, and no trouble. There was not a barbarian merchant who did not enjoy carrying on his business, so this became the point of concentration for barbarians."[90] Spoken like a true member of the Chamber of Commerce, but what a far cry from Yeh Ming-ch'en!

The proud Chinese were not humbled, but a few of them did begin to realize, somewhat bitterly, that the tables had been turned on them. "These barbarians for twenty years have contemptuously regarded us Chinese as being without leadership";[91] "their belittling of China is a matter of long standing."[92] They complained that the British "regarded the gentry as yamen runners and took good people for outlaws,"[93] and quoted an English journal published in China to the effect that "Chinese are hard to reason with and it is only by inspiring them with fear that we can gain our ends."[94]

By 1861, with the establishment of the Tsungli Yamen in Peking, Chinese officials had gone a long way from the childish concepts of red, white, and black barbarians. Western ships, steam engines, and cannon were not only admired but were being imitated in China. The Maritime Customs Service, set up under foreign inspectorship at Shanghai, was being extended to other ports at the request of Chinese officials.

The link between this early period and the later period of reforms and westernization was, perhaps, Tseng Kuo-fan. As early as 1861, he had abandoned the Chinese-barbarian concept of the world and was discussing intelligently the "Atlantic countries, England, France and America,"[95] as compared with Pacific countries like China and Japan.

Unfortunately, however, Tseng had illusions about the United

---

89 IWSM. HF 53;44a, 3-5.
90 IWSM. HF 30;44a, 8-44b, 3.
91 IWSM. HF 62;44a, 4-5.
92 IWSM. HF 54;33b, 1-2.
93 IWSM. TK 65;29a, 10-29b, 1.
94 IWSM. HF 7;21a, 5-6.
95 IWSM. HF 71;10a, 5-6.

States which were not borne out by the facts. "Americans," he wrote, "are of pure-minded and honest disposition and have long been recognized as respectful and compliant toward China."[96] He went on to cite instances of proffered American aid to China from 1839 to 1860, showing that they had consistently tried to pursue a policy separate from the English and French. Without knowing that the United States was already committed to the "cooperative policy" toward China, Tseng Kuo-fan went on to conjecture: "Probably by secretly blocking the Russian barbarians' overtures to China and preventing them from winning over the Americans' sympathies, the Americans could be made to realize that China is not the least suspicious of them, and might even be induced to turn around completely and draw nearer to us--one cannot tell."[97]

---

96 IWSM. HF 71;11a, 8-11b, 1.
97 IWSM. HF 71;12a, 2-4.

PART II

CHINESE DOCUMENTS DEALING WITH
UNITED STATES, 1841-1861

Chapter 1

China Discovers America, 1841-1842
Documents 1-34

The Chinese documents of this period, February 6, 1841 to December 12, 1842, comprise twenty-one memorials and thirteen edicts. The documents indicate a fairly lively interest in the problem of the United States on the part of the emperor. There are no formal or casual endorsements but there are three specific comments by the emperor and seven instances of interlinear or marginal notations in the emperor's hand. The memorialists are the coastal officials and generals involved in the First Opium War, then in its last stages in Canton, on the eastern seaboard, and the Yangtze valley. The period also covers the conclusion and initial operation of the Treaty of Nanking, concluded with Great Britain in August, 1842. Curiously enough, the one anti-Western memorialist during this period is a court official who was not personally involved in the war. Of the thirteen edicts, ten are addressed to the grand councillors, that is, they are important edicts involving state policy, either military or civil; three are of a routine character addressed to the Grand Secretariat. Two of these involve appointments and one involves denunciation and punishment of officials. As will be noted hereafter from time to time, the function of the Grand Secretariat during this period, insofar as it affects foreign relations, appears to be limited to the appointment, removal, and punishment of personnel. The grand secretaries are not concerned with the formulation or execution of foreign policy.

In content, the documents of this period deal with the trade and activities of Americans during the hostilities, and the status of the United States as a neutral. The discovery of the possibility of enlisting the sympathies and possibly the aid of the United States and France on China's behalf is the principal theme. The American consul, Delano, is mentioned, and suggestions as to the use of American trade as bargaining material are made. A British shipwreck on Taiwan (Formosa) results in depositions by the sailors and provides the occasion for an early Chinese attempt to distinguish among the various types of "barbarians."

The position of the United States in this period is indicated by the appearance of American naval units at Whampoa. This elicited pro-

posals for the building of an effective Chinese navy and experiments by
hong merchants in the construction of Western-type ships and in the
manufacture of under-water mines and torpedoes. Americans were
involved in these activities as potential allies of China, as friendly
neutrals with no love for the British, or as skilled technicians capable
of assisting China.

The Western materials parallel to the Chinese documents of this
period are summarized by Tyler Dennett, Americans in Eastern Asia,
in his chapter entitled "Americans and the Anglo-Chinese War," pages
91 to 113. Some of the pertinent American documents for the same
period are the "Memorial of R. B. Forbes and Others," U. S. Cong.
26:1, H. Doc. 40; "Memorial of Edmund Fanning," U. S. Cong. 26:1,
H. Doc. 57; "Canton Consular Letters," U. S. Cong. 26:1, H. Doc.
119; "Petition of Boston and Salem Merchants," U. S. Cong. 26:1,
H. Doc. 170; "Report of the Secretary of the Treasury on China Trade,"
U. S. Cong. 26:1, H. Doc. 248; "Canton Consular Letters," U. S.
Cong. 26:2, H. Doc. 71; and The Chinese Repository, Canton, for the
years 1832-1842, volumes 1-11.

TRANSLATIONS OF DOCUMENTS

1. February 6, 1841. MEMORIAL: Proposal to Use the Americans
Against the British.

I-li-pu further memorializes. Moreover, the attitude of
those barbarians now at Canton is extremely refractory. Your
slave[1] has received and read a communication from that province and was immeasurably depressed. The said barbarians,
after capturing the forts, again sent barbarian letters, stating
their demands seriatim. Although Your slave does not know
how many items were listed altogether or what the things they
asked for were concerned with, he still fears that those barbarians are using force in pressing their demands and that in
managing them, fingers are pricked at every turn.

---

1 Nu-ts'ai, bondsman or slave, is a term used by bannermen, who were sometimes
   Chinese but mainly Manchu officials, in addressing the emperor, instead of the
   first personal pronoun. It could be translated "I," but is preserved to distinguish
   it from ch'en, "Your official," third personal form used by Chinese officials who
   were not bannermen in memorials to the emperor. In these translations the terms
   "Your slave" and "Your official" have been preserved as more accurate. This clue,
   plus the form of their names, serves to distinguish Manchus from Chinese in the
   translations. Manchus had no family names and their given names were polysyllabic,
   indicated in transliteration by hyphens; e. g., I-liang, A-ching-a, Seng-ko-lin-
   ch'in. The same rule and form holds for Mongol names. In the case of Chinese names
   in the text, the family name is written first, followed by a given name in one or
   two syllables, e. g., Juan Yüan, Yeh Ming-ch'en, Liu Yün-k'o.

In devising means of restraining the enemy, we should not be afraid to inquire widely. Your slave has received a communication of Juan Yüan, recently occupying the post of Grand Secretary, saying:

> According to rumor, since Ch'i-shan reached Canton, the barbarians
> have not yet become tractable and I worry about it day and night. I
> have long since been aware that of the countries trading at Canton,
> besides England, the United States is the largest and most powerful.
> In this country the ground is level and rice plentiful. The English
> barbarians look to her for supplies and do not dare antagonize her.
> But the American barbarians at Canton have always been peaceable,
> not obstinate like the English barbarians. If we treat the American
> barbarians courteously and abolish their customs duties, and also
> take the trade of the English barbarians and give it to the American
> barbarians, then the American barbarians are sure to be grateful for
> this Heavenly Favor and will energetically oppose the English bar-
> barians. Moreover, the ships and cannon of the English barbarians
> have mostly been acquired by hire or seizure from other foreign
> states. If the American barbarians are made use of by us, then other
> countries will learn of it, and it will not be difficult to break
> them down. When the American barbarians have received (Imperial)
> Favor, the English barbarians will certainly not take it lying down.
> Probably one or two ports will be bombarded by them, but when their
> strength is expended and we have strengthened fortifications and
> purged the countryside, then we will meet them and it will not be
> hard to repel them. Still, this is a plan devised during sickness
> and I do not yet know whether or not it is practicable. Therefore,
> I have not ventured to put it into a memorial.

Your slave observes that the present situation at Canton is very critical. If we clash with them it is extremely difficult to predict whether or not we can win. If we conciliate them along the line requested in this letter, it is feared that their demands will be troublesome and many and, under the circumstances, hard to satisfy. But if we utilize the strength of the American bar- barians to curb the English barbarians, it would seem that the ef- fort would be halved and the result doubled.

Although, in view of the greatness of the Heavenly Court, to borrow the help of outside barbarians may not seem to be proper handling, still in the books of strategy there is the theory of "attack by conciliation" and the technique of "using barbarians to curb barbarians." From Han and T'ang times onward it is re- corded in history, not once but many times, that such has been done without loss of dignity. Moreover, considering the alter- natives of conciliating the English barbarians or utilizing the American barbarians, at least the latter is better than the former. It would seem that the device of Juan Yüan is not entirely without

perspicacity. The only question is whether or not the American
barbarians can curb the English barbarians; whether or not they
are willing to be used by us. That, besides these, there are no
other obstacles, Your slave as yet is not fully convinced. Even
so, Juan Yüan has been away from Canton for many years and it
is feared that there may be differences between then and now. It
is only right to append this secret communication and beseech Your
Majesty's judgment. If it meets Imperial approval, it is respectfully requested to charge the acting governor general of Liang-
kuang [i.e., Kwangtung-Kwangsi], Ch'i-shan, thoroughly to investigate the situation and execute in detail. (IWSM. TK 21; 21b,
1-22b, 8)

2. February 10, 1841. MEMORIAL: Report of Decline of Canton
Customs Revenue and Loss of Trade by England and Other Countries.
        Governor of Kwangtung, concurrently in charge of Canton
customs, I-liang, memorializes. It is found that the Canton Maritime Customs revenue, annual collection and surplus, totals over
899,000 taels, of which the barbarian customs form a large part.
The number of barbarian ships arriving each [sic, copyist's
error; should read "the present"] year has not been twenty
per cent of that of former years. Not only have the ships of the
English barbarians and the Indians[2] stopped trading, but also the
ships of other countries have been obstructed by the English barbarians and are unable to enter port. So after the sixth month
(July 18 - August 17), just when collections of revenues should
be the greatest, on the contrary there was a shortage. Not only
was there a great disparity with previous administrations, but
compared to the amounts collected during the past two years of
Yü-k'un's regime, it was again reduced by more than half.
(IWSM. TK 21; 38a, 4-10)

3. February 10, 1841. EDICT: Proposal to Capitalize on Resentment of Other Countries against England for Loss of Trade.
        Edict to the Grand Councillors. I-liang has memorialized on
(his) taking over the management of the Canton Maritime Customs
and the shortage in collections, in which he states that in the
Canton Maritime Customs revenue, the barbarian customs form
a major part; also that the number of foreign ships arriving in the
present year is not twenty per cent of that of previous years, be-

---

2   Indians refers to "country ships" from India, chartered by the English East India
    Company to trade with China. A large proportion of these "country ships" carried
    opium to China, thus technically absolving the Company from complicity in the opium
    trade.

cause the ships of other countries, being obstructed by the English barbarians, were not able to enter port. So, after the sixth month (July 18-August 17), just when collections of revenues should be the greatest, on the contrary, there was a shortage, etc.

Kwangtung precedent allows the various barbarians to trade. The respectful and obedient states naturally should trade as usual. The English barbarians are overbearing and tyrannical and have interfered with the livelihood of other countries. Are those states willing resignedly to lose their profits? (We) hereby charge I-shan, Lung-wen, and Ch'i Kung, on their respective arrivals at Canton, to investigate carefully the attitudes of the various countries, whether or not they are resentful of the English barbarians' interference with their livelihood or have any disappointment with the Heavenly Court for not yet being able to draw them in and pacify them, leaving them to be neglected and lose their trade, and to memorialize according to the facts. (IWSM. TK 21; 38b, 1-8)

4. March 6, 1841. MEMORIAL: Encouragement of Americans to Trade in Order to Alienate Them from the British.

Memorial of the already degraded Grand Secretary Ch'i-shan. ...Furthermore, at the present time, the American merchant ships coming to Canton are prevented by the English barbarians from entering port, falsely telling them the local officials would take their ships for war purposes. Your slave has already ordered the hong merchants to inform them that this circumstance does not exist. Moreover, he has issued a statement that the reason they cannot carry on trade lies entirely with the English barbarians, but that if they can devise means for entrance (to the port), the Heavenly Court authorizes trade with them as usual; in this way we can quiet their minds and cause them to feel resentful toward the English barbarians and grateful to the Heavenly Court. Thus, while they would not be used by us, there would still be no danger of their siding with evil and abetting treason.... (IWSM. TK 23; 33a, 8-33b, 3)

5. March 21, 1841. MEMORIAL: Proposal to Encourage Americans to Oppose the English Rebels.

[Imperial Commissioner, Governor of Kiangsu] Yü-ch'ien further memorializes. Moreover, these marine volunteers[3] are

---

3 *Shui-yung*, literally "water irregulars," is here applied to militia, commonly called "braves" in contemporary English accounts, recruited locally to put down uprisings. Here the usual term, *yung*, is qualified by *shui*, "water," to indicate that their service was for patrols in the rivers and on the coasts around Canton and to distinguish them from land forces. W. F. Mayers says that these "braves," enlisted and

all brigands. In Kwangtung they are called "ragamuffins." To use them against the barbarians would be like using poison to counteract poison. In case they are wounded or killed there will be no regrets; thus there will be no injury to the Heavenly prestige and, at the same time, a local evil can be removed. Furthermore, Your slave has ascertained that the various foreign countries, because the English rebels have stirred up trouble and trade has become slack, are all thoroughly angry and resentful. The strength of such countries as Europe, America, and France is separately equal to that of the (English) rebels. It is not worth while for the Heavenly Court to issue an Edict ordering them to render help, but in the proclamation offering rewards, there is no harm in making clear that no matter whether they be soldiers or civilians, marine volunteers or Chinese traitors, or barbarians of the various countries, all are authorized to kill the rebels and claim the rewards, and also to issue a manifesto informing the various countries:

> The Great Emperor as Sovereign over all under Heaven, looks upon Chinese and outsiders with the same benevolence. Those who obey, he soothes; those who rebel, he chastizes. England is rebellious and has resisted authority, and already troops have been sent to punish her. You various other countries are not involved, and are all allowed to trade as usual. If the English rebels brazenly dare to use force to stop you and interfere with your livelihood, you various countries are authorized to fire upon them on the open seas, or separately to use warships to attack their country, or anything else you like.

Thus the minds of the various countries can be pacified, and also the gall of the rebel barbarians be overcome. In addition, (we can) secretly summon the capable and dependable among the hong merchants and order them to act as though this were their own idea, to make use of the policy of disagreement and alienation to meet emergencies as they arise, and to play them off and encourage them until they destroy one another. Our army can merely be quiet and await the opportunity to move, until the said (English) barbarians are left isolated and embarrassed. Then the government troops and marine volunteers can take advantage of their weakened condition and attack them. Such an insignificant rebel can easily be eradicated with one stroke of the drum. (IWSM. TK 24; 36a, 9-37a, 6)

---

discharged according to circumstances, superseded the sedentary garrisons "on all occasions when active service is required." He adds that "the officers of these irregular troops are usually invested with rank as 'expectants' of appointments to posts in the regular service." Mayers, *Chinese Government,* Shanghai, 1878, p. 59.

6. March 21, 1841. EDICT: Americans to be Offered Rewards for Killing English Rebels.

Edict to the Grand Councillors. Yü-ch'ien has memorialized asking to offer rewards and recruit marine volunteers in order to dissipate the Chinese traitors and also to allow barbarians of the various countries as a whole to kill rebels and claim rewards. The rebel barbarians at Canton show a great deal of lawlessness. Now the various forces have been mobilized and I-shan and others ordered to attack them quickly. It is hoped that after those generals arrive, they can in one beat of the drum effect their capture and exterminate the evil lot. The government troops sent from various places are experienced only in land warfare; when it comes to going to sea and making captures or attacks, perhaps they are not as able as the marine volunteers. Now Yü-ch'ien's memorial suggests the posting of offers for rewards and the issue of proclamations for recruits to make up the deficiencies in military strength.

(We) charge I-shan and the others immediately to devise means of recruiting and to exert themselves to make them all useful to us in order to dissipate the traitorous bands and extinguish the flames of revolt. His separate memorial proposes, in the proclamations offering rewards, to announce that barbarians of the various countries are all authorized to kill rebels and claim rewards. Whether or not it is practicable, (We) also charge I-shan and the others to take counsel and manage accordingly. The two memorials of Yü-ch'ien are both ordered copied and sent to them for perusal. (IWSM. TK 24; 37a, 7-37b, 4)

7. April 6, 1841. MEMORIAL: Reports United States Consul Delano's Request for Trade on Behalf of the British Merchants. •

Military Assistant Governor Yang Fang memorializes. It is humbly observed that the English rebellious barbarians, on March 16, on board warships, steamers, and small boats, wished to enter the Canton River. The Feng-huang-kang government troops[4] exerted their strength to attack and expel them, and an express memorial was immediately sent regarding the occurrence. On the same day there was (the case of) the American consul, Delano.[5] As that country's trading ships were not among those forbidden to trade, Ch'i-shan had previously authorized them to enter Huang-pu (Whampoa) to trade. Then, when the

---

4 *Kuan-ping* are distinguished from the militia or "braves" and include both the Banner Forces and the Provincial Green Standard troops.

5 Edward Delano, of the American firm of Russell and Company, 1841-1846, was United States merchant consul at Canton. Eldon Griffin, *Clippers and Consuls*, Ann Arbor, 1938, p. 306.

English barbarians attacked Hu-men (called Bocca Tigris), they
were prevented from entering port. On hearing that the Feng-
huang-kang government troops had attacked and expelled the rebel
ships, he appealed to the military camp. On receipt of the report
of Brigade General Ch'ang Ch'un, Your slave charged the acting
prefect of Canton (Kuang-chou-fu), Yü Pao-shun, to take an
interpreter with him and make an inquiry. He received Delano's
statement:

> The English barbarians having been attacked and expelled, we do
> not venture to make further request, but consider that the taking
> up of arms and rebelling against authority are the evil doings of
> the English barbarians. Their merchant ships have never dared to
> participate in stirring up trouble, but in spite of this have been
> obstructed for more than a year and unable to trade. That their
> merchants have been implicated by the military leaders of their
> own country is not worthy of sympathy, but we, America and other
> countries, have been respectful and obedient and have not dared
> illegally to sell prohibited goods. For the receipt of the Great
> Emperor's gracious permission to trade as usual, we are extremely
> grateful. But on arrival at Canton for the past year, we have been
> implicated by England and unable to get into Whampoa to discharge
> cargo, to the end that goods have been ruined and trade decimated.
> We acknowledge the Heavenly Court's commiseration. Now we find that
> the English barbarian merchants are in a critical situation. Could
> you not in some way, after attacking and driving out their warships,
> for the time being allow their merchant vessels to trade without
> discrimination so that the various countries would not incur the
> hatred of England and escape being hindered or implicated? Then,
> with the English merchant vessels at Whampoa, her warships would
> have them to consider and would not dare start trouble. This
> would seem to be one way of subduing them.

Your slave then transmitted an order that, although what the
barbarian said was reasonable, he did not fully realize that the
barbarians of England had fomented rebellion and committed
murderous acts, that her guilt was onerous and great, and that
actually she had cut herself off from the Heavenly Court. Now
Your Majesty has ordered the army out and specially declared
the Heavenly punishment. Although he says that the barbarian
merchants have not helped the rebels, they are after all Englishmen, so how do they even dare request to trade?
After having sent this reply in proper language, on the same
day, although the rebel ships made no movement, it was learned
that they had withdrawn and anchored not far away. Your slave
predicts that sooner or later they will again come to cause trouble,
and has made adequate and stringent preparation. . . .
. . . But the barbarians of the various countries at Canton all
look forward to peace, saying that the English barbarians have

already restored Ting-hai and would not dare to make still
further demands; that with regard to trade, the Heavenly Court
for two hundred years has repeatedly shown its Favor and they
could not but on their behalf beg the exceptional favor of continuing according to the old regulations. They also presented
a written pledge made by Elliot[6] and others that they would not
ask for any other conditions and only seek permission to trade
as usual; that if they carried prohibited goods, then we could
confiscate their ships and cargo. This shows that their former
repeated demands and illegal plans cannot be repeated at this
time.

    But Your slave has been ordered to lead the troops and
knows only that military affairs are paramount. By no means,
because the various countries continuously make requests
[Vermilion endorsement: These are clearly subversive plots
of the English rebels.], will he relax the morale of the army.
Even as to the terms of their written pledge, although Your
slave has already examined them, it is still as though he had
never seen them. However, since these are the circumstances,
reason compels him to report them according to facts.

    As to the statement that the barbarian traders have also
had no share in causing trouble and that by letting their merchant ships enter port we can curb and reduce the barbarian
troops, Your slave secretly inquired and openly investigated,
and apparently this is not without foundation. Even from the
point of view of military strategy, there are also occasions
for giving leash as a means of getting control. If we stubbornly resist all the barbarians, it is feared it will lead to general
disappointment, and perhaps (we should) use discretion in
controlling them.... (IWSM. TK 25; 39b, 8-40b, 10...41b,
10-42b, 2)

8. April 6, 1841. EDICT: Opening of Trade Left to the Discretion
of the Local Officials.
    Edict to the Grand Councillors. (We) have received the
memorial (containing) the report of the American consul that,
throughout the year since his arrival at Canton, (the American
merchants) have been implicated by the English rebels and unable to unload their ships, and further that English merchant
vessels carrying goods likewise request permission to trade.
(We have) also received the pledges of Elliot presented by the
hong merchants, requesting on his behalf permission to trade.
    These are nefarious plots of those rebels to weaken our

---

6) Captain Charles Elliot was English superintendent of trade.

military spirit. But at present our main army is not yet concentrated and is inadequate for disposition. (We) charge Yang Fang
to devise means of parrying them so that they will not be able to
escape into the outer ocean, making it difficult in the future to
attack and suppress them. As to the present proposition of using
discretion in controlling them, We also shall not dictate from
this distance.

I-shan and Lung-wen presumably have reached Canton. (We)
charge them to manage properly and discuss secretly. As soon as
the troops and cannons successively transferred (to them) are adequate to make attacks, and marine volunteers and fast boats are
adequate for service, (We) charge them, continuing in conformity
with the Edicts, to cut off their rear, close in on all sides, and
recover Hong Kong in order to fulfill their assigned mission.
(IWSM. TK 25; 42b, 6-43a, 3)

9. April 14, 1841. MEMORIAL: Recommends Reopening of Canton
Trade to British Merchants.

Military Assistant Governor Yang Fang, [Tartar] General-in-
chief of Kuang-chou (Canton) A-ching-a, and Governor of Kuangtung
I-liang, memorialize. As to the vicious disposition of the English
rebels, and also the reasons for the American consul, Delano's,
request on their behalf to trade, we have already repeatedly
memorialized. On March 23, we received a communication from
the Grand Councillors, and on February 9, 1841, we received the
Imperial Edict: "On this day We received Ch'i-shan's memorial
stating that the rebel barbarians, hearing that the main army was
about to be assembled, were planning to stir up trouble. Respect
this." Your slaves thereupon respectfully read it kneeling, and
also read Ch'i-shan's original memorial. They secretly notified
the provincial commander-in-chief likewise respectfully to obey
and carry this out.

They find that since the rebels forced their way into the
Canton River on March 8, and then withdrew, there have been
no further developments for the last ten days. According to our
information, America and other countries have been allowed to
trade, and their merchant vessels have had continuous access to
Whampoa and have been reported daily by the hong merchants.
They find that previously the merchant vessels of these barbarians were obstructed by the English barbarians, causing
great loss and damage to their goods. Now since they are one
after another entering Whampoa and taking advantage of the opportunity to trade, all are pleased and enthusiastic and all
grateful for Imperial benevolence. Even the merchants of the
rebel English are all looking on enviously from the side.

Your slaves have investigated the present attitudes of these

English rebels and it seems that since our main army is being mobilized and the provincial capital is being effectively strengthened, they will not dare suddenly to start trouble. In addition, since the Americans, on their behalf, have asked for trade, and Your slaves have already reported it for them in a memorial, they are not without hopes. Therefore, for about ten days there has been no activity at all. But the rebel barbarians cunningly devise many plans. Our defenses on land and sea were previously destroyed by them; we have not been able to restore these immediately and can hardly guarantee that they will not seize the opportunity to return. The rigorousness of our defense must be even more thorough than when the rebel ships were in the river. The outside regions southeast of the province have extensive coast lines, and must be defended everywhere. Already Your slaves have directed the military and civil districts to engage many irregular troops, and also, at strategic places, to scuttle ships and sink stones, secretly fastening down concealed stakes to serve as obstructions, all as means of protection.

Previously, in the first month, Provincial General-in-chief of the Land Forces Kuo Chi-ch'ang, ordinarily stationed at Hui-chou, came to Canton. The former governor general, Ch'i-shan, because Hui-chou is primarily ocean frontier, ordered him to re-turn to Hui (-chou) and defend it. At Ch'ao-chou and Nan-o, further to the east of Hui-chou, Your slaves have charged the various military officials to defend rigorously and exert them-selves to coordinate their information and resources. In Canton the people who moved away are gradually coming back; the buyers of the various sections, who have relatively large capital, are still holding off. They must await the flow of commerce before they can secure their position and resume trade. (IWSM. TK 26; 18a, 8-19b, 1)

10. <u>April 14, 1841.</u> EDICT: <u>British Merchants Classified as Rebels and Not to be Allowed to Trade.</u>

Edict to the Grand Councillors. Today We have received Yang Fang's express memorial that the English rebels have withdrawn from the Canton River and that in accordance with the Edicts he is energetically planning defense and resistance. According to the memorial, America and other countries customarily allowed to have their trading ships enter Whampoa were taking advantage of the opportunity to trade.

The rebel barbarians causing the trouble have no connection with America and other countries; naturally (the latter) can be permitted to trade. Only the said minister's previous memorial had a petition of America and other countries saying that, as the English barbarians are in a critical situation, could they not like-

wise be allowed to trade and their warships given something to be
apprehensive about? The English barbarian merchant ships, although they have not participated in furthering rebellion, all belong
to the rebel English and can by no means be allowed to trade. On
this occasion, if the various trading countries have sold anything
to the rebels, or deceived or misled or (been guilty of) any such
malpractice, then We charge that they be thoroughly investigated
and dealt with. In no case can there be any compromising attitude,
causing the rebel barbarians to obtain their desire of carrying on
trade.

We presume that I-shan, Lung-wen, and Ch'i Kung by this
time have all reached the provincial captial. The troops dispatched from various places must also be continually arriving at
Canton. The said general on the one hand should defend the provincial capital, on the other, carry out (the campaign of) suppression according to circumstances.... (IWSM. TK 26; 22a,
2-10)

11. April 18, 1841. MEMORIAL: Reports Request by United States
and France for Reopening of Trade to Indian Ships.

Military Assistant Governor Yang Fang and Governor of
Kwangtung I-liang memorialize. Your slaves formerly received from the American consul, Delano, on behalf of India, a
request to trade. They did not dare to grant it at once. Already on March 22, they respectfully reported this by post in a
memorial and respectfully prayed instruction in this matter.
They now beg to note that the American trading ships originally
allowed to trade, because of the troubles caused by the English
barbarians last year, have been obstructed more than half the
time. On March 31, it was reported to the Throne that that
country's trading ships were allowed to enter Whampoa as usual
to trade. The American barbarians, having had their goods
stopped for a long time and then suddenly set in motion, were
all pleased and encouraged, and grateful for the Imperial
beneficence. The English barbarian merchants all stood by
enviously. That their real interest is trade can already be
clearly seen. Therefore, from the time of the memorial onward, the English barbarians have been quiet and have not
dared to cause trouble again.

Yesterday was received a request on their behalf from
America, France, and other countries, stating that India, although a dependency of the English barbarians, is more than
twenty thousand li from England, nor did she join in causing
trouble. [Vermilion endorsement: The following details
should not be discussed now. We only know one word, "Attack!"
Besides, they are entirely untrustworthy.] At this time the

trading ships of the other countries have all entered the port, and it
seems inappropriate for the innocent Indians to be forced into the
corner in order to show discrimination. Even Elliot told the American consul that the India merchants had no connection with England's
resort to arms; the English ships of the mother country were willing
to await the Imperial Edicts and would not dare enter port hastily,
and only India had innocently suffered and had her goods stopped;
actually this is discourteous to them, so he had the request made on
their behalf, to allow them to trade along with the others.

We find that India is a dependency of Great Britain. Previously
we memorialized its inclusion in the port embargo (of Canton). Now
we have investigated carefully the Indian barbarian merchants and
(find that) they have not participated in causing trouble. It is fitting
that in dealing with the obedient and the rebellious, we consider the
course of accommodation. Moreover, [underlined in vermilion:
i.e., by drawing a line parallel to the Chinese text] according to the
report of the hong merchants, among the India merchant ships were
nine cargoes of foreign rice, amounting to something over 30,000
piculs [1 picul = 133 1/3 pounds.]. Kwangtung, being cut up with
hill and sea, and the grain production not being large, has always
depended on supplies of Saigon and foreign Indian rice. [Vermilion
endorsement: This is the source of opium. Whom are you deceiving?
On reading this memorial, We are angry to the extreme!] Now
that the Indian barbarian merchants have again brought in rice, it
may be credible that they are not harboring evil in their hearts
[underlined in vermilion.] (Sic. No underlining appears in the
text but the implication is that the emperor regards this as incredible.). Moreover, there is real benefit to the sustenance of the
people, and in this way the populace can be pacified. It seems that
to allow the India merchant ships, one and all, to unload, while extending the Sage Sovereign's gracious kindness to those from afar,
would at the same time diminish the strength of England's following. (IWSM.TK 26; 36a, 3-37a, 4)

12. April 18, 1841. MEMORIAL: Recommendation of Appeasement
of the British by Restoration of their Trade.
Yang Fang and I-liang further memorialize. To continue: we
find that, as the Kwangtung coast faces the open sea, the various
foreign countries have traded (there) for over two hundred years.
Hu-men (Bocca Tigris) is the lock and key of Canton. The various
forts are also the barricades of the coast. Therefore, the problem
of controlling the outside barbarians actually depends on these.
Now Hu-men has already been lost. Near Canton, Lieh-te, Ta-
huang-chiao and other places have already been invaded. Other
than these, Canton has no barricade able to ward off (invaders). In
Canton, reserves of the various customs and provincial treasuries

altogether amount to over 4, 000, 0C0 (<u>taels</u>) in silver. The prisons
and granaries are all important places, and besides, the crowded
market places and thickly populated districts now on the outside
have no protection, and within, the people are stricken with secret
fear and are in a completely agitated condition.

In a previous memorial (we) reported the fall of Hu-men and
the memorial has been returned to Canton. We respectfully received an Imperial Edict stating that the (provincial) capital is the
headquarters, and that, being of the greatest importance, it must
be rigorously defended in order to provide for the unexpected. We
look up to the condescending regard of the Imperial Heart, and the
officials and people of the whole city are grateful to the point of
tears. Now although Imperial troops have been transferred from
Kweichow, Hunan, Kiangsi, and Szechuan, and those which have
successively arrived at Canton already number more than 8000,
still they are all unaccustomed to marine warfare. The barbarian
ships will fire their cannon on the water; our troops can only meet
the enemy on shore, and battle cannot be joined. Since there is no
good scheme which will provide circumstances certain of victory,
how can we dare to act quickly and forget the danger of painful
defeat?

During the last ten days the reason the English barbarians have
been quiet is that their minds are thoroughly devoted to trade. Now
while America and other countries have made firm requests on
behalf of India, the mother country ships of the English barbarians
still cannot enter port. It appears that they are still inclined to
dread punishment and willingly submit. Moreover, America and
other countries, with the Indian barbarian merchants, daily carry
on trade and mutually cooperate with one another, and under the
circumstances it is hard to distinguish the ships one by one. If
we are going to be deceived, would it not be better to exemplify the
(Imperial) favor? The minds of the merchants would then be at
ease and the gunboats could not act recklessly. But we find the
present temper of the English barbarians is one of chagrin, partly
because they have heard that the Rebel-pacifying General is
hastening from behind with a large army, incessantly arriving;
partly because Your slave, Yang Fang, on March 11, memorialized
asking to exchange the marine forces for land forces, to strengthen
the barriers, and to prohibit only the trade of those rebels. Formerly, relying on the superiority of their ships and cannon, they boldly
forced their way into the Canton River. If they had been able to
break through the city walls, then the whole city would have been
in their hands, and there would have been no occasion for request.
Later, seeing the city ready to defend and resist and no place to
display their cunning, thereupon they asked the other barbarians
to appeal for them and did not seek other terms. Compared with

the precedent of Ch'i-shan [Vermilion endorsement: The language
is different but the content is the same. It is really incomprehensi-
ble that (you) dare to make the attempt.], when they demanded
territorial compensation, there seems to be some difference. As
to the present situation, it seems wise at first to allow them to
trade as a temporary means of holding and leading them on, in order
to facilitate leisurely preparation. [Vermilion endorsement: We see
that you two men desire to follow Ch'i-shan's precedent. Therefore
A-ching-a did not attach his name.] Then we can hope that the outcome will be entirely safe.

    Vermilion endorsement: If trade were the solution of the prob-
lem, why would it be necessary to transfer and dispatch generals
and troops in this way, and why did We need to arrest Ch'i-shan?
These observations are entirely wrong. Edicts will be issued at
once. (IWSM. TK 26; 37a, 5-38a, 10)

13. April 18, 1841. EDICT: Unsuccessful Defenders of Canton are
Ordered to be Placed under Arrest.

    Edict to the Grand Secretariat. Formerly on account of the
English barbarians' reckless barbarity, wounding our high defense
officers, We have repeatedly issued Edicts ordering Yang Fang to
proceed, together with I-liang and others, to lead troops to attack
them, in order to proclaim the Heavenly punishment and satisfy
peoples' hearts. Today (We) received the memorial of Yang Fang
and others (to the effect that) the troops sent from the various
provinces to Canton already numbered over 8000. Still they do
not seize the opportunity to attack; they procrastinate and idle
about, and even go so far as to request authorization for the ships
of the English barbarians' dependency, India, to trade at Canton.
This is deliberate obstruction and demoralization of the army's
spirit. It is entirely unreasonable.

    Yang Fang and I-liang are ordered to be handed over to the
Board for strict determination of punishment. (IWSM. TK 26;
38b, 1-5)

14. April 18, 1841. EDICT: Repudiates Appeasement Proposals and
Orders a General Attack on the British at Canton.

    Edict to the Grand Councillors. On this day Yang Fang and I-
liang memorialized to allow the India merchant ships to carry on
trade, and also (presented) a separate memorial on the condition
of the Canton defense. On reading the memorial (We) were af-
flicted with the deepest indignation, and have issued an explicit
edict that Yang Fang and I-liang be immediately turned over to the
Board for rigorous examination. That the rebel barbarians are
by nature and appearance treacherous and unusually faithless, (We)
have long since discerned. If we do not punish them rigorously how

can we exemplify national prestige and eliminate future anxiety? Now that troops dispatched from various parts, numbering more than 16, 000, are successively reaching Canton, why did not Yang Fang prepare to attack vigorously? Still he procrastinated and idled and deliberately obstructed, eagerly using trade as a pretext. This following in the rut of Ch'i-shan, changing the words but leaving the content the same, is entirely inexplicable. Previously (they) memorialized, asking permission for the various countries to trade; We, out of deference to popular opinion, did Our best to accord their request. Now again, they dared to plead the case of the India ships on the grounds that they have not aided the rebels. If this were the solution, why should it be necessary to summon generals and put forth armies and transfer troops in great numbers? Moreover, those rebels have wounded our superior military officers and killed our soldiers in great numbers. How can their loyal spirits be comforted? Yang Fang and the others only know how to compromise and bring a matter to an end, without regard for the nation as a whole, completely failing to come up to Our expectations.

Then, what was said about the merchant ships carrying foreign rice, etc., is completely unbelievable; it is rather that the source of opium is found in them. Furthermore, how could (we) publish prohibitions for eradicating the evil? At this time, there must be no consideration other than of means of attack. I-shan and Lung-wen, who have received personally Our full instructions and are certainly able to understand Our point of view, have now reached Canton with adequate troops and supplies. Naturally they should cooperate wholeheartedly with Yang Fang and Ch'i Shen and exert themselves for the country, in order to receive great rewards. No reference to the word "commerce" will be tolerated, nor will idle loss of opportunities. The present documents are ordered distributed and read.

I-shan and the others, on receipt of this Edict, are charged forthwith to have the commanders order troops distributed for attack. It is imperative that not a single rebel sail should escape and that (the rebels) be made to revere and fear us. If the barbarian ships hear the rumors and hide far away, and we expand our military strength in vain, only the said generals will be held to account. Tremble! (IWSM. TK 26; 38b, 6-39b, 2)

15. April 20, 1841. MEMORIAL: New Commanders Report their Determination to Attack Despite the Hopeless Situation at Canton.

Rebel-pacifying General I-shan, and Military Assistant Governor Lung-wen memorialize. Your slaves, on March 25 and 27 respectively, received two communications from the Grand Councillors, as well as an Imperial Edict ordering them to proceed posthaste day and night, and also to assume direction of the lately

arrived government troops, keeping them in order as they proceeded; if possible, to seize the rebels from the rear, and to take
advantage of the opportunity to attack them.

Respectfully, they received the Sage Sovereign's instructions;
they heard them kneeling, with boundless admiration. Immediately
they on the one hand made haste, and on the other, dispatched word
to Chekiang to stop the continued transfer of 2800 government troops,
and to Kwangsi to order the 2,000 newly transferred government
troops to hasten southward. Further, they sent orders to the tao-
t'ai of Nan-Shao-Lien, Yang Chiu-wan, that, excepting for those
which have already crossed the Shao border enroute to Canton
and need not be stopped, the others, no matter from what province
they are coming, should all be detained, ordered to have their
military stores in order, and to await further developments.

Your slaves, on April 1, while crossing the border at Nan-
hsiung-chou, Kwangtung, received a report from the Nan-Shao-Lien
tao-t'ai saying that the Yunnan, Kweichow, Hunan, and Szechuan
government troops which were going from Shao to Canton numbered
over 8,000. Besides these, the government troops subsequently
raised in the various provinces have still not reached Canton, and
there are no troops to detain. Now we have sent the Shao-chou
brigade of 300 men as an escort. We also urged the 300 men led
by Lieutenant Colonel Ta-san of Hupeh, on their arrival, to accompany the others. The troops being transferred from Hunan,
Hupeh, and Kwangsi have not yet entered the province, and cannot
be awaited for long; while more than half of the Kwangtung cannons
have been scattered and lost, and, except for the defense of the
city, are inadequate for offense or defense.

Then, according to a letter from the governor of Kiangsi,
transmitting a report of his deputy, Fu-k'uei, more than ten of
the old iron cannons in Kiangsi, because of having been stored
for many years, could not be fired. Besides, as to those to be
sent from Hunan and Kwangsi, no reply has yet been received.
The saltpeter sent for has not yet reached Canton either. We are
just now burning with anxiety. We have learned that after the fall
of Hu-men (Bocca Tigris), the gunboats went directly to Whampoa
and that the Hai-chu-ssu fort (Dutch Folly) was also taken. The
merchant ships were anchored outside Canton city. The rebel
barbarians repeatedly fired cannons and rockets, and shot into
the city. In addition, traitorous Chinese took advantage of the
opportunity to burn and plunder. The merchants inside and out
fled in disorder.

At that time, the Americans were asking to trade. The high
officials in Canton temporarily put them off, and encouraged them
by promising to memorialize their request. Now the rebel barbarian warships are not willing to withdraw into the outer ocean

and are still at Whampoa in reserve. They let it be known that
after Your slaves arrived at Canton, they would immediately request
a settlement. [Vermilion endorsement: Detestable to the extreme!]
     Your slaves, on hearing these things, were filled with grief.
They personally know that since the beginning of the rebel barbarians' defection, they have seized forts and wounded our commanders. Wherever their ferociousness reaches, is it true that
no one dare resist it? On the whole, it is rather that prior to this
we have proposed conciliation, voluntarily removed the barriers,
causing them to take advantage of the opening to penetrate deeply
and press at our gates. Those ministers, acting as circumstances
required, could follow expediency, but Your slaves have received
(Imperial) command to attack. How dare they hesitate or equivocate and idly lose an opportunity, thus betraying (Imperially imposed) trust? [Vermilion endorsement: Take care not to follow
the example of those who are cowardly, compromising, and
conscienceless. We are wholly dependent on you.]
     But troops can hardly be collected hastily, and ammunition has
not yet arrived. If, on Your slaves' arrival at Canton, they were to
refuse trade, the barbarians would certainly attack the city with all
their strength. If there should be any unexpected danger and rescue
be too late, then, wishing to protect Canton, we would on the contrary be hastening its loss. Now the enemy's determination ought
not to be further fostered [pointed with vermilion; i. e. , by drawing
a small circle next to the Chinese text] the national [Vermilion
endorsement: Quite right] prestige ought not to be further injured
[pointed with vermilion]. We must devise thoroughly complete
plans, in accord with our Sage Instructions.
     At this time the governor general, Ch'i Kung, is crossing the
Mei-ling mountains. We are halting temporarily at Shao-chou, and
have dispatched a latter to the said governor general to hasten here
for a conference, to collect government troops from all regions,
and to occupy all the land routes and strategic places; to station
troops for defense, to urge the collection of powder, and secretly
to devise implements for defense and attack; to prepare ambushes
everywhere, to encourage the troops and volunteers, and to use
them in unexpected ways; to attack sharply the inner anchorages,
thus causing the rebel barbarians to lose courage, and in addition
to defend the various inlets of the river, in order to show that we
are always on guard. It is reported that the barbarian ships stores
are depleted, and an immediate battle would be to their advantage.
This is nothing more than anxiety to force the sale of goods to
supply their needs. If we strengthen our walls and purge the
countryside, then the Chinese traitors will have no profit to covet.
When their adherents are cut off, they (we) can send crack troops
to take their rear, lower rafts to fill up the river, and join land

and marine (forces) to capture and seize by different routes, so that not a single barbarian sail will return (home), in order to manifest Heavenly punishment and gratify men's minds.

Vermilion endorsement: These views are quite proper. We only await the news of victory with the greatest impatience. (IWSM. TK 26; 40b, 10-42b, 10)

16. April 28, 1841. MEMORIAL: Reports that the British at Canton are Waiting to Share United States Favor.

Military Assistant Governor Yang Fang memorializes. Now the Chinese traitors are gradually scattering, and the rebel ships have withdrawn from the Canton River, excepting for ten-odd rebel ships of various sizes anchored at Ta-huang-chiao. According to reports from Hu-men (Bocca Tigris), Hsiang-shan, Macao, and other places, at Sha-chiao there is one large three-masted warship anchored, and one large two-masted sampan; at Heng-tang, one large three-masted warship; at Yung-an, three large three-masted warships; at Ma-yung, one large two-masted warship; at Ta-hao-t'ou, one large three-masted gunboat; at Huang-pu-wei, three large three-masted warships; at Shen-ching, one large three-masted warship. The said rebels anchor irregularly. The (British) sail around, delay, and merely hope, along with the United States and other countries, to receive (Imperial) favor. In their eagerness in waiting for the bounty of the (Imperial) will, there still remain evidences of going about and spying.

Your slave still fears that the endangered city has only just been made secure and the popular mind is not yet freed from anxiety. Accordingly, he has already issued proclamations notifying the inhabitants to carry on as usual. At the same time, he has strictly ordered the cantonments and guardhouses of the various coastal districts to defend diligently, and has let the said barbarians know that we are prepared, in order to shatter their courage. In matters of defense and attack, he has taken such measures as circumstances require. Now the sores on Your slave's legs have again broken out, but he does not dare on this account to evade any of his responsibilities. He awaits the arrival of I-shan and Lung-wen at Canton, to cooperate wholeheartedly with them, and hopes that defense and offense will be complete without one chance in ten thousand of failure, in order to contribute to the Emperor's ultimate object of restoring peace to His borders and tranquillizing His people. (IWSM. TK 27; 14b, 9-15b, 4)

17. April 28, 1841. MEMORIAL: Reports that British are being Restrained by American Intercession on their Behalf.

Yang Fang further memorializes. On March 5, Your slave arrived in haste at the Kwangtung provincial capital (Canton). On

the twelfth, he went out on horseback from the Ta-fo-ssu Supreme
Military Headquarters within the city, into the small streets. The
streets were narrow and crowded with people. Suddenly a Chinese
traitor seized his left arm and almost unhorsed him. [Vermilion
endorsement: Odious.] He was seized by Your slave on the spot. On
being questioned, he made no other complaint, merely acknowledging his fault in confused words. Your slave immediately ordered
that his head be hung up and exposed--by killing one man, to strike
fear into the hearts of the populace.

After six days, the rebels pressed the gates of the capital.
Inside the city, orders were carried out and prohibitions enforced.
The Chinese traitors held their breath. The small boats plying
their trade in the Canton River were very numerous. On March
18-19, for two days and three nights, the rebel ships were anchored
at Pai-ho-t'an.

Although there were no wood supplies, Your slave hastened the
work on one hundred fire-boats and two large bamboo fire rafts,
originally intending to release them, lighted, with the tide, but the
said three-masted barbarian warships and armed steamers were
anchored at wide intervals, each [of the latter] protected by three-
masted warships, and more than a thousand small boats of the
Chinese traitors were going about over a radius of five or six li.
[Vermilion endorsement: Odious to the extreme! You certainly
should have totally exterminated them without regrets!] Elliot
[underlined in vermilion] stayed at night on a patrol boat and on
seeing the flames would certainly have withdrawn, so the fire
would not have served its purpose. So, on account of the request
of the Americans, they, the British, were temporarily restrained
and led on, in order to await the collection of troops from the rear
and to plan for defense and attack.

But there has long been the rumor that our marine forces received three hundred dollars for each unloaded cannon shot. Your
slave has investigated the death in the field of Kuan T'ien-p'ei.
Because the officers did not dare to force the soldiers to fire the
cannon, [Vermilion endorsement: Such utter uselessness. On the
whole, the military and civil officials are so many wooden idols.]
Kuan T'ien-p'ei himself took up a fuse, but water had already
seeped into the fuse hole of the cannon. Thus the degenerate
practice of soldiers and people in yielding to bribery will hardly
bear inquiry. If we do not cleanse their hearts and wash their
faces, repair the strings and get out of the rut, we can hardly
effect any reform.

As to curbing the Chinese traitors, Your slave proposes to
post proclamations setting forth the dangers. After the governor
of Kwangsi, Liang Chang-chu, has sent wooden rafts and large
stakes and the means of attack are prepared, he will again issue

proclamations, to curb the traitors' hearts and break the rebels' courage.   (IWSM. TK 27; 15b, 5-16b, 1)

18. May 11, 1841.   MEMORIAL: Reports the Resumption of Trade by all Non-belligerent Countries at Canton.
        I-shan, Lung-wen, and Ch'i Kung further memorialize. Your slaves, before leaving Peking, received a dispatch from the Grand Councillors, and on February 10, 1841, received an Imperial Edict:

> I-liang's memorial on the decrease in the revenue from the Canton customs states that in the Canton Maritime Customs revenue the barbarian customs form a large part, and that for the present year the number of barbarian ships arriving is not twenty percent, because the ships of the various countries have been obstructed by the English barbarians and have been unable to enter port, so that after the sixth month (July 18-August 17), which should have been the flourishing period for customs collections, there was on the contrary a decrease. Canton traditionally allows the various countries to trade. The respectful and obedient countries, naturally, should trade as usual. The English barbarians are imperious and domineering and have interfered with the livelihood of the various countries. How is it that those countries are willing resignedly to lose profits?
>
> (We) charge I-shan, Lung-wen and Ch'i Kung on their respective arrivals at Canton, to investigate the attitudes of the various countries, whether or not they are resentful of the English barbarians' interference with their livelihood or if they feel any disappointment toward the Heavenly Court for not yet being able to encourage and tranquillize them, causing them to stand in a corner and lose their business, and to memorialize according to the facts. Respect this.

        Looking up, they see that the Emperor is kind to those from afar, with infinite sympathy. Your slaves made haste to reach Canton and for several days secretly investigated and sent word to Governor I-liang to find out clearly the number of trading vessels of the various countries entering port, and to report to us for management. Your slaves have carried out a thorough investigation, and this is the situation: The old customs regulations of Canton traditionally authorize the trade of the various countries. Besides the trading vessels of the Portuguese barbarians who reside at Macao and unload their cargo at Macao, there are the merchant vessels of the United States, France, Holland, Spain, the Philippines, Cambodia (?), Denmark, Sweden, Prussia, Austria, England, and India, legally entering Whampoa for inspection and unloading. The distances from and routes to Canton are not the same. The number of ships coming to Canton each year varies from over one hundred to two hundred. From April 27 to June 30,

1840, there arrived only nineteen American and Spanish merchant ships. From this time on, no ships at all entered port. Because the English barbarians resisted authority, and their warships came and anchored in Canton seas, the merchant vessels of the various countries were all obstructed by the English barbarians and could not enter port. The English barbarians are imperious and domineering. The strength of the said countries is not sufficient to restrain them, and they are all deeply resentful.

On February 26 of the present year, when the English barbarians without authorization entered Hu-men (Bocca Tigris) and attacked and destroyed the Wu-yung guard station, the barbarian ships went direct to Whampoa. Therefore the merchant vessels of the United States, France, and India which were formerly allowed to trade, altogether forty-two vessels, were at last able to follow the British warships and enter port. They requested trade on behalf of the English barbarians.

Your slave, Yang Fang, together with Governor I-liang, has thoroughly investigated the situation, and memorialized clearly to continue to allow the respectful and obedient countries to trade as before. The said barbarians all gladly honor the Imperial grace and do not dare to be disappointed with the Heavenly Court. We have had the reports of the interpreters examined and they are all in agreement. Now although trade has already been opened, still the substantial buyers have all fled, and those doing business are extremely few. Your slaves have already issued proclamations ordering their speedy return, that all peaceful firms could trade with the respectful and obedient countries as usual, with no need for fear or doubt. In the last few days more are returning to their occupations, and the popular temper is a little more stable. (IWSM. TK 28; 4a, 4-5b, 5) ·

19.   January 16, 1842.   MEMORIAL: Reports Conditions at Ningpo, Chen-hai, and Ting-hai, with Observations on Barbarians.

I-ching and Wen-wei further memorialize. Again in the last few days, Your slaves have dispatched persons secretly to learn the rebel barbarian situation in the three cities of Ningpo, Chen-hai, and Ting-hai. They have carefully made a fair copy and respectfully present it for Imperial inspection.

1.   It is found that Ningpo, heretofore controlled by Gutzlaff,[7] now has changed to the Chinese traitor Liang Jen [underlined with vermilion]. All matters are entirely under his control. East of the city there is Hu-lang·Barrier. On the route connecting Chen-

---

7   Karl F. A. Gutzlaff (1803-1851), British German-born missionary, was attached to Sir Hugh Gough's staff.

hai and Ting-hai, the barbarians come and go continually. Now cannons have been placed at the prefectural capital, all facing west, in order to prevent the sudden arrival of our soldiers. The city gates are constantly watched and guarded, and ingress and egress is rigorously scrutinized. Money is not allowed to leave the city, and wood supplies are transported to the ships. In addition, behind the prefectural headquarters, (they) have torn down residences of the inhabitants, built walls on both sides, and opened a road in the middle leading to Yen-ts'ang Gate. At the side they have bored through the wall making another gate, which the people are not allowed to pass through. The barbarians themselves come and go freely, so that in the future there will be a means to escape from (government) troops. Now they have ordered artisans to construct equipment. The expenses are appropriated from the small shops and wealthy households. The cash thus accumulated, about 1,000,000 strings,[8] has already been thirty to forty percent expended. Each day collection of supplies is made from the homes. At this time the barbarian brigands within the city are something over two thousand; outside the city, the number of ships anchored is sometimes six or seven, sometimes eight or nine. They come and go irregularly. A month ago, when they seized and carried off fifty or sixty local fishing boats, it was falsely said that they intended to attack Hang ch'eng, Cha-p'u, and other places. At present there is no activity.

    2. It is found that at Chen-hai the barbarians are the most numerous. The Chinese traitors are also not few. The chief conspirator and barbarian leader is Robert Thom[9] [underlined in vermilion]. He is extremely cunning. Every day he uses Fan's T'ien I Ko Library, in Ningpo, [10] and the gazeteers of the various districts of Chekiang, which enable him to trace boundaries. The Chinese traitor named Li of Chin-hsien [underlined in vermilion] is of great assistance to him. The prefectural city has five

---

8 The cash or ch'ien was the only Chinese coin current at this time. "The piece is thin and circular, about three-quarters of an inch in diameter with a square hole in the middle for the convenience of stringing them." The nominal value of one cash was 1/1000 of a tael or ounce of silver, but had depreciated by 1849 to 1,680 or 1,700 to one tael. A string of cash was 1,000. S. Wells Williams, Middle Kingdom, 3rd ed., New York, 1849, v. 1, p. 156.

9 Robert Thom (1807-1846), interpreter and student of Chinese, was H. B. M. consul at Ningpo and attached to Sir Hugh Gough's staff.

10 This is a reference to the oldest and most famous private library in China, located in Ningpo, owned by Fan Mou-chu (1721-1780), and founded by his ancestor Fan Ch'in (1506-1585), eight generations before. See biography of Fan Mou-chu by Miss Tu Lien-che in Hummel, Eminent Chinese of the Ch'ing Period, Washington, 1943, v. 1, p. 230-231.

gates, but only one is open. They examine everybody going out and
coming in, just the same as they do at Ning-chün (Ningpo). Within
the city, they have set up a forge to make munitions, and on board
their ships they have done likewise. The residents who do not open
their shops are bombarded with cannons. Every day they seize
artisans and take them to Chao-pao-shan to build small houses and
to construct and operate foundries. The artisans are not allowed
to go behind the mountain and are constantly watched over by barbarians. They (the barbarians) repeatedly issue false proclamations.
They are anxious to acquire the clothes and belongings of a certain
Yü. In addition they have engaged from other countries a strong
force of over two hundred men [underlined in vermilion], to afford
protection, but for a long time they have remained on shipboard
and are not allowed to go ashore.

3. (We) learn that the barbarians at Ting-hai are not numerous within the city, the great majority being on board the ships.
The ships are mostly anchored at the various ports. Everywhere
communication is maintained and strategic positions are utilized,
only they dare not enter the villages, because formerly they were
beaten by the villagers and are very fearful. Now they do no
more than secretly sell opium to the [Chinese] traitors.

In general the barbarians are very suspicious and besides,
they covet petty gains. The white devils [Spanish or Portuguese]
are fond of women; the red devils [Dutch or English] are fond of
money; the black devils [Indians] are fond of wine [underlined in
vermilion]. The various leaders inside the city are not all of the
same mind nor do they all give the same orders. In general they
want to establish a shipping port on Chu-shan and trade with the
interior. Therefore, they treat the residents very very generously.
[Annotated in vermilion: i.e., by putting a series of short dashes
parallel to the Chinese text.]

The barbarian ships are two-ply, one layer outside and one
inside. Each layer is made of hardwood boards seven inches
thick, with sand in between. The outside is covered with copper
and iron, also in two thicknesses. When a cannon ball strikes
the ship, it moves a little and that is all. There are also several
small vessels with fifty or sixty wounded barbarians on board.
It is said they have come from Formosa to Chen-hai for medical
treatment [annotated in vermilion].

This is the situation in these three cities. In all cases, Your
slaves secretly sent responsible persons, and the gentry of the
said prefectures who are in service at the military encampments
secretly went inside and outside the three cities, made a minute
investigation, and reported truthfully what they saw. (IWSM.
TK 41; 22b, 2-25a, 6)

20. March 28, 1842. EDICT: Appointment of Ch'i-ying as Tartar
General of Hangchow.
        Edict to the Grand Secretariat. Ch'i-ying is ordered to pro-
ceed posthaste to Chekiang as acting Manchu General-in-chief
(Tartar General) of Hangchow. Ch'i-ming-pao is ordered to await
Ch'i-ying's arrival at Chekiang and then come to Peking and wait
for Imperial orders. (IWSM. TK 44; 35b, 5-6; cf. Chinese Repository, v. 11, p. 675)

21. April 4, 1842. EDICT: Demotion of I-li-pu and Hsien-ling and
Assignment to Posts under Ch'i-ying.
        Edict to the Grand Secretariat. I-li-pu is ordered to be given
the seventh rank; Hsien-ling is ordered to be given the fourth rank
Officer of the Guards. Both are ordered handed over to Ch'i-ying
to be taken to Chekiang for disposal; all to be done posthaste.
(IWSM. TK 45; 10b, 3-4)

22. April 13, 1842. MEMORIAL: Reports Rejection of a French
Offer to Mediate with the British on Behalf of China.
        Ch'i-shan and others further memorialize. It is noted that
France has borders contiguous to those of the English barbarians.
Each comprises a separate state, long known for its prowess.
Formerly, on account of disputed territory, they were at odds and
fought with one another for many years. Subsequently they made
peace. The said country (France) has also in the past traded with
Kwangtung.   During the twelfth month of last year (January 11-
February 10, 1842), word was received that recently one of the
said country's warships, with the officers Jancigny and Cécille[11]
in command, had come to Kwangtung and was anchored at Chien-
sha-tsui opposite Hong Kong. They also said that there were still
warships which had not yet arrived. Just in the midst of our
secretly ordered investigation, a report was received that the
French officer Cécille had come to Canton on board a small sampan
and taken up residence. We immediately gave secret instructions
to the hong merchants to make discreet inquiries, and received the
report that they had come to Canton wishing to meet government
officials personally; that they had matters to propose which they
were unwilling to state openly; and in addition that two priests,
Yü-ch'ao and I-li-ta,[12] thoroughly conversant with the Chinese

11 Colonel A. de Jancigny was officially designated "Agent of the government of the
    King of France on a special mission to China and Indo-China" (Chinese Repository,
    v. 13, p. 112) and arrived at Macao, December 8, 1841, on the ship-of-war Erigone,
    Captain Cécille commanding. Ibid., v. 11, p. 586.
12 These are French names transliterated in Chinese characters; the originals have
    not been identified. One may be Pere Callery, sinologue, who was interpreter in
    1842.

language, came with them and reported that the said country's army officers had military affairs to discuss secretly and would not use (Chinese) interpreters to transmit them, and begged to make a report in person.

Your slaves considered that as the said country had always traded and been uniformly respectful and obedient until the English barbarians took up arms, rebelled against authority, threw the ocean frontiers into disorder, and obstructed the business of other countries, they would not necessarily be without hatred for the English barbarians Now on receipt of their report, requesting a personal interview secretly to discuss military affairs, we could take advantage of the circumstances to keep them under control and lead them on to our advantage, as a policy of using barbarians to curb barbarians.

Immediately, Your slaves, I-shan and others, jointly examined the channel of the river, went by boat to P'an-t'ang, ten li from the city, and had them summoned there for an interview to inquire into their objects in coming. According to their statement, the said country is profoundly grateful for the Heavenly Court's generous favors. The king of the said country, on hearing that the English barbarians had taken up arms against China, feared that the commercial ships of his country would be implicated, and thereupon sent them to provide protection, and in addition ordered them on their arrival here to act as intermediaries for the settlement of the dispute. Your slaves instructed them as follows:

> His Imperial Majesty is well aware of the fact that your country has
> long been respectful and obedient. The English rebels are so obstinate
> and unregenerate, so reckless and overbearing, that in the future your
> country and others are sure to be injured by them. The king of your
> country has sent you here with ships-of-war. If you are really able to
> exert yourselves on our behalf, the present general-in-chief and others
> will certainly memorialize the fact to His Imperial Majesty to secure
> for you unusual kindness and special favors.

According to their statement (in reply):

> We and the English barbarians, once enemy states, have now recently
> made peace, so we cannot act rashly without any pretext. If we were
> to attack them without reason, we fear that other countries would be
> resentful. Would it not be better to conclude the affair and stop the
> fighting by making an early settlement?

On hearing this, we asked them what method they had of concluding the affair. They replied that they were willing to negotiate with the English barbarians. If they agreed, that would be the end of it; if they did not agree, then they would have a pretext for taking up arms against them.

Your slaves informed them that, as the English barbarians had

repeatedly defied authority and were now occupying Ningpo, Ting-
hai, and other places, they had caused the Emperor to become angry
and to select and commission awe-inspiring generals and military
governors of various districts to lead the government troops of
various provinces to deal with them. How could the present general
and others dare to take the initiative and authorize them to negotiate at this time?

They replied: "Since Your Excellencies do not dare to memorialize, we shall first go out and negotiate with the English barbarian
leaders on the high seas. If there are any developments, we shall
come back and report."

Then (Your slaves) distributed gifts of various kinds, and thereafter the said officers and priests took their leave for the high seas.

Furthermore, according to the investigation of the local police,
the rebel barbarian officer Pottinger,[13] during the twelfth month of
last year (January 11-February 10, 1842), secretly returned from
Chekiang to Hong Kong. Furthermore, they found that the French
officer came to Hong Kong and had two personal interviews with the
rebel barbarians. Subsequently we received the report of the Hsiang-
shan Assistant District Magistrate residing at Macao, Chang Yü,
that the French priest Yü-ch'ao and others had reported personally
that the military officers now had important business and on February 25 had set sail for the Philippines, going to look after the warships. They left word for Jancigny to go to Canton to petition in
reply. On March 16, Jancigny arrived at the factory and presented
a memorandum, still under the pretext of concluding peace, hoping
to be given the English rebels' wharf.

Your slaves investigated their activities. It seems that the
English rebels recently made peace with them, and the French barbarians desire to share in the gains, and also to share in the
territory; therefore, they mediated on their behalf. The barbarians
are by nature full of cunning. Although the said military officers
are apparently respectful and obedient, how do we know they will
not avail themselves of this to spy out conditions in the interior, or
otherwise cause trouble? Since at present the said barbarians,
along with the barbarian merchants of the United States and other
countries, have access to the Canton factories, carry on trade as
usual, and now with no reason seek peace, it is impossible not to
be suspicious.

Accordingly, (we) employed polite words to reject (their proposal) and also informed them that they should not help the rebels

13 Sir Henry Pottinger succeeded Captain Elliot in command of the British forces in
China, arriving at Macao, August 10, 1841, and remaining to negotiate the Treaty of
Nanking, August 29, 1842.

lest jade and stone be both destroyed, but if they could exert themselves on China's behalf, His Imperial Majesty would certainly bestow favors on their country. Besides our ordering land and marine
forces to make our defenses rigorous and to watch their movements, we have not dared to withhold from Imperial knowledge the
circumstances of the French military officers coming to Canton, but
have appended this account according to the facts. (IWSM.TK 45;
30a, 3-32a, 6)

23. April 13, 1842. EDICT: Orders Amity and Trade with France
but Rejects Mediation and Military Aid.
          Edict to the Grand Councillors. ... In addition, there was a
separate memorial that the king of France, on hearing that the
English rebels had defied authority, had sent military officers to
come to Canton to disperse them. Barbarians are by nature cunning.
What they call "favorable means of dispersing them," (We) fear can
hardly be depended on. Moreover, how are the said barbarians
going to explain to the English barbarians? Even the means by
which they could disperse them, they were unwilling to make clear
in their report. Besides, now that the collected troops in Chekiang
are making attacks, there is no reason to be in a hurry to make
peace at Canton. But as the said country has always traded, has
been consistently respectful and obedient, and has come to Canton
to make a petition, (We) charge the said general-in-chief and others
to transmit an order to the said barbarians to this effect:

> Your country has always been respectful and obedient and naturally
> will be allowed to trade as usual. If you are really able to exert
> yourselves on behalf of the Heavenly Court, His Imperial Majesty
> must naturally be highly pleased. As to protecting yourselves from
> being thrown into confusion by the English barbarians, or having a
> pretext for taking up arms, etc., China rightfully is not concerned.

The said general-in-chief and others shall continue diligently
and secretly to defend. Be sure not to fall in with their wicked
scheme. (IWSM.TK 45; 36b, 6-37a, 3)

24. August 21, 1842. MEMORIAL: Proposal for a Chinese Navy:
American Model Rejected on Comparison with Traditional Chinese Ships.
          Sub-director of the Grand Court of Revision, Chin Ying-lin,
memorializes. We consider that the ruthlessness of the rebel barbarians is entirely attributable to the weakness and unmanliness of
(our) maritime forces, resulting in defeats. I venture to think that
what the said barbarians rely on is ships. Last year Canton bought
a ship from the United States. On taking it apart and examining it,
we found the wood was very hard, covered with five layers of
leather, in addition to a copper and an iron covering, also in five

or six layers, making a thickness of something over one ch'ih (14.1 English inches) placed over the wooden frame. Thus even large cannon balls could hardly shatter it. The masts were of very hard wood and the tops could bear a number of men, while the cannons could shoot a great distance, thus causing people to be very afraid of them.

I consider these to be by-products of China. Formerly when Sui attacked Ch'ien, they constructed a mast fifty feet high. When enemy ships approached it, none escaped destruction. The barbarians have merely slightly changed this device; their covering of ships with leather also to some extent follows the device of our war-junks, and is nothing to be marveled at.

Now in discussing the southern provinces, Szechuan is usually taken as a basis. In Szechuan wood is cheap and the soldiers strong and, compared to those of Hu-kuang (i.e., Hunan, Hupeh, Kwangtung, and Kwangsi), more serviceable. Now if we ask Szechuan to make Szechuan ships and Hu-kuang ships, nominally for rice transport, they will serve as preparations in advance. Even if the said barbarians should secretly flee, this would still be an effective means of protecting the rivers. Fukien and Kwangtung provinces, also on the pretext of suppressing robbers, can each build ships as means of coordination.

As to the method of building ships, we must use their methods advisedly and adapt them. "The large can win over the small; the soft is not the equal of the hard." We may either adapt or build, depending on expediency.

As to the "mother-and-son" type of ship, the front section is two chang long (23 feet, 6 inches), the stern, one chang, five feet long (about 17 feet, 7 inches), thus totalling three chang, five feet (41 feet, 1 inch), with boards on either end and clear space in the middle. The back conceals small boats, all joined together; the hold of the "mother" ship is filled with oil and cannon. In front of the hold on both sides are hooked prongs. When the enemy is encountered, their prow is hooked, fires are set inside the holds, and (our ship is) burned together with theirs. Soldiers crouching in ambush release the "son" boats and return. These should be provided.

As to the "ships chained together" type, this consists of two ships, each forming one third, bound to the middle one with chains. The front carries large cannon, poison fire, and spirit smoke. The prow of the ship is imposing and has a hooked prong, and in the rear there is provision for several oars. When the troops meet the rebels, they nail their boat fast and set fires with the wind. It is never done without effect. After the front chain is severed, the back boat returns. These should be provided.

As to the "tower boat" type, on top of the ship is built a tower·

comprising altogether three stories. Each has separate gunwales
where flags and banners can be placed; openings for arrows and
spears, cannon carriages and felt guards, all are prepared; the
places for cannons, stones, and molten iron, give the appearance
of a little fort. They are so spacious that horses and chariots can
be driven onto them. If they encounter a storm, they can be kept
anchored and not taken out. These should be provided.

As to the "fast galley" type, above the ship's wall there is a
separate gunwale. The oarsmen used are all picked soldiers.
These (ships) are light as flying gulls and come and go with great
speed, taking the enemy unawares and suddenly attacking his ships.
In the back are provided many gongs and drums to be used for
signaling. These should be provided.

As to the "large war junk" type, it is one hundred twenty paces
(366 feet) long and carries two thousand men, the walls being made
of wood with four oar platforms. On top, horses can be driven; on
the prow is painted a strange beast to scare the River God. The
gunwales are high enough to half cover a man's body. In addition,
each has a covering even with the gunwales. In the back there is
an additional wall where warriors are also placed, with no cover
above. There are gongs and drums on either side. These (junks)
are lined up in the water and used for battles. These should be
provided.

As for the "sea gull" type, the bow is low and the stern is
high; fore large and aft small, like a gull. On top of the ship's
wall on either side are placed outriggers, as though the gull had
wings. These serve to keep the ship from listing when it encounters storms. The roof and both sides are covered with
leather. Forked pennants, gongs and drums are all in the usual
manner. These should be provided.

As for the "cruising punt" type, it also has no gunwales, the
oars being placed on the sides. It is large or small, long or
short, according to convenience. Sometimes it uses revolving
paddles to steer and turn it by churning the water. When the
forces retreat or change formation, it is as fast as the wind. If
we plan to use these, they will be advantageous wherever we go.
These should be prepared.

As for the "covered shed" type, it uses raw cowhide to cover
the prow and roof, and in addition has copper plates. In motion
or in position, arrows or stones can hardly attack it. It has
openings for archers and spearmen and when near the enemy
they attack him. The ship need not be large but depends on agility
and speed; it takes the enemy unawares and cuts off his retreat.
These should be prepared.

As for the "three-decker" type, it has a bamboo and wood
cover to ward off lances and stones. It has openings for guns and

arrows, to be used in attacking rebels. It is divided into three
decks, top, bottom and middle. The bow and stern have covered
compartments to afford communication from top to bottom. Inside
the middle deck are boards bristling with knives and nails. On the
sides are flying oars. It travels very fast. On encountering rebels,
it feigns defeat; as though abandoned, it comes alongside them. The
crack troops crouch below and wait for the rebels to board the ship.
With one turn of a lever, the rebels fall to the middle deck, where
they immediately encounter the knives and nails and are all completely prostrated. These should be prepared.

As for the "double-header" type of ship, it has rudders on either
end, fastened so they can alternate, and can go according to the
wind. The outside is covered with leather; the inside conceals
cannons. Used for ambushing, the enemy is very much in fear of
them. These should be provided.

As for the "decoy" type of ship, it has the appearance of a
board. It also has no side walls. The mast is in the middle, the
rudder at the stern, and the men are in the hold. The helmsman
on top is also well concealed. Water washing over the deck cannot
sink it. It travels very fast. Northerners are familiar with it.
These should be provided.

As for the "skin-boat" type, it is of raw horse or cow hide with
bamboo or wood frame. It gives the appearance of a box, dried
with fire and floated on the water. One boat carries two men; they
use poles to strike the water, helping one another to make it go.
These should be provided.

All the devices should be modified to make them useful, extended to make them comprehensive, each according to its fitness
and its full usefulness.

The Szechuan and Hu-kuang ships are adequate to control the
rivers; the Fukien and Kwangtung boats can protect the seas. This
is the policy of making preparation and having no worries.

As to the means of offense, first we should examine the direction of the wind. As the barbarians' cannon are mostly on the
sides, our armies should only attack the bow and stern. If the bow
of the barbarian ship is to the south, and the stern north, and there
is a north wind, then attack the stern; if there is a south wind,
then attack the bow. If the bow is to the east, and the stern west,
again if there is an east wind, attack the bow; if (there is) a west,
attack the stern. Thus getting the wind to our advantage and also
avoiding cannon fire, we can get in close to the stern or bow of the
barbarian ships. Furthermore, our ships must meet them obliquely.
The bows should be drawn close together and the sterns kept clear.
Then many ships can be placed together, and firearms will also
not be fired promiscuously. If the bow of the barbarian ship is
to the east, and the stern west, and our ships take advantage of a

west wind to attack their stern, then the bows of the ships approaching on the left must face the southeast, and those on the right have their bows facing northeast, always at an oblique angle; then our cannon-fire cannot strike our own ships; the rest can be deduced by analogy. It is essential that pilots be skillful in handling the rudder; those who are expert should be rewarded several times, whereas for those who are remiss, capital punishment should extend to themselves and their families. This must needs be practised beforehand.

Next we should examine the conditions of tides. With the tide coming in, we can succeed; with an ebb tide, we had best avoid (encounter). When our forces have the advantage and attack the rebel ship's bow and stern obliquely, in general have them employ the four-corner strategy. Each corner requires not more than four tugboats; if they are large, not more than three. Even with the four corners attacking simultaneously, there are not more than twelve to sixteen boats. Not a single barbarian ship we attack can escape immediate destruction. If we have more ships than this, they can be sent to attack other ships; it is not necessary to keep them in one place, causing much confusion.

The barbarian ships have a draft of over two chang (23 feet, 6 inches); our ships, not more then a few feet. If we come from a distance and turn around, we can certainly get the favorable wind. If we attack the bow, then we must first strike the point of it; if we attack the stern, then we must first strike the rear hold. The rear hold, having windows, is where the barbarian chief stays and where the powder is. When it is struck the powder will explode. Then the copper which encases the rudder can be hit with cannons and broken. With the rudder broken and the prow shattered, the whole ship will be completely out of control; the seamen who handle the sails, being mostly fore and aft, will be thrown into the sea, and the ship will be endangered. This must needs be practised beforehand.

To continue, we should make use of the device of burning; we should send out fifty "melon" boats (i.e. small rowboats), carrying dry grass and grass rope and covered with matting, secured with chains and capped with large nails. The extreme end is pointed and sharp. Several swimmers with their bodies half in the water, paddle alongside. The gunwale of the boat is very low, and the cannon fire of the barbarians cannot reach it. Once alongside, it is nailed to the wood (-en hull) and set fire to, and cannot fail to work destruction. From the top of our masts, we can also hurl fire-pots. We select two men, with bamboo helmets on their heads, their breasts protected with cane shields which are tied with ropes at the back; they carry two knives at their waists and are provided with fuses. One man is on the foremast, one on the second mast, and they go up until their heads are even with the sails.

At the bottom of each mast there are also two men to work the
pulleys, prepare fire-pots and draw them up. The man at the top
of the mast, at proper times, lights and releases them, but the
supply is not exhausted. The rockets at the bow are also handled
in this way. Our troops can board their ships and can surely win a
great victory. This must needs be practised.

In addition, there is the stratagem of "avoiding the empty and
attacking the full." The barbarian ships are large and their draft
very great. The gunwale does not protrude from the water.more
than two or three feet. The top is entirely empty. If we attack
them with artillery, every shot falls in empty space. If we only
attack the side of the ship, taking a low point as base, there would
not be a chance of escape.

Near the rebel ships, there is always noxious smoke. Licorice
and brown sugar held in the mouth give immediate relief.

When the barbarian ships go aground, we must entangle their
sails. Using our sails and spars to tangle up their sails, and holding them back with hooked poles, they will not be able to get away.
To use stones to attack their bows is also very fearful. This must
be practised.

Now the rebel barbarians, from the time they presented tribute
in the Chia-ch'ing era (1796-1821), have been arrogant in their
language and draw maps everywhere they go. They have harbored
mischief in their hearts for a long time. Having provocation, they
rebel, and without provocation, they also rebel. Now their low and
cowardly nature is worse than before. If we restrain them with
temporary measures, how can it last for long? If we sleep on firewood and taste bile [i. e., keep alive our spirit of revenge], eat
late and go without rest, what has been lost will be recovered and
success will not be slow in coming. If we are generous with our
time and persist whole-heartedly, if we do not spare heavy expense
or cling to "rules of grammar," the insignificant barbarians will
not be worthy of being conquered.   (IWSM. TK 58; 43a, 3-47a, 5)

25. August 21, 1842. EDICT: Orders Shipbuilding on Both Western
and Chinese Models at Canton.

Edict to the Grand Councillors. Formerly, because of resistance
on the ocean frontiers, warships were of primary importance and
(We) issued Edicts ordering Kwangtung province to consider building
(them), and also that Fang Hsiung-fei's proposal be copied and sent
for perusal. Subsequently (We) received Chin Ying-lin's memorial
requesting that more ships be prepared. His methods of building
ships of such types as "mother-and-son" ships, "chained-together"
ships, as well as "tower ships," "fast galleys," "war-junks," "sea
gulls," "cruising punts," "covered sheds, " "three-deckers,"
"double-headers," "decoy" ships, and "skin boats," are after vari-

ous patterns.

I-shan and others are charged to make careful inquiry, to determine which types among the various ships the said sub-director memorialized about are the most efficient, then to buy up supplies of strong wood and build them as quickly as possible, and in addition to memorialize fully on the charts and descriptions for the proposed designs for building ships. If, among the hong merchants of the said province, there are any thoroughly familiar with the methods of building ships and able to devise means of buying barbarian ships, Wen-feng is also charged carefully to seek them out and give them encouragement. The original memorials are ordered copied and given to them for scrutiny. Let this serve as a notification to I-shan, Ch'i Kung,[14] Liang Pao-ch'ang, and Wu Chien-hsün and also be transmitted for Wen-feng's information.
(IWSM. TK 58; 47a, 6-47b, 4)

26. August 22, 1842. MEMORIAL: Reporting British Shipwreck on Formosa.

Memorial of Brevet Provincial General-in-chief and Brigadier General of T'ai-wan (Formosa), Ta-hung-a, and Brevet Provincial Judge and Tao-t'ai of T'ai-wan, Yao Ying.

. . . We find now that the eighteen white barbarians captured include the leader, Denham,[15] and two accomplices, who are all red barbarians. There are in addition four other persons, one named Gully, one named Partridge, one named Newman, and one named Wilson, also red barbarians. Because their hair is slightly yellow, they are called red barbarians. Along with the eleven white barbarians, they are all natives of the English mother country. The previously received report of the battalion|of the sub-prefecture of T'an-shui regarding (the capture of) one red bar-

---

14 *Cf.* note on Ch'i Kung's shipbuilding activities in the *Chinese Repository* (v. 13, p. 390): "He took great interest in building ships of war, and gave the name Chingkih [*Cheng-chi*], the Fortunate, to the largest ship which has been launched. This vessel is a full rigged ship of about 600 tons, pierced for forty guns, and cost $60,000."

15 This probably refers to the English brig *Ann*, wrecked on Formosa, March 11, 1842. The British aboard were F. A. Denham, commander; G. Roope, chief officer; D. Partridge, third officer; S. Cowan, gunner; F. Newman, seacunnie; E. Wilson, seacunnie; J. Mills, seacunnie; W. Norris, seacunnie; and R. Gully, passenger. Six of the Englishmen and two others were liberated and sent to Amoy; 43 crewmen (Filipinos, Portuguese, and Lascars) were beheaded; the others making up the complement of 57 died or escaped. The survivors reached Amoy, November 24 and Hong Kong, December 5, excepting the carpenter, who did not arrive until April 2, 1843. The names of the Englishmen have been identified with the Chinese transliterations. *Chinese Repository*, v. 12, p. 113-121, 235-248. A seacunnie is defined as a white quartermaster or steersman on a ship manned by East Indian sailors.

barian was a mistake and must be corrected. In addition, there are
thirty black barbarians, all natives of Bombay. From their depositions the rebel barbarians' violent attitude is clear as a picture.
When they made their depositions our hair stood on end. These
island barbarians from ancient times forward have known only love
of gain and fundamentally are no different from dogs and sheep....
(IWSM. TK 59; 16a, 5-16b, 2)

27. August 24, 1842. MEMORIAL: Reporting French Captain Cécille
at Shanghai and his Proposal to go to Nanking.
        Governor General of Liang-chiang Niu Chien memorializes. I
have received the report of the tao-t'ai of Su-Sung-T'ai, Wu I-hsi,
stating that on July 31, there was a French warship anchored outside Wu-sung. The barbarian leader Cécille sent a letter on August
9, asking for an interview. The said tao-t'ai met him outside the
city to inquire into his object in coming.
        According to the translated report of the interpreter Chin Wan-
ch'üan, their country has in the past traded at Canton and been most
friendly to the Heavenly Court. Now the king of their country, hearing that the English barbarians are rebelling, has specially dispatched two warships to China to ascertain the facts. His ship
reached Canton in the tenth month of last year (November 13-
December 18, 1841). The other ship has not yet arrived. Coming
without making any promises to the English barbarians, if they are
favored with a memorial to His Imperial Majesty permitting the
English barbarians to set up a barbarian official in Peking to
manage their affairs [underlined in vermilion], the same as Russia
and other countries, they would be gratified. Now they wish to proceed to the Yangtze River and see first, Pottinger, and later, His
Excellency the Governor General, to induce the English barbarians
to cease hostilities. They said further that when their ships went
to the Yangtze they feared that the officials and populace would
consider their vessels as helping the combatants and a good deal
of misunderstanding result. They asked us to engage for them one
or two native vessels so that they could proceed immediately.
        The said tao-t'ai instructed him (Cécille) that engaging ships
for them must await a report to superiors for decision. The barbarian leader returned to his ship and sailed out of Wu-sung
harbor. This report and request for instructions are at hand.
        Now to comment on the contents of the said tao-t'ai's report:
France has traded at Whampoa, Kwangtung province, for two
hundred years and has been on very friendly terms with the
Heavenly Court. Now on hearing that the English barbarians are
rebelling in China, they wish to go to the Yangtze River to induce
them to cease hostilities. This is evidence of their respect and
obedience and worthy of some praise, but the English barbarians

are now at Canton, seeking trade, and have already sent a joint memorial asking (Imperial) favor.   Recently an Imperial decree was
received, and the English gunboats immediately all withdrew outside
the Yangtze.   We suppose that Cécille on hearing this must needs be
particularly pleased, as it does not set at naught his purpose in
coming so far to effect peace.

As to the suggestion that we memorialize His Imperial Majesty
to allow the English barbarians to install an officer at Peking, like
Russia and other countries, the English made this request in 1793.[16]
Because the matter was not practicable, Emperor Kao-tsung Shun
[of the Ch'ien-lung era] issued a special Imperial Edict to the king
of the said country, denying what was requested.   Now that England
is requesting a treaty and there is no such clause, there is surely no
need to discuss it.   But as Cécille, having traversed several oceans,
has heard news of England's cessation of hostilities, and as there is
no need of his going further to the Yangtze, which would involve a
troublesome journey, the said tao-t'ai must induce the said leader
to return at an early date, so as to avoid causing officials and
people to take his ships for belligerents, thereby causing a great
deal of misunderstanding.   This will be further evidence of the said
country's amicable attitude toward the Heavenly Court.

As to the said barbarian leader's commission to act as an intermediary, etc., on the one hand, the said tao-t'ai was instructed to
manage properly, and on the other hand, it is reported fully in a
memorial.

Another report was received from Wu I-hsi, that on the 13th
the said French barbarian leader on board a three-masted barbarian
ship carrying more than twenty barbarians, boarded one Wang Yü-
lung's "sand" boat, saying that he wanted to hire it to go to Nanking
to negotiate peace.   The sailors did not consent.   The barbarians
then forcibly weighed anchor themselves and sailed away to the
north.   All the (native) crew escaped by swimming, excepting one
man whom they took away.

We find that France in the former Ming dynasty (1368-1644) was
most powerful.   In firearms, the Frankish type was then introduced
into China from that country.   In recent years she has been comparatively weaker.   At Canton the (French) trade and pay duties and
have been regarded as respectful and cautious.   Now they come to
the Yangtze in ships, nominally to urge the English to cease
hostilities, but actually, we fear, to take advantage of the time before the fighting has ceased.   As to the said barbarian leader's
going out and mediating, it is hard to be sure that it is not simply
because he plans to appear friendly to the Heavenly Court, in the

---

16   This is a reference to the embassy of Lord Macartney to Peking in 1793.

hope of getting a pretext for making demands. [Vermilion endorsement: This is not without perspicacity.] Actually it is hard to
determine. But we have learned that England dominates the high
seas and all the foreigners recognize her leadership in all respects.
If this country obeys the Heavenly Court, the other countries all
keep quiet. Therefore when, on the occasion of the English barbarians' request for trade, (We) joined the Imperial Commissioner
Ch'i-ying in a memorial requesting Imperial favor, it was primarily to relieve the anxiety of the predicament of the interior, and
also to nip the opportunism of all the barbarians in the bud. Now
Cécille is in command of only one warship and will by no means
dare to assume perverse or unrestrained airs. As Canton allows
them to trade, he is not likely to be willing to forfeit their livelihood by making greedy demands unadvisedly. He was merely in a
hopeful frame of mind and therefore tried an experiment. Now he
has already commandeered a "sand" boat to come to Nanking. We
have only to wait until after his arrival, and then send a deputy to
interview the barbarian chief personally, explaining to him politely
our instructions on the matter in the report of the said tao-t'ai, Wu
I-hsi, and inducing him to return immediately to Kwangtung. The
said barbarian leader will have no pretext to rely on.

The English Consul Pottinger and others look up with gratitude
to His Imperial Majesty's surpassing Heavenly favor, and their
gratitude is an expression of perfect sincerity. Now their ships
are still anchored in the river and would be only too glad to be of
service to us. We certainly should instruct Pottinger to wait until
such time as Cécille arrives at Nanking and give him specific
instructions to return to a point outside Wu-sung harbor and then
to take his warship back to his own country, without allowing him
to tarry or cause additional trouble. (Pottinger will thus) reciprocate our Emperor's supreme purpose of restoring peace on the
frontiers. (IWSM. TK 59; 18b, 9-21a, 9)

28. August 24, 1842. MEMORIAL: Reports Pottinger's Willingness
to Deal with Cécille if he Comes to Nanking.

Niu Chien further memorializes. To continue, Your minister
sent a petty officer, Chang P'an-lung, to the English barbarians'
ship to discuss the affair. The subordinate leader of the said ship
told the said petty officer, "Since a French warship has come to the
Yangtze, it will be hard to avoid the development of false hopes,
but once the Heavenly Court and ourselves have concluded peace,
there will be complete, untroubled amity." The said officer then
inquired how they should be handled if they came. The said subordinate barbarian leader replied: "If France sends a ship here,
we shall not find it difficult to explain to them and induce them to
return."

Later on the said petty officer reported secretly to Your minister. At first he did not believe it to be true, but the said subordinate barbarian leader must have referred this matter to Pottinger and others and received their judgment before he talked with the said officer.

After the said military officer, Cécille, arrives, Your minister will send deputies to consult with the English barbarian leader and see what answer he gives then. Thereupon, he can manage according to circumstances.   (IWSM. TK 59; 21a, 10-21b, 8)

29. August 24, 1842. EDICT: Orders Ch'i-ying to Dispose of Cécille and Avoid Complications.

Edict to the Grand Councillors. On this day Niu Chien memorialized that the French barbarian leader wanted to go to Chiang-ning (Nanking) to urge the English to make peace and cease hostilities. On reading the memorial (We) were completely informed. Yesterday there was an Edict ordering Ch'i-ying and others to discuss and manage properly. Now according to their memorial, after their arrival they would send a deputy for a personal interview with the barbarian leader to give him guidance in polite words.

(We) charge Ch'i-ying and others as soon as Cécille arrives to inform him that his willingness to mediate for peace to stop hostilities shows fully his country's respectful and obedient intent; (but) now that England has already made peace with China and will never resume hostilities, the said barbarian leader should quickly return to Kwangtung and carry on trade as usual.

As to the matter of England setting up a barbarian official in Peking to handle her affairs, formerly in the Ch'ien-lung period (1736-1796) it was impossible to carry this out. Now in the three matters in which the English barbarians request (Imperial) favor, they were unwilling to allude to it, and besides, as this does not concern the said country (France), it is naturally unnecessary to give rise to additional complications.

In this way give explicit instructions in such a way that the said barbarians must turn sail and go away. (We) further charge them to send deputies to notify Pottinger:

China is now at peace with your country, having discussed the terms in detail and ceased hostilities forever. Now the French barbarian leader has come despite obstacles, declaring that he would urge your country to make peace. Actually what is his point of view? If it is sincere, then explain to him that now you are already at peace with China and will not bother the barbarian leader to state your case for you. Take care to make Cécille understand this and quickly sail back home. Still more, if Cécille's coming was nothing but a desire to get profits out of this, you should devise means to admonish him and to destroy his illusions, so as not to cause him to interfere and disrupt matters.

In a separate memorial regarding the matter of the sending of the officer Chang P'an-lung to the English barbarian's ship, it is stated that subordinate barbarian leaders said if any French ships arrived it would not be difficult to explain to them and induce them to go away. These various nefarious plots are very hard to fathom. The said high officials must, above all, manage properly according to the circumstances. Be sure not to fall in with their machinations. This is of the greatest importance. (IWSM. TK 59; 21b, 9-22b, 5)

30. October 28, 1842. MEMORIAL: Reports Visit of Chinese Officials to USF Constellation, Commodore Kearny, at Whampoa.
[Memorial of Barbarian-pacifying General I-shan, Governor General of Liang-kuang, Ch'i Kung, Governor of Kwangtung, Liang Pao-ch'ang, and Kwangtung Commander-in-chief of Marine Forces, Wu Chien-hsün, discussing the building of ships at Canton for use against the foreigners. The suggestions of Chin Ying-lin, and the various ships built and under construction at Canton are discussed. These latter were being built by private subscription by the hong merchants.]
... During the summer of the present year two American warships came to Whampoa to protect barbarian trade. The barbarians of the said ships notified the interpreters: "Our foreign warships are strong and large. If the officials of the Heavenly Court wish to come on board and inspect them, they are entirely free to visit."[17]

---

17 "The *U. S. A. frigate Constellation*, Commodore Kearney[*sic.*], and the *sloop of war Boston*, Commander Long, arrived off Macao on the same day" (March 23, 1842). *Chinese Repository*, v. 11, p. 183. The visit of "Admiral Wu" to the *Constellation* on May 9, 1842, has been described by an unidentified American: "...He [the admiral] was received by the commodore on the quarterdeck, and conducted to the cabin. The admiral, a native of Fukien was appointed to this station shortly after the battle of the Bogue, where his predecessor fell in storming one of the forts. Kwan bore a good reputation among his own countrymen; but in his appearance and whole bearing as a warrior, Wu is decidedly his superior. He is now 44 years of age, tall, well formed, has a high acquiline nose, a keen eye, and moved across the deck with an easy, but firm and manly step. He had hardly been seated in the cabin, before he begged that the men be put at their ease--he supposing that they were then, as when he came aboard, standing upon the yards. At his own request he was shown round the ship, and was afforded an opportunity of seeing the men at their quarters...

"It was nearly sunset when the admiral left the ships, evidently much pleased and well satisfied with his reception and the attentions shown him on board the foreign men of war. On Monday the 18th, two other officers, one the second in command to the admiral, visited the commodore. These men were from the northern provinces, and though they had been a year or more at Canton, had never before been on board a foreign vessel. They said they had supposed, from all reports, that the foreign men-of-war were strong, but till then they never realized them *so* strong as they now found them to be. They seemed astonished when told, that many English ships were far superior to the Constellation." *Chinese Repository*, v. 11, p. 333-334.

At the time Brigade General of Nan-Shao-Lien, Ma Tien-chia, and acting Grain Intendant Hsi-la-pen were in the eastern district to inspect volunteers, and together with Your slave, Wu Chien-hsün, and others, went on board their ship. The said military leader presented a small boat and an atlas of his country. Then we made them exceptional gifts in order to show a conciliatory attitude. Then we made a detailed inspection.

The said warship is divided into two decks, top and bottom, set with forty-odd cannon, all on movable carriages. They made trial shots and turned them around and were extremely dextrous. The most versatile feature was that the main mast in the middle and the masts fore and aft were all in three sections, as were also the sails. If they encounter a heavy wind they lower the top sections of the sail and mast. Compared to the masts of our ships, which are in one piece, they seem particularly practical. For instance, if there is a north wind and you are sailing from south to north, this is a head wind and is called tacking. Our ships are slow and clumsy and in tacking go back and forth like a shuttle. The barbarian ships turn their sails smartly and proceed by beating a little obliquely into the wind. Our ships have always used wooden anchors and coir rope. If they met a strong current or big waves and dropped the anchor, it would not reach the bottom. These barbarian ships make theirs entirely of iron, which is more efficacious. We should seek out skillful workmen and build ships after the style of these ships.

Your slaves all examined and consulted together. The rebel barbarians rely on the strength of their ships and the effectiveness of their cannon. Since our warships cannot go out into the high seas and engage them in battle, they act wantonly without fear. The undergraduate Fang Hsiung-fei says that for the quota warships the price was very low and that the contractors, unwilling to incur losses, used thin boards and few nails so (the ships) could hardly withstand wind and waves. This is the actual situation.

As to the methods of building ships, what the said sub-director said about being "generous with our time, and persisting whole-heartedly, not sparing heavy expense nor clinging to 'rules of grammar'" is particularly appropriate. Now if we seek to determine the most useful ships, it is certain that we must make them after the model of the barbarian ships; then we may be equal to the said barbarians. But the largest barbarian ships with cannon on three decks carry more than seventy large guns; the hull is about two hundred feet long and we would find some difficulty in building them. Now we propose taking their middle-sized ship as a model and building accordingly.

We have also taken up the various kinds of ships built by officials and gentry and discussed the various charts and drawings, which we respectfully present for Imperial scrutiny, humbly begging instructions for our guidance.

As to the collection of timber, last year a deputy went to the Ch'in-chou district to purchase. According to his report, the seas are not peaceful. The Annam lumber merchants are not willing to go out to sea and he had no means of making purchases. We learn that the lumber supplies are for the most part produced abroad. Now we are devising means of engaging merchants to collect them, and also have transmitted orders to the Canton Customs Superintendent Wen-feng to instruct the hong merchants to buy barbarian ships. Later, according to the said superintendent's report, in turn quoting the statement of the hong merchants,

> At present the barbarian ships at Whampoa have all come to Canton loaded with goods and, as before, must go back with goods loaded in the original ships and are not for sale. We are waiting to find out if, among the ships coming to Whampoa, there are any strong ones which are for sale; we shall then again devise means of purchasing them.

Now as to the battleship built by P'an Shih-ch'eng, the actual price is calculated at 19,000 taels. The said superintendent says he is willing to contribute from his salary and pay for it in installments, obviating the use of funds from the treasury. It is proper that this should also be reported to the Throne.

Furthermore in building ships we find that we must insist on good workmanship and sound materials, and not in the least begrudge heavy expenditure. We must first build thirty large type battleships, and then thirty or forty small ships. These will serve as auxiliaries to the large ships and will also serve to patrol the ocean. What is spent will actually be very great.

Your slaves have taken counsel together and propose that the Canton war junks, now due to be built for the regular building period, be temporarily held up, in the hope that the saving can be used for building large ships. However, the saving for each year is not a large amount. They will wait until they have secured funds and again memorialize as to procedure. (IWSM. TK 61; 38b, 10-40b, 9)

31. October 28, 1842. EDICT: Approves Building of Western-type Ships for Chinese Navy.

Edict to the Grand Councillors. I-shan and others have memorialized on the building of warships. According to their statement, the "fast crab," "drag-wind," "pull-net" and eight-oared ships can only be used in the rivers and inlets. The newly built ships are only prepared for patrolling inland waters and can hardly meet an enemy. But the ship built by the contributions of Senior Board Secretary P'an Shih-ch'eng, in retirement there, is very substantial. When

it was taken out for target practice, the gunners were extremely
proficient and the shelling very effective. In addition there is the
ship built on the model of the American warship. Now it is proposed
to build after the model of the English barbarians' middle class
ships, while also temporarily stopping the periodical repairs on the
war junks, and to use the saving for building big ships.

We consider that in the matter of protecting the seas, the building of ships and manufacture of cannon take precedence over everything else. The building of warships by the various provinces is
actually a mere sham and of no use in meeting an emergency. This
is extremely infuriating. Now as to ships which are being built,
we shall certainly not go so far as to cling blindly to the old types
which are of nominal rather than actual value. The memorial proposing to stop the building and repair of the war junks and instead
to build battleships, closely conforms to Our intention and (We)
charge all to act according to the proposal. But in the large sea-
going ships the cannon are fired from mounts. When the charge
explodes and the force necessarily goes toward the back buffer, how
can muzzle be kept level? According to the memorials of the said
governor general and others, the (gunners) are already skilled and
proficient. (We) charge them to memorialize again and in full
detail, on the matter of the method of firing.

The five charts and explanations forwarded are ordered copied
in triplicate and sent to the governors general and governors of
Kiangsu, Fukien, and Chekiang. On this day (We) have also issued
an Edict giving orders that each, according to the maritime conditions in his province, make careful inquiries as to which are
suitable for use, and then memorialize asking that they be built.
Also that the original be sent to Na-erh-ching-e for transmission
to T'o-lun-pu for perusal. If it suits the needs, in the future the
(ships) should be built in Kwangtung province and distributed to
other provinces.

According to the memorial, the ship built by P'an Shih-
ch'eng is sound and useful. As to subsequent ship building, (We)
charge that the said official be given full charge and that, above
all, the officials not be allowed to interfere, which, as before,
would result in carelessness and graft. The necessary wages are
authorized to be paid by the officials. Moreover, there must be
no limitation as to time, so as to afford them leisure to do sound
work and exert their utmost skill.

Furthermore, the English barbarians are now reconciled to
pacification and are trading. The Kwangtung seaports are on the
routes the barbarian ships must follow, and we must expend extra
effort to protect them. Battleships are already being built and,
aside from firearms and munitions, the question of whether they
are to be increased or diminished need not conform rigidly to

the old regulations. On the whole, excellence and utility are the
criteria.

As to the cannon and garrison troops at the ports, by no means
should you allow them to be kept in position at their posts throughout the year. Means must be devised to manage properly in the hope
of securing results. When the time comes for facing the enemy, how
can the successive ranks be reinforced and stratagems devised to
secure victory? As to the marine and land forces, how can they be
carefully selected and rigidly trained so as to attain proficiency?
On shipboard and on land, for each there is a proper time for
firing rifles and cannon, and these should also be gone into.
Further, how are the important places on the approaches to be
seized and strongly fortified?

In these various supplementary matters, (We) charge I-li-pu,
after his arrival at Canton, together with Ch'i Kung and others, to
make a thorough inquiry, discuss properly and memorialize fully.
(IWSM. TK 41; 40b, 10-42a, 4)

32. November 13, 1842. MEMORIAL: Formosa General Comments
on the United States and France.

Brevet General-in-chief, Brigade General of T'ai-wan (Formosa)
Garrison, Ta-hung-a, and Brevet Judicial Commissioner, Tao-t'ai
of T'ai-wan, Yao Jung memorialize. We, in accord with the
Imperial Edict, supervising and acting together with the Brevet
Tao-t'ai, Prefect Hsiung I-pen, Sub-prefect T'ung Pu-nien, and all
the deputy officials, again brought forward the barbarian prisoner
Denham and others and repeatedly and separately questioned them.

... Of all the countries in the seas, the strongest and largest,
and those which England fears are, first, America, which Chinese
call "Flowery Flag," to the west of Ti-hsi-shih, [18] and second,
France. The territory of each is larger than that of England and
their ships and cannon are the same. They also like trading and,
along with Holland, Denmark, and Portugal, all trade at Kwangtung and are rather respectful and obedient. The French ships are
few and in recent years have not come. This is the condition on the
ocean routes.... (p. 17a, 2-6).

... Southwest of and separated by an ocean from Madeira (?),
is a large country called America. The northern section of the
country is called in Chinese, the "Flowery Flag." From its northern
to its southern boundary, its territory is several times that of
England. Its ships and cannon are the same. The English, entering
China, must come by way of their (American) seas, and hence fear
them.... (p. 20b, 9-21a, 1.)

[The memorial records the deposition of the English prisoners

───────────────
18 Unidentified place name.

concerning the countries of the world and checks the data with the
K'un Yü T'u of Ferdinandus Verbiest and the Hai Kuo Wen Chien
Lu of Ch'en Lun-ch'iung.] (IWSM.TK 62; 15b, 7-25b, 9)

33. December 12, 1842. MEMORIAL: Reports Building of a Steamship and the Employment of an American Ballistics Expert at Canton.
    Memorial of Barbarian-pacifying General I-shan, Governor
General of Liang-kuang, Ch'i Kung, and Governor of Kwangtung
Liang Pao-ch'ang.
    ...As to the steamship type, already in the spring of this year
the prominent citizen, P'an Shih-jung, engaged barbarian artisans
to build one small ship and launched it on inland waters. It was not
particularly efficient. Fundamentally these ships must be ingenious-
ly and cleverly contrived before they are of use. Native workmen
are often not fully acquainted with their mechanism. It is reported
that there are still barbarian artisans at Macao rather skilled in
building. But with the barbarians, for each steamer they build, the
cost of labor ranges from several tens of thousands of dollars to
more than a hundred thousand dollars. In the future, should we
hire barbarian artisans to build copies or buy ships already built
by foreigners? Your official Ch'i Kung and the others will discuss
the case according to the circumstances and memorialize clearly
as to procedure.
    Furthermore, we find that in the sixth month of the present
year (July 8-August 6, 1842), a prominent citizen, P'an Shih-
ch'eng, raising money himself and not sparing expense, engaged
an American barbarian official, Jen-lei-ssu, living in out-of-the-
way, quiet monasteries, to concoct expolsives. He was also
skilled in making torpedoes. According to the statement of the
said citizen, a torpedo built by him is particularly ingenious and
efficacious. Your slaves have already sent men to him to learn
his skill. If in the future, after they have been completed, the
experiments prove successful, the said citizen will himself send
a man to forward them to the capital and await their inspection.[19]
(IWSM. TK 63; 15a, 6...16a, 8-16b, 8)

34. December 12, 1842. EDICT: Orders Abandonment of Steamship Building Project and Dismissal of Foreign Artisans.
    Edict to the Grand Councillors. Ch'i Kung and others have
memorialized....As to the steamship class, since those built in
that province have not proved useful, (We) charge them to dismiss

---

19 The *Chinese Repository* (v. 12, p. 108-109) notices these activities, including
   the employment of "an American officer" by "native gentlemen," but does not
   identify the American by name.

the foreign artisans who were building them, nor is there any need
to buy them.   As to the explosives and torpedoes which the prominent citizen, P'an Shih-ch'eng, has built, if the experiments when
completed are successful, (We) charge that they immediately be
sent to Peking and presented for (Our) examination.   (IWSM. TK
63; 16b, 9... 17a, 1-3)

Chapter 2

Admission of Americans to Trade under
the Nanking Treaty, 1842-1843
(Documents 35-64)

The Chinese documents comprising this chapter cover the period
from December 12, 1842 to November 15, 1843. There are thirty
items: twenty memorials and ten edicts. All of the edicts are addressed to the Grand Council, indicating that they are concerned
with important matters of state, rather than with routine affairs.
Personal endorsements by the emperor appear only five times in the
thirty documents. One of the vermilion endorsements is purely
formal, one is a specific comment, and three are interlinear notes
scribbled on the original memorial as the emperor read it. The
principal memorialists are Ch'i-ying, who was then imperial commissioner in charge of negotiations with the British; Ch'i Kung, the
Chinese governor general of Kwangtung and Kwangsi, better known
as Canton Viceroy; Liu Yün-k'o, governor of Chekiang; I-li-pu,
Manchu general in charge of military operations; and Mu-chang-a,
the Manchu chief of the Grand Council and virtual prime minister
and foreign secretary of China at this time. The American involved
is Commodore Lawrence Kearny, U.S.N., in command of the East
India Squadron.

The subject matter of the documents is unified. Almost every
document is concerned in one way or another with the problem of
British trade monopoly versus the opening of China's treaty ports
to all nations indiscriminately. American interests were ably represented by Commodore Kearny, who exploited every opportunity to
ensure the continuation and expansion of American trade in China.
The happy denouement was secured through the friendly efforts of
Ch'i-ying and Mu-chang-a.

More specifically, the documents are concerned with Kearny's
efforts to secure most-favored-nation treatment for the United States,
the trial voyages of American traders to Ningpo, Shanghai, Foochow,
and Ting-hai, and the parallel efforts of the French to secure the
benefits of the Treaty of Nanking for themselves. One memorial
continues the topic developed in Chapter 1, namely, the building of
Western ships by Chinese hong merchants at Canton. The period
ends with Ch'i-ying's decision to open the five ports to all traders
indiscriminately and the subsequent official approval by the Grand
Council of most-favored-nation treatment for all countries under
the British Supplementary Treaty concluded at the Bogue.

American materials for this period are summarized by Tyler

Dennett in his Americans in Eastern Asia, p. 108-113, and by Charles
Oscar Paullin, Diplomatic Negotiations of American Naval Officers,
1778-1883, p. 191-205. This problem is also treated by T. F. Tsiang
in an article entitled "The Extension of Equal Commercial Privileges
to Other Nations than the British After the Treaty of Nanking," Chinese
Social and Political Science Review, v. 15 (1931), p. 422-444. There
are three replies to Professor Tsiang's articles by a descendent of
the commodore, Thomas Kearny. The first is entitled "The Tsiang
Documents: Elipoo, Ke-ying, Pottinger and Kearny and the Most
Favored Nation and Open Door Policy in China in 1842-1844; An
American Viewpoint," China Social and Political Science Review, v. 16
(1932), p. 75-104, followed by a "Note in Reply" by T. F. Tsiang,
p. 105-109. Mr. Kearny's second article is entitled "Commodore
Kearny and the Open Door and Most Favored Nation Policy in China in
1842 to 1843," New Jersey Historical Society Proceedings, v. 50 (1932),
p. 162-190. The third article, "Commodore Kearny and the Opening
of China to Foreign Trade," was published in the T'ien Hsia Monthly,
v. 3 (1936), p. 323-329. The Kearny papers, 1842-1843, were
published by the United States Government in 1846, U.S. Cong. 29:1,
Senate Document 139, p. 1-47.

TRANSLATIONS OF DOCUMENTS

35. December 12, 1842. MEMORIAL: Ch'i Kung Reports Commodore Kearny's Request for Most-Favored-Nation Treatment.
          Ch'i Kung further memorializes. On October 13, 1842, a
letter was transmitted to me from the American barbarian leader
Kearny. Its object was to request a memorial on his behalf asking
for Imperial favor allowing the barbarian merchants of his country
to trade in the same way as the barbarian merchants of England.
Your official immediately took counsel with Rebel-pacifying General
I-shan and Governor Liang Pao-ch'ang and in reply ordered him to
wait until the Imperial Commissioner reaches Canton, when it will
be considered jointly and again be taken up and disposed of. Furthermore, on October 20, there was received a communication from a
barbarian of the country, Ball,[1] that, "being skilled in astronomy
and mathematics, he requests a memorial authorizing him to proceed to Peking to take up service." Your official again took counsel.
As the Western ocean barbarians who were formerly at Peking had
already received an Imperial Edict ordering them to return to their
countries, the present request is difficult to transmit in a memorial.

---

1 This is an approximation of the Chinese transliteration, Po-li; neither the person
   nor the incident has been identified in Western sources.

Orders were sent to the hong merchants to make this clear in explicit instructions to the said barbarian. Both (cases) are on record.
Further, Your official learns that the American barbarians have
always been fairly respectful and obedient and even now they have
used no unreasonable language. It is only that barbarians are by
nature extremely treacherous. Besides the matter of the said barbarian Ball's request for a memorial in his behalf to enter service,
which has already been denied, there is the affair of the barbarian
leader Kearny's communication regarding trade. He is still watching and hoping. (We) shall wait until Imperial Commissioner I-li-pu
reaches Canton to weigh the situation together, to consider the case
as a whole, to investigate accurately and consider carefully, and
then memorialize in full. (IWSM. TK 63; 17a, 4-17b, 6)

36. December 12, 1842. EDICT: Orders Strict Adherence to Regu-
lations--Most-Favored-Nation Issue Parried.
Edict to the Grand Councillors. Ch'i Kung has memorialized
on the written communication received from the American barbarian. The American barbarians have been regarded as respectful and obedient. "The said barbarian Ball being skilled in astronomy
and mathematics, begs to come to Peking to enter service." Ch'i
Kung has already in proper language ordered him stopped. As to the
matter of the barbarian leader Kearny's communication regarding
trade, (We) charge I-li-pu, after reaching Canton, to confer wholeheartedly with Ch'i Kung and in everything conform to the old regulations, which cannot be added to or changed. It may be that the
hong merchants are coercing the said barbarians. (We) charge
I-li-pu and the others to investigate carefully and post prohibitions
in order to show (Our) sympathy. If they dare to covet the establishment of ports and so forth, be sure to stop them with earnest and
sincere orders. Let there be no compromising. On the whole (We)
consider that in our commiseration for those from afar, it is essential to show them the fixed institutions of the Heavenly Court, so
that there be no fomenting of trouble. . . . (IWSM. TK 63; 18b, 4-10)

37. December 15, 1842. MEMORIAL: Ch'i-ying Reports Arrival of
an American Ship at Ningpo.
Ch'i-ying further memorializes. To continue, Your official
has now received a report from Lu Tse-ch'ang, the Ning-Shao-T'ai
tao-t'ai of Chekiang, that on November 27, a barbarian vessel arrived at Ningpo. Upon inquiry it was found to be a merchantman of
the "Flowery Flag" country, that is, America. It had a cargo of
foreign cloth, etc., and wanted to trade. The said tao-t'ai and
others gave orders that, although the English barbarians had received an Imperial Edict authorizing them to trade, since the regulations were not yet fixed, they were not yet trading, so the said

country, having customarily traded at Kwangtung, must as before
go back to Kwangtung. When he explained this, the said barbarians
were reasonably courteous and obedient. They immediately got
their sails and rigging in order and on the 29th, weighed anchor and
got under way.

Besides sending express word to the said tao-t'ai carefully to
investigate and not allow them to tarry and cause trouble, Your
official will reach Shanghai today and, if the aforesaid ship arrives
in the region, shall immediately order all the civil and military
officials to inquire in detail into their reasons for coming, and to
control them carefully.   (IWSM. TK 63; 29a, 3-10)

38. December 15, 1842. EDICT: Gives Instructions that American
Ships Coming to New Ports be Ordered to Return to Canton.

Edict to the Grand Councillors. Ch'i-ying ... in a separate
memorial (stated) that an American merchant vessel came to
Chekiang to trade, that the said tao-t'ai, Lu Tse-ch'ang, had
ordered it back to Kwangtung, and that now it has weighed anchor
and departed.

Previously, according to the memorial of Ch'i Kung and others,
there was the matter of the Americans at Canton presenting a request to trade. Already an Edict has been issued ordering I-li-pu
strictly and explicitly to order the said barbarians as before to act
in accordance with the old regulations. If it is a question of the
hong merchants coercing the said barbarians, investigate clearly
and put an end to it. By no means allow them to covet the establishment of wharves and such things. After the said barbarians came
to Chekiang, it is hard to be sure that they will not go to Kiangsu
and make requests.

(We) charge the said governor general earnestly to enjoin his
subordinates to make detailed inquiry of their motive in coming
and control them properly. If they make any demands, notify
them that, as their country has traded at Kwangtung for a long
time, they should naturally return to Kwangtung province and
trade as of old; that the laws of the Heavenly Court are established
and cannot suffer the least change. It is essential to show re-
strictive control.   (IWSM. TK 63; 29b, 1-30a, 4)

39. December 25, 1842. MEMORIAL: Liu Yün-k'o Reports an
American Ship at Ningpo is Ordered to Return to Canton.

The governor of Chekiang, Liu Yün-k'o, memorializes. On
December 1, Your official received a report of the Ning-Shao-T'ai
tao-t'ai, Lu Tse-ch'ang, and the acting prefect of Ningpo, Shu
Kung-shou, that on November 27, according to inquiry made at
Chin-hsien [in which Ningpo is situated], an American merchant
vessel came from Ting-hai to the prefectural capital and anchored

outside at San-chiang-k'ou.   Immediately the tao-t'ai and others
sent deputies in advance to question them. Subsequently, according
to the statement of the barbarian merchant, Po-na,[2] of the said
ship, and the interpreter, Hsü Chao, whom he brought with him,
the ship carried foreign cloth and other goods, and asked for a
customs declaration and trading facilities at Ningpo. The said tao-
t'ai and others then argued that America originally had an established
wharf in Kwangtung province and could not go to other places. Now
the English barbarians had respectfully received a Magnanimous
Edict authorizing them to trade at Ningpo but, as the customs regulations were not yet agreed upon, their ships were still anchored
at Ting-hai, waiting. The said barbarian had come without reason.
How could he in turn expect to declare for customs and dispose of
goods? He was ordered as before to return to Canton and not to
tarry in Chekiang.

The said barbarian, having no reply to this, thereupon returned
to the ship. The said tao-t'ai in addition carefully wrote out instructions ordering the interpreter in turn to explain to him. Then
according to the reply of Po-na and others, they had heard the
rumor at Canton that in the Ningpo district all countries were
allowed to trade, and had therefore came laden with goods for sale.
Now that they had received orders they would not dare to oppose
them. They only asked to remain a few days until their ships were
put in order and then they would leave. The report was transmitted to Your official.

Now we find that the said tao-t'ai's handling of the situation was
rather satisfactory; it was only that the said barbarians, on the pretext of repairing their ships, were earnestly seeking a little delay.
Probably they still retained the intention of watching for openings.
Moreover, it was feared that the merchants of the interior, because
the (American) ships are laden with foreign cloth and other goods,
would covet petty gains and secretly trade with them and start the
gradual process of the said barbarians' future penetration of
Chekiang. Consequently, the said tao-t'ai and others were ordered
strongly to urge the said barbarians to weigh anchor and also to
prohibit the merchants from buying goods illegally from the said
barbarians.

This done, it is now learned in addition from the tao-t'ai and
others that on the 29th they sailed out from San-chiang-k'ou to
Chao-pao-shan, and on the 30th again went from Chao-pao-shan
to Ting-hai. These are the two reports. As to whether or not
they have left for Canton, there is as yet no further notice from
the said tao-t'ai and others. Now as before Your official ordered

2 This name has not been identified in Western sources.

inquiries.

As to the various English barbarian ships at Ting-hai, there
are still more than forty vessels. The various barbarians from
time to time come on small boats to the prefectural capital to buy
food. Their dealings are fair. Moreover, when they went to the
customs to make declaration, Lu Tse-ch'ang, because the regulations were not yet fixed and also in view of the fact that the food
they bought did not amount to much and the duties were slight,
exempted them from paying. The barbarians were pleased and
jubilant and their gratitude increased. Their attitude was extremely complacent--sufficient to gratify the Imperial bosom.
(IWSM. TK 64; 3a, 5-4a, 10)

40. December 25, 1842. EDICT: Local Officials Ordered to Prohibit American Trade outside Canton.

Edict to the Grand Councillors. Liu Yün-k'o has memorialized
that an American merchant ship seeking to declare for customs and
trade at Ningpo was ordered back to Canton and was not allowed to
tarry in the Chekiang region. The said barbarian thereupon returned to his ship.

The United States has customarily traded in Kwangtung province
and originally had a fixed wharf. How can they go to Ningpo and expect to trade? Now the said merchant ship has gone out from San-
chiang-k'ou to Chao-pao-shan and again from Chao-pao-shan to
Ting-hai. Whether or not it has already left for Canton, (We) charge
the said governor to depute officials to make strict inquiry. If as
before they hope to trade at Chekiang, take pains again to give them
explicit orders. Moreover, give stringent orders to the merchants
of the interior to prevent any secret, illegal selling of goods to the
said barbarians, lest they start the gradual process of the future
penetration of Chekiang.... (IWSM. TK 64; 4b, 1-7)

41. January 12, 1843. MEMORIAL: Ch'i Kung Reports Purchase of
American and Spanish Ships at Canton.

[Memorial of Ch'i Kung and Liang Pao-ch'ang regarding the
building of ships after foreign models and the rehabilitation of Chinese warships.]

...As to the Imperial Edict we formerly received ordering the
Canton Customs Superintendent, Wen-feng, to transmit orders to
the hong merchants to devise means of buying barbarian ships, we
have received word from the hong merchants, Wu Ping-chien and
P'an Cheng-wei, that they had bought by subscription one American
and one Spanish barbarian ship. Your officials find on inspection
that the timber is solid and rather fit for service, only the ships are
are a bit small and are also rather old. Now as before, together
with Wen-feng, they have ordered the hong merchants carefully to

investigate and purchase according to the circumstances.... (IWSM. TK 64; 26b, 5-9)

42. January 17, 1843. MEMORIAL: I-li-pu Advocates Most-Favored-Nation Treatment for the United States and France.
      I-li-pu further memorializes. Moreover, previously on December 12, 1842, Your slave received an Imperial decree ordering him, on arrival at Canton, to take up for joint discussion the matter of the American barbarian leader Kearny's petition for trade. Respect this.
      He ventures to refer to the establishment of additional ports and the coming of all foreign ships alike to trade. Previously at Nanking, the barbarian chief Pottinger (said) that in case the various countries came to Fukien, Chekiang, and the various places to trade, whenever China was willing to give her consent, the said chief would by no means stop them in order to seek exclusive gains. Thus there is the view that he has already secretly invited the other countries likewise to come and trade. Moreover, American ships previously made requests at Chekiang; now they are also petitioning at Kwangtung. Previously, when France went to Ningpo, her purpose was probably also for trade. If we allow only England to establish additional trading ports and do not also allow other countries to come to trade in the same way, it is feared that as their ships and dress are not very different, it will be hard to distinguish clearly. Moreover, it is feared that prohibition would give rise to complications and perversely cause the various countries to complain on account of England. Furthermore, it is feared that if England joins them and all alike come to trade, it will also be hard for us to prevent them and, perversely, the kindness would derive from the (English) barbarian leader. Then the various countries would be well disposed toward England and resentful toward China. This will also be erroneous calculation. On this matter, he only waits until after he arrives at Canton to discuss it thoroughly and properly with the governor and governor general.
      Moreover, an understanding must be reached with the barbarian chief, Pottinger; then the discussion can be terminated, a joint memorial be (prepared) asking for an (Imperial) Edict, and action taken accordingly.... (IWSM. TK 64; 37a, 3-37b, 6)

43. January 17, 1843. EDICT: Orders Investigation of Formosan Shipwreck and Confirmation of Pottinger's Willingness to Extend Trading Privileges.
      Edict to the Grand Councillors. I-li-pu has memorialized that he has received an Imperial Edict and is waiting until after his arrival at Canton for its proper execution. Now the pacification has been completed and it is not worth causing fresh complication.

(We) charge I-li-pu, after reaching Canton, in accord with previous Edicts, first to take the Edict ordering I-liang to go to T'ai-wan (Formosa) to investigate and personally explain to the said chief: "It is the desire of His Imperial Majesty to right the wrongs of all of you. There is no need to doubt or fear." After I-liang has gone to T'ai-wan, investigate and get the facts. If the barbarian ships had no cannon and the barbarian sailors were unarmed, were really shipwrecked barbarians in distress, and without any appearance of causing disturbance, then he will mete out to Ta-hung-a the punishment he deserves. If the circumstances in I-liang's report and in the charges of the said chief do not coincide, We shall handle the affair on Our Own authority. I-li-pu should only explain circumspectly, take pains to make the said barbarian abandon immediately his former doubts, and not give rise to difficulties. (We) consider I-li-pu thoroughly familiar with the barbarian temper and certainly capable of stooping to get results.

According to the separate memorial, the United States, France, and other countries have likewise gone to the ports to trade and he (I-li-pu) is waiting for a personal interview with Pottinger to consider it carefully.... If we were to prevent altogether the various countries from participating in trade, it would cause the said barbarians to resort to subterfuge. Then the affection would be for the said barbarians and the resentment with the Heavenly Court. This would certainly be an erroneous calculation.

What I-li-pu memorializes is not without insight. But if we suddenly allow them to trade on the same basis, it is hard to guarantee that England will not, on account of having to share her gains with other countries, cause further trouble. (We) charge I-li-pu, when he meets and confers with the said chief, to discuss it in extenso and settle it properly. On the whole we hope that the concord will last for a long time and not give rise to mutual jealousy and quarreling. This will be the greatest good. Whether or not that which was memorialized on the subject of duties is practical, (We) also charge I-li-pu to discuss carefully, settle, and memorialize fully. (IWSM. TK 64; 38b, 2-39a, 5)

44. January 18, 1843. MEMORIAL: Ch'i-ying Confirms Pottinger's Statement and Advocates Most-Favored-Nation Treatment for United States and France.

Ch'i-ying further memorializes. To continue, Your official has received a dispatch from the Grand Councillors, and on December 15 received an Imperial Edict that an American merchant ship has arrived at Chekiang to trade and that Imperial Edicts have been issued ordering I-li-pu carefully and earnestly to instruct the said barbarians to act as before according to the old regulations. Respect this.

Your official finds that the American merchant ship after leaving
Ningpo immediately went to Ting-hai. Whether it subsequently returned to Kwangtung or not, he has no way of learning definitely.

Now an Imperial Edict has been received ordering I-li-pu to
notify the said barbarians that no covetousness will be tolerated.
I-li-pu is certainly capable of respectful obedience and careful
management and will not cause the development of fresh complications. How would Your official dare overstep propriety and speak
presumptuously? But during the seventh month [August 6-September
5] when Your official discussed pacification with the English barbarians, he had already become concerned that the other barbarians
might imitate them. So he questioned the English barbarian and
afterwards received his reply that all the countries of the outer
ocean were allowed to trade at Canton, that England would not seek
(Imperial) favor on their behalf, but that if His Imperial Majesty
graciously allowed other countries also to go to Fukien, Chekiang,
and Kiangsu to trade, England would not begrudge them in the least;
that access of the vessels of the various countries to Hong Kong
would also be unimpeded. However, when this has been discussed
thoroughly and sympathetically with I-li-pu after reaching Canton,
we shall investigate the attitudes of the various barbarians, reconsider, and request an Edict for our guidance.

Now the Americans have gone to the two provinces of Kwangtung and Chekiang and requested to trade. As to the benefits and
evils involved, (I) venture to address my Emperor. Now where
there is profit, there men are sure to rush after it. In the K'ang-
hsi period (1667-1723) the English barbarians originally built a
wharf at Ting-hai. Because the duties were troublesome and heavy
and the trading sparse, they could not count on any profit and returned to Kwangtung. There for more than one hundred years evils
stopped and conditions were good. The various barbarians appeared
respectful and throughout showed no domineering, untractable attitude. It was only after many years that evils developed. The hardships and burdens of the various barbarians became unbearable
and they cherished resentment in their hearts. The English barbarians thereupon took the lead in causing troubles which have
reached the present extremity. The rest of the barbarians, although outwardly respectful and obedient, in reality sat by to see
who won or lost. Should we succeed in overcoming the English
barbarians (the other barbarians) would then take over England's
benefits for themselves; but should it prove otherwise, they would
then throw in their lot with the English barbarians, adhere to and
join with them, and thus their profit would still be there.

For instance, when the English barbarians first defied authority, their battleships were not numerous. Later on they increased
day by day until finally numbering a hundred and several tens of

vessels. These barbarians are separated by successive oceans
several tens of thousands of li wide--how can it be said to be easy
to mobilize and distribute (forces)? If anyone says that they are
not in collusion with other barbarians and secretly helping each
other, Your official certainly dares not put much confidence in it.
Now the English barbarians have already got what they wanted, but
the other barbarians are still in Kwangtung, neglected and harassed.
Observing matters from their own angle, they may feel some in-
justice in their hearts: "The various barbarians have helped the
English barbarians; so then, how can the English barbarians fail
to help the other barbarians?" This is an inevitable consequence.
Even if the said barbarians do not dare openly to oppose authority
but, adhering to the English barbarians, secretly go to the various
ports to trade, how are we then going to keep watch over them? Thus
the English barbarians can in the end gain the gratitude of the other
barbarians and secretly seize the lever of our country's wealth. The
various barbarians not being able to expect favor from the Heavenly
Court will be bound to the English barbarians hand and foot. Consequently the cohesion of barbarian with barbarian will be daily
closer, while the estrangement between barbarian and ourselves will
will become daily wider. The English barbarians alone were enough
to cause damage to the frontier; how much more so all the barbarians if we cause them to unite? This is also necessarily a matter
for thorough consideration and deep concern.

If it is said that by diligently removing the accumulated evils and
giving all a new start, the various barbarians would trade peacefully at Canton and not be led erroneously to harbor expectations,
this is truly the policy of clearing roots and purging sources. But
the roots of the evil are already deep and can hardly be pulled up
suddenly. In addition it is feared that, once the evil clumps have
been removed, then former illegal exactions will be regarded as
something required by custom. The case is like that of the port of
Amoy in Fukien, which was originally a place where foreign merchant
ships trading with China congregated, whereas later, because the
illegal exactions were troublesome and heavy, and, though repeatedly
forbidden, become increasingly worse the more they were forbidden,
the foreign hongs eventually failed and foreign trade was stopped.
Fortunately the Chinese merchants were able to go wherever they
wanted and did not cause trouble. As to the barbarian merchants,
they legally had a definite port and could not go a foot or an inch
beyond. Men are the same in their feelings, so how would they be
willing to accept (this) complacently? This is also what Your official
has thought of on clear nights, unable to keep from worrying nervously.

Thinking it over and over, if America and other countries also
wish to establish separate ports in Fukien, Chekiang, and Kiangsu,
we certainly should use strict language to stop them in order to show

control. In case the English barbarians take the ports in Fukien,
Chekiang, and Kiangsu for themselves and are unwilling to let other
countries trade, then there will be occasion for fighting among
themselves. In that case we could "take their stratagem to effect
our plans." Now these barbarians are after all willing to compromise, and the other barbarians would also all gladly follow. When
a system is worn out it should be changed. If in dealing with them
we carefully preserve the old regulations, it will cause many pricked
fingers and is not as good as leading them advantageously according
to circumstances and treating all with equal kindness. If the United
States and other countries are determined to trade in Fukien, Chekiang, and Kiangsu, it would seem that we could allow them likewise
to draw up regulations and allow them to go where they will. But
outside of these there should be no coveting, nor should they be
allowed to establish ports of their own in Fukien, Chekiang, and
Kiangsu. Although the customs receipts in Kwangtung province
would not be without curtailment, still in Fukien, Chekiang, and
Kiangsu they would be augmented. What is drawn from one is
poured into the other and there would be no effect on national revenue. Moreover, Fukien, Chekiang, and Kiangsu provinces have
already admitted the English barbarians to trade, so it would
seem that to extend it to these other barbarians would not be objectionable. Moreover, if we could take the barbarian ships which
are congregated in one place and scatter them in five places, their
strength would be dissipated and their relations estranged. In the
matter of managing and curbing outside barbarians, this is not
necessarily a bad plan. (IWSM. TK 64; 43b, 1-46a, 1)

45. January 18, 1843. EDICT: Orders Ch'i-ying and I-li-pu to Consider Most-Favored-Nation Policy and Make Recommendations.
        Edict to the Grand Councillors. Ch'i-ying ... has also a
separate memorial (saying) that the United States and other
countries are determined to trade in Fukien and Chekiang, and it
would seem that we could allow them also to draw up regulations
as a policy of taking advantage according to circumstances.
Yesterday, an Imperial Edict was issued ordering I-li-pu to discuss
carefully and settle it. As to what the governor general said regarding "not letting them go beyond Fukien, Chekiang, and Kiangsu
or otherwise spy around, nor allowing them to establish ports of
their own" naturally, even though stooping to accord with the barbarians' wishes, it is essential to show restriction.
        (We) charge Ch'i-ying to consult freely with I-li-pu, devise a
perfect plan, and memorialize requesting an Edict. As to the
matters which the said governor general proposed as essential for
river defense, (We) charge him as before to follow the successive
Edicts and together with (General) Yu P'o to arrange thoroughly

and respectively carry them out, in the hope of preparing against
future regrets. This is of the utmost importance. (IWSM.TK 64;
46a, 2...9-46b, 5)

46. February 11, 1843. MEMORIAL: Liu Yün-k'o Reports Foreign
Ships at Foochow, Ting-hai, and Other Ports.

Liu Yün-k'o further memorializes. To continue: after returning to the provincial capital, Your official again received a report
from the acting sub-prefect of Ting-hai, Wang P'i-hsien, that now
there are only twenty barbarian ships anchored at Ting-hai harbor.
Compared to the time when Your official was at Ningpo, this is a
reduction of ten-odd vessels. But according to the statement of the
acting sub-prefect of Shih-p'u, Huang Wei-kao, on January 6 there
were two barbarian ships anchored before the said sub-prefecture.
Subsequently there were two barbarian leaders, one named Wei-
shih-pi, the other named Te-i-shih,[3] who presented cards at the
office and requested an interview. The said sub-prefect met and
talked with them. Wei-shih-pi and the other requested the dispatch
of two sailors to guide them to Foochow and to Teng-chou, Shantung.
The said sub-prefect replied that there were no sailors of this kind.
Wei-shih-pi thereupon returned to the ship.

Your official finds that Foochow is a place where the said barbarians are allowed to trade. As to their desire to proceed there,
it may be to inspect the country. Now in wishing to go on to Teng-
chou, what is their intention? The circumstances are rather
suspicious. Moreover, he finds that the English barbarians, in
coming from Canton to Chekiang, must have come by way of Fukien
and still have had ships anchored at Ku-lang-hsü [in Amoy harbor].
The various seas of Fukien must be thoroughly familiar to the said
barbarians. Furthermore, when the said barbarians in 1840 sailed
their ships to Tientsin, it was by way of Teng-chou, so they must
know the route to that place. How is it that they now again ask for
men to lead them there?

Now there are still anchored at Ting-hai two ships, American
and French. After all, whether or not Wei-shih-pi and his companion were English barbarian officials or Americans or Frenchmen
is rather hard to determine. Although the said sub-prefect refused
them, it is feared that they themselves will undertake to find persons
to lead them. Now he has sent express letters to Your officials, the
governor general of Min-Che [Fukien-Chekiang] and the governors
of Fukien and Shantung to order their subordinates to search care-

---

3 These names have not been identified in Western sources. There were various
   British surveys of the coast at this time. *Cf.* sailing directions in the *Chinese
   Repository*, v. 12, p. 401-434.

fully and to be on guard. Moreover, he wrote to Imperial Commissioner I-li-pu as well as to (Your) officials, the governors general of Liang-chiang (i. e. Kiangsu-Kiangsi) and Chihli, all to take notice. (IWSM. TK 65; 8a, 1-8b, 7)

47. February 11, 1843. EDICT: Orders Local Officials to Have the British at Ting-hai Send American and French Ships back to Canton.

[Edict to the Grand Councillors regarding Liu Yün-k'o's memorial.] ... As to the two American and French ships originally anchored at Ting-hai; also as to the difficulty of determining whether or not Wei-shih-pi and the other man are English barbarian officials or are Americans or Frenchmen: even if these be American and French ships, inasmuch as they have anchored at Ting-hai along with those of the English barbarians, (this means that) they too must listen only to the words of the said barbarian chief. If they are barbarians of his country, (We) charge you immediately to give Pottinger earnest and clear instructions to order them as before to return to Canton and await disposal. (IWSM. TK 65; 11a, 2-6)

48. March 6, 1843. MEMORIAL: Reports that United States and France are Awaiting Establishment of Customs Regulations.

[Memorial of I-li-pu, Ch'i Kung, and Liang Pao-ch'ang during the negotiation of the commercial regulations with England at Canton]. ... As to the United States and France, since Your official, I-li-pu, arrived at Canton, they have made no request to go to the various ports to trade. Certainly this is because the English customs regulations are still not clearly established and they are maintaining an attitude of watchful hoping. We beg leave to wait and observe the temper of the barbarians and act according to circumstances. Now in the Hong Kong ocean front, there are altogether twenty-one English barbarian warships anchored. They are indeed peaceful and quiet enough to tranquillize Imperial concern. (IWSM. TK 65; 27a, 1-5)

49. March 6, 1843. EDICT: Authorizes I-li-pu to Arrange American and French Trade after Customs Regulations are Established.

Edict to the Grand Councillors. ... As to the fact that the United States and France are at present making no request to go to the various ports to trade, if after the customs regulations of the English barbarians are settled, the said two countries do request to trade, (We) charge I-li-pu to examine the situation and arrange according to circumstances, and in everything to take pains to manage with the greatest safety so as to fulfil his commission. (IWSM. TK 65; 27b, 1-4)

50. March 8, 1843. MEMORIAL: Ch'i-ying Reports Movements of British, American and French Ships around Ting-hai and Ningpo.

... As to the barbarian ships anchored at Ting-hai, the original reports of the secret agents of Chen-hai-hsien were only brief accounts. Ever since the acting sub-prefect of Ting-hai, Wang P'i-hsien, took office, the said sub-prefect has reported every fifth day. He said in his report that from December 27 to 31 of last year there was one American vessel laden with foreign cloth and kerseymeres, and also one French vessel. Also according to the report, from January 11 to 15 there was one American ship carrying sixty or seventy men, and a French ship carrying over one hundred men. In view of the rather large number of men on these two American and French ships, Your official regarded the circumstances as somewhat suspicious. (In order to learn) whether or not they are the same as the ships formerly reported anchored at Ting-hai, he sent an express letter to the tao-t'ai of Ning-Shao-T'ai to find out positively and report. Moreover, he sent word to the various maritime provinces that if any barbarian ships were seen passing by, no matter whether coming from the south or going to the north, they should immediately send an express report so as to enable (him) to consider the case and act accordingly. Afterwards, according to a further report of the acting sub-prefect of Ting-hai, there were, from January 16 to 20, one American ship and one French ship laden with foreign cloth and other goods; according to a later report, the said two ships both sailed on the 15th for the south seas. Up to February 3 there were at Ting-hai altogether twenty-three barbarian vessels. This is also on record.

Further, on January 27, a communication was received from the governor of Chekiang, Liu Yün-k'o, saying that according to the statement of a distinguished citizen of Ting-hai sub-prefecture, Chin Shih-k'uei, and others, the English barbarians were constantly hostile to the people of Ting-hai, sometimes fining them, sometimes flogging them, and that they regarded the gentry as yamen runners and took good people for outlaws. The letter requested that Chief Pottinger be notified rigorously to restrain them.... [p. 28b, 5-29b, 1.

... As to the two ships of Wei-shih-pi and Te-i-shih and the ships which were seen on the Ch'uan-sha ocean front, are they the same as Sterling's two ships, and have the two American and French ships gone back to Canton? Hereafter, the barbarian ships at Ting-hai, if they expect to go south by way of the inner ocean, must be sure on coming near to notify the Ning-Shao-T'ai tao-t'ai and inform (the officials) en route in advance in order to dispel suspicions. He has earnestly and frankly notified Chief Pottinger to act carefully. This is also on record.

In general the barbarians' nature is rather suspicious and they also like action. Guarding against them too rigorously may easily

cause suspicion and dislike; to let them go where they will is also
entirely unthinkable, particularly as our military preparations are
still not well developed and the popular temper still not restored to
normal. It is impossible adequately to guard against them. It all
rests with various military and civil officials on the seaboard who
should take warning from former mishaps and sleep on firewood
and taste bile [i.e., keep their spirit of vengeance alive]. Let
them not take peace policies as necessarily dependable, nor, on
the other hand, as necessarily undependable. Especially let them
not show the least appearance of timidity nor be needlessly agitated
or alarmed, but let them work wholeheartedly together and, while
outwardly showing no suspicion, inwardly maintain care and discretion. If any barbarian ships arrive, they should forthwith go to them
and, explaining with the utmost sincerity and giving orders with
severity, expel their doubts and break through their cunning; maintaining their own calmness, restrain their activity. Although these
be wolf cubs with wild natures and we dare not trust that they will
not turn on us, still sincerity can accomplish wonders, and it would
seem that we could bring them under our sway. If not, we should
only be wasting proclamations and not be getting any real benefit.

Your official is now delegating Ch'en Po-ling, chiliarch of the
Hung-hu regiment, together with Sergeant Ch'iu Yung-an of the Nanking city garrison battalion -- these being thoroughly familiar with
the barbarian temper -- to make secret inquiry from the Kiangsu
seaboard region straight to Ting-hai, hoping in this way to get
(accurate information about) the actual situation in order to banish
all doubts.

Vermilion endorsement: These views are very sound; circumspectly carry them out. (p. 32b, 3-33a, 8) (IWSM. TK 65; 27b,
5-33a, 8)

51. March 22, 1843. MEMORIAL: Reports the Death of I-li-pu at
Canton.
Deprived of rank but retaining the duties of governor general of
Liang-kuang, Ch'i Kung, together with the Manchu Lieutenant
General of Canton, Yü-jui, and the Chinese Lieutenant General of
Canton, Kuan-wen, memorialize. Imperial Commissioner, General-
in-Chief of Canton, I-li-pu, on March 4 died of illness. They re-
quest an (Imperial) decree quickly making selection and appoint-
ment in order to continue the negotiations. (IWSM. TK 65; 45a, 3-6)

52. March 22, 1843. MEMORIAL: Ch'i Kung Reports on the Urgency
of Completing Trade Regulations.
[Memorial of Ch'i Kung. Pottinger has given assurance that Wei-
shih-pi and Te-i-shih are British officers sent to survey the coast and
had no intention of going to Shantung; his explanation appears reason-

able.] (p. 45b, 4-46a, 5.) ...As to the two American and French
merchant ships previously anchored at Ting-hai, it is now found
that both have returned to Kwangtung. Pottinger is now living at
Hong Kong and is extremely quiet. As to matters of trade and
customs, I-li-pu's arrangements are somewhat under way, but the
articles are numerous and each item must be discussed in detail.
As to the favorable or unfavorable attitude of the barbarians, all
depends on there not being at the present critical juncture, the
least procrastination. Your official, together with the Judicial
Commissioner of Kiangsu Huang En-t'ung, Imperial Bodyguard of
the Fourth Rank Hsien-ling, and Kwangtung Financial Commissioner
Collateral Relative Ts'un-hsing, has ordered delegates immediately
to take suitable action, and also informed the said barbarian chief
and others that although I-li-pu has died of sickness, the tariff
should be settled entirely according to the old arrangement and
the various items determined. Your official immediately memorialized fully on his behalf in order to set the popular mind at
rest. (p. 46a, 5-46b, 2) (IWSM.TK 65; 45a, 3-46b, 2)

53. May 21, 1843. MEMORIAL: Sun Shan-pao Reports American
Ships being Refused Permission to Trade at Shanghai.
          Acting governor general of Liang-chiang and governor of Kiang-
su, Sun Shan-pao, memorializes. It is humbly observed that on
March 3 of the present year, outside Wu-sung harbor, there arrived three barbarian ships intending to go to Shanghai to trade. It
seems that they were American ships. The military and civil
district (officials) notified them that as the tariff was not yet
fixed nor wharves built, it was not convenient to proceed to trade.
The said barbarians, because of having to repair the equipment on
their ships, anchored outside the harbor. Thereupon Your official
the governor general, Ch'i-ying, sent express orders to the tao-t'ai
of Su-Sung-T'ai to delegate officials to confer with the local officers
and have them in earnest and clear terms order (the barbarians) to
return immediately to Kwangtung and wait there until the Imperial
Commissioner had determined the tariffs and further memorialized
asking for an (Imperial) Edict.
          Later, on the 15th, another barbarian ship came. It seems that
it was also an American ship. Since after some delay it did not depart, again Your official, the governor general, ordered Grain Intendant and Sub-prefect Shen Ping-yüan to go there and together with
the local officials explain to them clearly. Two ships in all have
left and two are still anchored there.
          Later, on the 27th, two English barbarian ships arrived. The
said local officials learned that they came from Ting-hai to inquire
about news from Kwangtung. Then on the 30th, together with the
two barbarian ships previously anchored, they sailed away to the

outer seas.

On April 11 again a barbarian ship, taking advantage of the wind and a favorable tide, sailed from Wu-sung to the outskirts of the city wall of Shanghai. The said local officials went on board and found on inquiry that it was a "Flowery Flag, " that is, American ship, laden with goods and coming here from the Philippines to trade. The said officials explained that they still had no notice regarding the customs agreement. The said barbarians agreed to return to Kwangtung and wait for word. On the 15th they sailed away.

Later, a report was received from the acting tao-t'ai of Su-Sung-T'ai, Yen I-ao, saying that on April 20 an English steamer came to the Huang-p'u River. The said tao-t'ai was just considering going on board, together with the commandant and the magistrate, to make inquiries. The next day the barbarian leader, accompanied by an interpreter, came to the official residence. According to their statement the high officials of their country, hearing that ships from other places were tarrying at Shanghai, feared that they would cause trouble, so they came to compel them to return to Chou-shan (i.e., Chusan, on which Ting-hai is situated). They also presented a letter of the assistant general of the said country stationed at Ting-hai, named Hu, to the tao-t'ai of Su-Sung-T'ai. They immediately all opened and examined it and it was in general agreement with what they said, without any ulterior motive. They made a fair copy of the letter and reported fully to Your official.

Just while examining and acting upon this, a report arrived from the military and civil official of Pao-shan that the said vessel departed on the 22nd for the outer ocean.

Your official finds that the coming and going of barbarian ships, even though their purpose is trade, may still cause the residents of the seaboard to become suspicious and frightened on seeing them. Repeatedly orders have been given to subordinates carefully to restrain and patrol but to avoid the least alarm or confusion.

The barbarian chief previously resident at Ting-hai, fearing that the barbarian ships at Shanghai would cause trouble, commissioned a barbarian chief to bring them back in custody. This all shows that they are able to foster friendly relations. It is found on examination of the contents of this communication, that the expressions, although not particularly clear, are extremely mild and obedient. What he says also has no ulterior motive and is fairly plausible. On the day the said barbarian ship arrived, the various other ships which had come had already all left. Therefore, it immediately returned.

As before, Your official gave orders to the said circuit and prefecture officials that if any more ships came, they should always carefully issue proclamations ordering them to leave immediately and await the settlement of the tariff schedule at Canton. He has

memorialized clearly asking for an Imperial Edict to direct management.

Vermilion endorsement: Noted.   (IWSM. TK 66; 11a, 2-12b, 3)

54. May 31, 1843.   MEMORIAL: Pi-ch'ang and Sun Shan-pao Report
Enforcement of Trade Prohibition at Shanghai Pending Completion of
Tariff Schedule.

Provisional Governor General of Liang-chiang Pi-ch'ang and
Governor of Kiangsu Sun Shan-pao memorialize. It is humbly observed that during the second and third months of the present year
(March 12-May 10, 1843) barbarian ships came to Wu-sung, Shanghai, and other places wishing to trade, and also that an English
barbarian steamer delivered a letter to the Su-Sung-T'ai tao-t'ai.
They thereupon left one after another until by April 22 they had all
departed for the (outer) ocean. These facts have been fully memorialized and are on record.

But the ship which arrived on March 3 delayed until March 30
before leaving, thus lingering a long time. Fearing that uninformed, stupid people were secretly trading with them or engaging
in other evil practices, a secret investigation was immediately
ordered. At that time the Su-chou (Soochow) Grain Intendant and
Sub-prefect, Shen Ping-yüan, was returning from Shanghai to Su-
chou. Your official Sun Shan-pao questioned him about the proclamations issued by the acting tao-t'ai of Su-Sung-T'ai, Yen I-ao,
copies of which were presented for perusal; on examination, the
language employed was altogether ambiguous and might easily give
the people cause for complaint.

Just when examining and acting upon this, Your officials received further word from Imperial Commissioner Ch'i-ying en route
in Chekiang: "Formerly because the barbarian ships tarried and
did not leave, Shen Ping-yüan was secretly ordered to investigate
and report. Now the reports of the Su-Sung-T'ai tao-t'ai have been
received. Accordingly, you are requested to examine them and take
action." Your officials found these in agreement with the previously presented copies of the proclamations.

Moreover, on May 9 a report was received from the officials of
Pao-shan: "Outside the mouth of the Wu-sung (River) there arrived
one after the other five American and English ships, large and
small, including two American ships and three English. Among them
also were two ships which had come during the second month (March
1-31). The American ships declared that they came laden with goods
and awaited trade. The English ships stated that they came to inquire
about news of the opening of trade."

Your officials now beg to observe regarding the barbarians ships
up to the present time, that although they are divided into American
and English, the English barbarian had officially notified the Su-Sung-

T'ai tao-t'ai that he would compel the ships of the various countries to leave. So why have the ships of the said country which left in the second month (March 1-31) now brought with them another ship and together with the American ships arrived one after the other? The circumstances are quite contradictory. Your officials have sent a letter to Imperial Commissioner Ch'i-ying to notify Pottinger to make a clear investigation and reply fully. Moreover, they ordered Shen Ping-yüan, who is thoroughly conversant with barbarian conditions [Vermilion endorsement: Very true.], to go to Shanghai together with the local officials to explain clearly that they (the barbarian ships) must wait until after the Imperial Commissioner [pointed in vermilion] has reached Canton and arranged the tariff schedule with Pottinger, and then they can trade according to the regulations; that it is useless to wait; and to order them quickly to weigh anchor and go to Canton. At the same time he should make accurate inquiry and take strict precautions not to allow the traitorous people of the interior to enter secretly into collusion with them and cause further trouble.

It is only that trade at Shanghai is just beginning, and if there is the least discrepancy between the findings and the management, it might give both the people and the barbarians cause for complaint. Now the tariff schedule is still not published. The said acting tao-t'ai, because the barbarian ships which arrived during the second month wished to buy silver at the port, issued a proclamation. In the proclamation, after using the expression "definitely await the publication of the tariff schedule and then trade," he further used the words, "take advantage of the currency of these goods to effect a quick turnover." These are really ambiguous and unclear and could hardly fail to cause uninformed stupid people to seize the pretext to trade with them. Hereafter in the intercourse between people and barbarians, incidents will be comparatively numerous so it will be necessary that there be not the least carelessness in management.

The proclamation which the said acting tao-t'ai issued employed terms that were inappropriate. Having examined the man and the post, he is not particularly suited to it. Your officials memorialized requesting an Imperial Decree removing the acting tao-t'ai of Su-Sung-T'ai, Yen I-ao, from office.

Vermilion endorsement: Removal from office is not enough. There must be a rigorous trial. If there are other reprehensible circumstances, then he should be indicted according to the facts. Punishing one warns a hundred. Take care that there be no indulgence! (IWSM. TK 66; 13b, 5-15a, 10)

55. <u>May 31, 1843</u>. <u>EDICT</u>: <u>Orders Punishment of Shanghai Tao-t'ai</u>
<u>Who Permitted American Trade without Authorization</u>.
        Edict to the Grand Councillors. Pi-ch'ang and others have me-
morialized asking that the acting <u>tao-t'ai</u> of Su-Sung-T'ai who issued
ambiguous proclamations be removed from office. According to the
memorial:

> Previously, during the second month (March 1-31), two English ships came and
> left. But now they have returned, bringing along another (English) ship as
> well as (two) American ships. Ch'i-ying was notified immediately by letter
> to instruct Pottinger to make a full investigation and reply. The ships now
> remaining have been ordered to weigh anchor immediately and proceed to
> Canton. As before, an accurate inquiry was made at once and the traitorous
> people of the interior were strictly prohibited to act secretly in col-
> lusion with them and cause further trouble.

What has been done is very appropriate. As to trading regulations,
naturally they must await the determination of the tariff schedule in
Kwangtung, so that action in all the ports will be uniform.
        How is it that the said acting <u>tao-t'ai</u>, Yen I-ao, has issued pro-
clamations using the expression "when the tariff schedule has been
published then trade can be carried on," and elsewhere the words
"take advantage of the currency of these goods to effect a quick turnover in the hope of making profits?"[4] These seem ambiguous and
unclear. Actually they are mutually contradictory and it is feared
will be secretly ridiculed by the said barbarians. Moreover they
may easily give traitorous traders and stupid people a pretext for
beginning to trade. Let Yen I-ao immediately be removed from
office and then be rigorously tried by Pi-ch'ang and Sun Shan-pao.
In the matter of using ambiguous terms, what was his purpose? If
there are other reprehensible circumstances, let him be immediately
indicted in accordance with the facts, in the hope that by punishing
one, a hundred will be warned. Let there not be the least indulgence.
        The newly appointed <u>tao-t'ai</u>, Kung Mu-chiu, is urged quickly to
proceed to his post. Before he reaches his post, let Pi-ch'ang and
others select a suitable official to take charge. After Kung Mu-chiu
has taken office, ascertain carefully whether or not he is thoroughly
conversant with barbarian affairs and then take action.   (IWSM. TK
66; 15b, 1-16a, 3)

56. <u>July 30, 1843</u>. <u>MEMORIAL</u>: Ch'i-ying Proposes to Deal Sepa-
<u>rately with the United States and France</u>.
        [Memorial of Ch'i-ying on the negotiation of the supplementary

---

4 The last phrase in this sentence, "in the hope of making profits," does not occur
in the original memorial, *supra*, from which the quotation is taken. Either the
phrase was omitted by the copyist from the memorial or the Grand Councillors
added it on their own.

treaty and commercial regulations with the British at Hong Kong.]
... Again as to the United States and France, now a request is received to allow them to proceed according to the newly completed
regulations. Your slave begs leave, together with the governor
general and governor, after the regulations are ascertained, to make
a clear agreement with them and handle it as a special case. (IWSM.
TK 67; 3b, 6-8)

57. July 30, 1843. EDICT: Authorizes Ch'i-ying to Make Separate
Arrangements for Trade with the United States and France.
      Edict to the Grand Councillors.   ... Let Ch'i-ying, together
with Ch'i Kung, Ch'eng Yü-ts'ai and Wen-feng, examine comprehensively and take action. While necessarily stooping to accommodate barbarian opinion, they must especially safeguard the national
honor, forever stop corrupt practices, and enable the various
provinces to manage accordingly. This will be for the best. As to
the United States and France requesting permission to proceed according to the newly concluded regulations, after (the British)
negotiations are completed, make a clear agreement with them and
deal with them separately. (IWSM. TK 67; 8a, 9-8b, 2)

58. August 11, 1843. MEMORIAL: Trade Regulations Treating All
Foreign Countries Alike Submitted.
      [Memorial of Ch'i-ying, Ch'i Kung, Ch'eng Yü-ts'ai, and Wen-
feng, setting forth the tariffs and trade regulations for Canton and
the other ports, treats the trade of all the foreign countries alike,
with no discrimination in favor of the British.] (IWSM. TK 67; 40b,
4-45b, 8)

59. September 23, 1843. MEMORIAL: Ch'i-ying Reports General
Trade Regulations and Requests Modification of Tariff Schedule for
United States.
      Imperial Commissioner and Governor General of Liang-chiang
Ch'i-ying, Governor General of Liang-kuang Ch'i Kung, Governor of
Kwangtung Ch'eng Yü-ts'ai, and Canton Superintendent of Customs
Wen-feng memorialize. They venture to note that the United States
and other countries have presented at Ch'i Kung's yamen a request
that we on their behalf seek Imperial favor allowing them as well as
England to proceed to the various provinces to trade. Already Your
officials Ch'i Kung, Ch'i-ying, and I-li-pu have from time to time
memorialized and received an Imperial Edict: "The United States
and France\have requested to proceed according to the newly established regulations. After negotiations have been completed,
make a clear agreement with them and deal with them separately.
Respect this. "
      Your officials humbly observe that various countries come to

Canton to trade, but (the ships) of England and her dependency, India, are most numerous. Next, those of the United States are nearly as many. Besides these, only Holland has from three or four up to ten-odd merchant ships a year; France, Spain, Denmark, Sweden, Prussia, Austria, and Belgium sometimes have ships coming, sometimes not; sometimes many, sometimes few. In general each country has from one to two up to not more than five or six. Now the British commercial regulations have been concluded. As to the wharves at Shanghai and other places, they also dare not monopolize their advantages. Moreover, as Ting-hai and other places all have had American merchant vessels anchored along with those of the English barbarians, eagerly looking forward to the opening of trade, naturally trade should be discussed first with the United States.

However, previously at the <u>yamen</u> of Your official Ch'i Kung, they presented a letter of the barbarian leader Kearny who during the third month (March 31-April 30), previous to the arrival of Your official Ch'i-ying, had sailed back to his country. There was only an acting consul, King,[5] at Canton in charge of trading affairs. Again in Your official Ch'i-ying's presence, he petitioned asking to trade according to the new regulations. Your officials, leading them to advantage according to circumstances and exemplifying Imperial kindness, gave them permission to trade and pay duties according to the new regulations in the five ports in Fukien, Kwangtung, and Chekiang, in order to show conciliation.

Now according to the sincerely grateful petition of the (American) barbarians, it is stated that their imports include foreign ginseng and bulk lead produced in the said country. Formerly, because the duties were troublesome and heavy, there was often much smuggling. Now, although irregular exactions are eliminated, still the newly established duty on superior foreign ginseng is thirty-eight <u>taels</u> for each hundred catties and on inferior foreign ginseng is three <u>taels</u> five mace for each hundred catties; on black and white lead, it is four mace per hundred catties. According to the selling price, this is forty or fifty per cent. The said merchants would not only realize no profit but would suffer loss. They asked that, taking five per cent as a standard, the duty on superior foreign ginseng be four <u>taels</u> per hundred catties; on inferior foreign ginseng, two <u>taels</u>, seven mace per hundred catties; on lead, two mace per hundred catties. Your officials, because the customs schedule had been determined and reported by memorial, and because the said barbarian chief's initial request for revision, if imitated by many of the other countries, would result in rather unseemly procedure, forthwith expressed disapproval.

---

5 P. W. Snow, the American consul, was absent from Canton at this time; the reference is to Edward King, vice consul. *Chinese Repository*, v. 12, p. 18.

Thereafter, another petition was received from the said barbarian stating that foreign ginseng originally was not divided into
superior and inferior. Figuring each hundred catties to consist of
half of each, superior and inferior, they would temporarily conform
to the new rule and, as in the case of bulk lead, pay the duties according to verified facts. But at present the ships of the said country
have not all arrived. After the barbarian chief (consul) arrived, he
would see that the matter was settled.

Suspecting that his words were neither true nor complete, Your
officials immediately sent trusties into the market to buy (samples).
Superior grade foreign ginseng cost one tael four mace per catty.
On the basis of one hundred catties, it would amount to one hundred
forty taels. Furthermore, they found on careful investigation that
the price of foreign ginseng was high or low depending on whether
the importation was large or small. At times when it is cheap a
catty is not worth more than about one tael. Thus, what the said
barbarian requested was not presumptuous or exacting. Moreover
they found that the annual importation of superior grade foreign
ginseng was not more than four hundred-odd piculs; of inferior grade
foreign ginseng, not more than a thousand piculs; of bulk lead, not
more than two hundred-odd piculs. Thus to reduce the duty as they
requested would only amount to an annual reduction of a few thousand
taels. Considering that with heavy duties there would be smuggling
and moreover occasion for complaints, is it not better magnanimously to collect duties according to verified facts and avoid giving
rise to fresh complications? But now since France and the other
countries still have not reached an agreement, it is not appropriate
suddenly to inaugurate the system. Your officials beg leave to consider the case as a whole, reach a decision, and separately memorialize asking for an Edict.

As to France, although the number of her ships arriving each
year is not large, formerly she was one of the powerful states of the
West. Of the various countries now engaging in trade, the said
country has traded at Canton for the longest time and up to the
present time has never been willing to accomplish things through
others. Previously the barbarian leader Jancigny, who calls himself consul and resides at Macao, sent his assistant, Challayé,[6]
to Canton to present a separate petition discussing the formalities
of intercourse and also the customs regulations. He also stated
that this alone was not to constitute a basis. Your officials
immediately delegated officers to proceed to Macao to question

---

6 M. Charles Alexander Challaye, attache of the French Consulate at Manila, was made
   consul to China and arrived in China September 20, 1840. *Chinese Repository*, v. 12,
   p. 424.

Jancigny with complete frankness. Further, the barbarian leader Ratti-Menton,[7] considering that Jancigny was posing as consul and that Challayé acted rudely in Canton, has already removed Challayé from office and has twice sent petitions to Ch'i Kung's yamen asking for an interview with us. Your officials, because of the difficulty of distinguishing between true and false, are now secretly making an investigation. As soon as they get the facts, they will meet them and make an agreement. Probably within a few days it can be concluded.

As to Holland and the other countries, their ships have not arrived and it cannot be ascertained whether they are coming or not. Even if they do come from time to time, these other countries' ships are few and their strength isolated. They are commonly known to be respectful and obedient and have been favored by Your Majesty's uniform compassion. Naturally they will have no cause for dissent. This is a resumé of the conditions of the various countries which customarily anchor their ships at Whampoa, P'an-yü-hsien, where they tranship and then proceed to Canton to trade.

Besides there is the country of Italy [sic] of the Great Western Ocean, which from the Ming to the present time has occupied Macao in Hsiang-shan-hsien. A fixed number of their merchant ships, twenty-five, are allowed to go to various countries and buy goods, come to Macao, and sell them themselves. Their duties all come from the Chinese merchants who go to Macao to buy goods. The said country pays only tonnage dues, unlike the practice of the various countries trading at Canton. Fundamentally there is no need for a separate agreement. But it has been customary for the barbarians of the various countries trading at Canton, being cramped for space there, to go to Macao and rent residences from the Italians. Now the English barbarians live in Hong Kong. The newly-fixed regulations also allow trade at five ports. With the various barbarians scattered in all directions, Macao's rents are sure to become gradually less; trade also cannot be what it was and Italy will have her livelihood suddenly curtailed and her conditions straitened. Now their plea to devise means of dealing with this matter has been received. Your officials have carried out a detailed and thorough investigation and shall consider ways of revision. They have also delegated officers to proceed to Macao to confer at length with the said barbarian leader. It would seem that it can easily be effected. This is a brief summary of the conditions of the Italians trading at Macao.[8]

All in all, the various countries of the West take trade as their life. The Heavenly Court's secret in restraining and curbing them

---

7 Count de Ratti-Menton succeeded Challayé as French consul in China. *Chinese Repository*, v. 12, p. 503.

8 Throughout this paragraph the memorialists have written "Italians" for Portuguese, who had been in Macao since the 16th century.

lies entirely in maintaining absolute equality and should not be concerned with exacting demands. If we sedulously preserve general
propriety, then their refractory temper, being unrestrained, will
defeat itself. Moreover, the results we could get from taking a
little would be the same as if we took much. But Your officials,
braving criticism and complaints, can only abolish irregular exactions in order to relieve the barbarian's suffering and increase the
tariff in order to enrich the national revenue, all in the hope of
Chinese-barbarian concord and perpetual friendly relations, and in
order respectfully to supplement our Sovereign's supreme purpose
of pacifying the ocean frontiers.

    <u>Vermilion endorsement</u>: Do not be concerned with the immedi-
ate present. Above all it is important to consider what is large
and what is distant. After it is settled, memorialize fully.   (IWSM.
TK 68; 24b, 5-28a, 3)

60. September 23, 1843. MEMORIAL: Ch'i-ying Reports Increased
Revenue under the New Tariff Schedule.

    Ch'i-ying, Ch'eng Yü-ts'ai, Ch'i Kung, and Wen-feng further
memorialize. Your official Ch'i-ying, on account of England's
eagerness to trade, had separately memorialized that, according to
I-li-pu's previously fixed date, on July 27 Canton would be opened to
trade. He has received an Imperial Edict, "Let it be done as proposed. Respect this." His respectful compliance is on record.

    Your officials humbly note that merchant ships of the various
countries have in past years all come to Canton sometime after the
sixth month, selling goods and paying duties according to circumstances, and remained until the second or third month of the following year, when, laden with export goods, they one after another returned home. The ships arriving thereafter were not numerous.
Thus the prosperous period for the collection of customs at Canton
was the conjunction of fall and winter.

    Now from July 27, the date of the opening of the customs ac-
cording to the new regulations, up to September 3, altogether
fifty-three English and American merchant ships entered port, all
consigned to the ten-odd generally trusted hong merchants. They
exchanged their goods and paid duties. Chinese and barbarians are
both very content and quiet. The mart and the community are happy
and enjoying their pursuits and trade entirely as usual. Customs
collections amounted to more than 128,900 <u>taels</u>. Compared with
the amount collected last year from August 6 to September 14, this
is an increase rather than a decrease. Hitherto in the trading transactions of the merchant ships of the various countries exports exceeded imports. Now the foreign ships have just arrived and what
is collected is entirely import duty. What exports there are, are
in very small amounts. Very soon the export duties naturally must

be ample. In the future, after Foochow and the other ports are
opened, although the Canton Maritime Customs will be less than in
previous years, yet counting all the five ports together, the amount
of the customs will be increased. The indications already apparent
are sufficient to gratify entirely the Imperial concern.

But the Canton Maritime Customs port is scattered and vast;
its bays and tributaries are many and divergent. Many clerks must
be sent to make the rounds one by one. Duties are paid by the picul
and goods are weighed often amounting to several hundreds or
thousands of piculs. The porters required are actually not few.
Previously porters of this sort all received extralegal tonnage
money and did not receive wages. Now the irregular exactions are
entirely abolished and they are reduced to working on empty
stomachs. Under the circumstances we cannot but provide their
expenses in order, by filling their mouths, to stop corrupt practices.
...   (IWSM. TK 68; 28a, 4-29a, 5)

61. September 23, 1843. EDICT: Approves Principle of Most-
Favored-Nation Treatment for the United States and Other Countries.
Edict to the Grand Councillors. On this day (We) received the
memorials of Ch'i-ying and others, one outlining the conditions
with regard to the handling of the trade of the United States and
other countries, the other (saying that) since the opening of the
Canton Maritime Customs, Chinese and barbarians have been tranquil and trading as usual. (We) read the memorials and are fully
informed. The various Western countries take trade as their life.
The art of controlling and curbing them lies entirely in the maintenance of absolute fairness. Sedulously maintain general propriety
and above all properly consider permanence and ultimate consequences. Do not consider merely the immediate present. As
for any regulations for the trade of the United States and other
countries, let them, after discussing and settling them, memorialize fully....   (IWSM. TK 68; 29b, 2-6)

62. October 2, 1843. MEMORIAL: Liu Yün-k'o Reports Operation
of Trade Regulations at Ting-hai and Ningpo.
Governor General of Min-Che [i. e., Fukien-Chekiang], Liu
Yün-k'o, memorializes. On returning to the capital of Chekiang,
Your official learned on inquiry that the Ting-hai ocean front had
ten-odd barbarian ships of England and the United States at anchor,
and also that Tao-t'ou, Tung-kang, P'u-ssu, Wan-miao, and T'ien-
hou-kung all have had several residences built and have accumulated
goods. The barbarians occasionally take small boats and go to the
prefectural cities of Chen-hai and Ningpo to buy things. When their
business is finished they return without tarrying. Their attitude is
very quiet and peaceful. The residents are also tranquil and cause

no trouble. But apparently the trading regulations of the said barbarians and the tariff schedule have already been discussed and
settled by Imperial Commissioner Ch'i-ying and others and been
communicated to Chekiang. Your official also received a communication from the Boards. He has examined minutely the articles
Ch'i-ying and the others have concluded. They are thorough and
really adequate to aid national policy and conciliate the barbarian
nature.... (IWSM. TK 68; 35a, 7-35b, 5)

63. November 7, 1843. MEMORIAL: Ch'i-ying Advocates Strict
Limitation of British and American Trade to the Five Treaty Ports.
     Ch'i-ying further memorializes. It is humbly noted that from
last winter to the present, barbarian ships have been cruising about
in the Fukien, Chekiang, and Kiangsu ocean fronts. They are all
English and American merchant ships waiting for the opening of
trade; there are no ships at all of other countries. Previously, in
the fifth month (May 29-June 28), a two-masted barbarian merchant
ship came to the Cha-p'u, Chekiang, ocean front and wanted to
trade. After the Cha-p'u garrison colonel explained, it left. Your
slave immediately wrote to Pottinger demanding why the treaty was
disregarded. Later he received a reply saying that he would investigate immediately; that if they were his country's ships, he
would summarily prohibit and restrain them; that after the opening
of trade at Shanghai and other places, each port would have a barbarian leader in charge to control the immediate environs; and
that naturally they should act according to the treaty, but the
Chinese local officials must take pains to cooperate by preventing
traitorous people of the interior from engaging in illicit trade, so
that then (the controls) could be effective.
     In the Supplementary Treaty, furthermore, one clause says
clearly that if anyone goes to other places or ports on his own
authority, cruises about, and has both cargo and ship confiscated,
the said country cannot dispute it. This is to guard against incipi-
ent (troubles) and stop (them) at the outset.
     Now is received an Imperial Edict ordering that Wen-tang,
Jung-ch'eng, and Fu-shan-hsien in Shantung, and the vicinity of
the bar of the Lan River at Tientsin, be watched for barbarian
ships cruising about. Your slave immediately respectfully obeyed
and made inquiries. Also on October 8, when the treaty was
agreed upon, he personally interrogated him (Pottinger). He said:

> Actually, because barbarian leaders to take charge of affairs at Shanghai
> and other places had not yet reached the ports, the said Canton chief's
> whip was not long enough, and consequently the various merchant ships dis-
> regarded his prohibitions and went elsewhere. Now that the treaty has been
> concluded and the various ports are being successively opened, he would
> immediately issue proclamations. If there were still some who disobeyed,

we should request that they be handled according to the treaty. Thereafter it would not be necessary to give them food supplies. He also asked
us to forbid the people from dealing with them.

His manner and speech were very straightforward and sincere.
Your slave has taken the clause of the treaty that "barbarian ships
going to other places or ports should have both their ships and cargoes confiscated, " and sent it by letter to the various coastal
provinces as a general notification. Furthermore, he is impelled
to request an Imperial Edict ordering the respective governors
general and generals-in-chief of Mukden, Chihli, Shantung, Kiangnan,
Chekiang, Fukien, and Kwangtung, that if any barbarian ships hereafter come into a port not opened to trade, no matter what the
country or the ship, they should, in accord with existing treaties,
invariably confiscate both cargo and ship; if any fail to obey, they
are to find out definitely what country the ship belongs to and its
name, and notify the governor general of Liang-kuang by letter.
He will inform the said barbarian leader and thus ensure delivery.

Previously barbarian ships have never gone North. Since 1830
Mukden, Chihli, Shantung, and Kiangsu have still seen them only
occasionally. The two provinces of Fukien and Chekiang have
them coming and going continually throughout the year. After all,
they are all in collusion with the traitorous populace, and the soldiers
purposely connive and bring about evils which it is almost impossible to control. In law one must control himself before he is able to
control others. If traitorous people are not strictly forbidden to
act in collusion, and the evils of the purposely conniving soldiers
not stopped, then "where profit is, men are sure to go after it" and
"where things are rotting, worms will breed." In administration
there will be much obstruction, and there is also concern that
there will be a shortage in the customs on this account.

Your slave has received an Imperial Mandate to take charge of
barbarian affairs, and he will by no means shift his responsibility.
Success, however, depends entirely on the wholehearted cooperation
of the governors general and commanders of the various maritime
provinces in ordering the civil and military officers under them to
pledge themselves to public loyalty and strive for a policy of self-
control. If we strengthen our defenses, the said barbarians will
not be able to count on any profit and will by no means dare to disregard the prohibitions and go elsehere. If they still ignore the
treaty and act wantonly, the error will be with them and can be
handled according to the treaty. Then they will not dare but bow
their heads and obey. (IWSM. TK 69; 17b, 2-19a, 5)

64. November 15, 1843.   MEMORIAL: Grand Council Notes Most-
Favored-Nation Clause in Supplementary Treaty Concluded with Great
Britain.

[Memorial of Grand Councillor Mu-chang-a and others discussing
the terms of the Supplementary Treaty with Great Britain submitted by
by Ch'i-ying which was turned over to the Grand Council for discussion.]   ... The original document states in one article, "if the
merchants of the various foreign countries of the West are permitted
indiscriminately to go to the various ports to trade, then they are
the same as the British.   In the future if any new Imperial favors are
granted to other countries, they must be granted entirely equally to
the British."

The merchants of the various foreign countries were formerly
permitted to trade only in Kwangtung.   Now they have been allowed
to go to the various ports of Foochow, Amoy, Ningpo, and Shanghai
to trade.   This is a new favor of His Imperial Majesty, shared indiscriminately by Great Britain and other countries.   Moreover, the
tariff and complete regulations have now been determined and promulgated in the various ports.   Great Britain and the other countries
must all uniformly respect and obey.   There can be no unreasonable
demands....   (IWSM. TK 69; 29a, 10-29b, 6)

Chapter 3

The Cushing Mission, 1843-1844
(Documents 65-99)

   The documents of this period, dated November 15, 1843 to December
14, 1844, cover the first diplomatic mission of the United States to China
-- that of Caleb Cushing of Newburyport, Massachusetts. There are
thirty-five items in this group, twenty-one memorials and fourteen edicts.
All but one of the edicts are addressed to the Grand Council. The single
one addressed to the Grand Secretariat is that appointing Ch'i-ying as
imperial commissioner to negotiate with Cushing. This bears out the
generalization that the Grand Secretariat had degenerated to the rubber
stamp category, at least insofar as foreign relations were concerned.
There is no indication that the emperor was greatly perturbed by the
Cushing mission. There are only seven vermilion endorsements on the
memorials. Two of the endorsements are the formal Chih-tao-la ("Noted"),
only one is a specific comment, and four are interlinear jottings by the
emperor. Moreover, the interlinear endorsements are brief and formal
and the one comment proffered by the emperor is merely: "This is the
way to do it. We have understood it entirely," appended to Ch'i-ying's
memorial explaining the peculiarities of the American barbarians and the
impossibility of treating them like civilized Chinese.
   The number of memorialists of this period is very limited. The preliminary phase of the Cushing mission is reported by the acting governor
general of Liang-kuang, Governor Ch'eng Yü-ts'ai of Canton. The bulk of
the memorials (fifteen) are from Imperial Commissioner Ch'i-ying, who
was transferred to Canton to handle the negotiations with Cushing and who
remained as China's first "foreign minister." There is one memorial by
Liang Pao-chang, governor of Chekiang province, reporting on the barbarian
situation at Ningpo and Ting-hai. One of the most interesting and significant
documents of the group is that of Mu-chang-a, chief of the Grand Council,
and the other grand councillors, in which they present a critique of the
Treaty of Wanghia (Wang-hsia) or Cushing Treaty.
   The parallel American documents are summarized by Tyler Dennett,
Americans in Eastern Asia, in a chapter entitled "The Policy of Caleb
Cushing," p. 145-171. Some of the more personal aspects of the mission,
from the family papers, are recorded by Claude M. Fuess in his Life of
Caleb Cushing (2 v., New York, 1923). The Cushing correspondence has
been published by the government, U.S. Cong. 28:2, Senate Documents 58
and 67. Four of the Chinese documents have been paraphrased by P.C.
Kuo and published in his Critical Study of the First Anglo-Chinese War,
with Documents, Shanghai, 1935. Both the English and Chinese texts of the
Treaty of Wang-hsia, as well as notes on the negotiations, are found in

Hunter Miller, <u>Treaties</u> and <u>Other</u> <u>International</u> <u>Acts</u> of <u>the</u> <u>United</u> <u>States</u> of <u>America</u>, v. 4 (Washington, 1934) p. 559-662.

TRANSLATIONS OF DOCUMENTS

65. <u>November 15, 1843. MEMORIAL: Ch'i-ying Reports Interview</u> with <u>United States Consul Forbes at Canton--Cushing Mission Fore-</u> <u>shadowed.</u>
Imperial Commissioner Ch'i-ying, Governor General of Liang-kuang Ch'i Kung, Governor of Kwangtung Ch'eng Yü-ts'ai and Canton Superintendent of Customs Wen-feng memorialize.

They beg to comment on the case of the United States and other countries requesting to trade according to the new regulations. Previously, because the American barbarian leader, Kearny, had already returned to his country and there was only an acting consul named Kin, in charge of trade at Canton, and also because the French barbarian leader Jancigny was impeached as an imposter by the barbarian leader Ratti-Menton, Your officials could not distinguish between true and false and found it inexpedient to enter into useless negotiations with them. This is the general situation already presented in memorials for the Imperial notice and is on record.

Subsequently, according to the reports of our subordinates, a newly dispatched American chief, Forbes,[1] has already arrived in Canton, Ratti-Menton is the <u>bona</u> <u>fide</u> French barbarian leader, and Jancigny has already returned to his country. On questioning barbarians who have traded at Canton for a long time, all opinions coincided. Your officials have again investigated and found no disparity. Then Forbes and Ratti-Menton one after the other asked for interviews.

Your officials humbly find that heretofore when the barbarian leaders of the various countries made requests, instructions for their guidance were always transmitted by the hong merchants and linguists There were never any interviews granted. Opinions and conditions were segregated. The various barbarians often took the lack of personal contact as cause for resentment. Now on the occasion of changing the regulations, if we do not grant interviews and confer with them face to face, it is sure as before to cause a great deal of suspicion and innumerable retractions. This is certainly not the way to conciliate and curb the barbarians. Therefore, they first ordered Huang En-t'ung and Hsien-ling to meet them. Their attitude and language we extremely respectful and obedient. At the time, Your official Ch'eng Yü-ts'ai was supervising the provincial literary examinations, and

---

1 Paul S. Forbes, Esq., was the newly appointed American consul at Canton. *Chinese Repository*, v. 13, p. 9.

Your official Wen-feng was occupied with customs collections, and
could not get away. Your officials Ch'i-ying and Ch'i Kung, taking
with them Huang En-t'ung and others, granted separate interviews in
a public hall outside the city wall.[2]

According to the replies of the American barbarian leader,
Forbes, the merchants of his country, respectfully receiving the universal benevolence of His Imperial Majesty, and being permitted to
trade and pay duties at the five ports according to the new regulations,
are grateful no end for this kindness to men from afar. The chief of
the said country sent him to reside at Canton and supervise matters
of trade at the various ports. He only requested of the high officials
of the Heavenly dynasty special consideration and courteous treatment.
The chief of the said country had already separately delegated an envoy
to come to Canton and intended to request written (permission) to
proceed to Peking and respectfully regard the Heavenly countenance,
as a means of expressing the sincerity of his esteem. Ocean winds
being uncertain, he did not know when he would be able to arrive.

Your officials told him that his country(men) came from afar
only for purposes of trade. Canton had long traded, and in addition
the other ports were also successively being opened. All matters
were to be handled by the commissioner sent by His Imperial Majesty
to Canton, together with the governor general, the governor and the
customs superintendent. If they had anything to say, they should make
a factual report and await their decision. Moreover, his country's
previous respect and obedience had long since come to the attention
of His Imperial Majesty and would be sure to receive condescending
consideration. From his country to Canton he would already have
traversed many oceans for over seventy thousand li. To go from Canton to Peking, counting the distance both ways, would be another ten
thousand li and more. He certainly could not bear to have the envoy
of the said country proceed by circuitous routes to Peking and incur
additional labor and expense. Even if the envoy went to Peking with
matters of trade, he would be sure to receive an Edict of His Imperial Majesty ordering him to come back here and resume discussions,
and the laborious trip would have been in vain, so the said barbarian
chief should immediately stop him, and this would be brought to the
Emperor's attention for him. As the said barbarian leader was residing in China, in charge of trade at the various ports, if he was able
to force the merchants to trade equably and pay duties according to
the regulations without any leakage, all the ports would be notified to

---

2   An account of this meeting, from the *Canton Press*, is reprinted in the *Chinese
    Repository*, v. 12, p. 503. The *Repository* carries no account of Forbes' interview
    with Ch'i-ying.

respect him, so there would not be the least grievance.

The said barbarian leader replied that he would not dare wantonly make demands. He would take it upon himself to notify the envoy to prevent his going to Peking, but as he could not immediately receive the envoy's reply, he dared not be positive. If in the future the envoy should nevertheless come to Canton and the Imperial Commissioner had left, he would report to the high officials of Kwangtung province and await their decision.

The French barbarian leader Ratti-Menton only requested permission to proceed to the five ports and to pay,duties and trade accord ing to the new regulations. He also stated that previously Jancigny, posing as consul and without authority, presented a separate petition and willfully insulted the authorities. He would certainly report this to the king of his country and have him severely punished.

Your officials thereupon made clear the Imperial favor and authorized them to proceed to the various ports and engage in trade on an equal basis. In addition they ordered that, as the separate petition presented by Jancigny had no insubordinate terms, as he had dismissed the said barbarian leader Challayé who handed in the document, and as Jancigny had already returned to his country, the government of the Sacred Court, being magnanimous, would by no means take any notice of it. If later on there were other imposters there could not again be such accommodation. They also further stipulated that they (French) were only permitted to trade, rent buildings and reside at the five ports and were not permitted to go elsewhere. All regulations should be handled exactly as for the English. The said barbarian leader and the others went away thoroughly happy and exhilarated.

Besides, the one Belgian and two Dutch ships entering port had only merchants and no barbarian leader (on board). They joined the other countries and traded according to the new regulations. They were all extremely peaceful. The Spanish merchant ships have still not reached Canton. The number of ships of this country is not great and whether they come or not is uncertain. When they come they can merely trade like the rest without the need of a separate agreement.

As to the United States, they previously requested a reduction of the duties on foreign ginseng and bulk lead. At the time, Your officials considered that as the tariff was just settled, it was improper to issue orders in the morning and change them in the evening and bring about complications. Moreover, trade is the principal means of pacifying the frontiers. Certainly, according to Imperial instruction, it is important to consider majors and ultimates and not merely regard the immediate present and incur future criticism. Just then was received the statement of the said barbarian that the superior and inferior grades of foreign ginseng were not equal. On actual examination, out of a hundred catties only twenty catties were superior ginseng. They only asked for examination of goods for the payment of duties, whereupon the various foreign merchants would have no fear of losing their capital. They did not venture to ask that the regulations be changed nor will they in the future make further requests.

Your officials find that customs examinations must necessarily distinguish superior and inferior goods and determine the values in order to levy tariffs. The request received to levy duties on imports by actual examination according to the new regulations was in fact natural and reasonable. It has no effect on the national revenue, and the barbarian temper can be forever pacified. We have already approved and given orders accordingly.

As to bulk lead, the amount imported is not large and there is no need to discuss it. (IWSM.TK   69; 34b, 5-37b, 3)

66. November 15, 1843. MEMORIAL: Ch'i-ying Anticipates Cushing's Demand to Go to Peking.

Ch'i-ying and others further memorialize. The (representatives of) various Western countries, from the time the Italians, Adam Schall and Ferdinand Verbiest,[3] entered the service of the Heavenly Court until after Russia established a school for officials at Peking, have differed in ability and fame and have been proficient in different fields. Because the various other countries had not the same felicity, those hoping to be invited to China were not limited to one time nor to one person. There is a rumor that in the fall of 1840 the English desired to cease hostilities, make peace, and enter the (Hanlin) Academy to study. Last year at Nanking a French barbarian said that if the English barbarians were permitted, the same as Russia, to have their people reside at Peking, then there would be peace and no trouble.

Previously, during the negotiation of the Supplementary Treaty, Your official Ch'i-ying originally drew up a joint draft and sent it to the said chief ordering him to re-examine it. To the clause saying that other countries were allowed to go to the five ports to trade

---

3 Jean Adam Schall von Bell (1591-1666), native of Cologne, and Ferdinand Verbiest (1623-1688), native of Belgium, were famous Jesuit missionaries to China. See Couling, Encyclopaedia Sinica.

without discrimination, the said chief added the clause, "in the future any new favors extended by His Imperial Majesty to the other countries will be allowed equally to the English without discrimination." Your officials, suspecting that in regard to tariff and ports now determined there would be separate demands, ordered Huang En-t'ung and Hsien-ling repeatedly to question the (English) barbarian leader at Canton. According to his statement, "The tariff and ports being already determined, I shall not in the least dare to make separate demands. It is only that I have heard that the United States is seeking to go to Peking. If they receive His Imperial Majesty's permission, my country should also receive the favor."

Subsequently there was received the statement of the American barbarian leader, Forbes, that his chief had delegated an envoy to proceed to Peking to pay his respects to the Emperor. On asking him the reason for this, he insisted that it was only to show the sincerity of his respect and there was no other motive. Then it was recalled that in the ninth month of last year (October 4-November 3, 1842) there was another American, Ball, who presented a petition at Your minister Ch'i Kung's yamen, that "being proficient in astronomy and mathematics, he besought a memorial in his behalf (for permission) to go to Peking and serve (at the Court)." Ch'i Kung has already memorialized stating his refusal. Consequently, as today's request to go to Peking is, as before, in the hope of employment, it was plain that they would not memorialize for him. Therefore, being unwilling to state it openly, England in the statement added to the Supplementary Treaty, understanding clearly that there would be a request of the United States to go to Peking, secured a vantage point in advance. Even if it were clear that there was no mutual collusion, it is at least an artful experiment by the United States.

Furthermore, Your officials again ordered Huang En-t'ung and others to select and delegate able officers to explain carefully to the American barbarian leader, and also to tell him not to be duped by others. The said barbarian leader agreed to notify (the envoy) to stop. England's desire to make fraudulent use of Imperial prestige to outshine neighboring countries and induce the United States to act as scapegoat can already be clearly seen. (IWSM.TK 69; 37b, 4-38b, 9)

67. November 15, 1843. EDICT: Accepts Most-Favored-Nation Treatment of the United States but Specifically Forbids Access to Peking.

Edict to the Grand Councillors. We have received memorials of Ch'i-ying and others on the conclusion of the American trade regulations (t'ung-shang chang-ch'eng). We have read the memorials and are fully informed. Now that the English barbarians have been allowed to trade, whatever other countries there are, the United States and others, should naturally be permitted to trade without discrimination, in order to show Our tranquillizing purpose. Let them arrange carefully according to the proposals. Above all, they must consider ultimate and major (results) and cannot regard merely the immediate present and give cause for later abuse.

As to the statement that "the request of the United States to come to Peking for an audience," /and the (most-favored-nation) clause of England added to the Supplementary Treaty "as a prearranged point of advantage, even if it were known to involve no collusion, is a cunning experiment," let Ch'i-ying and the others make adroit explanations, saying that the Heavenly Court soothes and restrains the various countries and regards all with the same kindness; that no essential regulations can be expunged, no unessential regulations can be added; that if the various countries in large numbers ask to have audiences and to visit China, not only is there no such arrangement, but it is contrary to traditional regulations and it would be very hard to memorialize for them; that in already permitting them to trade without discrimination the Heavenly favor is magnanimous, and if they can restrain the merchants, trade fairly and pay duties according to the regulations without any smuggling, His Imperial Majesty will hear of it and will be sure to be greatly pleased.

On receipt of **this** Edict, Ch'i-ying shall immediately order Huang En-t'ung and others to issue clear instructions in accordance with it. Not the least equivocation is permissible, to give rise to other complications. This is of the greatest importance. This Edict is to instruct Ch'i-ying, Ch'i Kung, Ch'eng Yü-ts'ai, and is also to be transmitted to inform Wen-feng. (IWSM.TK 69; 38b, 10-39b, 1)

68. December 12,1843. MEMORIAL: Ch'i-ying Reassures the Court that the Cushing Mission is Still Indefinite.

Ch'i-ying further memorializes. Your slave has received a communication from the Grand Councillors that on November 15, 1843 they received an Imperial Edict:

Now that the English barbarians have been allowed to trade, whatever other countries there are, the United States and others, should naturally be permitted to trade without discrimination in order to show our tranquillizing purpose. As to the request of the United States to come to Peking for an audience and the statement of England added to the Supplementary Treaty as a preliminary vantage point and a cunning experiment,

let Ch'i-ying and others issue clear instructions and by no means allow
the development of other complications. Respect this.

Your slave humbly finds that the request of the American chieftain to send an envoy to Peking for an audience was entirely the oral
statement of the said barbarian leader, Forbes. When Your slave,
together with Governor General Ch'i Kung instructed Huang En-t'ung
and others repeatedly to notify him, they received the statement
that he (Forbes) intended immediately to tell him (Cushing) to stop,
but whether or not he could intercept him he dare not be positive.
Also he (Forbes) did not know when the said envoy could reach
there. If in the future the envoy did come to Canton and the Imperial
Commissioner had already left, he (Forbes) would immediately
notify the high officials of Kwangtung province and await their instructions.

When we examined the said barbarian Forbes, his language was
sincere and ingenuous, his attitude very respectful and obedient,
not to be compared with (that of) overbearing, intractable people.
Up to the present, there is still no news of the said envoy's coming
to Canton. Whether or not he has already turned back or if Forbes'
words were only empty phrases to feel out the way, it is difficult to
conjecture.

Furthermore, Your slave will find it inconvenient to remain in
Canton long and has now ordered Huang En-t'ung respectfully in accord with the Imperial Edicts to issue clear instructions letting it
be known that if any (American) envoy comes he will have made
the journey in vain. If they are content with trade, all can receive
substantial favors. If, due to the fact that ocean winds are irregular,
their letters cross each other, and as a result an envoy does come
to Canton, still in accord with previous memorials, it will be for
Governor General Ch'i Kung to order Huang En-t'ung adroitly to
explain things to him in the earnest hope of removing the covetousness of his heart, and order him to return home, in order to stop
any idea of other countries imitating him. (IWSM.TK 70; 17b,
4-18b, 1)

69. December 12, 1843. EDICT: Instructs Canton Officials to Block
Any Attempt of American Envoy to Proceed to Peking.

Edict to the Grand Councillors.... (We) have also received Ch'i-
ying's separate memorial, that "he has respectfully obeyed the
Imperial Edict and ordered Huang En-t'ung to give clear instructions
to the American barbarian leader, Forbes."

Now that Ch'i-ying has already returned to his post, if an envoy
of the said country does come to Canton, let Ch'i Kung and the others
immediately order Financial Commissioner Huang En-tung adroitly

to explain that the Heavenly Court conciliates and curbs outside barbarians entirely according to fixed laws. The said barbarians having never up to this time paid tribute, not only could the Kwangtung governor general or governor not memorialize the request for him, but if he came to the ports of Chihli they would not even permit the said barbarian to go ashore. Thus the said barbarian would make the voyage in vain. Rather than be ungrateful for His Imperial Majesty's intention of extending undeserved sympathy, would it not be better to be content with trade and receive substantial favors?

In this manner inform him clearly so as to destroy the covetousness of his heart and also stop any idea of other countries' doing likewise. Be sure that there is not the least equivocation to give rise to further complications.

This Edict will serve to inform Ch'i Kung and Ch'eng Yü-t'sai and shall be transmitted for the information of Huang En-t'ung. (IWSM.TK 70; 19a, 5-19b, 3)

70. April 9, 1844. MEMORIAL: Ch'eng Yü-ts'ai Reports Arrival of the Cushing Mission at Macao and Preliminary Exchange of Correspondence.

Acting Governor General of Liang-kuang, Governor of Kwangtung Ch'eng Yü-ts'ai memorializes. It is on record that in the eighth month (September 24-October 23) of 1843 there was received a report of the American consul, Forbes, that the chieftain of the said country had dispatched an envoy to come to Canton, intending to ask permission to proceed to Peking. Your officials Ch'i-ying and Ch'i Kung refused this in suitable words and also ordered the said consul to send word back to his country to prevent his setting out, and immediately reported fully in a memorial.

Later was received a communication from the Grand Councillors that on December 12 they had received an Imperial Edict:

(We) have received Ch'i-ying's separate memorial that, respectfully obeying the Imperial Edict, he had ordered Huang En-t'ung to give clear orders to the American barbarian chief, Forbes. If the said country does have an envoy come to Canton, let him immediately explain to him adroitly. Respect this.

Your officials forthwith transmitted this word to Huang En-t'ung to act entirely accordingly.

On February 28 of the present year, was received a secret report of the provisional sub-prefect of Macao, Hsieh Mu-chih, and others, that an American cruiser, having on board over five hundred barbarian troops and sixty-four guns, on the 25th of the same month, anchored at Chiu-chou. Before an investigation could be ordered, on March 2, a report was received from the consul, Forbes, saying that Cushing, an envoy of his country, had arrived at Kwangtung.

Considering that the envoy who was to be sent by the said country had already been stopped by a letter of the said consul, at Your minister, Ch'i-ying's, order, we wondered why he still came, and whether the envoy had already set out so that he did not receive the letter. Immediately the said consul was ordered to act in accordance with the original record. And also since there was a physician of the said country, Parker,[4] who had long resided at Canton, who was somewhat conversant with spoken and written Chinese, and who seemed rather trustworthy, immediately the magistrate of Yung-an-hsien, Ch'ien Yen-kao, was delegated to instruct Parker to go to see Forbes and inquire into the motive of his coming in the face of orders to stop.

Subsequently, according to the report of the said magistrate, he had questioned Forbes, and the said envoy still sought to go to Peking for an audience with His Imperial Majesty and had no other purpose. On being told of the repeated orders to desist, he said they had never reached him. In the meantime, further word was received in barbarian character that the said envoy, Cushing, was sending the barbarian leader, O'Donnell, to Canton, to ask through Consul Forbes for an interview. On examination, there is the following Chinese translation:

> He has received the appointment of the president of his country as Envoy Extraordinary and Minister Plenipotentiary of the United States of America, to come and confer with ministers of China on the terms of intercourse of the two peoples and to conclude a treaty of amity. He will proceed to Peking without delay respectfully to present the president's sealed letter containing various important matters for Imperial inspection. Within one month, when the warships are loaded with provisions, he will go to Tientsin and the mouth of the Pei-ho.

Your official, inasmuch as the said envoy was far away at Macao and had not come to Canton to seek an interview, had no means of talking with him and immediately delegated Financial Commissioner Huang En-t'ung, with the provisional prefect of Kuang-chou-fu, Liu K'ai-yu, on two occasions to explain clearly to the various barbarian leaders the various previous notices. In addition, in accord with the

---

4 Dr. Peter Parker (1804-1888), medical missionary to China, sinologue, and later United States Commissioner to China, 1856-1857.

previous Imperial Edict, they again questioned them, explaining the law and giving them clear reasons. In the process, they made adroit explanations, and intercepted them with appropriate language.

According to the said barbarian leaders' reply, "the envoy of their country had received a plenary commission and traversed eighty thousand l̲i̲ of ocean, taking nine months to reach China, solely to ask permission to go to Peking for an audience. Actually this proceeds from the utmost sincerity and he would be pleased not to be impeded." Our officers found his language extremely respectful and obedient but his purpose very obstinate.

The said official again told them that if the said country, having come far for a righteous cause, should suddenly go by warship to Tientsin, there would be some loss of righteousness. Besides, Tientsin was still some distance from Peking, which was hardly accessible by ship, and the local coastal (officials) could not allow them to go ashore. Thus first making a long voyage with the certainty of being turned back from Tientsin, how vain would be the trip His Imperial Majesty having always been considerate, they certainly could not lightly indulge in wanton activities or wilfully commit improprieties.

The various barbarian leaders all seemed to accept this but said that they could not make decisions. Then they immediately went to Macao to transmit the information minutely to Cushing and to report back again.

Examining the barbarian document for the so-called various items on important matters, (the barbarians) were further asked what the matters and items were. Previously when foreign countries had matters of complaint, they had to have the governor general or governor memorialize for them according to the circumstances and could not directly get Imperial attention. The said barbarian leaders replied that they were entirely friendly and well-intentioned and would not dare make improper demands. As to the separate items, they have not yet been ascertained and (the barbarian leaders) dare not indicate them carelessly. In general they insist on going to the North and communicating with an Imperial Commissioner. On inquiring two or three times, the answers were always the same.

Your official finds that America has come to Kwangtung to trade for more than a hundred years and has not yet paid tribute. Now the envoy, Cushing, requests to go to Peking and also uses the title of Minister Plenipotentiary and the words, "to discuss regulations of intercourse and conclude a treaty of amity." His purpose, to follow the English barbarians and also the desire to go beyond them, is already entirely apparent. The said country has traded up to the present and been extremely peaceful, never having the least pretext for

quarrelling. Naturally there should be no pretext for causing trouble
or other incidents. But the said envoy did not even come to Canton
and seek an interview. The barbarian ships with favorable winds
can reach Tientsin in ten days. If Kwangtung province had not reported in a memorial and the ports in the environs of the capital
suddenly saw a barbarian ship, some suspicions would be aroused.
Moreover it is feared that if the barbarian temper is obstructed it
may lead to trouble.

Your official, mindful that barbarian affairs had just been settled, and that present and past conditions are not alike, was impelled
to restrain them temporarily and then consider maturely how to get
them under control. Now he has already sent a perspicacious reply,
repeatedly pointing out their error, refusing their request in appropriate language. As before, he has used equivocal language to get
the said envoy to tarry in Kwangtung, whereupon the whole policy of
holding-in-and-giving-leash can be conveniently worked out.

Your official had a personal interview with the governor general, Ch'i Kung, and their views entirely coincide. But barbarians
are by nature impatient and without understanding of values. Whether or not they can be detained long is hard to predict with certainty.
We have investigated as time afforded and devised means to stop
them; we are still waiting until the day when the said envoy replies
again so as to report in a memorial, and we have immediately sent
a flying message to the governors general and governors of the
various coastal provinces fully apprising them. In addition to all
this, Your official fittingly memorializes by four-hundred li post
and also makes a fair copy of the said envoy's letter and of the official reply and respectfully presents (them) for Imperial scrutiny.

To continue, in the barbarian document, what is called A-mo-li-
chia (America) is another reading of Mi-li-chien (America). The
said country has twenty-six regions comprising one country and consequently has the name of United States (Ho-chung-kuo). What they
call the president is their national executive. It is also incumbent
on me to explain (these terms). . . . (p. 6b, 4-9b, 3. Text of Cushing's letter given in literal Chinese translation, p. 9b, 3-10a, 9.
Text of the governor general's reply, p. 10a, 10-12b, 2. IWSM.TK.
71; 6b, 4-12b, 2)

71. April 9, 1844. MEMORIAL: Ch'eng Yü-ts'ai Comments on the
Cushing Mission and Anticipates a French Mission.

Ch'eng Yü-ts'ai further memorializes. To continue, it is noted
that America, France, and England are the three large countries of
the West. In strength, no one is inferior to another. They look particularly to the character of their treatment by the Heavenly Court

as a measure of national status. Last year the trade of the English barbarians was arranged, but the American consul, Forbes, then made a request for an envoy to go to Peking. The French military leader, Cécille, sent a letter to Your official Ch'i Kung with a proposal to join China in attacking the English barbarians, and asked China to send an envoy to his country to inquire into shipbuilding and the making of munitions. Your official Ch'i Kung immediately replied and refused. Now the American envoy has already reached Canton, but France has still made no move. But there is received a confidential report of the Macao sub-prefect, Hsieh Mu-chih, that "the said country now has one cruiser anchored at Chiu-chou, and it is rumored that several cruisers are expected to arrive in two months. Moreover, there is an envoy coming to China expecting to go to Tientsin with the American envoy for an audience with His Imperial Majesty."

Your official again questioned the distinguished citizen and expectant tao-t'ai, P'an Shih-ch'eng, and what he has heard is substantially the same.

It appears that American merchant ships are gathering like clouds, in numbers equal to those of England. The coming of their envoy to Kwangtung is thus a reasonable development. But the French (ships) coming to Canton to trade are very, very few. Now, in again sending an envoy on board a warship and anchoring in Kwangtung waters, their purpose must be based on something. But as the barbarian leaders of the said country have not yet made any requests, it is improper for Your official to stop them beforehand. (IWSM.TK 71; 12b, 3-13a, 7)

72. April 9, 1844. EDICT: Commends Ch'eng Yü-ts'ai for Holding Cushing at Macao and Announces Appointment of Ch'i-ying to Negotiate.

Edict to the Grand Councillors. Ch'eng Yü-ts'ai has memorialized on his preventing the American envoy from coming to Peking. According to his statement, "The American envoy, because the official letter previously sent to stop him was never received, on February 25 sailed into Chiu-chou anchorage and intended to come to Tientsin and the mouth of the Pei-ho for an Imperial audience." We have received the provisional governor general's repeated explanations and the compliance of all the various barbarians. He has already notified the said envoy but the latter has not yet replied. In addition he proposed "to have the said envoy wait at Canton for mature deliberation and regulation."

What has been done is entirely satisfactory. Since America has never paid tribute, if (the envoy) were to arrive at Tientsin We should certainly order him to return. The request to conclude commercial regulations should certainly be discussed and settled as before with the commissioner of the original negotiations, and by no means should they on this account sail north to Tientsin and have specially appointed officials to negotiate with them. Now We have notified Ch'i-ying ordering him to proceed posthaste to Kwangtung. After the said governor general has received this he must needs soon reach Canton. Before Ch'i-ying arrives, let Ch'eng Yü-ts'ai, together with Huang En-t'ung, notify the said barbarian that the commissioner of the original negotiations, Ch'i-ying, has been transferred to the post of governor general of Liang-kuang, is proceeding posthaste to Kwangtung, and will arrive shortly. Order (the envoy) to wait quietly in Kwangtung and by no means to engage in irresponsible actions.

In view of the statement that with favorable winds foreign ships could reach Tientsin in ten days, (We) have ordered Na-erh-ching-e to act as circumstances require.

According to the separate memorial, "there is also a French cruiser anchored at Chiu-chou. Since they have made no requests it is improper to stop them in advance." France is to be treated in the same way as America. If the said barbarian leader makes any request, immediately refuse in accord with previous Edicts. Take care that in adroitly explaining to him you do not lose sight of the idea of refusing him in proper language. (IWSM.TK 71; 13a, 8-14a, 1)

73. April 9, 1844. EDICT: Orders Ch'i-ying to Proceed to Canton to Negotiate with Cushing.

Supplementary Edict. Today (We) received the memorial of Ch'eng Yü-ts'ai that "the American envoy, not having received the previously dispatched orders to stop, on February 25 sailed into Chiu-chou anchorage intending to go to Tientsin for an audience. The said provisional governor general has explained back and forth and ordered the barbarian leader to notify the envoy, but he has not yet replied. Moreover there is a French cruiser anchored."

Since various Western countries have never paid tribute, if they sail north to Tientsin (We) shall certainly order them to return to Kwangtung. As to their desire to discuss regulations, it must be arranged as before with Ch'i-ying and others. By no means will other commissioners be sent to negotiate with them.

Let Ch'i-ying, on receipt of this Edict, proceed posthaste to Kwangtung and, together with Ch'eng Yü-ts'ai, take suitable action. The said governor general is a man trusted by the various barbarians. After reaching Kwangtung he should explain adroitly, rely on reason to circumvent properly, control and curb, and not give rise to further

complications. Thus he will not betray his commission. Let the
original documents, the communication of the said envoy, and the
official replies be copied and sent for (his) perusal. (IWSM.TK 71;
14a, 3-14b, 1)

74. April 9, 1844. EDICT: Warns the Tientsin Garrison to Be on Guard against Any American Attempt to Enter the Pei-ho.

Supplementary Edict. Today (We) received the memorial of
Ch'eng Yü-ts'ai that "the American envoy is at Chiu-chou anchorage
in Kwangtung waters and intends to come to Tientsin for an audience.
The said governor general has explained and refused, and has ordered the barbarian leader to inform the envoy, but he has not yet
received a reply." It is hard to guarantee that the barbarian ships
taking advantage of the winds will not come to Tientsin.

Let Na-erh-ching-e order the Tientsin commandant and tao-t'ai
to make plans in advance. If barbarian ships arrive at Tientsin,
(let them) immediately send an express report to the said governor
general, and at once order the said barbarians to await the governor
general's arrival. If they have anything to say, considered action will
then be taken. Since the said country claims to be coming for an
audience, by no means open fire on them. What food and fresh water
they need let them buy, but do not allow a single man ashore. As to
the so-called discussions of regulations and such matters, after the
said governor general reaches Tientsin, let him say that Ch'i-ying,
the commissioner originally negotiating, is now transferred to be
governor general of Liang-kuang and will shortly reach Kwangtung,
and that the commercial regulations of the said country have already
been determined. Order them immediately to turn back to Kwangtung.
This place is unsuitable for negotiations. As to their coming to Peking for an audience, say that the Heavenly Court, in pacifying and
curbing outside barbarians, always follows old regulations, and that
it is improper to memorialize this request for them. Take care to
explain adroitly and depend on reason to cut them off. By no means
leave the least ambiguity. (IWSM.TK 71; 14b, 3-15a, 2)

75. April 9, 1844. EDICT: Alerts Coastal Officials of Possible Arrival of American Warships--Friendly Treatment to be Accorded.

Supplementary Edict. Today (We) received a memorial of
Ch'eng Yü-ts'ai saying that "the cruiser of the American envoy is at
Chiu-chou anchorage, Kwangtung, intending to go to Tientsin for an
audience." (We) have notified Ch'i-ying by five hundred li post, ordering him to proceed posthaste to Kwangtung. Western countries
have never paid tribute and will by no means be permitted to come to
Peking. But barbarian ships take advantage of the wind and their

routes are uncertain. Let this serve notice to Hsi-en, Pi-ch'ang, Sun Shan-pao, Liu Yün-ko, Liu Hung-ao, and Liang Pao-ch'ang to give orders to the officers at the various ports that if the cruiser of the American envoy anchors by no means to open fire on it. What food and drinking water is required, let them buy, but do not permit a single man to come ashore. Moreover, tell them that Ch'i-ying has already gone to Kwangtung, and order them to return to Canton waters and await disposal of the case. Take these,several Edicts as a notification. (IWSM.TK 71; 15a, 3-10)

76. April 22, 1844. MEMORIAL: Ch'eng Yü-ts'ai Reports Cushing's Insistence on Proceeding to Peking, Possibly via the Grand Canal.
　　　　Acting Governor General of Liang-kuang and Governor of Kwangtung Ch-eng Yü-ts'ai memorializes. It is humbly observed that the American envoy, Cushing, came to Kwangtung and requested to go to Peking. Your official delegated the provincial treasurer Huang En-t'ung and others, in respectful accord with Imperial Edicts, to explain and intercept him, and also sent a lucid reply successively refuting (his arguments), immediately making copies and memorializing fully by four hundred li (post), making clear that when the said envoy replied, he would again report in a memorial. This is on record.
　　　　Subsequently, on March 28, 1844, a reply was received from the said envoy. It is noted that it states:

> He came solely for the two objects of going to Peking for an audience and (negotiating) a treaty of amity. He has received instructions from the president not to discuss anything with the various ranks of officials and to negotiate only with an Imperial Commissioner. Because of the fact that he did not meet an Imperial Commissioner at the border province, he was greatly disappointed. Now he still desires to go to Peking. If he is not allowed to take a warship to the mouth of the Pei-ho then he is willing to go to Peking by inland waters to avoid arousing suspicion.

Your official finds that the said envoy, Cushing, after the previous explanation to stop him, still begs to go to Peking. Although his language is respectful and obedient, his purpose is rather set. But on reading his reply, we note the suggestion he makes of being willing to go to Peking by inland waters; although difficult to accede to, it means that he will probably not suddenly sail to the north. But it contains the statement that he will negotiate only with an Imperial Commissioner and will not discuss anything with officials of various ranks. It can be detected that his purpose is after all, a desire to outshine the English barbarians and, like them, to set up a treaty in order to show preferential treatment by the Heavenly Court. Thus,

he regards the trade regulations as of no particular importance.
Now although Your officials have ordered him to desist, it is
feared that he still has not acquiesced. The said envoy has traversed
many oceans, coming to China from afar. If he is not somewhat
soothed and curbed he will not be willing to go right back. But fearing that on this account disappointment, rather, would result, Your
official on receipt of the communication of the said envoy immediately secretly wrote to the governor general of Liang-chiang,
Ch'i-ying, to enable him to make arrangements in advance. Besides
notifying the said envoy to wait quietly in Kwangtung for an Imperial
Edict for his guidance and not to make any unconsidered move,
(Your official), in accord with reason, respectfully memorializes
by express post, and also makes a copy of the said envoy's letter,
which is respectfully submitted for Imperial examination. (p. 15b,
1-16b, 3). Text of Cushing's letter to Governor Ch'eng, p. 16b,
3-17b, 2 (IWSM.TK 71; 15b, 1-17b, 2)

77. April 22, 1844. EDICT: Instructs Ch'eng Yü-ts'ai to Detain
Cushing with Assurances of Ch'i-ying's Competence to Negotiate a
Treaty.

Edict to the Grand Councillors. According to the memorial of
Ch'eng Yü-ts'ai, the United States has submitted a reply and, as before, "begs to go to Peking, and moreover is willing to go by way of
inland waters." As to the request of the United States to come to Peking for an audience, (We) have already issued Edicts ordering
Ch'eng Yü-ts'ai, together with Huang En-t'ung, to issue orders to refuse it and have also ordered Ch'i-ying to go to Kwangtung to manage
carefully.

Now, as the said envoy still begs to come to Peking, let the said
governor again issue instructions that inasmuch as the treaty the said
country proposes is to be negotiated with an Imperial Commissioner,
Ch'i-ying has been transferred to the post of governor general of
Liang-kuang. Moreover, he has again been granted the official seal
as Imperial Commissioner with exclusive control over barbarian affairs, and is coming to Kwangtung without delay. If the (envoy) will
wait quietly at Kwangtung, it will be highly expedient to negotiate with
him. If he insists on going to Tientsin and the mouth of the Pei-ho,
there will be no Imperial Commissioner there and he cannot negotiate
a treaty at all. His Imperial Majesty must needs issue an Edict ordering him, as before, to go back to Kwangtung and deal with Ch'i-ying.
Why should he make a laborious journey in vain?

The said governor, on receipt of this, shall immediately order
Huang En-t'ung to explain clearly, saying that when the Heavenly Court
conciliates and curbs outside barbarians, none who have not custom-

arily been admitted to court will be granted this request. At this
time the said country, no matter whether by way of the high seas or
the inland waters, can not be allowed to come to Peking. Merely order
him to await the Imperial Commissioner in Kwangtung, and do not
allow the development of further complications. (IWSM.TK 71; 17b,
3-18a, 4)

78. April 22, 1844. EDICT: Instructs Ch'i-ying to Hasten to Canton in
Order to Quiet Cushing and Restrain him from Proceeding to Peking.

Supplementary Edict. Previously Ch'eng Yü-ts'ai memorialized
that the American envoy begged to come to Peking. Immediately an
Edict was issued ordering Ch'i-ying to double his haste in going to
Kwangtung and to manage carefully. Subsequently We received another
memorial of Ch'eng Yü-ts'ai stating that the said barbarian envoy had
submitted a reply and still intended to go to Peking. Moreover, the
envoy stated that because he did not find an Imperial Commissioner he
was greatly disappointed. Then (Ch'eng) again notified the said envoy
to wait for Imperial orders and not to take any inconsiderate action.

(We) trust that Ch'i-ying, on receipt of the previous Edicts, has
already set out for Kwangtung. Let Ch'eng Yü-ts'ai's original memori
al and American envoy Cushing's communication both be sent for his
perusal. After the said governor general receives them, let him first
give urgent notice that now the said governor general has received an
Edict to take sole charge of ocean border affairs and has also been con
ferred the official seal as Imperial Commissioner, authorizing him to
manage barbarian affairs personally. The said envoy should only wait
quietly in Kwangtung and not undertake a long journey. If he did go to
Peking he would certainly be ordered to return to Kwangtung. If there
are instances of subsidiary affairs which need to be submitted to the
Throne they will also be memorialized fully by the present commissioner. In this way carefully make everything clear, so that the said
envoy will not stubbornly cling to his former statements.

Let Ch'i-ying immediately proceed with redoubled speed. After
reaching Kwangtung, if the said country presents a letter proposing
an Imperial audience, say that China naturally has fixed regulations.
There can be nothing contrary to the law, and nothing can be added to
it. If there are demands contrary.to propriety, on the one hand refuse them, saying that they are difficult to incorporate into a memorial, and on the other hand secretly report them in a memorial. This
matter is to be handled entirely by the said governor general and he
should take care that the arrangements be entirely satisfactory and
free from contamination from beginning to end, so as not to give rise
to further complications and so as to justify Our hopes. (IWSM.TK
71; 18a, 6-18b, 8)

79. April 22, 1844. EDICT: Authorizes the Grand Secretariat to Issue the Official Seal of Imperial Commissioner to Ch'i-ying.

Edict to the Grand Secretariat. Ch'i-ying has been transferred to the post of governor general of Liang-kuang. The adjustment of residual matters relative to the trade of the various provinces is entirely entrusted to the management of the said governor general. Let him, as before, be granted the official seal of Imperial Commissioner. Let all dispatches relating to the management of trade in the various ports be authorized by his seal, in order to show care and gravity. (IWSM.TK 71; 18b, 9-19a, 1)

80. May 29, 1844. MEMORIAL: Ch'eng Yü-ts'ai Reports the Visit of U.S.S. Brandywine, Commodore Foxhall A. Parker Commanding, to Whampoa.

Provisional Governor General of Liang-kuang, Governor of Kwangtung, Ch'eng Yü-ts'ai memorializes. The circumstances of American envoy Cushing's reaching Kwangtung Your official has twice memorialized by express post. Subsequently there has been another communication from the said envoy inquiring when the Edict of His Imperial Majesty could arrive and when the Imperial Commissioner would reach Kwangtung. Your official again ordered him to wait quietly at Macao and not to take any unconsidered action. Later he learned privately that the said country's warship, which went to the Philippines, has returned to Macao. Then was received Cushing's communication to the effect that the military chief of the said ship, Parker,[5] wished to go to Whampoa. As Whampoa is inland (inside Bocca Tigris) where the merchant ships of the various countries trade, and as warships cannot enter the port on their own authority, Your official immediately set forth the law clearly.

After he had prepared a note clearly forbidding it, to his surprise the said warship on April 19 entered the harbor and anchored at Shenching opposite Whampoa. Moreover, according to a communication presented by the military leader, Parker, the said ship came to the port solely to restrain the merchants and sailors and to guard against pirates and had no other motive at all. He also asked for an interview at Your official's yamen. Your official again told him that warships could not anchor inside the harbor, and that the various barbarian leaders never entered the city for interviews, and ordered him to leave immediately. He also sent a letter to Cushing ordering him to restrain

---

5 Commodore Foxhall A. Parker, U.S.N., commanding the East India Squadron, had the frigate *Brandywine* as his flagship.

and stop (Parker).

Just while copying and dispatching (this), further word was received from Cushing that, as the said envoy had come to Kwangtung, China should afford courteous treatment. Your official considered that, as the envoy of the said country, Cushing, was living far away in Macao, there was no way to meet him. Even though Parker's ship is anchored at Shen-ching, how could there be personal intercourse? But these outside barbarians are by nature impetuous and rather suspicious. The said country has never come to Court or paid tribute. With the laws of the Heavenly Dynasty they are not yet fully acquainted. Therefore it is impolitic to accommodate them too much and increase their arrogance; yet we must restrain them somewhat and open their path to understanding. Now (Your official) has again explained the customary prohibitions, given him clear reasons, and prepared a perspicuous document notifying him to act accordingly.

Your official has not ventured to copy one by one the communications that have been exchanged from time to time, and present them for Imperial examination (lest this) cause annoyance. As before, he communicated with the commander of the naval forces, Lai En-chüeh, to be watchful and take precautions as occasions arise, and to make a full report of any move the said warship has made, as soon as it is gone. [Vermilion endorsement: Noted]   (IWSM.TK 71; 23a, 8-24a, 10)

81. June 22, 1844. MEMORIAL: Liang Pao-ch'ang Reports the Appointment of Henry Wolcott as United States Consul at Ningpo.

Governor of Chekiang Liang Pao-ch'ang memorializes. On May · 22 Your official received a letter from the acting governor general· of Liang-kuang, Ch'eng Yü-ts'ai, that on April 14 of the present year, according to the statement of the American consul Forbes, the said consul was sending a man, surname Wolcott, given name Henry, to manage consular affairs at the port of Ningpo,[6] that he would be required to take charge of all matters, and that this letter was transmitted as notification.

Apparently the merchant ships of the said country which were trading at Ningpo had previously left. (Your official) immediately

---

6 Griffin states, "On March 22, 1844, Consul Forbes at Canton authorized Henry G. Wolcott of Boston (like Forbes, connected with Russell and Company) to discharge the duties of vice-consul at Ningpo. The reason given to the Department (July 8, 1844) was the need of having someone to enter ships at the customhouse. Wolcott was consul at Shanghai from 1846." *Clippers and Consuls*, p. 298.

notified the tao-t'ai of Ningpo that once the said consul reached the
region, if there were commercial questions, he should immediately
make careful arrangements and report. To date no word of the said
consul had been received and no American barbarian ships have
arrived.

As to the Ting-hai ocean front, up to May 2 there were altogether
nine English barbarian ships there. Later, it was found that of the
ships formerly anchored, from May 3 to 13, three ships had left for
the south sea. There still remained six English barbarian ships.
From the 13th to the 19th there came, one after another, three merchant ships and four steamers and warships, carrying barbarian
troops, munitions, etc. Now there are altogether thirteen barbarian
ships anchored. While the number of men is somewhat increased and
there is some activity in drilling troops, their attitude is still tractable
and obedient. The residents are also very content.

April 25 a "Number 3" French barbarian ship came and it remains
anchored outside Chu-shan-men without contact with the English barbarians. Accordingly the second captain of the left battalion, Sun Tien-
kuang, and others were instructed to go and make inquiries. They
could not understand the language. According to the English barbarians' statement, the (French) ship set out from Canton and came to
inspect the various ports along the way and had no other motive whatever. Your official again ordered that the facts be found regarding
the French barbarian ship. On May 23 it had already left for the high
seas. Now, although the trade at the port of Ningpo is still slight, the
barbarians are all rather peaceful.   Vermilion endorsement: Noted.
(IWSM.TK 71; 29a, 3-29b, 10)

82. June 23, 1844. MEMORIAL: Ch'i-ying Reports Arrival at Canton
and Imminent Opening of Negotiations with Cushing near Macao.
    Imperial Commissioner, Governor General of Liang-kuang, Ch'i-
ying, memorializes. Previously, while en route, at Wu-chiang Your
slave received the official seal of Imperial Commissioner and thereupon travelled night and day. On reaching the provincial capital of
Kwangtung, he interviewed Governor Ch'eng Yü-ts'ai and Financial
Commissioner Huang En-t'ung and inquired fully about the American
envoy Cushing, who was still waiting at Macao.
    Your slave, knowing that barbarians are by nature somewhat
impatient and the said envoy had been waiting a long time, feared that
on hearing of Your slave's arrival at Canton he might take ship and
sail up the Canton River in the hope of a conference (here), which
might easily arouse popular suspicion. On the other hand, if Your
slave were to go immediately at Macao, without waiting to assume
office, he feared that false reports would quickly arise. So he had a

wholehearted discussion with Your official, Ch'eng Yü-ts'ai and, on
the one hand sent a communication to the said envoy informing him of
his arrival at Canton and early departure for Macao to confer with him,
to quiet his heart in advance and, on the other hand took over the seal
of office of Your slave's post.

After somewhat disposing of essential public business, he will
proceed to Macao, taking Huang En-t'ung along. The latter will be
ordered to meet the said chief in advance to find out his intentions and
devise means of controlling him. Then Your slave will personally
announce the Imperial grace and earnestly enlighten him. If he can be
brought into our scheme, naturally he will not persist in asking to
sail to the North. Outside of this, if there are requests, (Your slave)
will negotiate separately and act carefully. (IWSM.TK 71; 30a, 2-30b
3)

83. June 23, 1844. EDICT: Authorizes Ch'i-ying to Conclude Negotiations with Cushing and Report Actions to the Court.

Edict to the Grand Councillors. According to Ch'i-ying's memorial he has reached Canton and also sent a communication to the
American envoy that he would proceed immediately to Macao for a
conference. (We) have read the memorial entire.

Let the said governor general, together with Financial Commissioner Huang En-t'ung, proceed to Macao. First ascertain the said
chief's position and devise means of controlling him. Afterwards in
conference with him earnestly enlighten him. If he makes any requests
examine the importance of the matter, discuss it carefully in detail
and take action, then send an express memorial in accord with the
facts. By no means can other complications be allowed to develop.

Also (We) received yesterday a memorial of Liang Pao-ch'ang
stating that, according to Ch'eng Yü-ts'ai's dispatch, the American con
sul was sending Henry Wolcott to take charge of affairs at the port of
Ningpo. The said consul to date had not reached Chekiang nor were
any American ships arriving. As to the English barbarian merchant-
men, steamers, and warships now anchored in the Ting-hai ocean
front, there are altogether thirteen, and the number of men has increased. While there are some drilling activities, their attitude is
still complaisant.

Accordingly, let the said governor general investigate the various
items mentioned in the said governor's appended memorial as occasion presents itself. If there are any matters that should be discussed
or acted on, let them also be memorialized fully according to the
facts. Let the original and the supplement be copied and sent for
perusal. (IWSM.TK 71; 30b, 4-31a, 3)

84. July 17, 1844. MEMORIAL: Ch'i-ying Reports Negotiations,
Stressing Cushing's Reluctance to Abandon his Trip to Peking.

   Imperial Commissioner, Governor General of Liang-kuang, Ch'i-
ying, memorializes. On June 10, 1844, Your slave, accompanied by
Financial Commissioner Huang En-t'ung and other officers, set out
from Canton, arriving at Macao June 20th. On the 21st and 22nd they
met the barbarian envoy and the barbarian chiefs, Parker and Bridgman.[7] They were polite and very respectful but did not mention
going to Peking for an audience and the presentation of their credentials. For several days in succession Your slave has sent Huang En-
t'ung, with various other officials, to explain everything clearly, to
commend the envoy for having waited in Kwangtung peacefully, and
also to tell him that even if he went to Peking he would certainly be
ordered back, thus making the trip in vain. But the said envoy's reply
was vague. Then he presented the précis of a commercial treaty.
Although translated into Chinese, it was not clear and the phraseology
was uncouth, but the purport was in general like the recently fixed
regulations. Moreover, he said that they would not venture to follow
the example of the English barbarians in appropriating islands. Your
slave examined it carefully and there seemed to be nothing detrimental
to the general commercial picture. Only on the issue of giving up his
northern trip did he equivocate. But he urged that the trade regulations be quickly agreed upon, drawn up, sealed, and copies exchanged.
   Inasmuch as the envoy had crossed the wide oceans, Your slave
considered it reasonable to conclude negotiations, provided there were
no unreasonable demands outside the trade regulations. But on examining the said envoy's first communication to the former acting governor
general, Ch'eng Yü-ts'ai, the purport seems to be to conclude the
treaty first and then go to Peking. Now he insisted on a speedy signing
of the treaty, but it was feared that after the treaty was concluded he
would actually proceed to Peking. If he were not carefully blocked we
should fall into his trap.
   Consequently, the various trade articles which he presented were
acceded to or rejected discriminately, each one being discussed carefully. Huang En-t'ung was ordered to confer with him personally in the
hope of observing his attitude. The said envoy was also notified in
writing that, if the treaty could be concluded without delay, there would

7 Dr. Peter Parker and Rev. Elijah C. Bridgman, both of the American Board Mission at
   Canton, in China from 1834 and 1829 respectively, were made joint Chinese secretaries. Dr. Bridgman was also official chaplain of the Cushing mission. Dennett,
   op. cit., p. 113.

be no necessity of going to Peking and (was asked) when he cared to
hand over his credentials. Seeing his scheme foiled, the said envoy
reiterated his request to go to Peking. When the discussion had
dragged on for several days, Your slave, accompanied by Huang En-
t'ung, called on the said envoy in person and told him that the regulations of the Heavenly Court had never provided for (going to Peking)
and could not be amended; that since he respected and admired His
Imperial Majesty, he must humbly obey His Edicts and not make
obstinate demands. (Your slave) repeatedly broke him down with
reasoning and pointed out the pros and cons, arguing for half a day.
The said envoy apparently has some vestige of understanding, but he
made the excuse that he came under orders from his president and
had credentials which must be presented for Imperial scrutiny. He
argued interminably. (We) told him that if he ever had any requests
which he could not present to the Emperor himself, (we) could
memorialize them for him. He said that he sincerely desired to see
China, hoping to travel by inland waterways, and that he had no ulterior
motives. His attitude was alternately respectful and haughty; his position was extremely changeable. (We) cross-examined him thoroughly, leaving him "no place to put his beak" [i.e. no leg to stand on].
Then he said he would prepare a reply in writing to clarify the original conversation, rather than reach a hasty conclusion orally.

   Your slave humbly observes that the said envoy, Cushing, in submitting these regulations, hoped to trade according to the English
barbarians' new regulations; on hearing that the English barbarians
had a supplementary treaty, he wanted to emulate and outdo them.
This is only reasonable. His request for an audience was actually to
show off before the English barbarians. Moreover, he constantly used
the northern expedition as a threat. Now, Huang En-t'ung, accompanied
by the other delegates, has been ordered to find means to enlighten him

   On June 25, the said envoy finally told Huang En-t'ung et al. that,
after considering for several days what the Imperial Commissioner
said, it had become entirely clear that he could probably anchor at
Macao for a while and not go north. Since this was an oral statement
it cannot be relied upon. As soon as the said barbarian envoy's written reply is received and his position confirmed, it will be memorialized posthaste. (IWSM.TK 72; 1a, 3-2b, 9; cf. P.C. Kuo, A Critical
Study of the First Anglo-Chinese War, with Documents, Shanghai, 1935,
p. 299-301.)

85. July 17, 1844. MEMORIAL: Ch'i-ying Notes the Inadequacy of
American Interpreters and His Utilization of Local Chinese Experts.
   Ch'i-ying further memorializes. To continue, those associated
with Your slave last year in the management of barbarian affairs were

the tao-t'ai Hsien-ling and the garrison officers Ch'en Po-ling,
Chang P'an-lung, and Ch'en Chih-kang. This time none of them
accompanied him to Kwangtung. Among the Cantonese officials, besides Financial Commissioner Huang En-t'ung, only the expectant
sub-prefect T'ung-lin, and the degraded official on probation, Wu
T'ing-hsien, are thoroughly conversant with barbarian conditions.
Outside of these there are no experienced officials.

Just as he was worrying about the lack of competent men for
assistance, Your slave, on reaching Nan-hsiung (Kwangtung) en
route, met the former prefect of Chao-ch'ing, expectant ministerial
secretary Chao Ch'ang-ling, (who was) going from Kwangtung to Peking. Last year, when he discharged his commission in Kwangtung,
Your slave discovered that the said official's ability was extraordinary and his official reputation very good. Therefore he took him
back to Canton to await an official appointment.

After arriving at Canton, he inquired fully of Huang En-tung regarding the American barbarians' difficulty of understanding. It is
much greater than the English barbarians', because the English barbarians had Morrison[8] and others. Although they were artful and cunning they were somewhat conversant with Chinese written and spoken
language, and when there was business one could discuss it with them.
The American barbarians have only Parker and Bridgman, who do not
know many Chinese characters. They are only versed in Cantonese
local dialect, with the result that it is hard to understand each other's
point of view and a great deal of energy is consumed. Then it occured
to Your slave that the expectant tao-t'ai, P'an Shih-ch'eng, who has
long held a Board post and has exceptional judgment, was born and
reared in Canton and well versed in the local dialect. Moreover, in
the adjustment of postwar issues for several years, in connection with
the purchase of barbarian cannon and the employment of barbarian
artisans to construct torpedoes, he has become well acquainted with a
considerable number of American merchants and is generally highly
respected by the barbarians of the said country. Now this official had
not yet put aside mourning, but it was highly expedient to take advantage
of his proximity and to appoint him. So he was summoned to this office
and ordered, with Chao Ch'ang-ling and Huang En-t'ung, to assist in
handling barbarian affairs. (IWSM.TK 72; 3b, 1-4a, 5)

---

8 Rev. Robert Morrison, D.D. (1782-1834), first Protestant missionary to China, came
to Canton in 1807, served as Chinese translator for the English East India Company,
and assisted Sir Henry Pottinger in his treaty negotiations. See obituary notice,
Chinese Repository, v. 3, p. 176-184.

86. July 17, 1844. EDICT: Advises Ch'i-ying on Most Diplomatic Method of Dissuading Cushing from Proceeding to Peking.

    Edict to the Grand Councillors. Ch'i-ying has memorialized the general circumstances of his meeting with the American envoy. We have read both memorials and understand the situation. The articles of trade submitted by the said barbarian envoy and others, according to the detailed examination of the said governor general, are about the same as the recently settled regulations and on the whole are not an impediment to trade. They have been separately sanctioned or rejected Ch'i-ying has ordered Financial Commissioner Huang En-t'ung to confer with him personally and expects to conclude the matter shortly. The indefiniteness of the envoy's manner and speech and his repeated use of the trip to the North as a threat are rather cunning. The said governor general has earnestly explained the refusal of the northern voyage.

    If he (the envoy) querulously reiterates the request then he (Ch'i-ying) should say that in the northern provinces there are no interpreters and the interior officials do not understand barbarian language. Besides, at this place there is no commissioner specially charged with barbarian affairs. The long journey would be sure to be made in vain and they would as before be sent back to Kwangtung. Be sure not to leave the tracks too conspicuous and cause the said barbarian envoy to suspect that we are evading the issue, which would only give rise to a threatening attitude. This is of the utmost importance. As soon as any thing is decided upon, immediately memorialize fully according to the facts. . . . (IWSM.TK 72; 4a, 6-4b, 4)

87. July 22, 1844. MEMORIAL: Ch'i-ying Reports Cushing's Abandonment of his Northern Trip but Refusal to Relinquish His Credentials.

    Imperial Commissioner, Governor General of Liang-kuang, Ch'i-ying memorializes. As the barbarians have become more tractable since his last memorial, Your slave Ch'i-ying, together with Huang En-t'ung and other officers, spent the last several days endeavoring to enlighten the barbarian mind, employing the obvious to clarify the obscure, using the credible to expel their suspicion. The said barbarian envoy seemed to comprehend and promptly submitted a communication saying that, despite his original intention to proceed to Peking for an audience, because this was prohibited by Imperial Edict and after careful consideration of (our) advice, he had finally abandoned his plan to g north. But he insisted that in case any Western power sent an envoy to Peking his country must not be prevented from sending one; that in the present negotiation of commercial regulations he asked only fairness in negotiation; but that should there be any delay he would still insist on proceeding to the North.

Your slave notes that in this communication the said barbarian envoy has agreed to abandon his northern trip but brings in the case of other countries as a vantage point for the future, and also brings in the treaty to threaten us immediately. He has a very cunning mind. But the best way to deal with barbarians is to block their presumption first and then proceed to destroy their schemes. Since the said barbarian envoy regarded the treaty as vital, its prompt conclusion was agreed to. It was only necessary to make adjustments to ensure the mainte- nance of fixed regulations of the Imperial Court and to accord with international convention, justly and without discrimination, thus achiev- ing perpetual amity between China and the outside world, without any compromise to lead us into his trap.

Accordingly, along with Huang En-t'ung and the other officers, (Your slave) has argued with him for several days. The sections dealing with trade have been made to conform to the regulations set up last year, in order to avoid discrepancies. Those not concerned with trade which are found in the Supplementary Treaty of last year were also allowed. In the case of new regulations not included, but not impracticable and not involving vital issues, there was no harm in granting his requests. But anything at great variance with the Supple- mentary Treaty or contrary to fixed law was flatly rejected. The said barbarian envoy, although not without repetitious argument, was over- come with reason and in most cases agreed. But there are still four or five articles not decided.

Besides, it is to be noted that the said barbarian envoy stated at the outset that he has autograph credentials from his president which he wanted to present in audience; he finally abandoned the trip north but refused to say definitely whether or not he will hand over his cre- dentials. The barbarian chiefs, Webster[9] and others, in conference with Huang En-t'ung, spoke of requesting His Majesty to delegate an official to come here to receive them, but Huang En-t'ung personally repudiated this. As the treaty was discussed day after day, the problem of dealing with the credentials was probed, but his (the envoy's) ambiguous ex- pressions were inscrutable and there was no assurance that after the treaty was concluded he would still not act irresponsibly. Then, if he were categorically refused he would bring up the fact that he had no way of presenting his credentials as a pretext for renewing his request

---

9 Daniel Fletcher Webster (1813-1862), usually called Fletcher Webster, was the son of Secretary of State Webster, who had arranged the Cushing mission. Fletcher Webster was secretary of the mission. Dennett, *op. cit.*. p. 113.

to go north. This must needs be anticipated.

   The said barbarian envoy has also attempted to insert an article
in the treaty now under negotiation providing that a ministerial board
in Peking [pointed in vermilion] should receive communications from
his country, following the precedent set by Russia and other countries.
If we probe for his motive, it may well be found in his desire to go to
Peking to present his credentials. Therefore Your slave flatly refused
this [Vermilion endorsement: Right], but the said barbarian envoy keep
making the request incessantly.

   On second thought, the interest of the American barbarians is
trade, and regulations must needs be suitably negotiated; but Chief
Cushing is a very crafty man and no amount of precaution is superfluous. If everything is cleared up with him he will not be able to ask to
go north on the pretext of presenting his credentials. So Your slave
has decided to forego technicalities [Vermilion endorsement: Right]
and conclude the treaty with him. Then, as was done with the convention concluded last year with the English barbarians, it will, on the one
hand be copied and memorialized, and on the other be sealed and respective copies retained in order to prevent the said barbarian from
undue suspicion. But unless there is positive assurance (that he will
not go north), even after the treaty is concluded it will not be sealed,
thus blocking his covetousness and exemplifying our power to harness
him.   (IWSM.TK 72; 5b, 7-7b, 2; cf. Kuo, op. cit., p. 301-303)

   88. July 22, 1844. EDICT: Urges Ch'i-ying to Expedite Conclusion of
Treaty upon Cushing's Final Relinquishment of His Credentials.
   Edict to the Grand Councillors. Ch'i-ying has memorialized the
circumstances of the American envoy's handing over his official papers
and abandoning his northern voyage and also of the negotiation of the
treaty. (We) have read the memorials and understand the situation.
The said barbarian envoy has abandoned the matter of the northern voy
age but he cites the various Western countries as an argument to seize
a point of vantage.

   The Heavenly Court, in conciliating and curbing outside barbarians
sees all with the same charity. Now that an Edict has been issued stopping the envoy of the said country, naturally there will be no reason for
granting other barbarians audience. The said barbarian's aim is trade
Since the treaty is urgent, policy must needs be considered and the
treaty quickly concluded. On points not in conflict with the new regulations, there is no objection to showing some preference; as to those
concerning the fixed law, there cannot be the least accommodation to
give rise to further complications. The said governor general must
fully consider the whole aspect and establish the regulations carefully
in the hope that for a long time there will be no ills. As the various

articles are concluded, take care that the said barbarian is not led to
raise unreasonable hopes. Let the governor general immediately, on
the one hand, report in a memorial, and on the other, seal copies in
duplicate in order to accord with barbarian ideas. Unless there is
positive assurance (that he will not go north) do not take any chances
lest you fall into his trap.

As to the said barbarian's request for a ministerial bureau to receive the official communications of his country, not only has there
never been such an institution but the capital actually has no one conversant with the written or spoken language of the said country. (We)
trust that the said barbarian is also well aware of this. The said
governor general has flatly refused this and he was quite right in doing
so. He should as before explain to him in detail, to open the springs
of his understanding and cut off his covetous thoughts. This is of the
utmost importance. (IWSM.TK 72; 8a, 7-8b, 8)

89. July 28, 1844. MEMORIAL: Ch'i-ying Reports his Acquisition of Cushing's Credentials and the Signing of the Treaty of Wang-hsia.

Imperial Commissioner, Governor General of Liang-kuang, Ch'i-
ying memorializes. It is noted that the American barbarian envoy,
Cushing, had, in a previous dispatch, promised to abandon his intended
trip to the North, but he urgently requested a speedy negotiation of the
treaty and insisted that a ministerial board be set up in Peking to receive messages from his country, following the precedent of Russia and
other countries. Yet, in regard to the delivery of his credentials he
was completely noncommittal. Considering the fact that the said barbarian envoy persisted in keeping his credentials hidden and urged the
appointment of a ministerial board, Your slave became convinced that
his intention was to insert the latter as an article in the treaty and thus
have a pretext in the future for presenting his credentials in Peking.
It was essential to anticipate this. Accordingly, an early opportunity
was seized to memorialize an opportunistic handling of the matter.

On the other hand, together with Huang En-t'ung and other officers,
(Your slave) has endeavored to enlighten his mind, explaining that the
institutes of the Celestial Court are immutable, that the ministers in
Peking are not conversant with the situation, and that should anything
urgently require presentation it would be better for him to hand over
his credentials and have (us) memorialize for him, which would certainly ensure the Emperor's consideration. Finally, after repeated
argument for several days, 'the barbarian envoy consented to insert in
the' treaty the provision that in the future credentials should be presented to the Emperor for them by the Imperial Commissioner in charge of
barbarian affairs, the governor general of Liang-kuang, Min-Che, or
Liang-chiang. He also yielded to our opinion in regard to every one of

those trade regulations upon which there had not yet been any agreement.

Your slave still considered this inadequate, for, although the said barbarian envoy had yielded to our requirements he still refused to hand over his credentials. Accordingly, with Huang En-t'ung and other officers, we again interrogated him closely and every opportunity was seized to break down his obstinacy. Finally, the said barbarian envoy came to trust us without any suspicion, whereupon he handed over his credentials and the other papers he carried.

In retrospect, as to his motive, it appears that the said barbarian envoy insisted on going to Peking not on account of the treaty but on account of his credentials. His initial letter gives the clue. Governor Ch'eng Yü-ts'ai has already had this copied and presented for Imperial scrutiny. His reasoning seems to be that the treaty could be negotiated outside but the credentials must be presented in person at Peking. Consequently, as long as his credentials were not handed over his barbarian mind could not rest. Even after the treaty was concluded there was still no assurance that he would not go north. Now that the credentials have been handed over to be memorialized for him, he has no more hope of proceeding to Peking, and no trace of doubt or suspicion remains. But as the barbarian temperament is rash and over suspicious it was feared that delay would involve changes, so Your slave ordered that copies be made of the completed treaty, sent to the barbarian envoy for translation into barbarian character, and mutually checked for errors. Then a date was fixed for meeting the barbarian envoy and the seals were affixed. The envoy was rewarded with a banquet to show our bounty and confidence, and was greatly pleased. He is presently residing at Macao, entirely peaceable, thus providing some solace to the Imperial breast.

A copy of the treaty has been submitted in a separate memorial. The credentials, being in barbarian character, are hardly decipherable off hand, so Your slave will duly order linguists to translate them into Chinese, carefully consider how they should be presented, and then request an Edict for guidance.

After meeting the said barbarian envoy and affixing the seals to the treaty, Your slave, accompanied by Financial Commissioner Huang En-t'ung and other officials, set out and on July 7th returned to the provincial capital (Canton). (IWSM.TK 72; 13b, 9-15b, 2; cf. Kuo, op. cit., p. 303-305)

90. July 28, 1844. MEMORIAL: Ch'i-ying Analyzes the Treaty of Wang hsia and Compares it with the British Supplementary Treaty.

Ch'i-ying further memorializes. It is observed that the treaty originally presented by the said barbarian envoy contained forty-seven

articles. Some impracticable things were arbitrarily demanded
while other absolutely essential things had been omitted altogether.
Besides, the meaning was vulgar and the phraseology obscure; the
defects were various and innumerable.

Your slave Ch'i-ying, assisted by Financial Commissioner Huang
En-t'ung and other officers, argued back and forth with the envoy day
after day to distinguish what items should be allowed, what rejected,
what should be deleted, what added. Finally, thirty-four articles were
agreed upon. Whatever was reasonable was painstakingly pointed out
in order to break up his ignorance; whatever affected statute law was
argued down in order to prevent vain expectations. Moreover, whenever expressions were obscure, they had to be changed to make them
succinct so that there would be absolutely no doubt (as to their meaning). Altogether, the draft was changed four times before negotiations
were finally concluded.

It is noted that, in the précis originally presented by the said
envoy, there were ten articles which were entirely inadmissible but
which were stubbornly demanded. For instance, when the barbarian
consuls at the ports have any business to transact, they should deal
with the governor general or governor, but the said barbarian envoy
had a clause providing that they be allowed to go directly to the Censorate with it. When foreign buildings are burned they should be repaired by the merchants themselves, but the said barbarian, dragging
in the precedent of indemnity by the hong merchants, had a clause providing for indemnity by the (Chinese) government. When foreign cargoes have broken bulk and duties have been paid thereon, it is no concern of our government whether their sales be good or bad, but the
said barbarian envoy asked for a clause providing that the duties be
refunded if the goods were not sold after three years. Once the hongs
have been abolished, barbarian merchants themselves should find
means to trade with Chinese merchants, but the said barbarian envoy
had a clause providing that the Chinese government build warehouses
and store goods for them. Merchant vessels are allowed to trade only
at the five ports and are not to go elsewhere, but the said barbarian
envoy had a clause providing that the Celestial Court allow all countries, enemy and friend alike, to trade anywhere. Merchant vessels
anchoring in a port should be controlled by the consul, but the said
barbarian envoy requested a clause providing that the Chinese government provide protection for all, and if a third country caused damage
China should make restitution. When foreign powers are at war China
has no way of restraining them, but the barbarian envoy had a clause
providing that, should merchant vessels be seized by hostile forces,
China would recover and attack them respectively. Foreign warships
should anchor outside ports, but the said barbarian envoy had a clause

providing that as soon as a man-of-war arrived in port it would exchange salutes with the forts in order to show respect. Official papers
of foreign countries should be presented to the governors general or
governors of the coastal provinces, who will make suitable disposition of them, but the said barbarian envoy requested a clause providing that either the Grand Secretariat or some other ministerial
board receive official papers of his country. Treaties are primarily
for reconciliation or the prevention of trouble, but the said barbarian
envoy had a clause providing that if China and a third country were at
war, the merchants of his country be allowed to withdraw and escape
harm.

All these provisions were either impracticable or highly defec-
tive. Besides, there were not a few which were minute, far-fetched,
rapacious, or crafty. Your slave Ch'i-ying, together with Huang En-
t'ung and other officers, corrected them one by one, without daring to
make any compromise. The items were argued over and over, at
most more than ten times, at least five or six times. Not until his
logic broke down and words failed him did the said barbarian envoy
consent to scrap them.

Of the various articles in the treaty now concluded, about eight-
tenths are in conformity with the Supplementary Treaty concluded
last year [with Great Britain]. The article providing that a merchant
vessel which has paid tonnage dues and then, because her cargo is not
all sold, goes to another port to sell it, need not pay tonnage dues
again; another providing that a merchant vessel which comes into port
and wishes to depart without breaking bulk, provided it leaves within
two days, is not subject to duty or tonnage dues; and still another providing that a merchant vessel, having entered port and paid all duties
and tonnage dues and wishing to transport its unsold cargo to another
port for sale, is exempted from paying duties a second time--these
are all at variance with the Supplementary Treaty of last year. But
now that five ports are open to trade, the situation is different from
that when trade was restricted to the one port of Canton. That these
barbarian merchants, finding the market at one port unsatisfactory,
should seek to transship to another port, follows the natural pro-
pensity of brokers, so it seems unnecessary to impose arbitrary re-
straints or to exact duties again after they have been duly paid. Rather,
we should allow a certain compensation to accommodate the sentiment
of the merchants, and at the same time maintain a rigid inspection in
order to prevent smuggling.

To continue, Your slave, Ch'i-ying, at first refused to approve
the clause providing for the renting of land, construction of churches
and cemeteries at the treaty ports, and the clause providing for the
employment of Chinese scholars to teach the local dialects and to

assist in literary work and also for the purchase of all kinds of
books. But the said barbarian envoy replied that both the Europėans
at Macao and the British at Hong Kong could build churches for worship and select land for cemeteries, thus enabling the living to pray
for blessings and the dead to find burial; that the number of his
countrymen coming to China to trade is not great, nor have they dared
to ask for any grant of territory, and if they were not allowed to rent
land for construction they would really be in a quandary; that, as to
their engaging Chinese teachers and buying all kinds of books, this
was a practice of long standing and the demand for incorporation in
the treaty was to prevent the police from using it as a pretext for
starting trouble.

On thinking this over, since the said barbarians are to rent land
and build their churches and cemeteries themselves, this hardly
called for arbitrary refusal, but there must be clear restrictions
against forced rentals and appropriation in defiance of popular wishes.
If the gentry and people are unwilling to rent, the said barbarians
should have no pretext. Since the various countries have been coming
to Canton to trade more than two hundred years, there have been a
considerable number of Chinese slightly versed in learning, such as
linguists and clerks, whose services have been utilized for communication back and forth. And also when Westerners record the events
of a locality Chinese characters are often used; the fact that Chinese
dictionaries and thesauri have even been translated into Western
languages is ample evidence that the purchase of books has been a
common occurrence and is long since impossible of prevention.
Therefore, there was no harm in granting his request.

Besides these, the articles concerned not with trade but with amity
offered no obstacle to customary Chinese policy. A clause providing
that (American) merchants who venture outside the five ports to
trade, engage in smuggling, deal in opium or other contraband, shall
be subject to trial and punishment by Chinese local officials, was
added to the original draft. The fact that the said barbarian envoy
consented to this is enough to show that he is willing to observe the
laws of the Celestial Court and will not act without restraint. The
articles suggested by him that the consuls at the five ports submit at
the end of each year to the respective governors general for transmission to and inspection by the Board of Revenue, detailed reports of
the number of vessels and the amount and value of goods, is also
evidence of the willingness of the said barbarian to trade peacefully
and not allow any smuggling.

Finally, the said barbarian envoy accepted completely the tariff
schedule of last year; he did say that lead is produced in his country
and that a duty of four mace per hundred catties (picul), three times

that on iron, seemed excessive and asked for a reduction. Since lead
is not a main item of trade and since (Cushing's) request is also
quite reasonable, Your slave Ch'i-ying lowered it one mace, two
candareens per picul, making it two mace, eight candareens. The
barbarian envoy obediently agreed. (IWSM.TK 72; 15b, 3-18b, 5;
cf. Kuo, op. cit., p. 306-310)

91. July 28, 1844. MEMORIAL: Ch'i-ying Reports the Expected
Arrival of Lagrené and Compares France and the United States.

Ch'i-ying further memorializes. Your slave has thoroughly investigated the circumstances of the various barbarian countries. As the
interest of the United States was in trade, we could take advantage of
this importunity to control and restrain her. Although there were
several hitches, in the end they were gradually maneuvered into our
scheme. But France fundamentally does not regard trade as important. Her merchant ships coming to Kwangtung are not more than one
or two a year. Her situation is very different from that of the
American barbarians. The difficulty of handling them, compared to
the American barbarians, is at least twice as great.

According to what Your slave has heard, the said country (France
and England are neighbors, only separated by a sea. The English
barbarians were formerly under their control. Later when they
became strong and large they rebelled and set up a state themselves.
They were repeatedly at war. Although they ceased fighting and
concluded peace, neither has accepted inferiority to the other. The
United States was also a dependency of the English barbarians.
Because they were oppressed by the English barbarians, one of their
countrymen, Washington, led the people in a war of resistance. The
French barbarians sent troops to help them, whereupon the English
barbarians made peace and the American barbarians were enabled
to set up a nation. Therefore the French barbarians have a grievance
against the English barbarians but have greatly benefitted the
American barbarians. Thus, last year the English barbarians'
defiance of authority had absolutely no connection with the French
barbarians. . . . At this time the American barbarians had already
made a request to send an envoy to proceed to the capital, but the
French barbarians had not heard of this. It transpires that Ratti-
Menton even said that his country would not send an envoy to come to
Kwangtung. Unexpectedly in the spring of this year, when Ratti-Menton
and Jancigny went home one after the other, they sent word that a
French barbarian envoy would arrive shortly. At the time of Your
slave's interview with Cushing, he also stated that a French barbarian

envoy named Lagrené[10] would reach Kwangtung not more than a month
later. For several days (Your slave) had the expectant tao-t'ai
P'an Shih-ch'eng privately sound out the French barbarians residing
at Macao. He reported that Lagrené, in command of seven warships
and one steamer, had anchored in the Philippines, was buying up food
supplies, and whether he would come to Kwangtung for a temporary
sojourn or go directly to Tientsin was as yet uncertain. Although
this is not entirely trustworthy, it is not necessarily groundless.

It is noted that the French barbarians have never had any rupture
with China and also no great amount of trade. If they have an envoy
coming it must be, as before, on the pretext of making an alliance
with China to attack the English barbarians; they hope to see the
glories of our superior country, and expect Imperial Favor. Probably,
on hearing that the American barbarians have been denied an audience,
they will not make a second (attempt) to go North, but this is not
certain. If Lagrené comes to China, no matter to what port he sails,
means must be devised carefully to conciliate and curb him, then
further complications will be avoided. Your slave will wait for a
thorough inquiry into the situation and then memorialize fully as
occasions arise. (IWSM.TK 72; 18b, 6-20b, 2)

92. July 28, 1844. EDICT: Commends Ch'i-ying for Skillful Handling
of Cushing and Urges Him to Keep Lagrené from Proceeding to Peking.
       Edict to the Grand Councillors. Ch'i-ying has memorialized on
the American envoy's handing over his credentials, the abandonment
of the northern voyage, and the conclusion of the treaty. This has
been very well executed. The said barbarian envoy requested to come
North, with the idea of presenting his credentials in person. The said
governor general has thoroughly discovered the barbarian's nature
and repeatedly enlightened (him). Finally he got the said barbarian
envoy to hand over his credentials with the request that they be
memorialized for him and not to persist in the hope of going to Peking.
The text of the proposed treaty has also been determined article by
article and seals affixed in duplicate in order to dispel suspicion and
ensure fidelity. What has been done is entirely in accord with policy.
Let the credentials which were delivered, after having been translated,
be presented for (Our) inspection when convenient.

       There is a separate supplementary memorial dealing with a confi-
dential report that a French barbarian envoy, Lagrené, has seven warships and one steamer anchored in the Philippines. Whether he will

---

10 M. Th. de Lagrené, minister plenipotentiary and envoy extraordinary, charged with
    a special mission from the King of France, arrived at Macao August 14, 1844.
    Chinese Repository, v. 13, p. 447.

come to Kwangtung for a temporary sojourn or go directly to Tientsin, is still uncertain. The barbarians are by nature treacherous.
Naturally you should take special precautions. But as there are still
no indications, you cannot make a great stir beforehand and then
develop further complications. Kwangtung is an important route of
communication. The said foreign ships, no matter to what port they
are going, must pass through Kwangtung waters. Let the said governor
general secretly order his subordinates to reconnoitre with added
care and, if they see any traces of ships coming from the said country,
immediately send a flying report, find out their motive in coming, and
act according to circumstances. If there is actually evidence of their
going North, report immediately in a memorial and also send flying
word to the various coastal provinces to complete the defences.
Conciliate and curb them with care. Maintain your tranquility but
take pains not to lose sight of the objective of preparedness. This is
of the utmost importance. (IWSM.TK 72; 20b, 3-21a, 5)

93. August 15, 1844. MEMORIAL: Mu-chang-a and the Other Grand
Councillors Present Their Critique of the Treaty of Wang-hsia.
        Grand Councillor and Grand Secretary Mu-chang-a and others
memorialize. On July 28, the memorial of Ch'i-ying and others
regarding the conclusion of a commercial treaty with the United States
of America received the Vermilion endorsement: "The Grand Council
lors together with the Boards will quickly deliberate and memorialize
fully. Respect this."
        Your ministers find that trade in the five ports was originally
permitted to the various countries uniformly. Now the United States
of America has sent an envoy to Kwangtung insistently requesting a
clearly established treaty in order to cement friendly relations. The
said governor general instructed the provincial commissioners to
approve or reject items with discrimination and they agreed upon
thirty-four articles, made copies and affixed seals in duplicate in
order to show conciliation.
        Your ministers have repeatedly examined (them). The primary
objective was to defer to barbarian views and not to obstruct trade in
general. As to the fifteen articles concerned with customs, the Board
of Revenue finds various matters of trade agreed upon by the said
governor general, such as "all duties paid shall accord with present
practice," "outside the five ports there can be no promiscuous
cruising," "all kinds of goods are permitted to be transported and
sold," "baggage and the like shall not pay tonnage dues," "underlings
sent to take custody (of ships) cannot be extortionate," "imports and
exports shall be honestly examined," "measures and scales are to be

distributed by the Customs," "when duties and dues are paid in full, clearance papers are to be issued," "merchant ships at anchor are not to be illegally taxed," "the dissolution of the co-hong will facilitate intercourse and if the merchants incur losses, the government shall not reimburse them" -- altogether eleven articles. They find that there is no particular discrepancy with the new regulations drawn up last year and these should be executed as proposed.

As to the clause that "unsold goods transhipped to another port need not pay duties a second time," and the clause that "(a ship) entering port without breaking bulk and then wishing to go elsewhere, provided it leaves port within two days, shall not pay duties"; and the clause that "merchant ships entering port and paying full duties and taking goods which have been unloaded to another port shall be exempt from repayment," although somewhat different from the new regulations, (these items) have been discreetly adjusted after the said governor general and others carefully examined the situation.

As to the request that "after specific clearance papers have been sent to notify the various customs houses, (ships) cannot remain in port more than two days," and also "if on examination of the original package and original goods, there are no cases of tampering or changing contents, it will be permitted to enter them on the ship's register and turn them over to the said merchant," -- all in all, the various customs houses must examine assiduously and not allow the carrying of misrepresented goods and resultant smuggling, so that there will be no injury to customs or commerce.

As to the clause that "at the end of each year, clear reports of ships and the values of goods are to be made by the consuls of the five ports to the governors general of the respective provinces, and then transmitted to the Board of Finance," the object is to verify the amount of the customs; the said governors general should be ordered to make a special report at the end of each year to the Board in order to authenticate the examination.

In the nine clauses dealing with crimes and litigation, the Board of Punishments finds various articles decided by the said governor general and others, such as: "it is strictly prohibited for customs house runners and underlings delegated to take custody of ships to extort gratuities; violators will be dealt with according to the bribe"; "if there are cases involving (native) persons and barbarians, each is to be apprehended and tried by his own officials"; "if there are important Chinese-barbarian matters in dispute and they are found to be reasonable, then the officials are allowed to take them over for examination and disposal; if there is disagreement over an affair, it shall be mutually discussed and decided"; "if any of the said barbarians break the law and abscond to the interior to hide, they shall be

apprehended and delivered over to the said consular officers for
punishment; on the other hand if law breakers from the interior abscond to the establishments of the said barbarians or conceal themselves in merchant ships, the local officials shall notify the said
consular officials to apprehend and return them": "if there are brawl
involving mutual resort to force or careless use of firearms to wound
people, or serious cases leading to battery and killing, the local
officials and the said consular officers shall both take rigorous
action to maintain the law. There cannot be the least partiality";
"any of the said barbarians who go unauthorized to other ports not
opened to trade and engage in illicit trade or smuggling, or carry
opium or other kinds of prohibited goods to China, shall be subject
to trial and punishment by the Chinese local officials." In the above
six articles the object is either to prohibit the extortions of rapacious
underlings, to prevent controversies between (native) persons and
barbarians, or rigorously to guard against smuggling and illegal
carrying of prohibited goods, and they should all be put into effect as
memorialized.

As to the clauses, "officials are to investigate the plundering of
the said barbarians' ships and punish accordingly," and "it is strictly
forbidden for the people to violate barbarian graves or burn foreign
buildings," we find that as long as the said barbarians are content to
trade the local officials should naturally on occasion afford protection
It should be specified that hereafter if barbarian ships are plundered
in territory under Chinese control, (the owners will) be allowed to
submit requests to local officials to seize the plunder and the robbers,
and prosecute according to law. However, if plunder and robbers are
not entirely captured, there can be no indemnity for the stolen goods.

As to burial grounds within the area leased by the said barbarians
at the ports providing they are not forcibly leased or occupied or
illegally handled, if the Chinese residents precipitately violate the
graves or if incendiaries set fire to foreign buildings and seize
property, the local officials shall rigorously apprehend and punish
according to law.

Besides the above articles there are such provisions as: the
establishment of consuls, hiring of pilots, keeping of barbarians in
order and not allowing them to idle about and cause trouble; the
recognition of flags, which are not allowed to be borrowed or fraudulently used; if there is dispute with another country, they will be
allowed as usual to settle it themselves and seizures will be clearly
prohibited in order to avoid occasions for confusion; those encountering
storms or rocks are to be treated with special consideration; those who
come to get water or to buy food shall not be denied consideration;
presentation of credentials is to be by memorial on their behalf; for

transmission of letters there should be fixed forms for faithful communication and these cannot be lightly altered. Your ministers find these provisions are not in conflict at all with the port regulations previously established and they should be carried out entirely as proposed.

But the article regarding the engaging of scholars to teach and the purchase of all kinds of books is essentially contrary to law. Besides, being very indefinite, it will lead to many evils. The said governor general and others, because the said barbarian asked many times, followed the precedent of supplying linguists and clerks and allowed the barbarians to engage teachers. Also the fact that the West has dictionaries, thesauri and various books is evidence that they have already been buying books. Since we are temporarily obliged to acquiesce in order to conciliate the barbarian temper, naturally it is improper to make unconsidered and confusing changes and then cause the said barbarians to complain. Your ministers think that the key to control of the outside is the opportuneness of holding in or giving leash; the method of governing internally is thoroughness of observation. Now after the conclusion of the treaty, we should order the persons engaged by the said country to report their names, ages, families and places of residence to the said local officials to keep on record, before they are allowed to go to the said barbarian establishments. As to books purchased, each book shop should keep a separate list. Titles of books, number of copies, and price, after being sold, should be entered on the record at the time, and at the end of the year turned over in summary to the said local officials and presented to the governor general for examination, so that by examining the entries we can thoroughly discover miscreants and search out those from afar.

As to the persons engaged (as teachers), those who wish to go need not be prevented; but if any make excuses for not going, (the foreigners) cannot require the local officials on their behalf to induce them to go. As to buying up books, those who wish to sell may supply them. If they raise their prices extortionately, (the foreigners) cannot involve the local officials, to buy them by force. This is in conformity with the treaty and can be reported to those in authority.

Further, as to the clause authorizing the establishment of churches and cemeteries in the ports, it is noted that merchants in business are unlike registered residents. Although permitted to trade at the five ports, their comings and goings are uncertain. Compared to Macao and Hong Kong (the situation) is also entirely different. As to what is said of the living seeking blessings and the dead finding burial, it is feared that when they have bought and built much they will seize more land. The said governor general and others, because the said barbarians voluntarily proposed renting, found it improper to refuse absolutely.

Besides, it has been made clear in the treaty that "land sites are to
be jointly examined by the Chinese local officials, who are allowed to
settle rentals fairly. No forced renting or arbitrary encroachment
is to be allowed." The drawing up of a treaty is comparatively
strict and naturally there can be a compromise arrangement in
execution. Your ministers humbly consider that in the building of
churches barbarian practice is well established, but the matter is
untraditional. Notions readily raise doubts. Stupid people delight
in the new and dislike the old and it will be hard to prevent imitation.
This should be discussed by the said governor general with the
various governors to devise means of mitigating it. They cannot
propagate or practice among the people. Take pains to cause the
residents of the seacoast to understand that barbarian languages are
not to be imitated and barbarian rites are not to be practiced. These
points seem to be not without bearing on customs and morals.

The matter of burials has now been agreed to. On their part is
ignorance of the virtue of native burial; on our part there is accord
with the practice of the burial of bodies. From the point of view of
Imperial bounty it is certainly not objectionable. But once the sites
have been determined, the boundaries should be clearly defined and
ever after adhered to. After the various sites have been established
there cannot be further encroachment on the plea of being ¯cramped
for space. In this we should certainly, in conformity with the treaty,
make rigid prohibitions in advance.

Furthermore, the said governor general and others state in a
separate memorial that "foreign lead is a product of their country.
The tax of four mace per picul was undoubtedly rather high and they
asked that it be somewhat reduced, the tax on each picul to be
lowered by one mace, two candareens, fixing it at two mace, eight
candareens." The Board of Finance finds that the tariff fixed last
year has been agreed to in toto by the said barbarians. As foreign
lead is not a large item the matter of reducing the duty should still
be carried out as agreed upon, and also the various trading ports
should be ordered to act carefully in complete accord with the agreement.

EDICT: (Let it be done) as recommended. (IWSM.TK 72; 21a,
6-25a, 7)

94. September 17, 1844. MEMORIAL: Ch'i-ying Reports Requests of
Cushing and Davis for Permission to Visit the Treaty Ports.

Ch'i-ying further memorializes. To continue, the American
barbarian envoy Cushing previously asked to go to Amoy and the
other trading ports to investigate trade conditions. Express letters
have been sent notifying the governors general, governors, and

commandants of the seaboard, and a clear supplementary report has
been placed on record. Later, according to the personal report of the
expectant tao-t'ai P'an Shih-ch'eng, he has ascertained that Cushing
on account of matters within his country wishes to return home
immediately. Whether the trip to the five ports will be abandoned is
still difficult to predict.

Just as we were ordering the said tao-t'ai to make further
inquiry, a communication from the English barbarian chief, Davis,[11]
stated that he proposed on August 27 to go to the four ports of
Foochow, Amoy, Ningpo, and Shanghai to determine whether or not
the consuls there were upholding existing treaties; he expected to be
able to finish the trip within forty days and then return to Hong Kong.

Your official finds that England, the United States, and France do
not accept inferiority one to the other. They are constantly imitating
each other in order to extol themselves. Thus as soon as the English
barbarians had negotiated a treaty, the American barbarians sent
Cushing here. As soon as the American barbarians made a request
for an audience, the English barbarians immediately declared that if
His Imperial Majesty at any other time extended new favors to other
states they should also be granted to the said barbarians without
discrimination, and insisted that it be included in the Supplementary
Treaty. Even France, while her trade is actually not large, also
recently had a cruiser proceed to Ningpo, Shanghai, and other places
to interview officials. Although nominally this was to inspect the
ports, actually the purpose was to outdo the English barbarians. Now
that the American barbarian Cushing has asked to go to the four ports,
the English barbarian Davis also requests likewise; the purpose to
outshine is readily seen.

Your slave personally feels that as Foochow and the other places
have been authorized to trade we can hardly prevent their going.
Besides, since the various countries take the character of their treatment by the Heavenly Court as a measure of national prestige, a
possible means of restraint and control is found right here. [Vermilion
endorsement: Hardly practicable!] Naturally (we) should treat them
equally and not give rise to occasions for disappointment, encourage
admiration and gratitude among them, and further strengthen their
sincerity in turning toward civilization.

Besides sending express communications to the various governors
general, governors, and commandants of Fukien, Chekiang, and Kiangsu
to transmit word to the circuit and prefectural officials on the seaboard

---

11 Sir John Francis Davis succeeded Sir Henry Pottinger as British minister and superintendent of trade.

that upon the English barbarian chief, Davis, coming into port, they must exert themselves to show composure and to restrain him carefully, (Your slave) only awaits the confidential report of the expectant tao-t'ai P'an Shih-ch'eng, as to whether or not Cushing is returning to his country and what the present trouble in his country is, whereupon he will again memorialize fully. (IWSM.TK 72; 33b, 4-34b, 6)

95. September 17, 1844. MEMORIAL: Ch'i-ying, Announcing the Arrival of the Lagrené Mission, Notes the Imminent Departure of Cushing from Macao.

[Memorial of Ch'i-ying on the arrival of the French mission at Macao.] . . . Furthermore, there is received a communication from the American barbarian envoy Cushing, that the said envoy had set August 26 to begin his journey homeward.[12] The matter of his previous intention to go to the four trading ports and inspect trade has been abandoned. (IWSM.TK 72; 37b, 1-3)

96. September 17, 1844. EDICT: Admonishes Ch'i-ying to Certify Cushing's Departure and to Hold the United States and Britain to the Treaties.

(Edict to the Grand Councillors regarding the various topics on which Ch'i-ying had memorialized.) . . . Immediately take pains to learn discreetly and clearly whether or not Cushing has returned to his country and what the trouble within his country is, and memorialize according to the facts. As to the outside barbarians striving to outdo one another, this is the usual condition. Now in handling barbarian affairs, granting them a treaty allowing them to trade in the various provinces has been an extraordinary favor. The said barbarians should only respectfully abide by the regulations, enjoy in common the blessings of tranquillity, and not wantonly hope for advantages outside the various provisions agreed upon. The nation, in soothing and curbing outside barbarians, regards all with the same charity and never shows the least partiality for one or another to give rise to disputes. If the said barbarians continue to make requests, the said governor general and others should take pains earnestly to explain and sternly to reject them. Let there not be any vestige of ambiguity to give rise to further complications. (IWSM.TK 72; 38a, 3-9)

---

12 Caleb Cushing left Macao August 27th on the U.S. brig *Perry* direct for San Blas, to proceed through Mexico on his way to Washington. *Chinese Repository*, v. 13, p. 448.

97. October 29, 1844. MEMORIAL: Ch'i-ying Reports Cushing's
Departure and Parker's Plan to Visit the Ports, and Forwards Cushing's
Credentials.

    Ch'i-ying further memorializes. It is noted that the American
barbarian envoy Cushing previously wrote saying that on August 26th
he would start for home. This has been stated in a separate memorial
and is on record. But the said barbarian envoy first said that he was
going to the four ports to investigate trade conditions and then said
that he was going home. Whether or not there was an ulterior motive,
when Your slave went to Macao he made a detailed private inquiry.
The said barbarian envoy Cushing has actually gone home. When he
left he sent the barbarian leader, (Dr. Peter) Parker, to inspect the
four trading ports in his place. The said barbarian leader, Parker,
having encountered a storm en route and being unable to proceed, has
also returned to Canton and is now residing in the foreign buildings
of the Thirteen Factories, with no other purpose.

    The carefully copied American credentials, translated into
Chinese, are respectfully presented for Imperial inspection [p. 47a,
5-47b, 2; text of President Tyler's letter to the Emperor, p. 47b,
4-49b, 1. In the official translation of President Tyler's letter, the
word ku (孤 literal meaning, "orphan") is used to denote the first
person, i.e., Tyler. In feudal usage, ku is the word employed by the
head of an inferior state, vassal to a higher imperial overlord. The
use of this character clearly indicates the still prevalent attitude and
the belief in China's traditional position as the apex of a world hierarchy, which was not destroyed by the Opium War defeats or by the
treaties.] (IWSM.TK 72; 47a, 5-49b, 2)

98. November 23, 1844. MEMORIAL: Ch'i-ying Analyzes American and
European Customs and Comments on China's Diplomacy and Foreign Policy.

    Ch'i-ying further memorializes. To continue, Your slave has
written up from time to time and presented in memorials the circumstances of handling the affairs with the various barbarian countries,
as well as the reception of barbarian envoys and the control of them
according to circumstances. The various supplementary matters of
trade have also been discussed fully and the articles memorialized
for Imperial examination and commission to the Boards for investigation. These are on record.

    Now, to recapitulate, after the conciliation of the English bar-
barians in the seventh month (August 6-September 5) of 1842,[13] the

---

13 The reference is to the signing of the Treaty of Nanking, August 29, 1842.

American and French barbarians in the summer and autumn of the
present year followed on their heels. Within this period of three
years, the barbarian situation has changed in many respects. This
is not manifested uniformly. The method used to tranquillize and
control them must also be changed. Certainly it lies in rectifying
them through sincerity and still more essentially in controlling them
by artifice. Some can be made to follow and cannot be made to understand. Sometimes by showing that there is no suspicion refractoriness
can be dispelled. Sometimes by considerate treatment a sense of
gratitude can be aroused. Sometimes by trusting a people broad-
mindedly and not being too critical of them a situation can be saved.
As the barbarians were born and bred in the outer wilderness there
is much in the institutes of the Heavenly Côurt that they do not fully
understand, but as they always pretend to understand things, it is
hard to explain them reasonably. For instance, the Emperor's transmitted words are all passed on by the Grand Councillors, but the
barbarians respect them as Vermilion endorsements. If shown not
to be Imperial writings at all, then there would be no means of maintaining their trust. This then is something that should not be made
clear.

When the barbarians eat together it is called a banquet. They
always gather a large number together for a lavish feast and eat and
drink together for pleasure. At Hu-men (Bocca Tigris) and Macao
on several occasions Your slave gave dinners for the barbarians and
anywhere from ten-odd to twenty or thirty of their chiefs and leaders
came. When he, on infrequent occasions, met them in a barbarian
house or on a barbarian ship they also formed a circle and sat in
attendance and outdid themselves to present food and drink. He could
not but eat and drink with them in order to bind their hearts.

Besides, barbarian custom extols women. Whenever there are
honored guests they are sure to present the women. For instance,
the American barbarian Parker and the French barbarian Lagrené
both brought barbarian women with them. When Your slave went to
the barbarian houses to discuss matters, these barbarian women would
suddenly appear to pay their respects. Your slave was composed and
respectful but uncomfortable, while they were greatly honored. This
is actually the custom of the various Western countries and cannot be
determined by Chinese standards of propriety. If we condemn them
hastily there will be no means of dispelling their stupid ignorance,
and at the same time we would arouse their doubts. Furthermore,
all the barbarians came in complete amity and we cannot but treat
them with some cordiality.

When intercourse becomes more intimate there must be more
precautions. Thus in negotiating the treaties with the various countries

when it came time to conclude them, (Your slave) always ordered
the provincial commissioner Huang En-t'ung to make clear to the
said barbarian envoys that a Chinese statesman in charge of our
relations with other countries never crosses the barrier or has
personal intercourse. If presents are sent he can only firmly refuse
them. If they are accepted ambiguously, the laws of the Heavenly
Dynasty are very strict. Not only is it contrary to the constitution,
but it is also very difficult to evade the statutory regulations. The
said envoys respected the instruction and obeyed. But when we met,
if there were any small gifts, such as foreign wines or perfumes, the
value of them was very slight, and as the intent was rather sincere
it was improper to make a practice of rejecting them to their faces.
Your slave gave them in return only personal accessories such as
snuff bottles and pouches, to give the idea of returning more than
was received. Furthermore, the four countries, Italy, England, the
United States, and France asked for his picture. These were made
and presented to all.[14]

Although the various countries have rulers, their sex is not
uniform and their tenure is not the same--far removed from (our)
regulations. For instance, the English barbarians have a female
sovereign, the American and French barbarians have male sovereigns.
The English and French sovereigns are both hereditary, but the
American barbarians' sovereign is popularly set up by the people for
a four-year term, and after leaving office his rank is the same as
that of a commoner. Nor are designations uniform. In general they
plagiarize Chinese terms with a wanton display of boasting and
ignorant presumption. This veneration for their own sovereigns is
no concern of ours.

As to applying (to them) the forms of border dependencies, since
they do not accept our calendar and do not receive Imperial inves-
titure, they would by no means be willing to lower themselves to the
status of Annam or Liu-ch'iu. These people outside the pale are in
utter darkness in regard to designations and forms. If we use our
documentary forms to determine authoritatively their rank, even if
we wore out our tongues and parched our lips we could not avoid the
smiling response of a deaf man. Not only would there be no compre-
hension but also friction would immediately appear. Certainly there
would be no great advantage to the essential business of tranquillizing.
Rather than quarrel with them over empty words with no real result,
it is better to disregard a small matter to effect a large program.

---

14 The Cushing portrait of Ch'i-yung is now in the Boston Museum of Fine Arts.

The above observations are all based on thorough examination of the barbarian situation. A sure determination of the point which lies between triviality and gravity, delay and urgency, must provide a plan adapted to needs and permeating changes. Whether the situation be essentially trivial or immediately pressing, Your slave did not venture to make separate statements monotonously to importune the Imperial ear. Now that barbarian affairs have been generally concluded, it behooves him to state them clearly in a supplementary memorial.

Vermilion endorsement: This is the only way to do it. We have read it and understand the situation. (IWSM.TK 73; 18a, 8-20b, 2)

99. December 14, 1844. MEMORIAL: Ch'i-ying Makes Recommendations as to the Form and Content of the Emperor's Reply to the President's Letter.

Ch'i-ying further memorializes. Your slave begs to observe that previously he had the credentials of the American envoy Cushing rendered into Chinese and copied for presentation, and also asked that an Imperial Mandate be conferred to show control. This has been written in a confidential statement. On November 14, 1844 he received a confidential letter from the Grand Councillors that on October 29 they had received an Imperial Edict:

We have received Ch'i-ying's memorial confidentially stating according to the facts his thorough investigation of border conditions, and also a supplementary memorial stating that the American barbarian Cushing now presents his 'credentials and personally asks that, after they are presented for Imperial inspection, We graciously issue an Imperial letter for him to keep forever.

The said country is separated from ours by many oceans. In the hope of Imperial favor it sent an envoy to present his credentials. As his bearing and language are respectful and obedient, we should naturally favor him with praise to match his sincerity in according with our customs and admiring our principles. The said governor general asks that an Imperial Mandate be conferred on him to show control. This is not necessarily impossible. But to the said peoples living outside, our language is unintelligible. How should an Imperial Mandate issued by Us be expressed, in order to show the constitution of the Court?

Let the said governor general present a maturely considered proposal. After we have examined it, We shall affix the Imperial seal and turn it over to the said governor general to transmit for their respectful reception. Moreover, tell them to take pains to observe forever the treaties now concluded, to be content to trade, and to appreciate His Imperial Majesty's purpose of kind treatment. They must not undergo the hardship of a long journey or request an audience. Besides these (favors already conferred), there can be no further requests.

What is the purpose of the cake of vermilion contained in the bronze box in which

the credentials were forwarded? Let (the governor general) make a clear inquiry
and then memorialize according to the facts. Respect this.

Your slave begs to note that the location of the United States is
in the Far West. Of all the countries, it is the most uncivilized and
remote. Now they hope for the Imperial favor of a special Imperial
Mandate which can be kept forever. We have both commended the
sincerity of their love of justice and strengthened their determination
to turn toward culture. The different races of the world are all
grateful for Imperial bounty. It is only that the said country is in an
isolated place outside the pale, solitary and ignorant. Not only in the
forms of edicts and laws are they entirely unversed, but if the meaning
be rather deep they would probably not even be able to comprehend.
It would seem that we must follow a rather simple style. Our choice
of words and use of expressions should in general show that the
constitution of the Heavenly Court is to be respected.

Your slave has deliberated wholeheartedly and personally
considers that in the present Imperial Mandate, the style employed
should be simple and direct, the meaning used should be clear and
obvious. There is no use in adhering to forms, but it is absolutely
necessary to maintain the constitution. This will be appropriate.

It is noted that the executive of the said country is called Po-li-
ssu-t'ien-te; translated into Chinese this means president. Besides
this he has no other designation. It would seem proper therefore to
use this term to address him. When (the Mandate) is promulgated,
it would seem proper to write it in Manchu. This would be more
discreet. Besides, the people of the said country have occasionally
been to Russia to trade and place the greatest value on Manchu
letters. This will further move them to accept it respectfully. Your
slave respectfully proposes separate Manchu and Chinese drafts and
presents them for Imperial inspection. Your slave realizes that his
literary style is essentially commonplace and his translation (into
Chinese) even more rough and deficient, but as this is a proposal
confidentially presented he did not dare entrust it to others. As it
is entirely made up of everyday phrases which he has selected and
translated himself, he really fears that it is not without errors and
omissions, and his embarrassment is extreme. Still he begs that
it be authenticated to the Grand Councillors for examination and
correction, and thereafter (he) requests an Edict to enforce it.

As to the formal Manchu calligraphy, Your slave has not written
in it for a long time. Consequently the material now presented is in
the cursive style. He humbly asks that the Imperial Mandate issued
to the said country also not employ the formal Manchu characters but

be written in the cursive style. This is also suitable.

Moreover, previously when Your slave personally arranged the treaty with the barbarian envoy Cushing, it was definitely agreed that hereafter he must not request an audience nor could there be further demands. It would seem that there should be no further retraction.

As to the cake of vermilion contained in the bronze box of the said barbarian's credentials, it is a wax model of the seal of his country's sovereign, attached to the letter in order to show sincerity and respect, and has no other use. (Your slave) hereby makes this clear. (IWSM.TK 73; 28a, 8-30a, 7) (Chinese text of Imperial Mandate issued to Cushing which was drafted by Ch'i-ying and approved by the Emperor, p. 30a, 8-30b, 8.)

Chapter 4

First Years under the Treaties, 1845-1854
(Documents 100-124)

This group of twenty-five documents covers the period from
January 25, 1845 to April 19, 1854. Dr. Peter Parker, American
medical missionary, served much of this time as chargé d'affaires ad
interim, in the absence of any American commissioner resident in
China. Commodore James Biddle, U.S.N., commanding the East India
Squadron, exchanged the ratified treaties negotiated by Caleb Cushing;
Alexander H. Everett served briefly in China as American Commissioner;
John W. Davis and Humphrey Marshall each represented the United States
in China for brief terms.

The Chinese documents consist of eighteen memorials and seven
edicts, all but one of the latter being addressed to the grand councillors.
As these documents are scattered over several years and cover many
subjects, the number of memorialists is fairly large. Ch'i-ying, who
served as imperial commissioner at Canton until 1848, is responsible for
six memorials. The Manchu governor general of Liang-chiang, I-liang,
has two memorials, and the notorious "Viceroy Yeh," otherwise Governor
General of Liang-kuang Yeh Ming-ch'en, also has three. The remainder
of the memorialists have one each: Liu Yün-k'o, now governor general
of Fukien and Chekiang; Liang Pao-ch'ang, governor of Chekiang; Hsü
Kuang-chin, governor of Kwangtung and Ch'i-ying's successor in 1848;
Imperial Commissioner Hsiang Jung; the Manchu Yu-feng, provisional
governor general of Min-Che; and Hsü Nai-chao, governor of Kiangsu
province, spokesman for Shanghai Tao-t'ai Wu Chien-chang.

The subject matter of this group is diverse. Several events of minor
importance are covered. The exchange of the ratified treaties negotiated
at Wang-hsia, the formal reception of Chargé Parker and Commissioners
Everett and Davis at Canton, and the activities of American traders at the
ports are all reported by memorial. This period marks an important shift
both in Chinese policy and in American interest. Ch'i-ying was recalled
in 1848 and was replaced in Canton first by Hsü Kuang-chin and then by
Yeh Ming-ch'en. Both were non-cooperative and were backed up by a
strong anti-foreign war-party in Peking. This new attitude at Canton, combined with the increasing trade and the existence of a group of friendly
officials at Shanghai, brought about a new interest in the latter port. The
court and Imperial Commissioner Yeh continued to insist that all foreign
affairs be conducted at Canton, but by the end of this period it had already
ceased to be the situs of the real foreign minister of China. Characteristic
of this shifting emphasis was the reception of American Commissioner
Humphrey Marshall at K'un-shan, forty miles west of Shanghai. Minor

items memorialized in this period were the hiring of barbarian ships to be used against the Taipings, a resumé of American history, probably drawn from Cushing's memorandum and translated by Peter Parker, and the coolie traffic.

The American documents for this period are summarized by Tyler Dennett in his Americans in Eastern Asia, chapters IX, X, and XI, p. 175 to 224. In the published documents, John W. Davis' correspondence on consular courts appears in U.S. Cong. 31:1, S. Ex. Doc. 72; the correspondence of Humphrey Marshall is in U.S. Cong. 33:1, H. Ex. Doc. 123. Biddle's mission is treated briefly by Paullin, Diplomatic Negotiations of American Naval Officers, 1778-1883, p. 211-214; his unpublished correspondence occurs in the "East India Squadron Letters, 1845-1847" in the National Archives. The private papers dealing with Everett's China mission (unpublished) are in the Massachusetts Historical Society collection, Boston, Massachusetts, under the title "A.H. Everett Papers, Private, 1841-1857," in 16 cases, one of which deals with the China mission.

TRANSLATIONS OF DOCUMENTS

100. January 25, 1845. MEMORIAL: Liu Yün-k'o Reports the Inauguration of American Trade at Foochow.

Governor General of Min-Che Liu Yün-k'o memorializes. The English barbarian consul G.T. Lay,[1] during the fifth month of the present year (June 16-July 15, 1844) came to the port of Foochow to make arrangements for the opening of trade. Your official and others ordered Financial Commissioner Hsü Chi-yü to instruct the local officials in the Nan-t'ai district outside the city to inspect residences on their behalf to provide the said barbarians a place to live. The said barbarians, because the people and region of Foochow were strange to them and the commercial regulations had not been determined, asked to discuss these things when convenient. Your officials respectfully reported this in memorials and it is on record.

From the arrival of the said barbarian at Nan-t'ai onward, already half a year, the situation has been extremely quiet. But the said country has not had a single merchant ship enter port; therefore the commercial regulations have never been settled. In the eighth month (September 12-October 12), one American merchant vessel sailed into the harbor and anchored for over a month. Among the people, no one came forward to engage in trade. After the American traders had delayed a long time they wished to go to another port, but their supplies were completely exhausted and they could not set out. They proposed

---

1 George Tradescant Lay was the first British consul at Foochow.

to sell the cargo of black pepper, rattans, long-ells, foreign cottons, and other goods at reduced prices in order to cover their disbursements. Your officials found that although the commercial regulations of Foochow were still unsettled, the various duties could all be levied in accord with the current law. Since the American merchants wanted to sell their goods cheaply in order to make up costs of transportation, naturally we should allow them to dispose of them and make the barbarian temper complacent. The said barbarian merchants were then able to sell the black pepper and other goods at Nan-t'ai for several thousand foreign dollars. In the tenth month (November 10-December 10) they set sail and left port.[2]

G.T. Lay also sold one bale of long ells, one bale of cotton, and four bolts of cotton cloth, which was sent by English merchants, and like the American merchants paid all the duties and dues according to law. Outside of this there has been no merchant ship of any country enter port nor has there been any illicit trading among the people.

As to trading conditions at Amoy, they are the same as before, excepting that Consul Gribble[3] has resigned and returned to Kwangtung. Davis dispatched Alcock[4] there to take charge. On November 4 he reached Amoy and had an interview with the Hsing-Ch'uan-Yung taotai, Heng-ch'ang and others. This man also is intelligent, respectful, and obedient; enough to gratify the Imperial bosom.

Vermilion endorsement: Noted. (IWSM.TK 73; 39a, 10-40a, 10)

101. February 16, 1845. MEMORIAL: Ch'i-ying Reports the Receipt of the Emperor's Reply to the President and its Presentation to Peter Parker at Canton.

Ch'i-ying further memorializes. On December 30, 1844, an Imperial Mandate arrived by courier. After receiving it, Your slave immediately found that the American envoy Cushing had returned to his country and what matters of intercourse there were, were all to be handled for him by the barbarian leader Parker.[5] He accordingly ordered the expectant tao-t'ai P'an Shih-ch'eng to prepare a hall outside the city and notify Parker to come there on January 14, 1845. He immediately delegated Financial Commissioner Huang En-t'ung respectfully to receive the Imperial Mandate and personally hand it to

---

2 This may be the only record of the first American ship to trade at Foochow. Griffin, *Clippers and Consuls,* p. 295, cites as the first record of an American ship to that port, the journal of the American ship *Thomas Perkins,* New York, which was in port a year later, September 5-October 13, 1845.

3 Henry Gribble was the British officiating consul in 1844.

4 Rutherford B. Alcock became the first regular British consul at Amoy; Harry S. Parkes was his interpreter.

5 Dr. Peter Parker, medical missionary at Canton, was American chargé d'affaires ad interim.

the said barbarian leader, who should receive it reverently.

According to the statement of the said barbarian leader, "this country is maritime, uncultivated, and primitive; it has always known respect and admiration for the Heavenly Dynasty; now that it has received an Imperial Mandate conferred by the Great Emperor to be kept forever, its gratitude is excessive, its glory doubled; and he would respectfully treasure it until there is a ship to carry it respectfully back to his country, to be handed to the president, who would receive it reverently."

Vermilion endorsement: Noted. (IWSM.TK 74; 2b, 5-3a, 5)

102. July 8, 1845. MEMORIAL: Ch'i-ying Presents a Resumé of the History of the United States.

[Memorial of Ch'i-ying and Huang En-t'ung in answer to the report that had come to the Emperor that the United States was founded only sixty years before.] . . . As to the previous memorial of the Governor of Fukien, Liu Hung-ao, stating that the United States was only set up as a nation sixty years (ago), Your officials find that America was originally a large continent in the extreme West, its night and day the reverse of China's, a vast country with a sparse population. Before the Ming dynasty (1388-1644), no one knew the country. During the Hung-chih period (1488-1506) an Italian named Amerigo first came to this land, established residences, and gradually formed communities. Thus the name of the country became A-mi-li-ko also called A-mei-li-chia, and also Mi-li-chien, all approximate renderings of the barbarian sound and consequently not without ambiguity. Again in the T'ai-ch'ang period (1620-1621), several hundred Englishmen moved and settled there, and later called the country New England. In the Wan-li period (1573-1620) the Dutch seized the southern portion and called it New Holland. Again in the Shun-chih period (1644-1662) of our dynasty, the French seized the northern portion and called it New France. Later, England expelled the people of the two countries and took the country as her dependency. The population gradually increased and the cultivated area daily expanded. There were altogether twenty-six settlements. In the Ch'ien-lung period (1736-1796) England wanted to increase its customs duties. When the people did not obey, England taxed them more severely and besides harassed them with troops. The natives were angry and together set up Washington as military leader, united various settlements to form one nation, called it the United Provinces Country and did not submit to English control. England opposed them, and both held out seven or eight years without surrendering. Then France sent troops to help them and England could not hold out. So in the 49th year of Ch'ien-lung (1784) she made peace with them and allowed them to set up an independent country. These are the general circumstances of the establishment of the United States.

The northern boundary of the country is near England and Russia;[6] its southern boundary Mexico; its eastern boundary the Atlantic Ocean; and its western boundary the Pacific Ocean. The people generally emphasize agriculture and delight in labor. The principal product is cotton. They also monopolize the profits on salt and iron. Their production of cotton and woolen goods is rather large. Furthermore, they set the greatest value on trade. Hence, of merchant ships coming to Canton, seven-tenths are English and three-tenths are American. With France she is on the friendliest terms; with England she is outwardly friendly but actually resentful. Although she established her country not more than a few decades ago, her territory is broad, her people diligent and her products abundant. Hence of all the barbarian (countries) of the West which along with England and France are regarded as great powers, only the United States is noteworthy, while Holland and Spain, although established previously, on the contrary do not come up to the recent status of the said country. (IWSM.TK 74; 17b, 2-18b, 5)

103. January 17, 1846. MEMORIAL: Ch'i-ying Comments on the Diplomatic Importance to China of France and the United States.

[Memorial of Ch'i-ying on the policy of toleration of Catholicism brought up after the negotiation of the treaty with France.] . . Of the various commercial countries of the West, only France, the United States, and England are large. The French barbarians have long been at war with the English barbarians. The American barbarians also have an old feud with the English barbarians, but with China they have no quarrel at all. Compared to the repeated disturbances of the English barbarians, this is very different. If we wish to cause the English barbarians to have some respect and awe, we must first not lose the confidence of the French and American barbarians. But the said (French) barbarians' devotion to Catholicism is not unlike the belief of the Mongols in Lamaism. Now if an Imperial Edict is issued to converts, not only will the French barbarians be drawn in by it but even the American barbarians will be won over, and when the English barbarians hear of it it may even check somewhat their proud and domineering spirit. It would seem that in subsequent management of barbarian affairs, this would not be without a little benefit.

Vermilion endorsement: Conditions have changed to such an extent that if we cling rigidly to one view it will be still harder to accomplish things. We can only somewhat follow temporary expediency. (IWSM.TK 74; 44b, 1-8)

---

6 *I.e.*, Canada and Alaska.

104. January 17, 1846. MEMORIAL: Ch'i-ying Announces the Arrival
of Commodore James Biddle, U.S.N., and Date for Exchange of
Ratifications.
      Ch'i-ying and others further memorialize. Your slave has now
received a letter from the barbarian chief of the United States,
Biddle,[7] stating that "the said chief's ship has arrived at Hu-men
(Bocca Tigris), Kwangtung province, and immediately respectfully
inquires as to His Imperial Majesty's health. The treaty agreed upon
last year and the commercial regulations have now received his
sovereign's sanction and he has brought them to exchange with a high
commissioner specially delegated by His Imperial Majesty and hopes
that a date will be fixed immediately for a reply."
      His attitude and language were very respectful and obedient.
Now, on account of the two matters of Chu-shan and entrance to the
city (Canton), which Your slave was just devising means of handling,
it was hard to get away. But the said barbarians, while outwardly
friendly to the English barbarians, are inwardly resentful. At this
juncture in the scheming of the English barbarians, we could only
exchange ratifications with him immediately in order to bind his heart
to us. We prepared a written reply acknowledging his favor and fixing
January 7, at the office of the naval commander-in-chief of Hu-men
for exchanging ratifications, at which time, taking along the deputies
Chao Ch'ang-ling and P'an Shih-ch'eng we will go there.
      Vermilion endorsement: Noted. (IWSM.TK 74; 47a, 5-47b, 5)

105. February 18, 1846. MEMORIAL: Ch'i-ying Reports the Exchange
of Ratifications with Commodore Biddle at Puntong, Near Canton.
      Assistant Grand Secretary, Governor General of Liang-kuang,
Ch'i-ying, memorializes. Previously, (by arrangement) with the
barbarian chief of the United States, Biddle, January 7, at Hu-men
was set for the exchange of ratifications. Later, word was received
from the said chief that "he had come to Canton and was living at the
Thirteen Factories outside the city wall, waiting to exchange ratifications, and it was unnecessary to go to Hu-men." As the said chief
had come to Canton and was waiting, naturally Your official should
make the exchange with him at an early date in order to show our good
faith. Accordingly, together with Governor Huang En-t'ung and taking
along Acting Grain Intendant Chao Ch'ang-ling and Expectant Tao-t'ai
P'an Shih-ch'eng, he met the said chief and exchanged ratifications[8]

7 Commodore James Biddle, U.S.N., aboard the U.S.S. *Columbus*, to whom Alexander H.
   Everett, the regularly appointed American Commissioner, had delegated his powers,
   carried out the exchange of ratifications.
8 The meeting and exchange of ratifications took place at "Pwantang, Puntong, a
   country seat of Pwan Sz'shing," *i.e.*, P'an Shih-ch'eng. *Chinese Repository*, v. 14,
   p. 590-591.

on December 31, at a guild hall outside the city wall. Moreover, he prepared a dinner as an additional courtesy.

According to his (Biddle's) statement, his country was extremely grateful for Heavenly favor and would maintain the treaty forever without any other proposals whatever. His manner and language were very respectful and obedient.

Vermilion endorsement: Noted. (IWSM.TK 75; 1a, 2-1b, 1)

106. August 25, 1846. MEMORIAL: Liang Pao-ch'ang Reports the Visit of Commodore Biddle to Ningpo to Investigate Trade Conditions.

Liang Pao-ch'ang further memorializes. According to the report of Hsien-ling and others, "on the night of July 27, he discovered that a barbarian ship of Denmark, that is the Flowery-flag country which has formerly traded, sailed into Ting-hai and anchored. Thereupon the English barbarian Gutzlaff[9] conducted Captain T'u-shih[10] of the said barbarian ship ashore for an interview with the said tao-t'ai and others. Their manner was very respectful. They stated that they wished to go to Shanghai to trade. At Whampoa, Kwangtung, they had requested the Imperial Commissioner to notify the Shanghai tao-t'ai. As the Imperial Commissioner had gone outside the city to inspect troops, they returned to Hong Kong. Hearing that Chief Davis had come to Ting-hai to hand over Chu-shan, they hoped that Chief Davis would in turn ask the said tao-t'ai for a letter to carry to the Shanghai tao-t'ai to enable him to seek quarters for them.

The said tao-t'ai and others replied to them in accord with the treaty. Hsien-ling wrote out a letter, affixed the official seal, and gave it over to their keeping. Then on the 29th they left for northern waters.

Furthermore, according to the communication from Imperial Commissioner Ch'i-ying, "Chief Biddle of the United States would en route investigate trade conditions at the five ports and everyone should treat him courteously." After having sent orders to the Ningpo tao-t'ai and prefect to act accordingly, the report of the said tao-t'ai and prefect was received:

Chief Biddle on board a small gunboat arrived June 30th at Chen-hai, transferred to a native fishing craft, and came up to Ningpo. At that time the said circuit

---

9 Rev. Charles Gutzlaff (1803-1851), Protestant missionary in China, frequently served as Chinese secretary to various British offices, although he was a native of Prussia. *Chinese Repository*, v. 20, p. 511.

10 These are transliterated Chinese characters; the foreign name has not been positively identified. It may, however, be a reference to the Danish man-of-war *Galathea*, Captain Stern Anderson Bille, which came to China in 1846 on a scientific and exploratory commercial mission. The *Galathea* left Hong Kong in July, 1846, bound for Shanghai and intermediate ports. *Chinese Repository*, v. 15, p. 461-464.

officials Hsien-ling and Lin-kuei had both gone to Ting-hai, so the acting prefect of Ningpo, Yang Chu-yüan, had an interview with him. His manner was very
respectful. The said prefect prepared a dinner for his entertainment and the said
chief was extremely pleased. Then on July 1, he set out, as before leaving port
by way of Chen-hai, went on board his original gunboat, and departed for
southern waters.

It is noted that Denmark and the United States are both in the class
legally permitted to trade at the five ports. The said barbarian chief
T'u-shih and others, whether they sought a letter to go to Shanghai to
trade or went to the five ports to investigate trade conditions, were
both in conformity with the regulations previously agreed upon. The
said tao-t'ai and prefect in treating them kindly also acted advisedly.
Vermilion endorsement: Noted. (IWSM.TK 76; 13a, 8-14a, 8)

107. December 5, 1846. MEMORIAL: Ch'i-ying Reports Meeting with
United States Commissioner Alexander H. Everett near Canton.
Assistant Grand Secretary, Governor General of Liang-kuang,
Ch'i-ying, and Governor of Kwangtung Huang En-t'ung memorialize.
Your officials have received a communication from the American
barbarian chief Everett,[11] stating that his country had ordered him
to Kwangtung in the capacity of commissioner in charge of the commercial affairs of his country; that, moreover, he bore credentials to be
forwarded for the inspection of His Imperial Majesty; that now he had
arrived at Canton and asked to set a time and place for an interview.
A reply was immediately prepared setting October 27, at a business
office outside the city wall, for the interview. We also ordered
deputies to transmit instructions to him to bring his credentials to the
business office in order to facilitate their handling.[12]
At the appointed time, Your officials took along their subordinates
Chao Ch'ang-ling, P'an Shih-ch'eng, T'ung-lin, and Ning Li-t'i, and
went outside of the city for a personal interview with the said chief,
Everett. At first they used friendly language and disarming questions
to determine whether or not he had brought along the credentials. The
said chief produced a document translated into Chinese. On glancing
over it, its terminology and content appeared to be extremely respectful and obedient. Questioned as to the whereabouts of the original
letter, he (Everett) stated that "his sovereign had ordered him to
secure an audience and personally present it to His Imperial Majesty
and that it was improper at this time to produce it."
Obviously this was a repetition of the former chief, Cushing's, old

11 Alexander H. Everett of Massachusetts was United States Commissioner to China
from March 13, 1845 to June 28, 1847, although he did not arrive in China until
October 29, 1846. Dennett, op. cit., p. 189.
12 The account of the meeting which appeared in the China Mail is reprinted in the
Chinese Repository, v. 15, p. 624. Although the account does not say so
specifically, the meeting was apparently at P'an Shih-ch'eng's country villa.

trick of making inordinate requests.

Your officials find that formerly in concluding the treaty with the American barbarians--because it was feared that in the future, using the presentation of credentials as an excuse, they would attempt to go north--it was clearly stated in the treaty that thereafter if the United States had any credentials to forward to the Chinese Court, the original letters should be sent up in a memorial on their behalf by China's Imperial Commissioner in charge of foreign affairs, or the governor general of Liang-kuang. Now, since the said chief had credentials, naturally they should be handed over and memorialized for him. This would evince fidelity. It would be improper for him to present them himself and violate the original treaty. They again ordered Chao Ch'ang-ling to look up the treaty and let him examine it. Moreover, they explained to him in detail.

The said chief hung his head and had nothing to say. He agreed that after returning to his quarters he would deliver up the credentials with the request that they be memorialized for him. Then wine and food were prepared for his entertainment and we also proclaimed His Imperial Majesty's Gracious Bounty, ordering that "for the perpetual amity of the two countries and the mutual benefit of both peoples, all matters should be in conformity with the treaty, that merchants should be restrained and there could not be the least violation and that the said chief well knew how to appreciate this." According to his statement, "hereafter in all matters he would respectfully follow directions."

Then he returned to his quarters in the Thirteen Factories and delivered up the original letter which he had brought. The deputy, P'an Shih-ch'eng, was ordered to turn it over to someone who knew barbarian characters for corroboration, and it was found to be in agreement with the text translated into Chinese.

Your officials discover that the said chief is not particularly deceitful. In the future, if we manage properly it would seem possible to avoid causing adverse complications to develop.

As to the king of the said country's conforming to custom and admiring principle, specially preparing credentials, and dispatching the said chief to bring and present them, his motive was not at all ulterior. We have forwarded the original papers and the Chinese translation to the Grand Council for examination. In addition, whatever interviews Your officials have had with the said chief and the reasons for their actions have in conformity with right been respectfully memorialized for the Emperor's information.

Vermilion endorsement: What has been done is good and has been noted. The papers will be kept here. (IWSM.TK 77; 5a, 3-6b, 3)

108. February 3, 1848. EDICT: Orders Ch'i-ying to Give up his Post at Canton and Report to Peking for an Audience.

Edict to the Grand Secretariat. Ch'i-ying, from his appointment
to the post of governor general of Liang-kuang and assistant grand
secretary onward, has been expending his energies year after year
tranquilizing the borders, and has never come to Peking to report.
Let him set out in the warm spring days of the new year and proceed
to the capital for an audience in order to relieve (Our) anxiety. Let
the duties of governor general of Liang-kuang and the seal of Imperial
Commissioner both be taken over temporarily by Hsü Kuang-chin, and
for the governor of Kwangtung let Yeh Ming-ch'en act; for treasurer
of Kwangtung let Hsü Kuang-chin appoint an official to act. (IWSM.TK
78; 36a, 2-5)

109. February 3, 1848. EDICT: Appoints Hsü Kuang-chin Imperial
Commissioner and Governor General at Canton to Succeed Ch'i-ying.
Edict to the Grand Councillors. On this day it has been decreed
that Ch'i-ying come to Peking for an audience. The duties of governor
general of Liang-kuang and the seal of Imperial Commissioner are
both turned over to Hsü Kuang-chin to administer provisionally. We
had appointed Hsü Kuang-chin governor of Kwangtung and he has been
at the post for more than a year. Regarding local conditions and all
barbarian affairs, he naturally should be thoroughly accustomed to
adapting himself to circumstances and acting circumspectly. But in
provincial posts the emphasis is on keeping the people content. If
popular favor is not lost, then outside taunts can be obviated. Hereafter, when there are incidents involving relations between the populace and barbarians, he should not show favoritism or compromise at
the loss of popular favor. As to accommodating and consulting, it is
for the said provisional governor general to exert himself at the time
and to deliberate and investigate thoroughly, in the ultimate hope of
using sincerity to bind popular sentiment and constraint to manage
barbarian affairs. Thus he will not betray his commission.

Huang En-t'ung has held the post of governor of Kwangtung. On
various occasions of pacifying the barbarians, his management has
always been adaptable. We specially conferred on him the sixth rank
and turned him over to Ch'i-ying for allocation. The said official has
personally received great favor in being quickly selected for appointme
How grateful he should be for favors conferred and how energetic from
beginning to end. Now (We) have decreed that the said official be agai
turned over to Hsü Kuang-chin for appointment. If the said provisional
governor general takes advantage of his advice on matters, he can
secure useful assistance.

Hsü Kuang-chin, on receipt of this Edict, will immediately notify
Ch'i-ying and also transmit it to Huang En-t'ung for perusal. Hereafter, if Huang En-t'ung exerts himself energetically and shows perfec
sincerity, the said provisional governor general will naturally be able
to surmise his remorse and, relying on the facts, recommend him in a

memorial and await Our granting of favor. If he does not know how to
be diligent and relies on words to shirk responsibility, others cannot
help but be aware of it. In that event, let him be memorialized for
impeachment. (We) shall have to see whether or not Huang En-t'ung
is capable of meeting this serious punishment. Tremble! (IWSM.TK
78; 36a, 6-36b, 9)

110. November 18, 1848. MEMORIAL: Hsü Kuang-chin Reports Meeting
with United States Commissioner John W. Davis at Jen-chin Godown.

Governor General of Liang-kuang Hsü Kuang-chin and Governor
of Kwangtung Yeh Ming-ch'en memorialize. On August 24 a note was
received from the newly arrived American chief Davis,[13] proposing a
time for an interview. (Your officials) answered setting September 21
at Jen-chin godown, White Goose Tything, on the Canton River for an
interview. On that day, on account of being obstructed by storms on
the ocean, he did not arrive. On the 22nd he reached Canton and asked
for an interview on the 23rd. (They) thereupon expressed disapproval
saying that "a date having been fixed for a personal interview, agreed
to by both in an official letter, how was it he had not come and only today finally put forth 'obstruction by storm' as an excuse; that this was
actually an intentional breaking of his promise; and that just now public
business was pressing and we had no leisure for a meeting," to break
somewhat his proud and domineering spirit.

The said chief again prepared a letter confessing his fault and
reiterating that "as the weather on the ocean was unpredictable he was
really prevented by Heaven and there was no intentional breaking of
his promise at all."

He made repeated requests. (Your officials) consider that the way
to handle foreigners is none other than constraint. Now that he had
confessed his fault and repented, it would not be worthwhile to argue
with him. Therefore, October 8th was set, again at the original place,
for an interview.[14]

On this day Your officials took along Grain Intendant with Associate Duties as Provisional Salt Controller Po-kuei, Canton Prefect
I-t'ang, Deputy Prefect of Chiu-chou T'ung-lin, and Brigade Adjutant,
Colonel K'un-shou, and proceeded there. The said chief brought along
more than ten barbarian leaders. According to his statement, "the

---

13 John E. Davis of Indiana, United States Commissioner to China, January 3, 1848 to
     May 25, 1850, arrived in China August, 1848. Dennett, *op. cit.*, p. 190.
14 The meeting took place "at one of the warehouses of Howqua in White Goose Tything
     in the western suburbs of the city." The report comments on the "contrast between
     the hauteur and ignorance" of Hsü Kuang-chin and Yeh Ming-ch'en in contrast to the
     "inquisitiveness and affability" of their predecessors, Ch'i-ying and Huang En-
     t'ung. *Chinese Repository*, v. 17, p. 543-544.

barbarians at great risk crossed many oceans to trade and depended entirely on the favor extended and protection afforded by His Imperial Majesty." Your officials informed him of the Heavenly Dynasty's tranquillizing purpose, and said that "Chinese and outsiders are one family but that it was essential that among the various groups of merchants there not be the least partiality. Naturally if all could get on peacefully together trade would gradually become extremely prosperous." The said chiefs heard this and were unanimously grateful. They were rewarded with a banquet. The tenor of their speech was rather tractable and mild.

It is humbly noted that the United States is generally known to be respectful and obedient. Davis, personally, has been quiet. Since he made no demands on this occasion, it would seem that hereafter he will not go to the extent of causing unfortunate complications.

Vermilion endorsement: Noted. (IWSM.TK 79; 26b, 2-27a, 10)

111. March 11, 1849. MEMORIAL: Hsü Kuang-chin Reports Visit to U.S. Corvette Plymouth, Commodore Geisinger Commanding at Whampoa.

Hsü Kuang-chin further memorializes. To continue: previously, just as Your official was setting out for Hu-men, he received a note from the American barbarian chief Davis, saying that "now there was a warship anchored at Whampoa and could I come on board; that this might be considered as a return of the banquet proffered last fall and that I could also inspect their military set-up." The idea seemed to be that just because I was going to Hu-men for an interview with the English chief, he (Davis), unwilling to be inferior to him, also wished to invite me to his ship in emulation. It is noted that the said barbarians are generally regarded as respectful and obedient. Moreover, what he requested was no more than a display for appearance sake. Naturally his request should be granted in order to show control.

As my route conveniently passed through Whampoa, (Your official taking along Grain Intendant Po-kuei and others, went on board his warship.[15] The said chief fired a salute and displayed his troops to receive us, and prepared a banquet. He was urgently persuasive and extremely pleasant. No requests were brought up at all. (Your officials) prepared gifts of oxen and tea and distributed them to the barbarian soldiers in order to show their intention of tranquillizing. (IWSM.TK 79; 39a, 4-39b, 2)

112. March 15, 1851. MEMORIAL: Comment on Americans in China by the Shanghai Tao-t'ai.

[Memorial of the tao-t'ai of Su-Sung-T'ai (Shanghai), Lin-k'uei,

---

15 An account of Hsü's visit to the U.S. Corvette Plymouth, on February 14, 1849, is given in the Chinese Repository, v. 18, p. 110-112.

dealing with Chinese policy toward the British, especially with regard
to utilizing trade and opium as levers of control, and toward France,
with regard to Catholicism and cases involving missionaries and converts. (p. 7a, 7-11a, 1.)]

    . . . As to the United States, they do no more than follow in
England's wake and utilize her strength. As feelings are not really
cordial between them, they suspect and dislike each other. They (the
Americans) are not in the least worthy of our concern. . . (IWSM.HF
4; 9b, 9-10a, 1.)

113. May 28, 1853. MEMORIAL: General Hsiang Jung Reports on the
Possibility of Hiring Foreign Warships for Use against the Taiping Rebels.

    Imperial Commissioner Hsiang Jung and others memorialize. An
English barbarian steamer has arrived at Shanghai. Now is received
the report of the Su-Sung-T'ai tao-t'ai, Wu Chien-chang, 'that "Provisional Governor General Yang Wen-ting delegated the degraded
official, Cheng K'uei-shih and Lieutenant Colonel Chang P'an-lung to
deliver a note ordering him to consult with the various barbarian
chiefs on the matter of hiring warships and that the said tao-t'ai,
accompanied by Cheng K'uei-shih, went to the various barbarian establishments for personal interviews."

    According to the statement of the English barbarian consul Alcock,
his country's warships in sailing up to Nanking had no other purpose
than finding out the true situation of the rebels; they did not go up the
river to render assistance nor had they gone forth to make an alliance
(with the Taipings).

    The French consul also said that the commissioner had not yet
come and he could not assume responsibility.

    The American commissioner said that the warships from his
country which had come to take part in the war had gone to the mouth
of the river, struck shallows and returned. Now they had gone to fight
in Japan and could not be hired to fight rebels. As to the English ship
going to Nanking, all say that they do not understand its motive.

    The said tao-t'ai, considering that the various countries had no
ships that could be hired, turned the provisional governor general's
note over to Cheng K'uei-shih to return (to him).

    Furthermore, it is reported that none of the English barbarian
steamers scheduled to go to attack Burma has yet weighed anchor to
start.

    Your officials find that barbarians are by nature deceitful and
certainly must be rigorously guarded against. Now that our war junks
are gradually approaching full strength, they are adequate for war purposes; and as there are no outside barbarian ships for hire, the matter
must be dropped in order to preclude their using it as a pretext for
causing trouble.

    Vermilion endorsement: Seen. (IWSM.HF 6; 12a, 9-13a, 2)

114. June 16, 1853. MEMORIAL: I-liang Forwards Credentials and a Letter from United States Commissioner Humphrey Marshall from Shanghai.

Governor General of Liang-chiang I-liang memorializes. A report received from the tao-t'ai of Su-Sung-T'ai, Kiangsu, Wu Chien-chang, states that "on the first of the third month (April 8-May 8) of this year, the American commissioner Marshall[16] had personally handed to him a letter addressed to the Grand Secretaries, to be sent to the former provisional governor general of Liang-chiang, who would affix his seal and forward it." As the rebels were just then causing trouble, the said tao-t'ai urged delay.

The said commissioner and consul said that, inasmuch as they had a sealed letter of their sovereign to present, they first went to Kwangtung, only to find that the Imperial Commissioner was leading troops outside the city. Now they came to Shanghai just when the provincial capital, Nanking, was besieged. Their credentials had been transmitted long ago and there could be no further delay. Therefore, they addressed a letter to the prime minister and must find a way to forward it; they requested a memorial asking His Imperial Majesty to issue an Edict ordering it done. If it were not presented for them, then they would go to Tientsin and present it themselves.

On examining the nature of their contention, under the circumstance it cannot be controverted. It appears that Article 31 of the General Regulations for Trade includes this clause: "If the United States, that is, America, hereafter has credentials to be presented to the Court, they shall be sent up in a memorial for them in the original by China's Imperial Commissioner in charge of foreign affairs or the governor general of Liang-kuang or of Min-Che."

Now the said commissioner was not unreasonable in directing his letter to the Grand Secretaries. It was only that at that time some petty officers and minor officials were sending the barbarian-type ships, which had been hired, to the Yangtze; so the letter was turned over to these officers for transmittal. The former provisional governor general has now resigned, and it was improper to go out of the way to recall him and get the letter back. So the said tao-t'ai informed the said consul of the situation. Now a communication has arrived stating that "the new incumbent of the governor generalship is reported to be in Kiangsu," so he has taken the trouble to report fully and ask him to comply.

After receiving and examining this, Your slave instructed the said tao-t'ai to tell the said chief to repair immediately to Kwangtung as usual and deal with the Imperial Commissioner originally charged with

16 Humphrey Marshall of Kentucky was United States Commissioner to China from August 4, 1852 to January 27, 1854.

the trading affairs of the various countries, to determine after consultation and inquiry whether or not the letter ought to be sent for him. Moreover, he ordered the said tao-t'ai to make suitable explanations.

This having been done, on May 4th a report was received from the said tao-t'ai saying that "following his instructions, in a friendly discussion with the consul of the said country, Griswold,[17] he gave him (my) view (but he) did not agree. He (Griswold) insisted on having it transmitted for him at Kiangsu." Moreover, he said that "in the letter there was nothing objectionable whatever and if we examined the draft copy we could understand it completely. The said chief originally intended to ask to have the letter presented in Kwangtung. As at the time the Imperial Commissioner had not returned from an expedition outside the city, he had proceeded to Kiangsu to request that it be forwarded."

Therefore, we considered that if we again firmly refused to forward it, it would be hard to guarantee that he would not go directly to Tientsin. In the face of the violence of the rebels and the stringent measures of the various provinces, if the said barbarians were allowed to go to Tientsin it would inevitably arouse the suspicions of the people living along the coast. If, after all, we took the original letter and forwarded it to Peking for him, in what language are the contents of the letter expressed? In the final analysis, whether or not there is anything objectionable or impracticable, we cannot trust them implicitly. Therefore Your slave immediately sent the said chief's sealed letter to the Imperial Commissioner and governor general of Liang-kuang in charge of the commercial affairs of the various coun-countries, Yeh Ming-ch'en, to enable him at first hand to find out the actual nature of the contents of the said barbarian letter and thereby determine whether or not it should be transmitted for him.

Now a fair copy of the said tao-t'ai's draft of the original letter which he received from the said chief is respectfully presented for Imperial inspection. (IWSM.HF 6; 13b, 5-15a, 6)

115. June 16, 1853. EDICT: Orders I-liang to Have Marshall Instructed to Deal only with Yeh Ming-ch'en at Canton.

Edict to the Grand Councillors. I-liang memorializes that "he received a report of the Su-Sung-T'ai tao-t'ai, Wu Chien-chang, that in the present year the American commissioner Marshall handed to him personally a letter to transmit to the governor general of Liang-chiang for forwarding. The said governor general has now sent the original letter to the governor general of Liang-kuang and presented (to the Throne) a separate draft copy."

---

17 J. Alsop Griswold was United States consul at Shanghai from May 19, 1848 to December 30, 1851.

(We) have read the memorial and understand the situation. Communications to be presented by the said barbarians are ordinarily to be discussed and reported in a memorial by the Imperial Commissioner and governor general of Liang-kuang. On this day an Edict has been issued ordering Yeh Ming-ch'en immediately to open and read the said barbarian envoy's letter which I-liang has sent, to weigh the conditions, and memorialize clearly his actions.

The (barbarians of the) said country ordinarily maintain good faith. Let the said governor general, as before, order the said tao-t'ai, Wu Chien-chang, to tell them clearly to continue to observe the old rules and wait until the Imperial Commissioner and governor general of Liang-kuang can investigate and act. (IWSM.HF 6; 15a, 7-15b, 3)

116. June 16, 1853. EDICT: Orders Yeh Ming-ch'en at Canton to Receive Marshall's Letter and Act Discriminately.

Supplementary Edict. I-liang has memorialized that the American commissioner Marshall has handed over a letter to the Grand Secretaries asking him to forward it. Now the original letter has been sent to Kwangtung and a separate draft copy has been presented (to the Throne). Previously barbarian affairs have reverted to the Imperial Commissioner and governor general of Liang-kuang for deliberation and action. I-liang has sent the original sealed letter of the said chief to Yeh Ming-ch'en to investigate and handle. After the said high official receives it, let him immediately investigate barbarian conditions first hand, (determine) what their object is in sending the letter, how their request should be answered, and memorialize fully according to the facts. Above all, adhering firmly to the established treaty, prevent the development of further complications. This will be satisfactory. (IWSM.HF 6; 15b, 5-10)

117. July 20, 1853. MEMORIAL: I-liang Reports Meeting with United States Commissioner Humphrey Marshall at K'un-shan.

Governor General of Liang-chiang I-liang memorializes. Your slave stopped over at K'un-shan-hsien of Su-chou prefecture and the tao-t'ai of Su-Sung-T'ai, Wu Chien-chang, came for an interview. According to his statement:

> The United States usually is not much trouble nor is the said barbarian chief tyrannical or proud; fundamentally there was no objection to (my) having a personal interview with him at Shanghai; but it was feared that as other countries would imitate and come one after the other to request the honor of an interview with the new governor general, and as it would be hard to avoid the development of further complications, it would be better to have the said barbarian come here for an interview and have it over with.

In addition, Your slave received a note from the said chief
asking to set a place and a day in order to facilitate a personal interview, and (he) immediately replied. This done, he also ordered the
said tao-t'ai to prepare a public hall inside the city of K'un-shan for
a personal interview. The credentials presented and the separate
text translated into Chinese were both securely sealed. (Your slave)
received them personally and after remaining about an hour, (Marshall) withdrew. His language and manners were all quite respectful
and courteous. The said tao-t'ai also took the translated Chinese
draft and examined it in detail, and there were no parts contrary to
the treaty.

After the said chief had left the hall, Your slave, with the said
tao-t'ai, immediately took the sealed text in Chinese translation;
first breaking it open, they compared it character by character (with
the copy submitted separately), and they consistently agreed. (Your
slave) humbly thinks that the credentials presented by the said chief
are in essential agreement with regulations previously memorialized.
As to the said country's changing its commissioner to reside in China
and wishing to bring his name to the Emperor's attention and seeking
amity and trade as usual, these are matters of no consequence whatever. But in the letter there is one phrase, "ordered to have an
audience at court," which was neither in the request previously
memorialized nor contained in the treaty. It would seem hard to
carry out for a long time.

It is noted that the outside dependencies conquered by our dynasty
all have annual presentations, and that the liege officials of the
various countries paying tribute, after arriving at the capital, must
first practice the ritual of bowing and kneeling. Thereafter they are
ordered to be presented according to rank; none has been allowed to
have an (individual) audience. Now the United States has never been
subjected to our sovereignty but still they claim equal rank (with the
tributary states) and ignorantly puff themselves up. They are not
worthy of comparison. How can we treat them like the various
dependent states and cause the development of other difficulties? (On
the other hand), it is certainly impolitic to treat them with unusual
courtesy and cause the gradual budding of covetous desires. So we
merely urged them carefully to maintain the treaty and trade as of
old; for mutual amity it was not necessary for them to make the long
journey to the North.

But Your slave avoided proclaiming these details in advance in
order to show that matters in our Court all derive from the personal
decision of the Emperor and that ministers cannot have arbitrary or
private opinions. Therefore, when the barbarian letter was received,
(Your slave) only answered that it would immediately be memorialized for him, and ordered him as before to return to Shanghai and
quietly await news. The credentials in barbarian character delivered

by the said chief, and the text translated into Chinese, are hereby respectfully presented for Imperial inspection. (IWSM.HF 6; 24b, 6-26a, 5)

118. July 20, 1853. EDICT: Rejects Marshall's Requests for an Audience and Declines to Send a Letter in Reply.

Edict to the Grand Councillors. Previously We received I-liang's memorial that "the American commissioner Marshall personally handed him a document and also stated orally that he carried certain credentials which he sought to present." We have ordered the said governor general to explain and order him to continue to conform to the old rules and wait for the Imperial Commissioner of Liang-kuang to investigate and act. On this day We received another memorial from I-liang that "he has had an interview with the said barbarian chief at K'un-shan and also that he took the barbarian letter which was delivered, broke the seal, and forwarded it." We have perused it for thought and language and find it is no more than a matter of announcing the change of commissioners and as before seeking the usual amity and trade. As to the expression, "being commissioned to have an audience," although this is an empty phrase, its (impossibility) must by all means be explained clearly so as to stop wanton thoughts. As for issuing to him a letter in reply, it is out of the question.

The Shanghai tao-t'ai Wu Chien-chang is thoroughly conversant with barbarian conditions. The said governor general will immediately confidentially instruct the said tao-t'ai, adhering rigidly to the agreements, to explain to him carefully that only dependent states under Chinese control, who have annual presentations, and liege officers of the various tributary states are in the class admitted to audience. The said country lies far away across many oceans, is always honest and righteous, and generally knows well our Court and provincial institutions. But he must adhere rigidly to the treaty and trade as of old. Certainly it is not necessary to send an envoy for an audience in order to appear sincerely earnest.

Altogether use suitable language and adroit words to win him over and the said chief then will not cause further complications to develop. If he should make other requests which cannot be reasonably explained as before observe the previous Edicts. Inform him that the Imperial Commissioner is now in Kwangtung and order him to wait quietly for him to investigate and act. Immediately instruct Yeh Ming-ch'en to manage carefully and take pains to inform the said chief of the receipt of an Edict of refusal; that no governor or governor general of any province whatever will dare again memorialize for him. Threats and covetousness will avail nothing. Naturally they must trade quietly. Let the said governor general circumspectly carry this out. (IWSM.F 6; 26a, 6-26b, 9)

119. July 25, 1853. MEMORIAL: Yeh Ming-ch'en Explains his Previous Inability to Meet Marshall and Offers to Receive him on his Return
to Canton.

Imperial Commissioner and Governor General of Liang-kuang,
Yeh Ming-ch'en, memorializes. It is noted that the United States
formerly had a commissioner at Kwangtung. After May 15, 1850,
when the former commissioner, Davis, returned it was not until February 1 of this year that Marshall came to Kwangtung to take over the
management of the affairs of commissioner. According to the said
chief's note "he now has credentials to present (and wishes) to set
a time for a personal meeting and interview." Just then, Your official
was directing troops stationed at Shao-chou, so Governor Po-kuei
replied that after Your official returned to Canton he could have an
interview.

In the second month (March 10-April 8) of the present year, he
found that the said chief had gone to Shanghai. On hearing that the
rebels were drifting eastward down the Yangtze he had gone there to
protect trade and for no other reason. On April 8 Your minister
finally returned to Canton from Shao-chou and received a letter from
the barbarian chief addressed to the Grand Secretaries. As scruples
were impolitic, he immediately opened and read it. It is no different
from the draft presented at Chiang-nan. Because in the ninth month
of last year Your minister was previously occupied with troops outside Canton, there was no interview. Again this spring just when there
was trouble in Chiang-nan the said chief went to Shanghai and then
this discussion developed. It is no more than an experiment because
of his previous desire.

But the treaty of 1844 states that "if hereafter the United States
has credentials addressed to the Chinese Court they shall be memorialized for them in the original by the Chinese Imperial Commissioner
in charge of barbarian affairs or the governor general of Liang-kiang
or of Min-Che." Thus the said chief in wishing at this time to present
them in Chiang-nan was not entirely without justification.

On examination it is found that when Davis first arrived in Kwangtung he also wrote fixing a date for an interview. Your official, with
the former governor general Hsü Kuang-chin, had an interview with him
at Jen-hsin Godown, White Goose Tything, on the Canton River, and
also received the credentials from Chief Davis personally. As there
were no insubordinate expressions, he had them translated and sent
under seal to the Grand Council for examination. This has all been
memorialized fully and is on record.

Now Chief Marshall's coming to Kwangtung and seeking an interview, as well as requesting the transmission of credentials, is exactly
the same situation and naturally should be handled in accord with the
old rule. An express letter has been sent to have the governor general
of Liang-chiang, I-liang, order the Su-Sung-T'ai tao-t'ai, Wu Chien-

chang, to instruct Chief Marshall as before to return to Kwangtung
and that it is not necessary to remain in Kiangsu.
Vermilion endorsement: Noted. (IWSM.HF 6; 27a, 1-28a, 2)
[Text of Marshall's official note asking how his credentials should be
forwarded to the court, ibid., p. 28a, 3-29b, 7]

120. September 1, 1853. MEMORIAL: Yeh Ming-ch'en Discusses
Marshall's Letter and Advocates Strict Adherence to Existing Treaties.
    Imperial Commissioner, Governor General of Liang-kuang, Yeh
Ming-ch'en memorializes. Now the American chief Marshall came to
Kwangtung primarily to assume the duties of commissioner of the
said country and originally had no other motive. Then this spring the
said chief went to Shanghai, also only to protect trade and with no
other intention whatever. But after reaching Shanghai, because Chiang
nan (officials) proposed to the said chief the hiring of steamers, he
realized that China was in turn depending on foreign countries to ward
off insult, and from this he inevitably developed ideas. Therefore, in
the letter previously addressed to the Grand Secretaries there was
the statement "if matters of intercourse of the two countries were
discussed and settled at the capital as between friends rather than on
the frontier as between enemies or strangers, it would be immeasurably better." Thus the letter presented by the said barbarian took
this point of view, but it was no more than an opportunist experiment.
How can we be disturbed by it? If Marshall soon returns to Kwangtung
no matter what demands he makes, (Your official) will certainly, in
accordance with Imperial decrees, adhere firmly to existing treaties.
    But it is noted that the said chief is still in Shanghai. The present
situation is such that he is not subject to remote regulation. It is
further feared that if he remains there for long, traitorous people will
have occasion to urge him on and renegades will connive with him.
These matters are all still unsettled. (Your official) is impelled to
request that an Imperial Edict be issued to the governor general of
Liang-chiang, I-liang, that he order Shanghai Tao-t'ai Wu Chien-chang
to instruct Marshall immediately to return to Kwangtung. (IWSM.HF
6; 29b, 9-30b, 2)

121. September 1, 1853. EDICT: Orders Yeh Ming-ch'en to Handle
Marshall at Canton and to Prevent his Meddling in Chinese Affairs.
    Edict to the Grand Councillors. Yeh Ming-ch'en has memorialized
concerning his opinion of the explanation of the letter presented by the
said barbarian, and also asking that the governor general of Liang-
chiang be ordered to instruct the said chief to return to Kwangtung.
According to his statement:

    Marshall came to Kwangtung to take charge of the affairs of commissioner
    and had no other motive. When he went to Shanghai it was also to protect

trade. Then, because of Chiang-nan's proposal to hire steamers, he realized
that China was dependent on others to ward off insult. So his wish to present
his letter was planned as an experiment. Now he has remained in Shanghai a
long time and should be ordered to return.

On this day (We) have instructed I-liang to order Shanghai Tao-
t'ai Wu Chien-chang to instruct the said chief immediately to return
to Kwangtung. Let Yeh Ming-ch'en, after the said chief reaches Kwangtung, immediately devise means of blocking and controlling him as
circumstances allow. If there are further demands, hold rigidly to
the treaty as before and stop his wanton ideas. It is important not to
allow the development of further complications. (IWSM.HF 6; 30b,
3-10)

122. September 1, 1853. EDICT: Orders I-liang to Have the Shanghai
Tao-t'ai Send Marshall back to Canton Immediately.
      Supplementary Edict. Previously (We) received I-liang's
memorial that within the city of K'un-shan he had an interview with
the American commissioner Marshall, and also forwarding the barbarian letter presented by the said chief. An Edict was issued
instructing the said governor general confidentially to order Shanghai
Tao-t'ai Wu Chien-chang to explain carefully and notify him that the
Imperial Commissioner is now in Kwangtung and have him quietly wait
for him to investigate and act.
      On this day (We) received Yeh Ming-ch'en's memorial stating:

> The said chief went to Shanghai only to protect trade and had no other
> intent. But later, because of Chiang-nan's proposal to hire steamers, he
> realized that China was dependent on others to ward off insult and inevitably
> developed ideas. The letter he presented was therefore no more than an experi-
> ment. If Marshall returns soon to Kwangtung and makes any demands, the said
> governor general will certainly be able firmly to maintain the treaty and
> control him as circumstances allow.

Now the said chief has been in Shanghai a long time, and it is hard
to guarantee that there will not arise the evils of traitorous people
inciting trouble and renegades conniving. Let I-liang immediately
order Wu Chien-chang to instruct the said chief immediately to return
to Kwangtung for an interview with the Imperial Commissioner and
that there is no use remaining in Shanghai. After the said chief reaches
Kwangtung, Yeh Ming-ch'en can naturally devise means of explaining
and stopping his wanton ideas and not cause the development of further
complications. (IWSM.HF 6; 31a, 2-31b, 1)

123. February 26, 1854. MEMORIAL: Yu-feng Reports Mutiny and
Murder Aboard the American Coolie Ship Robert Bowne off Formosa.
      Provisional Governor General of Min-Che Yu-feng memorializes

A reply has been received from Imperial Commissioner, Governor General of Liang-kuang Yeh Ming-ch'en, (stating) that he had received a statement from the American chief Parker that "a merchant vessel of his country had had its captain, mate, and crew killed by Chinese passengers who stole the ship's cargo and escaped on shore. At that time a foreign warship pursued them to the place, captured several tens of those who went ashore and brought them back here for trial and punishment." The Imperial Commissioner had received several letters from the said chief.[18]

In addition, Ch'en Te-li and sixteen others have been brought to Canton and assigned to be tried in Kuang-chou-fu. According to their unanimous statement, they were all beguiled on board the barbarian ship as contract laborers by emigration agents and confined in the hold. They were altogether four hundred and seventy-five men. After the ship sailed, the said barbarian gave each man in the hold a contract of servitude. If he did not accept he was flogged. On reaching the Liu-ch'iu ocean front, the said barbarian suddenly seized all of them, brought them on deck one by one, and cut off all their cues. More than ten who were sick in bed and could not walk were immediately killed and thrown into the ocean. Everyone looked on horrified and as a result a clamor set up. The captain of the said barbarian ship was very frightened and escaped by swimming. The crowd of passengers then ordered the sailors to sail the ship to the coast of the islands, went ashore and hid. On being questioned by the Liu-ch'iu islanders they falsely stated that the ship leaked and was being repaired. The Liu-ch'iu islanders daily gave them food and drink. After a fortnight the said barbarian warship arrived, arrested Ch'en Te-li and others, more than seventy persons, forced them on board the barbarian ship and sailed back to Hong Kong. Later on they conveyed Ch'en Te-li and sixteen others to Whampoa and delivered them up to the officials for trial and punishment. Ch'en Te-li received no head money from the barbarians. The reported charges of murder of barbarians and theft of money and goods from the barbarian ship, which have already been recounted in successive letters of the said chief, were respectively disproved.

Further, according to testimony submitted by the said chief,

---

18 This is the famous "piracy" case of the ship *Robert Bowne*, Lesley Bryson captain, which left Amoy, March 21, 1852, bound for California with 410 coolies aboard. The coolies mutinied and went ashore on the "Magicosima Islands," i.e., Miyakoshima Retto, southernmost of the Liu-ch'iu or Ryukyu Chain, 300 miles east of Formosa. Surviving members of the crew of the *Robert Bowne* overpowered the Chinese left aboard and brought the ship back to Amoy on April 18. Other survivors were picked up and the "pirates" or mutineers were captured by the joint efforts of the U.S.S. *Saratoga* and H.M.S. *Riley* and *Contest*. The whole case is covered in Parker's correspondence, U.S. Cong. 34:1, *S. Ex. Doc.* 99, p. 120-183.

Hsieh Ting-mao and three others were also ordered tried in Kuang-chou-fu. According to their statement they were all with Ch'en Te-li at the time he was on the ship and he did not wound anyone. Among them, one Hai Ting, that is Su Yu, attacked one barbarian, who then slipped and fell overboard. Lo An and the thirteen others were all tried and there was no instance of bandits murdering barbarians. Ch'en Te-li and Su Yu will eventually be retried and (their cases) variously settled. (Your official) has given instructions that the witnesses, Hsieh Ting-mao and the three others, be sent back to the barbarian leader.

As to the seventeen miscreants delivered in custody, excepting Ch'en Sao, who died of illness, and Ch'en Te-li and Su Yu, who remain in Kwangtung for retrial, Lo Fu-an and thirteen others were ordered to return immediately to their homes.

As to the said Fukienese, Ts'ai Hsiang-ch'ing, and others detained in Liu-ch'iu, we have sent word asking that orders be transmitted to the Liu-ch'iu government to provide a ship to return them to their native place to resume peaceful pursuits in order to show commisseration.

Now according to Fukien Financial Commissioner Ch'ing-tuan, he has received a detailed account from the provisional assistant prefect in charge of coastal defense of Foochow, Lou Hao:

> In the case of Liu-ch'iu sending back in custody the distressed natives --Ts'ai Hsiang-ch'ing, Lin Yu, and one hundred and twenty-four others have arrived in Fukien.

> To summarize, the refugees Ts'ai Hsiang-ch'ing and others are all Fukienese who boarded an English ship wishing to go to California to make a living. On March 21, 1852, they set out from Amoy. On the sea they encountered storms, and on April 8 were driven into Liu-ch'iu jurisdiction, a rocky promontory in the waterfront of Pa-chung-shan Island. The ship struck a hidden rock. The English barbarian then placed the distressed people, Ts'ai Hsiang-ch'ing and others, three hundred eighty persons and one Englishman, ashore. Later on when the tide came in the ship floated, and the original ship of the said barbarian took advantage of the winds to set out to sea. The distressed people on the island were provided with quarters by the local Liu-ch'iu barbarian official and received food through charity. Later, on May 4-6, two English ships arrived one after the other.

Through the local barbarian official comes the oral statement of the English interpreter, Lo-yüan-hu:

> The said distressed people, Ts'ai Hsiang-ch'ing and others, the month before boarded a barbarian ship to go to California. Because the captain and five sailors were murdered at sea, the English official at Amoy sent a ship to the island to arrest them. They went ashore armed and seized five of the distressed people and shot three. Eighteen were frightened into submission, three committed suicide by hanging, the rest fled and hid in the mountains. The

English barbarians then took the twenty-three captured distressed people, as well as the one English barbarian on the island, placed them in the two ships, and on May 11 left, one after the other.

On May 22 another English barbarian ship arrived in pursuit, arrested fifty-seven refugees, took them on board, and left. They also said that later they would come back and seize all of them. The refugees hiding in the mountains were all again invited to return and receive food. Of them, twenty-three died at' one time or another, and two hundred seventy-one were left. The prince of the said country, as the tyranny of the English barbarians was extraordinary, greatly feared that if they were not delivered up immediately the barbarian ships would return, make an exhaustive search, and give rise to trouble.

Last year, when the (Liu-ch'iu) tribute ship came to Fukien, they asked for a settlement and received word from the prefect that they should follow the usual procedure and send officials to bring them in custody to Fukien. He specially delegated a barbarian official to go to the said island to interrogate the leader of the refugees, Ts'ai Hsiang-ch'ing, who had previously been arrested and returned. Besides those who were driven away, ninety-two persons, and Cheng Te and three others who had died of sickness or hanged themselves in the meantime, there remained only Lin Yu and others, one hundred seventy-five persons. With special permits of the prince of the said country, they dispatched the assistant interpreter, Cheng Chia-cheng, on board the first ship charged with the refugees, Lin Yu and others, one hundred five persons, and dispatched the assistant interpreter, Wang Chia-chin, on board the second ship charged with the refugees Ch'en Ch'ang and others, seventy persons. Among them Ch'en I, Ko Ch'i, and Huang Tao died in the meantime.

On November 1, 1853, they put out to sea from the said island. At sea the two ships were boarded by pirates and forty-seven of the refugees absconded. The actual number left was one hundred twenty-five. On November 14 they reached Foochow harbor and anchored at the place for foreign ships and were examined separately by the deputy officials. Then on the fifteenth they were housed in the post-station. The said distressed people were turned over to the magistrate of Min-hsien to investigate and provide for them, to examine and try them.

According to the joint account of the magistrates Min-hsien and Hou-kuan

The refugees sent by the barbarian official of Liu-ch'iu, Lin Yu and others, one hundred and five persons, together with those refugees being escorted by the deputy official of Foochow-fu, who absconded at sea, Li Chi, Ch'en Ch'ang, and Lin Shih, three persons, were investigated in detail. They all actually boarded an English barbarian ship, wishing to go to California to make a living. On the high seas they encountered storms and were driven into Liu-ch'iu jurisdiction, Pa-chung-shan Island. They went ashore and fled. From the local barbarian official they received care and relief and were returned in custody to Fukien. In all there was no case of wounding or killing barbarians.

The investigation tallies with the reply from Kwangtung and appear to be trustworthy. I am impelled to ask that the said refugees be divided up and returned to their respective native hsien for investigation and report at first hand, that they be strictly tried and variously punished.

Vermilion endorsement: Noted. (IWSM.HF 7; 14a, 1-17a, 4)

124. April 19, 1854. MEMORIAL: Hsü Nai-chao Reports on American
and French Cooperation against the Rebels at Shanghai.

Hsü Nai-chao [Governor of Kiangsu] further memorializes. To
continue, the English barbarians are arrogant and untractable and have
long been so. Since the opening of the five ports to trade they have
increasingly ignorantly vaunted themselves. The honest people of
Canton became steadily increasingly resentful. Repeatedly the mass
of people have wanted to take vengeance on the said barbarians. The
said barbarians also greatly feared them. From their arrival at
Shanghai, the popular temper has been mild, and the people have not
been antagonistic. The said barbarians are greatly pleased at this
situation, vastly different from Canton, and have constantly courted
popular favor. Their purpose is particularly questionable. Wu Chien-
chang is thoroughly conversant with barbarian psychology and understands them deeply. The American and French barbarian chiefs have
also repeatedly spoken of this. Wu Chien-chang has therefore secretly
allied with the American and French barbarian chiefs in order to
isolate the strength of the English barbarians. In recent years the
formalities of interviews, as well as the whole procedure of written
communication, are all made clear in fixed regulations to provide
limits. Even in the customs there has not been excessive smuggling
or deceit.

In the eighth month of last year (September 3-October 3) the
rebels began to attack officials. When the government troops first
arrived, the English barbarians regarded the north city wall as
entirely their province. It was agreed that troops would not be led
through there. The section from the North Gate to the Little East
Gate, where all the foreign residences were, being entirely in the line
of rebel communication, munitions, food supplies, and all necessities
were all brought through there. The recruited rebel bands also
entered by this way. The rebels regarded the barbarians as close
allies; the barbarians regarded the rebels as profitable customers.
The feeling of all English barbarians was merely fear that Shanghai's
hostilities would stop.

Furthermore, those who read Chinese books and knew a smattering of grammar published a journal called Hsia Erh Kuan Chen or
"News from Far and Near."[19] The language was inferentially sala-
cious, but regarding the motives and the actions of the Yang [Hsiu-
ch'ing, Taiping leader] rebels, on the contrary, the said journal
regarded them as rather well ordered. It was most mischievous.

---

19 The *Hsia Erh Kwan Chen* (News from Far and Near) was the title of a periodical
published in Hong Kong. Griffin, *op. cit.*, p. 85n.

Furthermore, there is a (barbarian) newspaper printed.[20] It makes the extreme statement that "Chinese are hard to reason with and it is only by threatening them with force that we can gain our ends." As it is circulated among the various countries, the barbarian chiefs get ideas therefrom. Up to the present time its harm has been most extreme.

It is noted that trade at Shanghai began with the English barbarians. In this trade the English barbarians are the greatest and the American barbarians are second to them. The French barbarians regard religion as most important and their interest is not in gain. The lesser countries, adhering to England, the United States, and France, are about five or six. They are not uniformly good or bad, but the English barbarians are the most inscrutable and most difficult to manage. . . [A description of relations of the British with the Government troops and the rebels during the past year, occupies the rest of the memorial.]   (IWSM.HF 7; 20b, 1-21a, 10)

---

20 The *North China Herald,* a weekly newspaper, was inaugurated August 3, 1850, at Shanghai, with Henry Shearman as publisher and proprietor. *Chinese Repository,* v. 19, p. 462.

Chapter 5

First Attempts at Treaty Revision, 1854
(Documents 125-194)

The seventy documents making up this chapter are dated May 17 to
December 14, 1854, and cover the attempts of American Commissioner
Robert M. McLane, in collaboration with Sir John Bowring, to negotiate revision of the Treaty of Wang-hsia. The Chinese record comprises thirty-four memorials and thirty edicts, all but one of the latter
being addressed to the Grand Council. The interest in foreign affairs
of the new emperor, Wen-tsung of the Hsien-feng period, is attested
by twenty-two vermilion endorsements. Eleven of these are the laconic chih-tao-la ("Noted") notation and two more are general, non-
factual endorsements. There are, on the other hand, seven specific
comments and two interlinear notes in the text of the memorials. Outside the memorial-edict pattern, there are six notes exchanged between
China, Britain, and the United States.

    The memorialists of this period are divided into three groups,
corresponding to the three geographical centers of diplomatic interest.
At Canton, there was Imperial Commissioner Yeh Ming-ch'en, stubborn and uncooperative as ever. At Shanghai, there were I-liang,
governor general of Liang-chiang; Hsü Nai-chao, governor of Kiangsu, who was the patron and memorialist for Wu Chien-chang, the
energetic tao-t'ai of Shanghai; and Chi-er-hang-a, who became governor of Kiangsu when Hsü Nai-chao was dismissed. The bulk of the
material centers around Tientsin, where McLane and Bowring, with
their Chinese secretaries Parker and Medhurst, attempted to negotiate treaty revision. The Tientsin memorialists were Former Ch'ang-
lu Salt Controller Ch'ung-lun; present encumbent of the same post,
Wen-ch'ien; and Tientsin Garrison Brigade General Shuang-jui. Minor
memorialists were Deptuy Lieutenant General of Shanhaikwan Fu-lo-
tun-t'ai and Governor of Shantung Ch'ung-en.

    The content of this group of memorials all centers around the
single topic of treaty revision, allegedly due in 1854, according to the
involved legalistic process of applying the twelve-year revision clause
of the Treaty of Wang-hsia (1844) to the Treaty of Nanking (1842).
Though the latter contained no revision clause, the British claimed
revision was applicable because of the comprehensive most-favored-
nation clause in the supplementary Treaty of the Bogue (1843). This
complicated reasoning confused the Chinese, who were determined to
resist any but "minor alterations" in the existing treaties and who
claimed that by simple arithmetic revision was not due until 1856. At
Canton, there was non-cooperation of officials and the violent opposition

of an incited populace. At Shanghai, there was friendly intercourse, but the officials had no authorization to negotiate and were severely reprimanded for transmitting foreign credentials and communications, as they were specifically authorized to do under the Cushing treaty. At Tientsin, there was polite evasion and reference of the foreign envoys back to Yeh Ming-ch'en, where the futile merry-go-round would start all over again. About all that was accomplished was the placing of the British and American précis on treaty revision before the Grand Council, and the Chinese versions of these recommendations are reproduced in this group of documents, here re-translated into English.

The American documents of this period are summarized by Tyler Dennett in his Americans in Eastern Asia, chapter on "The Policy of Commissioner McLane," p. 225 to 240. The voluminous McLane correspondence is published in full in U. S. Cong. 35:2, S. Ex. Doc. 22 (2 v.).

TRANSLATIONS OF DOCUMENTS

125. May 17, 1854. MEMORIAL: Hsü Nai-chao Reports Meeting of the Shanghai Tao-t'ai with United States Commissioner McLane.

Governor of Kiangsu Hsü Nai-chao memorializes. There is received a report from Wu Chien-chang stating that "on May 1 he learned that an American war steamer came to Shanghai. Later he received a letter from the consul of the said country, Murphy,[1] stating that the American commissioner, McLane,[2] had arrived and had matters to discuss personally. Because it would be improper for him to call on the (Chinese officials) in the garrison quarters, could the honorable tao-t'ai come for an interview?" The said consul also sent a letter of the same general purport to Chi-erh-hang-a.

On the third, the said prefect and tao-t'ai went together and received the personal statement of Chief McLane:

> The various countries had received His Imperial Majesty's Heavenly favor of trading in the ports of China, enabling them to be benefited, and were actually deeply grateful. Now rebels were harassing Shanghai, causing impediments to the Chinese customs and losses to the trade of the various countries. It was actually very deplorable. Because the merchants and officials of the various countries were unable to cooperate in subduing the rebels, they were still more ashamed. Things actually had reached the point of violent popular suspicion but the United States had no intention of helping the rebels.

1 Robert C. Murphy of Ohio was officially United States consul at Shanghai from July 21 1853 to June 25, 1857, although he did not reach Shanghai until March 4, 1854. Griffin, op. cit., p. 364.

2. Robert M. McLane of Maryland was United States Commissioner to China from October 18, 1853 to December 12, 1854.

Now the present minister has personally come to Shanghai and wishes to go
to Chen-chiang and other places to investigate the rebel situation. If there
are any means of being of assistance, they can be discussed. Furthermore, he
wishes to set trade in order and enable the Chinese customs to reap benefits
rather than deficits. Thus will his mind be at rest. The present commissioner
must have a personal interview with the honorable governor general in order
to express his opinion. Moreover, there are a great many matters of benefit
to China which must be discussed personally.

The former commissioner, Marshall, was a man of the greatest integrity. The
king of our country originally wished him to request an audience with His
Imperial Majesty to make proposals. Then, because this did not receive Imperial sanction, it was not carried out. Now the present commissioner has come
here to make a sympathetic study of conditions. By the 16th of the present
month he would proceed to Chen-chiang. He hoped that the honorable governor general would be requested on his behalf to set a time and place for a
meeting.

In short, what he wished to say was entirely beneficial to China and he had
no intention whatever of making demands. If a conference could not be
arranged, the only alternative was to delegate someone to go to Tientsin and
present a memorial in order to express his sincere feelings. He hoped for a
definite reply. He further asked that the marine garrisons of Chen-chiang be
notified not to fire or attack by mistake.

Wu Chien-chang considers that while the English and French
barbarians had previously gone to Chen-chiang without giving any
notice, now the American chief first sent word asking that the
governor general be informed; in language and intention both, he
was extremely respectful and obedient. Furthermore, he observes
that since the rebel disturbances the trade of the various countries
has actually suffered losses. The said chief's insistence in requesting to see the governor general may be a real wish to set
trading matters in order, but one cannot be sure. As to his decision to go up the (Yangtze) River, although urged to desist, he
has not finally complied. He (Wu) has immediately and fully reported the circumstances to the governor general and will await
and carry out his instructions.

Your official notes that of the various countries trading at Shanghai the British consul and vice-consul, Rutherford B. Alcock and
Thomas Wade, are most crafty. Last year American Commissioner
Marshall told Wu Chien-chang confidentially that their attitude was
inscrutable. Now Chief McLane's statement of violent "popular
suspicion" alludes to the affair of the English chief on April 3.[3]
It is noted that although there are some American barbarian traitors
who secretly furnish supplies to the rebels, it is nothing more than

3 The British and French consuls, with United States Consul Murphy, protested the establishment of the Chinese customs house in the interior and refused to recognize it.

the desire for petty gain, and besides there are not many of them.
Nor did the barbarian chief know the facts. Now he has prohibited
such activity. As the barbarians think only of profits, the statement
he makes "of benefit to China" cannot be entirely believed. However,
it is noted that his language and motives seem unlike those of the
English chief. The confidential report previously received from Wu
Chien-chang is at hand. Your official has also inquired of Chi-er-
hang-a, and what he observed on that day is substantially the same.
(IWSM. HF 7; 29b, 5-31a, 5)

126. May 17, 1854. EDICT: Instructs the Shanghai Officials to Handle
the Americans Carefully and to Send Them back to Canton.
    Edict to the Grand Councillors. I-liang and Hsü Nai-chao have
memorialized on the various circumstances of handling the suppression campaign at Shanghai. (We) have read both memorials and understand the situation. Now the region is not yet quiet. An American
warship has arrived at Shanghai; it will do no more than observe our
condition and so forward their nefarious plans. We must maintain
extreme calm and cut off the gradual development of their covetousness
When I-liang has conferences with the said barbarian he should take
pains to explain things to him clearly and, instructing him in the great
principles, order him to proceed to Kwangtung and await the investigation and disposal of his case. On the one hand notify Yeh Ming-ch'en
and on the other, ascertain the various conditions the said barbarian
chief spoke of, and quickly memorialize in full. (IWSM. HF 7; 31a, 6-1

127. May 17, 1854. EDICT: Instructs Yeh Ming-ch'en to Hold McLane
Strict Adherence to the Existing Treaties.
    Edict to the Grand Councillors. Hsü Nai-chao has memorialized
stating the barbarian situation at Shanghai. According to the report of
Wu Chien-chang and others: "There is an American barbarian chief.
Because the rebels are investing Shanghai, trade at the port has suffer
losses. The said chief wishes to go to Chen-chiang and other places to
investigate the rebel situation and also wishes to set trading affairs in
order. If the governor general and governor do not grant an interview,
he will prepare a full memorial and take it to Tientsin for presentation
    Barbarians are by nature inscrutable. Now the rebellion is not
yet quieted, and there is no assurance that he will not develop ideas
of coveting and spying. (We) have ordered I-liang to explain to him
clearly and, according to precedent, order him to go to Kwangtung
and wait for the Imperial Commissioner to investigate and act. Yeh
Ming-ch'en, after the said barbarian reaches Kwangtung, must take
pains to enlighten him with fundamental principles. While encouraging
and appeasing outside barbarians he should, as before, firmly maintain the treaty. By no means can he listen to any other of his demands
and cause the development of complications.... (IWSM. HF 7; 32a, 5-3

128. May 24, 1854. MEMORIAL: I-liang Reports McLane's Request
for Permission to go up the Yangtze and for an Interview (with I-liang).
Governor General of Liang-chiang I-liang memorializes. On
May 8 a report was received from Su-Sung-T'ai Tao-t'ai Wu Chien-
chang stating that:

> On May 1 American commissioner McLane, on board a war steamer, came to
> Shanghai and asked for interviews with the said *tao-t'ai* and Chi-erh-hang-
> a. According to his statement, the various countries receiving the
> Heavenly favor of His Majesty allowing trade at Chinese ports and enabling
> them to reap benefits, were extremely grateful. Now rebels are investing
> Shanghai and there are obstructions to trade and customs. The said chief
> wishes to go to Chen-chiang and other places to find out how he could be
> of assistance, which can then be discussed. He also wishes to set trading
> affairs in order and cause the Chinese customs to yield benefits rather
> than deficits. It is essential to have a personal interview with the
> governor general in order to reveal his intentions. If they cannot meet,
> the only alternative is to proceed to Tientsin and present a memorial in
> order to express his sincerity.

Your slave considers that, as Chen-chiang is now occupied by
troops and is primarily not an outside barbarian trading port, the
warships of the various countries need not go there. Examining the
treaty, there is no provision for commissioners of foreign countries
to go directly to Tientsin to present memorials. As to the trading
affairs of the various countries, they have always reverted to the
Kwangtung Imperial Commissioner for execution. Last year Marshall
went to Kwangtung. Because the Imperial Commissioner was leading
an army outside the city, according to his statement he waited several months without securing a personal interview. Therefore, I
yielded to pressure and saw him instead, memorialized, and received
an Imperial Edict ordering me to have him return to Kwangtung and
wait for the Imperial Commissioner to investigate and act.
This year the Kwangtung Imperial Commissioner has not left his
office at all. If (McLane) has public business, naturally he should go
to Kwangtung and state it personally.
After instructing Wu Chien-chang to make this clear, then on May
15, I received from Wu Chien-chang a draft copy of the said chief's
note stating:

> The said chief bears credentials to be presented to His Imperial Majesty.
> According to the treaty, credentials should be sent to the honorable
> governor general to be forwarded on his behalf. Therefore he must rely on
> the honorable governor general (*i.e.*, I-liang), because when he arrived
> at Kwangtung and notified the governor general (*i.e.*, Yeh Ming-ch'en), the
> latter excused himself on the ground of public exigency. Now (McLane) sets
> May 20 or thereabouts to go in person to Chiao-shan, bringing the official
> letter for transmission, and hopes that His Excellency will be present and
> afford a personal interview, in order to show personally the mutual respect

of His Imperial Majesty and of the United States, and also afford a thorough
discussion of all the recent difficulties of the two countries.

There was also received Wu Chien-chang's report that "the said
chief wished to go to Chen-chiang and that his determination in requesting an interview was very earnest. Now he has gone first by
ship to Ningpo, then he will go to Chen-chiang, and again return to
Shanghai."

Your slave finds that, although the said chief is bearing credentials, in the treaty there is no provision for discussions with the
governor general of Liang-chiang. Last year Marshall forwarded
his credentials and handed over a second copy. Now it is not clearly
stated whether or not there is a second copy and, not having clear
notice, Wu Chien-chang has been ordered to make inquiries and,
after the said chief returns from Ningpo, if he passes through Shanghai, to have him remain in Shanghai; there is no need for him to go to
Chen-chiang. As soon as there is a report from the said tao-t'ai it
will be possible to send a reply.

Vermilion endorsement: Noted. (IWSM. HF 7; 32b, 9-34a, 9)

129. May 24, 1854. MEMORIAL: I-liang Suggests the Advisability
of Meeting McLane if he Insists on an Interview.

I-liang further memorializes. To continue, last year on the occasion of forwarding Marshall's credentials, an Imperial Edict was
received ordering him to go back to Kwangtung immediately and see
the Imperial Commissioner. This situation naturally ought to be
managed the same way, but Chief McLane used the pretext that Yeh
Ming-ch'en evaded him on grounds of public exigency. If Your slave
were to refuse him summarily it would cause the said leader on the
contrary to use it as a pretext for going directly to Tientsin. At
present there is fighting in Chihli; besides, just now junks for the
ocean transport of rice are continually going to Tientsin and there
would inevitably be many difficulties.[4] On this occasion, after Your
slave has rejected (his proposal), if the said chief is willing to return immediately to Kwangtung there is nothing to be considered. If
he repeatedly seeks an interview and is continually refused, he can
say that Your slave is avoiding him and will feel some discourtesy.
Only there is the Vermilion endorsement received last year to the
effect that the competent man manages according to circumstances.
When Your slave meets him, if he recklessly proposes further
changes or makes other demands in matters of trade and customs,
Your slave can only rely on justice and insist that, as before, he go

---

4 The transport of tribute rice to Peking was at this time done by sea, due to the
interruption of the Grand Canal and other inland routes by the Taiping Rebellion.

to Kwangtung and wait for Yeh Ming-ch'en to investigate and act in
order to avoid the development of further complications.
    Vermilion endorsement: What is memorialized is right. Let it
be executed accordingly. By no means encourage the development of
further complications and still less allow the matter to end in
compromise. In no case can weakness be shown; but if the restraint
is apparent it will just serve to start the demands of the said barbarians. (IWSM.HF 7; 34a, 10-35a, 2)

130. June 24, 1854. MEMORIAL: Yeh Ming-ch'en Anticipates British
and American Demands for Treaty Revision in 1854.
    Yeh Ming-ch'en further memorializes. The American chief
Marshall returned to his country on January 27 of this year. McLane,
who took over the charge, arrived in Kwangtung on April 24 of this year.
Unexpectedly the English chief in charge, Bowring,[5] also came to
Kwangtung April 23, and Bonham[6] left for home on the twenty-fifth. As
the commissioners of the two countries were changed at the same time,
there must be some reason. At first they appeared secretive, and
only after repeated inquiries was it learned that it was all because of
the statement that twelve years from 1842, when the treaty was concluded at Chiang-nan [i. e., Nanking], it should be revised. On
August 29 of the present year, the period will have expired. The kings
of the said countries each sent a commissioner to Kwangtung just on
account of this. (We) venture to ask why, in that year when the Treaty
of Chiang-nan was concluded, this twelve-year period was set? It was
clearly a ground purposely prepared so as to enable them to make
complaints now. Your official will explain as occasion is afforded
and devise means of constraint.
    Vermilion endorsement: Memorial read and situation understood.
(IWSM.HF 8; 4a, 3-4b, 2)

131. June 24, 1854. EDICT: Erroneously Attributes Twelve-year
Revision Clause to the Treaty of Nanking and Plans to Resist Demands
for Revision.
    Edict to the Grand Councillors.... As to the American and
English chiefs, McLane and Bowring, being changed at the same time,
according to the said governor general's information it was because
previously, when the treaty was concluded at Chiang-nan, there was
the phrase: "to be again revised after twelve years." Therefore, the
said barbarians' intention is to make demands. By no means should
you give any indication, but take defensive measures. But when the

---

5 Sir John Bowring was British superintendent of trade and governor of Hong Kong
    succeeding Sir Samuel George Bonham.
6 Sir Samuel George Bonham was British superintendent of trade and governor of Hong
    Kong, 1848-1854.

time expires some changes may be necessary according to circumstances, in order to intercept their nefarious plans. Yeh Ming-
ch'en has been in Kwangtung several years, is thoroughly conversant with conditions, and (We) trust he can find means to curb them
and not wait for repeated injunctions. (IWSM.HF 8; 4b, 3-9)

132. July 7, 1854. MEMORIAL: Hsü Nai-chao Reports British Offer
of Aid against the Shanghai Rebels and Notes Wu Chien-chang's Trip
with McLane.

Governor of Kiangsu Hsü Nai-chao memorializes. As to the
strength of the Shanghai rebels, just now their funds are daily being
depleted and their adherents daily scattered. In our management
this is an occasion for gaining confidence. In the middle of this
month English commissioner Bowring and Admiral Sterling, with
five warships, large and small, came to Shanghai. They said that
they were going to Japan and Siam to expel the Russian barbarians.
Then there was a note requesting interviews with Your official and
Chi-erh-hang-a, saying that there were important matters to be discussed personally. Just at that time Your official was suffering from
a cold and refused on that ground.

Wu Chien-chang refused also, because he was going with the
American commissioner McLane to K'un-shan to visit Governor
General Chi-erh-hang-a. On June 21, (Chi-erh-hang-a) had an interview with Bowring and, according to the said chief's oral statement,
"as the rebels at Shanghai after all this time are still not tranquillized, it has caused the ruin of British trade, so we will agree
to get rid of the rebel bands if you are willing not to question where
they were sent. Then the city will be restored to your honorable
country."

Chi-erh-hang-a answered that expelling the rebels and restoring
the city were good intentions of the honorable country, but the two
rebels who had killed officials, P'an Hsiao-ching-tzu and Hsieh An-
pang, could not properly be set at large. Moreover, if the honorable
country sent off the said rebels probably there would be other troubles,
in turn defeating the honorable country's originally good intentions.
They (the rebels) must be sent to a definite place, then there will be
no regrets.

The said chief said, "If you wish to raise these difficulties then
I shall go by steamer to Tientsin and inform His Imperial Majesty by
memorial directly."

Chi-erh-hang-a answered, "We will do only what is right. His
Imperial Majesty (treats) Chinese and foreigners as one family and his
acts always accord with reason. We do not rebel against propriety and
even if you memorialized no one would oppose you. "

The said chief continued to argue vehemently. Subsequently he
said further that this matter must be reported and discussed with the

governor. Thereupon I returned to the garrison and agreed to see him again the next day at noon.

In the afternoon (3-5) of the same day the rebels went out of the west and north gates, about a thousand men from each. The Ch'ao [i.e., Swatow] irregulars chased the rebels as far as the broken wooden bridge when the barbarians met them and opened fire. As the Ch'ao irregulars also, on the nineteenth, had chased the rebels to this point and four persons had been killed by the barbarians, when the barbarians again opened fire, the Ch'ao irregulars thereupon returned several volleys and scattered. The barbarian troops received no injury.... [Recounts further British activities at Shanghai.] (IWSM.HF 8; 9a, 5-10a, 4)

133. July 7, 1854. EDICT: Removes Hsü Nai-chao from Office for Relying on Wu Chien-chang and Pandering to McLane.

[Imperial Edict removing Hsü Nai-chao from his post for failure to recapture Shanghai or to cope successfully with the barbarians, and appointing Chi-erh-hang-a in his place.] ...Hsü Nai-chao has memorialized separately that an English barbarian ship sailed into the river off Chiao-shan on June 18. He learned that it wished to go to Nanking. But previously Ch'i-shan had memorialized that he had also received a letter from Hsü Nai-chao stating that an American barbarian ship would enter the river and asking him not to fire on it. Thus, Hsü Nai-chao's confidence in the barbarians was great. It is no wonder the said barbarians disregarded rules and sought trouble.

Previously Shanghai barbarian affairs were all in Wu Chien-chang' charge. At this time the said official again went with the American chief, McLane, to K'un-shan to meet the governor general. He was not personally involved and it is hard to guarantee that the said official did not know the barbarian situation in advance and intentionally withdraw; also it is hard to guarantee that it was not Wu Chien-chang's evil management which caused those who were under the control of the said barbarians to blame Hsü Nai-chao. Thus the reports successively memorialized were only based on Wu Chien-chang's statements.... (IWSM.HF 8; 12b, 8-13a, 5)

134. July 7, 1854. EDICT: Enlarges on the Charges against Hsü Nai-chao and Orders Yeh Ming-ch'en to Defy the British and Hold Them to the Treaties.

Supplementary Edict. (We) have received I-liang's memorial stating that an American barbarian ship had gone to Chen-chiang for a personal interview with the governor general. Subsequently Ch'i-shan memorialized:

The said barbarian ship proceeded from Chen-chiang and anchored at P'u-k'ou. Moreover, it stopped at Kua-chou and had illicit dealings with the rebels.

The English barbarians at Shanghai are obstructing us at every turn and are extremely malicious. Whenever our troops drive the rebels out, they fire on our Swatow irregulars, and then demand that our headquarters surrender those who returned their fire. They also say they want to move the Shanghai rebels to some other place and, if we do not agree, threaten to proceed to Tientsin.

Hsü Nai-chao, fearing that if the barbarians moved the rebels elsewhere other areas would be thrown into turmoil, told them that the two rebels who had killed officials must be surrendered to him. The said barbarians refused and had someone draft a communication on behalf (of Hsü), stating that "apparently our (Chinese) troops opened fire first so we were obviously the guilty ones and that if we did not agree, they would attack our headquarters the following day." They were extremely arrogant and the said governor, fearing that they would make an issue of it and start trouble, actually wrote the communication according to (this draft). This amounts to giving the others a weapon against us. Hsü Nai-chao has already been impeached for cowardice and incompetence, but this has not solved the Shanghai problem. It has been mismanaged despicably.

As to Chinese ports outside the five treaty ports, barbarian ships have never been allowed entry, but recently barbarian ships have arbitrarily gone where they pleased, sometimes to Chenchiang, sometimes to Nanking, and they have had intercourse with the rebels in open defiance of existing treaties. Why do these barbarians, who are on friendly terms with China, have intercourse with the rebels? Their motive is certainly not friendship. Right now, if they suffer casualties incident to the hostilities on the Yangtze, our troops cannot be held responsible.

Let Yeh Ming-ch'en point out to the barbarian chiefs Bowring and Sterling, in preemptory and lucid terms the risks involved, and nip their malice in the bud. Bowring just came to Canton on April 13, and then on June 21 he went to Shanghai with a warship. At Shanghai on June 18, he dispatched the barbarian chief Medhurst[7] to Chenchiang with a steamer. If the (British) are really at war with Russia, how can they go back and forth about the interior so freely? That they are concealing some evil design can be clearly seen.

Yeh Ming-ch'en is in sole charge of the management of barbarian affairs. Let him immediately, on the authority of the existing treaties, enjoin the Shanghai barbarians that they are not to cruise about at will and give them orders that, as the Yangtze ports are all

---

7   Walter Henry Medhurst, Jr. (1823-1885), son of the famous missionary (1796-1857), accompanied his father to China in 1839 and within two years was employed by Captain Elliot as Chinese secretary. He served in various secretarial and consular posts in China until his retirement from service in 1876.

crowded with troops at the present time, if they disregard the treaty
and suffer casualties from our forces it will be the said barbarians'
own responsiblity, not ours. This will let the barbarians know that
we are not afraid to fight, and will put an end to their daily increasing audacity. We trust the said governor general will be able to
exert himself to accomplish this and nip calamity in the bud. He is
also charged to admonish both the American and French barbarians
sternly.

If there is any reliable information at Canton as to what the
Russian barbarians are up to, he is ordered to memorialize it immediately. (IWSM. HF 8; 13b, 8-14b, 10; cf. Wade's translation
and notes, U.S. Cong. 36:1, S. Ex. Doc. 30, p. 449-451.)

135. July 15, 1854. MEMORIAL: I-liang Reports McLane's Trip
up the Yangtze and Interview (with I-liang) at K'un-shan.

Governor General of Liang-chiang I-liang memorializes. Your
slave has received Su-Sung-T'ai tao-t'ai Wu Chien-chang's report
that the American barbarian chief, McLane, has come to Shanghai
in command of two steam warships and demanded an interview, and
that after delivering his communication, he proceeded to Ningpo and
Chen-chiang to inspect conditions. Subsequently he received reports
from the magistrates of Tan-t'u, Shang yüan, Liu-ho, Chiang-p'u
and Tang-t'u that the said barbarian ships passed through Chen-
chiang, Chiang-ning, Ho-chou, and Wu-hu successively and then returned to Chiao-shan to anchor. He has sent a communication via the
Chen-chiang Maritime Battalion of the Banner Forces requesting
Your slave to come there for an interview.

As the Yangtze River is not a treaty port area and barbarian
ships are not allowed to go there, Your slave felt that if the said barbarian wished to present his credentials personally, as Marshall
did last year, he should return immediately to Shanghai and wait for
Wu Chien-chang to conduct him to K'un-shan for an interview. When
this reply was made, the said chief departed immediately aboard a
native craft.

On June 20, Wu Chien-chang, with Lan Wei-wen, the assistant
prefect in charge of coast and river defenses at Sung-chiang-fu,
accompanied (McLane) to K'un-shan. Your slave, accompanied by
Acting Prefect of Su-chou P'ing-han, who has long resided at Su-
chou and is thoroughly conversant with conditions there, set out
from Su-chou on June 19th and arrived at K'un-shan on the 20th.
The next day he sent word to the said chief to meet him at a public
hall in K'un-shan. The said chief conducted himself respectfully,
saying:

> The receipt of His Majesty's Heavenly favor allowing us to trade at the
> five ports is a great boon, but in recent years the Yangtze has not been
> open and business has collapsed. Consequently, I should like to request a

memorial begging Imperial favor to allow us to trade along the entire
course of the Yangtze River. We ourselves are willing to protect all goods
entering the Yangtze. If this is not memorialized for me, I shall go personally to Tientsin.

Your slave instructed him that, as the treaty providing for
trade at the five ports had been authorized by Imperial Edict in 1844,
Chinese and foreign officials and gentry must all abide by it forever;
that moreover, the treaty clearly stated that "subsequently no state
(i. e., country) should send officials for separate negotiations,"[8] and
as his present request was contrary to the original treaty it could
hardly be memorialized. As for Tientsin, since the Canton rebels
had penetrated to the borders of Chihli [mod. Hopei Province], the
local populace was hostile; the militia numbered more than a hundred
thousand and if barbarian ships were to proceed recklessly, and
should the populace misunderstand and possibly inflict casualties, it
would be no concern of the government; the governor general of
Chihli was not responsible for handling barbarian affairs and would
certainly not consent to an interview, so that even if the said chief
went to Tientsin he would accomplish nothing. As for recent military
developments in the North (the Imperial forces) had met with a
number of victories and the defeated rebels north of the Yellow River
had all been exterminated, so that it would not be difficult to reduce
them to submission in time: once the Yangtze was cleared, business
would revive spontaneously without the need of special negotiations
for extension.

The said chief said that since he realized that China's military
affairs were unsettled he would not insist on going to Tientsin immediately to beseech Divine favor, but that the treaty provided for
reconsideration and revision after twelve years and now the date was
approaching; that since the Shanghai Customs (House) had been moved
to Woosung, contrary to the old regulations, there were many inconveniences; that as plenipotentiary of his country, he could easily
negotiate and if the governor of Kiangsu could not officiate because
it was contrary to the treaty, then he would request a memorial that
an Imperially delegated plenipotentiary be sent to facilitate personal exchange of credentials and the conclusion of negotiations.

Your slave instructed him as follows. As provided in the treaty,
the clauses concerning trade and the high seas might be slightly
modified after twelve years, provided agreement was reached fairly

---

8 *Vide* Treaty of Wang-hsia (Wanghia), Article 34: "...and no individual State of
the United States can appoint or send a minister to China to call in question
the provisions of the same."

and justly,[9] but the clause dealing with the "high seas" did not include inland waters such as the Yangtze and Yellow Rivers, and "slight modifications" implied nothing more than certain adjustments at the five ports necessitated by changed circumstances, certainly not major changes, and least of all did (the treaty) allow a single ship to go to another port. Furthermore, if there were violations of this prohibitory order, ships and cargoes must be forfeited to the Chinese government, such situations being covered by a special clause which is most explicit.[10] As for the new customs house at Woosung, it was set up temporarily on account of military uprisings and not for any purpose of double taxation, and as soon as the city was recaptured the old regulations would be followed as usual. If barbarian trade suffered any obstructions, there was nothing to prevent his taking them up with the Kiangsu Maritime Customs. In the institutes of the Heavenly Court, the Sovereign is exalted, the minister base, and there is no such thing as "minister plenipotentiary." Besides, the Canton Imperial Commissioner in charge of the affairs of all countries is an Imperial Commissioner and we cannot act independently or make importunate requests.

The said chief stubbornly held to his former statement and persistently made demands. Finally, at nightfall, he departed.

On the 22nd he sent a duplicate copy of his credentials, which are about the same as those Marshall presented last year, but made no mention of the request to go to the Yangtze River to trade. He also sent a communication, the phraseology of which is confused, the characters faulty, and the meaning ambiguous. The purport is the same as what he said, but he adds that if we will memorialize for approval (the Americans) would be willing to assist China in eradicating the rebels; otherwise he will memorialize his own government and take steps to act independently; that if he is unable to carry out his plan to completion, the blame will be with the Chinese government. He also asked that the new customs house at Shanghai be abolished.

Your slave humbly thinks that the American barbarians ordinarily speak respectfully but are taking advantage of the present situation to make demands; while they speak of "helping to put down rebellion," absolutely no faith can be placed in them. It is feared that the said barbarian made his proposal first and (if he succeeded) the English and French barbarians would try to imitate and excel him afterwards. The Yangtze River is a natural barrier, and if other countries are allowed to encroach on it it is certain to lead to disaster. On the other hand, of late the English barbarians at

---

9   *Vide* Treaty of Wang-hsia, Article 34.
10 *Vide* Treaty of Wang-hsia, Article 3.

Shanghai have repeatedly clashed with our forces; if the said barbarian's requests are not memorialized for him or even transmitted
by letter for him, it would certainly be an over-hasty decision, for
if he goes directly to the Yangtze there will be no way of bridling
him.

Your slave has considered this over and over and, in accord
with the Imperial Edict in re Marshall last year, can only order him
to return to Canton and wait for Yeh Ming-ch'en to investigate and
act, thus allowing the latter time to bridle and control him. Wu
Chien-chang has also been ordered to take up the Shanghai customs
question immediately, discuss it at length, and make a suitable
settlement, so as not to leave the various barbarians any pretext.
(IWSM. HF　8; 18b, 3-21, 10; cf. Wade's translation and notes, U.S.
Cong. 36:1, S. Ex. Doc, 30, p. 452-456. Wade records two paragraphs of the original not incorporated by the compiler of the IWSM.)

136. July 15, 1854. EDICT: Commends I-liang's Management of
McLane and Reiterates that Canton is the Only Place to Handle Foreign
Affairs.

Edict to the Grand Councillors. Previously, because the English
chief at Shanghai wantonly used coercion, Hsü Nai-chao had a weak
and compliant policy. He was degraded, and Yeh Ming-ch'en was
then directed to order the barbarian chief at Canton, in accord with
existing treaties, to see that the barbarian merchants at the various
ports did not penetrate the inland waterways. Now (We have) received I-liang's memorial stating that the American chief, Robert
McLane, has had an interview with the said governor general at
K'un-shan and presented his credentials and a communication; that
he insists on the twelve-year treaty revision so as to authorize
trade on the Yangtze River; and that he also used the fact that the
Shanghai Customs House had been moved to Woosung as a pretext
for asking that it be abolished. None of the various demands made
in his communication is mentioned in his own credentials. Moreover, his phraseology contains some haughty expressions. The
communication which I-liang sent refuted him with logic, without
any of Hsü Nai-chao's loss of dignity. It is simply that commercial
matters of the various countries have always reverted to the governor
general of Liang-kuang for exclusive control, so I-liang had the said
barbarian's credentials and communication copied and sent to Yeh
Ming-ch'en for disposal and ordered the said chief to leave K'un-
shan immediately and proceed to Kwangtung; he could not linger
there at will and delay investigation and settlement.

Yeh Ming-ch'en must needs rely strictly on the existing treaties
to instruct him in stern language and to nip his evil designs in the bud.

Today is received Hsü Nai-chao's memorial stating that in the
last few days the management of the Shanghai rebels and the bar-

barian chief has got completely out of hand. He also states that he
has agreed on a date to meet the said chief and "in case there is anything beneficial to China, he will not venture to hold to preconceived
ideas." This means that he has already made up his mind to give in
to him. The said governor has now been dismissed. Even though he
appeased the barbarian chief and was taken in by his deceit, order
I-liang and Chi-erh-hang-a to cut him [McLane] off sternly and not
be confused by his reckless arguments. Furthermore, order him
sent to Kwangtung to await Yeh Ming-ch'en's disposition.   (IWSM. HF
8; 22a, 5-22b, 9; cf. Wade's translation and notes, U. S. Cong. 36:1,
S. Ex. Doc. 30, p. 456-458; a final paragraph of the original memorial
given in Wade's translation has been deleted by the compiler of the
IWSM.)

137. August 8, 1854. MEMORIAL: I-liang Reviews in Detail his
Handling of McLane at Shanghai and at K'un-shan.
          Governor General of Liang-chiang I-liang memorializes. Your
slave I-liang went to K'un-shan and summoned the American chief,
Robert McLane, to an interview, so the (English) barbarian chief,
Bowring, ordered Wu Chien-chang to request an interview for him.
As this was not in accord with the treaty, it was not granted. Subsequently, on July 16, Wu Chien-chang reported that the English
barbarian consul, Alcock, had transmitted a letter from Bowring
requesting an interview with Your slave, and that Bowring would
bring state papers for presentation.
          On perusal, Your slave observes that the letter states that he
has credentials issued by his country and has important matters requiring a personal discussion with an Imperial Commissioner before
they can be produced; that previously, in dealing with the Imperial
Commissioner at Canton, he had been intimate and friendly but had
been repaid with discourtesy; that now mutual friendship is essential,
and if an Imperial envoy were named to discuss Chinese and foreign
affairs it would greatly strengthen amity. He made no demands.
          Your slave is of the opinion that since the Canton Imperial
Commissioner in charge of Barbarian Affairs is an Imperial envoy,
there was no call for importuning (Your Majesty) with his request,
and besides, at present China has nothing whatever to discuss with
any outside country. As to the manner in which the Imperial Commissioner treated the said chief, (we have) no way of knowing.
After all, China and the outside have been on friendly terms for a
long time and good faith should be maintained. As to the question
of etiquette, whether it should be intimate or formal is a matter
for public opinion to decide. The said chief charges others to be
polite; we trust he can treat others politely and not develop new
complications.
          Since the drafting of this reply, Wu Chien-chang has brought in

another communication from the American chief, Robert McLane, requesting an Imperial Commissioner to discuss matters of mutual benefit to China and the United States; if (this request) is not memorialized for him he intends to go to Tientsin with the English chief and present his views to the Court; as to the Shanghai customs, he has delegated the consul to make a suitable settlement with the Su-Sung-T'ai tao-t'ai; and hereafter he will certainly admonish the merchants of his country to abide faithfully by the treaty.

Your slave is of the opinion that all commercial matters of the five ports revert to the Canton Imperial Commissioner. Not only is Your slave not an Imperial Commissioner, but also the said chief still did not produce the original of his credentials, so there is no occasion to memorialize them. This arrangement is in conformity with the treaty, without any discrepancy. Otherwise, the whole situation has been explained to him minutely in person as follows.

> The said chief had said that he would not presume to go to Tientsin. How is it that barely twenty days later he talks about accompanying the English chief to Tientsin? Not only is this contrary to his previous statement; it is also a treaty violation. The said chief must needs consistently cooperate in reaching a satisfactory settlement of the customs and also instruct the merchants of his country hereafter to abide faithfully by the treaty for perpetual amity and for the benefit of his country. It is not necessary to go to Tientsin. If there are matters that require personal negotiation, he can go to Canton and await the Imperial Commissioner's disposition. In handling matters of foreign relations, Chinese officials rely solely on the treaties; anything outside the treaties is beyond their cognizance, so it is useless to hold them responsible.

This was put in writing to make it conclusive. Wu Chien-chang was also charged to point out the advantages and disadvantages and to make suitable explanations. At such time as the said tao-t'ai's report is at hand, the matter will be taken up again. (IWSM. HF 8; 26a, 7-27b, 9; cf. Wade's translation and notes, U. S. Cong. 36:1, S. Ex. Doc. 30, p. 458-460; three paragraphs of the original memorial included in Wade's translation have been omitted by the compiler of IWSM.)

138. August 8, 1854. EDICT: Anticipates McLane's Attempt to Come to Tientsin and Orders Him Sent back to Canton to Deal with Yeh Ming-ch'en.

Edict to the Grand Councillors. I-liang has memorialized on the present circumstances of handling barbarian affairs. He has received word from the American chief of his intention to accompany the English chief to Tientsin. The said barbarians rely on circumstances to press demands. Such is their habitual cunning. What they say is no more than empty words for experiment.

On this day (We) have instructed Yeh Ming-ch'en to maintain control
firmly and clearly and manage properly. The said governor general
will immediately order the barbarian chief to proceed to Kwangtung
to await disposition and avoid the development of complications.
(IWSM. HF 8; 27b, 10-28a, 3)

139. August 8, 1854. EDICT: Instructs Yeh Ming-ch'en to Hold
McLane and Bowring to the Existing Treaties and to Block Revision
Demands.
          Supplementary Edict. Previously, as the English and American
barbarian chiefs in Kiangsu demanded interviews with the governor
general and governor to impose their will on them, Yeh Ming-ch'en
was ordered to charge the said chiefs sternly to abide by existing
treaties, in order to nip their mischief in the bud.
          Now I-liang has memorialized the receipt of a state paper from
the English chief Bowring, to the effect that when he was at Canton
the Imperial Commissioner treated him discourteously; I-liang has
also received a communication from the American chief, Robert
McLane, stating that he intends to accompany the English chief to
Tientsin.
          Barbarians are inherently cunning and malicious. They know
perfectly well that all commercial affairs revert to Canton for
settlement but persist in going to other ports and making inordinate
demands. I-liang has been instructed to order the said chiefs back
to Canton to await a settlement.
          Order Yeh Ming-ch'en, in accord with previous Edicts, to de-
vise means to enlighten them, and to instruct them to abide faithfully by existing treaties. By no means is he to let them bring up
the twelve-year treaty revision or exercise their covetousness.
Furthermore, he is to explain that the port of Tientsin is so involved
in defense preparations and so crowded with troops that if the said
chiefs went there in defiance of orders, it is feared their ships
might suffer damage and that they would bring disaster upom themselves.
          As to the forms to be observed by the said governor general in
receiving the various chiefs, he must by all means maintain the old
regulations; he is not to make the least concession just because the
said barbarians request somewhat better treatment, lest he thereby
dispel their fear of us.
          Previously Yeh Ming-ch'en memorialized that he has learned
confidentially that the Russian barbarians have declared war on the
English barbarians and have even seized their cargo ships at Hong
Kong. Thus hard pressed, how can these barbarians turn around
and stir up trouble with China?
          In all probability these rumors are unfounded. In handling this
situation the said governor general must use extraordinary care; by

no means can he allow the fact that the Russian barbarians are fighting the English barbarians to throw him off his guard. Order him to memorialize all current developments by express courier. (IWSM. HF 8; 28a, '5-28b, 1; cf. Wade's translation and notes, U. S. Cong. S. Ex. Doc. 30, p. 461-462; a final paragraph of the original edict, preserved by Wade but not concerned with foreign affairs, has not been incorporated by the compiler of the IWSM.)

140. August 17, 1854. MEMORIAL: I-liang Reports McLane's Postponement of His Tientsin Trip and His Departure for Canton.
          Governor General of Liang-chiang I-liang memorializes. Via Chi-erh-hang-a comes a communication from Chief McLane addressed to Your slave stating:

> His proposal to go to Tientsin with the English chief has been temporarily abandoned. On July 29 he will proceed to Kwangtung. If there is difficulty in negotiating with Governor General Yeh he will still have to go to Tientsin and negotiate with the high officials of Peking. Around the intercalary seventh month (August 24-September 22) he will return to Shanghai.

          A letter has also been received from Chi-erh-hang-a, stating that he has learned that Chief McLane's ship has already set out and that it is reported that Bowring also will soon go to Kwangtung. Chi-erh-hang-a has repeatedly explained, but the said chiefs both say: "Whether or not Governor General Yeh will consent to an interview is still uncertain. If he again rejects our affairs which demand action, we shall still be compelled to memorialize asking that an Imperial Commissioner come to Shanghai to negotiate."
          Vermilion endorsement: Noted. (IWSM. HF 8; 28b, 10-29a, 8)

141. August 30, 1854. MEMORIAL: Chi-erh-hang-a Reports Bowring's Claim to Most-Favored-Nation Treatment, Citing the Cushing Treaty of Wang-hsia.
          [Memorial of Governor Chi-erh-hang-a of Kiangsu regarding his conversations with Sir John Bowring, in which he makes clear that England's claim for revision is based only on the clause in the American treaty, the benefit of which she claims by the most-favored-nation clause.]
          ... The said chief (Bowring) also said that,

> As the United States is offering to aid in suppression (of the rebellion), requesting access to the Yangtze for trade, and is also insisting on the payment of last year's customs deficit, his country desires a like settlement. Now public matters at Hong Kong are troublesome, and he proposes to return temporarily to set them all in order. If Governor General Yeh is not willing to see him personally he will as before be compelled to come to Shanghai. Probably he will be able to return in about forty days.

Your slave then told him that what the United States requested
had never been conceded. If what they said was reasonable, Governor General Yeh, when they went to Kwangtung would by no means
reject them or refuse to see them. If they relied on empty words to
leave and come back here, even if they had written proof of Governor
General Yeh's refusal to receive them, he (Your slave) still could
not memorialize for them. The said chief, on August 6, weighed
anchor and left port. . . .   (IWSM. HF 8; 31b, 2-9)

142. August 30, 1854. MEMORIAL: Chi-erh-hang-a Reports
McLane's Return to Canton and His Continued Insistence on Treaty Revision at Tientsin.
        Chi-erh-hang-a further memorializes. Since the opening of
Shanghai to trade, America's trade has been the largest and her
attitude has always been respectful and obedient. After the fall of
Shanghai the barbarian customs which the various countries are required to pay have been repeatedly demanded, and so far without
result. In the fifth month of this year (May 27-June 25) the American barbarian chief, Robert McLane, came to Shanghai to investigate trading conditions. The former Su-Sung-T'ai tao-t'ai, Wu
Ch'ien-chang, asked him on his behalf to urge payment. The said
chief said orally:

> The king of his country had sent him here pledged to do something of great
> benefit to China in order respectfully to reciprocate His Imperial Majesty's
> generous favor in opening the five ports to trade. Now he finds that China
> has long been under arms and her food supply is very short. The old and
> new customs which the merchants are required to pay must all be paid in
> full. He only asks their excellencies the governor general and governor to
> memorialize on his behalf, in the hope that His Imperial Majesty may know
> that Robert McLane's management is not erroneous and thereafter he can
> continue to exert himself on behalf of China.

Your slave and former Governor Hsü Nai-chao, although realizing
that he was using fine words to beguile us, still in this period of many
troubles could not but lead him to our advantage according to circumstances, in order to avoid outside annoyance and secure military
stores. Before long the said chief made the trip to Chen-chiang and
Nanking. When he returned to Shanghai he also went to K'un-shan to
meet the governor general. He presented his dispatch and other
papers and sought commercial changes. Since Governor General
I-liang ordered him, as before, to return to Kwangtung and await
investigation and action, the said chief returned to Shanghai. He said:

> Previously at Kwangtung he asked to see the governor general but to the
> last never had an interview. Thus there could be no negotiation whatever
> at Kwangtung and he was determined not to go there again. Now the Shang-
> hai region for several years has not been quiet and goods are tied up.

> He wished to transport various goods to Chen-chiang, Nanking, Hankow and
> other places for sale. If it should please His Imperial Majesty to com-
> mission an official with full powers to act as he saw fit and conclude an
> agreement, his country was willing to join the government forces and,
> starting at Shanghai, deal with one faction of the rebels and open up
> the Yangtze River. As long as Shanghai or other places had one rebel un-
> subdued, they dared not go to that point. But if the governor general of
> Liang-chiang would not memorialize his request for him, his country,
> rather than ruin its own trade, would independently enter the Yangtze.

Because his language was not complaisant as it had been when
he first came, Your slave and the former governor, Hsü Nai-chao,
ordered that word be transmitted to the said chief.

> In the original treaty, although there was the statement that after
> twelve years changes could be discussed, there was no mention of addition-
> al ports. As Chen-chiang and the other ports are places where the said
> barbarians were never allowed to go, it is extremely hard to comply. The
> military affairs of the Heavenly dynasty are matters in which the said
> barbarians can not participate. If the trade regulations of the five ports
> need to be changed, the governor general of Liang-kuang is the Imperial
> Commissioner in sole charge of barbarian affairs. They should therefore
> follow the personal advice of the governor general of Liang-chiang, re
> turn immediately to Kwangtung, and present their request for investi-
> gation and decision.

The said chief then said: "If he were in the end denied, both he
and the English chief Bowring would board the warships of their
countries and go to Tientsin to report the whole matter to the Court."
    While they were explaining back and forth, Hsü Nai-chao and Wu
Chien-chang both lost their posts. After Your slave came into office,
Chief McLane again presented a brief, asking that it be memorialized
for him. What it said was in general the same.
    As to the barbarian customs due, a paltry forty thousand taels
silver has been paid, (but) because Wu Chien-chang has left office,
there is again an attitude of hesitancy. Your slave told him (McLane)
that when the Heavenly Court installs an officer and imposes duties
all matters are charged to the man holding the office at the time.
Although Tao-t'ai Wu has left office, Prefect Lan has been deputed
to act temporarily in his place. The said barbarian duties are
primarily the amount the various merchants should have paid, and
they ought, as before, to be handled according to the original agreement. There cannot be the least equivocation because of the change
of personnel in the office. If payments can be made in full as computed, approximately the same as in past years, and also last
year's back customs be made up as per account, (we) shall certainly
memorialize His Imperial Majesty calling attention to this faithful
adherence to the treaty and unerring administration of affairs. As

to trading affairs, (we) have received an Imperial Edict to order him (McLane) to return to Kwangtung and await investigation and action without the least tarrying, needlessly dragging out the time. Then the brief which he presented was returned.

The said chief said further that if, on reaching Kwangtung, Governor General Yeh still would not see him personally, he would be impelled to come to Shanghai again and then go to Tientsin. He figured that he could reach here about September 15. He would order the various merchants to meet current customs payments due. The old duties to be made up would, he said, be subsequently investigated and reconsidered. The said chief set July 31 to weigh anchor and leave port.

Your slave ventures to observe that, although Chief McLane's language and actions, compared to those of the English chief, Bowring, were fairly respectful and obedient, his attitude is still inscrutable. The temper of the Kiangsu people is mild, without concern for the future. Interested parties say that what the English barbarians asked for at first was only Hong Kong, and then they became very arrogant, and five ports were opened to trade before they were satisfied. Now Chief McLane insists on the promise of revision after twelve years and wishes to establish ports along the Yangtze up to Hankow. In our position there is no way to stop him. It would be better to take advantage of circumstances to perfect a plan. If Your Majesty commissions a minister of long experience and great distinction to come and conclude suitable regulations, it will satisfy his request. Thus the circumstance of the American barbarians' respectful request to open the riverway, compared to the English barbarians' defiance of authority to get the five ports, appears to be different. Besides, the English and American barbarians being outwardly friendly and inwardly jealous, we can temporarily use the Americans to oppose the English. If, instead, there is a sudden rupture, they will take advantage of the time before Nanking is recovered to force their way into the Yangtze, and none of the matters will be brought up again for discussion. Our every move will be restricted by them. One mistake leads to another. The Yangtze will be an additional great sorrow.

Your slave considers barbarians inconstant by nature. If we are lenient with them they hate and distrust one another; if we are importunate, they unite as one. For instance, the French and American barbarians originally were joined as one spirit in their war with England. Now because the Russian barbarians are at war, the French also join England against Russia. Their relations are still close.

Besides although there is no provision in the English barbarian treaty for revision after twelve years, there is the clause that should His Imperial Majesty extend any favors to other countries

the English should share them equally. The American barbarians'
inability to keep the English barbarians from entering the Yangtze
would be similar to inability of the English barbarians to prevent
the American barbarians from going to the five ports. As to the
situation of the Americans at Shanghai, although they did not give
aid to the rebels themselves, yet before their eyes the English barbarians were furnishing supplies, meddling, and variously causing
trouble, and they could not stop them. Taking advantage of China's
many difficulties (the Americans) seek to go up the Yangtze to trade.
Besides (McLane) said that if we did not memorialize for him asking
that an Imperially appointed high official be sent to investigate and
act, he would either go direct to the Yangtze or would accompany
the English chief to Tientsin.

At present he and the English chief have one after the other returned to Kwangtung. What they ask is also about the same. Are they
outwardly friendly and inwardly jealous or rather outwardly jealous
and inwardly friendly? Although Your slave is most stupid and extremely ignorant, by no means dare he be moved by promiscuous
argument to take a wolf into the house. But whatever his views, he
dare not but report them clearly beforehand according to the facts.

Vermilion endorsement: Noted. (IWSM. HF 8; 32b, 6-36a, 1)

143. October 7, 1854. MEMORIAL: Chi-erh-hang-a Reports that
McLane and Bowring Have Not yet Returned to Shanghai.

Governor of Kiangsu Chi-erh-hang-a memorializes. Previously
Your slave repeatedly memorialized on the status of English and
American barbarian trickery and respectfully received the Vermilion
endorsement: "Manage carefully and calmly but by no means be
coerced by them. In the case of the American chief, although he says
that on August 15th he will return to Shanghai, this is probably an
empty threat. Respect this."

Now August 15 has passed and there is as yet no indication of
the return of the said two chiefs. Because the barbarian chief
(consul) now at Shanghai sees our troops moving camp and attacking
rebels with repeated success while the rebels are still relying on the
barbarian houses for places of refuge, he really fears that our
troops will cross the moat in pursuit and cannot but make some complaint. While (the barbarians) have not yet become arrogant their
hearts are inscrutable. It remains only for Your slave to obey Imperial Edicts, remain calmly on guard, and curb them as occasions
arise, in the hope of avoiding the development of further complications

Vermilion endorsement: Noted. (IWSM. HF 9; 1a, 2-1b, 1)

144. October 15, 1854. MEMORIAL: Chi-erh-hang-a Reports the Arriv
of Bowring, Bourboulon, and McLane and Urges Negotiations at Shanghai.

Governor of Kiangsu Chi-erh-hang-a memorializes. It is humbly

noted that the English barbarian chief Bowring and the American barbarian chief Robert McLane during the fifth month (May 27-June 25)
came to Shanghai and at Your slave's office presented a brief asking
for the Imperial appointment of a high official to take charge of revising trading arrangements. Your slave returned the brief and,
obeying the Edict, ordered them to return to Kwangtung and wait for
Governor General of Liang-kuang Yeh Ming-ch'en to investigate and
act. Moreover, the said barbarians' various artifices have been
reported confidentially time and again. Then because the time expired and the said chiefs did not arrive, a separate report was made,
which is on record.

On September 28-29, just after the previous document had been
submitted, Chiefs Bowring and McLane and the French barbarian
chief Bourboulon[11] arrived with their ships in close order. On the
30th Your slave received them politely and inquired of their object
in coming. According to their statement, Chiefs Bowring and McLane
obeyed instructions and went to Kwangtung, and with Chief Bourboulon all sent notes to the governor general of Liang-kuang. Not
only did Governor General Yeh not meet them; Chief Bourboulon did
not even receive an answer. He (Yeh) merely notified Department
Magistrate Chang Ch'ung-k'o and District Magistrate Ch'en I-chih to
see the interpreters personally and tell them orally that Governor
General Yeh had not yet received Imperial instructions to handle the
matter of revision. The reply of Governor General Yeh subsequently
received by Chiefs Bowring and McLane said merely: "The lower
ministers of the Heavenly Court have no authority and can only
preserve the treaty faithfully. Matters of great concern must be
memorialized to request an Edict. Further, he has no authorization to memorialize for them." They waited a number of days
and left. So they had to come here for an interview. Now they intend to proceed to Tientsin to request an audience with His Imperial
Majesty and the Grand Secretaries in order to make a full statement.

In the brief previously presented the things requested were not
mentioned, but according to Chief Bowring's statement: "The twelve-
year period has expired. The provisions previously fixed are en-
entirely inadequate for our needs. " Further, according to the
statements of Chiefs McLane and Bourboulon: "At Hong Kong we
received orders from the kings of our countries to confer and act
with Bowring in all matters."

As the said chiefs had united as one and the situation was not
like that of the seventh month (July 25-August 24), Your slave replied:

The regulations originally concluded with the English barbarians were
nominally an agreement for perpetual amity and originally had no provision for revision after twelve years, and thus should be adhered to

---

11. The French minister was M. de Bourboulon, then at Macao.

> forever. Chief Bowring should not indulge in irrelevant talk. The
> American and French barbarians, although they had a twelve year re-
> vision agreement, made no mention of a separate conclusion of new
> regulations. If they wish to go to Tientsin, they must await a me-
> morial to His Imperial Majesty and (His) authorization before they
> can set out. Otherwise there would be nothing more than an interview
> with the brigade general and tao-t'ai of Tientsin, and as before they
> would have the trip for nothing. It is also possible to have their
> request presented in the previous brief, memorialized for them, and
> then respectfully to await Imperial decision.

The discussion lasted all day without any conclusion being reached.

On October 3, the said three chiefs, with the interpreter Walter
Medhurst, and four other persons came back for a meeting. ' According to their statement:

> The trip to Tientsin had already been memorialized to their respective
> kings. If His Excellency the Governor memorialized for them and His Im-
> perial Majesty again ordered them to return to Kwangtung and they still
> went to Tientsin, it would repudiate the orders of His Imperial Majesty;
> if they returned to Kwangtung, it would repudiate the orders of their
> own kings. It was really a dilemma.

Your slave further explained to them repeatedly. According to
their statement:

> If this time they received Imperial authorization for the appointment of
> two or three high ministers with large powers to come and negotiate,
> the advantages to China and foreign states would be substantial. If as
> before they were ordered to return to Kwangtung, they would certainly
> lose face. They would not immediately venture to raise other discussions,
> however, and would only report the circumstances of utter futility to
> the kings of their countries and await orders to act. What would happen
> thereafter would be difficult to predict. They had chosen October 9 to
> weigh anchor and go.

Your slave repeatedly explained, but the said chiefs were
stubbornly adamant and got up and left.

Your slave begs to observe that previously, when the said
chief presented his brief, he said orally that if they received the
Favor of an Imperial Commissioner assigned to a trading locality
and there were rebels in the place, they would certainly join in
exterminating and tranquilizing the rebels and would also order
the merchants to make up the back duties in order to provide
military stores. Although this cannot be implicitly believed, his
words were very cogent. When he arrived at Shanghai this time,
however, he avoided mention of it. Thus what he said about aiding authority and opposing rebellion was no more than a plan he

relied on to secure revision of the regulations. If they were to help
the rebels and oppose authority, now that the Yangtze is occupied by
rebels, what would prevent their taking the opportunity to act wantonly? However, in their going to Kwangtung, to Shanghai, and even to
Tientsin, they have always acted only after receiving Imperial orders.
It would seem that they may not be motivated by evil at all.

Considering these circumstances, if we do not somewhat gratify
their expectations, it is feared that they will take advantage of China's
many troubles and, using the back customs as financial support,
unite the strength of the various barbarians under a separate banner,
not accept control or pay customs, and find a pretext to take steps
toward independent action. This is certainly a proximate danger. If
at present they dare not display violent or oppressive action, it is because they have received the deep favor of nurture from our Dynasty,
and because their pledges are still ringing in our ears. Therefore,
they expressly beg for Imperial favor in order to show their own
respect and obedience. If they ask in vain, they will certainly concoct
other nefarious plans. As to the statement that they will memorialize
the kings of their countries and await orders to act, this would probably take half a year to accomplish.

Barbarians are by nature cunning and vicious. Judging from
previous experience they must get all they ask for before they stop.
In the American and French treaties there are twelve-year revision
clauses. In the English treaty there is the statement that should
favors be extended to other countries Englishmen shall share them
equally. Could not a high official be Imperially commissioned and,
together with the governor general of Liang-kuang, properly investigate and act? If their requests are permissible, nothing prevents our stooping to show magnanimity in granting what they ask; if
they are very perverse and extravagant, nothing prevents our refusing them in plain language and removing their covetousness. But
if, as before, we send them back to Kwangtung causing them to cross
land and sea, endure wind and wave, there will be no conclusion to
the discussion for a long time. The barbarian heart still will not be
appeased, and it is feared they will cause further trouble.

The brief previously presented and returned has been copied
entire for the record and, respectfully copied according to the
original, is now presented for Imperial inspection. (IWSM.HF 9;
1b, 2-4b, 1)

145. October 15, 1854. EDICT: Instructs Chi-erh-hang-a to Block
Tientsin Trip and Warns against an Allied Diversion up the Yangtze River.

Edict to the Grand Councillors. Chi-erh-hang-a has memorialized
that the barbarian chiefs of England, the United States, and France,
with their combined fleets, have arrived at Shanghai and firmly maintain that they intend to go to Tientsin. Previously, when the English

chief at Shanghai availed himself of a pretext to make demands, Chi-erh-hang-a refused him in appropriate language. Now Hsü Nai-chao has been deprived of his duties and replaced as governor by Chi-erh-hang-a with instructions to manage and curb properly. Subsequently, at K'un-shan the American chief presented credentials and a communication, and I-l'iang replied according to what is right. The said barbarian, seeing his error and failing for arguments, at every turn used going to Tientsin as a threat.

The previous two occasions of their coming to Tientsin resulted in nothing but failure and return. This time the English chief Bowring, the American chief Robert McLane, and the French chief Bourboulon, with combined fleets, have come to Shanghai and, stubbornly holding to their previous statement, demand changes in trade arrangements and say they wish to proceed to Tientsin. They set October 9 to weigh anchor. Do not the said chiefs know that the port of Tientsin is not navigable by large ships?

Besides, there is the statement that "if as before they are ordered to return to Kwangtung they will not immediately raise new arguments. This is the present condition of arrangements, and even the said barbarians can recognize it. Chi-erh-hang-a should immediately earnestly enlighten them and tell them that there is no advantage in coming to Tientsin; the labor of the voyage would be in vain. How can he hastily believe their insistent statements of expelling rebels and making up customs, and then say that they have no evil intentions? Moreover, he says "if we do not gratify their hopes they are sure to develop other nefarious plans... probably in half a year the matters can be arranged." Thus the said governor has profound confidence in them. He frankly says that "it is impossible not to grant what they ask." Then why does he also say that "if their requests are perverse and extravagant, there is nothing to prevent our refusing them in plain language"? The said governor is in personal charge of his province and cannot shift his responsibility of controlling the populace and expelling outsiders. But, unable to reduce them by arguments, he must await the Imperial appointment of a high official! Of what further use are you governors general and governors to Us?

The said governor also says "if they were ordered as before to return to Kwangtung, for a long time there would be no settlement; the said barbarians' hearts are not yet appeased and in the end it might cause trouble." This is plainly requiring that "We must grant their requests and then it will be all right." What kind of language is this that the said governor has finally uttered? On seeing the memorial We were infuriated.

Looking through the said barbarian communication there is the utmost praise for the cordial treatment of the Shanghai officials and there is also the admission that the customs tao-t'ai discussed the revision of the rules with the various consuls. Thus in this

matter of the barbarians, Wu Chien-chang's long participation in
their plans was greatly depended upon, and so in the various affairs
memorialized by the said governor he must have been either imposed
on by others or deceived by them. The said tao-t'ai has long since
been arrested and cannot as before be allowed to interfere in military affairs and cause obstruction to action.

As to the trip of the said barbarians on October 9, perhaps it
can be stopped. As before, let Chi-erh-hang-a manage according
to circumstances, show favor by conciliating and pacifying, and,
prevent the further development of wanton ideas by breaking their
dominating spirit. This will be satisfactory.

If they have started, it is feared that in their demoniac cunning
they will "say east and go west." At this time of many troubles on
the Yangtze, let T'o-ming-a, Hsiang Jung, and I-liang give strict
orders to the various officials in charge of troops along the (Yangtze)
River to make secret barricades in the section of the Yangtze below
Ch'en-shan Barrier, to guard the mouth of the river and not let the
barbarian ships enter unauthorizedly and make illicit alliances with
the rebels. If they should spy about the mouth of the river, they can
by no means engage them on slight provocation. They must devise
means of setting up barriers and not allow them to pass in and out
freely as they have been doing.

I-liang is now at Ch'ang-chou   Let him as before confer with
Chi-erh-hang-a on means of controlling and curbing, in order to
avoid later regrets and satisfy the hearts of the people. As to the
Tientsin situation, orders have been issued notifying Chihli to
make full preparation. (IWSM.HF 9; 4b, 2-5b, 10)

146. October 15, 1854. EDICT: Alerts Tientsin Military Officials
Against Possible Aggressive Action by the British, French, and
Americans.

Additional Edict. Chi-erh-hang-a has memorialized that "the
barbarian chiefs of England, the United States, and France want to
go together to Tientsin to revise the treaties. The said governor
has repeatedly explained to them and is unable to stop them." (We)
have secretly ordered Wen-ch'ien and Shuang-jui, if the said barbarians arrive, on the one hand immediately to send an express
memorial, on the other, to notify Kuei-liang and to discuss means
of properly explaining to them. When Chi-erh-hang-a sent his
report he was still uncertain whether he could stop the said barbarians before they weighed anchor. At this time the important
place is the provincial capital [i.e., Pao-ting] and the said governor
general need not necessarily hasten to Tientsin. Wen-ch'ien is very
competent in ordinary management of defense but in barbarian affairs
may not yet have become well versed. In 1850 the barbarian Walter

Medhurst came to Tientsin. Some of the officers present at that time must be in the provincial capital.

Let one or two carefully chosen, competent officers be sent to Tientsin, under pretense of other business, and, together with Wen-ch'ien, discuss in advance defense measures. These are secret precautions prior to the events. At this time when the environs of the capital are not yet quiet, there cannot be the least confusion to give rise to incidents. Furthermore, as occasion demands, let deputies be sent to Tientsin to investigate the situation and send express memorials in accord with the facts. Let the original memorial and the brief presented by the said barbarian both be copied and sent for perusal. (IWSM.HF 9; 6a, 2-6b, 2)

147. October 15, 1854. EDICT: Instructs Tientsin Officials to Recruit "Barbarian Experts" to Assist in Dealing with the British, French, and Americans.

Additional Edict. Chi-erh-hang-a has memorialized that the barbarian chiefs of England, the United States, and France have one after the other arrived at Shanghai saying that they wish to revise the treaties. Because the governor general of Liang-kuang was unwilling to see them, they fixed October 9 to proceed to Tientsin. Chi-erh-hang-a has repeatedly explained. The said chiefs are stubbornly adamant, and under the circumstances it is hard to stop them.

The said chiefs since the fifth month (May 27-June 25), at Kwangtung and Shanghai, have repeatedly talked of revising the treaty. The said governor general and governor did not consent, so finally they declared their intention of going to Tientsin. This was largely empty threatening, and it was not yet certain that they would dare to carry it out. But this time the three chiefs are united as one. Chi-erh-hang-a has used the expression, "under the circumstances it is hard to stop them." There is no assurance that they will not come direct to Tientsin, and we cannot do otherwise than secretly take precautions.

Let Wen-ch'ien and Shuang-jui make rigorous and secret defense preparations at all the land approaches and port fortresses. If the said barbarian ships arrive at the port, on the one hand immediately memorialize with great haste and secrecy, and on the other notify Kuei-liang and together discuss means of admonition. Take care not to make any stir which would arouse the fears and the suspicions of the residents.

When the said barbarians come, if it is necessary to meet them, there is no call for either overbearing or servile deportment. Explain to them in proper language and stop their covetous desires. Tientsin is not primarily a place where the said barbarians should come.

Previously, the English barbarian Walter Medhurst[12] came from Kiangsu. Let Wen-ch'ien and the others consult thoroughly according to circumstances with the local officials of the said place who had personal contact with him in this affair, as to how they should be disposed and how repulsed, and memorialize clearly what they have done. As to what Chi-erh-hang-a requested in his memorial, they can by no means go so far as to carelessly discuss (terms) with the said barbarians for fear of becoming their tool.

Let Chi-erh-hang-a's original memorial as well as the brief presented, both be copied and sent for perusal. This memorial was sent October 4, before the said barbarians had weighed anchor. If the said governor was finally able to stop them, after ten days there must be a memorial reporting it. At that time further instructions will be issued. By no means let this be noised abroad beforehand. (IWSM.HF 9; 6b, 4-7a, 10)

148. October 17, 1854. MEMORIAL: Tientsin Military Officials Report the Arrival of Foreign Ships off Ta-ku Bar.

Ch'ang-lu Salt Controller Wen-ch'ien and Tientsin Garrison Brigade General Shuang-jui memorialize. (We) hastened to the port to investigate and manage the (possible arrival) barbarian ships. On the sixteenth of the present month we received the report of Provisional Colonel of Ta-ku Hung Chih-kao stating that according to the information of agents he had sent out, in the afternoon (3-5) of the fifteenth two strange looking ships arrived outside the bar of the Lan River and orders were sent to the coastal officials to take rigorous measures of defense. (We) also received a report from Acting Sub-prefect in charge of Coastal Defense Ch'iao Pang-che stating: "They are barbarian ships and the said sub-prefect has personally gone to the bar outside the Lan River to ascertain clearly and will make another report later."

Just when Your slave was considering going to the port in person to investigate, he received via the Grand Councillors an Imperial Edict stating that "Chi-erh-hang-a has memorialized that the barbarian chiefs of England, United States, and France have one after another arrived at Shanghai. Respect this." Your slave Wen-ch'ien, together with Tientsin Tao-t'ai Ch'ien Hsin-ho, set

---

12 H. B. M. steamer *Reynard*, with Walter H. Medhurst, Jr., interpreter of the Shanghai British consulate, aboard, visited the mouth of the Peiho in June, 1850, and delivered a letter from Lord Palmerston addressed to the Emperor of China. The *Reynard* did not proceed up the river to Tientsin but visited Shanhaikwan before returning to Shanghai and Hong Kong. *Chinese Repository*, v. 19, p. 344; 403.

out the same day from Tientsin and proceeded to the port of Ta-ku to investigate. If these really were the British, American and French barbarian ships, Your slaves had only respectfully to obey the Imperial Edict, take rigorous and secret precautions, watch the movements of the said barbarians, and take such action as the situation demanded. While devising means to explain to them, (they would) refuse them in explicit language. As soon as they arrive at the port they will investigate conditions, make confidential reports according to circumstances, and memorialize asking for an Imperial Edict to follow.

But the Lien-chen rebels are besieged and are hard pressed. The Tientsin defenses are also of vital importance. Now Ta-nien, the brigadier general of Tu-shih-k'ou whom we memorialized had been retained in Tientsin and sent to take charge of the Ko-ku defenses, has been recalled to the Tientsin district. We have ordered the soldiers and volunteers under his command to be stationed at Shao-chih-k'ou garrison for defense. As to the prefectural capital, if a critical situation develops, Your slave Wen-ch'ien has ordered the prefect of Tientsin to take advantage of his proximity to ask T'an T'ing-hsiang, prefect of the Metropolitan Prefecture and stationed at Tientsin to examine the rice, to advise and manage.

Vermilion endorsement: We have read the memorial and understand the situation. The circumstances of management are to be quickly memorialized in full. Let Wen-ch'ien quickly report this situation in a secret letter to Seng-ko-lin-ch'in for his information. (IWSM. HF 9; 9a, 3-9b, 10)

149. October 18, 1854. MEMORIAL: Tientsin Military Officials Report Preliminary Conversations with Medhurst and Parker.

Ch'ang-lu Salt Controller Wen-ch'ien and Tientsin Garrison Brigade General Shuang-jui memorialize. After humbly dispatching the confidential memorial, Your slaves set out from Tientsin and travelled day and night to Ta-ku. In the fourth watch (1-3 a. m.) of the 17th, at Ko-ku while en route, they received a report from Colonel Hung Chih-kao of Ta-ku stating that First Captain Ch'en K'o-ming and Provisional Sub-prefect Ch'iao Pang-che, whom he sent out to sea to make inquiries, returning in the afternoon (5-7) of the 16th had reported orally:

They saw on the ocean English and American ships, three large and two small, carrying altogether three hundred and several tens of men. The first captain and others went on board a large vessel and saw the English interpreter Walter Medhurst and the American interpreter Parker, and inquired their object in coming. According to their statement. "Because goods at the five ports were hard to dispose of, we have had a conference with Governor Chi [i.e., Chi-erh-hang-a] to discuss it. As he was not in charge of barbarian affairs, he ordered us to go to Kwangtung for settlement. We then went to Kwangtung and to our surprise Governor Yeh [i.e., Yeh Ming-ch'en] would not even give us an interview. It seemed that in these circumstances our only alternative was to proceed to Tientsin. If the Tientsin officials also evade responsibility we will go to T'ung-chou and to Peking, pay our respects to the ministers of the Heavenly Court and arrange for them to memorialize on our behalf."

The captain and others replied that they should wait and request a high official to come to investigate and act. The said barbarians finally agreed to wait; they also produced passports of their respective countries. After the said officers returned to the port, to their surprise Walter Medhurst suddenly appeared in a small boat. The captain and others again went on board his boat and repeatedly urged him to stop, but he would not obey respectfully. The said barbarian small boat sailed more than half a *li* beyond the fort and anchored.

The complete report is at hand.

On hearing this news, Your slaves were very much perturbed and with flying speed reached Ta-ku port in the early morning (5-7). They first sent Ch'en K'o-ming to see Walter Medhurst and tell him that the high officials had both arrived and to order him to take his boat back and await investigation and disposal. The said barbarian then agreed to a meeting in the forenoon (9-11). Your slaves feared that, although Walter Medhurst's oral statement that "they intended to go beyond the fort by sea and river directly to Tientsin" was an empty boast to make a show, we could not but take rigorous precautions. We sent Provisional Sub-prefect Ch'iao Pang-che to the Hsin-ch'eng district to determine the narrow places in the river, first to use bamboo wattle and iron chains placed crosswise in the river channel and then to engage native ships to build bridges in the river and mount guns. We ordered defenses prepared at Ko-ku to guard against them. If and when the said small barbarian ship arrived they were not to allow it to pass the bridges and proceed.

In 1850, when Your slave Shuang-jui was provisional brigade general of Tientsin, he had an interview with Walter Medhurst, and well knows that the said barbarian's trickery is extraordinary. Therefore, it was mutually agreed that Your slave Shuang-jui, with Provisional Tao-t'ai of Tientsin Ch'ien Hsin-ho, would go first for a personal interview with Walter Medhurst. Later, when they had agreed on the time for an interview, Wen-ch'ien would also meet him in order to show him some discrimination in procedure. If there were occasion for breaking off (negotiations) we could then indicate a change [in personnel, i.e., shift the responsibility; "pass the buck"].

The said barbarians, Walter Medhurst and Parker, accompanied by two barbarian officials and fourteen barbarian soldiers, each carrying a rifle, came aboard two small punts for an interview before the fort. Your slave Shuang-jui, with Ch'ien Hsin-ho, inquired why they came to Tientsin. What the said barbarians answered was about the same as what Captain Ch'en K'o-ming reported. Then we repeatedly explained to them, giving notice that Tientsin.is not the place to handle matters of barbarian trade; if there were matters that required discussion, they should as before return to Kwangtung and await investigation and disposal. The said interpreters again said, "We have repeatedly gone to Kwangtung and Governor General Yeh makes unreasonable excuses; under these circumstances we accomplished nothing and could not but come to Tientsin to state our case."

After repeated arguments over a period of several hours they were again told that the governor general of Chihli had never had charge of barbarian affairs, but if they made a factual statement of their case, there was now at Tientsin an Imperial Defense Commissioner who might consider transmitting their request. But it would be necessary first to withdraw away from the fort the punts on which they first came. Then it would be possible to ask for an interview for them. The said interpreters then took the punts down below the fort.

Your slave Shuang-jui discovers that the said barbarians, on this trip to Tientsin, are very earnest in manner and speech, somewhat different, it would seem, from 1850. As to how they should be handled, he humbly looks to the Emperor's instructions for guidance. (IWSM.HF 9; 10a, 1-11b, 9)

150. October 18, 1854. EDICT: Orders the Local Officials at Tientsin to Turn the Foreigners back and to Strengthen their Military Defenses.

Edict to the Grand Councillors. Wen-ch'ien and Shuang-jui have memorialized on the circumstances of their hastening to the port to investigate and dispose of the barbarian ships. According to the memorial, the English and American barbarians named in Chi-erh-hang-a's original memorial were still not the principal chiefs of the said two countries. They were interpreters sent ahead to come and feel the way and observe our attitude and then later make demands. This was unquestionably their purpose. Shuang-jui and Ch'ien Hsin-ho first went to meet them, intentionally leaving Wen-ch'ien behind in order to have grounds for refuting (the barbarians).

This management has some merit. If our troops first opened fire it is gravely feared difficulties would develop. But the port fortifications and the troops in the city should both make secret preparations in advance. If there is the slightest display of weakness it is sure to augment their desire to use force. Otherwise things will be hard to manage. The said barbarians are tyrannical, proud, and cunning. During the summer at Shanghai they destroyed our cantonment and also wished to lead the Shanghai rebels to another place. They have by no means the intention of making respectful and obedient requests. Even in their repeated statements about revising treaties, they do not point out in detail the things they have in mind and wish to say; they go so far as to request the appointment of an Imperial Commissioner invested with an official seal authorizing discretionary powers. Their objectives are still more inscrutable. Wen-ch'ien and the others in their meetings with them must break their vainglorious spirit and stop the beginnings of their cunning arguments. By no means can they lightly acquiesce.

What they say of intending to go to T'ung-chou is clearly an empty phrase to cause alarm. By no means allow yourselves to be coerced by them. Such evasion of issues as Chi-erh-hang-a's entertaining their requests and then temporarily restraining them by such statements as "memorializing on their behalf requesting an Edict," (We) will not allow to be uttered by you. In the ninth month (June 25-July 25), I-liang at K'un shan refused the American chief's requests. His language was very proper. Wen-ch'ien and the others, then, can in general imitate him and devise suitable phraseology. First find out the said barbarians' real object in coming, then you can induce them to yield according to circumstances. If you merely order them to return to Kwangtung and are still unable to expose their secrets and leave them as bewildered as lost (souls), then, although the said barbarians acquiesce, it will not be an end of the matter. Wen-ch'ien and the others can surely appreciate this idea.

Building ships and mounting guns in inland waters, as well as placing successive barricades, are all vitally important. The Tientsin Volunteers are famous for their discipline and there is no objection to letting the said barbarians know that once they enter the interior, not only will there be nothing gained but rather they will suffer loss. Find out the said barbarians' real situation. Wen-ch'ien and the others, no matter how they manage, will confidentially and quickly memorialize for (Our) information. Let I-liang's memorial be copied and sent for perusal.   (IWSM. HF 9; 11b, 10-12b, 8)

151. October 18, 1854. MEMORIAL: Kuei-liang Reports on the

Paucity of Experienced Diplomats Available at Tientsin.
        Governor General of Chihli Kuei-liang memorializes. It is
noted that of the various officers in charge of barbarian affairs in
1850, besides Ch'ien Hsin-ho and Shuang-jui there are also the
present Provisional Commander-in-chief of Chihli, Chang Tien-
yüan, and Substantive Tientsin Tao-t'ai Chang Ch'i-yüan, but these
two officials are now at military camp, just at a critical stage of the
fighting, and it was impolitic suddenly to recall them. Of the various other officers, some have died, some are of rather low rank,
serving merely as runners, and could hardly be appointed to important posts. Whether or not the said barbarians' proposed journey
to Tientsin can be stopped is still uncertain. Now when the metropolitan area is still not pacified it is even more important that there
not be the least confusion. Your slave proposes, as before, to ask
to have Ch'ien Hsin-ho and Shuang-jui secretly make arrangements
with Wen-ch'ien, immediately send a flying report, and then deliberate and act.
        Vermilion endorsement: Now that barbarian ships have arrived
at the port, you must send in reports. Above all, manage with composure; there cannot be any panic. Although for the defense of nearby places there are Hung Chih-kao, Ta-nien, Shuang-jui, and others,
if there are places where more should be sent, arrange secretly in
advance. Hung Chih-kao, although (he served) in T'ai-wan (Formosa)
many years, is, it is feared, superannuated. (IWSM. HF 9; 12b,
9-13a, 8)

        152. October 18, 1854. EDICT: Reviews China's Recent Foreign
Policy and Orders I-liang's Memorial Sent to Tientsin for Guidance.
        Edict to the Grand Councillors. On this day We received Kuei-
liang's memorial on the various aspects of management to prevent
the barbarian ships coming to Tientsin, in accord with Imperial
Edicts. Endorsement has been made on the memorial ordering
that, while remaining calm, he must also make preparations in
advance, deliberate carefully, and act according to circumstances.
        (We) have just received the express memorial of Wen-ch'ien
and others:

> After the English and American ships arrived at the port of Ta-ku, Captain
> Ch'en K'o-ming and others went on board to inquire fully about the situation.
> Unexpectedly, the English.chief Walter Medhurst suddenly boarded a small
> boat and came inside the port, going more than half a *li* beyond the fort.
> Subsequently, Shuang-jui and Ch'ien Hsin-ho argued back and forth with
> him. The said chief finally withdrew his punt from the fort and anchored.

        The said barbarians at Shanghai and K'un-shan repeatedly made

requests which were not complied with. Now, on the pretext that
Kwangtung was unwilling to act in their behalf, they come simultaneously to the North. After all, what they want has not been clearly
expressed. Besides, since the rebels invaded the Yangtze (valley)
last year, these barbarians have from time to time gone to Nanking
and Chen-chiang and consorted with the rebels. The inscrutability of
their hearts has become apparent.

Now Wen-ch'ien first sent Shuang-jui and Ch'ien Hsin-ho to meet
them. When the barbarian punt had withdrawn, they interviewed the
said chiefs; the reason for this was observance of protocol. But at
this interview it is not known whether or not the said barbarians hung
their heads and submitted and whether or not Wen-ch'ien alone was
equal to the occasion. The said barbarians' statement that "should
the Tientsin officials again shift their responsibility they would go to
T'ung-chou" cannot be readily credited as fundamentally true. Still
we cannot but take precautions.

On this day (We) have specially ordered Wen-ch'ien and others
on the one hand to make clear to them the advantages and risks and
explain the whole situation, by no means to show weakness and further
induce the said barbarians' spying tendencies; and on the other hand,
within and without the Tientsin area, to give strict orders to land
and water forces to increase their defense preparations, so that
there will be nothing the said barbarians can covet. This will be
satisfactory.

As the matter of the Pao-ting defenses is of vital importance,
Kuei-liang will scrupulously adhere to previously received Edicts and,
as occasions arise, send capable officers to assist in the transactions, and as before send flying word to Wen-ch'ien to be handed
down to the said garrison commander and tao-t'ai to stop them in
explicit terms. It is important not to cause the development of
further troubles. I-liang in his previous meeting with the barbarian
chief at K'un-shan used words that were very appropriate. Let the
original memorial be copied and sent for perusal. (IWSM. HF 9;
13a, 9-14a, 8)

153. October 19, 1854. EDICT: Orders the Mukden Military Officials
to Put the Defenses of South Manchurian Ports in Order.

Edict to the Grand Councillors; special Edict to Mukden Military
Governor Ying-lung. Yesterday (We) received Wen-ch'ien's memorial on the barbarian ships going to the port of Tientsin. Orders have
been issued to Kuei-liang and the said salt commissioner carefully to
devise defense preparations; it is above all important to use explicit
language to refuse them. Previously (We) received Chi-erh-hang-a's
memorial: "the English, American, and French barbarians set out
at the same time from Shanghai to come north." At present the ships
arrived at Tientsin are only those of England and the United States,

three large and two small, with not more than three-hundred-odd men.   Their object in coming is none other than the desire to revise existing commercial treaties.   This can by no means be done.   (We) trust that Wen-ch'ien and the others will certainly be able to manage properly in accord with the Edicts.

But the said barbarians are following a treacherous course and their wanderings are unusual.   Once Wen-ch'ien has exhorted them to return there may be a succession of ships combining to come north.   Altogether it will be hard to guarantee that they will not rush up the coast.   The various strategic positions of Mukden, Chin-chou, and Shan-hai-kuan should all have their defenses set up beforehand in the hope of being prepared.

Let the said military governor, military deputy lieutenant general of the Metropolitan Prefect, and others rigorously and secretly take precautions in all the various ports under their jurisdiction, and also as occasions arise delegate carefully chosen subordinates to make very thorough secret inquiries and memorialize confidentially according to the facts.   But there cannot be the least display of confusion, lest popular feeling become nervous and suspicious.   As to Teng-chou, on the Shantung coast, (We) have also ordered Ch'ung-en carefully to make thorough preparations.   (IWSM. HF 9; 14a, 9-14b, 9)

---

154.   October 19, 1854.   EDICT: Alerts the Military Officials on the Northern Coast of Shantung against Possible Foreign Attack.
Additional Edict.   Yesterday (We) received Wen-ch'ien's memorial that English and American ships had arrived at the port of Ta-ku.   An Edict has been issued ordering Kuei-liang and the said salt controller rigorously and secretly to set up defenses and carefully manage.   But according to what the said salt controller memorializes, the ships of the said barbarians which have reached Tientsin are five, large and small, with some three-hundred-odd men.   It is hard to guarantee that no other barbarian ships will successively arrive.   Besides, after Wen-ch'ien has earnestly explained things, if they immediately hoist sail and go southward, what requests they will make for foodstuffs and such at the ports at which they call, cannot yet be known.

Let Ch'ung-en quickly send strict orders to the military and civil officers of the port of Teng-chou to lead out their troops and make preparations in advance; he must take pains to place successive barricades and not allow the barbarian ships to seize an opportunity to enter.   In this time of many troubles (We) are still more apprehensive of their devilish trickery of "saying east and going west."   They know well that the port of Tientsin is not navigable to large ships, yet they might linger in other places

and not go away, relying on exigencies to make demands. The said
governor, without giving any indication, should order all those in
his jurisdiction to take rigorous and secret precautions. There cannot be the least confusion lest the popular mind become suspicious.
Moreover, first thoroughly investigate the current conditions of the
port and quickly send an express memorial.   (IWSM. HF 9; 15a, 1-10)

155. October 20, 1854. MEMORIAL: Tientsin Officials Report on
Their Second Conversation with Medhurst and Parker at Ta-ku.
     Ch'ang-lu Salt Controller Wen-ch'ien and Tientsin Garrison
Brigade General Shuang-jui memorialize. It is respectfully noted
that on the 17th (October), Your slaves, Shuang-jui and Tientsin
Tao-t'ai Ch'ien Hsin-ho, had a preliminary interview with the English
interpreter Walter Medhurst and the American interpreter Parker.
On the 18th, Your slave Wen-ch'ien and others all met the said barbarians in front of the forts for an interview. Your slave Wen-ch'ien
informed them that Tientsin is not a treaty port and asked them why
they had come there unauthorized. The said barbarian, Walter
Medhurst, said:

> As there were commercial matters which must be changed, they had gone. to
> Kwangtung and requested interviews with His Excellency Yeh [Yeh Ming ch'en],
> who never did meet them; they had then gone to Shanghai and had seen His
> Excellency Chi [Chi erh-hang-a], telling him plainly that they intended to
> go to Tientsin. His Excellency Chi had repeatedly tried to stop them and
> urged them to hand over the brief which they had prepared, that he might
> memorialize it for them. They were apprehensive of delay, so they had come
> directly to Tientsin, and requested us to memorialize His Imperial Majesty
> for permission for the two ministers, Bowring and McLane, to come to Peking,
> meet the ministers of the Heavenly Court, and state the whole case for
> treaty revision. Actually this would benefit both China and foreign
> countries. If we were not willing to memorialize for them, they would have
> no alternative but to return immediately to the South and report in person
> to the sovereigns of their respective countries, and the previously es-
> tablished "Treaty of Perpetual Amity" would have become waste paper.

Your slave replied:

> All commercial matters were determined at that time in Kwangtung and al-
> though they were not thoroughly understood in these parts, he did know
> that they were agreed to in perpetuity and should always be followed, so
> how could they ask to have them changed? Even the twelve-year treaty of the
> Americans had not yet expired. Besides, on their return to Shanghai from
> Canton, when His Excellency Chi offered to memorialize their prepared brief
> for them, they should have handed it over to him and awaited action on it.
> What was the necessity of proceeding to Tientsin with importunate requests? As
> for the request for permission for the ministers, Bowring and McLane, to go
> to Peking to state their case, not only was there no provision for it, but
> also the present officials could not even memorialize it for them.

The said chiefs then said that what they wanted was not necessarily to have Tientsin opened to trade but rather, since they had a
host of utterly insufferable things to complain of, they wanted to go
to Peking to state their case.

It is noted that Your official, Governor General of Chihli Kuei-
liang, transmitted various memorials on the management of barbarian affairs in Kiangsu province, with secret instructions to Acting
Tientsin Tao-t'ai Ch'ien Hsin-ho that, in case the barbarians came
to Tientsin, he was to observe the treaties faithfully and act accordingly.

With this authorization, Your slaves argued with them over and
over and tried repeatedly to make them see the light, but the said
barbarians were consistently evasive and stubbornly demanded a
memorial. If we had not allowed them some latitude and agreed to
memorialize for them, while the said barbarians would not have
ventured to proceed directly (upriver), it was feared that they
would hoist sail for the South and then use (our refusal) as a pretext
(for retaliation).

In such an important matter, Your slaves would never dare to
cling to preconceived ideas. However, the barbarian nature is
extraordinarily malicious and they could not but guard against the
development of future trouble. There was no alternative but to
make a straightforward report of the facts. (Could not Your
Majesty) either name an Imperially Commissioned Minister or order
Your governor general, Kuei-liang, to go to Tientsin and issue explicit instructions for them to return to some specific place and
await investigation and settlement?   (IWSM.HF 9; 15b, 1-16b, 8;
cf. Wade's translation and notes, U. S. Cong. 36:1, S. Ex. Doc. 30,
p. 463-465.

156. October 20, 1854. MEMORIAL: Tientsin Officials Supplement
their Report on the Medhurst and Parker Conversations.

Wen-ch'ien et al. further memorialize. There is noted on
perusal of the original memorial of Governor of Kiangsu Chi-erh-
hang-a, the statement, "the three chiefs are united as one," but the
barbarian ships at the port of Ta-ku are only those of England and
America. There is a report that the French ship came part way,
encountered storms, and was wrecked, but whether this is
accurate or not there is no way of knowing.

As to the interview itself, of the items brought up by the barbarians, Medhurst himself initiated the great majority, while the
other three did little more than second his motions. Sizing up the
situation, Medhurst is the most crafty. Although they said they
came to Tientsin for treaty revision and to present a bill of
grievous wrongs, what goes on in their minds is inscrutable; there
is no assurance that they are not hiding some evil plan and are

intentionally picking a quarrel with us.

Yesterday they wanted to come ashore for a walk, but Your slaves informed them that as the Tientsin volunteers were very numerous and the temper of the people violent, there might be some misfortune and then their friendly purpose would be lost. The said barbarians thereupon desisted.

Twenty soldiers have now been sent in a small boat alongside the barbarian ships, nominally for their protection but actually to watch their every move. But the native craftiness of barbarians has many facets and if, after braving the seas to come here, they are sent back to Canton without accomplishing anything definite, they would have had their whole trip for naught and will certainly be disappointed. Even if, when they sail south, they dare not make any great display of violence, some secret plan of collusion will almost inevitably be hatched.

Your slave has received Imperial favor bounteously and now in this troublous time he still cannot but bare his heart and estimate the whole situation thoroughly.

It is noted that barbarian ships have long traded at Shanghai. Moreover, these barbarians have said that they have the greatest respect for the governor general and governor of Kiangsu. Could not an Imperial order be sent to Kiangsu for the governor general and governor to make a suitable investigation and settlement, possibly sending another high official there to assist them in conferences and negotiations? Then Your slave, in respectful accord with Imperial Edicts, could order them back South to wait, leaving the said barbarians with nothing for a pretext; nor would this occasion any further proposals. (IWSM. HF 9; 16b, 9-17b, 5; cf. Wade's translation and notes, U. S. Cong. 36:1, S. Ex. Doc. 30, p.466-467; a formal paragraph at the end, included by Wade, has been omitted by the compiler of IWSM.)

157. October 20, 1854. MEMORIAL: Chi-erh-hang-a Reiterates the Importance of the Shanghai Merchants and of the Back Customs Issue.

Governor of Kiangsu Chi-erh-hang-a memorializes. As to the barbarian chiefs of England, the United States, and France coming with a combined fleet to Shanghai, refusing reasonable instruction and insisting on proceeding to Tientsin, Your slave has respectfully submitted an express memorial which is on record. After presenting the memorial, he humbly recalls that the said barbarian chiefs' expenses for all activities are drawn entirely from the merchants. But the said barbarian merchants will not meet their demands without orders from the king. The said king has known how to avoid trouble and sympathizes with the merchants. But the chiefs who are invested as commissioners or admirals consistently fan the flames when trouble arises and turn it to their own advantage.

Still, without asking instructions from the king they dare not make any wanton moves. Therefore, they had to find a pretext for a quarrel to rouse their king's ire. Only thus could they get what they wanted. The said chiefs' statement that "on this expedition to Tientsin if they received orders to return to Kwangtung they would certainly lose face and would have no alternative but to inform their respective kings and await orders," is patently juggling truth and falsity to get profit therefrom.

As to the back customs, last summer they agreed to devise means to hand them over. Then they postponed a settlement until they returned from Kwangtung. Now they do not make the slightest mention of it. Thus they are openly shielding the merchants' repudiation of the duties, while actually in secret they are luring the merchants with profit as a scheme for future extortion. Therefore, Su-Sung-T'ai <u>Tao-t'ai</u> Lan Wei-wen, who handled the matter, was ordered to ask the reason for their not being able to keep their word.

According to their reply:

> From September 7 of last year to February 9 of this year, the matter was managed by the former English chief Bonham. Chief Bowring originally proposed to devise means of clearing up the matter. Now we unexpectedly receive a letter in English saying that when Bonham went home he said personally that as the interior was in turmoil the various merchants all suffered serious losses. "The Shanghai commercial companies have all taken steps to protect themselves. The conditions of mutual intercourse are not satisfactory." The king of the said country was considerably displeased. Therefore he tore up and discarded the customs receipts handed over by the various merchants prior to February 9. The said chief, Bowring, regards Bonham's statement as not very reliable. He has memorialized his king that he will wait for orders to act upon, but it is essential that the barbarian merchants be allowed to import and export goods and that trade be kept open. Then the said chief will be able to manage.

Your slave again questioned this on the grounds that even if the customs due under Bonham's administration must await orders, for the customs due from February 10 to August 11, one day before the opening of the customs house, there was no possible pretext, and these should then be paid as computed.

He received the reply: "If, without waiting for orders from his king he proceeded to make a retroactive settlement, he really feared the merchants would be recalcitrant and it would actually cause waste and delay." His language was still respectful and obedient. Now on October 10 he has weighed anchor and left port.

On the whole, the back customs due are at the most one million (<u>taels</u>) and at the least seven or eight hundred thousand. If the country is short this amount it will be a great inconvenience. But on the other hand, if the said barbarians rely on this to prose-

cute their nefarious plans, it is still more to be feared that causes
of rupture will repeatedly arise.   The new customs will also cause
apprehension.   Apprising the circumstances and considering our
strength, Your slave is actually secretly worried.   Since there is
an agreement for revision in twelve years, should we not lead them
to our advantage according to circumstances, in the hope of removing troubles before they sprout?   (IWSM. HF   9; 17b, 6-19a, 2)

158.   October 19, 1854.   EDICT: Ch'ung-lun is Appointed as Deputy
Negotiator under Kuei-liang.

Edict to the Grand Secretariat.   The former Ch'ang-lu salt
controller, Ch'ung-lun, is ordered to report to Kuei-liang, for
service as a deputy.   (IWSM. HF   9; 19a, 3)

159.   October 19, 1854.   EDICT: Instructs Chi-erh-hang-a on the
Utilization of Ch'ung-lun's Services and the Necessity of Firmness with
the Foreigners.

Edict to the Grand Councillors.   Send this Edict to the governor
general of Chihli, Kuei-liang.   Formerly when English and American
ships sailed into Ta-ku, orders were issued and given Wen-ch'ien et
al., suitably to instruct (them) that there should be no ready acquiescence.   Now We have received the memorial of Wen-ch'ien and
Shuang-jui stating that on (October) 10th they had a personal interview
with the said barbarians.   The barbarian Medhurst spoke only of
commercial matters and the necessity of treaty revision but did
not state his real intentions in detail.   He did say that if they would
not memorialize for him he could only report back immediately to
his country and that the treaties previously agreed upon would have
become waste paper.

At this time Bowring et al. have not arrived at Tientsin.   Medhurst et al. are no more than linguists but still they dare to threaten
us with empty phrases.   Their deceitful nature can already be clearly
seen.   Although Wen-ch'ien et al. have repeatedly undeceived them,
they were still unable with logic and admonitions to get the said barbarians unqualifiedly to assent; they bluntly ask that an Imperial
Commissioner go to Tientsin to clarify instructions (to the barbarians).   We can read Wen-ch'ien's mind and recognize that he
does not have the situation under control.

According to the former treaties, Tientsin was not a place to
which the said barbarians could come; the various provincial
governors and governors general could have interviews with them
only in the five treaty ports.   But now the situation is critical and
the said governor general should either go in person to Tientsin
or devise a suitable plan for handling them and order Wen-ch'ien
to carry it out.   The said governor general has had considerable
experience in extra-routine duties and will certainly be able to

improve the general situation. Even though he does go in person
to Tientsin, he must by no means lightly agree to an interview with
the said barbarians, but must, as before, order Wen-ch'ien et al.
to elucidate consequences and inculcate principles; under no circumstances show any weakness to cause the said barbarians to make unscrupulous demands, nor even let the barbarians know that the said
governor general is in Tientsin. Such will be satisfactory.

As to the barbarians' statement that "they did not seek to trade
at Tientsin and that actually there were absolutely intolerable
grievances," determine which of their demands are absolutely
necessary to pacify them, and memorialize clearly asking for instructions. If they involve general policy, refute them with discreet words. Be sure not to assent through fear as Chi-erh-hang-a
did in making requests on their behalf.

Today the former incumbent of the Ch'ang-lu Salt Administration,
Ch'ung-lun, has been sent to the said governor general for service as
a deputy and is ordered to proceed to Tientsin. The governor general
can instruct the said official to work with Wen-ch'ien toward a satisfactory and speedy settlement. Although the barbarian nature is
cunning in the extreme, if we adhere strictly to the existing treaties,
refute them with reason, and at the same time maintain such a
strong defense system ourselves, they will have nothing to hope for.
Once the said barbarians have sailed south, what further pretext
can there be?

Today another memorial of Chi-erh-hang-a has been received
stating that "the said barbarian envoys and military officers have
tried to juggle fact and falsehood to their own advantage, the back
customs dues have not been paid over, and it is still feared that
trouble will again develop. The new duties are also unsatisfactory."
Critical examination of his memorial shows that the purport is to
effect a compromise in the hope of collecting the customs. This
view is very narrow. In coming to Tientsin at this time, it is
feared the barbarians have other schemes than merely the customs
duties. If the said barbarians' customs duties have suffered losses
because of the Shanghai disturbances, there is no objection to having I-liang et al. investigate and arrange a reduction in order to
show sympathy. Only we must be sure to wait until Bowring et al.
have initiated the request; then we can clarify the whole matter
and order the said chieftains to return to Shanghai and wait for
I-liang to investigate and arrange. At this time the said governor
general need not notify Wen-ch'ien.

As to the situation of which Wen-ch'ien has memorialized,
first deliberate carefully and, as soon as a decision has been
reached, memorialize secretly. Wen-ch'ien's supplementary memorial and Chi-erh-hang-a's memorial are both ordered copied
and distributed for perusal. (IWSM. HF 9; 19a, 4-20b, 1)

160. October 19, 1854. EDICT: Reviews Demands of the Foreign
Envoys and Orders the Tientsin Defenses Strengthened.
      Additional Edict. Formerly, when barbarian ships came to
Tientsin, Wen-ch'ien et al. were ordered to find out the barbarians'
purpose in coming and with proper language reduce them to submission. Today a memorial has been received stating that he
(Wen-ch'ien) has had an interview with the barbarians and, although
he repeatedly undeceived them, he was ultimately unable to stop
them with proper language. Besides, he did not state item by item
what they wished to discuss but bluntly asked that an Imperial
Commission be sent first, or possibly have Kuei-liang go to Tientsin to give the explicit instructions. It is obvious that Wen-ch'ien
et al. in their interview with the barbarian linguists were rendered
speechless and were cowed by their threats. In what he says about
having the governor and governor general of Kiangsu take charge,
there is unquestionably the intent to evade responsibility in the
hope of compromise. Cowardice and lack of ability are evident here.
      These barbarians wish to revise the treaties. Exactly what are
the revisions? Can you not ask them to enumerate (the items) clearly? If they are such as to involve general policy or if they are impossible to agree to, refute them with proper language. If we are
right and they are wrong, even if they sail back to the South, what
further pretext can there be? If there are any that can be discussed,
there is no objection to receiving specific items pending instructions
for settlement. How is it that the salt controller is unable to memorialize and must wait for a special Imperial Commissioner?
Moreover, these barbarians are unusually cunning. On this trip to
Tientsin, if we do not make them reveal their intentions and after
ascertaining these clearly formulate a proper plan of procedure,
and if instead we carelessly let them slide and see only what is
before our eyes, the covetousness of these barbarians will certainly increase daily. If their demands are unobstructed, where will
they end?
      Today (We) have secretly ordered Kuei-liang to decide if it is
necessary to go in person to Tientsin to settle matters satisfactorily
and have ordered Wen-ch'ien et al. on the one hand to instruct the
said barbarians without the slightest display of weakness, and on
the other hand to await Kuei-liang's decision.
      As to defense measures, they must be arranged in strict secrecy
but without any remissness. Whether or not Kuei-liang is to go to
Tientsin, still cannot be decided; even if the said governor general
goes to Tientsin, he should by no means readily consent to an
interview with the barbarian chieftains. It is essential that Wen-
ch'ien and the others should not let the said barbarians know that
Kuei-liang is proceeding to Tientsin lest it augment their tendency
to make demands. As to whether or not Bowring is coming to

Tientsin or merely sending Medhurst and Parker ahead to reconnoitre, Wen-ch'ien is ordered to make careful inquiry and memorialize secretly.

Today there has already been an order for Ch'ung-lun to go to
Tientsin and, together with the said officials, carry out the negotiations satisfactorily.   (IWSM.HF 9; 20b, 3-21a, 10)

161.   October 21, 1854.   EDICT: Kuei-liang is Ordered to Utilize
Ch'ung-lun and to Avoid a Personal Interview as Long as Possible.

Edict to the Grand Councillors.   Yesterday, because ships of
the two countries, England and America, sailed into Ta-ku, the
question of the necessity of Kuei-liang going in person (arose) and
instructions have been given for the said governor general, after
due deliberation, to handle it.   Ch'ung-lun was also sent to act under
the commission of the said governor general.

The barbarian chieftains, not conforming to existing treaties,
recklessly make demands.   If the governor general is afraid that
his coming to Tientsin will tend to arouse the barbarians' covetousness, he need not go himself but can instruct Ch'ung-lun to proceed
to Pao-ting on commission.   If, on personal inspection of the situation, it proves necessary to go in person to negotiate together with
Wen-ch'ien, he is to send express orders to Ch'ung-lun to go direct
to Tientsin.   After the said governor general has reached Tientsin,
he is to deliberate and reach a satisfactory settlement.

Today (We) have given oral instructions to Ch'ung-lun to wait
for the said governor general to give orders and to abide by his
decisions.   Kuei-liang must, therefore, obey the former Edict:
if he does go he should by no means lightly consent to an interview
with the said barbarians, in conformity with regulations, but should
order Ch'ung-lun et al. to give them explicit instructions not to
start trouble.   This is of the utmost importance.   (IWSM.HF 9;
22a, 8-22b, 5)

162.   October 22, 1854.   EDICT: Warns the Tientsin Military Officials
against Panic in the Face of the Foreign Threat.

Edict to the Grand Councillors.   Ships of the two barbarians, the
English and Americans, have come to Tientsin on the 24th (October
15).   After Wen-ch'ien interviewed and undeceived them, they still
did not sail back.   Yesterday further orders were given to Kuei-liang
to consider whether or not it was necessary to go first, and to decide
secretly.

It is feared that if the governor general leaves the provincial
capital, the region will inevitably sprout rumors.   The coming of
the barbarian chieftains is prompted by nothing more than the desire
for treaty revision and is not a matter for war.   If there are any in
the army who spread news of doubt or fear, order Seng-ko-lin-ch'in

to keep them in control and not allow rumors to spread. As conditions become known, memorialize secretly from time to time.
(IWSM. HF 9; 22b, 6-23a, 1)

163. October 23, 1854. MEMORIAL: Kuei-liang Proposes to Divert
Bowring and McLane by Sending Orders to Yeh Ming-ch'en to Negotiate at Canton.

Kuei-liang, governor general of Chihli, memorializes. It is our
humble opinion that the barbarian chiefs coming at this time and
speaking of treaty revision, have not clearly expressed their purpose;
feeling that the officials who met with them rejected their requests
peremptorily, they said, "if there was not a memorial on their behalf, they would immediately return to their countries and the previously established treaties would have become waste paper," completely ignoring the fact that the previously established treaties
specified "ten thousand years." How can they wantonly discuss
revision?

Wen-ch'ien et al. have had to instruct them in proper language
and also ascertain their motive for coming. If they violate the treaty
with frequent demands we must confront them with righteousness.
Moreover, commercial matters have been placed in the charge of
the governor general of Liang-kuang. At present, treaty revision is
definitely not permissible. If, because Shanghai bandits have caused
trouble, barbarian commercial gains are somewhat reduced, they
should by all means go to Kwangtung and await investigation and
settlement. The court in its magnanimous practice of granting the
boon of trade has issued as compensation a uniform customs schedule.
The situation must be investigated personally by the governor general
of Liang-kuang, who will memorialize requesting reductions or
exemptions as circumstances require, nor can he hastily give his
assent lest it give rise to further covetousness.

On scrutinizing the contents of Chi-erh-hang-a's memorial, it is
concerned only with the customs. It is indeed, as Imperial Edict
says, a very narrow view. At the present time we must consider
first of all the general welfare. If these barbarian chieftains use
Yeh Ming-ch'en's refusal to see them as a pretext, it is proposed
to have Wen-ch'ien first send a communication to Canton for them,
and then personally notify the barbarian chieftains that previously
when they went to Canton they had taken the initiative for an interview, therefore Yeh Ming-ch'en did not negotiate with them. Now
having the Tientsin officials write ahead for them, he will certainly
consult, investigate, and act, so it is unnecessary to make additional
requests for dignitaries. Thus clearly enlightened, the barbarian
chiefs will have no opportunity to show their craftiness.

Furthermore, the acting magistrate of I-chou, Ch'eng Jen-chieh,
has been delegated to come to the provincial (capital) to carry out

this policy.   We have ordered him to go at once to Ta-ku to take part
in the transactions.   (IWSM. HF 9; 23a, 2-23b, 7)

164.   October 23, 1854.   EDICT: Orders Kuei-liang to Block the Envoys Authoritatively and Finally in order to Avoid Future Reprisals.
        Edict to the Grand Councillors.   Kuei-liang memorializes that he
has deliberated on barbarian affairs and has sent an additional representative to Tientsin to cooperate.   The original memorial has been
copied and sent to Wen-ch'ien et al. to enable them to act according
to his decision and clearly enlighten (the barbarians).
        In addition, abstract the 1843-1844 commercial treaties and send
them all out for examination.   If Wen-ch'ien et al. are able to sway
them with proper language and get them to sail back without delay,
the said governor general need not proceed; this will also serve to
quiet popular clamor.
        Ch'ung-lun is now daily expected to arrive at the provincial (capi-
tal) and it will be necessáry, if there are any explicit orders, that you
immediately direct the said official to hasten to Tientsin to manage in
accordance with instructions.
        As to whether or not Wen-ch'ien et al. are able to handle the
situation satisfactorily from day to day, have secret inquiry made as
occasion requires and forthwith secretly memorialize.   The utmost
care is necessary.   If there is anything unsatisfactory in Wen-ch'ien's
handling, the said governor general may yet have to go there himself to
quench popular agitation.   At the present time some delay is permissible.   These troubles with barbarians are chronic affairs!
        Now, although the clamor of arms is not yet stilled, if we are to
be able to manage satisfactorily according to circumstances, new
techniques must neccessarily be devised.   If you employ empty words
opportunistically to cause (the barbarians) to return to Canton, it is
actually just to get them out of Chihli province and have it over with.
We think you are not that stupid.   After the barbarians return home
this time, if they come back again due to other causes, it will be
(something) beyond your calculations.   But if they come again because the Chihli authorities have been negligent in the present situation, and bring unceasing complaints, We shall certainly hold you
responsible.   Observe (this Edict) with care!   (IWSM. HF 9; 23b,
8-24a, 9)

165.   October 23, 1854.   EDICT: Refutes the English Claim for Treaty
Revision in 1854 and Spells Out a Plan to Block them.
        Additional Edict.   Since the memorial of Wen-ch'ien and others
reporting their interview with the barbarian Medhurst et al., no further
memorials have been received.   We have been deeply concerned
whether ultimately the said barbarians were discouraged and turned
back or if they have found pretexts for more demands.

Today Kuei-liang's memorial on the state of negotiations and management is received. The intent and phraseology are all extremely involved. If Wen-ch'ien et al. can do as well in involving the barbarians, he can surely handle them.

Moreover, in the treaties originally concluded the commercial convention had a clause to the effect that if any slight modifications were necessary, negotiations would be renewed after twelve years. The American (treaty) was concluded in the seventh month (August 14-September 12), 1844; the French was concluded in the tenth month (November 10-December 10), 1844; the exchange of (ratifications) of both treaties took place in 1845. Thus the period is still far off. These barbarians should not at this time wantonly make fresh demands. In the terms of the English treaty there is not this provision, and since it is called a perpetual (ten-thousand year) treaty it should be adhered to forever. It states that if Our Court bestows favors on any country, Englishmen shall be favored entirely equally. America and France themselves cannot, before the expiration of the period, propose changes. How can the English barbarians thus go beyond them? Wen-ch'ien et al, can rightly use this argument to shut the mouths [lit.] of the said barbarians.

This trip to Tientsin was made by the English and American linguists. Whether or not the barbarian chiefs of the three countries, Bowring et al., are still coming should be clearly and carefully determined.

Further, instruct them on ocean-port (treaty port) affairs as follows. It was originally agreed that these should be handled exclusively by the Imperial Commissioner of China in charge of the management of foreign affairs. These barbarians' visits, even though apprised by memorial, must needs be diverted to the five open ports, to await investigation and report. As there is nothing whatever to be gained, these barbarian chiefs certainly should not undertake the long and toilsome voyage. Thus the barbarian leaders will realize that repeated trips to Tientsin are useless, and hereafter will not be sailing back and forth for this purpose.

Kuei-liang is now proceeding leisurely to Tientsin. After Ch'ung-lun shall have arrived at the provincial (capital) to negotiate, he is instructed to precede him there. Wen-ch'ien and the others are now ordered to negotiate forthwith and manage according to circumstances without waiting for Ch'ung-lun or causing delays and errors. They are to state things as entirely their own idea without mentioning the governor general. This is absolutely essential and will put a stop to subsequent endless requests.

In addition, order the local civil and military officials on the one hand to take adequate defense measures and, on the other hand to investigate secretly any seacoast traitors to prevent their furnishing the barbarians with grain and food. It is also forbidden to buy

foreign goods or to distribute or sell opium for them. You can thus
entirely circumvent their covetousness and make them withdraw in
short order. Report by express memorial each matter that is done
during the day. Kuei-liang's memorial and excerpts from the commercial treaties of the three countries are ordered copied and sent
out for perusal. (IWSM. HF 9; 24b, 1-25b, 1)

166. October 24, 1854. MEMORIAL: The Tientsin Officials Report
a Third Meeting with Medhurst and Parker and Present Their Proposals in Detail.
          Ch'ang-lu Salt Commissioner Wen-ch'ien and Tientsin Garrison
Commander-in-chief Shuang-jui memorialize. Your slaves humbly
state that on October 17 and 18 they interviewed the two barbarian
linguists, English and American, Medhurst and Parker. (Your
slaves) asked the present whereabouts of the barbarian chiefs, Bowring and McLane, and were told that they are now anchored outside
the bar awaiting word.
          Your slaves then delegated an officer to go out and reconnoitre.
He found that there are three steamers and one sailing vessel
anchored outside the bar. Your slaves, realizing that if they had
them come to see them here it would mean one more barbarian ship
in port, feared that if they went outside to see them it would be a
violation of customary law. They had two interviews with the said
barbarians Medhurst et al. and asked their motive in coming. Medhurst produced a projet and Parker produced two, including the one
previously submitted to the governor general of Liang-chiang, Your
official I-liang. They noted that in general the various proposals
made were mostly preposterous statements, very difficult to put
into practice; so they severely reprimanded them and immediately
returned the (documents), not daring to take the responsibility of
receiving them.
          Yesterday was received the Imperial Edict transmitted by the
Grand Secretariat, to the effect that Wen-ch'ien, et al. were to meet
them and must positively put a stop to their arrogance and block their
cunning schemes. Your slaves thereupon agreed to a meeting. On
account of the violence of the north wind, the barbarians were unable
to come ashore.
          On October 21 there was another conference with Medhurst and
the others to determine their actual motive in coming to Tientsin and
to get them to explain according to fact. The barbarians reiterated
that it was really because the country was disturbed and goods were
hard to sell that they were asking for treaty revision, and they again
produced the various items of the previously presented projets.
          Your slaves went over them together and refuted separate items,
such as their desire to build homes, buy land, erect factories, and
establish godowns anywhere in China. Your slaves explained that

outside the five ports, ships are still forbidden to enter any harbor, so how could they build factories and erect godowns? And besides, the Chinese people, knowing the severity of the law, would not dare to sell privately even an inch of ground to outside barbarians.

Then there was the request to have a plenipotentiary reside in Peking, China, to handle the exchange of public documents. Your slaves explained that according to the original treaties the various countries were not allowed to send officials. In commercial matters what public documents would there be to handle? Besides, the Heavenly Court and Chariot Hub is an important place. How could outside barbarians be allowed to scramble into it? These requests were all preposterous, could by no means be granted, and must not even be discussed.

Other items of revision which they requested concerned mostly a private arrangement opening the Yangtze valley to trade. Your slaves, conforming in general to I-liang's memorial, cut them off in no uncertain terms, explaining that in the original treaties nothing whatever was said of allowing them to trade in the Yangtze Valley, that penalties for treaty violations are very severe "as you (barbarians) must know," that this heedless request for revision of existing treaties is actually a violation of trust and impossible to accede to.

Furthermore, at this juncture there were some of the items of the projet which we took pains to scrutinize in detail. For instance, the statement that the leasing of residences in the five ports has been much obstructed; that when merchants have contracted debts the local officials have not stood security; that having been robbed by brigands and pirated on the high seas, they have appealed to the Chinese officials for handling, but so far (the evils) have not been eradicated; that because Canton has been besieged, as has Shanghai, several million (dollars) worth of goods remain unsold at the five ports; that lacking official management they had come north to complain.

Your slaves explained that in matters of renting buildings, whether the people wished to rent or not depends upon their convenience and even the officials could not force them. If debts were owing and they had reported them to the officials, how could there be any question of their following them up? As to being robbed and pirated, Chinese laws are very severe and the jurisdiction of local officials very great, so how dare they fail to apprehend and arrest in good faith? If anyone anywhere is remiss, redress must be sought on the spot. At the present juncture there is no case to proceed on. As to the Kwangtung districts, great military successes are now reported, peace will shortly be restored, and trade can be carried on as usual. There is no need of further concern.

(We) thus enlightened them in proper language, explaining two and three times. Medhurst et al., having no rebuttal, maintained that they merely presented letters and that the matters concerning all the demands in the projets, which had been handed over, must await a personal conference with Bowring and McLane before they could be settled. If we did not agree to memorialize, they would report to their barbarian chiefs and return to the South.

Your slaves explained that they were willing to negotiate personally with Bowring et al., but Medhurst et al. said that unless there were an Imperial Commissioner they could hardly confer, and expressed various other devices and deceits until the sun went down and we dispersed.

As to their desire to go to T'ung-chou, we had already explained that if they dared proceed the officials would not obstruct them, but as the Tientsin trainbands and militia numbered more than 100,000, and as public sentiment was very volatile, it was feared that they would suffer injury along the way, beyond official control. Medhurst said: "The Tientsin rebels were expelled by the militia a year ago. Even we in the South heard of it." (So) the matter was dropped.

Reverting to the incident of the barbarian ships entering the ports, Your slave Wen-ch'ien, in accord with Imperial Rescript, secretly reported to Assistant Military Governor Seng-ko-lin-ch'in and yesterday received word from him that he has deputed Acting Provincial General Chang Tien-yüan, at the head of over three thousand men, to go at once to the Tientsin district to cooperate in defense.

Vermilion endorsement: Examination of the memorial is enough to reveal the empty threats of the barbarians. They are not very clever. After Ch'ung-lun arrives, you must all cooperate to negotiate and manage. You are to memorialize speedily and secretly (if) the barbarian ships continue to advance, and as to the activities of the said barbarians. (IWSM.HF 9; 25b, 4-28a, 3)

167. October 24, 1854. MEMORIAL: The Tientsin Officials Report that a Foreign Boat Has Penetrated the Bar and Been Ordered Outside.

Wen-ch'ien et al. further memorialize. According to a report of the acting lieutenant general at Ta-ku, Hung Chih-kao, the small boat outside the bar sailed up to the mouth of the river on October 23. He immediately delegated an officer to go to the barbarian boat and investigate. Altogether there were nineteen of the barbarians. They said that because of the strong wind for several days this boat had gone aground on the bar. It dared not anchor there and, taking advantage of the tide, came inside.

Your slaves immediately personally instructed Hung Chih-kao that although the men on the boat were not many he should not allow them to come into the river to anchor, but should order them

back outside the bar.
    Vermilion endorsement: Read.   (IWSM. HF 9; 28a, 4-10)

  168. October 25, 1854. MEMORIAL: Kuei-liang Reports the Situation Well in Hand and that He Will Negotiate at Tientsin if Necessary.
    Chihli Governor General Kuei-liang memorializes. On October 23, 1854, the Imperial Edict was respectfully received: "Kuei-liang memorializes that he has sent additional officers to Tientsin to co-operate in the handling of barbarian affairs. Respect this." He (Kuei-liang) begs to note that since the English and American chiefs arrived at Tientsin they have not been willing to make a clear state-ment of their intentions. This is a cunning position. Your slave immediately instructed Wen-ch'ien et al. that they must ascertain the real reason in the hope of devising means of enlightening them.
    It is noted that Ch'ung-lun will shortly reach the provincial capital, whereupon he will be fully instructed to proceed forthwith to Tientsin to reconnoitre as circumstances allow. If the barbarian officials cannot be brought to terms, Your slave will immediately memorialize clearly and set up official residence at Tientsin to assume control, hoping to take advantage of the situation to tran-quillize them and block their stupidity, not daring to let things go by before his eyes and give rise to future trouble and incur the blame himself.
    Vermilion endorsement: You do not need to be so disturbed. When Ch'ung-lun arrives he will manage suitably as a matter of course. You must not allow it to leak out whether or not you are go-ing to leave the provincial (capital). If you do leave the capital and still do not have an interview with the barbarian chiefs, it is better not to let them know you are in Tientsin. In case you find it neces-sary to leave the capital, transfer Wu T'ing-tung to the post of judi-cial commissioner; Keng-ch'ang will open mail and act in your place. (IWSM. HF 9; 28b, 1-29a, 2)

  169. October 27, 1854. MEMORIAL: The Tientsin Officials Report the Receipt of a Note from Medhurst and Parker and that the Situation is Quiet.
    Ch'ang-lu Salt Commissioner Wen-ch'ien and Tientsin Garrison Commander Shuang-jui memorialize. Your slaves ventured on the 25th, during the eleventh watch (7-9 p. m.), to receive a communi-cation from Medhurst and Parker, immediately conferred together, and sent a reply, a separate detailed memorandum of which is respectfully presented for Imperial scrutiny.
    Reverting to the barbarian boat which came into port on the 23rd, it is now anchored alongside Medhurst's vessel and has caused no trouble. (IWSM. HF 9; 29a, 3-7)

170. October 27, 1854. EDICT: Chides the Tientsin Officials for Temporizing and Orders Ch'ung-lun to Meet the Envoys and Settle the Issues.

Edict to the Grand Councillors. Wen-ch'ien et al. have memorialized that they received a communication from the barbarian chiefs and sent a reply. Previously Wen-ch'ien said that he had refuted the barbarians, maintaining a stern terminology and manner, but if these barbarian chiefs evade an interview it is hard to be sure that they do not have some ulterior plan. Even if they are forced to return South it will not be the end of it.

On this occasion Wen-ch'ien et al. sent a communication ordering the barbarians back to the five ports to await settlement. This amounts to replying with empty words. In final analysis, to what port are they ordered to return? The Kwangtung Imperial Commissioner is now occupied with military affairs. If he is not able to make a settlement at once it will certainly afford another pretext to come north. Besides, at Shanghai, the barbarian chiefs have already said that they are unwilling to return to Kwangtung. If means are not found in the North to stop them and block their cunning schemes, we shall by no means be able to subdue the barbarians' hearts. To send an Imperial Commissioner would offer a myriad of difficulties. Ch'ung-lun has been ordered to Tientsin as the official to handle barbarian affairs. If the barbarian chiefs, Bowring et al., arbitrarily make wanton demands, he should enlighten them with high principles and circumvent them with proper language.

Ch'ung-lun is instructed, on receipt of this Edict, to investigate secretly and quickly. If the barbarian chiefs are actually aboard ship, he should either order them to come to see him or devise other means of having an interview with them, and then, with Wen-ch'ien, negotiate a suitable settlement. If the chiefs are in the end unwilling to see him, he should make it clear that this time the failure to negotiate personally is the barbarians' own fault and they cannot use unwillingness of the local officials to see them as an excuse for further complaints.

Wen-ch'ien previously stated that if he went outside the river to meet them he feared that it would violate customary law. His view is correct. If Ch'ung-lun et al. have an interview, they are instructed to memorialize immediately.

Was the barbarian boat which came into the river on the 23rd included in the previous enumeration? If another has come, the orders are to investigate clearly and memorialize. (IWSM. HF 9; 29a, 8-30a, 2)

171. October 27, 1854. BRITISH-AMERICAN JOINT NOTE: Ultimatum that Arrangements for Negotiations Must Be Completed by
October 27th.
        English-American communication. We take this occasion to
explain. We respectfully acknowledge the receipt on this day of a
letter from the provincial officials, the Tientsin patrol commander
and the local authorities, saying that they had already memorialized
that "when the present ministers came to Tientsin their intention
was to proceed to the capital to request that an Imperial Commissioner be delegated to confer at the capital on national affairs."
Then ten days elapsed, which was regarded as adequate for the receipt of a reply. The said ministers agreed to wait until the 25th
of the present month, the eleventh watch (3-5 p. m.), at which time,
if an Imperial Edict had not arrived from the Court granting permission to proceed to the capital, they would sail back on the
morning of the 27th and report (to their superiors). It is hoped
that there will be no further delay.
        Naturally, they (English and American representatives) should
prepare this letter notifying the (Chinese officials) of what had
occurred so that the latter might act accordingly. Hence this
communication.
        Vermilion endorsement: Read.   (IWSM. HF 9; 30a. 3-30b, 2)

172. October 27, 1854. REPLY TO BOWRING AND McLANE:
Rejects Negotiations at Tientsin and Orders the Envoys Back to Shanghai and Canton.
        Reply to the English-American communication. In reply, it is
noted that the originally concluded commercial regulations contain
the statement that all countries subsequently having credentials to
transmit to the Chinese Court must have the originals memorialized
for them by the Chinese Imperial Commissioner charged with the
management of foreign affairs or by the governor general of Liang-
kuang, Min-Che, or Liang-chiang. Now the honorable envoys'
coming to Tientsin is not in accord with the original treaties. Now
that the present ministers, in consideration of the fact that they
have traversed distant and stormy seas to reach here, have had
memorials presented (for them), they must return to the five ports
and wait while the present (Chinese) ministers quickly prepare a
statement notifying the Imperial Commissioner charged with handling
foreign commerce to investigate and act. Herewith the reply which
is duly made.
        Vermilion endorsement: Read.   (IWSM. HF 9; 30b, 3-31a, 2)

172. October 27, 1854. MEMORIAL: Military Official at Shanhaikwan
Reports his Defense Preparations against Foreign Ships.
        Deputy Lieutenant General of Shanhaikwan Fu-lo-tun-t'ai me-

morializes. Your slave makes bold to state that on October 20 of the present year he received a Court Letter from the Grand Secretariat saying that on October 19 they had received an Imperial Edict to the effect that "barbarian ships had come to the port of Tientsin and that Kuei-liang et al. had been ordered to make suitable defense plans and pointing out the necessity of using proper language to cut them off. Respect this."

Your slave begs to note that Shanhaikwan is close to two ports, one at Shih-ho-k'ou, one at Ch'in-wang-tao ; that English barbarian ships have already come on two occasions and on both they were sternly ordered to return. But now the barbarian ships have come to Tientsin, accessible to Shanhaikwan by water in one day's sail. Although we have sent out reconnoitering parties they have been inadequate for the occasion. In accord with Imperial Edict we have deputed the competent Captain Ch'ing-nien to lead ten-odd soldiers, without causing any stir, to scout night and day in strict secrecy and, if any barbarin ships arrive, to report immediately. Your slave on the one hand will issue proclamations to quiet the people, endeavoring to maintain morale and keep the peace as usual, and on the other hand, (should the barbarian ships arrive) will go personally to the port to elucidate general principles and strongly urge them to sail back forthwith. He will secretly memorialize the status of the said barbarians' activities, truthfully and in detail, not daring in the least to gloss over.

But it is noted that in Shanhaikwan, in accord with an Imperial Edict to make preparations, using government troops to defend the barrier city, from the ninth month of last year (October 3-31, 1853) up to now, drilling has been continuous without a single day of respite. (Your slave) has secretly made suitable preparations and as soon as the alarm is sounded will spring into action. Now he has ordered Captain T'a-ch'ing-an, Imperially commissioned to take charge of defeated and transferred troops, to assume command and await orders.

Your slave Fu-lo-tun-t'ai is directing troops for defense, giving orders from headquarters and has also secretly ordered the acting magistrate of Lín-yü [i.e., Shanhaikwan], Tsao Lien-ch'eng, and the acting colonel of Shan-Yung, First Captain Li Hsiang, to cooperate in everything, secretly to make rigorous defense measures, but by no means dare to act abruptly, in the hope of fulfilling to the utmost the repeated orders of our Sacred Lord (Emperor).

Vermilion endorsement: Such noising about! Still talking about secret negotiations and secret plans! Who believes it? Your histrion disposition is still unchanged! Further orders will be sent to you! (IWSM. HF 9; 31a, 3-32a, 3)

174. October 27, 1854. EDICT: Chides the Shanhaikwan Military
Official for His Blustering Officiousness.
    Edict to the Grand Councillors. Previously, because barbarian
vessels came to Tientsin, Fu-lo-tun-t'ai and others were ordered
each at his own port to make careful defense, without the least
confusion. Now a memorial from Fu-lo-tun-t'ai says that he has
sent officers to lead out troops and keep watch night and day; on the
one hand, he is issuing proclamations to reassure the people and
on the other, personally going to the ports and ordering reserves to
support the official army to be drilled continuously and await transfer.
    These various activities are actually deliberately noised abroad
and yet the said brigade general himself speaks of secret negotiations
and secret plans! In the orders he originally received, he has not
even recognized their true import. How can he be so pleased with
affairs? Since the barbarian leaders arrived at Tientsin, Wen-ch'ien
and others have explained to them in correct language; they have not
yet sailed back to the South but We trust they will not cause further
complications.
    Fu-lo-tun-t'ai is ordered, as regards the local ports, to recon-
noitre intensively; no false moves will be tolerated. If any barbarian
ships arrive, he must secretly send an express memorial, await
orders and act in accordance with them. He must not act rashly
and arouse public sentiment to cause further trouble. Tremble!
(IWSM. HF 9; 32a, 4-32b, 2)

175. October 29, 1854. MEMORIAL: The Governor of Shantung Reports Foreign Ships Sighted off the North Coast Bound for Tientsin.
    Governor of Shantung Ch'ung-en memorializes. Previously, on
October 14, Your official received a communication from the governor
of Kiangsu stating that the English and American envoys left Shanghai
by steamer on October 9, proceeding to Tientsin to request revision
of trade regulations and for no other reason. Now as these barbarian
ships were going from Shanghai to Tientsin they must needs pass
through Shantung waters. According to a report of the acting garrison commander, Ch'en T'ing-fang, ocean patrol officers have reported
that, "early on the morning of October 14th, in the waters of Miao
Island, P'eng-lai-hsien, under the jurisdiction of Teng-chou-fu, they
saw clearly in the outer ocean three barbarian ships, large and small,
sailing due west, far out from the Miao Island coast, nor did they
enter port." Naturally these are the ones proceeding to Tientsin.
    Between the number of barbarian ships coming north and those
arriving at Tientsin there is a slight discrepancy. It would seem that
as they were sailing on the high seas in the dead of night, the patrol
officers failed to discern the whole line. Whether or not any ships have
come since, no reports have been received.
    As to the ships which came to Tientsin, they will either obediently

return south or, if their wants are not met at Tientsin, make further
demands on the Shantung coast, according to (Your official's) conjecture. Secret orders have been given the said commander and
tao-t'ai, on the pretext of defense against local brigands, to distribute
troops and without any demonstration carefully protect the coast.
Should they discover any barbarian ships passing, if they only want
to buy food and fresh water, they should weigh the circumstances and
allow only the small boats to do business outside, and keep careful
watch to prevent the development of further trouble. If there should
be any other pretext for demands, or if (the English and Americans)
should present letters, they are, on the one hand, to report by express
post to Your official for decision and execution and, on the other, to
negotiate and reason with them. They must prevent making a commotion beforehand which would give them opportunity to spy on us.
(IWSM. HF 9; 32b, 3-33a, 8)

176. October 29, 1854. EDICT: Warns the Shantung Governor that
Foreign Ships May Still Make Demands at His Ports en route to Shanghai.
    Edict to the Grand Councillors. Previously when the barbarian
ships of England and America came to Tientsin's Ta-ku port, there
was no assurance that there would not be other barbarian ships to
follow. Orders have been issued Ch'ung-en to give strict instructions
to the military and civil port authorities to make defense preparations
in advance.
    Now the said barbarian pretexts for demands at Tientsin are no
more than empty threats to intimidate us. Wen-ch'ien and others
have stopped them with appropriate words and repeatedly enlightened
them, and the said barbarians have exhausted their arguments and
expended their vocabularies and can no longer argue back. But if
their wishes are not accorded at Tientsin, there is no assurance that
they will not make further demands at Shantung ports.
    Ch'ung-en is ordered to give secret instructions to the garrison
commander of Teng-chou and others to ascertain if any barbarian
ships come, and should they submit any letters evincing further
aspirations, by no means to receive them, and further strictly to
forbid the coastal population to buy the said barbarians' opium or
other goods or to supply them with food. The said governor must
not make any outward show, making his defense preparations in
strict secrecy so as not to cause popular apprehension. This is of
the utmost importance. (IWSM. HF 9; 33a, 9-33b, 6)

177. November 1, 1854. MEMORIAL: The Tientsin Officials Report
a Plan to Have Ch'ung-lun Meet Bowring and McLane at Tientsin.
    Ch'ang-lu Salt Controller Wen-ch'ien, Garrison Commander
Shuang-jui, memorialize. Your slaves beg to note that after drafting
their reply of the 26th (October) to the barbarians, the said barbarians

on the 28th, between 9 and 11 a.m., sent a communication by
patrol officers and also proffered Your slaves a gift of 36 bottles of
barbarian wine, which was promptly refused. They were not allowed
to bring the wine ashore because in the said barbarians' communication there were reckless expressions. On joint consultation, a
reply was composed and the said barbarians' original letter was also
returned. They (Your slaves) have separately made fair copies and
respectfully submit them for Imperial perusal.

But the said barbarians stubbornly maintained that they were
respectfully awaiting an Imperial Rescript. Your slaves did not
dare lightly to make promises, yet if they continually argue with
empty words, truly, as Sacred Edict has stated, it will be no way to
end the matter.

Further, it is reported that the said barbarians wish to weigh
anchor and return South on the 30th. With much deliberation, in their
reply to the said barbarian letter on this occasion, Your slaves have
analyzed their expressions to ascertain their motivation before re-
formulating a policy of management. Now it is not difficult to send
them away for the time being; the difficulty is after they have gone
not to have new troubles develop. As soon as Ch'ung-lun arrives at
Tientsin, Your slaves will again deliberate and decide about a meeting
with Bowring and the other barbarian chieftains in the earnest hope of
checking their covetousness and subjugating the hearts of the said
barbarians.

The small barbarian vessel which subsequently entered the harbor
was one of the five steamers which came previously, and since then
no other barbarian ships have arrived.

Vermilion endorsement: The various circumstances described in
this memorial have been noted.   (IWSM.HF 9; 33b, 7-34a, 10)

178.   November 1, 1854.   MEMORIAL: The Tientsin Officials Report
a Meeting of Their Deputies with Medhurst and Parker.

Wen-ch'ien and others further memorialize. After Your slaves,
between 7 and 9 a.m., on the 29th (October), had sent their answer
to the reply of Medhurst and the others, the said barbarians requested a personal interview. Your slave Wen-ch'ien, on the pretext that the barbarians' communication contained reckless expressions, replied that he would not see them. Your slave Shuang-jui
and Your official Ch'ien Hsin-ho, went to the interview and reprimanded them righteously. Medhurst and Parker bowed their heads
and said nothing, acknowledging their error. They also said that
since some high officials would shortly come to Tientsin to investigate, hereafter feelings would be friendly and that they held absolutely no resentment ["although they die there would be no resentment"].
Their manner was very embarrassed and their speech extremely respectful and conciliatory. Your slaves, Shuang-jui and others, reiter-

ated the absolute necessity of the envoys, Bowring and McLane, (being present) before an interview could be held. Medhurst said: "It would be impolite for the envoy of my country not to consent to an interview, and when I have gone outside and notified Bowring I can give you an answer." Then they separated.

Between 5 and 7 in the evening, according to the report of the colonel of Ta-ku, Hung Chih-kao, Medhurst and Parker, accompanied by ten-odd barbarians, left the harbor in a small boat.

It is noted that the water is running low in the Pei-ho, the wind has been from the North for several days and the weather is getting colder. The said barbarians dread the cold and are also apprehensive of being frozen in, so when they talked about going to Peking it was clearly an empty phrase noised abroad. The circumstances made a prolonged wait impossible, but we have sent them back humbled, without a leg to stand on; if there is to be any revision at all, they still must return south to negotiate. Having been enlightened with reason, the said barbarians could do nothing but acquiesce. Analyzing their position on this occasion, since they made no demands they will not dare cause further trouble. (IWSM.HF 9; 34b, 1-35a, 4)

179. November 1, 1854. EDICT: Orders Ch'ung-lun to Meet Bowring and McLane and to Forestall All Future Attempts to Negotiate in the North

Edict to the Grand Councillors. Wen-ch'ien and others have in the last few days memorialized various items concerning the circumstances of the barbarian chieftains, saying that the said chiefs, after receiving a reply to their communication, asked for a personal interview. Since the said barbarians' communication contained some reckless expressions, Wen-ch'ien did not meet them. When Shuang-jui and others admonished the said chiefs righteously, Medhurst and the others bowed their heads and said nothing, acknowledging their error. These chiefs are not really clever; they are merely making pretexts for demands and using empty words to threaten us.

By this time Ch'ung-lun should have reached Tientsin. He is ordered to plan carefully and consult maturely with Wen-ch'ien and the others. When they meet Bowring and the others they must by all means stop them with suitable words and, as occasion demands, give reasoned orders to bend the barbarians' will so that they will not dare wantonly to develop covetousness. This will be right and proper. (IWSM.HF 9; 35a, 5-35b, 1)

180. November 3, 1854. MEMORIAL: Ch'ung-lun Reports the Completion of Arrangements to Meet Bowring and McLane in Front of the Ta-ku Forts.

Former Ch'ang-lu Salt Controller Ch'ung-lun, Ch'ang-lu Salt

Controller Wen-ch'ien, and Tientsin Brigade General Shuang-jui
memorialize. On the 25th (October), Your slave Ch'ung-lun went
to the provincial capital, Pao-ting, and called on Governor General
Kuei-liang to acquaint himself with Kuei-liang's present deliberations
on affairs and get his policy in person. He was ordered to go to
Tientsin and, setting out from the capital on the 27th, arrived at Ta-
ku on the 31st. He notes that in the period from 1840 to 1850, when
barbarians came to the ports they were always received in tents in
front of the forts. This time it naturally must be handled as before.

On (November) 1st Medhurst asked for an interview. When Your
slaves, Shuang-jui and Ch'ien Hsin-ho, proceeded to the fort, the
said barbarian said: "Now Imperially commissioned officials have
come to Tientsin; the envoys Bowring and McLane are plenipotentiaries
of their countries. Bowring being elderly and McLane in bad health,
and as along the coast the wind was strong and they dreaded the cold,
could they go to Tientsin for the interview?" Your slaves, Shuang-jui
and the others, told them that although the port of Tientsin was
originally not a place to which barbarians could come, they realize
that (the envoys) had come far and so had memorialized for them; but
now Imperial Commissioners have been sent to Ta-ku and the meeting
must be there--how could they go on to Tientsin for an interview? If
they vacillate like this it will really be difficult to grant them what
they want.   Medhurst replied: "The bar is more than twenty li from
the forts and large ships cannot enter. Besides, the negotiations will
take time and the envoys will have to have some place to stay. The
small barbarian boats which have entered the port cannot provide living
quarters. If it is not agreed that they go to Tientsin, living quarters
must be found at Ta-ku in order to facilitate negotiations." In reply
Your slaves refuted them twice and three times: "If you do not agree
to the old arrangements and the present subjects for negotiation cannot be discussed personally, the fault will be with you barbarians, not
with the local officials." The said barbarians continually used
threatening language and insisted on finding living quarters before
they would consent to meet. Your slave Shuang-jui, putting on a stern
countenance and standing up, told them that now high officials had
come to negotiate, and if they quibbled disrespectfully like this they
would have to leave immediately and not loiter around here. The barbarians, seeing that it would be hard to recover their position, finally
agreed. November 3rd was finally set for the barbarian chiefs to enter
port, with the place of meeting in front of the forts, as usual.

At the time of the general meeting on the 3rd, (Your slaves) will
ascertain what matters they wish to bring forward and what changes
they want in the treaties. If they wilfully make wanton requests,
these will naturally be answered righteously and stopped with proper
language; but even if their position is pardonable, Your slaves will
not dare lightly to grant what they ask, but will only carefully report

the facts and ask for an Imperial Edict to handle it.
Vermilion endorsement: Noted.   (IWSM. HF 9; 35b, 2-36b, 6)

181.   November 5, 1854.   MEMORIAL: Ch'ung-lun Describes in Detail
the Meeting with Bowring and McLane in Front of the Ta-ku Forts.

Former Ch'ang-lu Salt Controller Ch'ung-lun, Ch'ang-lu Salt
Controller Wen-ch'ien, and Tientsin Garrison Commander Shuang-jui
memorialize.   Your slaves beg to report that on the 3rd of November,
between 11 and 1 o'clock, the barbarian chiefs McLane and Bowring,
at the head of 167 barbarians, entered the port in seven small boats
and came ashore with the interpreters Medhurst and Parker; each
person bore arms and they came in procession with a band playing.
Your slaves were in the open blue-cloth tent in front of the forts,
surrounded by troops standing like a wall.   They also arranged civil
and military officials in two wings, standing in orderly attendance
to make a good showing and an impressive display.   The said barbarians advanced to the tent and Your slaves, Ch'ung-lun and the
others, met them immediately.

The barbarian chiefs, McLane and Bowring, conducted themselves very respectfully, saying that on coming to Tientsin, they
were greatly indebted to His Imperial Majesty for sending high officials there; that in getting a personal interview the envoys were
overwhelmingly fortunate.   Your slave Ch'ung-lun then informed them
that even though Tientsin was not a place to which foreigners should
come, realizing that they had braved the seas, this meeting had finally been agreed to, and that any matters requiring discussion would
be entertained according to the facts and if, regarding the original
treaties, there were anything reasonable, the present officials would
take it up personally.

McLane answered first that the original treaties had been in
operation a long time and that, as present conditions had changed
materially, they had first gone to Kwangtung.   Governor General Yeh
would not see them, so they came to Tientsin to seek settlement.   He
also produced the précis which had been submitted before.   The purport of it was approximately the same as that which Your slave Wen-
ch'ien has repeatedly memorialized.

Your slave Ch'ung-lun then rejected specifically several items
in the précis: the request to get houses and rent land in the interior,
the establishment of godowns, and the sending of barbarians to
reside in Peking to handle official correspondence.   The said barbarians had no word of argument.   They said that the previous précis
had not been complete.   Now that Imperially appointed officials had
finally come to Tientsin and could undertake this heavy responsibility,
the various requests of all countries could be included in a detailed
treaty.   If they did not have full powers, then there was no need for
further discussion.   Your slave Ch'ung-lun replied:

In our country all officials are inferior and dare not act without
authority. Everything awaits the Monarch's mandate for execution. There
has never been such a term as "full powers." Now if the things which
your countries are asking for benefit both parties, or if they benefit
foreign countries and do not injure China, they can all be discussed
and memorialized for execution. If they would do serious injury to
China and the present officials agreed to memorialize them, Our Emper-
or would certainly regard it as an offense of trespass. However, you
can present any items you like and after examination they can then be
deliberated upon reasonably.

The barbarian chief McLane turned to Bowring, Medhurst, and
Parker, and they consulted together for a long time and finally each
presented a separate copy of treaty revisions. Your slaves, Ch'ung-
lun and Wen-ch'ien, examined the articles they presented. Most of
them concerned the general situation, involving matters of no little
consequence, and had to be immediately and trenchantly rejected,
thus effecting a defeat of the said barbarians' will.

By this time it was nearly dark and if the barbarians were prevented from leaving the port there would be still another complication.
Besides, England has Medhurst who interprets for Bowring; this barbarian is unusually treacherous and we were afraid that (his interpretation) might not be complete. So we said that most of the things
they asked for in the document were rash and could hardly be noted
reasonably at once; that after the present officials had discussed the
original document in detail and rejected seriatim those articles
absolutely impossible to agree to, they would prepare a reply; that
even if the present provisions were suitable and could still be discussed, this was not the place to handle barbarian affairs; that there
were no records to refer to — customs affairs particularly had
different aspects in each locality; so the best thing to do was to
memorialize clearly asking that the provincial governor general
Imperially commissioned to manage barbarian affairs examine the
original treaties, weigh the situation and take action with possibly
some small improvement to foreign trade.

The said barbarian chiefs then asked, (now that) they had submitted a treaty (proposal), how soon they could get an answer. Your
slaves said that it would have to be deliberated in detail and returned
to them on the 8th (November). The barbarians immediately agreed
and, leading the barbarians who came with them, boarded the small
boats, left the harbor, and returned to their ships.

Now we have copied the documents submitted by England and
America and respectfully present them for Imperial examination.
Among the items presented are clauses on "the exchange of
communications with governors general and governors," "the
necessity of personal interviews being held in official yamens,"
"that in controversies between Chinese and foreigners, after a

joint investigation by officials of the two countries, the parties shall return to their respective countries for trial," "that governors general having interviews with barbarians shall treat them as equals," "cooperation in devising means of exterminating coastal pirates," and "that Englishmen being cheated in money or goods by natives can demand immediate investigation and arrest" -- these items, although negotiable, all concern (our) dignity and institutions. Besides, they wish to use gold in payment of customs, to have customs debts cancelled, to use foreign silver and foreign currency. These items concern customs affairs of various places with which Your slaves are not thoroughly familiar. If we were to discuss them superficially with the barbarians we were afraid of being taken in by them.

Now these barbarian chiefs went first to Kwangtung, where Yeh Ming-ch'en did not give them an audience; then they went to Shanghai, where, although they had an interview with Chi-erh-hang-a, they were unable to have the things they asked for brought to Imperial notice. Now, having come direct to Tientsin, and having finally had officials delegated to examine them, the gratitude and pleasure in the barbarians' hearts was revealed in their words and in their faces. Although the various items of treaty revision requested are very rash, if we make absolutely no concessions we are sure to send them away resentful and angry. Although they would not dare commit any reckless acts of violence, if they should covertly undertake any craftiness while the Southern disaffection is still unsettled, we would be sure to prick our fingers in handling them.

It is noted that among the various items which the said barbarians brought up there are some that could be discussed, but here we have no records to refer to and investigation and decision would involve delay. In no time ice will be forming and, as barbarians dread cold, it will be impossible for them to wait here. So why not take the draft submitted by the barbarians and, determining the articles which can be extenuated by circumstances, select several items and have the governor general and governor in charge of barbarian affairs check them with the original treaties, deliberate wholeheartedly, and take suitable action in order to demonstrate that our desire to cherish those from afar has come from Imperial decision? (IWSM.HF 9; 36b, 7-39b, 4)

182. November 5, 1854. MEMORIAL: Ch'ung-lun Comments Adversely on the Précis Submitted by Bowring and McLane.

Ch'ung-lun and others further memorialize. The English barbarians' craftiness is manifold; their proud tyranny is uncontrollable; the Americans do nothing but follow their direction. The précis submitted is mostly selfish in its view and not within reason. Your slaves have duly consulted with one another regarding this document to pick out those items which can be considered. Those of no importance they have relegated to whichever of the five treaty ports they wish to go to for settlement. Your slaves will memorialize for Imperial orders to the respective governors general and governors to investigate the situation, consult together and manage, and to have the barbarians ordered to return and wait.

The other articles will be refuted and rejected in toto. When we shall have received the Vermilion Rescript, we shall again issue a reply for the said barbarians to follow and fling the original précis back at them. If they still wilfully obstruct, we can merely disregard them, but (we must) covertly make careful preparations and wait sword in hand. We are straight and they are crooked, so they will have no pretext. Since it is the nature of Southern [i.e., uncivilized] barbarians to respect strength and ridicule weakness, if we do not show some might it may be hard to restrain their covetnousness. In our reply we plan to generalize briefly, vaunting our National prestige and curtailing their wicked plans.

As to the original précis, we did not tell them we were including it in our memorial, only that we were taking it to ascertain if it benefited both parties. What harmed neither side we would deliberate and memorialize asking for an Edict for them; the rest, reckless proposals which were obstructive and hard to carry out, we would then repudiate item by item. On the 8th (November) we shall return it, still without letting the barbarians know that we have copied and presented it for Imperial examination. (IWSM.HF 9; 39b, 5-40a, 9)

183. November 5, 1854. EDICT: Rejects the Major Items of Treaty Revision and Accepts Three Minor Ones for Future Adjudication.

Edict to the Grand Councillors. Ch'ung-lun and others have memorialized that the American and English barbarians came into the port for a personal interview, that they questioned their motives, deliberated and took action. On the 3rd (November), Ch'ung-lun and others met the barbarians McLane and Bowring and talked to them within the bounds of proper decorum. The separate paper giving various aspects is also very thorough and compact.

As to the draft of revisions submitted by the barbarians, its various items are all extremely rash and must be rejected seriatim in order to stop their insatiable demands. For instance, in the matter of intercourse with Chinese local officials, we have established statutes. Every high local official has his own responsibilities; how can he lightly grant interviews wherever the barbarians happen to be? As to leasing or buying houses and land and transporting goods for sale, they must abide by the old treaties; we can by no means allow them to build wherever they like, come and go as they please, least of all on the Yangtze River, which has never been accessible to barbarian ships. While coastal fishing and prospecting have nothing to do with trade, actually the intention is further to spy out and encroach on land outside the five ports. As to future payment of duties, it has long been possible to pay either in sycee or in foreign currency computed in sycee but we have never used a gold standard and Chinese taxes have never been computed in gold. Besides, what they said of keeping goods temporarily in government warehouses, which the foreign merchant and the Chinese Customs House would jointly guarantee, is entirely unreasonable. The capital is the hub of the Empire and Tientsin is adjacent to the Imperial Domain. The desire of these chiefs to send barbarians there to sojourn and carry on trade is utterly perverse.

Bowring's reiteration of statements about paying duty on opium and wishing to enter Canton City is extremely odious. His other articles, compared with the American chief's, are even more fundamentally obstructive and must accordingly be repudiated in proper terms to curb his wanton demands.

As to controversies between people and barbarians, the original treaties can be referred to. Whether or not the local officials decide unjustly (We) shall allow them to ascertain from the governors general and governors, who will act with justice. As to the trouble caused by insurgents at Shanghai -- although originally not the least cancellation was allowed, if barbarian merchants have suffered thereby and wish to cancel back customs, We (who) govern and cherish Court and province and deal compassionately with those from afar, will agree to some adjustment. This must be investigated and handled by the provincial governor general and governor. As to the Kwangtung duty on tea, which they say is two mace too much on each picul, there are no records in Tientsin by which to check and it must be handled by the governor general and governor of Liang-kuang.

As to the above three articles which they are authorized to investigate and act upon, and the others which they are to repudiate entirely, Ch'ung-lun and the others shall act as if on their own initiative and rely on reason to enlighten them, on the one hand agreeing to memorialize for them, and on the other hand ordering them to return to Canton. If the barbarians are obstinate and refuse to return, they may be allowed to go to Shanghai, where negotiation and management will be conducted by I-liang and others, but this consent must not be given readily. In the end, ordering them to return to Kwangtung will be most suitable. It can be added that Tientsin cannot be compared with the five ports. On this occasion, since the barbarians had braved the storms of land and sea, it was agreed to memorialize for them. But if they vacillate and are disobedient, and if they ever come to Tientsin again, it will be absolutely impossible to treat them thus generously.

Furthermore, the précis presented by the barbarians is to be returned. After repudiating the barbarian chiefs, Ch'ung-lun and the others shall send an express memorial reporting their attitude. They are also to take careful defense measures to prepare for the unforeseen.   (IWSM. HF 9; 40a, 10-41b, 5)

184. November 5, 1854. BRITISH NOTE: Summary of Précis Submitted by Sir John Bowring.
          Articles submitted by the English barbarian chief, Bowring:
          1.   England to commission a minister to reside at the capital.
          2.   Permission for Englishmen to go anywhere they wish in the interior and to any city or town on the seacoast.
          3.   Tientsin to be made a trading port and a consul sent to reside there.
          4.   English plenipotentiaries meeting with high officials of the various coastal provinces must be received in official residences and treated as equals.   English consular officers must also be civilly received in official residences if they have necessary business to transact.   The capital of Kwangtung is included in this article.
          5.   The two countries to send representatives to draw up amendments and changes in the trading regulations.   Furthermore, opium to be allowed uniform entrance with a published duty jointly agreed upon.
          6.   In all trading ports, English ships to be allowed to load and move goods in and out without interference.
          7.   On all imports being moved to the interior, and exports being moved to the coast, excepting for the duties paid according to published schedules at the five ports, no additional duties shall be levied at interior customs-houses; these goods must be allowed to move without any impediment.
          8.   The value of all kinds of foreign money, whether it be fine or gross sycee or foreign silver or foreign dollars, to be accepted by weight according to mace and taels and carat.
          9.   Cooperation in means of exterminating piracy along the coast.
          10.   Cooperation in means of establishing regulations regarding Chinese natives emigrating to foreign countries, affording complete control and strict inspection.
          11.   Request for special Imperial orders to the various provincial high officials that whenever Englishmen buy land they must help them get a clear title and a deed drawn up in writing and duly recorded.
          12.   Request for special Imperial orders to the various provincial high authorities that the persons, lives and property of Englishmen are to be protected.
          13.   Request for special Imperial orders to the various provincial high officials that whenever an Englishman is cheated in money or goods by a Chinese native or is otherwise wronged, the

offender is to be immediately arrested and redress given.

14. The surtax of 2 mace per picul which has been added at
Canton to all tea used, to be stopped, the revenues which have been
collected to be returned to England and deducted from the back
customs due at Shanghai.

15. In the second (Chinese) month (March 17-April 14) of
1847, former commissioner Ch'i-ying agreed to a definite date to
allow Englishmen to enter the capital city of Kwangtung; we request
that His Imperial Majesty issue a special edict ordering compliance
with this agreement.

16. After the establishment of the new treaty, if there are
urgent grounds necessitating revision, then the new treaty shall
again be discussed and revised; otherwise, after a period of twelve
years it shall again be discussed and concluded.

17. At the various trading ports means shall be devised to
establish official warehouses for temporary housing of goods awaiting sale, so that goods which are not all sold can be exported and,
if eventually sold, duties will be paid according to the schedule.

18. In the present treaty the English version shall be standard,
with perhaps both parties affixing signatures to Chinese and English
texts to prevent deception. (IWSM.HF 9; 41b, 6-43b, 3)

185. November 5, 1854. AMERICAN NOTE: Summary of the Précis
Submitted by Robert McLane.

Articles submitted by the American barbarian chief, McLane:

1. According to Article 4 of the Treaty of Wanghsia, when
Chinese and United States officials at the five ports have intercourse,
whether personal interviews or interchange of public documents, both
parties must be equal. Subsequently when the United States sends a
commissioner to one of the five ports he must communicate with the
local provincial governor general and governor; if there is an interview, the meeting must be in the official yamen of either China or the
United States in order to preserve intact the genuinely friendly feeling
between the two countries. The Chinese officials have never once
been willing to exchange visits, thus engendering not a few difficulties.

2. Article 17 of the treaty states that citizens of the United
States trading at the five ports, whether permanent or temporary,
are allowed to rent houses or lease land and build houses, as well
as to establish hospitals, churches, and cemeteries. The repeated
difficulties encountered in trying to take advantage of this article
have been given in detail in the précis. Hereafter, a special rule
must be laid down allowing citizens of the United States to lease
dwellings and business houses or to lease land and build, the same
as natives of China.

3. Article 24 of the treaty concerns the settlement of controversies between Chinese and nationals of the United States.

Hereafter, when there are such occurrences, the officials of the two countries at the said port must make a joint investigation, arrest and bring the two parties to court, get absolutely indisputable proof. After the inquiry is completed, the two parties will go to their respective officials for sentence and punishment. The details of the case must then be reported to the said country's high officials.

4. According to Article 20 of the treaty, American goods in the five ports on which duty has been paid can be moved to another of the five ports for sale without payment of additional duty. Hereafter, this clause must be extended to allow specially designated cargo boats, which have received a permit to come and go at will, to carry goods from one port to another, but only among the five ports.

5. According to Article 13 of the treaty, duties can be paid in sycee or in foreign silver. Hereafter, silver of all countries must be accepted according to fineness and weight. Gold coin of the United States must also be accepted according to fineness. If pure silver and pure gold be exchanged it should be at a ratio of 15; for instance, one pound of pure gold (that is 12 ounces) should be changed for 15 pounds of pure silver. Accordingly, all gold of any degree of fineness could circulate by weight. English, French, American, Philippine, Mexican (that is, the "Eagle Silver" country) Peruvian, Mo-li,[13] or African gold or silver coin could all be accepted for payment of customs according to fineness and allowed to circulate. Therefore, at this time the Court of China should have officials, appointed by the Emperor, confer with officials of the three powers and determine the value of silver and gold coin of various kinds for circulation, according to the fineness and weight of pure gold and pure silver.

6. The tariff schedule fixed at the time the treaty was drawn up must be revised. Hereafter, the duty on exports cannot exceed one percent ad valorem, and duty on imports must not be over five percent.

7. Hereafter, whenever the Great President of the United States notifies His Imperial Majesty, if both act reasonably, the treaty shall be reconsidered at any time.

8. All goods brought to the five trading ports by merchants of the United States shall be allowed to be stored temporarily, without payment of duty, in government warehouses under the protection of the said merchants and the Chinese Customs House, but the deposit must not exceed a period of three years. Within three years, full customs, storage, and carrying charges having been paid, the goods can be removed, and the merchants can, according to the treaty, deposit or dispose of them as they wish.

---

13 Unidentified place name.

9. As to the duties demanded by China in the Shanghai area,
from September 7 of last year, 1853 (i. e., 3: 8.5) to July 12, 1854
(i. e., 4: 6.8), since there were no Chinese officials at the said port
and no officials of the United States to assist, it was impossible to
handle the customs. Consequently, merchants of the United States
recorded in the books of their country's consul the amount owed (in
foreign dollars) for those particular duties. These His Imperial
Majesty should rescind. Since the merchants of the United States
have a claim against the Chinese officials that their countrymen
were overcharged two mace per catty on tea exported at Canton in
1849 (i. e., Tao-kuang 29), this country does not care to discuss it.
Further, while in the port of Shanghai imports have been stored and
are hard to sell, they cannot be moved to any part of the interior for
sale. Besides, the price of silver has gone up, causing the merchants of the United States to lose their capital and increasing as
much as three times the price of tea, silk, and other Chinese
products and goods. Altogether, losses on imports have amounted
to no less than [word missing in the original.] one million (foreign
dollars).

10. After having paid duty on goods at Shanghai, merchants
of the United States should be allowed, either using their own ships
or leasing Chinese ships, to move them into the Yangtze River
basin without limitation or hindrance. The United States will provide them protection herself. It must be assured that neither the
merchants of the United States nor those of other places who thus
enter waters of the interior to trade shall disgrace the flag of the
United States. Chinese officials must also cooperate with those of
the United States in protecting the lives and property of these
merchants trading in accordance with the treaty. And further,
since it is our desire firmly to establish the friendship of the two
countries, it is necessary that citizens of the United States, whether
in matters of trade or other things, act in accordance with the
established laws of His Imperial Majesty. We ask that passport
certificates be issued enabling them to come and go or to live any
place in the interior, always looking to China for protection, and
also allowing them to rent houses and build residences, establish
hospitals, churches and cemeteries, just as provided in the original treaties for the five trading ports.

11. Hereafter, to avoid misunderstandings between the
officials and peoples of the United States and China as well as to
avoid future difficulties, it is essential that permission be given
for the United States, whenever she likes, to send high officials or
other officials with power to act, to reside at the capital of China,
if circumstances warrant, to enable them and the prime minister
either to exchange notes or meet personally for the joint conduct
of business and, should it meet His Imperial Majesty's pleasure,

to deal directly with the Court.

12. The revised customs regulations must be set up clearly. Hereafter all products and manufactures of the United States and China are to be brought into the ports at will by the people of both countries without payment of any duties. Furthermore, Chinese coastal enterprises shall also be extended to citizens of the United States with equal advantages; that is to say, Chinese coastal, peninsular, and insular fishing and prospecting privileges, handled necessarily according to Imperial orders, shall be extended equally to citizens of the United States. The Chinese already have these two enterprises, and if there can be mutual cooperation these undertakings will naturally increase daily, while Chinese trade and customs must needs also increase daily.   (IWSM. HF 9; 43b, 4-47a, 8)

186. November 6, 1854. MEMORIAL: Kuei-liang Reports the Arrival of Count Kleskowsky as Deputy Representative of France.

Governor General of Chihli Kuei-liang memorializes. On the third of the present month (November) the English and American chiefs came for an interview. They submitted a précis of several pages, containing mostly things hard to grant, although the phraseology was respectful and compliant. Now they have left the harbor and await a letter.

In addition, a French representative, Kleskowsky,[14] (came) saying that his country's envoy came in the same spirit as the English and Americans, but, being detained by a damaged ship, had sent him ahead to look for a place to carry on negotiations. He had no other request. His country's twelve-year treaty, beginning in 1844, has been in force ten years, and he was instructed to come alone to register complaints.

Your slave notes that the précis submitted by the barbarian chiefs has not yet been copied and sent to him by the said general and tao-t'ai, but assumes Ch'ung-lun and others must have memorialized them.

Vermilion endorsement: Noted.   (IWSM. HF 9; 47a, 9-47b, 6)

187. November 8, 1854. MEMORIAL: Chi-erh-hang-a Reviews the Shanghai Back Customs Situation and Urges a Settlement at Canton or Shanghai.

Governor of Kiangsu Chi-erh-hang-a memorializes. It is humbly considered that the only method of handling barbarians is that of our gratefully received Imperial Edict -- holding firmly

---

14 Count Michel Alexandre Kleskowsky (Kleczkowski) (1818-1885), native of Galicia, became a naturalized French citizen in 1850 and was attached to the French legation in 1854. Couling, *Encyclopaedia Sinica*, p. 276.

to existing treaties, to exemplify them with good faith, humble them with reason, and mollify them with favor--these three, outside of which there is no good plan.   What the barbarians now say of helping us expel rebels is intrinsically incredible, but there is someting demonstrable in the matter of customs.

When Shanghai fell last year, barbarian customs had already defaulted.   After English Chief Bowring, during the fifth month (June 7-July 5), came to Shanghai and established a new schedule, the old schedule was ordered adjusted and the deficiency made up.   Then he went to Canton.   After he returned to Shanghai, he stated that the English chief formerly at Canton, Bonham, had gone home and stated emphatically that China had been unable to protect English chieftains, that none of the five ports was peaceful, and that goods could not be extensively sold.   Therefore, his sovereign had ordered that the deficiency according to the old schedule need not be paid.   Now Bowring, out of consideration of China's just treatment and unbroken friendly relations, has notified his sovereign that payments would be made according to the new schedule, as usual, in order to fulfill their agreement.   He has also asked that the deficiency according to the old schedule be entirely made up, and now awaits his country's reply with instructions to act.

From July 12, when the Custom House opened, this being the midst of the trading season, it is estimated that over 400,000 taels have been collected under the new schedule.   Besides the barbarian customs, there are no funds to count on.   It is much feared that these barbarian leaders will find a pretext to start trouble, as Bonham did, and refuse to pay duties.   Then, not only will the Shanghai garrison have its supplies cut off but the Nanking, Ching-k'ou and Hung-tan-ch'üan garrisons will all likewise be without support.

It is observed that the request of these barbarian chiefs to have Imperial Commissioners sent to discuss treaty revisions is not fundamentally a rash utterance, and (Your slave) makes bold to bring it secretly to the Imperial ear.   Nor has he been coerced by the barbarians and wrongly acceded to their requests in thus memorializing.   On other occasions when these barbarians made unseemly requests, Your slave stopped them with reason nor could they persist in their arguments.   These people in their hearts are secretive while outwardly they persistently assume the role of reason, but if their reason is deficient and ours is straight, they must needs fail.

Now they say that the treaty has run its twelve years and should be revised, and they also complain querulously because the governor general of Liang-kuang will neither act nor respond.   Your slave does not know how things have been done in Canton and has said merely that the port of Tientsin will hardly accommodate large ships and that the governor general of Canton at this time has many troubles but after a little will certainly investigate and manage, thus adroitly enlightening them. They stolidly refused to listen and Your slave had no means of stopping them, not daring to use force to prevent their going North. In Your slave's stupid way of thinking, while the barbarians thus talk conciliation we should promptly control and make use of them.

If it pleases Your Majesty to appoint a high official to act with the governor general of Liang-kuang to make a slight revision of the trade regulations which have run twelve years, in order to justify their hopes, their inclination to help the rebellious and oppose the righteous can be curbed. Then afterwards (if we) find means to insist on their paying up the back customs and continuing to pay the new duties, and all the needs of the army are supplied, the minds of soldiers and people will be gratified and the general welfare can be protected without apprehension. Besides, water transport of tribute rice will not be delayed. With careful timing it may be feasible. This is just Your slave's restricted view, nor is he coerced or hoodwinked by others.

In the barbarians' communication they spoke especially of the generosity of their treatment by the Shanghai officials. It is noted that when the governor general and Your slave met the barbarians, everything was in accordance with the old regulations, without the least additional generosity. The generosity they speak of must refer to their being afforded an interview, and so they said we were generous. Further, the statement about the customs tao-t'ai and the various consuls, in accordance with the treaty, negotiating revision of the regulations, refers to the loss of the records after the fall of Shanghai and the setting up of a new customs house, while delaying the payment of barbarian customs, stating that if there were any variation from the original treaty, complete adjustment should be made to accord with its regulations.

Now what the barbarian chiefs request may still be considered as obedient and begging Imperial favor. If we continue to soothe them there will be no loss of prestige. To wait until there is contradiction or until insubordiantion develops and then try to conciliate is not as good as to use the plan of cherishing those from afar. (IWSM.HF 9; 47b, 7-49b, 4)

188. November 8, 1854. EDICT: Chides Chi-erh-hang-a's Naiveté and Orders Settlement at Shanghai of the Three Items Determined Negotiable by the Court.

Edict to the Grand Councillors. Chi-erh-hang-a has memorialized a secret account of the barbarian situation. The said memorial aims basically at preserving intact the customs revenue; but to compromise endlessly is the way to become coerced by others. Barbarian shipping trade, counting from 1844 when the

treaties were exchanged, has not yet run twelve years, but these
barbarians have already made a pretext for revision. Their motives
are certainly perverse. Now Bowring and McLane have each presented a précis at Tientsin; the purport of both is false and rash and
the items impossible to accede to are legion, but that of the English
barbarians is much the worse. Among the items, only three are
relatively insignificant: the request for settlement of disputes between
the populace and barbarians, the request for remission of back
customs in the Shanghai affair, and the request to terminate the
additional duty of two mace per picul levied on tea in recent years
at Canton. Orders have been given Ch'ung-lun, Wen-ch'ien, and
others to explain reasonably and order them to return to Kwangtung
or Shanghai for settlement. The other items, clearly contrary to
the existing treaties, are entirely repudiated.

But the said governor abruptly states that the request of the barbarian chiefs was only that Imperial Commissioners be appointed and
was not perverse or rash; how is it that Chi-erh-hang-a never mentions
the various articles presented by the barbarians? It is not that We
consider the said governor rash in memorializing for (the barbarians),
but We think him undiscerning in being unable to stop them.

On this occasion have not Ch'ung-lun, Wen-ch'ien and others on
the one hand flung back the barbarian document and on the other hand
managed to memorialize it? But their reasoned explanations and conflicts were all done as on their own initiative, making the barbarians
realize that inordinate requests cannot be presented with impunity.
And even the above-mentioned three items were not immediately accepted. Besides, ordering them back to Kwangtung or Shanghai to
await settlement is the way to effect revision. What need is there
to appoint Imperial Commissioners? Now there is a slight clue in
the settlement made at Tientsin. If they actually go back to the South
as ordered, I-liang and Chi-erh-hang-a shall, even in the matter of
these three articles, take due pains that the settlement show our
control and not permit the development of further complications. We
think that Ch'ung-lun, Wen-ch'ien and others, when the barbarians
go back, must needs give the said governor general and others a
full-detailed account of the circumstances of the several days' cross-
questioning, so that they can conscientiously make a thorough investigation and reasonable settlement.   (IWSM. HF 9; 49b, 5-50b, 2)

189. November 12, 1854. MEMORIAL: Ch'ung-lun Reports His Reply
to Bowring and McLane and the Satisfactory Conclusion of the Affair.

Former Ch'ang-lu Salt Controller Ch'ung-lun, Ch'ang-lu Salt
Controller Wen-ch'ien, and Tientsin Garrison Commander Shuang-jui
memorialize. Your slaves, after thorough deliberation, have refuted
the said barbarians' willful and rash requests item by item. Although
we conceded them the consideration of three clauses we did not give

our consent readily. As to the contents of our communication to the barbarians, we said merely that there might be something negotiable. Then after sending the dispatch of the 8th (November), we received replies from both the barbarian chiefs, McLane and Bowring between 7 and 9 in the morning of the 10th. We find they say that, because the various items requested were not all granted, whether or not they would subsequently be memorialized was not indicated at all and the barbarians wanted to return to their sovereigns before they decided on future procedure. So Your slave prepared replies for the barbarian chiefs' guidance, specifying the three items which had been decided upon as negotiable and which under the circumstances we agreed to memorialize fully: that tea duties pertained to Canton, the back customs to Shanghai, to which places they would have to repair, and that on their arrival the governors general and governors of those places would have received Imperial Edicts authorizing them to investigate and manage.

Furthermore, between 11 and 1 (noon) a report was received from the acting lieutenant general of Ta-ku, Hung Chih-kao, that two barbarian ships weighed anchor from their original anchorage and left port between 9 and 11 a.m. of the 10th.

It is noted that on this occasion the English and American barbarian chiefs, McLane and Bowring, came to Tientsin and presented copies of their requests, and that although these were successively rejected, there were still three items negotiable. Examining their objectives, the emphasis was upon the Shanghai back customs, the Canton excess tea duty, and trade in the Yangtze basin. The other items were no more than empty talk noised abroad. Although it is the nature of barbarians to be extraordinarily persistent, we were able to circumvent their cunning schemes, but we are obliged to request an Imperial Edict ordering the governor general of Liang-kuang, the governor general of Liang-chiang, and the governor of Kiangsu, when the barbarian ships of McLane and Bowring arrive, on the one hand to make stringent defense plans, and on the other hand to take the three items which they are allowed to handle, consider the circumstances, make settlement and memorialize fully, making clear to the barbarians that Tientsin has never been the place to handle barbarian affairs, in order to remove the possibility of their coming back later on. (IWSM.HF 9; 50b, 3-51b, 1)

190. November 12, 1854. EDICT: Commends Ch'ung-lun's Diplomacy and Orders I-liang and Yeh Ming-ch'en to Manage the Envoys in the South.

Edict to the Grand Councillors. Ch'ung-lun and others have memorialized their refutation of the various requests of the barbarian chiefs, making out a report for Our perusal, and also the departure of the barbarian ships from the port. We have examined

the memorial comprehensively, and the rejected items were handled
entirely properly. Today orders have been given I-liang and Yeh
Ming-ch'en to deliberate properly and secretly after the barbarians
go South. They are only authorized to consider the three items,
calculate their importance and how best to effect control. Ch'ung-
lun and the others are also ordered to send the original records of
the various aspects of the present negotiation, distinguishing between
particular and general, to the governors general and governor of
Liang-kuang and Liang-chiang, for examination and use. Whether or
not the barbarian ships, even though they have weighed anchor and
left harbor, do go South, they are further instructed to ascertain
immediately and memorialize fully by courier.

The separate memorial states that the French barbarians had
prepared a note asking for the release of a barbarian missionary.
The established regulations do not authorize the barbarians to venture
into the interior, outside of the five trading ports. How is it that in
the vicinity of Chou-chih-hsien, Shensi, there is this barbarian
missionary? If he was seized by the said local officials, how should
the affair be investigated and settled? Ch'ung-lun and others shall
notify Wang Ch'ing-yün to ascertain if there is such a case and decide
it according to the old regulations; on the other hand, he should stop
them with suitable language and order these barbarians not to tarry
in Tientsin, so as to avoid the development of further complications.
(IWSM. HF 9; 51b, 2-52a, 2)

191. November 12, 1854. EDICT: Instructs the Shanghai and Canton
Officials to Continue Negotiations on a Strictly Commercial Level.
      Additional Edict. Ch'ung-lun and others have memorialized that
the English and American barbarian ships have weighed anchor and
left port. Assuming that within a few days they will be able to sail
to the South, orders have been sent Ch'ung-lun and others to send a
comprehensive account of the Tientsin negotiations to the Kwangtung
and Kiangsu governors general and governors.

This time, when the barbarian chiefs came North, they insisted
that it was to ask for the appointment of high officials and did not
dare to make their objectives clear. They waited until Ch'ung-lun
and the others had met them and explained repeatedly before they
submitted their requests. Their rashness and obstruction are un-
bounded. We have secretly ordered Ch'ung-lun and the others to
repudiate them entirely. Only three items -- the controversies
between people and barbarians, the Shanghai back customs, and the
Kwangtung tea duty -- are allowed to be investigated and disposed of.
Furthermore, Ch'ung-lun and the others answered the barbarians
as of their own opinion. As the barbarian chiefs suspected that no
memorial had been sent, Ch'ung-lun and the others consented to
memorialize for them and ordered them to return to Canton and

await investigation and settlement. Then only did the barbarians speak of weighing anchor.

Considering their going South to mean, if not Shanghai, then Kwangtung, and regarding what they said about returning to their countries for instructions as not more than empty talk, Yeh Ming-ch'en, I-liang, and Chi-erh-hang-a are ordered closely and secretly to spy them out at the respective ports. If the barbarian chiefs return with more requests, tell them that Ch'ung-lun and the others have memorialized the reasonable items, but that the back customs are at Shanghai, the tea duties in Kwangtung, and the controversies between people and barbarians are necessarily at the trading ports, and although their memorials could be sent from Tientsin their (grievances) could not be settled there; that an Imperial Edict has been received transferring the investigation to Shanghai and Kwang-ung, where a just settlement must be made. As to the other items, not only can they not be memorialized from Tientsin but not even the Commissioner of Barbarian Affairs would dare lightly to memorialize them. If they did ignorantly and rudely petition, the memorializing official himself would incur severe reprimand, while there would be no benefit to the said barbarians' trade.

These barbarians think only of profit; in their rushing back and forth, their purpose does not go beyond matters of trade and customs. Therefore, if we grant a little of what they ask they will certainly be tamed into silence. But the item which Ch'ung-lun points out in his memorial regarding trade in the Yangtze River must be rigorously intercepted, nor can the barbarians be allowed to know that this idea has been memorialized, lest it provide them with the excuse of waiting for an Edict or waiting for an Endorse-ment. The said governors general and governors must by all means study the circumstances and make a proper settlement. The time of arrival and the circumstances of the interview they are ordered to memorialize speedily and secretly.

As to the French barbarian Kleskowsky's coming to Tientsin, he did not mention matters of trade. Whether he did not further protest because the English and American barbarians' ruse failed, or whether it was actually not his objective, Ch'ung-lun and the others are to tell him plainly to return South. The respective governors general and governors are to scrutinize his various movements and find means to control him.

Today's memorial and supplement of Ch'ung-lun and the others, as well as the seven memorials of Ch'ung-lun, Wen-ch'ien and the others of October 10, 24, November 1 and 5, and the secret Edict to Ch'ung-lun and the others of November 5, are all ordered copied and sent for their examination. (IWSM. HF 9; 52a, 4-53a, 7)

192. November 12, 1854. CH'UNG-LUN'S NOTE TO BOWRING:
Formal Notice of the Three Items to Be Negotiated and Rejection of
the Rest.

Communication to England. By way of communication: a few
days ago when the present ministers met with you, we stated fully
to the honorable envoys that anything not detrimental to either
(country), beneficial to both, or beneficial to one country and not
harmful to China could be discussed; that anything entirely selfish
or not within reason would be virtually impossible to accede, with
which the honorable envoys entirely agreed. We recognize their
profound intelligence and broad understanding.

The present ministers (then) took with them the précis, opened
and read it carefully. Take for example the three items, the desire
to reside at the capital, to travel freely in the interior, and to reside
and trade in Tientsin. The capital city is the sanctum of the Imperial Court, Tientsin borders on its suburbs, and as to penetrating
the various parts of the interior, there has never been a foreigner
in there. May we ask if your honorable country could give China a
foot or an inch of its territory? It is entirely unnecessary to discuss.

To continue, as to the desire to communicate with Chinese
local officials, rules have already been negotiated and established.
The ranking officials of our country have their respective official
duties; how can they flit about to interviews wherever the honorable
envoys go? As to the revision of the customs schedule and the
entry of opium with a published duty, we find that the honorable
country's treaty is for ten thousand years, and it would seem that
there is no need of further discussion. The clause providing for
unimpeded loading and transfer of goods at the ports is extremely
difficult to grant. As to imports and exports on which duties have
been paid at the five ports, not being subject to further duties at
customs barriers in the interior, we find that Chinese customs
houses all have their duties established long ago. How can old
regulations be suddenly changed? As to the payment of customs
either in sycee or foreign silver or foreign dollars, weight standards
all have fixed regulations and cannot conveniently be changed. Besides, the desire to establish government warehouses, delayed sale
of goods, etc., must all be done according to the old treaties, as it
would be extremely difficult to revise them at will. As to the desire
to enter the capital city of Kwangtung, it is even more difficult to
accede. As the above several items are very injurious to our
country, they are all virtually impossible to accede. Since the
present ministers are not even able to consider these requests,
how dare they memorialize them?

As to controversies between Chinese and the various nationals,
the original treaties can be referred to. If the local officials have
recently given unfair judgments, the governors general and governors

of the said provinces must be appealed to for just investigation and settlement. The request to cancel the back customs because the Shanghai local banditti have caused trouble, making trade difficult and causing merchants to suffer losses, is somewhat detrimental to China, but His Imperial Majesty, who soothes and controls Court and province and pacifies those from afar by comforting them, might be able to reduce (the indebtedness) somewhat, as usual by having the said provincial governor general and governor deliberate and memorialize asking Imperial grace. As to the Kwangtung tea surcharge of two mace per picul, there are no records at Tientsin to refer to and it also must be determined by the governor general of Liang-kuang. Although the above three items are somewhat to China's detriment, they are still within reason and negotiable. But on customs affairs the present ministers are not fully informed nor are there any records to examine, and besides this is not the place to handle foreign trade. Only consideration of the fact that the honorable envoys are all responsible officials of their respective countries and have come far through wind and wave to ask for a memorial on their behalf, has led the present ministers, after thorough investigation, to discard the articles detrimental to Our Country, delete those they dare not memorialize, and, disregarding the rashness it involved, memorialize those somewhat reasonable and negotiable items, (and) ask to have the governor general of Liang-kuang carefully examine the circumstances resulting in losses and possibly somewhat reduce them. So the honorable envoys must naturally return to Kwangtung and wait.

Besides, in the original regulations it is the American and French (treaties) which contain the twelve-year revision clause. As your honorable country concluded a ten-thousand-year treaty and has nothing excepting the clause that "if Imperial favor is shown other countries all shall participate equally," you certainly cannot take the lead in starting separate negotiations contrary to the former treaty.

On this occasion of the honorable envoy's coming to Tientsin, the present ministers have in all respects treated him courteously; even those items which were rejected were discussed reasonably and, besides, those requests which could be compromised were selected and memorialized for adjustment. Nothing has been done that is not in the spirit of complete friendliness. If the statements made previously are stubbornly adhered to, the present ministers will not even meet him. Therefore this document is prepared for communication. This is that communication.

<u>Vermilion endorsement</u>: Seen. (IWSM.HF 9; 53a, 8-55a, 10)

193. November 12, 1854. CH'UNG-LUN'S NOTE TO McLANE:
Formal Notice of the Three Items to Be Negotiated and Rejection of
the Rest.

    Communication to America. By way of communication. At the
recent interview the present ministers carefully stated to the
honorable enovys that anything beneficial to one or the other (country)
and not detrimental to both, or beneficial to the various countries and
not harmful to China could be discussed, but that which was entirely
selfish and not within reason would be virtually impossible to accede.
For instance, the honorable envoy is now envoy plenipotentiary with
discretionary powers; suppose we asked if he could give a foot or an
inch of his honorable country to our China? Isn't it entirely unreasonable? Although the various countries are beyond the seas,
men's hearts are alike in this and would, we trust, alike recognize
this reasoning. If action is to follow desires, disregarding good faith
and principle, the present ministers cannot abide such unreasonable
requests themselves, so how could they memorialize them? The
honorable envoys have treated us courteously and speak of friendly
relations between our two countries, so we trust they will believe
what the present ministers say.

    The précis has been scanned minutely. Of the various items in
the document, let us take for instance the one concerning communication with Chinese local officials. We have fixed regulations; the
ranking local officials all have their duties, so how could they constantly give interviews wherever they (the foreigners) go? As to
the lease and purchase of dwellings and land and the movement and
sale of goods, this must accord with the old treaties. It would be
impossible to allow promiscuous building and travel. The Yangtze
River is by no means a place where the various countries should
go; coastal fishing and prospecting have no connection with trade
but are extraordinary propositions outside the five ports. Would
China be allowed to invade at will the territory of the various
countries? As to future duties being payable in either sycee or the
equivalent in foreign silver, this has long been the practice, but
there has never been a gold standard; even Chinese land taxes have
never been paid in gold. Nor has the proposed temporary lodgment
of goods in government warehouses under the joint protection of the
various states and the Chinese customs house ever been our policy.
The capital city is the sanctum of the Imperial Court and foreigners
have never intruded therein. The present ministers have separately
investigated the various above items for rationality and find them
all virtually impossible to accede.

    As to controversies between Chinese and various foreigners,
there are the original treaties to refer to. If the local officials have
judged unfairly, it will be necessary to ask the said governor
general and governor to make a fair adjustment. Whether or not

the trouble caused by the Shanghai banditti has brought difficulties to trade and losses to merchants, we are not thoroughly informed. Although the request for cancellation of back customs dues is detrimental to China, His Imperial Majesty, who soothes and controls Court and provinces and pacifies those from afar by comforting them, may be able to reduce them somewhat, as usual having the respective governors general and governors investigate them clearly and memorialize for Imperial grace. As to the Kwangtung tea duty surcharge of two mace per picul, there are no records at Tientsin for reference and it must also be handled through the governor general of Liang-kuang. Although the above three items are rather detrimental to China, their content somewhat approaches reason and they are negotiable. Although customs matters are not thoroughly understood by the present ministers, nor are there any files to examine, nor is this the place to handle foreign trade, they still realize that the honorable envoys are responsible to their countries and have come far by land and sea to ask for a memorial. The present ministers have investigated carefully, discarding those items very injurious to Our Country, and even to those which they would not venture to memorialize, they have given due consideration. They have memorialized the three negotiable articles, at great risk to themselves, asking to have the governor general of Liang-kuang examine the actual losses and determine whether or not they can be partially rescinded.

The honorable minister must therefore return to Kwangtung and wait. If not, the present ministers cannot see him again in any case. On this occasion of the honorable envoy's coming to Tientsin, the present ministers have in all matters treated him courteously; even those articles rejected were discussed reasonably, and from those of their requests which could be adjusted they selected three for memorializing, to fulfill their purpose of friendliness. Therefore a document has been prepared for communication. This is that communication.

Vermilion endorsement:. Seen. (IWSM.HF 9, 55b, 1-57a, 9)

194. December 14, 1854. MEMORIAL: I-liang Reports Meeting of Chi-erh-hang-a with Bowring and McLane at Shanghai.

Governor General of Liang-chiang I-liang and Governor of Kiangsu Chi-erh-hang-a memorialize. It is noted that Bowring and McLane, on November 16 and 17 respectively, came to Shanghai. They have made no further move, but it was reported that Chief Bowring wanted to interview Your slave Chi-erh-hang-a. It was learned further that he had set the nineteenth for weighing anchor and returning to Canton and would not return here. At that time (Your slave) had not received the Imperial Decree and did not know the facts of the Tientsin settlement. Fearful of some mistake, Your slave, Chi-erh-hang-a, took advantage of the report that

Bowring wanted an interview and met them on the eighteenth at a business office.

The two chiefs, Bowring and McLane, said:

> Imperial Commissioner Ch'ung, who graciously came to Tientsin for a conference, considered only three items, none of them of much significance. The really important matters were not memorialized. They would not bother the Chinese officials again. Having already memorialized their sovereigns fully of the facts, they would wait for a reply and then act accordingly. For the time being they would not venture to interfere, nor was there anything further to discuss.

Furthermore, they produced the rough drafts of the communications exchanged with Ch'ung-lun and others for me to examine. Your slave Chi-erh-hang-a saw that the requests made were very different from the précis presented at Shanghai, and he interrogated them. They said that the précis presented at Shanghai concerned matters prior to the seventh month [i.e., before July 25]; that since returning to Kwangtung in accord with an Imperial Edict, having also received mandates from their own sovereigns to draft a treaty, they had returned to Shanghai and then gone to Tientsin; hence they had been unable to show the précis to us; that, as the treaty which they had shown to the Imperial Commissioner had not been memorialized, their responsibility was terminated; whatever the subsequent arrangement, they would not venture to act on their own authority.

Since the chiefs have increased their demands several-fold with each visit, Your slave, Chi-erh-hang-a was impelled to ask about the Shanghai back customs. The said chiefs originally said that they had instructed the merchants to make up the payments as computed and added that if their mission depended on it the old customs would be recovered. With these words ringing in our ears, how could they immediately ask for cancellation as soon as they arrived at Tientsin? With such inconsistency, any contingency may develop. Chief Bowring said bluntly that the Imperial Commissioner had been without full powers and that they were really embarrassed [without face]; that since the cancellation of the old duties had been authorized, they need not be mentioned again. His expression reflected disappointment. Although Chief McLane's words were affable, he was no more discursive. He said merely that minutiae need not be discussed again, but he asked that another Imperial Commissioner be sent to negotiate important matters, in order to consolidate friendly relations, and he said that it could not be delayed until 1856.

Your slave Chi-erh-hang-a told them that, as an Imperial Commissioner had already investigated and memorialized fully, their trade would be greatly improved, but that Chinese customs receipts had been curtailed, that His Imperial Majesty's self-denying

magnanimity, cherishing those from afar, was immeasurably deep
and vast; that if we again memorialized an imprudent request for the
appointment of another Imperial Commissioner, the present govern-
or would personally incur heavy punishment, and their trade would
not be benefited in the least. The discussion went on for two hours.
They said that since (Your slave) would not memorialize for them
they would wait until next year, when their countries' replies came,
to renew negotiations, and dispersed.

Now, what these chiefs meant by important matters were particularly admission to Yangtze trade, the import of opium on payment of duty, and such rash proposals. Only by cutting them off
with stern language could Your slaves possibly have stopped their
covetousness.

Early on the 19th (of November), Chief Bowring boarded ship and
weighed anchor. Chief McLane left for Canton on the 27th, but the
French chief Bourboulon has not yet promised to return to Canton.
Although the French barbarians' trade is not large, their military
strength is very great. Whenever the outside barbarians need
soldiers they all make use of their strength. Their nationals in
China are engaged only in the propagation of Catholicism. It has
long been their desire to have a Catholic Church established at the
capital, to get permission to preach in the North, and to travel
throughout the interior. Hence they were summarily intercepted. On
this occasion, Kleskowsky went north to deliver in person a public
letter with no other objective than this. Whether or not he has returned South has not yet been learned with certainty.

Vermilion endorsement: Noted. Everything must be handled
calmly. Do not entertain their requests. If you take special pains
to control them rigidly and to check them courteously, how far will
these barbarians' cunning get them? (IWSM. HF 10; 1a, 2-3a, 4)

Chapter 6

Shanghai, Liu-ch'iu, and the Minor Ports, 1855-1856
(Documents 195-206)

This small group of miscellaneous documents covers the period from December 19, 1854 to February 14, 1856. There are twelve items --eight memorials and four edicts. There are five Vermilion endorsements preserved on the eight memorials in this group. Two of these are the routine endorsement "noted"; two are general indications that the document has been read by the emperor; only one is a specific comment, appended to a long memorial of Yeh Ming-ch'en and indicating clearly that his policy at Canton had the unqualified personal approval of the emperor.

The memorialists, besides Imperial Commissioner Yeh at Canton, were I-liang, governor general of Liang-chiang; Wang I-te, governor general of Min-Che (Fukien-Chekiang); Huang Tsung-han, governor of Chekiang; and Chi-erh-hang-a, governor of Kiangsu.

The more important topics in this group are the stalemate of diplomacy at Canton, with Yeh Ming-ch'en's justification of it, and the local rebel situation at Shanghai: the problems of recovery, the possibilities of foreign aid, and the disruption of customs. Minor, but interesting, items memorialized are the report from the ruler of the Liu-ch'iu Islands (Okinawa) of Commodore Perry's visits and demands, the revelations in the case of the fallen Shanghai diplomat, Wu Chien-chang, and the transmission of four American shipwreck victims from Korea to Shanghai.

Some of the American material paralleling the Chinese documents in this chapter is included in the McLane correspondence, cited in the previous chapter. The Perry correspondence is published, U.S. Cong. 33:2, S. Ex. Doc. 34; and Francis L. Hawks' Narrative of the Japan Expedition, is published as U.S. Cong. 33:2, H. Ex. Doc. 97, in four volumes. In addition there are the Consular Letters in the National Archives and the excellent summary by Eldon Griffin, Clippers and Consuls, Ann Arbor, 1938.

TRANSLATIONS OF DOCUMENTS

195. December 19, 1854. MEMORIAL: Chi-erh-hang-a Reports on British and American Interest in the Taiping Rebel Situation in Shanghai.
Governor of Kiangsu Chi-erh-hang-a memorializes. It is humbly reported that the Shanghai insurgents have withdrawn to their lair undefeated. This is due to (the fact that) the whole district outside

the walls, from the northeast corner of Yang-chin-pin southward to
the northwest corner of San-mao-ke Bridge, is interspersed with the
temporary residences of the barbarian merchants of the various
countries, and they have repeatedly made the government troops agree
not to enter the area so as to avoid endangering their property and lives
by rifle and cannon fire. Consequently the rebels have utilized the
barbarian houses as hiding places. As soon as they are defeated by
government troops they scurry in back of the barbarian houses. When
the government troops pursue them to the area, barbarian soldiers
open a fusillade of rifle fire and a clash between troops and barbarian
results, enkindling incidents which can hardly be quelled. So Your
slave had a trench dug around the irregular boundaries of San-mao-ke
Bridge and did not allow the government troops to cross the trench,
and in addition forbade the various barbarians to afford the rebels
hiding places. Although clashes were stopped, the rebels still had
free access to and from Yang-chin-pin by way of the Little East Gate
and the North Gate. They came and went as they pleased, and our
soldiers never had a chance to intercept and rout them. Supplies of
arms, ammunition, grain, and foodstuffs also came in by this route.

In the eighth month (September 22-October 21) the governor of
Chekiang, Huang Tsung-han, informed me by letter of a native of
Ningpo who had asked leave to return home. He was a Hanlin bachelor
named Chang T'ing-hsüeh, related to one Yang Fang, who was waiting
for an appointment as magistrate and operating a foreign goods store
at Yang-ching-pin, and who could negotiate with (the foreigners).
Your slave thereupon delegated the prefect of Chia-ting-hsien, Wu Hsü,
to consult with Chang T'ing-hsüeh and Yang Fang and make careful
plans for building a wall along the river bank outside the North Gate,
something over 500 chang (5875 feet) long, completely blocking the
bridges and roads, thus enabling us to intercept supplies and leaving
the rebels no place of refuge. But this place was very near the city
wall and the plan could not be carried out without the support of the
barbarians.

At that time, the English, French, and American barbarian chiefs,
Bowring and the others, had come to Shanghai from Canton. Your slave
immediately communicated with the said chiefs to order their respective consuls to cooperate in the arrangement. As the two chiefs,
Bowring and McLane, had gone to Tientsin, the American consul, Murphy,
led the opposition, saying that his country's admiral would not act
under his orders. The English consul, Alcock, seconded and exceeded
him. But the French chief, Bourboulon, and the French consul, Edan[1]
consistently made no objection. Therefore, the section adjoining the

---

1 M.B. Edan was chancellor at the French consulate at Shanghai in 1851. *Chinese Repository*, v. 20, p. 17.

French barbarians' settlement, south of Yang-ching-pin to Lo-hung-ch'iao near the North Gate, was constructed first. The Little East Gate supply route was thus cut off. When Bowring and the others returned from Tientsin, Your slave further pressed them personally. Chief McLane took personal charge of the affair and on November 22 concluded an agreement to construct the wall, to delegate American and French barbarian soldiers to guard it, and not to admit supplies of ammunition, etc., nor allow barbarians to enter the city wall promiscuously.

Who could have known that the secondary leader of the rebels, Ch'en A-lin, disguised as a barbarian, would slip into the barbarian quarter to beg for mercy and ask for help? In addition he asked the use of an American barbarian vessel to flee elsewhere. When Wu Hsü and the others learned this and secretly reported it, Your slave ordered him sought and seized, but he had slipped away. It then occurred to Your slave that even barbarian chiefs know how to simulate loyalty and justice, and could make a reasonable judgment, whereas consuls, whose villainy has a hundred manifestations, are hard to reason with so he gave orders to take advantage of the time before McLane left, working from morning till night.

When the construction reached San-mao-ke Bridge on North Gate Road, the barbarians, on the pretext that the twenty-sixth (Sunday, November 26) was a day of worship, would not operate. On the 27th, Chief McLane boarded ship and we had to see him off, and as there were no soldiers left to guard, the work had to stop. Your slave realizes that San-mao-ke Bridge, where the American barbarian residences are concentrated, is outside the wall at the North Gate, where the bringing in of supplies is convenient and escape is easy. Such is the obstructiveness of these barbarians that they might take advantage of McLane's departure to block the building of the wall at that point.

Your slave, accompanied by Lan Wei-wen and Wu Hsü, thereupon interrogated Chief McLane personally. During the discussion the barbarian admiral[2] came in holding a rifle bullet and said that the government troops had crossed the trench contrary to agreement and clashed with the rebels, causing the bullet to fly into a barbarian residence, and he demanded an investigation. As San-mao-ke Bridge was the place their troops were defending, how could they fail to see that the wall which had been built must needs have stopped a bullet (from that direction)? Actually, the bullet which he was holding had been fired by the rebels into the newly built wall and had been dug out by the barbarian soldiers, for there was a carpenter present who witnessed it.

---

[2] Probably a reference to Commodore Joel Abbott, U.S.N., commanding the United States squadron on the China station.

When Your slave saw this situation his eyes split with anger. He insisted that if the government troops crossed the trench contrary to agreement they could be court martialled, but if the rebels used foreigners' houses for refuge why didn't (the foreigners) chase them out? Where was the justice in getting angry at government troops and harboring rebels? When McLane saw the gravity of Your slave's words, the accuracy of his principles, and the severity of his tone and expression, he realized that his case was lost. He said that he only hoped that hereafter there would be no incursion by either side, and on this occasion he asked that we not investigate too thoroughly for the sake of friendship. He then agreed to the closing of San-mao-ke Bridge and immediately notified the admiral to act accordingly. He said further that everything must be done entirely in accordance with established regulations of the existing treaties, and that the slightest infraction would not be tolerated. The admiral promptly obeyed, fixed the 29th as the date for the closing of San-mao-ke Bridge, and left.

Since his words were now within reason, Your slave relaxed his expression somewhat and inquired what his motive was. He said that when the former chief, Marshall, went home he insisted that in China the beacon fires were lighted everywhere [a state of war], that the Yang (i.e., Yang Hsiu-ch'ing) rebels had taken Nanking and had already cut the country in two. He urged his king to formulate a different policy, so the king ordered him (McLane) to come out and investigate the situation. When he first reached China he visited the five ports, as well as Nanking and Chen-chiang, and made careful inquiries. Rebel Yang's conduct was plainly that of a bandit and he was not worth talking to, while the Chinese officials and people preserved law and order. Thus he recognized that His Imperial Majesty was the truly ordained Son of Heaven, so he informed his king that he wished to give his support to legitimacy and show his loyalty. Therefore he had obeyed the Imperial Edict and returned to Canton. When Governor General Yeh would not see him, he went to Tientsin. But his meeting with Imperial Commissioner Ch'ung was superficial and he could not fully express what he wanted to, and besides, as (Ch'ung-lun) did not dare to memorialize his true feelings for him there was nothing for him to do but memorialize the facts to his king and wait for orders to proceed. He said that this statement was really from the heart.

Your slave told him that his recognition of His Imperial Majesty as the truly ordained Son of Heaven was enough to attest his deep understanding of right and wrong, but his comings and goings were uncertain and the consuls arbitrarily hold our elbows and cause the dying agonies of the rebels to be prolonged, and in effect, to degrade their country's flag. The barbarian chief answered that he would certainly specifically enjoin adherence to the treaties and not allow the least transgression.

Then on the 27th he went aboard ship to return to Canton. On the 28th the rebels left the city by the Little East Gate, followed the wall around North Gate to San-mao-ke Bridge, and rushed on our encampment. As soon as the government troops attacked they retired behind the barbarian houses and raised a clamor of shouting, taunting our soldiers to cross the ditch and destroy them. The American barbarian soldiers, nominally to protect the barbarian houses, leveled rifles, moved cannon, and waited. Fortunately our men obeyed orders, stopping west of the ditch and waiting in perfect order. Not a man crossed the ditch.

On the 29th, when my representatives gathered masons and proceeded to San-mao-ke Bridge to extend the wall, the American barbarians also obstructed. Your slave immediately sent a note to the consul questioning and reprimanding him sternly, and also ordered Lan Wei-wen and Wu Hsü to have Alcock and Murphy appear at the Customs House and explain their reasons for blocking the building of the wall.

They said that the wall west of San-mao-ke Bridge was still unfinished, but once it was built to the bridge head, thus completing the barrier, there would certainly be no further argument. As to the barbarian soldiers waiting with leveled rifles and cannon in position, the purpose was to protect the barbarian houses and not to shield the rebels. In addition, they sent to Your slave's barracks the interpreter, H.N. Lay,[3] who repeated what had been said before. Your slave then said that the soldiers not crossing the ditch was certainly in accord with the agreement. If the rebels took refuge around the barbarian houses and the barbarians did not immediately drive them out, we would have to cannonade them across the barrier trench. If they seized the pretext to start a quarrel and injured our troops, they must realize that the resentment of soldiers runs deep and everyone would be outraged. Let them not say that our Chinese soldiers are no match for theirs, and then after the conflict discuss right and wrong, talking of reason and doing good deeds, when they already had the worst of it. At present the fact that our troops did not cause them trouble is explained by the present officials' orders, not by any fear. Let them think this over soberly.

As to the wall at San-mao-ke Bridge, we yield to their demand, permitting construction from the west to close the gap in the middle, and have had orders sent to Murphy not to obstruct again. On December 2 the gap at San-mao-ke Bridge was closed and supplies by way of the North Gate could also be stopped. There were still some 10 chang

---

3 Horatio Nelson Lay, son of George Tradescant Lay who died at Amoy in 1845. H.N. Lay was later Inspector General of the Chinese Maritime Customs.

(117 1/2 ft.) west of the bridge where it was essential to extend the wall. This place is the English barbarians' route in and out. Now a date for the beginning of construction has been set, and once it is finished we shall seize the opportunity to push our attack without delay.

But note these barbarians' malice behind their fair countenance, their profiting from our China's many troubles, and their seizing of the occasion to act presumptuously. For instance, after the rebel Yang (Hsiu-ch'ing) appropriated Nanking, these barbarians went back and forth to Nanking and Chen-chiang by no means infrequently. When the rebel Liu (Li-ch'uan) appropriated Shanghai, the various barbarians were not numerous and they had only a few soldiers, living in peace right near the city wall, without being disturbed the slightest. When our soldiers gathered like clouds they asked that they not attack the North, leaving this opening for bringing in supplies and for escape. So up to the eighth month of this year (September 22-October 21, 1854) they confined themselves to holding our elbows secretly, coercing us in a hundred ways. Therefore, Your slave, disregarding rashness, asked that an Imperial Commissioner be sent to Kwangtung to investigate and manage, as a means of getting them under our control; once Shanghai was recaptured new devices could be made. Since returning from Tientsin, Chief Bowring has said nothing except that he was deeply grieved. Chief McLane, on the other hand, said plainly that he was undecided which way to turn. The intercourse between the consuls and the rebels gradually transpired. The situation was almost impossible to handle. If we were severe it would certainly create a crisis; if we were lenient, advantage would be taken of us. Further, we feared another storm like the former one of 1848, stopping our ocean transport and leaving us without adequate means of coping with it.

As to the French barbarian Kleskowsky, he has gone South to ask out of justice for the old Catholic church site at Sung-chiang and also to request the release of the missionary named Fang in Shensi. Besides these things, he has nothing to ask. The French chief Bourboulon weighed anchor for Canton on December 5.

As to the present situation, although the barbarians' speech is still respectful and agreeable, their nature is that of dogs and sheep, so not much faith can be placed in it. It was necessary to make these further clarifying statements. (IWSM.HF 10; 3a, 5-7b, 7)

196. <u>December 19, 1854</u>. <u>EDICT</u>: <u>Scorns Foreign Aid and Advocates a Strong, Sovereign Policy toward the Foreigners at Shanghai.</u>

Edict to the Grand Councillors. Chi-erh-hang-a has memorialized a secret account of the activities of the various barbarians at Shanghai and also the status of present management. (We) have examined this memorial in detail. Because the Shanghai insurgents have made a practice of using the barbarians as blinds, and the same barbarians

have used the insurgents for purposes of intimidation, when our soldiers were building a wall along the river outside the North Gate, with
the nominal collaboration of the barbarian chiefs, the consuls manifested cunning in a hundred ways and obstructed everything. Actually
the barbarians are in secret conspiracy with the rebels. The evidence
is clear. Their statements of collaboration and devotion to Our cause
do not merit an ounce of belief.

At this time our one need is to collaborate with officers and soldiers in a vigorous campaign to recover the district capital (Shanghai).
There is no need to get help from these barbarians and furnish them
with pretexts. Since even the rebels' occupation of the capital (Nanking) is no reason for not proceeding to attack, how can we hesitate
because the barbarians make difficulties? The barbarians' dog-
sheep mentality is awed by strength and scorns weakness. If our
army scares at heads and scares at tails, and the unconquered Shanghai bandits make a further display of violence and oppression, these
barbarians will certainly sprout new schemes.

As for the present situation, to treat them mildly and have them
take advantage of us is not as good as to be stern and induce some
fear. Our great army is chastizing rebels, its honor is bright, and
its mission fair; it has not a hair's connection with the barbarians.
This North Gate district is still Chinese soil, not barbarian territory.
If they still dare to make open obstruction, the fault is with them,
and the quarrel not of our starting. If you tell them so plainly, (We)
think these barbarians will not dare destroy the treaties themselves.
On this occasion the governor's various reports on the suppression
situation are all verbose and evasive as well as inaccurate. If he
makes pretexts of barbarian obstruction and is unable to destroy the
bandit lair, how can the crime of delay be repeatedly condoned?
(IWSM.HF 10; 7b, 8-8b, 2)

197. January 12, 1855. MEMORIAL: Yeh Ming-ch'en Reports his
Summary Dealing with Requests for Treaty Revision at Canton.

Imperial Commissioner, Governor General of Liang-kuang Yeh
Ming-ch'en, memorializes. According to the barbarians' communication, August 29 of the present year (1854) marked the completion of
the twelve-year term of treaties and it would be necessary for them
to have an interview at my yamen to reopen negotiations. Your official
immediately replied that he could receive them either on the Canton
river or at Hu-men (Bocca-Tigris), but as for the yamen, which is
inside the city-wall, the question of access to the city was closed six
years ago. How could there be another repetition of the arguments
given before?

Immediately afterwards he heard that the barbarian chiefs went
to the ports of Amoy, Ningpo, and Shanghai to inspect trade conditions.
When in the seventh month (July 25-August 23) the said barbarians

returned to Canton, they again sent a communication and also sent to the provincial capital a minor barbarian leader who said that there were now important matters to negotiate and consent must be given before they could be presented in person. Your official immediately replied that if everything was to be done according to treaty regulations, why did they ask my consent now? But if there were to be any slight changes they would all have to be memorialized clearly and an Edict requested. Certainly Your official, a subordinate, would not dare to act on his own authority.

Thereafter, he never learned what their demands were. Now he hears that the said barbarian chiefs returned to Shanghai in the eighth month (September 22-October 21), and there is an indirect report that they will proceed to Tientsin. If these barbarians do go straight to Tientsin, no matter what their demands are, he urges that Imperial orders be given the governor general of Chihli to send the barbarian chiefs back immediately to Kwangtung, where he will enlighten them according to circumstances and find means to control them, in the hope of seeing His Majesty's anxiety relieved.

Vermilion endorsement: It has been so ordered. (IWSM.HF 10; 14a, 8-15a, 3)

198. January 21, 1855. MEMORIAL: Chi-erh-hang-a Reports American Sympathy for the Taiping Rebels at Shanghai.

Governor of Kiangsu Chi-erh-hang-a memorializes. When the wall was built at Yang-ching-pin to cut off supplies, only the French barbarians complied at first, nor did they make any other objections. This was because these barbarians' trade is not large and they have no material interest. Inside the walls the Catholic missionaries, surrounded by the rebels, were not entirely content.

The American barbarians openly gave help to and glorified the rebels. Their previous compliance to the building of the wall at San-mao-ke Bridge was given under pressure of circumstances and was unavoidable. Therefore, no sooner had construction begun than (the rebels) dug a tunnel under Ta-kou Bridge, passing underneath the wall directly to the back door of the barbarian establishment. The barbarians also acquiesced in the insurgents' building a dugout hard by the barbarian residence, and then, on the pretext that the barbarian homes had no one to protect them, demanded idemnity from the government, complaining endlessly. Only when his representatives, Wu Hsü and others, had discovered the tunnel and reported, and Your slave had questioned and reprimanded them severely, did they board it up.

The English barbarians maintained an ambiguous position, not obstructing the building of the wall, but not sending soldiers to defend it, thus bringing about the affair of the night of December 19th, when the rebels pushed down the wall. When the insurgents constructed the dugout, the three countries mutually evaded responsibility and all disregarded it. Although the dugout was nearest the American barbarians' residences, the land lay in a crescent, so that once our troops opened fire the houses of the French barbarians would be in direct line. Therefore we told the French admiral La-e-erh[4] that since the rebel dugout was completed we could not but cannonade it, and as his country's consulate was right in line it must be evacuated in order to avoid casualties; besides, as we analysed the rebels' motives, it was certain that since they regarded (the French) as the leaders in building the wall, thus incurring their anger, (the rebels) hoped to make use of us to destroy their property and lives, but we would not fall in with this scheme. The admiral bristled and said angrily "had you not pointed (this) out to us, we should almost have fallen into the rebels' trap!" He asked us to send two hundred laborers under the direction of his officers to demolish the dugout, destroying their evil plans and protecting the barbarian consulate.

But when the rebels, firing from the top of the wall at our workmen, wounded the barbarian soldiers, his anger was aroused, and a bitter clash developed which the English and Americans were not able to mediate. So Your slave himself secretly sent a dependable person under cover of night to set fire to the two American barbarian houses ordinarily used by the rebels as refuges, destroying the bandits' nest. The barbarians never discovered where the fire came from. Since it was a place our soldiers did not go to, the English barbarians, figuring that the rebels were now causing trouble for the barbarians, voluntarily agreed to allow the government troops to attack the North Gate from the Ch'en-chia Bridge district, and did not venture to hold stubbornly to their former position.

Vermilion endorsement: (We) have read the memorial and understand the situation entirely. (IWSM.HF 10; 15a, 4-16a,8)

199. January 21, 1855. EDICT: Warns against Reliance on Foreign Aid in Suppressing the Taiping Rebels in the Shanghai Area.

Edict to the Grand Councillors. Chi-erh-hang-a has memorialized on the successive attacks on the insurgents. The French Admiral La-e-erh's destruction of the rebel-built dugout, as well as his firing on the rebels, is a beginning in creating enmity between the barbarians and the insurgents, and advantage can be taken of this to attack them; but barbarian cunning has a hundred expressions, and there are still missionaries inside the city. Besides, the English and American barbarians are still in contact with the rebels. The method of control at this time lies in using the circumstances to advantage and by no means to rely alone on the help of these barbarians. If we trust them

---

4 A transliteration of the Chinese characters; the French name has not been identified.

unquestioningly the barbarians will change their minds and secretly connive with the rebel followers inside the city. Therefore beware of falling into their trap.

The said governor must order his troops and braves to attack immediately, and must recapture the prefectural capital of Shanghai within this year [i.e., by February 16, 1855]. If days are wasted in inaction, allowing that insignificant lone city to remain occupied by rebels, the governor will have committed a crime of procrastination and can hardly expect pardon.   (IWSM.HF 10; 16a, 8-16b, 6)

200. February 12, 1855. MEMORIAL: Fukien Officials Transmit an Okinawan Account of Commodore Perry's Visit to Naha.

Governor General of Min-Che Wang I-te and Governor of Fukien Lü Ch'üan-sun memorialize. According to a dispatch from Heir Apparent Shang-t'ai, via Prince (Regent) Chung-shan of Liu-ch'iu:

On January 21, 1854, an American admiral[5] on board a steamer accompanied by two other vessels came to his state and said through an interpreter that on the 15th of that month they had put out from Hong Kong, Kwangtung, and sailed with the winds directly to Liu-ch'iu, and that in a few days three other ships would arrive. Then on January 24th, two other ships did come. The admiral stated that on February 3rd he would conduct his officers and soldiers to the palace for a personal interview with the Heir Apparent and his ministers for New Year's felicitations and other purposes. The officials were repeatedly instructed to request that the meeting be solemnized with the ministers at the T'a-pa (Naha) yamen, but the barbarian would not agree.

On the 3rd he did force his way into the palace at the head of his troops. The ministers were then ordered to meet them. The barbarians paid their respects and led their troops away in silence. Then one minor official and five sailors came ashore to reside, to replace the 15 minor officers who had been left before; these, as well as the Englishman Bettleheim's[6] wife and son and the interpreters, Ch'ien Wen-ch'i and Chin Shan-ming, were taken on board the two accompanying ships and on the 7th and 8th, respectively, departed. One vessel remained. On the 14th again, an Englishman, Moreton,[7] with his wife, arrived on board an ocean-going vessel to replace Bettleheim, came ashore, and lived in the same house with him. After a while the ship returned.

On July 1st the admiral returned aboard the same ship accompanied by one other vessel. The admiral stated that "hereafter if any American ship came it must

---

5   Commodore Matthew C. Perry, U.S.N.
6   Rev. B.J. Bettleheim, M.D., went with his family to the Liu Ch'ius in 1846. *Chinese Repository*, v. 15, p. 160. Perry's comment on Bettleheim is that he was "a converted Jew, and by birth a Hungarian, not however in holy orders, but a Christian layman. He had become a British subject by naturalization, and the husband of an English woman." Hawks, *Narrative*, v. 1, p. 225.
7   G.H. Moreton and his family replaced Dr. Bettleheim as Protestant missionary on Okinawa.

be received courteously, allowed to buy anything in the markets,
and any fuel and water required should be supplied on receipt of
payment; if an American vessel encountered a storm and was driven
there and the vessel wrecked, the local officials must by all
means send persons to rescue the men and keep them until a vessel
appeared to take them home; if there were any dead, they should
furnish ground for burial." The officials were forthwith ordered
to give temporary consent. The admiral was pleased, relieved the
one minor officer and five sailors he had left behind, loaded his
store of coal, also took the Englishman Bettleheim on board and,
with the one ship which had been left behind, departed one after
the other on July 15th and 17th. This is truly what the Emperor's
virtue and prestige has effected and the whole country is grateful
no end.

As to the said barbarians, the Moretons, they still wilfully loiter
about, and for the things of their daily use they employ a great
deal of extortion, exhausting the country and embittering the people.
And even worse, they insist that we must accept Christianity, are a
constant annoyance, and there is no telling what kinds of calamities
they will induce. Our anxiety is so great that we can hardly eat or
sleep. Please tell the English chief to send a ship for Moreton and
his family and take them home so that there may be peace and quiet.

The present officials find that the English barbarian Bettleheim
and his family have long remained in Liu-ch'iu, that the American
warships have frequently caused anxiety, and on several occasions
the heir apparent of that country has begged us to restrain them.
Although the English Bettleheims, who have long remained in Liu-
ch'iu, and the American warship have departed, there are other
English barbarians, the Moretons, residing in Liu-ch'iu who act with
reckless abandon, try to force acceptance of Christianity and endlessly cause all manner of trouble. Now that the heir apparent of that
country, Shang-t'ai, has begged us to investigate and act, it is essential that his request be accorded.

We quickly notified Imperial Commissioner, Governor General of
Liang-kuang Yeh Ming-ch'en to investigate, examine the situation
there (at Canton), and give instructions as circumstances require,
urging the English chief to dispatch without delay a ship for their return, in order to evince conciliation.

Vermilion endorsement: Noted. (IWSM.HF 10; 18b, 10-20b, 4)

201. March 18, 1855. MEMORIAL: The Fukien Officials Report the
Establishment of a Foreign Residence District in Foochow.

Governor General of Min-Che Wang I-te, and Governor of Fukien
Lü Ch'üan-sun memorialize. The merchants of the various countries
of late have come increasingly to Fukien to trade, but all the tea markets

are outside the city in the Nan-t'ai district. Since barbarian traders were coming to Fukien in increasing numbers and the consular residence was far away, making it hard to investigate or control, the consul Caleb Jones[8] asked to lease the vacant plot behind the Shuang-chiang-t'ai of T'ien-an Monastery in Nan-t'ai, on which to build an office. He also asked in the meantime to lease for a temporary residence the part of Chen-ju Convent which had been confiscated. The barbarian merchants who have come to Fukien to trade, whenever they lease buildings or land for storing goods or for residences, ask to have the seal of the local officials on every lease contract in order to make it respected.

We beg to observe that the treaties state that barbarian consuls are allowed to live in cities and towns and that the place of residence for barbarian traders in Foochow is fixed south of Ta-ch'iao; that rates for leasing buildings or land must be fair, Chinese not being allowed to extort nor barbarian merchants to rent forcibly. Now that the remote barbarian comes within the pale he must be afforded legal residence. As to all the lease contracts being sealed, they are like tax receipts with us, the object being a guarantee. If the request is not met it would seem like not showing adequate consideration. But the temperment of the Fukienese is avaricious and quarrelsome. Whenever the barbarians negotiate a property lease they always raise prices and drive hard bargains. The barbarians do not relish extortion, have repeatedly said that it would spoil friendly relations and have used it as a justification for their own pressure. For instance, in the eighth month of this year (September 22-October 21, 1854) the English barbarians' tea customs dues of over 14,000 taels were withheld for three months before they finally paid them, because their leases were not settled. The barbarian temperament is inconstant, always looking for a quarrel. In matters of relations between the people and barbarians it is only by faithfully observing the treaties that both parties can obtain justice.

Now we find that the barbarian merchant Hsi-li-wei-shih-lin[9] and others have made leases from the civilians Lin Sen, Hung Ch'i-yüan, Chou T'ing-ch'i, Lin Jui-ch'üan at Kuan-ying-ching and Hsia-ting-t'ung in Ta-ch'iao and Fan-ch'uan-pu, Chung-chou-wei and other places, totalling six properties. In all cases both parties agreed to the lease, and now the contracts have been drawn. The property that the barbarian asks for, Shuang-chiang-t'ai in T'ien-an Monastery, has been arranged clearly. Every month they are to pay 50,000 cash rental to the local gentry for common use. Subsequently, when other barbarian merchants come and want to rent houses, the local officials will be ordered to

---

8 Caleb Jones of Richmond, Virginia, was appointed United States consul at Foochow on August 11, 1853, and reached his post by November, 1854. Griffin, *op. cit.*, p. 293.
9 Name of this foreign merchant' has not been identified.

manage in the same satisfactory way. (IWSM.HF 10; 20b, 5-21b,6)

202. March 18, 1855. EDICT: Approves of the Arrangements for
Foreign Residences at Foochow but Warns against Friction with Local
Inhabitants.
        Edict to the Grand Councillors. Wang I-te memorializes that the
barbarian tea traders ask permission to lease buildings for residences.
Because the tea traders could not come in, Fukien province has only
recently been opened to trade, but the various barbarian merchants
are now coming increasingly to trade. In view of the extensive receipts
of tea duties and the pressure of popular opinion, the said governor
general and governor allowed the barbarian consul to rent the vacant
land behind Shuang-chiang-t'ai in T'ien-an Monastery, Nan-t'ai, and
also allowed the barbarian merchants to rent Kuan-yin-ching and
Hsia-ting-t'ung south of Ta-ch'iao, and other places, totalling six, for
warehouses and residences. The citizens and barbarians were both
willing and besides, on all leases drawn, seals were affixed. This was
done in accordance with the former treaties.
        These barbarians come into the pale from afar and must be
furnished quarters, to show consideration. But when the residences
of citizens and barbarians are intermingled there must be even more
rigid control. Besides, the Nan-t'ai district is very near the capital
city wall. Now that it is leased for residences, the said governor general and governor are ordered to instruct the barbarian consuls,
Caleb Jones and others, to investigate and restrain and to order the
local inhabitants to live with them peacefully and without disturbance,
avoiding the development of enmity. This will be satisfactory. As for
subsequent barbarian arrivals who want to rent houses, the local officials shall be instructed to make like arrangements. (IWSM.HF 10;
21b, 7-22a, 6)

203. April 3, 1855. MEMORIAL: The Governor of Chekiang Reports
on Wu Chien-chang's Taiping and American Connections at Shanghai.
        Governor-elect of Chekiang Huang Tsung-han memorializes. A
Court Letter to the Grand Council has been received stating:

    A certain person has memorialized concerning *Tao-t'ai* of Shanghai, Kiangsu,
    Wu Chien-chang's association with the barbarians to aid the rebels and
    saying that (the Council) had received an Imperial order for me to send
    an officer, on the pretext of some other business, to Shanghai, unobtru-
    sively to investigate clearly the various charges made in the memorial and
    memorialize factually by express.

At the time, Your official was collecting rice for transportation
to Tientsin. He had not finished, so he immediately deputed Yen Tuan-
shu, to go to Shanghai nominally to impress ocean transport, and make

a thorough inquiry. He also selected the important items and sent
them to the Shanghai deputy prosecutor, Magistrate of Chin-hua Prefecture Shih Ching-fen, to be investigated secretly on the spot. From
time to time he has received secret reports from these representatives. He has also carefully probed the barbarian-bandit situation
with Chekiang gentry and merchants going back and forth to Shanghai
for substantiating evidence.

The Imperial instructions received were to investigate the charge
that Wu Chien-chang and Liu Li-ch'uan are fellow villagers, that when
Liu Li-ch'uan started trouble the tao-t'ai was the first to know it and
took his family to live temporarily in a barbarian ship, that the district treasure of no less than 300 or 400 thousand taels was all left
for the rebels, that he also went into partnership with others in Shanghai and opened the Ch'i-ch'ang Hang,[10] that the food supplies and bullets of the rebels inside the city were all supplied from here, that of
late the rebels often went on board ship to confer with the said tao-t'ai
and from there entered the city.

According to what Your official has heard from his representative
and the gentry and merchants, the said tao-t'ai is actually from the
same village as Liu Li-ch'uan, and their relationship has usually been
very intimate. In handling the defenses of Shanghai the volunteers
recruited by the said tao-t'ai were under the control of Liu Li-ch'uan.
Liu Li-ch'uan knew well that there was much silver in the district
treasury and secretly hatched plans to conspire with the volunteers in
training to start a rebellion. On September 26, early in the morning,
the rebels crowded directly into the tao-t'ai's yamen and plundered it
thoroughly. Later some barbarians entered the yamen and conducted
the tao-t'ai and his family in safety out of the city, concealing them in
the barbarian consulate. The silver in the treasury and the personal
property were all taken by the rebels.

The Shanghai Ch'i-ch'ang Hang was originally opened by American
barbarians. The firm has operated for many years, but its ownership
has changed from time to time. The barbarian merchants now operatir
it are on friendly terms with the tao-t'ai and a good deal of money goes
back and forth, consequently before the fall of Shanghai there was a
great deal of talk about the said tao-t'ai and the barbarians operating
Ch'i-ch'ang Hang in partnership. Although merchants guilty of furnish
ing supplies to the insurgents were not confined to the one Ch'i-ch'ang
Hang, the Ch'i-ch'ang Hang's furnishing of supplies was incontrovertib

During the sixth month of this year (June 25-July 24) the Ch'i-
ch'ang Hang had a munitions ship carrying 148 t'iao (bars) of lead fror
Soochow to Shanghai by way of Tung-hsiao. Your official's representative had it stopped there and searched. After the search, the lead was

---

10 This firm was a subsidiary of the well known American firm of Russell and Company.

held, lest it be given the rebels for bullets. Later the tao-t'ai ordered
the Ch'i-ch'ang Hang to file securities and the lead was released. On
investigating the destination of this lead, it was never established
whether it was really to line tea chests or to supply the insurgents.

As to the tao-t'ai's conferences with the insurgents, most of the
Chekiang officers and soldiers of the Shanghai South Battalion have
heard about it. On May twenty-ninth of this year (1854), outside Ch'i-
ch'ang Hang, onlookers crowded there raised a general hubbub, stating unanimously that Liu Li-ch'uan and the said tao-t'ai entered Ch'i-
ch'ang Hang together and then went from the rear of the shop on board
a steamer for conference, the shop door already having been closed.
Every merchant in Yang-ching-pin understood (the significance of
this) without asking.

The above items, all extremely pertinent to the charges, Your
official investigated as herewith indicated. The Imperial instructions
were also to investigate the charges that the said tao-t'ai's hiring of
fishing-tug crews, nominally as a private contribution, was actually
paid for out of customs; that during the spring of this year a Kwangtung cargo boat came to Shanghai and, because (the owner) was an old
acquaintance of the said tao-t'ai, duties amounting to some 40,000
taels silver were waived, causing the other barbarian merchants to
complain; that the said tao-t'ai reported customs amounts as he
pleased, and that his hoarded silver was all carried to his native
village by coastal transport. Regarding the one item of his sending
hoarded silver from customs receipts to his own village by sea, nothing has been learned after extended search. However, the tao-t'ai's
hiring of fishing-tug crews is reported to have been done originally
by subscription, the crews being recruited from Canton. In the spring
of last year, when they first arrived at Shanghai, the insurgents' boats
at Whampoo were all burned, thus clearing the sea approach. After
that, because their demands for money were insatiable and they were
unwilling to fight, the tao-t'ai dismissed half of them and retained the
other half, comprising 15 vessels, with four other chartered foreign-
rigged vessels to protect Woosung so that the rebels were unable to
escape by sea. But the fishing-tug crews were innately intractable.
Not only did they go ashore to whore and loot until people could not
bear the pain, but the hired Cantonese braves whom the tao-t'ai had
used in the city had all turned rebel. His marines on the water-ways
were also all Cantonese. Every time the government forces attacked
the city the marines and rebels in the city secretly communicated
by letter, and they were prepared in advance. It was actually on this
account that we were unable for so long to capture it.

As to the Shanghai customs, from the beginning of collections in
the last ten days of the first month of this year (February 16-26, 1854)
to the first part of the third month (March 29-April 6), when the cargo
boat of the barbarian merchants of Kung-p'ing Hang entered port with-

out paying duties, the said tao-t'ai, being an old friend of their's, did
not punish them and ordered only half the duties paid, causing the rest
of the merchants to complain. Hence customs matters were stymied.
Only after the various consuls went to K'un-shan to interview Govern-
or General I-liang were customs paid as before. The above circumstances Your official has ordered investigated and they are as described.

As to whether or not there were three or four hundred thousand
(taels) of silver in the district treasury, whether or not the money
which the tao-t'ai used to hire fishing tugs was later indemnified from
the customs, and also whether the customs collections have or have
not been falsely reported and appropriated, after the imminent recapture of Shanghai, an examination of the account books of the said tao-
t'ai's administration, as well as his files, will determine the truth or
falsity of the charges and the amounts in detail. They cannot be determined by the present investigation.

Whether or not he had any contract with the American barbarian
partners in operating the Ch'i-ch'ang Hang, what he discussed with the
rebels when he went from Ch'i-ch'ang Hang on board the steamer,
whether or not the evasion of customs by the cargo boat actually a-
mounted to several thousand taels, what were his various dealings with
the barbarians, it is impossible to prove positively by probing. But
after the said tao-t'ai was dismissed, not only did Governor Chi-erh-
hang-a remonstrate with the various barbarians in proper language
and humble them greatly, but the Chekiang deputy, Shih Ching-fen,
whose loyalty and courage are respected even by the barbarians, the
Ningpo gentry and merchants, Hanlin bachelor Chang T'ing-hsüeh,
tao-t'ai by contribution,[i.e., by purchase] Yang Fang, together with
the present governor's deputy, have had discussions with the barbarian
and have reached the conclusion that the insurgent cause is daily approaching exhaustion. Then the criminal charges against Wu Chien-
chang certainly cannot escape Imperial cognizance. (IWSM.HF 10;
25a, 2-28a, 2)

204. April 3, 1855. EDICT: I-liang and Chi-erh-hang-a are Ordered
to Press the Charges against Wu Chien-chang at Shanghai.

Edict to the Grand Councillors. Previously because a certain perso
memorialized several charges of Wu Chien-chang's connections with
barbarians in supporting the rebels, Edicts were issued to I-liang and
Chi-erh-hang-a to examine rigorously one by one the charges as broug
to determine the punishment, and memorialize fully. In addition Huang
Tsung-han was ordered to send a representative to make inquiries.

Now Huang Tsung-han's memorial is at hand stating that he has
established definitely that Wu Chien-chang is actually a fellow villager
of Liu Li-ch'uan, that when that rebel started trouble Wu Chien-chang
and his family took refuge at a barbarian consulate and all the silver i

the treasury went to the rebels; besides, he went into partnership with barbarians to operate the Ch'i-ch'ang Hang, that all the marines he hired were Cantonese, and whenever there was an attack on the city it always leaked because the marines and the Shanghai rebels were in communication; but as to whether or not there were 30,000 or 40,000 (taels) of silver in the treasury, whether or not the money Wu Chien-chang used to charter fishing tugs was compensated from customs, whether there were false reports and embezzlement of customs receipts or whether he had any contract with the American barbarian partners to operate the Ch'i-ch'ang Hang, or what he discussed with the rebels on board the steamer, or whether the customs evaded by the cargo ship were actually several thousand taels, no positive proof is available.

I-liang is nearby in Kiangsu province and observes at first hand, and Chi-erh-hang-a has been at Shanghai with Wu Chien-chang for a long time, so they can hardly plead ignorance. The said tao-t'ai was held for questioning long ago and there is still no indication that the said governor general and governor have investigated and memorialized fully on the several original charges. Now Shanghai is recaptured and all the people and evidence to be examined will not be hard to get together; they are ordered to examine them one by one. Moreover, if besides these there are any other evidences of corruption, they will make rigorous examination and jointly memorialize according to facts. Let there not be the least concealment. The original memorial is ordered copied and sent for their scrutiny. (IWSM.IIF 10; 28a, 3-28b, 6)

205. September 28, 1855. MEMORIAL: Yeh Ming-ch'en Reports his Refusal to See Bowring and McLane at his Yamen and Comments on Treaty Revision.

Imperial Commissioner, Governor General of Liang-kuang Yeh Ming-ch'en memorializes. According to several secret reports, the English chief Bowring and the American chief McLane, one after the other, returned to Hong Kong during the tenth month (November 20-December 19, 1854). First McLane came to Canton in the middle of the month; in the latter part, Bowring, with several warships, also came to Canton, and sent a man to give notice and to fix a date for an interview, insisting that it be in the yamen to accord with propriety. Your official answered that he was really so desirous of a meeting that, no matter where the place, he should consent, but as the yamen was inside the city it was virtually impossible to agree. They stayed in Canton some three weeks but never came back to repeat the request. These barbarians never mentioned that they had gone to Tientsin and never indicated what their requests were.

Just at that time, at the various river ports adjacent to Canton, the rebel ships were particularly powerful. The chiefs became exceedingly curious and every time there was fighting insisted on going up to find out if the government troops won or lost. Moreover, (they) had the barbarian soldiers bruit it about, that if the Chinese officials asked their assistance it would not be hard to wipe out the rebels. Actually the barbarians secretly furnished the insurgents cannon and powder and also sold their loot for them. This is known positively. During the eleventh month (December 20, 1854-January 18, 1855), when Bowring heard that Fo-shan (Fatshan) was recaptured and saw the various ports near Canton succumb to our victorious arms one after the other, he went on board his gunboat and returned to Hong Kong. McLane also left Canton for home.

As the chiefs, on their return to Canton, never notified Your official what requests they had made at Tientsin, he could not take the initiative and repudiate them. But whatever these chiefs actually wanted when they went together to Tientsin, it was essential for him to know the whole background before he could verify the facts. So Your official personally instructed detectives, promising them large rewards, to find out exactly every one of the various requests made by the chiefs at Tientsin and to report back. By the fourth month of the present year (May 16-June 13, 1855), after extensive bribing and searching, they got the articles copied out by the secretariat in the barbarian headquarters. Except for the three articles on controversies between citizens and barbarians, insistence on entrance to the city, and the tea warehouse surcharge of two mace, which have been argued back and forth at Canton and all repudiated seriatim, none of them had been mentioned here. How is it that when they were at Canton they never breathed a word about the other items? They seem not to have come from these chiefs at all. Your official suspects that when they were at Shanghai some corrupt people of our own country utilized them for their schemes, but he cannot be sure.

Upon receipt of the Imperial Edict, Your official carefully investigated the three articles still left for settlement. After deliberation, we feel that the articles on controversies between citizens and barbarians in the established treaties are very explicit. It is noted that, as a general rule, the populace has never quarrelled with barbarians without cause; (controversies) always arise out of the fact that barbarians purposely and unreasonably illtreat the people, who are unbearably insulted, and public indignation is thus aroused. Then the barbarians claim that the local officials judge unjustly. For instance, in Canton prior to 1847, incidents arose repeatedly; every month several outbursts occurred and the clamor could not be stilled. The more (the foreigner were conciliated the more intractable they became. But during the eight years since 1848, the barbarians have not ventured to act outrageously, and so the people have so far kept the peace. The renewal of these discussions by the barbarians at this time is nothing more than the desire to renew their overbearing attitude. Without regard for right or wrong they try to force the local officials to accept their views. If the least thing is not according to their wishes they use every means to terroriz

obviously wishing to cause a cleavage between officials and people,
they are not happy until they get what they want. Their mentality is
most inscrutable.

Then, as to the desire to cancel the Shanghai back customs:
naturally Your official cannot examine carefully the circumstances
of customs in Shanghai, but he hears that after the city fell, the imports and exports of the barbarian merchants could not be examined
and the amount of smuggling was enormous. In the winter of 1853,
the former tao-t'ai of Shanghai repeatedly negotiated with the English,
American, and French consuls until in the spring of 1854 there was
finally established a uniform customs, entirely managed for him by
the various consuls without waiting for examination by (our) officials.
Whether or not the payments were in accord with the treaties is so
far not clear. But if they are now decreased it will greatly affect the
customs in all the five trading ports. Judging from the annual customs at Canton, the amount of the exports and imports of the various
countries is very great. If we take the principal items, in export tea
is the greatest; in import cotton is the greatest. In the course of a
prosperous year tea customs will total 700,000 or 800,000 taels, cotton customs will bring 200,000 or 300,000 taels, and the customs of
these two items constitute 8 or 9 tenths, all other goods not amounting to more than 1 or 2. If there is a general reduction, the barbarians will certainly bring up these two items first. If in the future there
is to be a settlement, in any case they must be ordered to make suitable adjustments at Canton, to avoid obstructing the situation as a whole.

Then, as to the Canton surtax on tea of two mace on each picul, it
is noted that in the past the hong merchants trading with the tea agents
from the interior added a certain number of mace on every picul for a
common fund[11] exclusive of the price agreed on. This outlay was a
fixed practice with the hongs and fundamentally had no connection
with the regular duties which the Canton Customs House charged the
barbarian merchants. Later, during the trouble stirred up by the
English barbarians, the hong merchants soon began to make advances
of various kinds to the government, and with the years the accumulated
deficits (of the hongs) to the public funds became very great. As long
as there were payments to the consoo fund there could be liquidations
from time to time. But after the Co-hong was abolished the consoo
fund payments were no longer made. It was left for annual arrangements to make up the deficiency.

In 1849 the former hong merchants presented a joint petition to
the former governor general's yamen when Your official was governor.
It is noted that this petition presented the following arguments:

---

11 The so-called Consoo Fund under the Co-hong system.

Customarily debits to the public funds were made up from the funds of the commercial hongs by installments. Now that the hong fund has been abolished it would seem to be hard to reestablish it. If means were not found to apply for adjustment, public monies would certainly never be paid. Going back to the Ch'ien-lung period (1735-1795), all tea was handled by the hong merchants, distributed only to reliable tea wholesalers who acted as agents; they furnished deposits and held a monopoly. The established tea fund was to pay the expenses. For a hundred and several tens of years there was continuous peace. The tea wholesalers were restricted to a few families, inspection was very convenient, and hence smuggling was very slight. Now that the hong merchants are eliminated, the new warehouses are chaotic and unregulated and tea is openly smuggled. That no improvement of customs can be expected is directly attributable to this. We are impelled to ask that hereafter tea wholesalers be issued official permits before they are allowed to operate, and that regulations be specified in accord with the old practice. Although black tea and green tea are not the same, a levy of two mace would be placed on each picul to make good debits to government funds, as the tea fund formerly levied by the hongs compensated the deficiencies in public monies. Thus it has reasonably developed from circumstances; it would add no burden to the tea agents and not have the slightest connection with the barbarian merchants. If a man offered his services and his sincerity could be fully relied on, he would be given bond by the said merchants and petition the magistrate for a permit allowing him to operate. If he were disloyal or violated the rules his dismissal would also be petitioned for by the merchants. Thus, along the tea routes there would be government warehouses that could be inspected, and on the export side, security merchants with double responsibility. Thus the tea trade would probably not develop unrestricted smuggling, the new taxes would promise daily increase and the old funds have a chance of liquidation.

At that time the former governor general, Hsü Kuang-chin, and Your official agreed to grant their request. After the sanction was posted, Bonham sent eleven communications requesting that this be abolished. His communications were all answered and his arguments refuted. Thereafter, Bonham never brought the matter up again.

Now at this time Bowring wants to take this fund already collected at Canton to indemnify the customs deficits in Shanghai, without at all realizing that a levy paid by the tea merchants in the interior and the customs paid by the barbarian merchants of foreign countries have not the least connection with one another. Actually, since for the last few years there has not been quite as much smuggling and customs evasion as they would like, the barbarian chief has seized upon this pretext, hoping by confusing the issue to be able to arrest development and thus perhaps satisfy his gluttony.

As to the French barbarian Kleskowsky's coming to Tientsin and then not mentioning matters of trade, neither the French barbarians trading at Canton nor their barbarian ships coming each year are really numerous. In the one item of tea, the barbarian traders of this country do not trade much with the interior merchants. After persistent inquiry it has been learned that this country's everyday hot drink is called coffee and is produced in barbarian lands. This can take the place of Chinese tea (in France) but England and America cannot get along without Chinese tea. On this occasion at Tientsin if the English and Americans had got any of their requests, the French barbarians, besides insisting on entirely equal treatment, would probably have had other requests.

As Your official estimates their intentions, the only thing the French barbarians care about is Catholicism. He finds that when they were permitted in 1846 to preach in the five ports, they also built churches and people in the interior who practiced their religion were exempt from punishment. Consequently the interior banditti practiced the same rites, and as soon as they were arrested many of them said they were converts of the religion of that country. In my humble opinion the confusion which has spread over several provinces for several years all started with the Shang-ti Hui[12] in Kwangsi, and that Shang-ti Hui is another name for Catholicism.

In 1849, a communication was received from the French barbarian Rouen[13] saying that he had seen Minister Ch'i [i.e., Ch'i-ying] who had repeatedly promised him that in the future China's published laws would print the Imperial (Toleration) Edict of February 20, 1846, but that they had bought the 1847 edition of the laws, looked for the clause, and it was not printed there; on the contrary, there was the law prohibiting Catholicism with no abrogation of the prohibition. What was the explanation? Subsequently, whenever a missionary was held in Szechwan, Yunnan, Kiangsi, or Shansi, the French barbarians all knew about it and urgently pressed for his release, saying that once they were allowed to preach, how could they then be seized? Your official has completely refuted their unreasonable language and unreasonable requests one by one.

After the Kwangsi Shang-ti Hui disturbance reached Hunan, Hupeh, Anhwei, Kiangnan, and Chihli provinces, the French barbarians sent a communication and used the (treaty) phrase about "missionaries exhorting men to do good." Your official upbraided them sternly saying that "if their missionaries exhorted men to do good, why had they always produced conspirators and rebels?" Only then did the barbarians realize that their arguments were distorted and weak. Compared to their former position, they seemed somewhat deflated, nor was their language expansive, but probably in their hearts there was some discontent.

Thus whether their coming to Tientsin and never speaking of trade was on this account, (Your official) cannot be sure. He realizes that

---

12 A reference to the "Society for Worshipping God," inspired by Protestant Christianity and organized by Hung Hsiu-ch'uan, who led the Taiping Rebellion and later became the Taiping "Emperor."

13 The French envoy to China was Alexandre Forth-Rouen.

when they were allowed to preach at the five ports it was an arrangement made as a temporary expedient. Who imagined the unobstructed
flow of poison would be so great? It is noted that the French barbarian military leader is Bourboulon. Whether or not Kleskowsky, who
went to Tientsin, was sent by Chief Bourboulon, or if after being sent
back, he came to Canton or remained in Shanghai, the French barbarians have never made any announcement. However, it is reported that
both the American barbarian McLane and the French barbarian Kleskowsky had promised the English barbarian Bowring to go to Tientsin.
It is entirely credible that the French barbarians, having reached Tientsin later than the English and American barbarians and seeing that
those barbarians' cunning was bootless, decided not to repeat their
arguments.

Vermilion endorsement: We observe that what the honorable official memorializes on the circumstances of the barbarians is really
lucid. Furthermore it is a worthy expression of Our purpose of exemplifying dignity, not only stopping their interminable requests but
also preventing other unexpected developments to disturb the general
scene. The honorable official must carry on until the military situation is tranquillized. When supplies are again abundant and strength
renewed, We shall certainly not tolerate their cunning endeavors and
persistent spying. (IWSM.HF 11; 15b, 5-20b, 10)

206. February 14, 1856. MEMORIAL: I-liang Reports Delivery to
American Consul at Shanghai of Four American Escapees from Whaler
"Two Brothers" off Korea.

Governor General of Liang-chiang I-liang memorializes. Word
·has been received from the Board of War that the Board of Rites memorialized that the King of Ch'ao-hsien (Korea) had forwarded four
shipwrecked barbarians to Peking by special envoy.[14] On questioning
these barbarians through an interpreter, it was found that they are men
of the Flowery Flag country, one named Thomas McQuire, one Edward
A. Brailey, one David Barnes, and one Melville Kelsey. (The Board)
recommended that in accord with the regulation covering distressed
barbarians forwarded from Korea, they be handed over to Your slave
for positive examination, and if there were at Shanghai or some other
place any people of that country coming into port to trade, they should
be sent home. An Imperial Edict of approval has been received.

The Board of War sent the distressed barbarians to Ch'ang (i.e.,

---

14 A reference to the adventure of four young Americans who left their ship, the American whaler *Two Brothers*, John Childs, master, off the coast of Korea. They were
passed along by Korean and Chinese officials to Peking, where they remained twenty
days, and on to Shanghai, where they were turned over to United States Consul Robert
C. Murphy. Griffin, *op. cit.*, p. 85. The depositions of the four sailors are preserved in the *Shanghai Consular Dispatches*, v. 3, National Archives, Washington, D.C.

Ch'ang-chou-fu). Your slave immediately sent the Su-Sung-T'ai tao-t'ai to take charge of them and has now received a detailed report from Acting Tao-t'ai Lan Wei-wen. He says that the four distressed barbarians, when questioned through an interpreter, said that they are all men of the Flowery Flag country, served as sailors on a barbarian trading ship (captained by John) Childs, and came from their country to our country to trade. At sea they encountered a storm, were rescued, and were sent from Korea to Peking. This report is at hand.

Your slave finds that Flowery Flag is the same as American, that these barbarians trade at the five ports and have a barbarian leader at Shanghai to handle that country's commercial affairs. He has ordered these distressed barbarians turned over to the said barbarian chief for custody, to await his convenience to return them (to the United States) in accord with the Divine Son of Heaven's purpose of cherishing faraway people.

Vermilion endorsement: Noted. (IWSM.HF 12; 24b, 5-25a, 9)

Chapter 7

Peter Parker as Commissioner, 1856-1857
(Documents 207-223)

The seventeen documents of this chapter cover the period of Dr. Peter Parker's ineffective tour of duty in China as United States commissioner, March 24, 1856 to April 23, 1857. There are six memorials and eleven edicts, including one addressed to the Grand Secretariat. Something of the insignificance of Parker's efforts in China may be indicated by the fact that there is but one vermilion endorsement in this group. It is appended to a report on the Shanghai back-customs question, i.e., the customs dues defaulted by Americans during the rebel occupation, and says simply, "As recommended."

The memorialists are I-liang, governor general of Liang-chiang, Imperial Commissioner Yeh Ming-ch'en, at Canton; Wang I-te, governor general of Min-Che; and Metropolitan Circuit Censor Han Ch'ing-yün.

The topics memorialized are mostly concerned with Parker's abortive efforts at treaty revision and the successful conclusion of the Shanghai back-customs question. Minor incidents include the reception of Parker by the governor general of Min-Che, Wang I-te, who transmitted his credentials and recommendations for treaty revision to Peking. These were rejected by the court, returned to Yeh Ming-ch'en at Canton, and Wang I-te was severely reprimanded, although the latter's actions were in conformity with the Cushing Treaty. Incidental items are the alerting of the China coast against Parker's threatened visit to Tientsin and the persistent Chinese conviction that Dr. Parker was a scheming adventurer and dangerous character. The really important developments of this period are outside the American frame: the incident of the lorcha Arrow at Canton and the resultant breaching of the city walls by the British in October, 1856.

Tyler Dennett has a chapter on "The Policy of Dr. Peter Parker-- Formosa," p. 279-291, in his Americans in Eastern Asia. The Parker correspondence is published with the McLane correspondence, U.S. Cong. 35: 2, S. Ex. Doc. 22, p. 610 ff. There is a biography of Parker by G.B. Stevens and W.F. Marwick, Life, Letters, and Journals of Peter Parker, published in 1896; a more recent biography is included in W.W. Cadbury's history of Canton Hospital, At the Point of a Lancet, Shanghai, 1935, p. 19-100.

TRANSLATIONS OF DOCUMENTS

207. March 24, 1856. MEMORIAL: I-liang Reports the Arrival at Canton

311

of Peter Parker as United States Commissioner to China.

Governor General of Liang-chiang I-liang and Governor of Kiang-su Chi-erh-hang-a memorialize. Your official Chi-erh-hang-a, on February 3, 1856, received a report from the acting tao-t'ai of Su-Sung T'ai, Lan Wei-wen, that the American consul Fish[1] had presented him a communication from that country's barbarian chief Parker, stating that the said chief had succeeded to the post of commissioner for that country, that he had arrived at Canton and awaited the arrival of a war steamer from his country to proceed to Shanghai to discuss treaty revision. A reply was immediately sent that all matters of trade at the five ports must be handled by the Imperial Commissioner, the governor general of Liang-kuang, and that (the governor of) Kiangsu province could not interfere. If there were matters to be discussed, requests should be made by the said barbarian there, for the governor general of Liang-kuang to settle. It was unnecessary to make a fruitless trip here and back.

Now there is another report from Lan Wei-wen that the English barbarian customs superintendent, H.N. Lay, notified him personally that the treaty regulations of the various countries must be revised; otherwise he feared trouble would result; Kwangtung Governor General Yeh had been so extremely uncooperative that the envoys of the various countries were absolutely unwilling to address his office again.

Your officials find that in the winter of 1854, when the envoys of the various barbarian states stopped at Shanghai on their way back from Tientsin, they said that they would come again in 1856 to negotiate. Now the American barbarian chief has taken the initiative and the English barbarians have utilized the customs superintendent to give notice for them. Although their language seems respectful and compliant, the intent is still to coerce. Their nature is truly inscrutable.

At present, military affairs in Kiangsu are still unsettled and we are impelled to request an Edict ordering the governor general of Liang-kuang, Yeh Ming-ch'en, to devise means to control them and not let them rush up north to pull our elbows any more. (IWSM.HF 12; 29a, 3-29b, 8)

208. March 24, 1856. EDICT: Orders Parker to be Relegated to Canton and Treaty Revision to be Limited to Slight Modifications.

Edict to the Grand Councillors. I-liang and Chi-erh-hang-a have memorialized that the American and English barbarians demand a revision of the treaty regulations. The American chief Parker has sent word to Kiangsu that he is only waiting for a ship to go to Shanghai to reconsider the treaties. The English Chief H.N. Lay has also said that

---

1 Dr. M.W. Fish was acting vice-consul at Shanghai from January 1, 1856 to August 6, 1856.

the treaties of the various countries must be revised, that (the governor general of) Kwangtung has been so extremely uncooperative that the envoys of the various countries are absolutely unwilling to address that office again.

His purpose is to come to Shanghai to use coercion, so he uses the pretext that Kwangtung has been unreceptive. The situation is clear. Although the treaties opening the five ports to trade do have the clause for revision in twelve years, this only meant that if in time abuses developed or there were obstacles, there would be nothing to prevent minor adjustments. The general provisions were not intended to be alterable. The various requests which the barbarians previously made at Shanghai and Tientsin were all absolutely impracticable and Ch'ung-lun and others personally refuted them. The barbarian chiefs themselves realized that they were in the wrong and did not renew the argument. Now they say that Kwangtung is so uncooperative they are going to Shanghai. The governor general and governor of Kiangsu, not having charge of barbarian affairs, naturally cannot accede to their request. If they insist on coming to Tientsin, it will be an act of great impropriety.

Yeh Ming-ch'en is ordered to investigate the situation thoroughly and bridle them suitably. If the revision the barbarians want is really confined to details, there is no objection to negotiating and memorializing the facts, but if their slight modifications are anything like their previous rash demands he will forthwith cut them off in suitable terms. He must make use of both magnanimity and intimidation to frustrate their idea of coming North. He must not stubbornly refuse to see them and thus give these barbarians a pretext.

I-liang and Chi-erh-hang-a are also ordered to instruct Lan Wei-wen to send word to the various barbarian consuls that commercial affairs of the five ports are all handled at Kwangtung and that other provinces cannot trespass. If the barbarians are not willing to address the Kwangtung office, other provinces cannot act for them; while the contents of their present communication have been incorporated in a memorial, they can only be passed on to the Imperial Commissioner at Canton for investigation and action. The said governor general and governor are not authorized to entertain even matters that need to be discussed, but by enlightening them with persuasive words, must send them back to Kwangtung so as not to allow other complications to develop. This is most essential.

The original memorial of I-liang et al. is ordered copied and sent to Yeh Ming-ch'en for perusal. (IWSM.HF 12; 29b, 8-30b, 7)

209. July 23, 1856. MEMORIAL: Yeh Ming-ch'en Analyzes Peter Parker and Comments on Treaty Revision.

Imperial Commissioner, Governor General of Liang-kuang Yeh Ming-ch'en memorializes. It is humbly noted that English, American,

and French barbarian chiefs previously went to Tientsin intending to
revise the treaties. The special Imperial delegate ordered them back
to Canton. After the barbarian chiefs returned to Canton, more than
a year elapsed and they said nothing.

But after the American envoy McLane went home, last winter Parker
replaced him and came to Canton. This chief was originally an American physician, had been in Canton for twenty years, and was generally
regarded as crafty. In 1854, when the Cantonese rebels were making
trouble, this chief had secret relations with the various rebel leaders
and, besides, he boasted to various barbarian merchants that the rebels were sure to succeed. Then when the government troops reduced
the various rebels to complete submission, the chief lost so much face
that in the summer of last year he went home of his own accord. Unexpectedly, after McLane went home on account of illness, the king of
that country, as he (Parker) had been in Canton for many years, sent
him back to Canton to take over the duties of envoy. Chief Parker
still cherished resentment in his heart and was determined to find
expression for his personal views and to silence people's ridicule.

A communication has now been received saying that he finds that
the 34th article of the treaty states that "after 12 years both countries
shall appoint officials for equitable deliberation," that on July 3rd of
this year the time will be up, and he gives special advance notice, hoping that it will be soon memorialized for him. Now he wishes to visit
the various ports and sometime in the first part of July he will be
ready to start for Peking.

A communication has also been received from the English envoy
Bowring, stating that in Article 34 of the treaty previously negotiated
with America at Macao, there was the provision that "after 12 years,
revision of the treaty could be discussed," and that he finds that on
July 3 of this year the time limit will be exactly up; furthermore, that
Article 8 of the English supplementary treaty specifies that "additional favors acquired by other countries will also be extended to his
countrymen with complete equality." He asks that all these sentiments
be promptly memorialized.

A communication has also been received from the French envoy
Gros[2] stating that he has now received notes from England and America
saying that the regulations negotiated with China must now be reconsidered by both parties; that between England and America and his
country, friendly relations are most cordial and their arrangements
in China coincide entirely with the views of his country. He notes that
Article 35 of the established treaty of his country states that "if in the

---

2 Jean Baptiste Louis Gros, made a baron in 1829, was sent as Special High Commissioner
to China in 1856, signed the Treaty of Tientsin for France, and in 1860 entered Peking with the Allied forces. Couling, *Encyclopaedia Sinica,* p. 218.

future China shows any Special Imperial Favor to other countries, his country will be treated likewise."

Now Your official notes that in the fall of 1854, when England, America, and France successively went to Tientsin intending to renew the treaties, the English chief Bowring was the trouble maker. On this renewal of discord it seems to be the American chief Parker who is fanning the fire. Now it is only Parker who wants to proceed to Tientsin, and he has been stopped forcibly; England and France have not even mentioned it. But as Parker is naturally very crafty, there is real danger of his tricking Bowring and Gros into returning North with him. Considering the dog-sheep mentality of the barbarians and their insatiable greed, how will they ever be discouraged?

In retrospect, the treaties with the various states were made successively rather than simultaneously. The first English (treaty) was made in the ninth month (October 7-November 5) of 1839 [sic. actually August 29, 1842] at Nanking, and the supplement in 1843 at Hu-men. In neither of these is there any provision for treaty revision after 12 years. In the American treaty of the 5th month (June 16-July 14) of 1844 [signed July 3, 1844] Article 34 states that "as conditions in the different ports vary, and the clauses relating to trade on the seas may have to be changed somewhat, after 12 years both countries shall appoint officials to discuss equitable adjustments." In the French treaty (exchanged) in the 7th month (August 3-September 1) of 1845, Article 35 states that "if in the future there are any of the provisions which need to be changed, in 12 years, figured from the date of the exchange of the treaties, negotiations with China can be renewed, but if in the future China grants any special Imperial favors, exemptions or protection to other countries, France will be treated likewise."

Thus the year when the American and French treaties containing the twelve-year revision clause were signed was after the principal settlement with England. Why was the settlement not uniform? As it is, the treaties of these two countries retain this indeterminate feature, which the countries subsequently use as a pretext. As an example, in the summer of 1850 the English barbarian Bonham sent a chief[3] to Tientsin. In the fall of 1854 the barbarian chiefs of England, America, and France respectively went to Tientsin. On both occasions all looked up with covered faces toward the Sacred Sovereign's Heavenly Omnipotence and Uninterrupted Effulgence, and they were sent back to Canton to await a settlement.

For the last seven years the various ocean frontiers have remained tranquil, but it is feared that if a request is rejected here, other requests may be made there [in Tientsin]. Subsequently, regardless of what province they go to, if the barbarian chiefs present any requests

---

3   Interpreter Walter Medhurst.

to be memorialized, by all means order them back to Canton to await
a settlement, and Your official will immediately comply with the reiterated Imperial intent to hold fast to the treaties so as to manage
them as occasion requires, and find ways to force submission and make
it possible to nip calamities before they bud. (IWSM.HF 13; 11a, 4-
13b, 2)

210. July 23, 1856. EDICT: Identifies Parker as Instigator of Treaty
Revision and Collaborator with the Rebels, and Orders Him Blocked.
          Edict to the Grand Councillors. Yeh Ming-ch'en memorializes
that England, America, and France are asking to revise the treaties,
and that he has found ways to enlighten and stop them. He reports that
the American barbarian Parker has said in a communication that Article 34 of the treaty regulations states that after 12 years both countries
shall appoint officials to deliberate, that in the sixth month of this year
(July 2-31, 1856) the period will have expired, and he has asked for a
memorial in his behalf. The English barbarian Bowring and the French
barbarian Gros have also sent communications one after the other.
          In previous years these barbarian chiefs came to Tientsin and pre-
sented various requests full of extravagances. Ch'ung-lun and others
repudiated their requests in suitable terms, (on the grounds that) they
were difficult to memorialize. Among them, only the Shanghai back
customs, which was not previously considered, the Canton tea duty, which
was added later, and cases of controversy between citizens and barbarians, which were originally provided for in the treaties but we fear
have not been well administered, were allowed them for settlement. At
that time Yeh Ming-ch'en and I-liang were ordered to deliberate and
execute.
          Now these barbarian chiefs, at the end of the twelve-year period,
request memorials in their behalf, and the American chief Parker further speaks of setting out for Peking. Although Yeh Ming-ch'en has
forcibly stopped him, there is the fear that Parker will sow his trickery
among the others and induce Bowring and Gros to come north again.
This must be prevented. Although the barbarian treaties do say that
after twelve years there will be an equitable deliberation, this clause
was inserted in case conditions might be different in the future and
require some slight modifications; but the main body (of the treaty) was
by no means to be altered, hence they were all called "Ten-thousand-
year Treaties." Besides, the favor of discussing the cancellation of
customs and other items was added previously at Tientsin. The Court's
purpose of cherishing and comforting far-away people cannot be called
ungenerous. If they again seize a pretext to annoy (us) with petitions
it will be impossible to accede to them.
          Yeh Ming-ch'en has only to rely on reason to enlighten them and
restrain their greed. If they hold fast to this 12-year arrangement, the
said governor general and others can even select those items which

border on reason and which are not injurious to our constitution, consent to the change of one or two clauses, memorialize clearly and await an Edict, in order to keep them in control.

If these barbarian chiefs do go to Shanghai and other ports and make perverse requests for memorials on their behalf, I-liang and the others are ordered to tell them that the governor general of Liang-kuang is Imperial Commissioner in charge of barbarian affairs, and no matter what the trouble is, they must go to Canton to present requests. The governor general and governor of Liang-chiang cannot memorialize for them.

If they still talk about wanting to come to Tientsin, Yeh Ming-ch'en and others are further ordered to tell them that Tientsin is not a trading port, that when they came before it was in clear violation of the treaties, as the Imperial Commissioner told them clearly on the former occasion at Tientsin, and that if they ever return to Tientsin there will certainly be no minister appointed to confer with them. In this way notify them explicitly, thereby stopping their perversity.

As for Parker at Canton, since his mentality is inscrutable, if he comes to Shanghai at this time, I-liang and the others must secretly make preparations to prevent his conspiring with the Cantonese rebels, in order to prevent the development of other incidents. (IWSM.HF 13, 13b, 3-14b, 5)

211. August 6, 1856. MEMORIAL: Wang I-te Reports His Interview with Parker and the Transmission of His Credentials to Peking.

Governor General of Min-Che Wang I-te memorializes. On July 12th of this year, upon receipt of a communication from the United States envoy Peter Parker requesting a date for an interview, Your official replied that, as the problems of the barbarian leaders of the various countries are of little consequence, it was inconvenient to come in person to a conference. (Your official) then ordered the prefect of Foochow in charge of trade, Yeh Yung-yüan, to go and intercept him. He has reported back that the said barbarian envoy, inasmuch as his country's barbarian sovereign had prepared credentials and ordered him to convey them, he begged to present them. Since the mentality of the barbarians of foreign countries is inscrutable and if some civility is not shown them they use it as a pretext, Your official could not but consent to his coming to call on the 15th, between 7 and 9 in the morning.

So the barbarian envoy Peter Parker, accompanied by several barbarians, came to the yamen and presented a casket containing the original and duplicate national credentials, altogether four items. As credentials presented by foreign countries must first be opened and examined by Your official, who, if there are no improper expressions, would then agree to present them for him, the barbarian envoy first opened the two copies for perusal.

Your official scanned them carefully and they contained no improper expressions, but in several places the character chen [person-
al pronoun "We" used exclusively by the Emperor] occurred. This
was really not according to propriety, but the said barbarian envoy
had been instructed by the barbarian sovereign to convey the credentials and he did not dare change them. Besides, it was asked that
ministers of the United States stationed in China should reside near
the Court [under the Imperial chariot-wheel] and that Your Majesty
should appoint ministers to reside at the capital of their country, Washington. Your officials told him that as the intervening oceans and seas
are very extensive this would be inconvenient for both parties. And
besides, since neither the capital nor its environs are places for the
residence of barbarian chiefs, he feared that his requests could hardly
be granted.

He also proposed likewise to open the original national credentials
and read them, but as they bore the seal of the barbarian sovereign,
the barbarian envoy would not venture to open them himself, and as
the language therein was identical with the copy, he asked that they be
respectfully forwarded for him. If at that time Your official had insisted on opening them, it would certainly have grated the barbarian's
teeth.

So, merely in accordance with Article 31 of the perpetual treaty,
which states that "if the United States subsequently has any credentials
to present to the Court the original documents shall be forwarded for
them by an Imperial Commissioner or by the governors general of
Liang-kuang, Min-Che, or Liang-chiang," Your official respectfully
presents the credentials submitted by the barbarian envoy for Imperial
scrutiny. (IWSM.HF 13; 16a, 7-17b, 2)

212. August 6, 1856. EDICT: Condemns Wang I-te for Receiving Parker's Credentials and Précis for Treaty Revision, and Orders Him to Return Them.

Edict to the Grand Councillors. A memorial has been received
from Yeh Ming-ch'en saying that the American chief Parker and the
barbarian chiefs of England and France each presented communications
at Canton requesting treaty revision, and that Parker also said that he
wanted to proceed North. Yeh Ming-ch'en has already refused him and,
anticipating his demands at other places, has asked that orders be given
that subsequently, no matter to what province the chiefs may go, if they
request the memorializing of requests, they be sent back to Canton for
settlement. Orders were sent I-liang to act accordingly and to make
suitable preparations.

Today Wang I-te memorializes that the American chief presented
credentials to be forwarded for him; that he examined the materials
presented, and found that they were mostly about treaty revision and
the requests were virtually impossible to concede. When Wang I-te

received this material, he should have rejected it in proper language, told (the American chief) that all barbarian affairs are handled at Kwangtung and other provinces could not present memorials, and ordered him to present the originals at Kwangtung, meanwhile copying and secretly memorializing them without letting the barbarians know. This is the proper procedure.

In previous years, when these chiefs came to Shanghai and Tientsin, I-liang and Ch'ung-lun handled them like this, and the chiefs finally bowed their heads in submission and weighed anchor for the South. Now Wang I-te has forwarded the credentials. It now only remains for him to find some means to enlighten the (American chief) and again send him back to Kwangtung, saying that although he has sent a memorial for him this time, since this is not a matter for the governor general of Min-Che to handle, he could not execute what he had memorialized and is returning the originals to (Parker); that if he were to send another memorial he would certainly be punished for a grave offence to His Majesty and would still do their country no good; that last year the former (chiefs) went to Kwangtung to await settlement after making an entirely fruitless trip to Tientsin. Now at Foochow there was a similar situation and he (Wang I-te) has memorialized but the Throne could hardly sanction it.

These barbarians are naturally crafty and trouble-making. Although we cannot be too stubborn and cause an outburst, still how can we continually compromise and give them the whip hand? Wang I-te is ordered to return all the barbarian credentials which he presented for them in the original casket. Nor can he present them again later. After returning them, he is ordered to memorialize promptly and secretly whatever movements the barbarians make and whether or not they obey orders and go to Canton. (IWSM.HF 13; 17b, 3-18a, 9)

213. <u>August 6, 1856</u>. EDICT: <u>Orders Copies of Parker's Papers Sent to Yeh Ming-ch'en, Who is Instructed to Block Treaty Revision</u>.

Supplementary Edict. We previously received Yeh Ming-ch'en's memorial that the barbarian chiefs had again asked to revise the treaties and also spoke of wanting to go to Peking. We have notified the said governor general to enlighten them rationally and also to prevent their getting to Tientsin again.

We assumed that the governor general would certainly be able to fulfil this purpose by mature deliberation and suitable action, but the American chief Parker has gone to Fukien, presented his credentials, and asked that they be forwarded. Wang I-te transmitted the originals for presentation.

We find that the main purport is that they want to send someone to reside at the capital and, as before, ask for treaty revision. These requests are utterly impossible. But in Yeh Ming-ch'en's previous memorial there was no mention of these barbarians having any credentials at Kwangtung. It is perfectly apparent that in Kwangtung there was nothing to be gained, so they were unwilling to present them at Kwangtung. And besides, since in previous years at Shanghai and Tientsin there was no chance to try their schemes, they hoped to give Fukien a try. Their inscrutable mentality is apparent without inquiry.

Today (We) have returned the original papers to Wang I-te with orders to explain to the chief that he is to return to Kwangtung as usual.

All the translations of the barbarian credentials are ordered transcribed and a copy sent for Yeh Ming-ch'en's perusal. When these barbarians return to Kwangtung he is ordered, in accord with previous Edicts, to explain to them suitably. If he were able to hold fast to the treaties without any changes, this would be best; but this is out of the question, so he can select those things which do not obstruct the constitution, discuss them, and change one or two items. If they say anything about sending someone to Peking, that is improper and unreasonable, and We assume Yeh Ming-ch'en will find means to refute it himself and not need constant instruction from Us. (IWSM.HF 13; 18b, 1-19a, 3)

214. October 10, 1856. MEMORIAL: I-liang Reports the Final Adjustment of the American Back Customs at Shanghai and Asks for Imperial Approval.

Governor General of Liang-chiang I-liang and Acting Governor of Kiangsu Chao Te-ch'e memorialize. It is humbly observed that when the rebel Liu occupied Shanghai on September 7, 1853, the former tao-t'ai of Su-Sung-T'ai, Wu Chien-chang, agreed to have the consuls of the various countries assume control and collect for him whatever foreign customs were due. At that time the rebellion was violent and the foreign merchants, taking their valuable goods with them, settled temporarily in the Yang-ching-pin district. The foreign consuls found means to protect the goods for them but the expense was not inconsiderable. Not until July 12, 1854, when the government troops had gathered like clouds, chastised the (rebels), and got the situation in hand, was trade normal and the newly established customs house collecting as usual. The unpaid duties of the American merchants from September 7, 1853 to July 12, 1854 amounted to 354,149 taels, 8 mace, 3 candareens, 7 li; and through the defaults of bankrupt merchants, which there was no hope of collecting, totalling over 80,000 taels, they would actually pay only 81,592 taels.

Since the duties paid for which there were receipts but no clearance certificates issued, 27,000-odd taels, came during Wu Chien-chang's administration, Your official I-liang and the former governor, Chi-erh-hang-a, ordered a treasury representative to bring Wu Chien-chang in custody to Shanghai and, with an official from the tao-t'ai's

office, went over the accounts in the presence of the three witnesses.
As there were no errors, we agreed to their deduction, to be adjusted
in the records handed over by Wu Chien-chang.

As for the losses incurred by the said country's trade, he was
impelled to request Imperial favor to contemplate aid; but the said
country will pay only one third of the old duties owed. Inasmuch as
defaults of merchants included in the present deduction constituted
a loss to the government revenues, he ordered the tao-t'ai of Su-Sung-
T'ai, again to make a suitable representation. Now according to the
acting tao-t'ai of Su-Sung-T'ai, Lan Wei-wen, a detailed account of the
successive consuls of that country, Murphy and Fish, presented by the
present envoy, Parker, states that business is not yet up to standard
and asks that a detailed memorial be forwarded according to the
original agreement.

Your officials beg to observe that at the time of the Shanghai disturbances the merchants of that country individually went to the expense of protecting their goods, and business was curtailed. This was
the true state of affairs. Your Majesty soothes and controls China
and the outer world with a uniform benevolence. The Shanghai land
taxes and tribute rice have by Imperial favor been discriminately
reduced or rescinded; this country's unpaid back customs must needs
secure Your Majesty's benevolence for a like settlement.

May We then request that Heavenly favor graciously remember
the grievous complications of business and entirely remit the American
unpaid back customs of more than 354,000 taels, and all other unpaid
monies, exclusive of the 81,592 taels, and also of the duties paid before
the capture, for which clearance certificates were not issued (taels
27,673: 8: 3: 7), so as to show conciliation?

Vermilion endorsement: As recommended. (IWSM.HF 13;26a,2-27b,2)

---

215. October 10, 1856. EDICT: Officially Approves I-liang's Adjustment
of the American Back Customs at Shanghai.

Edict to the Grand Secretariat. I-liang and Chao Te-ch'e have
memorialized to reduce the American back customs. All countries
trading at Shanghai are required to pay duties at the Shanghai Customs
House. Because of bandit disturbances last year trade was abnormal
and business was grievously affected.

We had already ordered the said governor general and governor
to consider reduction. Now they report definitely that the American
accumulated back customs are 350,000 taels. The envoy of that country
is willing to pay 81,500-odd taels. There are also 27,600-odd taels of
customs that have already been paid. The amount of these unpaid customs is very large, but we recall that that country's business was handi-
capped. This is the true state of affairs.

All the American back customs prior to July 12, 1854, exclusive of
those already paid, are ordered entirely remitted, by Special Favor, in

order to show compassion. (IWSM.HF 13; 27b, 3-10)

216. October 11, 1856. MEMORIAL: I-liang Reports that Parker Has Come to Shanghai and is Threatening to go to Peking for Treaty Revision.
    Governor General of Liang-chiang I-liang and Acting Governor of Kiangsu Chao Te-ch'e memorialize. A report has been received from Lan Wei-wen that the American barbarian Parker, on board the gunboat generally used by his country,[4] arrived at Shanghai on August 1st. On the 18th he called on Lan Wei-wen but did not bring up either his request to revise the treaty or his desire to go to Tientsin.
    It had been learned from private sources that there was an admiral of that country on board another steamer[5] still at Canton being repaired on account of a damaged hull. On September 16 Admiral James Armstrong[6] arrived at Shanghai on board a steamer.[7] Further secret inquiry brought out that still another steamer would arrive shortly and that as soon as this vessel arrived Parker would go to Tientsin. Since on his previous visit Parker had said nothing of going to Tientsin, the said acting tao-t'ai, Lan Wei-wen, feared that he would go without notice.
    The now dismissed Su-Sung-T'ai tao-t'ai, Wu Chien-chang, was in Shanghai at the time arranging for steamers to assist in the Yangtze River campaign. So on September 23rd it was arranged for Wu Chien-chang to call on Parker together with (Lan) and ask his intentions. He [Parker] said:

> As the twelve-year period had expired, his sovereign had given him credentials and he had to go to Peking and personally notify His Imperial Majesty of some items to be discussed. Before leaving Canton he had sent a communication to Governor General of Liang-kuang Yeh saying that he would go direct to Tientsin. Because of a storm he had called at Foochow and now he was awaiting at Shanghai the repair of a steamer, hence this slight delay. Now that the steamer had arrived he must forthwith go North.

    The acting tao-t'ai and the other told him that Tientsin was not a trading port; that because Envoy McLane and the others in 1854 had gone there in ignorance, and had come so far by land and sea, His Imperial Majesty had appointed an Imperial Commissioner to meet them. This was an exceptional display of Imperial conciliation. It was made clear to him that if they went to Tientsin they could under no circumstances expect again the appointment of an Imperial Commissioner to confer with them; that Governor General of Liang-kuang Yeh, as Imperial Commissioner, had exclusive charge of the trade of the five por

---

4 U.S.S. *Levant*.
5 U.S.S. *San Jacinto*.
6 Commodore James Armstrong, U.S.N., commanding United States Naval Forces, East India and China Seas.
7 U.S.S. *Portsmouth*.

and no matter what the affair, he must repair immediately to Canton, present his requests and await settlement, rather than make a fruitless journey.

He [Parker] replied:

> He had received a mandate from his sovereign to maintain friendly relations with China and was especially concerned that both parties be benefited. He had passed through England and France and conferred with their ministers, and all had agreed that there must be another Imperially authorized conference. If he were again ordered back to Kwangtung to confer with His Excellency Yeh, he would "have his head cut off before he would go." If he were to go to Tientsin and was unable to see His Imperial Majesty personally, he would be without recourse and the best he could do was to come back. If he were not allowed to go to Tientsin, he could merely ask that the governor general and governor of Liang-chiang memorialize for him asking that an Imperial Commissioner come to Chekiang for a conference, and he would wait there.

Lan Wei-wen and the other repeatedly explained to him, arguing for several hours, but he was stubbornly adamant. They then sent a hasty appeal (to us).

Your officials find that this barbarian chief Parker had come to Shanghai and remained a month without saying a word about wanting to revise the treaties or going to Tientsin; that he was waiting without saying a word, knowing full well that we would certainly prevent his going until the steamer should arrive, and would then go without notice. Then, when Lan Wei-wen found out about it and questioned him, he used threatening language. His mentality is certainly inscrutable.

If Your officials are too abrupt he will certainly go straight to Tientsin; if they do not grant what he asks his vexation and shame will turn into anger, and he may cause further trouble. At present matters of trade are handled uniformly for England, America, and France, and the said chief said he visited England and France to confer with their ministers and they agreed that there must be another Imperial Commissioner to negotiate. At present the English and French envoys are both in Kwangtung, and are not coming along but we have the prospect of only the one chief going to Tientsin. If England and France negotiate separately at Canton, then we should have trouble in two places and it would be very awkward. Therefore Your officials did not venture to memorialize for him, but suggested that Lan Wei-wen and the other explain things to him again in the hope of preventing his going north and of blocking his rash ideas. But barbarian nature is crafty and deceitful and whether or not he will go straight to Tientsin, because of Your officials' refusal to memorialize for him, there is no assurance. (IWSM.HF 13; 28a, 1-29b, 10)

217. October 11, 1856. EDICT: I-liang is Instructed to Order Parker

back to Canton and to Keep the Fears of the Court from Him.
     Edict to the Grand Councillors. I-liang and another have memori-
alized that the American chief wants to go to Tientsin and that they
have for the present found means to restrain him. We see from the
circumstances memorialized that this barbarian is extremely crafty
and perverse. Now that Lan Wei-wen et al. have ordered him back to
Canton, it is essential that (they) reaffirm this decision and also order him back to Kwangtung.
     Previously We received Yeh Ming-ch'en's memorial that this chief
Parker, was in secret communication with the leaders of various bandit groups in Canton in 1854 and boasted that the Cantonese bandits
were sure to succeed. When the government troops subjugated the
bandits, the said chief lost face, and the barbarian merchants even
regarded him as an outcast. Now on his return he still nurses his
resentment and wants to vindicate his own views in order to silence
the ridicule of his fellows. Hence his desire to go to Tientsin is actually not shared by the English and French barbarian chiefs. Although
the barbarian chiefs of those two countries presented a communication
at Kwangtung, as soon as Yeh Ming-ch'en intervened, they did not proceed to Shanghai. Besides, the merchants regard the English barbarians as leaders and the Americans and French both trail along and
acquiesce. They would not be willing to have the American chief take
the initiative.
     We have received Wang I-te's memorial that he has returned the
credentials which this barbarian had presented and ordered him back
to Kwangtung, that now he is again in Shanghai and requests that an
Imperial Commissioner come to Chekiang to confer. This is all contrary to current treaties and extremely improper. The provincial officials have already carefully explained to him. If he complains again,
let them completely disregard him.
     Today We have notified Kuei-liang that if this barbarian chief com
to Tientsin he need not send a high official to meet him but he should
strictly prohibit the corrupt coastal inhabitants from trading with him
privately. We have also notified Ch'ung-en to take similar precautions
in the Shantung ports, thus removing all hope of profit, in order to
block his intention to come North.
     But I-liang should merely tell him that trading matters can only
be memorialized by Kwangtung, and that other provinces dare not repo
them. If he continues obstinate and insists upon going to Tientsin, it
is not necessary to restrain him too much, lest this chief think that we
are afraid to have him come North and thus have one more pretext for
threatening us. We assume that I-liang and the others will surely be
able to appreciate this view and control him adequately. The things
memorialized this time and those that may be reported subsequently
must none of them be allowed to reach this barbarian's ears. All admonitions shall be made as if on the provincial officials' initiative.

This is most essential. (IWSM.HF 13; 30a, 1-30b, 9)

218. October 11, 1856. EDICT: Kuei-liang is Ordered to Defend the Tientsin Area against Parker and to Be Prepared to Refute Him Diplomatically.

Supplementary Edict. I-liang and another have memorialized that the American chief wants to go to Tientsin and that for the present he has found means to control him. He says that the American barbarian chiefs, Parker and James Armstrong, have come one after the other to Shanghai. When acting Su-Sung-T'ai tao-t'ai Lan Wei-wen asked his (Parker's) intentions he stated that the twelve-year period has expired and his sovereign had given him credentials and ordered him to go to Peking and present them, and that there are still matters to negotiate which require his going to Tientsin.

Today We have ordered I-liang and another to say, as of their own volition, that matters of trade must be settled at Kwangtung, that Tientsin is not a trading port, and that if the barbarian chief comes there again now, he regrets that he cannot ask for the appointment of an Imperial Commissioner to meet him, as he did last time, and his trip would have been in vain; thus making an appropriate explanation.

This barbarian wants to go to Tientsin under pretext of making requests, but actually to undertake the private sale of prohibited goods. Should the Kiangsu provincial (officials) be unable to restrain him and should he actually come North, Kuei-liang is ordered to instruct local military and civil officials to make careful, secret defense, and not allow the coastal inhabitants or trading or fishing boats to sell goods illicitly to these barbarians. All supplying of foodstuffs by corrupt inhabitants is strictly prohibited. If he enters port to present his barbarian credentials it is not necessary to appoint a high official to meet him. Order reliable civil and military underlings to tell him that this place is not a trading port, that last year the barbarians came contrary to the treaties and received exceptional favors from His Imperial Majesty who sent officials to entertain them, but if he should return now, the present provincial governor general dare not memorialize and under no circumstances can an Imperial Commissioner be delegated to come. Tell him that if he has any credentials to present he is, in accord with the treaty, to go (to Canton) and ask the governor general of Liang-kuang to memorialize them.

Explain everything like this and memorialize secretly and by express post whatever movements he makes. You are also ordered to arrange and execute carefully whatever preparations are necessary at Ta-ku and other ports, nor can there be the least confusion. The military and civil officials at the port are to seize and punish corrupt people who sell the (barbarians) anything whatever. If the said military and civil officials are not able to promulgate warnings in advance, or if they do not enforce the prohibitions, they are ordered to be rigorously impeached. If these barbarian chiefs cannot count on any profit, their determination to come North may be blocked. In the important matter of coast defense, Kuei-liang must make thorough plans. Let there not be the least dilatoriness. (IWSM.HF 13; 31a, 1-31b, 9)

219. October 11, 1856. EDICT: Shantung Officials Are Warned against Parker's Anticipated Attempts to Call at Coastal Ports en route to Tientsin.

Supplementary Edict. Today we received I-liang's memorial that the American barbarian Parker had come to Shanghai requesting treaty revision and wanting to go to Tientsin. We have ordered I-liang and others to find means of explaining things to him suitably, and have also ordered Kuei-liang to make rigorous secret preparations not to send a high official to meet them if the barbarian ships come, and also strictly to prohibit coastal inhabitants from trading.

These barbarians' mentality is inscrutable, and they use threatening language. There is no assurance that they will not arbitrarily visit various places along the coast. The barbarian nature is avaricious. Were corrupt people to carry on clandestine trade with them, these barbarians would be sure to regard (the place) as a commercial center and find pretexts to come back, and the evil consequences would be innumerable. There must be the most stringent and secret prohibition (against trading). If on this occasion the barbarian ships do not heed the explanations of I-liang and others and do come straight north, they will pass by Shantung.

Ch'ung-en is ordered to give secret instructions to local military and civil officials to make stringent and secret preparations, and not to allow either coastal inhabitants or trading or fishing boats to exchange goods with the barbarian ships. If they cannot count on any profit they will certainly be disappointed and turn back. Furnishing of foodstuffs is absolutely prohibited. Let there not be the least negligence. (IWSM.HF 13; 32a, 1-9)

220. December 12, 1856. EDICT: Commends Yeh Ming-ch'en for Conduct of the Early Stages of the Arrow War at Canton.

Edict to the Grand Councillors. Yeh Ming-ch'en has memorialized that during the ninth month (September 29-October 28) because (our) marine forces arrested the bandits, Li Ming-t'ai and others, in a small boat,[8] the English barbarian consul Harry Parkes seized the pretext to start a quarrel, boldly dared to enter the Canton River, and harrassed Lieh-te Fort. He also fired empty cannon shots at Ta-huang-chiao Fort, and from October 27-29 attacked the city wall, setting fires at

---

8 Reference to the lorcha *Arrow* case at Canton, resulting in the so-called *Arrow* or Canton War in 1856.

Ching-hai Gate, Wu-hsin Gate, and adjacent houses, burning them
completely. On the 29th, when he gathered together two or three hundred men and scaled the wall, Lieutenant Colonel Ling Fang and the
gentry, Ou-yang Ch'uan, met and hurled them to their death. On November 6, when the barbarians came out from the Thirteen Factories
anchorage and pounced on Tung-ting Fort, our troops blew up a warship, killed their admiral Michael Seymour,[9] and killed or wounded
more than 400 barbarians and rebels.

Now the provincial authorities have fortified the old city wall,
and mobilized 20,000 soldiers and marines, sufficient to obstruct and
scatter them. The gentry and citizenry are all showing righteous indignation, and even the American and French barbarians and the other
Western-ocean countries all realize that these barbarians are unreasonable and are sure not to aid them. They are quite isolated. Yeh
Ming-ch'en understands barbarian affairs thoroughly and can certainly
find means to control them, so he is ordered to act as circumstances
require.

As to the barbarian chief's harboring resentment and making a
pretext of never having been given access to the city, and last year the
English barbarians at Shanghai also saying that the governor general
of Kwangtung refused to see them, speaking resentfully and making
threats everywhere--We regard all these as attempts to further their
advantage. The barbarian mind is inscrutable. In this instance of
hostilities, if we had been unsuccessful it would have been very regrettable and it would also have injured the country; but since we succeeded, the barbarians are sure to take revenge or perhaps go to the
various ports just to state their grievances. This is the habitual device of rebel barbarians. As at present the interior is still disturbed,
how can we have another disturbance on the coast? Leniency and severity both have their difficulties.

As Yeh Ming-ch'en has long held office on the ocean frontier, we
trust he will be able to manage satisfactorily and relieve somewhat
Our indignation and anxiety. If these chiefs, having been defeated repeatedly, acknowledge and regret their wrongs and come to beg an
armistice, the said governor general can himself find means to handle
them in order to end strife. If they are still tyrannical, there can be
no compromise settlement to give rise to a train of demands. (IWSM.
HF 14; 14b, 6-15b, 3)

221. December 12, 1856. EDICT: Notes American Position in the Arrow
War and Warns Coastal Officials against Possible British Attacks.

---

9   Sir Michael Seymour, 1802-1887, was placed in command of the China station in 1855,
    and on the occurrence of the *Arrow* incident, took the Bogue Forts and then Canton.
    He later took the Taku Forts at the mouth of the Pei-ho, was made admiral in 1864,
    and lived to a ripe old age. Couling, *Encyclopaedia Sinica*, p. 506.

Supplementary Edict. Yeh Ming-ch'en has memorialized that the English barbarians have seized a pretext to start a quarrel, and that our forces have been successful in two encounters. In the ninth month (September 29-October 28), because the Kwangtung marines apprehended a boat load of robbers, the English barbarian chief Harry Parkes chose to make it an excuse for renewing the issue of entrance to the city and actually dared to open hostilities, attacked the city wall, and set fire to shops and dwellings. On October 29 and November 6 successively, our soldiers joined battle and twice won victories. The casualties of barbarians and rebels were over four hundred, and besides, the chief of the barbarian marine forces was killed. The Canton gentry volunteers are filled with righteous indignation, while the barbarians' ardor is cooled. Already more than 20,000 (of our) land and water forces have been mobilized.

Even though these barbarians are extremely crafty and perverse, once defeated, We trust they will not dare to be violent again. Besides, America, France, and the other Western countries all know that the English barbarians were in the wrong in starting this quarrel and are unwilling to help them, so they are isolated. Should the English barbarians repent their error, cease hostilities, and swing around of their own accord, orders have been given Yeh Ming-ch'en today that he need not be too vindictive. If they are as obstinate as ever, circumstances prevent any compromise settlement to give another wedge for demands Yeh Ming-ch'en has long held office on the ocean frontier and thorough\ understands the barbarian temper. We assume that he will be able to manage judiciously.

Since the coastal regions of Kiangsu, Chekiang, and Fukien are on the accustomed routes of the barbarian steamers, there should be preparation in advance in case the barbarians, having failed to get what they want in Kwangtung, make trouble again in other ports. I-liang, Chao Te-che, Wang I-te and Ho Kuei-ch'ing are ordered to give secret instructions to their respective local officials, in case barbarian ships should arrive, to make adequate preparations without affecting external appearances. If the barbarians come to report the circumstances of the conflict at Canton, they are also ordered to rely on reason to refute them, giving them to understand that there is no pretext available, so that they will be disappointed and leave. As usual there cannot be the least confusion to alarm the populace. (IWSM.HF 14; 15b, 5-16a, 9)

222. December 15, 1856. MEMORIAL: A Peking Censor Comments on the Canton Situation and Urges All-Out Popular Force against the British.
Metropolitan Circuit Censor Han Ch'ing-yün memorializes. It is humbly observed that ever since the English barbarians defied authorit in 1841, they have been extremely violent. The only place where they have not been able to do as they please is Kwangtung, because the Cantonese are a substantial people accustomed to English barbarian chi-

canery. Besides, the barbarian traders all regard Kwangtung as
most accessible, so as soon as the English barbarians squirm, trade
is held up and the other barbarians are sure to intervenc to end the
trouble. Hence, in 1849 the English barbarians discussed entrance
to the city but in the end did not force the issue. If the governor general has method in his management, perpetual peace can be secured.

Your official has just received letters from Canton and Hong Kong
saying:

> On October 21 an English cargo boat [the lorcha *Arrow*] had on board three
> bandits. Government forces, having bought a witness, waited until it en-
> tered the river and arrested the whole crew of twelve Chinese. As the
> governor general had not given prior notice, the English barbarians were
> greatly perturbed. Seven times they sent notes to the governor general
> to release the men. The governor general did not accept the letters but
> did return the twelve prisoners to the barbarian establishment. The bar-
> barians said that some of the men were spurious and asked the governor
> general to see them personally to distinguish real and false. The gover-
> nor general would have nothing to do with them, nor did he make any de-
> fense preparations.
>
> On October 23 the barbarian admiral, with three warships, suddenly entered
> the river, seized and occupied Lieh-te, Kuei-chiang, Feng-huang-kang,
> Hsi-ku and Hai-chu forts and raised the Red-head's flag [*Hung-mao ch'i-
> hao*, i.e., the British flag.] On the 25th patrols were dispatched to all
> streets; two of them were shot dead by the English barbarians. On this ac-
> count the people's hearts were incensed and they wanted to burn down the
> Thirteen Factories, but the governor general explicitly forbade it. On the
> 29th the barbarian troops opened fire outside the city wall and forced
> their way into Ching-hai Gate. Their cannon fire spread to several tens of shops
> shops and residences. On the 28th the barbarian soldiers scaled the outer
> wall and fought their way to the street behind the governor general's
> *yamen*, where they were killed or routed by the volunteers. On the 30th
> they carried the outer wall by assault and burned the governor general's
> *yamen*. The governor general fled to the inner city and ordered Messrs.
> Wu Ch'ung-yao and Su T'ing-k'uei to go outside the wall and discuss terms
> with the English barbarian consul. The barbarians continued to cannonade
> the city for several days, and no ships could come in or go out.

Your official begs to observe that on this occasion the governor
general merely sent soldiers on board a barbarian ship to seize bandits; as he failed to notify them, he gave the barbarians a pretext. If
on the other hand he had ordered the coastal forces to defend the forts,
he would not have been taken unawares. As for present plans, since
the Chiang-Hu provinces [i.e., Kiangsu, Chekiang, Hunan, Hupeh] are
both still carrying on trade, how can we again start a border quarrel?
But the barbarian temper is inscrutable. As they cannot be transformed
by virtue they should be intimidated by force. They conspire with bandits and harbor renegades, wilfully enter the interior, kill troops and
volunteers, burn forts, fire yamens, and even incite the populace by

saying that their fight is with officials and that they are not enemies
of the people. They try to frighten the provincial officials into paying bribes to maintain peace, and the provincial officials have to
suppress the populace, bow their heads in agreement, and let them
do what they will. Their ability goes no further than this.

Your official has received a letter from Kwangtung saying that
the English barbarians have no real ability. Although they have captured the provincial capital they cannot defend it. But the officials
fear them like tigers. Now the gentry of ninety-six villages in Ta-
li, Nan-hai, are drilling more than 10,000 volunteers, providing their
own supplies, and it is rumored that during the middle decade of the
tenth month (November 7-17) they will fight it out with the English
barbarians. Eight or nine out of every ten men formerly hired by
the barbarians have returned to their villages. Lieutenant Colonel
Wei Tso-pang and Sub-prefect Lin Fu-shen both led soldiers to the
provincial capital.

Since November 7 it is not known what the conditions are like,
but as everybody is filled with enmity, the courage of the English
barbarians must needs fail. In case the English barbarians repent
their wrongs and again consider peace terms, then we must establish clear regulations, ordering the former hong merchants, who
thoroughly understand the barbarian temper, to cooperate in the settlement. By no means can we sacrifice our constitution or injure our
prestige and thus depress popular morale. If they are as tyrannical
as ever, we should publish and punish their crimes. Their ships are
stalwart and they are good at maritime warfare, but if we wait until
they land, with our hundred against their one, we cannot but win.
(IWSM.HF 14; 16a, 10-18a, 5)

223. April 23, 1857. EDICT: Urges Yeh Ming-ch'en to Seek American
and French Support against the British at Canton.
    Edict to the Grand Councillors. Yeh Ming-ch'en has memorialized
on his success in warding off the English barbarians and the present
status of administration. We have read and thoroughly understood
this memorial. After having driven the English barbarian ships out
of the Canton River, the government forces attacked and routed them
again in succeeding weeks, repeatedly burning ships and killing the
rebels. The defense has been so rigorous that the barbarians have
made no move in the three weeks since their rout. Naturally the offensive should be temporarily slowed up, but the deployment of land
and water forces cannot yet be relaxed at all so as to weaken the soldiers' morale.

As for that country [England], the story that Bowring and Harry
Parkes were replaced at Canton by other barbarian chiefs because they

gratuitously started a quarrel with China is based on hearsay, and its truth or falsity cannot be ascertained. Even if it is true, the barbarian chiefs who are sent (to replace them) would not get to Canton before summer. At present We should determine a policy in advance as a basis for future negotiations. If the men sent this time do talk reasonably they should be received courteously and not be given another pretext for a change of attitude.

As to the merchants of America and France, their goods having been held up and their factories burned, they must be resentful. The reason the English chief is not willing to return to Hong Kong is that he is afraid the other barbarian merchants will demand indemnity. When the new chief arrives, he will not only negotiate with China but is sure also to discuss matters with America and France. Now those two countries have no quarrel with China. On this occasion, the circumstances of Harry Parkes starting trouble being apparent to all the barbarians, they are sure to reason justly who is right and who is wrong. You should send intelligent people to explain carefully to the American and French chiefs in advance to clarify their minds, so that when the English chief comes he will not be misled by the fabricated account of Harry Parkes and others. This is most suitable.

In the face of China's many troubles and the dearth of supplies, Yeh Ming-ch'en must plan thoroughly and look to the future in terminating this incident. But fixed objectives cannot be compromised merely for immediate circumstances, nor anything granted which will be hard to live up to and lead to other border troubles. The said governor general is so thoroughly conversant with barbarian affairs that we trust he can manage suitably with great discretion and not evade his responsibility. (IWSM.HF 15; 10b, 3-11a, 9)

Chapter 8

Reed and Preparations for Treaty Revision, 1858
(Documents 224-259)

The thirty-six documents included in this chapter cover the period
from January 17 to April 5, 1858. There are seventeen memorials and
eighteen edicts, sixteen of the latter addressed to the Grand Council
and two to the Secretariat. There are only two vermilion endorsements,
one of which is the laconic chih-tao-la ("Noted") and the other a specific endorsement. The latter is a shocked comment, appended to the
report of the fall of Canton to the British and the capture of Yeh Ming-
ch'en. In addition to the memorials and edicts, there is one American
note.

The principal memorialists include Yeh Ming-ch'en, who in a final
fourteen-page account of the developments at Canton, involving principally the British, shows himself as a serious and intelligent, though misguided, student of China's foreign relations. His information regarding
British activities, much of it from foreign sources, is outstanding among
all the Chinese officials of this period. The other principal memorialists are Canton Tartar General Mu-k'o-te-na and Governor of Kwangtung
Po-kuei, who took over when Yeh Ming-ch'en was taken prisoner by the
British. Other memorialists are Ho Ching, circuit censor of Kiang-nan
(i.e., Kiangsu-Anhwei); Canton Customs Superintendent (Hoppo) Heng-
ch'i; Lo Ping-chang, governor general of Fukien and Chekiang; Ho Kuei-
ch'ing, governor general of Liang-chiang; and Governor General of
Chihli T'an T'ing-hsiang.

The subject matter of the documents in this chapter is almost entirely centered on the developments at Canton, in which the British
completely dominated the picture. The American figure is William B.
Reed, first United States minister to China, with the possible exception
of Cushing, after a series of commissioners. Reed came to China to
secure treaty revision by peaceful methods and was personally inclined,
at the outset, to sympathize with the Chinese in their unequal struggle
with the British. His experiences in these months at Canton, however,
led him to request permission to join the British and French in the use
of force. This request was refused. Reed was an observer at Canton,
and the United States was a neutral power in the hostilities which resulted
in the occupation of the city by the British and French and the capture
of Yeh Ming-ch'en. Reed did succeed in transmitting his recommendations on treaty revision to Peking.

The events of this period are only lightly touched on by Dennett. The
Reed correspondence, including his reports on this Canton phase of his
mission, are published, U.S. Cong. 36: 1, S. Ex. Doc. 30. Most of this

material deals with the Tientsin treaty negotiations which are covered in the following chapter.

TRANSLATIONS OF DOCUMENTS

224. January 17, 1858. MEMORIAL: Yeh Ming-ch'en Reports the Arrival of Elgin, Gros, and Reed and Reviews the Canton War and Diplomacy at Length.

Imperial Commissioner, Grand Secretary, Governor General of Liang-kuang Yeh Ming-ch'en memorializes. It is reported that since the English chief Elgin[1] returned to Canton from Bengal during the eighth month (September 18-October 17), a French envoy, Baron Gros, and an American envoy, William Reed[2] came to Canton during the first and middle decades of the ninth month (October 18-27, 28-November 4) respectively.

It is learned privately tha during the seventh month (August 20-September 17), when Elgin was defeated in Bengal, he fled overland and was pursued to the coast by the Bengal barbarians. Just then a French warship was passing by, and not until it opened fire did the Bengal barbarians withdraw and Chief Elgin escape from danger.[3] Because of his gratitude to Chief Gros for saving his life, when (the latter) arrived at Canton, Chief Elgin invited him to a feast to thank him. He also discussed with him the ultimate solution of the present Chinese situation. Chief Gros said:

> Last year when this affair began, I was not here to witness it but the accounts current in China are most detailed and exhaustive. To wit, when the ten-odd places had been captured (by the British), there was still no resistance, and when several thousand residences and shops were burned there was still no conflict. Indeed, not until (the foreigners) were right on the city wall were the Chinese soldiers and volunteers willing to join battle, nor were they ever unsuccessful. It would appear that the strength of the Chinese troops was not insignificant. They certainly had well-laid plans before they took a stand. Former and present circumstances are vastly different and the determination of who was right and who was wrong must be left to my own judgment. The pretext which existed in the opium affair more than ten years ago is no longer tenable.
>
> On my part, when I left my country my sovereign said plainly that, as Eng-

---

1 Lord Elgin, Earl of Elgin and Kincardine, was appointed British High Commissioner and Plenipotentiary and arrived in Hong Kong, July 2, 1857. Couling, *Encyclopaedia Sinica,* p. 158.

2 William B. Reed of Pennsylvania was United States minister to China from April 18, 1857 to December 8, 1858.

3 This is an apochryphal account of the Indian Mutiny.

land was at war with China, he was sending me to Kwangtung to be on hand
to maintain the treaties and to mediate, but he would not allow me to help
the belligerents. I was not to cause China to regard the French as criminals
or mean men, to the detriment of previously negotiated treaties. When Your
Excellency (the English minister) came to China, I am confident that your
sovereign personally laid down the policy which you were to follow.

When Chief Elgin heard this, he agreed somewhat, but he still
wavered and no decision was made.

Just at this time America also replaced her envoy. This country
well knew that the English disturbance last year was actually the
result of Parker's secret machinations, for which he had been recalled. While William Reed was still in his own country, the decision
was made to trade as usual and he was ordered not to bring about
further complications. After his arrival at Canton on November 5,
the English barbarians feared that his communication to the provincial
capital would precede theirs and used many devices to prevent this,
but Chief Reed did not listen to them. Consequently, on November 23
he sent a communication through the sub-magistrate of Macao, and we
replied on the 24th. On receiving and reading this, Chief Reed was so
very gratified that he had our reply printed and distributed to the other
countries. He also said that it was apparent that his country and China
were friendly and without enmity, that he regarded such treatment by
the high Canton officials as handsome, even more glorious than previous receptions, and that American merchants were without exception
rejoicing in the streets.

When the English officials heard this they were startled and breath-
less. All the English merchants then became angry with Chief Elgin
for allowing the American envoy, not yet one month in Canton, to get
first place, while their envoys one after the other had come to Canton
twice, and in more than half a year not one word of communication
had passed between them. How would it ever be settled?

Chief Elgin had to do something. He again went to confer with the
French chief Gros. They recalled that in the practice of ten-odd years,
new envoys of the various countries arriving in Kwangtung had always
first sent communications to Canton and then the provincial government
had replied. China had never made the first move.

The French chief Gros really reached Kwangtung before the American chief Reed; but all the English officials told him that a letter could
not be sent directly and that even if he went to deliver it, it would not
be received, or if it were received, would certainly not be answered,
and would this not be a loss of dignity (for France)? Chief Gros was
a newcomer and foolishly believed this talk. When he heard about the
American chief Reed, he realized clearly his great mistake.

They (the English and French) both agreed to send communications,
and on December 11 a report was received from linguist Wu Ch'üan that

the English interpreter Thomas Wade[4] had now ordered him to present one communication, each, from the former English envoy Bowring and the former French envoy Bourboulon [sic]. He further said
that on the afternoon of the twelfth an English steamer and two sampans, each with white flags on their masts and also the inscription
"Cease Fighting," and with three English officials and two French officials on board, would come to Pai-ho-t'an waterfront in the Canton
River to deliver the communications of the new envoys of the two
countries. He asked that a representative receive them, after which
they would immediately return.

Your official immediately opened and read the two communications from Bowring and Bourboulon. They said that their countries
had each sent a new envoy, who would come to Kwangtung to assume
duties, and that hereafter when they sent communications they hoped
for replies. Besides this they had nothing to say.

To receive the barbarian chiefs, it seemed essential to have an
official who was thoroughly familiar with barbarian nature, and was
neither overbearing nor servile, who could meet them face to face.
It was noted that a certain expectant assistant sub-prefect, Assistant
Magistrate of Nan-hai Hsü Wen-shen, for years in charge of communications on barbarian affairs, formerly deputy magistrate of the sub-
district of Chiu-lung (Kowloon), was, in all his many dealings with
the Hong Kong barbarian chiefs, consistently spoken of as trustworthy;
so by noon of the twelfth we had him waiting at the Pai-ho-t'an waterfront.

At one o'clock there were seen three ships, steamers and sampans
coming in with the tide. The steamer carried a large, square white
flag, and the sampans each carried three-cornered white flags, all
with the two characters "Cease Fighting" written large. The English
officers were one brigade general, one lieutenant general, and one
interpreter; the French officers were one brigade general, and one
interpreter. When the vessels came alongside, they came on board
for the interview. All the chiefs had removed their hats and wore
swords, and their manners were very respectful and correct. After
exchange of civilities and a short stay, the communications were received, and all the chiefs returned to their respective ships and sailed
back.

Your official finds on careful examination that the literary style
is scarcely intelligible and the characters and sentences are hard to
decipher. In general, Chief Elgin's communication asked why, of

---

4 Thomas Francis Wade (1818-1895) came out to China as a British army officer but
   entered the foreign service in 1847, became a translator and Chinese secretary, and,
   in 1871, minister to China. He is best known for his Wade system of romanizing Chinese characters. Couling, *Encyclopaedia Sinica*, p. 591.

China's five ports, Canton alone should not allow entrance to the
city? He also asked that China specially appoint an officer of equal
rank to carry on separate treaty negotiations, that Englishmen and
English subjects suffering hardships in last year's disturbances all
be duly idemnified. He also wanted English forces stationed on Ho-
nan Island [opposite Canton] and the various forts. If the above articles were agreed to, all the gunboats in the area would withdraw and
Chinese and foreigners could trade as usual.

Your official replied immediately, item by item:[5] that according
to (Elgin's) current communication, four of China's ports were alike,
and only one did not conform, that conditions in other places were all
correct and only one was not. It was observed (in reply) that his
honorable country had come to Kwangtung to trade for more than a
hundred years with only one port, at Kuang-chou (Canton), and there
had been no mention of four ports; that only after the treaties were
set up in 1842 and 1844, respectively, were the four ports opened;
since in the beginning there was just the one port at Kwang-chou, it
had old regulations fundamentally different from the four ports.

As to the question of entrance to the city of Canton, in neither of
the former treaties of 1842 and 1844 did this clause occur; it was only
in 1847, during the second month (March 17-April 14) that Envoy Davis
suddenly brought up the question of entrance to the city, first placing
the time limit at two years. Before a year had passed, merchants returning home made complaints because of the troubles, and he was
recalled. Then in his place Envoy Bonham came to Kwangtung and in
1849, in correspondence with former commissioner Hsü, closed the
question of entrance to the city. Envoy Bonham posted notice in the
factories forbidding foreigners to enter the city. Therefore, as the
English themselves had closed the question of entrance to the city, the
present official, formerly in the office of governor, joined former commissioner Hsü in memorializing the late Emperor Hsüan-tsung [Tao-
kuang] on the matter, and they respectfully received an Imperial Edict:

Walls are built to safeguard the people, and if the people are safeguarded
the country is secure. Where the hearts of the people point, there will
the Heavenly Mandate go. Now the people of Canton are of one mind and of

---

5 Yeh's long quotation in reply to Lord Elgin, as well as his subsequent quotation of
his reply to Baron Gros, is partly in direct address, in honorific second person to
the foreign envoys, and partly in the third person, reporting indirectly what he said
to them in his memorial to the emperor. In this translation, the whole has been placed
arbitrarily in the third person, with consequent violation of Chinese grammar. The
alternative, however, of placing it in direct quotation, would also involve contra-
dictions, so the present form against the better judgment of Dr. E-tu Zen-Sun, is
preserved.

China's Management of the American Barbarians

fixed determination in not desiring foreigners to enter the city wall, so
how could We give them coercive decrees? China cannot thwart its people
to please those from afar, and the foreign countries ought also to study
popular feelings to increase their business.

We also reminded him that a newspaper of his honorable country had
stated in 1850:

The sovereign's instructions to Bonham have arrived in Hong Kong stating that
that his reports of conditions in Tientsin and the five ports of China
had all been noted. The said military head was obviously able to know the
crux of affairs, and besides knew that Governor General of Liang-kuang Hsü
had secretly evolved a plan, and that the governor of Kwangtung was also
in on it and had jointly notified Peking, China, secretly to dispatch So-lun
[Heilung Kiang] troops to defend Tientsin. Although their warships would
not find it difficult to land troops and fight them, still Bonham understood affairs of state wnd was thoroughly familiar with Chinese customs.
His present trip to the various Chinese ports amounted to a secret spying
to observe the prosperity or decay of the regions of China. If they had to
fight, the Chinese people would all say that their countrymen (the English)
were in the wrong. It was apparent that their military head, Bonham, had
handled affairs admirably and in the future should have no unusual trouble.[6]
He was very admirable, and in fact should be designated *Wei-li-pa*.[7]

Besides, a medal was pinned on him and he was very glorious.
At this time the English officials and English merchants in Hong Kong
all put on formal dress to congratulate him; thus his honorable country
merchants all regarded Envoy Bonham as right and disapproved Envoy
Davis. Now that the honorable envoy has come with his mandate he
naturally should prefer the actions of Envoy Bonham and not imitate the
conduct of Envoy Davis.
  According to his letter, when an officer of equal rank was appointe
to negotiate with him and draw up a separate treaty--which must be in
duplicate and be sent to his country and to China for the affixing of
seals--then he would withdraw his troops.
  We replied that in 1850 Bonham had gone personally to Shanghai
and had sent man to Tientsin to repeat his request for entrance into
the city. In 1854 Envoy Bowring had also gone to Tientsin to request
entrance to the city as well as treaty revision and other things. His
Imperial Majesty, because the treaties of 1842 and 1844 had both been

---

6 Sir Samuel George Bonham was H.B.M. Plenipotentiary and Chief Superintendent of Trade
   from March 20, 1848 to April 12, 1854. Couling states that "the Government was pleased
   with his diplomacy, promoted him from C.B. to K.C.B., and gave him at the same time a
   baronetcy, November 22, 1850." *Encyclopaedia Sinica*, p. 53.
7 This is a transliteration of Chinese characters for an unidentified English term.

designated by the late Emperor Hsüan-tsung as ten-thousand-year treaties in the hope of perpetual friendship, would allow no changes. Ever since, Chinese and foreign trade had mutually benefited; everything had been done according to the treaties, as was really suitable and proper. We said further that His Imperial Majesty, as the question of entrance to the city was closed, has received and has before him the late Emperor's Edict, and as the ten-thousand-year treaties had also been determined by the late Emperor, He could not readily change either of them. Therefore, although on the two previous occasions his honorable country (men) went to Tientsin and Imperial Commissioners received them, they never consented to discuss the treaties but sent them back to Canton to continue to manage according to the treaties. Now no official in China of any rank would dare disregard the Sacred Edict.

The communication also said that Englishmen and English dependents who had incurred losses during the recent disturbances should all be duly indemnified. (We replied that) the trouble during the ninth month (September 29-October 28) began because, when China seized native outlaws, Consul Parkes, relying solely on the testimony of the lorcha captain, said that government troops came on board to arrest bandits and tore to pieces the English flag, without knowing that when the government soldiers went on board they never saw a flag. For even according to the unanimous testimony of the sailors who were seized, since the boat was not under way when the government soldiers came to seize them, the flag was kept in the hold. Thus it is clear beyond a doubt that the flag was never torn down.

The said lorcha was built by a native, Su Ya-ch'eng, who chartered it to the said captain, who took over his license. Therefore the sailors on board were all native bandits. Li Ming-t'ai and Liang Chien-fu, who were seized, have both been generally known as pirates, and there is the testimony of Wu Ya-jen that they are really great robbers. Because of the many letters received from Consul Parkes, we finally returned the twelve outlaws to him. Sentiment and right were both fully satisfied, but Consul Parkes would not receive them and abruptly and without justification began hostilities, destroyed various forts, bombarded the city wall day after day, and also thrice sent English soldiers to set fires, burning contiguous buildings everywhere. The damage incurred by the Chinese merchants and people was much greater than the losses of his honorable country. Now the gentry within and without the city and suburbs are flooding this office with petitions, beseeching the present official to send a communication to the honorable envoy demanding a just inquiry and settlement, but he has not yet complied. If (the British) did not believe this, the present official would send another reply enclosing copies of the various petitions received for the honorable envoys to peruse and determine their disposition.

As to Ho-nan Island, the population is large and very violent. In

1847, the fourth month (May 14 to June 12), some of his honorable country's merchants wanted to rent land on Ho-nan. The local gentry and people signed a petition (in protest) and only when it was answered by Envoy Davis did the clamor subside. According to their communications, Ho-nan Island and the forts along the river now are to be occupied by troops. Land on Ho-nan, previously leased to build a warehouse, was withdrawn before (the warehouse) was finished, so how would it be possible to station troops? The forts along the river were all built by popular subscription to serve as protection against bandits, and if his honorable country tried to station troops there it is feared it would cause trouble.

It has always been said that the honorable envoy was experienced and discriminating and that everyone in the country respected him; that now that he had come to Kwangtung, what his honorable country most desired of him was a termination of this affair, not to come here and stir up trouble; (we said) that we thought the honorable envoy was reasonable and perspicacious and would do nothing unjust, nor did this derive merely from the present official's approbation.

As to the statement in his letter that China and the outside would trade as usual, it was quite apparent that the honorable envoy understood the situation clearly. Ever since the signing of the commercial treaties all Chinese merchants had acted courteously. Only since the ninth month of last year (September 29-October 28, 1856) had the trading ships of the various countries not come, but it was not China that stopped them. Now the honorable envoy has proposed that China and the outside trade as usual, and it was hoped that an exchange of correspondence would effect a suitable agreement and settlement. Thus Your official answer English chief Elgin's communication article by article from beginning end.

As for the French chief Gros' communication, because in the spring of last year a missionary, Father Ma [Abbé Chapdelaine], [8] was arrested and executed by the magistrate of Hsi-lin, Kwangsi, he wanted the Hsi-lin magistrate punished and an indemnity paid. Also, under Article 35 of the treaty, he wanted officials appointed for separate negotiations everything that was burned in their Canton factory last year should be indemnified; inasmuch as England was now requiring China to pay indemnity, Ho-nan and the various forts should be turned over to France and England who would send troops to garrison them; and only when terms were negotiated would troops be withdrawn.

Your official immediately replied in detail. According to his present communication the missionary Abbé Chapdelaine had been arrested in

---

8   Auguste Chapdelaine, an *abbé* of the Missions Etrangères was "most brutally tortured and murdered" at Hsi-lin, Kwangsi, February 29, 1856. Couling, *Encyclopaedia Sinica* p. 89. Abbé Chapdelaine is referred to in the Chinese documents as Father Ma.

Hsi-lin-hsien, Kwangsi, and died from beating to extort confession.
But before receiving Envoy Bourboulon's letter (Your official) had
received a report from the provincial judge of Kwangsi that Acting
District Magistrate of Hsi-lin-hsien Chang Ming-feng had reported
on February 24, 1856, that there was no record of the arrest of Abbé
Chapdelaine and his death by torture, but during the second month
(March 7-April 4) of the same year, the militia leader of Chien-k'o
village reported a rebel, Ma Tzu-nung, who came to the village and
aroused the people with weird tales, collected crowds to worship, and
also ravished women and plundered stockaded towns, and such. (The
said villager) and a military officer immediately led the militia to
arrest him and then Ma Tzu-nung was captured. This is on record.
According to Ma Tzu-nung's testimony, he was a Cantonese of the same
party with (the rebel) Lin Pa and Teng A-hsiu; Lin Pa and the others
were then in Ling-yün-hsien to collect adherents to worship; nor did
he deny in his testimony robbing and raping. After this trial, (his case)
was entered among the bandit-suppression reports, and this is on
record. Now he (the provincial judge) had received orders to investigate; actually there was only the arrest and execution of Ma Tzu-nung,
whose name is not the same as the Father Ma [Abbé Chapdelaine] in
the inquiry, nor did his nativity coincide.

The present official received this, and his previous reply to Envoy
Bourboulon is on record. He observed that the Catholic religion is
primarily to exhort men to do good; Article 23 of the treaty regulations
states that "if any Frenchman crosses the boundary and penetrates far
into the interior, he will be subject to arrest by Chinese officials but
must be sent under custody to the nearest consul to receive jurisdiction;
no Chinese official shall injure or mistreat him." Thus the envoy's
honorable countrymen had traveled contrary to the treaty, repeatedly
going beyond the boundaries into the interior to preach.

For instance, in the eighth month (September 20-October 19) of
1846, two men, Gabet and Huc were returned under escort from Tibet
to Kwangtung;[9] in 1848, Lo-ch'i-cheng[10] was escorted from Szechwan
to Kwangtung; in 1850, the eleventh month (December 4-January 1, 1851),
Ni-chi-li-li and Hua-ling-chia-li were escorted from Mongolia to Kwangtung; in 1851, the fourth month (May 1-30), Meng-te was escorted from
Kiangsi to Kwangtung; in 1855, the ninth month (October 11-November 9)
Ya-shui-ming was escorted from Chia-ying-chou to Canton; and in the

---

9   The Lazarist missionary priests Evariste (Huc) and Gabet arrived in Canton from
Lhasa, September 25, 1846. They had worked with the Mongols and reached Lhasa in
December, 1844, remained for some time but were eventually compelled by the Chinese
Resident to leave. They were given safe conduct to Canton. *Chinese Repository*, v. 15,
p. 526.

10   These and the subsequent transliterations of the names of priests have not been
identified.

fourth month of this year (April 24-May 22, 1857) a French missionary, who when asked his name spoke unintelligibly, was escorted from
Jen-hua to Canton. These were all turned over to his honorable country's
consul for disposal, and all are on record; they were all missionaries
of his honorable country who had gone far into the interior and all were
questioned and delivered over. This could be said to be a fulfillment
of courtesy and right. Now Kwangsi is outside the five ports, actually beyond the border and far inland. If Father Ma were found to
be a Frenchman he would certainly have been transported back to
Kwangtung. But the Catholic religion exhorts men to do good and as
there are rapine and plundering involved, it could not have been done
by one who was exhorting to do good. Thus it was obvious that this
was not Father Ma (Abbé Chapdelaine).

The present dispatch also said that his countrymen and those under
his protection at Canton who had had all the goods in their hong burned
should be duly indemnified. It is found that in the ninth month of last
year (September 29-October 28, 1856), England had begun hostilities
without justification, burned the buildings in the Hsi-kuan (Western
suburb) district; that several hundred thousand people witnessed it and
even among the foreigners there was not one but fully understood that
the English soldiers set fires and did the burning and that the various
foreigners should negotiate with England; it was also reported that
Consul Parkes had promised indemnification and that this was clearly
not China's responsibility.

His present note also said that according to Article 35 of the treaty
regulations they again requested the appointment of officials for a separate negotiation. We replied that in 1845, when the two countries established the regulations, they received the late Emperor Hsüan-tsung's
[i.e.,Tao-Kuang] approval of a ten-thousand-year treaty in the hope of
preserving forever friendly relations and there was no provision for
revision; that His Imperial Majesty, the present Emperor, inasmuch as
this ten-thousand-year treaty had received the late Emperor's ratifica-
tion, had issued a perspicacious decree which everyone implicitly
obeyed; that now no Chinese official of any grade would dare say anything
different so how could there be another appointment of officials for a
re-negotiation?

As to his statement about England requiring China to indemnify her,
We replied that the trouble of the ninth month of last year (September
29-October 28, 1856) involved England's unjustified bombardment of
Canton, the destruction of the various forts, and the burning of the
houses of several blocks and that Chinese citizens incurred this damage;
that each country could decide justly who was right and who wrong. In
the tenth month of last year (October 29-November 27, 1856) a letter
was received from Envoy Kleskowsky stating that "when your honorable
country is at war with another country, the present envoy is properly
not concerned." This showed that Envoy Kleskowsky clearly understood

morality and wanted no connection with English affairs. We thought
the honorable envoy would also see the situation in a clear light and
thus would certainly not disagree with what Envoy Kleskowsky said.
He must not listen to the excitations of outsiders or allow them to destroy the honorable envoy's fundamentally steadfast heart. The Ho-nan
Island citizenry are numerous and known to be fierce, and if their
honorable soldiers were stationed there it was feared there would be
trouble. As the two countries were friendly and any matters of mutual trade could be arranged suitably, the present official hoped that he
would not be misled by rumors and induced to take on the troubles of
others.

Thus, Your official replied to the French chief Gros' note, item
by item from beginning to end. He notes that England, France and
America are all traditional rivals, none willing to be beneath the other
but whenever they become involved with China they league together as
one, so that with their strength united their power is increased for
combined coercion.

Last year when the English caused trouble it was merely due to
the machinations of the American, Parker, and at first they were not
willing to resist openly. When in the first decade of the eleventh
month (November 28-December 7, 1856) they finally opened hostilities at the various forts on the eastern route, they seriously blunted
their lance. When his country [America] heard of it, it agreed that
according to precedent, when a foreign country is engaged in hostilities with China, other countries could not intervene and that Parker's
gratuitous assistance was really meddlesome; hence his recall.

At this time the American envoy, Chief Reed, has come to Canton.
Since his country has accidentally had a difference with China, it was
feared petty enmity would develop detrimental to trade. So, in the
middle decade of the sixth month of this year (July 31-August 9, 1857)
when the American merchant Sturgis,[11] et al. came to Whampoa and
asked to open trade, consent was given immediately. Also in (Your
official's) reply to Chief Reed's note, he never mentioned Parker's
insurgent activities here last year and thus gave him a chance to change
his face. The American chiefs have all regarded China as genuinely
magnanimous and have all expressed gratitude.

As to the French chief Gros, he has urged the English chief Elgin
to consider means of closing the affair; how can he turn right around
and be utilized by him? This is actually because Bowring was still
in Hong Kong and repeatedly begged him, saying that, although England

---

11 R.S. Sturgis and Edward Cunningham of Russell and Company went to Whampoa,
    July 31, 1857, in the steamer *Antelope* to confer on the resumption of trade
    with all friendly powers, the English excepted. U.S. Cong. 35:2, *S. Ex. Doc.*
    22, p. 1417.

was not willing to lend troops to help him, his country still had the Abbé Chapdelaine case, so why did he not argue the case (with China) and at the same time make use of this to augment his prestige a bit. Actually the Abbé Chapdelaine case occurred in the summer of last year when the former acting envoy, Kleskowsky, was in office; his communication was answered clearly and for the last half year nothing more had been said: Then in the summer of this year (1857), Bourboulon and Wade returned to Kwangtung and, although the case was reopened, it was explained in communications over and over and the whole affair was put to rest.

Now Chief Gros' incessant complaints are actually because of Chief Bowring's egging him on from the sidelines and seem not at all of his own conviction. Who would have thought that the American chief Reed on hearing this would ridicule the French chief Gros for sending a joint note when he did not have to cling to the English barbarians, and make a joke of it? The situation has all been written up and published in the newspapers for all countries to see, and Chief Gros is greatly mortified

But England, France, and America, since the signing of the treaties have been still more insatiably greedy. Aiding each other like a pack of wolves, their will to coerce is practically impregnable. Now means have been found to oppose (this united front) which have already led them to differ, and resulted first in the isolation of England. It is definitely known that other countries have changed their views. Besides, the English barbarians are perverse, violent, wilful·and cruel and actually for more than a hundred years all the foreign countries have been accustomed to look askance at them. Now in China they have started hostilities with both sides holding out for more than a year; actually it is a case of riding a tiger and not being able to get off. The said Chief Elgin had been in Kwangtung almost half a year and never sent a communication, just for this reason.

Fortunately (Elgin's) instructions from that country's female sovereign reached Hong Kong by steamer in the middle decade of the tenth month (November 26-December 6, 1857) and it has been learned through spies that they say:

> In the troubles reported from China, jealousy and suspicion must be laid
> aside in order to provide for lasting mutual friendehip. He (Elgin) must
> not rely on force or use coercion. Those things which China has been unable
> to concede should be amicably considered, reported in accord with facts, and
> action withheld until a national edict is issued. Under no circumstances will
> she sanction arbitrary use of arms again to cause loss of national prestige
> along the coastal provinces.

The fact is that lately, English newspapers have been kept even more secret, being arranged in order and locked in a safe, and excepting during conferences, even the barbarian officials cannot see them and they cannot be bought at all outside. Hence, we secretly sent to the barbarian residence a man accustomed to dealing with them and whom they trust unquestionably, and who understands barbarian language and also reads barbarian writing. Whenever they hold a conference, he meets them as if by chance, mixes around among them, watches and listens, and has finally procured complete details.

In this communication, although Chief Elgin as usual made various demands, since they had been repeatedly repudiated he knew full well that under the circumstances they could not be acceded to, making it obvious that there was some ulterior motive involved. First, if on arrival at Kwangtung he were completely to disregard the requests of his predecessors which had not been acceded to, he feared that at home there would be talk behind his back, so it was better to repeat the requests whether they be granted or rejected, just for the record. Second, last year these barbarians set fires inside and outside the city and suburbs three times, spreading and burning a thousand buildings. The losses suffered by Chinese merchants and people were greater than those of the barbarians. How could he but know that if all of them turned around and probed him and demanded indemnity, he would have no argument. Third, the said country is already completely exhausted. They have just had a rebellion in Bengal and no supplies are forthcoming. Even if all the items were not granted, judging from former occasions, it was possible to get a silver (indemnity) which would relieve somewhat the immediate need. His fiendish chicanery and avaricious secret plans, in our opinion, do not go beyond this. Your official, since replying on December 14, analyzing his requests item by item, has to date received no further communications.

In retrospect, our previous consent for entrance to the city after two years and revision of the treaty after twelve years were originally only devices of expedience. Who realized that they contained potential woes, transmitting a train of troubles to the present? If we still fail to take advantage of this occasion, when their measure of iniquity is full, their schemes run out and their strength depleted-- to take all their various and repeated demands and once for all cut off all their manifications in order at one stroke to gain lasting ease --having got an inch they will want a mile and there will be no stopping them. Not only will the present anxiety be unrelieved but it is feared that later the poison will spread.

But the barbarians are naturally extraordinarily argumentative and their wickedness has a hundred manifestations. Now that success is but one step away, Your official must needs make his defenses still stronger, outwardly showing compassion but not daring to be the least bit careless or to weaken our general position. Once their local gunboats have all withdrawn and a date is set for the opening of foreign trade, he will send an express memorial to report it, in the hope of early relief of Imperial anxiety.   (IWSM.HF 17; 25b, 8-37b, 3)

225. January 17, 1858. EDICT: Commends Yeh Ming-ch'en's Policy at Canton and Expresses Confidence in Elgin's Ultimate Defeat.
Edict to the Grand Councillors. Yeh Ming-ch'en has memorialized concerning the English and French communications and his reasoned replies. Although the said chiefs realized that their argument was faulty, they boldly made requests hoping for some gain. The said official refuted them reasonably and explained matters adroitly. His rhetoric was entirely appropriate. We trust that the said chiefs have no place left to stick their beaks.
Previously it has been the English and American barbarian chiefs who have repeatedly connived in evil at the five ports, and the French have not taken part. Their cooperation in coercion at this time is clearly due to Chief Elgin's inveigling. Although Chief Elgin is committed to Chief Bowring's policy, fortunately the queen of that country does not approve of being at odds with China, and before many days a change of attitude should take place. Yeh Ming-ch'en has probed and destroyed their machinations, so that the barbarians' cleverness has come to naught.
Should there be other communications, our general attitude can be roughly defined: the (demands for) entrance to the city, payment of indemnity, and treaty revision must be exterminated in all their ramifications in order at one blow to gain lasting peace. If the said barbarian gunboats all withdraw and a date is fixed for the opening of foreign trade, he is ordered to send an express memorial. At this time the immediate need of military supplies in the various provinces is very great, and the said governor general must needs manipulate affairs to our greatest advantage. (IWSM.HF 17; 37b, 4-38a, 3)

226. January 27, 1858. MEMORIAL: Canton Officials Report Reed's Proposal of Mediation and the Subsequent Fall of Canton and Capture of Yeh Ming-ch'en.
Kuang-chou (Canton) Tartar General Mu-k'o-te-na, Governor of Kwangtung Po-kuei, Deputy Lieutenant Generals Shuang-hsi and Shuang-ling, Superintendent of Customs Heng-ch'i, Kwangtung Financial Commissioner Chiang Kuo-lin, and Judicial Commissioner Chou Ch'i-pin memorialize. After Your slave Po-kuei returned to Kwangtung he made a careful investigation of last year's English barbarian fracas. Governor General Yeh Ming-ch'en mobilized soldiers and volunteers and steadfastly resisted; he also stopped foreign trade. Although the houses and forts along the river were burned and there was no little commotion, the English barbarian losses were also great. There was a stalemate for a long time, until finally they withdrew their warships from Canton River. Then no barbarian of any nationality dared regard us lightly. During the delay of more than half a

year, although no communications were sent, still they made no move. Your slave and the governor general decided, if the barbarians sent a communication, to turn the situation to our advantage and avail ourselves of the overture.

In the tenth month of the present year (November 16-December 15, 1857) the governor general received a communication from the American barbarian chief (Reed) asking for an interview and a formal presentation of credentials. The governor general replied that as previous barbarian interviews had been in the Jen-hsin Godown of the former hong merchant, Wu I-ho, and as this godown was burned last year by the English barbarians, although he had the desire to see him he had not the place to effect it, and so he declined. At the time the governor general did not notify (me) at all.

Afterwards, when Your slave finally learned of this, he was greatly astonished and called on the governor general to inquire about the matter. He said that if he saw the American barbarian, the English barbarians would seize the opportunity to make trouble, and it would be improper. Besides, the English barbarians prohibited the American barbarian's entrance to the port, so how could he see him? Your slave said that as the American barbarian did not dare to oppose authority openly but rather asked for an interview, how did he know it was not to arrange terms for the English barbarians? Even if he did not see him personally, he could send a representative. The governor general replied that as he had not asked for a representative it could hardly have been necessary; that in less than a month he could certainly bring the trouble to an end.

Your slave has worked with the governor general for years and knows that he works cagily and secretly, and when he spoke this way must have things under control. Moreover he had received various provincial officials and said emphatically that he could guarantee that there would be no trouble. Consequently, everyone kept his mouth shut. Anyway, as no symptoms had developed, Your slave could not oppose him outright.

Then unexpectedly, on December 16, ten ships of the various barbarians sailed up Canton River. The governor general sent orders that unless the barbarians made a move the soldiers and volunteers were not to pick a fight. There was a stalemate for several days, and then on the 24th the barbarians sent a communication to the five provincial officials, Tartar general, governor general, governor, and the two deputy lieutenant generals. Again the governor general consulted no one and it is not known how he replied. Then on the 27th the barbarians again communicated with the five officials, and still the governor general gave us no notice. Moreover, he sent orders to various gentry that they were not to go unauthorized on board the barbarian ships, and if they disobeyed they would be specially punished. Consequently these gentry, Wu Ch'ung-yüeh and others, just looked on.

On the 28th cannons roared on all sides. The governor general
finally mobilized the village trainbands, but they were not all assembled by the 29th when, between 7 and 9 in the morning, Kuan-yin
Shan inside the city and the forts both inside and outside the North
Gate were occupied by the barbarians. Your Slaves then sent for Wu
Ch'ung-yüeh, who along with various gentry, went to the barbarian
ships to find out what they wanted. The barbarians' language was
proudly contemptuous. They said that none of Your slaves could handle
this affair; that this demonstration occurred because the governor
general's obstinacy had gone too far and there was nothing they could
do but take action; that matters had reached the point where the only
thing they could do was proceed to Tientsin and ask His Imperial
Majesty to appoint a competent Imperial Commissioner to handle
things right; that the provincial capital would not be occupied long.
In their conversations with Wu Ch'ung-yüeh and other gentry, they
held stubbornly to this statement.

Suddenly, on January fifth, the barbarians burst into the yamen
of Your slave Shuang-hsi, seized the governor general and led him to
a barbarian ship. Your slaves were grieved beyond measure and sent
Wu Ch'ung-yüeh and other gentry to intercede for him. The barbarians
would not even let them see him but sent word that he would not be
injured. They also asked Your slave Mu-k'o-te-na and Your slave
Po-kuei to go to Kuan-yin Shan, merely telling them to repress troops
and populace inside and outside the city, and not a word more.

After much thought Your slaves have concluded that the barbarians in the city will find it impossible to occupy it very long; but they
have burned up the more than 100,000 (catties) of gunpowder stored
in Kuan-yin Shan, and people are frightened. Naturally it is important
to quiet the people. Besides, pacifying barbarians has never been anything but management. So they sent Wu Ch'ung-yüeh and other gentry
to explain to these barbarians and if possible to prevent them from
going to Tientsin. When this plan has shaped up, they will memorialize
again, express.

They only request the Imperial favor of the immediate appointment
of an Imperial Commissioner to come to Canton to mollify those from
afar and quiet popular unrest. Although barbarian affairs are not Your
slaves' particular responsibility, having rendered assistance ineptly
and taken inadequate precautions, they (i.e., we) are all deservedly
guilty, and must ask for an Edict instructing the Boards to adjudge Your
slaves' crimes rigorously. With uncontrollable fear they await the arrival of the Decree.

Vermilion endorsement: Deeply shocked on reading this memorial
There is a separate Edict.　(IWSM.HF 17; 38b, 3-40b, 7)

227.　January 27, 1858.　EDICT: Repudiates Yeh Ming-ch'en's Action at
Canton and Orders his Degredation; Other Canton Officials to Be Tried

Edict to the Grand Secretariat. Mu-k'o-te-na, Po-kuei, and others have jointly memorialized express on the barbarians' furtive entrance into the provincial capital. If Yeh Ming-ch'en, as Imperial Commissioner in charge of barbarian affairs, could not accede to the unreasonable demands of the barbarians, he should have found means of bringing them around and, on the other hand, discussed suitable plans for their management with the Tartar General,governor, et al. Twice when the barbarians sent communications to the Tartar General, the governor general, governor, and deputy lieutenant governors, the said governor general not only did not discuss his action with them, but even kept the contents of the communication secret and gave no notice. He procrastinated a long time and so antagonized the barbarians that they stormed the provincial capital.

Patently obstinate, smug, perverse in administration and unworthy of the responsibility entrusted to him, Yeh Ming ch'en is ordered immediately degraded. Kuang-chou (Canton) Tartar General Mu-k'o-te-na, Governor of Kwangtung Po-kuei, Deputy Lieutenant Generals Shuang-hsi and Shuang-ling, Kwangtung Superintendent of Customs Heng-ch'i, Provincial Financial Commissioner Chiang Kuo-lin and Provincial Judge Chou Ch'i-pin are all guilty of lax defense, but as the said governor general did not confer with them they can be somewhat condoned. Their request for rigorous trial and punishment is ordered changed by special favor to investigation by the Boards. (IWSM.HF 17; 40b, 8 -41a, 6)

228. January 27, 1858. EDICT: Grand Councillor Huang Tsung-han Named to Succeed Yeh Ming-ch'en and Ordered to Proceed Immediately to Canton.

Additional Edict. Huang Tsung-han is ordered appointed governor general of Liang-kuang, to proceed immediately by mounted stage. He is also ordered to take over the seal of Imperial Commissioner in charge of barbarian affairs. Until Huang Tsung-han reaches his post the duties of Imperial Commissioner and governor general of Liang-kuang are ordered handled temporarily by Po-kuei, those of governor of Kwangtung, by Chiang Kuo-lin. (IWSM.HF 17; 41a, 8-10)

229. January 27, 1858. EDICT: Names Governor Po-kuei Acting Imperial Commissioner to Salvage the Canton Situation and Notes Reed's Offer.

Edict to the Grand Councillors: Mu-k'o-te-na, Po-kuei and others have memorialized jointly that the barbarians took advantage of circumstances and entered the city, and ask for an Edict and trial. Upon reading the memorial We were certainly shocked. On this day specific orders have been sent for the degradation of Yeh Ming-ch'en. The case of Mu-k'o-te-na, Po-kuei and the others was transferred by special favor to the Boards for discussion. We also ordered Huang

Tsung-han appointed governor general of Liang-kuang to proceed by
mounted stage. Until he arrives at his post, Po-kuei was ordered to
act as governor general of Liang-kuang.

Yeh Ming-ch'en repeatedly reported that the English barbarians
were making trouble, but his management seemed to have it under
control. He memorialized during this month that the English and
French chiefs had sent communications and he had replied reasonably and hoped that from then on things would be different and they
could get along peaceably as before. Unexpectedly the said governor
general was obstinately over self-confident in his stubborn rejection
of the American barbarian's request for an interview. Twice the barbarians sent communications to the five (provincial) officials and he
did not even discuss them with the Tartar General or the governor.
In addition he ordered the gentry not to go on board the barbarian
ships without permission, and so antagonized the barbarians that they
occupied Kuan-yin Shan inside the city and the forts inside and outside the North Gate and also carried off the governor general to a
barbarian ship. Even though they said they would not harm him, it
is a complete violation of propriety.

Yeh Ming-ch'en has managed miserably and cannot deny his guilt.
But the barbarians have taken him to a barbarian ship with the idea
of extortion and are sure to come out with rash demands. The Tartar
General and acting governor general can tell them that Yeh Ming-ch'en
has been degraded and is beneath consideration, so the barbarians will
have no ground for extortion and realize that it is useless to hold him.
The barbarians have admitted that they would not occupy the city long,
but if they do withdraw of their own accord they are sure to make
endless demands.

As these barbarians have no standing enmity toward Mu-k'o-te-na
or Po-kuei and as Po-kuei is now acting governor general, he is
ordered to explain plausibly and see if they have any feeling of remorse
If the barbarians withdraw from the city and ask to trade, the said
Tartar General and acting governor general can act according to circumstances so as to show management. If the barbarians bring up
indemnity for goods destroyed by fire, tell them that the Chinese forts
and residences which they burned are very numerous and if we discuss
indemnity, their account would not equal ours. Besides, it was the barbarians who started hostilities and all nations are free to decide who
was right and who was wrong.

If in the end they are not willing to evacuate the city and are still
obstreperous, the only thing to do is mobilize soldiers and militia and
fight them. Do not let them stay in the city long. Besides, the Cantonese gentry have a sense of justice and the courage of the people can
be relied on. Po-kuei and the others must cooperate with gentry and
people, arouse popular indignation and create common hostility and
antagonism and then, when the barbarians are driven out of the river,

make terms with them. In handling this matter, the said Tartar General, governor and others must neither fail from being too rigid and create a crisis like Yeh Ming-ch'en, nor fail from being too lenient and create among barbarians a disrespect for China. This is most essential.

In the interval required for Huang Tsung-han to go from Peking to Kwangtung, military affairs cannot be postponed. It rests entirely with the acting governor general to formulate a line of action and take the initiative in planning and execution and if there are any new developments, memorialize express in order to relieve Our anxiety. He will also ascertain whether or not the official seals have been lost and memorialize accordingly. (IWSM.HF 17; 41b, 1-42b, 6)

230. January 27, 1858. MEMORIAL: The Canton Tartar General Reports the Loss of the Great Seal of the Imperial Commissioner.

Mu-k'o-te-na further memorializes. So on the 27th (December, 1857), the barbarians on the one hand bombarded and on the other engaged handarms. Your slaves Mu-k'o-te-na and Po-kuei took counsel and fearing the forces at the forts were inadequate called up more government forces, both bannermen and governor's garrison, and fought bitterly for one day and night. There were casualties among officers and men of the troops and militia.

As to the governor general and salt gabelle seals, as well as the great seal of Imperial Commission, the governor general in his haste was unable to give any notice. If a new Imperial Commissioner is sent to Kwangtung, he requests an Edict ordering the Board to have both seals and a great seal at once cast and forwarded to facilitate administration.

Vermilion Endorsement: Noted. (IWSM.HF 17; 42b, 7-43a, 4)

231. February 1, 1858. EDICT: Suggests the Possibility of American Aid and Orders the Recruitment of Trainbands in Canton Area to Repel the British.

Edict to the Grand Councillors. Because the barbarians formerly entered the capital of Kwangtung by stealth, until such time as the newly appointed governor general of Liang-kuang, Huang Tsung-han, shall arrive at his post, We ordered Po-kuei to take over the great seal of Imperial Commissioner and the duties of governor general of Liang-kuang and also sent instructions to the acting governor general and others to study the situation for opportunities and to take action in advance [i.e. before the new incumbent's arrival].

This time the violence of the barbarians' feelings is primarily because Yeh Ming-ch'en's obstinacy, self-sufficiency, and bad management exasperated them. But ever since the barbarians have traded, these ten-odd years, they have continuously disregarded treaties, occupied our walled cities, humiliated our high officials, and acted like rebels. How can they be said to be innocent? If at this time we were to cut off trade and proclaim their crimes for punishment, it would be entirely fitting and proper. But we realized that although the trouble was begun by the barbarians, Our own officials' management was not entirely proper. Consequently, we delayed somewhat using troops and reasoned with them first but this was neither from fear of their evil spearhead nor from willing acquiescence. Cantonese and barbarians of other countries must all appreciate the justice and un-selfishness of Our motives.

In 1849, the fact that the English barbarians dared not to enter the city was in reality because of the strength of gentry and people. Today, Yeh Ming-ch'en has not only failed to control the barbarians but has also failed to arouse the village militia and move it to popular indignation, causing loss of national prestige. This really merits bitter condemnation.

Po-kuei and Mr. Lo Tun-yen are ordered to communicate Our sentiments secretly to the various village trainbands. If the barbarians are remorseful and evacuate the city, the past can still be forgiven as a manifestation of clemency. If they remain stupidly unrepentant and continue to occupy the city, there is no alternative but to mobilize troops and militia from various cities, unite them as one man, and expel the barbarians from the city so they will not dare belittle China. Thereafter we can thresh out with them the right and wrong as a basis for future cooperation. This will conform with national dignity as well as stop their demands.

According to Huang Tsung-han's memorial, he fears that local bandits will take advantage of the outside barbarian conflict to start trouble and that in-view of the present situation it is essential to guard against local bandits in order to be basically secure. He also fears the barbarians will conspire with them and unfathomable evils will ensue and we must somehow detach defense troops to dissipate internal troubles. Order Po-kuei and the others to consider this carefully and act accordingly.

Also, according to Huang Tsung-han's memorial, when he served as governor of Chekiang he worked with Mu-k'o-te-na and knows that, in the capacity of Deputy Lieutenant General of Ch'a-p'u, he was not only able to maintain the morale of the soldiers but also very successful in maintaining that of the people. Now that barbarian affairs are crucial and the various rebels are not entirely exterminated the said Tartar General must consult thoroughly with the said acting governor general and others, on methods of pacifying the internal and expelling the external (rebels) and not cause other troubles.

Previously Yeh Ming-ch'en memorialized that the English forces were weak and that their sovereign did not want trouble with China. He also memorialized that an American, Sturgis, and others came to Whampoa and asked to open trade. When Yeh Ming-ch'en replied, the

American chief felt very grateful. Now according to Mu-k'o-te-na's memorial, when the American barbarians asked for an audience, Yeh Ming-ch'en stubbornly refused. Thereafter the forts were occupied.

Order them to find out and memorialize fully whether or not the American barbarians, because the English barbarians were powerless to indemnify their burned goods, used their soldiers to help the evildoers in the hope of demanding indemnification from China.

Dispatch the great seal of Imperial Commissioner today and order it first turned over to Po-kuei in solemn trust. Order the old misplaced great seal, if it is not lost, kept in bond and when convenient sent by an official and delivered to the board for presentation. (IWSM.HF 17; 44a, 6-45b, 3)

32. February 3, 1858. MEMORIAL: A Circuit Censor Urges an Immediate Land Attack on the British at Canton.

Circuit Censor of Kiang-nan [i.e. Kiangsu-Anhwei], Ho Ching, memorializes. It is humbly observed that the barbarian bandits have seized a pretext to start trouble and have sneaked into the provincial capital of Kwangtung. There is a rumor that Governor General Yeh Ming-ch'en has been driven out by the barbarians; also that the Tartar General, governor, and deputy lieutenant generals have been invited by the barbarians to Kuan-yin Shan with the idea of coercing the population and that they plan to continue their occupation of the city. These are unexpected developments which never occurred before.

It is his humble opinion that the temperament of the Cantonese people is generally regarded as vigorous and steadfast while that of the distant barbarians is contemptible and fundamentally lacking in ability. It is all because Yeh Ming-ch'en managed things badly that soldiers and civilians were so divided that the barbarians were free to do whatever they pleased without fear. If at this time we do not overawe them with military power and still wrongly indulge them on the pretext of being lenient, the English barbarians will become even more tyrannical, America, France, and the other countries are sure to vie with them head over heels, and our house cannot be put in order. Thus at present barbarian affairs in Kwangtung are actually in a state that makes attack imperative.

Kwangtung has been disturbed by bandits for many years and although they have been repeatedly wiped out, the remaining evil is ever greater. Now Canton, an important center, is occupied by the barbarians and if we do not speedily drive them out but procrastinate day after day, the local bandits will get wind of it and rise on all sides, assemble their hordes and tyrannize; prefectures and districts will have no unity and law will be thrown to the winds; mobilization and development will be impossible, resulting in an unsupportable explosion and everything reduced to chaos. Thus also at present the matter of attacking barbarians is actually such that haste is imperative.

Now Huang Tsung-han has been Imperially selected as governor general of Liang-kuang. It is assumed that this governor general will need several months to reach Canton and mobilize his forces and it is gravely feared this will be too late. Although the acting governor general Po-kuei has taken over the great seal of Imperial Commissioner, the barbarians have occupied the inner city and the governor and others are under their control, and are certainly unable to handle this. Thus, our only procedure is to bring in troops from outside. Then we can get control.

Of high officials in charge of troops outside the province, there are only the two commanders-in-chief of the sea and land forces. Commander-in-chief of Sea-forces Wu Yüan-yü must be ordered to pick ships and men to defend the coast, but need not move up the river. We make bold to ask for an Edict ordering Commander-in-chief of Land Forces K'un-shou to select troops under him and transfer them immediately to San-shui, Fo-shan and other strategic places, as well as speedily to order the militia of nearby villages to collect around the city and await orders and, on the other hand, send a stiff note to the barbarians reprimanding them for defying authority and giving them a few days to get out of the city.

As to the items in their communication, have them wait quietly until the governor general gets to Canton to take them up. If they dare resist and fail to comply, lead the troops to attack and send orders to Canton residents to consolidate warlike fervor and cooperate with the army inside and out. Anyone capturing and bringing in a barbarian will be heavily rewarded. Even though the Tartar General, governor, and other officials are still at Kuan-yin Shan, there must be no feeling of "not throwing at a rat because it endangers a vase."

It is estimated that the barbarian bandits who have entered the city are not more than a few thousand men. If we overwhelm them with ten times that number, can we fail to demolish them? Fearing the might of the thunderous Imperial Army without and apprehensive of the people gouging them from within, the barbarians will be in circumstances like the wolf "looking about him and losing his grip" and be sure to flee. After the city has been recovered we can determine who was right and who was wrong. If we act with force and virtue the barbarians are sure to bow their heads and obey, and the general situation can be definitely vouchsafed. (IWSM.HF 17; 45b, 4-47a, 3)

233. February 3, 1858. MEMORIAL: The Circuit Censor Urges the Punishment of all the Canton Officials in Addition to Yeh Ming-ch'en.

Ho Ching further memorializes. The mismanagement of the high officials of Kwangtung province has fomented a great calamity. The stupid perversity of Yeh Ming-ch'en needs no discussion. Although Governor Po-kuei makes the excuse that he was not consulted, he was right in the same city. How could he be completely unaware? If Yeh Ming-ch'en was obstinate and self-sufficient, the governor should have admonished him suitably; if he stubbornly refused to comply, he was obligated to impeach him according to the facts. How could he place himself outside, sitting idly and criticizing?

Besides, the governor is personally in charge of his frontiers and the area is solely his responsibility. When barbarian ships entered Canton River and Yeh Ming-ch'en was unprepared, the governor should immediately have dispatched his own garrison and also called upon the militia of surrounding villages to unite their influence in order to be ready on the outside and, on the other hand, joined the Tartar General and deputy lieutenant generals in sending word to the banner forces to mount the parapets for defense to hold the inside. If deployment had been coordinated, how could the barbarians have succeeded in their wicked plot? Why did he stand on the sidelines with his hands in his sleeves and open the doors to greet the robbers, so that they left their boats, landed and went right through the double walls? If the governor general let them take him hands down, the governor also willingly accepted their control. Thus did Po-kuei betray Imperial Favor and fail the state; his guilt is the same as that of Yeh Ming ch'en.

As to Tartar General Mu k'o-te-na and Deputy Lieutenant Generals Shuang-hsi and Shuang-ling, all the banner forces under them were originally set up as a defense garrison. Now when the barbarians entered the inner city they had to pass through Banner Street to get to Kuan-yin Shan, and in the entire battalion of banner troops not a man opposed them. If (the troops) were completely dumbfounded and let (the barbarians) occupy as they pleased, of what use was the defense garrison?

Previously Ch'i-shan and I-shan were punished with degradation because their management of barbarian affairs failed, but then the barbarians did not even enter the city. Now both inner and outer cities are occupied by the barbarians and they have brought even more shame on the country. Although Yeh Ming-ch'en has been degraded and Po-kuei and the others have been referred to the Boards for investigation, Imperial Favor has been magnanimous and is not exacting in reprimands. But those officials' crime merits execution and cannot rightly be evaded.

In Your official's stupid opinion, the governor general and the governor should be punished severely, Yeh Ming-ch'en's estate confiscated to furnish military supplies, and the Tartar General rigorously investigated. Hereafter it will serve as a precedent for law fulfilment so that we will not fall into the same rut again.   (IWSM.HF 17; 47a, 4-48a, 4)

234. February 4, 1858. MEMORIAL: The Canton Hoppo Reports on the

Canton Situation and Commends the Competence and Experience of Po-kuei
    Kwangtung Superintendent of Customs Heng-ch'i memorializes.
This is a humble report on the present status of barbarian affairs in
Kwangtung.

    The governor has repeatedly conferred with the barbarian chiefs
personally; his attitude has been so rigorous and his righteousness so
convincing that the barbarians dare not disrespect him. The barbarians are well aware that of all Kwangtung officials only the Imperial
Commissioner has charge of barbarian affairs and no one else can
take the lead and, although the governor has repeatedly questioned them
they have never committed themselves. Their purpose is to wait until
an Imperially Instructed Commissioner arrives at Canton before agreeing to negotiate.

    But they have already occupied the provincial capital for more than
ten days. Although they did not injure the people, the inhabitants of the
city were apprehensive and have evacuated. Already nine out of ten
houses are empty. If they were to persist in waiting until and Imperially Instructed Commissioner comes to Canton, a long delay would be
inescapable. Not only would uprisings of local bandits cause apprehension, but it was also feared other barbarian complications would
develop which would be still more unthinkable. It was absolutely necessary at this time for the governor to negotiate with the barbarians in
advance in order to stabilize popular feeling and prevent the outbreak
of further trouble.

    It is noted that Governor Po-kuei has risen gradually to his presen
position from district and prefectural (posts) of Kwangtung and has
been in Kwangtung altogether for nearly twenty years. He is generally
known to be thoroughly conversant with barbarian affairs. Moreover,
in 1852 when he was Imperially-appointed governor of Honan he remained temporarily in Kwangtung. While he was performing the duties
of governor, as the governor general and governor were both leading
troops outside the province, he also took over the great seal of Imperial Commissioner, memorializing as is on record. If at this time
there were an Imperial Edict ordering the governor to make the necessary decisions until an Imperial Commissioner reaches Canton further
to discuss peace, popular feeling in Kwangtung province could be quiete
earlier and rigid adherence to the views of an individual be avoided.

    Your slave, charged with the management of the customs, has been
extremely hard pressed and since the first of this year has repeatedly
conferred with the governor general. But since the governor general
was the official in sole charge of barbarian affairs and even the govern
although personally in charge of frontiers, could not get a word in,
whatever imperfect knowledge Your slave, lacking any territorial juris
diction, might have, must needs be given even less consideration. But
customs payments of Chinese and foreign merchants have been held up
for a year, neither money nor goods circulating, involving increasingly

grievous losses. The sooner there is a settlement the sooner the
straits of the merchants will be relieved.

At present only the southwest corner of the city is open, Kuei-te
Gate in the inner wall and T'ai-p'ing Gate in the outer. The barbarian is by nature inscrutable and his cunning is unique. Besides, where
Chinese and barbarians are thrown together over any length of time,
there is no telling what kinds of complications will develop. (IWSM.HF
17; 48a, 5-49a, 10)

235. February 4, 1858. EDICT: Reviews Ten Years of China's Foreign
Policy and Orders Lo Tun-yen to Mobilize the Populace against the
Occupation.

Edict to the Grand Councillors. Previously, until Huang Tsung-
han had time to reach his post, Po-kuei was ordered to take over the
great seal of Imperial Commissioner and the duties of governor general of Liang-kuang. It was further ordered that the acting governor
general and others take prior action in managing barbarian affairs.
Today is received Heng-ch'i's memorial, sent by express post because
of the critical situation. What he requests is exactly what has been ordered in previous Edicts. Po-kuei is to act as Imperial Commissioner
and barbarian affairs are to be solely his responsibility. His authority
to conciliate or attack must never go beyond the two words "reasonable need."

Our China, in the more than ten years since the conclusion of
peace with the barbarians, has never been willing to start trouble herself or make arbitrary use of force. Now the barbarians burn down
private dwellings outside the city and lead their hordes to attack the
walls; taking the lead in violating treaties, their guilt is obvious. If
they say Yeh Ming-ch'en handled affairs badly, the fact that We have
degraded the governor general is evidence of absolute justice and the
barbarians must be repentent. If they still do not acknowledge their
guilt and wilfully make requests, how can we tolerate their wilfulness
and trade as usual? Po-kuei has repeatedly had personal interviews
with the barbarian chiefs and they still dare not disrespect him; he
can therefore argue with them reasonably and on the other hand mobilize troops and cooperate with gentry and volunteers to strengthen prestige and maintain national integrity.

In addition to the previous instructions to the acting governor
general to guard rigorously against bandits seizing the opportunity for
clandestine acts, and also to Vice-president Lo Tun-yen and others to
arouse gentry and people, they are hereby ordered to take suitable
action accordingly. Commander-in-chief K'un-shou has been directing
the attack on Wu-chou and if he has not returned to Canton, order Po-
kuei to send a suitable officer to Wu-chou to take charge of the troops
and transfer K'un-shou to Canton to take command of the regular army
of pacification. Commander-in-chief of Sea-forces Wu Yüan-yü is

stationed at Hu-men (Bocca Tigris) with the responsibility of defending the mouth of the river. This time when the barbarian ships came
up the Canton river, why was there no plan of defense? Order Po-
kuei to investigate and memorialize.

We have also received the memorial of Censor Ho Ching that as
the barbarians have entered the inner city he fears Po-kuei and the
others are being coerced and asks that K'un-shou be ordered to transfer troops to San-shui and Fo-shan, station them at strategic places,
quickly mobilize the militia of neighboring villages to surround the
city, and send a stern summons to the barbarians demanding their
withdrawal from the city. The barbarian bandits are not more than a
few thousand, and overwhelmed by ten times their number, they are
sure to flee. After the city is recovered, matters of right and wrong
can be determined and the barbarians will certainly bow their heads
and obey. The memorial is not without bearing.

Order Po-kuei and the others to examine his proposals thoroughly,
deliberate and execute. (IWSM.HF 17; 49b, 1-50a, 10)

236. February 9, 1858. MEMORIAL: The Governor of Hunan Reports
Independently on the Foreign Occupation of Canton.
Governor of Hunan Lo Ping-chang memorializes. It is humbly
observed that since the English barbarians renewed hostilities, no
communication has been received from Kwangtung on the various
developments of barbarian affairs. Governmental affairs are secret
and outside gentry and merchants do not necessarily know their workings; but recently there have been reports that the rebel barbarians
have seized and occupied the provincial capital. Your official heard
this, but ventured to think, as the capital is an important place, it
would naturally be strongly defended. Besides, as the rebel barbarians
are the embodiment of inscrutability and have long looked for trouble,
"how could there be no preparations at all, allowing them to become
violent?" He did not dare believe them. But for the last several days
the reports have become more numerous, so several times he sent
spies to question Cantonese merchants in Hunan and, finding that letters coming to the Canton Guild Hall since the twenty-eighth of December are in fairly close agreement, he was astonished beyond words.

Examining the dates of documents passing through, after the
600-li dispatch of Governor General Yeh Ming-ch'en on December 27,
there have been only the two 600-li dispatches of the Canton Tartar
General and the governor of Kwangtung on January 7 and 13, respectively. Thus outside reports that the governor general of Liang-kuang
went to a barbarian ship on January 6 and never came back, and that
the Canton Tartar General, deputy lieutenant generals and the governor
were invited by the barbarians to Kuan-yin Shan, seem not without
foundation. Whether or not these documents were sent while they were
at Kuan-yin Shan, there is no way of knowing, but the matter is of great

significance and it could not be withheld from the Imperial ear.
(IWSM.HF 17; 51a, 4-51b, 7)

237. February 9, 1858. EDICT: Encourages Governor Lo Ping-chang
of Hunan, a Cantonese, to Advise the Court on Foreign Policy.

Edict to the Grand Councillors. Lo Ping-chang has memorialized
on the rebel barbarians' occupation of the capital city of Kwangtung.
On January 27, there was a joint memorial from Canton Tartar General Mu-k'o-te-na and others that on December 29, the rebel barbarians occupied Kuan-yin Shan and the forts outside and inside the North
Gate and on January 5, forced their way into Deputy Lieutenant General Shuang-hsi's yamen, took Yeh Ming-ch'en and led him off to a barbarian ship. As Yeh Ming-ch'en was stubborn and self-sufficient and
unable to manage barbarians, We have issued an Edict degrading him
and ordered Huang Tsung-han to fill out the term as governor general
of Liang-kuang and take over the great seal of Imperial Commissioner
in charge of barbarian affairs. Until he arrives at his post, Po-kuei
was ordered to handle the duties of Imperial Commissioner and governor general. Repeated instructions have been given the said acting
governor general and others to take preliminary action. If the barbarians evacuate the city and want to trade as before, the past can
still be forgiven; if they continue obstreperous, he has but to mobilize troops, proclaim their guilt and administer punishment. Further,
orders have been sent Vice-president-on-leave Lo Tun-yen and others
secretly to notify the village militias and the volunteers and garrisons
of the cities to unite as one man, expel the barbarians from the city,
and argue with them afterwards as to the status of subsequent intercourse.

Later, on February 4th, the memorial of Superintendent Heng-
ch'i was received stating that Po-kuei had had repeated conferences
with the barbarians and asking that Po-kuei be authorized to make a
preliminary negotiation of barbarian affairs. Po-kuei has received
the previous Edict but no answer has yet been received. Whether or
not the barbarians are holding him on Kuan-yin Shan and will not let
him go back, the detailed situation is not fully known.

Today Huang Tsung-han inquires about the rumor that Po-kuei
and the others have discussed three items with the barbarians: first,
allowing them to build a barbarian consulate on Honan Island; second,
allowing treaty port merchants to levy likin,[12] using the first few
million taels to rebuild residences, the rest to go to the barbarian

---

12 Likin (li-chin), a tax on the inland transit of goods, was first introduced in 1852,
as a special tax to raise funds to suppress the Taiping Rebellion. It was extended
throughout China by 1863. It was originally one tenth of one percent of the value of
the goods.

consulate; and third, allowing those having public business to enter the city to call, but without allowing barbarians to enter promiscuously. Although this news is current it is not known whether or not it is true. The present handling of this affair will prick many fingers.

Lo Ping-chang is a native of Kwangtung and able thoroughly to understand various Chinese-barbarian situations. Any opinions he has, he is allowed to report according to the facts, for consideration; subsequently if he hears any news of Kwangtung, order him to memorialize at any time. (IWSM.HF 17; 51b, 8-52b, 6)

238. February 15, 1858. MEMORIAL: The Canton Officials Report Further Developments of the Foreign Occupation of the City.

Canton Tartar General Mu-k'o-te-na and Governor of Kwangtung Po-kuei memorialize. Recently the barbarians have deployed troops and occupied the northeast city wall and the Yüeh-hsiu Shan [i. e. Kuan-yin Shan] district and also sent troops to patrol various streets. Although they say this is to pacify the people, actually the motive is fear that we have secret intentions against them. As for Hsi-kuan [western suburb], it is the prosperous district of Canton with merchants and people as thick as clouds. There are always several tens of barbarian soldiers going in and out among them without causing any commotion. Popular feeling is not tense. Barbarian soldiers have not gone to the Fo-shan district and it remains completely quiet.

Your slaves thereupon secretly consulted officials and gentry to figure out a general mobilization of sturdy braves outside Canton, and will offer extraordinary rewards in the hope of effecting a speedy recovery. But the barbarians now have more than twenty gunboats of various sizes stationed up and down the Canton River, and Yüeh-hsiu Shan and the forts to the north and south are all occupied. It was feared that any move would be "sketching a tiger without filling in" (i.e. it would backfire). The several hundred thousand souls of Canton are completely ground to dust; besides, it was feared that they would deliberately stir up trouble in the districts along the whole river-front, thereby doing even greater damage, and it was also feared that local bandits would seize the opportunity to rise unexpectedly; under these circumstances it is hard to be circumspect.

Your slaves were not afraid for themselves, but out of regard for general welfare could not but endure patiently for the time being and devise means to get control. They have repeatedly sent Mr. Wu Ch'ung-yüeh and others to see the barbarian consul at Canton and inquire what conditions they require. According to their reports of the barbarians' statements, they insist that barbarian affairs have always been the sole responsibility of the Imperial Commissioner, that the governor is a territorial official and cannot suitably negotiate. Besides, they still want to go to Tientsin and ask His Imperial Majesty to delegate a minister competent to discuss everything with the idea of effecting a ten-thousand-year friendship.

Your slaves figured that the barbarians' concern is trade. If trading were resumed at an early date, not only could the people's livelihood and business be facilitated, but also the barbarians would not be disposed voluntarily to disrupt that which they hold dear. Whereupon, Your slave, Po-kuei, sent communications to barbarian chief Elgin and the French chief Baron Gros suggesting that whatever they had to discuss they could talk over freely with Your slave in advance, and also urging them to withdraw their gunboats before the port could be opened.

On February 19, the French chief replied that what he had said at the Yüeh-hsiu Shan conference was entirely with the idea of mutual pacification of the people; that as soon as the Emperor named a commissioner and there were suitable negotiations the city would be restored. The entire purport was delay until the English barbarians made up their minds before he could answer.

The English barbarian replied on February 20 that heretofore His Excellency Yeh [i.e. Yeh Ming-ch'en] would neither accede to their requests nor confer with them and had been so rude that there was nothing to do but fight; that whenever the Emperor appointed a commissioner competent to negotiate treaties with England and France, he could withdraw his troops and restore Canton; that he was now sending a consul to reside at Canton with full authority, without any intention of harming the people but with the hope of reassuring merchants and people, and that reinforcing Chinese and foreign friendly relations was was really a capital plan.

Your slaves scanned the replies of the two chiefs and there were no insubordinate expressions except their insistence on an Imperial Commissioner coming to Canton to negotiate before they were willing to withdraw their soldiers. In the matter of trade, it would probably not be difficult to bring them around. Your slaves again ordered Mr. Wu Ch'ung-yüeh and others to interview the barbarian chiefs and they repeatedly explained; when they pointed out the losses, the barbarians gradually came to their senses. At present they are anxious to rebuild the barbarian factories as places for trade, and if in the next few days means can be found to bring negotiations to a conclusion and the port is opened first, popular feeling will be further stabilized. Your slave Po-kuei on several occasions has received the consul who was very complaisant; he has only to discover his personality and moral scruples and explain vigorously to find means of opening trade and quieting the populace without giving rise to complications.

At present military operations on the West and North Rivers are uncompleted and a branch commissariat has been established at Fo-shan. Salt Controller Ling-ch'un, and Grain Intendant Wang Tseng-ch'ien have been ordered to that place to take charge of the trainbands and defend against various groups of local bandits. Financial Commissioner Chiang

Kuo-lin and Provincial Judge Chou Ch'i-pin continue in charge of
Canton.

As to Governor General Yeh Ming-ch'en, since he went on board
on February 4, when gentry have gone to see him, the said chief never
lets him receive them personally and they can only see his face through
a window. It is reported that the barbarians are still treating the
governor general respectfully and that they are disposed to return him
as soon as the treaty is concluded. The great seal and ordinary seal of
governor general and salt controller respectively have not been located.
(IWSM.HF 18; 1a, 2-3a, 4)

239. February 15, 1858. MEMORIAL: The Canton Tartar General Reports the Seizure by the Allies of China's Foreign Office Files at Canton.

Mu-k'o-te-na and others further memorialize. To continue, when
the governor general went on board ship the draft copies of documents
dealing with barbarian affairs of several years, located in the governor
general's yamen, were all taken by the barbarians. At present, in governmental matters our movements are confidential and once they leak
out they are spied out by the barbarians and the executive's elbow is
shoved still more. Hereafter, for all documents relating to barbarian
affairs, it is urgently requested that Imperial Edicts be transmitted to
the Grand Council which will issue Court Orders, rendering proclamation unnecessary, and that none of Your slaves' memorials need be
copied, so as to secure strict secrecy.

As to the barbarians' intention to go to Tientsin, Your slaves have
made a secret investigation. Just now there is a north wind and the
river is cold, making sailing difficult, but if it is found impracticable
to grant their requests, it is feared that in the spring when it warms up
the barbarians will certainly go to Tientsin to make requests. When the
time comes, whether an Imperial Commissioner is sent to negotiate or
they are again sent back to Kwangtung to await the appointment of a new
Imperial Commissioner to investigate and act, rests with Your Imperial
Majesty. (IWSM.HF 18; 3a, 5-3b, 5)

240. February 15, 1858. EDICT: Condemns the Helplessness of the
Canton Officials and Urges the Mobilization of the Populace.

Edict to the Grand Councillors. Mu-k'o-te-na and others have
memorialized repeatedly reporting the state of barbarian affairs. We
have read these memorials and the whole situation is obvious. On this
occasion the English barbarians, in clear violation of the treaties,
have raised troops against authority, captured our provincial capital
and kidnapped our high official. Strictly speaking, we should stop their
trade and raise troops to chastize them, at once fulfilling the wrath of
heaven and gladdening the hearts of men. Previously Po-kuei was
notified that if the barbarians evacuated Canton the past could still be
forgiven, but if they continued in occupation of the city he could only

raise troops and expel them, settling details with them afterward.

Now a memorial is received stating that the barbarians want to wait until regulations are concluded before they evacuate Canton. Their coercion is apparent, and still Po-kuei and the others were willing to consider the building of a barbarian factory and prior opening of the port. How can they have become as helpless as this? Recently it is reported that the barbarians wanted to establish a barbarian consulate on Ho-nan Island and also to collect likin at the ports and Po-kuei was willing to grant everything. We thought Po-kuei had been in Kwangtung a long time, thoroughly understood barbarian mentality, and would not have to compromise like this.

On reading the present memorials, the rumors seem not entirely without foundation. Why should this not-throwing-at-a-rat-for-fear-of-the-vase attitude be held, just because Yeh Ming-ch'en is there? Yeh Ming-ch'en disgraced his country, brought misfortune on the people, and were better dead than alive. Besides he has been degraded so why should he be considered? Even Mu-k'o-te-na, Po-kuei, and the others all have the loss of Canton on their heads. Our leniency in turning them over to the Boards was primarily because We wanted them to devise a solution and never thought they would end up in the palm of the barbarians' hand and, annoyed at the loss of trade, hope to effect an opportunist settlement. Now, until Huang Tsung-han arrives, Po-kuei will act as Imperial Commissioner and the barbarians in discussing trade with him are sure to use a lot of coercion. If he agrees to their building a barbarian factory on Ho-nan, right next to Canton, peaceful relations cannot be maintained in the future. As to Chinese likin, the purpose is the immediate need of military supplies and when military operations are over, it will stop automatically. Now the barbarians want to levy likin, but there is no terminal date and it is feared it would not meet the wishes of the merchants. Whenever the barbarians have wanted to enter Canton City they have been stopped by the popular indignation of the Cantonese and Po-kuei must know this. Now Canton is captured and still the Cantonese have not risen en masse to deliver it. We assume this is because Yeh Ming-ch'en's obstinate self-sufficiency has dissipated the hearts of the people.

Now that Po-kuei and the others cannot leave the city to lead troops to battle personally, it has never occurred to them to activate the gentry militia to augument the punitive force. Their tribulations are self-inflicted. Without the least resourcefulness, their timorousness and lack of ability are far beyond Our expectation. On this occasion the barbarians have violated treaties and seized our provincial capital, nor was it China who started the quarrel. If the Canton gentry and people are aroused by moral indignation to raise militia and punish the crime, Po-kuei and the others are not to prohibit them. If the strength of gentry and people can be utilized to inflict the punishment and drive the barbarians out of the city, they will realize that the will

of people cannot be opposed and their ferocity will be slackened.
Afterwards Po-kuei and the others will emerge as mediators. Thus
they can be brought into our bailiwick and not develop their endless
inordinate demands.

In short, Po-kuei and the others are to use both firmness and
leniency but not agree to everything, injuring national prestige and
losing popular confidence. As to the barbarians wanting to come to
Tientsin, We have Our plans and they need not worry any more about
that. (IWSM.HF 18; 3b, 6-5a, 1)

241. February 15, 1858. EDICT: Authorizes the Mobilization and Arm-
ing of the Populace to Recover Canton from Allied Occupation.
  Supplementary Edict. Because Mu-k'o-te-na and others previousl
memorialized express that the barbarians had violated treaties and
occupied the city, We immediately ordered Po-kuei to act temporarily
as Imperial Commissioner and together with Mu-k'o-te-na and others
mobilize soldiers and volunteers and drive the barbarians out of the
city, and further ordered Lo Tun-yen and others to assemble the militia to assist in the fighting.

The main reason the barbarians did not succeed in entering the
city in the Tao-kuang period was the utilization of the strength of gentr
and people which merited an Imperial Edict of commendation. On this
occasion, the barbarians have violated treaties, occupied the provincia
capital and even abducted Yeh Ming-ch'en, and nothing has been heard
of the gentry and people of the city having a common war spirit. We
have assumed this is because Yeh Ming-ch'en's bad management has
dissipated peoples' hearts, but recently Po-kuei and others, with an
eye on immediate trade, according to rumor, issued proclamations to
the people saying that means were at hand for handling barbarian affairs and there was no occasion for rash acts. It is feared that Po-kue
and the others were coerced and are without resource. Previously an
edict was sent to Lo Tun-yen, Lung Yüan-hsi and Su T'ing-kuei, secret
to transmit to the various village trainbands notice of Our desire to
drive the barbarians out of Canton, but it is feared that this was intercepted by the barbarians and has not been publicized.

Now we are specially ordering Lo Ping-chang to pass on a court
letter for the said vice-president and others' information, ordering
them to send orders to the various gentry and people to assemble trair
bands by the myriad to punish the crime of attacking the city in violati
of treaties and expel the barbarians from the city. If the barbarians da
resist, our soldiers and volunteers can then mercilessly exterminate
them. They are not to hold a not-throwing-at-a-rat-for-fear-of-a-vas
attitude because Yeh Ming-ch'en is there. The governor general has
disgraced his country and brought calamity on the people and were bet*
dead than alive. He is not worth considering. Besides this affair is
one of barbarian violation of treaties as they were the first to resort t

force, and if the gentry and people can unite their wills like a
fortress to administer punishment, opportunely augmenting national prestige and according popular feeling, We shall certainly not
reprimand them as wilfully starting border trouble. Do not lag
behind from timorousness! If they can expel the barbarians from
the city and prevent their tampering with officials and people, the
strain of governing will be somewhat relaxed.

When that time comes, use the argument of indemnity for the
people whose buildings, numbering several thousand, were burned,
to refuse trade at Canton and they will certainly realize the fallacy
of their argument. Afterwards the officials of the locality will e-
merge as mediators. Thus they can be brought into our power and
there will be some respite from inordinate demands. The said vice-
president and others have only to respect Our wish and exert them
selves for the country. Let them not be misled by random talk. This
is most essential. (IWSM.HF 18; 5a, 3-6a, 2)

242. February 15, 1858. EDICT: Orders Lo Ping-chang to Assume
Leadership of Popular Mobilization and to Act Secretly while Canton
Officials are Captive.

Additional Edict. Previously on receipt of Lo Ping-chang's express memorial on the barbarian occupation of the capital of Kwangtung, We immediately issued Edicts ordering all Kwangtung events
memorialized express at the time of their occurrence.

Today We have received successive reports on the state of barbarian affairs from Mu-k'o-te-na, Po-kuei, and others. Some twenty
rebel barbarian warships are still stationed along Canton River and
according to report not until after the arrival of a new Imperial Commissioner at Canton will they withdraw from the river or turn over
the city. Their making of interminable demands is now apparent.
Recently it is reported that they want to build a barbarian factory on
Ho-nan, levy likin at the ports, and enter the city in sedan chairs.
On receipt of the Edict to take over the duties of Imperial Commissioner, Po-kuei was to make preliminary arrangements, but according to
his memorial he, in his anxiety for immediate trade in order to pacify
the people, inevitably failed through over leniency. Moreover ming-
ling with barbarians inside the city, probably everything is done
under pressure making it impossible to cooperate with gentry and
people to deliver it.

In Our opinion the reason the barbarians did not get into the city
before was due entirely to the strength of the Cantonese gentry and
people. On this occasion the barbarians in their angry ferocity have
captured the provincial capital and We have not heard of the local
gentry and people emerging to recover it. This is primarily because
Yeh Ming-ch'en's inept management destroyed people's confidence.
Now it is reported that the said Tartar General and acting governor

general have even issued proclamations saying that barbarian affairs had been arranged and forbidding adverse movements among the people. This is not the way to arouse righteous indignation to defend the land.

Although We have sent successive Edicts ordering them and former Vice-president Lo Tun-yen, Director of the Court of Sacrificial Worship Lung Yüan-hsi, and Junior Metropolitan Censor Su T'ing-kuei to consult about arousing the village irregulars to help the military forces expel the barbarians from Canton River and reason with them afterwards, when the barbarians see that mass fury cannot be defied they may restrain their ferociousness somewhat, and when we are not completely under their control, administrative direction will certainly be facilitated.

Now We have issued secret instructions ordering Lo Tun-yen, Lung Yüan-hsi, and Su T'ing-kuei to send secret notices to the village units setting forth Our wishes and to take suitable action. Order Lo Ping-chang on receiving this to reseal it and send it by messenger express to Kwangtung to be duly delivered without letting the barbarians know or have a chance to intercept it. This is most important. (IWSM.HF 18; 6a, 4-7a, 1)

243. February 22, 1858. MEMORIAL: Foochow Governor General Reports All Quiet in Fukien Ports and a Rumor that Canton has been Recovered.

Governor General of Min-Che Wang I-te and Governor of Fukien Ch'ing-tuan memorialize. It is humbly observed that since the ninth month of last year (September 29-October 28, 1856) the English barbarians have used pretexts to foment enmity in order to induce an incident; defense is of the utmost importance and we have secretly instructed military and civil officials along the coast accordingly. There cannot be the least show of confusion. Then we received the Edict saying that, as Yeh Ming-ch'en had memorialized, the English barbarians had seized a pretext to start a fracas and that our army had won two battles; in case any barbarian ships should come to Chekiang or Fukien, we were to make suitable defense.

We have acted accordingly and have received successively secret reports from the Min-Che commander-in-chief of sea forces and the brigade general that Chinese and barbarians in the port districts were trading as usual and there seemed to be nothing to fear.

Now in the first decade of the twelfth month of this year (January 15-24, 1858), it is reported that the English barbarians at Canton have defied authority and their attitude is very refractory. While investigating this, further reports arrived from Acting Commander-in-chief of Sea Forces in Fukien Lai Hsin-yang and Kwangtung Nan-ao (Namoa) Brigade General Ch'en Ying-yün, that it was reported by spies that on December 29, 1858, the village units of the vicinity

came to the rescue and recovered it, but when a survey was made
of officials some forty or fifty of them were missing. Whether or
not these were reliable was still undetermined.

On reading these how can we express our alarm? It is humbly
observed that if Kwangtung barbarian defenses were rigorous, the
people's morale firm, and mass determination like a stone wall,
how could they let them sneak in and rout the place? As to village
units of the vicinity having already come to the rescue and recovered
it, from the nature of the situation we assume that it could not be
occupied by the barbarians long. What actual conditions in Kwangtung are or what the present campaign is, Kwangtung has not informed
us and we know no details.

In the Fukien ports, Chinese and barbarians have a thorough
mutual understanding. In case of an accidental clash we have ordered the officials in charge to make an immediate investigation
and force the barbarians into submission, not allowing them to make
inconsequential matters an excuse for starting a quarrel. In the
first decade of the present month (January 15-24) it was reported
that a barbarian steam warship was cruising about in Fukien waters
and then left without venturing to come far in. Should Kwangtung
hostilities become critical and, with designs on neighboring frontiers,
the barbarians come to Fukien to spy about, we have only to charge
them to uphold the treaties and overcome them with reason. Although
barbarians are very crafty they will not be likely to cut off the
avenues of trade. Then on the other hand we secretly instructed
the Min-Che commander-in-chief of sea forces, the brigade general,
and the civil and military officials along the coast, to make secret
defenses, with no remissness at all allowed. (IWSM.HF 18; 7a, 2-8a,
2)

244. February 22, 1858. EDICT: Orders Huang Tsung-han to Confer
with Fukien Officials en route to Canton.

Edict to the Grand Councillors. We have received a memorial
from Wang I-te and others on the barbarians throwing the capital of
Kwangtung into confusion and the present secret defense plans on
the Fukien border.

The Canton barbarians occupy the provincial capital and Yeh
Ming-ch'en is still on board a barbarian ship. We have appointed
Huang Tsung-han governor general of Liang-kuang and, until he reaches
his post, ordered Po-kuei temporarily to take over the great seal of
Imperial Commissioner. Recently We have received a series of
memorials from Canton Tartar General Mu-k'o-te-na and others
that affairs are still out of hand, that if the barbarians can admit
their faults and reform, by withdrawing from the city it will still be
possible to talk reason with them, but if they continue knavery and
squat there indefinitely, it is feared a forceful settlement cannot be

avoided.

Fukien waters are contiguous and naturally must be rigorously defended but the defenses must be planned in secret, without allowing the barbarians to detect any inklings. When Huang Tsung-han passes through Fukien en route to Kwangtung, Wang I-te and the others must confer with him and determine the most advantageous way to maintain the general set-up.

As to the barbarians now in Canton, the governor general's statement that it was thrown into confusion on December 29 and recaptured by the village units of the vicinity on January 5, We think is a false report. As usual, order anything that is heard about developments in Kwangtung reported fully from time to time. (IWSM. HF 18; 8a, 3-8b, 2)

245. February 22, 1858. EDICT: Arranges to have All Recent Canton Memorials Copied and Transmitted to Huang Tsung-han en route to Canton.

Additional Edict. February 15, We received another express memorial from Mu-k'o-te-na and others that the barbarians still occupied the provincial capital. While they insisted on the conclusion of treaty regulations before they were willing to withdraw, Po-kuei actually discussed with them the erection of a barbarian factory and prior opening of the port in the hope of closing the matter. His timorousness and lack of ability exceeding Our expectations, We issued orders that Po-kuei and others must utilize the strength of the gentry and people to expel the barbarians and explain to them afterwards in order to show conciliation. We also ordered Lo Tun-yen, Lung Yüan-hsi, and Su T'ing-kuei to transmit secret orders to the various village units manifesting Our desire for the immediate expulsion of the barbarians from the city. The Edict has been sent via Governor of Hunan Lo Ping-chang to be delivered by special messenger.

Huang Tsung-han is now en route and must make inquiries from time to time concerning the present status of Canton administration, but it is feared that indirect reports will not be reliable and cause him doubt and worry, so the successive memorials of Mu-k'o-te-na and the three letters and Edicts are all ordered copied and sent for his perusal. (IWSM.HF 18; 8b, 4-9a, 1)

246. March 3, 1858. MEMORIAL: Ho Kuei-ch'ing Reports Shanghai Intelligence of Allied, American and Russian Plans to go to Tientsin.

Governor General of Liang-chiang Ho Kuei-ch'ing and Governor of Kiangsu Chao Te-ch'e memorialize. To continue, when Your officials previously heard that the English barbarians had forced entrance to the capital of Kwangtung and abducted Governor General Yeh Ming-ch'en, since Shanghai and Kwangtung are interrelated, and, if, affected by this calamity, ocean transport, customs and <u>likin</u> are all obstructed, the consequences will certainly not be slight, they immediately secretly ordered <u>Tao-t'ai</u> of Su-Sung-T'ai Hsüeh Huan to make a secret inquiry. They also sent word to the barbarian chiefs in Shanghai that Kwangtung affairs must be settled in Kwangtung, that as Chinese and barbarians in Shanghai had no enmity trade must naturally continue as usual, and not to be at all alarmed.

For more than a month now, all is quiet except for the statement of the French, English and other barbarian consuls to Hsüeh Huan, that with this year's spring thaw the envoys of the various countries intend to go by way of Shanghai to Tientsin to ask His Imperial Majesty specially to appoint a minister of state to negotiate matters of trade and amity. Although their word is not entirely reliable, we must be prepared.

Your officials again gave secret instructions to Hsüeh Huan. If the barbarians come and wrangle, he is to tell them that His Imperial Majesty has sent another Commissioner to Kwangtung to investigate, manage, and duly regulate, and to order them back to Kwangtung. We are still awaiting the time when Huang Tsung-han reaches Soochow or Ch'ang-chou, so as to discuss the matter thoroughly with him according to Your officials' observations. But the barbarian temper is inscrutable.

It is also reported that a Russian barbarian ship has passed between Japan and Hong Kong but her intentions are unknown   (IWSM. HF 18; 9a, 2-9b, 6)

247. <u>March 3, 1858. EDICT: Orders Ho Kuei-ch'ing to Confer with Huang Tsung-han and to keep the Court Posted on Canton Developments</u>.
Edict to the Grand Councillors. Ho Kuei-ch'ing and Chao Te-ch'e have memorialized that they have given explicit orders to the barbarian chiefs to trade as usual. The English barbarians have defied authority and forced their way into the capital of Kwangtung and they rightfully should have their trade at the various ports stopped. Mindful that the inception of this quarrel was Yeh Ming-ch'en's obstinacy and self-sufficiency, letting administration get out of hand and getting the barbarians so annoyed that they started trouble, we are reluctant to resort to hostilities. We have repeatedly instructed Po-kuei and others that if the barbarians repent and withdraw from the city they can still be forgiven the past, but if they rely on their strength and will not change, then (Po-kuei and others) are to mobilize soldiers and volunteers and expel them from the city and then reason with them.

As the Chinese and barbarians in Shanghai have no quarrel, they should naturally trade as usual. Ho Kuei-ch'ing and others have sent Su-Sung-T'ai <u>tao-t'ai</u> Hsüeh Huan to notify them that Kwangtung affairs must be handled in Kwangtung and also, as England and France said that they intended going to Tientsin to ask for the appointment of

a high official to reconsider trade, they (Ho Kuei-ch'ing and others)
have ordered Hsüeh Huan to notify them that another Commissioner
had been appointed and was proceeding to Kwangtung to arrange
matters. The language used is all appropriate.

At present barbarian affairs at Canton are still inchoate, but as
the Shanghai barbarian chiefs remain quiet they can only be kept in
control like this. When Huang Tsung-han passes through Kiangsu the
said governor general and others will see him and can inform him
of the circumstances of which they have memorialized. As Shanghai
always has steamers going back and forth, order them to spy on the
barbarians in Kwangtung and report fully in memorials from time
to time any movements they make. (IWSM.HF 18; 9b, 7-10a, 8)

248. March 5, 1858. MEMORIAL: Lo Ping-chang Discusses Foreign
Policy and Recommends the Establishment of a New Provincial Administration Outside Canton.

Governor of Hunan Lo Ping-chang memorializes. Your official
is of the opinion that all western barbarians rely on the efficacy of
cannon and the strength of ships; sailing the seas and trading for a
living, they use false strength to take advantage of others. Ever
since the former dynasty it has been like this although then the evil
was not great. The advantage of their ships and cannon is on the
sea. When they use them in the rivers they are afraid of rocks, of
shallows, and of fire. Barbarian soldiers are accustomed to naval
warfare but when used in land battles they are afraid of flanking and
of ambush. When victorious they cannot penetrate deeply; when defeated they cannot easily retire.

Annam overcame the Dutch with ya-ch'uan,[13] which is a case
of small overcoming large. Japan overcame the Dutch in land
battle, which is a case of host overcoming guest. Ming Police Magistrate Wang Ch'eng-en burned five barbarian ships and the barbarians did not dare be arrogant. Cheng Ch'eng-kung [Koxinga]
forced the Dutch to retire and then appropriated Taiwan, which is
a case of unexpected ejection. Barbarians are naturally arrogant
and anxious to excel, crafty and greedy for gain, but once badly
beaten they refrain from opposition. This has been the uniform
experience of the past.

Ever since their former rebellion, while familiarity with the
cowardice and weakness of the coastal forces of Kwangtung, Fukien,
Chekiang and Kiangnan has aroused their militant spirit, they have
recognized thoroughly the vulnerable positions on the coast. With
their cruising range of a thousand li, our Imperial Army cannot fend
them off and as Tientsin is a strategic place near the capital it can

---

13 This is literally "crush boats"; it apparently refers to some type of small craft but
the exact term has not been identified.

be used as an underhand threat against us. Hence they are always
looking for pretexts to start trouble in the hope of getting what they
want.

As popular feeling in Canton is powerful, in the past whenever
the barbarians have made demands the officials felt they could not
grant, they utilized popular opposition to reject them. The barbarians
knew that although the Imperial Army was afraid to fight, the village
people were eager for battle and that although they could get their
own way for a while, they would have trouble in the end, so they did
no more than threaten. There have been four popular uprisings since
1854, and most of the rebel chiefs have taken refuge in the Hong Kong
barbarian lair.

Yeh Ming-ch'en never sought out and supported those who really
exerted themselves among the trainbands, never organized the naval
and land soldiers and volunteers, and was out of touch with military
and popular opinion. He trusted former Provincial Judge Shen Ti-
hui and allowed the present financial commissioner Chiang Kuo-lin
to extort subscriptions. Since his appointments and execution were
confused and corrupt, popular support was undependable. When barbarian affairs reached a crisis and consensus was needed for the general good, Yeh Ming-ch'en regarded profound silence and complete
inactivity as essential. Making no arrangements whatever, he merely
divined in sand for oracles to appear and hoped for divine aid. When
the barbarians entered Canton River and bombarded the city there
were no defenses on the walls, so barbarians and Chinese traitors
placed their ladders and climbed up, engendering this great calamity.
Thus the catastrophe to the capital of Kwangtung derived from Yeh
Ming-ch'en's habitual failure to stabilize popular opinion and his
immediate failure to take precautionary measures, rather than from
any impossibility of resisting barbarian cunning. Since it was not
until preparations went wrong that the barbarians were free to spring
in, it was not entirely due to Yeh Ming-ch'en's stolid obstinacy.

After the rebel barbarians entered the city they were gradually
free to flaunt their ferocity. They took Yeh Ming-ch'en on board a
barbarian ship, and held the Tartar General, the lieutenant general,
and the governor at Kuan-yin Shan. Not until January 9 did they return the Tartar General and the governor to their offices, and then a
barbarian officer and barbarian troops were ordered to guard them.
They took over the weapons of the city garrisons and of the village
units nearby, and gave over all the armed ships in Canton River to
barbarian officers' command, as well as stationing barbarian troops
at the city gates. Proclamations bore the joint authority of the four
barbarian chiefs and also the Tartar General and governor. Obviously
afraid of the Kwangtung military and civil population plotting against
them, they coerced high officials to endorse them; afraid that peaceful
negotiations would not be speedily concluded or would not completely

satisfy their desires, they forced high officials to act as hostages. Such are their cunning deceits.

According to a detailed report from Financial Commissioner Wen-ko, he has received word from the Kwangtung financial commissioner that the great seals of the governor general of Kwangtung, salt controller, and Imperial Commissioner are all missing and that in communications he must guard against forgeries, not realizing that even though the great seals of the Tartar General and the governor are affixed, their official letters must all pass inspection by the barbarians before they are sent, so even the seals of the Tartar General and the governor are not enough to warrant faith.

What the rebel barbarians request is on the whole limited to demands for supplies for their soldiers, reduction of duties, and such. Not only are these rebel barbarians inconsistent but also their demands are virtually impossible to meet. There are no funds available to pay a military indemnity, and if we reduce customs, other provinces will all follow suit and reduce them still more. If we refuse their requests it is almost certain the present situation cannot be maintained, and if we grant their requests it is feared many complications will develop later. Reasoning back and forth one dare not make a hasty decision.

At present Po-kuei is already collaborating with the barbarian chiefs and they are all occupying one office, so whatever Po-kuei reports must be entirely inspired by the barbarian chiefs. If the barbarians evacuate the city and again ask for trade, naturally we can forgive the past, but if they are as arrogant as ever, as oppressive as ever, what are we to do about it?

Your official stupidly thinks that the main idea of the rebel barbarians in occupying the city and coercing high officials is that as Canton is the most important place in the province and the Tartar General and governor are the highest officials in the province, they can, if they seize and hold them, demand what they please.

Now it is reported that the residents of the city fear a catastrophe and nine out of ten of them have fled, that most of the dependents of civil and military officials have also moved out, that the financial and judicial commissioners have temporary offices outside the city, that the grain intendant's office is located in Fo-shan, that military stores, weapons, and treasure have all been plundered, and that all the cannons have been spiked so that all that is left of Canton now is an empty city of no importance whatever. The high officials have undergone such humiliation that without, they are not respected by barbarians, and within, they have not at all justified the hopes of the military and civil population of Canton. They are completely dominated by the barbarian rebels and their subordinates do not know where to turn. It seems essential to have an entirely new set-up and give them a new start.

May I suggest Imperial Orders to the newly appointed Imperial Commissioner and governor general of Liang-kuang to choose a place for temporary residence and also issue him a new great seal with orders, on the one hand, to manage barbarian affairs and, on the other, to take over the trainbands, mobilize naval and land forces, and wait in readiness.

As to the posts of Tartar General and governor, (Your official) is impelled to ask that great seals be given to persons Specially Chosen (by the Emperor) for their judgment and ability. On arrival at their respective posts they will notify all the subordinates accordingly. Thus the rebel barbarians having lost their lever for coercion, will be somewhat dampened in ardor; officials and people having something to respect, confidence will gradually be restored, and decisions of pacification and aggression will derive from our own authority and not be dictated by barbarians.

It is reported that the expenses of the English barbarians for war supplies are very heavy and therefore they cannot use many troops nor use them long; that continuous fighting with various foreign states in recent years has gradually exhausted and impoverished them; that in this rebellion, real barbarians and Chinese traitors together were not more than a few thousand, so the French gang came in at their bidding, not at all of their own volition. So if this is handled properly, restoring popular confidence and gradually raising the soldiers' morale, what harm can the rebel barbarians do?

As for Hong Kong, it has long been a barbarian nest and there are even Chinese who have taken up residence there and trade back and forth. In the three districts of Hsiang-shan, Tung-kuan, and Hsin-an popular feeling is very strong and it will require only one or two good magistrates to organize them secretly, offer them heavy rewards, have them form secret affiliations and, without letting the news leak out, descend like a whirlwind, taking advantage of the barbarians' absence in Canton to strike their empty lair and seize their important forts. How can the barbarians, in their haste to get back, occupy Canton long or be in a position to make threats? Never was there such a device for handling the barbarians.

In case rebel barbarian plots should suddenly be turned against Fukien, Chekiang, and Kiangnan to threaten them, it would seem necessary to forewarn the various coastal provinces to issue secret instructions to their best veterans on land and sea to strike as occasions arise in inland waters. At Tientsin it is absolutely essential to select a veteran of many battles to command the crack cavalry and infantry to make preparatory plans. The Tientsin inland river is narrow and not to the advantage of the barbarian ships. If we can only get them on land and beat them badly once or twice they will not dare get reckless and try to coerce.

To summarize, we must deal with barbarians either in inland

waters or on land and must not contest the ports with them. Whether or not Your official's limited views are correct, he cannot but present the facts. From the letters from Canton, he copies excerpts and respectfully appends them and presents them for Imperial inspection.
    A letter from Kwangtung of January 23 says:

On January 9, the rebel barbarians finally returned the Tartar General and the governor to their *yamen*. Barbarian officers in charge of several hundred barbarian soldiers are living in the official *yamen* with them and force them to issue proclamations to pacify the people. They intend to have His Excellency Po to continue in his office as governor.

The judicial and financial commissioners are now outside the city. The salt controller and grain intendant have both gone to Fo-shan to take charge of the commissariat and issue military supplies for the West and North River (districts). The Cantonese have got accustomed to obeying orders of officials for their every move. As the governor is still in the city, it is reported unofficially that he has sent an express memorial asking the Emperor to appoint a Commissioner to take charge. They dare not make any move.

Now all the city gates are guarded by barbarian soldiers. The barbarian leaders are repairing the Tartar General's *yamen* and intend to move there from the governor's office. They still send barbarian officers to the governor's office every day to attend to correspondence and transact business.

They have divided the city into five banners, east, west, north, south, and west suburb, and send barbarian troops to cooperate with the local government troops in patroling the area. They have also inventoried and sealed the arsenal of the third regiment of the Canton Brigade and taken over all the arms of the Banner Forces. They have also asked the governor to recall all cruisers and tow-boats and turn them over to the command of barbarian troops to assist them in capturing bandits. Any marine volunteers who are in the city are forbidden to wear uniform or carry arms.

They do not allow the use of the two words "Foreign Devil" *(fan kuei)* and proclamations of the Imperial Commissioners of Great England and Great France are put up everywhere. Barbarian officers and men armed with rifles are constantly wandering about in the city and suburbs.

It is noted that while the barbarian ships anchored between Whampoa and Canton harbor number some thirty or forty, real barbarian soldiers do not exceed some 3,700 men, or Chinese traitors more than 2,000. The English barbarian so-called Imperial Commissioner is Elgin; the so-called Admiral is Seymour; the Consul, Thomas Wade.

Chief Elgin has come only recently; Chief Seymour is by nature tyrannical and proud; Consul Wade is personally fairly approachable, but the former consul, now the so-called Ambassador, Harry Parkes, is thirty-odd years old, grew up in Macao and can speak Chinese. He is deceitful and cruel and thoroughly understands Chinese conditions. The fundamental reason for starting war and the instigation of operations are entirely his handiwork. He is most difficult to handle.

So-called "Great France," that is *Fo-lan-hsi*, also has a so-called Imperial Commissioner and an admiral, and they all have come at England's bidding.

At present wielding authority in the barbarian office are a Chinese traitor named Wang Tao-ch'ung, native of Chia-ying-chou, and one named Li Hsiao-ts'un, Fukienese. Wang understands foreign characters and foreign speech and is extremely treacherous. Li has no ability but is of a sinister nature. Both wear "devil" clothes and "devil" hats and are staying for the time being in the governor's compound and know everything that goes on. Until Wang and Parkes are disposed of, Kwangtung will never have a quiet day!

(IWSM.HF 18; 10a, 8-15a, 6)

249. <u>March 5, 1858.</u> EDICT: <u>Orders Lo Ping-chang to Recruit Cantonese "Barbarian Experts" to Assist in the Campaign to Recover Canton.</u>

Edict to the Grand Councillors. Lo Ping-chang has confidentially reported on the Kwangtung barbarian situation and has copied letters and presented them for Our inspection. Today We have ordered Huang Tsung-han to proceed with all haste and to bring troops to station in places adjacent to the provincial capital, and to act according to circumstances.

Since Po-kuei has taken on the duties of governor general he has never memorialized. If he and Tartar General Mu-k'o-te-na are both being coerced and merely do whatever the barbarian chiefs say, We can only appoint another, competent official to proceed and collaborate with Huang Tsung-han.

Previously a court letter was issued ordering Lo Ping-chang to delegate someone to deliver it in Kwangtung to Lo Tun-yen, Lung Yüan-hsi, and Su T'ing-kuei, ordering them secretly to assemble village bands and plan to take the capital. We assume it has been duly delivered. If the said vice-president and others can manage properly and take it unawares according to the stratagem Lo Ping-chang memorialized, they should be able to snatch the rebel barbarians' soul. What worries Us is that although their prestige is more than adequate, their resourcefulness may not be, and so they may find it hard to carry out the plan.

If at present there are in Hunan any Cantonese in the lower brackets of officials or among expectant officials, thoroughly familiar with the country and with the state of barbarian affairs, with administrative ability, who could serve in this capacity, order Lo Ping-chang to select and send two or three to Kwangtung to assist Lo Tun-yen and the others in the various matters of arranging to collect volunteers and mobilize soldiers, in order to increase efficiency. (IWSM. HF 18; 15a, 7-15b, 7)

250. <u>March 5, 1858.</u> EDICT: <u>Deplores Po-kuei's Weakness and</u>

Instructs Huang Tsung-han to Raise Troops en route to Canton for a
Liberation Campaign.

Additional Edict. Today We have received Lo Ping-chang's memorial secretly reporting Kwangtung citizen-barbarian conditions and
enclosing copies of letters. According to his statement the barbarians
have returned the Tartar General and governor to their offices and
ordered barbarian officers and soldiers to guard them, have taken
over the military supplies of the various Canton regiments and of the
village units around the city; the warships in the Canton River are
commanded by barbarians; they are guarding the city gates and have
issued proclamations under the joint authority of the barbarian chiefs,
the Tartar General and other officials.

The rebel barbarians have forced entrance to the capital city of
Kwangtung and coerced high officials. Po-kuei is working with the
barbarian chiefs and they are all living in one compound so everything
he reports must needs be entirely dictated by barbarians. He is entirely devoid of authority. Since the Tartar General and the governor
are both under restraint and have no troops at their command in the
government, and the gentry and village units can hardly operate alone
without support from government forces, order Huang Tsung-han to
proceed posthaste and not delay any longer.

If in the country the said governor general passes through he
sees available troops, let him, on the one hand, notify by memorial
and on the other, arrange to conduct them and, on arrival in Kwangtung, station them as rear guard reserves. He must not take false
confidence in what people tell him and enter the city lightly, repeating the mistake of his predecessor. After making camp he shall
immediately and speedily mobilize land and sea forces and assemble
the trainbands of various places, determining secretly his offensive.
He must not evade the issue because Po-kuei and the others are in
the city; after all the important consideration is general policy. If,
as Lo Ping-chang memorializes, recent conditions are as rumored,
that is, if the said acting governor general and Tartar General have
administered wrongly just like Yeh Ming-ch'en, We must appoint other
high officials to go there and work with Huang Tsung-han in the various posts. They will plan to attack opportunely so as to make the
barbarians lose what they have. With the initiative in our hands, we
can still recover.

Lo Ping-chang memorializes that this time, true barbarians and
Chinese traitors do not exceed a few thousand, that the French gang
came in at their bidding, not of their own will, so if we manage
properly, what harm can the rebel barbarians do? He also says
that in the three districts, Hsiang-shan, Tung-kuan, and Hsin-an,
popular feeling runs highest and if one or two competent officials
secretly organize them, offering large rewards and getting them to
form secret affiliations, and take advantage of the time when the

barbarian troops are at Canton to seize their Hong Kong hideout, then the barbarians will not be able to get back fast enough and so cannot continue in occupation of the provincial capital; that until the barbarian Chief Harry Parkes and the Cantonese Chinese traitor Wang Tao-ch'ung are both eliminated Canton will never know a peaceful day.

Order Huang Tsung-han to plan to take suitable action. Order the letters Lo Ping-chang submitted to be copied and sent for his perusal. (IWSM.HF 18; 15b, 9-16b, 9)

251. March 10, 1858. MEMORIAL: Ho Kuei-ch'ing Reports Meeting of British, French, and American Representatives with the Governor of Kiangsu at Soochow.

Governor General of Liang-chiang Ho Kuei-ch'ing and Governor of Kiangsu Chao Te-ch'e memorialize. On February 23 a report was received from acting Coast Defense Assistant Prefect Li Huan-wen that the English barbarian consul Robinson and others, inasmuch as the barbarian chiefs had sent communications regarding the Kwangtung trouble to Shanghai, wanted to come to the governor's yamen at Soochow to deliver them in person. On February 24, Your official Chao Te-ch'e received letters from the barbarian leaders Contrades [M. de Contrades, French Secretary] and Oliphant [Laurence Oliphant, British Secretary], informing him that they had arrived at Soochow. He replied that the barbarian leader should turn the documents over to Hsüeh Huan who would present them and they need not come to the capital. On the twenty-fifth, he received a report from Li Huan-wen and Fu-an that the barbarian chiefs could not wait and had left Shanghai on the twenty-fourth.

Just when Your official, Chao Te-ch'e, was thinking about packing up to go to K'un-shan to receive them, the barbarian leaders arrived in Soochow. Your official, Chao Te-ch'e, and the two commissioners ordered Acting Prefect of Soochow Ts'ai Ying-tou accompanied by Hsüeh Huan to go on board the barbarian ship and order them to wait outside the city, but the barbarian leaders, on the grounds that they were bearing important public documents, insisted on coming to the office to deliver them in person, and under the circumstances he could hardly refuse.

Then on the twenty-sixth, between three and five in the afternoon, the English, American, and French consuls, Robinson, Freeman,[14] and Min-t'i-ni,[15] as well as Oliphant, came to the office for an interview and to deliver public communications of their English, American, and

_____

14 Albert L. Freeman acted as American vice-consul at Shanghai from January 23 to March 8, 1858.
15 The name of the French consul has not been identified.

French barbarian chiefs addressed to the present officials; enclosed were three communications addressed to Grand Secretary Yü-ch'eng which they asked Your official to forward to Peking. Your official, Chao Te-ch'e, questioned the barbarian chiefs. They said that the communications presented concerned the Kwangtung affair and were very important; that the various envoys had determined to come to Shanghai during the second month (March 15-April 13) and if the Grand Secretary had not replied by that time they would go immediately to Tientsin.

Your official Chao Te-ch'e told them that as an Imperial Commissioner, Huang Tsung-han, was on his way to Canton to officiate, they should wait quietly, but the barbarian leaders said nothing else. Since they had come a long way to present them and if we did not agree to deliver their letters it would lead to other complications, we wrote three replies for them so they could report fulfillment. The barbarian leaders went away pleased and on the twenty-seventh they departed from Soochow. We instructed the tao-t'ai of Su-Sung-T'ai, Hsüeh Huan, accompanied by our representative, to escort them back to Shanghai and the situation continues quiet.

Your official Chao Te-ch'e at once consulted Ho Kuei-ch'ing confidentially by letter, and also opened and read the document addressed to Grand Secretary Yü-ch'eng. Observing its purport, Yeh Ming-ch'en's maladministration needs no comment but the barbarians' self-confessed violence is also apparent and it is enough to stand one's hair on end. Besides they said they wanted an Imperial Commissioner to be in Shanghai to negotiate before April 10 and included exaggerated threats. To the American barbarian's note was appended a Russian barbarian communication to the Grand Council, the spirit and phraseology of which were about the same.

Your official begs to comment that the barbarian chiefs, unable to get their way in Kwangtung, wanted to come to Shanghai to negotiate. Their minds are basically inscrutable. Since Shanghai is the tribute route port as well as the place where customs and likin are concentrated, if complications develop on account of rejecting their demands, it is greatly feared there would be many inconveniences.

Computing that since leaving Peking, Huang Tsung-han should have reached the Ch'ing-chiang district in Shantung, Your officials immediately copied the four communications and sent them secretly by night and day express post, notifying Huang Tsung-han to deliberate and take action. (IWSM.HF 18; 16b, 10-18a, 10)

252. March 10, 1853. EDICT: Orders Yü-ch'eng to Reject and Ho Kuei-ch'ing to Repudiate a Joint Foreign Request for Treaty Revision made at Soochow.

Edict to the Grand Councillors. We have received a document from Ho Kuei-ch'ing and others confidentially reporting that English,

American, and French barbarian chiefs had presented public communications. On this occasion the barbarians have used force to
resist authority, occupied the capital city of Kwangtung and now they
come to Shanghai to deliver communications. They even say that
they intend to come to Tientsin but this is obviously an empty threat
intended to implement their endless demands.

Heretofore barbarian affairs have all been the special province
of the governor general of Liang-kuang. Huang Tsung-han has been
sent to Kwangtung to take charge, but the barbarian chiefs, without
even waiting for a settlement, proceeded to Soochow to deliver communications, including a communication addressed to Grand Secretary
Yü-ch'eng. All their annoying complaints are completely one-sided
and unreasonable.

Besides instructing Yü-ch'eng that he is not to reply to the barbarians, order Ho Kuei-ch'ing and the others to explain seriatim and
in full detail the various items in the communication to Yü-ch'eng,
telling them that Shanghai is not really the place to manage barbarian
affairs, and that since China has a man specially charged with barbarian affairs, the said barbarians are to return to Kwangtung and
wait for Huang Tsung-han to make arrangements, thus doing as they
should. The said governor general can certainly comprehend Our
wish and instruct his subordinates to act accordingly, so as to maintain national prestige and avoid occasion for violence. (IWSM.HF
18; 18b, 1-19a, 1)

253. March 19, 1858. AMERICAN NOTE: Reed Presents American
Grievances and Demands Negotiations at Shanghai.[16]
By way of communication. The present minister has received
edicts and credentials from his government personally and come to
China to present them for His Imperial Majesty's examination. He
has discretionary plenipotentiary powers to negotiate various regulations with Chinese ministers of equal rank. He now specially
communicates with the Grand Secretaries and begs them with un-
biased minds to read fully, in detail and with discrimination. Any
documents coming from any of China's ministers or the Emperor,
the president and cabinet ministers will be glad to receive without
exception.

The present minister arrived in Kwangtung, China, November 5,
1857, and soon realized that the provincial capital was about to have
war because the western countries, France and England, could not
but resort to arms to redress their grievances. When fighting began

16 This is a translation back into English of the communication of William B. Reed addressed
to Grand Councillor Yü-ch'eng and presented by Consul Freeman to Ho Kuei-ch'ing at the
Soochow meeting and thence forwarded to Peking. The original is published in U.S. Cong.
36:1, S. Ex. Doc., 30, p. 171-175. It is dated at Macao, February 10, 1858.

nationals of the present country rigidly maintained neutrality [lit. faith and courtesy] without intercourse with either side. Basically the [Imperial] ancestors of the present country and the high officials who founded the dynasty left as a heritage that peace with all countries under heaven was most precious, with no discrimination between mine and thine. Therefore there is no wish to go to war with the various provinces of China or to invade her borders.

Lest it be assumed that necessarily the United States has no grievances in China, not knowing that actually there are several occasions for grievance, they are now briefly set forth.

First, since the signing of the treaties your honorable officials have hindered trade on many, many occasions.

Second, there are many nationals of the present country residing in the ports who have had their persons plotted against by murderers who make no distinction between worthy and unworthy, and who are bold enough to cut to pieces or poison. Therefore people are alarmed and very apprehensive.

Third, various imperial commissioners of the present country who have come to handle foreign affairs and trade at the five ports with Chinese Imperial commissioners have repeatedly been insulted, put off, and on several occasions have been unable to gain interviews or answers to state papers.

Fourth, the great discourtesy was last year when, since there was an Imperial autograph letter, permission was given to send it by government post to Peking to be presented to the Emperor for inspection. Unexpectedly, it was suddenly returned with the seals broken and was never answered. This is a matter of great discourtesy and people were infuriated.

But mindful that the present country always desires to have continuous friendly relations with China, how could even these grievances large or small postpone a settlement? Besides, it proposed mediation between the two parties which might have saved the capital city the catastrophe of a war and the people any anxiousness of danger. The present minister was certainly at one with his countrymen in this hope.

The present high official several months ago sent two or three communications to His Excellency Governor General Yeh asking for an interview with him in order to deliver personally an Imperial autograph letter and ask him to send it to Peking for him in a memorial and to discuss amicably various matters, large and small, of interest to our respective countries; but His Excellency Governor General Yeh would never receive him. By defeating our plan to arbitrate between the two sides, he brought about a clash of arms. When calamity came upon his country, he allowed the city to be lost and taken over by others, was arrested hands down, and placed in confinement.

This kind of conduct the present high official has experienced and observed, but greatly fears that the Emperor living in the depths of his cabinet may not fully know everything that develops in distant parts. Now the French and English military and civil officials control the forces at Canton. The people in the city want peace and there is no more resistance. As soon as merchants are allowed to open trade the Imperial Commissioners of the two countries will go direct to the Court to try again to negotiate in order to avoid subsequent concern. They have invited the present minister and the Russian Imperial Commissioner to negotiate with them. All want peace and justice for everybody, which accords with the humanity of the Holy Commandment of Jesus.

Russia is one of the great countries under heaven; she is north of China and is her neighbor. To the east and across a large ocean is the United States, thus China and the United States are really separated only by an ocean. Although our two countries [Russia and the United States] have somewhat different laws, in peace and friendliness they are as one. Speaking generally, our two countries and China should be friendly nations.

As to the present country and Great Britain, their intercourse is of the longest standing. Since they are of a common origin, their books in the same script and their speech of the same sound, they always cooperate. Since both have a great mutual trade in China which is daily becoming more prosperous for both, he must ask that there be no interference with it.

As to France and the present country, from ancient times to the present there have been cordial relationships without any barrier, as examination of a long series of past events will prove. But France and China previously established the ruling that no Catholic priests coming to the country be harmed without cause, and to her surprise, last year a missionary was arrested, tortured, and cruelly put to death. Now a minister has come to Canton specially instructed to redress the grievance and forgive the sin, thus it is apparent that the emperor of that country is benevolent and princely.

The present minister deeply hopes that China will lay a solid foundation for friendship with western countries by negotiating treaties. If treaties of amity are firmly established China and the world will never be worried with spoliation of their frontiers. The present minister has been sent to renew an old friendship and negotiate regulations. Although in the present document it is not convenient to itemize what the treaties should be, our various western countries have no ulterior motives nor does any one country demand special favor. While the present country agrees in general with the other three countries, still the present country's grievances ought naturally to be set forth. As soon as convenient they must be explained item by item and investigated clearly.

As one instance, the goods stolen from merchants of the present country several years ago should, by right, be indemnified. Although

382 China's Management of the American Barbarians

these merchants are not smugglers they have suffered losses; while engaged peacefully in business, encountering the fighting of other countries with which they had not the slightest concern, they have never been protected.

Now to secure indemnity for their losses, it is necessary to notify the Grand Secretaries that on this occasion he has gone direct to Shanghai in the hope of a Patent by Command for one or two ministers with full powers, of rank equal to that of the present official, to come to the port to meet him and suitably discuss matters, large and small, by March 30, 1858. Should there be any desire to shift the place to Kwangtung as has been proposed in previous years or to some other port further removed from Peking, the present minister after much thought must regard this as an evasion of treaty negotiations. But mindful that the Grand Secretaries of China are the pillars of the state, he is sure they will not reject this excellent proposal.

If they fail to arrive by the appointed day, the present minister as soon thereafter as convenient, without further notice, without delay, and without further explanation will either himself take up residence near the capital, or with the Imperial Commissioners of the other western countries go to reside near the capital, or wait until he memorializes the throne to see what instructions there are. If this takes place how can China take exception and how can she prevent it? By way of communication. This is a necessary communication. (IWSM.HF 18; 26b, 8-29b, 8)

254. March 21, 1858. EDICT: Rejects Shanghai Negotiations and Orders Huang Tsung-han to Treat at Canton and Mobilize Chinese Forces to Attack.

Edict to the Grand Councillors. According to the previous memorial of Ho Kuei-ch'ing and others, the English, American, and French barbarian chiefs submitted communications addressed to Grand Secretary Yü-ch'eng wanting to revise treaties at Shanghai. Ho Kuei-ch'ing was immediately notified that Yü-ch'eng could not reply. We also instructed the said governor general and others to make it clear to the barbarians that they were to wait as usual at Canton for Huang Tsung-han to take action. We figure that by this time Huang Tsung-han has reached Ch'ang-chou, conferred with Ho Kuei-ch'ing and fully understands the situation. The various statements of the barbarians are entirely one-sided. They know well that in the inauguration of hostilities, the fault was theirs but they continually make Yeh Ming-ch'en the pretext, determined to put the blame on China so as to implement their covetousness.

When We look at their attitude it seems impossible to reason with them. Heretofore We sent orders to Lo Tun-yen and others to organize the gentry-led bands to drive the barbarians out of the city and reason

with them afterwards. If gentry and people work together the barbarians will feel some apprehension.

After Huang Tsung-han arrives, with a show of military force
without, and relying on the efforts of the people within, he can point
out to them the advantages and hazards, and the point of vantage can
still be turned in our favor. If the barbarians do not follow his reasoning and do come to Shanghai, that is the headquarters of Imperial transport and customs and, unlike Kwangtung, cannot be defended. Order
him, then, to discuss with Ho Kuei-ch'ing suitable means of making
them return to Kwangtung. He must not let word of mobilization leak
out and cause the barbarians to create other complications.

As to the content of the barbarian communications, besides the
statement in Yü-ch'eng's answer to Ho Kuei ch'ing "to consider the
matter discriminately and reply," the Chinese translation of the barbarian text states that "indemnity for military expenditures will be
considered." On this occasion hostilities were started by the barbarians. The private dwellings and goods in Canton destroyed by them must
run into the millions. While these citizens have never been indemnified,
for the barbarians to turn around and want indemnification for war
expenses is most unreasonable. If the barbarians propose this, say
that China's goods which were burned must be indemnified first, for
while His Imperial Majesty is magnanimous and would not bargain
with them, the people and merchants of Canton would never be satisfied. Moreover, it is reported that goods of the French barbarians
were all burned up in the fires started by the English barbarians but
their chief, instead of demanding indemnification of the English barbarians, demands of China payment for her war expenses, in complete disregard of reason. These are arguments for future discussions. Whether
or not they can be propounded now must depend upon Huang Tsung-
han's estimate of the exigencies and order of administration.

As to the Russian barbarians, they have had friendly relations
with China for years but have never traded on the seacoast. Suddenly
now there are these (Russian) documents in Manchu, Chinese, and
barbarian characters, presented appended to the American barbarian
papers. Their intention is to help the English and French barbarians
but actually that affair does not concern them. We have notified Urga
and Heilungkiang to send word to that country's Senate Yamen to come
to an agreement with them on the matter of their request for a boundary
survey. The present Kwangtung affair has absolutely no connection with
that country.

The American barbarians, even though in self-vindication they
make it clear that they were not involved in the fall of Canton, support
the demands in their papers. This situation must be turned to our advantage by preventing their alliance with England and France. Thus we
deal with them separately.

As to the port of Tientsin, We have notified T'an T'ing-hsiang to order his subordinates to lay secret plans for defense. The Edict addressed to Ho Kuei-ch'ing and others, Yü-ch'eng's reply to Ho Kuei-ch'ing, the Chinese texts of the two communications of the English barbarians, the Chinese text of two French barbarian communications, one French barbarian document which has been translated from the barbarian text, the Chinese text of three American barbarian documents, and the Chinese text of one Russian barbarian document, dated March 11, are all ordered copied and sent for his perusal. (IWSM.HF 19; 1a, 3-2b, 2)

255. March 21, 1858. EDICT: Alerts Tientsin Military Officials against a Possible English-American-French Attack.

Additional Edict. There have been received successive memorials from Ho Kuei-ch'ing and others reporting that the English, American, and French barbarian chiefs had presented communications and that they intended in the middle decade of the second month (March 24-April 3) to come to Shanghai to discuss matters. They said further that should we not negotiate with them at that time they would proceed from Shanghai to Tientsin. We forthwith ordered Ho Kuei-ch'ing and others to explain in detail and get them to wait in Canton for a settlement. The barbarians have occupied the capital of Kwangtung and abducted the governor general and We have already appointed Huang Tsung-han governor general of Liang-kuang, to hasten to Kwangtung and act according to circumstances.

The barbarians say in their communication that they intend to go to Tientsin, and although this is obviously an empty threat to implement their demands, since they do say it, there is no assurance that it will not take place. Should they one day appear at Tientsin, We fear that it will not be under the same peaceful circumstance it was before. Tientsin is a vital capital suburb, a hub of commerce, and must be rigorously defended in order to avoid any slip.

Order T'an T'ing-hsiang to send word to Wu-lo-hung-e to collaborate with the Tientsin brigade general and tao-t'ai in a rigorous defense program for various strategic places at the port without making any outward show. If barbarian ships arrive, they must first strictly forbid the coastal inhabitants to supply food or to trade illicitly, to make it impossible for them to remain long, and on the other hand, delegate a suitable official to reason with them and get them to return to Kwangtung and await a settlement. When the time comes, observe their movements and secretly memorialize asking for an Edict. (IWSM.HF 19; 2b, 4-3a, 5)

256. March 26, 1858. MEMORIAL: T'an T'ing-hsiang Reports Confidently on the Defense of the Tientsin Approaches from the Sea.

Acting Governor General of Chihli T'an T'ing-hsiang memorializes It is noted that the sea outside Tientsin is clear for a thousand li with no islands for anchorage. Near the port, at thirty-odd <u>li</u> is the bar hazard. While large steamers dare not enter, small ships and sampans can readily come and go. There are forts on the north and south sides of the port but the fort on the north shore is right on the main channel.

As the situation demanded early action, Your official first sent an officer to get the lay of the land in order to facilitate the subsequent repair of the barracks and official compound. He then ordered the brigade general to map out the troops, arms, and horses which need to be moved and has ordered Colonel Ta-nien, now taking over the duties of the said brigade general, to go there and take charge. This officer has been in Tientsin several years and understands the situation thoroughly, so it was fitting to charge him with the duty of co-operating with Tientsin <u>Tao-t'ai</u> Ying-yü and his deputies in making suitable plans secretly and speedily. The Tientsin division continger.', including old and new troops, is over 7,000, much more than other divisions, so besides the thousand men on campaign and sent out as garrisons, there are enough left for deployment. Firearms and other supplies are also abundantly supplied. It seemed necessary to have Acting Tientsin Brigade General Ta-nien specially assigned to the port and Commander-in-chief Chang Tien-yüan to take his seal and transfer to Tientsin as a defense measure.

As to the port, it is five or six <u>li</u> from Ta-ku and 180 or 190 <u>li</u> from Tientsin; in between is the new city of Ko-ku with an assistant prefect for coast defense and the Ko-ku battalion with a major in residence. Heretofore this has been an anchorage inside the port for commercial ships. Beyond this, villages are sparse and the channel crooked, and it has been proposed to entice the barbarians into the upper river and then annihilate them.

Your official thinks that inasmuch as the barbarians are strong on water and weak on land, being naturally wily they would never be willing to give up a strong position for a weak one. Besides, using sampans and small ships to come up with the tide, the situation would be very simple, and once on the upper river the people would be thrown into a panic. Thus our defense policy is to make the water course the first consideration, and to prepare a land route behind the forts, thus making it comprehensive.

Last year Your official had the Tientsin <u>tao-t'ai</u> raise subscriptions for a pontoon bridge at Ta-ku, but as the harbor is extensive the expense was too great and funds were not at once available. He then temporarily rented ships and placed them across the river to connect the roads on the north and south banks. If salt junks and old ocean-going ships were used to block this and soldiers sent to guard it, it would be still more effective. Orders have been given the Tientsin <u>tao-t'ai</u> secretly to arrange its defense.

The Tientsin trainband was rather efficient, but since the recall

of the regular troops expenses have been excessive and besides the
gentry in charge have been very busy. Your official finds that there
is a former tao-t'ai of P'ing-Ch'ing-Ching, Kansu, one Fei Yin-chang,
who has returned on account of the death of a parent. He is bright
and competent, and is suitable to command trainbands. The Tientsin
tao-t'ai has been instructed secretly to confer with him and, in accord
with the old regulations, duly to cooperate with the gentry.

It has always been essential to defend without by first coordinating
within. The Tientsin populace is naturally volatile and self-seeking
with people from the five directions jumbled together indiscriminately,
thus such measures are necessary to restrain popular feeling. It is
still more essential to muster all ships in the port so that in case of
trouble supplies from without can be intercepted. Your official has
secretly sent a deputy to the port to make a careful, advance inventory of trading and fishing vessels large and small as well as to exhort and regulate the Ta-ku trainbands, hoping to tranquillize the interior. Besides, the port of Pei-t'ang in Ning-ho-hsien and neighboring places where commercial and fishing vessels call will all be
managed likewise. (IWSM.HF 19; 5b, 10-7a, 9)

257. March 26, 1858. EDICT: Orders T'an T'ing-hsiang's Defense
Plan Executed and Tientsin Officials to be Prepared to Negotiate.
Edict to the Grand Councillors. T'an T'ing-hsiang has memorialized on the matter of handling Tientsin coastal defense. The port
of Tientsin, although not accessible to large barbarian ships, can be
readily visited by such boats as sampans and it is of the utmost
necessity to set up a rigorous defense in order to be ready for the
unforeseen. The acting governor general has delegated acting Tientsin Brigade General Ta-nien to reside at the port, transferred
Commander-in-chief Chang Tien-yüan to Tientsin, and also ordered
Tao-t'ai (on leave) Fei Yin-chang to collaborate with the gentry in
organizing trainbands, as well as making an inventory of fishing
ships and intercepting supplies.

As his arrangements are entirely satisfactory, order his proposals executed immediately. These barbarians are extraordinarily
cunning. If they come to Tientsin, they will first insist on presenting
barbarian documents, observe our movements, but not necessarily
start trouble, so the acting governor general will confidentially
instruct the brigade general and tao-t'ai, along with Wu-lo-hung-e,
to delegate the civil and military officers who went on board the barbarian ships last year to go and reason with them, devising means to
handle them. If it is absolutely necessary for the acting governor
general to go in person, order him to memorialize for an Edict and
act in accordance.

At present Tientsin and Ta-ku are prepared against danger, but
it is necessary to show composure while defenses are being made

secretly; there cannot be the least show of confusion. This is most
essential. (IWSM.HF 19; 7a, 10-7b, 9)

258. April 5, 1858. MEMORIAL: Canton Officials Report Reduction of
Occupation Forces, the Reopening of Trade, and Review American Neutrality and Good Offices.

Canton Tartar General Mu-k'o-te-na, Acting Governor General
of Liang-kuang Po-kuei, Canton Customs Superintendent Heng-ch'i
memorialize. It is noted that since January 5, 1857, Your slave Po-
kuei has explained continually and even the barbarians have recognized reason. The warships anchored in Canton River and the barbarian troops occupying Yüeh-hsiu Shan in the northeast city are being
gradually reduced. The barbarian chiefs, Elgin and Baron Gros, have
also returned to Hong Kong, leaving only five barbarian leaders resident at Yüeh-hsiu Shan, inside the city. Barbarian troops remaining
are only a few hundred. Soldiers and civilians come and go as usual
without the barbarians causing any trouble. Shops are gradually
opening and the barbarians buy and sell normally without any cases
of seizure by violence.

On hearing that the former governor general, Yeh Ming-ch'en,
was degraded, the barbarians were profoundly grateful. On being
told to move out of the city, however, they refused on the grounds
that the Imperial Commissioner had not reached Canton and conditions
were unsettled.

As we analyze their position, since the barbarian soldiers are
not numerous, they are afraid if they were moved outside the city
other uprisings would occur. Thus externally arrogant, at heart they
are really fearful. When the new governor general, Huang Tsung-han,
arrives in Canton, as soon as there is any indication of a settlement,
they will retire altogether. Since the citizens and barbarians were
already getting on, it seemed possible at this time to get rid of them
gradually in order to avoid repeated uprisings.

As to commerce, it would normally have to wait until this (evacuation) was complete before it was taken up again, but trade has already
been suspended for more than a year. Capital is greatly depleted and
many goods have rotted. At present bandits on the West and North
Rivers have not yet been suppressed and operating expenses are wanting.
As Sino-barbarian trade has been long stopped, sailors, stevedores,
and all the poor people have lost their jobs and, lacking means of
making a living, are constantly turning bandit.

Moreoever since the stopping of customs, October 27, 1856, now
more than a year, the dishonest merchants who have taken up smuggling
are by no means few. By comparison, open prohibition and secret
trade with a useless loss of national revenue is not as good as adjustment to circumstances and getting a real supply of much needed provisions. Moreover, opening trade in foreign grain might equalize

market prices.

Just while this was being considered, a report of Mr. Wu Ch'ung-yüeh and other gentry was received that some barbarian merchants of different countries who used to trade, Fu-ssu-tsan, Tien-tien-ti,[17] and others had asked them to present a petition that, as it was not easy for the said merchants to transport goods across the ocean this distance, and now that there was a stalemate and merchant ships had been waiting to enter port for more than a year, they earnestly entreated the said gentry to find a way to transmit their plea for permission to trade immediately.

When these items, respectful and compliant in letter and spirit, were presented, Your slave Po-kuei communicated the sentiments of the barbarian merchants, utilizing the consensus of the barbarian merchants to commit the barbarian chiefs. Then on February 2, he received the reply of the French barbarian chief, Baron Gros, stating that on receiving and reading the letter he was indescribably delighted; that if hereafter merchants were to prosper as before, it was essential to make suitable arrangements to protect native and foreign merchants peacefully and without hazard. Then on February 5, he received English barbarian chief Elgin's reply to the effect that he had received and read the letter and would be profoundly relieved to have trade as usual and both parties at peace; so he hoped that we would conscientiously explain and reiterate to the masses that outside guests entering their boundaries should not be regarded as enemies; that this was his fervent hope.

So it was agreed to open the port on February 10, and all merchant: Chinese and foreign, without exception danced for joy. Your slaves, Po-kuei and Heng-ch'i, immediately issued orders to the Chinese and barbarian merchants to trade as usual, present their goods for examination at the various ports and pay duties as specified. Between February 24, when customs examination and collection began, and March 10, the Canton customs house made three collections totaling over 5,700 taels, and hereafter the amount should increase daily and expenditures can be met.

As to the matter of former Governor General Yeh Ming-ch'en's refusal of the American barbarians' request for an interview leading to the subsequent occupation of the forts: it is noted that the primary motive of the Americans in asking for an interview was to mediate and the former governor general did stubbornly refuse; that although the American barbarians' good intentions were thwarted, the barbarian ships entering Hu-men (Bocca Tigris) bore the flags of England and France, and on no occasion did the American barbarians assist in the evil.

---

17 The names of these foreign merchants have not been identified.

The Hu-men forts are the most important entrance to Canton
River and if defended energetically barbarian ships could not get in
without flying. The commander-in-chief of sea forces stationed
there has sole responsibility for its defense. It is noted that since the
ninth month (September 29-October 28) of 1856, when the barbarians
started trouble, the said commander, Wu Yüan-yü, has never exerted
himself to defend them so the troops for the defense of the forts have
scattered. On two occasions barbarian ships have entered just as
they pleased and the forts and gun positions have all been demolished
by barbarians.

This is real ingratitude for Imperial Favor and failure of duty
and we are compelled to ask for an Edict to the Boards turning Kwangtung Commander-in-chief of Sea Forces Wu Yüan-yü over for strict
punishment and a warning.   (IWSM.HF   19; 7b, 10-10a, 3)

259. April 5, 1858. EDICT: Orders the Degradation of Admiral Wu
Yüan-yü for Failure to Defend Canton.

Edict to the Grand Secretariat. Po-kuei and others have memorialized that in accord with Imperial Edict they have investigated the
lax defense of the commander-in-chief and ask that he be ordered
tried.

Order Kwangtung Commander-in-chief of Sea Forces Wu Yüan-yü
degraded immediately, to continue in office temporarily, and charge
him to defend the port vigorously in order to mitigate previous guilt.
(IWSM.HF   19; 10a, 4-5)

Chapter 9

Reed and Ho Kuei-ch'ing at Shanghai, 1858
(Documents 260-277)

The eighteen documents making up this chapter cover the period from April 5, 1858, to April 16, 1858, and represent the Shanghai preparatory phase of treaty revision to be carried out immediately afterward at Tientsin. There are seven memorials and ten edicts, all of the latter addressed to the grand councillors. There are only four vermilion endorsements, all of them of a formal or general nature; there are no real expressions of imperial will or opinion. In addition to the memorials and edicts, there is one informal memorandum.

The principal memorialist of this period is Ho Kuei-ch'ing, governor general of Liang-chiang and spokesman for Hsüeh Huan, who had taken over the active execution of foreign affairs at Shanghai after the fall of Wu Chien-chang. The second memorialist is Canton Governor General Huang Tsung-han, who made a long report on conditions in Canton under British-French occupation. Minor memorialists are T'an T'ing hsiang, governor general of Chihli (Hopei), and General Chang Tien-yüan, in command of the Chihli provincial army.

The theme of this chapter is the emergence of Ho Kuei-ch'ing as a major statesman and virtual foreign minister, without authority to perform any conclusive act in that capacity. Governor General Ho was ably assisted by Hsüeh Huan, who had succeeded Wu Chien-chang as Su-Sung-T'ai tao-t'ai. Hsüeh Huan assumed actual charge of foreign affairs at Shanghai, but it was his able superior, Ho Kuei-ch'ing, who memorialized for him, formulated and made palatable to the reactionary court his realistic policy, and did his best to avert the series of tragedies which were to develop in the North. Ho Kuei-ch'ing was one of the first Chinese officials to recognize the fallacy in trying to play off one barbarian against another--a policy, conceived as early as Han times and popularized during the Sui dynasty, which continued to plague China through the nineteenth century and is still a factor in Chinese foreign policy today. He realized that foreign rivalry was at best a negative defense, that it could become very dangerous for China, and that China's only hope lay in building up a strong and wealthy nation. He advocated a positive program of increasing the national revenue and buying up Western ships and arms, until such time as China could produce her own. The position of American Minister William B. Reed, in Shanghai, offered unusual possibilities for independent action, but both his and Ho Kuei-ch'ing's instructions precluded such action. At the same time that this ineffective sparring was going on at Shanghai, preparations were being made to carry the negotiations to Tientsin. One Manchu and

391

one Chinese envoy, Ch'ung-lun and Ch'ien Hsin-ho, were sent to Tientsin
to receive the Western representatives. At the same time, China tightened
her northern defenses by alerting her generals from Ta-ku Bar to Shanhaikwan against possible foreign attack.

The Shanghai phase, like the previous Canton phase, is not adequately covered by Dennett. Reed's negotiations with Hsüeh Huan and Ho Kuei-
ch'ing are, however, included in his correspondence, published by the
United States government, U.S. Cong. 36: 1, S. Ex. Doc. 30.

TRANSLATIONS OF DOCUMENTS

260. April 5, 1858. MEMORIAL: Ho Kuei-ch'ing Reports the Imminent
Arrival of the British, American, French, and American Envoys and
Threats toward Tientsin.

Governor General of Liang-chiang Ho Kuei-ch'ing and Governor
of Kiangsu Chao Te-ch'e memorialize. To continue, Your officials
received the dispatch from the Grand Councillors stating that on
March 11, 1858, they had received an Imperial Edict that Ho Kuei-
ch'ing and others had secretly reported on the English, American, and
French barbarians' presentation of communications and state papers.
Respect this.

Your officials immediately obeyed and had the communication
copied and, since turning them over to the tao-t'ai of Su-Sung-T'ai and
the barbarian-language-speaking expectant tao-t'ai, Wu Chien-chang,
to deliver to the respective consuls, have as yet received no replies.
But they have received a report from the said tao-t'ai and others that
there have arrived one after another three steamers of not more than
some four feet draft, and in addition, two English barbarian warships
and one Russian warship are anchored outside Woosung. It is reported
that the three English, American, and French chiefs may arrive any
day and that the Russian chief Poutiatine[1] is now on board the warship, but there is still no activity.

Your officials find that in the winter of 1854, the English and
American barbarians proceeded to Tientsin, presented requests for
treaty revision and received an Imperial Edict ordering them to return
to Kwangtung for settlement; that when the American chief returned
to Shanghai he told former Governor Chi-erh-hang-a that the treaties must be revised and could not go beyond the twelve-year period;
that if settlement were put off he feared friendly relations would be
strained. This has been memorialized and is on record. Now having
raised troops and opposed authority in Kwangtung they have come on to
Shanghai and presented communications asking that an Imperial Commis

---

1 Count Euphemius Poutiatine was the Russian envoy to China.

sioner negotiate with them at Shanghai by March 21.

Their mentality is really inscrutable. Your officials secretly
instructed Hsüeh Huan and others, when the barbarian chiefs arrive,
to be neither arrogant nor servile, to treat them courteously and
tell them that Kiangsu province is not familiar with the matters discussed in the communications they presented, so they were forwarded for them and the reply of the Grand Secretary received; that
there has been no refusal to receive or forward. This is a plausible
explanation but the nature of dogs and sheep is difficult to analyze.

Shanghai is a place where people from the five directions are
jumbled together and the temper of the populace is fundamentally
unstable. During the eleventh month of last year (December 16, 1857-
January 14, 1858) when we got the shocking news of the fall of Kwangtung, trade was stopped for several days. Not until Hsüeh Huan had
explained elaborately and duly exerted pressure was it possible to
trade as usual. Now that barbarian warships are coming one after
the other the alarm is even greater. Tribute rice leaving the port
is reduced to one half and sand junks offered for hire for grain transport are still inadequate and recently very few have come into port.
If the barbarians make any rash demands one cannot bear to ask the
state Shanghai will be in.

What is even more disturbing, in 1854 these barbarians originally asked to establish ports at Chen-chiang and other places, and
now they also state that if there is no Imperial Commissioner at
Shanghai they will do as they please. Although Chen-chiang and Yang-
chou are in ruins they are still the north-south bottleneck and must
be defended. Your officials have notified Ho-ch'un and Te-hsing-a
by secret letter that if there is any word of barbarian ships entering
the river they must present a formidable force without joining battle,
but whether or not troops are available for deployment, there is still
no way of knowing.

Vermilion Endorsement: Noted. (IWSM.HF 19; 10a, 6-11b, 5)

261. April 5, 1858. EDICT: Orders Shanghai Officials to Send the
Foreign Envoys to Canton with Promises of Trade and Arrival of an
Imperial Commissioner.

Edict to the Grand Councillors. Ho Kuei-ch'ing has memorialized on the status of barbarian affairs in Shanghai and asked that
orders be given for rigid defense of Tientsin. The memorial has been
read and comprehended. Shanghai is the receiving point in tribute
transport so naturally means must be found to control the barbarians
and prevent their causing trouble. Today Po-kuei and Mu-k'o-te-na's
memorials have been received on various aspects of Kwangtung administration. Orders have been sent Huang Tsung-han to deliberate
and take action. At present in the capital of Kwangtung the barbarian
troops are being gradually reduced and the barbarian chiefs have

moved to Hong Kong. Moreover, because the various countries
earnestly requested commerce, the port has been opened to trade.

If and when the English, American, and French chiefs reach
Shanghai, order officers sent immediately to tell them that Canton
has already opened its mart to trade and the situation is not like
that of last month; that when the new governor general arrives he
will naturally have a solution; that Shanghai fundamentally has no
quarrel with the barbarians; and get them back to Canton for a
settlement. If the barbarians want to go to Tientsin, simply say
that it would be effort wasted without benefit. It is not necessary
to go so far as to prevent them, lest it indicate a feeling of fear.
But the mental processes of barbarians are inscrutable, so at the
same time order local officials to take suitable precautions without giving any outward evidence.

In addition, urge the loaded sand junks to put out to sea at once.
There must be no delay or friction.

Order the original documents of Po-kuei and others copied and
sent out for reference. (IWSM.HF 19; 11b, 6-12a, 6)

262. April 5, 1858. EDICT: Instructs Huang Tsung-han to Hasten
to Canton and Accomplish its Recovery by any Means Available.

Additional Edict. Previously because the barbarian chiefs
presented communications and wanted to come to Shanghai, Ho Kuei-
ch'ing and others were immediately notified to find means to get
them to return to Canton and take up the matter again with Huang
Tsung-han. Today Ho Kuei-ch'ing's memorial has been received
saying that three steamers as well as two English barbarian warships
and one Russian barbarian warship have arrived one after the other
at Shanghai and are anchored outside Woosung, but have still made
no move. This fits in with the statement in today's memorial of Po-
kuei and others that the barbarians were setting out one after the
other. At present Po-kuei and the others at Canton have opened the
mart to trade with the barbarians. Moreover, according to his
memorial the barbarian chiefs have all left voluntarily and now only
a few hundred barbarian troops are still in the city; but that these
are unwilling to move out of the city and insist on waiting until conditions are settled before they will withdraw.

Shanghai is an awkward place to confer with them and they can
only be ordered to return. Secret instructions have been sent Ho
Kuei-ch'ing to manage accordingly. But as Kwangtung is already
trading with them it is not the same situation as last year. Previously We ordered Lo Tun-yen and others to assemble militia to expel
them and these many days have seen no reply. We gather that Po-
kuei and the others are afraid to provoke hostilities and will not allow
any hasty move, or it may be that the barbarians heard of this move
and fearing they would suffer loss left Canton for Shanghai, while

Po-kuei and the others believed it was because people and barbarians were harmonious.

In any event it is essential that Huang Tsung-han reach Canton quickly. Then he can act as the situation requires. Order today's papers of Po-kuei and the others copied and sent to Huang Tsung-han for reference. He must take into consideration in his administration both the program previously sent him and present circumstances in that province, nor will We bind him from this distance.

At present the country has many problems. Troops and supplies are both deficient. Shanghai is right on the transport route and certainly appeasement there would be to our advantage, but when national prestige is involved, how can we accede to their demands and thus create in other countries the desire to emulate them?

When Huang Tsung-han arrives, he still cannot enter the city thoughtlessly. Since Wu Ch'ung-yüeh has negotiated with the barbarians to open trade, he can have him spy out the intentions of the barbarian chiefs. If they still have the idea of demanding military expenses, tell them that the buildings and goods of merchants and residents which were destroyed by fire must be indemnified first, utilize the influence of gentry and people to block their extortion at the outset, and afterward manage according to circumstances; using both firmness and compliance we can pull the strings. He cannot altogether compromise, causing us to lose prestige while he antagonizes them.

Commander-in-chief of Sea Forces Wu Yüan-yü whose lax defense enabled the barbarian ships to invade Canton River has been ordered degraded, to continue in office temporarily. When the said governor general arrives, he will order him to defend the portal vigorously as a strong frontier is important. (IWSM.HF 19; 12a, 8-13a, 8)

263. April 6, 1858. MEMORIAL: Reports Conferences with Ho Kuei-ch'ing and Military Conditions Observed en route to Canton.

Imperial Commissioner, Governor General of Liang-kuang Huang Tsung-han memorializes. On the seventh (March) Your official sailed south from Ch'ing-chiang [Kiangsi] and en route heard that the barbarians had gone direct to Soochow to present documents. Your official immediately transferred to a (Yangtze) River boat and with a favorable wind entered Tan-t'u. On the fourteenth at Ch'ang-chou he received a letter from the governor of Kiangsu, Chao Te-ch'e. Copies of the English, American, French, and Russian barbarian chiefs' communications to Grand Secretary Yü-ch'eng, and a draft of the said governor general's memorial were referred to Your official for examination and disposition, charging Your official to proceed leisurely and wait for Vermilion Endorsed Memorials before leaving Kiangsu, because since the barbarians came to Kiangsu, the people of the province were naturally feeling somewhat suspicious and apprehensive. Some said that if he did not go to Shanghai to meet them he might talk with them in Kiangsu.

They seemed to think that if Your official were in charge here the
barbarians would not be likely to make trouble for Kiangsu.

Your official thereupon conferred two or three times with Governor General Ho Kuei-ch'ing. After all, Shanghai is not the place for
barbarian affairs and, although Your official is the person in sole
charge of barbarian affairs, this is no time to rush things. That is
to say, not having reached Kwangtung and being completely ignorant
of conditions, how could he negotiate with only one side of the argument? Besides Po-kuei is acting and it is not known what he has
agreed to or what he has memorialized. If he met them at Shanghai
or Soochow, failed to comply with any of their demands, and they
again used coercion, it would not merely agitate Kiangsu province
but even more involve general conditions. By no means should there
be a settlement en route.

Furthermore, on this occasion the barbarian communications
were sent January 31, with the idea of asking for another Imperial
Commissioner in the absence of Yeh Ming-ch'en. At that time Kwangtung had not received the Imperial Edict degrading Yeh Ming-ch'en
and delegating Po-kuei to take over his duties. Now that it had arrived, he is of the opinion that their coming to Shanghai by March 31
is not necessarily certain, and even if they come according to schedule, it need only be explained adroitly that Your official is proceeding
to Canton by 24-hour stage to get them to return to Canton. If the barbarians do not .agree, they can do no more than use it as a pretext for
going to Tientsin.

The Shanghai customs are certainly the vital source of the Kiangnan war chest. Besides, being the vortex of trade with foreign countries
it is not likely that the barbarians would ever want to start trouble
there. Moreover, as he judges barbarian motives, embittered with
Yeh Ming-ch'en for keeping the requests they made in their communications from the knowledge of the Emperor, they made copies and appended them, still hoping for future Imperial Favors. For the present
they are not likely to intercept tribute grain and it would seem there
is no need of undue concern.

On the twenty-ninth, on board ship at Tan-yang, he received a
confidential Court Letter from the Grand Councillors that they had
received an Imperial Edict to order Your official to proceed at all
speed to make preliminary arrangements; and if in the country he
passes through there are any available troops, on the one hand to
memorialize and on the other to arrange to take them and on reaching Canton select a place to encamp them, and not thoughtlessly enter
the city. Respect this.

His Majesty's concern is most comprehensive and His official
must respectfully act accordingly. But at present the military situation in Kiangnan is that all government forces are besieging Nanking
and although (our position) has been consolidated on the north and

south, the attitude of the rebels is most ferocious. When he passed
through Ch'ang-chou, he heard Ho Kuei-ch'ing say that he feared
that forces were inadequate and was deeply concerned, so it was impossible to propose transfer of troops to him. Besides, whether or
not the English, American, and French barbarian chiefs will come to
Shanghai at the end of March is still uncertain so it would be inexpedient to transfer troops to hold Kwangtung and let them use it as a
pretext.

In Chekiang the defense of both Ningpo and Ch'u-chou is of strategic importance, but in the Ch'u-chou area there are several tens
of thousands of rebels who are just now closing in on Kuang-feng-
hsien, Kiangsi, which <u>hsien</u> adjoins Ch'u-chou in Chekiang. Your official, Governor Yen Tuan-shu has ordered the brigade general and
<u>tao-t'ai</u> to lead several thousand troops to its relief and also to defend
Ch'ang-shan. He has also expressed dispatches to both Fu-hsing and
Chang Fei to transfer government troops for a joint expedition. Thus
actually none of the Kiangsu-Chekiang forces can very well be transferred to Canton at present.

Your official has sent an express dispatch to Governor General
of Fukien-Chekiang Wang I-te; if the Chang-ch'uan area has any troops
available he is to mobilize them in advance, and when your official
passes through he will on the one hand take them with him and on the
other, report to the Throne. Otherwise, he can only respectfully follow Imperial Edict and, on entering Kwangtung, mobilize and enlist
Ch'ao [then Ch'ao-chou-fu, now Ch'ao-an-fu] and Chia [then Chia-ying
chou, now Mei-hsien] land and sea regulars and militia along the coast,
and station them in previously selected places, as well as assembling
trainbands of various districts, and secretly plan a campaign in order
to get the situation under control.

As to the Canton letters submitted by Lo Ping-chang, they were
written on February 2, and recount events of January. In Kiangsu,
Your official examined copies of letters received by Wang Yu-ling
from Cantonese merchants in Shanghai and copies of various letters
received by his secretary Pi Ch'eng-chao and others, no less than
twenty-odd in number. As they are all similar to those submitted by
Lo Ping-chang, there is no need to present them again. But in the
summary of barbarian affairs submitted by Expectant Prefect Yang
Ts'ung-lung, the narrative is rather lucid and there are also copies
of two letters from Cantonese merchants in Shanghai written since the
middle of January, which are somewhat different. These are respectfully copied in an appendix and respectfully submitted for Imperial
inspection.

Your official can only proceed posthaste and on reaching Canton,
taking precautions at every step, speedily assemble a number of
competent officials of the province to come to his aid, unite officials
and citizens, and act as occasion requires in the hope of meeting the

heavy responsibility imposed by his Sovereign. (IWSM.HF 19; 13a,
10-15b, 10)

264. April 6, 1858. MEMORANDUM: Narrative of Canton Events Prepared by an Expectant Prefect and Presented to the Court by Huang Tsung-
han.

Expectant Prefect Yang Ts'ung-lung submits a memorandum on
barbarian affairs in Kwangtung. During 1842 and 1843, barbarian affairs were settled and treaties negotiated for a fourteen-year [sic]
period. After seven years they were to enter the capital city of
Kwangtung (Canton). In the spring of 1849 the barbarians again
broached the subject of entrance to the city. At that time the governor general and governor, Hsü and Yeh, so rewarded and aroused the
gentry and rewarded the braves that popular sentiment formed an
effective barrier, determined to resist entrance. The English heard
reports and dropped the proposal. A memorial elicited an Imperial
Decree liberally rewarding gentry and officials and erecting p'ai-lous[2]
at the four corners of the city to commemorate the event.

In 1854, Red Turbans (bandits) and pirates sprang up on land
and sea. After a campaign of more than a year the affair was terminated but in annihilating the bandits, more than 47,000 were hunted
down and killed. In this number not a few innocent suffered. Stupid
people in their ignorance flocked to Hong Kong and Macao and sought
refuge as laborers on barbarian ships. In the fall of 1856, they were
still not all rounded up. On October 11, the chief runner of the P'an-
yü-hsien yamen, Chang Shun, arrested 16 bandits on board a barbarian
ship and turned them over to the office for trial and punishment.[3] The
English barbarians sent six or seven communications demanding these
men but His Excellency Yeh would not consent. Not until October 22,
when he heard that they were about to attack the city did he send Nan-
hai Assistant Prefect Hsü Wen-shen to deliver the arrested bandits
to the barbarian ship. The barbarians would not receive them so they
were brought back to P'an-yü and held in confinement.

Between the twenty-third and the twenty-sixth, they seized our
east and west forts; on the twenty-seventh and twenty-eighth, they set
fires and burned down more than 90 residences and shops outside
Ching-hai Gate and also cannonaded the governor general's compound
inside the wall. At this time His Excellency Yeh was also holding the
governor's seal, so he moved to the governor's compound. There

---

2 A *p'ai-lou* is a memorial arch erected to commemorate some meritorious act or great
   event, such as a Chinese victory over an enemy. The important feature of the
   p'ai-lou is the tablet bearing the characters *yü chih*, "by Imperial Decree." *Cf.*
   Couling's *Encyclopaedia Sinica*, p. 417.
3 This is another reference to the incident of the lorcha *Arrow*.

followed more than ten communications, all of which he ignored. On
November 4, the Lin braves recovered the east fort and then lost it
again, and it was levelled to the water. From November on, there
was daily cannonfire, sometimes several tens of shots, sometimes
less than ten and never more than about a hundred, so it was not of
much significance. On January 21, the foreign factories were burned
by our forces. The barbarians then used rockets to set fire to our
Mai-ma Street. Not until the end of the year (February 13, 1857)
when the government war-junks assembled did the barbarian ships
retire to Feng-huang-kang.

In the fifth month (May 23-June 21) of 1857, at Whampoa and
Ch'en-ts'un, they burned eighty percent of our fleet and after this it
was never restored. From this time on our maritime forces were
completely disbanded. Of the more than ten thousand land irregulars,
eighty percent were dispersed. The remainder, 700 Lin braves, 800
Tung braves, and several hundred Ch'ao braves, does not amount to
more than 2000 men.

At the beginning of the trouble, a Cantonese gentleman, Wu Ch'ung-
yüeh, and others agreed with the barbarians to set up a barbarian
office in Chang-shou Monastery so that in case of Sino-barbarian
trouble, they could meet there. His Excellency Yeh did not consent.
From about April to about September, Wu Ch'ung-yüeh repeatedly
asked for a prior opening of trade with the various countries but the
English barbarians wanted to wait until the trouble was settled and
then trade and His Excellency would not consent to this either.

At this juncture, France found a pretext to begin hostilities.
There suddenly arrived a communication saying that someone in China
whose name they did not know had killed one of their aged teachers[4]
and demanded the offender of His Excellency; that if he were not produced in three days they would attack the city. They joined the English
barbarians and on December 12 more than ten war steamers of the
two countries suddenly appeared flying white flags with the two characters "Cease Fighting" and delivered three communications demanding
five things: (1) entrance to the city; (2) the island of Ho-nan;
(3) treaty revision; (4) indemnification for war expenses; and (5)
trade; giving fourteen days for a reply and if any item were refused,
they would attack the city. On December 26, they extended the period
48 hours.

His Excellency replied, agreeing to trade but rejecting all the other
items. The Commissioners, tao-t'ai, and the two prefects all asked to
increase the braves on defense. His Excellency said that they (barbarians) could not be equalled on water where even if we had many troops
it would do no good, and he would give his bond that the barbarians would

---

4 This is another reference to Father Ma or the Abbé Chapdelaine.

never dare come on land; that if anyone wanted to increase troops or muster braves, let them raise money themselves; he would not author- ize the expenditure. Nor would he allow the garrison and banner troops to defend or even allow the gentry and people of the various wards to prepare defenses. Because of previous assessments the gentry were rather disorganized and because of subsequent skimpy rewards none of the trainband braves of the various wards were will- ing to exert themselves. And then he even issued orders that he would not allow any promiscuous killing of barbarians! On land or water there was not the least preparation.

To his amazement the English and French barbarians secretly gathered together several hundred rebels, concealed them in their ships and, on December 28, between 5 and 7 in the morning, opened fire. The sound was like thunder and bullets fell like rain; in the midst of it they dropped rockets and set fire to Shuang-men Ti, went straight for the Great South Gate and burned two-thirds of Ta-hsin Street. By the fourth watch (1-3 A.M.) on the twenty-eighth the barbarians had landed and pitched camp at Tung-chiao-ch'ang so that even though our headquarters proposed increasing the irregulars they did not arrive in time. By nine o'clock on the morning of the twenty-ninth, it was estimated that seven or eight thousand shrapnel shells had entered the city. The people fled in disorder westward, out of the city. Neither soldiers nor irregulars, officials nor gentry had any will to resist.

Between 7 and 9, the barbarians scaled the east wall with ladders. At first not more than a few tens entered, then as there was no one to oppose them, a great company came right in and occupied Kuan-yin Shan [Goddess of Mercy Hill], that is, Yüeh-hsiu Shan, and the various city gates. After the thirtieth, although Wu, P'an and other gentry and merchants made overtures the barbarians would not even listen.

On January 5, (1858), they suddenly appeared at the treasury, seized 227,000 taels and carried it to the barbarian ships; they also went to the governor's, Tartar General's, and lieutenant general's compounds and took the governor general, governor, and Tartar General to Kuan-yin Shan. On the seventh they took His Excellency on board a steamer and released the Tartar General. The governor was taken to his compound and cooperated with them in administration. The great hall and second hall were quartered with foreign devils; the third and fourth halls were occupied by Governor Po, and all officials had access to him.

On January 16, although various gentry and citizens offered to gather braves to attack the city to try to recover it, Governor Po sent word that anyone daring to find a pretext to raise volunteers would be court-martialled, so the proposals were shelved.

On February 10, the barbarians opened trade. After January 29, the gentry of 96 villages had posted red placards saying that they were going to attack the city, hence the barbarians changed the date [to the above].

At present Canton River, with the exception of Hua-ti, continues quiet. Outside the city there are only barbarian ships, our large privately owned ships still not daring to approach. Since January 5, Financial Commissioner Chiang has had his office at Chiu-tou-lan in the seventeenth Ward; Judicial Commissioner Chou, in the Ch'ang-shou Monastery in the Western Suburb; the Salt Controller and Grain Inten- dent at Shih-lu-k'ou in Fo-shan (Fatshan); Expectant Prefect Shen Pao-i is at the Fo-shan Trainband (headquarters) and the Finance Com- missioner has habitually gone to Fo-shan to confer with him; the Can- ton Customs was on Shih-pa-p'u (Eighteenth Street) but Kuang-chou Prefect Wu, about the middle of September (1857), had gone to Ch'ing- yüan on a bandit expedition and the provincial examiner had already set up examination booths at Nan- (ao), Shao- (chou) and Lien- (chou) Of Kwangtung officials capable of leading militia, only Expectant Pre- fect Liu Fu-sheng is outstanding, but alas, during the fall (the militia) was dispersed and practically abolished.

This is a general outline of things heard and seen in Canton prior to the end of January (1858). Respectfully submitted. (IWSM.HF 19; 16a, 1-19a, 3)

265. April 6, 1858. EDICT: Repeals Contradictory Instructions to the Canton Officials to Arouse the Populace and to Negotiate with the Foreign- ers.

Edict to the Grand Councillors. Yesterday was received a me- morial of Po-kuei and others reporting the state of barbarian affairs during the first month (February 14-March 14). The original document has been copied and sent to Huang Tsung-han for reference. Instruct him to hasten to Canton and act as occasion demands.

Today according to a memorial from Huang Tsung-han, when he reached Ch'ang-chou, Kiangsu, because Shanghai after all is not the place to handle barbarian affairs, he was afraid once he was detained, the barbarians would use coercion to gain their requests and thus create a disturbance in Kiangsu. His views are eminently correct. At present the said governor is already on his way from Chekiang. Since there are no available troops along his route, and the government forces of Fukien have been Imperially ordered transferred to relieve Kiangsi, it is feared there are none to spare. If in the Chang-(-chou) Ch'uan(-chou) area there are any trained braves, let him order them to accompany him. This will be an advantage. As Kwangtung is now without military equipment, he can also arrange to bring it from Fukien for use.

The copies of letters presented for examination contain the state- ment that Po-kuei prohibited volunteers. It is obvious that he was being coerced and could not but concede something to gain control. Later as

soon as the barbarians heard that villages were putting up red posters
they changed the date for opening the mart and the barbarian chiefs
even returned to Hong Kong, so they are still not without fear in their
hearts. When the said governor general reaches Canton he must
again utilize the strength of gentry and people. When he frightens
them with empty clamor he can make them have some dread.

Previously in the ninth month (September 29-October 28, of 1856)
the barbarians burned nine thousand of our peoples' houses. On this
occasion of their entering the city, the number again was not small.
Why not ask the barbarians how these are to be indemnified? If they
do not make unreasonable demands of China then this matter can
naturally be arranged differently; but if there continues to be talk of
replacing barbarian goods and demands for military indemnity, he
(Huang) has only to let gentry and merchants demand indemnity of
them, and when they all start making them trouble, not afford the barbarians any protection.

As for the barbarians resenting Yeh Ming-ch'en's rebuffs, getting angry and resorting to force, this in itself was a treaty violation.
Then after they entered the city, although Po-kuei appeased them in
every way, the barbarians plundered the treasury, released prisoners,
took over war material in the garrison, and acted altogether like robbers. Besides, intentionally insulting China by having their chair
bearers wear red buttons and peacock feathers [official insignia] was
even more obnoxious. We hear that this is all Harry Parkes' doing.
These barbarians have assaulted a city because Yeh Ming-ch'en was
overbearing and allow their national, Harry Parkes, this defiance of
right! What punishment does he deserve? How is it we have not heard
of his punishment? This kind of material can be used to argue with
them.

As to Po-kuei's present trade arrangement, it was Wu Ch'ung-
yüeh who intermediated. Although this gentleman is thoroughly
familiar with barbarian affairs, he is after all a hong merchant and
has many connections with barbarians so his plans cannot be entirely
relied upon. If secrecy is called for, negotiation and decision must be
by the governor general himself. It is important not to disclose them
in advance. (IWSM.HF 19; 19a, 4-20a, 5)

266. April 8, 1858. MEMORIAL: Ho Kuei-ch'ing Reports the Determin
ation of the Envoys to Proceed to Tientsin and Urges an Imperial Commission to Negotiate.

Governor General of Liang-chiang Ho Kuei-ch'ing and Governor
of Kiangsu Chao Te-ch'e memorialize. The English and American
chiefs arrived at Shanghai on March 26, and the various barbarian ship
fired cannon to welcome them, the reverberations continuing to shake
our ear drums for more than an hour. Hsüeh Huan and the others
remained as if they had heard nothing, meeting the situation with calm-

ness. On the 27th, the chiefs conferred and there is a rumor that they are unwilling to return to Kwangtung and, as soon as the French chief arrives, will start trouble at Shanghai.

Wu Chien-chang, knowing that whatever the barbarians did they always first inquired of the barbarian merchants, acting only when they were of the same mind; (and also knowing) that the barbarian merchants had come a long and arduous way for the objective of profit and were all concerned about their investments, (he) there-fore sought means to explain suitably to these barbarian merchants, as well as to spy out what the real intentions of the barbarian chiefs were, and whether or not any more barbarian ships were coming later on. Hsüeh Huan also sent reliable men to spy around secretly and their information has been collated. The consensus is that the French barbarians have no great concern with trade, but are active in propa-gating Catholicism, but that their soldiers are able and their cannon effective and whenever any western country takes up arms against anyone, these barbarians hire themselves out to assist them, collect-ing payment for their subsistence.

Since the opening of the five ports to trade, the English barbarians have collected every year on tea, pongee, Ma-la-hua,[5] and other items, gross duties of more than 4,000,000 taels, used to defray military ex-penses for their arbitrary acts in China and elsewhere. Now that they are illegally holding Kwangtung their military expenses are multiplied, and they are anxious to open trade and collect duties. They were really afraid that the arrival of the Imperial Commissioner at Canton would be delayed. So on March 10 they opened the mart at Canton to pacify the hearts of the barbarian soldiers, and came to Shanghai to negotiate. They hoped for a speedy termination, (so they could) de-mobilize troops and stop expenses.

Then when they reached Shanghai, since the Imperial Commissioner had passed Kiangsu for Kwangtung, pursuing a slow route, they did not know when or where to negotiate. Unable to meet their military ex-penses, they would naturally give vent to their animal [dog-sheep] instincts and cause trouble in Shanghai, and then figure that after cre-ating a disturbance, if there still were no Imperial Commissioners to negotiate they would have to go to Tientsin. This would take a long time so they have decided to go to Tientsin as soon as the French chief ar-rives and implore His Imperial Majesty's Favor. If they do not meet Imperial Approval, they will create incidents at Tientsin and along the river and coast, before we can get our hand in, to get what they want.

Up to March 28, nine English, American, and Russian warships and steamers had arrived, drawing variously from four to seven feet

---

5   *Malwa* was a common trade name for opium. The text does not distinguish export and import items.

of water. It is reported that the French chief has now gone to the
Philippines to borrow warships and that, counting them altogether,
there will be forty or fifty, carrying four or five thousand barbarian
soldiers.

Your officials find that heretofore when barbarian chiefs arrived
at port, the tao-t'ai of Su-Sung-T'ai was always notified by their respective consuls and a date fixed for their coming to call. When they
came this time they first fired cannon to awe us. Not only did they
not notify the tao-t'ai of Su-Sung-T'ai, but they have not even answered
the communication of Your officials promptly. Their nature is certainly inscrutable. Hsüeh Huan and Wu Chien-chang have constantly
watched conditions and although there is much of false-alarm threatening, still the barbarians, on account of onerous military expenses, are
anxious to open trade and unwilling to return to Canton, and we fear
that the talk of wanting to go to Tientsin is not entirely baseless. Your
officials have sent express letters to Hsüeh Huan and Wu Chien-chang
to make suitable explanations; but it is really feared that the barbarian
chiefs, without either responding or seeing them, will eventually go
to Tientsin.

Anytime after March 22, the tribute rice (barges) will be at
Shih-hsiao on Ch'ung-ming (Island) and will take advantage of winds
and one after the other, set sail for Tientsin. Although the crews
know that they are to run for cover if they meet a foreign ship, if
this should happen when they are in port or where there is no island
for refuge, there would really be something to worry about. Before
interior bandits are subdued, border troubles have again developed.
Should the barbarians display their wantonness at Tientsin and along
the coast and river, it would be particularly difficult to manage.

Your officials venture to think that since the barbarians drew
arms and opposed authority at Canton but have not ventured to display
their arrogance at Amoy, Foochow, Ningpo, or even Shanghai, it is
because they still have some qualms of conscience. To see if we can
take advantage of this to our advantage, it is requested that an Imperial
Edict be issued to the governor general of Chihli, if the barbarian
ships come to Tientsin, to devise suitable means to manage them
temporarily, and on the other hand Imperially Commission a high official thoroughly familiar with barbarian affairs to settle general
matters with them at first hand, getting them to restore the city and
cease hostilities, and then order them to go to Kwangtung to make
suitable treaty arrangements separately, utilizing this to maintain
national prestige and avoid hostilities.

In addition, according to a secret report of Wu Chien-chang, in the
barbarian trade the three items, tea, pongee silk and Ma-la-hua form
the bulk. When negotiations take place, naturally a heavy duty should
be placed on these articles while on other items it can be reduced or
removed, by juggling the duties around there can be a positive gain

without any loss. Just now when military needs are multifarious,
must we not act adventitiously? We respectfully await Imperial Decision. (IWSM.HF 19; 20a, 5-22b, 2)

267. April 8, 1858. EDICT: Orders Special Treatment of the Russian
and American Envoys as Distinguished from the British and French.
    Edict to the Grand Councillors. Today a memorial of Ho Kuei-
ch'ing and Chao Te-ch'e has been received that the English and
American chiefs arrived at Shanghai on March 26, and intended as
soon as the French chief arrived to go to Tientsin; that up to the
twenty-eighth, nine English, American, and Russian warships and
steamers had arrived and it was reported that the French chief had
gone to the Philippines to borrow warships, which they estimated
would bring (the total) up to forty or fifty ships and four or five
thousand barbarian soldiers; they asked that orders be given the
governor general of Chihli, if the barbarians arrived at Tientsin, to
find means to handle them.
    The rebel barbarians came to Shanghai and finding that Imperial
Commissioner Huang Tsung-han had passed through Kiangsu, wanted
to come direct to Tientsin. The communications of Ho Kuei-ch'ing
and others, moreover, were not answered immediately. Their atti
tude is certainly inscrutable. The port defenses of Tientsin have
been secretly arranged by T'an T'ing-hsiang but if the barbarians
come to Tientsin they will not necessarily immediately start trouble.
Today, Ch'ung-lun has been sent to Tientsin to take charge of ocean
transport (of tribute rice). Order (T'an T'ing-hsiang) to send word
to Financial Commissioner Ch'ien Hsin-ho to proceed posthaste to
Tientsin for a full discussion with Ch'ung-lun.
    Last year when the Russian chief came to Tientsin, his papers
were not received at first, but afterwards Wen-ch'ien and others went
to receive them. If on this occasion of the barbarians' arrival, Ch'ien
Hsin-ho and the others rush out to meet them, it is feared the Russian
barbarians would have a pretext, so at first some competent officers
must be sent to say that as the Kwangtung high official managed badly,
His Imperial Majesty has appointed another Imperial Commissioner
to Kwangtung to investigate and manage; that it is also reported that
Acting Governor General Po-kuei, at the earnest request of the various
countries, has authorized trade and if they will go there a fair discussion and reasoned settlement can be had; that Tientsin is not a
treaty port, nor is there any official assigned to handle barbarian
affairs, so no negotiations can be conducted here. See what their reaction is and memorialize for instructions.
    As to the Russians' presenting a public document last year pur-
porting to oppose the English barbarians and now joining those same
barbarians in their infamy, their hearts are even more hypocritical.
But there has been Sino-Russian friendship for more than a hundred

years without any cleavage,[6] quite different from (our own experiences with) the English and French barbarians. Their treatment must
also be somewhat different. If Poutiatine is received he must be
treated affably and told that as there is a long record of friendship,
he need not associate himself with unjust acts of England and France.

The American barbarians in Kwangtung never helped the evildoers and can be congratulated for their fidelity to make them grateful and submissive. If we first separate the Russian and American
chiefs to prevent their helping the rebels, the position of the English
and French will be isolated. Then we can look over their demands
and negotiate advantageously.

The crime of the English barbarians is unpardonable; the French
barbarians have joined in their evil and are also detestable but at
present China is unsettled and (tribute) transport is by sea, so once
there is trouble there will be much obstruction. We cannot but plan
to be lenient with those from afar as a means of keeping them under
control. Chang Tien-yüan and Ta-nien are now making secret defenses without any outward indication. If the barbarian ships come,
they must then deploy many troops and make a noisy display to prevent the barbarians belittling us. That the said governor general
also order local officials to prohibit unscrupulous people along the
coast from private trade with them and from furnishing them food,
is essential. (IWSM.HF 19; 22b, 3-23b, 8)

268. April 8, 1858. EDICT: Orders Coastal Officials along the Route
to Tientsin to Forbid Local Trade with the Foreign Ships.

Additional Edict. Today has been received from Ho Kuei-ch'ing
and Chao Te-ch'e a memorial of secret findings on barbarian affairs,
saying that the English, American, and Russian chiefs had agreed
that they were unwilling to return to Kwangtung and when the French
chief arrived they would go to Tientsin to implore Imperial Favor.
If they did not meet with approval they would cause trouble at Tientsin and along the river and coast. The said governor general and
others have sent express communications to Fengtien and Chihli
provinces as well as ordering various coastal garrisons to make
rigorous defense.

The said barbarians now have nine warships and steamers and
it is reported that the French chief has gone to the Philippines to
borrow warships, estimated (to total) some forty or fifty, carrying
four or five thousand barbarian soldiers. Although these are empty
threats to facilitate their demands, since there is the report, it is
hard to guarantee that it is baseless. Fengtien is an important
coastal position and must be rigorously prepared to prevent regrets

---

6 Russia and China signed the Treaty of Nerchinsk in 1689 and the Treaty of Kiakhta in 17

for laxness.

Order Ch'ing-ch'i and Hsi-la-pu to instruct various officers
along the coast to make secret defense preparations at various strategic ports, without any outward indications. If any barbarian ships
arrive, strictly prohibit the coastal inhabitants' supplying them food
or trading privately with them and on the other hand take precautionary measures. Let there not be the least confusion. This is most
essential. (IWSM.HF 19; 23b, 10-24a, 9)

269. April 12, 1858. MEMORIAL: T'an T'ing-hsiang Reports in Detail
on the Military Preparations in the Ta-ku and Tientsin Areas.

Acting Governor General of Chihli T'an T'ing-hsiang memorializes. In the matter of Tientsin coastal defense, Your official has
obeyed Imperial Edict and managed secretly. At the present time
Acting Brigade General Ta-nien has gone personally to the port and
Commander-in-chief Chang Tien-yüan should soon reach Tientsin.

As to the necessary officers and men, the special regiment was
originally proposed for transfer to the fort on the north shore, half
of which original contingent of 700 men has been ordered from the
territorial regiment to cross the river first and take up position, the
half from the brigade to be transferred gradually. Besides this, there
are still left one thousand and several hundred soldiers of the original
command of the colonel at Ta-ku, specially charged to defend the south
bank. Separate orders have been sent the Tientsin brigade general to
select 1500 men, choose their officers, prepare military supplies, and
await transfer. At the port of Pei-t'ang near Ta-ku, the T'ung-yung
brigade general has also been ordered to send a force of 300 men to
Pei-t'ang to defend the fort and have another 500 to 700 men ready for
transfer. In addition, Expectant Tao-t'ai Ch'un-pao is appointed to go
and assist in arrangements.

As to the Tientsin trainbands, Salt Controller Wu-lo-hung-e along
with the brigade general, the tao-t'ai, and the tao-t'ai in mourning for
a parent, Fei Yin-chang, have already sent invitations to gentry and
merchants Huang Shen-wu, Chia Chao-lin, Hua Shang-lin, Chang Chin-
wen, Wang Chia-hsi, Liang Feng-chi and Hsiao Chen, on the one hand
to exhort (the populace) to action and on the other to take subscriptions.
We may expect to tranquilize popular opinion and get real results.

The requisite Ta-ku pontoon bridge has been prepared following
the decision of the brigade general and tao-t'ai. In the matter of requisition and collection of supplies, Your official has ordered Expectant
Tao-t'ai Chen-lin, Expectant Prefect Ch'ang-chi and the prefect of
Ts'ang-chou, Pien Pao-shu, who went on board the barbarian ships last
year, whether managing transport, registering merchant ships, or repairing barracks, to act under cover.

There is now received the Imperial Edict appointing Ch'ien Hsin-ho
to proceed; he can carry the load with ease and confidence and all

things will be properly handled. In this crisis, Your official could but plan carefully and urge his commissioners meticulously to respect Imperial instructions to consider being lenient to those from afar as a means of controlling them, while making rigorous defense plans with the general-in-chief and brigade general, and to deploy many troops for a noisy display to keep the barbarians from belittling us, that he might meet the Sovereign's supreme desire to tranquillize the ocean frontier.

Vermilion Endorsement: Memorial read and comprehended. (IWSM.HF 19; 26b, 1-27b, 2)

270. April 13, 1858. MEMORIAL: The Chihli Provincial Commander Recommends Detail to Improve the Defense of Tientsin.

General-in-chief of Chihli Chang Tien-yüan memorializes. In Accord with the Imperial Edict to defend the ocean frontier, it can be said that south of the prefectural capital (Tientsin) there is Ma-chia-k'ou connecting the city with the sea by land and water routes. He proposes utilizing this for a flanking route from the sea, placing an artillery base here and stationing troops.

Vermilion Endorsement: Noted. (IWSM.HF 19; 27b, 3-6)

271. April 15, 1858. MEMORIAL: Ho Kuei-ch'ing Reports a Concentration of Naval Force, Analyzes the Four Powers, and Advises on Tientsin Negotiations.

Governor General of Liang-chiang Ho Kuei-ch'ing and Governor of Kiangsu Chao Te-ch'e memorialize. According to various reports of Su-Sung-T'ai Tao-t'ai Hsüeh Huan, on March 30 the French chief also arrived at Shanghai on board a three-masted steam warship. Their movements are kept very secret but false stories abound. There are rumors that they intend to intercept the ocean transport (of tribute rice) and stop customs payments in order to demand the establishment of a port at Hankow, and that they will go to Hu-chou (in Chekiang) and Ch'ung-an to buy pongees. The people are very apprehensive and local bandits are itching to be on the move.

Your officials flashed word to Hsüeh Huan to collaborate with Expectant Tao-t'ai Wu Chien-chang to send word to various barbarian merchants that should these moves be made, Chinese merchants would be forbidden to ship goods to Shanghai or to transport foreign goods inland, and when Shanghai trade was cut off, the unemployed would be deprived of all resources, their investments of several millions would certainly be subject to plunder, and they should not do something they would regret; that they had traded peacefully here for more than ten years and we could not but tell them this in advance. The barbarian merchants felt grateful for the warning and the false stories ceased. Then we ordered Transport Headquarters to receive and ship tribute rice immediately, as soon as a ship was loaded to rush it out to sea for

Shih hsiao, Ch'ung-ming. At present collections are seventy percent
complete.

Hsüeh Huan also told the barbarian consuls that heretofore when
their envoys came, visits were exchanged and as this time there had
been no intercourse, the procedure seemed unfriendly, in order to slow
down their procedure. The English, American and French barbarians
answered that sometime later they would set a date for an interview,
but the Russian barbarians first sent a secretary, Ming-ch'ang[7] to the
tao-t'ai's office to agree on a time for an interview with the barbarian
chief Poutiatine at a public place. At the appointed time Hsüeh Huan
went with elaborate retinue and formality. The barbarians received
and dismissed him with cannon-fire and band music and were very
respectful and compliant. The conversation consisted of pleasantries
about the weather, so Hsüeh Huan left without being able to talk with
them seriously.

The English consul, Robinson, accompanied by his country's naval
commander Sawyer, and lieutenant commander Lo-pi,[8] came to the
Su-Sung-T'ai tao-t'ai's office on April 6 and presented a communication to Your officials and also returned our previous reply ordering
them to return to Canton, enclosing a communication addressed to
Grand Secretary Yü-ch'eng. They said they intended going north immediately and nothing more.

Privately it has been learned that the English chief's name is
Elgin, the American chief, Reed, and the French chief, Gros, and that
during the night of the fifth one English warship weighed anchor and
put to sea, going ahead to chart the course; that on the sixth two more
left for Tientsin; that the rest of the ships were scheduled to follow
the English barbarians north on the afternoon of the seventh; and that
altogether there are ten warships and steamers of various sizes,
carrying perhaps one thousand, several hundred barbarian soldiers.
It is also reported that the English barbarians have another high
military leader in command of several vessels who will go by sea
direct to Tientsin without calling at Shanghai.

Your officials humbly observe that the four chiefs who have come
with joined masts to Shanghai have acted very obstreperously. The
English barbarians actually returned Your officials' reply ordering
them to go back to Canton and await a settlement, and went direct to
the north. Neither the American and French barbarians have replied.
Their attitude is indeed detestable. It is reported that the English barbarians have come after a decision was reached in their country; that
the French barbarians are in their pay and will join them in making
trouble; that the Americans and Russians are taking advantage of the

---

7 The name of this person has not been identified from the Chinese transliteration.
8 The name of this British officer has not been identified.

strife to follow in their wake hoping for benefits gratis. They (the Americans and Russians) are crafty and fraudulent in the extreme. On examining the (English) communication to Grand Secretary Yü-ch'eng, there are no improper expressions, but they regard the fact that "ministers have no intercourse with foreigners" as a slight to them and use this as an excuse for wanting to go to Tientsin. It is obvious that although these barbarians are mercenary they have an air of false pride and are afraid that others will belittle them. May we not beg Your Majesty, with Heavenly grace, to seize this wedge to formulate a plan and send an Imperial Commissioner to Tientsin to flatter them a little, discuss the general situation with them personally, and then send them back to Canton in order to avoid other complications?

Your officials, after opening and reading the English barbarians' communication to Grand Secretary Yü-ch'eng, inasmuch as these barbarians returned their communication, felt that if they again transmitted one for them they would become even more arrogant, and so instructed the tao-t'ai of Su-Sung-T'ai to return it to the barbarians. (IWSM.HF 20; 2b, 2-4b, 1)

272. April 15, 1858. MEMORIAL: Ho Kuei-ch'ing Dissipates False Military Hopes and Urges Appeasement of the British and Alienation of the Russians and Americans.

Ho Kuei-ch'ing and others further memorialize. It is humbly recalled that at the end of the first and beginning of the second month (March 4-5 circa), newly appointed Governor General of Liang-kuang Huang Tsung-han passed through Soochow and Ch'ang-chou and Your officials discussed barbarian affairs with him. He said that he was afraid he would have to fight first and conciliate afterwards, and as Kiangsu and Chekiang formed Kwangtung's rear line, in the future his troops and supplies would have to be borrowed from there.

Your officials think that fighting first and conciliating afterward is no easy matter. At present in eleven provinces, Hunan, Hupeh, and Fukien being only recently tranquillized and the spirit of rebellion not far off, mobilization and deployment are frequent, and besides, there is always the fear of reoccurrence. Although Chekiang is considered completely restored, soldiers are mobilized and braves assembled to defend against Kiangsi and Fukien on the southwest, and Kiangsu and Anhwei on the northwest. On the east is the broad ocean and the trading port of Ningpo, where the local bandits are always itching to be on the move, so with fending without and pacifying within it is almost like the provinces which are fighting. Moreover, in the north the Nien-fei[9] appear and disappear along the Anhwei-Honan border

9 The Nien-fei were troops of mounted bandits and rebels, independent of the Taipings. They ravaged the northern provinces from 1853 onward. Nien means "twisted" and the name is supposed to derive from the coiled turbans worn by the rebels.

attacked in the east they flee west, suppressed in the south they rise
in the north. In the event of another coastal conflict, interior banditry
and external grief will both be upon us and how will we handle them?
So much for the state of the empire.

Turning to the state of barbarian affairs, although Your officials
are not thoroughly versed, the past can be studied. In the Tao-kuang
period, when Lin (Tse-hsü) and Hsü (Kuang-chin) held the office of
governor general, their ability and energy were enough to control the
barbarians. As there was no outlet for barbarian schemes, they used
their chicanery to oppose us at Ting-hai and from then on their actions
were unpredictable; they were in arms several years; no place along
the rivers or coasts but felt their violence and Kiangsu suffered especially. Not until after the five ports were opened to trade was it
terminated.

Now the barbarians have repudiated treaties, occupied our (provincial) capital city, abducted our high official and every red-blooded
man is gnashing his teeth in bitter anger, wanting to eat their flesh
and use their hide for blankets. The Cantonese are naturally quick-
tempered and mercenary. At the beginning of the occupation, before
the barbarians had strengthened their position, popular fury was such
that if anyone bared his arm and gave one whoop, followers would
certainly have taken up the echo and, wiping out their ugly kind, recovered the city as easy as a twist of the wrist. Now that it has been
put off for three months, it is reported that the barbarians have re-
built the forts within and without the city and have a strangle hold on
strategic positions. The Tartar General and governor under duress
issued notices to dissipate popular feeling and opened the mart to trade,
so while public spirit is starved, public greed is gratified. Even if a
public-spirited gentry and a law-abiding people were to arouse popular
indignation all day long, there is no one competent to do the fighting.
It is greatly feared that the good people of Canton now are not to be
relied on as they were a few months ago.

Someone has said that if we seize their Hong Kong lair, we would
not have to worry about their restoring the provincial capital, so Your
officials made a careful inquiry. Hong Kong is suspended in the open
sea and the barbarians' patrol and defense are rigorous. If our troops
go with rifles and cannon, they will intercept them with steamers and
warships and certainly prevent their landing; and if they go empty-
handed, how are they to meet rifles and cannon? So much for the state
of public morale in Canton.

If we send Chekiang's able officers and skilled troops away on a
punitive expedition, not only is the attack of Nanking hanging in the balance and cannot be relaxed and San-ch'u a most important place whose
defense cannot be neglected, but also with the long journey over land
and sea the soldiers would be exhausted and rations would not be forthcoming. Even if we speedily collected funds, rushed to Kwangtung and,

relying on our Holy Sovereign's Heavenly fortune, proclaimed victory at the first beat of the drum, we fear that the barbarians, having at this time received the Grand Secretary's letter ordering them to return to Kwangtung and await settlement, on receiving this chastisement would certainly come back to Shanghai and, saying that we had broken our promise, take up arms against us to work off their spleen. While Shanghai would be the first to suffer, other places along the rivers and coasts would be sure to fend and fend in vain. Chekiang and Kiangsu provinces would have no troops to mobilize, no supplies to commandeer, and if they were then to ask help from Canton, it would be too late. Even if Kwangtung took up arms we could hardly be sure of success, and if we remained deadlocked or even suffered some losses, the barbarians' situation would be even better and a reversal even harder. The bandits in various parts are also about to swarm. Even if Shanghai is fortunate enough to escape trouble, the source of supplies will be cut off, then with the fate of our great Nanking force sealed, how dare we ask about the empire? So much for Kiangsu and Chekiang's inability to furnish Kwangtung with troops and supplies.

Given these three conditions, the present policy for the management of barbarian affairs is self-evident: employ soft to manage hard; devise means to manage in accord with Imperial Edict; and not talk promiscuously about going to war.

Now the English, American, French, and Russian barbarians have joined masts and come to Shanghai, and their prowess is very great. If we had not agreed with Wu Chien-chang to use the plan of pulling the fire from under the pot, diminishing somewhat their arrogance, Your official could not even bear to think of (the outcome). Under the circumstances their going to Tientsin can hardly be prevented, but kowtowing at the gate and asking for Imperial Edicts is the common practice of outside barbarians begging mercy. It is humbly requested that Your Majesty's Heavenly Favor condescend, as His officials have requested, to appoint an Imperial Commissioner to meet them, flatter them a little so that they will have no quarrel to pick, settle general conditions by negotiation to get them to cease hostilities and restore the (provincial) capital, and then tell them to return to Canton and discuss treaty provisions separately, in order to relieve the immediate crisis. When internal banditry is somewhat settled and provisions are abundant, after sleeping on firewood and sipping gall [so as not to forget vengeance], and selecting and training naval forces, then will be the time to seize an opportunity to overcome our country's enemies and mete out Heavenly punishment.

Now we hear that the countries at present trading with us are actually legion, not limited to just England, America, and France; that while the five ports were established by the English barbarians, the American barbarians have been able to plant their own flag and renounce English domination; that the French barbarians, as the mother country of Catholicism, came to China earlier than the English and Americans and so claim precedence for themselves; that all the countries coming to China to trade are distributed under the names of these three barbarians and fly their flags so these three barbarians levy heavy taxes on their goods, ten or twenty times the amount of our customs, as a means of mustering soldiers and vying for precedence; that in general the English barbarians get seven-tenths, the Americans get three-tenths, so the French barbarians do not even get one-tenth and because of this discrepancy in profits, although united when there is trouble, when there is no trouble they cannot get along at all; also that Russian barbarians trading at the five ports under the auspices of the English barbarians for years have resented the heavy exactions of the English barbarians, but never having received a grant from the Heavenly Court did not dare establish their own wharves and hence their earnest request for intercourse.

It is noted that the Russian barbarians' previous presentation of a communication to the Grand Council was enclosed in American barbarian papers and not in the English barbarian papers. This is clear evidence that the English and Americans cannot get along and that the Russians have left the English and approached the Americans. As dogs and sheep are naturally inconstant, it should not be hard to separate them and, using barbarians to control barbarians, sow mutual disaffection and gradually weaken them.

If we used only this means of controlling them, the fall of one would mean the certain ascendancy of another, so this is not a good policy. What the barbarians rely on are strong ships and efficient cannon. Our government ships can hardly meet them in battle. We have only to seize what they rely on and turn it to our advantage, to be able to determine their life or death. Since these barbarians care only for profits, even their strongest and most effective things should not be hard to buy for a heavy price. If, when our innate vigor is adequate, we use the plan of playing one against another and buying their ships and cannon, supporting the weak ones so that they will help us, weeding out the strong so that they will not dare run wild, then barbarian troubles will be quieted and frontier strife suppressed.

From the present viewpoint, this seems to be the situation but if subsequently the situation is changed, we cannot speak dogmatically. So it is up to the Imperial Commissioner in charge of barbarian affairs in the five ports to consider the general situation comprehensively, moving as occasion demands, and not be concerned merely with the one province of Kwangtung. Then however clever these barbarians are, they will accomplish nothing.

Vermilion Endorsement: This memorial is very lucid. (IWSM.HF 20; 4b, 2-8a, 5)

273. <u>April 15, 1858</u>. <u>EDICT</u>: <u>Orders Ch'ung-lun to Negotiate at Ta-
ku and Shanghai Officials to Strengthen their Defenses.</u>
        Edict to the Grand Councillors. Ho Kuei-ch'ing and others have
memorialized that the barbarian chiefs did not accept their explanation and have gone direct to Tientsin; they also secretly report that
the present management of barbarian affairs calls for temporary
postponment of hostilities. His memorial is very lucid. Today a
memorial is received from Wu-lo-hung-e and others that on April 13
two Russian steamers, one large and one small, came to Tientsin,
saying that they had favorable matters to discuss and that the said
Salt Controller had delegated an officer to go and make inquiries.
Orders have been given Ch'ung-lun, accompanied by Financial Commissioner Ch'ien Hsin-ho, to go and elucidate, watching their movements and managing accordingly.
        Shanghai is an important centre for ocean transport and customs,
particularly unsuited to war purposes; but as the barbarians talk of
wanting to go to Hu-chou and Ch'ung-an, we cannot but make secret
defense. The said governor general must outwardly show leniency
and not let any clues leak out, but on the other hand prepare selected
places to guard against a barbarian change of heart. (IWSM.HF 20;
8a, 6-8b, 3)

274. <u>April 15, 1858.</u> <u>EDICT</u>: <u>Orders Preliminary Talks with the
Russians Giving Assurances that the Defenses are against the British
and French.</u>
        Additional Edict. Today a memorial is received from Ho Kuei-
ch'ing and others that the various barbarian ships at Shanghai, from
April 5-7, sailed for Tientsin; that altogether there were 10 warships coming to Tientsin. There is also received a memorial from
Wu-lo-hung-e and others that on the thirteenth a Russian war steamer
came to the seven-armspread depth outside the Bar to present an official document, and that they had delegated an officer to go and make
inquiries.
        As the Russian barbarian ship, before reaching Tientsin, said that
there were favorable matters to discuss personally, naturally they are
not likely to start hostilities immediately and only want to intrude
their mediation, hoping to profit from their position. As the said
Salt Controller and others have sent an officer there, order him to
talk to them suitably and find out what their intentions are. If their
proposal is not just a blind for the English and French barbarians or
if there is nothing detrimental to the general scene, order him to
memorialize secretly and quickly and await an Edict for decision.
        As to mobilizing troops and assembling militia, if these barbari-
ans detect it, tell them that it is being done entirely on account of the
English and French; that China has been friendly with the (Russian)
barbarians for years and will by no means resort to war.

Ch'ung-lun has been ordered to leave immediately and Ch'ien Hsin-ho should have reached Tientsin. Order T'an T'ing-hsiang to leave his capital at once and either establish his residence in the prefectural capital of Tientsin or stay temporarily some place near Tientsin and subsequently when Ch'ung-lun arrives, they can memorialize jointly on the ground. If there are important matters of mobilization or defense the said acting governor general will be in more convenient calling distance. However, he need not go personally to the port, thus avoiding barbarian demands for interviews. (IWSM. HF 20; 8b, 5-9a, 7)

275. April 15, 1858. EDICT: Orders Mongol Cavalry to Proceed to Shanhaikwan to Defend it against Possible Foreign Attack.

Additional Edict. Today a memorial is received from Ho Kuei ch'ing and others that the English and other barbarian chiefs intend to proceed from Shanghai to Tientsin and have already weighed anchor.

Shanhaikwan is an important place and it is vitally important to prepare defenses. Order Hsi-ling-a to select a crack cavalry corps of 2000 from the troops at Chahar and equip them with uniforms and arms; then order the said military lieutenant governor to take personal command and proceed immediately by way of Mi-yün to Shanhaikwan and act as occasion demands. He need not go by way of Peking.

At present the Peking regiment is in need of horses, so order him to select 2000 from contributions [as tribute] at Chahar and during the fourth month (May 13-June 10) send them by easy stages to Peking to be ready for use. After Hsi-ling-a leaves, order Ch'ing-yün to take over the seal and duties of military lieutenant governor of Chahar. (IWSM.HF 20; 9a, 8-9b, 5)

276. April 15, 1858. EDICT: Orders Peking Troops to Shantung to Protect the Route between Shanghai and Tientsin.

Additonal Edict. Order Kuo-jui, Chu-lo-heng and Fu-lo-tun-t'ai to determine and take command of a suitable number of Peking troops and proceed to the Shantung area to suppress bandits and protect the (Yellow) river banks. (IWSM.HF 20; 9b, 7-8)

277. April 16, 1858. EDICT: Orders Manchurian Military Officials to take Measures to Defend Shanhaikwan.

Edict to the Grand Councillors. Yesterday a memorial was received from Ho Kuei-ch'ing and others that the barbarian ships at Shanghai have successively sailed for Tientsin; that there are altogether 10 warships and steamers and later there will be several more barbarian ships. A memorial was also received from Wu-lo-hung-e and others that on April 13, a Russian barbarian steamer came to the seven-armspread depth outside the Bar to present an official document.

On this occasion the English and French barbarians defied authority

in Kwangtung and then with the Russian and American barbarians
left for Tientsin by way of Shanghai. Primarily, this is nothing but
an empty threat to implement their demands, but barbarian mentality is inscrutable so we cannot but take precautions. Shanhaikwan
is on the route the barbarian ships must take for Tientsin and so
must be prepared.

     Order Ting-fu to supervise the officers at that place and work
out secret defense without giving any outward indication. Let there
be no laxness. If funds are needed order him to instruct Superintendent Ch'ing-ch'un to estimate and supply the necessary amount from
customs receipts. (IWSM.HF 20; 9b, 10-10a, 7)

Chapter 10

Reed and Treaty Revision at Tientsin, 1858
(Documents 278-378)

After the preliminary sparring at Canton and Shanghai, the negotiations for treaty revision were finally carried out at Tientsin. One hundred
and one documents, dated from April 17, 1858, to July 9, 1858, cover
this important period. Of this large number of documents, fifty-eight
are memorials and thirty-six are edicts, all but three of the latter being
addressed to the grand councillors.

The personal interest of the emperor is attested by fourteen vermilion endorsements. Four of these are the laconic chih-tao-la ("Noted")
scrawled at the end of memorials, two more are formal acknowledgments,
but several are specific and detailed comments on the subject matter of
the memorials. In addition, there is one vermilion edict personally
written by the emperor. This autograph edict pronounces sentence on
Ch'i-ying, calling for his death by suicide. In addition to the usual memorials and edicts, new types of documents are included in this chapter,
indicating that China's foreign relations are assuming new importance
and developing new techniques. There are elaborate instructions issued
by the Grand Council to the Chinese commissioners charged with the negotiations; foreign memoranda, including American and Russian, are reproduced; the letter of President James Buchanan to the Emperor of
China is reproduced in Chinese and here retranslated into English; and
finally, the testimony and charges against the tragic figure of the aged
Ch'i-ying are incorporated to record the denouement of the drama of
China's first "foreign minister."

The principal memorialists of this period are divided into three
groups. The most important, of course, are the Tientsin negotiators.
Preliminary negotiations were carried out by Ch'ang-lu Salt Controller
Wu-lo-hung-e and Chihli Financial Commissioner Ch'ien Hsin-ho, under
the supervision of the governor general of Chihli [Hopei], T'an T'ing-
hsiang. To this group were added Ch'ung-lun, now superintendent of
imperial granaries, and Wu-erh-kun-t'ai, sub-chancellor of the Grand
Secretariat. The final negotiations were carried out by Imperial Commissioners Kuei-liang and Hua-sha-na. The second group of memorialists is that set up to try Ch'i-ying, headed by I-hsin Prince Kung of the
imperial clan court, and including Prince Hui, Prince I, and Prince Cheng.
The third group comprises miscellaneous memorialists like Ho Kuei-
ch'ing from the Shanghai scene, Lo Tun-yen from Canton, and Wang Mao-
yin and Yün Shih-lin, both representing opinions at the court in Peking.

The content of this important chapter is the bifurcated expedition
to the North, with Great Britain and France as military allies determined

to exert whatever force was necessary to secure wholesale treaty revision and extension, and with Russia and the United States thrown together because of their separate instructions to remain neutral and to
secure whatever treaty revision could be effected by peaceful means.
Britain and France were represented by Lord Elgin and Baron Gros, respectively. The Russian envoy was Count Poutiatine. The United States
Minister to China was William B. Reed of Pennsylvania. Preliminary
negotiations at the mouth of the Pei-ho proved unsatisfactory and were
followed by hostilities carried out by Britain and France, with the
Russians and the Americans hanging back as neutrals. Separate negotiations were then carried on by the four powers at Tientsin, resulting
in four separate treaties of Tientsin, of which the British was the most
comprehensive, being agreed to by the Chinese imperial commissioners.
Minor themes are the attempts of the Chinese to utilize Poutiatine and
Reed as mediators, the intimidation of the Chinese negotiators by the
British secretaries, the confused disgust, sympathy and frustration of
Reed, and the frantic attempts of the Chinese to keep the barbarians out
of Peking.

    The American documents are well summarized by Tyler Dennett
in a chapter entitled "William B. Reed and the Treaty of Tientsin," in
his Americans in Eastern Asia, pages 311-331. The Reed correspondence
as previously noted, is published in U.S. Cong. 36: 1, S. Ex. Doc. 30.
The fullest account of the Tientsin negotiations from the American point
of view is found in "The Journal of S. Wells Williams," who acted as
Reed's Chinese secretary, edited by F.W. Williams and published in the
Journal of the North China Branch of the Royal Asiatic Society, volume
XLII (1911), pages 3-232. Another American participant, W.A.P. Martin,
has published his impressions in a volume entitled, A Cycle of Cathay,
published in 1897.

TRANSLATIONS OF DOCUMENTS

    278. April 17, 1858. MEMORIAL: T'an T'ing-hsiang Reports the
Arrival of Russian Ships off Ta-ku Bar and the Recruitment of Local
Trainbands.

    Acting Governor General of Chihli T'an T'ing-hsiang memorial-
izes. According to the report of Corporal Feng En-fu and others of
the coastal and river patrol, on April 13, between five and seven in
the afternoon, two unusual ships, one large and one small, were
sighted. They immediately boarded boats and went out to meet them.
A small sampan threw a package to them, which on examination
proved to be a Russian communication saying that there were favorable matters which they wanted Tientsin local officials to come and
discuss. The barbarian ships are now anchored outside the bar.

    As to port defense arrangements, according to a report from

Ta-nien he had posted 3200 men to defend the north bank and the coastal area and arrangements were completely tight. Later Commander-in-chief Chang Tien-yüan, inasmuch as 400 troops originally at Tientsin remain at K'ai-chou and cannot return to the barracks, and feeling'that the present force was scanty, filled it out from the Ching-hai and other garrisons and even added 500 Ho-chien troops as reserves as well, to make a good showing.

But Your official hears that in Kwangtung the barbarians did not not fear the soldiers so much as the people. If popular feeling is strong, soldiers are more effective. Tientsin is a melting pot and the people turbulent, so it is even more essential to have order within as a means of harmonizing without. Your official knew of the present magistrate of the independent department of Ting-chou, Wang Yung-chi, and the now acting prefect of Chiao-ho, Wang Lan-kuang, who formerly held office in Tientsin and commanded general popular respect, and also of the magistrate of T'ang-hsien, Ch'en Chao-lin, native of Kwangtung who has been in charge of the Fukien-Kwangtung Guildhall at Tientsin. Consequently, he ordered these three officials to proceed, in cooperation with gentry and merchants, to manage among them the trainbands of the port and the prefectural capital and also to check on the Fukien and Kwangtung residents (in Tientsin) When the interior is well ordered, foreign invasion cannot come in of itself. From the customary district, household, and port militia, it requires only some adroit manipulation to bring in several thousand men at a moment's notice. This is in general the situation as to mobilization of troops and use of militia.

Vermilion Endorsement: Noted. There is already an Edict ordering you to Tientsin, but now 2000 Peking troops are being transferred and should shortly reach Tientsin with no one to lead them. They are all ordered turned over to you for disposition. When Kuo-jui and others reach your headquarters, inform them fully of this Vermilion Endorsement. (IWSM.HF 20; 10a, 8-11a, 8)

279. April 19, 1858. MEMORIAL: Tientsin Officials Report Preliminary Talks with the Russians and Efforts to Alienate them from the British and French.

Ch'ang-lu Salt Controller Wu-lo-hung-e, Chihli Financial Commissioner Ch'ien Hsin-ho, and Acting Tientsin Brigade General Ta-nien memorialize. According to reports of patrol officers and men, two more barbarian ships have arrived, totaling six, including one steamer, and have come inside the bar. Your slave Ta-nien and Tientsin Tao-t'ai Ying-yü immediately sent Second Captain Chang Chen-hsiung to go out and stop them, and Your slave, Wu-lo-hung-e, and Your official, Ch'ien Hsin-ho, both went to the fort to investigate. Before the said captain reached them, the barbarian ships suddenly turned around and went out of the harbor; several sampans (from the ships) also left after taking soundings.

It is noted that our deputies Pien Pao-shu and Ch'en Kuang-ming had put out to sea, sending Corporal Liu Yung-kuei ahead to tell the barbarian chiefs that the said deputies were in Tientsin to take charge of ocean transport and, as their ships had arrived, were coming to see them. The barbarians were delighted and said, "They will be very welcome for we have really important matters to discuss." As there was a strong south wind they could not come alongside the barbarian ship and had to return to the port to wait out the storm.

Your slaves immediately sent for these deputies and informed them secretly of Imperial Edicts and urged them to go quickly and act in respectful accord with them. The said deputies put out to sea the same night and between three and five on the morning of the 17th, approached the barbarian ships. As there was a strong wind against them, they were still unable to come alongside at eight. When the barbarians sighted them they sent Ming-ch'ang[1] in a sampan to meet them and bring them on board. Throughout the interview they were respectful and compliant. The deputies inquired why they had asked for the appointment of an Imperial Commissioner to discuss matters last year and, seven months having elapsed, never made their appearance; and why, now that Governor General Huang had been sent to Kwangtung to take charge of barbarian affairs, they did not go there? Why must they come to Tientsin?

They said: "We have received a mandate of our country's sovereign on the Heilungkiang matter and fear that it can scarcely be concluded." They continued, "We four countries, on our arrival at Shanghai, heard that His Imperial Majesty had sent Governor General Huang to handle barbarian affairs, but we do not care to negotiate with him, so we have all come to this port and shall proceed together to Peking."

The deputies told them, "If there are matters that are admissible, they can be negotiated anywhere. What is the need of going to Peking?

The barbarians then said: "We greatly fear that there is an unwillingness to memorialize for us according to the facts, that our humble affairs never reach the high places, so we must insist on going to Peking to discuss matters with the Grand Councillors and Grand Secretaries in person. We request that a factual memorial be sent immediately; then we will await Imperial Edict. When negotiations are concluded, we shall set a date to return. All the matters to be discussed are beneficial to both parties and there are no ulterior motives. We shall by no means resort to arms. We now have an official document which we request be forwarded to the capital. We

---

1 Ming-ch'ang was the Russian interpreter. He is subsequently identified as a "Russian barbarian" but his Russian name has not been determined.

shall await a prompt reply."

The deputies told them that Tientsin officials could not memorialize, that it must be sent to Pao-ting-fu with a request for the governor general to memorialize for them, and that the round trip would require at least ten days. The barbarians insisted, "As the matter is important, speed is essential in order that the main business not be impeded."

The deputies answered, "As your honorable country has been friendly for years and habitually understands decorum, your official document should naturally be presented for you. But as for the English and French barbarians, they are from boorish countries and we are not concerned with their affairs. Besides, last year your honorable envoy said he had come to oppose the English barbarians. With these words still ringing in our ears, how can we forget? Why have you now come with them?"

The barbarians then said: "We have made careful inquiry of the English-French incident in Kwangtung and actually Governor General Yeh had been dilatory for years. On several occasions he did not answer communications. He did not accede to requests for interviews. He also burned the buildings of that country without leaving a scrap of tile. He perpetrated this action by being absolutely intolerable. As we are already on friendly terms, we can tell you this with exceptional frankness: do not by any means ruin matters by procrastination." Then they delivered their official document. They also said that four English ships had arrived and invited the delegates to come and call on them.

The deputies replied that they had come to see them because they were amicable; but as for the English barbarians, they would certainly not condescend to go to their ships. The (Russian) barbarians were afraid, "If you do not go, we shall lose face. Besides, we have no ulterior motives. If you are too uncommunicative and develop a blood feud, we cannot restrain them (the English)." Then they ordered (their interpreter), Ming-ch'ang, to accompany them there. Ultimately, because of the storm they could not go, but agreed on another day, saying: "No matter what officers go with us to their ships, we shall find out their motives and tell you according to the facts."

The deputies also told them that as they had not come to memorialize for them, now while they (the Russians) were waiting for a reply, they must not let their ships enter port and bring calamity on them. The barbarians replied that the quicker the replies arrived the better; that if they were delayed they were afraid they could not wait. The deputies respectfully obeyed the Imperial Edict and devised means to explain for three hours, returning between five and seven in the afternoon. They sought to alienate them (from the English) but could not.

It is noted that these barbarians are remarkably changeable and their minds are fundamentally inscrutable, but from the reports of these deputies it is observed that their expressions seem to reveal

their thoughts with complete straightforwardness. Although they
are temporarily under control, the implications are enormous and
we dare not fail to report according to facts. (IWSM.HF 20; 11a,
8-13b, 3)

280. April 19, 1858. MEMORIAL: The Tientsin Officials Send a
Personal Deputy to Peking to Explain the Gravity of the Foreign Threat
at Ta-ku.

Wu-lo-hung-e and others further memorialize. To continue,
Your slaves have closely questioned their deputies and these barbarians are not making empty threats. They (Your slaves) venture the
opinion that the capital is a vital place and they must never be allowed
to enter Peking. Your slaves respectfully received the Imperial Edict
to exploit leniency to those from afar as a means of bringing them
under control, but alas, their deputies used feeling and reason to explain to them repeatedly and the barbarians were as determined as
ever. How in the end should they manage to avoid giving them any
pretext to turn around and make us more trouble?

Your slaves are very fearful of losing the opportunity by waiting.
The phraseology and viewpoint of the barbarians were told in detail
by deputy Pien Pao-shu, some of which cannot be adequately expressed
in a memorial. Being a matter of important concern, Your slaves, at
the risk of being considered rash, are ordering the said deputy to proceed posthaste to Peking, await summons from the Grand Councillors
for complete questioning; they can then memorialize what he says, or
else receive a special grant for an Imperial Audience so that he can
report factually and in person the attitude of the said barbarians.
(IWSM.HF 20; 13b, 4-14a, 3)

281. April 19, 1858. EDICT: Instructs Ch'ung-lun to Meet the Russians
after a Suitable Delay and to Deal with Russia and the United States Separately.

Edict to the Grand Councillors. Wu-lo-hung-e and others have
memorialized that they sent officers to see the Russian chief who
presented an official document. When Deputy Pien Pao-shu and others
called on the Russian chief and the barbarian presented his official
documents, his concern was for a speedy reply, but the deputies said
that if they asked the governor general to memorialize it for them it
would take ten days.

Now, although Ch'ung-lun has reached Tientsin, he must not see
them at once. After a minimum of five or six days he shall send an
officer to tell them that the official document they sent to the Grand
Secretary has been delivered to him by the governor general of Chihli;
that now a high official to examine and receive the ocean transport (of
tribute rice) is in Tientsin; as he is an Imperially commissioned official any important matters can be discussed with him and the said

minister will memorialize them fully.

When they shall have replied, Ch'ung-lun, Wu-erh-kun-t'ai and Ch'ien Hsin-ho can arrange a date for a meeting, and say that when they came to Tientsin last year, recalling their years of friendship, Ch'ien Hsin-ho and others transmitted a letter for them when they left and told them to go to Heilungkiang and arrange with the Imperial Commissioner for a boundary survey. This year (they) also presented another letter in Kiangsu, concerning which the Court of Colonial Affairs has notified their Senate Yamen. Now an official letter has been presented for them to Grand Secretary Yü-ch'eng; they hear that as usual it was turned over to the Court of Colonial Affairs for reply, and they think they should receive an answer shortly. The Kwangtung affair is fundamentally no concern of their country. England and France took up arms and violated treaties and now an Imperial Commissioner is proceeding to Kwangtung to make an equitable settlement. Tientsin is not the place to handle barbarian affairs, but their honorable country has always been friendly so if there is anything they want to say, the said vice-president can memorialize for them, asking for an Edict. Year before last when England and America came to Tientsin, it was Ch'ung-lun who met and memorialized for them

As for Russia, although they have long had an envoy in Peking, he is not a minister.[2] Last year when the honorable envoy asked permission to come to Peking and Ch'ien Hsin-ho and others stopped them, it was actually because no minister of the honorable country had ever come to Peking and there was no established precedent to follow as to reception ceremonies, so we were afraid they would be inadequate and result in a rupture of friendship. Nor was there any other motive. Last year the honorable minister was likewise stopped midway. Now as he merely insists on explaining at Tientsin on account of the English-American [sic] affair, it will certainly be possible to reach an agreement by negotiation. He must needs realize that China, in dealing with them, will respect existing treaties and always maintain perpetual friendship.

Explain to him in this way, watch what his reactions are, lead him around as occasion offers, and join with T'an T'ing-hsiang in a secret memorial.

If the English and French barbarians present state papers addressed to the Grand Secretaries, tell them that as the English barbarians re-

---

2 The Russian Ecclesiastical Mission, actually more of a language and political mission, was founded in 1727, to serve the Russian prisoners from Albazin in Peking. Under the terms of the Treaty of Kiakhta (1727) negotiated by Vladislavich, the Orthodox Church in Peking was recognized and four Russian priests were allowed to live in the capital, together with six young students of the language. They had no diplomatic status.

turned the reply of the governor general and others in Kiangsu, and neither the American nor the French barbarians replied, on this occasion at Tientsin, China cannot receive the documents they present; but as the American barbarians have not helped the evildoers, (the officials) can meet with them and treat them courteously; that England and France must go to Kwangtung and await the equitable settlement of the Imperial Commissioner.

If the American barbarians should apologize for England and France, he can give them face by agreeing to memorialize for them. The official letter of the Russian barbarians must be answered as usual by the Court of Colonial Affairs.[3] When Pien Pao-shu shall have arrived, question him carefully on the situation and then give him confidential instructions for administration. Wu-lo-hung-e, We trust, has returned to the prefectural capital. (IWSM.HF 20; 14a, 4-15a, 9)

282. April 19, 1858. MEMORIAL: T'an T'ing-hsiang Reports his Departure from Pao-ting to take up Temporary Residence at Tientsin During the Crisis.

Acting Governor General of Chihli T'an T'ing-hsiang memorializes. An Imperial Edict was received on April 15, 1858, stating that T'an T'ing-hsiang was ordered to leave the provincial capital at once and take up residence either in the prefectural capital or in Tientsin. Respect this.

Your official begs to note that barbarian nature is inscrutable and defenses must be rigorous. But as they say they have favorable things which they want to discuss personally, truly as per Sacred Edict, they will not necessarily precipitate hostilities, so we must seize the opportunity to explain everything clearly first, treating them with courtesy and moving them with sincerity. At present Ch'ien Hsin-ho has gone to the port and Your official, summarily dispatching essential matters, will set out from the capital the eighteenth of this month, traveling by the land route to facilitate reception and disposition of reports en route. He expects to be able to reach Tientsin on the twenty-first. He plans to make his residence in the prefectural capital to facilitate direct consultation with Ch'ung-lun and others. (IWSM.HF 20; 16a, 7-16b, 4)

283. April 19, 1858. MEMORIAL: T'an T'ing-hsiang Reports the Arrest of a Chinese Catholic Christian at Tientsin and the Seizure of Foreign Papers.

T'an T'ing-hsiang further memorializes. A deputy has arrested

---

3 The *Li Fan Yüan*, sometimes called the Mongolian Superintendency, handled Russian affairs in Peking.

one Ch'iu Yün-t'ing, a native of Nan-hai-hsien, Kwangtung, who has opened a medicine store in Tientsin and is a practicing Catholic. A crucifix and a Bible, as well as barbarian books and barbarian letters have been seized. Inquiry brought out that Bishop Meng of Shanghai ordered him to go out and do good, distribute medicine, and heal the sick, and that he did not proseletize or deceive.

Your official finds that Ch'iu Yün-t'ing is a follower of Catholicism, which is an ordinary matter; but whether the barbarian books and barbarian letters seized have any other significance cannot be determined, so he must be examined carefully. At this time it is not convenient to try him at Tientsin and he has been sent in custody to the provincial capital for rigorous trial and punishment.

Vermilion Endorsement: This matter is of great significance. We fear this type of rebel is not limited to this one man and he must be thoroughly interrogated; in no case must he be tortured or put to death. Order these instructions passed on to Ch'ing-sheng. (IWSM. HF 20; 16b, 5-17a, 2)

284. April 19, 1858. MEMORIAL: A Mongolian Governor Reports his Dispatch of Cavalry and Archers for the Defense of Shanhaikwan.

Military Lieutenant Governor of Chahar Hsi-ling-a memorializes. April 16, between nine and eleven at night, a secret court letter was received from the Grand Council to the effect that on April 15, an Imperial Order was received saying that on that day a memorial had been received from Ho Kuei-ch'ing and others that the English and other barbarian chiefs intended to proceed from Shanghai to Tientsin and had already weighed anchor; that Shanhaikwan was a strategic place and defenses must be prepared. Respect this.

Your slave, Hsi-ling-a, has selected from among the commandants of the Eight Banners at Chahar, four officers who are experienced and able, delegating Commandant of the Bordered Yellow Banner T'e-k'o shen, Commandant of the Solid Red Banner Seng-ko-ta-erh, Commandant of the Solid Blue Banner Chu-k'o-tu-erh-p'a-mu, and Commandant of the Bordered Blue Banner Na mu-chi-lo-to-erh-chi, each officer to command 500 men. Of these 2000 men selected from the Chahar troops of Your slave Hsi-ling-a, 50 men constitute a squadron, totaling 40 squadrons; each squadron has three officers, totaling 120 officers; he is also sending 300 grooms.

As mounts for the said troops, he asks that from the levies of the Imperial Pastures of the Court of the Imperial Stud at Shang-tu, 2300 fat, strong horses be selected ready to mount. In this contingent of 2000 men, 1000 are fusiliers, 1000 are archers. Now there have been levied 1000 fowling pieces, 1000 bows, 50,000 plum-point arrows, and 1000 quivers, and ordered carried for use.

He has also ordered the said commandants to divide into four units and lead their commands quickly to the port. Your slave Hsi-ling-a

will lead the first unit of government forces and start out ahead, go
direct to Shanhaikwan by way of Mi-yün, and deploy as occasion demands. (IWSM.HF 20; 17a, 3-17b, 8)

285. April 19, 1858. EDICT: Orders Kalgan Horse and Camel Cavalry,
Fusiliers, and Archers to Garrison Shanhaikwan under Chinese Command.
          Edict to the Grand Councillors. Hsi-ling-a has memorialized on
his compliance with Imperial Edict in ordering government forces
transferred to the port and immediate setting out in command. He
says that he is accordingly sending 2000 Chahar troops, 1000 as
fusiliers, 1000 as archers, divided into four units, ordering four officers, Commandant T'e-k'o-shen and others, to divide the command,
and transferring 2300 fat, strong horses selected from the levies in
the Imperial Pastures of the Court of the Imperial Stud at Shang-tu
to be used as mounts. He is also taking funds from subscriptions held
in the treasury to make 600 sets of camel saddles and blankets and
transferring 600 camels from the Shang-tu herds to be ready for use
by the government troops. The said military lieutenant general at the
head of the first unit of government troops is starting out ahead, direct
for Shanhaikwan by way of Mi-yün, to arrange the defenses.
          Order everything done as he proposes. As regards his request
that the governor general of Chihli be ordered to prepare hostels, food,
hay, and carts for carrying munitions for use in the places passed
through en route from Kalgan to Shanhaikwan, order T'an T'ing-hsiang
to consult previous records and order his subordinates to issue
warrants accordingly, in order to expedite the trip. After Hsi-ling-a
starts, the later units of government forces must be ordered to proceed continuously. No delay will be tolerated.
          After the said military lieutenant governor reaches Shanhaikwan,
he will dispose in whatever way occasion demands. Also order him to
report by memorial from time to time. As Mongol troops at the fort
are mostly stupid and it is feared that should barbarians land, they
would fall to and demolish them, they must be strictly disciplined to
avoid the development of complications. If there are any particularly
conscientious officers or men in the Kalgan garrison, they can be
selected and taken along. Orders have been given the Board of Works
to arrange remittances for the necessary bullets and powder. (IWSM.
HF 20; 17b, 9-18b, 3)

286. April 21, 1858. EDICT: Urges the Utilization of the Americans to
Estrange the Russians from the British and thus Strengthen Chinese
Foreign Policy.
          Edict to the Grand Councillors. . . . The delegate Pien Pao-shu
has today come to Peking and been received in audience. His personal narrative was in general the same as Wu-lo-hung-e and others had
memorialized. Although the Russian barbarians and the English bar-

barians cannot be estranged at once, barbarian nature is changeable
and prone to vie for precedence. If by word and manner, we make
them understand that China's treatment of them is entirely different
from (her treatment) of England, we will be in a position to utilize
them to tame and subdue the English barbarians. Since the American
barbarians did not help the evildoers, they can be used to bring them
around.

In general barbarians are covetous. As the English barbarians
have vested interests in the five ports, the other barbarians look at
them longingly. Not only was the French barbarians' assistance to
the evildoers prompted primarily by their desire to share the profits,
but the Russian barbarians risked a long voyage over many seas to
come and mediate for no other reason than to gain the gratitude of
England and France and in the future get a share of their profits.
When Ch'ung-lun meets them he will see what they want and then
memorialize secretly asking for an Edict.

As to the Russian barbarians wanting to enter the capital, this
was denied reasonably last year. At present Imperially Commissioned
Ch'ung-lun is in Tientsin and they can speak freely whatever they
have to say and it will certainly be memorialized for them.

As for the English and French barbarians, if they want interviews,
he need not be too adamant. Say that he was just wanting to talk to
the said barbarians about the Kwangtung affair and now that they are
here, right and wrong, crooked and straight can be analyzed; that
when Yeh Ming-ch'en mismanaged they could have spoken freely at
their leisure; why go to the extent of occupying our provincial capital?
Say that last year the English barbarians set fire to and burned nearly
10,000 civilian houses but Heaven willed to change the wind and burn
barbarian houses; that now the hearts of the Cantonese are filled with
hatred and if there is not a favorable settlement there will never be
harmony. Now that all the countries are here there can be a general
discussion.

When these barbarians see that we are not afraid to meet them,
their hauteur will naturally be somewhat reduced. Then, making use
of the mediation of the Russian and American barbarians, gradually
bring them under control. This may give a clue to the settlement.
Previously Ch'ung-lun met the English barbarians and completely
maintained our prestige. If he sees the English and French barbarian
chiefs this time, there cannot be the least disparity lest these barbarians be led to disrespect.

As to the dispatch of the government forces of the Peking Battalion,
they have been turned over to T'an T'ing-hsiang for disposition. Order
him to send word to Kuo-jui to discipline them properly. It is essential not to develop further complications. (IWSM.HF 20; 19b, 1-20a, 9)

287. April 21, 1858. MEMORIAL: A Peking Official Observes the

Strength of Foreign Arms, the Vulnerability of Tientsin, and Despairs
of Peking's Defense.
        Senior Vice-president of the Board of War Wang Mao-yin me-
morializes. Hearing that barbarian ships have come to Tientsin, Your
official is immeasurably anxious. Barbarian nature is inscrutable;
their wily schemes always exceed our expectations; their wickedness
always catches us where we are unprepared. Between the capital of
Kwangtung and Hu-men there are forts all along and defenses everywhere, but what they suddenly took advantage of was our unpreparedness.
        Now Tientsin is only 200 li from Peking, a day's trip with no
passes that can be closed. Although, as the barbarian ships are still
in the outer ocean they cannot suddenly land, and as barbarians are
very different in face and physique they cannot come secretly to Peking, still trade has been going on in the five ports for more than ten
years and there is no lack of corrupt people available at every port.
If they secretly intruded corrupt people inside the walls and, placing
their usual effective firearms at various places, fired them simultaneously in the middle of the night, civilians and soldiers with their
ordinary lack of preparation would suddenly be thrown into confusion
and flight and, in addition, the downtrodden and starving masses would
take advantage of it to create a disturbance among them. Thus a few
tens of men would be the equivalent of myriads and even though there
were no great calamity, still they would laugh at us.
        Now it is windy and parched and within three weeks there have
been numerous fires, almost as if Heaven were issuing a warning.
Obviously there must be rigorous defense within the city wall, but
the Imperial Gardens outside the wall cannot even be compared with
the inner city. Although all gates are closed tight, it is feared that
what is more than sufficient in peaceful times will prove inadequate
in time of trouble. Because of the unusual aspect of the sun during
the first month (February 24-March 14), Your official has felt un-
controllably anxious and has not dared express fully his inner thoughts
He hopes Your Majesty and his ministers will take early secret counsel and prepare.
        In the present crisis observers are inclined to think that Your of-
ficial is over-anxious, but in the past unusual calamities have usually
sprung from not feeling the need for anxiety or not being anxious
enough. These stupid views he respectfully ventures to state confidentially. (IWSM.HF 20; 20a, 10-21a, 7)

        288. April 23, 1858. MEMORIAL: The Tientsin Officials Report Pre-
liminary Friendly Contacts with the American Ship off Ta-ku Bar.
        Acting Governor General of Chihli T'an T'ing-hsiang, Superinten-
dent of Imperial Granaries Ch'ung-lun, Sub-chancellor of the Grand
Secretariat Wu-erh-kun-t'ai, and Chihli Financial Commissioner

Ch'ien Hsin-ho memorialize. According to the brigade general and
tao-t'ai of Tientsin, on the nineteenth they sent Acting Major Ch'en
K'o-ming and Corporal Chang Chen-hsiung to go on board the Russian
barbarian ship. The interpreter, Ming-ch'ang, said that two American
ships had arrived and asked that they come to call.

The major and the others then went on board the American barbarian ship. These barbarians said, "We have just sent someone to
announce our arrival and your coming to call is very good." They
also went to the English barbarian ships to investigate. These barbarians also welcomed them but their attitude seemed to reveal a
feeling of insolence. Between three and five in the afternoon of the
same day, American barbarians on board a small foreign cargo boat
and followed by a small row boat came direct to the fort and presented two notes, asking that food be purchased for them; they also
took soundings. They were told that there were still no traders on
the sea and that now no fishing boats could leave port. The Americans
were in small boats and as there was a strong south wind, they lay
over for the night under the fort and then sailed back. It is computed
that altogether 10 barbarian ships have arrived, comprising seven
large steamers and three warships.

Vermilion Endorsement: Memorial read and fully understood.
(IWSM.HF 20; 21a, 8-21b, 9)

280. April 24, 1858. MEMORIAL: Ho Kuei-ch'ing Reports Final Visit
of American and Russian Representatives before their Departure for
the North.

Governor General of Liang-chiang Ho Kuei-ch'ing and Governor
of Kiangsu Chao Te-ch'e memorialize. According to various reports
from Su-Sung-T'ai Tao-t'ai Hsüeh Huan, he has found that the barbarians kept postponing their date of departure because they were
waiting for news from Canton.

Furthermore, the American barbarian leader Shih-t'ing-po-erh,
interpreter, T'ai-chen-hsi; French Consul Min-t'i-ni,barbarian chief
K'ung-ch'uan-fu-pien-fei-mo, and translator Li-mei,[4] and Russian
secretary Ming-ch'ang came to the tao-t'ai's office and each presented a communication to Your officials, each enclosing a document
addressed to Grand Secretary Yü-ch'eng. The Russian chief, Poutiatine,
left port March 11; the English chief Elgin left port on the twelfth; the
American chief Reed left port on the fourteenth; the French chief Gros
left port on the fifteenth; all sailing for Tientsin. There are still two
warships left anchored at Shanghai.

Your officials opened and read the communications of the American,

---

4 These names have not been positively identified; W.L.G. Smith was the American consul
   at Shanghai.

French, and Russian barbarians addressed to them. They merely
asked to transmit the communications to the Grand Secretary and not
a word more. In the communications to Grand Secretary Yü-ch'eng
they said that since he had not sent a reply they intended going to
Tientsin. As there were no improper expressions, they naturally had
to be transmitted for them. Besides our communication to the Grand
Council, their communications to Your officials have been copied and
are respectfully presented for Imperial inspection. As to the barbarians originally fixing the seventh for sailing and then delaying for
several days, we do not know what their motive was.
    Vermilion Endorsement: Noted. (IWSM.HF 20; 22a, 8-23a, 4)

    290. April 26, 1858. MEMORIAL: T'an T'ing-hsiang, on the Advice of
the Russians, Receives English, French, and American Notes at Ta-ku.
    Acting Governor General of Chihli T'an T'ing-hsiang, Superinten-
dent of Imperial Granaries Ch'ung-lun, Sub-chancellor of the Grand
Secretariat Wu-erh-kun-t'ai, and Financial Commissioner of Chihli
Ch'ien Hsin-ho memorialize. . . . At this time the English, French,
and Americans came up in sampans. We ordered Ch'en K'o-ming
and others to stop them, not allowing them to come ashore. The barbarians each presented an official document. At first Your officials,
Ch'ien Hsin-ho and others, were unwilling to receive them, but on
account of Ming-ch'ang's repeated and urgent entreaties on their behalf, they received them with compliments and smiles. In addition
they received a document presented by the Russian barbarians, making four altogether. Then on the twenty-second, two more French barbarian steamers arrived and one American barbarian steamer, making altogether thirteen anchored outside the bar.
    Vermilion Endorsement: Memorial read and fully comprehended.
(IWSM.HF 20; 29b, 1-7)

    291. April 26, 1858. EDICT: Notes Conciliatory Policy of Reed and
Poutiatine as Opposed to the Hostile Position of the Allies and Hopes to
Isolate Elgin.
    Edict to the Grand Councillors. Today T'an T'ing-hsiang and
others have memorialized that the Russian barbarians presented an
official document; they also submitted the official letters of the
English, American, and French barbarians. The Grand Councillors
have opened and read the letters which the barbarians presented to
T'an T'ing-hsiang, and they are all asking him to transmit communications to Grand Secretary Yü-ch'eng. Not knowing that the said
governor general has come to Tientsin, all the dispatches to Yü-ch'eng
contain requests that an Imperial Commissioner come to negotiate,
but the object of both Russia and America is to mediate and placate,
so we can take advantage of their request and devise means of getting
them under control. Ch'ung-lun and others were instructed to meet

these barbarians but can not see them at the same time and must see
them successively.

As the Russian barbarians have been friendly with China for years,
he must receive them first, treat them with company manners, and
tell them that the English and French barbarians occupied the capital
of Kwangtung and abducted our high official with an utter lack of propriety; that as His Imperial Majesty, mindful that Yeh Ming-ch'en had
managed badly, degraded him, and sent another Imperial Commissioner
to investigate and manage, He could be said to be most just and most
enlightened; that now the honorable envoy's purpose is to mediate and
if there is nothing harmful to China's dignity, there is no objection to
complying and memorializing for him, begging Imperial Favor; that
if they are not repentant and still make improper demands, we cannot
memorialize for them, or if we did memorialize, such could not be
granted.

As the American chief never helped the evildoers, he can be
received affably, given the unreasonable position of the English barbarians and asked to determine right and wrong. If he intervenes on
behalf of England and France, tell him also that anything not harmful
to China's dignity can still be memorialized for him.

To the French chief, (say) that in 1854, when they helped the
government forces in Shanghai in exterminating rebels, the governor
memorialized asking the Imperial Favor of commendation, and now
His Imperial Majesty is mindful of their previous respectful conformity;
that last year's Kwangtung affair was not of their origination, it is
only that they did not have to help the evil doers; that if they are repentant, we can still go out of our way to forgive, but they must never
again help the English barbarians in evil. Then we can trade with them
as of old.

As for the English barbarians, (say that) in last year's fighting
in Kwangtung, they were certainly the chief miscreants and the number
of private and business buildings burned reached nearly ten thousand;
that at present the people of Canton are unanimous in their hatred of
them. Even if they trade at Canton later, they will certainly suffer
harm and whatever arrangement is made for permanent friendly relations must be made by the high officials in Kwangtung. See what they
answer and then decide what to say.

But in these few days have Ch'ung-lun and the others met the barbarians or not? If they have not yet met the barbarians and they insist
on waiting for another high official to be sent to Tientsin to meet them,
then before the twenty-ninth someone can be sent to say that, as regards
the document they presented, Yü-ch'eng has memorialized and received
an Edict. As T'an T'ing-hsiang is nearby reviewing troops, he will also
be sent to Tientsin to meet them along with Ch'ung-lun and the others.
In case Ch'ung-lun and the others have met the barbarian chiefs and
the barbarians have presented letters asking that another high official

be sent and are hoping for a reply, they can still say that T'an T'ing-
hsiang is also being sent to meet them, but that Chinese institutes
require that everyone ask for Edicts and act according to them and
no one can act on his own initiative; that Ch'ung-lun and the others are
really Imperial Commissioners and were originally delegated to negotiate if trouble arose, but due to Russia's urgent request, T'an T'ing-
hsiang, who is of higher rank, has been ordered to come and negotiate.

    As for the things the barbarians requested, they are not yet
clearly formulated. We have now received from the Grand Councillors
the results of their deliberations and various proposals, asking Us to
examine and decide, and send them to the said governor general and
others to keep to themselves and be ready to answer as occasion demands. If the barbarians do not bring them up, they are by no means
to initiate them. It is inevitable that (they should bring up) additional
unreasonable requests. These must all be deliberated realistically and
rationally on the spot and the situation explained. It is difficult at
present to hypothesize. All developments are to be reported by express
memorial. All is to be carefully and secretly put in readiness; there
must be no carelessness.

    Order the barbarian documents addressed to Yü-ch'eng to be
copied and sent to them for reference. The official paper sent to T'an
T'ing-hsiang is also sent herewith for perusal.

    Today an Edict has been issued appointing T'an T'ing-hsiang gover
nor general of Chihli. (IWSM.HF 20; 30a, 5-31b, 7)

292. April 26, 1858. INSTRUCTIONS (Excerpt): The Grand Councillors
Advise the Chinese Commissioners to Listen to American Mediation but
not to Rely on it.

    . . . On meeting the Americans, if their chief says he wants to mediate
for the English and French, you can say that as the honorable envoy in
Kwangtung did not assist the rebels in attacking the capital, His Imperial Majesty commends his loyalty and righteousness and thus on
this occasion of his coming to Peking has ordered the present governor
general and others to receive him. Now he wishes to mediate on behalf
of two countries, but we do not know whether or not they acknowledge
their error. If they are not repentant, we can hardly reason with them;
if they do feel repentant and have asked the honorable country to come
forward and discuss peace, it is only necessary that the matters be
practicable and not harmful to our institutes, and they will certainly
be memorialized for them, begging His Imperial Majesty to bestow
favors. If they speak of customs affairs, say that there are no means
by which the matter can be investigated at this place; that now there
is a newly appointed Imperial Commissioner in Kwangtung who can
certainly make a just settlement so the honorable country can obtain
advantage. (IWSM.HF 20; 32b, 3-10)

293. May 1, 1858. MEMORIAL: T'an T'ing-hsiang Reports the Unwillingness of Poutiatine to Exert Himself against the British and French.
        T'an T'ing-hsiang and others further memorialize. To continue,
although the Russian barbarians are extremely respectful and obedient
they still inevitably shield all barbarians. Judging from their manner
and expression, it seems that they do not want to have any trouble that
will prevent the granting of their requests and therefore are highly in
earnest.
        As to the English and French barbarians using small steamers
to come and go inside the bar, gradually forcing entrance, their hearts
are inscrutable; but the barbarian ships are all anchored on either side
of the port, barely leaving a channel for passage, and while the ocean
tribute-rice transports pass through every day, they have never interfered with them. Apparently they know we are prepared and dare not
risk a sudden rupture. Although outwardly adamant, inwardly they
are anxious to expedite their schemes. If at this time we do not get
them under control promptly and put off from day to day, it would be
the worst policy. Your officials all figure that on account of the
Kwangtung affair the barbarians' attitude is very expansive and ordering them to go back would be no easy matter.
        Now seven more steamers, large and small, have arrived, which
added to those which had successively come in, make up 17 large
steamers and three small vessels, which is no small number.
        As to the Russian chief wanting to have Lama Pa-la-ti[5] and others
who are living in Peking come to Tientsin, he says that there is no
message to be transmitted; but since he has not seen them for several
years, he begs His Imperial Majesty to grant the favor of allowing
them a personal interview, and that actually there is no other reason.
Can this be granted or not? (IWSM.HF 21; 3b, 1-4a, 2)

294. May 3, 1858. MEMORIAL: The Tientsin Officials Report Conversations with Russian and American Deputies but Failure to Contact the
British and French.
        Governor General of Chihli T'an T'ing-hsiang, Superintendent of
Imperial Granaries Ch'ung-lun, Sub-chancellor of the Grand Secretariat
Wu-erh-kun-t'ai, and Financial Commissioner of Chihli Ch'ien Hsin-ho
memorialize. Your officials originally agreed for the English barbarians to come for an interview on the first. To our surprise they still
had not arrived by midday so we sent deputies, Prefect of Ts'ang-chou
Pien Pao-shu and Acting Major Ch'en K'o-ming, to the Russian ship to
inquire.
        Poutiatine told them that the four countries were all agreed that

5   This is a reference to one of the Orthodox ecclesiastics at the Russian Mission
    in Peking.

this trip north was really necessary, because for years matters reported were not acted upon or answered and they suspected that the true facts never reached the Imperial Ear, so they set a date during the second month) March 15-April 13) to meet an Imperial Commissioner in Shanghai; that unexpectedly Governor General Huang never came in person and there was nothing to do but come to Tientsin; that if their requests were not granted, the English and other barbarians would demand permission to go to Peking and it would be extremely difficult to stop them; moreover, that what the English and other barbarians asked were mainly two things which would seem to present no difficulties.

The deputies asked what these things were and were told that one was trade; that although nominally conducted at five ports, now by secret collusion trade was not restricted to the five ports. If trading places outside the five ports were fully opened to commerce, China's customs receipts would daily increase and other countries would all be benefited and permanent friendly relations would be assured. Asked what other places outside the five ports, they said that this was primarily the English barbarians' proposal and must be discussed with them personally.

The other issue was Catholicism; that although nominally released from proscription, various provinces still make wilful arrests and the extremity of the oppression was unbearable and all barbarians harbored resentment; that they would ask again for general orders for strict prohibitions to prevent persecution; that outside these requests, everything was a matter of detail, none of which could not be discussed; that the Kwangtung affair could also be discussed personally when they met the English barbarians.

Judging from their attitude and speech, the (Russians) are actually tied up with the English and French barbarians, firmly and inseparably, and their original professions of help and mediation cannot be relied on at all. Later in the afternoon the American barbarians sent someone with a letter stating that the four countries had agreed that they must wait until the third before fixing a date for a meeting. As the English barbarians never did come, Your officials figure their reasoning is that the troops and volunteers in the port are at their posts and they will be very cautious about going far into important territory. Moreover, it is reported that more ships are expected later. It is possible they are waiting for them.

Your officials humbly think that barbarian knavery is inborn and that they think only of profits, so we cannot reason with them, still less engage in a battle of words. For several years, means have repeatedly been sought to find excuses for sending them to Kwangtung to wait, but Kwangtung has completely disregarded them. While Shanghai has barbarian goods for a shield and barbarian merchants as hostages, Huang Tsung-han passed them up and left, bringing on their machination and arrogance. Having come direct to Tientsin and Ta-ku, the bar cannot entirely block steamers and their proximity is enough to make us fear redoubled coercion.

It is reported that warships have been borrowed from other countries and that their expenditures are not insignificant; that they have come united with the idea that we will have to do as they wish; that both coal and grain were completely prepared at Shanghai so that we can hardly control their fate by cutting off their supplies, so how can we expect them to be willing to sail back at once?

Your officials have thought it over and over. As Your Majesty cherishes clemency for those from afar, could we not take their requests, deliberate on them first and discriminate with them beforehand so as to give them something to hope for, and perhaps succeed gradually in bringing them to submission? Tientsin is now involved with ocean transport and the rice-tribute boats are gathered like clouds, so it is certainly no time to resort to war. As all military operations are not over in the five ports, how can we bring on still more trouble? They respectfully ask that Imperial omniscience quickly grant a Heavenly decision to enable them to proceed. (IWSM.HF 21; 9a, 10-11a, 3)

295. May 3, 1858. MEMORIAL: T'an T'ing-hsiang Reports Conversations with the Russians Urging an Increase in the Number of Treaty Ports.

T'an T'ing-hsiang and others further memorialize. The Russian barbarians state that there has been clandestine trading outside the five ports. It has been discovered that as various barbarians have traded for a long time there must have been smuggled goods going back and forth everywhere; but local miscreants have extorted and obstructed and made it impossible for them to do as they like; consequently they ask for an open increase of ports to afford them monopolistic control of profits. As this is their motive, this, therefore, is also the means of controlling them. But barbarians are naturally insatiable and there must be still further investigation.

Whether the barbarians, in the twelfth month of last year (January 15-February 13, 1858), in Kiangsu, presented an official letter to Yü-ch'eng, and whether they received a reply, Your officials are not completely informed. They request an Edict ordering the Grand Council to copy and send the documents to use for reference. (IWSM.HF 21; 11a, 4-10)

296. May 3, 1858. EDICT: Urges Utilization of the Russians to Impress China's Views on the British and Authorizes Concessions in regard to Customs.

Edict to the Grand Councillors. T'an T'ing-hsiang and others have memorialized that thorough investigation shows barbarian temper unpredictable and ask for an Edict allowing their requests to be deliberated

first. Because the English barbarians did not come for a meeting on
the first, T'an T'ing-hsiang and others sent deputies to inquire of
the Russian barbarians. They were told that the requests of the
English and other barbarians were limited to two things.

T'an T'ing-hsiang and others originally agreed to fix a date today for seeing the English, French, and American barbarians. We
wonder what the situation is, and we expect that it is surely difficult
to reason with them. All they can do is to tell the Russian barbarians
that the English and other barbarians in Kwangtung occupied the provincial capital, abducted a high official, acted like rebels, and were
fundamentally not worth talking to. Since Russia came along to mediate we postponed the use of force and even allowed them to meet the
Imperial Commissioner. This exemplifies China's cherishing clemency
for those from afar with complete magnanimity and complete justice.
Since the provincial capital of Kwangtung has not been restored and
Governor General Yeh has not been returned, what reason is there for
not imposing punishment rather than granting favors? If England and
France had come by themselves we could only have ignored them completely, not even allowing them to anchor quietly in the port. Now that
Russia was willing to intercede, she must leave China some face so
that both will be satisfied. If she unfairly listens to England, France,
and America's side of the story, it would be awkward for China and
would even obstruct a settlement.

On the subject of trade, in the Tao-kuang period (1820-1850)
treaties of perpetual amity were established, restricting it to the five
ports. Now the demand to add other places of trade outside the five
ports is not in conformity with the old treaties. In the more than ten
years since peace negotiations, China has never resorted to arms in
defiance of treaties; if they want another negotiation to add places to
trade, the previous perpetual treaties of peace were set up in vain,
and how could they inspire China's confidence? So it is entirely useless to discuss this matter.

However, as Russia has come in friendship, if there are any
instances of recent maladministration of trade in the five ports, we
can still consider adjustments. For instance, the statement in the
English barbarians' communication that goods transported to the interior encounter exactions and bribes in addition to the payment of
customs: if this is the case, China must certainly investigate and
stop it. The statement that because of decreased valuations in recent
years they want to negotiate customs reductions, is also within reason;
but if there are reductions, there must be increases; that is only just.
There must not be reduction without increase, which (would be) designe
only for the self-interest (of the barbarians).

As this arrangement necessitates a complete understanding of trad
in the ports, we cannot at this point make long range proposals, but the
hub of the five ports has always been in Kwangtung and all tariff

schedules have originally been fixed by Kwangtung. At this time the provincial capital is still occupied. How can China consider granting favors? Nor can she very well approve their requests in advance. We can only impose on the Russian minister to convey this sense to the English barbarians and urge them to return to Kwangtung and on the other hand, to restore the capital and return Governor General Yeh. With the enmity of the Cantonese somewhat abated and the two countries not concerned about suffering losses, then His Imperial Majesty will have something to say of granting favors.

As to Catholicism, it has also been settled before and incorporated in the treaties that anyone going out of bounds or going far into the interior would be subject to arrest by Chinese officials, to be returned in custody to the consul at the nearest port for disposal. We, China, have faithfully maintained the old regulation and over the years, whenever barbarian missionaries have been encountered they have been returned and turned over to their respective consuls. There has never been any instance of maltreatment. Now because the Cantonese bandit, Ma Tzu-nung, defied laws in Hsi-lin-hsien, Kwangsi, and was severely punished, the French barbarians, suspecting that it was their missionary Father Ma [i. e. Abbé Chapdelaine], started a quarrel. If they do not believe (the reports), they have only to ask for an Edict again instructing the new governor general to make an impartial investigation. How can they say on partial evidence that China is barbarous? For example, these two countries abducted Governor General Yeh and now that their envoys are coming ashore, what is to prevent China from taking revenge? As China treats others with confidence, she does not do this unreasonable sort of thing.

The various foregoing items, T'an T'ing-hsiang and the others can tell the Russian barbarians and have them pass them on to the English and French barbarians. See how they reply and then deliberate and act. Matters of trade are what are significant to these barbarians. As on this trip the Russian barbarians are outwardly respectful and compliant, we can take advantage of this to control them. As they ask for trade at the ports, promise that after general conditions in Kwangtung are settled, you could certainly memorialize for them requesting Imperial Favor, but as all matters of trade at the ports are alike for all countries, they must also go to Kwangtung for a settlement; that there will certainly be an Edict notifying the new Imperial Commissioner and governor general beforehand.

We are afraid that T'an T'ing-hsiang and the others in handling this matter will not complete it in one or two interviews with the barbarians; they must keep level heads and even tempers in reasoning with them. Now that they are caging the Russian barbarians to keep the English and French from breaking loose, the Russian barbarians, because of hope for trade, must needs exert themselves.

The outcome will certainly be to let them profit from barbarian customs and not send them back disappointed. Although this means a loss on our part, compared to an increase of ports without any restriction whatever, there is the saying that given two evils, choose the lesser. We expect that the said governor general and others are able tacitly to comprehend this.

Order the letter presented by the barbarians to Yü-ch'eng in the twelfth month of last year (January 15-February 13, 1858), and also Yü-ch'eng's reply to Ho Kuei-ch'ing and others, and the various letters and memorials all copied and sent for reference. (IWSM.HF 21; 11b, 1-13b, 3)

297. May 5, 1858. MEMORIAL: T'an T'ing-hsiang Reports Continued Use of the Russians and Americans as Mediators and Poutiatine's Warning of Allied Strength.

Governor General of Chihli T'an T'ing-hsiang, Superintendent of Imperial Granaries Ch'ung-lun, Sub-chancellor of the Grand Secretariat Wu-erh-kun-t'ai, and Chihli Financial Commissioner Ch'ien Hsin-ho memorialize. As the English barbarians broke their promise and failed to come, on the third we ordered deputies Pien Pao-shu and Ch'en K'o-ming to go back to the Russian barbarians' ship and say that since they were interceding for the English barbarians, they should not have allowed them to break their engagements, and still less need they come inside the bar with them and anchor their ships; that obviously they did not want to make peace and their previous request for Imperial Favor had become practically impossible to act upon. Furthermore, they told them that troops and militia are now mobilized and land and sea are both defended, that the hearts of the entire populace are filled with animosity because the steamers had come inside the bar and are demanding an attack on them; that because our ministers, mindful that their country came to mediate, were unwilling to start hostilities immediately; that the Tientsin watercourse is narrow, entirely unlike that at Canton; that northern crack troops are much stronger than southern, as the extermination of the Canton rebels in 1853 and 1854 clearly demonstrated. The implication is dangerous and let their country not deceive itself.

The chief, Poutiatine, said that they were entirely displeased by England and France's reliance on force but once hostilities began, even if England and France went away defeated, they were sure to return in later years and the evil of protracted warfare would never be ended; that actually they did not wish it but it was absolutely essential that our ministers agree to negotiate here, then they could make explanations; otherwise, there was nothing they could do; that they would immediately send someone to order the French barbarians to take it up again with the English barbarians; that if in the future there were a rupture, they would certainly withdraw outside the bar and not cooperate with them.

Judging from their attitude and speech, this is somewhat different from what they said yesterday but it cannot be relied on. We shall
see how they intercede and then decide.

Then the American barbarians sent someone to deliver a letter
asking for an interview. Your officials agreed to have their envoy
come to the port between three and five in the afternoon, received him
courteously and made it clear to him that His Imperial Majesty commended his country highly for not being willing to help the English
and French in Kwangtung, but what was the real reason for their arriving with the English and French now? They were told that the
Kwangtung affair was no concern of theirs; that he and the Russian
and French (envoys) proposed to intercede for the recently arrived
envoy, Elgin, as well as those who made trouble last year, hence he
came to ask for an interview. Your officers replied that they were
just about to send a communication to them asking those two countries
(Russia and America) to arbitrate (the rights and wrongs of) the case.
The said chief agreed.

Then he repeatedly asked earnestly whether Your officials would
have authority to decide matters of the two countries. Your officials replied that the regulations of the Heavenly Court had never
provided for a minister plenopotentiary, free to act as he pleased;
that they were Imperially assigned to this place and if matters were
reasonable could memorialize them asking for an Edict. The barbarians then said that twelve years had elapsed since the establishment of
the treaties, and several articles in them must be changed; that they
had received orders to come and act; that in addition, the credentials
from their sovereign were presented in Min-Che in 1856, with the request that they be memorialized for them. Unexpectedly the original
wrappers were broken and afterwards they were returned to them and
their sovereign had lost face terribly, so they asked that they be presented. They forthwith brought out the credentials for us to see.

Your officials replied that they did not recognize barbarian characters. They then produced translations into Chinese character, stating
that "the Emperor of the Great United States of America sends a letter
to His Majesty the Great Emperor and has delegated T'u-liang[6] to come
to China to arrange matters of perpetual friendship between the two
countries." He said that he must request a sealed letter of His Imperial
Majesty in reply as an evidence of friendship of the two countries.

Your officials replied that credentials were not the same as official letters, that they could not accept them blindly, and must wait
and ask for an Edict and act accordingly. When asked what the changes

---

6 This transliteration of Chinese characters has not been identified.

were, they said that after their credentials were accepted they could
discuss them. They also said that on February 10 of this year, in
Kiangsu, they besought the governor to transmit an official letter to
Grand Secretary Yü, which stated them clearly and we must have
copies of the original text sent for reference within a few days; and
further, that when they and Russia interceded and explained for
England and France they would bring up this matter again. Then they
sailed back.

Your officials observed that their attitude and speech were still
respectful and compliant. Your officials have memorialized asking
for an Edict ordering the Grand Council to copy and dispatch last
year's letters presented to Grand Secretary Yü-ch'eng. Whether the
credentials they presented can be accepted and forwarded or not,
Your officials dared not assume authority. They await an Edict and
will act accordingly. Further, the English and French barbarians
must wait until the Russian and American barbarians shall have clari-
fied matters to them before they can be received. (IWSM.HF 21;
13b, 4-15b, 4)

298. May 5, 1858. EDICT: Discredits Poutiatine and Urges the Commissioners to Utilize Reed to Mediate and to Limit Treaty Revision to
Slight Modifications.

Edict to the Grand Councillors. T'an T'ing-hsiang and others
have memorialized on their questioning the Russian barbarians and
receiving the American barbarians. The Russian barbarian Poutiatine's word cannot be relied on so it is necessary to explain the situation to the American chief and see how he can be brought around.

In 1854, the American and English barbarians came to Tientsin
together and it was Ch'ung-lun and others who went to interview them.
Those countries had failed to pay customs duties at the ports. Because
bandits had caused trouble, and trade was in a grievous state, these
duties were rescinded by special Favor. Also the two matters of the
Canton tea duty and Chinese-barbarian controversies were both turned
over to Yeh Ming-ch'en to consult records and settle. Yeh Ming-ch'en
was also instructed to notify the barbarians that the settlement of these
three items fulfilled the twelve-year revision clause and outside these
there could be no further negotiation. Now the American barbarians
tell us that in the old treaties there are still places which must be
changed. They have not pointed out what clauses. Order T'an T'ing-
hsiang and others to question the American barbarians again.

As to the credentials they presented in 1856, since the governor
general of Min-Che is not Imperially commissioned to handle barbarian
affairs, he did not accept them, telling them as a matter of course to go
to Kwangtung to present them. Now they tell us that Yeh Ming-ch'en
was willing for them to present them but would not meet them personally, therefore they did not present them. Thus, their country stopped of

its own accord. Now that they have come to Tientsin, since T'an T'ing-hsiang and the others are Imperially commissioned, they can allow them to be presented and memorialized for them. Also have them translated into Chinese characters to facilitate recognition.

As for Poutiatine, he is fundamentally outside the picture and what he says is not reliable.

If the American barbarians continue fairly reasonable, you can offer them some inducement to get them to act as go-between. Tell them that in regard to the former agreement on revision in twelve years, it was primarily limited to slight modifications and did not provide for extensive revision. Anything reasonable would certainly be memorialized for them, but in the treaty port trade all countries were equal; that at present England and France occupied the capital of Kwangtung and had not been expelled. Although Acting Governor General Po-kuei had proposed opening the port beforehand, popular sentiment was apprehensive and merchants did not gather in numbers. In addition the English barbarians burned private dwellings and aroused popular animosity. The village bands were always contemplating revenge. Although their country did not help the English barbarians, trade was stopped and they suffered great losses; so it was essential to bring the Kwangtung affair to a speedy conclusion. Then they could memorialize asking for changes in procedure and the various countries would all be benefited. After they have presented their credentials, (say that) His Imperial Majesty commends their country and that there will certainly be a reply. Talk to them plausibly like this, see how they respond, and then act as occasions arise.

As to the Russian and American barbarians, since both say they are explaining to the English and French, the Russian barbarians should have a reply by this time. Study their attitude and speech, report again in a memorial, and wait for an Edict. (IWSM.HF 21; 15b, 5-16b, 6)

299. May 7, 1858. MEMORIAL: T'an T'ing-hsiang Reports the Inability of Either the Russians or Americans to Curb the Allies and Urges Appeasement.

Governor General of Chihli T'an T'ing-hsiang, Superintendent of Imperial Granaries Ch'ung lun, Sub-chancellor of the Grand Secretariat Wu-erh-kun-t'ai, and Financial Commissioner of Chihli Ch'ien Hsin-ho memorialize. For several days the English and French barbarians have not been very active; the Russian and American chiefs, nominally respectful and compliant, harbor schemes for making demands. If we were lenient, they would adhere to England and France in the hope of gain; if we were severe, they would withdraw support from England and France to keep out of harm. To utilize our ability to unite or divide to turn the tide was actually a plan of mollification.

But at present the English chief is very confident and is utilizing
France. Russia and America merely hope to benefit from the achievements of others. They cannot actually curb their violence and intercede for us. Thus, controlling the enemy is still the objective for us
to look to and we can never meet the situation with empty talk.

Now on both sides of the port, small arms and artillery are arranged and 8 to 9,000 soldiers and militia are deployed, making a
rather formidable array. In the rear, 1000 cavalry are stationed in
Hsin-ho and Hsin-ch'eng districts, ready to be called in time of need.
As not many troops were left inside Tientsin, Your official has added
his garrison of 300 men to the encampment outside the east gate, to
cooperate with the merchant volunteers and household volunteers in
patroling and keeping order, so it is fairly secure.

But the barbarians' eight steamers and three small ships anchored
five or six li in front of the forts are spying night and day. Should they
suddenly force entrance they could not easily be stopped. Besides in
less than a month, food supplies and such have cost 40,000 or 50,000
taels, and if after a useless stalemate these give out, there will be
still more to be concerned about.

Your officials have deliberated seriously over and over; without
devising a plan for controlling the enemy, there can hardly be an effective expulsion of the enemy. We beg to think that for England and
France to occupy our provincial capital and abduct our high official
in Kwangtung, and then unite all the barbarians on a military expedition in the North while Shanghai, Ningpo, Foochow, and Amoy trade
as usual, is to mock China without the slightest fear. As for present
policy, it seems we should put up a bluff, sending word to barbarian
merchants in the various ports that on account of this northern venture in disregard of treaties, on such-and-such a day of such-and-such
a month, goods will be placed under seal and customs closed, relations
will be completely broken off, and we will not trade with them. On the
one hand, charge the governor general of Liang-kuang to plan a speedy
recovery of the capital, so that when the barbarians hear it they will
have reason to regret and stand in awe; then Your officials will inform
them of the plan to stop goods and close customs on a certain date.
On the other hand, explain and get them to agree among themselves,
with a chance of gradually getting them into our bailiwick. If we
merely wrangle, we are afraid that it will go on indefinitely. Plans
for controlling barbarians necessarily make trade their resting place
but a mere adjustment of customs schedule is not enough to satisfy
their demands; if there is a prolonged stalemate, we very much fear
the development of awkward complications.

In the matter of ports, if we can prevent addition, there is no need
of discussion, but if we cannot, may Your officials be allowed tentative-
ly to make careful calculation as to what places might be considered
and ask for an Edict for guidance? As to the barbarians' requests,

they must wait investigation and action in Kwangtung, but if the general scheme is not determined in Tientsin, the barbarians will suspect the old rut of evasion and a conclusion will be practically impossible. (IWSM.HF 21; 17b, 2-18b, 9)

300. **May 7, 1858**. MEMORIAL: Reports Separate Negotiations with the Russians and Requests Receipt of Reed's Credentials by the Court.

T'an T'ing-hsiang further memorializes. To continue, yesterday Your officials sent communications to the Russian and American chiefs to explain the English-French Kwangtung question for us. Then on the fifth we delegated Pien Pao-shu and Ch'en K'o-ming to go and sound out the Russian chief.

He told them that he had conferred with the English and French for several days and expended a great deal of plausible talk; that now the position of the French barbarians had taken shape. He discussed it with our deputies and their separate report is respectfully presented for Imperial inspection but the Russian chief wants to have his country's requests decided first. Your officials will have him explain the English-French problem clearly and then memorialize asking extraordinary Imperial Favor. They also told him that since the said chief's request to have Lama Pa-la-ti and others leave Peking to see him has no connection with public affairs of the two countries, they had memorialized and received Imperial permission and they should arrive shortly, as a means of showing control. The said chief was profoundly grateful.

As to the American chief's request that his credentials be presented, its wording is very laudatory. We find his object does not go beyond the hope of receiving an Imperial Rescript in reply, to give him glory at home. If we do not receive them, it would be hard to give an excuse; and besides, it is no obstacle to the main problem. [The French précis follows.] (IWSM.HF 21; 18b, 10-19a, 10)

301. **May 7, 1858**. EDICT: Rejects Proposal to use Bluff against the British but Offers to Appease them with the Russians and Americans as Guarantors.

Edict to the Grand Councillors. T'an T'ing-hsiang and others have memorialized that barbarian affairs are unsettled and ask that both Imperial Favor and Imperial Awe be employed. Their proposal of sending orders to the various ports to stop goods and close customs and also charging the governor general of Liang-kuang speedily to recover the provincial capital, is one way of curbing barbarians, but to arouse them now while the ocean (tribute) transport is en route is to court trouble.

Huang Tsung-han has not yet reached Kwangtung and Po-kuei has succumbed to the coercion of the barbarians and cannot speak his own mind. If we bluff without being able to carry it through, it will on the contrary be exposed and exploded by the barbarians and make them still more arrogant.

Since the English and French barbarians do not care to come, it is not necessary to set any more dates with them, but go on transmitting messages through the Russian and American barbarians. Say that their two countries have unceremoniously disregarded treaties and fundamentally do not deserve to have us meet them; that the only reason dates were arranged for interviews was regard for Russian and American face; that now that they have twice missed appointments, their coming or not coming will depend on their own volition; that yesterday you memorialized and received an Imperial Edict insisting that the two countries restore the capital city of Kwangtung and repent sincerely before detailed negotiations can be concluded; that His Imperial Majesty fixed the end of the fourth month (June 10) as a limit for the restoration of the capital of Kwangtung and if it were not restored by this time, hostilities would be started the beginning of the fifth month, the capital attacked, and the barbarian troops of the two countries in the city would certainly be annihilated; let them not hesitate now and be sorry afterwards; that now His Imperial Majesty is convinced that the English barbarians are the principal evil-doers, even burning business houses and private dwellings and arousing popular animosity, and in the future the port of Canton would certainly not admit them to trade; that although the French barbarians helped the evil-doers, in view of their previous aid in exterminating rebels in Shanghai, if they would withdraw from the provincial capital, they could still be forgiven; but that if the capital of Kwangtung is not restored and Yeh Ming-ch'en not returned, besides opening hostilities and attacking the city, we will order the five ports to stop English and French trade; that if the Kwangtung affair is brought to a speedy conclusion, not only can the French barbarians be somewhat forgiven, but the present high officials will also memorialize for the trade of the English barbarians in Kwangtung, requesting Imperial indulgence.

As for tariff reductions, they are unmitigated losses to China. But since no additonal ports have been granted despite America's respect and compliance, His Imperial Majesty will give them benefits in the customs schedules in the five ports. But as England and France still occupy Canton, how have they the face to ask Imperial Favor? However, His Imperial Majesty having conferred the Favor on America, in the future all countries would benefit alike, and when England and France shall have repented and resumed trade, they will be treated the same without further negotiation. As to the extent of tariff reductions necessary, we cannot make proposals at this distance; they must be determined by Kwangtung. But after they are made clear, we shall not eat our words, Russia and America will be witnesses.

Whether or not England and France terminate the Kwangtung affair on schedule, Russia and America must also act as neutral guarantors, so when this matter has been settled in outline the countries can go back. On the day that the negotiations of the three countries are concluded, you can memorialize asking for trade for Russia, so that they can all go to Kwangtung together and negotiate treaties with Governor General Huang.

Barbarians are naturally crafty so how can the word of deputies be relied on? If the English and French chiefs come in person, negotiate with them yourselves; otherwise, have the Russian and American chiefs come for interviews and have them transmit word. Since it is the word of high officials it can be trusted; there is no use having deputies wear themselves out carrying word back and forth.

Considering now the matter of tariff reduction, although detrimental to China, it is better to talk of maintaining existing treaties, than to open more ports and make the barbarians' attitude more arrogant. Since we will not increase ports, we will allow them tariff revision as a means of control. Although it is said that where there is reduction, there must be increase, since barbarians are greedy by nature, the reductions will have to be large and the increases small. There is nothing to fear in their getting a little profit.

Although most of the various itemized French requests transmitted by the Russian barbarians have been rejected by the deputies, they cannot speak for the Imperial Commissioners. We now order the Grand Council to issue specific replies item by item, so that when the time comes the said governor general and others can repudiate them [i. e. the French requests]. These will be in general agreement with previous Edicts.

Now that (tribute) transports are gathering in clouds, this is where the barbarians can bring pressure; this is also where we must be apprehensive. These (barbarians) have come North from Shanghai without any trace of insurrection, so the said governor general and others are not to initiate hostilities just because their forces are adequate. Even if they succeeded at Tientsin without any difficulty, if they (the English and French) were to throw other places into confusion, we fear it would not be the same as at Tientsin. The governor general and others must consider the situation as a whole and make suitable adjustment.

As to the American barbarian's credentials, a previous Edict authorized their presentation and We trust T'an T'ing-hsiang and the others will have received them and acted accordingly. (IWSM.HF 21; 21a, 3-22b, 10)

302. May 7, 1858. MEMORIAL: Ho Kuei-ch'ing Reports Shanghai Rumors of French and American Developments of Significance to China's Foreign Policy.

Ho Kuei-ch'ing and others further memorialize. To continue, just as Your official was preparing his memorial he received a secret

report from Acting Tao-t'ai of Su-Sung-T'ai Hsüeh Huan that it is
rumored in the barbarian hongs that a man plotted the assassination
of the King of France; word leaked out and he fled into English territory; France demanded he be given up but he was not, whereupon both
parties assembled warships and are on the verge of conflict. He also
heard that America was calling her warships back home and would
not allow them to create enmity with China. He questioned barbarian
merchants generally and all said the same.

Vermilion Endorsement: Seen. (IWSM.HF 21; 25b, 1-6)

303. May 8, 1858. EDICT: Utilizes Russian and American Envoys to
Transmit China's Rejection of the English and French Terms at Ta-ku.

Edict to the Grand Councillors. T'an T'ing-hsiang and others
have memorialized that the English and French chiefs presented communications. . .

The documents presented by England and France are despicably
perverse and erroneous. Yesterday's Edict instructed you to notify
the Russians and Americans to transmit word to these barbarians of
a time limit for the restoration of the Kwangtung capital and if it
were not restored by that time, on the one hand, the customs would be
closed, and on the other, hostilities begun. We assume that T'an T'ing-
hsiang and others on receipt of this immediately notified the Russians
and Americans to send the word to them. If on this account the English
and French reverse their policy, the matter of discretionary action
need not be brought up again.

If they insist on an answer, you can say that Russia and America
are speaking for us first and that an answer is forthcoming; say that
previously Ch'i-ying and others at Kwangtung received Edicts of the
Late Reign allowing them discretionary action, probably because they
were far away and communication wasted time; but Ch'i-ying and the
others still memorialized all matters, never acting on their own
authority; that as China does not have this office, subsequent Kwangtung
Imperial Commissioners without the term "discretionary action" were
still able to act, were they not?

For instance, in 1854, when Ch'ung-lun was sent to Tientsin to
meet the English and American envoys, did he have "discretionary
action" specified? Still he was able to memorialize all the items of
remitting back customs for them and petition for approval. How is
it that the Imperial Commissioner this time is held in such contempt?
Matters that require settlement have been communicated through
Russia and America and since they (England and France) did not come
to us there was no use coercing them. This place is not primarily a
trading port. Previous negotiations took place originally in Kwangtung
and their starting hostilities in defiance of treaties was entirely without reason. Since Russia and America interceded for them, His Imperial Majesty, generous as Heaven, specially ordered High Officials

to see them both, certainly an extraordinary Favor. Now that they do
not appreciate our good intentions and even dare to deprecate us, the
present minister has memorialized according to the facts. Let them
go back to Kwangtung and await a settlement rather than have regrets
later.

As to T'an T'ing-hsiang and others fearing that they will take
advantage of the tide to come up the river, if they merely sail around
it will not hurt us any; should they start hostilities, we would have an
excuse to return fire. The hostilities must in no case be started by
us. We assume they know we are prepared and that they will not dare
act presumptuously. (IWSM.HF 21; 28b, 5-29b, 3)

304. May 9, 1858. MEMORIAL: Tientsin Officials Report the Continued
Use of Russian and American Mediation and Reed's Request for Separate
Negotiations.

Governor General of Chihli T'an T'ing-hsiang, Superintendent of
Imperial Granary Ch'ung-lun, Sub-Chancellor of the Grand Secretariat
Wu-erh-kun-t'ai and Financial Commissioner of Chihli Ch'ien Hsin-ho
memorialize:. . . When Your officials have a plan of action, they can
reply to the (British and French) and on the other hand find means to
get the Russian and American chiefs to explain, so they will realize
that we are not indulging in empty talk. Then the situation can be
saved. Your officials, not fearing to be considered rash, have taken
their humble views and made a list of them for Your Majesty to see
whether or not they can be allowed, and ask for an Edict to guide their
actions.

Today the American chief sent someone to present a document,
also setting a six-day limit and agreeing to negotiate separately.
Allow us to wait until we have met them and then make observations.
(IWSM.HF 21; 35a, 4-9)

305. May 9, 1858. EDICT: American Credentials Accepted--Authorizes
Consideration of her Requests and Use of U.S. to Prevent Outbreak of
Hostilities.

Edict to the Grand Councillors:. . . As the American chief's
credentials have been allowed to be presented, if he has any other requests, order them handled the same as those of the English and
French barbarians. As to the Russian barbarians' requests for a
boundary definition and for trade in the five ports, the governor general
and the others having received yesterday's Edict, have, we assume,
made suitable reply. Although at present you have hopes of the English
and French barbarians coming under control, you must still have the
Russian and American chiefs devise means to explain to them, to prevent the development of other complications. The governor general
and others can, we assume, deliberate and act conscientiously. (IWSM.
HF 21; 36a, 7-36b, 1)

306. May 9, 1858. MEMORIAL: T'an T'ing-hsiang Reports Meeting
with Reed and Poutiatine, the Futility of Dependence on them, and Urges
Appeasement.

T'an T'ing-hsiang and others further memorialize. Your officials
have met both the Russian and American chiefs, but not the English
and French chiefs; nor have officers been sent to (see) them. Upon
careful daily observation, (it is found that) the barbarians' attitude is
not uniform. The English and French defy reason and while the
Russians and Americans are affable, yet the desire to satisfy their
demands is the same among them all. At present with Canton unre-
covered, the English and French still daring to resort to hostilities
and invest our ports, it is no different from their entering the Yangtze
River in the Tao-kuang period, so they hope to utilize Ch'i-ying's
policy to facilitate their extortion.

Thus while Russia and America realize English and French
tyranny and presumptuousness, they do not prevent it; on the contrary
they both condone their acts, sitting by to get the fisherman's share.
[Reference to the fable of the kingfisher that seized a clam which
in turn closed on the kingfisher's bill, so it could not get away. Meanwhile a fisherman came along and took both of them.] As Your official
respect the Imperial Decision, they have repeatedly tried to captivate
them, to make them happy and get them into our power. If we speak
of outward appearance they are very different from the English and
French, but if we probe their hearts they are just like the English and
French.

Now the Russian chief's case must be postponed until the three
countries are humbled and negotiations concluded. Then (Poutiatine's
request can be) memorialized asking him to go along to Kwangtung,
which he and the three other chiefs are now equally unwilling to do.
Will he be willing to exert himself? And even if he does exert himself to intercede, will the other three chiefs acquiesce? (Your official
feel) rather uncertain about the plan of manipulation.

Besides, yesterday the said chiefs all set a time limit of six days,
when relations can be broken off immediately if no reply is forthcomin
Your officials realize that once there are hostilities, ocean (tribute)
transport will be blocked immediately, the countryside thrown into
alarm, and when Tientsin is in confusion anything can happen. But for
such a pressing situation, this kind of rebellious, uncivil chief (Poutiatine) has not the slightest regard and certainly cannot be brought to
his knees with mere words, or obey our wave of the hand. If we did
not report straightforwardly according to facts our crime would be gre

Your officials dare not be cowardly or influenced by them, but at
this critical juncture, ideally they must maintain national prestige,
practically they must mollify barbarian belligerency, and the advantag
and disadvantage to each must be considered. They humbly ask that
Your Majesty deign to bear in mind that the local responsibility is

extremely great and, from the items previously memorialized by His
officials, condescend to make a selection, and consider beforehand
how much Favor will be granted the Russian chief. Besides, as ports
cannot easily be increased, consider some other consolation. We
beseech a Heavenly decision to act upon. (IWSM.HF 21; 38a, 10-39a,
10)

307. May 9, 1858. AMERICAN MEMORANDUM:[7] United States Minister
Reed Lists his Proposals for the Revision of the Treaty of Wang-hsia.
    1. Since China has never had silver currency, payment of customs
and tonnage dues is very troublesome. If the Chinese nation, as Japan,
Annam, and Siam have recently done, were willing to use minted coins
current according to value, the difficulty would be removed. If in this
matter they got men of ability to direct skilled workmen, it could be
easily accomplished and would avoid in the future the continual irrita-
tion of the past.
    2. The Envoy of the United States is most anxious to use all his
energies to prevent the entrance of opium, but it is essential that
Chinese officials, as provided in Article 33 of the treaty, cooperate
before anything can be accomplished.
    3. Recently residents of South China have often been enticed and
carried to foreign countries in great numbers to do hard labor in
strange lands. If Chinese coastal officials are willing to cooperate,
means can certainly be found in accord with the wishes of China to
negotiate the cessation of this kind of evil practice.
    4. Citizens of the United States bringing charges against the
Chinese state demanding indemnity, whether on account of arbitrary
confinement, pirating and destroying ships and cargo, burning residences and warehouses, or robbery, as well as many matters relating
to local officials accumulated over a period of years, have repeatedly
been brought to the attention of the governor general of Liang-kuang
and none of them have ever been satisfied. Now they must be redressed
immediately. If the Court is willing to send a special officer, complete evidence to support the charges will be presented for his scrutiny,
as well as the amounts clearly itemized--a matter of not more than
some 600,000 taels.
    5. The specially appointed Imperial Commissioner of the United
States should either be allowed to reside in Peking or to go and come
at will. When western countries send Imperially commissioned officials to another country this practice is always followed. Then if
the officials or people of the two countries have disputes or matters
to discuss, they can go immediately direct to the court and arrange

---

7 This is the Chinese version of Reed's memorandum to the Chinese commissioners. No
   memorandum in this form has been located in the American documents. The items have
   been numbered for clarity.

matters suitably. This is the long-standing practice of all countries and the benefits are great. Because China has not permitted the Imperial representatives of friendly countries to communicate with the Court, coastal governors general and governors have not been willing to grant interviews, as everybody knows, so that long-standing disputes are unsettled. If Chinese high officials had personal intercourse with foreign envoys they could study their governments and customs, and in case Chinese nationals were injured by foreign countries, they could notify their respective envoys, clear it up and get redress. Thus it is apparent that if this item is Approved, both parties will benefit. For instance, in social intercourse it is necessary to see one another face to face to achieve permanent friendship. In 1856, if there had been an American minister in Peking the Canton catastrophe could have been avoided. Looking at present developments, it is feared China will suffer, but were there today a minister resident there he could prevent calamity and restore friendship.

6. The Special Imperial Commissioner of the United States should be allowed direct communication with the Chinese Court. It can be done either through a specially designated president of the Board of Rites, Grand Councillor, or Grand Secretary, by special transmission by coastal governors general and governors, or presentation by his own deputy. Heretofore, there have often been matters they wished to reach the Court, but since the coastal authorities had no power to act, nothing was accomplished.

7. Hereafter, China must increase the coastal ports trading with foreign countries. Now there are several places which have begun trading privately. Could these immediately be made legitimate trading ports, merchants would go about their business and China would be benefited. For instance in Kwangtung, Ch'iung-chou, Tien-po, and Sha-t'ou in Ch'ao-chou; in Fukien, Ch'uan-chou; T'an-shui on T'ai-wan; and in Chekiang, Wen-chou, although not authorized to open their ports, have considerable trade and the natives have profited greatly. If these ports, as well as others, were all opened at once and regulations established, national revenue could be increased and illegal traders suppressed.

8. Ships of the United States should be allowed to go to the Yangtze River and to the Pearl River in Kwangtung and all their tributaries, in accord with regulations agreed upon, to trade and reside in the marts along them; but ships plying inland waters must be under the jurisdiction of Chinese officials; they must also be provided with pilots and allowed to procure food and things for their use.

9. According to the previously negotiated treaty, ships of the United States pay heavier tonnage dues than other countries because the method of measuring hulks to compute tonnage is different from that of other countries. That is to say, the United States takes 40 cubic feet as one ton while other countries take 50 cubic feet. Hereafter, (we

should) establish that every ton of 40 standard feet will pay 4 mace, to match the ships of other countries using 50 standard feet to the ton and paying 5 mace. (It should) also be agreed that hereafter all ports must spend 1/4 of their tonnage dues to improve and inspect the watercourse of the said port. Heretofore, with the exception of Woosung, Chinese officials at the various ports have not inspected them thoroughly so that at Foochow and Ningpo, due to the lack of lighthouses and marker buoys, the number of ships wrecked is not small, so China does not get the revenue from these ships. In other countries all the ports either build long-range light houses, or erect watch towers, markers, and floating buoys, and also publish accurate survey charts to facilitate communication. China must also utilize its tonnage receipts likewise.

10. Hereafter, Chinese who have accepted the religion of Jesus Christ cannot be punished on this account by Chinese officials. In 1844, the Imperial Commissioner memorialized and received an Imperial Edict granting that since the Catholic religion urged men to do good, its proscription was abolished. This will be but an extension of that clause.

11. Several clauses contained in the Treaty of Wang-hsia (Wanghia) have been repeatedly demonstrated to be not conducive to the improvement of benefits to the peoples of the two countries nor to friendly intercourse.

After all the above items have been negotiated, we must have the articles in the treaty which must be revised copied out and presented to the honorable ministers for scrutiny. That is to say that although the treaty established between our two countries is to maintain perpetual amity, still, after continued trial, it must be improved and revised.

Hereafter China will find it entirely impossible not to have intercourse with foreign countries and it would be better as in the K'ang-hsi period (1662-1723) to throw open all places in the country to free intercourse and thus abolish bigotry and the unwillingness to treat with the etiquette of equality which is bringing on China the evil of disruptive warfare. If Chinese officials are willing to accept these suggestions it will certainly enable China to move on a basis of complete equality with all western countries as well as to receive benefits.

12. The Chinese Imperial Commissioner has already agreed with the minister of the United States that hereafter, whatever honors, favors, or benefits the Great Ch'ing Dynasty extends to other countries, whether they concern ships, the high seas, trade and commerce, or political relations, which the said countries have not heretofore held, must all be allowed to citizens of the United States to benefit equally, just as if they had been specified in the treaty of their own country. (IWSM.HF 21; 41a, 4-44b, 8)

308. <u>May 9, 1858</u>. EDICT: Considers American Proposals and Author- izes Two Additional Ports, Adjustment of Tonnage Dues, and Rejects the Rest.

Edict to the Grand Councillors. Today T'an T'ing-hsiang and others have memorialized that barbarian affairs seem to have reached a turning point, and having made a list of the requests of the English and French barbarians, ask for an Edict. These have been either ap- proved or rejected and orders sent to the said governor to so reply to them.

Now is received a memorial of T'an T'ing-hsiang and others, that on the seventh they received the Court letter and Edict; that on thorough investigation of the barbarian situation, it is not easy to finesse; and that they are presenting for inspection the original text of the items requested by the American barbarians.

The trade of the American barbarians is fundamentally the same as that of other countries, and as we see their requests they would inevitably bring about complications, but now that we want to pursue a policy of finessing, we cannot but calculate how to choose among them. As to the proposal to increase trading ports, trade at five ports is incorporated in the treaties for perpetual observance, so when orders were given previously not to allow addition discussed, the proposal was made to reduce customs. Now that the governor general and others, unable to turn them down, again memorialize the barbarians' requests, how could they expect assent? However, there is no alter- native but to consider adding one small port in each province adjoining the ports in Fukien and Kwangtung. Orders must also be given the governors general and governors of those two provinces to make suitable investigation for putting this in operation. Beyond this, discussion is useless.

There is also the request on computing tonnage dues. They say that their country takes 40 feet as one ton in measuring a hulk and other countries take 50 feet as one ton, so that their tonnage dues are heavier. The Heavenly Court governs outside barbarians with uniform charity and if the said country pays heavier dues, naturally they can be reduced to restore equality, as usual waiting until orders have been given the governor general of Liang-kuang to investigate and send word to the five ports to act likewise.

His request to build lighthouses, etc., is without precedent and need not be discussed. As to his country's minister residing in Peking and documents going direct to the Board of Rites and Grand Secretariat this practice has never existed and the said governor general has been told repeatedly that it can not be allowed. His request for indemnity for his country's goods and ships stolen and burned should all have been settled in accord with treaty provision at the time of loss; when a long time has elapsed, how can individual items be liquidated? Besides, as their goods were destroyed last year by fires set by the English barbarians, how can they turn to China for reimbursement. This must also be repudiated. As to the proposal to mint coins, China still uses sycee[8] silver and fundamentally does not favor silver coins. The two items on the prohibition of opium and enticing Chinese from the ports are both matters which local officials must handle, nor do they have to wait for these barbarians to ask them.

As the above requests of the barbarians are hereby either approved or rejected, order T'an T'ing-hsiang and the others to reply to them accordingly and also explain carefully that this is extraordinary Favor.   After the matter of increasing ports has been investigated and acted upon, allow England and France to trade equally but do not let them ask for other ports. Customs revision has been granted to the various countries to be handled simultaneously and, since the American barbarians are respectful and compliant, it must naturally be treated accordingly in agreement with the treaty provision for complete uniformity of benefits.

These various modified benefits fulfil the treaty provision for twelve-year revision. The barbarians' statement that after all these items were considered, various clauses in the treaty must be corrected is really an excess demand. The said governor general and others can only repudiate it, still conforming to the previous Edict requiring that the Kwangtung affair be terminated within the fourth month [i.e. by June 10]. The period cannot be extended.

Since the Russian barbarians are willing for us to use them, give orders that their request to trade at the five ports need not be argued with them, but allow them to trade the same as other countries. Since we have granted repeated favors, in the matter of the Heilungkiang boundary survey they must needs administer fairly as has been explained in detail in a previous Edict. The said governor general and others must make it clear to Poutiatine that from now on friendship is solidified.

If the American, English, and French barbarians make more demands, they must be rejected in no uncertain terms. They cannot be allowed interminable requests. This is most important. (IWSM.HF 21; 39b, 1-41a, 3)

309. May 12, 1858. MEMORIAL: T'an T'ing-hsiang Reports Russian Perfidy and the Favorable Development of American Negotiations and Mediation.

Governor General of Chihli T'an T'ing-hsiang, Superintendent of

---

8 *Sycee (hsi-ssu)* means literally "fine silk." Chinese unminted silver of standard 9/10 fineness was called *Sycee.* Couling says this is because when heated the silver could be drawn out into silk-like threads. *Encyclopaedia Sinica,* p. 537. It seems more plausible that the term might derive from the fact that silver was substituted for tribute silk and the old term for tribute carried over.

the Imperial Granary Ch'ung-lun, Sub-chancellor of the Grand Secretariat Wu-erh-kun-t'ai, and Financial Commissioner of Chihli Ch'ien
Hsin-ho, memorialize. . . . As we estimate their (the Russians') objective, they are determined to take our left bank of the river and are
utilizing our need for them to intercede with the English and French
to press their demands. Their inconstancy is entirely despicable. If
we were to continue positive negation they would be even more arrogant so we now propose a little breathing spell and then, making use
of flattery, reason with them again.

When the American barbarians came for an interview, Your officials immediately arranged with them personally to have them
reason with the (British and French). As to the various requests of
the American barbarians, we have threshed them out thoroughly with
them and they were fairly reasonable. On the matter of trade at
various ports, Your officials have not been willing to agree immediately. Enlarging upon the indemnity clause, they ask to withhold
future customs receipts, which Your officials rejected emphatically.
It is now agreed to resume discussions on the twelfth. When that time
comes, we shall watch circumstances and deliberate. The English
and French chiefs' six-day period has elapsed and we have now sent
them a dispatch, as well as telling the American chief to intercede.
We cannot tell whether they will come around or not. (IWSM.HF 21;
49a, 9-49b, 7)

310. May 12, 1858. EDICT: Approves T'an T'ing-hsiang's Policy of
Utilizing the United States and Authorizes Continued Finesse.

Edict to the Grand Councillors. T'an T'ing-hsiang and others
have memorialized on the Russian chief's vacillation and his two
meetings with the American chief. . . . As to the American barbarians coming for another interview, the said governor general and
others did not agree to his additional ports immediately. Diplomacy
has its proper timing. Now they have agreed to another conference on
the twelfth. After having met the said chief, memorialize fully on the
situation. Let the American credentials be presented and await reply.
(IWSM.HF 21; 50b, 10-51a, 2)

311. May 13, 1858. MEMORIAL: T'an T'ing-hsiang Reports Continued
Favorable Negotiation with Reed but no Contact with the British and French

Governor General of Chihli T'an T'ing-hsiang, Superintendent of
the Imperial Granary Ch'ung-lun, Sub-chancellor of the Grand Secretariat Wu-erh-kun-t'ai, and Financial Commissioner of Chihli Ch'ien
Hsin-ho memorialize. . . . In the discussions with the American barbarians, only the two topics of trade and indemnity remain to be settled.
These people, compared with the Russian barbarians, are trustworthy
and their speech rather reasonable but they are very suspicious and
obstinate. We must continue meeting them and explaining.

As to the English and French barbarians, we sent communications to them yesterday. There has not been a reply.

In the last few days eight more steamers have arrived, totalling 26 with the previous ones, besides three small boats. Of them, except for the large steamers which cannot come inside the bar, the others do not draw much water and can all come right up in front of the forts. Your officials conjecture that the barbarians are sure to line up their ships, use their strength as a threat, and then send letters fixing a date for reply to expedite their demands without the necessity of an interview. There has been no news since ordering the Americans to bring them around yesterday. Probably once the affairs of the American barbarians are settled, we can certainly negotiate with the English and French.

But the American barbarians' request for Ch'uan-chou, Ch'ao-chou, Wen-chou, and other places has not been entirely accorded and (they are) particularly cunning and obstinate on the indemnity item. The hopes of England and France are still more extravagant. Between the horns of the dilemma the places to prick one's fingers are really legion. When we meet the American barbarians, we shall manage as occasions arise. (IWSM.HF 22; 1b, 10-2a, 10)

312. May 13, 1858. EDICT: Approves Continued Negotiations with Reed and Poutiatine and the Utilization of One or the Other to Finesse the Allies.

Edict to the Grand Councillors. Yesterday a memorial of T'an T'ing-hsiang and others was received. . . . Since the language of the American barbarians is fairly reasonable, order (T'an T'ing-hsiang) after meeting them to watch their attitude and handle them accordingly. If the Russian barbarians can be brought into our provenance, he can use Russia to control England and France; if America is more advantageous than Russia, then there is no objection to giving up Russia and using America. In this finessing the said governor general and others, we assume, can recognize when to be rigid and when to be expedient, and manage accordingly. (IWSM.HF 22; 3b, 2-5)

313. May 15, 1858. MEMORIAL: T'an T'ing-hsiang Reports his Conviction that All Foreigners are Unreliable but Continues Contacts with Reed and Poutiatine.

Governor General of Chihli T'an T'ing-hsiang, Superintendent of the Imperial Granary Ch'ung-lun, Sub-chancellor of the Grand Secretariat Wu-erh-kun-t'ai, and Financial Commissioner of Chihli Ch'ien Hsin-ho memorialize. At present England and France openly show their malice, America and Russia secretly foster crime. While their strength and weakness vary, they are all in one category in their insatiable greed. In the two days since we replied to England and France there has been no response. Sometimes they send small boats around the ports to reconnoitre, sometimes they send small boats near the mouth of the river to spy around, suddenly appearing and as suddenly leaving; when patrol boats pass they fire empty volleys. They have also erected boards on the shore for target practice, constantly egging us to fight. Your officials are completely passive as if they did not hear nor see, as usual secretly ordering officers and men to maintain strict discipline and send out detachments every day to exhibit their martial prowess. When their letters arrive we shall take them into consideration.

(Our) position with regard to Russia and America is similar. When the Russian chief's desire to place the boundary on our left bank was not accorded, he seemed inclined to break off relations and Your officials were not in communication with him for two days. Then yesterday they sent someone to invite a deputy to talk; we sent Pien Pao-shu, told him what to answer and to find out what he could.

The American chief agreed to come and present his credentials in person on the twelfth, but when the time came we were suddenly notified that the envoy was taken ill and was sending the assistant envoy, that he did not dare ask to meet the Imperial Commissioner but had something he would like to talk over personally with Your official, Ch'ien Hsin-ho. The latter received the official document he presented in which the items Your officials had rejected were again argued. Your official, Ch'ien Hsin-ho, explained to him decisively; Your officials have also replied, distinguishing between those items which they could agree to and those they could not. In regard to credentials, they said that the reply must be in terms of equality, and that when they saw the Imperial Edict they would be willing to present them, in order to remove the shame of the previous breaking open and return (of their communications). They only await an Edict and will act in accordance. (IWSM.HF 22; 7a, 6-8a, 3)

314. May 15, 1858. MEMORIAL: T'an T'ing-hsiang Reports Poutiatine's Warning of Imminent Hostilities if Entrance to Peking Continues to be Denied.

T'an T'ing-hsiang and others memorialize further. . . .As to the affairs of the English barbarians, the Russian chief said that he was afraid they would make trouble in a day or two and that it was decidedly to our advantage to be friendly. Our deputy answered that it was because of the intercession of his honorable country that China had not opened hostilities before and that we were waiting from day to day fully prepared. The chief said that of the English and French requests, that for entrance to Peking was most important and if, when there were important matters, perhaps at intervals of several years, we would allow them to come to Peking with not more than a small retinue, what would China have to fear?

If this were agreed to, he would undertake to bring the other matters to a conclusion; otherwise he would not open his mouth and that we must answer immediately in order to prevent estrangement. Your officials recall that ever since the beginning of barbarian relations, whenever there were any commercial requests at the five ports they have always been passed on to Kwangtung, while Kwangtung has either shelved them without answering them or procrastinated, white-washed, and failed to report the real facts to the Emperor until they have been driven to this, and fear that in the future mere words will not suffice. Heretofore men of the western ocean, Verbiest[9] and others, served their whole lives on the Imperial Astronomical Board. Now they only ask to be allowed to go to Peking once in several years or when they have important business. If restricted to a small retinue and perhaps required to come by land, not allowing them to use the Tientsin sea route so that we could control them properly and avoid coastal troubles, it is not an impossible way to mollify the barbarians.

Vermilion endorsement: The honorable ministers know their ones but don't know their twos. The Russian barbarians' reason for wanting the land route is certainly to spy out Khalka to facilitate their plans for future gradual encroachment. England and France's request to come to Peking at intervals of several years or when they have important business, is not at all analagous to former times. Their words seem plausible but their hearts are inscrutable. That is to say, in former times foreigners resided in Peking because they were students of mathematics and we controlled them, so there was no fear of disaster; but now they would come and go as they wish and their greed is insatiable. If we think only of concluding the affair there will be hidden sorrow in the end. And besides, if we allowed them to come to Peking the Kwangtung Imperial Commissioner would be superfluous. Not only is this no better than Yeh Ming-ch'en's disaster-breeding violence, but it is no more feasible than Ch'i-ying's short-sighted compromising. There will be a separate Edict. (IWSM.HF 22; 8b, 3-9b, 1)

315. May 15, 1858. EDICT: Vehemently Denies Access to Peking on Traditional Grounds and Forbids Any Extension of the Scope of Treaty Revision.

Edict to the Grand Councillors. T'an T'ing-hsiang and others have memorialized on their thorough investigation of the barbarian situation and present plans of control, and also added a postscript that the Russian barbarians want to go to Heilungkiang by land and transmitted the request of the other barbarians to come to Peking.

---

9 Ferdinand Verbiest (Nan Huai-jen), 1623-1688, was a famous Jesuit who served for many years in the court at Peking under the Manchus.

The impossibility of acceding to these has been set forth in a note on the original postscript. . .As to foreigners coming to Peking, they are all vassal officials bearing tribute. As the various commercial countries are primarily motivated by profit, in recent years all port matters have been settled on the frontier. There is no precedent whatever for negotiating in Peking.

Were the barbarians to come to Peking, whether the number be large or small, what would China have to fear? It is really because it is not in accord with fundamental law. Last year when Chief Poutiatine asked permission to come to Peking, he was stopped because there was no previous provision for a form of reception. Is there not more reason to stop the English and French barbarians, who have raised arms against authority and cannot even be compared with respectful and compliant countries? Allowing them to meet high officials on this occasion is already extraordinary (favor). How can they be allowed to come to Peking?

Now, with tariff reduction and additional ports, His Imperial Majesty's consideration for foreign countries is expended. If Chief Poutiatine does not intercede, we can only await the English and French replies; if these are not reasonable, China will not even treat them courteously. T'an T'ing-hsiang and the others have also exhausted their energies and cannot treat again. If England and France, not having gained much, still have expectations, tell them definitely that as you cannot memorialize their requests for them, their opportunity is in Kwangtung. Whether tariff reductions are to be large or small is not a matter that can be determined at Tientsin and they will have to take it up with Kwangtung's newly appointed Imperial Commissioner.

As to the Americans wanting to transmit credentials, permission has been granted for their presentation. As to their insistence at this time on seeing the Imperial Edict before they are willing to present them, order T'an T'ing-hsiang and others to tell them that according to the fundamental law of the Heavenly Court all credentials of non-tributary nations have a fixed form of transmission and that there is absolutely no disrespect intended; on the contrary, now that America comes with courtesy, there is no reason whatever for suspicion. T'an T'ing-hsiang and others can copy out this passage and show it to these barbarians and tell them that they received an Imperial Authorization to do so.

After all, the demands of the barbarians are entirely insatiable. Last time when they came to Tientsin they laid down many items and when we agreed to one or two they sailed back. This time, although the situation is different, how can detailed provisions be agreed upon at Tientsin? For instance, the amount of tariff and value of goods cannot be understood except at the various ports. To add small ports in Kwangtung and Fukien also, one must go there

and investigate locally before he can determine the place. It is only
that if a thing is agreed to at Tientsin, the Heavenly Court will
certainly not eat its words; the detailed items will await determination in the outside provinces, but the general picture will not be
changed. This is a positive principle.

As to giving them everything they want and sending them away
happy and satisfied, we fear this will never be. As T'an T'ing-
hsiang and others have continuously had directions on strategy, We
trust they will not be affected by their threats or show the slightest
feeling of fear. If they let these rebels detect a flaw they will make
still more demands. (IWSM.HF 22; 9b, 2...10a, 1-11a, 3)

316. May 17, 1858. MEMORIAL. T'an T'ing-hsiang Tactfully Urges
the Opening of Peking as an Alternative to Military Invasion of Tienstin
and Peking Areas.

Governor General of Chihli T'an T'ing-hsiang, Superintendent
of Imperial Granary Ch'ung-lun, Sub-chancellor of the Grand Secretariat Wu-erh-kun-t'ai, and Financial Commissioner of Chihli Ch'ien
Hsin-ho memorialize. While the Russian situation can be gradually
rounded out, at present it is still not completely settled. Since the
Americans are joined to the Russians while secretly following England
and France, we should of course use the Russians to get at the Americans in order to control the English and French, in accord with the
Imperial Edict to use both orthodoxy and expediency as a means of
finessing, hoping not to miss our opportunity.

While the requests of the barbarians are not entirely the same,
all of them are disadvantageous to us. We have no alternative but to
choose among them and we must place support of national prestige
and repression of subsequent evils foremost. For example, the
matter of coming to Peking is fundamentally very objectionable and
Your officials have already rejected it, but we gather that the main
idea is simply that because the governor general and governor of
Kwangtung tried to govern them by not governing them [i.e. to
neglect their needs entirely], failed to report any of the actual
circumstances of the starting of hostilities to the Throne, and
constantly procrastinated and evaded, they were finally driven to
this. Actually they are asking a favor of us and it involves no loss
of prestige. If we seize this opportunity to get them under control
and govern ten thousand li from our own doorstep, facts from below
will get through without being intercepted and can be settled on the
spot. This is still not an impossible way of controlling barbarians.
If they should be disrespectful or disobedient, we would have the
power to seize their people, declare their crime, close customs and
stop goods; they would have a stake to be fearful and apprehensive
about and the control would be in our hands.

It would seem that, compared to having an army come to the

capital and then talking mollification, there is as much difference as between obedience and rebellion, difficulty and ease. So your officials after having rejected their persistent requests have secretly reported them according to fact. Now because this matter could not be conceded, we find on inquiry that more steamers are coming to apply coercion. If it is said that they certainly dare not attack the forts, Your officials actually have not this assurance and can only constantly maintain rigid defense and wait quietly for developments.

In our humble opinion, England and France deliberately joined together and came North without evacuating Canton; their conduct was very perverse and our not exterminating them at once but talking mollification was due to the extraordinary Favor of Your Majesty. Due to last year's drought and locusts in Peking, poor people have lost their livelihood and are easily aroused, while provincial ports and regions are not entirely tranquillized. Besides, the ocean transport is just arriving and the complications are even greater, so it is neither the time for using force nor is this the place for using force. Therefore Your officials repeatedly, after mature deliberation, pushed the Russians and Americans in order to contact England and France and find means of managing them. Our temporary consideration for them and compromise of the main issue was not voluntary acceptance of coercion.

As to their requests, the Russian barbarians' desire to use the (Amur) river as a boundary and occupy our territory was repudiated and they have agreed to a fair survey. The other three barbarians' addition of ports and indemnity are both things that have been done before. The greed of the barbarians is insatiable. As they encroach step by step we can hardly agree to everything. We can only plan to use force to stop them and watch their movements for a chance to bring them around. As Your officials see the whole situation, in their present arrogant attitude it is hard to bring them under control, but there is no sense whatever in using the haphazard methods of recent years to settle the matter. (IWSM.HF 22; 12a, 3-13a, 8)

317. May 17, 1858. EDICT. Charges the Tientsin Officials with Hysteria and Urges them to Persuade the Powers to be Satisfied with Existing Treaty Machinery.

Edict to the Grand Councillors. T'an T'ing-hsiang and others have memorialized that the barbarian situation is hard to get under control. The impossibility of acceding to the barbarians' persistent requests to come to Peking has been pointed out clearly and in detail in the Court Letter and Edict of the fifteenth, as well as in the marginal Endorsement on the memorial. The governor general and others, in sending this memorial before those were received, reveal undue agitation. At this time the English and French barbarians have made no reply and items of their arbitrary demands cannot be accu-

rately known, so you must wait for their answer and then take
counsel and memorialize what you do.

T'an T'ing-hsiang and others repeatedly ask that they (the barbarians) be allowed to come to Peking, seeming to think that once
this request is granted they will not be bothered with discussing the
others. How were they to know that the request to come to Peking
was made in part because the Russian barbarians were not granted
their request and took advantage of England and France to exert
pressure? In the end, what England and France are interested in
is profit and they do not necessarily put all their weight on this
matter, so it must be examined analytically. Now that (the requests)
of Russia and America have not been entirely accorded, how could
we grant those of England and France?

Anyway, see how they reply. If they are really afraid that facts
cannot reach the Emperor, you can say that this is a distant worry,
for some future time; that if they are concerned with immediate
problems they must go to Kwangtung to settle them; that in the future
should there be anything Kwangtung would not settle, there are still
Fukien, the governor general of Liang-chiang, the governor of
Chekiang, any of whom they can ask to memorialize for them, so that
they will not be blocked again. Thus their argument will be defeated.
But you must also study the English and French replies and if they
are obstinate, use this reasoning as a way out. It is not necessary
to bring it up first.

As to the statement that the addition of ports and payment of
indemnity are things that have been done before, previously when
we acknowledged indemnity it was because China burned 2000 [sic]
chests of their opium; but on this occasion the barbarians set the
fires themselves and burned the houses of our people, so they are
the ones who should indemnify. Russia and America are both at
Tientsin so there can be a general discussion. Were China to
acknowledge the indemnity it would certainly be without reason.

As there has never been a proposal for additional ports in the
more than ten years since trade began, and now having agreed to let
them add two, how can the governor general and others say that the
methods in recent years have been haphazard? There are continual
Court Letters and Edicts, very detailed and exhaustive, and T'an
T'ing-hsiang and the others have only to interpret them conscientiously; they cannot make plans on the spur of the moment. The
matters of tariff reduction and additional ports, it must be made
clear to them, can be arranged only after the Kwangtung matter is
concluded.

As to wanting to stop them by force, it has been made clear in
successive Edicts that if the barbarians start hostilities there is
absolutely no reason for not retaliating; but if we resort to arms
first they will have even more pretext for flaunting their arrogance

and it will be harder to conclude the matter. Are not all the coastal provinces Our territory? How can they fail to consider matters as a whole? Let the governor general and others not readily believe the words of military officers whose object is to win renown and who do not think of consequences. (IWSM.HF 22; 13a, 9-14b, 1)

318. May 20, 1858. MEMORIAL: T'an T'ing-hsiang Reports his Receipt of Reed's Credentials and his Conviction that All Four Powers are Acting in Collusion.

Governor General of Chihli T'an T'ing-hsiang, Superintendent of Imperial Granaries Ch'ung-lun, Sub-chancellor of the Grand Secretariat Wu-erh-kun-t'ai, and Financial Commissioner of Chihli Ch'ien Hsin-ho memorialize. The American barbarians sent someone to report on the transmission of their credentials, that they would be presented personally by their officials, Dupont[10] and others.

Your officials received them immediately and treated them courteously. The said official asked us to determine when they could hope to receive the Imperial reply to facilitate a respectful reception. Your officials replied that they could not propose a definite time, but when an Imperial Edict was issued they would send a communication. The official said that today they would only present credentials but would come back later to discuss business, and immediately sailed back. The original letter and casket are respectfully forwarded to the Grand Council for reverent presentation for Imperial Inspection.

At present the English, French, and American chiefs are all outside the bar and only the Russian chief is inside the bar. We have learned that the English and French chiefs, whenever they enter port, invariably confer personally with the Russian chief on board ship and that the Russian chief sometimes goes out to sea to talk with them; that they are closely allied and news is always current. The Russian chief asked on behalf of the English and French to go to Peking and was flatly refused and, although the said chief says he will write further on their behalf, he cannot be relied on with certainty. Nor can we repeatedly press him with questions lest their obstinacy be increased.

We can hardly be sure that the sudden presentation of the credentials of the American barbarians is not a scheme to shift positions for intercession. But Your officials have been at loggerheads with these barbarians ever since the twenty-ninth of last month, now more than twenty days, during which time the situation has changed kaleidoscopically. In general the Russian chief is secretly the chief conspirator, England and France rely on their

---

10   Captain S.F. DuPont commanded the United States steam frigate *Minnesota*.

power to coerce, while the American chief goes along with them both.
The affairs of one country are fully known to all. Their manifold
schemes combine plots against us.

It has been seven or eight days and the English and French replies have still not arrived. They are constantly sending small boats
to take soundings in the mouth of the river or climbing the masts to
spy on conditions in the countryside with telescopes, but grain ships
arriving from time to time have not been stopped. It must be that
they are merely awaiting the outcome of Russian and American
affairs to determine their action. (IWSM.HF 22; 19b, 4-20b, 2)

319. May 20, 1858. EDICT: Rejects the American Request for Diplomatic Residence in Peking and Chides the United States for Presumptuousness.

Edict to the Grand Councillors. T'an T'ing-hsiang and others
have memorialized on the transmittal of the credentials of the American barbarian. Having examined the credentials presented by the said
barbarians, one text in Chinese character and one in barbarian
character, on the pretext of fostering friendship and inquiring about
Our health, they want to send their minister plenipotentiary to live
in Peking.

As with the Russians' like desire, there are insurmountable
obstacles to acceding. Now that we have allowed them to be presented,
we must naturally grant a letter in reply as a means of controlling
them. If the barbarian chief asks about the time of replying, say that
"His Imperial Majesty commends them for not having helped the
rebels in Kwangtung and within a few days will prepare an honorific
reply." It is not necessary to divulge anything else.

If the said barbarian brings up the matter of coming to Peking,
T'an T'ing-hsiang and the others, in the words used previously to
answer the Russian barbarians, will say that, "in the fundamental law
of the Heavenly Court the only foreigners allowed to come to Peking
are vassal officials bearing tribute. As America is a friendly state,
no precedent is included for the etiquette of receiving her, and since
there is no ruling to follow, it is feared that the formal etiquette
would be incomplete and in turn detrimental to friendly relations, so
we are afraid this matter can hardly be conceded."

On additional ports and reduction of tariff there has been an
Edict; the English and French problem must be settled and then all
can share the benefits.

Examining the context of the credentials submitted, the king of
that country actually refers to himself as Chen [i.e., the Imperial
We, restricted to the use of the Emperor, the use of which by anyone else being regarded as presuming upon the authority of the
Emperor]. This is really the self-importance of Yeh-lang [i.e., an
aboriginal tribe which occupied the territory to the west of modern

Kweichow during the Han dynasty. When an envoy of Han came to
the place, he was asked by the local chieftain which state was larger,
Yeh-lang or Han. The expression is now used for one who ignorantly
exaggerates his own importance.], and induces an involuntary smile.
Whether or not this corresponds with the credentials which the barbarians copied and gave T'an T'ing-hsiang and others to examine,
we are now having the Chinese text of the barbarian credentials
copied and sent to the said governor general and the others to determine. But neither of the barbarian documents has the seal of its
sovereign imposed. In the Chinese text there is merely written in
ink the two characters "National Seal," so in replying this time we
shall not use the Precious Seal either, in order to show reciprocity.

As to the English and French chiefs constantly going to the
Russian ship for personal conferences, and the Russian chief also
going out to sea to communicate, there can be no doubt they hang
together like one breath and the view of T'an T'ing-hsiang and
others not to press them further is quite appropriate. If the American barbarians, on the pretext of presenting credentials, shift to
the position of intercessor, you can ascertain the bearing of the
various countries in order to effect a turnover. (IWSM.HF 22;
20b, 3-21a, 8)

320. May 20, 1858. CREDENTIALS: President Buchanan's Letter to
the Emperor Presenting Reed as United States Minister to China.

President of the Great United States of America,[11] James
Buchanan, specially transmits this respectful letter to his Greatly
Esteemed good friend His Majesty the Great Emperor of Ta-ch'ing.
We (Chen) have selected a capable and sagacious gentleman,
William Reed, and send him to reside near the Court, to serve in
the capacity of Envoy Extraordinary and Minister Plenipotentiary.
This official has a thorough understanding of all policies that
concern the fostering of benefits and removal of ills of our two
countries, is long familiar with matters of friendly intercourse of
our two countries, and is also fully cognizant of Our constant
desire to consolidate the perpetual peace of the two countries. We
know that this official has always been loyal, honest and good and
will expend his mind and energy to augment the benefits of both
countries, and urge His Majesty to welcome him. Furthermore,
this official specially bears his country's friendly good wishes to
the Great Emperor, only hoping that His Majesty will condescend
to receive him favorably and give all his representations full
credence, without suspicion. We only pray God to protect the
Great Emperor in happiness and long life forever. This is re-

---

11 This translation of Reed's credentials is incorporated into the Chinese documents
    without any heading or explanation.

spectfully presented, respectfully asking after His Precious Health.

The Year after the birth of Our Lord Jesus 1857, April 22, that is Ting-chi[12] year, the third month, the twenty-fifth day. Respectfully written by Grand Secretary of the United States, Lewis Cass, at the capital city, Washington, having received the order of the Great President.   (IWSM.HF 22; 21a, 9-22a, 6)

321. May 21, 1858. MEMORIAL: T'an T'ing-hsiang Reports Meeting between S. Wells Williams and Ch'ien Hsin-ho and Hostile Movements of the Allied Fleet.

T'an T'ing-hsiang and others further memorialize. Between eleven and one o'clock on the nineteenth of this month the American barbarians sent Vice-minister Williams[13] and others to bring the treaty here and asked for an interview with Your official, Ch'ien Hsin-ho, saying that he wanted first to discuss in general the provisions that had to be changed after twelve years, to be later deliberated impartially by their envoy and Your officials.

Your official, Ch'ien Hsin-ho, went immediately to meet him and, taking up the various items previously proposed, explained clearly why some could be granted and others could not be granted, and that besides these, no changes could be made. The vice-minister was very understanding, took careful notes, and agreed to discuss again later, but he said that the English and French were not very reasonable and he was afraid if the matter of coming to Peking was not conceded trouble could hardly be avoided. Your official, Ch'ien Hsin-ho, replied:

"Previously you set dates for interviews but you broke them and did not come. Later when we received your communications and answered fully, asking you to fix a date for a conference, you also shelved them without replying. You have never stated clearly what your other requests are, and since your honorable country is an intermediary, we must find out what your ultimate objectives are in order to facilitate negotiations." The said vice-minister agreed and went away pleased.

As for the Russian barbarians, we first sent someone to make inquiries and then ask them to send a representative to come and resume negotiations.

Then, between 5 and 7 in the evening, eight English and French steamers suddenly came inside the bar and anchored alongside the eight steamers already anchored there. Drums rolled and flags

12 This is the Chinese cyclical year designation, according to the sixty year cycle used in Chinese chronology.

13 S. Wells Williams, 1812-1884, was Reed's first secretary. Williams came to China in 1833, with the American Board Mission and had a long and distinguished career in China. He is best remembered for his *Middle Kingdom,* first published in 1851.

were hoisted. Some twenty-odd sampans also came up and their
attitude seemed to indicate an intention to start hostilities. Actually,
they were going to make demands by force. Your officials had already anticipated this situation, but so long as they did not start
firing, would certainly not order our forces to raise a hand first lest
they start a brawl. If the barbarians sent someone to talk peace or
had the Russian and American barbarians talk peace for them, (Your
officials) would watch for a chance to hold them. If they actually
sunder relations, then we will fight.

 Vermilion endorsement: Noted. (IWSM.HF 22; 22b, 4-23b, 1)

322. May 21, 1858. MEMORIAL: T'an T'ing-hsiang Reports the
Opening of British and French Attack on the Ta-ku Forts and China's
Reply in Kind.

 T'an T'ing-hsiang and others further memorialize. The rebel
barbarians started hostilities, attacking the forts. Our big guns on
the north and south banks opened fire simultaneously and damaged
four barbarian ships. To our surprise, the said barbarian ships
came straight ahead en masse and pushed into the river. Bursting
shells brought down a great many (of our) soldiers and militia,
who could not withstand them and had to withdraw. The forts were
immediately occupied and now there is nothing in the rear to stop
them, which is of vital significance for Tientsin.

 Your officials Ch'ung-lun and Wu-erh-kun-t'ai quickly went to
its defense. Your official, T'an T'ing-hsiang, is in the Hsin-ch'eng
sector, to hold this position against them. They have also ordered
Your official, Ch'ien Hsin-ho, to devise means to scuttle ships along
the channel as a means of stopping them. Your official, T'an T'ing-
hsiang, in command of the forces has been unable to restrain or
defeat them; he is undeniably guilty, and asks for an Edict punishing
him severely. (IWSM.HF 22; 23b, 2-8)

323. May 21, 1858. EDICT: Orders Manchu General T'o-ming-a to
Tientsin to Assume Command of Defense Operations.

 Edict to the Grand Secretariat. Order T'o-ming-a given the
rank of Senior Bodyguard of the First Rank, to proceed posthaste to
Tientsin to cooperate with T'an T'ing-hsiang in handling barbarian
affairs. (IWSM.HF 22; 23b, 9-10)

324. May 23, 1858. MEMORIAL: T'an T'ing-hsiang Reports Allied
Possession of the Ta-ku Forts and Asks Leave to Use the Russians and
Americans as Mediators.

 T'an T'ing-hsiang and others memorialize further. At present
the barbarian ships are anchored at the forts and have not proceeded
in, nor have they done any damage to the villages, but the Tientsin
populace is already alarmed and fleeing in disorder. There was no

alternative but to go in person to reassure them, as well as to distribute troops en route for defense, but the prefecture has no
defensible vantage point. With nothing to rely on, the consequences
to millions of souls are very grave.

Now there are still Russia and America as mediators, and although they are sure to make insatiable demands, still, compared to
fighting, this has its advantage. We can only humbly ask for Heavenly Favor to bear in mind that this is a vitally important place and
allow Your officials first to draw Russia and America close to us,
showing continued appeasement. After T'o-ming-a arrives, they
will duly discuss and arrange.

As to building banks to constrict the water or breeching the
boom to divert the current, the Hai-ho is very deep, the tide
constantly ebbing and flowing, unlike other rivers, so these would
seem difficult to accomplish. Allow us to reconsider and make
plans. (IWSM.HF 22; 29b, 5-30a, 3)

325. May 23, 1858. EDICT: Authorizes the Use of Reed and Poutiatine
as Mediators and Announcement of the Opening of Two Additional Ports.

Edict to the Grand Councillors. T'an T'ing-hsiang and others
have memorialized on the fall of the forts and also of the Russian
and American barbarians still being willing to intercede and asking
permission to get them under control. . . .When Russia and
America interceded before the matter was never concluded. Since
they are now willing to intercede again, naturally you can make use
of them to bring the others around as a scheme for delaying hostilities [i.e. gaining time].

As T'an T'ing-hsiang and others have never told the American
barbarians about the additional ports, he should tell them now. As
the demands of England and France, that is, to send envoys to
Peking and to permit barbarian missionaries to travel in the interior,
are no benefit to them and would only disturb China, it is practically
impossible to concede to them. Besides these, where the matter
concerns only profits, there can still be discussion and settlement.
Anyway, see how Russia and America transmit this and then memorialize Us. . . . (IWSM.HF 22; 30a, 4-5...30b, 9-31a, 4)

326. May 24, 1858. MEMORIAL: T'an T'ing-hsiang Reports Sending
Deputies to Reed and Poutiatine to Ask The British and French to Open
Negotiations.

Governor General of Chihli T'an T'ing-hsiang memorializes.
. . .As for waiting until defeated in battle and then talking restraint,
the difficulties would be even greater; but as the tribute ships have
not been stopped, it would seem that there is a possibility of being
able to mollify them. Of two evils take the lesser; so we could not
but reconsider. It is not that Your officials wanted to mollify them

for want of courage, but because they realize that if unable to fight or defend they were still to meet them with force, one could not bear to think of the consequences.

Therefore they again sent deputies, Pien Pao-shu and Chang Chen-hsiung, to go and find out if the Russians and Americans would intercede and also sent them communications, saying that since the fighting all the things previously proposed must await a separate Edict, and then we could act accordingly.

Now it is reported that barbarian sampans are gradually coming in to sound out the channel. We have instructed the commander-in-chief and Tartar General to stop them in the lower course and Your official will cooperate in the upper course.

He is ordering Your official Ch'ung-lun to go to Peking to report personally the details of the situation and await Imperial direction as to strategy. (IWSM.HF 22; 31a, 9...32a, 2-32b, 1)

327. May 24, 1858. EDICT: Orders T'an T'ing-hsiang to Supervise Military Leaders and Warns against Russian and American Plot to Extend Hostilities Inland.

Edict to the Grand Councillors: . . .Today a memorial has been received from the said governor general saying. . .that the barbarians are sounding out the watercourse. As these are all sampans they are not as speedy as steamers and so can easily be stopped. Besides it is feared that this kind of survey boats have also Russians and Americans among them so that their talk of bringing the others to terms has been empty words. It is necessary to supervise the work of the commander-in-chief and brigade general with the utmost care to defend. . . . (IWSM.HF 22; 32b, 10. . .33a, 2. . .33a, 8-33b,1)

328. May 24, 1858. MEMORIAL: Leaders of the Canton Irregular Forces Comment on Terminology: Barbarian versus Foreigner.

Former Vice-president of the Board of Revenue Lo Tun-yen, Former Director of the Court of Sacrificial Worship Lung Yüan-hsi and Former Junior Metropolitan Censor for the Board of Works Su T'ing-k'uei memorialize. [re. recruiting militia in Kwangtung] . . .As to Your officials' previous statements regarding the cutting of a great seal to furnish a recruiting caption, it was because popular indignation against barbarians was great. Yet ever since the barbarians entered the city the local officials have forbidden any use of the term "barbarian affairs" (I-wu), even going to the length of referring in writings and public documents to "barbarian affairs" as "ocean affairs" (Yang-wu), and as "the affairs of foreign countries" (wai-kuo shih-chien), not daring to revile them with the the term "barbarian". Your officials, after repeated deliberation, insisted on cutting on the seal the inscription "Management of Barbarian Affairs" (Pan-li I-wu) to enable us to arouse popular feeling.

Now the cutting has been completed and it has been affixed as occasions arose. (IWSM.HF 22; 37b, 9. . .39b, 3-8)

329. May 24, 1858. MEMORIAL: Lo Tun-yen Reports the Subservi-
ency of the Canton Officials to British and French Control.
      Lo Tun-yen and others further memorialize: . . .Acting Governor
General Po-kuei has repeatedly issued proclamations explaining to
merchants and populace that "Chinese and foreigners are one family";
the barbarians, on the contrary, belittle and revile him, who, along
with the Tartar general and brigade general, is under their control.
Salt Controller Ling-ch'un and Grain Intendant Wang Tseng-ch'ien in
the twelfth month of last year (January 15-February 13, 1858), transferred their offices to Fo-shan in Nan-hai-hsien, to carry on departmental affairs and only thus are still able to act independently.
(IWSM.HF 22; 40b, 1. . .41a, 3-7)

330. May 27, 1858. MEMORIAL: T'an T'ing-hsiang Reports the
Russian and American Demand on Behalf of the Allies for Negotiations
at Tientsin or Peking.
      Governor General of Chihli T'an T'ing-hsiang, Sub-chancellor of
the Grand Secretariat Wu-erh-kun-t'ai, Senior Imperial Bodyguard of
the First Rank T'o-ming-a, and Financial Commissioner of Chihli
Ch'ien Hsin-ho memorialize. . .As to the deputy sent in advance to
the Russians and Americans, he was delayed because of the blockade
of the port, and we have just received a reply in Manchu (sic.,
"Ch'ing") characters, the purport being either to have a minister
with full powers sent to Tientsin or grant permission to go to Peking,
still adhering to their previous statement. We respectfully present
the original text for Imperial inspection. (IWSM.HF 23; 1a, 2. . .
1b, 1-4)

331. May 27, 1858. RUSSIAN REPLY: Poutiatine Transmits Joint
Demand for Treaty Negotiations in Tientsin and Subsequent Reception
in Peking.
      As the present official has been asked to negotiate, he duly sends
his reply. First, the envoys of the four countries insist on coming into
into the city of Tientsin to negotiate matters; and second, after
everything is settled, they insist on going to Peking, not necessarily
seeing His Imperial Majesty personally, but to confer with the Grand
Secretaries. The request to send a minister with full powers to
Tientsin to discuss matters is vital, nor is the envoys' coming to
Peking anything to be afraid of. The number of persons in the
retinue would not be large. Otherwise, it is feared that England and
France will bring troops and enter forcibly. Other than these there
are no items to be taken up. He hopes they both will be examined
carefully. (IWSM.HF 23; 1b, 5-10)

332. <u>May 27, 1858. EDICT: Expresses the Fear that the Demand for Negotiation is a Ruse for Foreign Occupation of the City and Blames the Tientsin Officials.</u>

Edict to the Grand Councillors. T'an T'ing-hsiang and others have memorialized on the barbarian ships coming up the river and also submitted a letter from the Russian barbarians. On reading the memorials We are most indignant. The barbarians having started hostilities and carried their defiance so far, speaking reasonably, we cannot talk terms with them at all but can only order them back to Kwangtung and settle with them there. Our waiting for the reply of Russia and America was because we were mindful that Tientsin is a vital place near the capital, hence our plan for bringing them around as a means of delaying hostilities.

Now the letter from the Russian barbarians holds to the proposal to come to Peking and wants to confer in the prefectural capital of Tientsin. If we let the barbarians occupy it by force, will we not be falling into the Kwangtung rut again? These are all ten-thousand times impossible matters.

When the governor general and others say "get them under control", exactly how are they going to do it? Are they going to grant them everything and "get them under control" that way?. . .
(IWSM.HF 23; 2a, 9-2b, 5)

333. <u>May 28, 1858. MEMORIAL: T'an T'ing-hsiang Reports the Arrival of Foreign Steamers at Tientsin and Demand for Newly Appointed Imperial Commissioners.</u>

Governor General of Chihli T'an T'ing-hsiang, Sub-chancellor of the Grand Secretariat Wu-erh-kun-t'ai, Senior Bodyguard of the First Grade T'o-ming-a, and Financial Commissioner of Chihli Ch'ien Hsin-ho memorialize. On the twenty-sixth, four steamers came straight up to the Tientsin harbor-limit with four more behind which came in and joined them. They have still not come ashore to cause trouble.

Then according to the interpreter of the English barbarians, H.N. Lay, they wanted us to send the prefect and district magistrate to see them. Your officials immediately ordered the prefect and magistrate to go. H.N. Lay told them orally that they must report the matters which his country was to negotiate to us, who were to memorialize asking Your Imperial Majesty separately to appoint two ministers of the highest rank capable of assuming responsibility to come immediately to confer; that they could not see again the ministers appointed before; that otherwise they still intended to go to Peking and would also bombard the prefectural capital; that they would expect a reply within two days and that they must see the forthcoming Imperial Commissioners' Imperial Edict before they would be willing to believe.

As we observe his position, it is about the same as that of the letter from the Russian barbarians. In our humble opinion, because previously at the port Your officials did not fulfil all the items memorialized for them, through Russia and America, they insist on asking for other ministers to come and confer. Although their attitude is again arrogant, after all they are still asking for trade and if we handle them properly, the matter of coming to Peking may not have to be brought up again.

At this critical juncture when both offense and defense are difficult, we can only beseech Heavenly Favor to agree to send ministers of higher rank with an Imperial directive on tactics to Tientsin immediately and it is necessary that they arrive before June 1. At that time Russia and America must certainly come also and we will again duly treat with them and may perhaps be able to smooth things over immediately. Their dog-sheep temper is fundamentally difficult to subdue and if there is again delay and hostilities are precipitated, we are afraid the people will be caused to suffer and it will be even harder to restore order. (IWSM.HF 23; 6a, 10-7a, 7)

334. May 28, 1858. EDICT: Appointment of Two Manchus, Kuei-liang and Hua-sha-na as Commissioners to Negotiate at Tientsin with the Four Powers.

Edict to the Grand Secretariat. Order Grand Secretary Kuei-liang and President of the Board of Civil Office Hua-sha-na appointed to proceed posthaste to the port of Tientsin to investigate matters and act. (IWSM.HF 23; 7a, 8-9)

335. May 28, 1858. MEMORIAL: A Hanlin Academician Deplores Appeasement and Favors a Militant Policy Utilizing Popular Citizen Armies.

Expositor of the Hanlin Academy P'an Tsu-yin memorializes. It is ventured that ever since the English barbarians defied authority in the Tao-kuang period (1821-1851), only with Lin Tse-hsü at Canton were the barbarians unable to have their way; thereafter, the first blunder was when Ch'i-shan handed over Hong Kong; the last blunder was when Ch'i-ying consistently repressed the people and extolled barbarians. Therefore at the time of Your Majesty's enthronement he dismissed Ch'i-ying and published his guilt to China and the outside world and all officials and people raised hands to forehead and approved. . . .

More recently, Yeh Ming-ch'en, who has been degraded, did not realize that the strength of the people could be utilized and consistently feared barbarians so as to increase the greed of the barbarians, thus fomenting China's greatest humiliation in two hundred years. This is what pains the hearts and racks the brains of all officers and people within the seas.

Now that these barbarians have come to Tientsin and are exerting pressure wilfully, if we use pacification with them, the flames of

rebellion will burst forth more than ever, national prestige be even
more diminished, and the subsequent unknown calamities will be un-
speakable.

It is Your official's stupid opinion that as a present policy, using
pacification is not as good as using warfare, and using soldiers is not
as good as using citizenry. . . . [Goes on to expound how the natural
hostility of the Tientsin populace to barbarians could be utilized to
defeat them as it had in Canton.]   (IWSM.HF 23; 8a, 5-9...3-8)

336. May 28, 1858. MEMORIAL: Prince I Analyzes the American Items
for Treaty Revision and Recommends Action for Each.

Tsai-yüan Prince I and others memorialize.[14] Your officials now
list the items of the various barbarians to be approved or rejected and
submit them:. . .

4. The American barbarians' request for additional ports: it has
been conceded that to each of the commercial ports in the provinces of
Fukien and Kwangtung, we will consider adding one small port, for all
countries equally.

5. The American barbarians' proposal as to the computation of
tonnage dues: it has been agreed to administer it the same as other
countries.

6. The American barbarians' request to build lighthouses and
signal towers: we find there is no precedent and it need not be discussed.

7. The American barbarians' request to reside at the capital and
to send communications direct to the Board of Rites and Grand Secretariat is the same as that of the Russian barbarians. There is no provision for this.

8. The American barbarians' request for money indemnification:
the said country's ships and goods stolen or burned must all be
handled according to treaty at the time of loss; as the matters are of
many years' standing there is no obligation to indemnify them.

9. The American barbarians' request to mint silver coins:
China has always used sycee silver and there is no need of coins
besides.

10. The American barbarians' request for the prohibition of
opium and of enticing people from the ports [the coolie trade]:
these are both prohibited by Chinese law and must be administered
by local officials. . . .

21. The American barbarians have been conceded a reduction of
tonnage dues, but their request to make good more than 10 years'
losses, some five or six hundred thousand taels, has not been agreed

---

14 This is the recommendation of the Grand Council to the emperor; Prince I was the Chief
Councillor or what foreigners called the Prime Minister of China at this time. The
items have been numbered for clarity.

to; but as the American barbarians did not help the English barbarians oppose authority and are still respectful and compliant, we
must figure on treating them well in order to win them over. If they
make the above request again, they can be allowed, according to the
Shanghai precedent, to compute and remit customs duties for three
or four months. The claim of more than 10 years' losses is many
years old and there is no means of investigating it, so there is no
need to discuss it. . . .

26. The old treaties have long been in operation and revision at
this time is all to the advantage of the various countries with no advantage to China. China does not wrangle over profits but if the old
treaties are changed, there are in them several items unsatisfactory
to China which must also be changed in order to restore reciprocity.
After (they) return to Kwangtung (this will be) gone into and discussed. . . . (IWSM.HF 23; 10b, 1-13a, 5)

337. May 30, 1858. MEMORIAL: T'an T'ing-hsiang Reports Approaching Negotiations at Tientsin and Comments on the Neutral Position of
Russia and the United States.

Governor General of Chihli T'an T'ing-hsiang, Sub-chancellor of
the Grand Secretariat Wu-erh-kun-t'ai, and Financial Commissioner
of Chihli Ch'ien Hsin-ho memorialize. Inconstancy is a fundamental
trait of barbarians. Although we have already talked pacification they
are still constantly spying in the North River. Your officials, knowing the North River is extremely shallow and steamers could not
possibly enter, originally had no apprehension but, lest they transfer to small ships to pry in, decided to have Your official T'o-ming-a
transfer residence to Yang-ts'un. Now one small steamer of the
English barbarians has come up the North River to Wang-chia-chuang
where it encountered shallow water and, finding it impossible to proceed north, gradually withdrew; so their interest in coming to Peking
has somewhat abated.

Now that ministers are Specially Appointed to proceed they can
readily reason with them. The Imperial Edict has been respectfully
copied and communicated to them with orders to wait quietly. The
barbarian ships are all standing at anchor outside the wall of Tientsin
and have not made any trouble. Were we to try to force them to withdraw downstream several tens of li, they would certainly not consent,
so we are constrained to ask permission to select a place for a
conference gound outside the city wall in order to pacify them.

The Russians and Americans will arrive shortly. Actually their
motive is to draw advantage from their middle position without any
real willingness to intercede on our behalf, still we cannot but
utilize them to bring the others around. Besides this, those of the
gentry from southern provinces who are of use have been secretly
called upon by Your officers, to spy out barbarian affairs. . . .

(IWSM.HF   23; 17a, 1-17b, 2)

338. June 1, 1858. MEMORIAL: T'an T'ing-hsiang Reports the Arrival of Reed and Poutiatine as Neutrals and Mediators at Tientsin.
        Governor General of Chihli T'an T'ing-hsiang, Sub-chancellor
of the Grand Secretariat Wu-erh-kun-t'ai, and Financial Commissioner of Chihli Ch'ien Hsin-ho memorialize. . . .The barbarian envoys
of Russia and America came yesterday. We sent deputies to question
them and were told that they still wished, as originally proposed at
the port, wholeheartedly to intercede for England and France.
        As for the English and French barbarians, we also sent officers
to see them and say that Imperially Appointed Grand Secretary Kuei-
liang and others should reach Tientsin in a few days and for them to
wait. The barbarians had nothing further to say except that the two
characters "full powers" (ch'uan chuan) were absolutely necessary
before anything could be agreed upon.
        Twelve barbarian ships, large and small, are anchored together
at San-ch'a-ho with a considerable number of men. Lest they make
the purchase of water and vegetables a pretext for coming ashore,
we ordered a Volunteer Headquarters established and placed Train -
band-leader Chang Chin-wen and others to take charge. It is still
quiet, but as there are many men on board the ships and the weather
is hot, the barbarian envoys seeing that there are several empty
rooms in the Wang-hai-lou, insisted on occupying them temporarily.
We forbade them but they would not listen and since we had proposed
mollification, we could not but temporarily bind their hearts until
Grand Secretary Kwei-liang and others come to conclude negotiations
with them.
        Vermilion endorsement: Noted. The residence is really an-
ticipating a place to trade. There is no word of the population rising
up to oppose them. With popular feeling like this, We cannot but sigh
deeply in sorrow. (IWSM.HF 23; 32a, 6. . .32b, 6-33a, 7)

339. June 1, 1858. MEMORIAL: T'an T'ing-hsiang Reports the Insistence of the Powers on "Full Powers" like those of Ch'i-ying in 1842
and 1844.
        T'an T'ing-hsiang further memorializes. The four barbarians,
English, French, Russian, and Americans, have handed over to our
deputy, Pien Pao-shu, four official documents with the Honorable
Grand Secretary Yü's name and title written on the top and told him
to deliver them to Peking.
        The said deputy inquired of the Russian barbarians what the
contents were and was told that the position of the English and other
chiefs was, viz.: Now that is was reported that Imperially Commissioned Grand Secretary Kuei-liang and Board President Hua-
sha-na were coming, if like the previous Grand Secretary Ch'i-ying

they had the designation "full powers to act discriminately" as soon
as they saw the Imperial Decree, everything could be decided either
to concede or to reject. Otherwise, he could not assume responsibility and they must still come to Peking. As the watercourse was
difficult they must needs come by the land route; if no one resisted
them they would not make further trouble, but if they were resisted
they must needs retaliate.

With the barbarian temper so obstinate, certainly they cannot
be appealed to with reason. (IWSM.HF 23; 34a, 1-8)

340. June 1, 1858. EDICT: Recognizes the Threats of the Powers and
Authorizes the Duplication of Ch'i-ying's Credentials for Kuei-liang and
Hua-sha-na.

Edict to the Grand Councillors. We have lately received memorials from T'an T'ing-hsiang and others that the barbarian ships
have retired to San-ch'a-ho and are quietly awaiting the Imperial
Commissioners to negotiate and also, according to letters presented
from the four countries, the Imperial Commissioners must be
designated as having "full powers to act discriminately", like those
previously held by Ch'i-ying, before they can negotiate; that otherwise they still intend to come to Peking, actually coming by the land
route; and that if anyone obstructs them they will retaliate.

The barbarians' defiance and lack of reason certainly makes
one's hair stand on end. Now that we have appointed Kuei-liang
and Hua-sha-na to go and reach an agreement, the situation is
different from the time when T'an T'ing-hsiang met them at the
port of Ta-ku. At that time the barbarian ships were still at the
port, had not started hostilities, and there was still hope of using
reason to overcome their arrogance. But now that their threats are
even greater and they display more ferocity, we can only first resolve their suspicions and then reason with them.

A separate Court Letter is being sent, duplicating the credentials
given to Ch'i-ying and I-li-pu in the Tao-kuang period, with only a
few necessary changes. If the barbarians demand to see it, you can
show them this Edict and say that since you have this Court Letter,
how can you be unable to act discriminately? If there are unreasonable and irrelevant matters which are practically impossible
to agree to, the present high officials are free to reject. "Full
powers" does not necessarily mean that we must agree to everything.

As the barbarians have a large company and many ships there
may be danger of arbitrary seizure if their wishes are not accorded,
so we cannot but be prepared. On meeting them, T'an T'ing-hsiang
must order troops to accompany the high officials and protect them
rigorously and amply notify the bodyguard to be prepared for
emergencies. If there is the least laxness leading to any unexpected
reverse, T'an T'ing-hsiang's guilt, with one blunder on top of another,

will be inescapable. Likewise, if Kuo-jui, Chu-lo-heng and Fu-lo-tun-t'ai do not defend energetically, their crime will certainly be severely punished. On the matter of defense of the land route, orders have been given Seng-ko-lin-ch'in and others to take suitable action. (IWSM.HF 23; 34a, 9-35a, 3)

341. June 1, 1858. EDICT: Instructs Kuei-liang and Hua-sha-na to Explain the Extent and Limitations of the Chinese Version of "Full Powers."

Additional Edict. Previously because the various countries made requests and T'an T'ing-hsiang and others managed badly, Kuei-liang and Hua-sha-na were specially appointed to hasten to Tientsin, duly negotiate and act, but We have received communications from these states, still doubting if Kuei-liang and the others are able to assume authority.

Order Kuei-liang and Hua-sha-na to explain concisely that if they act within reason and sincerely cease hostilities, anything not harmful to China can certainly be agreed to, and that it is not necessary to harbor any more doubts or suspicions. We have specially appointed Kuei-liang and the other and they must uphold the national constitution, secretly study men and events, and except for improper and irrelevant articles, are required to act discriminately, that is to say, they are ordered to act as occasion demands. Let them do their best. (IWSM.HF 23; 35a, 5-10)

342. June 2, 1858. EDICT: Orders Ch'i-ying Restored to Brevet Rank of Board Vice-president to Assume Charge of China's Foreign Affairs.

Edict (to the Grand Secretariat). Order the brevet rank of board vice-president conferred on Ch'i-ying, to take charge of barbarian affairs. (IWSM.HF 24; 1a, 6)

343. June 3, 1858. EDICT: Orders Ch'i-ying to take charge of Foreign Affairs and Requests Explanation of "State Seal" on the American Credentials.

Edict to the Grand Councillors. Kuei-liang and Hua-sha-na set out May 31, and should have reached Tientsin June 2 and, with Ch'ung-lun, have met the barbarian chiefs of the four countries. Whether or not Russia and America still adhere to their former statement and what the English and French chiefs demand, we suppose the said Grand Secretary and others must have memorialized a detailed account en route.

Yesterday an Edict was issued conferring on Ch'i-ying the brevet rank of board vice-president to take charge of barbarian affairs, because in the Tao-kuang period, the conclusion of the treaties with the English and other barbarians was all managed by the said official. Therefore he is ordered to go and take charge

again this time. Kuei-liang and the others can have deputies notify
the said barbarian chiefs and also covertly find out what the state
of barbarian affairs is.

As to the various demands of the barbarians, since they can
hardly be settled all at once, could they not be delayed until Ch'i-
ying has reached Tientsin and then discussed and settled?

In the credentials forwarded by the American chief, there are
only the two characters "State Seal" written in ink in a square and
no seal of the said country affixed. We do not know the reason. As
this matter was handled by Ch'ung lun, he can ask the American chief
when he sees him and memorialize fully at his convenience. (IWSM.
HF 24; 9b, 4-10a, 2)

344. June 3, 1858. EDICT: Orders All Necessary Assistants and
Documents Supplied to Ch'i-ying who will use the Seal of the Governor
of Chihli.

Additional Edict. Yesterday an Edict was issued to send Ch'i-
ying to Tientsin to take charge of barbarian affairs. Order whatever
civil or military officers he may need sent from the Chihli local
headquarters for his use. For all memorials and papers he will use
the seal of the governor general of Chihli for convenience. Whatever
matters are proposed for pacification will revert to Ch'i-ying exclusively for handling. T'an T'ing-hsiang need not take part.
(IWSM.HF 24; 10a, 4-7)

345. June 3, 1858. EDICT: Orders Two Former Canton Officials to
Proceed to Tientsin as Special Assistants to Ch'i-ying.

Additional Edict. Regarding former Governor of Kwangtung
Huang En-t'ung and Former Judicial Commissioner of Kwangtung
Chao Ch'ang-ling: order the said governors to send word to these
officials to set out immediately from their residences, proceed to
Tientsin, and submit themselves to Ch'i-ying for commission and
use. They need not come to Peking. (IWSM.HF 24; 10a, 8-10)

346. June 6, 1858. MEMORIAL: Prince Kung Protests the Appointment of Ch'i-ying as a Return to the Policy of Appeasement of 1842 and
1844.

Prince Kung memorializes. I venture to observe that barbarians
are naturally insatiable. All the time they have traded at the five
ports they have vacillated and repeatedly caused differences, culminating in their disturbance in Kwangtung last winter, occupying our
provincial capital and abducting our high official, and still they dare
proceed North in a body straight to the port of Tientsin. Although
Your Majesty, magnanimous and lenient, treated them courteously,
the barbarians, because their demands were not fully met, on May 20
abruptly seized the forts, forced their way to the gates of Tientsin,

entered the North Canal, and had not their boats been turned back by shallow water, the barbarian ships would have attacked T'ung-chou. While Your Majesty is pained by the present difficulties, His commiseration extends even to them, and He has ordered Kuei-liang and Hua-sha-na to go and settle with them; and now Ch'i-ying is reinstated to take charge of barbarian affairs. Venturing to pry into Imperial Judgments, there must have been no alternative.

Your official is of the opinion, however, that in Ch'i-ying's previous handling of barbarian affairs, if he did not humble himself to give in to them, he mumbled what was taken for consent, feared barbarians like tigers and treated the people like grass, and brought about a great disaster with evil consequences to the present. This time, if he acts as he did before and gives them whatever they ask, why Kuei-liang and Hua-sha-na could do that. As to not acting as he did before, if Ch'i-ying was timorous before, there is no assurance that he can pull himself together now.

Therefore, it rests with Your Majesty's sovereign authority to decide that on items which must not be agreed to, even if demanded a hundred times, there cannot be, on account of Ch'i-ying's appeals for mercy for them, the least compromise; as to the items which can be granted, if when the barbarians bow their heads and accept authority, we bind and not break with them, there is no objection to using him to bring it about.

I am impelled to ask that Ch'i-ying be given strict Imperial orders that he must define terms and make condemnations: first charge them with causing disturbances in Kwangtung province and pressing defiantly at the gates of Tientsin; then tell them that, although unsettled for several years, China can by no means endure this kind of barbarian coercion and that if they stubbornly refuse to conform we will resort to closing customs, stopping trade, and mobilization of soldiers and militia, to decide the issue.

First break their spirit in this way and then bend their wills to conform. Thus pacification will have been effected without falling into the old rut. If complete weakness is manifested it may result in a slovenly settlement and then there will be only Ch'i-ying to blame....
(IWSM.HF 24; 16b, 6-17b, 6)

347. June 6, 1858. EDICT: Instructs Kuei-liang to Use Reed's Good Offices and Orders Ch'i-ying to take a Strong Position toward England and France.

Edict to the Grand Councillors. Kuei-liang and Hua-sha-na have memorialized that after arriving at Tientsin they notified the various barbarians that they would see them on separate days. On June 4 they had an interview with the English chief, Elgin. The chief showed them his credentials and seal given by his sovereign. Kuei-liang and the others told them that China had never used credentials and seals

in the management of affairs. The said chief cherished some doubts
and did not bring up the matter of demands.

Kuei-liang and the others propose using the Russian barbarians
to explain for them but when the Russians have interceded it has
actually been conditioned on their request for trade. Then when we
allowed them to trade, they said that the English and French barbarians insist on coming to Peking and if it is not allowed they will
not undertake to intercede. Thus the Russian barbarians have already approved of their demand and are completely unreliable. If
we still depend on these barbarians to intercede we fear it will be
fruitless endeavor with no benefit.

The American barbarians have traded at the ports the same as
the English and French for many years. On this occasion in meetings
at Tientsin with T'an T'ing-hsiang and others they have never had a
refractory attitude. If Kuei-liang and the others will reason with
them they may be able to induce England and France to conclude the
affair. After they have met them on the sixth, let them study the
situation thoroughly and figure out how to manage.

Yesterday Ch'i-ying was appointed to take charge of barbarian
affairs primarily because the previous establishment of treaties has
all been the work of this one man and besides, having been in Canton
for many years, he is thoroughly familiar with the attitudes of the
various countries, and it was hoped he would have an advantage.

Now is received a memorial from I-hsin Prince Kung, asking for
a Rescript instructing Ch'i-ying that he must charge the barbarians
with causing disturbances in Kwangtung and pressing defiantly at the
gates of Tientsin, first breaking their spirit and then bending their
wills to compliance; that there could not be a constant show of weakness causing us to fall into the old rut.

This memorial is not without perspicacity. On this occasion
having disregarded Ch'i-ying's error and restored him to office, We
have instructed him repeatedly and in detail in the sincere hope that
he will perform his duties wholeheartedly and somewhat mitigate
imminent disaster in order to atone for his previous mistakes. It is
assumed that Ch'i ying must needs be grateful for this Grace and
apply himself assiduously.

At this time when he meets the English and French barbarians he
will first demand why they took up arms in repudiation of treaties in
Kwangtung and, on arrival at Tientsin to talk terms, unaccountably
started hostilities and forced their way up river; that it was not
expected that the treaties of perpetual amity previously concluded
would lead to this today. As Ch'i-ying was the man orginally in
charge, he can reason with them explicitly, break their arrogance,
and later find means to get them under control, thus making it
possible to maintain national prestige and restrain war spirit.

As for asking Favor in their behalf on matters that are absolutely impossible, (We trust) that Ch'i-ying has a conscience and will not act as expected by some persons. Now that We have restored Ch'i-ying to office and elevated him to a responsible position, We cannot but instruct him explicitly and hope that he respects fully Our desires. Let him tremble at this and take heed! (IWSM.HF 24; 20a, 2-21a, 3)

348. June 6, 1858. MEMORIAL: Kuei-liang Proposes to Proceed with Negotiations without Waiting for Ch'i-ying in the Hope of a Quick Settlement.

Kuei-liang and others further memorialize. To continue, on the fourth was received and acknowledged the confidential Court Letter from the Grand Council that an Imperial Edict had been received and a Rescript issued the day before, conferring the brevet rank of board vice-president on Ch'i-ying to take charge of barbarian affairs. Respect this!

But in our opinion barbarians are very suspicious by nature and cross-question us when anything arises. Now that dates have been arranged for meetings, if we send deputies to notify them to wait until Ch'i-ying arrives to act, we are afraid it will make them even more suspicious. As the consequences are great we dare not be the least arbitrary. We propose to wait until the meetings with the barbarians are completed and all matters are somewhat settled and then discuss the method of settlement with Ch'i-ying.

Your slaves have heard for some time that the Kwangtung gentry have set a date for attacking barbarians, but there has been no conclusive evidence and we have not ventured to memorialize it. Now we hear that two of the English barbarian ships at Tientsin have withdrawn, possibly because there is trouble in Kwangtung or for some other reason. When we have determined definitely, we shall memorialize express.

Just now the Russian and American barbarians are both willing to conclude negotiations at an early date and as the French barbarians are merely the English barbarians' yes-men, their arrogant disposition being comparatively somewhat less, it is only the English barbarians who are empirically perverse, inconstant, and undependable. Your slaves were impelled in respectful accord with repeated Imperial Edicts, secretely to watch developments for a chance to lead them to our advantage and order deputies to make inquiries from time to time in the ultimate hope of an early peace settlement, and have not dared undue delay.

Vermilion endorsement: Noted. (IWSM.HF 24; 21a, 4-21b, 6)

349. June 7, 1858. MEMORIAL: Kuei-liang Reports Reed and Poutiatine's Good Offices in Persuading Elgin to Accept the Credentials

of the Chinese Commissioners.

Imperially Commissioned Grand Secretary Kuei-liang and President of the Board of Civil Office Hua-sha-na memorialize. Previously we heard that English Chief Elgin, after returning to his ship, transferred more infantry with the idea of occupying Tientsin and leading forces to invade the interior.

Your slaves secretly sent their deputy Pien Pao-shu to go to the Russian and American ships to enlist their good offices. According to the said deputy's report, Russia and America had already informed the English chief of the reasons for China's Imperial Commissioners not being given seals and credentials, and the said barbarian chief's suspicions were somewhat resolved, and so he had not broken off relations. . . . (IWSM.HF 24; 27a, 5-10)

350. June 7, 1858. MEMORIAL: T'an T'ing-hsiang Explains the Use of the Term "State Seal" Appearing on the Translated Copy of the American Credentials.

T'an T'ing-hsiang further memorializes:. . . As the American barbarians have repeatedly pressed our deputy for reply, he asked them the reason for the two characters "State Seal" being written in with ink, and was told that on the actual letter the original seal of their sovereign appeared; that they had translated the Chinese text separately and so had written in ink where the state seal should be, and that there was no other reason. They also begged that the request be memorialized on their behalf, that the reply be issued so that they could respectfully carry it home. (IWSM.HF 24; 30b, 9. . .31a, 4-7)

351. June 7, 1858. EDICT: Authorizes T'an T'ing-hsiang to Inform Reed that the Emperor's Reply to the President's Letter is Forthcoming.

Edict to the Grand Councillors: T'an T'ing-hsiang has memorialized:... In regard to the American barbarians' request that a reply be issued, the said governor general can tell them that a reply has been written and should be dispatched to Tientsin within a few days so that they can take it back with them. . . .   (IWSM.HF 24; 32a, 3. . .32a, 4-5)

352. June 9, 1858. MEMORIAL: Kuei-liang Reports the Bold Attitude Assumed by Reed but Hopes that Ch'i-ying will be able to Appease the Four Envoys.

Imperially Commissioned Grand Secretary Kuei-liang and President of the Board of Civil Office Hua-sha-na memorialize. Between five and seven on the morning of the seventh, we met the American barbarians and to our surprise the language of these barbarians was insolent. They utilized the English barbarians to frighten us and acted as middlemen to argue querulously their various demands. The items they proposed were many more than those presented by T'an T'ing-hsiang and it is impossible to think of having them intercede for us with England and France.

At this time the French barbarians wait for the English barbarians to get the word and the Russian and American barbarians merely want to get the fisherman's [i.e., the third party's] profit. Since the opening of hostilities on May 20, the English barbarians have wanted to invade the interior, but fortunately T'an T'ing-hsiang secretly sent officers to find means to restrain and delay them. Later, when they were convinced that Your slaves were Imperially Appointed with power to act discriminately, they were finally willing to wait for a settlement.

As Your slaves carefully study the situation, should relations be broken off again, once the barbarians opened fire, not only would Tientsin immediately be thrown into confusion but the barbarians would lead their forces to invade the interior, of which we feel even more apprehension. If we gradually get them more into our meshes and show the barbarians we will not allow them to go to Peking, they will be afraid to break off relations (for fear of losing what concessions they have). Later, we can on the one hand negotiate the treaties and on the other destroy their determination. Even if we should consent (to their coming to Peking), we would insist on waiting until negotiations are concluded and the barbarians' ships have withdrawn to the high seas and then let them come to Peking, each barbarian being allowed only a few men and those not allowed to bear arms. Inside the capital, proclamations would be issued beforehand so the populace would not be alarmed. We would delegate officers to escort them en route, who would also secretly protect us against them. Evaluating the situation we assume there would be nothing more to fear.

Now the English barbarians, seeing that Your slaves treat them courteously, have already somewhat relaxed their suspicion. Should these barbarians, out of gratitude, come to repent and be willing to give up going to Peking, would not this be too perfect?

Today Ch'i-ying arrived at Tientsin and Your slaves have acquired in their negotiations a man whom they recognize as most suitable. But the barbarians, seeing that Your slaves do not carry seals, have been skeptical all along and yesterday they brought out the letters formerly given in Kwangtung bearing seals and sent them to us in a communication which we have already adroitly answered.

Dare we not beg of Your Majesty the extraordinary Heavenly favor of issuing an Imperial Commissioner's seal, with officers appointed speedily to bring it to Tientsin so as to enable Your slaves to control the (barbarians) as occasion presents itself? It would certainly be an aid to state affairs and as negotiations are concluded, we could affix it as occasion requires as an evidence of care and gravity. (IWSM.HF 24; 33b, 9-34b, 9)

353. June 9, 1858. EDICT: Authorizes the Cutting of a Great Seal of Imperial Commission for the Joint Use of the Three Negotiators at Tientsin.

Edict to the Grand Councillors. Today has been received Kuei-liang and Hua-sha-na's memorial on meeting the various barbarians and the present state of negotiations. We have read the memorial in its entirety.

As to the request to confer an Imperial Commissioner's seal, orders have been given to have it cut and within two or three days it should be issued. If the barbarian chiefs inquire about this matter before it comes you can say you have already memorialized their request and, if approved, the seal should arrive shortly.

As to the credentials presented previously by the American barbarians, a reply has already been authorized and today the answer to the autograph credentials of the American barbarians has been sent by post. When it arrives, Kuei-liang and the others will send word to the said envoy so he can receive it respectfully, and be able to go back to his country and report fulfillment of commission. . . . (IWSM. HF 24; 34b, 10-35a, 5)

354. June 10, 1858. EDICT: Extends Broad Powers to Ch'i-ying to Act Independently of Kuei-liang and Hua-sha-na and Indicates Permissable Concessions.

Edict to the Grand Councillors. Previously a confidential Edict was sent Kuei-liang and Hua-sha-na, first to conclude negotiations with the various barbarians, making a preliminary approval and rejection; then if they were not satisfied, they could arrange for Ch'i-ying to make a few more concessions in the capacity of one who knows this matter thoroughly. We assume that they have received and read this.

Today is received a memorial from Kuei-liang and others that the barbarians want to trade in the Yangtze, to allow anyone bearing a passport to travel in the interior, and to establish consulates at important places. If these matters were once agreed to, the consequences would be infinite. They are entirely unreasonable. As to the matter of coming to Peking, they must also find means to nullify it.

As Ch'i-ying has reached Tientsin and has still not met the various barbarians personally, he should fix a date for meeting them. Ch'i-ying is the original negotiator of the treaties, is Imperially Commissioned the same as Kuei-liang and Hua-sha-na, and as soon as the seal is conferred will use it equally. On any matters requiring discretion in handling, Ch'i-ying does not necessarily have to consult with Kuei-liang and the others but can explain to the barbarians personally.

Among the various items requested, figure on agreeing to

several in order to avoid breaking off negotiations, and find means
to block the two items of trade in the Yangtze and travel in the interior. Ch'i-ying has long been thoroughly cognizant of the position
of these barbarians. Tientsin being close to the capital, the situation is urgent, so we cannot but be opportunistic, but if on the two
matters which are practically impossible to concede, the barbarians
insist on being obstinate, it will be clear they have no real desire to
make peace and there is nothing to prevent Ch'i-ying's telling the
English barbarians so. Watch them for any point of advantage and
then figure how to fish in the troubled waters. As to what can be
done, and what cannot be done, Ch'i-ying will certainly have the
situation well in hand and We shall not bind him from afar. (IWSM.
HF 24; 38a, 9-39a, 2)

355. June 12, 1858. MEMORIAL: Kuei-liang Reports Ch'i-ying's
Reception by Reed but Repudiation by Elgin and Gros with Increasing
Defiance of China.

Imperially Commissioned Grand Secretary Kuei-liang, Board
President Hua-sha-na, and Ch'i-ying, with the brevet rank of Board
Vice-president, memorialize. Since Your slave Ch'i-ying arrived
at Tientsin, Your slaves Kuei-liang and Hua-sha-na have respectfully followed Imperial Edicts to negotiate discriminately to carry
out the policy of control. To our surprise the barbarians were unusually cunning and perverse and they get their information very
fast.

Your slaves Kuei-liang and Hua-sha-na sent a deputy to inform
the various barbarians that His Imperial Majesty was now sending
Ch'i-ying to handle the affairs of the four countries. The barbarians
had already seen through our device and so were unreceptive; they
said moreover, that only a minister with full powers could act
discriminately and they could hardly treat with him. Your slaves,
without calculating its rashness, sent an officer to say that as he
had received an Imperial Decree to come to Tientsin, he could act
as occasion demanded. Nevertheless the barbarians' suspicion
was too great to be shaken.

Your slave, Ch'i-ying, arrived in Tientsin on the eighth, and on
the ninth went to pay his respects to the various barbarians. The
Russian and American chiefs were willing to see him, but the
English and French chiefs either replied by communication or made
excuses by letter. The communications they sent were still addressed to the two officials Kuei-liang and Hua-sha-na.

Between three and five this morning was received and acknowledged the confidential Court Letter of the Grand Council that
an Imperial Edict had been received, Imperially commissioning
Ch'i-ying, as well as Kuei-liang and Hua-sha-na, and that a seal
would be issued immediately for all to use alike. Respect this!

Your slaves notified the various barbarians to enable them to see and believe. Hereafter, whether or not they will continue to be suspicious is still unpredictable.

Today from Financial Commissioner of Chihli Ch'ien Hsin-ho comes a confidential letter of Ho Kuei-ch'ing of May 27, which has been copied and respectfully presented for Imperial scrutiny. It is apparent that these barbarians' intention to rely on force to trade in the interior has long been a secret ambition. Your slaves fully realize the regrettable consequences and can by no means consent to it, but at this time the four barbarians are insistent and it is feared that a host of prohibitive treaties would not be able to stop them.

For days we have deliberated carefully with our subordinates without daring to be the least careless, but since the (barbarians) have broken through our defenses with ease, it is hard for us to bring them into our power. Our considered judgment is that compared to a future invasion culminating in a vindictive occupation, it were better to act expediently and grant Imperial Favor, cultivating their pride and our resentment and later, when the military affairs in various provinces are quieted, devise means to stop them. Although compared with not having given consent at all this is greater expenditure of energy, still it is better than taking the offensive and not being able to follow it up. Having repeatedly computed values and exigencies we figure there is no alternative and fear we cannot but offer this mediocre plan.

If worst comes to worst we might allow them to trade in one or two designated places in inland waters, making clear that they wait until China's military affairs are quieted before the arrangements are made. If we do not do as they want and thereby antagonize the barbarians, not only can we offer no relief for Imperial anxiety, but Your slaves would deserve punishment worse than death. We can only act as the situation requires and exert our efforts to control them and, as soon as negotiatoins are concluded, have the barbarians speedily withdraw their warships in order to quiet popular feeling and preserve general conditions.

At present the Russian barbarian treaty has been concluded. Today the American barbarians at Hai-kuang Temple respectfully received the Imperial Autograph letter and personally concluded a treaty. Excepting for the Abbé Chapdelaine and other missionary items, (the French treaty) is about the same as those of the other countries and can also be easily concluded. Only the English barbarian (treaty), on account of the items concerning Yangtze trade and travel in the interior, cannot be concluded readily and has been argued in all directions.

Yesterday the barbarian H.N. Lay tried to force acquiescence and was discourteous to the extreme. We talked adroitly to stall

him off temporarily. Today we again asked the Russian and American barbarians to consult the English chief, Elgin, personally. When
we have had a reply we shall memorialize fully. As to the matter of
coming to Peking, we are still trying to find means to prevent it and
having had an Imperial Edict on the subject, will not dare to give our
consent readily. (IWSM.HF 25; 3a, 4-4a, 8)

356. June 12, 1858. MEMORIAL: Kuei-liang Acknowledges the Receipt of the Emperor's Reply to the President for Transmission to Reed.
        Kuei-liang and others further memorialize. On June 10 was re-
ceived an Imperial Autograph letter Imperially issued to the American barbarians through the Board of War, for the envoy of the said
country respectfully to receive. As soon as it was received, Your
slaves notified T'an T'ing-hsiang and Ch'ung-lun, between eleven
and one o'clock on the eleventh at Hai-kuang Temple, to turn it over
for the American minister respectfully to receive. . . . (IWSM.HF
25; 6a, 9-6b, 3)

357. June 12, 1858. EDICT: Instructs Ch'i-ying to Offer Two Additional Ports to Block British Demands for Trade and Travel in the
Interior of China.
        Edict to the Grand Councillors. Previously memorials were
received from Kuei-liang and others that the English barbarians
wanted to trade in inland waters and also wanted to travel in the
interior but as the evil consequences would be infinite, consent had
not been given and further, as Ch'i-ying had not met the barbarians,
ordered him to reason with them personally and find means to block
it. Today they memorialize again saying that the English and French
chiefs made excuses not to meet Ch'i-ying, and that the barbarian
representative, H. N. Lay, was still pressing for assent to the above
two items.
        This is deliberate coercion, singling out the matters utterly
impossible for us to concede in order to be obstructive. Actually
they have nothing but greed. As Ch'i-ying has likewise been given
an Imperial Commission and as a seal was issued yesterday, we
assume that both have been received, and you can so inform the
barbarians in order to resolve their doubts of your not being able
to act discriminately. Further, order Kuei-liang and Hua-sha-na
to refuse them first and not to agree readily to any additional requests of the barbarians; then when Ch'i-ying comes forward to reverse them, the barbarians must needs have confidence in Ch'i-ying
and not dare make excuses.
        Previously Kuei-liang and others were authorized to consider
adding two small ports outside the five ports. Now that their demands
are insatiable, order Ch'i-ying to consider giving them one large
port in the Fukien-Kwangtung area; if they are still not satisfied he

can also consent to another large port. It is essential that they be
in the Fukien-Kwangtung area; he cannot on his own authority agree
to any place in inland waters.

Ch'i-ying has long been familiar with barbarian affairs and
must know where their profit lies and without any great disadvantage
to China can still let the barbarians make a profit. He can easily
calculate how to bait them in order to avoid another calamity.

In the articles which Kuei-liang and others have concluded, if
the American request for fifty or sixty thousand taels has not been
agreed to, in accord with the precedent of customs remission in
Shanghai, consider abolishing a few months' duties after the port of
Canton has been opened. This item will serve to bait the American
barbarians. While the English and French have no items of this
kind there are certain ones which there is no harm in considering
conceding, but any which are very harmful to China cannot be agreed
to. . . .   (IWSM.HF 25; 6b, 7-7b, 3)

358. June 12, 1858. MEMORIAL: A Circuit Censor Deplores the Appeasement Record of Ch'i-ying and Urges Imperial Action to Block its
Repetition.

Shansi Circuit Censor Yün Shih-lin memorializes. It is now
reported that the barbarian temper is gradually becoming tractable
and it is possible to talk conciliation; but what articles are now being discussed, those outside the Court have no grounds for speculation. Your official judges from past events that there are some
which can never be agreed to.

Your official is a native of Kiangsu and in 1844 went to Shanghai.
At this time trade had just begun. A barbarian consulate was
established outside the city wall and barbarians in groups of three
or five entered the city to pay calls. Inquiring from natives, it was
learned that in the barbarian consulate the men and women servants
employed were all local inhabitants, receiving four dollars foreign
money per month and there were some (Chinese) who even taught
them (the foreigners) to read. The barbarians also preached
Catholicism and those who followed this religion the barbarians
subsidized every year with silver, with 30 taels as a minimum.
Poor people are greedy for gain, so they increased from day to day.
The local officials did not dare to stop it. Recently it is reported
that the provincial capital of Soochow and also Chia(-ting), Hu(-chou),
and other places all have barbarians coming and going.

Tientsin is only two hundred-odd li from Peking. If we allow the
establishment of a barbarian consulate, it will be no different from
Shanghai; the harm to men's minds will be inexpressible and besides, they will gradually get to T'ung-chou; eventually to Peking!
If they are prohibited, it will start trouble; if they are not prohibited, our laws will be nullified, and what recourse will local

officials have? They must needs endure silently and conceal, allowing them to come and go freely. Under the circumstances, there is
certain to be proselyting and coercion. In all probability the (barbarians) will manifest their dog-sheep nature and suddenly back-bite,
so the evil is one which one cannot bear to speak of.

Previously Ch'i-ying was in charge of barbarian affairs and
readily conceded everything the barbarians asked. To take one item,
he allowed them to enter the capital city of Kwangtung and the barbarians turned around and charged us with repudiating treaties. The
present hostilities actually derive from this. Thus Ch'i-ying's complete lack of vision and statesmanship has long been within the
Divine Intelligence and Insight, so in Ordering him to manage barbarian affairs on this occasion, the Divine Mind must have had a
stratagem into which Your stupid official dare not himself intrude.
It is only that the establishment of a barbarian consulate at Tientsin
is of no little consequence. If the barbarians are actually requesting
this, it is humbly asked that Your Majesty personally determine to
repudiate it immediately. Nor can they be allowed to trade at ports
near the capital.

The sole objective of war is not the hope of one day's peace but
to stop interminable future injuries. Some may say that as the barbarian ships have come right to Tientsin and our troops have lost
their vantage, this is a situation which demands conciliation. But
Your official is of the opinion that this is actually the time we have
the tiger in a trap and can plan to catch him. Excepting at high tide
the barbarian ships cannot leave the port and the large ships out in
the ocean cannot come to their relief; actually they are like fish
swimming inside a pan.

Seng-ko-lin-ch'in has massed troops at strategic places and
deployed adventitiously; if he now arouses the population along the
river and coordinates the trainbands, completely encompassing them
in a pocket, barbarian morale will be broken before the fighting
starts and when we consider granting requests they will be sure to
be amenable to pacification.

Thus it is essential to use war to expedite conciliation; we cannot for the sake of conciliation, ruin our plans for war. (IWSM.HF
25; 9b, 10-11a, 7)

359. June 14, 1858. MEMORIAL: Kuei-liang Reports Ch'i-ying's
Embarrassment by Reed and Humiliation by H. N. Lay and Urges Permission for his Return to Peking.

Kuei-liang and Hua-sha-na further memorialize. After Ch'i-
ying arrived at Tientsin, the English and French barbarians did not
meet him and were very suspicious. Ch'i-ying went to the Russian
establishment and got to see Poutiatine who said that if he went on
board the English ship he must be careful. Ch'i-ying did not under-

stand why and went to pay his respects to the English chief who, true enough, was unwilling to see him.

Later, at the American quarters he suddenly was shown the seal copy of the treaties previously concluded. Ch'i-ying was amazed and asked how they came by this document. He was told by the American chief that when the English barbarians captured Canton and Yeh Ming-ch'en was taken prisoner, they took China's "Management of Bar-barian Affairs Yellow Chest" [vault]; not only did it contain their American treaty, but also several years' accumulation of Edicts and memorials which were all taken by the English barbarians. Moreover, they asked him, as seal copies of treaties must be kept at the capital, how it was they remained at Canton? Ch'i-ying said he supposed that in order to collate important matters, request had been made by memorial for the Emperor to send them for exami-nation. After Ch'i-ying returned to his official residence he became more nervous.

Yesterday between seven and nine in the evening, the English barbarian, H. N. Lay, sent a threatening communication. Your slaves and Ch'i-ying met him together and just when we were arguing the treaty, the English barbarian Thomas Wade brought before us a document. It was Ch'i-ying's secret memorial on the state of bar-barian management for that year. The language greatly disparaged barbarians. Besides there was a <u>Vermilion endorsement</u> of Emper-or Hsüan-tsung (Tao-kuang).

Your slaves were astonished beyond measure. For several days they have heard reports that the English barbarians, because they had previously been deceived by him, wanted to take revenge. His ill fate is unfathomable.

As Your slaves think that Ch'i-ying's personal fate actually in-volves national prestige and if these barbarians are allowed to have their way with Ch'i-ying it will be a great impediment to a peaceful settlement, rather than wait for this to happen and be left helpless, it were better to plan ahead in order to block their wicked and dangerous scheme. They can only beg Your Majesty's extraordi-nary Heavenly Favor of allowing Ch'i-ying to come to Peking and report on barbarian affairs personally, thus enabling them to avoid unpredictable worries and him to present a detailed account of the present barbarian situation in Tientsin. (IWSM.HF 25; 18b, 6-19b, 7)

360. <u>June 14, 1858.</u> EDICT: Challenges Request for Ch'i-ying's Re-call and Demands Explanation for the Omission of his Name from Kuei-liang's Memorial.

Edict to the Grand Councillors. Previously because Ch'i-ying had long been familiar with barbarian affairs a special Rescript was issued dispatching an Imperial Commissioner's seal for him, along with Kuei-liang and Hua-sha-na, to receive together and use equally,

and ordering him to explain personally to the barbarians in the hope
of bringing about a change. Now is received a memorial from Kuei-
liang and others that after Ch'i-ying arrived at Tientsin, the English
and French barbarians would not meet him and were very suspicious.
The memorial asks that he be ordered back to Peking.

Ch'i-ying is the negotiator of the original treaties, long familiar
with all the circumstances of these barbarians, by Us on this occasion forgiven his errors and restored to office, given responsible
post by Imperial Commission in sole charge of barbarians. An
Edict had been issued that he need not handle everything with Kuei-
liang and others but, discussing the acceptability of the requests of
the various barbarians, having made sure that there was no harm
to China, consider granting them. Now, although Kuei-liang and
others are likewise Imperially Commissioned, on barbarian affairs
as a whole they are not as well-informed as Ch'i-ying; how is it that
they memorialize on his behalf asking for his recall to Peking?
What is the meaning of not appending Ch'i-ying's title (to the memorial)?

Order Ch'i-ying to consult carefully and memorialize fully the
ultimate meaning of this affair and how it is to be handled. (IWSM.
HF 25; 19b, 8-20a, 6)

361. June 15, 1858. MEMORIAL: Princes and Ministers Report Ch'i-
ying's Dereliction of Duty, Charge him with Cowardice, and Transmit
his Letter to Court.

Princes and Ministers of Reserve Forces Prince Hui, Tsai-
yüan Prince I and Tuan-hua Prince Cheng memorialize. Your
minister Mien-yü [i.e., Prince Hui] set out on the fourteenth from
Seng-ko-lin-ch'in's camp for Peking. En route, Seng-ko-lin-ch'in
sent by special messenger a letter he had received from Ch'i-ying,
informing us that Ch'i-ying had already returned from Tientsin.

Your official, Mien-yü, on opening and reading it was immeasurably horrified. He then took the original letter to Reserve
Headquarters and secretly showed it to Your officials Tsai-yüan and
Tuan-hua. They were both amazed. Your officials, being of the
humble opinion that Ch'i-ying was thoroughly versed in barbarian
affairs, had secretly asked that the Emperor send him to Tientsin
to handle barbarian affairs. As the said official was a man under
punishment, having received Imperial Favor overlooking his error
and restoring him to office, was he not obliged to manifest his
natural goodness and negotiate wholeheartedly? Unexpectedly, as
the barbarian attitude was inscrutable, without even making a start
at settlement, he has made this pretext to unload his responsibility
and, without having received a Special Edict, actually dared to return to Peking. His cowardice and lack of ability, repudiation of
Imperial Favor and betrayal of his country, merit him our complete

contempt.

Further, examining the said official's letter, he says that he can reach Seng-ko-lin-ch'in's military headquarters between seven and eleven on the morning of the fifteenth. Your officials propose that Imperial orders be sent Seng-ko-lin-ch'in, after questioning Ch'i-ying at his headquarters, to inflict capital punishment as a drastic warning to others.

As Your officials were remiss in their judgment of this man and recommended carelessly, their guilt is inescapable, and must request an Edict to punish severely Your officials Mien-yü, Tsai-yüan, and Tuan-hua.

[Ch'i-ying's letter]:   "Between three and five in the afternoon of the twelfth your [Seng-ko-lin-ch'in's] letter was respectfully received. I have received gratefully your gracious inquiry of barbarian affairs, but the English barbarians continue extraordinarily arrogant. Yesterday the barbarians were provocative and it looked like there was going to be a clash. Having gratefully received the Emperor's Heavenly Favor, I pledged myself to recompense fully or die.

"On the eleventh, the English barbarian interpreter sat in the office of His Excellency Kuei and demanded a communication and also produced and let everybody look at the transmitted records which they acquired at the capture of Kwangtung, containing my confidential memorials on barbarian affairs with the Vermilion endorsements. I was completely astounded. Then we held a consultation.

"In sending me to Tientsin, His Majesty originally felt that as I was conversant with barbarian affairs and had been trusted, I could find means to restrain them. Unexpectedly they displayed the documents, entirely made up of my statements of that year reviling barbarians. There had previously been reports that the barbarians were wolves in sheep's clothing and were planning revenge. My personal rise or fall, life or death, was of no consequence whatever, but negotiations were just at the point of being, but still not, concluded. Probably the barbarians calculated that once they sprang this device the whole situation would be affected. Brought to this regrettable extremity, there was absolutely no way out.

"Today this affair has been secretly memorialized, so I am returning to Peking immediately and plan to wait at T'ung-chou. I should arrive beneath your banner between seven and eleven on the morning of the fifteenth, and shall make a full report personally."

Vermilion endorsement: Order Prince Hui and the others, together with Prince Kung, Prince Tun, and the Grand Counsellors to examine this memorial and attached letter and come to a decision. (IWSM.HF 25; 22b, 5-24a, 5)

362. June 15, 1858. MEMORIAL: Prince Kung and Others Recommend that Ch'i-ying be Tried by the Imperial Clan Court and that his Sponsors be Punished.

Prince Kung, Prince Tun, and Grand Councillors P'eng Yün-chang, Po-chun, Mu-yin and Tu Han memorialize. Today we gratefully received from Your Majesty the memorial of Prince Hui and others, (incorporating) Ch'i-ying's letter and respectfully received the Vermilion endorsement ordering Prince Hui and others, together with Prince Kung, Prince Tun and the Grand Councillors to examine this memorial and letter and come to decision. Respect this!

Your officials find that Ch'i-ying, having by Imperial Favor had his faults disregarded and restored to duty as the officer in charge of barbarian affairs, did not gratefully manifest his native goodness. While negotiating along with Kuei-liang and others he actually dared, without waiting for an Imperial Edict, to return to Peking on his own authority. This is real ingratitude for Imperial Favor. Prince Hui and others asked, after he has been tried, that capital punishment be imposed. Actually his crime deserves this.

Your officials propose either that an Imperial Commissioner proceed to T'ung-chou and together with Seng-ko-lin-ch'in carry out a rigorous trial and memorialize fully or that Imperial Orders be given Seng-ko-lin-ch'in to delegate an officer to bring Ch'i-ying to Peking under custody and turn him over to the Imperial Clan Court and the Board of Punishment for rigid trial and request for an Edict to execute the decision.

As to the request of Prince Hui, Tsai-yüan [Prince I], and Tuan-hua [i.e. Prince Cheng] for punishment of themselves, Your officials P'eng Yün-chang, Po-chun, Mu-yin, and Tu Han can hardly deny their guilt and must request that they all be punished. They respectfully await Imperial Judgment.

Vermilion endorsement: We overlooked Ch'i-ying's error, restored him to office, and put him in charge of the management of barbarian affairs. Now timorous and without ability, before a general settlement is reached and without waiting for an Edict, he arbitrarily returns to Peking. Not only is he ungrateful for Our favor but he is also unable to face his country. Actually he has asked for his own death.

Order Seng-ko-lin-ch'in to send an officer to bring Ch'i-ying in chains and under guard to Peking and turn him over to the Ministers of Reserve Forces and the Imperial Councillors, who together with the Imperial Clan Court and the Board of Punishments, will try him rigorously and memorialize fully.

Our using Ch'i-ying on this occasion was from desperation but we hoped for his success. Although Prince Hui and others memorialized recommending him, the actual decision lay with Us! For our lack of foresight, We are very deeply ashamed but the princes' advice was without direction. If they are not given some slight punishment how can public opinion be met?

It is ordered that Prince Hui is not to have charge of Chung Cheng Tien [Buddhist Chapel within the Forbidden City], or Yung-ho Kung [Lama Temple]; order both Tsai-yüan [Prince I] and Tuan-hua [Prince Cheng] dismissed as Chamberlains of the Imperial Body-guard and both, along with Prince Hui, turned over to the Imperial Clan Court for examination; and order P'eng Yün-chang, Po-chun, Mu-yin and Tu Han all turned over to the Board (of Civil Office) for examination. (IWSM.HF 25; 24a, 6-25a, 9)

363. June 15, 1858. EDICT: Charges Ch'i-ying with Cowardice and Ingratitude and Orders him Brought to Peking in Chains to Await Trial and Punishment.

Edict to the Grand Councillors. We have received the memorials of Prince Hui and others impeaching Ch'i-ying for returning to Peking on his own authority and also the letter they presented.

On reading the memorial, We were greatly surprised. Ch'i-ying was originally a degraded official. Previously because Prince Hui and others memorialized asking that he be sent to Tientsin to take charge of barbarian affairs, We, mindful that only he was versed in barbarian affairs, forgave his past and, overlooking his errors to restore him to office, had him negotiate and act with Kuei-liang and Hua-sha-na. He should have gratefully manifested his native goodness and exerted himself to make retribution; even if the rebel barbarians were per-verse and not readily open to reason, he was still obliged to devise and plan wholeheartedly.

Yesterday Kuei-liang and Hua-sha-na memorialized on his be-half asking (permission) to return to Peking. Before permission was given, without even waiting for an Edict or Rescript, he returned from Tientsin to T'ung-chou. Reading his letter to Seng-ko-lin-ch'in, his timorousness, lack of ability, and disregard for the general situation in placing himself outside of affairs, are really very despicable. There has already been a Vermilion edict ordering Seng-ko-lin-ch'in to send an official to bring Ch'i-ying in chains and under guard to Peking and turn him over to the Ministers of Reserve Forces and others for rigorous trial. The said minister on receipt of this Edict will delegate an official and set out with Ch'i-ying under custody.

At present the pacification program is not completed and there is no assurance that the barbarians will not act rashly and renew hostitlities, so we must be beforehand with plans of offense in order to prevent haste and confusion. The said minister is stationed at T'ung-chou very near Tientsin and must reconnoitre from time to time and make immediate arrangements. . . . (IWSM.HF 25; 25a, 10-25b, 10)

364. June 18, 1858. MEMORIAL: T'an T'ing-hsiang Reports Pouti-atine's Tractability and Reed's Increasing Arrogance--Negotiations Proceeding.

Governor General of Chihli T'an T'ing-hsiang memorializes. For several days Your official, Grand Secretary Kuei-liang, and others have sent officials to discuss treaties with the various barbarians and they are still not all concluded. Of the various barbarians, only the Russian chief is still respectful and compliant. The American chief is gradually more overbearing, while the English and French are as obstinate as ever.

Several days ago one of the Swatow irregulars employed by the Americans came ashore with a barbarian soldier and forced his way into a private house. The irregular was bound by the man of the house and the barbarian soldier escaped. The American interpreter with ten-odd men came to the headquarters of Kuei-liang and others and reported. An officer was sent immediately to tell him that it was the irregular who caused trouble, that he had been bound but was ordered returned to them for punishment. The said barbarian acknowledged his fault and went away. . . .[15]   (IWSM.HF 25; 33b, 6-34a, 2)

365. June 20, 1858. MEMORIAL: Kuei-liang Proposes the Granting of Restricted Residence in Peking in order to Avoid Breaking off Negotiations.

Imperially Commissioned Grand Secretary Kuei-liang and President of the Board of Civil Office Huà-sha-na memorialize. . . . At present the Russian and American treaties have been concluded. The English and French barbarians are always thinking of going into the city to live and, while they have not occupied the villages, they have forcibly taken over private residences and are constantly stirring up trouble. Every day the complications increase and the more inextricable our worries become. True, as Sacred Edict has it, we cannot but plan the outcome in advance.

In Your slaves' stupid opinion, barbarian nature is essentially that of dogs and sheep. In the past they have been most irked by China's contempt and so want to acquire residence in the capital as a matter of prestige. If we could just send officials to look after them suitably they might repent out of gratitude and be able to resolve their former suspicions; even if they did not meet their obligations, their numbers would not be great and we could still manage them. But these barbarians have many cunning devices and whether or not they are harboring any subtle motives, Your

---

15 For the American version of this incident, see "The Journal of S. Wells Williams, Ll.D.", *Journal of the North China Branch of the Royal Asiatic Society*, v. 42 (1911), p. 63.

slaves do not venture to claim firm control of them. From this
dilemma we see no escape.

Speaking of the immediate situation, we can by no means allow
them to break off relations and can only ask the Emperor's Heavenly
Favor of a secret strategem, so Your slaves can act in accordance.
As soon as the Imperial Will is expressed negotiations will be
speedily concluded to preclude further discussion. (IWSM.HF 25;
36b, 10. . .38a, 9-38b, 9)

366. June 20, 1858. MEMORIAL: Kuei-liang Reports Russia's Offer
of Rifles and Cannon to China to Strengthen her Defenses against Foreign
Aggression.

Kuei-liang and others memorialize further. On the eighteenth,
Department Director Su-chang-a brought the Russian ecclesiastic (Ta-
la-ma) Pa-la-ti to Tientsin. An official was sent to conduct him to
that country's ship.

At this time the Russian barbarians, moved to gratitude for Your
Majesty's extraordinary Heavenly Favor, offered to give China 10,000
rifles and 50 pieces of cannon of various kinds, to be sent to the port
of Ta-ku and received by local officials with cargo boats, in order to
show their desire to reciprocate, and asked Your slaves to memorialize on their behalf. They also said that hereafter there must be
stringent preparations against barbarian troubles, that the forts at
the ports could not be relied on at all; they proposed writing a letter
home to have officials skilled in the construction of forts, drilling of
troops, and able to identify outcroppings of gold and silver, sent out
to China to make complete preparations for her; that this was planned
as an actual expression of gratitude, without any other motive whatever, and there was no need to be suspicious.

Having seen these barbarians for several days and discussed with
them seriously, we feel this is proposed with the utmost sincerity.
When the barbarian chief prepares the letter for us to make the request for him, we propose to memorialize for him according to the
facts.

After the contingent of barbarians ships has withdrawn, measures
must be taken at once to fortify the coast. The various ports along
the coast must be energetically reconstructed so as to fix the fence
even after the sheep are lost. (IWSM.HF 25; 38b, 10-39a, 9)

367. June 20, 1858. EDICT: Urges the Commissioners to use
Desperate Efforts Including Russian Good Offices to Dissuade Elgin
from Impossible Demands.

Edict to the Grand Councillors. Kuei-liang and Hua-sha-na memorialize that the English barbarians are about to fall in line and
now ask for a document showing full powers (to accept their terms).
Every one of the items requested by the English barbarians will have

evil consequences.

Take the matter of trade in the interior. It was originally proposed to arrange it when military operations were over; now the barbarians want to build a wharf at Chen-chiang first and one can see
their gradual encroachment. Their demands are endless. At present
the barbarians disturb the ports, ocean (tribute) transport has become difficult to manage, and under the circumstances we cannot but
change to canal transport. If we let them occupy Chen-chiang again,
even canal transport will be difficult to manage. This is a real
calamity and you can explain clearly. Say that as the Chen-chiang
district has been subject to pillage for several years, popular feeling
is still unsettled, nor are there any prosperous merchants there, that
if the barbarians build a wharf immediately, establish godowns and
stock goods, not only will they not sell, but there is no assurance that
there will be no disputes. Should there be quarrels, it would indeed
injure our friendly relations, therefore (we) must wait until the
military campaigns are finished before deciding on this. This is not
wilful delay on pretext.

Take also the matter of travel in all provinces and divisions.
Although it is specified that they carry passports, if they quarrel or
fight with the people or get lost or die, China is large and populous
and cannot be searched. You must make it clear to them in advance
so that disputes can be avoided afterwards.

As to admission to the capital, what other countries propose is
merely access when they have business, but the English barbarians
insist on remaining at the capital and even presume for themselves
the title of imperial commissioner. The objections are still more
impossible to express. Your must say that as access to the capital
on business has been granted, in case there are important matters
they can come to Peking and plead in person, so what is the need of
leaving anyone to reside far away in the capital? If they insist on
residing in Peking, since the precedent of the Russian barbarians
consists entirely on being able merely to send students to reside,
they could not have the title of imperial commissioner, would have
to adopt Chinese clothes and caps, obey Chinese regulations, could
study only mechanical arts, and could not be consulted on public
matters, so there would be no great advantage to their country [i.e.
England]. Besides, each trading port has a governor general and
governor and if subsequently there are important matters, where-
ever they are, they can all be transmitted by memorial for them by
the governor general and governor of the local province without the
necessity of arguing with the Kwangtung Imperial Commissioner.
Provided there is no evasion, this is as convenient as residence in
Peking. From all the above items, they can be allowed to choose.

Kuei-liang and the others have utilized the Russian barbarians
to effect a coup for them and, no matter how difficult it is, must

block this [i.e. residence in Peking] affair. The Russian barbarians
have exerted themselves out of gratitude and their love of pre-
eminence can surely be aroused, so say to them that their country
has been friendly for many years and still has only students in Peking, never having had a resident Imperial Commissioner; that now,
before the English barbarians have restored Kwangtung, how can
they propose entrance to the city without taking precedence over
Russia? Get them to find means to intercede. Even if the proposal
to come to Peking cannot be blocked, the Kwangtung affair must be
terminated and then determine meticulously the rules of etiquette.
Only with both parties cooperating can the treaty be concluded.

As to the port of Tientsin, they can never be allowed access. In
the future in coming to an agreement on entrance to Peking, they can
only come north from Shanghai overland, escorted by Chinese officials, fully provided and all managed by China, it being unnecessary
for them to pay their own expenses. Subsequently they will come to
Peking once in three years or once in five years; it is not necessary
to make the trip every year. If it is possible to get the Russian barbarians to bring this about, it will then be unnecessary to pursue
their talk of coming to Peking first to decide on residences and the
renting of houses in Tientsin.

As to establishing a wharf at Chen chiang, the matter of tribute
transport being impeded need not be represented to the Russian barbarians. The Russian barbarians want to present rifles and cannon.
Since this is done with sincerity, you can tell them that when they
bring them they will certainly be received and that in the future there
will certainly be gifts in return. Actually this can be utilized to
implicate them and to show we are not suspicious in the hope that
they can be utilized by us. You are not to give any indication that
China sorely needs these things to arouse a feeling of condescension.

As to their wish to have men come to give instruction in mechanical arts and to survey mineral deposits, you are ordered to make a
plausible reply. It is essential that you do not agree. (IWSM.HF 25;
39a, 10-41a, 2)

368. June 21, 1858. MEMORIAL. The Princes and Ministers Present
Three Depositions of Ch'i-ying in Extenuation of his Conduct at Tientsin.

Princes and Ministers of Reserve Forces Prince Hui and others
memorialize. On the fifteenth of this month a Vermilion Edict was
received ordering Seng-ko-lin-ch'in to send an officer to bring Ch'i-
ying in chains and under custody to Peking, turn him over to the
Princes and Ministers of Reserve Forces and the Grand Councillors,
and for them to cooperate with the Imperial Clan Court and the Board
of Punishments for a rigid trial. Respect this!

Your officials directed and cooperated with representatives of
the departments in a trial, lasting several days. According to Ch'i-

ying's testimony, it was actually because the English barbarians
bore him malice, and that he was therefore afraid that negotiations
were endangered, and because he had things to report personally
that, after having Kuei-liang and Hua-sha-na memorialize for him,
he returned to Peking; that after reaching T'ung-chou he received
the Grand Councillors' Court Letter containing the Imperial Edict
of June fifteenth, and at T'ung-chou he prepared a memorial reporting according to fact. Then because Seng-ko-lin-ch'in received
a Stern Edict to bring Ch'i-ying to Peking in chains and under custody
and also to bring back Ch'i-ying's original memorial, now he was being tried, and he could only beg the Emperor's Heavenly Favor to
punish him, Ch'i-ying, severely.

Your officials have opened Ch'i-ying's three personal depositions and the original memorial he sent from T'ung-chou, read them
in court, and respectfully present them all for Imperial Scrutiny.

Vermilion endorsement: Order I-hsin Prince Kung and I-tsung
Prince Tun, together with the Grand Secretaries, the Six Boards, and
the Nine Dignitaries to come to a just decision and memorialize fully.
Have Ch'i-ying's depositions and memorial turned over to them for
reference. (IWSM.HF 26; 1a, 2-1b, 6)

369. June 21, 1858. DEPOSITION: Ch'i-ying Describes his Humiliation and Abuse by H. N. Lay and the Circumstances of his Return to
Peking from Tientsin.

Ch'i-ying respectfully and fully testifies. On June 8 he went to
Tientsin and saw that barbarian intercourse and wilful causing of
trouble could not be stopped by reason nor could they be overcome
by awe. As barbarian tyranny was increasing day by day, it was
genuinely feared that popular feeling could not endure it and once a
quarrel was started, the whole situation would be lost. As to the
actual conditions (of barbarian tyranny), not only are they unfit to
be reported on paper, but also they cannot be told by word of mouth.
It was truly a difficult situation to manage.

On June 11, H. N. Lay and the assistant interpreter, Thomas
Wade, came to Kuei-liang and Hua-sha-na's temporary quarters and
demanded that they be allowed to send a communication. Their attitude and expression were both threatening. They also produced the
memorials with Vermilion endorsements of that (former) year confidentially reporting barbarian affairs, for everybody to open and
read, full of expressions reviling barbarians. These barbarians
were suspicious and hateful and throughly displeased. Furthermore,
according to the reports of our deputies, the English barbarians
harbored resentment and were determined not to see Ch'i-ying.
Consequently Kuei-liang and Hua-sha-na concluded that as the
English barbarians hated Ch'i-ying, he was of no use in Tientsin and,
if a break were precipitated on account of him, it would be even

harder for them to function, so it was agreed that he should return
to Peking and keep negotiations intact by avoiding a split. These are
the actual circumstances of Kuei-liang and Hua-sha-na's memorial
asking to have Ch'i-ying return to Peking.

Then on the twelfth there was a general conference. On that day,
Kuei-liang being sick, Kuei-liang's deputy was present, so Ch'i-ying
said to Hua-sha-na and the deputy that, as the memorial was asking
Ch'i-ying to return to Peking, he would not dare affix his signature
lest it cause suspicion; that if, as Ch'ung-lun (suggested), he should
leave as soon as the memorial was sent, it was feared people and
barbarians would be suspicious and it would be very awkward. Hua-
sha-na said that if the barbarians asked about it, they could say,
"As Ch'i-ying's views do not coincide with yours and as you envoys
are not willing to see him, His Imperial Majesty has recalled Ch'i-
ying". Ch'i-ying said that if local business men and people asked
about it, they could reply that he had left on official business and
would return to Tientsin after a few days, in order to allay general
suspicion. After the conference was concluded, Kuei-liang and Hua-
sha-na added a postscript to their memorial begging His Majesty's
extraordinary Heavenly Favor of allowing Ch'i-ying to come to
Peking. The real motive was to afford an opportunity to report
personally the whole situation of the management of barbarian affairs.

It is humbly observed that even though Ch'i-ying has been away
from court for many years and is decrepit and foolish, how could he
not know that whenever he reports by memorial he must wait until it
has received the Vermilion endorsement before he dares act upon it?
Now having heedlessly returned to Peking without waiting for the
Vermilion endorsement, actually according to the Sacred Edict he
was inviting his own death. But his desire to report personally
actually concerned the general security of the nation and, suspecting
that the barbarians have many eyes and ears and Chinese traitors
were reporting his every move, it was absolutely necessary for
him to report personally, he by no means would dare commit (his
views) to writing, so disregarding the risk of death he returned to
Peking, hoping that Imperial Edict would vindicate him. These are
the actual circumstances of his leaving Tientsin on his own authority,
without any idea of evasion.

As the barbarians at Tientsin wilfully aggravate, populace and
militia are in a state of desperation and if there is any provocation
there is danger of an immediate rupture. So the defense of the T'ung-
chou area must be adequately planned.

On the fourteenth, Ch'i-ying passed through Yang-ts'un, had an
interview with T'o-ming-a, and discussed the military situation in
detail.

On the fifteenth, he reached T'ung-chou, met Seng-ko-lin-ch'in,
and informed him of barbarian affairs in Tientsin in detail: that there

must be thorough investigation and planning, looking toward both punishment and pacification in order to meet the situation. He also gave him a white gunpowder rocket [or arrow] as a model for manufacture. In fighting with fire it is a rather effective instrument. He [Seng-ko-lin-ch'in] said that he proposed within a few days to memorialize on the whole defense situation; that, as to the necessity of defending the river-course, he was sending orders for the governor general to find means to effect it.

Ch'i-ying, in risking death to come from Tientsin to Peking, actually intended to report personally the general plan of barbarian affairs and did not dare think of his own life. He respectfully makes this personal deposition and humbly asks that it be memorialized for him. He begs His Majesty's Heavenly Favor of inflicting heavy punishment on Ch'i-ying. This is a true personal deposition. (IWSM. HF 26; 1b, 7-3b, 6)

370. June 21, 1858. DEPOSITION: Ch'i-ying Reports his Views on British Demands for Access to the Interior and his Desire to Discuss this Orally at Court.

Ch'i-ying further testifies. It is noted that of the items which the English barbarians insist on, only the two items of trade in the interior and travel in all provinces and districts with the selection of places to establish consulates, actually concern the general welfare of the nation. There must by no means be a hasty compromise to give rise to endless future troubles. Although we agree now, after military matters are terminated we shall reconsider the matter, so it is no more than a temporary sop to quiet them. If these barbarians want to go immediately to undisturbed areas they are certain to excite alarm and commotion. If we wait until the time of signing the treaties to insert even a slight retraction, it is certain to cause a rupture. It is absolutely necessary to make plans in advance and take precautions clause by clause. Once this leaks out, it is certain to bring about hostilities immediately.

As actions must be kept strictly secret and time is at a premium, he did not dare commit this to paper nor did he dare discuss it with outsiders; so he rashly returned to Peking, hoping to visit the Court, make a complete report and humbly ask His Majesty for directions for him to follow, and also ask that Secret Orders be sent officials in charge of troops as well as local civil and military officials to make preparations at strategic land and water positions without divulging the least inkling to mar the stratagem. These are the real circumstances of Ch'i-ying's insistence on returning to Peking to report personally.

He humbly thinks that Ch'i-ying in the evening of his life, having received His Majesty's infinite mercy to overlook his errors and restore him to office, even though he pledge to exert himself to the death he could not recompense it in one-ten-thousandth part. How would he dare use a pretext to shirk duty and devise a plan to absent himself? His present return to Peking at risk of death is really stupid and he can only beg His Majesty's Heavenly Favor to punish Ch'i-ying severely. This is an additional true deposition. (IWSM.HF 26; 3b, 7-4b, 3)

371. June 21, 1858. DEPOSITION: Ch'i-ying Reports the Hostile Moves of the Allies at Tientsin and Warns against a Reopening of Hostilities.

Ch'i-ying further testifies. On June 10 he went to see the barbarians of the four countries. The barbarian chiefs of England and France sent word by interpreters that they would not receive him. At the American and Russian interviews, (their) manners and speech were fairly respectful and compliant.

Now the four barbarian chiefs have moved on land and are far removed from the large ships outside the port. The barbarians have brought from the port more than two hundred iron picks and shovels, more than two hundred tents, and in Tientsin have obtained over three hundred reed mats. At the mouth of San-ch'a-ho they have also taken Wang-hai-lou, the Han family residence, and various houses in Chin-chia-yao. The four barbarian chiefs occupy separate house in Chin-chia-yao and have stores of munitions and such things. They have also sent five or six sampans to sound the water in the South Canal and mounted our fortifications to look out with telescopes.

Their statements that they will not fight again are only to weaken our morale. Their harbored malice is also very apparent. Ch'i-ying does not dare entirely to believe that they will withdraw their ships and cease hostilities as soon as their terms are settled. The barbarian ships now anchored at San-ch'a-ho come and go irregularly. When they come, popular feeling is aroused; when they go, merchants and people are immediately quiet.

Examining the barbarian attitude thoroughly, it cannot be compared with previous years, nor is it entirely mercenary; there is now disclosed an attitude of spying and plotting. For instance, the barbarians first wanted to occupy Tientsin; then they did not insist and everyone said this was fine; then they asked to trade in the interior. Might we ask if Tientsin is not also in the interior? First they asked to come to Peking; now this can wait, and they change their request to trade in the interior and travel in the various provinces and subdivisions, but is not Lu-ho [i.e. T'ung-chou] also in the interior? With all kinds of treachery, how can faith be implicit? It is essential to plan comprehensively to determine our future procedure.

Respectfully presented, this is an additional true deposition. (IWSM.HF 26; 4b, 4-5a, 9)

372. June 21, 1858. MEMORIAL: Ch'i-ying's Report Prepared at
T'ung-chou. en route to Peking, Presented as Evidence in his Trial by
the Imperial Clan Court.

    Ch'i-ying memorializes. After sending communications to the
various barbarians, although the English and French barbarians
sent interpreters to Your slave's temporary quarters to call, they
returned after only a few words.

    On June 10 he went to Wang-hai-lou where the English and French
barbarians lived, hoping primarily to interview the barbarian chiefs
and find means to explain to them, but they were stubbornly unwilling
to see him and made excuses to put him off. Then that evening the
English interpreter, H. N. Lay, came to the temporary quarters of
Your slaves, Kuei-liang and Hua-sha-na, pressed demands for various treaty provisions, and insisted that every item be agreed to.
Then when the subordinates politely equivocated, the said barbarian
immediately became indignant and wanted to leave. His language
was defiant and most hateful. As the general situation was involved,
Your slaves, although filled with indignation, could not but humble
themselves and mollify (him) in the hope of bringing him around.
Unwilling to receive the communication we had prepared for him, he
finally left in anger.

    The next day H. N. Lay returned with Interpreter Thomas Wade
to the temporary quarters of Your slaves Kuei-liang and Hua-sha-
na, and again demanded that they agree to sanction a communication.
His expression was thoroughly severe. He also produced Your
slave's confidential memorials on barbarian affairs, with their Vermilion endorsements, of that (former) year for everyone to open
and read, concerned for the most part with reviling barbarians.

    Now with the capture of Canton and seizure of the governor
general's yamen all the files of barbarian affairs are in the hands
of the barbarians and the stratagems of that year are all penetrated
by the barbarians. Your slave really fears that it is now virtually
impossible to get them under our control or to induce them to trust
us again.

    Moreover, according to the report of the subordinate officials,
they found that the English barbarians harbored malice. Their inner-
most thoughts are inscrutable. Their stubborn refusal to treat with
Your slave and their disclosure of the documents clearly reveals the
resentment they cherish. As enmity already existed we could not but
temporarily remove the object of their venom to safeguard the general situation.

    Besides, the barbarians are always going about the city streets
in groups of three or five and arousing the inhabitants, even to the
extent of forming bands for wilful action and there is real danger of
another incident arising. Kuei-liang and Hua-sha-na repeatedly discussed it with Your slave and agreed that the barbarian temper

is fundamentally very suspicious and besides they are cherishing a grudge. If Your slave held to the letter and insisted on an interview, in case anything happened, not only would there be no benefit to the general situation but it was even feared that it would precipitate a break which would be hard to close.

So Your slaves Kuei-liang and Hua-sha-na added a postcript to their memorial begging Heavenly Favor to allow Your slave (Ch'i-ying) to come to Peking in order to memorialize completely in person. How would he dare to adhere to personal views to the detriment of policy. If Your slave had deliberately shirked duty, lost his mind and suppressed his better nature, disregarded the precarious state of the nation, and thought only of his own fate, how could he escape the omniscience of the Divine Intelligence?

The day after the memorial was dispatched, Your slave set out and has now arrived at T'ung-chou. He has confidentially and thoroughly discussed the whole barbarian situation with Seng-ko-lin-ch'in personally, hoping to arrive at a coordinated plan and then go to Court, and kneeling, listen to Divine Instructions and respectfully act accordingly. (IWSM.HF 26; 5a, 10-6b, 6)

373. June 24, 1858. EDICT: Urges Commissioners to Substitute Occasional Visits to Peking for Permanent Residence and Accepts War as the Alternative.

Edict to the Grand Councillors. Kuei-liang and Hua-sha-na have memorialized that negotiations have reached an absolute crisis and ask for a definitive Edict.

Because the English barbarians wanted residence at the capital, a previous Edict instructed Kuei-liang and the others to say that in case of important business they could easily come to Peking and report personally; that it was unnecessary to leave anyone to reside remotely in the capital city or, according to the precedent of the Russian barbarians, merely send students to reside who could not be designated as Imperially Commissioned, must adopt Chinese clothes, obey Chinese laws and not be allowed to report official affairs; that they must wait until the Kwangtung affair was terminated and then determine detailed articles of conduct. It is entirely agreeable that in the future when they come North by the inland route perhaps once in three years, perhaps once in five years, China will send officials to escort them and it will not be necessary for them to pay their own expenses. Thus the English barbarians' proposal to come to Peking will not be completely rejected. If Kuei-liang and the others explain clearly and the barbarians get this prestige, how can they say that we merely procrastinate?

The letter from the Russian barbarians says that they have explained the two matters of entrance to Peking and inland waters for us, but on questioning the English barbarians, they say that this was never done. In this affair, it cannot be determined whether the Russian barbarians did not transmit the message or the English barbarians deliberately lied.

As to these barbarians' request for a wharf at Chen-chiang and that of the French barbarians at Nanking, the agreement of Kuei-liang and the others to reconsider both, when military affairs were completed, was primarily merely a device to delay hostilities. When the time comes means must still be found. If in the matter of coming to Peking we also have to accede to their request, it will be because Kuei-liang and Hua-sha-na in the management of barbarian affairs have no principles whatever, are consistent cowards, and have never thoroughly comprehended the Court Letter and Edict of the twentieth.

The communication of the English barbarians says that we merely procrastinated and if again there were no definite statement they could only move their armies northward. After all, what is indefinite? How is it that Kuei-liang and others have never told them explicity? In the last few days memorials from princes, ministers, and censors have agreed that the barbarians can by no means be allowed to reside in Peking or to trade in inland waters. Can it be that Kuei-liang and others do not know the consequences? They have only to manage suitably in accord with the Court Letter and Edict of the twentieth and make the barbarians realize that we will not repulse them entirely nor will we agree to everything they ask. If we get them involved like this, it may not come to an open break.

The requests of the French barbarians must by no means be rejected and can only be handled likewise. If these barbarians insist on sending Imperial Commissioners to Peking and erecting buildings for permanent residence, tell them that this is practically impossible to concede; that if you granted it on your own authority, His Imperial Majesty would certainly punish you severely and even the items which have been granted would all go by the board.

As to what action you shall take, wait for the replies of the English and French chiefs and on the other hand notify the Russian and American barbarians to withdraw their ships from the inner waters immediately to avoid unintentional damage during the fighting and also send an express communication to Seng-ko-lin-ch'in to make due arrangements immediately. Talk as though you were breaking off relations and see how they react. If they actually take up arms we can only fight them; but if they look upon what Kuei-liang and others have conceded as not insignificant benefits, they will surely turn around and get the Russian and American barbarians to come out as mediators. Then we can reconsider without being entirely coerced, with its endless consequences. (IWSM.HF 26; 25b, 7-27a, 2)

374. June 26, 1858. MEMORIAL: Kuei-liang Reports Conclusion of Russian and American Treaties and the Inevitability of War if Britain's Terms are Refused.

Imperially Commissioned Grand Secretary Kuei-liang and President of the Board of Civil Office Hua-sha-na memorialize. On this occasion, the English and French barbarians, since entering Tientsin harbor, have been perverse beyond description in attitude and appearance and, having exposed all of China's weakness, have flaunted their arrogance.

Bitter and desperate, Your slaves have forcibly staved off (calamity) for more than twenty days, more and more strongly pressed for an immediate settlement. The difficult position of Your slaves cannot be fully appreciated excepting by an eyewitness, primarily because having calculated over and over, they have recognized that while the consequences of acquiescence were endless, the catastrophe of a rupture was even greater. If we consider consequences, not only entrance to Peking and the inland waters demand circumspection but also the various customs provisions are very harmful to China. Therefore, this was something Your slaves had to endure and they willingly acknowledge their guilt. That is to say, at this critical juncture they feared that once barbarian sentiment changed, Tientsin would be immediately lost to us, thence a northern invasion, which would be of great concern.

The present English and French treaties can by no means be taken as actual commitments; they are nothing more than a few pieces of paper useful for the moment to drive their warships from the harbor. If in the future we want to repudiate the agreement and give up friendly relations, it will require only the punishment of Your slaves for the crime of mismanagement to make waste paper out of them.

Yesterday this barbarian (H. N. Lay) came to headquarters with a self-made treaty of 56 articles and pressed Your slaves to agree to it. His pride and anger everyone with eyes could see. Not only could there be no discussion but not even one word could be altered. The gunboats were close by and if we let him leave, Your slaves certainly had no assurance it would not cause a rupture. The best they could do was agree to conclude negotiations within two or three days.

At this time the Russian and American treaties have been concluded. As the treaties of the English and French barbarians included the items of entrance to Peking and trade in inland waters, their demands were too extravagant; besides they also wanted to reside in Tientsin. As we had not reached any conclusion (ourselves) we could not treat satisfactorily (with them). The word of the Russian barbarians is not to be relied on and as the American barbarians are anxious to set sail, these two barbarians are actually in the same category as the English and French, so to get them to intercede could hardly be of any advantage.

At present we are, on the one hand, sending an express communi-

cation to Seng-ko-lin-ch'in to make arrangements immediately, and
on the other hand, calling on the Chinese assistants and clerks of
the barbarians secretly to devise means. If in the end we cannot re-
tract, the best we can do is to let them break off relations. If
entrance to Peking is permissible after one year without sending
Imperial Commissioners, perhaps following the regulations of the
Russian students, if trade at Chen-chiang is permissible after the
termination of military operations and wharf established; all customs
rates to be settled at Shanghai; no residence at Tientsin, perhaps
shifting it to another place--then we can make a settlement in accord
with circumstances. The English and French are exceptionally arrogant and we cannot lightly try their sword-point; of this Your slaves
are absolutely certain. So for the time being the effective plan is to
rely on concession to effect an immediate conclusion. (IWSM.HF
26; 28a, 10-29b, 4)

375. June 26, 1858. MEMORIAL: Prince Kung Reports the Verdict that
Ch'i-ying be Confined in the Imperial Clan Court Pending Strangulation.

Prince Kung and others memorialize. We note that Ch'i-ying was
a degraded official, forgiven and restored to office by Imperial favor;
how must his native goodness be brought out in an effort to recompense? Although he has testified that he returned to Peking to report
personally a line of action and Kuei-liang and others separately memorialized in explanation, that it was not a pretext to evade duty,
nevertheless, in setting out without waiting for an Imperial Edict, his
rashness and stupidity are certainly irrational. Truly as the Sacred
Edict has said, he virtually asked for his own death. However, this
official was not in command of troops and besides his return to Peking
was from fear of disrupting negotiations, which is different from
arbitrary withdrawal without reason.

We have examined the laws thoroughly and there is no specific
clause saying what punishment a minister receives for returning to
the capital on his own authority. It is inappropriate to determine his
crime on the provisions for deliberate refusal to follow orders, for
arbitrary flight from posts by officials in the face of danger, or
for taking immediate action on matters which have been memorialized
but not reported back, and thus give rise to casual interpretation.

Your officials have considered together the circumstances of his
misconduct and must ask that the proposal of Prince Hui and others
that Ch'i-ying be immediately executed, be reconsidered and somewhat lightened. (They recommend that he be) consigned to prison
to await strangulation according to law, turning him over to the Imperial Clan Court for temporary confinement until Court Session,
when he will be handled as a capital offender. Whether or not this is
correct, we respectfully await Imperial confirmation. (IWSM.HF 26;
31a, 9-32a, 1)

376. June 26, 1858. MEMORIAL: A Court Official Protests the Verdict of the Imperial Clan Court and Urges that Ch'i-ying be Summarily
Executed.

President of the Court of Colonial Affairs Su-shun memorializes.
In (my) humble opinion Ch'i-ying, because his previous handling of
barbarian affairs was improper, incurred most serious guilt. Now
by Extraordinary Imperial Magnanimity forgiven and restored to
office and charged with the management of barbarian affairs, how
obliged was he to manifest his better nature to recompense Supreme
Generosity? Now on arrival at Tientsin, with the first empty threat
of the barbarians, disregarding general conditions, he immediately
rushes back trumping up a story of memorializing in person.

Now Your slave sees that Ch'i-ying's deposition is mostly whitewash, nor is there anything which could not have been reported fully
by memorial. Thus his cowardice and lack of ability, the cunning in
his heart, truly as Sacred Edict says, virtually invite his own death.
If he is not immediately executed and only committed to await
strangulation, then that will afford a delay of months or years and
will appeal to his ignoble clinging to life. If he has the good luck to
die of sickness and save his neck, how will the law of the land be
manifested, and how official depravity be admonished? Besides,
there are still officials in charge of barbarian affairs; if they all
follow his example and cowardlike, secretly flee, what a sorry state
will things have come to?

In Your slave's stupid view, it is necessary to ask for an Edict
ordering Ch'i-ying's immediate execution in order to discourage
official depravity and carry out the law of the land.

Vermilion edict: Today Prince Kung and others, as well as Su-
shun, have memorialized. We must still consider this in detail. Order
the assembled Princes and ministers all to come to the Summer
Palace on the twenty-ninth and await the Edict. (IWSM.HF 26; 32a,
2-32b, 5)

377. June 29, 1858. EMPEROR'S AUTOGRAPH EDICT: Reviews Ch'i-
ying's Case and Orders his Suicide in the Death Chamber of the Imperial
Clan Court.

Vermilion edict. Previously the request of Prince Hui and others
was received that Ch'i-ying be court martialed so he was ordered to
Peking for rigorous questioning. Later when tried, he prepared his
testimony. Then I-hsin Prince Kung, and others were ordered to
come to a just decision. Now is received their memorial stating that
Ch'i-ying's failure to wait for an Edict was stupid and rash and proposing imprisonment awaiting strangulation and, at Court Session, to
be among the capital offenders. The proposal is not inept but while
it states the case for catching the culprit it says absolutely nothing
about punishing his heart, so this must be set forth clearly.

Ch'i-ying, a degraded official, was restored to service in the hope of some achievement in his old age of benefit to affairs. Moreover, when that official took his leave from the Throne he personally memorialized that he would try to surmount his difficulties and for Us to watch how he performed. He did not seem like one who had blinded his better nature in confusion. Moreover after Ch'i-ying's arrival at Tientsin, June 8, there were a Court Letter and an Edict that he need not agree with Kuei-liang nor be at all cramped, so that he could develop his own plans to devise a second line of negotiation. Our use of Ch'i-ying cannot be said to have been lacking in confidence; Our protecting Favor cannot be said to have been ungenerous.

When Kuei-liang and others memorialized to have the said official return to Peking, We assume that Ch'i-ying was certainly not ignorant of the reason. There is still suspicion that there was some coercion. With a Court Letter and Edict ordering him to remain in Tientsin to participate in negotiations, if Ch'i-ying had a conscience how could he fail to drench his back with sweat? Unexpectedly that official, after the dispatch of the memorial, returned to Peking on his own authority on the pretext of reporting an emergency in person. May we ask, if there were to be a personal report, why he didn't memorialize secretly under his own name?

He also said that under the circumstances he could hardly commit everything to writing. How is it that on receiving the Edict to remain in Tientsin he hastily prepared a memorial? May we ask, besides that contained in his testimony, what other emergency there was?

This repeated annoyance with petitions is nothing more than a neck-saving device. Moreover, as the statements in the said official's deposition are somewhat plausible, those who do not thoroughly understand underlying motives may still feel that the offense is light and the punishment heavy, not knowing that We and Our ministers had already arrived at the policy he proposed. Moreover, coming from anyone else, it would be possible; coming from Ch'i-ying, it is impossible. Why? Because Ch'i-ying was party to the negotiations and whatever views he had could have been put into practice. How is it that given one matter to handle jointly, he could do nothing to save the situation beforehand and uselessly tells Us all about it afterward?

If it is said that punishing whom the barbarians hate is falling right into their trap, it is a case of Ch'i-ying using this to whitewash his own motives, not only to remove entirely former stains but even trying to put the blame on others. His motives will not even bear inquiry. He thought to himself that for arbitrarily leaving his post he would only be removed from office which was exactly in accord with his personal plans to loiter about at home. Having long received (Our) hospitality, he can still bear to do this! Moreover, if we search his heart, there is not just this! When he agreed with Kuei-liang and Hua-sha-na to send communications, they faced each other before the window and wept, not knowing in the morning if they would die by evening, but we have not heard of his devising any better plan in accord with the previous Edict.

When he was leaving Tientsin he told Hua-sha-na, as he was afraid his departure would alarm popular feeling, to pretend he was leaving Tientsin temporarily on business. Arriving at T'ung-chou he received the Court Letter and Edict but we have not heard that he hastened back. He was only afraid of not getting away fast enough and treated Our Edict like a boy's cap [i.e. with scant respect, as the boy is eager to discard the mark of his childhood and assume that of his manhood]. Cunning and false all along, he intentionally deceived. Even though (he be) executed at once with the common herd, a hundred mouths will not be able to deny the justice of it.

But the original indictment of Prince Hui was too heavy, nor was Su-shun's memorial proposing capital punishment correct. Our turning the case over for discussion was just because, his crime being serious, We wanted the ministers to weigh facts and reach a verdict and publish it to all. If he was to be executed what was the need of bringing him to Peking? or what was the need of making proposals? The further statement that if there is a delay of months or years he might die of sickness and save his neck, is even less pertinent. This is the terminology of bandit suits and cannot be wrongly applied to Ch'i-ying.

We have deliberated carefully several days and though We should like to forego his death, actually it cannot be done. While according to I-hsin's [Prince Kung] proposal that it was necessary to register his name in Court Session, We could never bear to have him publicly executed. There was no alternative but to think out a method satis-fying to both sentiment and law.

Order Senior Assistant Controller of the Imperial Clan Court Jen-shou, Senior Director of the Imperial Clan Court Mien-hsun and President of the Board of Punishments Lin-k'uei to proceed imme-diately to the Death Chamber of the Imperial Clan Court, show Ch'i-ying Our Vermilion Edict, and transmit the Decree for him to take his own life, in manifestation of Our ultimate purpose of carrying out the law and extending Favor. (IWSM.HF 27; 28b, 5-30a, 7)

378. July 9, 1858. MEMORIAL: A Court Official Recommends Wei Yüan's World Geography for Officials Dealing with Foreign Affairs and Urges Military Reform.

Senior Vice-president of the Board of War Wang Mao-yin memo-rializes. The observation is ventured that since the beginning of bar-barian affairs, all commentators have said that there is no way of handling them; secretly suffering, we have relied entirely on

conciliation. Although conciliation is now completed, our difficulties
are not over, so it is up to us to find a way to handle that of which
they say there is no way of handling.

Your official finds that there is a book called Hai Kuo T'u Chih,[16]
("Illustrated Gazetteer of Ocean Countries") in 50 chüan, giving a
complete and detailed account of the boundaries, conditions, customs,
and characteristics of all the countries beyond the seas but most detailed on England. The author, sighing over the lack of policy in past
acts, proposes various policies for the future. Policies of defense,
of offense, and of treatment are all discussed in great detail. Although the offense policy requires more time, the defensive policy
is comparatively easy. If possible to defend the ports according to
this plan, the English barbarians would not dare come near.

(Your official) is not sure whether or not this book has come to
Imperial notice. If it has not, he asks that Orders be given the courtiers to purchase it and present it. He hears that this material was
gathered by the former High Official Lin Tse-hsü while he was in
charge of barbarian affairs in Kwangtung. After his office was terminated, it was taken over and completed by the late department magistrate Wei Yüan. The book blocks are in Peking; if Your Majesty
should find it has merit, he asks that it be Ordered reprinted so that
a copy can be in the house of every prince and minister; and also
order the Imperial Clans and Eight Banners to teach it, to study it,
so that they will realize that while it is hard to resist barbarians,
it is not impossible to find means of resisting them. If people understand the plans of resistance and are constantly filled with ardor,
then the methods of this book will come forth and what may be lacking in its methods, the people will certainly strive to supplement and
it will be possible to remove the evil of "nothing to do about it."

As methods depend on men for execution, the method of finding
men is even more essential. Your official notes that in 1842, as men
were wanting for barbarian affairs, Emperor Hsuan-tsung (Tao-
kuang) specially called upon Governor General of Kwangtung Ch'i
Kung to search out ability and talents above the average and to probe
the military strategists. Ch'i Kung memorialized in reply that if
we wanted to secure the services of capable men in military affairs
We must first inaugurate a method of selecting military officers
so he asked to change the selective examinations: questions put on
the third day of examinations (for the second degree and above) to
be changed to topics in five fields--knowledge of history, dealing
with a thorough familiarity with military tactics, ability to make
instruments and understanding of mathematics, deep knowledge of

16 *Cf.* accounts of the *Hai Kuo T'u Chih* in the biographies of Wei Yüan and Lin Tse-
    hsü (p. 511-514) written by Miss Tu Lien-che in Hummel, *Eminent Chinese of the
    Ch'ing Period*, v. 2, p. 850-853.

weather forecasting, and a thorough understanding of geography. (His theory is that) if we search out real scholarship and encourage true talent, probably genius will constantly appear.

That this proposal was blocked without being put into operation, (Your official) ventures to regret. When (Your official) filled in as censor, he memorialized that the English barbarians' hidden resentment might burst forth any day, and since the Empire was suffering from want of talent, we must find ways to search out talent; that for seeking talent through examinations, there was nothing better than Ch'i Kung's memorial to put questions in five fields to encourage scholars to study military affairs; that for seeking talents outside the examinations, there was nothing better than widespread recommendation so that we will have talents stored up for selection for military affairs. An Edict was issued turning (this memorial) over to the Board of Rites for discussion and recommendation.

Later it was reported that the Board decided not to carry it out. Then (Your official) carefully analyzed the sections not discussed exhaustively by the Board and memorialized them again, feeling that if put into operation at once the results would be felt ten years later; if the day were lost without putting them into operation, he was afraid we would later wish in vain for a (Lien) P'o and a (Li) Mu [two generals of the state of Chao in the Period of Contending States during the Chou Dynasty, 1122-255 B. C.]; that while Your official's suggestions were unworthy it was still essential to find a good plan; they could not be put aside without any consideration. The memorial was presented but received no Imperial Rescript so he could not speak further.

Now that there is an earnest desire to find real talent, it would seem difficult to dispense with the two previous plans. He is impelled to ask for Orders to the Grand Councillors to ferret out Your official's memorials of November 11, 1851 and February 9, 1852, respectively, and reconsider them carefully. In them the statement that the Imperial Clan and Eight Banners study military tactics and generalship to constitute the shield and buckler of the Imperial person, calls for special attention. When the Board discussed them, they repudiated the questions in five fields saying that scholars were ordinarily comprehensive and did not need to be specialists. (Your official) would like to ask who are the munitions makers and mathematicians today? Who are the expert strategists? The Board discussed and rejected the general recommendation saying that there were both civil and military, provincial and metropolitan examinations and all those with scholarship or talents above the average or skills in military arts were selected for promotion without fail. He should like to ask why none of the generals who have slain bandits and captured cities in recent years, like Lo Tse-nan, Wang Hsin, Yang Ts'ai-fu and Li Hsü-pin were got through examinations? How did the selection miss them? As this is evidence of the incompleteness of the previous consideration, the necessity of careful consideration now is apparent. This is the permanent method of getting men. Even if we need men for an immediate crisis, this is still not impossible.

In Your official's opinion, for knowing men like a mirror no one equals Former President of the Board of War Tseng Kuo-fan, who, when (Your official) first met him in 1851, discussed the abilities of men and, citing the prominent personages of the day, dismissed one after the other as useless. At first Your official did not dare to believe but later everything was as he said. As to the generals developed recently in Hunan, not one but was unrecognized and raised from the masses. Thus his (Tseng Kuo-fan's) knowledge of men and of using them to advantage is by no means commonplace.

Now Tseng Kuo-fan has received an Imperial Rescript to go to Chekiang to take charge of military affairs. If there is a genuine desire to find talent immediately, all that is necessary is to ask for Orders to ministers and officers of all ranks to recommend whom they know and send them all to Tseng Kuo-fan's headquarters for him to examine one by one, and we can certainly get men to meet our needs and thus eliminate the dearth-of-men hazard.

Even a plan of action and men to put it into effect, able to lead forces against the barbarians, are not enough. With the intention of finding a plan of action, if we are fearful that the plan cannot be inaugurated quickly or feel that conciliation will afford a little respite, then the plan will certainly fail. With the intention of finding men of action, if we are fearful that they cannot be entrusted with responsibility because they are not relatives of the Emperor or feel that those who are given responsibility should still be schooled in essay-writing, poetry, and copying, then men of real talent will certainly not come forth. That is to say, the empire follows precepts; it does not follow facts.

Moreover, Your official has heard that in fighting, victory depends entirely on morale and the morale of troops must be stirred daily to be maintained, must be stimulated forcibly to be developed. If soldiers feel in their hearts that everything depends on chance and favoritism, their morale is immediately dissipated and they are useless. Of old, T'ien Tan (a general of Ch'i in the period of Contending States of the Chou Dynasty, 1122-255 B. C.) attacked the Northern barbarians and Lu Chung-tzu predicted that he could not conquer them, saying that formerly when (T'ien Tan) was at Chimo (in modern Shantung), his generals were ready to die and his officers and men had no will to live, so he defeated Yen; that now as his generals were pleased with life and had no desire to die, he could not succeed. This is the last word of the strategists and also an important determinant for future order or chaos, prosperity or decay. Hence when Wu (one of the Contending States) determined to take revenge on Yüeh, men were sent daily to exhort in the central court; Yüeh determined to take revenge on Wu and went to the extent of sleeping on firewood and tasting gall--thus did the hegemon develop his superior morale.

Now the countries beyond the seas are daily striving for mastery. Although as man sees things, there are differences between China and the outside; as Heaven sees things, there may be no difference at all. The Book of History says: "High Heaven has no favorites; It helps only the virtuous."[17] Your Majesty has received from His Predecessors the heavy commission of being China's Sovereign; to make the barbarians of the four quarters willing to submit, he must magnify his luminous virtue in order to solidify the base and build up a solid morale in order to develop morality. When this is effected, policy and execution can achieve success.

The chapter of the Great Learning on "Empire" speaks of three things to be gained or lost: first, the hearts of the people; next, the Mandate of Heaven; and last, the heart of the Prince. That is to say, binding the hearts of the people to maintain the Mandate of Heaven rests entirely with the maintenance of loyalty and the banishment of proud self-confidence from the heart of the Prince. In other words, from Son of Heaven to commoner, self-cultivation is equally fundamental to all. Your Majesty's learning is daily renewed; Your Majesty's virtue is daily expanded and fundamentally His stupid official's heart is pressed with worry and fear without outlet for his earnestness; therefore, he respectfully puts forth his stupid fears for the Emperor's critical selection. (IWSM.HF 28; 45b, 9-49a, 10)

---

17 Legge's translation, v. 3(II), p. 490.

Chapter 11

Reed and the Supplementary Negotiations at Shanghai, 1858-1859
(Documents 379-404)

The twenty-six documents of this chapter, dated July 15, 1858 to January 29, 1859, cover the period of negotiations at Shanghai, following up the treaties concluded at Tientsin. There are fifteen memorials and eleven edicts; of the latter, nine are addressed to the grand councillors, one to the grand secretaries, and one to the imperial commissioners sent to Shanghai to continue the negotiations. There are fourteen vermilion endorsements, indicating the emperor's concern in modifying the treaties which were forced upon the commissioners at Tientsin. Five of these imperial endorsements are formal, chih-tao-la ("noted") acknowledgments that the memorial has been read; five are specific comments; three are interlinear comments, inserted by the emperor, and one is a vermilion edict, drafted by the emperor personally. This autograph edict is of particular interest because it authorizes the exchange of the ratified treaties in Peking, as specified at Tientsin. The British envoys at Shanghai and Ta-ku questioned China's good faith on this point and suspected the Peking court of repudiating this treaty provision.

The memorialists of this period are Ho Kuei-ch'ing, the liberal and realistic governor general of Liang-chiang, and Kuei-liang, the Manchu who headed the Imperial Commission sent to Shanghai from Peking. The other names appearing on the memorials are those of the additional members of the commission: Hua-sha-na, Ming-shan, and Tuan Ch'eng-shih. The leading figure is clearly Ho Kuei-ch'ing, who took a bold and aggressive interest in foreign affairs and who was finally made imperial commissioner in January, 1859. Behind the scenes at Shanghai is still the energetic Hsüeh Huan, now promoted to financial commissioner, commonly called vice-governor, of Kiangsu.

The negotiations at Shanghai, in which Reed still represented the United States, were originally arranged to draw up tariff regulations, supplementary to the Tientsin treaties. The emperor and grand councillors, however, were so distressed by the broad concessions forced on the commissioners at Tientsin, particularly the opening of Peking to permanent residence of foreign diplomats and the opening of the interior to foreign travel and trade, that they determined to utilize the Shanghai meeting to secure the drastic modification of the Tientsin treaties. The result was the so-called "Secret Plan," hatched at court, by which the commissioners were authorized to offer free trade--that is, the abolition of all customs duties--at the ports, in exchange for the abrogation of the four most obnoxious provisions of

515

the British treaty, including permanent residence at Peking. It should
be noted that occasional visits to Peking, including those provided for
the exchange of ratifications, were specifically authorized, even by the
war party at the court. The documents reveal the bold repudiation of
this plan by Ho Kuei-ch'ing and Hsüeh Huan. It was never submitted to
the foreign envoys and, most remarkably, both Ho Kuei-ch'ing and Hsüeh
Huan not only kept their heads, but even their political positions.

The meagre American documents on this second Shanghai phase of
treaty revision are covered by Tyler Dennett, Americans in Eastern
Asia, pages 326-330. Reed's correspondence, already cited, U. S. Cong.
36:1, S. Ex. Doc. 30, is the best American source. The Chinese documents have been utilized by Professor T. F. Tsiang in an article entitled "The Secret Plan of 1858," published in the Chinese Social and
Political Science Review, volume 15 (1931), pages 291-299.

TRANSLATIONS OF DOCUMENTS

379. July 15, 1858. EDICT: Appointment of Four Imperial Commissioners Headed by Kuei-liang to Negotiate the Tariff Supplement at
Shanghai.
       Edict to the Grand Secretariat. Order Kuei-liang, Hua-sha-na,
   Chi-p'u and Ming-shan to take the seal of Imperial Commission and
   proceed posthaste to Kiangsu and with Ho Kuei-ch'ing duly discuss
   matters of trade and tariff. Order whatever staff officers they need
   to proceed likewise posthaste. (IWSM.HF 29, 8a, 1-3)

380. September 14, 1858. MEMORIAL: Ho Kuei-ch'ing Reports Pre-
liminary Negotiations at Shanghai on the Tariff Schedule and Awaits
Imperial Commissioners.
       Governor General of Liang-chiang Ho Kuei-ch'ing memorializes.
   It is noted that the various barbarians, on receiving the Imperial
   Edicts which Your official respectfully copied and sent in his communication, seemed fairly compliant.
       Since August 18, as there was no news of Imperial Commissioners
   coming to Kiangsu, there has gradually been complaint. On August 23,
   Your official received a note from the American chief saying that as it
   was already August 18; and the Imperial Commissioners had still not
   come, he did not understand why and when would they actually come;
   that his communication is still unanswered. Your official had just received the reply of Kuei-liang and the others to the English chief and
   knew that Revised Orders had been received for Tuan Ch'eng-shih and
   Ming-shan to start out ahead on August 19; he immediately replied to
   this effect and also confidentially order Hsüeh Huan to take up miscel-
   aneous minor items in the tariff schedule and discuss them one by one

as a means of keeping them under control.

Then the American and French chiefs said if the Imperial Commissioners did not come at once negotiations would have to be broken off and they would either go back to Tientsin or go home temporarily and come back at the end of the year to resume negotiations. At that time the English chief was still in Japan, so Hsüeh Huan made plausible explanations to English chiefs Thomas Wade and H. N. Lay and, on the other hand, cleared up item by item the schedules which needed to be discussed in order to quiet their doubts.

After stalling for ten days, the previous Edict was respectfully received. Then on September 2, the English chief returned to Shanghai and, after consulting with the American and French chiefs for three days, wanted to weigh anchor and go home without saying why or without a word about when he would be back to negotiate.

Hsüeh Huan realized that it was already autumn and the rivers would soon go down and we would not have to worry about their going to Tientsin, but that the most important principle in controlling barbarians is confidence and if they were allowed to go away, as soon as waters rose next spring they would have a pretext for starting more trouble, so he must find means to prevent their leaving in order to consolidate the general situation; so he again explained in various ways. The English chiefs were somewhat moved but he was afraid they would not believe without evidence and petitioned Your official for a communication stating that an Imperial Edict has been respectfully received to the effect that Ming-shan and Tuan Ch'eng shih left Peking August 19, that Kuei-liang and Hua-sha-na had fixed the twenty-first for leaving Peking, and that they were ordered to wait quietly at Shanghai.

As to the American and French chiefs, they both intend to go to Hong Kong for awhile, weighing anchor within two or three days. Hsüeh Huan repeatedly insisted on an understanding and they agreed to return to Shanghai within the eighth month (September 7-October 6). Your official has prepared communications for each of the English, American, and French chiefs, and sent them to Hsüeh Huan to transmit to them. The Russian chief has not yet arrived. These are the various things Hsüeh Huan has done on various occasions, in order to show our good faith and to find means of controlling them in the hope of getting them into our bailiwick.

Your official feels that while His Majesty's only levers for swaying the Empire are good faith and capital, depositing wealth with the people is the fundamental axiom of economics. Now the treaties agreed to at Tientsin allow the (barbarians) to travel anywhere in the empire and to buy and sell any kind of goods; thus they can even trade in our native goods in the interior. No monopoly of profits could be as serious as this. For instance, while the cream of all Kiangsu province is concentrated at Shanghai, its so-called affluence comes from the ten percent profits on the north and south carrying trade. Now if we let these barbarians carry Shanghai goods to Newchwang and goods from various places to Shanghai, their capital is great and with no losses from wreck or piracy, all shippers will be glad to use them and Shanghai shipmasters and sailors will all lose their livelihood. It will not be many months before destitution will appear. Using this as an analogy, it is apparent the economic lever of the Empire will be entirely in the hands of the barbarians and our device for diverting wealth to the people defeated. When the people's resources are exhausted they have no perseverance. The calamity is one which we cannot bear to speak of. Therefore, Your official and Hsüeh Huan consulted Governor Chao Te-ch'e and Financial Commissioner Wang Yu-ling, who urged us to show good faith and seize an opportunity when they were submissive to get the economic lever and then gradually make plans.

Now, a month after the Imperial Commissioners received their Rescript, they are finally setting out but there is still no certainty as to when they will reach Kiangsu. If their [the barbarians'] dog-sheep mentality is not amenable to manipulation and they are actually rash enough to leave, the Imperial Intelligence can naturally determine what means can be found hereafter to restrain them.

In no time grain transport will begin and if, as the ministers propose, it is to continue by canal, the Kiangsu-Chekiang tribute rice, amounting to one million, five or six hundred thousand catties, will require some five or six thousand ships and it is feared that number of ships cannot be chartered. Even if there are ships, they would not constitute a fleet, would not be of the same size, and the sailors would be irresponsible, unlike the transport ships' enrollment of sailors by ships and assigning officers for a fleet proceeding in convoy, with the consequent responsibility. Adulteration, fraudulent sale, separate anchoring, crowding, starting of incidents, are all conceivable.

Besides the northern branch of the Turban Bandits (<u>Nien-fei</u>) are out and in irregularly, and when the transport ships come north there is no assurance that they will not covet them. If the barbarians intend to make trouble for us, they may intercept them at the mouth of the Yangtze or block them at Tientsin between the north and south canals, all of which cannot but be anticipated. If we rashly continue sea transport they may even stop it at crucial points of transfer, then how are we to handle this?

Your official has contrived exhaustively with Governor Chao Te-ch'e, Judicial Commissioner Wang Yu-ling, and Financial Commissioner Hsüeh Huan and failed to find any completely satisfactory plan. Thinking it over and over, he can only beseech Your Majesty by Heavenly Favor to condescend to be mindful of the present difficulty and order Kuei-liang and the others, traveling early and late at

double speed, to proceed to Kiangsu to conclude the tariff schedule,
as a policy of temporary constraint, to the great benefit of the Empire and the great good fortune of general conditions. (IWSM.HF
30; 28a, 10-31a, 2)

381. September 14, 1858. EDICT: Orders the Four Commissioners
to Proceed Posthaste to Shanghai because of the Increasing Impatience
of the Foreign Envoys.
        Edict to the Grand Councillors. Ho Kuei-ch'ing has memorial-
ized asking that Kuei-liang and the others be urged to come on the
double to Kiangsu. As there was no news of Kuei-liang and others
coming to Kiangsu, the various barbarians made it a pretext for
being anxious to return. Means have been found to explain to them.
The English chief is willing to wait temporarily at Shanghai; the
American and French chiefs will go temporarily to Hong Kong but
have agreed to come back to Shanghai during the eighth month
(September 7-October 6).
        The barbarians' disposition is still compliant so give orders
instructing them to await settlement. At present Ming-shan and
Tuan Ch'eng-shih should have reached Kiangsu and Ho Kuei-ch'ing
can secretly discuss plans with these officials. There is no need
to wait until after Kuei-liang and Hua-sha-na arrive to resume
negotiations. Today an Edict has been sent Kuei-liang and Hua-sha
na to proceed double-time to Kiangsu, and on the other hand notice
has been given the said governor general to inform the barbarians
so they will be willing to wait quietly.
        As to the present proposals of method, after Ming-shan arrives
he must inform the said governor general fully. After a settlement
is reached, economic power will not revert entirely to the barbarians, so do not be over timorous. (IWSM.HF 30; 31a, 3-10)

382. September 14, 1858. EDICT: Orders Ho Kuei-ch'ing to Start
Preliminary Negotiations at Shanghai when the First Two Commissioners Arrive.
        Additional Edict. Ho Kuei-ch'ing has memorialized that the
barbarian chiefs are anxious to go home and asks that the Imperial
Commissioners be ordered to hasten double-time to Kiangsu. He
says that the English chief originally wanted to weigh anchor for
home and only when Ho Kuei-ch'ing had sent a communication, saying that the Imperial Commissioners had already started, was he
willing to wait quietly at Shanghai; that the American and French
chiefs still intended going to Hong Kong temporarily, weighing anchor the first part of the month, and after Hsüeh Huan insisted
repeatedly on a date they had agreed to return to Shanghai within
the eighth month (September 7-October 6).
        By now Kuei-liang and Hua-sha-na should have arrived at

Ch'ing-chiang (Kiangsu), so order them to proceed double-time without the slightest delay. The said ministers on receipt of this Edict will send word ahead to Ho Kuei-ch'ing that they are coming immediately so that the governor general can notify the barbarian chiefs to rest easy and wait quietly. Today orders have been sent Ho Kuei-ch'ing, when Ming-shan and Tuan Ch'eng-shih arrive, to consult secretly on preliminary plans, so that as soon as Kuei-liang and the others arrive, they can all confer and reach a settlement. (IWSM.HF 30; 31b, 2-9)

383. September 21, 1858. MEMORIAL: Ho Kuei-ch'ing Reports that Reed and Gros are in Japan but will Return to Shanghai when the Commissioners Arrive.

Governor General of Liang-chiang Ho Kuei-ch'ing memorializes. . . . As to the American and French chiefs, it is learned privately that they are actually in Japan and did not go to Hong Kong. The consuls of their respective countries have stated that on the day the Imperial Commissioners arrive they will send a steamer for them in order to prevent delay or misunderstanding.

Vermilion endorsement: Noted. (IWSM.HF 30; 32b, 5. . . 33a, 10-33b, 3)

384. September 24, 1858. EDICT: Orders the Procurement of a Cantonese Ts'ai Chen-su Reputed to be a Foreign Expert for Service in Peking.

Additional Edict (to the Grand Councillors). Someone has memorialized that Ts'ai Chen-su of Kwangtung, promoted by purchase to tao-t'ai, is thoroughly familiar with barbarian affairs. Just now there is a dearth of men to handle barbarian affairs. Order the governor general to instruct the said official to come to Peking immediately and be formally presented by the Board of Civil Office. Let there not be the least delay. (IWSM.HF 30; 38a, 5-6)

385. October 5, 1858. MEMORIAL: Ho Kuei-ch'ing Expounds his Foreign Policy Based on Conciliation of Foreigners and National Defense along Western Lines.

Governor General of Liang-chiang Ho Kuei-ch'ing memorializes. Your official observes that Shanghai's management of barbarians has consisted of taming them by catering to their moods. If the barbarian mood was avaricious, we feigned indifference to money; if the barbarian mood was proud, we treated them with deference; if the barbarian mood was crafty but had a false front of sincerity, then we showed trust in them. Therefore, for more than ten years there has been mutual accord and no trouble. There was not a barbarian merchant who did not enjoy carrying on his business, so this became the point of concentration for barbarians.

The barbarian chiefs, Elgin and others, previously requested the appointment of an Imperial Commissioner instructed to negotiate at Shanghai, March 31. This request was not necessarily exorbitant, so Your official importuned Huang Tsung-han to make the most of the opportunity and devise means for a settlement, which is what I call taming them by catering to their mood.

When Huang Tsung-han was ordered back to Kwangtung and it was said that there was no need to prevent their going to Tientsin, the first file was cast [i.e. the first blunder made]. Your official apprehended that they would not return to Kwangtung but would go to Tientsin and were certain to display their arrogance and make arbitrary demands; so he corresponded secretly back and forth with Ho-ch'un, Hsü Nai-chao and Chang Kuo-liang. All agreed that the troops, supplies, and tactics for exterminating Kwangtung rebels were all inadequate for resisting barbarians and that it was necessary, after recovering Nanking, for Chang Kuo-liang to go personally to the various river and ocean ports to study conditions and reform the manufacture of munitions and the drilling of troops and, after one year, there would be some advantage; that nevertheless there must still be metropolitan-provincial harmony and cooperation among the various ports before we could control their destiny; that it was not a responsibility one or two people could shoulder.

As Your official judged the above statements these were surely the mature plans and valued estimates of army veterans but too slow to meet an emergency; therefore, he asked for a temporary postponement of hostilities. After the fall of the port and the immediate occupation of Tientsin, Kuei-liang and Hua-sha-na were without generals or troops and vainly defended with empty words. To block by force of arms their request to proceed to the Palace Door would have been no easy matter, but commentators all regard the treaties they concluded as detrimental and so still gossip on the outside; if they themselves were placed on the inside, they would probably have no way of expelling the barbarian ships either.

Now that affairs have reached such a pass, there is only the negotiation of the tariff schedule as a means of correcting the balance and salvaging the wreckage; it would seem that we cannot abruptly repudiate our previous agreement and give them a chance to charge bad faith and start another tempest.

Your official is concerned about customs collection, which is called examination and collection, i.e., examination of imports and exports for contraband and collection of the duties. If we did not collect import and export duties, there would be no inspection. This would mean allowing the barbarians to take our native products and trade in the interior; turning over the economic lever of the empire to the barbarians while our people perish and our capital is depleted. It is Your official's stupid opinion that we must recover the economic lever, and tariffs cannot be lightly abolished.

H. N. Lay is the most crafty of the barbarians. In the winter of 1855, the former governor, Chi-erh-hang-a, sent an offer to that chief to employ him as Shanghai Customs Commissioner with generous pay. The barbarian still feels grateful and looks out for smuggling for us, so in recent years barbarian customs have been three or four times as much as when the port was opened. The said barbarian was afraid of being disliked by various other barbarians, so he also accompanied them to Tientsin and made a great display of violence and ingratiated himself with the barbarian chief in order to show his public spirit. When he returned to Shanghai he was as compliant as ever in our employ. "Who bells (the tiger) can remove the bell;" so we must continue to hold him responsible for all the barbarians.

When Your official has rear defense matters somewhat arranged, he will proceed at once to Shanghai and with Kuei-liang and others arrange means to settle matters of first importance in order to set up supplementary regulations as a diplomatic coup de grace.

As to the matter of the tariff schedule, Hsüeh Huan, directing and cooperating with expectant Prefect Wu Hsü, has already singled out the leads and it can be arranged with just a few words. Although there is no word of the American and French chiefs' returning to Shanghai, once the English barbarians sign, the other barbarians will sign and we need not worry about their changing their minds. Having called Kuei-liang and others to witness, our views are in general agreement. (IWSM.HF 30; 44a, 9-46a, 4)

386. October 5, 1858. EDICT: Reviews the "Secret Plan" for Rescinding Tariffs in Exchange for Closing Peking and Chides Ho Kuei-ch'ing for Opposing it.

Edict to the Grand Councillors. Previously because Ming-shan and others memorialized that the complete removal of tariffs should not be announced until after explanation had been made to the barbarians, orders were given Kuei-liang, Hua-sha-na, and Ho Kuei-ch'ing to continue to act according to original instructions. Yesterday a memorial was received from Kuei-liang and others that they were cooperating with Ho Kuei-ch'ing and had discussed the general situation. We again gave detailed instructions and assume that when the said ministers receive it they will take care to act accordingly and not stubbornly hold to their own views.

Today Ho Kuei-ch'ing memorializes that as the economic lever must be recovered, tariffs cannot be lightly abolished. In the said governor general's own locality this national revenue is coveted for the nation, so he is not willing to rescind barbarian duties. His reasoning is actually a short-sighted view rather than a method of settling once and for all. Moreover, if, according to the plan of the Secret Edict, they can only trade at the five ports and discussion of

all requests is stopped, how can the barbarians still get complete
economic leverage? If we withdraw only one or two items, and on
the others still insist on discussing the tariff schedule separately,
how can we be sure they will agree to everything?

The previous Edict and Vermilion endorsement were most detailed and exhaustive and there can be no further instructions. Ho
Kuei-ch'ing has received Our Generous Favor and certainly cannot
have other motives; but We fear his subordinates are afraid that,
after the duties are abolished, there will be no means of lining their
pockets and so find pretexts to confuse the issue, which is an inevitable occurrence. The said governor general must adhere rigorously
to fixed views and not be moved by others' talk. If there are disadvantages to local conditions, slight changes have been authorized and
also the disadvantageous items must be reported in detail. He must
not carry out his own views to the detriment of general conditions.
(IWSM.HF 30; 46a, 5-46b, 7)

387. October 9, 1858. MEMORIAL: Ho Kuei-ch'ing Clarifies Terminology and Argues his Case against the "Secret Plan" and in favor of
Treaty Fulfilment.

Governor General of Liang-chiang Ho Kuei-ch'ing memorializes.
Those barbarians who trade back and forth are called "barbarian
merchants" [I-shang]; those who superintend the trading affairs of
the various ports and take the surplus for their country's use, were
first called "public envoys" [Kung-shih, present term for minister],
now they presumptuously call themselves "cabinet ministers" [ta-
ch'en, a term applied to the highest officials in China, such as Imperial Commissioners and Grand Councillors], while we call them
"barbarian chiefs" [I-ch'iu]; the "consuls" [ling-shih] and such
are the subordinates of the barbarian chiefs. Thus barbarian chiefs
and barbarian merchants are in two separate categories.

In the collection of the Shanghai barbarian customs, formerly
an invoice of goods was made by the barbarian merchants and declared to the consul who in turn reported it to Customs for examination and collection. The records were made openly and both China
and the foreign (consul) had copies for reference, nor was there any
corrupt practice of overcharge or collecting more and reporting less.
Even if fraud was detected, the barbarians did not suffer any loss,
but neither barbarian chiefs nor barbarian merchants felt any gratitude. The duties come from the merchants and the barbarian chiefs
are not involved.

If we were to abolish import and export duties, the barbarian
merchants would certainly heartily agree, but the barbarian chiefs
would still not be grateful. Although we prohibit opium they still
deal in it. Now it is proposed to change the name and remove the
prohibition so the rebels in the interior will have no occasion to

collect in bands to convoy it and breed serious troubles. The advantage will be with us and there will be neither loss nor gain to the barbarian merchants.

The reason for their raising arms against authority was that the
barbarian chiefs could not enter the provincial capital of Kwangtung
or meet the Imperial Commissioner. Thus their treacherous seizure
of Kwangchou (Canton) and desire to go to the Palace Door is entirely
a matter of the vanity of the barbarian chiefs and is no concern of the
barbarian merchants.

In order to manage barbarians it would seem that we must investigate the cause of the incidents and tame them by conforming to their
mood; then we shall have a point of vantage. Otherwise, they in turn
will regard the treaties negotiated by the Imperial Commissioners as
undependable, stiffen their demands for audience, and start further
hostilities with by no means insignificant consequences.

Your official first notified Ming-shan and Tuan Ch'eng-shih in
detail, but when Tuan Ch'eng-shih reached the Yangtze crossing, he
sent his own deputy ahead to Shanghai to make a secret investigation
but had no means of accomplishing anything. After Kuei-liang and the
others reached Ch'ang-(chou), Your official also conferred with them
carefully and secretly and they were of the same view. At present we
are separately planning a coup de grace, finding means to settle the
most important items in the hope of assuaging Imperial worries.

Vermilion endorsement: Noted. There are already a Court Letter and Edict ordering continued negotiation according to Palace decisions. In case there are obstacles, they still must report them
clearly and in detail. (IWSM.HF 31; 18a, 9-19b, 1)

388. October 13, 1858. EDICT: Insists on carrying out the "Secret
Plan" against Apparent Weakening under Pressure of the Commissioners
at Shanghai.

Edict to the Grand Councillors. Previously Kuei-liang and others
memorialized on the general policy of negotiating barbarian affairs,
and Ho Kuei-ch'ing also memorialized that neither the abolition of tariffs nor removal of (opium) prohibition was any concern of the barbarian chiefs. Strict and pertinent Endorsements have been made on
each of the memorials and also Edicts informing Ho Kuei-ch'ing that
he must strenuously maintain his position; in case there are any
slight changes he must report the points of difficulty in detail and
cannot act on his own views. Kuei-liang and others on receipt of the
Endorsements and Edict must needs adhere scrupulously to the program originally determined.

Now today Prince Hui and others present letters received from
Ho Kuei-ch'ing and others, actually saying that the removal of tariffs
would be of no advantage to general conditions and that the proposal
to remove the prohibition (of opium) was also of no advantage; that

on the matter of residence in Peking, they had a clue; that the matter
of entering the Yangtze could hardly be retracted and they could only
refuse to allow them trade in native goods in the interior; that if the
barbarians could not expect profits, we could get them to give up the
idea.

On reading this We were very surprised. Although Ho Kuei-
ch'ing's concern about customs furnishing military supplies is excus-
able, he had already received a confidential Edict with Vermilion endorsement repeatedly warning him that he must not persist in contrary
views. Moreover, Kuei-liang and others received a Mandate when they
left as to how they must scrupulously follow Our Edicts and strive to
arrange a settlement.

Now before they even meet the barbarian chiefs their ideas have
shifted. What is the idea? Moreover, even if there were objections
to removing customs, they must needs analyze the items and report
them in detail. How can they change policy arbitrarily? Moreover,
if the (barbarians) are allowed to enter the Yangtze, how can we prohibit their trading in native goods in the interior? Previously at
Tientsin, Kuei-liang and the others agreed to too many of the barbarian demands. Now with the present chance to retrieve losses, if
they again act carelessly without settling once for all and hereafter
barbarian troubles recur, even if Kuei-liang and the others are punished severely, how will national affairs be remedied?

On the customs removal question, they say that while the barbarian merchants would be pleased, the barbarian chiefs would not even
be grateful. But if it benefits barbarian merchants, why shouldn't the
barbarian chiefs be pleased? This time at Tientsin was not the request that the president of the Board of Revenue go to Shanghai to draw
up the tariff schedule the wish of the barbarian chiefs? Besides, the
present desire to collect Chinese customs is primarily to compensate
the loss of barbarian customs. If it is handled as Kuei-liang and others
propose, why should we get a bad name to gain such a slight advantage
and then suffer endless consequences? When that time comes regrets
will get us nowhere.

Order Kuei-liang and others conscientiously to reconsider another
feasible plan of negotiation and if possible settle once for all and make
sure that there will be no barbarian troubles hereafter. If there is no
positive assurance, We can hardly give our consent and they must continue to adhere scrupulously to the original proposal and carefully
follow Our repeated suggestions. There can only be slight changes;
the general situation cannot be altered nor will We allow, as previously
at Tientsin, presumptuous acquiescence and the mere use of the four
words "punish our crime severely" as a loophole to evade responsibility. Tremble at this! (IWSM.HF 31; 21b, 6-22b, 9)

389. October 18, 1858. MEMORIAL: The Four Commissioners Report
Arrival at Shanghai and Immediately Reflect Local Arguments against the
"Secret Plan".

Imperial Commissioner, Grand Secretary Kuei-liang, President
of the Board of Civil Office Hua-sha-na, Director of the Imperial
Armory Ming-shan, Brevet Director of the Fifth Grade, Second Secretary of the Board of Punishments Tuan Ch'eng-shih memorialize.
Your slaves, Kuei-liang and Hua-sha-na arrived at Soochow, September 28; Ming-shan and Tuan Ch'eng-shih had arrived before us on the
twenty-fourth, and having received word from Your slaves Kuei-liang
and Hua-sha-na to wait temporarily at Soochow, did not go immediately
to Shanghai. Later, on October 1, they left Soochow together and arrived at Shanghai on October 4. Governor General Ho Kuei-ch'ing and
Financial Commissioner Wang Yu-ling arrived October 5th and 6th
respectively, and we agreed immediately to send a communication to
the English barbarians to send men to negotiate. Shortly thereafter
we received the barbarians' communication still harping on the Kwangtung question, so it is copied out and presented for Imperial Inspection.

Your slaves, Kuei-liang and others, ordered Judicial Commissioner
Acting Tao-t'ai of Shanghai [sic] Hsüeh Huan to sound out the barbarians on the articles originally proposed (at Peking), see how they re-
acted, and report back immediately.

They received the said judge's personal statement that barbarians
are naturally cunning and perverse and that we could not lightly discuss
the treaties; that our abolition of customs dues would do no more than
make the barbarian merchants grateful, while if we asked them to give
up the whole treaty, under the circumstances they would certainly not
agree. (Vermilion endorsement: Without seeing the barbarians, how
do they know that "under the circumstances they would not agree."
Actually Hsüeh Huan's conduct is traitorous.) Besides, the barbarians
are very suspicious and if we were too adamant he feared it would
cause a rupture.

It is our humble opinion that because Your slaves arrived late,
(the barbarians) had already been wrangling. On seeing that the Emperor sent four Commissioners and fearing we would insist on revision,
they made a pretext of the statement in the Imperial Edict that the barbarian ships blocked entrance to Teintsin, to send a communication and
start a tiresome argument. Thus the difficulty of discussing with them
is quite apparent. The said judicial commissioner has not even had a
chance to take up seriously the key question. Although we have used
many means to influence them, whether or not we can pacify them is
still uncertain, but the matter is of great significance so Your slaves
must needs exert their utmost efforts. They have charged the financial
commissioner and others with the responsibility of finding a means of
settlement in the hope of assuaging somewhat Imperial care.

Examining carefully the barbarians' communication, the emphasis is not on profits and it is not certain that we can move them by using customs as bait. If at this time we suddenly divulged it, it is feared that the barbarians for mercenary motives would pretend to agree, then after one or two years either again make demands on us which we could not meet, on the basis of treaty provisions, or perhaps cause other complications, either of which cannot but cause us concern. Then when we want to recover our economic advantage where can we get any handhold?

Yesterday was received from the Grand Councillors a confidential Court Letter that on September 29, 1858, they had received an Imperial Edict, etc., Respect this. On respectfully reading it, our fright was indescribable. Your slaves received a Mandate to negotiate a tariff schedule and also gratefully received the Emperor's tactical directive, and naturally must manage accordingly. However, having investigated thoroughly barbarian attitudes and placing them alongside present conditions, they dare not regard the one and lose sight of the other, to the detriment of general conditions. (Vermilion endorsement: You do not understand the meaning of the two characters, i wu ["detriment"; Emperor's reading: "bequeathing error"]. If the matter is compromised now, is not this bequeathing error? In the future the inherited error will be worse than today's.) Having considered and reconsidered, we could only make the most of existing circumstances to balance the scales and salvage losses by working together for a settlement, hoping in any case not to fail Your Majesty's trust. Allow us to wait for a cue and then report immediately.

It must be explained that as Governor General Ho Kuei-ch'ing has some matters he must memorialize on military affairs north of the Yangtze, he has not affixed his name to this memorial. (Vermilion endorsement: Since Ho Kuei-ch'ing went to Shanghai, why did he not join in the memorial? Having received an Edict to cooperate, this exhibition of bad temper is as though he were actually ill-favored. Show this to the said governor general.)

Vermilion endorsement: Suppose it is settled as the said governor general wants, may We ask if the governor general can give his head as security? If so, the governor general has a real grip and We shall be only too pleased to assent. (IWSM.HF 31; 29b, 6-31a, 8)

390. October 18, 1858. EDICT: Repeats the Sentiments of the Vermilion Endorsements and Urges Repudiation of the Most Obnoxious Treaty Provisions.

Edict to the Grand Councillors. Today Kuei-liang and others have memorialized on the state of their discussions and arrangements. Their statements that "barbarians are naturally cunning and perverse and they cannot lightly discuss treaties," that "removal of duties would do no more than make the barbarian merchants grateful and if we wanted them to abandon the whole treaty, under the circumstances they certainly would not agree," are mistaken management as has been noted on the memorial.

In sending Kuei-liang and others to Shanghai to negotiate with the barbarians on this occasion the primary objective was to settle once for all. Heretofore, there have been successive Edicts ordering management according to Palace decision and on the thirteenth of this month again there was a rigid and explicit Court Letter and Edict. On receipt of these successive Edicts, Kuei-liang and others must needs have had their consciences stirred to strive to effect a recovery. If they still have not the least grip and only hope to evade responsibility, it may be asked what punishment they deserve.

In the barbarian treaties the four provisions most injurious to China are: sending officials to reside at Peking, trading in inland waters, traveling in the interior, and indemnification for military expenses before evacuation of the provincial capital of Kwangtung. If Kuei-liang and the others could entirely eliminate these four provisions We could barely accommodate Ourself to acceptance; if they only recovered one or two items the other impossible features would still engender untold consequences and it would be impossible for Us to acquiesce. As Ho Kuei-ch'ing has received Our bounty and was obligated to confer with Kuei-liang and others to work out a satisfactory solution, how could he merely take his subordinates' word and incriminate himself?

As to the statement in the English barbarians' communication about (our) opening fire and wounding men in Hsin-an-hsien, a memorial was received previously from Huang Tsung-han that because the English barbarians attacked the said hsien city, the magistrate had trained volunteers to drive them off and that our troops had not inaugurated hostilities; even less had officials caused them trouble. Lo Tun-yen and two others were especially ordered to manage the trainbands and exterminate bandits. Since the Tientsin negotiations, orders have been given the said secretary (Lo) and others to discipline the braves and not let them antagonize the barbarians. If the barbarians without provocation go to villages and cause trouble, moving the inhabitants to popular indignation, under the circumstances the said gentry can hardly stop them. But hereafter there must not be antagonism so there can be permanent friendly relations. (IWSM. HF 31; 31a, 9-32a, 5)

391. October 19, 1858. MEMORIAL: Ho Kuei-ch'ing Reviews Foreign Policy since 1838 and tries to Separate Economic and Diplomatic Issues Involved.

Governor General of Liang-chiang Ho Kuei-ch'ing memorializes. Your official begs to acknowledge the receipt of an Imperial Edict and respectfully noting Your Majesty's ultimate wish, Heaven-determined and inexorable, to get the barbarians to acquiesce willingly and sincerely, he is awed and respectful beyond measure and must naturally strive, in reverent accordance, for a settlement once for all. But barbarians are naturally cunning and having gained one step they want to go on, and it would seem necessary to clear the source and dam the flow before there is a vantage point.

Looking back to the time when Canton was the only place to trade, there were no envoys or consuls living in the interior at all; movements and trade of the barbarian merchants were all determined by the Thirteen Hong Merchants at Canton. These hongs, in addition to overcharging and extorting, were heavily in debt to them. The foreign merchants with no place to file complaints were naturally squirming for a change. When we burned their opium, the barbarian merchants turned their combined resources over to the barbarian chiefs and took up arms against authority. Therefore, when the treaties were concluded at Nanking in 1842, they asked for the abolition of the hongs, indemnification for commercial losses and for the value of the opium. The source of trouble was the barbarian merchant.

Since the opening of the five ports to trade, barbarian merchants and individual Chinese merchants traded with one another without the evils of foreign hong monopoly. The duties to be paid were declared by the barbarian merchant to his consul, who in turn declared them to the customs, which examined and collected them, without any extortion or squeeze; opium was openly traded in with no means of prohibiting it and the barbarian merchants had no complaint whatever.

Therefore, the recurrence of hostilities against authority was because of the vanity of the barbarian chiefs. Because they could not enter the provincial capital of Kwantung or interview the Imperial Commissioner, in the treaties concluded this year at Tientsin their first request was for formal rules of intercourse, while there was not a word about extortion or squeeze in the customs. Their wish to revise the customs schedule is because present and former commodity values are not the same. As to the 2,000,000 taels indemnity for commercial losses, they stated clearly that the maladministration of Canton authorities had caused English people to suffer losses. Moreover, none of the other ports were like this. Thus the present difficulty derives from the barbarian chiefs and does not affect the barbarian merchants, unlike the situation in the Tao-kuang period. This is the occasion for Your official's request to clarify the source.

Although these barbarians have all the characteristics of human beings, they are unusually cruel and cunning and depend on the strength of their ships and the superiority of their cannon. If we bind them with favors they will think we are afraid of them; if we threaten them with our might they will immediately break off relations. If we abolish import and export duties, the benefit will go to the barbarian merchant and their 2,000,000 taels of commercial

losses at Canton may not have to be paid; but the barbarian chiefs
will not be affected and there will still be their military expenses.
Once Your Majesty's good intention is announced, (Your official) ventures to fear that they will display still more perversity, thinking that
this is a Special Flood of Gracious Words from Your Imperial Majesty
in addition to the Tientsin treaties, while the aspirations of the barbarian chiefs will be still more extravagant and, not only can all the
items agreed to not be retracted, but not even one or two items can
be suppressed. Making this a pretext for demands, they will then
branch out.

As to removing the opium prohibition or not, the benefit and harm
are both ours and is neither here nor there to the barbarian chiefs or
barbarian merchants, as Your official has carefully reported. If,
when they got what they want, they sailed away, it would really be the
end of the matter for all time, but subsequently, poachers will not be
restricted to the five ports; if we do not utilize customs collection to
examine them, there will be no control over them whatever and troubles
will develop before mid-morning. This is the situation Your official
referred to when he said the flow must be dammed.

As Your official ponders the policy of controlling barbarians, from
ancient times to the present there has never been an efficacious scheme
When the army is strong and supplies adequate, we thrash the barbarians on our four frontiers like using our own hands; as soon as China
Proper is in difficulties, they seize the occasion to rise and none but
feel their scourge. Today the barbarians pretend to trade in good
faith and fairness, therefore Your official wants to show them good
faith and, taming them by conforming to their mood, get them into
our power.

Although frankly we cannot guarantee that there will be no wrangling (Vermilion endorsement: If you do not have any assurance your-
self, why raise all this fuss?), yet if we abolish customs, while we
might be able to bend their heads to receive the Mandate, we cannot
be certain that they will actually obey. Besides, since (the beginning
of Taiping) hostilities, the Eight Banners and Green Standard[1] government forces' pay and rations have not been issued regularly, nor
have they been adequate. Their plight has become desperate. The
barbarians have sent out Chinese traitors to gather information for
them by extending petty favors. For instance, Your official first
learned in detail the policy determined by the Court after an interview
with Ming-shan and Tuan ch'eng-shih, but the barbarian merchants
had already heard it. Thus, there must have been Chinese traitors

---

1 These two branches comprised the Manchu military organization (including Mongol
   and Chinese Banner Forces) and the Chinese provincial forces respectively.
   Cf. W. F. Mayers, *The Chinese Government*, Shanghai, 1878, p. 51f and 59f.

who pretend to advise us while being secretly in communication with the barbarians. Probably many of these are even Court officials who have bought offices and mingle in the capital. Your official, besides being shocked, is gravely apprehensive.

Vermilion endorsement: Successive Court Letter, Edicts, and Vermilion endorsements have been explicit and detailed. There is no need of another Edict. (IWSM.HF 31; 33b, 6-36a, 2)

392. October 21, 1858. MEMORIAL: The Shanghai Commissioners Report that the Envoys are Defiant and Already Suspect Treaty Repudiation--"Plan" Delayed.

Imperial Commissioners Grand Secretary Kuei-liang, President of the Board of Civil Office Hua-sha-na, Governor General of Liang-chiang Ho Kuei-ch'ing, Director of the Imperial Armory Ming-shan, and Brevet Director of the Fifth Grade, Second Secretary of the Board of Punishments Tuan Ch'eng-shih memorialize. Although the barbarians have made many complaints since the beginning of autumn because Your officials were a little late in reaching Shanghai, still there was no indication that their attitude was reckless or perverse until we sent communications to them, on October 7, for them to send someone here to negotiate and, to our surprise, the barbarians ignored it. Then the same day they sent a communication complaining at length about Kwangtung affairs.

Your officials first issued proclamations to the inhabitants and then wrote to Governor General of Liang-kuang Huang Tsung-han not to continue with his proclamations and to order the gentry, Lo Tun-yen and others to cease hostilities temporarily until they received word from Shanghai. To our surprise the barbarians were far from pleased. Their reply of the ninth was arrogant in spirit and phraseology and extremely discourteous. It is copied separately and presented for Imperial Inspection.

Your officials have consulted wholeheartedly with the financial and judicial commissioners and it is really difficult to reach a satisfactory program. If we do not grant what they ask, not only can other matters not be arranged but there is danger of an immediate rupture. Besides, the barbarians, seeing us four officials come together, already suspect that our purpose is to repudiate the treaties. There is constant talk of a northern campaign. In all probability they would go to Tientsin again, and how dare we think of general conditions? If we do grant what they ask, we dare not heedlessly agree to what affects national prestige. There was no alternative but, out of the insoluble, to make a solution for the immediate emergency. We immediately prepared a reply to prevent their becoming suspicious, saying that according to current rumor the whole administration of the governor general of Liang-kuang was unsatisfactory and that a memorial had been written impeaching him.

At present, whether or not the barbarians will wait quietly for an Imperial Edict or proceed to the discussion of other matters, we await their reply before we can be certain. It is only hoped that complications will not develop, so that Your officials may devote their whole energy to the elimination of the most important matters. Furthermore, in the matter of the customs, (we are to) explain that the indemnity is to be paid by annual (customs) rebates, so as to induce them to restore the Kwangtung capital.

Concerned for the moment with the immediate situation confronting us, other matters can only gradually be thought out. If at this time we followed the provisions originally decided on, disregarding the fact that the barbarians would never be willing to give up (the treaties) entirely, economic advantage would all go to the foreign countries and hereafter the transactions of barbarian merchants would not be subject to any scrutiny whatever. As the saying goes, if you held T'ai-ya [a famous sword], backwards and gave your opponent the handle, the calamity would be indescribable. Besides, not to tax barbarians while we do tax (Chinese) merchants would leave us with still more obstacles

Your officials will not dare adhere stubbornly to prejudiced views, and if they can make some adjustments, never failing to follow in principle the regulations originally agreed on, in their petty stupidity, they trust they can invite the understanding of the Sacred Intelligence. (IWSM.HF 31; 36a, 3-37a, 10)

393. October 21, 1858. MEMORIAL: Kuei-liang Reports Reed's Return from Japan and Prospects for Early Inauguration of Negotiations.

Kuei-liang and others further memorialize. Just as the memorial was sealed, the reply of the barbarians was received stating that as soon as an Imperial Edict is received, to send it for them to see.

Your officials have sent Financial Commissioner Wang Yu-ling and Judicial Commissioner, Acting Shanghai Tao-t'ai Hsüeh Huan to meet with the officials sent by the barbarians between one and three this afternoon, and as soon as anything develops will memorialize forthwith. Heretofore, when the barbarians have sent a communication in the morning they have always dated it the day before.

We have also Judicial Commissioner Hsüeh Huan's report that the American barbarian chief has now returned to Shanghai from Japan, which we announce parenthetically.

Vermilion endorsement: Seen. (IWSM.HF 31; 39b, 4-10)

394. November 14, 1858. MEMORIAL: Ho Kuei-ch'ing Develops his Foreign Policy, Noting McLane's Repudiation of the Taipings, and Calls for Statesmen to Meet China's Greatest Crisis in Two Hundred Years.

Governor General of Liang-chiang Ho Kuei-ch'ing memorializes. This is the greatest crisis in barbarian affairs of the past two hundred years of our Dynasty. Your humble official, having received Imperial

Grace in great measure, would not even in the ordinary course of
public business dare to be the least biased, how much less so in the
handling of barbarian affairs which determine our security or
danger?

Ever since the trouble in Kwangtung last year, Your official
has been worried. When in the first month of this year (February
14-March 14, 1858) the barbarians came to Shanghai and presented
communications with the request for Imperial Commissioners to
negotiate with them at Shanghai by March 31, their requests were
still not extravagant. They also said if this was not agreed to they
would go to Tientsin and do as they liked. Therefore, when Huang
Tsung-han passed through Ch'ang-chou, (I) wept bitterly pleading
with him to settle the matter at Shanghai in the hope of minimizing
somewhat Your Majesty's arduous cares.

Now if there had been adequate control since the opening of the
five ports to trade, friendly relations without trouble would have
been possible, but because the barbarian chiefs could neither enter
the provincial capital of Kwangtung nor meet the Imperial Commissioner, they started hostilities. Having been suppressed for ten
years, they waited until after our military operations were under
way and seized the occasion of our many troubles to develop antagonism. They repeatedly entered the Yangtze to investigate the activities of the Hung [i.e., the T'ai-p'ing Rebels, followers of Hung
Hsiu-ch'uan] Rebels. Later it was the American chief McLane who
decided that as the Hung Rebels had none of the five relationships
[or moral obligations; the five human relationships between prince
and minister, father and son, husband and wife, older brother and
younger brother, and between friends], nor even a criminal law,
they were not worth consideration and shifted policy in our direction. He proffered a request to enter the Yangtze to help in their
eradication and to allow him to establish a wharf at Sung-chiang
(Kiangsu). He also asked for an examination of the Tao-kuang
commercial regulations with a view to changing tariff rates, all of
which former Governor Chi-erh-hang-a has memorialized and is
on record.

It is noted that the treaty concluded at Nanking in the Tao-kuang
period was called a Ten-thousand-year Peace Treaty. It was a definitive document, never to be changed. The one concluded in Kwangtung was called a Trade Convention, stating clearly that after 12
years revisions would be discussed.[2] All the officials in charge of
barbarian affairs ever since have only known the term, Ten-thousand-
year Peace Treaty, without seeing the text, and thus mistaking the
Trade Convention for a ten-thousand-year Peace Treaty have vainly
wagged their tongues in argument. None of the requests which they

---

2 *I. e.*, the Treaty of Wang-hsia (Wàng-hiya).

memorialized could they explain in detail; when they received Court
Letters containing Edicts, they did not dare divulge them, so the
barbarians formerly thought the officials did not report their grievances (to Your Majesty) and their accumulated suspicions piled up.

Then when Kwangtung fell they inevitably seized the records and
all our previous methods were exposed. If they are allowed to go to
Tientsin and the ministers Imperially commissioned to treat with
them are all men without previous experience or have not made a
detailed study, they are sure to take even more advantage of them,
with nothing to fear. Huang Tsung-han is a native of Fukien, has
served as governor of Chekiang and as tao-t'ai in Kwangtung understood things in detail; he would have had no difficulty splitting them
open as they met his blade. But this was not done and the file has
been cast [mistake made]. This immediately engendered the barbarians' desire to reside in Peking, thinking that if everything could
be settled with Your Imperial Majesty personally, Court and provincial officials would have no chance to employ their wiles.

When Your official ventures to regard the items agreed upon
at Tientsin, in the clause on residence in Peking, the countries involved and the forms laid down cut his heart like a knife. Because
of their clamorous attitudes and the proximity to the capital, Kuei-
liang and the others could not but acquiesce and memorialize asking Approval of their proposals as a scheme for getting their troops
withdrawn, while hoping later to repudiate these proposals as a plan
of settlement once for all.

This can by no means be accomplished with words nor can it
be effected by promise of petty gains. It is only possible by use of
force, but if we use force we must be in a position to be sure of
success beforehand. If we turn them back this year, next year they
are certain to come back in force. If we could be victorious three
years in succession and have every place prepared, then they might
bow their heads to authority. But if we look at present conditions,
internal banditry is rampant, popular distress is unrelieved, maritime forces are still untrained, so it would seem necessary to wait
for a time to move when the outcome will be satisfactory.

As to our overall situation, there are certainly Chinese traitors
everywhere to ferret out information for them. Therefore after the
barbarians returned to Shanghai, Your official ordered Judicial
Commissioner Hsüeh Huan on the one hand to make a thorough investigation of Chinese traitors and on the other hand, find means
to keep (the barbarians) under control. For three months the good
fortune of their not going North has been because Shanghai procedure
has prevented Chinese traitors from delivering letters for them.
When Kuei-liang and others respectively reached Ch'ang-chou, Your
official urged them to go direct to Shanghai and meet the chiefs in
order to show their confidence, rather than stay in remote

Sung-chiang and give an appearance of weakness. Moreover, he issued drastic orders for the seizure of all Chinese traitors so they could not undermine us.

We dare not stake everything on one throw. But actually if this were not done there was no adequate way to display national prowess or control popular sentiment. While the barbarians' arrogant attitude, having lost those they relied on, was not what it was at Tientsin, their firm reliance on the treaties was still unshakeable. Your official conferred thoroughly and intimately with Kuei-liang and others to discover an opportunity to explain (to the barbarians) . Then when a month had passed, just when military affairs were especially vital and exigencies hanging in the balance, Your official could not but anticipate the crisis and, in obedience to the Imperial Edict, return to Ch'ang-chou and then determine his future course of action. (He) instructed Financial Commissioner Wang Yu-ling to remain temporarily in Shanghai, to find means of settlement along with Kuei-liang and the others. If they can not get everything to suit our needs, as the situation is still fraught with difficulties, Kuei-liang and the others cannot but do their best with what can be recovered, eliminate the worst, and draw up an itemized account for presentation. Whether or not Heavenly Favor can be expected to condescend to give assent in order to avoid an immediate rupture, he respectfully awaits a Sacred Decision.

If Imperial assent cannot be given, then while war is inevitable, at this time we still must give no outward indication lest we make them suspicious. When our land and water preparations at the port of Tientsin have been completed, Your official will certainly exert himself to help somewhat with military supplies and, when they come to Tientsin next year to exchange ratifications, we can exterminate them en masse.

The present aspect of things is ominous. No one who uselessly gives vent to his feelings or talks airily about statesmanship but is without real capacity can undertake this affair; nor is it something one or two men can recover. (Your official) humbly asks His Majesty to search widely for those good and virtuous men whose statesmanship and learning have been manifested in conduct and who have given evidence of achievement, and place them at Your right hand. Thereafter, with court and country of one accord and cooperating in support, there can be perfection without flaw. Otherwise one mistake will lead to another and stop only after it has become irreparable.

Your official, having repeatedly received Mandatory Edicts and being overcome with fear, still dares again to offer up grass and reeds [worthless advice] for Imperial selection, because when the Sovereign is a saint His officials become upright. If by Imperial Grace Your official is allowed to wait until military operations are somewhat settled and humbly go to Court and look upon the Heavenly Countenance so he can report everything in person, relying upon loyalty such as a horse or dog shows his Master, he will be fortunate indeed.

Vermilion endorsement: Having read it with Prince Hui, this memorial has considerable significance. Order a thorough deliberation. Yesterday Prince Hui personally memorialized a program which is practicable. We think that to postpone and let things get worse is not as good as to make the first move and get control. (IWSM.HF 32; 5a, 9-8b, 6)

395. November 14, 1858. EDICT: Adheres Firmly to the Repudiation of Four Obnoxious Treaty Provisions and Threatens War as the Alternative.

Edict to the Grand Councillors. As to barbarian policy, since Kuei-liang and others reached Shanghai, We have repeatedly made Vermilion endorsements on the memorials themselves and basically there can be no further Edicts. Today Ho Kuei-ch'ing's memorial is received stating that he has returned to Ch'ang-chou and again explaining in detail the pricklish state of barbarian affairs.

At this difficult juncture We assume these officials, having received Our great bounty, would not dare deliberately betray their better nature in the hope of concluding the matter by compromise. But weighing present conditions, not only must the sending of officials to Peking be energetically opposed, but all of the important items, viz., trade in inland waters, travel in the interior, and indemnity for military expenses (before) the evacuation of the capital of Kwangtung, must somehow be blocked. Kuei-liang and others are in sole charge of barbarian affairs and can by no means evade responsibility, while Ho Kuei-ch'ing himself is high territorial official and, having received this charge, is obligated to strive for a solution.

Order them to continue in accord with previous Edicts and finesse to rescind these four items. Using force afterwards is not as good as eradicating the evil immediately. If we discuss tariffs now, the barbarians are sure to have something to gain; this will give us a handhold and prevent a rupture. If the four items are reversed, the rest can be handled according to provisions agreed upon at Tientsin and Shanghai. If the barbarians sincerely want everlasting friendship and will give up these four items, there can be real assurance of permanent peace.

As to the barbarians' purpose, originally they wanted to transfer the Imperial Commissioner to Shanghai. If the discussions are concluded eliminating the four items, then Kuei-liang and the others may agree to the transfer to Shanghai of the Imperial Commissioner in sole charge of commercial affairs. Thereafter, any country having a commercial problem will settle it at Shanghai. Kwangtung will

continue to trade as before; after the barbarians withdraw from the
capital (Canton), suitable regulations will be established by the governor general of Liang-kuang so as to prevent conflicts between
populace and barbarians.

If after everything is settled, barbarian ships again come to
Tientsin, this being a treaty violation, they cannot be treated as they
were this year. But at this time general conditions are unsettled and
this must not be divulged prematurely. Kuei-liang and the others
shall keep this in mind and tell them when the time comes. If they
have not made it clear when the barbarians leave and, in the twink-
ling of an eye, next spring the barbarian ships come back to Tientsin, there will be only Kuei-liang and the others to blame.

As to the statement in Ho Kuei-ch'ing's memorial that, although
promiscuous travel cannot be prohibited, there must be rigid regulations to maintain discipline, it is feared that once travel is allowed
there will be no means of limiting it. While at this time We are willing to waive rigid adherence to the plan agreed on at Court, the said
officials must display loyalty and sincerity and exert themselves
for retraction as a plan looking toward future national policy and
popular livelihood. We trust that Kuei-liang and the others will certainly be able to comprehend Our meaning. (IWSM.HF 32; 8b
7-9b, 8)

394. November 14, 1858. MEMORIAL: Ho Kuei-ch'ing Reports on an
Old Collision Claim in Shanghai and Proposes a Plan to Salvage the
Tientsin Treaties.

Ho Kuei-ch'ing further memorializes. In the second month (February 27-March 28) of 1854, the ship Herbert Compton, chartered by
former Su-Sung-T'ai Tao-t'ai Wu Chien-chang collided with and
damaged the trading vessel, Mermaid, owned by an American barbarian,[3] whereupon the barbarian merchants reported to the tao-t'ai
and demanded damages, estimating the cost of repairs at not more
than three or four hundred dollars, foreign money. Later the respective barbarian consul sent a communication to Wu Chien-chang
proposing damages of $3000 foreign money. Then the captains of
the Chinese and barbarian ships were ordered to make a voluntary
settlement, which is on record.

Suddenly on October 26 of this year, the tao-t'ai of Su-Sung-
T'ai received a communication from the American chief stating that
the former tao-t'ai had long since agreed to indemnify, but as the
treasury was low it had not been paid and $250 per day must be
added for interest, starting from March 28, 1854, and that now the

---

3 This case is mentioned by J. K. Fairbank, "The Creation of the Foreign Inspectorate of Customs at Shanghai," Chinese Social and Political Science Review, v. 20
(1936), p. 88. The Mermaid was owned by Heard and Company.

equivalent of the interest and capital must be settled immediately or else customs would be deducted to the full amount of interest and capital. At present we have had Wu Chien-chang determine the whereabouts of the Chinese and barbarian captains and make a suitable settlement.

We find that while the ship captain should pay an indemnity, the demand made on the official is unreasonable. The estimated cost of repairs was not more than three or four hundred dollars while the indemnity demanded is $3000 and besides, drawing interest at $250 foreign money per day for a period of four years and seven months, the interest would total more than $412,000. Certainly this is unthinkable. Were there actually excess customs collections, we cannot even imagine what methods they might adopt. Hence the reason why Your official has not ventured to disclose the Court Letter and Edict previously received to investigate the losses and grievances of the various barbarians, is for fear it would inspire unmanageable and unsubstantiated demands.

As to matters of Chinese-foreign intercourse, there are some which cannot be decided by law, depending entirely on treaties for definition. If we did not collect customs it would not be in conformity with the ten-thousand-year treaties of amity or the regulations concluded originally in Kwangtung. When one item is discarded, a hundred others collapse of themselves, so with the Tientsin treaties terminated it would actually amount to letting them do as they pleased. If we wanted to conclude separate regulations with them, the barbarians would then seize the pretext that the ten-thousand-year treaties of amity had been cancelled and there was no need of further negotiation and, without any means of subordination, it would be impossible to get a handhold.

This is merely discussing barbarian affairs as barbarian affairs without considering the concerns of the people, the merchants, or the army. As soon as Kuei-liang and the others arrived in Kiangsu, a great enlightenment burst upon them, that while they were thinking out remedial means, they would first strive, no matter how hard it was, to rescind the matter of permanent residence at Peking in order to comfort the Sacred Breast. As to the economic advantage of merchants, it must also be recovered, so that the millions of souls in Kiangsu, Chekiang, Fukien, Kwangtung, may have the means to dress and eat and not plant the seeds of rebellion; the tariff being neither increased nor diminished can be relied on to help out present straits; as to promiscuous travel, although it cannot be prohibited, it must be strictly regulated to afford discipline; and the capital city of Kwangtung must be restored by a certain time. All this is aimed at the maintenance of national prestige, while relying on the treaties to hold everything together. Your official, Financial Commissioner Wang Yu-ling, and Judicial Commissioner

Hsüeh Huan estimate their strength as possibly still adequate, but
at present the military situation has changed greatly, security and
danger are in the balance, and as Your official's distress is like a
flame, he actually cannot produce another plan.

At present the barbarian chiefs of all three countries are in
Shanghai; if there is not a speedy conclusion and they leave, the
situation will have been terminated without being closed. Then
when the water rises next spring, (the situation) will be something
Your official cannot anticipate.

Vermilion endorsement: Seen. (IWSM.HF 32; 9b, 9-11b, 1)

397. November 24, 1858. MEMORIAL: The Shanghai Commissioners
Report Reed's Offer of Cooperation and Propose Treaty Modification
rather than Repudiation.

Imperial Commissioners, Grand Secretary Kuei-liang and
President of the Board of Civil Office Hua-sha-na, Governor Gen-
eral of Liang-chiang Ho Kuei-ch'ing, Director of the Imperial
Armory Ming-shan, and Brevet Director of the Fifth Grade, Second
Secretary of the Board of Punishments Tuan Ch'eng-shih memori-
alize.

A few days ago the English Chief Elgin told Your officials that
judging from the recent attitude, official business in the future could
be handled very nicely, while America and France both want permanent friendship also. Today the American chief, William Reed, in a
communication on official business, made the statement that whatever occasion China had to make use of America, there would certainly be cooperation and support. It is apparent that the present
temper of the barbarians is not that of Tientsin (Vermilion endorsement: How can this kind of talk be believed? If it goes no further
than urging us to use them and if we use barbarians to restrain barbarians, then it is possible.) and we can somewhat reassure Imperial concern; but they hold firmly to the treaties and it is impossible
to discuss revision. After a whole night of fevered thought, we have
no advantageous plan. Your Majesty's Favor was magnanimous and,
in charging his officials with four items, did not force the impossible
upon them. If they cannot somehow abolish them, not only can there
be no evasion of responsibility but none can face his Sovereign.

However in the management of barbarian affairs at this time
when a settlement has just been made, it is very difficult to get
one's hand in. If we insist on open revision they will regard it as
repudiation of the treaties. For instance, the matter of residence
at Peking was brought up repeatedly before they were willing to
forego permanent residence. Moreover, as this clause contained
two conditions, the original wording was not specific and their arguments stalled. If other clauses are reopened, under the circumstances
they are certain to fail. Your officials have discussed it thoroughly

with the financial and judicial commissioners repeatedly, and can
only accept the insoluble and propose a policy of "pulling the fuel
from under the pot."

The barbarians by entering the Yangtze hope to get profit from
Huai Valley [Honan-Anhwei] salt. As these duties and various
charges plus the profits of the merchants amount to several tens of
millions per year, those who depend on it for their livelihood are innumerable. Once the (barbarians) are allowed to seize it, traders
will be destitute, poor people will be out of work, and conditions will
be unbearable to think of. Hence, without waiting for them to make
the proposal, we insisted in advance that they would not be allowed
to trade in it. Again the barbarians held out for it tenaciously. When
we had talked for more than ten days, we finally got their voluntary
assent. Now table salt is placed in the category of prohibited articles, and they are not allowed to transport it. If in the future there
is violation of the prohibition it must be dealt with severely when occasions arise, to stop gradual encroachment of the outer barbarians.

No arms or ammunitions are allowed imported. In the two ports,
Teng-chou in Shantung and Niu-chuang (Newchwang), beans and bean-
cake are the principal items. Heretofore they were all carried by
Kiangsu, Chekiang, Fukien, and Kwangtung merchants and shippers
and sold in the southeastern provinces and their profit was enormous.
Ships for this trade number altogether over 2000. Ocean transport
of tribute rice is dependent on them for the trip north. Those dependent on this for their livelihood are no less than several tens of millions. Your officials proposed that beans and bean-cake at Niu-chuang
and Teng-chou were not to be allowed carried out of port in English
vessels; only after heated argument was their assent finally gained.
Thus our merchant ships can trade as usual and not have their livelihood cut off and ocean-transport tribute rice can still be loaded --
a real benefit both to taxation and to people's livelihood.

Previously it was reported that barbarian ships laden with goods
went to Niu-chuang and Teng-chou to sell, but the local merchants
were only willing to supply them with food and not willing to trade
with them. The barbarian merchants returned disappointed. Two
more (such) trips should be enough to discourage them, while if
we try to negotiate with them at once, they will certainly not be willing to assent.

On the matter of travel and trade in the interior, we made clear
that excepting for Peking where they were not allowed to go at all, no
matter where they went, they must be reputable persons before the
respective consuls could issue them passports, which would be examined and stamped by Chinese local officials on presentation wherever they went. Requirement of examination could thus eliminate
promiscuous barbarian renegades. Moreover those who travel are
mostly missionaries. (Vermilion endorsement: At first they prop-

agate gospel; later their motives become inscrutable.) ... Originally they were not prohibited by law; now with passports, we can examine them (Vermilion endorsement: Even if they are examined every-where, how does that help the situation?). Barbarians naturally are most resentful of annoyances and if these accumulate perhaps even-tually they will be discouraged. (Vermilion endorsement: To hope that they will discard their former attitude is really to talk in one's sleep.) In this way, the best we can do is one at a time to think of ways to eliminate them eventually. Your officials stupidly think that when the barbarians' temper is compliant, we can press negotiations when occasion arises; while the barbarians' temper is antagonistic it is very hard to get a handhold for managing them. Only when China's army is efficient, supplies adequate, artillery effective, and ships strong can we do as we please and repudiate anything. Speak-ing for the present, we can only eliminate the worst and call it a day.

At present, the English and American barbarians' tariff schedules have been concluded on the eighth, and that of the French barbarians can be settled within a few days. As the commercial regulations and various Canton items are still undecided, we do not venture to me-morialize them hastily.

A few days ago the English, American, and French barbarians all spoke of wanting to go up the Yangtze. Financial Commissioner Wang Yu-ling and others told them that trade must await the termi-nation of hostilities. The barbarians all said that this trip was only to look over the ground, not to remain there, nor was there any other motive. When he told them that the route was infested with bandits and was entirely impassable, they promptly said they were not afraid and that it certainly would not lead to any trouble. While we repeat-edly refused, their determination to go was very firm. (Vermilion endorsement: Even if they did not cause trouble, they would be sure to make contacts [with the rebels]. Why did you not think of this?) Your officials negotiated with them personally, urging them this way and that, over and over again, and finally cut them off with forthright argument. The American and French barbarians, blankly dispirited, accepted our advice not to go up the Yangtze at once. But the English barbarians were stubbornly adamant, and no matter how we argued maintained that in not more than twenty days they would return to Shanghai to resume negotiations on the Kwangtung situation.

It is Your official's humble opinion that the barbarians' steamers come and go as they like and since 1853 have made several trips. As there is no way of stopping them it was better to show them that we were not suspicious, using their protection en route as a pretext for immediately notifying the tao-t'ai to delegate suitable officials with credentials to follow them up and watch their movements. As according to their statement they could make the round trip within 20 days, and being unfamiliar with people and country and with no goods to trade, it was quite certain that they could not remain long.

Your official, Ho Kuei-ch'ing, on first receipt of the news sent express letters notifying the various governors general, governors and generals in command of troops in advance to avoid alarm and suspicion.

Your officials are still at Shanghai quietly waiting for the barbarians to return to negotiate on Kwangtung affairs and also to discuss several clauses with them. Because multifarious affairs of taxation and military supplies were very pressing, Financial Commissioner Wang Yu-ling returned posthaste to Soochow on the eighth. All matters to be done now at Shanghai are being duly handled by Your officials, directing and cooperating with Judicial Commissioner Hsüeh Huan and various subordinates and deputies, as well as by correspondence with Governor General Ho Kuei-ch'ing.

Vermilion endorsement: On reading this memorial, We were involuntarily vexed. Even more exasperating, in your negotiation you not only have been unable to abrogate (the treaties), but even beyond the original treaties have actually allowed the English barbarian steamers to go up the Yangtze. If they do not return, how will you manage? (IWSM.HF 32; 15a, 8-18a, 6)

398. November 24, 1858. EDICT: Accepts the Tariff Schedule, Deplores the Weakness of the Shanghai Commissioners, and Suggests a Shanghai Foreign Office.

Edict to the Grand Councillors. Kuei-liang and others have memorialized that tariff schedules are concluded and barbarian temper is gradually being placated. As We read the memorial, it was most exasperating and detailed comments have been made in the text. When Kuei-liang and others receive them they must needs be ashamed. Why are English barbarian steamers lightly allowed to go into the interior? Kuei-liang and others readily assented and even said that they showed them that they were not suspicious of them. If We upheld our views rigorously, We should certainly charge that they be stopped, but We fear that as Kuei-liang and the others have already assented they cannot stop them forcibly and We can only let them go once. If when they return to Shanghai they still want to go back and forth as they please or if other countries emulating them follow them there, they must not be accommodated again.

As bulk salt was originally restricted to each locality in the interior and bulk beans are the principal item of trade of Fengtien ports, they must needs be restricted. As to travel in the interior, how can reliance on passport examination be adequate? This is the worst plan. Our not finding further fault at this time is only lest Kuei-liang and others, through want of ability, bring about a rupture, which is not saying We can bring ourselves to approve. The issue of residence at Peking to the barbarians is merely that Kwangtung is far away and

they fear that ordinary events do not reach the Throne. Previous
Court Letters and Edicts have sanctioned the removal of the Imperial
Commissioner to Shanghai. This was just the argument to use to
block their proposal to reside at Peking. If they are even allowed to
come and go on occasion, how can there be permanent harmony?
Give further orders to make clear to them that when the barbarians
set sail, if they come to Tientsin our forces will open fire immediately. Give them something to fear and not be led to try any schemes
again.

When the capital of Kwangtung is evacuated, it is of real advantage to both parties that the populace not cause the barbarians trouble
and that they can open up trade. When the barbarians come back and
want to discuss this matter, order this explained adroitly to provide
a turning point. Not one of these items but can be argued. It is entirely up to Kuei-liang and the others to bring out their better natures
and apply themselves energetically to the problem. Every item they
are able to abolish dispenses with the evil consequences of that item.
If they futilely talk about "pulling the fuel from under the pot" while
actually doing nothing to salvage the situation, how have Kuei-liang
and others the face to look at Us? (IWSM.HF 32; 18a, 7-19a, 4)

399. November 27, 1858. MEMORIAL. Kuei-liang Reports Improvement
in Foreign Relations and Hopes for some Slight Modification of the Treaty
Terms.

Imperial Commissioners Grand Secretary Kuei-liang and President
of the Board of Civil Office Hua-sha-na, Director of the Imperial Armory Ming-shan, and Brevet Director of the Fifth Grade, Second Secretary of the Board of Punishments Tuan Ch'eng-shih memorialize.

The circumstances of the barbarian ships going up the Yangtze
have been clearly detailed in a previous memorial. This time as the
barbarians are entering the ports of their own volition if inadvertently
they suffer damage they cannot blame China. Moreover, when Your
slaves made this clear to them they had nothing whatever to say. On
the possibility of rebel ships following them, it seems there is nothing
to fear. Although barbarians have the feelings of dogs and sheep, they
still have regard for their interests and if it were possible to form an
alliance with the rebels, the damage would have been done long since.
Therefore their insistence on going up the Yangtze was certainly in
view of contemplated profits in the future establishment of wharves
and that they had no other motive seems credible.

Previously at Tientsin when your slaves, Kuei-liang and Hua-sha-
na, because of the great crisis had no alternative but to ask Imperial
Favor on behalf of the barbarians, it was merely a device to get them
to withdraw their troops. The barbarians insisted on waiting for an
Edict of assent before they were willing to withdraw from the port.
Your slaves had actually exhausted their resources.

This time having received a special Imperial Mandate to come to
Kiangsu to arrange the tariff schedule with an opportunity to "win
back in the west what was lost in the east," how would they dare regard them as disparate? It is really as stated in Imperial Edict:
"Sending Kuei-liang and others to Shanghai and also ordering Ho Kuei-
ch'ing to cooperate in negotiations, how can they concern themselves
exclusively with tariff schedules?" As to thinking merely of bringing
the affair to a conclusion, it is certainly something Your slaves never
dared to contemplate.

When they arrived at Ch'ang-chou and met Governor General Ho
Kuei-ch'ing, he told them that the articles decided on at Court were
extremely difficult to execute. While Your slaves still felt that he
was stubbornly adhering to his own views, at the time they prepared
a joint memorial according to the governor general's views. After
Your slaves returned to the ship they decided between themselves
that when they reached Shanghai and saw what the situation was, they
would report the facts and request an Edict for guidance.

Later when they got to Shanghai, after open investigation and
secret inquiry, they realized that even if they abolished customs it
would still·be hard to abrogate the treaties and therefore did not
dare to divulge it readily. Sincerely fearing that even complete
abolition of customs would not improve the general situation, they
felt they had seriously miscalculated and even realized that the governor general's idea of present negotiations was fairly accurate.
As to Financial Commissioner Wang Yu-ling's coming to Shanghai
at this time, Your slaves actually wrote for him to come. Last month
when the governor general returned to Ch'ang-chou, the said commissioner also wanted to return to Soochow; but as nothing was yet
in shape Your slaves retained him for several days.

Now that an explicit Edict is received they dare not refrain from
reporting facts straightforwardly. Judicial Commissioner Hsüeh
Huan, having previously received an Edict ordering him to mollify
the barbarians, remained in Shanghai. Because residence at Peking
is of the utmost importance, the commissioner told H. N. Lay and
others that in Peking there was much dust and wind, the land frozen
and the weather cold; that for them to bring up matters themselves
in Peking for investigation and settlement, compared with having the
governors general and governors memorialize requests, would involve even more delay. By this lateral attack, he hoped to discourage
the barbarians and get them to change their minds. H. N. Lay and
the others immediately made the pretext that they had already memorialized their sovereign and feared they could hardly arrange it.

Just now, although the barbarian temper is gradually becoming
docile and they all say they are sincerely desirous of amity, once
the treaties are brought up they suspect abrogation. We must naturally negotiate seriatim the four items on which successive Edicts

have been received, but whether or not satisfactorily, can hardly be
guessed. Besides these four matters, those which are extremely
harmful must also be changed when there is a chance and means
found to abrogate them. Truly as Sacred Edict says, "Every ounce
of energy expended removes an ounce of harm from the Empire."

There is still no news of the English barbarians since they
went up the Yangtze. As they said they would return after twenty
days, they should be back in Shanghai within the month. These few
days we have been negotiating with the French barbarians on the
tariff and also on the Kwangtung affair, but on the whole these
barbarians cannot take any initiative and we still must await the
return of the English chief before negotiations are concluded.

Huang Chung-yü is not in Shanghai. At first Your slaves gravely
suspected he was in hiding; later seeing in Huang Tsung-han's memorial the statement that the said official was now in Kwangtung,
wearing the button and sash of the fifth rank and conducting separate
negotiations, we were convinced that he had returned to Kwangtung.
Liang Chih is now in Shanghai. A few days ago, when we stopped
the American barbarians from going into inland waters, it was he
who carried the word as an outsider.

It is Your slaves' private conjecture that if we can gradually
placate the barbarian temper at present, further complications can
be avoided; later if an advantageous future technique can be slowly
worked out it would seem more satisfactory. Anyway, it is essential for the army to be fit, supplies adequate, and the national situation strong before we can hope to settle once for all.

Vermilion endorsement: Noted. (IWSM.HF 32; 22b, 7-24b,
10)

400. January 9, 1859. MEMORIAL: The Shanghai Commissioners
Propose a Plan for Exchange of Ratifications at Shanghai with Modification by Separate Articles.

Imperial Commissioners, Grand Secretary Kuei-liang and President of the Board of Civil Office Hua-sha-na, Governor General of
Liang-chiang Ho Kuei-ch'ing, Director of the Imperial Armory Ming-
shan, and Brevet Director of the Fifth Grade, Second Secretary of
the Board of Punishments Tuan Ch'eng-shih memorialize. An official communication has been received from Governor General of
Hu-kuang [i.e. Hunan-Hupeh] Kuan-wen saying that on the twelfth
(December), all the English barbarians weighed anchor and left the
province and he figured that they should reach Shanghai by January
13.

It is Your officials' humble opinion that as it is not long until
the New Year (February 3), if they wait until the barbarians return
to Shanghai to submit both sets of treaties to the Throne, there may
be even more delay; if the barbarian treaties shall have arrived we

can discuss exchange of ratifications, while if our treaties are not here in time, then an opportunity will be lost. At present, tariff increases and deductions have been discussed fully and the seals affixed and they are merely waiting for the barbarians to return to Shanghai to discuss important matters. Your officials Kuei-liang and others have consulted together and propose dispatching the Tientsin treaties and the newly concluded customs schedule to Peking in advance and presenting them for Imperial inspection.

The treaties concluded at Tientsin have all been dispatched to their respective countries to be ratified. If later on it is necessary to revise or abridge any articles, allow us to wait until the barbarians return to Shanghai and then draw up separate articles, retaining copies of everything. Whether or not Your officials can be allowed to send the two sets of treaties by specially delegated officials to Peking as a means of expedition, they humbly await Imperial Edict for direction.

If in the future, after the (treaties) have been returned to Shanghai, we can exchange ratifications here, the barbarians' going to Peking can be dispensed with. If they adhere stubbornly to their previous statement, Your officials must needs find means to explain to them.

None of the barbarians want to go to Kwangtung to negotiate. When the various matters have been settled and ratifications exchanged, the Imperial Commissioners at Shanghai will again ask for an Edict of confirmation, so that the barbarians will understand that there is someone in sole charge of foreign affairs [N.B., wai-kuo shih-wu, not barbarian affairs, i-wu] and not be constantly proposing to go north.

The former Chekiang Salt Controller, Brevet Financial Commissioner, P'an Shih-ch'eng, who was summoned from his retirement in Kwangtung, reached Shanghai on December 10, and notice is hereby given. (IWSM.HF 33; 14b, 3-15b, 4)

401. January 9, 1859. MEMORIAL: Kuei-liang Reports British Relinquishment of Residence in Peking and Repeats Plan to Exchange Ratifications at Shanghai.

Kuei-liang and others further memorialize. To continue, according to a personal report of Judicial Commissioner, Acting Shanghai Tao-t'ai Hsüeh Huan, the English consul came to his office on other business and said that he had no news of Elgin and the others since they entered the Yangtze. He said further that on their return to Shanghai from Tientsin his country's treaties had been dispatched home and that he now heard that they had been ratified by the sovereign of his country and thought they would shortly arrive at Shanghai.

Your officials, lest that country's treaties reach here first, venture to ask that, after the Tientsin treaties and the tariff schedule now concluded shall have been presented for Imperial Inspection, they be Promulgated and dispatched posthaste to Shanghai to facilitate negotiations with the barbarians for exchange of ratifications at Shanghai. Except for permanent residence in Peking, which has been definitely denied, the status of the remainder of the four items must wait until negotiations are concluded, when separate articles must be drawn up and filed with the rest.

Vermilion endorsement: Seen. (IWSM.HF 33; 15b, 5-16a, 5)

402. January 9, 1859. EDICT: Approves Exchange of Ratified Treaties at Shanghai with Subsequent Articles Rescinding the Four Items.

Edict to the Grand Councillors. Kuei-liang and others have memorialized that the English chief will soon return to Shanghai and ask that the treaties be available there. The previous Edict for Kuei-liang and others to present the treaties, originally ordered them to rescind four items and, when this had been negotiated, to present them for inspection. Now their memorial proposes dispatching the two sets of treaties by special messenger in advance.

Issue orders in accord with their request allowing the presentation in advance of the Tientsin treaties and the tariff convention now concluded and, after separate articles rescinding the four items are drawn up, have them presented later. When We have determined what can be granted, they will be ratified altogether, promulgated, and delivered to Kuei-liang and the others to exchange with the barbarians.

Although they say that the barbarians will not reside permanently in Peking, their occasional entrance to the capital has not been blocked. How the three items of trade in inland waters, travel in the interior, and restoration of the Kwangtung provincial capital are to be handled, is by no means made clear in the memorial. As to the need of sending an Imperial Commissioner to Shanghai, it is also necessary to wait until everything is concluded and then reappoint.

At this time the barbarian ships have not returned to Shanghai. Actually where are they lingering? It is feared that Kuei-liang and the others are being fooled and put off, and as soon as spring comes the barbarians will again come secretly to Tientsin. Previously, notice has repeatedly been given that if the barbarians come north our troops will certainly open fire. Since Tientsin is not established as a port by treaty, there is no necessity for the barbarians to call there, and if we use force it will not be unreasonable. If Kuei-liang and the others have not divulged this, in case it is not convenient to tell Elgin personally, they can either have representatives tell him or transmit it through another country. As long as he knows, any means is permissible.

After all, since it is proposed to have the Imperial Commissioner transferred to Shanghai, in the matter of coming to Peking, not only is permanent residence not permissible but even occasional trips are uncalled for. The distance from Shanghai cannot be compared with that from Kwangtung, so what cannot be presented? What is the barbarians' real motive in insisting on the former proposal? Kuei-liang and others cannot even explain, so how can they say they have exerted themselves to the utmost?

At this time Kuei-liang and the others have only to find means to stop them and memorialize how far they are able to negotiate. No empty talk or glossing over which would misconstrue our policy, will be condoned. If with customary ineffectiveness they still allow the barbarians to come to Tientsin, previous Edicts have made clear that Kuei-liang and the others can hardly be able to face this heavy guilt. (IWSM.HF 33; 16a, 6-17a, 4)

403. January 29, 1859. MEMORIAL: The Shanghai Commissioners Submit the Tientsin Treaties and the New Tariff Schedules to the Grand Council for Approval.

Imperial Commissioners, Grand Secretary Kuei-liang and President of the Board of Civil Office Hua-sha-na, Governor General of Liang-chiang Ho Kuei-ch'ing, Director of the Imperial Armory Ming-shan, and Brevet Director of the Fifth Grade, Second Secretary of the Board of Punishments Tuan Ch'eng-shih memorialize. In accord with the Edict, the original four Tientsin treaties and the English, French, and American tariff schedules just concluded have been sent by four specially delegated officials to the Grand Council to be respectfully presented for Imperial Inspection and they have also respectfully copied out their detailed comments on the newly determined articles of the schedule and present them for Inspection.

In the Tientsin treaties, is it necessary to retain the Russian one at Peking? In the present negotiation of tariffs there was not a single Russian at Shanghai; besides, that country has never traded at the five ports and so has no tariff schedule to discuss. What special arrangement may be necessary in the future, the Imperial Mind will naturally conjecture. But if Russia comes to Peking to exchange ratifications, England, France, and America will certainly not be willing to exchange them outside. Although at this time the negotiations with the three countries are not concluded, if we want to prevent their going to Peking it is necessary to make clear that the treaties are to be exchanged outside, before we have anything to get hold of. In case the matter is settled in two ways, even after negotiations are concluded it is feared further complications will be unavoidable. This is something that must be thought through.

The English chief Elgin returned to Shanghai January 1. As Your officials, accompanied by Judicial Commissioner Hsüeh Huan, went to the barbarian house in Yang-ching-pin to meet him on the seventh, the said chief Elgin came to pay his respects on the tenth. His attitude was fairly compliant. Brevet First-class Sub-Prefect, District Magistrate Huang Chung-yü, previously recommended, also arrived at Shanghai January 1 from Kwangtung.

Of the four items for the reversal of which Imperial Orders have been received, on that of inland waters, orders are now given Huang Chung-yü to find means to intercede, to find out what objectives the barbarians still have. If in the end it can be blocked and wharves not established, that will be perfect. Even a nominal change reducing the number of places by one or two, even having the Chinese operate them for them, with the barbarians sending out only a few men for general supervision, all deferred until the conclusion of hostilities before the wharves would be opened, is also a modus operandi. There is still no reply on this item and it is not known whether or not it can be handled this way.

On the matter of travel in the interior, England, France, and America have all sent communications, stipulating that persons must be self-respecting and suitable before they would allow their respective consuls to issue passports, which would then be examined and stamped by local officials. With this system and rigid inspection as occasion arises, certainly not many will go out and we presume will not cause trouble. This item can only be handled in this way.

The matter of residence at Peking has been eliminated already. As to occasional visits, Your officials ordered Judicial Commissioner Hsüeh Huan to reason repeatedly with H. N. Lay without success. Now that Huang Chung-yü has come to Shanghai, Your officials have also had him use every sort of analogy with Elgin and carefully search out that barbarian's motives. In all probability he will not go, but he is absolutely unwilling to say so openly. For the removal of this item, even at the expenditure of all our energies, we shall still negotiate with them.

Your officials have also had their subordinates divulge to the barbarians the statement in the Edict previously received, that if the barbarians came to Tientsin again, they could not be treated as they were last year and that we should certainly open fire. They still said they were not afraid. In Your officials' stupid opinion, if this matter is temporarily dropped and we can negotiate to get the treaties exchanged outside, the desire to go to Peking will gradually disappear; so we can only wait awhile and then think out a plan. Meanwhile if there are any developments in the Kwangtung situation, with later deliberation item by item, it may be possible to resolve it readily.

As to the restoration of Canton, in the midst of the negotiations the barbarians suddenly received a letter from Hong Kong saying that the officials and gentry of Canton were still making trouble for them. The barbarians were very angry and immediately sent us a communication and also appended an Imperial Edict received by the gentry.

Although in their hearts suspecting it to be false, (the barbarians) were still somewhat disturbed. After receiving it, Your officials examined it carefully and certainly it is not like ordinary Imperial Edicts. They immediately dispatched a reply to the barbarians that it was really forged. Now they submit copies of the original communication and the copied document for Imperial Inspection.

Moreover, as the barbarians have asked whether or not an Edict has been received regarding their previous request for a memorial removing Huang Tsung-han and the three gentry, Your officials, after replying to the barbarians in accord with the Edict received October 21, are surprised that the barbarians still suspect Your officials of never having memorialized for them. They said further that if we did not agree to remove him they would go to Kwangtung themselves and make trouble for Governor General Huang and the three gentry by expelling the officials from the provincial capital; that they would collect the Canton customs themselves to meet the military expenditures of the two countries.

Recently they have been very quarrelsome, actually as if they did not want friendly relations. Your officials have now secretly ordered Huang Chung-yü to talk them out of going and, on the other hand, are cooperating with Judicial Commissioner Hsüeh Huan to devise suitable action. Your officials since arriving at Shanghai have written twice asking about Kwangtung affairs and Governor General of Liang-kuang Huang Tsung-han has never answered. Your official Hua-sha-na also sent a special letter of inquiry which was also unanswered. Your officials asked P'an Shih-ch'eng and he said that while the governor general was unable to pacify the barbarians, he was also unable to satisfy the people. On hearing this they were furiously angry. Without an alternative, they finally wrote this month to inquire of Governor of Kwangtung Po-kuei and Customs Superintendent Hang-ch'i, hoping to get an answer to facilitate the settlement of the Canton-restoration question.

A long time has passed since Your officials came to Shanghai and if they do not state their position soon, it is feared that delay will produce trouble. At this time the barbarians stick to their own view that if the governor general and the three gentry are not removed, they will not negotiate with us. Your officials have deliberated from morning until night without arriving at any really good solution. The barbarian steamers, without regard for winds, swiftly sail the seas and almost always leave without notice. If in the end they do go to Kwangtung and start trouble again, the implications will not be slight. Your officials and Huang Tsung-han have not the slightest difference of opinion, but the matter is of great importance and they dare not refrain from reporting facts confidentially and asking for an Edict for guidance.
(IWSM.HF 33; 28b, 6-31b, 3)

404. January 29, 1859. EDICT: Accepts Treaties but Urges the Commissioners to Use the Canton Issue to Finesse for Modification of the Four Obnoxious Items.

Additional Edict. Kuei-liang and others have memorialized their advance submission of the successive treaties and also reported the present state of negotiations. They state that the barbarians insist on removing Huang Tsung-han's Imperial Commission and also the trainbands of Lo Tun-yen and others before they can negotiate with us. The friction arises from the forged Edict. An Edict has been promulgated ordering Huang Tsung-han secretly to arrest the forger and punish him severely in order to dispel the barbarians' suspicion and discontent. Moreover, as the Imperial Commissioner is now transferred to Shanghai, another Edict orders Huang Tsung-han to appoint an officer to convey the seal to Kiangsu and turn it over to Ho Kuei-ch'ing.

As to the removal of the four items, Kuei-liang and the others have hardly touched them as a whole, nor have they reached a positive decision. As to residence in Peking they have only been able to deny permanent residence, still allowing them to come and go on occasion. If this results in this one coming and that one going interminably, how does it differ from permanent residence? Kuei-liang and others memorialize that if they can agree to exchange the ratified treaties outside, the desire to come to Peking will disappear of itself. Now that permission has been given to exchange (ratifications) at Shanghai, if in the matter of coming to Peking it is possible to finesse as the situation affords, what cannot be got by negotiation?

As to trade in inland waters, since the barbarian ships have struck shallows everywhere, this can be brought out to get them to recognize the difficulty and withdraw. In the memorial, the phraseology is ambiguous and, while it is stated that if it is possible to block them, it will be perfect, it is also stated that even if the change is nominal it is still feasible. It is already apparent that they still have no point of vantage.

As to travel in the interior, although stated in the treaty that the capital is not included, the barbarians are sure to point out that since places near the capital such as Shun-t'ien [the district in which Peking is located], and other parts of Chihli [now Hopei] are not mentioned in the treaty, this is no restriction whatever.

The officials and gentry trainbands of the Kwangtung provincial capital were set up primarily to eradicate bandits, not specifically for barbarian affairs. Besides after the Tientsin negotiations, successive memorials were received from Lo Tun-yen and others reporting that many (of the trainbands) had been dispersed and that in this period the cases of injuring barbarian soldiers all arose from the barbarian troops going outside the city and stirring up trouble. If they restore the city at once, there will be no occasion for this trouble. Since there is this fear of the gentry and people of Kwang-tung, this is just the thing for a talking point to bring the (barbarians) around to repentance.

The foregoing matters are all important. Since Huang Chung-yü is thoroughly trusted by Kuei-liang and the former is now in Shanghai, he can be prevailed upon to exert himself for the reversal of these items. Every article repudiated reduces the ill effects by one. Order wholehearted efforts continued. Just because the treaties have been presented they must not think their duty done.

As to the treaties previously taken to Shanghai, besides those of the three countries which have agreed to exchange ratifications at Shanghai, since the Russian barbarians had no one at Shanghai, that country's treaty must be kept temporarily in Peking and then later sent to the commissioner at Urga to take to that country's Senate yamen for exchange of ratifications.

Ming-shan having been granted leave, allow him to come to Peking. (IWSM.HF 33; 33a, 8-34b, 1)

Chapter 12

Ward Exchanges Ratified American Treaty at Pei-t'ang, 1859
(Documents 405-476)

The seventy-two documents comprising this chapter, dated February 13 to September 2, 1859, cover the breakdown of friendly relations between China and the Allies and the successful exchange of ratifications by John E. Ward, representing the United States. There are twenty-eight memorials and twenty-eight edicts; twenty-five of the latter are addressed to the grand councillors, two to the grand secretaries, and one to the imperial commissioners. There are fourteen vermilion endorsements on the memorials: five three-character acknowledgements, four slightly longer but still formal notations, four specific comments by the emperor, and one marginal notation in the text of a memorial. As in the documents covering the Tientsin treaty negotiations, a large amount of documentation outside the memorial-edict pattern is included. There are communications of the Grand Council, communications to and from the American envoy, Ward, and to and from the Russians. There is also a letter from the emperor to the president of the United States and a reply. These materials make the Chinese files resemble more and more the normal modern foreign office documents of Western countries.

The principal memorialists are the imperial commissioners entrusted with the arrangements for the exchange of ratifications, namely, General Seng-ko-lin-ch'in, Prince of Korchin, who was also in command of the Chinese military forces, and Heng-fu, governor general of Chihli; the name of another Manchu, Wen-yü, also appears as acting governor general of Chihli. The members of the Shanghai Imperial Commission are still active in this period, so the names of Kuei-liang, Hua-sha-na, Ho Kuei-ch'ing, and Tuan Ch'eng-shih also appear among the memorialists. There is also one short memorial on military affairs by the Shansi circuit censor, Ch'en Hung-i.

The representative of the United States of this period was John E. Ward of Georgia. His single function was to exchange the official copies of the Sino-American treaty of Tientsin, which had been ratified by the Senate and the emperor respectively, and to enable the treaty to be put into force. This simple task, however, involved him in the hostilities in which the British and French engaged the Chinese forces at Ta-ku Bar, in an ignominious overland trip from Pei-t'ang to Peking, in an unsatisfactory four-day confinement within the walls of the Tartar City of Peking, and in a final successful exchange of ratifications at Pei-t'ang. Ward's credentials were presented in Peking to Kuei-liang and Hua-sha-na and received by the Grand Council. The backdrop of this little drama is the battle of the Pei-ho, in which Prince General Seng-ko-lin-ch'in inflicted an unexpected but decisive defeat on the

British and French fleets. Prince Seng is the hero of China for 1859, and everything else in the Chinese documents is subordinated to this exhilerating but, for China, ultimately disastrous victory. Minor themes are the return of a supposedly American prisoner (actually a Canadian) to Ward, the relationship of the Russian and American missions, and the bad feelings aroused between the United States and Great Britain. Ward's mission had a temporary importance because, as it was the only one of the Tientsin treaties to be ratified, the British and French were forced to request most-favored-nation treatment for a year under the American treaty. The United States Navy had its innings in this phase of American diplomacy because of the gallant but un-neutral actions of Commodore Josiah Tattnall.

The American documents are summarized by Tyler Dennett in a chapter entitled "Ward and Tattnall-Exchange of Ratifications" in his Americans in Eastern Asia, pages 333 to 345. The Ward correspondence is printed, in part, in the same volume with Reed's, U.S. Cong. 36:1, S. Ex. Doc. 30. The journal of S. Wells Williams, cited above, covers both the Ward and the Reed missions. The Ward mission to Peking is put into historical perspective by William W. Rockhill in an article entitled "Diplomatic Missions to the Court of China," in the American Historical Review, volume 40 (1897), pages 627 to 643.

TRANSLATIONS OF DOCUMENTS

405. February 13, 1859. MEMORIAL: The Grand Councillors Present the Ratified Tientsin Treaties and Shanghai Tariff Schedules for Imperial Inspection.

The Grand Councillors memorialize. In accord with Imperial Edict, Your officials have resealed the Yellow Text[1] of the English barbarian tariff schedule, one copy; the Yellow Text of the French barbarian tariff schedule, one copy; the Yellow Texts of the American barbarian tariff schedule, two copies, submitted by Kuei-liang and others, and present them all for Imperial Inspection. On all the originals of the Tientsin treaties, one case, and on the English French, and American tariff schedules, one case each, Your officials have fixed their seals and sent them to the Record Office [An-shang] for preservation to secure caution and secrecy. (IWSM.HF 34; 11b, 4-9)

406. February 13, 1859. EDICT: Orders the Imperial Commissioners to Continue Negotiations for Modification of the Four Items by Separate Conventions.

Edict to the Imperial Councillors. According to a previous

---

1 I.e., the original text.

memorial from Kuei-liang and others, they are submitting two sets of treaties in advance. An Edict was immediately issued granting permission and also ordering that, when the four articles had been rescinded and separate articles drawn up, they all be sealed and returned at once.

On the eleventh of this month, the treaties and schedules were delivered by the special officer of Kuei-liang and others, and the Grand Council presented them on their behalf for Our inspection. But the separate articles of repudiation, when the barbarian chief shall have returned to Shanghai, must be concluded as soon as possible and presented immediately, so they can be sealed together with the treaties now submitted and promulgated to the various countries to avoid long delay.

Kuei-liang and the others must not conclude the affair with mush in their mouths and shirk their duty just because the treaties have been submitted. At this time, the turn for good or bad depends entirely on the separate articles to save the day. Order Kuei-liang and the others to consult wholeheartedly, recover the situation to the best of their ability and then memorialize express.

Order Kuei-liang and the others, when they receive the Edict issued January 29, to memorialize fully how they transmit it to the barbarians, how the barbarians react when they receive it, as well as what news there is of the barbarian ships going to Kwangtung. (IWSM HF 34; 11b, 10-12a, 8)

407. March 29, 1859. EDICT: Accepts Exchange of Ratifications in Peking as a Last Resort and Names Ho Kuei-ch'ing Imperial Commissioner of the Five Ports.

Edict to the Grand Councillors. Yesterday a memorial was received from Kuei-liang and others on the inscrutability of the barbarians. They say that the matters of exchange of ratifications at Shanghai and the drawing up of separate articles have never been discussed with the barbarians. Thus, in the handling of this affair, the said ministers up to now have no point of vantage at all.

At present Chief Elgin has long been in Kwangtung. If he returns to Shanghai shortly, the said ministers shall still negotiate with the said barbarians to exchange ratifications there. Kuei-liang and the others all have better natures, and must needs do their best to save the situation. But barbarians being naturally obstinate and the said ministers being pressed by circumstances constitutes a dilemma. We have fathomed the difficulty faced by the ministers. But as residence in Peking is regarded as having the most dire consequences, it cannot possibly be agreed to. As to coming to Peking to exchange ratifications, if by utmost effort it can be prevented so much the better.

If the barbarians stubbornly refuse, the (ministers) shall make

absolutely clear to them that when they come from the port to the
capital the number of attendants allowed will not be more than ten,
that they cannot bear arms, and on arrival at the capital, in conformity with the regulations of outside countries coming to the capital, they cannot ride in chairs or have attendants, and when the
treaties have been exchanged, shall return immediately, not being
allowed to remain in Peking. If they are willing to conform to the
foregoing terms, you will on the one hand memorialize and on the
other, return to the capital first to determine a date. After you are
in Peking, their ships can proceed to Tientsin without having a long
wait in the port. If you explain clearly like this the barbarians
must needs bow their heads and obey.

The three other matters can be elucidated when occasion affords
and if one can be eliminated, hereafter there will be one less hardship to bear. If complete abrogation is not possible, restrictions
must be placed on the three clauses to keep the barbarians from
making endless demands.

Ho Kuei-ch'ing is Imperial Commissioner of the five ports and
cannot shirk responsibility. As soon as he hears of the barbarians'
return to Shanghai he will proceed to Shanghai with Kuei-liang and
the others, and is obliged to deliberate even more diligently. Wang
Yu-ling, Hsüeh Huan, and Wu Hsü can all understand barbarian affairs thoroughly, so order them sent there first, in accord with
Imperial Edict, to take suitable action as things come up.

If the barbarians insist on coming to Peking to exchange ratifications, Ho Kuei-ch'ing will delegate two of the three officials,
Wang Yu-ling, et al., who with Kuei-liang and the others will come
to Peking posthaste to take charge, so as not to afford the barbarians any excuse for lingering.

At Tientsin last year, when Kuei-liang and the others glibly
gave their consent for the barbarians to come to Peking, they assumed
a responsibility they cannot evade. Then it was hoped by sending them
to Shanghai they could gradually retrieve the situation. Now after
several months there is still no positive relief. Allowing them to come
to Peking to exchange ratifications this time is certainly a case of being left with no possible alternative.

If the said ministers can personify Our mind, then they must exchange the treaties at Shanghai, which will be suitable. We assume
that Kuei-liang and the others will not think that, just because of
Our Edict, they can compromise or evade responsiblity. (IWSM.HF
35; 40a, 7-41a, 9)

408. March 29, 1859. EDICT: Orders Prince Seng-ko-lin-ch'in to
Strengthen the Ta-ku Defenses but still Hopes to Keep the Envoys at
Shanghai.

Additional Edict. Previously on account of the memorial of Kuei-liang and others that they had learned that barbarian sentiment was set on coming to Peking, Seng-ko-lin-ch'in was ordered to redouble his vigilance. The original memorial of Kuei-liang and others and the newspapers they presented were also copied and sent for his inspection. We assume that Seng-ko-lin-ch'in has conferred with Wen-yü in making advance plans.

At present it is still uncertain whether or not Chiefs Elgin and Bruce are going to Shanghai. If the barbarian ships do come to the port of Tientsin, the said ministers shall in accord with previous Edict delegate competent officers to meet them, saying that at this juncture they are only waiting for word from Shanghai and if Imperial Commissioners Kuei-liang and others did give notice to allow them to enter port, this time they would certainly not be prevented; that if there was no agreement at Shanghai, they could by no means be allowed to come into port without authority and would have to go back to Shanghai and await a settlement.

If with this explanation the chiefs are willing to return, then there can be no need of starting hostilities. If by any chance they should not listen to reason, your deputies will tell them that they will report back to the local officials to ask for an Edict on their behalf, and order the barbarians to wait there. If they have the audacity to open fire, Seng-ko-lin-ch'in and others have made preparations and can watch their chance and then strike, frightening them with their military force. We assume that Seng-ko-lin-ch'in can certainly comprehend Our meaning.

Today there is also an Edict notifying Kuei-liang and the others to deliberate duly and manage. As soon as they memorialize as to what the situation is, another Edict will be issued notifying Seng-ko-lin-ch'in and the others, so they can consult and act. (IWSM.HF 35; 41b, 1-42a, 2)

409. April 11, 1859. MEMORIAL: The Shanghai Commissioners Report the Massing of British, French, and American Forces with Little Prospect of Blocking Them.

Imperial Commissioners, Grand Secretary Kuei-liang, President of the Board of Civil Office Hua-sha-na, Governor General of Liang-chiang Ho Kuei-ch'ing, Brevet Director of the Fifth Grade, Second Secretary of the Board of Punishments Tuan Ch'eng-shih memorialize .... For several days now there has been definite news of 2000 English barbarian troops and more than 10 ships to go direct to Tientsin. America and France are sure to do the same. We hear that the American barbarians' ships are not more than 2 or 3, nor are their troops many, that the number of the French barbarians' ships and troops is rather more than the Americans'. Thus France and England are still cooperating in evil. When the French barbarians say that where a settlement is made and where things are

to be settled, only they and England can determine, it is still more
boasting. They are full of iniquity.

Your officials' affability and humility, from the receipt of the
Mandate to handle barbarian affairs to the present, which observers
are sure to revile, has been primarily with a view to the general
condition of the Empire. With barbarian temper as it is, extremely
arrogant, it is feared that words alone cannot win them over. Ponder-
ing early and late, still without any really efficacious plan, Your officials must merely on the one hand keep a vigilant watch and on the
other wait until the (barbarian chiefs) return to Shanghai and explain
duly, urging them to exchange the treaties at Shanghai (Vermilion
endorsement: This is splendid. Only with this policy of "pulling the
fuel from under the pot" can we possibly hope for recovery.); then
if they do not consent, have the Chinese merchants and the various
barbarian merchants explain and exhort them to reform and, in all
probability, it will be possible to stop them. By no means will we
dare relax the least bit.

Now it is proposed to send subordinate officials to Shanghai in
advance duly to discuss means of persuasion with the acting tao-t'ai.
As soon as there is word of the barbarians coming to Shanghai, (Your
officials) will immediately size up the situation and act as occasion
offers in order to accomplish a general policy of conciliation.
(IWSM.HF 36; 12b, 8... 13b, 3-14a, 6)

410. April 11, 1859. EDICT: Accepts the Inevitable Entrance of
Foreign Missions to Peking and Seeks to Limit Numbers and Specify
Conditions.

Edict to the Grand Councillors. Kuei-liang and others have memorialized on the report of the barbarian chiefs' determination to
come to Peking and also presented copies of communications for
Our inspection. These barbarians are fickle and inconstant, perverse in feelings and words, not by any means to be managed by
mere words. The said ministers propose, when the barbarians
come to Shanghai, first to explain to them, then if they do not agree,
have the Chinese merchants and the various barbarian merchants
explain to them. This is the plan to "pull the fuel from under the
pot." As barbarian conduct is largely determined by merchants,
there may be some hope of recovery.

With things in this state, We assume that Kuei-liang and others
must still exert themselves to hold firm and not compromise as before. If actually they cannot stop them they must, in accord with the
Edict of March 29, arrange with them the number of men, making
clear that after ratifications are exchanged they will not be allowed
to remain, that they cannot bear arms nor ride in chairs nor have
attendants, before they can consent to their coming to Peking.
Permanent residence at Peking certainly cannot be allowed.

If as Kuei-liang and the others have learned, the English barbarians have 2000 troops and over 10 ships and the American barbarians and French barbarians both have many warships, their
purpose is to pick a quarrel so we can hardly let them penetrate,
with the possibility of open hostilities. It is absolutely essential to
exchange ratifications in Shanghai and thus eliminate this calamity.
Thus the Edict of March 29 was a plan of absolutely last resort and
the said ministers are not to regard it as fixed policy.

The fear that England and France will not return to Shanghai but
proceed direct to Tientsin makes handling difficult. Order Kuei-
liang and the others to send communications immediately by steamer
to Chief Bruce[2] and Chief Gros inviting them to come to Shanghai
first, saying that there are important matters to discuss with them,
and maybe they can be stopped half-way. If they find that the said
chiefs have sailed for Tientsin, the said ministers will, in accord
with previous Edict, bring along the Kiangsu officials and proceed
posthaste to Peking to take charge so as to avoid delay.

As to the copy of a forged document in the communication of the
French barbarians, it is barbarian character translated into Chinese
character and it is feared that a foreign traitor forged it. Since
China is already hunting down the man who forged the Edict, the
foreign countries should likewise investigate in order to dispel
suspicion. Order Kuei-liang and the others to notify the barbarians clearly to this effect. (IWSM.HF 36; 14a, 7-15a, 4)

411. April 14, 1859. MEMORIAL: Prince Seng-ki-lin-ch'in Acknowledges Oral Instructions from Prince I and Specifies Pei-t'ang
Route for the Envoys.

Imperial Commissioner Seng-ko-lin-ch'in, Prince of Korchin,
and Acting Governor General of Chihli Wen-yü memorialize. On the
eleventh of this month, Tsai-yüan Prince I and Director of the
Imperial Armory Ming-shan arrived at the port and Your slave,
Seng-ko-lin-ch'in, kneeling, heard Imperial Instructions, as well as
all the strategic plans of conciliation and attack. Your slave will
certainly take them into consideration and take suitable action.

He personally thinks that if the barbarians insist on coming to
Peking to exchange ratifications, entering the river from the port of
Ta-ku, there is a water-way straight to T'ung-chou, which is very
convenient, but at the port of Ta-ku arrangements have been kept
strictly secret; not only can they not be allowed to pass through, but
they can not even be allowed to spy.

He notes that from the port of Pei-t'ang, by going up the river
60 li to Lu-t'ai, disembarking and going by land through Hsiang-ho

---

2 Frederick William Adolphus Bruce, made K. C. B. in 1862, brother of Lord Elgin,
was sent to China to exchange the ratified Tientsin treaties in 1859.

and T'ung-chou, one can also reach Peking; or perhaps by land from
Pei-t'ang to Tientsin and by boat to the vicinity of T'ung-chou.   This
should be decided at the time by Imperial Commissioners Kuei-liang,
Hua-sha-na, and their attendant officers, and orders given the local
officials to make due arrangements.

It is also proposed to have the barbarian ships, large and small,
all anchor outside the bar and use local boats to carry them up the
river; thus by strict precaution the development of other complications can be prevented.   (IWSM.HF 36; 17b, 7-18a, 8)

412. April 14, 1859. EDICT: Approves Pei-t'ang Route and Authorizes the Missions to Land and Proceed to Peking to Exchange Ratifications.

Edict to the Grand Councillors.   Seng-ko-lin-ch'in and Wen-yü...
add a supplementary memorial stating that at the port of Ta-ku, the
arrangements are strictly secret and they cannot allow the barbarians
to spy.

If barbarian ships arrive at the port, the said ministers, in
accord with Imperial Edict of April 2, will first send officers to
explain; then, when there is an Edict allowing them to come to Peking
to exchange ratifications, have them anchor outside the bar and use
native boats to carry them into the river and proceed by land from
Pei-t'ang to Tientsin, and then by water to T'ung-chou.   It will be
enough to deliberate and act when the time comes.   (IWSM.HF 36;
18a, 9...18b, 7-19a, 1)

413. April 30, 1859. MEMORIAL: The Shanghai Commissioners
Report Plans to Publish the Treaties to Allay Suspicion and Request
Originals Sent to Shanghai.

Imperial Commissioners Grand Secretary Kuei-liang and President of the Board of Civil Office Hua-sha-na, Governor General of
Liang-chiang Ho Kuei-ch'ing, and Brevet Director of the Fifth Grade,
Second Secretary of the Board of Punishments Tuan Ch'eng-shih me-
morialize.   In the matter of exchanging ratifications at Shanghai,
Your officials proposed to wait until the barbarians should return
to Shanghai and then explain adroitly, but greatly feared they would
not be willing to agree; so they also proposed to have the Chinese
merchants and the various barbarian merchants explain to them.
They sent Independent Department Magistrate Yang Ch'un-hua to
Shanghai to confer personally with Acting Su-Sung-T'ai Tao-t'ai
Wu Hsü on methods of handling.

Yesterday was received Wu Hsü's report that he has covertly
told Chinese merchants Yang Fang, Hsi K'uan and others to discuss
arrangements secretly and devise means to persuade (the barbarians) to desist without giving evidence of official inspiration.   But
the Chinese merchants said that the desire to go to Peking would
gradually cool if we could have the Tientsin treaties published

beforehand, to make them realize that we Chinese are acting entirely in accord with the new regulations; then the merchants could exchange ratifications at Shanghai and facilitate the early inauguration of the new regulations. Otherwise it is feared they will say we are stalling. Using this to stimulate them, it may be easier to get results.

Your officials note that the Tientsin treaties have been printed and distributed by the barbarians. Eventually they must be published. They therefore ordered the acting tao-t'ai to make a show of activity, but need not complete the publication. When the said chiefs come, what they see and hear will lead them to believe that China is doing everything promptly according to treaty and we may be able to hope for their assent.

As to permanent residence at Peking, the barbarians have said clearly that they would choose another place to live, and Your officials will certainly not let them change their minds. But in their opinion, it is the nature of barbarians to be impatient. Probably when these barbarians come to Shanghai, either Your officials will persuade them to stop or the Chinese merchants will, and ratifications can be exchanged in Shanghai. But the treaties are in Peking. If (Your officials) immediately memorialize requesting the Emperor to send them, the round trip would take 20 days and if the barbarians were unwilling to wait, the opportunity might be lost.

May they implore Your Majesty's Heavenly Favor to send out the treaties in advance, to be conveyed quickly by officers duly appointed from the Board of War to Kiangsu for Your officials' respectful receipt. If the barbarians are willing to exchange ratifications in Shanghai, they will be readily available; if the barbarians are adamant and insist on going to Peking to exchange them or proceed direct to Tientsin, and Your officials see that under the circumstances they cannot stop them and there is no possibility whatever of recovery, they will have the treaties sent back to Peking by special messenger. When the barbarians get to Tientsin, we can see what the barbarians' attitude is and act accordingly. Whether or not the English, French, and American treaties can be sealed in advance and sent to Your officials to facilitate devising means of tying them up, they humbly await Sacred Enlightenment to point out the way.

While writing this memorial, they have received a report from Expectant District Magistrate Huang Chung-yü that he has learned Bruce is expected at Hong Kong May 3 and 4, definitely; that after arrival he will not tarry long and should come to Shanghai around the twelfth; that just now Hong Kong has sent out eight small warships, each with about 70 marines, to be in Shanghai shortly, to be used to convoy Chief Bruce to Tientsin; that France also has warships coming but the number and date of arrival are not known; that moreover, there is a report that the ships have advance orders to go to the bar and wait.

Your officials beg to observe that for the barbarian chiefs of the various countries to come from afar over the seas and bring troops to protect themselves, if the numbers are not large, does not mean necessarily that they are coming bent on picking a fight. In all probability the barbarian ships will go direct to the port of Tientsin. On learning this, Your officials must needs make it clear that such warships and men can only be stationed outside the port and cannot be allowed to go up river, in order to show control. But since they are said to have ordered their warships to go to the bar first, it would seem that we cannot but make secret preparations and request must be made that Orders be sent to Tientsin to act accordingly. (IWSM. HF 36; 38a, 2-39b, 6)

414. April 30, 1859. EDICT: Rejects Proposal to Send the Treaties to Shanghai and Insists upon Prior Modification of the Four Items by the Commissioners.

Edict to the Grand Councillors. Kuei-liang and others have memorialized on present arrangements and reports of barbarian affairs. On the matter of coming to Shanghai it may be possible to get the barbarians to settle at Shanghai.

But at this time the four items of residence at Peking, et cetera, have not been withdrawn. If the treaties are sealed in advance and sent to the said ministers, should the barbarians be arbitrary and go direct to Tientsin, Kuei-liang and the others would be still more without a quid pro quo. To forward the treaties back at that time would also be a useless waste of time. If the barbarians are impatient and will not wait, they have only to tell them in advance that the round trip of 20 days would still not make them wait long.

The barbarians should reach Shanghai about the twelfth. When the time comes, Kuei-liang and the others will go immediately to Shanghai and deliberate wholeheartedly to find means to rescind the four items. They cannot just go to a nearby place and depend entirely on representatives to manage. If the four items are made clear and separate articles drawn up and the barbarians agree to exchange ratifications at Shanghai, memorialize express and then the treaties will be sent.

If the barbarians insist on coming to Tientsin, then Kuei-liang and the others, in accord with previous Edict, will select two from the three officials, Wang Yu-ling, Hsüeh Huan, and Wu Hsü, to accompany them and proceed posthaste to Peking to take charge, in order to avoid delay and suspicion.

As the barbarians have said plainly that they will select another place to live, the matter of residence at Peking can be eliminated, but it is not pointed out (where this will be). The said ministers must also confer beforehand. They cannot be allowed to live in the Chihli area, lest there will be damage to general conditions.

All in all, since there is word of Chief Bruce coming to Shanghai, Kuei-liang and the others can only do their best to stop him
and to rescind the various articles and must not hesitate for fear of
difficulties.

As to the intention of having the barbarian ships go first to the
bar and wait, today orders have been given Seng-ko-lin-ch'in and
others secretly to ready defenses.   (IWSM.HF   36; 39b, 7-40b, 1)

415.   April 30, 1859.   EDICT: Notes Concentration of Allied Forces
at Shanghai and Orders Prince Seng-ko-lin-ch'in to Complete his Ta-ku
Defenses.

Additional Edict.   Today an express memorial is received from
Kuei-liang and others that they have learned that the English barbarian chief, Bruce, is definitely expected to reach Hong Kong the
first part of May and should reach Shanghai about the 12th; that Hong
Kong has sent out 8 small steamers, each with about 70 marines, to
go to Shanghai shortly, to be used to convoy Chief Bruce to Tientsin.
It is further reported that the various ships are ordered in advance
to go to the bar and wait.   Kuei-liang and the others propose to
wait until the said chief reaches Shanghai and then settle with him
that this kind of warships and men only be allowed to anchor outside the port and cannot sail up the river.

At present Heng-fu has reached Tientsin, taken over his seal,
and it is assumed that within a few days will have gone to the port
of Ta-ku.   Order Seng-ko-lin-ch'in to confer carefully with the
governor general and secretly plan defenses.   If there is actual
word of the barbarian ships coming to the bar, they are ordered to
delegate responsible officers to go and make inquiry, saying that
this time we only await the arrival of letters from Shanghai.   Follow
entirely the Edict of April 2, and act as circumstances require.
(IWSM.HF   36; 40b, 3-41a, 1)

416.   June 6, 1859.   IMPERIAL COMMENT: Gives Definite Permission for the Envoys to Exchange Ratifications and Implies Acceptance of Residence in Peking.

Vermilion endorsement: [Appended to a memorial of Kuei-
liang, Hua-sha-na, Ho Kuei-ch'ing and Tuan Ch'eng-shih, reporting
the arrival of the English fleet at Shanghai and their announcement
of intention to proceed to Tientsin to exchange ratifications at
Peking; they had no news of France and America.] After all, the
exchange of ratifications at Shanghai is the most important consideration; but if there is no alternative but to stoop to an inferior
plan, anchoring outside the bar and (bringing) a small number of
attendants is quite suitable.

It is still more essential that the said chiefs come to Peking in
person; they cannot be allowed to substitute some military leaders

with the idea of stirring up trouble. They are coming to Peking
primarily to exchange ratifications and must not be allowed to stay
long. If the said chiefs want to live in Peking, Hsüeh Huan must be
kept in the capital as permanent director.

Although at this time the Ch'ing-Huai [i.e., the waterway of the
Ch'ing and Huai rivers through Kiangsu and Shantung to the north;
hence, the inland water route from Shanghai to Peking] route may be
obstructed, if We entrusted this to someone who does not understand
barbarian affairs he would be sure to be unable to manage satisfactorily. You ministers, who have undergone many tribulations and
worked tirelessly for two years, must needs want to see an early conclusion. Their request need not be discussed. The time required to
go to Tientsin is just the argument to use as a lever to get them to
exchange ratifications (at Shanghai). (IWSM. HF 38; 2b, 10-3a, 6)

417. June 7, 1859. EDICT: Orders Tientsin Officials to Notify the
Envoys that the Shanghai Commissioners are Proceeding to Peking to
Handle Exchange of Ratifications.

Edict to the Grand Councillors. Yesterday was received a memorial from Kuei-liang and others that on May 27 they received a
communication from the English chief stating that Bruce was going
to Peking to pay his respects and would shortly proceed to Tientsin
by ship; that he hoped that at Tientsin coolies, boats, and carts
would be prepared to facilitate going to the capital and also, inside
the capital city, spacious quarters would be selected as the barbarians are bringing attendant officials and officers with them.

Kuei-liang and the others have replied to the said chief (urging
him) not to go direct to Tientsin; that it is essential to come to
Shanghai to negotiate. They also sent District Magistrate Huang
Chung-yü to the port to arrange to exchange ratifications at Shanghai when the barbarian ships arrive. But barbarians are naturally
stubborn and it may be hard to detain them.

If they will not be dissuaded and do come direct to Tientsin,
Seng-ko-lin-ch'in and Heng-fu can only follow the previous Edict,
send officers to explain, have them anchor outside the bar, and say
that Kuei-liang and the others have set out from Shanghai and will
shortly reach Tientsin, when they can meet and settle everything;
say also that the port is fully fortified and they must refrain from
coming in promiscuously and suffering damage, in order to preserve friendship.

If the barbarians ask us to send other officials, they can say
that the treaties of the various countries have all been handled by
Kuei-liang and others and that other people cannot understand them
thoroughly. Thus explain clearly and have them wait quietly.
(IWSM. HF 38; 4b, 4-5a, 4)

418. June 18, 1859. MEMORIAL: The Shanghai Commissioners Report Ward's Personal Willingness to Exchange Ratifications at Shanghai.

Imperial Commissioners Grand Secretary Kuei-liang, President of the Board of Civil Office Hua-sha-na, Governor General of Liang-chiang Ho Kuei-ch'ing, and Brevet Director of the Fifth Grade, Second Secretary of the Board of Punishments Tuan Ch'eng-shih memorialize. ... Your officials have met the American chief, John Ward. This chief is personally very peaceable as well as very approachable. Previously because the time for exchanging ratifications was near, Your officials told him that, as we were already friendly, it did not matter whether they were exchanged within a year or not. The said chief did not disagree. Originally, he was willing to exchange ratifications at Shanghai but, since the English and French chiefs were determined to go north, he is also certain to want to go along. Your officials originally proposed using him to persuade them to stay but, while he will never be much trouble, his ability is inadequate for use as a middle man to dissuade them. (IWSM.HF 38; 13a, 1...15b, 4-9)

419. June 18, 1859. PROCLAMATION: The Grand Council Notifies the Metropolitan Prefecture to Locate Housing for the British, American, and French Envoys.

The Grand Council, by way of communication. At present England, America, and France propose to exchange ratifications, whether at Shanghai or coming to Peking being as yet undecided. If they come to Peking, naturally, according to the rules of barbarians paying court and paying tribute, they should be provided an official residence to stop at. The present Imperial Commissioners received Imperial Edict personally to order the Metropolitan Prefecture to find out if, .anywhere outside Cheng-yang Gate [i.e. Ch'ien Men, the main front gate in the wall of the Imperial city, opening out into the Chinese city to the south, in which the foreign envoys were to be housed, rather than in the Imperial City itself.] there are three buildings with vacant rooms to provide for their use. Respect this.

Accordingly notice is sent the honorable Yamen to make due search outside the three front gates; if there are buildings with vacant rooms, whether school, guild hall or what not, of something more than 50 or 60 chien [house units, not necessarily rooms, as one large room may be several chien large] up to 70 or 80 chien, and notify the Grand Council in advance so that when it is needed they can ask for an Edict and act accordingly. By way of due notice. (IWSM. HF 38; 21a, 4-21b, 1)

420. June 18, 1859. PROCLAMATION: The Grand Council Shifts
Reception Plans from the Chinese City to the Area Outside the East
Gate of Imperial City.

        The Grand Council, by way of communication. Having received
the honorable Yamen's note saying that they have duly investigated
five sites in Lung-wang-t'ang and other places which can be prepared for use, today the Grand Council took the original note, presented it to the Throne, and received in person an Imperial Edict
to order the Metropolitan Prefecture to find three other spacious
vacant buildings in the eastern suburbs outside the (Imperial) city
wall and prepare them for use. Respect this. Accordingly the
honorable Yamen is notified, if outside Ch'ao-yang Men or Tung-
chih Men there are any buildings such as temples, with vacant
rooms of 50 or 60 chien up to 70 or 80 chien, to report them to the
Grand Council so that when they are needed, they can ask for an
Edict and act accordingly. By way of due notice. (IWSM. HF 38;
21b, 2-9)

429. June 29, 1859. EDICT: Authorizes the American and French
Envoys as Neutrals to Proceed to Peking via Pei-t'ang to Exchange
Ratifications as Planned.

        [After hostilities on June 25th]
        Edict to the Grand Councillors. Heng-fu has memorialized that
as the barbarians' attitude is bellicose and he can hardly pacify them,
asks us to send a minister to take charge. . . . Last year since Tientsin
was lost we lost at the peace conference; now, fortunately, we have
won a victory and blunted somewhat the point of their ferocity. If
we take this occasion to explain to them it should be easy to get a
lever. As the English chief opened fire first and brought defeat on
himself, he will certainly have no face to come and talk peace.
        As to America and France, since they did not follow him against
authority, order Heng-fu to cooperate with Wen-yü, go and take up
residence at Pei-t'ang at once and either send officers to meet or
send communications to the two countries, saying that since the two
countries were coming to exchange ratifications and China has always
valued fidelity and right, although official residences have already
been prepared at Tientsin, still it is necessary to wait awhile until
Kuei-liang and the others shall have arrived, when ratifications can
certainly be exchanged; that as the port defense was already there
[i. e. at Ta-ku], it was originally proposed to receive them at Pei-
t'ang; that unexpectedly the English barbarians violated the treaties
beforehand, pulled up our iron chains [t'ieh ch'uang], and attacked
our forts, forcing our troops to become angry and fight back; that
fearing the present conflict had damaged the ships of their two
countries [i. e. America and France], this special proclamation is
now issued. If they wish to wait outside the bar, they must with-

draw somewhat; if not, fix a date for us to send someone to meet
them at Pei-t'ang and conduct them to Tientsin in order to confirm
friendship. It is not necessary, however, to bring a large retinue
lest our people be excited and cordiality be disrupted; that the
English barbarians' unceremonious repudiation of treaties, rejecting China's sincere reception, was really unexpected; that although
inimical to us for several days, we still sent them a communication
to dispel their doubts; that while we are continuing to act in good
faith, it is feared that they are obstinately foolish and deluded and
as this might interfere with the exchange of ratifications of the two
countries, we specially inform them of it.

See if they will come or not and how they respond. If the American and French barbarians intercede for the English barbarians,
then be guided by circumstances and fit speech to occasion, temporarily restraining them, until after Kuei-liang and the others arrive,
and then discuss the exchange of ratifications again. Heng-fu and
the others having received this heavy responsibility, must needs
devote themselves to its execution in order to complement Our
heart.... (IWSM. HF 38; 54b, 6... 55a, 3-55b, 8)

422. June 30, 1859. EDICT: Notes "American" Prisoner of War and
Authorizes the Reception of Ward and Gros at Peking and Negotiation
with Bruce at Shanghai.

Edict to the Grand Councillors. This time the barbarian chiefs,
Bruce and others, came to Tientsin to exchange ratifications, brought
warships and wanted to enter Ta-ku harbor. Orders had been given
for them to anchor outside the bar and wait quietly until Kuei-liang
and others got to Peking to take charge. Fearing that as the barbarian temperament is impatient they would not be willing to wait
long, orders were also given Seng-ko-lin-ch'in and Heng-fu to have
them enter the port by way of Pei-t'ang and stay temporarily at official residences provided at Tientsin, still waiting until after Kuei-
liang and others arrived to take charge.

Unexpectedly the barbarians would not accept our communications
nor follow reasonable instructions and repeatedly removed and destroyed many of the iron defenses and other things placed in the harbor. On June 25th the barbarian ships forced entrance, initiated
hostilities and government forces could not but fight back. After
many of the barbarian ships were damaged, they still fought with
foot soldiers. Their attitude was very fierce. Our troops killed
several hundred barbarian soldiers and captured two alive [one
English, one "American", cf. IWSM. HF, ch. 38, p. 43b, line 6 in
Seng-ko-lin-ch'in's account of the fighting at Ta-ku.]; all the rest
were defeated and fled. It is estimated that the barbarian ships
which came up the river totaled 13 and only one escaped outside
the bar.

According to the testimony of the barbarian soldiers captured alive, the whole thing was the idea of the English barbarian, styled "admiral", Hope [Admiral Sir James Hope]; that on that day because a broken mast crushed his leg, Hope could not move; that at present the ships are anchored outside the bar.

The English barbarians have repudiated treaties by violence and initiated hostilities, so it is not China who has broken faith. But it is recalled that in ancient times, control of barbarians always eventuated in conciliation. If we try to use force exclusively, it will never be settled. Now while continuing Seng-ko-lin-ch'in in charge of military affairs, We are also sending Heng-fu to cooperate with Wen-yü in arranging conciliation. As the English barbarians have opened hostilities in defiance of treaties, they can hardly be reasoned with. Although the Americans and French came with them, they did not necessarily cooperate in defying authority and can still be effectively conciliated. Let them come by way of Pei-t'ang to Tientsin, stay there temporarily until Kuei-liang and the others come, and then negotiate. What the attitude of these two countries is, Heng-fu and the others have still not memorialized.

Since the English barbarians were defeated, the warships they have outside Tientsin cannot be numerous. They must have gone either to Shanghai or to Kwangtung to get more warships and come back for revenge. Order Ho Kuei-ch'ing secretly to send reliable officers to Shanghai to find out what activities there are and make secret defense plans. They are not to mention the defeat at Tientsin. If the barbarians do bring steamers to Shanghai and want to come North en masse to defy us, they can have the local Chinese merchants and the barbarian merchants say that if hostilities are renewed and the treaties negotiated last year are so much effort wasted, will it not be a shame? Ask the merchants to intercede to dissuade them or perhaps ask the American and French barbarians in Shanghai to persuade the English barbarians for them, to refrain from military acts and to wait at Tientsin for Kuei-liang and the others to make a settlement; thus all countries will benefit alike. This is also a means of preserving the peace.

But this idea must come from the merchants and cannot be divulged by officials; still less can there be a communication on this matter in advance. As Ho Kuei-ch'ing is responsible for the management of barbarian affairs, he must be notified at once if there are any developments. (IWSM.HF 39; 1a, 3-2a, 6)

423. July 1, 1859. MEMORIAL: Prince Seng-ko-lin-ch'in Reports Victory of June 25th Including the Capture of a French Flag and an "American" Prisoner of War.

Imperial Commissioners Seng-ko-lin-ch'in, Prince of Korchin, and Governor General of Chihli Heng-fu memorialize. Since the 25th

we have been fighting furiously with the barbarians night and day and
fortunately have won a complete victory. The barbarian ships which
were damaged went outside Chi-hsin-t'an and anchored for repairs.
The four vessels which were sunk all have barbarian soldiers guarding them. When our soldiers swam out to the ships the barbarians
fired rifles and cannon simultaneously and would not budge.

The night of the 27th, we sighted a number of barbarian sampans collecting ceaselessly alongside the sunken vessels all night.
The morning of the 28th, between 5 and 7 o'clock, the steamers
outside Chi-hsin-t'an spouted smoke and fire; all we could see of
the sunken vessel was the upright mast going along the surface of the
water. Apparently the barbarians were secretly using a silk line
fastened to the front ship to pull the two wheels along the bottom as
if traveling on land and they were soon outside Chi-hsin-t'an. Between 1 and 3 in the afternoon, our troops swam out and burned one
ship; many foreign cannon are being brought up to the barracks. For
three days the barbarians have only been able to squat motionless,
deadlocked with our army; they dare not invade.

On being questioned, the two captive barbarians said that Bruce
and the envoys of the various countries were on board the large
steamers anchored outside the bar, not venturing to enter on account
of the shallow water. In the battle of the 25th, a French flag was
captured and an American barbarian soldier; although the starting
of hostilities was by the English barbarians, France and America's
cooperation in the melee is also inescapable.

Examining the situation, this time the barbarians brought warships and came up the river, nominally to exchange ratifications,
actually with the intention of occupying Tientsin and using it as a
lever for coercion. If, after the government forces have soundly
thrashed them, officers were sent immediately to negotiate, under
the circumstances it would certainly be impossible (to get them)
to agree. The Tientsin tao-t'ai has been ordered to communicate
with the barbarians making everything clear and to return the captive
American barbarian, making them feel remorse by a show of
magnanimity. If there is any opportunity that can be taken advantage of, we must needs finds means to bring them around.

As to the Pei-t'ang garrison and artillery, they have just been
transferred to the barracks. If they are brought back to set up
defenses, not only will the moving be cumbersome and a useless
expenditure of energy, but also in the area behind the Pei-t'ang
forts, there are villages with private dwellings one against another,
with no strategic point where resistance could be made, so it would
not be a policy of cautious defense.

Your slaves have written Hsi-ling-a to post many scouts to
reconnoitre night and day. If barbarian ships enter Pei-t'ang they
are not to prevent their anchoring but, once they come ashore, to

lead the cavalry forces forward to block them, in order to prevent a surprise attack on our rear. They having lost the advantage of their ships and cannon, our troops can employ mobile strength and the defense of Pei-t'ang will be even more effective.

In the future barbarian chiefs entering Peking will continue to come by Pei-t'ang, so it can be reserved as the place for future conciliation.

In this conflict with barbarians, the arrangements of half a year and the unanimously heroic efforts of the troops of the various garrisons have made possible some meting out of Heaven's punishment. After gaining this voctory, army morale being even better and popular sentiment hostile, the defense of Ta-ku can naturally be expected to be increasingly effective, so as to allay Imperial anxiety.

Imperial Clansman Kuo-jui is being sent to bear this memorial to Peking. This official has served in Court and understands the present conflict personally, so can report in person in full detail.

As to the Edict authorizing the commendation of officers and men who distinguished themselves in this day's fighting, still more evidence of Your Majesty's certain recognition and discriminating reward of efforts however small, Your slaves have accordingly scrutinized carefully the various officers and men who distinguished themselves in the fighting on the 25th, respectfully made a list of them, and request Imperial decision. (IWSM. HF 39; 2a, 8-4a, 1)

424. July 1, 1859. EDICT: Commends and Rewards the Victorious Officers of Ta-ku and Authorizes Magnanimous Conciliation of the Defeated British.

Edict to the Grand Councillors. Today Kuo-jui arrived at Peking and was immediately summoned for an audience and questioned for a full description of the battle. We have also read Seng-ko-lin-ch'in and Heng-fu's memorial on the combat of the last few days with the barbarians, and the recommendations to reward outstanding officers and men. Although they report a victory of arms, the said officials are still trying to conciliate, which is eminently suitable. We are deeply relieved.

Since their defeat, the barbarians are still crouching outside the bar, in contact with our forces but not daring to move inside. On interrogation, the captured barbarians testified that Bruce and the other envoys were aboard the large steamers, all anchored outside Ta-ku. Seng-ko-lin-ch'in and others ordered the Tientsin tao-t'ai to communicate with the said barbarians, giving them explicit instructions to utilize the captive American barbarian to deliver their messages, in an attempt to bring them around. He also sent a communication to Hsi-ling-a saying that, if the barbarian ships came to Pei-t'ang, he was not to prevent them from anchoring but as soon as they came ashore, to lead out his cavalry and cut them off.

What the said officials have done is in exact conformity with
Our previously issued Edicts. Order them to take such action as
occasion demands in the hope of an early termination of the matter.

Seng-ko-lin-ch'in, in charge of coastal defense, has arranged
everything carefully regardless of the effort and fatigue involved.
Order a preliminary gift of one pair of Imperially-used snuff bottles
and one pair of watches to be carried back by Kuo-jui for Seng-ko-
lin-ch'in's respectful acceptance. His recommendations for ele-
vation in rank, for award of peacock feathers, and for field promotions are all to be carried out as proposed. Honors for (Prince)
La-mu-kun-pu-cha-pu will be promulgated by separate Edict after
the conclusion of affairs.

Matters which have not been promulgated can be transmitted
orally after Kuo-jui reaches Tientsin. The captive American barbarian has already been utilized to carry communications for us.
See how the barbarians reply and if they show any inclination to
swing around. If they do not reply at all, it may mean that all three
countries are equally arrogant. Order them by all means to weigh
the situation carefully and then determine what action should be
taken.   (IWSM. HF 30; 1a, 0 5a, 1)

425. July 2, 1859. MEMORIAL: Prince Seng-ko-lin-ch'in Reports
the Arrival of Ward at Pei-t'ang and Preparations to Open Negotiations
with him.

Imperial Commissioner Seng-ko-lin-ch'in, Prince of Korchin,
memorializes. At present the ships previously damaged are still
anchored at the bar. As there had been no activity for several days,
Your slave, with Heng-fu and Wen-yü, originally proposed on the 29th
(June), to have the captive American barbarian returned in advance,
in order to get some news of the barbarians.

Then early on that day one barbarian ship was sighted sailing
northward. By mid-morning (9-11) it reached the port of Pei-t'ang.
Then according to the findings of the cavalry led by Hsi-ling-a, that
day at a place called Ch'eng-t'ou-ku northwest of Pei-t'ang, a sampan appeared with 8 barbarians aboard. Three of them came ashore
and wanted to go to the village. Seeing that there were government
troops, they went back on board. The government troops picked up
a document of the American barbarians in Chinese character addressed to Governor General Ch'ing[3] and five name cards and
speedily turned them in at the garrison.

Your slave consulted with Heng-fu and ordered a reply sent by

---

3 The addresse of this American note has not been identified. Williams refers to
him as "Governor General King", *op. cit.*, p. 130-131. The governor general of
Chihli at this time was the Manchu, Heng-fu.

the <u>tao-t'ai</u> of Tientsin; he also delegated officials to prepare rice, flour, pork, mutton, and other foodstuffs and take them from Pei-t'ang out to the vessel occupied by the American barbarians outside the bar, as an evidence of hospitality. Whether or not the barbarians are amenable to conciliation will be respectfully memorialized when the delegates return.

It is now proposed to postpone temporarily the return of the American barbarian. The captive English barbarian is seriously wounded. It is proposed to guard them both carefully and Huang Hui-lien has been ordered to fraternize with them as a plan of inducing them to conciliate (for us).

On this occasion of the barbarians coming to Tientsin, the large cannon carried on the warships were very numerous and they were wilfully reckless; certainly (they were) not really intent on friendship, nor is it certain that they were not designing to occupy Tientsin as another plan of coercion. The battle of the 25th has just been fought. If we talk peace with them now, just when the barbarians are resentful, they are certain not to accept our silken bonds; while even if we force them into conciliation it is certain not to be secure or permanent.

Now since the American barbarian ship is at Pei-t'ang, it is they who are coming to us and they may be somewhat easier to handle. It is Your slave's humble opinion that the barbarian nature is inscrutable. If at this time Heng-fu and Wen-yü were to go promptly to Pei-t'ang and there were any negligence, it would involve national prestige; so it would seem necessary to wait until the deputies return to the garrison, calculate the barbarian situation carefully, and then determine the place for negotiations. Moreover, just after the rupture we must be doubly cautious. If we once stoop down, the barbarians are sure to become arrogant again.

We have finally come to the conclusion that in conciliation, the slower the better. Therefore, (Your slave) personally ordered Heng-fu and the others to postpone going and wait for news of the deputies, vigilantly directing the troops to maintain defences suitably, in order to prevent the barbarians from hatching other schemes. If the barbarians are transferring troops from Kwangtung and Shanghai to Tientsin, steamers are so fast that it would not take long. At present, on the one hand, we are pushing conciliation and on the other, repairing fortifications. Your slave is transferring the cannon set up at Shuang-kang to the garrison; also the cannon brought from Tientsin and Peking as well as captured barbarian cannon are all set in position, so defenses seem adequate.

In accord with Edict, Heng-fu has further transferred 500 government troops from the governor general's garrison and encamped them at Hsin-ho to relieve the north bank of Ta-ku. When the Kuei-hua and Sui-yüan troops reach Tientsin, it is proposed to send them to Shuang-kang. When the Eight Banners' cannon arrive from Wu-ch'eng and Yung-ku they will also be set up there to form the back line of Ta-ku.

On the 25th, Provincial Commander-in-chief Shih Jung-ch'un, at the central fort on the south bank, and Colonel Lung Ju-yüan of the Ta-ku Brigade, at the front fort on the south bank, led troops in attack. The said commander and colonel both led their men personally and fired the cannon themselves and, when shot from barbarian ships fell in the fort, were killed in action.

The ten large ships of English Chief Bruce are still anchored together outside the bar, which is duly memorialized in addition. We have also had the barbarian communication, as well as the reply which he ordered the Tientsin tao-t'ai to send, copied and respectfully presented for Imperial Inspection.

Vermilion endorsement: Execution completely satisfactory. (IWSM.HF 39; 6a, 8-8a, 4)

426. July 2, 1859. AMERICAN NOTE: Ward Formally Requests Transportation from Tientsin to enable him to Exchange Ratifications at Peking.

By way of communication: Whereas the present minister has respectfully received appointment from the Great President, bears his autograph credentials respectfully to present to His Majesty the Great Emperor of China, and also personally received his instructions to present his expression of sincere friendship to the Court of this honorable country; on arrival at Shanghai he notified Imperially Commissioned Plenipotentiaries Kuei, Hua, Ho, and Tuan and asked to come to the Capital to exchange the treaties drawn up at Tientsin. Article 5 of said treaty states that for the American minister's passage from the port of Tientsin to Peking, carts, horses, men, official residences, services, etc., will all be prepared by local officials of the various places along the way. Now the present minister on board the steam warship Powhatan has anchored outside the port and ventures to ask the honorable minister, in accord with the treaty, to order the preparation of everything en route to enable the present minister and his suite to set out immediately for the capital city. Hoping for a prompt reply, this is by way of communication and it is duly communicated. (IWSM.HF 39; 8a, 5-8b, 8)

527. July 2, 1859. CHINESE NOTE IN REPLY: Governor General Heng-fu Acknowledges Ward's Note, Presents Gifts, and Offers him Escort to Peking.

Communication to the Americans. By way of communication: June 30, the honorable country's state paper to His Excellency the Governor General was communicated from Pei-t'ang and it was

learned that the honorable country's Imperially Commissioned barge
had arrived at the port of Tientsin. An Edict of His Imperial Majesty had been received ordering His Excellencies the Governor General and the Financial Commissioner to look after the honorable
country's commissioner's trip from Pei-t'ang to Peking to exchange
ratifications. The present tao-t'ai having made preparations for
sending official gifts, presents them on board the state barge and
begs their acceptance. This is by way of communication. (IWSM.
HF 39; 8b, 9-9a, 4)

428. July 2, 1859. MEMORIAL: Governor General Heng-fu Reports
Plans to Receive Ward at Pei-t'ang and Escort him to Peking.

Governor General of Chihli Heng-fu memorializes. Your slave
proposed going to Pei-t'ang with Financial Commissioner Wen-yü.
Just when he was packing up to leave, Seng-ko-lin-ch'in (decided), as
barbarians are naturally inscrutable, to wait until the return of the
officers sent by the Tientsin tao-t'ai to deliver a communication and
provisions to the American barbarians and then go, as that minister
has memorialized under his own signature.

Your slave humbly thinks that the control of outside barbarians
ultimately reverts to conciliation. Truly as Sacred Edict says, how
can the issue be terminated by force alone? Whatever official
residences it was necessary to prepare in Tientsin and all their needs
en route, the local officials have been ordered duly to prepare. Now
the communication submitted by the American barbarians is ante-
dated the 24th, before the hostilities. Whether or not this involves
fear or possibly some more chicanery is practically unfathomable;
nevertheless, (Your slave) hopes that once he gets them under control, he can utilize the situation to swing them around, in order to
stabilize general conditions.

As soon as the officers return and there is definite news of the
barbarians' reaction on receipt of the tao-t'ai's communication, Your
slave, together with Financial Commissioner Wen-yü, will proceed
immediately to Pei-t'ang. If the barbarian temper is amenable to
conciliation, in accordance with Edict he will either send officers to
interview them or send a communication saying that treaty affairs
must wait until after Kuei-liang and the others arrive, before there
can be an exchange, thus hoping to act as opportunity offers to involve them temporarily and hold them until Kuei-liang and the others
get to Peking and take over.

As to the one American barbarian and the one English barbarian
(prisoners), orders are being sent the Tientsin tao-t'ai to send officers to guard them properly, give them food and drink, and keep
them as a basis for conciliation.

The English barbarian chief, Bruce, according to the testimony
of the captive barbarians, is still outside the bar and there are

altogether ten ships anchored as before. There is still no activity.
Vermilion endorsement: Noted. (IWSM. IIF 39; 9a, 5-10a, 1)

429. July 3, 1859. MEMORIAL: Two Court Officials Deplore Ward's
Reception in Peking and Urge Stringent Precautions against Espionage.
   (President of the Board of War) Ch'uan-ch'ing and (Superinten-
dent of Government Granaries) Lien Chao-lun further memorialize.
The official residences just now being selected in Tientsin are reported to be the places prepared for the barbarians coming from
Pei-t'ang to Peking.
   (Your officials) make bold to think that to come to Peking from
Pei-t'ang, there is no necessity of coming by way of Tientsin. Now
we even prepare residences for them! To what extent will the barbarians' nefarious cunning not go? They may, after getting to Tientsin, prolong their stay to spy out our military affairs, or perhaps on
the pretext of sightseeing, send someone direct to the Ta-ku area
to ascertain our position. At that time we cannot allow them nor
can we stop them and as Tientsin, with the exception of the Ta-ku
crack troops, has not much defense, once this is detected it will be
a serious matter.
   Besides the barbarian temperament is most suspicious and most
crafty, and when they come to Peking they will not necessarily be
amenable to our restraint and bring a small suite, so unless troops
are placed strategically, they will certainly be inadequate to ward
them off or to rely on for suppression. If Heavenly Favor does grant
them audience, preparations for their entrance to Peking from Tientsin must be even more stringent than for meeting a strong enemy.
As for "treating courteously while showing prowess," one must preclude the development of perverse ideas before one can sincerely
make friends. After all, the natures of scorpions and wolves can
never be treated with human reason.
   Vermilion endorsement: Seen. Before the battle, defenses are
indispensable; when the battle is over, even greater care is required,
but not the slightest evidence of it must be revealed. (IWSM. HF 39;
13b, 7-14a, 9)

430. July 5, 1859. MEMORIAL: Heng-fu Reports Contact with S.
Wells Williams at Ta-ku and Suspicions of American Collusion with the
British.
   Heng-fu further memorializes. On the 2d, between 7 and 9 in the
evening. Lieutenant Jen Lien-sheng returned to Ta-ku and reported
personally that on the first, he was unable to go out on account of a
high wind. Early on the second, he did get outside the bar. The
American barbarian steamer is anchored alongside the ships of the
other barbarians. When the said officer presented the document,
the barbarian soldiers stood in formation on board the ship and

ordered the said officer to wait more than an hour. Only then did they receive the pigs, sheep, and other things. They gave him a communication in Chinese character and a red name card. According to appearances, it would seem that they secretly exchange information with the English barbarians. They also agreed orally to go to Pei-t'ang on the fifth for an interview.

Your slave and Financial Commissioner Wen-yü scrutinized it together and it is a communication from the American barbarian vice-minister in charge of translations, Williams, to the Tientsin tao-t'ai; the contents correspond with the report of Jen Lien-sheng.

In our humble opinion, the English barbarians provoked trouble and so after this punishment can hardly show their face. If the American barbarians are really willing to accept conciliation and go to Peking to exchange ratifications, Your slaves will treat them courteously and find means to involve them. If we can get them under our thumb, France's wavering position can possibly be recovered and England's arrogance will be isolated. While there is any opportunity that can be exploited, we must needs try to manage accordingly. But these barbarians' ships are alongside those of the English barbarians and they secretly exchange news. Besides, these barbarians asked the officer orally about the report that at present it is Prince Seng at the head of the troops stationed at the port of Ta-ku.

On the fifth they intend to come aboard a steamer and asked us to send an experienced pilot to lead them into port. Whether or not they are actually coming to exchange ratifications or if there is some other scheme, can hardly be determined definitely. Your slave agreed with Financial Commissioner Wen-yü to add to the communication that at Pei-t'ang the water is shallow and that his country's ships could hardly enter port; that on the fifth, officers would be sent to prepare boats to receive them. This communication we likewise sent Lieutenant Jen Lien-sheng to go to their ship and deliver and again make careful observations.

Financial Commissioner Wen-yü will proceed to Pei-t'ang on the third to make suitable arrangements. Your slave proposes on the fourth to go to Hsin-ho and wait until the fifth, when he will meet the barbarians. If the barbarians marshall troops to come ashore, our army will receive them in formation to augment prestige. If the barbarians do not bring many men and the steamers do not enter port, we must needs order the troops to disguise themselves and keep our defenses secret. Eventually we hope to be prepared for anything without giving any outward evidence, in order to maintain a policy of conciliation.

Vermilion endorsement: Memorial read and understood fully.
(IWSM. HF 39; 15b, 3-16b, 5)

431. <u>July 5, 1859.</u> EDICT: <u>Orders Military Preparations at Ta-ku Against Allied Treachery in connection with the Ward Negotiations at Pei-t'ang.</u>

Edict to the Grand Councillors. . . . Heng-fu separately memorializes that he has arranged an interview with the American barbarian chief on the fifth at Pei-t'ang. Barbarians are naturally crafty and violent and it is not certain they can be brought under our thumb.

Order the said governor general to go back to Ta-ku after the interview and discuss plans with Seng-ko-lin-ch'in. (IWSM.HF 39; 16b, 6. . . 17a, 4-6)

432. <u>July 5, 1859.</u> AMERICAN NOTE: <u>S. Wells Williams Acknowledges Gifts and Sets Date for Ward's Interview at Pei-t'ang on July 5th.</u>

By way of communication: June 30 one official document and one lot of official gifts was received from the honorable tao-t'ai for which there is infinite gratitude. Now are received orders from his country's envoy extraordinary and minister plenipotentiary resident in China, Ward, to reply, giving notice that on the fifth of the present month, he will meet His Excellency the Governor General of Chihli Ch'ing on shore at Pei-t'ang and asks that a pilot thoroughly familiar with the Pei-t'ang channel be sent to guide this country's steamer into the port, which it is hoped will be granted. This by way of necessary communication. (IWSM.HF 39; 17a, 7-17b, 3)

433. <u>July 5, 1859.</u> CHINESE NOTE IN REPLY: <u>Heng-fu Presents China's Case Against Great Britain and Arrangements for the Pei-t'ang Interview on July 5th.</u>

By way of communication: June 30 an Imperially authorized communication was received by way of Pei-t'ang and it was learned for the first time that the honorable country's Imperial Commissioner was traveling by ship and had reached port.

The present governor general previously respectfully received His Imperial Majesty's Edict to take charge of the various honorable countries' Imperial Commissioners coming to Peking by way of Pei-t'ang to exchange ratifications and on June 25, sent a communication to Imperial Commissioner Bruce of Great Britain, as is on record. Just then was received a reply from Great Britain's First Chinese Secretary Wade. Without waiting for a delegate to deliver the communication, they had the warships open fire and start hostilities.

When the present governor general heard this he was surprised beyond measure, because he was mindful that the coming of Great Britain's Imperial Commissioner was for the purpose of entering Peking to exchange ratifications, not to make trouble. Our country's defense of Ta-ku was originally to repress the countryside, nor was there any other motive. So the present governor general received Imperial Orders to direct the provincial treasurer to take charge of all arrangements for the entrance of the Imperial Commissioners of the honorable countries to Peking by way of Pei-t'ang, but the Imperial Commissioner of Great Britain insisted on going to Ta-ku and, destroying the fortifications at the bar, conceived the idea of browbeating. In this, the right and wrong, true and false, must be clear to all.

Now the communication received from your honorable country's Imperial Commissioner proposes entrance to Peking to exchange ratifications. The present governor general has directed the financial commissioner to instruct the local officials to prepare carts, horses, bearers, and post-houses, duly taking care of everything. Whether the honorable Imperial Commissioner stays on board ship or in Pei-t'ang, he will wait until our country's Imperial Commissioners, Grand Secretary Kuei and President of the Board of Civil Office Hua, arrive at Tientsin; they will arrange with the honorable Imperial Commissioners for entrance to Peking and exchange of ratifications. As our country and the honorable country are known to be friendly without any differences, the Financial Commissioner must needs be directed respectfully to receive Imperial orders and make suitable arrangements.

Just when the communication was posted, July 2, the Tientsin tao-t'ai presented an official document from the vice minister of the United States of America officially appointed to reside in China, concurrently in charge of translations, Williams, notifying us that the honorable Imperial Commissioner set the fifth of this month for an interview with the present governor general at Pei-t'ang and we were very pleased.

It is pointed out that the harbor at Pei-t'ang is shallow and the honorable country's ships will find it difficult to enter. On that date Lieutenant Jen Lien-sheng will be sent to prepare ships to meet the honorable Imperial Commissioner and conduct him to Pei-t'ang for the interview. As our two countries are peaceful, they ask him as a token of old friendship not to bring a large retinue to avoid agitating the residents. This is most essential.

This is a necessary communication. (IWSM. HF 39; 17b, 4-18b, 9)

434. July 5, 1859. MEMORIAL: Prince Seng-ko-lin-ch'in Approves the Pei-t'ang Meeting with Ward but Warns Against a New Allied Ruse.

Imperial Commissioner Seng-ko-lin-ch'in, Prince of Kor'chin, memorializes. After being chastised, the barbarians stood off for several days; then the American chief John Ward presented a communication. Governor General Heng-fu first ordered Tientsin Tao-t'ai Sun Chih to answer him and then ordered Financial Commissioner Wen-yü to proceed to Pei-t'ang to keep him occupied and, on the other hand, sent a communication to the American chief to come to Peking by way of Pei-t'ang to exchange ratifications. He also agreed to an

interview on the fifth. It is reported that the American chief has
been tractable and can perhaps be managed according to Edict; but
whether or not he is allied with the English barbarians and is being
managed by them, cannot as yet be determined.

As the plan of the defenses of Pei-t'ang is the same as Ta-ku,
Your slave has withdrawn the soldiers from the fortifications lest
the barbarians come in to spy and be enabled to ascertain the situation at Ta-ku. Thus, laying land mines inside the camp and locking
the gate, he ordered the guards to notify the barbarians and prevent
their entering.

Heng-fu, in sole charge of pacification, cannot but confer with
the barbarian chief; but as the Pei-t'ang garrison, adjoining the barbarian ships, is withdrawn, some carelessness is feared so he must
reside at Ta-ku and fix a date for meeting. The distance is not great
and he can go back and forth to negotiate. Above all let us have a
plan for controlling barbarians so these barbarians will not take
advantage of our weak spots. This is best.

This time the English barbarians have been punished and their
resentment must be deep. Most of the barbarian warships which
came up the river were damaged. They are sure to go to Kwangtung and Shanghai, collect warships, and plan revenge. As the
American and French barbarians are in the same category, they may
pretend to make peace with us and dampen our military zeal in order
secretly to advance their schemes, so we cannot be too apprehensive.
Your slave has expressed a communication to the governor general
of Liang-chiang, notifying him that many barbarian ships have been
destroyed and the barbarians defeated and dispersed; if he learns of
any barbarian ships coming north to let him know by fast mail.

The Ta-ku fortifications are somewhat damaged and have been
ordered repaired immediately, hoping by arousing martial spirit
and rigorously managing defenses to forestall the revenge of the barbarian ships, not daring, because plans of conciliation are in progress
at Pei-t'ang, to relax our main objective.

On the twenty-fifth, we sank four barbarian ships; the barbarians
recovered one from the bottom, our troops burned one and bombarded
the other two for several days, completely destroying them, nor are
there any barbarian soldiers stationed outside the chain blockade on
guard. Our troops have salvaged seven cannon of various sizes from
the water and mounted them on the fortress wall. These cannon weigh
three or four thousand catties. [4] There are large cannon of ten
thousand catties and up, which we sent sailors to salvage. If (these
salvage crews) are attacked or resisted by the barbarians, or if the
barbarians come secretly to seize the cannon, our troops will in turn

---

4 One cattie (*chin*) is equivalent to one and one-third pounds avoirdupois.

open fire and attack.

Outside Ch'i-hsin-nan we attacked and damaged eight barbarian ships. The barbarians worked all day to repair them, first righting two ships and sailing them outside the bar. Between 5 and 7 the afternoon of the third, pulling each ship in front and pushing behind, they rode the tide out, and shortly they were all outside the bar. The ships at anchor total 17 or 18. This accounts for the barbarian ships successively withdrawing outside the bar.

This time the barbarians have been chastized and suffered humiliation. The proposal to go to Peking to exchange ratifications was primarily a ruse which perhaps we can eventually intercept. The American chief has sent two communications, both to Governor General Ch'ing, by name and rank, so their deliberate indirection is apparent, nor are they sincerely seeking peace. Eventually they may augment their warships and again foment trouble. We can only wait for some later clue and then memorialize.

Vermilion endorsement: Your fears are certainly apt. We are only waiting until after today's interview between the governor general and the American chief when We can get the whole picture, to give a detailed Edict for you to follow. (IWSM. HF 39; 19b, 9-21b, 2)

435. July 6, 1859. EDICT: Approves Arrangements for Pei-t'ang Meeting and Orders the Shanghai Commissioners to Peking for the Exchange of Ratifications.

Edict to the Grand Councillors. ...Now it is reported that the American barbarians have sent someone to Pei-t'ang, presented a communication, and Heng-fu and Wen-yü have set the fifth for an interview with them at Pei-t'ang. At present we have not received any memorial from Heng-fu et al.

If the American barbarians are willing to bring them around for us, they can manage as circumstances warrant. If those barbarians are not willing to enter port by way of Pei-t'ang, it is virtually impossible to remove the defenses and allow them to come in by way of Ta-ku. Besides, battle has been joined and present circumstances. are not the same as previous negotiations.

Let Kuei-liang and the others first order Hsüeh Huan and Huang Chung-yü to go direct to Tientsin and wait at Seng-ko-lin-ch'in's headquarters for further orders for their disposition as the Commissioners see fit. Kuei-liang and the others are still to hurry back to Peking. No matter who arrives first, order him to memorialize and be prepared for an Imperial Audience to receive personal instructions on policy. (IWSM. HF 39; 22a, 9...22b, 7-23a, 3)

436. July 6, 1859. EDICT: Authorizes Ward's Coming to Peking if he is Unwilling to Exchange Ratifications at Pei-t'ang and Anticipates Mediation with Bruce.

Additional Edict. Yesterday was received Heng-fu's memorial that the fifth was set for an interview with the American chief at Pei-t'ang. Order was given for the said governor general, after the interview, to return to Ta-ku and consult with Seng-ko-lin-ch'in on the results of the meeting with the chief. It is assumed that the commissioners have memorialized and are en route.

Today Kuei-liang and others memorialize that they have decided to have Hsüeh Huan, accompanied by Expectant District Magistrate Huang Chung-yü, proceed from Ho-chien direct to Tientsin. They are also sending a special delivery communication to Tientsin for Seng-ko-lin-ch'in and the others to transmit to the barbarians, in order to quiet their minds. They also say that barbarians are naturally very suspicious and to make them wait long at the port is inadviseable under the circumstances. They ask to order Heng-fu and others to explain clearly to the barbarians and allow all those who are going to Peking to exchange ratifications, to go to Tientsin first and reside outside the city wall. Have the others wait quietly outside the bar. As for anchoring near Pei-t'ang, in all probability these bar barians will not be willing to proceed by that route and it would seem necessary to consult (with them) and act accordingly.

What they memorialize must have been written before they knew that the barbarians had opened hostilities. The situation is not what it was. When Hsüeh Huan and Huang Chung-yü shall have reached Tientsin, have them await commission at Seng-ko-lin-ch'in's headquarters. Whether or not the communication they sent coincides with present developments must also be determined before it is submitted.

As soon as the barbarians reach the port, have them proceed to Tientsin via Pei-t'ang and remain temporarily outside the city-wall, quietly awaiting Kuei-liang and the others. Now the barbarians have disobeyed Imperial Edict and precipitated fighting. At the time Kuei-liang and the others memorialized, they still feared that the barbarians would not be willing to proceed via Pei-t'ang and proposed to take counsel and act accordingly; the idea still being to have them go to Tientsin via Ta-ku. This was an impossibly excessive compromise, in ignorance of the present violence of the barbarians. It is even more essential to intensify our defense. How can we destroy our own barriers to please the enemy?

Now the American chief is willing to go to Pei-t'ang for an interview with Heng-fu. If his attitude discloses that he is also willing to bring the English chief around or that France and America are willing to exchange ratifications first, order the governor general to instruct Wen-yü to take advantage of the situation to draw them out. As the

French barbarian sided with evil, we can only pretend ignorance to get him into our provenance first, isolating the English chief. Then management will be a simple matter. As to coming to Peking, if the American chief does not bring it up first, do not propose it to him. When Kuei-liang and the others shall have arrived it will be time enough to speak. (IWSM. HF 39; 23a, 5-24a, 3)

437. July 7, 1859. MEMORIAL: Heng-fu Reports Postponement of the Pei-t'ang Interview to July 8th and Presents Evidence of American Belligerency at Ta-ku.

Governor General of Chihli Heng-fu memorializes. Between 3 and 5 on the morning of the fifth, Your slave, accompanied by Financial Commissioner Wen-yü, as well as the tao-t'ai's of T'ung-Yung, Tientsin, and Ch'ing-ho, and followed by various civil and military officers, went from Ta-ku to Pei-t'ang to wait on the said barbarians for an interview. Seng-ko-lin-ch'in dispatched 500 government cavalrymen and Your slave sent 400 men from his garrison to the region around Pei-t'ang and, without making any outward show, took rigorous defense measures. Hostels to receive the barbarians were suitably arranged. They repeatedly sent officers and men to mount the lookouts, but no barbarian sail was seen.

At five o'clock in the afternnon, Jen Lien-sheng finally returned to Pei-t'ang and reported that because on the fourth the weather was unfavorable, he could not get there. Early on the fifth he finally reached the barbarian ship and delivered the communication. The barbarians asked to set the eighth, and to arrange inland boats to meet them and pilot the barbarians' one steamer into port; if the harbor depth was insufficient to float it, to let them know where they could anchor; that they could not tarry at Pei-t'ang but would proceed to Peking to exchange ratifications. They also asked when Kuei-liang and the others could be there and said that in the recent fighting, their chief had energetically opposed England and France to avoid breaking off friendly relations, but England and France, relying on their force, would not listen to persuasion. Then they produced a communication in reply and gave it to the said officer to bring back.

Your slave and Wen-yü opened and read it together. The purport was about the same as what the officer reported. As the said barbarians had already changed the date there was nothing to do but wait for them, so Your slave took the financial commissioner and the rest and went back to Ta-ku.

He ventures to think that when the American barbarian, John Ward, previously proposed coming to Pei-t'ang on the fifth for an interview, Your slave sent a communication to the said barbarian either to remain on board ship or to stay in Pei-t'ang until Kuei-liang and the others reached Tientsin to discuss the matter of going to Peking to exchange ratifications. Now comes this barbarian's letter and his statement to Jen Lien-sheng. There is still no answer to that document but he still wants to go to Peking. His determination is very fixed.

Your slave consulted wholeheartedly with Wen-yü. Although the American barbarian's expressions are respectful and compliant and he has never been tyrannical or proud, in the battle on the twenty-fifth, American barbarian ships certainly burst into the port at the same time as those of England and France, as the captured American barbarian John Powers'[15] deposition can verify. Now the barbarian falsifies the date of a communication and also says he energetically opposed England and France to cover up his share in the plot. Whether this is because, since Seng-ko-lin-ch'in defeated them, he fears our martial might or that he has some other scheme, it is rather difficult to believe him. Besides in going to Peking via Pei-t'ang on the eighth, the date is too close. It is hard to be sure that he is not harboring some coercive intent under cover of a peace move.

At present how far have Kuei-liang and the others come? Your slave and Seng-ko-lin-ch'in previously wrote by 600 li post and to date have not received a reply. We are daily impatiently watching.

(Your slave) is proposing in a communication to the said barbarian to interview him at Pei-t'ang on the eighth and have him wait awhile for news of the arrival of Kuei-liang and the others at Tien-tsin. But whether or not this barbarian can be got to take orders and let us manage him is still hard to guess.

As to the number of his retinue, in the barbarian's communication he says he will bring along a few subordinates; he also told Jen Lien-sheng personally that he would bring subordinates and servants totaling thirty-odd persons. If the barbarian is sincerely conciliatory, naturally he cannot bring barbarian soldiers; but he still wants his steamer to anchor in Pei-t'ang harbor, so complete restraint and investigation must be applied with double care. There cannot be the least bit of negligence.

The said barbarian's communication and also Your slave's communication to the barbarian, John Ward, are both copied and respectfully presented for Imperial scrutiny. If the said barbarian is unwilling to wait, whether or not to allow him to proceed to Peking, an Edict is requested for guidance. (IWSM.HF 39; 24a, 4-25b, 8)

438. July 7, 1859. EDICT: Authorizes Heng-fu to Arrange Ward's Visit to Peking for Exchange of Ratifications and Hopes to Alienate

---

5 John Powers, one of the two British captives, was a Canadian by birth who said he had claimed to be an American for the purpose of "getting clear". Williams, "Journal", op. cit., p. 205.

France from Great Britain.

Edict to the Grand Councillors. Heng-fu memorializes that he has received a communication from the American barbarians requesting permission to come to Peking and that he proposes to restrain them temporarily. On the fifth, Heng-fu was unable to interview the American barbarian. The said barbarian sent a communication asking him to arrange for boats to meet him on the eighth; after reaching Pei-t'ang he would proceed to Peking to exchange ratifications. He also said that he would be accompanied by several subordinates.

As the American barbarians want to come to Peking to exchange ratifications, it is not necessary to obstruct them too much and thus arouse their suspicions. He needs merely to say that Kuei-liang and the others have not reached Peking and they are either to wait at Pei-t'ang or, if they want to go direct to Peking, they will have to wait there until after Kuei-liang and the others arrive before they can exchange ratifications. As the said barbarian is desirous of bringing a few followers and coming to Peking first, the governor general will send one tao-t'ai and one lieutenant colonel to conduct them, take proper care of them, and escort them to Peking.

As to the French barbarians, although they joined the English barbarians in the invasion, we can still affect ignorance, so order Heng-fu and the others to send them a communication saying that he hears that the said country's ships have also arrived outside the bar, that the American barbarians are being allowed to come to Peking to exchange ratifications, that this time it is only the English barbarians who have without justification caused trouble and violated the peace. China has not broken faith. He thinks that France is certainly unwilling to repdudiate treaties and she can either exchange ratifications with America or wait until the English affair has been settled and exchange them with that country.

Send this sort of a communication and see how they reply. Also make it clear in the communication to the French barbarians that they are to wait until Kuei-liang and the others have reached Peking before arrangements are made; that Kuei-liang and the others will reach Peking sometime after the nineteenth of this month.

To ensure complete restraint and investigation when the American barbarians anchor at Pei-t'ang, Seng-ko-lin-ch'in and the others must make rigorous defense plans as usual. Let there not be the least bit of negligence. (IWSM. HF 39; 25b, 9-26b, 3)

439. July 7, 1859. CHINESE NOTE TO THE AMERICANS: Heng-fu Accepts July 8th Interview with Ward and Anticipates Kuei-liang's Return from Shanghai.

By way of communication: This is to acknowledge the communication of July 5th of the honorable country's Imperial commissioner,

changing to the eighth of this month the date of coming to Pei-t'ang.
The present governor general naturally must, as agreed, order the
local officials on the eighth to prepare boats and go to the entrance
to the bar and receive the honorable country's commissioner coming
to Pei-t'ang for an interview.

As to entering Peking, a Rescript was previously received ordering Grand Secretary Kuei and President of the Board of Civil Office
Hua to come to Tientsin from Shanghai, to arrange with the honorable
country's commissioner a date for coming to Peking and, at the appointed time, prepare all necessary carts, horses, bearers, and
hostels. The present governor general naturally must obey this Rescript and with the financial commissioner take suitable charge. By
way of communication. This is a necessary communication. (IWSM.
HF 39; 26b, 4-27a, 1)

440. July 7, 1859. AMERICAN NOTE: Ward Accepts July 8th for
Meeting at Pei-t'ang and Specifies Immediate Departure for Peking.

By way of reply: Acknowledging the honorable governor general's letter of July 3, the contents have been read in full. The present
minister, on July 8, between 11 and 1 o'clock, accompanied by a few
subordinates, will proceed to Pei-t'ang and thence to Peking. He is
desirous that all traveling requisites shall have been prepared, enabling the present minister and suite to set out on the journey.

Previously at Shanghai he was informed specifically by Imperial
Commissioners Grand Secretary Kuei and President of the Board of
Civil Office Hua that dignitaries were certain to be at Tientsin to receive him. Therefore the present minister sees no necessity for
suspicion or delay. It is his real and sincere hope that he may set
out at once as previously granted. This by way of reply. This is a
necessary communication. (IWSM.HF 39; 27a, 2-9)

441. July 9, 1859. EDICT: Orders Reception of the Russian Mission
by the Li Fan Yüan--Traditional Agency for Dealing with Tributary States.

Edict to the Grand Secretariat. Now Russia is sending an envoy
to Peking. Order President of the Board of Revenue in charge of the
affairs of the Bureau of Dependencies Su-shun and President of the
Board of Punishments Jui-ch'ang to arrange a date to meet the said
envoy. (IWSM.HF 39; 27b, 1-2)

442. July 11, 1859. MEMORIAL: Heng-fu Reports Meeting at Pei-
t'ang and Ward's Willingness to Ride in a Cart and to Await the Arrival
of Kuei-liang.

Governor General of Chihli Heng-fu and Financial Commissioner
Wen-yü memorialize. Between 3 and 5 on the morning of the eighth,
Your slaves with various civil and military officers, at the head of
two divisions of Mongol cavalry comprising 500 men and 400 men

from the governor general's garrison, proceeded to Pei-t'ang. Lieutenant Jen Lien-sheng had been sent ahead to prepare private ships to
meet them at the edge of the bar.

Then the barbarian chief arrived on board a private ship towing
two small sampans and came ashore between 9 and 11. The said barbarian saw carts and horses prepared on shore and was unwilling to
mount because he had brought along one green cloth sedan chair and
one blue cloth sedan chair. He demanded of Lieutenant Jen Lien-
sheng sixteen chair bearers so that his country's envoy and the admiral could ride. Your slaves then sent First Class Sub-prefect of
Kuang-p'ing-fu Po-to-hung-wu and Expectant Department Magistrate
Ts'ao Ta-shou to go and say that just now the port was run down and
there were no bearers, so all military and civil officials including
the governor general were to ride horseback. When the chief and the
others heard this they came ashore, mounted horses, and came.

Your slaves met them altogether at the hostel. They are the
American envoy, John Ward, the admiral, Chief Tattnall, and Chief
Interpreter and Assistant Envoy Williams. The interpreter said on
Ward's behalf that he had received his sovereign's order to bear his
credentials to Peking and to exchange ratifications. He arrived at
Shanghai June 3rd and met Kuei-liang and Hua-sha-na twice, then set
sail and on June 21st reached the port of Ta-ku. It had already been
more than half a month, so he would take advantage of the bearers
and horses prepared and go to Peking to exchange ratifications.

Your slaves then said that Kuei-liang and the others had set out
from Shanghai and could arrive within a month; also that they were
reported to have sent Kiangsu Judicial Commissioner Hsüeh Huan
to take care of them, so they could rest assured and wait quietly.

The said chief said that due to stormy seas he could hardly remain long, so wished to go to Peking first and wait. He also said
that he would take only twenty subordinates and ten secretaries and
servants to Peking. All the rest would wait on board ship.

Your slave said that he would have to wait until we asked for an
Edict and then send another communication. The said chief acquiesced, but repeatedly asked the date. Your slaves replied, at
latest not more than ten days. The barbarian added that with the
strong wind and spring tide their large steamer could remain outside the bar, but their small steamer should anchor at the mouth
of the Pei-t'ang river to be protected from storms; that the soldiers
on board would go out themselves and buy all their foodstuffs.

Your slaves said that since there was peace, there was no objection to the small steamer anchoring in the river but the soldiers
could not go ashore on their own authority; that in the local forts
and camps there were ambushes set to protect the locality and in all
probability his followers would get into camps by mistake and be injured; that the local officials would not assume the responsibility.

As to all foodstuffs, the officials could procure and send them. The barbarian agreed not to let the barbarian soldiers go ashore. So much for the American barbarian's desire to conciliate.

As to the English barbarians' repudiation of Imperial Edict and opening of hostilities, Your slaves questioned him closely. Why did they reject our communication? Why would foodstuffs not be accepted? Since they were together he must know the details. Our China treated people with sincerity and trust and never took up arms recklessly, out of compassion, but for years His Imperial Majesty's gracious treatment of England had been more than generous. Now in permitting them to come to Peking to exchange ratifications, since Ta-ku and Pei-t'ang are equi-distant, what was the objection? Besides as they were coming to exchange ratifications and the motive was peaceful, what was the reason for destroying our defenses and attacking our forts? The crooked and straight, right and wrong in this should be clear to all.

The said chief replied that although he had not seen the communication presented on the twenty-fifth, he knew there was one. As for England and France, since they were not actually at Pei-t'ang, they insisted on going via Ta-ku and therefore clashed with government troops. Now the English envoy had set sail on the sixth, and the French envoy had set sail on the fifth, both returning to Shanghai. There were still ships anchored outside the bar. In existing treaties there was a mutual good offices clause and if they could be induced to return, he was certainly willing to do his best, but it was essential that our country and both England and France all authorize him. Then he could compromise as an intermediary.

Your slaves replied that as the trouble was not started by us, if England felt remorseful and acknowledged error there was nothing to prevent making peace as before. If she was as violent as ever, there was nothing to do but resume hostilities. Your slaves noted his attitude and he seemed to be speaking for the English and French but, whether allied or separate, he was unwilling to be involved on his own responsibility. But barbarians are naturally cunning and it is actually difficult to detect clues. This is the general situation of the English and French barbarians' inability to accept conciliation immediately.

The American barbarian talked (with us) for more than an hour in the hostel at Pei-t'ang and his bearing was very respectful and compliant. On leaving they produced a barbarian letter which was addressed to Russia, and charged Your slaves to deliver it to the Peking Russian office. Then between 1 and 3 o'clock, they got back in their carts and went to the river bank, boarded their own sampans and left.

As regards going to Peking, Your slaves (feel) that this barbarian is very impatient and they should not detain him long and give

rise to complications. Just as they were drawing up the memorial,
a Court Letter with Edict (attached) was received. Your slaves
accordingly returned immediately to Ta-ku and discussed the above
events wholeheartedly with Seng-ko-lin-ch'in.

They estimate that Kuei-liang and the others will not reach Peking until after the nineteenth. About the fourteenth they propose
to send the said barbarian a letter, agreeing to send suitable civil
and military officials on or about the nineteenth to conduct the barbarian chief John Ward up north. The routes of travel are: starting from Pei-t'ang to Tientsin and from Tientsin by canal to T'ung-
chou; or starting from Pei-t'ang to Hsiang-ho and from Hsiang-ho by
canal to T'ung-chou. Both routes are passable, but Tientsin is
densely populated and if the barbarians come to Tientsin it is feared
(the populace) will be alarmed and it would be better to go by way of
Hsiang-ho. If the barbarians are unwilling to go via Hsiang-ho, (we
shall) let them take the Tientsin road and determine arrangements
at the time, settle everything and send deputies specially charged
with this matter, in order by a show of courtesy to placate the barbarians.

Although the English and French chiefs, according to John Ward's
statement, have returned to Shanghai, it is very difficult to believe
that they actually have. However, after the battle started these barbarians withdrew outside the bar. If we propose to send a communication to the French barbarians it would be difficult to deliver. Besides if we make overtures first they are sure to be more haughty.
It is better to go a little slow and perhaps the American barbarians
can bring them around. If the French barbarians come to terms,
the English barbarians will be isolated, without even a trace.

Although this chief John Ward is unwilling to assume responsibility for English and French affairs, he did say that as the three
countries were all to exchange ratifications, if his country went via
Pei-t'ang the other two countries could do the same. At this time
it is most essential to be firm, wait for them to come to us, and
make the most of the situation. This is the safe and suitable
(course). (IWSM. HF 39; 34b, 4-37b, 5)

443. July 11, 1859. MEMORIAL: Heng-fu Advises Against Delivering Kuei-liang's Letters to Ward but Accepts Russian Letter for Transmission.

Heng-fu and others further memorialize. Seng-ko-lin-ch'in on
the seventh, received a communication from Kuei-liang and the
others sent en route from Su-ch'ien and also three (enclosed) communications. Your slaves all read them together. The communications were written prior to the beginning of hostilities. Now as
the American chief is permitted to enter the capital, there is no
use giving him these communications; as England and France are

just in the midst of their wrangle, they seem even more unreceptive. The previous communications it would seem must be temporarily withheld.

As to the Russian letter which the American barbarians gave us today, when it has handed over Your slaves feared that as it was their first meeting if they did not accept it, they would become suspicious, so they temporarily put it aside. Now they propose when convenient to return it saying that as they are going to Peking shortly, they can take it themselves.

Vermilion endorsement: Noted.   (IWSM. HF 39; 37b, 6-38a, 3)

444. July 11, 1859. EDICT: Instructs Heng-fu as to Ward's Route and Schedule from Pei-t'ang to Peking and Accepts Possibility of American Mediation.

Edict to the Grand Councillors. Heng-fu and others have memorialized on their meeting the American chief and on the proposal to postpone the date for the said chief to go to Peking.

On the eighth, American Chief John Ward had an interview with Heng-fu and others at Pei-t'ang. His attitude was respectful and compliant. Since he is now permitted to come to Peking to exchange ratifications, whether he is to start from Pei-t'ang, go to Tientsin, thence by canal to Peking, or follow the Hsiang-ho to Peking, above all let the barbarian decide for himself. By no means can he be ordered that he must go via Hsiang-ho lest he become suspicious. But he cannot bring a large suite. The various localities must also be ordered to make rigorous defense plans. The circumstances along the way can hardly be spied out hurriedly. Starting out after the nineteenth, Kuei-liang and the others should have arrived by the time they reach Peking. But Hsüeh Huan and Huang Chung-yü previously had a Rescript authorizing them to proceed to Tientsin. As officials have now been sent by Heng-fu to escort the said barbarians to Peking, there is no need of Hsüeh Huan and the others going to Tientsin, so order Heng-fu to notify Hsüeh Huan and the others en route that they are to come to Peking and need not report at Seng-ko-lin-ch'in's headquarters.

As to the said barbarian's statement that the English and French chiefs had both gone to Shanghai, it is fundamentally hard to believe. But in the American barbarian treaty there is the statement that if there are disputes with other countries, the said country is to interpose its good offices. If he wishes to intercede for these two countries, you can take advantage of the circumstances to bring them around. Order Seng-ko-lin-ch'in and the others to deliberate wholeheartedly and act according to circumstances.

Today Ho Kuei-ch'ing has been notified by Edict to find out about the English and French chiefs; if they are in Shanghai, (he is) to send a communication first to enlighten the French chief. As to the

Russian barbarian letter transmitted by the American barbarian, it is not necessary to reject his request. Order Heng-fu and the others, when convenient, to send it to Peking where it can be transmitted to the Russian barbarians. (IWSM. HF 39; 38a, 4-38b, 8)

445. July 11, 1859. EDICT: Orders Ho Kuei-ch'ing to Sound out the Possibilities in Shanghai for Alienating the French from the British.

Additional Edict. Previously, after the barbarian ships were damaged at Tientsin, although there were not many anchored in the outer sea, it was feared that they had gone to Shanghai and Kwangtung and would come back for revenge. An Edict (was issued) ordering Ho Kuei-ch'ing to delegate officers to observe their movements and possibly to induce merchants and American and French barbarians in Shanghai to intermediate for an armistice.

Today is received a memorial from Heng-fu and others that on July eighth [mistakenly written June 9], they had an interview with American barbarian Chief Ward at Pei-t'ang. His bearing was still respectful and compliant and he was willing to bring only a small party and come to Peking to exchange ratifications; but he said that the English and French envoys had set sail on the fifth and sixth and both returned to Shanghai. He (Heng-fu) did not know whether his statement was true or false.

Order Ho Kuei-ch'ing to send an officer to ascertain secretly if the English and French chiefs are actually in Shanghai. As the English chief started the trouble, we can hardly address him first; but if the French barbarian is in Shanghai, order Ho Kuei-ch'ing to send him a communication saying that as the Tientsin trouble was started by the English barbarians, it is reported that the American barbarians have gone to Pei-t'ang to set a date for exchange of ratifications. As his country has not opposed authority, it is in the same category as America. Why doesn't he wait at Tientsin until Kuei-liang and the others come, also going by way of Pei-t'ang with a small suite and with the same arrangements as America, proceed to Peking, exchange ratifications, and return?

Lead them out in this way. If the French barbarians repent and come around, the English barbarians will be isolated and it is hoped can gradually be brought into line. If it is possible to utilize the influence of Chinese and barbarian merchants to intermediate, order them also to manage suitably according to circumstances. (IWSM. HF 39; 38b, 9-39b, 1)

446. July 14, 1859. MEMORIAL: Prince Seng-ko-lin-ch'in Reports the Departure of British and French Ships from Ta-ku and Insists that Ward Bypass Tientsin.

Imperial Commissioner Seng-ko-lin-ch'in, Prince of Korchin, memorializes. Previously Your slave memorialized fully on the barbarian ships going outside the bar. After the trouble with the barbarians, ten days passed before any more was made. According to the statement of the American barbarian chief in an interview with Governor General Heng-fu on the eighth, the English and French envoys returned to Shanghai on the fifth and sixth. For several days we could see that the barbarian ships outside the bar were still anchored as before. Beginning on the ninth they began to set sail and by 9 to 11 o'clock on the eleventh, none was visible on the seascape. There are only the two American steamers, one large and one small, anchored in Pei-t'ang harbor.

As we see the situation, they realized somewhat the failure of their position and withdrew without means; whether to return home to prepare another start or to anchor somewhere else and create further complications, cannot be known. On this trip these barbarians actually used friendship to fool us and secretly displayed their cunning schemes. If they came only to exchange ratifications, what was the use of more than 20 warships, more than 160 barbarian cannon, and several thousand barbarian soldiers? That they intended to use violence and coercion is clear without argument.

In the battle of the twenty-fifth, strength opposed violence and the humiliation of these barbarians was certainly deep, so they will collect troops and ships and plan revenge. If they are severely thrashed two or three times by Chinese military force, the hollow arrogance of these barbarians, unable to stand more setbacks, will certainly be visibly blunted and suppressed. Then China can be assured several decades without trouble. If the barbarians have any remorse, we can lead them around according to circumstances to get them under control. The subdued heart is loyal and when it appears spontaneously, pacification will be secure. This is Your slave's evaluation of the English and French situation. If we gradually offer inducements, undue haste is unnecessary, and the situation will actually be like this.

As to the American barbarians entering Peking to exchange ratifications, there has been received the Imperial Edict of July 11, 1859, detailing Imperial concern. Everything shall, of course be managed in respectful accordance. But Tientsin is densely populated and last year when barbarian ships anchored outside the city, it did not fail to start trouble. This time when the barbarian envoys crossed our frontier, the inhabitants, possibly because of the fighting, have been so violent in speech that (their coming by way of Tientsin) seems inadvisable so we must require them to bypass Tientsin and then get back to their ships, in order to make the situation fairly secure.

The three barbarian countries are all fellow conspirators. There is no such thing as the two countries being defeated and returning, and allowing one country, the American barbarians, to go ahead and exchange ratifications. It is feared there is a scheme involved. When the Americans were interviewed, they did not admit fighting us; the communication they sent had both the date and title muddled. It is certain that there was a satisfactory agreement with France and England to keep them (the Americans) at Tientsin as a turning-around place.

Deputies Ts'ao Ta-shou and Po-to-hung-wu went to the American barbarian ship to interview the barbarians' assistant envoy, Williams, and he was not even willing to acknowledge the American barbarian captured on the twenty-fifth. Besides, he stated that the soldiers of the three countries are interchanged, that America contained English-men and Frenchmen and when there was fighting the flag was the only criterion. Moreover, in regard to going to Peking overland via Pei-t'ang, the said barbarian prepared sedan chairs, bearers to be supplied from the locality. He also had over 100 pieces of baggage, requiring more than 100 bearers, and was unwilling to ride in a cart. The said barbarian was merely using the trip to Peking to exchange ratifications as an excuse to disclaim fighting and have it as a talking point with the English and French barbarians in the future.

As to the Cantonese who remained in Tientsin last year, Huang Hui-lien, he says the custom of outside barbarians, when two coun-tries have war and make peace, is that military expenses must be paid by the party who asks for peace. Previously these barbarians have repeatedly made demands of China and that they always propose military indemnity is evidence of this. This time the barbarians were defeated. If they ask peace of us, they are afraid we will de-mand military expenses; if we ask peace of them, the barbarians are certain to make ships and cannon they lost a pretext for demanding military indemnity. This sort of situation must be guarded against in advance. Therefore, at the meeting on the eighth, Your slave had military officers charge the American chief to transmit demands for military expenses to the English barbarians, the whole idea being to forestall their demanding military expenses of us.

The crux of the English and French peace situation lies entirely with the American chief. But we must wait until he intercedes of his own accord and gives a clear judgment so there will be no spread of corrupt practices. Then it will be perfect. This, then, is Your slaves' estimate of the situation of the three countries: while using benevolence to get them involved, we ought not continually to compro-mise and accede to requests.

The Russian barbarian letter sent by the American barbarian will naturally, in accord with Edict, be sent to Peking for transmission. But it is recalled that last year while England and France started the trouble, it was actually the Russian barbarians who stood in the middle and fanned the flames. This time if we allow them to com-municate with the American barbarians, it is feared the two countries will agitate and other complications develop. It would seem just as

well that they not communicate. The original letter handed over is
still retained by Governor General Heng-fu. After the said barbarians have arrived at Peking, he can deliver it to them himself.

Whether or not Your slave's stupid views are correct, he
humbly awaits Instructions to direct him.

As to the three sunken vessels of the English barbarians, their
hulls are broken, but inside several hundred bronze wheels of various sizes, made of beautifully refined bronze, are all undamaged.
Twelve barbarian cannon of various sizes have been successively
salvaged; four cannon of over ten thousand catties, one of which has
an 8-inch [11.28 English inches] bore; the hollow ball more than an
inch [1.41] thick has an estimated weight of over 60 chin [80 pounds].
If solid balls were used they would weigh 100 chin [133-1/3 pounds].
The barrel is so large and the balls so heavy it is feared they cannot
be moved. Now there are enough barbarian cannon captured to supply
our needs.

As to the eight large cannon disbursed from the Metropolitan
Banner Force as well as the successively transferred Kuei-hua and
Sui-yuan government forces of 1000 men, it is proposed to wait until
they have arrived at Tientsin and order them quartered in the various
Shuang-kang camps in order to relive the rear line. (IWSM. IIF 39;
39b, 3-42a, 3; cf. slightly abridged translation by T. F. Tsiang,
AHR 35 (1929). 80-82.)

447. July 14, 1859. EDICT: Orders Continuation of Defense Measures
at Ta-ku and Specifies Conditions of Ward's Imminent Visit to Peking.

Edict to the Grand Councillors. Seng-ko-lin-ch'in has memorialized on the English and French ships all leaving and on arrangements for escorting the American barbarians to Peking.

The English and French barbarian ships began leaving on the
ninth and by the eleventh all had gone. This departure of the barbarians, whether to Shanghai or to Kwangtung to mobilize warships
in the hope of revenge, cannot yet be determined. Moreover, it is
feared that the barbarians will continue plotting and scheming and,
hiding on nearby islands, collect warships and taking advantage of
our unpreparedness, under cover of darkness or storm, make a
secret invasion, so it is even more essential to make rigorous
defense plans.

Order Seng-ko-lin-ch'in to continue to cooperate with the officers and urge them to increase their attentiveness to defense, and
also to find means to spy on the barbarian ships. Let there not be
the least carelessness.

As to the American barbarian's coming to Peking, it is virtually
impossible to allow him to ride in a chair within the city; but from
the Pei-t'ang landing, overland, there is no objection to allowing
him to ride in a chair. As to going around Tientsin and then traveling

by canal, after reaching T'ung-chou let him ride in a cart or a mule
litter; in entering Peking, do not let him ride in a chair. Order
Heng-fu and Wen-yü to explain to the said chief in advance in order
to avoid obstinacy when the time comes.

   The said commissioner is afraid that the Russian barbarian
letter sent by the American barbarian is a conniving artifice. His
fears are justified. But this letter will eventually have to be transmitted to the Russian barbarians, so it is better for the government
to be the agent and prevent the evil of personal intercourse. Order
Heng-fu to send the letter he has received from the American barbarians to the Grand Council, to be turned over to the Bureau of
Dependencies for transmission to the Russian barbarians. Compared
to having them deliver it themselves, this seems more satisfactory.
(IWSM. HF 39; 42a, 4-42b, 6; cf. translation by T. F. Tsiang, AHR
35 (1929). 82-83.)

   448. July 17, 1859. MEMORIAL: Excerpt from a Memorial of Heng-
fu Reporting a Russian Request made at Ta-ku for an Audience in Peking.
   [Heng-fu memorializes that four Russians have appeared at Pei-
t'ang on a chartered American ship and ask to come to Peking. Permission is given by Vermilion Edict to exchange ratifications on the
same terms as the Americans, the Russians to wait until after the
American visit is concluded.] (iWSM. HF 40; 1a, 4-2b, 9)

   449. July 17, 1859. MEMORIAL: Heng-fu Discounts American
Mediation Value and Reports Detailed Route of Ward's Trip to Peking
Bypassing Tientsin.
   Heng-fu and others further memorialize. With regard to the
matter of the route of travel, Your slaves have conferred with Seng-
ko-lin-ch'in. The American barbarians going ashore at Pei-t'ang
will be sent by land to Chün-liang-ch'eng, then from Chün-liang-
ch'eng direct to Pei-ts'ang by boat, and deputies were ordered to
so notify them. The said chief was very pleased with it. It is noted
that Pei-ts'ang is 20 li from the prefectural capital of Tientsin.
When the barbarian chief leaves the road to board ship, although he
traverses the Tientsin area, he will be some distance from the city
to preclude his spying on the condition of the rear line, nor is it a
circuitous route. After reaching T'ung-chou, he will resume his
journey into Peking.

   We observe that Brevet Salt Controller, Tao-t'ai of Ch'ing-ho,
Ch'ung-hou, and Brevet Colonel, Expectant Lieutenant-colonel of
the Central Army, Hsüan-hua Brigade, Major Chang Ping-to, are
well qualified to escort them. We propose sending them to lead
and direct deputies to see that the various local officials take
proper care of them along the way. When they reach Peking they
will be turned over to the prefect of the Metropolitan Prefecture to

receive and take charge of. After exchanging ratifications we shall
send the said tao-t'ai and others to escort them out of Peking to
Pei-t'ang and on board ship, in order to have them in experienced
hands.

The number of persons the said barbarian chief is to take to
Peking has been memorialized clearly before, it being decided that
he is to bring only twenty subordinate officials of his country and
ten servants and American Chinese secretaries, altogether thirty
persons.

Again orders have been given the deputies and civil and military
officials en route, without making any outward sign, secretly to
make defense plans.

As to Kiangsu Judicial Commissioner Hsüeh Huan and Expectant
District Magistrate Huang Chung-yü, Your slave, Heng-fu, with
special alacrity, sent orders to the said commissioner and his companion Huang Chung-yü, no matter where they were, to go direct to
Peking, without going around to Tientsin, in the hope of expedition.

Your slaves for several days have used a telescope to look
from the top of the forts and have seen only the two American
steamers, large and small, anchored in the vicinity of Pei-t'ang
harbor. Of the English and French ships, no sail can be seen but
it is learned from a merchant ship in from Newchwang that on the
13th there were sighted in Shih-pa-t'o waters more than two hundred
li from the port of Tientsin, nine barbarian ships at anchor. Whether
they are a relief squadron intending revenge or are hiding in the
islands with some other scheme is equally difficult to conjecture.
Orders have been sent by Seng-ko-lin-ch'in to the various military
officers to continue rigorous defense plans in order to be prepared
for the unexpected.

Between 11 and 1 o'clock on the twelfth, the American assistant
envoy, Williams, with an interpreter, on board a small steamer
sailed into Pei-t'ang River and asked for a representative to discuss
matters. Your slaves sent the first class sub-prefect of Kuang-p'ing-
fu, Po-to-hung-wu, and Expectant Prefect Ts'ao Ta-shou to go and
meet him. The barbarian said that they had heard privately that
there was an Edict authorizing them to go to Peking on a certain
day and were anxious to get the communication.

Your slaves beg to think that, although the letter from the
American barbarian a few days ago referred to the clause in the
treaty providing for mutual mediation, he is unwilling to assume
responsibility in this matter. In the interview with the representatives, his statements were now here now there and very difficult to
get hold of. At this time they have merely to bow to his request and
allow him to start north on the 19th, to avoid arousing suspicion.

On the 14th a communication was sent to the American barbarian
and the said barbarian has replied. Your slaves opened and read it

together. It set the 20th of this month to start north from Pei-t'ang.
Orders have been sent to inform Ch'ung-hou and others that they
must make suitable preparations, as well as secret instructions to
allay his progress by canal and road, calculating the time so that
Kuei-liang and the others will certainly be able to reach Peking first.

Your slaves also consulted with Seng-ko-lin-ch'in and, as the
American barbarians want to go to Peking and there is no positive
news of the English and French barbarians, propose to send the
American barbarians another communication, as a means of bringing them around, see how they reply, and then send an express
memorial.

Also, the next day after Your slaves met the American chief on
the eighth, deputies presented them pigs, sheep, rice flour, and
vegetables. The said chief then made out a list enjoining the purchase of all foodstuffs and accordingly a bill has been made out and
sent. All has been received and is attached hereto and presented.
(IWSM. HF 40; 2b, 10-4b, 6)

450. July 17, 1859. EDICT: Notes Arrival of Kuei-liang at Peking
to take charge of the Exchange of Ratifications and Urges the Conciliation of France.

Edict to the Grand Councillors. Heng-fu and Wen-yü have memorialized on sending officers to escort the American barbarian on
his departure. On the twentieth of the month the American barbarian
will proceed to Peking from Pei-t'ang, according to the proposal of
the said governor general and others, going from Chun-liang-ch'eng
direct to Pei-ts'ang and by boat to T'ung-chou. As usual Ch'ing-ho
Tao-t'ai Ch'ung-hou and others have been secretly ordered to guard
him carefully and the local officials en route to take due care of him.

Today Kuei-liang and the others reached Peking, so there will
be experienced hands for the exchange of ratifications.

As to the English and French barbarian ships, all have left and
there is still no word of them. Now according to a Newchwang merchant ship, nine barbarian ships were sighted in Shih-pa-t'o waters
some 200 li from Tientsin harbor. These barbarians are hiding
nearby, either waiting for word from the American barbarians or
collecting warships to plot revenge. If they return and display their
ferocity, their evil thrust will be even worse than before. Order
Seng-ko-lin-ch'in to redouble his defenses. Let there not be the
least carelessness.

Previously since the American barbarians were willing to go to
Pei-t'ang for an interview with Heng-fu, successive orders were
sent for the said governor general to have Wen-yü seize the opportunity to lead them to our advantage and get the French barbarians
into our provenance, the object being to isolate the English barbarians. Now Heng-fu and others have sent a communication to the

American barbarians to have them contact England and France and if they are desirous of patching things up and coming to Peking to exchange ratifications, they can go to Pei-t'ang to discuss. Some slight discrimination is unavoidable. While the French barbarians abetted evil, we can pretend ignorance; but the English barbarians took the lead in precipitating hostilities and if we initiate overtures, we are afraid it will increase their arrogance and make them even harder to handle. These exigencies have been misrepresented. At present as it is not certain whether or not the English and French chiefs are capable of repentance and willing to come to Pei-t'ang, if we try to get the American barbarians to bring them around, naturally different terms must be given, so they (Heng-fu et al.) can ask for an Edict and act accordingly. (IWSM. HF 40; 4b, 7-5b, 1)

451. July 17, 1859. CHINESE NOTE TO THE UNITED STATES: Heng-fu Officially Notifies Ward of Arrangements for his trip to Peking and Proposes American Mediation with England.

By way of communication: Acknowledging the reply of the honorable country's imperial commissioner received yesterday setting the twentieth of the present month to proceed to Peking to exchange ratifications, now the present governor general and commissioner are instructing representatives and local officials to provide suitable escort.

They note that in the treaty of last year it is provided that if any other country causes trouble, the honorable country will always act as mediator. Now the English and French ships are still anchored in the high seas. Whether or not they are in communication, there is no certain knowledge. They are impelled to ask the honorable country's imperial commissioner to get in contact with them. The hostilities of the twenty-fifth certainly derived from the English warships forcing entrance to the harbor and the quarrel was not of our starting. In case they cherish hard feelings regarding past hostilities, the Ta-ku defense corps must needs wait quietly. If they acknowledge their own error and are desirous of resuming old friendship and come to Peking to exchange ratifications, they can proceed to Pei-t'ang harbor and discuss everything. The present governor general and commissioner will certainly memorialize for them asking for an Edict to consummate friendly relations. How it is to be settled is entirely up to the decision of the English and French commissioners. They still hope for the honorable country's reply according this. By way of communication. This is a necessary communication. (IWSM. HF 40; 5b, 2-6a, 3)

452. July 17, 1859. MEMORIAL: Heng-fu Reports Discussion of the Privilege of Riding in Sedan Chairs and Ward's Agreement to Ride in a Cart.

Heng-fu and others further memorialize. As regards the Ameri-

can barbarian's request to ride in sedan chair, yesterday Deputies
Po-to-hung-wu and Ts'ao Ta-shou discussed it personally with the
said chief at Pei-t'ang, telling him that none of the countries coming
to Peking had ever ridden in chairs. The said chief said that as
those countries were all dependencies, his country's situation was
rather different. The said deputies reiterated that while other
countries might be different, at present all the Russians in Peking
rode in carts and never rode in chairs and as his country was in
the same category as Russia, it would seem hardly convenient to
have two rules. After repeated explanations the said barbarian
finally agreed.

Now it is proposed to have him go ashore at Pei-t'ang and start
out by cart; nor will he ride in a chair from T'ung-chou overland to
Peking.

As to the Russian letter which the American chief gave us, Your
slaves' original proposal to return it was with the idea of preventing
collusion. Now in respectful accordance with Edict, Your slave
Heng-fu is preparing a communication to have the original letter
presented by the said chief sent to the Grand Council, to be turned
over to the Bureau of Dependencies to transmit to the Russian barbarians.

Vermilion endorsement: Noted.   (IWSM.HF 40; 6a, 4-6b, 4)

453.   July 20, 1859.   MEMORIAL: Heng-fu Reports Note and Conversation with S. Wells Williams and Final Arrangements for Ward's Trip
to Peking.

Governor General of Chihli Heng-fu and Financial Commissioner
Wen-yü memorialize. On the seventeenth, Expectant Assistant
District Magistrate Huang Hui-lien and Lieutenant Jen Lien-sheng
brought an American barbarian communication back from the barbarian ship. Your slaves and Seng-ko-lin-ch'in opened and read it
together. The purport was that as the English and French ships had
already returned south, there was no means of contacting them. In
the future after the said barbarian had exchanged ratifications and
returned to Shanghai from Peking he would certainly notify them.
He also said that at present there was no conflict whatever.

Further questioning Huang Hui-lien, he stated that the American barbarians said that the English chief, Bruce, had now gone
south and would also go to his own country as well as to the Five
Indies [India] to collect troops for revenge. He was still waiting
for word from his sovereign. If there were action, it would be
either during the ninth and tenth months (September 26-November
23) of the present year or in the spring of next year, it could not be
told which. The French barbarians also went south first. This
spring these barbarians had a clash of arms with the Ottoman Turks
and seeing their condition it would be easier to talk terms with them

than with the English barbarians. When John Ward returned to
Shanghai there would still be time to compromise or possibly when
he reached Peking he would put in a word for the two countries in
advance.

The American barbarian also questioned Huang Hui-lien regarding the present status of the prisoners of that country and England.
Huang Hui-lien replied that the governor general, respecting His
Imperial Majesty's pose of treating people with compassion, had now
sent persons to treat them generously. The said barbarian was very
grateful.

Also according to the deputies' questioning of the Russian barbarians, these barbarians said that around Sang-tao [an island on
the north coast of Shantung] several English and French steamers
had been seen and that they were anchored there for repairs.

Your slaves beg to note that the English and French barbarians
after being thrashed this time are not likely to be reconciled willingly.
If the American chief Ward's statement about returning to Shanghai
to compromise, is reliable, it is still not impossible to recover
something. So we must needs obey Edict and have the American
chief set out on the twentieh for the capital to enable him to exchange ratifications as soon as possible and return quickly to Shanghai.

Along the route of the said barbarian chief from Pei-t'ang to
the capital, boats, carts, and hostels have been duly prepared. We
note the tao-t'ai of Ch'ing-ho, Ch'ung-hou. In the fighting this time
at Ta-ku and the negotiations at Pei-t'ang this tao-t'ai has been
intimately associated with Your slaves in this affair and thoroughly
understands its true origins. Hence he is sent as escort. Orders
have been given this tao-t'ai and Major Chang Ping-to to proceed to
Pei-t'ang, to wait for and look after them, and also have him impress
on the said chief, John Ward, that after he goes to Peking and the
steamers are anchored outside, whatever barbarian officers or
interpreters he leaves to facilitate interviews with the deputies on
business, and the barbarian soldiers and sailors of the said ship,
are all forbidden to go ashore. All necessary foodstuffs will be
supplied by officials and it is not necessary for them to go out to
buy them.

Vermilion endorsement: Memorial seen and comprehended.
(IWSM.HF 40; 15a, 1-16a, 5)

454. July 20, 1859. MEMORIAL: Heng-fu Reports Failure of Local
Efforts to Utilize the Americans as Mediators and the Continued Defense
of the Ta-ku Area.

Heng-fu further memorializes. To continue, the English barbarians defied authority, disobeyed decrees, and attacked our forts.
Their violence has long borne Imperial understanding. Your slaves,

consulting with Seng-ko-lin-ch'in, sent a communication to the
American barbarians by officer messenger to determine these barbarians' temper, whether or not they can find means to bring them
(the British and French) around, as usual making clear that if they
want to fight, the Ta-ku defense corps would be waiting quietly, not
daring to manifest any weakness. Now are received Confidential
Instructions, pointing out general and particular and weighing slow-
ness and speed. Those who abetted evil can still be condoned; those
who started trouble must be discriminated against. Your slaves,
in their desire to seize the opportunity for conciliation, were not
able to avoid making inappropriate statements, and they are indescribably distressed. The purport of the reply received from the
American barbarian has been brought out in detail in the body of
our memorial. Hereafter, if there are occurrences, we must needs
request an Edict and act accordingly, by no means risking any tactical blunders.

As to port defenses, Seng-ko-lin-ch'in has as usual ordered all
divisions to guard carefully night and day and in case of storms and
darkness, to redouble their diligence to thwart retaliation. Now express orders have been sent by Your slave, Heng-fu, to the various
local army posts along the coast to report immediately if they see
any barbarian sail.

Vermilion endorsement: Noted.   (IWSM. HF 40; 16a, 6-16b, 8)

455. July 23, 1859. MEMORIAL: Prince Seng-ko-lin-ch'in Points
with Pride to the Subservience of Russia and America and Urges Maintenance of China's Prestige.

Imperial Commissioner Seng-ko-lin-ch'in, Prince of Korchin,
memorializes. It is noted that the American barbarians are willing
to go to Peking via Pei-t'ang. Not being allowed to ride in chairs,
the said barbarians agree to take carts. The Russian barbarian ships
went direct to Pei-t'ang harbor, sent persons out to present communications and never even went to Ta-ku.

This attitude, compared to last year, seems very compliant and
indicates that they are not yet without fear of our might. Taking
advantage of this opportunity, our means of gaining requisite control
is to state our broad policy clearly and raise our national prestige.
Once this opportunity is lost it can hardly be recovered. During last
year's conciliation, the deep penetration of the barbarian ships left
us with no room for action. Actually, however, it was a failure
through over-leniency and it only increased the contempt of all barbarians for China. Therefore, this year the ferocity of the English
and French barbarians was greater than last year.

This time as soon as the American barbarians came, they presented the Russian barbarians' letter and the Russian barbarians are
taking advantage of the American barbarians coming to Peking to

follow their lead. Thus they are in collusion and the details of their scheme are already discernable. After these two barbarians get to Peking they are sure to enlarge upon the overbearing attitude of England and France, talk big to scare us, and bring pressure on their behalf. These two barbarians will utilize this to fish for advantage. If we still compromise in everything they will think even less of China and display their threats in the hope of getting everything they want. Then in subsequent management, it will be even harder to be effective.

Your slave regards Kuei-liang and the others as devoted exclusively to compromise and can hardly envisage rousing them, so it is necessary to send a high official with courage and experience to collaborate with them in suitable management. Speech must be stern and principles correct to humble their hearts. On the other hand, an Imperial Edict should be promulgated publishing far and wide the English and French perennial violence. If these barbarians know shame,. China should not be too hard on them and still allow friendly relations; if they refuse to recognize their folly, their trade should be cut off. All these barbarians think of is profit, so perhaps they can be brought to submission. As the American and Russian barbarians recognize Your Majesty's Heavenly might and tremble with awe, if we attack (England and France) we can control the outcome and then a peace negotiator will be able to subdue somewhat their ferocity.

As to the American barbarian prisoner, John Powers, after John Ward gets to Peking, an Imperial Edict is requested returning him to the said country to make the barbarian grateful for Your Majesty's innate virtue and also as an adroit means of implicating him (i.e. Ward).

As to the English and French barbarians having met defeat and being intent on revenge, it is inevitable under the circumstances; but that they will harass China from a distance of 70,000 li, is not entirely certain. They will certainly not be willing to undertake it lightly. If they are punished once more, circumstances will not enable them to recover.

According to the statement of English captives questioned by Huang Hui-lien, when that country's warships go out to do battle, the minimum is twenty to thirty vessels, the maximum seventy to eighty vessels. Just now in the opium districts of India they are engaged in war and hostilities have not yet ceased. In view of the general situation, it stands to reason that they are not putting forth their entire effort in China. Even if these barbarians commit themselves to revenge, at present our camps are being strengthened and cannon secretly placed; of the various government armies, all are dauntless enough to meet an assault and can allay Imperial concern. We have only to have the French barbarians accept conciliation first to cut off their allegiance and those barbarians may also seriously consider making peace. Since the American and Russian barbarians want to mediate, we should have them make overtures to us; we cannot stoop to them. If they bring up the affairs of England and France, we should only discuss right and wrong according to circumstances, without antagonizing or agreeing, to try to control the outcome. If we make barbarians cherish virtue and fear might, we can hope for permanent friendly relations from this one stroke.

To continue, Second Class Compiler Kuo Sung-tao, since arriving at camp has been associated with Your slave in all arrangements working from morning till night and in the various matters of fighting and conciliation is thoroughly conversant with everything. In the negotiations with the American barbarians at Pei-t'ang, July 8, this official was at hand and eye-witnessed the situation. Hence this memorial is turned over to this official to carry to Peking and memorialize, to facilitate an oral report in outline. (IWSM.HF 40; 18a, 3-19b, 8)

456. July 23, 1859. EDICT: Commends Prince Seng's Militant Policy and Expresses Confidence in China's Ability to Conciliate and Divide the Western Powers.

Edict to the Grand Councillors. Seng-ko-lin-ch'in has memorialized on the general situation of handling the conciliation of barbarians, namely an interplay of rigidity and softness, and had Kuo Sung-tao bring his memorial and present it. We have read it carefully and also summoned Kuo Sung-tao for an audience, questioned him thoroughly on the said minister's plans for war and conciliation, and both are satisfactory.

This time the English barbarians defied authority and the said minister led his troops to attack; certainly enough to freeze rebel gall and delight the hearts of the people. Now the port cantonments are arranged even more compactly, so if the said barbarians plan retaliation, he can certainly meet the onslaught. As to the alternatives of war and conciliation, neither is fundamentally perverse in practice, for if the said minister decides to fight, he has the lever; while in conciliation, he will not have to resort to compromise.

Today is received a memorial of Ho Kuei-ch'ing that the English and French chiefs have one after the other returned to Shanghai. At present Chinese merchants and barbarian merchants are devising means to disperse. The whole situation has been communicated to Seng-ko-lin-ch'in to see how to manage. After the said minister has received it, it is assumed he will go into it thoroughly. Orders have already been given Ho-ch'en effectively to prevent the barbarians from joining up with the Nanking rebels.

Ho-Kuei-ch'ing is also ordered to delve into these barbarians' activities. If the Chinese merchants and barbarian merchants are

willing to distinguish true and false and the barbarians acknowledge
their error, he can take advantage of the circumstances to lead
them to our advantage; but he is not to make the mistake of stooping
and increasing barbarian arrogance. Ho Kuei-ch'ing can certainly
figure out how to manage. It is not yet certain whether or not the
said barbarians can bring themselves to repent and withdraw their
forces.

As to the American barbarians coming to Peking to exchange
ratifications, their demeanor is still respectful and compliant and,
compared to the English and French barbarians, they are easy to
control, so continue Ho Kuei-ch'ing in sole charge of managing them.
There is no need to send another dignitary.

As to Seng-ko-lin-ch'in's request to publish the perversity of the
English barbarians far and wide and also, after John Ward comes to
Peking, to issue an Edict returning the captured American barbarian,
John Powers, to the said country, the issuance of a proclamation
after the American barbarians reach Peking will suffice. Order the
newspaper copied and presented by Ho Kuei-ch'ing, recopied and
sent out for reference. (IWSM. HF 40; 19b, 9-20b, 5)

457. July 23, 1859. MEMORIAL: Heng-fu Reports the Landing of
Ward's Party at Pei-t'ang and Departure for Peking in Carts on July 20th.

Governor General of Chihli Heng-fu and Financial Commissioner
Wen-yü memorialize. On the eighteenth, Your slave Heng-fu ordered
Tao-t'ai of Ch'ing-ho Ch'ung-hou and Major Chang Ping-to of the Hsüan-
hua Brigade of the Central Army, to proceed to Pei-t'ang and take due
care of them. Your slave, Wen-yü, on the nineteenth, also went to
Chün-liang-ch'eng to wait.

Between 5 and 7 in the evening of the nineteenth the said chief
on board a small steamer entered the mouth of Pei-t'ang River.
Ch'ung-hou and Chang Ping-to, together with the tao-t'ai of T'ung-
yung, Te-ch'un, all went on board and talked with the first barbarian envoy, John Ward, the assistant envoy, Williams, and the interpreter, W. A. P. Martin,[6] and found that their admiral, Tattnall, because of his age had been left on board ship and would not be taken to
Peking. (Your slaves) told them that, as to the large vessel out at
sea, all necessary foodstuffs could be listed and ordered and (they
were) not to let sailors or soldiers go ashore. The barbarians
promptly agreed. They also presented a complete list of the names
and titles of the thirty persons going to Peking.

---

6 William Alexander Parsons Martin, 1827-1916, was a Presbyterian missionary, came
to China in 1850, was attached to Ward's mission as Chinese secretary, and later
became interpreter for the American legation at Peking. He is best known for his
founding of the T'ung Wen College in Peking and is the author of several books on
on China.

Between 5 and 7 on the morning of the twentieth, they came
ashore and one after the other got in the carts. It was very peaceful. At exactly 7 o'clock, all the carts got under way. By noon
they reached Chün-liang-ch'eng. Your slave Wen-yü met the said
chief, John Ward, and announced that His Imperial Majesty treats
men with sincerity, with profound grace and generous favor. The
said chiefs felt profoundly grateful and said that after going to Peking and exchanging ratifications, they would certainly intercede for
England and France. Your slave, Wen-yü said, as the English and
French ships had all gone south, how could they put in their good
word? The chief replied that England and France still had three
vessels anchored waiting for orders in the vicinity of Miao Island,
Teng-chou, Shantung, and now having received His Imperial Majesty's favor high as heaven and thick as the earth, they would certainly,
if in their power, intercede in their behalf. Your slave, Wen-yü
answered him speciously not to give an impression of hasty acquiescence.

At dawn on the twenty-first, Your slave Wen-yü waited until the
said chief had set out and then returned to Ta-ku. Ch'ung-hou and
Chang Ping-to escorted the barbarian chiefs in their carts and proceeded west in front of the dike to Pei-ts'ang and, with Tientsin Tao-
t'ai Sun Chih, took charge of embarkation. All the horses, bearers,
boats, carts, and hostels provided for the several days were in order.
The said barbarian and his suite were all greatly pleased. Their
admiral, Chief Tattnall, remains on board a large steamer, with
twenty barbarian officers, two hundred and sixty soldiers and
sailors. A small steamer has five barbarian officers and seventy
sailors. The large steamer comes and goes at will; the small
steamer still anchors inside or outside the bar. If there is a storm,
it comes up river to anchor.

Your slave Heng-fu has notified the tao-t'ai of Yung-chen, leading and cooperating with the civil and military, to investigate and
repress as occasion requires; that there cannot be the least carelessness.

We humbly think that last year when the American barbarians
came to Tientsin, they were equally guilty with England, France and
Russia; this year they successively arrived at the port of Ta-ku and
on the day of the battle, there was also an American barbarian, John
Powers, captured. That they were likewise resiting authority, there
is not the slightest doubt, but their present expressions are compliant.
Whatever the prohibitory regulations are, they have always been able
to accommodate themselves and obey. Naturally, this is due to the
battle of June 25; they fear our military prowess and do not dare be
arrogant as before.

But on the eighth Your slaves had an interview with them at Pei-
t'ang. At the time the English and French ships were still outside the

bar; but the said chief stated that the French chief and the English
chief on the fifth and sixth respectively, went south. On the fifteenth,
when they delivered a communication, the said chief repeated that the
English and French had returned south and there was no means of
reaching them; that when they returned to Shanghai from Peking they
would inform them. How is it that on meeting them this time, they
suddenly say that the English and French still have three vessels in
the vicinity of Miao Island awaiting instructions? Within ten days
their various statements do not tally. Their deviousness is extremely hard to anticipate.

The paper the said barbarian presented, listing the number and
ranks of those going to Peking, respectfully prepared in clear copy,
is respectfully presented for Imperial scrutiny.

Further, while Your slave Wen-yü was at the Chün-liang-ch'eng
hostel, the barbarian chief, John Ward, took off some glasses he
was wearing and presented them. Your slave, Wen-yü, replied that
as the envoy was now going to Peking, he must needs wear them himself and wait until he returned from Peking to give them away, refusing them repeatedly. The said chief said that the reason he gave
them was so that after we parted it would still be as though he were
before my eyes. His expression was very insistent so Your slave
was afraid of opposing his will and causing later complications. He
respectfully encloses them in his memorial to the Grand Council for
presentation.

Vermilion endorsement: Memorial read and fully comprehended.
(IWSM.HF 40; 23a, 7-25a, 7)

458. July 29, 1859. MEMORIAL: Prince Seng Reports a Conversation with Commodore Tattnall and Describes Safeguards against
American Trickery.

Seng-ko-lin-ch'in and others further memorialize. Your slave
Heng-fu agrees with Seng-ko-lin-ch'in that while the American chief,
John Ward, has gone to Peking the barbarian admiral is still at the
port of Pei-t'ang and he must be suitably controlled.

As to necessary fresh water and foodstuffs, a list came and
deputies have collected everything and sent it. Also orders have
been sent by Your slave, Heng-fu, dispatching Assistant District
Magistrate Huang Hui-lien and Lieutenant Jen Lien-sheng to present melons, fruit, vegetables, ice, et cetera, to the admiral's
large vessel as an excuse to sound out his attitude and also to investigate his activities.

Now, according to the oral report of Huang Hui-lien and the
other on their return, the said barbarian admiral, Tattnall was very
grateful. Huang Hui-lien took occasion to inquire if the English and
French barbarian ships had actually gone and the said chief stated
that the English barbarians really had three vessels waiting in the

vicinity of Miao Island, Shantung, and that he was still expecting
word to come North, but, on being questioned when it might arrive
and what its purport might be, stated that he did not know for certain.
Huang Hui-lien and the other also inquired about the Russian ships to
find where they were bound. The said chief said that they were going to Japan on business by way of Miao Island but, as Huang Hui-
lien stated, Japan is in the north and Miao Island in the south. If
they were going from this port to Japan, Miao Island was not along
the course. His statement could hardly be believed.

At present the large steamer on which the said chief is and one
large Russian steamer are both anchored out at sea. The small
American barbarian steamer constantly comes and goes inside Pei-
t'ang River and the whole situation seems to be peaceful.

The said barbarian admiral has sent Your slave Heng-fu one
letter in barbarian character and also sent three foreign rifles and
one rug for Huang Hui-lien and the others for presentation or return.
The barbarian letter has been translated into Chinese character by
Huang Hui-lien and is copied and respectfully presented for Imperial scrutiny. Whether the foreign rifles and rug sent by the said barbarian are to be accepted or not, they ask for an Edict for guidance.
(IWSM.HF 40; 37a, 8-38a, 6)

459. July 29, 1859. EDICT: Notes Reports of Rebel Situation and
Urges Separation of Domestic and Foreign Problems and Continued
Defense of Ta-ku.

Edict to the Grand Councillors. Today Seng-ko-lin-ch'in and
others have memorialized on the issuing of equipment and rations
to the Shantung and Anhwei cavalry and also the fact that the American and Russian vessels are quietly at anchor. The memorials have
been read and fully comprehended. They express the fear that the
barbarians intend to connive with the Nanking rebels to get the
Canton rebels and Nien-fei to join forces and come north, in the
hope of involving us while the barbarians bring up their reserves,
planning to go to Tientsin again for revenge when we are not free
to meet them.

These fears are naturally very apt. At present there is no
proof that the Canton rebels are in collusion with the barbarians,
besides they are still a long way from the north front. The Anhwei
Nien-fei are always planning northern invasions; the Hsü-chou
rebels have never been silenced. Repeated defense measures
have been taken and while for the time being we are free from the
threat of invasion, there is one district of Ts'ao-shan in Shantung
where the bandits appear and disappear and our only reliance is
on the defenses of Te-leng-e's one army. The said minister will
spy around from time to time in the hope of being prepared against
calamity. If there is word of a northern incursion, let him me-

morialize at the time and send someone to present it.

As to the troops at Tientsin, they are reinforced solely as a defense against barbarians. Just now, whether or not the barbarian temper can be brought into line is still undeterminable, so it is inexpedient to transfer them elsewhere leaving this important place empty.

The American and Russian barbarians have, one after the other, reached Peking. The whole situation continues quiet. The American barbarian, Tattnall, presented Heng-fu various gifts, so order Heng-fu that it is all right to accept them. (IWSM. HF 40; 38a, 7-38b, 8)

460. August 1, 1859. MEMORIAL: Ho Kuei-ch'ing Reports Shanghai Reactions to China's Victory at Ta-ku and the Completion of Tribute Transport to Peking.

Imperial Commissioner, Governor General of Liang-chiang Ho Kuei-ch'ing memorializes. It is noted that the recent Tientsin incident was the happiest event in more than twenty years. After receiving word, the barbarian merchants felt very uneasy and in their confusion called in their capital and the Shanghai area closed up shop. Acting Tao-t'ai of Su-Sung-T'ai Wu Hsü and Restored Prefect Lan Wei-wen transmitted word to the English barbarian, H. N. Lay, and the French barbarian, Edan, that while Bruce, headstrong and reckless, had brought shame upon himself, there was no blame on others since His Imperial Majesty's grace was commensurate with heaven. Since there were previously established treaties, they would certainly request an extraordinary show of Favor and there was no need of apprehension. The two barbarians assented and withdrew.

Wu Hsü and others also had the Chinese merchants explain clearly to the barbarian merchants. The barbarians all felt grateful, resented Bruce's bad management, and the minds of the merchants were finally composed. There was talk of not paying duties but it was not referred to again.

Wu Hsü and the others saw that there was an opportunity to be seized. As the Shanghai area had already heard that the American barbarian at Tientsin had decided to exchange ratifications, (they) ordered the Chinese merchants, as though it was their own idea, to inform the barbarian merchants that Elgin [sic] had sought for more than a year to exchange ratifications, which was a great waste of energy; that His Imperial Majesty, in permitting access to Peking to exchange ratifications, was treating him not ungenerously; that the mistake on the previous occasion was that he had gone North hastily, without a personal agreement with the Imperial Commissioner at Shanghai and also without knowing that the governor general of Chihli was waiting at Pei-t'ang, so actually there was no premeditation on either side; that the Imperial Commissioner should have reached Peking and the American barbarians would certainly manage as arranged. If the English and French barbarians would return and talk reasonably, they would certainly be treated hospitably as before; but if they pressed the matter it was sure to lead to war and concomitent evil results, waste time and lose the issue. Besides success or failure could not be assured and all benefits of the articles negotiated last year would be lost entirely, which would inevitably cause regret.

The said barbarian merchants thereupon argued these ideas back and forth. But the English chief stated that, although what they said was reasonable, China started the hostilities, that several hundred barbarian officers and men were killed or wounded and if he did not retaliate, he was afraid all the barbarians in Shanghai would laugh at him. Besides he could not take the initiative, so he intended to ask his sovereign for another settlement. The French chief then said that his country also had casualties and could not but make an arrangement like the English chief's.

In view of their attitude, we could not urge a settlement at once. It is inexpedient to be over hasty, for when or how they would retaliate, the chiefs were unwilling to say clearly, and even pointed to the American barbarian's chicanery to taunt us. The English barbarian's idea was to find a pretext for trouble. Not knowing that our ocean (tribute) transport had been completed, on the thirteenth, they took the steamer on which the chief was returning south and sailed back to Tientsin, hoping to prevent our sand junks from entering port. On the fifteenth, there was another steamer sailing southeast on the high seas; it has been ascertained that the English and French chiefs are sending messengers (by this steamer) to carry letters back home.

Your official observes that the French and American barbarians have been entirely subservient to the English. Now the English barbarian's desire for revenge is still strong and the French chief plays the sycophant. The American chief has gone to Peking and will certainly exchange ratifications first; but if, after the exchange of ratifications, we open ports in accordance with the new regulations, it is feared that England and France will use it as a pretext and it may be an obstacle to conciliation.

Imperial Commissioner Kuei-liang must have arrived before now and already deliberated (the above items). Further, it has also been proposed that as the English and French barbarians are reported to be having troubles themselves at home, we could use this as a plan for separating them. This does not take into consideration the fact that fighting among barbarians is a constant occurrence; but in matters involving China they always shield one another. Moreover, it is not yet certain whether or not the con-

flict really exists. The French barbarians are generally regarded
as pugnacious. Whenever the countries of the Western Ocean go to
war they turn to her for support, so these barbarians, using this to
their own advantage, sit back and get rich like so many merchants.
Thus we fear the hope of using the Americans and French to bring
them around is hardly reliable.

This time the English barbarians' intention to intercept our
present contingent of ocean (tribute) transport has already proved
futile. They are now anxious about their Indian troops and the replies from their home governments, neither of which will arrive
for several months. The situation will certainly be changed by
winter or next spring. The next tribute grain transport may be intercepted and it is impossible to change back to canal transport on
short notice. In Shanghai, prior to July 7, duties on foreign opium
amounted to 7000 taels; the barbarian duties of all countries were
only some 20, 000 taels, less than one-third those of the past. After
the eighth, although trade was not stopped, it might just as well
have been. There are no funds to procure military supplies and
popular feeling is increasingly apprehensive. Money and transport
are both risky. It is not so much the fear that these barbarians are
tied up with the Canton rebels, but the obstruction of both money and
supplies is indescribable. The consequences dare not be conjectured.

It is now reported that the English chief intends to raise a lot of
money and buy the draft copy of Imperial Commissioner Seng-ko-lin-
ch'in's memorial. They seem to suspect that we plan to close
customs and break off relations. If he is not informed of the facts,
their suspicions will increase daily and it is feared Chinese renegades
and barbarian rebels will again, as in Kwangtung, forge an Imperial
Edict and use it to deceive. This fear is by no means unfounded so
Your official, in accordance with his special Imperial Instructions,
but acting as if on his own initiative and pretending not to know that
the French barbarians have also helped the rebels, sent a communication to Bourboulon to go North immediately and follow the example
of the American barbarians in exchanging ratifications and also getting
him adroitly to lead Bruce out in order to dispel his suspicions.

Since barbarians have the instincts of dogs and sheep, really fearing that they had put it aside without answering, (Your official) again
gave secret orders to Wu Hsü and others to send word to Bourboulon,
the mutually trusted barbarian leader (Consul) Edan, and the interpreter Marques, and explain to each in succession, saying that Your
official is sending a communication; see how they respond, and then
hand it over. (IWSM.HF 41; 5a, 9-7b, 10)

461. August 1, 1859. EDICT: Abandons Hope of Alienating the French
and Authorizes Separate Agreements at Shanghai Along the Lines of the

American Treaty.
          Edict to the Grand Councillors. Ho Kuei-ch'ing has memorialized
that the English and French rebels' shame and anger is not quieted and
that he is now laying plans for management. Previously Ho Kuei-
ch'ing was instructed to draw out the French barbarians to bring the
English barbarians around and, as conciliation had already been decided upon, to handle the matter with the utmost leniency and with discrimination. Now, the English barbarians are afraid all the barbarians
will laugh at them because of their defeat. Their will to retaliate is not
dead. The French chief also adheres blindly to the English chief and is
not willing to come and exchange ratifications like the American barbarians. Since he is an aider and abettor of evil it is not necessary to
ask him again to effect a change.
          Ho Kuei-ch'ing asks to pretend ignorance of the French barbarians'
helping the rebels and send a communication to Bourboulon to come
north at once. It is really feared that barbarians are by nature dogs
and sheep and cannot be trained to obedience. Tientsin is prepared to
fight and there is nothing else to worry about. Since the French barbarians are allied to the English barbarians, after they receive Ho
Kuei-ch'ing's communication, if there is a chance of bringing them to
their senses, he can only make the same arrangement for trade at the
various ports contained in the treaty of the American barbarians. Discussion of the treaties which were sent to Peking last year is to be
dropped.
          As to the English barbarians' two trips to Tientsin, on both they
started hostilities. As to their initiative in violating treaties this
time, their actions were intolerable. If they repent and ask terms,
charge then with starting the quarrel and say that China had many
casualties among officers and men, her military expenditures would
probably be some 10,000,000 (taels); besides repudiating the 6,000,000
(taels) previously proposed by England and France, she must still
demand several million (taels). See how they react. At that time
again Ho Kuei-ch'ing, acting as on his own initiative, will request
Favor on their behalf to consider a reduction. When the time comes
he will act according to circumstances, as We can hardly decide in
advance.
          In the future the English barbarians are merely to trade at the
seven ports like the American barbarians. Ho Kuei-ch'ing will draw
up a separate treaty with their chief as well as a separate treaty
with the French barbarians, both to be exchanged at Shanghai and
not give permission again for these two countries to come to Peking
nor have Kuei-liang and the others come back to Shanghai. The
method of settlement of this affair, the said governor general will
keep to himself, not divulge it in advance, and only discuss it when
the time comes.... (IWSM.HF 41; 9a, 7-10a, 2)

462. August 2, 1859. RUSSIAN NOTE: The Russian Minister Protests China's Policy of Isolating the Russian and American Missions in Peking.

...Furthermore, as to China's statement that at present it was unnecessary for them (the Russians) to meet the Americans; to wait until after the exchange of ratifications before they have intercourse. This prohibition is certainly hard to understand. This country and China have long had intimate and firm friendly relations, so for our nationals to meet the Americans would do no harm to China. Forbidding us to see them is clear proof that China suspects us.

When they met previously, the present minister expressed the desire to send an officer to see the American envoy. Their excellencies Su and Jui did not agree, but allowed him to write a letter and give it to the director for transmission. As long as our nationals have lived in Peking they have never acted arbitrarily. Nor has the present minister up to now sent anyone to the Lao-chün-t'ang hostel, just to avoid suspicion and to prevent conflict.

But on the twenty-seventh, the day the Americans came to Peking, the present minister wrote a letter and sent it to them. The letter contained only greetings and 'should the said envoy or others have letters to send to his country, the present country now has a man going to Pei-t'ang and he could take them.' Now after three days, the Americans have not replied to this letter. The present minister's man charged to go to Pei-t'ang cannot wait and now at noon, July 29, will set out and when he reaches the said country's vessel, without bringing any letters, will certainly tell the reason, thus confirming suspicion that China is not sincerely maintaining friendly relations. How can this be allowed? He begs the Grand Councillors not to prohibit this country's and America's nationals from seeing one another and also from transmitting their communications. By way of communication. (IWSM. HF 41; 11b, 7...12a, 7-13a, 2)

463. August 2, 1859. CHINESE REPLY TO THE RUSSIANS: The Grand Councillors Chide the Russian Minister Ignatieff for Irregularity and Insist on Dealing through Channels.

The Grand Councillors in charge, by way of communication. There is now received from the Board of Rites a communication informing us that hereafter the honorable minister will not receive communications through the Bureau of Dependencies and that he also wishes to meet the Americans and communicate with them.

It is noted that according to a letter from the Metropolitan Prefect, July 24, his deputy in charge of the hostel of the American envoy in Lao-chün-t'ang reported that your honorable countryman, named P'ing, came there to look around and said that he wanted to move in. This sort of thing is a routine affair of the hostel and so

was communicated through the Bureau of Dependencies to the honorable minister for notice. When there are important matters naturally
they shall be sent, according to treaty, from the present Council direct to the Board of Rites for transmission to him or from the Imperial Commissioner in charge of communications.

As to the American envoy now come to Peking to exchange ratifications, arrangements have not as yet been concluded. If America
has any replies that need to go to Pei-t'ang, naturally they will be
handled by Imperial messenger. The honorable minister states that
he has not sent anyone to see them, specially to avoid suspicion and
prevent conflict. He has a deep understanding of decorum. The
matter of communication must also wait until ratifications have been
exchanged and then suitably arranged. By way of reply. (IWSM. HF
41; 13a, 3-13b, 5)

464. August 5, 1859. MEMORIAL: Ho Kuei-ch'ing Anticipates the
Dependence of the Other Powers on the Ratified American Treaty and
Discusses British Isolation.

Imperial Commissioner, Governor General of Liang-chiang Ho
Kuei-ch'ing memorializes. In matters of trade, the English barbarians
hitherto have been the leaders and the American and French barbarians
have followed. At present the American barbarians have gone to Peking to exchange ratifications first and when they return South are
sure to demand action according to the new regulations. The English
and French barbarians and the barbarian merchants of the various
dependent countries are also certain to bring forward the statement
in the treaties of the Tao-kuang period that, "should His Imperial
Majesty grant favors to another country, each country shall share
alike, " and make complaints. If we do not concede, the barbarian
merchants will harbor a grudge and not lend themselves to our use.
Not only will there be no possibility of a policy of "pulling the fuel
from under the pot," but merchants will be working hand in hand with
chiefs to make it hard for us. There will be war and concomitant
calamities and, under the circumstances, no place to stop.

If we bow to merchant feeling and open trade opportunistically,
then the new treaties of the English and French not having been ratified and the old treaties having become waste paper, there will be no
treaties to follow. The consuls, interpreters, and customs officials
can all lower their hands and engage in graft and the barbarian merchants, with profit in sight, will also disregard the treaties. Thus
with barbarian affairs even more unbearable, there will still be no
basis for a general conciliation.

This winter, ocean (tribute) transport is sure to have more
interference. If we expect the American barbarians to be mediators,
the English and French barbarians already despise their chicanery.
Moreover, last year at Tientsin, the English barbarians' falling in

with our schemes was due entirely to the personal manoeuvering of Imperial Commissioner Kuei-liang and the others. Although the American barbarians talked about mediation, no results were apparent.

Thinking this over and over, sending a communication to the French barbarians this time was certainly the great key to the barbarian situation. So going back and forth for secret consultations with Governor Hsü Yu-jen, a draft was determined upon and sent to Acting Su-Sung-T'ai Tao-t'ai Wu Hsü. Choosing just the time that the barbarian merchants had a grudge against Bruce, (Your official) had the Chinese merchants send word to the barbarian merchants that in the Tientsin affair this time, the fracas was started by Bruce personally and had no connection with the treaty, was merely an obstacle to trade, and was certainly useless. Moreover, "when he first came to Shanghai, Imperial Commissioner Kuei-liang and the others waited for more than a month; he agreed to see them and didn't, agreed to negotiate and didn't. When he got to Tientsin, he would accept neither communications nor supplies, forced entrance to the port, bombarded the barrier, and pulled up stakes. We should like to ask if it is reasonable to do this to a friendly country? That Imperial Commissioner Seng-ko-lin-ch'in did not completely demolish all his ships was not due to inability, but to pity for his stupid obstinacy! Now he has received a little punishment and it is assumed that you all realize that Imperial Commissioner Seng-ko-lin-ch'in's manoeuevering is marvellously quick and our forts very strong. If both parties are unwilling to yield, your property and goods will all become worthless and what will have been accomplished?

The barbarian merchants all regarded this as correct and discussed it variously. Therefore, Bruce also got word of it, finally realized that popular indignation is hard to oppose, and gradually felt remorse. The Chinese merchants also had various merchants send letters home with a statement of Bruce's starting of the quarrel, spreading it back and forth in order to quench Bruce's fabrications which were calling for a hearing. Then Wu Hsü, having an opportunity that could be taken advantage of, sent word to Edan, Marques, and even via Marques to the barbarians intimate with and closest to Bourboulon, notifying them that Your official still did not know that the French barbarians also had casualties and that there was a communication ordering them to go to Tientsin to exchange ratifications. He also had this transmitted to the English chief.

With merchants feeling like this, when their sovereign hears of it he (Bruce) is sure to incur punishment. Bruce, it is true, has brought the blame on himself, but for Bourboulon, it is really not worth the price. At the outset he was uncertain, but in the end he

saw the light. He replied that in what was said the right was with us
and if the governor general sent him a communication he would
certainly not put it aside unanswered, but he did not know how he
(the governor general) would put it. Moreover, the English barbarians belong to a large state and if Bruce had his heart set on revenge,
he (Bourboulon) could hardly take the lead himself. The best he could
do was gradually to put in a word, and if Governor General Ho could
also send a letter to Bruce, it would be easier to talk. Marques then
told Wu Hsü to deliver the letter. After receiving it, Bourboulon sent
his reply, which was brought by Wu Hsü and the others.

Your official has examined the reply carefully. The expressions
are still respectful and compliant but he uses his inability to take the
lead as an excuse; he also says that he and Bruce are without the
slightest mutual suspicion. Guessing his intent, he seems to want
Your official to send a letter to Bruce also. Your official thinks
that while Bourboulon wants to get Your official's letter to Bruce as
a talking point, he is not powerful enough to bring him around and
we must rely on the might of the Heavenly Court to control him. His
(Bourboulon's) own words give him away. At first Bruce displayed
his violence to give it a trial. Then after being punished and incurring
anger of the merchant group, his spirit has flagged. This is very
apparent.

If this affair must be concluded by conciliation, to rely exclusively
on the strength of the Americans and French and leave footholds for
pretexts in the future is not as good as complying with Bourboulon's
request to send a communication to Bruce also, to the effect that before we charged them with not waiting for an interview at Shanghai,
now in Bourboulon's communication there is the statement that there
is not the least suspicion, and ask whether or not he is going to Peking to exchange ratifications. We will not mention the Tientsin
affairs. A reply would then be sent to Bourboulon, saying that a
communication had been sent to Bruce, still secretly ordering Wu
Hsü and others to have Marques and others, as well as the barbarian merchants, again devise means of recovery, particularly to augument national prestige and not give the impression that we are asking
for terms. Then we shall see if Bruce replies or not, and act
according to circumstances.

To sum up the present situation, since the American barbarians
have gone to Peking to exchange ratifications, and the French barbarians have been contacted, the position of the English barbarians
has been isolated. As to Bourboulon's statement that he has memorialized his sovereign and must wait for a reply to act, this is
still within reason, but the barbarian merchants have written letters
home so their sovereign will certainly have word of Bruce's reliance
on force and wanton action. Then if there is still back talk, we can
argue with them according to the replies of the various chiefs and

perhaps be able to close the affair and avert hostilities.   (IWSM. HF 41; 15b, 10-18b, 8)

465. August 5, 1859. EDICT: Authorizes Revision of the British and French Treaties at Shanghai to bring them into Conformity with the American Treaty.

Edict to the Grand Councillors. Ho Kuei-ch'ing has memorialized on his estimate, in accord with Edict, of the barbarian situation and his sending communications to the English and French barbarians. He also had the communication he received copied and presented for examination. Both have been read in full.

The French chief after receiving the communication said that he still must await a reply from his sovereign; the English chief had not answered. These chiefs started unprovoked trouble and incurred punishment. That they now must wait for word from their sovereigns is only natural. Ho Kuei-ch'ing has sent communications, the barbarian merchants have explained, and these chiefs seem to be repentent, so wait until they come around of their own accord and then consider action. It is not necessary to make further advances and thus make it appear that China is asking terms.

As these barbarians took the initiative in repudiating treaties, we must seize this occasion for revision of those terms in last year's treaties which are absolutely impossible to carry out. On the first of this month, detailed instructions were given Ho Kuei-ch'ing that the treaties of these two countries could only be exchanged at Shanghai, both, like the American barbarians, to trade at seven ports and they must indemnify us for military expenses. When the said governor general has received this, he must act accordingly. If some advance clue is not given now, it is feared that these chiefs will consider things still according to previous agreements without any change and when, in the future, they hear of our program, will certainly be greatly disappointed.

Order Ho Kuei-ch'ing to go on having Wu Hsü and the others send word to the Chinese merchants to contact the barbarian merchants, saying that after the English barbarians defied authority, they have heard that the princes and ministers in Peking decided not to allow them to come to Peking to exchange ratifications, to break off discussion of all the previous proposals, and also to demand indemnity for military expenses before they would trade with them. Fortunately some of the ministers recalled that the barbarian merchants would lose their livelihood, and that their population was large. If in the future these two countries repented and asked for terms, these ministers could certainly entreat His Imperial Majesty's Favor and ask for trade like the American barbarians at seven ports and exchange of ratifications at Shanghai, in order to avoid their returning to Tientsin. As China was unwilling to

remove her defenses at Ta-ku and the said chiefs were unwilling to
lose face and go by way of Pei-t'ang, they realized that it was difficult. In this way divulge gradually to the two chiefs the foregoing,
see how they react and then go into the matter.

Outside of the seven ports of the American treaty, those added
by the English and French are only Newchwang, Teng-chou, T'an-shui
(Tamshui) and the ports on the Yangtze. T'an-shui is on the island of
Formosa (Taiwan) which also has (the port of) T'ai-wan, so they can
do without T'an-shui. The Teng-chou district is unproductive and
goods are very scarce. At Newchwang the profit is in bean cake; on
the Yangtze the profit is in the transport of salt. Now it has been
explained that bean cake and salt are not being transported, so the
Yangtze ports and Newchwang are practically worthless. Moreover,
last year barbarian ships went up the Yangtze, encountered shallows
everywhere in the river, and when they returned to Shanghai felt
rather frustrated. Now with barbarian merchants, the object is to
sell more goods. If ports were increased and the sale of goods did
not increase, it would certainly be a loss rather than a gain. The
above items are only to be brought up when there is occasion, at
which time have them duly explained.

After all, England and France acted violently without reason.
If we allow them to exchange ratifications at Shanghai and trade like
the Americans at seven ports, it is already unusual lenience. As
to how to ask for indemnity for military expenses and all such demands when in the future he gets to the point of conclusion, everything is up to the minister's thorough consideration and energetic
execution.

In the treaties concluded last year at Tientsin, there is a clause
that within four months after the treaties go into effect both parties
will promulgate them for the full understanding of the merchants.
Now although the American barbarians exchange ratifications today
there still must be four months before there is action according to
the new regulations. With such a long period, the English and
French barbarians should have time to get replies from their
countries, so there should be no mutual difficulties.

Since at present we are relying on the barbarian merchants to
explain to them for us, we can assume that the various countries
will go on trading at Shanghai as usual. Also order the said official to memorialize at his convenience for our information.
(IWSM. HF 41; 18b, 9-20a, 9)

466. August 5, 1859. CHINESE NOTE TO THE FRENCH: Excerpt
Illustrating the Use for the First Time of the Modern Respectful Term
for the United States.

[Chinese Court uses the modern term for the United States,
Mei-kuo in letter to French; in the same letter uses Ying and Fa

for England and France respectively, in the old derogatory terminology.] (IWSM.HF 41; 20b, 4)

467. August 9, 1859. EDICT: Terminates Ward's Mission by Acknowledging Receipt of his Credentials and Authorizing Exchange of Ratifications at Pei-t'ang.

Edict to the Grand Secretariat. Last year English vessels came to the port of Tientsin and inaugurated hostilities, wounding our officers and men. Consequently Seng-ko-lin-ch'in, Prince of Korchin, was ordered to carry out rigorous defenses at the port of Ta-ku. This time the various countries came to exchange ratifications. Kuei-liang and Hua-sha-na had told them at Shanghai that Ta-ku was defended and they must proceed by way of the port of Pei-t'ang. Then in the fifth month (June 3-July 1) of this year England's Bruce came to Tientsin, disregarding the original agreement with Kuei-liang and the others, and ultimately wanted to force entrance into Ta-ku and destroy our defenses. On June 24 he sailed up to Chi-hsin Shoal and used bombs to shatter the chain-barrier. Our troops still did not engage his. Governor General of Chihli Heng-fu and others sent an officer with a communication of the Tientsin tao-t'ai. England did not even receive it and finally dared to open hostilities and bombard the forts. Our forces finally opened fire and returned the attacks, sinking many of that country's battle ships and killing several hundred infantrymen who came ashore. The defeat of the English troops was certainly self-invited, nor did China break faith.

At the time the American envoy, John Ward, still respecting the original agreement with Kuei-liang and others, sailed to the port of Pei-t'ang and asked permission to come to Peking and present his credentials. Heng-fu and others have memorialized fully. In this country's communication the expressions were respectful and compliant, so We consented to let him come to Peking and present his credentials. Today Kuei-liang and Hua-sha-na present the communication of the American envoy, John Ward, to the said ministers, for perusal. Apparently the expressions and purport are very respectful and derive from perfect sincerity. The credentials presented by the said envoy are allowed to be presented and Kuei-liang and the others sent to receive them.

For the exchange of ratifications, he really should return to Shanghai for exchange but We, mindful that he braved the seas and came from afar, give special permission to commit the sealed treaty to Heng-fu to exchange with that country's envoy at the port of Pei-t'ang and, after the exchange of ratifications, declare eternal friendship and trade to show Our tenderness for those from afar and ultimate purpose to exalt faith and justice.

Order Kuei-liang and Hua-sha-na to proclaim this Edict to American Envoy John Ward for his information. (IWSM.HF 41; 28b, 9-29b, 7)

468.   August 9, 1859.   EDICT: Orders Heng-fu to Exchange Ratifications with Ward at Pei-t'ang and to Return the "American" prisoner
John Powers to Him.

Edict to the Grand Councillors.   Send orders to Imperial Commissioner Seng-ko-lin-ch'in and others that now the American barbarians are in Peking and are rather respectful and compliant and
today are presenting their credentials.   The said country's treaties
have by Special Favor been allowed to be exchanged at the port of
Pei-t'ang.   When the said barbarians set out, send the treaty by
post to Heng-fu.   After the said governor general receives it, he
can exchange ratifications with the said barbarians at the port of
Pei-t'ang.

As for the captured barbarian John Powers, since he is an
American he can be restored to that country in order to show commiseration.   The English barbarian captive, being severely wounded,
need not be retained and may perhaps be turned over to the American barbarians for them to take by ocean vessel back to Shanghai,
turned over to Ho Kuei-ch'ing to be restored through the Shanghai
tao-t'ai to the English chief, Bruce.   This can also be utilized to
obligate him somewhat.   Instruct the said minister that it will be
sufficient to act with deliberation.   (IWSM. HF 41; 29b, 8-30a, 5)

469.   August 18, 1859.   EDICT: Orders the Emperor's Reply to
President Buchanan Delivered to United States Minister Ward at Pei-
t'ang.

Edict to the Grand Councillors: ... John Ward should have
reached Pei-t'ang.   The reply to his country's autograph letter is
now being sent by post to Pei-t'ang to Heng-fu, to be handed
personally to the said envoy to be received with respect.   If John
Ward, after exchanging ratifications has already sailed away,
order Heng-fu that he is to send it by post to Ho Kuei-ch'ing for
transmission.   (IWSM. HF 41; 35b, 9...36a, 8-10)

470.   August 18, 1859.   EMPEROR'S REPLY TO PRESIDENT
BUCHANAN: Official Autograph Letter to be Delivered to the President by Ward.

His Majesty the Emperor in return inquires after the health of
the president of the United States of America.   On July 27 of the
present year, Envoy John Ward came to Peking and presented
letters.   On reading these, the expression and purport are seen to
be frank and earnest and also recalling our perpetual and far-
reaching friendship, Our heart was really overjoyed.

The treaties drawn up last year have all been Imperially sealed
and specially sent by minister to the envoy for reception.   We have
respectfully received the Mandate of Heaven to cherish the wide
world within and without (China) as one family without any discrimi-

nation and, from this treaty establishment on, desire firm and lasting friendly relations with the president, to be enjoyed mutually,
which We trust must needs delight both greatly.   (IWSM.HF 41;
36b, 1-6)

471. August 18, 1859. PRESIDENT BUCHANAN'S LETTER TO
THE EMPEROR: Ward's Credentials as United States Minister Re-
translated from the Chinese Text.
        James Buchanan, President of the United States of America
respectfully sends several special letters to His Majesty the
Emperor of Ta-ch'ing. Now We have specially chosen John Ward,
an upright man of intelligence and unusual ability, and commissioned him to go to your Honorable Country and reside near the
Court in the capacity of American minister plenipotentiary resident in China.
        This official is thoroughly versed in the relations of our two
countries and can fully embody Our customary and long firmly
established desire for peace and friendship; besides he has a deep
understanding of loyalty and sincerity, which led to his appointment
to this post, and must needs respectfully perform its duties. Acknowledging the impressive Favor received at the hands of His
Majesty the Emperor, in his conduct he must do his best to guard
diligently the cherished perpetual friendship and peace of the two
countries in the hope of mutual happiness. He sincerely hopes His
Imperial Majesty will extend him gracious courtesy, particularly
in giving full credence to the various matters he presents on behalf of America. It is of the greatest importance that he present
to the throne America's true aim of friendship and sincere desire
for the perpetual peace of your honorable country.
        We only beseech the True God to grant that His Imperial Majes-
ty long enjoy the three blessings [i.e. prosperity, longevity, and
male offspring] in abundance. This is our fervent prayer. This
is reverently presented with respectful greetings.   (IWSM.HF 41;
36b, 7-37b, 4)

472. August 20, 1859. MEMORIAL: Heng-fu Describes the Exchange
of Ratifications with Ward at Pei-t'ang on August 16, 1859, and Return
of the "American" Prisoner.
        Governor General of Chihli Heng-fu and Financial Commissioner
Wen-yü memorialize. On the fourteenth the American chief reached
Pei-ts'ang. The said chief, John Ward, sent Your slave, Heng-fu,
a communication setting the 16th for the exchange of ratifications, so
Your slaves went from Ta-ku to Pei-t'ang on the fifteenth. At the
time, Director of the Board of Punishments Ch'ing-ming and Second
Class Secretary of the Board of Civil Office Mei Ch'i-chao brought
from Peking a communication from the Grand Council, stating that

an Edict regarding the American treaty had been received in audience. They also brought the treaty, the commercial regulations, and the supplementary treaty which Your slaves respectfully retain. As the said Director of the Board of Punishments Ch'ing-ming and the other had been associated with Kuei-liang and Hua-sha-na at Shanghai in handling barbarians and understood the situation, they temporarily retained these two officials at Pei-t'ang until the exchange of ratifications.

On the sixteenth, Tao-t'ai of Ch'ing-ho Ch'ung-hou and Major Chang Ping-to of the Left Patrol of the Hsüan-hua Battalion, escorted the American envoy, John Ward, in (from the ship). Your slaves immediately prepared a banquet at the hostel and received the said envoy. His speech was entirely respectful and compliant. Then they exchanged ratifications, saying that as Your Majesty, with virtue like Heaven unusually sympathetic, recalled that the said chief had come far across many seas and allowed him to present his credentials and exchange ratifications, that hereafter they might trade in peace and forego hostilities forever.

The said envoys were grateful for Imperial benevolence and pleased no end. After ratifications were exchanged the chief went back on board, and was very peaceable.

As to the captured American barbarian John Powers and the English barbarian Che-shih Mo-ko-shen, [7] Your slaves have agreed fully with Imperial Commissioner Prince Seng-ko-lin-ch'in that as the American barbarians have exchanged ratifications, the captive barbarian should be returned in order to show Your Majesty's ultimate desire for generous benevolence and compassion. The English barbarians are not yet pacified and if there were simultaneous restoration, there would seem to be no discrimination. It is noted that from Tientsin to Shanghai, ocean vessels come and go continuously, so if we wait until that country acknowledges its error and submits and then return him, it would be more suitable. The American, John Powers, has been personally handed over to the said envoy, John Ward, and others to take back. These barbarians were most pleased. The English barbarian Chi-shih Mo-ko-shen is being held temporarily and an officer sent to take suitable care of him.

Vermilion endorsement: Noted. (IWSM.HF 41; 39a, 1-40a, 3)

473. August 20, 1859. MEMORIAL: Prince Seng-ko-lin ch'in Reports his Qualified Execution of Imperial Orders in dealing with Ignatieff and Ward.

Imperial Commissioner Seng-ko-lin-ch'in, Prince of Korchin, memorializes. On August 9-10 were respectfully received the Edicts

---

7 The name of this second English prisoner has not been identified.

of August 8-9, 1859, to the effect that Su-shun and others had memorialized that the Russian barbarian Ignatieff[8] stated that on behalf of the envoy of his country, Muraviev,[9] he had come to Pei-t'ang by ship and also that articles were being brought, so Your slave was ordered to send an officer to escort him; and further, that the American barbarians presented credentials at Peking and their treaty was allowed to be exchanged at Pei-t'ang, so the captive barbarian, John Powers, could be restored to his country and the English barbarian prisoner might be turned over to the English [sic] barbarians to be taken back to Shanghai and returned to Bruce. Your slaves were further ordered to act according to their discretion.

Respectfully obeying in their entirety the comprehensive Sacred Orders, they immediately ordered Department Magistrate Ts'ao Ta-shou and First Class Sub-prefect Po-to-hung-wu to proceed to Pei-t'ang, wait until the Russian barbarian ship reached port, and then go and inquire their motive; if it was to send someone to Peking, then in obedience to Edict, send officers to take charge of protecting their journey. As this chief, Muraviev, has occupied territory in Kirin, whether or not he has ulterior motives cannot yet be determined, so on the other hand we should secretly make defense plans and above all not allow him to come ashore and spy on our condition. Several days have elapsed and there is as yet no news.

The American chief, John Ward, returned to Pei-t'ang on the sixteenth and Heng-fu received him, exchanged ratifications, and early on the eighteenth used river boats to transport them out to sea. These ships also went up the river to meet him and, after trans-shipping, got out to the anchorage of the large steamer between three and five in the afternoon. Early on the nineteenth, gazing out over the ocean, they saw that the vessel had set sail.

The captive American barbarian, John Powers, was restored by Heng-fu and the others to the said chief who received him. If the English barbarian prisoner were turned over to this chief to conduct, it would not seem to exemplify Your Majesty's virtue of kindness. It is necessary to wait until the English and French barbarians at Shanghai are pacified and negotiations concluded, then send him by ocean vessel to Ho Kuei-ch'ing who will proclaim the Imperial Edict and restore him. This would seem more in accord with the logic of the case, while Your Majesty's innately perfect virtue could also be clearly manifested to cause them to feel grateful.... (IWSM. HF 41; 40a, 4-41b, 5)

---

8 Nicholas Ignatieff was the Russian minister to China, succeeding Count Poutiatine.
9 Count Muraviev (Mouravieff) Amurski was the Russian governor general of Eastern Siberia and the Russian envoy, Ignatieff, was bearing a letter from him to Peking. Cf. two letters of Ignatieff to Ward in the latter's correspondence, U. S. Cong. 36:1, S. Ex. Doc. 30, p. 614-616.

474.   August 22, 1859.   MEMORIAL: Prince Seng and Heng-fu Report
the Dispatch of the Emperor's Letter to the President to Shanghai for
Delivery to Ward.

Imperial Commissioner Seng-ko-lin-ch'in, Prince of Korchin,
and Governor General of Chihli Heng-fu memorialize. It is noted
that the two American barbarian steamers set sail on the night of
the eighteenth, so the Imperial Autograph letter which was sent to
the said barbarians was re-sealed by Heng-fu and sent by post to
Governor General of Liang-chiang Ho Kuei-ch'ing. When the
American chief, John Ward reaches Shanghai it will be turned over
for his respectful reception in order to display Your Majesty's desire to restore peace and treat kindly.... (IWSM.HF 41; 42b, 6-10)

475.   September 2, 1859.   MEMORIAL: A Circuit Censor Suspects
Anglo-American Collusion and Urges the Strengthening of Tientsin
Defenses against Retaliation.

Shansi Circuit Censor Ch'en Hung-i memorializes. It is noted
that after the barbarian ships sailed South in the fifth month of last
year (June 11-July 10, 1858) the Ta-ku forts had been repeatedly
repaired in preparation, while the Pei-t'ang forts some 30 li to the
north of Ta-ku were also repaired, and besides the cantonments
30-odd li north of Pei-t'ang river, four forts had been repaired and
1000 cavalry stationed. Ta-ku is in the south, the cantonments are
in the north, Pei-t'ang in between; the three places are mutually
complementary, so naturally they could support one another.

In the fifth month of this year (June, 1859), when barbarian
ships came north it was desired to have them enter port here and
all the cannon located at Pei-t'ang were moved back to the cantonments so that they would have nothing to fear. The English barbarians did not follow instructions and finally opened hostilities at
the port of Ta-ku, destroying our defenses. Seng-ko-lin-ch'in,
Prince of Korchin, leading and in command, attacked and destroyed
more than ten of their steamers, killed and wounded several hundred
barbarian soldiers, and quickly annihilated their infantry on the
beach. While the defeated barbarians retired south, certainly intending to increase their supplies and soldiers and then plan revenge,
the American barbarians were outwardly respectful and compliant,
entered port by way of Pei-t'ang and exchanged ratifications.

Your official ventures to think that the American barbarians
and the English barbarians are partners in crime. In view of the
tight Ta-ku defenses they could hardly pursue their wicked plans
and, under the circumstances, they certainly reported secretly to
the English barbarians the depth at the mouth of the Pei-ho, the
distance of the route, as well as the fact that defenses were withdrawn so that they could make plans.

The English barbarians are unusually cunning. Previously when

they fought at Ta-ku, they fully realized their defeat and our victory,
so they are sure to revise their plans and contemplate action, in all
probability returning to Ta-ku and engaging Prince Seng in open
battle, while secretly sending troops to land by night at Pei-t'ang to
prevent our garrison troops from crossing the river to bring up
reserves, and then hasten south behind the Ta-ku forts. Invested
front and rear, Ta-ku would be in a greivous state. Even though the
intervening Hsin-ho district also has defense troops, proceeding to
Ta-ku from Pei-t'ang, they (the English) could still skirt outside
Hsin-ho village. Besides, it is feared that the troops in that place
might be taken off guard or be startled, causing them to hinder
general operations.

This is something that cannot but give us concern. (Your official) is impelled to ask for an Edict ordering the minister at the
head of troops to investigate the lay of the land and transfer the
troops and artillery back to the northern port and instruct the commanding officers to guard rigorously so that barbarian schemes will
have no play. This is a comprehensive plan. Perhaps the restoration of the garrison troops to Pei-t'ang is still more strategically
important. (IWSM.HF 42; 19a, 9-20b, 1)

476. September 2, 1859. EDICT: Approves the Censor's Warning
Advice and Orders the Strengthening of Ta-ku and Pei-t'ang Defenses.

Edict to the Grand Councillors. Someone has memorialized,
asking orders for rigorous defense of Pei-t'ang. He says that during June of this year, barbarian ships came north and since we had
them come in by way of Pei-t'ang, the fortifications and guards were
removed to the cantonment; that now the English barbarians have been
chastized and gone south, they are sure to plan to come back for
revenge; that in all probability they will engage battle again at Ta-ku
and secretly land at Pei-t'ang, intercept our garrison, and then
hasten south behind Ta-ku forts, investing it front and rear; that
although there are guards at Hsin-ho, the barbarians can still bypass it and he fears that the troops might be taken by surprise, thus
hindering general operations. He asks orders for rigorous defense.

The Pei-t'ang district and Ta-ku are equally important. Previously Seng-ko-lin-ch'in secretly placed defenses and placed
cavalry for relief from a distance and the deployment is still satisfactory. Now although the American barbarians have gone south,
the Russian barbarians are still on the seas, spying. Pei-t'ang is
the rear defense of the Ta-ku north forts and, however the artillery
is set up and the transferred guards placed, there cannot be the least
carelessness.

Order Seng-ko-lin-ch'in to investigate the situation thoroughly
and make secret defense plans and not let these barbarians spy out
our condition. This is most essential. (IWSM.HF 42; 20b, 2-21a, 1)

Chapter 13

Ward and Ho Kuei-ch'ing at Shanghai, 1859
(Documents 477-494)

The eighteen documents which comprise this slight chapter on the negotiation of a supplement to the American treaty of Tientsin are dated September 5, 1859 to January 15, 1860. There are thirteen memorials and five edicts, all of the latter addressed to the grand councillors. There are eight vermilion endorsements, six of them uncritical acknowledgments, one a specific comment evincing serious concern for the transport of tribute rice to Peking, and two other expressions of the imperial will. The memorials in this group are principally from Ho Kuei-ch'ing, who is now imperial commissioner, as well as governor general of Liang-chiang, and virtual foreign minister of China. The others are from Lao Ch'ung-kuang, governor general of Liang-kuang, and are concerned with the extension to Canton of the Shanghai system of maritime customs collection by foreign inspectors. The American representative in China is still John E. Ward.

The subject matter of these memorials is the routine negotiation of a convention revising tonnage dues and opening the two new ports provided for in the American treaty, Ch'ao-chou and Taiwan (T'ai-nan). The relationship between Ward and Ho Kuei-ch'ing, represented by the able Shanghai tao-t'ai, Wu Hsü, was friendly and was climaxed by a meeting of the American minister and the Chinese imperial commissioner at K'un-shan in Kiangsu province, forty miles west of Shanghai. The Canton-Shanghai relationship here represented in the extension of the Chinese Maritime Customs system to Canton shows a beginning of a broader national view of commercial matters in China.

These routine matters are not mentioned by Dennett but are included in the Ward correspondence cited in the previous chapter, U. S. Cong. 36: 1, S. Ex. Doc. 30.

TRANSLATIONS OF DOCUMENTS

477. September 5, 1859. MEMORIAL: Ho Kuei-ch'ing Reports Shanghai Views of American Policy and his Concern for Customs Revenue and Tribute Transport.

Imperial Commissioner, Governor General of Liang-chiang Ho Kuei-ch'ing memorializes. ... [In the opinion of Chinese merchants in Shanghai,] the American barbarians at Tientsin last year concluded their treaty first; in the affair at Tientsin this year, realizing that the English barbarians were unwilling to go, they merely

planned to improve their position and agreed to mediate, still following last year's wisdom and exchanging ratifications first. Their motives are certainly deceitful. [These merchants are convinced] that
it would not be easy to make use of them.

Furthermore, Wu Hsü and others have had newspapers translated, copied, and forwarded. Your official sees by these newspapers
that English barbarian ships, before their departure, observed the
lay of the water and took soundings in the Pei-ho district; thus the
nefarious plan of these barbarians is to sketch plans of the Tientsin
forts. The reason that the American chief at Peking was not grateful
for our generous treatment is because he had brooded over it and
could not forget revenge, for it is perfectly apparent that Americans
and English, while divided on the surface, are one at heart.

But on July 15th, Bruce and others sent a vessel with letters
home and according to the period ordinarily figured for the round
trip, there should be a reply about November. Now the matter must
be fully discussed and cannot be settled hurriedly so it is feared that
it will be late winter or early spring before there is a reply. Although a communication from Imperial Commissioner Kuei-liang and
others has been received stating that the American chief has agreed
to an exchange of ratifications at Pei-t'ang, the date for the opening
of trade must be discussed likewise with England and France and it
is still necessary to come to Shanghai for further discussion to prevent inequality.

There is also received Imperial Commissioner Seng-ko-lin-
ch'in's communication, stating that the American chief, John Ward,
on August 17th, weighed anchor and sailed south from Pei-t'ang.

During this half year, since both parties have been unwilling to
yield, customs are hardly expected to improve. Moreover, after the
ninth month (September 26-October 25) ocean transport must be
considered and in case the barbarians prevent coasting vessels from
leaving port, there will be further obstruction. It may be suggested
to shift to the canal route temporarily. But this route has been
abandoned for many years and if we are suddenly asked to restore
it, canal beds and barges would take several months to prepare;
nor are there any funds for this. Moreover, the Nien-fei (rebels)
north of the Yangtze are on the increase and glare like tigers and
we dare not make a reckless move. Or it may be proposed to continue sea transport, changing the route to come out at the Liu River.
They must not know that to go out to sea from the Liu River is impossible without flying over the port of Woosung. When the route
was changed to the Liu River in 1854, because the Liu (Taiping)
rebels occupied Shanghai, the distress was only at Shanghai and the
port of Woosung was unaffected. Now barbarian ships are anchored
within and without the port of Woosung, so what difference would
changing the route make?

Your officer, tossed in the middle of the night on the two horns of the dilemma, is like one who knows the cause of a man's sickness without knowing what medicine to use to cure him.

The American chief, John Ward, returned to Shanghai August 23, is staying at a foreign factory and has as yet made no move.

Vermilion endorsement: Noted. There must be suitable deliberation. Next year's ocean transport (of tribute) is fraught with difficulties. Nevertheless, we must compute the total amount and requisition scows, then we will have a lever. If the barbarians make any trouble, we can still secure arrival at Tientsin. We shall certainly have the Inspector of Grains explore the situation with the said gentry and ask for an Edict conferring Favors. (IWSM.HF 42; 22b, 7...23b, 6-25a, 3)

478. September 18, 1859. MEMORIAL: Ho Kuei-ch'ing Reports Shanghai View of Ward's Humiliation at Peking and Preliminary Conversations on the Convention.

Imperial Commissioner, Governor General of Liang-chiang Ho Kuei-ch'ing memorializes. It is noted that after the American chief, John Ward, returned, for several days he had secret conversations back and forth with the English and French chiefs, not leaving before nightfall.

The English Consul, Medhurst, while pressing for the arrest of criminals for the assault and murder of English barbarians, told Wu Hsü that Tientsin constituted a trap, enticing his people into the harbor, leading to the loss of many lives; that when the American chief went to the capital he was treated like a captive chieftain and then sent back to Pei-t'ang to exchange ratifications; that under the circumstances the American chief could not but acquiesce, but the merchants of the various countries were all furious and next spring planned to go to Tientsin to retaliate; that originally there was no trouble at Shanghai when suddenly the talk of seizing men [impressing coolies] was fabricated in order to get the populace to start trouble; that the real culprits were not arrested was clear indication that the Chinese officials deliberately incited the populace to evil and were determined to incite a general rebellion.

As his speech was incoherent, Wu Hsü and the others replied that when the American barbarian went to Peking he was treated with courtesy and even received an autograph letter promulgated by His Imperial Majesty, a superlative favor; that England and France, had they not instigated trouble, would certainly have received Exceptional Favor likewise; that now since they had covetously become jealous and made these unorthodox remarks in the hope of perverting truth, even a babe in arms could recognize and refute this kind of deceit, and there was no advantage in uttering it; that as to the impressment case, although their country was not involved (in the Shanghai riots),

the masses were ignorant, so how could they distinguish who belonged
to what country? Once passions were aroused, a public made indignant was hard to oppose. If it had not been for due repression and
protection by the local officials, they feared the grievances would not
have been confined to this. Since they had agreed to arrest the culprits, they certainly would not eat their words, but it was a mob affair, nor was there any instigator, and it was necessary to devise
means of interrogation and arrest. While there had never been any
useless indulgence, arrests could not be made immediately, nor could
they be parties to their oppressing the people. As there was nothing
Medhurst could reply, he left.

Then was delivered a communication from John Ward that after
ratifications were exchanged, trade should be inaugurated according
to the new regulations and asking that word be sent to the five ports
and also the two newly opened ports, Ch'ao-chou and T'ai-wan (T'ai-
nan), notifying the merchants. His complete omission of any reference to his previous correspondence at Peking with Grand Secretary
Kuei-liang and the others is clearly induced by the English and French
with the idea of an experiment.

Your official immediately consulted the records and replied. Then
the said chief sent another communication falsifying and distorting the
Peking correspondence, and demanded that Your officer, on September
15, proceed to Shanghai for a conference on the payment of tonnage
duties according to the new regulations and also on the prior opening
of the new ports, Ch'ao-chou and T'ai-wan, to trade, the rest to be
effected gradually. Moreover, he told Wu Hsü that if Your official
did not come to Shanghai, the said chief would go to Ch'ang-chou, and
as this matter was of great importance it could not very well be arranged with Deputy Lan Wei-wen and the others. Wu Hsü and the
others argued back and forth, resolutely refused to agree, but delivered his communication (to me).

Your official finds that the original treaties negotiated at Tientsin,
inasmuch as the duties on goods carried into the interior had not been
agreed on, set a period of four months for the issuance of proclamations. Later, the tariff schedule agreed on at Shanghai, that is, the
supplementary treaty, stated clearly that Article 28 need not be discussed. Thus the four month period is in the category that is not to
be discussed. John Ward first rudely asked to inaugurate the new
regulations and when Your official rejected this, requested only two
items, but once these are granted, having gained one step, he will
advance a step. Under the circumstances, this is inevitable.

It is also noted that Kuei-liang and the others previously told
him (Ward) in a communication that trade at the various ports was
not just a matter of his honorable country. At present the English
and French treaties had not been concluded and there could not very

well be discrepancy lest trade in general be obstructed, so it would seem necessary to wait until England and France likewise agreed and then inaugurate the new regulations. Whatever the settlement, he hoped that it would be discussed and arranged with the ministers in charge. The statement was entirely lucid, but the said chief's reply expunged the part "that it was not just a matter of his honorable country," leaving only the statement "that the trade at the various ports must be handled alike," cut the text to suit his case, and replied ambiguously leaving the basis for the present haggling. Your officer has now prepared a reply that he must wait to ask for an Edict to guide his actions, and will see how he (Ward) responds and then devise plans.

But Kuei-liang and the others in a communication to the said chief made a statement about conferring with Your official. If he insists on seeing Your official [me] and is flatly refused he is sure to go straight to Ch'ang-chou to terrify people's senses. Besides, the English and French chiefs remain in Shanghai and if Your official went there and did not meet them personally, their resentment would be increased. So he has determined when the time comes, to travel lightly with a small suite and, following the precedent of former Governor General I-liang in meeting the American chief, set a date to proceed to the K'un shan district for a meeting with him.

As to the two matters requested, if they can be handled the same as with the English and French it will be most satisfactory; if not, he will study the whole situation and if they are not completely obstructive, he will memorialize asking Instructions. In case (Ward uses this as) an excuse to speak on behalf of England and France, (Your official) will wait until there is an advantageous situation and seize it to advantage, by no means daring to compromise in the least.

To continue, he has learned that the Imperial autograph letter on August 30 was entrusted to Governor General of Chihli Heng-fu to send to Your official. He immediately prepared a communication and delegated a sergeant respectfully to deliver it to Acting Su-Sung-T'ai Tao-t'ai Wu Hsü, who reported that the American chief had selected a propitious day and would respectfully receive it on the 11th (September).

Shanghai populace and barbarians are now as usual. The local officials are still charged with the speedy arrest of the criminals (involved in the riots) and to prohibit the export of coolies. (IWSM. HF 43; 4a, 8-6b, 8)

479. <u>September 18, 1859</u>. EDICT: <u>Rules that the Operation of the</u>
<u>American Treaty Must Await Ratification of the British and French</u>
<u>Treaties</u>.

Edict to the Grand Councillors. Ho Kuei-ch'ing has memorialized the request to pay tonnage dues according to the new regulations and to open Ch'ao-chou and T'ai-wan to trade in advance. The
memorial has been read and fully noted. The American chief, John
Ward, returned to Shanghai and, falsifying and distorting the Peking
dispatches, asked the said governor general to go to Shanghai to discuss paying tonnage dues according to the new regulations and also
opening the two ports of Ch'ao-chou and T'ai-wan to trade in advance.

Trade at all ports must wait until the English and French
treaties are concluded before the new regulations are inaugurated.
Kuei-liang and the other's communications to the said chief were
expressed lucidly. Now that John Ward wants to start trade at
Ch'ao-chou and T'ai-wan in advance, if we give in at once, he is
sure, having gained a foot, to advance a foot. Ho Kuei-ch'ing has
now prepared replies and is awaiting his reply. If he insists on
seeing the said governor general, he can go to the K'un-shan district for an interview with the said chief. His request to pay tonnage dues seems admissible. As to Ch'ao-chou and T'ai-wan, originally not included in the five ports, it is necessary to wait until
the general English and French situation is settled before this can
be handled. They cannot possibly be opened to trade before.

If John Ward utilizes this to speak for the English and French,
the said governor general will still comply with the previous Edict.
He is not to discuss important matters with him in advance and give
the impression that we are asking terms. If these barbarians sincerely repent, let them make request themselves and then we will
be in an advantageous position, able to bind and loose. It is entirely
up to the said governor general to manage at the time.

As to the trade of the various countries at Shanghai, since tea
is the main item and at present the English and French are talking
about going to Tientsin to retaliate and are not willing to accept our
control, it is absolutely necessary to devise means of restraint on
the principle of "pulling the fuel from under the pot."

Order Ho Kuei-ch'ing to give secret orders to the Shanghai
<u>tao</u>-t'ai to ascertain in advance which countries the tea merchants
trade with, then if next year the said barbarians obstruct ocean
(tribute) transport, we can prohibit tea export. If the barbarians
of other countries demur, tell them that because the English barbarians are making trouble for China, it is inconvenient to trade
with other countries and encourage misrepresentation. If we handle
it like this, other countries may fear stoppage of trade and be resentful toward the English barbarians and thereby make it easy to
bring them around. But this is uncertain and it is merely a future

technique. Ho Kuei-ch'ing must be careful not to divulge it. (IWSM.
HF 43; 6b, 9-7b, 6)

480. October 4, 1859. MEMORIAL: Ho Kuei-ch'ing Explains Ward's
Bitterness in re his Peking Mission and his Desire to Open the New
Ports as Compensation.

Imperial Commissioner, Governor General of Liang-chiang Ho
Kuei-ch'ing memorializes. The American chief, John Ward, previously received a communication from Grand Secretary Kuei-liang
and others making clear that when the English and French treaties
were concluded trade at the various ports would then be carried on
according to the new regulations and at the time made no objection.
Then as soon as he got back to Shanghai he tried to experiment. Although fully aware that he was egged on by the English barbarians,
it was essential to investigate secretly what his motives were, then
we could act according to circumstances.

Having ordered Acting Su-Sung-T'ai Tao-t'ai Wu Hsü and his
deputy, Prefect Lan Wei-wen, to devise means to investigate, it is
finally learned that when John Ward was in Peking, unaccustomed
to the diet and accommodations and besides being in a solitary, isolated position, he was anxious to return south and therefore did not
venture any demands. Actually he deeply regretted this failure to
realize his heartfelt desires. When he returned to Shanghai, the
English and French barbarians felt that if they could not operate
according to the new regulations, why was it necessary to go to
Peking to exchange ratifications. (They implied that) his treatment
seemed no different from that of an official letter-carrier, much
beneath the dignity of an envoy, and that he was utterly incompe-
tent. In the future he would still be compelled to rely on the support of their great countries. Thus they ridiculed him.

Badgered by the English and French, John Ward requested
payment of tonnage dues according to the new regulations and also
the advance opening of Ch'ao-chou and T'ai-wan to trade, his principal concern being the opening of Ch'ao-chou and T'ai-wan, as evidence of his ability. In his communication he says that to wait for
an English and French agreement to inaugurate the new regulations
would make America dependent on other countries. This is what
was behind everything he had to say! The said barbarian, after receiving Your official's reply, sent another communication citing
Article III of the treaty that after the exchange of ratifications,
trade at the various ports would be operated uniformly, as an excuse for querulous argument and for changing the date from September 10 to the 20th, for his interview with Your official. Your
official has replied as is on record.

As to receiving the Autograph letter Graciously issued to the
said country, Su-Sung-T'ai Tao-t'ai Wu Hsü and others, after it

arrived, asked the said barbarian about a suitable reception ceremony. He replied requesting that it be respectfully brought forward
by the Su-Sung-T'ai tao-t'ai. He also, through the consul, W. L. G.
Smith, set September 9 as a propitious day to receive it. On the appointed day, Wu Hsü and the others respectfully prepared Imperial
Insignia and bore it reverentially to the barbarian consulate. The
said barbarians doffed hats and stood at attention, respectfully handling the affair as courteously as they could. Now according to
W. L. G. Smith's acknowledgement and also a reply from John Ward,
the latter has now gone to Japan, expecting to be able to return by
October 10.

The English and French chiefs have still made no move. The
barbarian ships formerly taking soundings at Tientsin and other
places, it is now learned from English barbarian interpreters, were
the ships of that country left in the North. Now on August 13th one
returned to Shanghai, still leaving two which are reported to have
gone to Hong Kong. The French barbarians, having been at war
with a neighbor state, have now made peace. The 3000 barbarian
soldiers which were withdrawn are awaiting orders at Hong Kong.
The English and French chiefs on returning to Shanghai sent letters
home and should have replies about November or December, but
how it is to be handled depends on public opinion and will require
another month or two before decisions on the various matters can
arrive.

Your official notes that although the American chief, John
Ward's, vascillation was instigated by the English and French barbarians, he is unusually cunning. This is his basic nature. In his
present communication he is still disposed, having gained a step,
to advance a step. His proceeding to Japan was merely that he
realized his position was weak and he could not hold out against
us. Also fearing the ridicule of the English and French, it is a
plan for temporarily leaving the country so he can eventually resume the negotiations. If he does not return on schedule, Your
official will examine the situation and in respectful accord with
Imperial Instructions proceed to the K'un-shan district for an interview with the said chief and act according to circumstances.

The culprits involved in the Chinese-barbarian controversy
have been arrested. The notorious Chinese traitor who impressed
citizens for the barbarians, Ni A-p'ei, has also been caught and
executed. The Shanghai populace and barbarians are getting along
without trouble.

The two communications exchanged with the American barbarian, John Ward, as well as the said chief's reply on receipt of the
Imperial autograph letter and the acknowledgment of Consul W. L.
G. Smith, are copied and respectfully presented for Imperial inspection.

Vermilion endorsement: Memorial read and fully noted. (IWSM.
HF 43; 17a, 5-19a, 5)

481. November 9, 1859. MEMORIAL: Ho Kuei-ch'ing Reports Ward's
Insistence on Implementation of the Treaty and Recommends Immediate
Opening of Two Ports.

Imperial Commissioner, Governor General of Liang-chiang Ho
Kuei-ch'ing memorializes. It is noted that the American chief, John
Ward, previously asked to open trade according to the new regulations
and notify the merchants. Your official has repeatedly sent special
memorials which are on file. When he received the Imperial Edict
of September 18, 1859, John Ward had just gone to Japan. Your official calculated that the said chief would return, so prepared a communication in advance saying that the matter of tonnage dues could
still be memorialized begging His Imperial Majesty to confer Favor.

On October 17th, the said chief returned to Shanghai, received
and read the communication and ordered the barbarian leader, W. L.
G. Smith, to go see Wu Hsü and others and say that after the exchange
of ratifications, there were three items requested: (1) authorization
to visit various ports along the coast as soon as American ratifications were exchanged and before paying duties according to the new
regulations and opening Ch'ao-chou and T'ai wan; (2) to fix a date
immediately for the payment of tonnage dues in accord with the new
regulations; and (3) permission to open the two ports of Ch'ao-chou
and T'ai-wan within two months. These were all items within the
treaty and must be carried out, so why had they been changed?

Wu Hsü said that in Peking His Imperial Majesty's allowing
John Ward to exchange ratifications first was an extraordinary show
of Favor; that the said chief's reply to His Excellency Kuei agreed
to uniform execution and also to a conference with the Superintendent
of Trade and, as the present decision was being executed according
to brief, what change was there?

The said barbarian leader stated that what was to have been deferred in execution was the Shanghai Supplementary Treaty, not the
original treaties drawn up at Tientsin, glossing over and arguing
until it seemed like there had been a complete reversal. Wu Hsü
and the others refuted him over and over. He finally said that he
requested only the granting of these three items in the Tientsin
treaty; the others need not be mentioned. Having argued at length
from three o'clock until nine, he withdrew.

As Wu Hsü and the others saw the situation, his mind was made
up. They forwarded a communication from John Ward which was
presented. Your official has examined the document and the phraseology is not clear, nor is the meaning consistent, containing statements that "the two ports must be opened," that "in the past, the
present and the future, ships have actually been trading there as the

honorable minister (i.e., Ho Kuei-ch'ing) must have heard," thus
clearly indicating that illicit trading has been going on at Ch'ao-chou
and T'ai-wan. His nature is extremely cunning.

It is humbly noted that during July Your officer heard rumors
that in the Ch'ao-chou-Swatow area there was an English barbarian,
Su-li-wan,[1] pretending to be in charge of customs and in collusion
with local gangsters, squatting there and fraudulently collecting customs. Notice was sent the Kwangtung governor general and governor
and the Canton customs superintendent to prohibit this entirely. Now
a communication is received from the acting governor general of
Kwangtung [sic] Lao Ch'ung-kuang, regarding the collection of likin
for military supplies at Ch'ao-chou and Swatow, that he has received
a report from his deputy Yü En-heng that there is a foreign merchant, Sha-li-yün, who has helped detect smuggling and is quite
rigorous. The Su-li-wan of the present letter resembles the sound
of Sha-li-yün. Whether or not the report is a repetition or if there
is another person, the tao-t'ai of Hui-Ch'ao-Chia has been ordered
to investigate and act.

Further, in August a communication was received from Governor General of Min-Che Ch'ing-tuan that there were barbarian ships
trading in the T'ai-wan district and that he was having the prefect of
Foochow send a communication to the English and American consuls
to send word to their respective merchants not to go to T'ai-wan
again. The English barbarian, Medhurst, replied that English merchants were not trading under the new treaties and that this did not
concern the said consul. He asked to send a communication to his
chief to order it stopped, so Your official sent a communication to
Bruce to wait until the treaties were concluded before he allowed
merchant ships to go. Up to now there has been no reply.

Besides, according to Wu Hsü and others, they have learned
that at Ch'ao-chou and T'ai-wan the various countries have traded
illicitly for more than three years without paying any duties; that
previously it was clandestine but recently ships have arrived at
Shanghai saying openly that they were from Ch'ao-chou and T'ai-wan.

Your official ventures to think that Ch'ao-chou and T'ai-wan,
now that ratifications have been exchanged, must eventually be
opened to trade. These are what the American chief originally
asked for. But the said chief wants to cover up the fact that illicit
trade has been going on there for a long time and so is urging a
prior opening. Thus he still has respect for the Heavenly Court
and his heart remains respectful and compliant. If we do not accord
his request, these chiefs' ships already trading at Ch'ao-chou and

---

1 This name reproduces the Chinese transliteration; the Englishman referred
to has not been identified.

T'ai-wan will certainly not be willing to withdraw and so these barbarians will then be able to do as they please indefinitely without any restrictions whatever. If we allow them to start in advance, the English and French merchants, relying on the old rule of the Tao-kuang period of equal benefits [i.e. most favored nation clause], are sure to go along with them, but the new tariff regulations which have not been ratified will by no means be allowed to be dragged in irrelevantly. It seems that major control would still be in our hands and not lead to any transgression of bounds.

As to the American barbarians' tonnage dues under the new regulations, there is a slight discrepancy with those of the English and French barbarians. We have the American chief's statement that he will certainly not bring up anything else. If he is granted prior opening of the two ports and we proclaim clearly the reasons why, after exchange of ratifications, it was necessary to pay tonnage dues and open Ch'ao-chou and T'ai-wan in advance, he will realize that it is an exceptional Favor emanating from His Imperial Majesty. Thus these barbarians would not be acting as they please and would have the utmost respect for our institutes.

As the letter now received made no request for a meeting, while the reply sent still provided for setting a date for a meeting at K'un-shan, Your official, fearing that having gained a step he would advance a step, insisted on a clear agreement with him. Now is received the said chief's communication setting November 3 for the trip. After writing this memorial, Your official will set out today, the journey not requiring more than a few days. When he meets the said chief he will make it perfectly clear that outside the three matters he cannot expect anything else. While it is possible to memorialize for him asking for an Edict, whether or not it can be granted, Favor emanates from His Imperial Majesty and it is necessary to wait until an Edict is received and act accordingly. When Your official has returned to Ch'ang-chou he will memorialize in detail.

To continue, the English and French chiefs have still made no move, but it is learned privately that the Canton barbarian merchants have accused Bruce of maladministration and the various barbarian merchants conjecture that their sovereign is sure to send someone else to negotiate peace. As they are also afraid that China will make further objections, they are certain to prepare warships to come along. Their place for starting trouble may not be Tientsin but Mukden and Shanhaikwan. They figure the time is probably next spring. (IWSM.HF 44; 19b, 8-22b, 10)

482. November 9, 1859. EDICT: Reverses the Previous Ruling (477) and Authorizes the Opening of Two Ports under the American Treaty.
     Edict to the Grand Councillors. Ho Kuei-ch'ing has memorial-

ized the American chief's urgent request for the advance opening of
Ch'ao-chou and T'ai-wan to trade.

At Ch'ao-chou and T'ai-wan, the various countries have traded
illicitly for more than three years. The present supplication of the
American chief for advance opening of trade is just because, trade
having long been going on, he wants to cover up the tracks of illicit
operations. As he is still respectful and compliant at heart, it is inexpedient stubbornly to refuse him.

When Ho Kuei-ch'ing has had an interview with the said barbarian
and duly agreed to memorialize for him, an Edict will be promulgated
clearly proclaiming the opening of Ch'ao-chou and T'ai-wan to trade
and also the prior payment of tonnage dues; beyond these, if the barbarian makes any demands, he will as usual refute him with reason;
he must not readily assent.... (IWSM.HF 43; 24a, 3-8)

483. November 15, 1859. MEMORIAL: Ho Kuei-ch'ing Reports Meeting with Ward at K'un-shan on November 3 and Agreement on Implementation of Tientsin Treaty.

Imperial Commissioner, Governor General of Liang-chiang Ho
Kuei-ch'ing memorializes. On November 3 Your official went to K'un-
shan. The said envoy, bringing with him Interpreter Jenkins[2] and
others totaling nine officials, also arrived on time. Your official
on the same day, in the public hall of the Temple of the City God,
accompanied by Acting Su-Sung-T'ai Tao-t'ai Wu Hsü and Prefect
Lan Wei-wen, had an interview with him.

The said envoy firmly requested the previous three items. Your
official repeatedly insisted on an agreement that on all items beyond
these, including the Shanghai Supplementary Tariff Convention, action
should be postponed, in accord with previous agreement, before he
would memorialize for him asking Imperial Favor and await the
arrival of an Edict of authorization. If Ch'ao-chou and T'ai-wan
were allowed to be opened to trade in advance, China would then
establish customs houses to collect duties and also order the local
official to arrange with the consuls suitable places to trade, in the
hope that there would be no damage to the general situation. The
said envoy nodded assent to everything, but asked that the Generous
Favor be speedy to ensure permanent harmony.

This is in conformity with the said envoy's communication. If
he receives an Edict agreeing to prior inauguration of trade and the
payment of tonnage dues according to the new regulations, the other
tariffs of the new convention are to be delayed until England and
France conclude negotiations before they go into operation. The

2 F. H. B. Jenkins of Charleston, South Carolina, acting vice consul at Shanghai,
January 5, 1858 to January 23, 1858, served as assistant interpreter, with
W. A. P. Martin, to the Ward mission. Williams, "Journal", op. cit., p. 6.

original American treaty and the reasons for the arrangement must naturally be sent for the notification of the various ports.

After the meeting the said envoy had nothing more to say and there is no cause for him to get out of hand. But the inauguration of the new regulations cannot be done without authority. Whether or not there can be this extension of Favor, he begs to await the Sacred Decision. (IWSM.HF 44; 33b, 8-34b, 4)

484. November 15, 1859. MEMORIAL: Ho Kuei-ch'ing Further Reports on the Details of the Agreement Reached with Ward at K'un-shan.

Ho Kuei-ch'ing further memorializes. To continue, after setting out Your official prepared a communication for the American chief, John Ward, agreeing to the meeting as scheduled and also to the previous exchange of ratifications, as a record for reference as well as to avoid a lot of palaver.

When he arrived at K'un-shan for the interview, John Ward said that if the three things requested could be enacted immediately, everything else could be easily agreed upon; otherwise, there was no use of further discussion. Your official replied that he could only memorialize for him asking for an Edict, not daring to agree to such an act unauthorized. John Ward also argued that in Peking His Excellency Kuei(-liang) had replied, in a communication dated August 10, that after ratifications had been exchanged everything should be managed according to the treaty.

Your official said that, as the exchange of ratifications at Pei-t'ang was agreed upon and the memorial reported afterwards, the proposal for complete implementation in His Excellency Kuei's communication should rightfully be entirely postponed, but mindful that their tonnage dues were really slightly different from those of England and France, and that the ports of Ch'ao-chou and T'ai-wan were also agreed upon with the said country in advance, therefore, in conformity with His Imperial Majesty's purpose of mollifying those from afar, he had agreed to this meeting and also prepared a paper stating explicitly that the rest of the treaty and the Shanghai Supplementary Tariff Schedule should not go into effect until England and France concluded negotiations, agreeing, when his reply was received, to memorialize and if an authorizing Edict were received, it would be an extraordinary display of Favor and would absolutely preclude further demands, nor could there by any contradiction. He argued with him repeatedly and when John Ward had no more objections, he wined and dined him and departed.

Later the reply was delivered and it was in complete conformity. He merely asked that after November 24th, all his country's ships should pay tonnage dues according to the new treaty and also asked that within two months from November 3rd, trade should be inaugurated at Ch'ao-chou and T'ai-wan. As for tonnage dues, an Imperial Edict had been received to the effect that consent might be given, so Your official replied that the date of activation as well as the opening of Ch'ao-chou and T'ai-wan must both be memorialized and an Edict of authorization requested.

Hearing that, after receiving the reply, John Ward proposed proceeding immediately to Kwangtung. Your officer, with Wu Hsü and Lan Wei-wen, made a thorough investigation and explained clearly to him that operation of the Supplementary Tariff Schedule was deferred and that the prior opening of the two ports and the payment of tonnage dues would be no impediment to the general situation; that if (the Emperor) agreed to his request, the said chief was expected to be grateful. Whether this memorial, besides that separately submitted, is acceptable or not, he must beg His Majesty to confer an Edict of clarification to enable him to act accordingly.

To continue, as John Ward made no reference to the English and French situation, it is apparent that he was not acting as their stooge. Your official did not want to give the least impression of asking terms and so did not ask him. As to the English and French, after their punishment, the earliest return mail would be received November or December, and when there is definite news, he will again memorialize confidentially.

Vermilion endorsement: Noted. (IWSM.HF 44; 34b, 5-36a, 5)

485. November 15, 1859. EDICT: Officially Authorizes the Opening of Two Ports and Payment of Tonnage Dues according to the American Treaty of Tientsin.

Edict to the Grand Councillors. Ho Kuei-ch'ing has memorialized that the American envoy asks to have the treaties promulgated at the various ports and trade inaugurated in advance at Ch'ao-chou and T'ai-wan. Ho Kuei-ch'ing had an interview with the American envoy at K'un-shan and the said envoy insistently asked for the promulgation of the three items of the treaty; the other clauses and the Shanghai Supplementary Tariff Schedule all to be postponed as previously agreed. The said minister and envoy made a clear agreement and while the said envoy asked that the Favor be expedited to ensure perpetual friendship, his attitude remained respectful and compliant.

As a special Favor, order it done as he requests, permitting America to open trade in advance at the two ports of Ch'ao-chou and T'ai-wan and also to pay tonnage dues according to the new regulations; the other duties to be temporarily deferred. The said minister will immediately notify the various ports to handle everything in accordance. As the ports of Ch'ao-chou and T'ai-wan must set up customs houses to collect duties, order him duly to discuss the regulations with the respective governors general and governors and memorialize. (IWSM.HF 44; 36a, 6-36b, 4)

486. December 4, 1859. MEMORIAL: Ho Kuei-ch'ing Reports
Arrangements for Opening the Two New Ports and Accepts Most-
Favored-Nation Status for England and France.

Imperial Commissioner, Governor General of Liang-chiang Ho
Kuei-ch'ing memorializes. It is noted that computing from Your
official's interview with John Ward, the termination of the period
of the said chief's request of November 24 for the payment of tonnage dues is only twenty days off and, while Fukien and Kwangtung
are rather distant by land, fortunately they are accessible by sea.

According to a detailed report of Acting Su-Sung-T'ai Tao-t'ai
Wu Hsü, the treaty provision providing for the payment of tonnage
dues has been copied. Communications have been sent to the gov
ernors general and governors of Liang-kuang and Min-Che, and to
the customs superintendents of Kwangtung and Fukien, and orders
given to the Ning-Shao-T'ai tao-t'ai, for the five ports, Kwang-
chou (Canton), Foochow, Amoy, Ningpo, and Shanghai to act accordingly when the period expires. Thereupon, Imperial Favor is
requested to allow Ch'ao-chou and T'ai-wan opened to trade in
advance.

Further, since John Ward asked that trade be inaugurated
within two months after November 3, that makes the date January
2 also quite near and customs houses must be set up to collect
the duties. If we waited to confer back and forth with Kwangtung
and Fukien it was feared it would cause delay; so when Your official received the Imperial Edict on November 22, he immediately
rushed a communication to the governors general and governors
of Liang-kuang and Min-Che to investigate the situation. Whether
or not it were necessary to make a separate request for an Imperial Appointment of a customs superintendent for the two ports of
Ch'ao-chou and T'ai-wan or if the duties should be taken over by
the Kwangtung and Fukien customs houses for management or have
the nearby tao-t'ai of Hui-Ch'ao-Chia take charge of the port of
T'ai-wan, (they are) to determine immediately and prepare memorials asking for an Edict of authorization. If they had not received
the Edict when it was time to open trade, they were to determine
on the spot whether or not to delegate the tao-t'ai of Hui-Ch'ao-
Chia and the tao-t'ai of T'ai-wan or to delegate other high officials
to take respective charge temporarily and submit a joint memorial
for retroactive authorization.

As to the American barbarians' new treaty, altogether thirty
articles, all are to be deferred except for the three items. As to
present trade at the seven ports, only tonnage dues are allowed to
be paid according to the new regulations; other duties must still
be handled uniformly in accord with the regulations concluded in
the Tao-kuang period. There cannot be the least discrepancy.
Communications were also sent the governor of Chekiang and

orders given the customs superintendents of Kwantung and Fukien and the tao-t'ai of Ning-Shao-T'ai that they were all to promulgate the American barbarian treaty in advance in order to reflect integrity.

On November 12 John Ward went to Kwangtung. We have duly sent a communication to the said chief to make him feel gratitude and awe.

As to the English and French barbarians, if they cite the uniform enjoyment of favors [most-favored-nation] clause and ask to go to Ch'ao-chou and T'ai-wan and to pay tonnage dues like the American barbarians, Your official can not very well refuse but will compel them and the American barbarians both to pay duties according to the old schedule and not under any circumstances allow them to drag in the new schedule irrelevantly. If the said chiefs send no more communications we can still avoid discussion in order to avoid the appearance of asking terms. Although implications are probably unavoidable, they will still be unable to exceed the regulations.

The Shanghai barbarian situation prior to November 19 has been specially memorialized express on the twenty-first. There is now received a report of Wu Hsü and others that the English chief, Bruce, since receiving letters from home, is rather crowing over his success and has several times summoned the merchants to confer, on account of which rumors are springing up everywhere and sentiment in Shanghai is increasingly apprehensive. As soon as anything positive is learned to show the direction of his purpose, means will be found to oppose it. Examining the Hong Kong newspapers which have been forwarded, they state that at Calcutta, which is a port of India, warships are continually arriving. There must be some scheme afoot, but we can only hope that every day their arrival at Shanghai is delayed, one more day's tribute transport leaves port. Otherwise it will be too late and everything will be subject to coercion, which is really unthinkable.

Vermilion endorsement: Noted. (IWSM.HF 45; 10b, 8-12b, 2)

487. December 19, 1859. MEMORIAL: Ho Kuei-ch'ing Asks for an Imperial Ruling on Most-Favored-Nation Status for England and France under American Treaty.

Imperial Commissioner, Governor General of Liang-chiang Ho Kuei-ch'ing memorializes. It is humbly noted that the American envoy, John Ward, after the exchange of ratifications, asked to pay tonnage dues according to the new regulations and Your official has memorialized for and received an Edict authorizing trade at the five ports carried out accordingly as is on record.

Now is received a communication from the English envoy, Bruce, and the French envoy, Bourboulon, that according to the consuls resident at Shanghai, Medhurst and Edan, as American merchant vessels at the customs barrier pay only four mace per ton in tonnage dues, their countries should be charged the same and ask that word be sent the customs houses at the various ports that English and French tonnage dues be charged accordingly.

Your official notes that in the Tao-kuang period the English and French commercial regulations state that if in the future His Imperial Majesty extends any New Favors to other countries, Englishmen must also be allowed to enjoy them equally, as evidence of justice; if any other countries receive by Special Favor, rights, exemptions, or protection, France will receive them likewise. Now American tonnage dues are being levied according to New Favor, while England and France are trading as usual. As these envoys rely on precedent in their request, it would seem that we should defer to merchant sentiment by extending Imperial Favor and not leave them in the corner. (IWSM.HF 45; 26b, 1-27a, 4)

488. December 19, 1859. EDICT: Cites Precedent of the 1842-1844 Treaties and Officially Authorizes Most-Favored-Nation Treatment of England and France.
Edict to the Grand Councillors. Ho Kuei-ch'ing has memorialized that England and France request to pay tonnage dues according to the American regulations and asks for an Edict of authorization. China in her treatment of outside countries consistently maintains faith nor was the affair at Tientsin this year a quarrel of China's starting. Now the English envoy, Bruce, and French envoy, Bourboulon, as American ships at the customs barrier now pay under the new regulations only four mace per ton, tonnage dues, have sent a communication to Ho Kuei-ch'ing asking that their two countries be charged tonnage dues accordingly. In the Tao-kuang period it was said that if in the future there were any new favors they would be extended to the various countries equally so we should defer to merchant sentiment and act uniformly.

Order Ho Kuei-ch'ing to send orders to the five ports where trade is carried on that England and France both be charged tonnage dues according to America's new regulations, allowing them to pay four mace per ton, in order to show that Our Favor to the various countries has for its ultimate aim equal justice to all. (IWSM.HF 45; 27a, 5-27b, 2)

489. December 19, 1859. EDICT: Advocates Policy of Alienation of France from England by Offering Exchange of Ratifications at Shanghai on American Plan.
Edict to the Grand Councillors. Ho Kuei-ch'ing has memorialized that England and France, on the basis of the American regulations, ask to pay tonnage dues at four mace per ton and an Edict has been sent the said governor general authorizing uniform administra-

tion. Later has been received a separate memorial stating that the English chief's determination to make trouble is at variance with the views of the French barbarians. The memorial has been read and fully noted.

The chief, Bruce, previously exhorted the barbarian merchants not to pay customs duties; the barbarian merchants, having been enlightened by the Chinese merchants, feared it would obstruct trade and did not agree. The newly transferred commander of Indian troops, realizing that the Tientsin terrain is restricted and military operations would be useless, advised that the port be blockaded but the barbarian merchants were not certain to agree to that. Since the French envoy, Meritens, feels resentful toward the English chief and the newspapers say that the English and French are not willing to join forces for fear of rivalry between themselves, it is just the time for us to take advantage of their nominal unity and inner difference, and devise means to split them.

Order the said governor general to order Wu Hsü and others to explain personally, saying that when France came to Tientsin this year she did not help England in the hostilities and China actually searched for the French envoy at Tientsin, wishing to negotiate the same as with America but the said country's ships had gone South and the arrangement did not take place. If they are really friendly they will be regarded the same as America and there will be no difficulty in exchanging ratifications at Shanghai. Secretly moving him in this way, it may be possible to prevent his helping the rebels [England].

As to the tonnage dues of the two countries, it had been agreed to levy them like those of the American barbarians, but we can still take advantage of the situation to draw them closer to us, perhaps ordering the Chinese merchants to tell the barbarian merchants confidentially that if in the future the English barbarians should repent, the said minister could certainly memorialize asking His Imperial Majesty, on the precedent of the American barbarians, to exchange ratifications at Shanghai. If so, it should be oral, dropping a hint, and can not be committed to a communication indicating that we are asking terms and showing weakness. If the two countries are capable of gratitude, the said minister will memorialize for further tactical instructions. By playing them back and forth, we think Ho Kuei-ch'ing can manage entirely satisfactorily. At present we need not reveal everything. (IWSM.HF 45; 30b, 1-31a, 6)

490. December 21, 1859. MEMORIAL: Lao Ch'ung-kuang Reports the Adoption at Canton on his own Initiative of the Shanghai Inspectorate of Customs.

Lao Ch'ung-kuang (Governor General of Liang-kuang) further

memorializes. As to Canton maritime customs, in recent years collections have not shown improvement partly because barbarian affairs have not been settled, but also because of excessive smuggling. It is noted that the port of Canton is cut up in several reaches and man's nature is perverse; corrupt people of the interior are in collusion with foreign merchants for smuggling. When examination is slightly lax, leakage is unrestricted; but when apprehension is too strict, it readily gives cause for trouble, so administration is unduly hampered.

After Your official arrived at his post, he inquired into the situation thoroughly and discussed everything with Superintendent Heng-ch'i, and agreed that we could only imitate the Shanghai system of using foreigners to administer for foreigners. Their common language, the fact that their true background is fully known, and that there is no possibility of their being in secret connivance with corrupt Chinese, is certainly advantageous to our customs service. So he had Heng-ch'i write to former Acting Tao-t'ai of Shanghai Wu Chien-chang and present Acting Tao-t'ai Wu Hsü to inquire into the system. Your official also wrote to Governor General of Liang-kiang Ho Kuei-ch'ing discussing it.

So Ho Kuei-ch'ing appointed the Englishman, H. N Lay, Inspector General of Customs. He has assisted in the management of the Shanghai Customs for years and been manifestly effective. He has visited all five ports and has been responsible for suppression of smuggling. He received Ho Kuei-ch'ing's sealed credentials and also brought the Shanghai regulations to Canton. Your official and Heng-ch'i met this man, discussed customs affairs with him and as he was lucid and intelligent, (Your official) immediately ordered him to start operating experimentally according to the Shanghai regulations beginning October 24.

Now having been tried for a full month, the change in the customs is gradually becoming apparent. As conditions at the various ports are not uniform, it is still necessary to modify the Shanghai regulations up and down somewhat. Heng-ch'i retired immediately afterwards. After the new incumbent to the superintendency, Yü-ch'ing, arrives and we have duly deliberated with him, there should be further improvement.

Vermilion endorsement: Noted. (IWSM.HF 45; 37a, 3-37b, 9)

491. January 6, 1860. MEMORIAL: Ho Kuei-ch'ing and Lao Ch'ung-kuang Report the Promulgation of the American Treaty and the Opening of the Ports to Trade.

Imperial Commissioner, Governor General of Liang-chiang Ho Kuei-ch'ing and Governor General of Liang-kuang Lao Ch'ung-kuang memorialize. In accordance with the Edict to promulgate the American treaty at the five ports and to allow the said country to open trade at Ch'ao-chou, Kwangtung, in advance and allow payment of tonnage dues according to the new regulations, Your official, Lao Ch'ung-kuang, received the communication and immediately proceeded to promulgate the American treaty and also sent a communication to the Canton customs superintendent to allow the said country to pay tonnage dues according to the new regulations. The various other items still to be charged according to the old regulations set up in the Tao-kuang period, are not to be confused with the new regulations. He also authorized him, in accordance with the original proposal, to inaugurate trade at Ch'ao-chou on January 1, of this year.

It is noted that in the Ch'ao-chou district, the Kwangtung maritime customs originally established sub-stations with An-fou as the main port, Swatow and other places as subsidiary ports, having sent customs guards and collectors to collect duties on goods of native ships for years. Now American ships are beginning to come to trade and, although customs dues are somewhat different from those on native ships, still as this place has been established as a port of entry administered from the Canton customs house for years as one unit, it can easily be handled as usual. Naturally, it should be joined to the Canton Customs House, managed in accordance with the general Canton customs regulations for the collection of barbarian customs. It is not necessary to inaugurate further expansion at the expense of uniformity, but when the port is first opened to trade it is essential to appoint an additional deputy to go and conduct an investigation to ensure caution.

Your official, Lao Ch'ung-kuang, notes that Yü Ssu-i, the district magistrate of Ling-shui, has had long experience and is suited for the commission and, along with the official originally delegated to carry out the job, further supervision will be exerted on the spot by the Hui-Ch'ao-Chia tao-t'ai and the customs collected will be reported quarterly to the main customs house and filed. It is noted that, according to the customs regulations, these are held to the end of the year and then reported jointly, as usual rigorously examined from time to time by the said superintendent to prevent smuggling, augment military supplies, and respect the customs administration.

The different ports of this place previously collected 21,900-odd taels a year and also paid over rice boat money, 36 or 37 thousand taels Now that barbarian ships are starting to trade and the annual collections cannot be determined in advance, it is essential to have them collected and forwarded in full, and actual findings reported, not allowing the least swindling. When a year has expired, we shall see what the situation is and memorialize discriminately on the execution.

As to the American envoy, John Ward, he has come to Canton from Shanghai. When he came to Your official's yamen and asked for an interview, Your official received him, proclaimed Your Majesty's charity and managed him suitably. The said envoy stated that he had abundantly received His Imperial Majesty's extraordinary Heavenly Favor and the people of his entire nation were grateful. From his demeanor, his respectfulness and compliance were expressions of complete sincerity.

As to his request to inaugurate trade at Ch'ao-chou from January 1, the time is almost here so Your official, Lao Ch'ung-kuang, personally told the said envoy to delegate a consul to go there to take his country's merchants and sailors in charge and to be careful not to develop incidents. On the other hand Your official, together with the Canton Customs Superintendent, issued proclamations ordering the merchants and people of that place to comply uniformly. As to any other unfinished business, if it becomes necessary to make any changes up or down, we shall from time to time deliberate and memorialize.

Vermilion endorsement: Noted. (IWSM.HF 46; 17a, 9-19a, 1)

492. January 6, 1860. MEMORIAL: Lao Ch'ung-kuang Reports British and French Requests for Most-Favored-Nation Treatment at Canton and Recommends Compliance.

Lao Ch'ung-kuang further memorializes. To continue, the English and French barbarian merchants who are at Canton, seeing the tonnage dues of America have begun to be levied according to the new regulations, were overcome with jealousy. Their chiefs came to Your official Lao Ch'ung-kuang's yamen, asked for an interview, and besought like treatment. Your official replied that as America had exchanged ratifications and their two countries had not exchanged ratifications, how could this be cited as a precedent? The said chiefs answered that the previous treaties provided for uniform enjoyment of favors, that his Imperial Majesty was impartial and must certainly be willing to treat all with the same charity and they only asked that the facts be memorialized.

Your official observes that while their minds are made up, their expressions are still compliant, so he must needs entreat Heavenly Favor to allow them uniform treatment in order to show control.

Vermilion endorsement: There has been an Edict. (IWSM.HF 46; 19a, 2-9)

493. January 15, 1860. MEMORIAL: Fukien Authorities Discuss the Various Formosan Ports and the Opening of American Trade on the Island.

Governor General of Min-Che Ch'ing-tuan, Foochow Tartar General Tung-shun, and Governor of Fukien Jui-pin memorialize. It is noted that T'ai-wan prefecture in Fukien province is isolated out in the sea and five sub-prefectures and four districts under its jurisdiction are separate islands. Formerly government and merchant vessels in their voyages and anchoring used the three ports of Lu-erh-men in T'ai-wan hsien, Lu-tsai-kang in Chang-hua hsien, and Pa-li-ch'a in T'an-shui t'ing, as regular ports of entry. Hu-wei harbor inside Pa-li-ch'a is also an anchorage for merchant vessels. Hu-wei's nearby Meng-chia district is also used as a place of trade by the various merchants.

Now that America has been authorized to open trade at T'ai-wan and customs house established to collect duties, we must in accordance with the original memorial, after the consul of said country arrives, make suitable arrangements with the local officials to proceed with the opening of trade and collection of duties. But it is noted that these barbarians' original request was to go to T'ai-wan to open trade within two months from November 3. Now this period has nearly expired. Although express word has been sent to the respective tao-t'ai and prefect in charge of the port to make suitable arrangements and act discriminately, still they are far away beyond the sea, the winds are variable, communications are hardly dependable, and if we wait for a return report, it is really feared the period will have expired. As that entire region borders the sea and is accessible at all points, it would seem necessary to determine the wharf in advance to avoid any confusion.

The acting financial commissioner of Fukien, Yü-to, who, when formerly serving as tao-t'ai of T'ai-wan, made a survey of the different ports, states that Lu-erh-men is near the prefectural capital, that Lu-tsai harbor is crowded with shipping and the channel narrow and shallow, and neither is suitable as a gathering place for barbarian vessels. He notes that there is only the one harbor of Pa-li-ch'a or Hu-wei. It is situated near the open sea and the trade gathered there justifies its being opened to trade and also the establishment of a maritime customs house at the nearby strait to levy duties according to regulations as evidence of commiseration. But when management is in the initial stage, pacification and repression are prerequisite, so it is necessary to delegate an experienced official to proceed to that port and consult duly and systematically with the tao-t'ai and prefect of T'ai-wan, then as soon as the said consul reaches T'ai-wan, they can confer and take action.

It is noted that there is a Fukien expectant tao-t'ai, Ou T'ienmin, intelligent and capable, with comprehensive discernment and penetration, capable of being sent on this commission and handling painstakingly all commercial matters, so this tao-t'ai was sent to assume full charge. It is also asked that hereafter new appointments be considered annually in order to equalize the exertion. His salary will depend on his execution of public business. If the said official manages really efficiently, then he will be retained another year to take advantage of his experience, after a record of his achievements has been made and an extension of Imperial Favor requested. Whenever there are matters of Chinese-barbarian relations the said official is required to confer with the tao-t'ai of T'ai-wan and manage as they arise, as a matter of precaution.

As to the duties to be collected, it is noted that the customs houses originally set up at Amoy and Foochow in Fukien province have been administered jointly by the Foochow Tartar General's yamen, sending officers to each port to take charge of collections. Although originally T'ai-wan had no maritime customs house it will

collect the same duties and so must likewise be administered by the
Foochow Tartar General of the Fukien Customs, a commercial tao-
t'ai being commissioned for the job every year to handle customs
affairs jointly. The customs receipts are to be submitted quarterly
and deposited separately by the Foochow Tartar General and, according to precedent, at the end of the year reported to the Court
for liquidation. There is no need of a separate request for Imperial
appointment of a superintendent, thus effecting an economy.

At present the barbarians are about to inaugurate trade. Before
having memorialized and receiving an Edict of instruction, the said
tao-t'ai, Ou T'ien-min, has been sent to take charge temporarily
and, in collaboration with the tao-t'ai and prefect of T'ai-wan, set
up a customs house and begin collections according to regulations,
in order to avoid delay.

Vermilion endorsement: Let the Board of Revenue confer immediately and memorialize. (IWSM.HF 46; 28b, 6-30a, 10)

494. January 15, 1860. MEMORIAL: A Circuit Censor Discusses the
Implications of British Defeat and American Peaceful Settlement for
China's Foreign Policy.

Shantung Circuit Censor Lin Shou-t'u memorializes. Your official ventures to discuss confidentially the military situation in various sectors. In the fundamental problem, the rebels are more important than the barbarians but in the immediate situation the barbarians loom larger than the rebels. Your official is of the opinion
that the satisfaction of Court and countryside over Seng-ko-lin-ch'in's
Ta-ku victory is unwarranted; and that the satisfaction of Court and
countryside over the peace settlement of the American barbarian,
John Ward, is also unwarranted. When the American chief made
peace he realized that we were merely appeasing him because our
military strength was inadequate. England and France also realized
that we would try to appease them. Therefore, although they have
been defeated, their treachery is undiminished and the more we reason with them the more we accelerate their revenge.

Previously Your official worked in the Grand Council and repeatedly read Imperial Edicts which were issued, ordering Ho Kuei-
ch'ing to lead on the barbarian merchants with trade and inviegle the
French barbarians with a treaty, hoping to use the American treatment on the French and then use the French treatment on the English
and thus nip the calamity in the bud, making use of both Favor and
Force.

If this plan is workable, it is really excellent. In Your official's
view, he ventures to fear that it is not. Although we are temporarily
using peaceful methods we cannot neglect the arbitrament of war.
Only by holding firmly to our determination to renew hostilities can
we stimulate martial morale. Now although Shanghai is angling for

peace, Tientsin is all set for war. If we are to fight again next year, what we have to worry about is Seng-ko-lin-ch'in, the nation's principal statesman. From Your official's observation, he is now our ace in the hole. The port of Tientsin constitutes the rampart of Peking and is of the most immediate urgency. The sea approach to Tientsin, the defenses blocking the river, the forts lining the coasts, have all been observed and are understood by (England) who is certain to work out a complete plan of action. Will they be willing to bring about their own defeat with similar rashness?

Your official assumes that they are sure to come both by sea and by land, will attack all quarters by night and by day. If we enlist more Ch'ao braves to resist their spearhead, secretly place cavalry to be ready for the onslaught, they will either, if our troops are turned by the success of their former venture, pretend cowardice in order to take advantage of our weakness or, if our troops are worn out by dispersion, rotate their forces in order to make continual attacks. As to Seng-ko-lin-ch'in, his excellent strategy, tireless loyalty and diligence, and comprehensive deployment, really defy description. But last year, if our enemy arrogantly belittled us and without knowing our real situation was able to pierce our forts, destroy our military officers, and throw our ranks into confusion, we can realize what their fury will be next year.

This year the Mukden-Shanhaikwan area can hardly be counted on to stop them, nor has the Pei-t'ang area enough troops for disposition. Leading the various regiments there are only Lo-shan, Kuo-jui, Hsi-ling-a, Jui-hsi et al., some military, some civil; some brave, some cowardly. In case our two armies join battle, when affairs are critical and reenforcements fail, our troops may withdraw.

As to Seng-ko-lin-ch'in, his personal defiance of arrows and stones is a thoroughly rash and foolhardy plan. Your official observes that Lieutenant General Sheng-pao is naturally firm but boastful, determined but mean-natured, and perhaps unsuited to fill the post of Tartar General [i.e., replace Seng-ko-lin-ch'in]. Even though he goes forth to meet the enemy bravely and faces him without fear, still his real forte is field warfare. Have him remain temporarily in the Pei-t'ang area. Then Mukden and Shanhaikwan will cooperate in defense and we can certainly destroy the enemy successfully. Besides these, the Chiang-nan [Yangtze Valley] divisions still have many able generals, such as Li Jo-chu, Chang Yu-liang, and Feng Tzu-ts'ai, and the ablest must be selected in advance. So let your Majesty instruct Ho-ch'un and Chang Kuo-liang to discuss the expediency of transferring them to Seng-ko-lin-ch'in for commission. Then after barbarian affairs are somewhat settled return them to their posts.

Vermilion endorsement: Read this with Prince Hui and others; also discuss it thoroughly with Seng-ko-lin-ch'in. (IWSM.HF 46; 30b, 1-32a, 2)

Chapter 14

Ward and the Anglo-French Hostilities of 1860
(Documents 495-544)

The fifty miscellaneous documents of this final chapter are dated
March 10, 1860 to June 6, 1861. There are twenty-eight memorials and
nineteen edicts, all but two of the latter being addressed to the grand
councillors. There are eleven vermilion endorsements, six of them
formal acknowledgments, four of them specific comments, and one
interlinear notation. In addition, there are two Chinese and one American notes.

The principal memorialists are Hsüeh Huan, now promoted to governor of Kiangsu, imperial commissioner, and virtual foreign minister
of China up to the time of the establishment of the Tsungli Yamen;
Prince General Seng-ko-lin-ch'in, who was in command of Chinese
forces; Prince Kung, who acted for the emperor after the latter's
flight to Jehol; and Marquis Tseng Kuo fan, representative of the new
"liberal" group of Chinese statesmen just emerging at this time.
Minor memorialists are Yüan Hsi tsu, acting junior vice president
of the Board of Revenue and sub-chancellor of the Grand Secretariat;
Kuei-liang and Wen-hsiang, acting with Prince Kung in the peace negotiations and in the new Tsungli Yamen; Yüan Chia-san, military imperial commissioner in Anhwei; and Kuan-wen, associate grand secretary.

The subject matter of the documents included in this chapter is
almost entirely outside the sphere of American activities, but the
events are so important to the United States that these documents
cannot be ignored. The major events are the Anglo French hostili
ties, resulting in the occupation of Peking, the flight of the emperor
to Jehol, and the burning of the Summer Palace. After the hostilities,
there are peace negotiations, to which the United States was not a
party, and the establishment of the Tsungli Yamen in Peking to handle
China's foreign relations. These catastrophic events are also marked
by the emergence of three important Chinese figures in the field of
foreign relations: Hsüeh Huan, new imperial commissioner at Shanghai; Prince Kung, head of the new Tsüngli Yamen; and Marquis Tseng
Kuo-fan, elder statesman and advocate of the westernization of China's
military organization and of a strong China.

American participation in this climactic year was purely peripheral. John E. Ward remained in China as American minister until
late in 1860. Throughout the period, Chinese hope for American mediation and good offices continued. When the Summer Palace was burned,
the original copy of the American treaty was lost and there was much
concern on the part of the Chinese officials for fear this would cause

further international trouble for China.

　　This period is dealt with in two articles by Professor T. F. Tsiang, "China, England, and Russia in 1860," in the Cambridge Historical Journal, volume 3 (1929), pages 115 to 121; and "Origins of the Tsungli Yamen," in the Chinese Social and Political Science Review, volume 15 (1931), pages 92 to 97. The Ward Correspondence, cited above, also contains some material on this period, U. S. Cong. 36:1, S. Ex. Doc. 30.

TRANSLATIONS OF DOCUMENTS

495. March 10, 1860. EDICT: Appoints Hsüeh Huan Governor of Kiangsu and Assistant Commercial Administrator of the Five Ports.

　　Edict to the Grand Secretariat. Chiang-ning Financial Commissioner Hsüeh Huan is ordered to take over in addition the rank of governor, to assist in handling commercial affairs of the Five Ports. (IWSM.HF 48; 26a, 5)

496. June 8, 1860. EDICT: Appoints Hsüeh Huan Acting Imperial Commissioner in charge of Commercial Affairs of the Five Ports.

　　Edict to the Grand Secretariat. Financial Commissioner of Kiangsu Hsüeh Huan is ordered to take over the seal as Acting Imperial Commissioner, in charge of commercial affairs of the Five Ports. (IWSM.HF 51; 26a, 3-4)

497. June 26, 1860. MEMORIAL: Hsüeh Huan Reports from Shanghai Ward's Determination to go to Tientsin with England and France.

　　Financial Commissioner of Kiangsu, with temporary rank of Governor, Hsüeh Huan memorializes: ... The American chief, John Ward, has now also returned to Shanghai and has had an interview with Your officials. He said that he, the said chief, would also have to go to Tientsin. Your officials tried to stop him, saying that his country's affairs had been concluded; but the said chief said, "If the English and French go to Tientsin I shall have to go too."

　　As we observe the said chief's attitude, while he has no desire to do harm, he cannot exert himself on our behalf.... (IWSM.HF 52; 12b, 9...14a, 2-6)

498. June 26, 1860. EDICT: Urges Hsüeh Huan to Dissuade Ward from Coming to Tientsin with the English and French.

　　Edict to the Grand Councillors: ... As the American barbarians have exchanged ratifications, why do they also want to come to Tientsin? They are obviously in secret collusion with the English and French barbarians. If on arrival at Tientsin any harm comes to the vessels of these barbarians it is sure to afford them a pretext. Order Hsüeh Huan to explain to them in detail and not let them come. This is most essential. (IWSM.HF 52; 17b, 6...18a, 10-18b, 2)

499. June 30, 1860. MEMORIAL: The Governor of Fukien Reports the Arrival at Amoy of an "American" Steamer with Three Hundred Foreign Troops Aboard.

Governor General of Min-Che Ch'ing-tuan and Governor of Fukien Jui-pin memorialize: ...Also on May 18, an American (Flowery-Flag) three masted steamer carrying more than three hundred barbarian troops arrived at Amoy from Hong Kong, and then on May 26, left port, sailing north.... (IWSM.HF 52; 36b, 5...37a, 2-4)

500. July 13, 1860. MEMORIAL: Hsüeh Huan Reports the Suspicion that Ward and Ignatieff are in Collusion with Lord Elgin and Baron Gros.

Acting Imperial Commissioner, Temporarily Acting Governor General of Liang-chiang, Governor of Kiangsu Hsüeh Huan memorializes. Your official ventured to memorialize express on June 13th that England and France were in close collaboration and that Elgin and Gros were still coming to Shanghai, as is on record.

Now on June 16th the American chief, John Ward, came to see your governor general, Ho Kuei-ch'ing, and notified him that the Russian envoy Ignatieff had left Peking, proceeding on board a steamer and on June 16th arrived at Shanghai. When Ho Kuei-ch'ing inquired on what business the Russian envoy came to Shanghai and how many ships he brought, the said chief replied sketchily, saying only that he was bringing the Shanghai resident consul, that there were altogether two steamers, one setting out from Peking, one coming from his native Russia, that there were several others that should arrive shortly, and that Ignatieff had resided at Peking for eleven months.

It is noted that the Russian envoy arrived unexpectedly and his intentions had not been learned. When several days passed without his coming to ask for an interview, orders were sent the Chinese merchant Yang Fang and others to make secret inquiry. According to their report, the said merchants had both deliberately and casually reasoned with Chief Bruce and Chief Bourboulon, urging that it was not necessary to lead troops north now, while they were energetically consulting and planning. The Russian chief arrived and strenuously egged on the English and French to fight. He also said that having been in Peking for a long time, what he said about the defenses at the capital, Tientsin, and Ta-ku was indisputable. He repeatedly told Bruce and Bourboulon that they should not be misled by the words of others advocating various views; that eventually they would have to go to Tientsin and fight and would have to destroy the Ta-ku forts before peace negotiations could be brought about. Chief Bruce and Chief Bourboulon, under his influence, were more determined than ever to fight and there was a proposal to go North immediately without waiting for Elgin and Gros to arrive. The

Russian chief also asked to go with them.

Your official observes that the barbarians are changeable, fundamentally vascillating and fickle. Now that the Russian chief has come to Shanghai and also steps in to make trouble, we find them even more difficult to handle. While Elgin and Gros are reported unofficially to be arriving shortly, so far they have not made their appearance. As it is reported that these two chiefs are coming on the same ship, they are already in alliance. Although now secretly using a policy of sowing discord, it is feared their secret plans are firmly interlocked and for the time being can hardly be dissociated.

Moreover, the American chief had just arrived when the Russian chief came on his heels, so these chiefs clearly came by arrangement, are exchanging information, are copartners in crime, planning to exhort and coerce. The barbarian nature is inscrutable and rigorous defense is absolutely necessary.

Your official and Governor General Ho Kuei-ch'ing must needs continue to devise means to prevent them from using force and, as soon as Elgin and Gros arrive, watch their movements, see what they are up to, and settle as opportunity offers, particularly exerting ourselves to prevent their going North. Then if it is possible to make a settlement at Shanghai, Your officials will again memorialize, asking for an exceptional show of Imperial Favor and commiseration so these barbarians will respect might, submit to virtue, and not give rise to further complications, then both Court and province will be very fortunate.

Vermilion endorsement: There is a separate Edict. The Russian barbarians' egging on the English and French is merely to profit from a middle position. At this time secret orders should be given the Chinese and barbarian merchants to find means of separating them. (IWSM.HF 52; 42b, 10-44a, 9)

501. July 13, 1860. EDICT: Charges Hsüeh Huan to Break up the Solid Diplomatic and Military Front at Shanghai by Sowing Discord among the Foreign Envoys.

Edict to the Grand Councillors. Previously because Ho Kuei-ch'ing and others wanted to borrow barbarian troops to recover Soochow, there were repeated instructions for Hsüeh Huan to put a stop to it. Now is received Hsüeh Huan's memorial that the Russian chief has reached Shanghai and is egging on the English and French to come North and fight and also that he [Hsüeh Huan] is recruiting braves and hiring barbarian braves and personally leading them to attack.

The Russian envoy Ignatieff has gone to Shanghai and is energetically egging on the British and French to fight; Chief Bruce and Chief Bourboulon, influenced by him, are more fixed in their determination to fight and there is a disposition to come north without waiting for Elgin and Gros to arrive; the Russian chief also asks to come along. Thus it is crystal clear that the various barbarians are in mutual agreement, exchange views, and are copartners in crime, while the Russian chief hopes to profit from a middle position.

At present we can only use a policy of sowing discord, secretly ordering the Chinese and barbarian merchants to interpose as occasion offers, saying that when the Russian chief was in Peking he frequently spoke of helping China and this time it is not certain that he is not enticing the English and French to come in order to get them chastised, hoping to get in good with China; that they cannot give credence to Russian barbarian advice to the detriment of peace negotiations; that Tientsin is fully prepared and if they come to fight they are not sure to succeed and will have expended their effort unprofitably. Besides last year's fracas was started by them, so if they will withdraw the four articles, conclude a treaty at Shanghai, then exchange ratifications, and thereafter have eternal peace, isn't that best?

At present, do not merely appease Chief Bruce and Chief Bourboulon and prevent them from coming suddenly to Peking, but when Chief Elgin and Chief Gros arrive you must also find means to stop them, explaining to them adroitly

Hsüeh Huan is now acting governor general of Liang-chiang, Imperial Commissioner to the Five Ports; the authority lies in his person alone and the responsibility cannot be shifted. He cannot plead inability to detain them, repeating Ho Kuei-ch'ing's reason for debasement, and thus fail his commission.... (IWSM.HF 52; 44a, 10-45a, 4)

502. July 14, 1860. EDICT: Orders All American Communications Presented Outside the Five Treaty Ports Rejected by Chinese Coastal Officials.

Edict to the Grand Councillors: ...To continue, today according to a memorial from Seng-ko-lin-ch'in and others, a Russian barbarian vessel anchored at Pei-t'ang to deliver letters and also delivered a letter for the American barbarians. Russia's established treaties have a clause allowing them to communicate at Pei-t'ang, but America does not come under this rule. Orders have been sent Heng-fu to receive Russia's letters. As to America's letters, have him say that they must be presented at the office of the Imperial Commissioner in-charge-of trade at the Five Ports.

At present at Yen-t'ai (Chefoo) and other ports we suppose the Americans who have come are not few and although Tientsin is closed they will doubtless still try to present communications there. The said governor will secretly instruct port officials to reply in accord with this Edict, making them as usual go to Shanghai to present them. He is not to receive them. This is most essential. (IWSM.HF 53; 26b, 10...27a, 10-27b, 6)

503. July 14, 1860. MEMORIAL: Prince Seng-ko-lin-ch'in Reports the Arrival at Ta-ku of a Russian Ship Bearing Two Letters from Ward for Delivery to Peking.

Imperial Commissioner Seng-ko-lin-ch'in, Prince of Korchin, and Governor General of Chihli Heng-fu memorialize. ...On the 9th of this month (July) between 7 and 9 in the morning, from the top of Ta-ku forts was sighted out at sea a three-masted barbarian vessel sailing northward. It hove to outside Pei-t'ang, anchored, and remained. Immediately officers were sent out to investigate. On the 10th was received the report of Acting Second Captain Jen Lien-sheng that between 7 and 9 that morning, a sampan carrying eleven sailors and two barbarian officials came into the mouth of the river and beached. The interpreter, named Pa-t'u,[1] said that it was a Russian vessel and presented the card of interpreter Ming-ch'ang, saying that between 9 and 11 the morning of the 11th, Ming-ch'ang would enter port and had urgent matters to discuss with Representative Te (i.e. Te-hsiang). Jen Lien-sheng replied that as he did not know whether or not Representative Te had a commission it was not certain if he could be there the next day. When the conversation was over they returned to their boat and left the port.

On the 11th Your slaves sent Assistant Department Director Te-hsiang and Tientsin District Magistrate Yao-hsü both to Pei-t'ang for an interview with the barbarian. On the same day Te-hsiang and Yao Hsü returned to camp and reported that Interpreter Ming-ch'ang said that they were from Shanghai, were going to Japan on business, and their route passed this place. They had two letters, one from the envoy of his country, one from the American chief, John Ward, which they wanted to send to Peking to the Board of Rites for transmission to the Grand Council.

Your slave ventures to recall previously reading Hsüeh Huan's original memorial that the Russian chief came to Shanghai and energetically egged on the English and French to fight, also saying that having been long in Peking, what he told them of the defenses of Peking, Tientsin, and Ta-ku was incontrovertible, resulting in a strengthening of the resolve of the English and French for revenge and increasing their arrogant manner. Thus the Russian barbarians are at heart as inscrutable as the English and French. Now if we continue to let them bring letters back and forth, it is even more to be feared that it will do the situation no good.

Your slaves find that on June 4th, these barbarians left Pei-t'ang saying they were going to Japan on business and from Japan, return home, and now they are already back. It was really feared that they would make demands on behalf of the English and French. So when Te-hsiang and the other went to Pei-t'ang, Your slaves

---

1 The name of this Russian interpreter has not been identified.

instructed Te-hsiang and Yao Hsü, if these barbarians had letters to
send to Peking, they were not to receive them. If they brought up the
affair of England and France they were not to discuss it with them
either. They also had them give the letter previously left by Ming-
ch'ang back to them in return.

So Te-hsiang and the other, in accordance with Your slave's
instructions, did not receive the letters. Because the letters he
sent were not received, Ming-ch'ang was very angry. When asked
what subjects were involved, his reply was entirely irrelevant. When
Te-hsiang and the other returned from Pei-t'ang to camp, Ming-
ch'ang was still there, not having returned to his ship. Now orders
have been sent for the local military and civil officials to take proper
charge of everything.

Vermilion endorsement: Noted. (IWSM.HF 53; 27b, 7...29a,
2-30a, 7)

504. July 14, 1860. MEMORIAL: Seng-ko-lin-ch'in Proposes that the
Governor of Shantung be Ordered to Deflect Ward and Gros at Chefoo.

Seng-ko-lin-ch'in further memorializes. Yesterday Your slave,
Heng-fu, received a letter from Governor General of Liang-chiang
Hsüeh Huan saying that at this time the English and French barbarian ships were coming North and the American barbarians had
ships coming too. Now a Russian barbarian ship has come to Pei-
t'ang and presented letters and also has a letter of the American
barbarian, John Ward, to the Grand Council.

Your slaves thought that since the port of Ta-ku should be rigorously defended and the Russian barbarians are inscrutable at heart,
the proffered letters should not be readily accepted, giving them a
chance to spy around; they are also mindful that as there are French
barbarian ships at Chefoo, there must be American barbarians
among them. The governor of Shantung, Wen-yü, was in charge at
Tientsin last year and met the American chief, John Ward, personally. As the barbarian ships are now at the eastern borders, the
said governor can send a well-trained deputy to say that, as to the
American chief's turning over a letter to the Russian barbarians
to transmit to the Grand Secretaries in Peking, hoping to deliver
it at Pei-t'ang, since the Grand Secretaries are still not handling
foreign affairs, it was not received for transmission, nor was the
letter of the Russian barbarians received; that now the acting governor general of Liang-chiang, Hsüeh Huan, has received Imperial
Mandate to act as Imperial Commissioner in-charge-of commercial
affairs and, if there are matters that need to be discussed, he can
go to Shanghai and discuss them personally.

If John Ward is not yet acquainted with Hsüeh Huan, they can
even send an official from Shantung to go with him. Also have the
deputy tell the American chief in advance that if the English and

French are intent on using force, they will have to go to Ta-ku; if they want to discuss peace then they should still go to Shanghai, but they could by no means readily believe what the Russian barbarian says and fall in with his schemes.

In case the American chief has not come, he can have the said deputy explain to the French chief as occasion offers. Wen-yü can also send a communication to the American chief saying that as France has no differences with China, this letter is given them to transmit to the American chief, John Ward. Thus finding means to sow discord, it would seem possible to foil the Russian barbarians' nefarious plans. He can get information about the English and French. If this receives Imperial approval, he prays that Orders be sent Governor of Shantung Wen-yü to act accordingly at once.

Your slaves (feel) that as the American chief has letters to send to Peking, to have the governor of Shantung send a letter to the American chief would be a reasonable arrangement and can be utilized as a scheme for effecting a coup. Whether or not this stupid view is correct, they humbly beg Sacred decision and instruction. (IWSM.HF 53; 30a, 8-31b, 1)

505. July 14, 1860. EDICT: Orders the Acceptance of Russian Letters at Tientsin but Insists that American Contact be Limited to Shanghai.

Edict to the Grand Councillors. Seng-ko-lin-ch'in and Heng-fu have memorialized that they have accordingly transferred government troops to the defenses and that a Russian barbarian vessel has anchored at Pei-t'ang and presented American barbarian letters.

...As to the Russian barbarians' letters for Peking, order Heng-fu to send an officer to receive them and transmit them to the capital. As to the American barbarian's letters for transmission, in the treaty there is no clause providing for America to present them at the port of Tientsin, so they can hardly be received. Should an American officially commissioned vessel arrive, he can say that as their country has exchanged ratifications, it must needs act in accordance with the treaty and have no further discussion. If they want to intercede for England and France, they still must confer at the office of the Imperial Commissioner in-charge-of the Trade of the Five Ports at Shanghai and thus preserve treaty channels....
(IWSM.HF 53; 31b, 7-8...32a, 4-9)

506. July 17, 1860. MEMORIAL: Hsüeh Huan Reports the Departure of British, French, Russian, and American Ships from Shanghai en route to Tientsin.

Acting Imperial Commissioner, Temporarily Acting Governor General of Liang-chiang, Governor of Kiangsu Hsüeh Huan memorializes.... Now it is learned that the French chief, Montaubon,[2] on July 3 weighed anchor for Shantung; Elgin also weighed anchor the same day; but Gros still had to wait a few days to start. The American chief, John Ward, and the Russian chief, Ignatieff, that is, I-na-hsüeh also went along with them.

Your official observes that these barbarians are all banded together but are not fundamentally averse to negotiating peace. They seem to regard going to Tientsin to discuss matters as a distinction, but negotiating at Shanghai as a disgrace. Although Your official has devised means to explain and prevent their going North, there is no denying the barbarian temperament is unyielding and they have stubbornly refused to comply. It is clear that, relying on the adequacy of their military strength, they want to flaunt their violence. The French barbarians' determination to fight is even firmer than that of the English barbarians'.... (IWSM.HF 53; 40b, 5...42b, 3-9)

507. July 17, 1860. MEMORIAL: Hsüeh Huan makes a Reasoned Argument for Negotiation and Peaceful Settlement with the Allied Powers at Tientsin.

Hsüeh Huan further memorializes. The method of controlling barbarians consists entirely in conforming to their nature to tame them. Now these English and French barbarians are planning together to come at the head of many troops and in full anger. There are only two ways of handling; one, to arouse our officers and men, spur them to attack and make them fear our martial might; the other, to dispose troops like a wall and send officials to negotiate, making it impossible for them to spy out our strength. Both are plans for success. But to use force it is necessary to have the leverage for certain victory, otherwise it is unthinkable; to discuss peace, it is still necessary to have the force of military might, otherwise there is nothing to rely on.

Now in our country's autumn of many troubles, everybody knows that peace is precious; but if peace is the least bit careless, the consequences are infinite. But to get everything we want, under the present circumstances, our strength is still inadequate.

Your official in several days has agreed secretly with Wu Hsü, Lan Wei-wen, and the Chinese merchant, with the rank of salt comptroller and expectant tao-t'ai, Yang Fang, that since these chiefs are not willing to arrange a peaceful settlement with the governors general and governors of outer provinces, if some adjustment is not made, it is feared there will be another rupture, so we can only conform to their nature in the hope of effecting a peaceful settlement. They are impelled to ask that Your Majesty immediately send two officials, Grand Secretaries or Board Presidents, raised to

---

2 General Montaubon was in command of the French forces under Baron Gros.

brevet rank and additional authority making them Imperial Commissioners, one to handle English negotiations, one to handle French negotiations. If Grand Secretaries are sent, they should be sent for both countries; if Board Presidents are sent, they should also be sent for both countries, to avoid giving these chiefs a pretext and still enable them to confer with each other secretly. They must be fearless and confident, to enable them to evoke submission at their appearance. Then it will be easy to bring them around.

As soon as the two chiefs, Elgin and Gros, arrive at Tientsin His Excellency the Governor General of Chihli can first give each of the chiefs a communication, making clear that His Imperial Majesty has appointed such and such person as minister to treat with the English chief, and such and such official to treat with the French chief, and that they will receive them suitably and will set out from Peking shortly; they are to wait a few days and (the officials) will come there to meet them and discuss everything. The warships which their countries brought must anchor outside the bar. If the conversations were not satisfactory, they can still resort to arms.

It would seem that such explanation would not damage our national prestige and yet might effect their submission, but when we negotiate with these barbarians it is essential to have someone thoroughly familiar with the barbarian temperament in the hope that, in the exchange of civilities, everything will be in order. Besides, the wording of our state papers is full of meaningless conventions. It is always from these trivialities that calamities develop, so we should consider everything carefully.

Your official has sent Tao-t'ai, Expectant Prefect, Lan Wei-wen, accompanied by Expectant District Magistrate Huang Chung-yü and one or two Chinese merchants, to go to Tientsin on board a Shanghai coastal patrol steamer, go ashore at Pei-t'ang, and await disposition by the governor general of Chihli. He is impelled to ask that Your Majesty instruct Governor of Chihli Heng-fu that if Lan Wei-wen and others on board a patrol steamer arrive at the port of Pei-t'ang, he need not be alarmed, but have them come ashore and await disposition. On the other hand, Your official prepared a communication for the governor general of Chihli to hand over to the said officials for presentation in order to afford credence and avoid suspicion. (IWSM.HF 53; 43a, 2-44b, 1)

508. July 17, 1860. EDICT: Authorizes Local Officials to Permit England and France to Proceed to Peking via Pei-t'ang According to the American Precedent.

Edict to the Grand Councillors. Today is received a memorial of Hsüeh Huan that Elgin and Gros arrived in Shanghai and on the same day sailed North and also that he is sending officials to Tientsin to await disposition. Hsüeh Huan, after assuming the duties of

Imperial Commissioner, sent communications to the four chiefs, English, French, American and Russian, and the English and French did not reply. Elgin and Gros arrived at Shanghai, merely placed their munitions and baggage on board -- including bamboo ladders, carts, horses, and dummy barbarians carved out of wood -- and within a few days set out for the North. When Chinese merchant Yang Fang and others urged them to see Hsüeh Huan, the chiefs replied that they were only concerned with going to Peking, not with seeing provincial officials. Elgin weighed anchor the same day, Gros was still delaying a few days, and the American and Russian chiefs were also coming along with them.

These barbarians are united as one breath in their determination to come North. Hsüeh Huan had no means of dissuading them. The Ta-ku defenses are formidable and it is presumed the barbarians will not venture to enter them lightly. In case they should either cruise about outside the bar or go direct to Pei-t'ang, order Heng-fu to send someone adept at expression to ask their intentions. If the barbarians say that they want to come to Peking to exchange ratifications, not wishing to precipitate hostilities, or to present documents, the said governor general need not refuse, but can say as his own idea that last year the American barbarians went to Peking by way of Pei-t'ang to exchange ratifications. Now that they are here, if they wish to act like the American barbarians, not bringing warships and with a small suite, and will send a communication, he can memorialize it for them. It is entirely possible that His Imperial Majesty, governing all countries with uniform charity, will consent to their coming to Peking.

If the barbarians say they will resort to arms, the said governor general will on the one hand memorialize immediately and on the other, delegate suitable officials, still expressing his own view, to explain carefully that last year while England was the first to start hostilities, France did not assist her and His Imperial Majesty, by extraordinary show of favor, can still agree to a reduction of her tonnage dues, to show that China is not ungenerous. Now if they insist on resorting to arms, not only will the forces of both countries suffer, but there will also be no benefit to commerce. With this argument it may be possible to gain some advantage. Reason in this way, see what they have to say, and memorialize asking for an Edict. He must not reveal any idea of taking the initiative in asking terms, but should take advantage of circumstances and cannot lose this opportunity.

Hsüeh Huan is now sending Expectant Prefect Lan Wei-wen accompanied by Expectant District Magistrate Huang Chung-yü and one or two Chinese merchants to Pei-t'ang on board a patrol steamer to await commission. When they arrive there is no need to be alarmed, but have them come ashore and turn them over to Heng-fu for disposition.

As barbarians are naturally crafty, they may on the pretense of changing ratifications spy out conditions, or Russia and America may come first to intercede with the idea of delaying hostilities, putting us off guard, and then suddenly display their ferocity. We cannot but be rigorously prepared.

As usual, order Seng-ko-lin-ch'in and others to redouble their precautions. We cannot fall into their schemes. Although Seng-ko-lin-ch'in's responsibility is for hostilities, in conciliation he should secretly cooperate with Heng-fu for a suitable administration. This is most important. The original memorial is copied and sent for reference. (IWSM.HF 53; 44b, 2-45b, 7)

509. July 19, 1860. MEMORIAL: Prince Seng-ko-lin-ch'in Reports the Arrival of Russian and American Ships at Pei-t'ang and British and French Ships at Ta-ku.

Imperial Commissioner Seng-ko-lin-ch'in, Prince of Korchin, and Governor General of Chihli Heng-fu memorialize. On July 13th, was received a confidential Court letter from the Grand Council that on the 11th it received an Imperial Edict to order Seng-ko-lin-ch'in and others to make preparations for rigorous defense. Then on the 16th, was received a confidential Court letter from the Grand Council that on the 14th it received an Imperial Order for Chihli to transfer 4000 government troops, besides those distributed at T'ang-erh-ku and Huan-hao forts, for defense, as additional transfers.

Your slaves immediately delegated Assistant Department Director Te-hsiang and First Captain Teng Ch'i-yüan to proceed to Pei-t'ang to receive the letter of the Russian barbarian and also explain to Ming-ch'ang why they would not receive the letters of the American barbarians originally sent. Subsequently Te-hsiang and the other returned to camp and reported that the Russian interpreter Ming-ch'ang, on learning that only Russia's letter was to be received, was very agitated and said that the American chief gave it to him to deliver and now if it were not received, when he returned how could he face the American chief? Te-hsiang and the other argued back and forth and finally he (Ming-ch'ang) took back the American barbarian letter. Ming-ch'ang was still at Pei-t'ang, not having withdrawn, but said that when the tide rose he would leave port.

Previously, between 11 and 1 o'clock of the 14th, there was sighted out at sea from Ta-ku another barbarian ship approaching. It sailed to Pei-t'ang and anchored alongside the Russian barbarian ship. Ming-ch'ang also on the same day collected his baggage and accompanied the barbarian who came originally, out of the port in a sampan, went to his country's vessel and departed.

Between 5 and 7 on the morning of the 15th there were sighted out at sea two more steamers sailing toward Ch'i-k'ou. On the same day two other steamers were seen one after the other coming due west and went straight to Pei-t'ang. When the ships approached the Russian vessel they exchanged salutes. Furthermore, the Pei-t'ang officials reported that between 11 and 1 on the same day, Ming-ch'ang and the others came back into the harbor in a sampan; between 1 and 3 in the afternoon another sampan of the Russian barbarians followed them in; they also came ashore and entered a temple where they met Ming-ch'ang. The said local officials questioned them and Ming-ch'ang said that they were delivering letters to him and that afterward there would be two more vessels come here. When the delegates questioned Ming-ch'ang further as to the nationality of the two steamers that arrived today, he said that they were American ships.

Your slaves venture to note that as the ships now anchored at Pei-t'ang are Russian and American, the ships cruising about Ch'i-k'ou must unquestionably be English and French. Thus the barbarian chiefs of the four countries are following on each other's heels. That they are all in communication, like devil--like ogre, is already apparent. Besides, the English and French barbarian ships in the vicinity of Ch'i-k'ou come and go suddenly, cruising back and forth giving the impression of spying out our condition, and also are taking soundings at Kao-sha Mountain and Lu-chu River. Furthermore, people who seemed to be Cantonese came ashore and asked the direct route to Tientsin. These barbarians' attitude is certainly inscrutable and we must needs have rigorous defense plans....
(IWSM.HF 54; 1a, 2-2a, 10)

510. July 19, 1860. MEMORIAL: Prince Seng Anticipates Hostilities but Requests T'an T'ing-hsiang and Ch'ung-lun be Appointed for Preliminary Negotiations.

Seng-ko-lin-ch'in and others further memorialize: ...Now it is noted that outside Pei-t'ang there was previously a Russian vessel. Yesterday it was reported further that the American barbarians also had a ship arrive and it is assumed that the English and French barbarians' ships will also follow them in.

Looking over this situation, the Russians and Americans are outwardly receptive and secretly defiant, so the English and French are plotting with them to assist in the evil. The situation is obvious. It is also feared that it will be like the spring of 1858. Your slave, Seng-ko-lin-ch'in, in charge of military activities, has only to make rigorous defense; Your slave Heng-fu is responsible for the area so how can he make any excuses? After arrival at his post last year he has only had to arrange matters of defense with Your slave, Seng-ko-lin-ch'in, as is thoroughly understood by the barbarians.

If peace negotiations are managed by one person, Your slave

Heng-fu, the barbarians are sure to regard it as an evidence of weakness and have their pride stimulated. Besides the situation is not at all like the American exchange of ratifications last year. If when the ships of the English and French barbarians arrive, they find there are no people whom they have seen before to talk with, they are sure to regard China as repudiating the revision clause and have a pretext for wrangling. It will be difficult to explain and so will be an obstruction to peace negotiations.

Your slaves have considered time and again whether or not it would be possible for either T'an T'ing-hsiang or Ch'ung-lun to be Imperially sent to Tientsin to confer with Your slave Heng-fu on barbarian affairs. To the general barbarian situation, this would seem beneficial.

Vermilion endorsement: There is a separate Edict. Seng-ko-lin-ch'in is familiar with the general situation and has the complete confidence of his troops. When war is the arbiter he is absolutely flawless and in conciliation he is certainly capable of making a decision. Since Heng-fu is a high provincial official with the added responsibility of defense, whether considering war or conciliation, both concern the people of the Empire, so how can he insist on having his own way? If he still insists on going back to old views, we can only revert to the winter of '57 before the loss of Canton and We should like to ask if this is possible? (IWSM.HF 54; 2b, 8...4b, 7-5b, 4)

511. July 26, 1860. MEMORIAL: Hsüeh Huan Reports his Failure to Prevent Ward's Going to Peking Despite Repeated Argument and Threats.
Acting Imperial Commissioner, Temporarily Acting Governor General of Liang-chiang, Governor of Kiangsu Hsüeh Huan memorializes: ...As to the American chief, John Ward, Your official also had the Chinese merchants tell him repeatedly that he positively could not go North. The said chief replied that as they (the English and French) were going as friends, with no other motive, he would not be deterred. As to the Russian chief, Ignatieff, since there were none of the Chinese merchants who knew him, there were no means of stopping him. It is learned that these two chiefs also weighed anchor for the North on the eighth. This is appended as a postscript. (IWSM.HF 54; 22b, 9...25a, 1-4)

512. July 30, 1860. EDICT: Proposes Exploitation of the Misunderstanding Regarding Russia's Delivery of American Letters to Sow Discord Among the Four Powers.
Edict to the Grand Councillors. Today is received at the Grand Council Seng-ko-lin-ch'in's letter to Prince Hui saying that the said minister sent a deputy to investigate the American barbarian ship and to tell them why the said country's letter previously transmitted was not received. The said barbarian was very surprised and

accompanied the deputy to the Russian vessel to investigate. The
Russian barbarian Ming-ch'ang said that the letter had been presented for him. Thus it is clear the Russian barbarians are intervening to pervert truth with the intention of provoking hostilities
and hoping to profit. It is most essential to take advantage of circumstances to separate them, in order to thwart their wicked
schemes. The said minister proposes sending an officer to the
American vessel to say that the governor general could receive
official letters and clear up the previous statement that the letter
was not received.

The proposal hits at the very crux of the matter. But no one
intimate with the Russian barbarians, like Te-hsiang or.Yao Hsü,
can be sent. It is essential to select carefully a reliable official to
proceed to the American vessel and say:

> As the honorable country previously gave Russia a letter to transmit
> and China did not receive it, it is now in the hands of Russia and the
> honorable country should demand it of her. If Russia says she has a reply
> from China, no matter what she says, it cannot be credited at all. If
> China had a letter for the honorable country it must needs, in accordance
> with the treaty, be sent through the Imperial Commissioner's office in
> Shanghai. Now that Russia has committed untruths it is feared that it will
> mar the friendship of certain countries and China, not only thus with their
> honorable country but also with regard to England and France. It is feared
> that Russian mediation also contains false statements to make the various
> countries question China's integrity. If the said two countries do not be-
> lieve their humbug and wish according to the honorable country's precedent
> of last year, to come to exchange ratifications, His Imperial Majesty will
> certainly forgive the past and it is still possible to arrange a settle-
> ment without any use of arms. It is feared the honorable country and
> England and France, not knowing what Russia has done, would believe all
> her statements and bring about some injury to their friendship with China,
> whereas it is not China who is suspicious. Actually, thanks to this matter
> of sending letters, Russia's falsity is clearly revealed and she can hardly
> be trusted, and therefore we could not but send a man to explain and thus
> enable them to profit from the occurrence.

Explain concisely in this way, see how they respond and then act
according to circumstances. The whole point is to cause Russia and
America and England and France all to suspect one another; then the
Russian barbarians' plan to egg them on will have no effect; nor in
English-French pacification will it be without benefit. (IWSM.HF 54;
27a, 6-28a, 6)

513. July 31, 1860. MEMORIAL: The Governor of Shantung Reports
that he is Investigating to Determine if any American Ships are Anchored
at Chefoo.

Governor of Shantung Wen-yü memorializes. Your official begs to state that en route to Ch'ing-chou he received a confidential Court letter from the Imperial Councillors that on July 14th they had received an Edict to the effect that Seng-ko-lin-ch'in had memorialized that a Russian barbarian vessel anchored at Pei-t'ang to deliver letters and also delivered a letter for the American barbarians.

Your official notes that the barbarian ships coming to Chefoo and other ports this year, according to statements of the respective officials, are those of the French barbarians and no mention is made of any of the American barbarians. Now is received the Edict of instruction aforesaid and accordinly word is sent the defense tao-t'ai to notify the respective civil and military officials to investigate carefully whether there are any American barbarians mixed in with them. In case request is made to present letters, they must, in accord with Imperial Edict, say that they should be presented at the office of the Imperial Commissioner in-charge-of the commerce of the Five Ports at Shanghai, and not agree to receive them. When replies arrive he will memorialize.... (IWSM.HF 54; 28a, 7-28b, 5)

514. July 31, 1860. EDICT: Authorizes Ward to Offer Elgin and Gros the Opportunity to Come to Peking Following the American Precedent.

Edict to the Grand Councillors. Wen-yü memorializes on the management of coastal trainbands, the dispatching of volunteers, the establishment of various defenses, and also on his continuing to instruct representatives to explain to the barbarians. In P'eng-lai and Fu-shan districts on the Shantung coast, the respective local officials have been urged to take charge of trainbands, comprising more than 10,000 men, and the said governor has also stationed volunteers he has mustered at Ta-shan, Li-ching, and other places. Order everything done as proposed.

After the American barbarians arrived at Tientsin, Heng-fu sent an officer to say that the letter from the said barbarians to be presented by the Russian chief was not received. But the Russian chief said the letter the American barbarians gave him had been delivered for them, hoping, as we did not answer, to arouse the anger of the American barbarians. Thus their purpose to provoke hostilities is apparent. At this time there is a communication of the American chief to Heng-fu clearly revealing his desire to mediate for the English and French, but not requesting a reply. Thus he wants China to ask for mediation so as to enable him to use coercion. At present, Heng-fu has not given him a reply.

Today orders have been sent the said governor general and others to reply to the American chief and have him notify the English and French that, if they want to exchange ratifications, they must follow the precedent of America's exchange of ratifications last year, having the said chiefs with small suites come to Peking by way of Pei-t'ang, and after the various articles that need to be discussed have

been settled, carry out a mutual exchange of ratifications. But barbarians are naturally crafty and may, when Tientsin does not fall for
their trick, return to Shantung for a trial, but this is uncertain.

Wen-yü is now having his representative Tung Pu-yün return
from Teng-chou. Order him secretly to instruct this official if he
ascertains that there really are American barbarian vessels at Chefoo or other ports, to find means to tell them that if these barbarians
want to mediate for England and France, outside barbarians are
treated well at the Heavenly Court and we can forgive the past, but
that they must conform to the pattern of America in exchanging ratifications before. Provisions that need discussion must also be determined after they reach Peking, and then ratifications can be exchanged. Russia, since she has spoken falsely regarding the delivery of America's letter, must also be using empty words to pervert
truth with regard to the French and English and it is feared the
honorable country and France and England, not knowing what Russia
has done, would believe everything she said, effecting injury to
China's friendship, and therefore he could not but explain for the
benefit of both parties.

Enlighten them carefully. If the American barbarians have not
come there, the said delegate may get to see the French barbarians
and can still use this line to explain to them, as usual doing it as
Tung Pu-yün's own view. In spreading this word, it cannot leak out
that he was officially directed. See how they respond and then we
can act according to circumstances.

If we can only get these barbarians not to listen to the humbug
of the Russian chief, it is not impossible to prevent the development
of hostilities. Wen-yü must be able to comprehend this Edict and
manage suitably.... (IWSM.HF 54; 31b, 2-32b, 4)

515. July 31, 1860. MEMORIAL: Prince Seng-ko-lin-ch'in Reports
American Offers of Mediation and the Arrival of a Large Allied Fleet
off Ta-ku Bar.

Imperial Commissioner Seng-ko-lin-ch'in, Prince of Korchin,
and Governor General of Chihli Heng-fu memorialize. Your slaves
beg to state that from July 17 to 28, they have received dispatches
from the Grand Councillors that they have respectfully received six
Imperial Edicts and Your slaves have respectfully perused them.
The handling of barbarian affairs is limited to the two alternatives
of war and peace, while under the present circumstances the lever
of war and peace rests not with China but with the barbarians.
(Inserted Vermilion endorsement: Even though the lever lies with
the barbarians, if we anticipate the lever and take the lead or meet
the lever and act, the controls are still in our hands. We cannot
merely follow the line of least resistance in order to avoid difficulties.)

If the barbarians have stored up resentment in their hearts and are determined on war, their ships may attack the port directly or their infantry land for a surprise attack. Your slaves must encourage their officers and men to exert themselves to ward off attack. In case the barbarians have it in their hearts to ask for peace, there is something we can take advantage of. (Inserted Vermilion endorsement: If the barbarians intend to ask for peace, we can be sure they have some means of exerting pressure.)

Your slave, Heng-fu, has only trembling to follow repeatedly received Imperial Edicts and find means of conciliation and, making the best of the situation at hand, get the barbarians into our control. Your slave, Seng-ko-lin-ch'in, is secretly assisting him to facilitate a peaceful settlement and early relieve Imperial Care. But barbarians are naturally dogs and sheep and it is feared cannot willingly accept submission. Besides, their belittling of China is a matter of long standing and if they mean to make peace they are sure to rely on force to coerce us. The terms they ask will be virtually impossible to accede to. Once thwarted, a break is sure to result. Thus peace negotiations in the end are sure to be difficult.

At this time if there are only the communications of the English and French barbarians, or perhaps the Russian and American chiefs speaking in behalf of the English and French, Your slave Heng-fu will promptly send a communication to ask those barbarians to conform to the precedent of the American barbarians and come to Peking to exchange ratifications; he will also ask them to go to Pei-t'ang to discuss everything. No matter whether the barbarians comply or not, this puts us in the position of first offering courteous treatment. (Inserted Vermilion endorsement: Very good. This is a clue to conciliation, but we cannot let it determine the issue of war or peace.)

It is noted that in Hsüeh Huan's original memorial he said that Expectant Magistrate Lan Wei-wen and others, on July 14th, set out overland for Tientsin and should be able to be here sometime after August 6th. If it is necessary to send officers to the barbarian vessels to carry word or if the barbarian interpreters' sampans enter Pei-t'ang harbor, (we shall) have Lan Wei-wen and the others receive them. If the barbarians want to come ashore for an interview at Pei-t'ang, then Your slave, Heng-fu, will go.

At the English and French chiefs' first interview, if their attitude is arrogant, it cannot be avoided and Your slave, Heng-fu, has only to keep a level head and even temper and reason with them. After all it is necessary first to win their hearts and make these barbarians recognize right from wrong, before peace negotiations can succeed. If we merely conclude the affair lightly it will not prevent future consequences.

In case the barbarians want to go to Peking to exchange ratifications [Underlined with Vermilion Brush], we must still conclude

the treaty at the port first to avoid other demands after they reach
Peking.

Your slaves' deputy, Hsieh Ch'i-ch'ing has returned to camp
reporting on the attitude of the American barbarians. They appeared
not to know of the previous failure to receive the letter of these barbarians and it was feared the Russian barbarians are concealing evil
intentions with the idea of bringing about hostilities. Therefore, another officer was sent to explain the original error. Now is received,
by this officer who has returned, a special American barbarian communication to Your slave, Heng-fu, merely intimating their desire to
mediate. If we reply immediately it will make it appear that China
wants to ask terms. If the English and French really do not want to
use force, the Russian and American barbarians will certainly have
word forthwith.

Of the five barbarian vessels anchored outside the port of Pei-
t'ang on the 19th, one has set sail; between 9 and 11 on the morning
of the 25th, seven more sailed in, all anchoring at Pei-t'ang harbor.
The next day they cruised about in the vicinity of Ta-ku, sometimes
looking through telescopes, sometimes using sampans to take soundings. On the 28th, from the forts, several tens of barbarians ships
were dimly visible outside the bar. The next few days merchant
vessels entering port reported in Tung-tion waters more than a hundred barbarian vessels anchored there. Thus the barbarians' big
fleet of warships has arrived en masse. Your slaves have only to
give stringent orders to the various divisions of cavalry and government troops to redouble their vigilance to defense, and not dare
to be the least bit careless.

During the day the barbarian ships have slowly approached. As
the Ta-ku and Tientsin situation is doubly critical and the Shantung
area is somewhat relaxed, at this time it is proposed to transfer the
government troops stationed at Ch'ing-hsien here and station them
on the defenses in the hope of consolidating military strength.

Vermilion endorsement: There is a separate Edict. Since the
American barbarians have sent a communication, it is necessary to
reply to avoid future pretexts. It can merely say that China has
never had any intention of insisting on war; do not give them the idea
that we are depending on them to ask for terms. (IWSM.HF 54;
33a, 1-34b, 9)

516. July 31, 1860. EDICT: Orders Local Officials to have Ward
Notify the Allies of China's Willingness for them to Come to Peking
Following American Plan.

Edict to the Grand Councillors. Today is received a memorial
of Seng-ko-lin-ch'in and others that one after another more than
ten barbarian ships have come to port and that the communication
received from the American barbarians was copied and presented

for inspection. Already in the memorial clear notations have been made. Since the American barbarians this time have sent a communication clearly indicating their wish to mediate for the English and French, this gives an opening for conciliation and we can make the best of the situation. The said minister proposes, when the English and French communications arrive, to send a reply to the said barbarians, through Heng-fu, for them to follow the precedent of the American barbarians in coming to Peking to exchange ratifications and asking them to go to Pei-t'ang for a conference, so that we will be in the position of treating them courteously first.

What he says is very apt under the circumstances. As for his statement about concluding the treaty at the port, it is not entirely necessary. If the barbarians intend to ask for peace they are sure to use complete coercion. If conversations at the port are not satisfactory, they will return to their ships and use their numbers and naval strength to coerce at will, so one denial will mean certain renewal of hostilities. It is still better to follow the precedent of the American barbarians, let them come to Peking to negotiate and then, when they are few and isolated, we may be able to have them at our mercy.

Order Heng-fu to take advantage of this opportunity to send a reply to the American barbarians, informing them that if England and France are truly desirous of friendship and come to exchange ratifications, His Imperial Majesty, showing His kindness and forgiving the past, will allow them, according to the American precedent of last year, to come to Peking with a suite of ten to twenty persons by way of Pei-t'ang to exchange ratifications. See how they respond and whether the English and French send communications or not; then act according to circumstances.... (IWSM.HF 54; 34b, 10-35b, 2)

517. August 2, 1860. MEMORIAL: Prince Seng-ko-lin-ch'in Reports a Hundred Allied Ships firing "Aimlessly" Outside the Bar--Fight First and then Negotiate.

Imperial Commissioner, Seng-ko-lin-ch'in, Prince of Korchin, and Governor General of Chihli Heng-fu memorialize. Your slaves beg to state that on July 31st they received a confidential Court Letter from the Grand Councillors that on July 30th they had received an Imperial Edict that the Russian barbarians were perverting the truth and it was of the utmost necessity to seize the occasion to sow discord in order to thwart their wicked schemes....

Although more than a hundred barbarian ships have arrived at port, at present they merely fire cannon night and day, their only idea being the hope of frightening us. Outside of this there is no activity. It has not been learned whether the two chiefs, Elgin and Gros, have arrived or not and at this time it is not convenient to send an officer to find out. As the barbarians' ships are many, their bearing will necessarily be expansive and their will proud. If we immediately sent out an officer, these barbarians would develop even more disrespect. Previously we sent a petty officer to the large vessel of the American barbarians and there was a man of the southern provinces who told the said officer that the purpose of the English and French barbarians was to fight first and negotiate later, that among these barbarians this was discussed every day.

It is noted that last year as soon as the barbarian ships arrived, sampans came to the shore and presented communications. This time the barbarian ships have been here several days without a sign of any word. It is enough to show the extremity of the barbarians' hauteur. At present there are no conversations in which we can reason so we have had to wait quietly.

When the American barbarians' communication comes, we shall immediately seize the occasion to bring them around. On the 30th Your slave Heng-fu sent Lieutenant Feng En-fu to present food to the American barbarians. As the wind and waves are unfavorable he has not yet returned to camp. (IWSM.HF 55; 1a, 2-5...2b, 1=3a, 1)

518. August 2, 1860, EDICT: Authorizes Immediate Opening of Negotiations with England and France Holding Prince Seng's Military Might in Reserve.

Edict to the Grand Councillors. Seng-ko-lin-ch'in and Heng-fu have memorialized that barbarian ships have arrived en masse and the defense of Tientsin and Ta-ku is of vital importance. A hundred and several tens of barbarian vessels are all anchored outside the bar not more than 30 or 40 li from the port. Seng-ko-lin-ch'in is transferring cavalry and government troops and stationing them in various sectors and, in the Ch'eng-tzu-chuang district, has placed cavalry to provide temporary interception. It is assumed his arrangements are complete.

Last year the English barbarians came to Ta-ku port to destroy our defenses; Seng-ko-lin-ch'in led his forces to the assault and gained a great victory, so these barbarians were not necessarily without fear and resentment in their hearts. This time they have assembled warships, spread the word that they are coming by land and sea for the purpose of revenge, but actually to use force to secure peace. Lao Ch'ung-kuang and Hsüeh Huan have both ascertained that the barbarians want to negotiate peace. The American barbarians also want to intermediate. That the English and French chiefs are not intent on war has become apparent.

Now that the barbarian ships have anchored outside the bar,

there cannot be prolonged delay so order Heng-fu to delegate a suitable officer to ask them their motive and also send communications
to the said chiefs, first instructing them, according to American
precedent, to go to Peking by way of Pei-t'ang with a small suite
and exchange ratifications. If the barbarians reply to the said governor general and want peace, even though their attitude is arrogant,
however slight the clue, the said governor general can seize the
opportunity to enlighten them this way and that and gradually get
them into line.

If it is said that sending a communication first will indicate
weakness, this ignores the fact that last year these barbarians were
defeated and that they have been greatly humiliated. Taking the initiative this time to send a deputy with communications for the English, French and Americans, indicates that China is magnanimous
and not cowardly asking for peace.

We feel that although Seng-ko-lin-ch'in's port arrangements
are complete, his prestige also commands the respect of the barbarians and it would not be intrinsically difficult to make the barbarians take another beating. Nevertheless, mindful that after a
rupture all the evil results of war follow ad infinitum and, although
immediate settlement is achieved there are future consequences,
how can we bear to have the coastal inhabitants suffer this calamity?

Heng-fu, personally responsible for the area, is obliged to exemplify Our will and cannot, just because port defenses are rigorous, persist in the idea of war first and peace afterwards. The
said governor general, on receipt of this Edict, must above all
regard conciliation as vital. He cannot be blocked from fear of
difficulty in the fulfilment of duty. In the matter of how to communicate with the said chiefs, order Heng-fu duly to consider and
act promptly. He cannot be the least prejudiced to the detriment
of the general situation. (IWSM.HF 55; 3a, 2-4a, 2)

519. August 3, 1860. MEMORIAL: Prince Seng Reports Use of
American Intelligence and Mediation as the Allies make Initial Land-
ings at Pei-t'ang.

Imperial Commissioner, Seng-ko-lin-ch'in, Prince of Korchin,
and Governor General of Chihli Heng-fu memorialize. On the first
of this month was received a confidential Court Letter from the
Grand Councillors that they had respectfully received an Imperial
Edict. On grateful receipt of this expression of the Imperial Will,
Your slaves respectfully read it and will act according to circumstances.

On the first, Lieutenant Feng En-fu returned to camp and reported that he had presented the foodstuffs to the American barbarians. The said barbarians accepted all of them and in return presented Your slave, Heng-fu, two cases of foreign wine. The said

barbarians said that the English and French barbarians intended to seize Pei-t'ang and then make a surprise attack on Ta-ku from the rear. Other than this they said nothing at all.

Between 1 and 3 o'clock in the afternoon of the same day, more than thirty barbarian vessels were sighted from the forts. Flying red flags, smoke and steam filling the sky, they sailed up to the mouth of Pei-t'ang River with the tide. Then some barbarians and horses landed and occupied a village.

It is noted that last year the barbarians were originally ordered to go to Pei-t'ang for interviews and these barbarians stubbornly refused to go. This year as soon as the ships sailed in they went to the mouth of Pei-t'ang River and anchored. Thus their intention to occupy Pei-t'ang is already apparent.

Your slaves at once ordered the respective local officials to order the inhabitants of their respective districts to evacuate immediately and now many have moved out, leaving only scattered small householders. Now that the barbarians have landed and occupied a village, whether it is war or peace is hard to predict. Your slaves have dispatched cavalry to encamp at a distance. If the barbarians advance in mass formation, whether they strike directly at Ta-ku or even attack Tientsin, we must wait until they are a good ways from Pei-t'ang and then intercept them; we cannot attack first and provide the barbarians with a pretext.

As to the barbarians' occupying a village, whether it is to use troops to demand a peaceful settlement still cannot be determined. As soon as an opportunity is available, Your slave Heng-fu will send an officer there to ask their intentions. If these barbarians are willing to follow the precedent of the American barbarians, going to Peking to exchange ratifications with a small suite, Your slaves have only to make suitable arrangements, in respectful accord with successive Imperial Edicts. If these barbarians want to come to Peking in sedan chairs and bring a large suite and stubbornly refuse to back down, even though Your slaves place adroit obstructions, this may be just the spark to start hostilities.

Your slaves must needs find means of reasoning in the hope of averting disaster and stopping hostilities. They are now sending Lieutenant Feng En-fu with a reply to the American barbarians and must await his return to camp. Whether or not there is a reply from the American barbarians, besides memorializing again posthaste, they are respectfully copying Heng-fu's reply to the American barbarians and reverently offering it for Imperial reading.

To continue, on July 30th Your slave Seng-ko-lin-ch'in ordered K'o-hsing-e to lead his troops here to the defenses. Now he reports that on the 31st he set out from Ch'ing-hsien for Tientsin. Now he has sent a dispatch urging him to come by forced marches in order to furnish defense. (IWSM.HF 55; 4a, 3-5a, 9)

510. <u>August 3, 1860</u>. EDICT: <u>Urges More Prompt and Effective Use</u>
<u>of American Mediation to Prevent the Outbreak of Hostilities</u>.

Edict to the Grand Councillors. Yesterday, as the barbarians'
vessels were outside the bar, there were orders for Heng-fu to take
the initiative by sending a communication to their chiefs to bring a
small suite and come to Peking to exchange ratifications. Today is
received a memorial of Seng-ko-lin-ch'in and others that more than
30 barbarian vessels have come to Pei-t'ang river-port, that barbarians came ashore and occupied a village. Heng-fu has now sent a
communication to the American chief to in turn invite the English
and French barbarians to Peking to exchange ratifications.

What has been done is fairly satisfactory but when the communication of the American chief was received, he should have replied
immediately. Now that the English and French have landed at Pei-
t'ang, belatedly to reply to the American chief is already manifestly
behind time. If the American chief does not reach the English and
French immediately, hostilities are sure to begin at once, so order
Heng-fu to prepare communications immediately and send them directly to the English and French chiefs. These English and French
communications need not mention last year's hostilities. Merely
say that as they have on this occasion come to Pei-t'ang, it is evidence enough that they have come in sincere friendship and desire
to exchange ratifications. If they wish to come to Peking to exchange
according to American precedent, he will certainly memorialize for
them and when an Edict granting permission is received, they can go
north from there.

In the communication to France, say that as their country did not
assist England in hostilities last year, His Imperial Majesty commends
them deeply; that this time coming to Pei-t'ang to exchange ratifications can reenforce permanent friendship. In this way communicate
with them discriminately, see how they respond, and immediately
memorialize express.

If these barbarians are willing to come to Peking according to
American precedent, the matter of riding in sedan chairs and bringing a small suite need not be mentioned specifically therein. If the
barbarians insist on riding in chairs to Peking, it is unnecessary to
object overmuch. Merely say that it is only possible to ride in chairs
outside the city. This small matter need not hinder the general situation. In subsequent communications, he (Heng-fu) must keep a level
head and an even temper and treat them courteously. He need not
divulge the least hint of using arms to make it difficult to bring these
barbarians around. This is most important.

As to the rear of Ta-ku and the city of Tientsin, order Seng-ko-
lin-ch'in to continue rigorous defense. Let there not be the least
carelessness. (IWSM.HF 55; 5a, 10-6a, 6)

521. August 3, 1860. CHINESE NOTE TO THE AMERICANS: Notifies Ward that Chinese Forces have been Withdrawn from Pei-t'ang and Authorizes him to Offer the Allies Safe Conduct to Peking.

By way of reply. On the 6th of this month [sic], was received the honorable minister's communication in which it was stated that the honorable minister had received his honorable country's mandate, when England and France should arrive in Pei-ho waters, suitably to adjust the two countries' differences. This proves that the honorable country is genuinely mindful of old friendship, that it specially sends the honorable minister here from afar to act as intermediary and its good will is deeply appreciated.

By way of observation, last year when England came to exchange ratifications, why did she bring warships, initiate hostilities and destroy our defenses to the detriment of friendly relations? His Imperial Majesty, Our Emperor, magnanimous and virtuous, fundamentally is not desirous of war for fear the soldiery of both countries would suffer without any benefit to commerce and trade. Now the ships of England and France have collected on the seas, whether for war or peace is not known. If they are intent on war, our country can only meet them with marshalled troops; if their motive is peaceful negotiation and they are sending the honorable minister to mediate, naturally we must discuss matters fairly without any partiality.

Our defenses have now been withdrawn from Pei-t'ang. It is asked that he transmit word on our behalf that they come to Peking to exchange ratifications according to the honorable country's precedent of last year and it is also asked that he extend an invitation to the envoys of both England and France to come into port immediately and select a place for a general conference.

By way of reply. This is a necessary reply. (IWSM.HF 55; 6a, 7-6b, 10)

522. August 4, 1860. MEMORIAL: Prince Seng-ko-lin-ch'in Reports the Failure of American Mediation and the Inauguration of Hostilities on Land.

Imperial Commissioner Seng-ko-lin-ch'in, Prince of Korchin, and Governor General of Chihli Heng-fu memorialize. On the 3rd of this month, between 5 and 7 o'clock in the morning, Lieutenant Feng En-fu returned to camp with a communication from the American barbarians; the purport seemed to be that there was no way of managing. Moreover they told the said officer that there were now at Pei-t'ang 5000 Cantonese rebels and 3000 black barbarians [Indians] and they intended a surprise attack on the Ta-ku forts from the rear.

Between 7 and 9 in the morning, a spy reported that the Pei-t'ang barbarians were in battle formation, perhaps several thousand strong, with several mandrawn, carriage-mounted cannon and were making a direct assault on the T'ang-erh-ku garrison. From the forts Your slaves could see these barbarians' cannon going forward in unbroken succession. Whereupon, Te-hsing-a leading and assisted by Senior Bodyguards Ming-an, Cho-ming-a, T'o-lun-pu, Te-ch'eng, Captain Shu-t'ung-e, Lieutenant Colonel Ch'ang Shan-pao, leading the Kirin and Heilungkiang Cherim League and Chao Uda League and the Kuei-hua City cavalry and government troops, met the attack head-on. By noon (11-1) the barbarians finally returned to the village. Three of our soldiers were wounded and several horses were wounded. The mounted and foot barbarian rebels both suffered casualties.

This days' engagement, since the barbarians were in close formation and went out from the village more than 10 li, was designed to attack the garrison and we could not but marshall troops and meet it. Since the barbarians returned to the village, Your slaves still propose to send the communication to the American barbarians, for them in turn to get the English and French barbarians to cease hostilities and be friendly. But since there have been hostilities, it was hardly suitable to reiterate mild terms in the wording.

The American barbarian communication as well as Your slave Heng-fu's communication in reply to the American barbarians, are copied and respectfully presented for Imperial inspection. (IWSM. HF 55; 12b, 2-13a, 6)

523. <u>August 4, 1860</u>. <u>EDICT</u>: Notes Opening of Hostilities but is Confident of Victory and Magnanimously Offers the Allies Entry to Peking on American Precedent.

Edict to the Grand Councillors. Seng-ko-lin-ch'in and others memorialize that the American barbarians said in a communication that England and France wanted hostilities and later that barbarian rebels went out of the village in mass formation intent on attack. The American barbarian communication to Heng-fu said that the situation had become hopeless. Thus that country cannot act as intermediary. The said governor general still sent them a communication to in turn get the English and French barbarians to cease hostilities and be friends. The phraseology is fairly suitable. As the American barbarians want to back out, he naturally had to send communications to the English and French chiefs directly showing that China is magnanimous and possibly making them feel a little remorse.

Now these barbarians have gone out of the village to attack and have been repelled. For us to send them a communication, while it has the appearance of conciliation, is no evidence of weakness. As for the barbarians, they fear our military prowess and have dread in their hearts, so this is just what we can take advantage of to enlighten them with reason and inspire them with gratitude and awe.

Order Heng-fu to continue in accord with previous Edicts and immediately send separate communications to the English and French chiefs, to come to Peking for exchange of ratifications following the precedent of the American barbarians. Moreover he must keep a level head and an even temper and, as in the communication to the American barbarians this time, the phraseology should be neither antagonistic nor compliant, but should explain adroitly; nor is it necessary to allude to hostilities and make it impossible for them to come around.

Seng-ko-lin-ch'in's arrangements are correct and (We) are not afraid of not being victorious at arms. The fear is that after defeat the barbarians will sail away and hide. In which case not only will the various ports be unable to have peace, but the Ta-ku defenses cannot be withdrawn and there will be no prospect of a speedy termination of barbarian affairs. So in the end it is not a perfect plan. Previously issued Edicts have explained in great detail and it is assumed the said ministers are able to embody Our will. (IWSM. HF 55; 13a, 7-13b, 9)

524. August 4, 1860. AMERICAN NOTE: Ward Bluntly Informs Governor General Heng-fu that Peaceful Settlement is Hopeless and War is the only Determinant.

By way of reply. The honorable governor general's letter of the 3rd instant has been received and read. The honorable country and England and France are now ill-disposed. The cause of the disagreement, the crooked and straight, right and wrong, the present minister cannot discuss with the honorable governor general, because this country is normally friendly with his honorable country, nor has she any differences with England and France. If it were possible to adjust satisfactorily the various controversial matters, would not everybody be pleased? But actually this is not possible. Now we can only, in accordance with the honorable governor general's request, convey his wishes to the two countries. This is by way of reply. This is a necessary reply. (IWSM.HF 55; 13b, 10-14a, 6)

525. August 4, 1860. CHINESE NOTE TO THE AMERICANS: Heng-fu Discusses with Ward the Allied Coercion of 1858, the Futility of Agreements Secured by Force of Arms and Presents a Three-day Ultimatum.

By way of a second reply. On the 3rd instant was received the honorable minister's reply stating that the contentions of England and France have become insoluble, that he can ask the envoys of the two countries to act according to the letter transmitted, but fears that before this letter is received the two countries will have started hostilities. The present governor general recalls the incident of 1858. England wounded our officers and men, demolished our forts, and her warships went to Tientsin. His Imperial Majesty begrudged

the several myriad lives of the people of Tientsin and cherished great
virtue rather than maintain a small trust. Therefore England coerced
at will, and at the time got what she asked. But fixed treaties must be
agreed upon by both parties before they are binding. How can they
rest on arms, might, and coercion?

When in 1859 the treaties were to be ratified, it was only necessary to come with one or two vessels. Why did they need to bring
so many warships and troops? When the English and French ships
came, our country sent communications to them in advance to go to
Pei-t'ang to exchange ratifications, but there was no reply. Suddenly
they swarmed against the port and started hostilities. At that time
our strength was estimated at not one tenth that of England, but that
we were able to gain victories on land and sea was actually because
England oppressed us too much and brought about her own ruin,
while His Imperial Majesty, Our Emperor, magnanimous and broad-
minded, still Imperially sent ministers to Shanghai to arrange commerce and complete old friendships. Thus our country did not want
to use force and one would think the various countries could all appreciate His Imperial Majesty's vast compassion.

Yesterday, on hearing that England and France were arriving,
our country withdrew the defending forces from Pei-t'ang to provide
a place to land and discuss peace. Unexpectedly, having been at the
port several days without even sending a communication to our country, suddenly on the 1st, coming with both land and sea forces, they
came ashore en masse and occupied a village near Pei-t'ang. The
residents were alarmed. On the 2nd they suddenly drew up their
troops in formation, but our country did not want to precipitate a
battle. On the 3rd their army again faced ours, opened fire, and
our country could not but meet the attack, but still ordered the officers leading the troops only to meet the enemy and did not permit
offensive action, exemplifying His Imperial Majesty's leniency, wishing to preserve old friendships.

But it is either war or peace; we cannot have both. If the main
idea is peace, why is it necessary deliberately to use force as a
policy of coercion? A date could easily be mutually agreed upon to
go to Peking and exchange ratifications according to the honorable
country's precedent of last year and it would certainly save trouble.
If England and France are rigidly set on war, our forces are prepared both on land and sea. Although they occupy our Pei-t'ang, it
will not be difficult to lead our forces to attack. It is only feared
that if England and France again suffer casualties, subsequent friendship will be difficult. It must be admitted that for several days our
country's yielding and restraint has been unlimited.

Since the honorable minister is here for friendship, convey this
idea to England and France and take advantage of this time so that
both parties, unharmed, will withdraw troops and conclude the affair,

still coming to Peking to exchange ratifications according to last
year's precedent, in order to perfect friendly relations. Then the
merchants of the various countries will all become prosperous. If
the honorable minister does not contact them for us, England and
France still do not hold the lever of certain victory and when they
again suffer casualties, it is feared the honorable minister can
hardly face England and France, nor will his relations with England
and France be truly good.

Now, if within three days England and France make no reply,
our country will have no alternative but war. Moreover, to use
troops on land is not like the high seas. If England and France misunderstand our army's yielding and again use force, our country's
chief general has only to alter his tactics. If the French and English troops are again defeated, not only will it greatly obstruct
peaceful negotiations, but the English and French envoys will also
be embarrassed to return home and report.

This is the requisite second reply. This is a necessary reply.
(IWSM.HF 55; 14a, 7-16a, 4)

526. August 8, 1860. MEMORIAL: Prince Seng-ko-lin-ch'in Interprets Allied White Flags as Admission of Defeat and Suspects their Use
to Cover an Ambush.

Imperial Commissioner Seng-ko-lin-ch'in, Prince of Korchin,
Lieutenant General of Chahar Hsi-ling-a and Governor General of
Chihli Heng fu memorialize. Your slaves beg to state that they received a dispatch from the Grand Councillors that on July 25th they
respectfully received an Imperial Edict, which Your slaves have
reverently read.

They note that on the 3rd, after marching forth and retiring,
barbarian ships sailed to the port of Pei-t'ang, only a few li from
the encampment and forts. Your slave, Hsi-liang-a, had provided
wooden rafts for attack with fire and lined them up in the river. On
catching sight of them, the barbarians returned. In the period of
excitement, two steamers grounded. When a large number of barbarians tugged, one rode the tide out, but the other has still not
been able to move.

Between 9 and 11 in the evening of the 4th, Your slave, Hsi-
ling-a learned from Captain Ting-an and Platoon Captain Lien-hsi,
who came to camp and reported, that between 11 and 1 o'clock of
the same day, two barbarians on board the grounded steamer went
ashore north of Pei-t'ang, each bearing a white flag, with the two
characters "Cease Fighting" written on them, as well as bolts of
white cloth. When Ting-an and the other asked their intentions and
whether or not they had any written orders, they said they had no
official papers, but that our cavalry was stationed too close and
it was feared that they would damage the explosives on board and

thus destroy harmonious feeling. If either party had occasion to send persons to communicate, they must carry white flags and must not be harmed.

Ting-an and the other replied that their ships in the river must leave the port at once. Since they occupied Pei-t'ang, the people who fled from there were in great distress and had demanded several times that they set fire to the vessels, which the governor general had refused to do. Once resistance got under way it would cause damage and would do more harm than good. The barbarians, having no answer, flung the bolts of white cloth on the ground, saying they would leave them for us to use in communication. Then they returned to the ship. Ting-an and the others, seeing that on the white cloth were traces of Chinese and barbarian characters, reported back to Your slave, Hsi-ming-a, and presented it at camp.

Between 1 and 3 o'clock in the afternoon of the 6th, Second Captain Ch'iu Jui-hsiang and Lieutenant Feng En-fu returned to camp with an American barbarian communication. From its purport, although evasive, they were still willing to communicate with the English and French barbarians. Ch'iu Jui-hsiang and the other watched these barbarians have copies made and sent to the various ships.

Your slaves all agreed that as the English barbarians sent white flags, although they could not be relied on, actually these barbarians were admitting defeat and so proposed to send a communication to these barbarians fixing a time for an interview. But in communicating this time, they sent Ting-an with it to these barbarians' grounded vessels. If the barbarians on board dared not receive it on their own authority, he was to have them send someone with him out of the port direct to Chief Elgin's vessel.

As these barbarians' trickery has a hundred manifestations, their two characters "Cease Fighting" were almost certainly intended to dampen our martial ardor, catch us unprepared, and wait for a chance to cause trouble. So orders were immediately sent to cavalry and infantry regiments to intensify their guard and not allow the least carelessness. They respectfully copy the American barbarian communication, make a replica of the "Cease Fighting" white flags and respectfully present both for Imperial Inspection.

To continue, K'o-hsing-a reached the defenses on the 3rd; his cavalry and government troops are distributed at the garrison city and on the two shores of Ta-ku, to cooperate in defense. (IWSM.HF 55; 20b, 3-22a, 1)

527. <u>August 18, 1860</u>. EDICT: Orders that Captured Allied Prisoners be Screened for Americans for Possible Use in Negotiation or Mediation.

Edict to the Grand Councillors. There is received the report of findings of Tsai-yüan Prince I and others, presented at Ta-ku, in which it is stated that on the 14th, Imperial Body Guard Pu-erh-ho-te handed over fifteen barbarians that had been captured, including ten Kwangsi Long-haired [Taiping] Rebels.... If among the five captured barbarians there are any Russians or Americans, they must not be harmed. Send officers to escort them back, and also send communications to the two countries that, being on friendly terms with China, their countrymen are certainly not assisting in the fighting and that we consider them included by mistake, and see how they respond.

When the English and French barbarians receive their communications, if there is any reply, also order them memorialized immediately in order to relieve worry. (IWSM.HF 56; 7b, 3-4: ...8a, 2-5)

528. August 18, 1860. MEMORIAL: The Governor of Shantung Reports No American Ships at Chefoo and No Attempt to Deliver American Letters at Shantung Ports.

Governor of Shantung Wen-yü memorializes. Your official begs to state that he received a confidential Court Letter from the Grand Councillors that on July 31st they had received an Imperial Edict that Wen-yü is now having his deputy Tung Pu-yün return immediately to Teng-chou, so order him confidentially to instruct that officer if he discovers there really are American barbarian vessels at Chefoo, he must find means to explain to them in detail. If American barbarians have not come there and he is able to see the French barbarians, he must make the same explanation to them.

It is noted that before Delegate Tung Pu-yün returned to Chefoo from Teng-chou he sent sub-district Magistrate Yen Kuo-jeng to see the barbarian chief and arrange a date for an interview. The barbarian chief, Montaubon, would not consent to a meeting and later went North on board ship, leaving only the so-called third general to guard Chefoo. Tung Pu-yün then again returned to Teng-chou.

Your official, having received the Edict that as the barbarian ships at Chefoo were very numerous, it was feared there were American barbarians among them who delivered letters, immediately sent word for a detailed investigation. According to the findings of the brigade general, tao-t'ai, prefect, and district magistrate, there are only French barbarians and no American barbarians, nor was there any delivery of letters.... (IWSM.HF 56; 8a, 6-8b, 6)

529. September 21, 1860. MEMORIAL: Peking Court Official Urges Summary Execution of Allied Prisoners and a Relentless Military Policy Against Foreigners.

Acting Junior Vice President of the Board of Revenue, Sub-chancellor of the Grand Secretariat Yüan Hsi-tsu memorializes. Your official begs to state that he has heard of Seng-ko-lin-ch'in's capture of a number of barbarian chiefs and their delivery to Peking.[3] He has since

3 This presumably refers to the capture and detention of Sir Harry Parkes and Henry Brougham Loch and their party.

respectfully read the Imperial Edicts repeatedly proclaiming this far and wide and has witnessed Your Majesty's simultaneous employment of virtue and might. The accomplishment of such a meritorious act in the space of one day certainly calls for the Emperor's facing the Imperial South Gate with (Seng-ko-lin-ch'in) presenting the captives to His Majesty to exemplify National Law and please the populace.

He also asks that Imperial orders be sent Seng-ko-lin-ch'in to take advantage of his victory to press toward Ta-ku, burn their ships, exterminate all that are left of their vile sort, and sow the seacoast with awe, as a policy of perpetual security.

It may be said that from ancient times in plans for pacifying barbarians, subduing their hearts is preeminent. Your official ventures to think that in the present situation this is not so at all. Of old, barbarian troubles were mostly on distant frontiers and as no whip was long enough to reach, we could only use artifice to restrain them. Now, Tientsin is near the capital and if we allow them to erect wharves and trade unafraid, in future year to year defenses not only will supplies be squandered and a long train of difficulties ensue, but barbarians are naturally changeable, not consistently peaceful, and therefore from a wound in the arm we would sustain a vital injury. This can never be.

In the previous Kwangtung affair, seizing Yeh Ming-ch'en and imprisoning Po-kuei, they acted violently and regarded the Heavenly Court lightly. In this extremity, Imperial Edicts still looked toward these barbarians' awakening, recognizing their guilt, and giving themselves up, apparently in the desire to leave them a loophole. This exemplifies Your Majesty's magnanimous charity. But Your official considers that letting them off so easily not only will be no comfort to the spirits of successive generations of ancestors above but even here below, how can it satisfy those officials who sacrifice their lives? Besides, if Seng-ko-lin-ch'in captures and the Emperor releases, in all probability the flame of rebellion will rekindle and how will the Mongol troops again be willing to obey orders?

Now the English barbarians' causing China trouble is not a matter of a day. Ever since Li Hung-pin conceded Hong Kong to the barbarians in the Tao-kuang period, the barbarians' status has gradually increased. Your official has heard that Governor General of Liang-kuang Lin Tse-hsü held the barbarian chief Eliot captive. Thereafter, Ch'i-shan, Ch'i-ying and Niu Chien spoke only of conciliating barbarians and voluntarily released him. Thus Chenchiang and Ting-hai were successively lost and 21 millions of China's treasure went to enrich the enemy, one consequence following another down to the present day. The Tao-kuang Emperor always regarded this with bitter regret.

These barbarians for twenty years have contemptuously regarded us Chinese as being without leadership; getting an inch, they take a foot. Now at last they dare harass T'ung-chou with a force of four or five thousand. If Heaven had not snatched away their courage and Seng-ko-lin-ch'in had not captured the barbarian chief, with the vital capital district so nearby, the very thought of it is enough to chill one's heart.

According to Your official, deep thought and careful planning are not as good as summary execution to eradicate the roots of the evil. It may also be said that the rebel barbarians have the manpower of four countries and if we now carry out general executions, in the future the four countries will league together and there will be no end to hostilities; that the consequent general opening of border troubles cannot but be feared. This is a misunderstanding of the barbarian temperament. Last year Your official returned from leave. As most of his clansmen are in Shanghai in trade, Your official discussed barbarian affairs with them repeatedly from morning till night and got thoroughly acquainted with barbarian affairs.

The English barbarians, being strong but not wealthy, regard steamers as their long suit. Their ballistic skill is actually hard to oppose. But their tradesmen form one group, their military men, another, and the two do not work together. The English barbarians' annual expenditure for hostilities depends entirely on commerical strength. Further egged on by native traitors and told that China's soldiery is pitiful, they seized the opportunity to precipitate hostilities. Then fearing their own strength inadequate, they formed a league of four countries to aid and abet them in crime. That they dare be thus violent is because the high officials of the outer provinces, as profits of barbarian customs are not inconsiderable, covet gain and indulge them, thus producing the present (crisis).

Actually, there are Chinese products which the outer ocean requires. Not only are rhubarb and tea vital for the lives of the barbarians but actually, if we did not trade with them, the commercial barbarians would defy the military barbarians completely, so in the end China would still have her profit from barbarian customs.

Your official heard Cantonese say that last year after the English barbarians were thrashed, their spirits did not recover and this year when they went to collect people to come to Peking, most of them were unwilling. When they threatened them with force, some were still unwilling to come, even to the point of death. Therefore they recruited Cantonese irregulars and collected Teng-chou bandits, assembling three to five thousand men to flaunt their arrogance, staking everything on one throw. Now that the principal rebel is captured, popular sentiment will immediately be dissipated.

Moreover, Your official hears that the barbarians' capital investment in steamers is very great; the large ones cost two million gold; small ones, one million gold, and now that these barbarians are without a leader, popular sentiment is very disturbed. Once Your

Majesty has offered heavy rewards, among the "harbor rats" some can certainly be found to sink them. He asks that an Imperial Edict be sent Seng-ko-lin-ch'in to move his camp forward and publish rewards in Tientsin, the money for the rewards to be paid by Seng-ko-lin-ch'in's headquarters. If by this most timely order it is possible to prevent a single steamer from returning, then even giving the barbarians ten years to collect forces and ten years to drill, their strength would still be inadequate. This is a plan to settle once and for all.

This matter is of such great significance to the nation's security that Your official in expressing his own views has scrupulously limited himself to those the consequences of which he understands. So he beseeches Your Majesty to issue orders for the Princes and Ministers, the Six Boards and the Nine Ministers to discuss them, each giving his view in the hope of fusing them into one and achieving perfection. For an early settlement of Imperial counsels, there cannot be as heretofore vascillation between peace and war and constant delay with loss of advantage. This is truly for Your Majesty's own decision to be made at an early date. (IWSM.HF 62; 42b, 9-45b, 6)

530. November 17, 1860. MEMORIAL: Prince Seng-ko-lin-ch'in Reports the Loss of the Ratified American Treaties During the Allied Burning and Looting of the Summer Palace.

Prince Kung and others further memorialize. Then as to the treaties and tariff schedules of the various countries kept in the Board of Rites, as it was necessary on October 5th, to memorialize the English and French treaties asking that the Imperial Seal be affixed, they were taken from the Board of Rites to Shan-yüan Temple for examination.

Then unexpectedly on the 10th the barbarian troops attacked Hai-tien. Your officials ordered secretaries and palace attendants to convey the documents and records inside the city. As time was pressing and there was a shortage of carts, when the "Records of the Four Barbarians" and the "Daily Correspondence" were transported, Your officials went ahead with them. The remaining boxes of treaties were later loaded on the carts but the main body of barbarian troops arrived before they were checked. Later, after the barbarian troops withdrew, when the monks of the place were questioned, they said that on that day the barbarian soldiers looted everything and there was no means of checking.

Subsequently, (Your officials) have repeatedly interrogated the chiefs of those two countries and have recovered from Chief Parkes only the file copy of the English treaty in Chinese and barbarian character. As to the file copy of the French treaty, also the treaties which America and Russia returned, and the credentials and tariff schedules of those two countries, the said barbarians both said they had not taken them and stubbornly refused to confess.

Your officials venture to think that even if the (English and French) barbarians stole them, they would have no use for them. Probably seeing later that they belonged to other countries, they immediately burned them. Now Heng-ch'i is again ordered to find means of recovering them at Tientsin.

As to the missing treaties and tariff schedules of the various countries, copies of all are on file for reference; only the credentials of America and Russia are unaccounted for. They must wait until the report of Heng-ch'i and the others comes in and then memorialize again.

Vermilion endorsement: Noted. (IWSM.HF 69; 17b, 1-18a, 6)

531. November 18, 1860. EDICT: Orders Diligent Effort to Accomplish the Return of the American and Russian Treaties from the British to Avoid Embarrassment.

Edict to the Grand Councillors.... As to the Russian and American treaties and credentials seized by the barbarians at Hai-tien, it is feared that when these two countries find they have been lost they will have a pretext. Order Heng-ch'i instructed to find means to recover them from Chief Parkes. It is essential to have the original copies returned, to avoid future wrangling. This is most important. (IWSM.HF 69; 23a, 3...23b, 1-4)

534. November 23, 1860. MEMORIAL: Prince Kung Reports Russian Offer to Assist China in Rebel Suppression and Tribute Transport and Recommends the Latter.

Imperial Commissioner Prince Kung, Grand Secretary Kuei-liang and Senior Vice-president of the Board of Revenue Wen-hsiang memorialize. It is noted that when the Russian barbarians exchanged ratifications, Chief Ignatieff already had word to return home. At the time the date of departure was not set. Now the Russian chief Balluseck[4] set out first on the 17th; Ignatieff set out the 22nd, going home by way of K'u-lun [i.e. Urga].

On the afternoon of the 19th, the latter came to take leave. Your official, I-hsin [Prince Kung], together with Pao-chün, Lin-k'uei and Ch'eng-ch'i met him at Kuang-hua Temple. The said barbarian's speech and demeanor were rather compliant during the discussion, apparently, the treaties having been ratified, taking pains to be friendly. As he has the appearance of a man and the heart of a beast, Your officials certainly did not dare believe him, but it was

---

4 Balluseck was aide-de-camp to Major General Ignatieff and served as captain of the guards. *Journal* of the North China Branch of the Royal Asiatic Society, v. 2 (1860), p. 128.

not the occasion to flout utterly his feelings. They thanked him as occasion demanded and the said chief was pleased.

But he also mentioned that in 1858 he had wished to present China
with 10,000 rifles and 50 cannon to be transported from his country by
land and sea, proposing to send them to Peking. As China had not been
willing to receive them they were gradually returned. Your officials
said that there had been a note from the Bureau of Dependencies for
them to be sent by land to K'u-lun and turned over to the officials in
charge there, who would take delivery and then send them to Peking,
but that there had been no reply. The said chief said that this communication never had been seen. His speech was very crafty and not
very credible.

The chief went on to say that as China was inexperienced in the
manufacture of firearms, as well as of bombs, torpedoes, mines, and
in their operation, he wished to send several of his country's officers,
with artisans, to China to instruct us. But fearing if France and England heard of it they would not allow them to help, he asked that China
send a number of officers and soldiers to a place some distance from
Peking, either west or north, the place to be determined by China. If
the Long-haired Rebels [i.e. Taipings] in Kiang-nan and other places
were not suppressed, the country could not recover, but if we would
agree to cooperate with the barbarians [i.e. Russia] against the
rebels, our government troops leading the attack with heavy forces
by land and the barbarians sending 300-400 men to cooperate by sea,
it would certainly be effective.

He also said that he feared next year's tribute to Peking might be
obstructed en route. When he was in Shanghai, some American merchants and Chinese Canton merchants said that they were willing to buy
up Formosan and foreign grain at a fixed price and send it to Tientsin.
If we would let him send word to the Shanghai consular officials, in the
future both foreign ships and sand junks could be loaded and, flying
Russian and American flags, be perfectly safe. Due to their sincere
desire for friendship, these two countries were willing to place confidence and exert themselves (on China's behalf).

As barbarians are naturally crafty with rich promises and honeyed
words, Your officials could hardly be sure they were not harboring
other pruposes. On the matter of presenting firearms, they said that
for holding this good will, His Imperial Majesty would certainly be
appreciative, but whether or not they could take advantage of it, they
must, after investigation, ask for an Edict for execution.

As to assistance in bandit suppression they said that the high officials leading the troops in the various sectors were in command of
several hundred thousand soldiers and militia and so could exterminate
them one after the other. As his country's clothing and language were
both unlike China's, they feared they could not suppress the rebels but

would rather agitate the populace. The said chief then said that while Chinese soldiers and volunteers were very numerous, their equipment was not entirely effective. On the matter of southern tribute transport, (Your officials) said that the means for bringing it to Tientsin in the future could hardly be determined at this time and they would have to settle it when the time came.

They venture to think that barbarians presenting firearms is not a matter to be considered casually. If we say that these barbarians are truly submissive and are doing this to testify the sincerity of their homage, we cannot but be taken in by them. But the desire to be friendly and distinguish themselves from the English and French barbarians to get us to give them special treatment seems to be sincere. Now sending them to a place some distance from Peking, to be determined by China, and limiting the barbarians to a small number, would do no immediate harm, but Your officials did not venture to assume responsibility and must request an Edict and act accordingly.

As to wealth and revenues in the Kiangsu-Chekiang region, the country has been ravaged several times and the soldiery is inadequate for bandit suppression. If the rebels are not reduced shortly, not only will the region be unable to recover, but if we want to withstand insults from without, our strength does not measure up. Your officials' will to revenge remains unabated, not daring the least relaxation. If we borrow the strength of barbarian troops to expel the rebels, our original rigor will gradually recover, while theirs, if they are successful, must necessarily be diminished. If they fail, it will at least reduce their arrogance. But it is feared that what these barbarians covet is profit. On the pretext of cooperating in bandit suppression, they will give vent to their wolfish and piggish desires and do more harm than good, while our losses would be even greater.

In handling conciliation, although Your Officials have become somewhat familiar with barbarian affairs, on military affairs in Kiangsu and Chekiang they dare not make a decision. Could not secret Imperial Instructions be sent the respective governor general and governors of Liang-chiang, Kiangsu and Chekiang to make a thorough joint investigation? If the advantage is great and the risk small and it is still a means of saving the situation, they can memorialize immediately for the issue of an Imperial Edict urging (Russia and America) to check their plans of helping the rebels and prevent their idea of staying in Tientsin. Nor would this seem to be without advantage.

Their transport of southern tribute rice for us can hardly be predetermined now and should be handled by the governor general and governor of Chekiang when the time comes. (Your officials) are impelled to ask that an Edict be sent the respective governor general and governor of that province to consider the circumstances and then memorialize asking for an Edict for final decision.

When he took his leave the said chief asked that notice of the
treaty be sent to Urga and other places. As this matter concerns
trade, Your officials agreed to send word to the various places,
which is hereby duly reported. (IWSM.HF 69; 28b, 9-31a, 8)

533. November 23, 1860. EDICT: Authorizes Establishment of a Russian Military Program at Kiakhta but Refers the Other Proposals to
General Tseng Kuo-fan.

Edict to the Grand Councillors. Today is received a memorial of
I-hsin Prince Kung and others concerning their meeting with the barbarian chief. The memorial has been read with care.

Regarding the Russian chief's statement that his country wishes
to present firearms to China, previously a letter from the Bureau of
Dependencies ordered them sent by land to Urga. This time he
wishes to send several officers of his country, accompanied by artisans, to China to give instructions, at a place north or west some
distance from Peking and asks China to send several officers and
soldiers there to study methods of manufacture and use. I-hsin
(Prince Kung) and the others, fearing barbarian word to be unreliable, asked for an Edict to act in accordance with. Since the barbarians have this idea they must want to be friendly and should not be
cut off abruptly.

Order I-hsin (Prince Kung) and the others, on the one hand, to
notify the Russian chief to send the firearms to Kiakhta, whence they
will be carried from the frontier to Peking by our officers to save
them expense, in order to show our friendly feeling and, on the other
hand, from the Peking garrison choose soldiers experienced in firearms and memorialize for the appointment of a high official to conduct them to Kiakhta and there make an earnest study of methods of
manufacture and use. They are to be changed in rotation, in the hope
of becoming thoroughly proficient. Managing thus, everything is under control and we also maintain the idea of complete defense.

The said chief's offers to suppress rebels and transport southern
tribute for us have been sent by Edict to Tseng Kuo-fan and others
for due consideration and execution. (IWSM.HF 69; 31a, 9-31b, 10)

534. November 23, 1860. EDICT: Instructs Tseng Kuo-fan to Study the
Russian Proposals to Assist China in Rebel Suppression and Tribute
Transport.

Supplementary Edict. In the autumn of this year England and
France led troops against the capital city and, the treaties having
been exchanged, withdrew their troops. The Russian envoy, Ignatieff,
also exchanged ratifications after them. The said chief saw I-hsin
(Prince Kung) and others and said orally that the Long-haired Rebels
were obstreperous in the Chiang-nan area and asked to have the
Chinese government forces lead the main attack on the rebels by

land and his country would send 300 or 400 troops to cooperate by
sea, which was sure to be effective. He also said that he feared
next year's southern tribute-rice transport to Peking might be obstructed en route and that when he was in Shanghai, some American
merchants and Chinese Canton merchants were willing to buy up
Formosan and foreign grain at fixed prices and send it to Tientsin.
If we would authorize him to write to the consuls in Shanghai, in the
future both foreign ships and sand junks could be loaded and, flying
the Russian or American flag, would be absolutely safe.

China's bandit suppression and tribute transport certainly cannot depend exclusively on foreign assistance. But realizing that the
Kiangsu-Chekiang district is reduced to a pulp and military strength
is inadequate for suppression, if we borrowed the strength of Russian troops to assist in the settlement, the sooner the rebels are
suppressed, the sooner our constitution will recover. But it is
feared what the said country covets is profit and on the pretext of
cooperating in bandit suppression may again make inordinate demands and we cannot but anticipate consequences. When the French
were in Peking, they also made this request.

Order Tseng Kuo-fan and the others to make a thorough joint
investigation If the advantages are greater than the risks and it is
still a possible means of saving the situation, memorialize immediately and await an Edict for final decision.

As to their carrying southern tribute-rice for us, the Kiangsu-
Chekiang district is devastated; whether or not it will be able to
manage new transport next year cannot yet be determined, but tribute grain is absolutely indispensable and cannot be diminished.
Whether or not what the said chief says about buying up and shipping
to Tientsin is feasible and what considerations and arrangements
are necessary to execute it, also order Tseng Kuo-fan, Hsüeh Huan,
and Wang Yü-ling to consider circumstances and memorialize immediately. (IWSM.HF 69; 32a, 1-32b, 7)

535. December 2, 1860. MEMORIAL: Prince Kung Reports Failure
to Recover Original Texts of American and Russian Treaties but Russia
has Expressed Unconcern.

Prince Kung and others further memorialize. Previously because the Russian and American treaties had not been found and returned, Heng-ch'i and others were ordered to devise means at
Tientsin of questioning the English and French and recovering them.
Recently a letter from Heng-ch'i and the others states that they
have repeatedly interrogated the said barbarians and they said that
as they were not their countries' treaties and at that time peace
had not been concluded, they were either discarded or burned, it
was hard to tell which. Now that peace had been restored they
would make an exhaustive investigation.

Your officials note that the Russian and American treaties have been published and circulated and the various original texts are now useless. The said barbarians cannot use China's loss of them as a pretext for wrangling. If they had wanted to use this to create further complications, the French barbarians would not have been willing to return them. When Your official I-hsin (Prince Kung) met the Russian Chief Ignatieff, that chief, knowing the original texts were lost at Hai-tien, said that as they had been published they were of no further use and there was no need of investigating. If they were gathered up and taken away by the English barbarians and they had secreted them, not wanting to return them, in the future after the said chief returned home he could certainly find means to extort them and then send them to Peking.

Thus what the Russian chief emphasizes is publication and distribution; the preservation of the original copy is of no importance. As the American barbarians are far away in Shanghai there is no way of explaining to them but these barbarians, inasmuch as the printed copies are distributed to the various provinces, surely cannot make this a matter of contention. While at present there is no trace of them, there is no necessity of making further demands of the said barbarians. (IWSM.HF 70; 6b, 9-7b, 1)

536. December 2, 1860. EDICT: Orders Hsüeh Huan to Sound Out the American Consul at Shanghai Regarding the Lost Originals of the American Treaties.

Edict to the Grand Councillors. Previously was received a memorial of I-hsin Prince Kung and others that the Russian and American treaties exchanged in 1858 and the American credentials had all been lost due to the English and French disturbance in Tien-yüan [i.e. Hai-tien]. Now is received a memorial saying that Heng-ch'i has repeatedly interrogated the said chiefs, who told him that under the circumstances it was not certain whether they were discarded or burned. It also states that the Russian chief, Ignatieff, told I-hsin (Prince Kung) that after a treaty had been published, (the original) was of no further use and there was no need of investigating.

As it is assumed the Americans far away in Shanghai still do not know of it, order Hsüeh Huan to notify the American chief immediately saying that as his country's credentials and original texts of treaties and tariff conventions were kept at Hai-tien, they were lost when it was sacked by England and France. After investigation there was no trace, but now printed editions of the treaty have been distributed to the various provinces. In the future all matters involving the two countries can be verified according to these and whether there is an original copy or not is of no importance. Thus explain to them in advance and avoid future wrangling. This is most important. (IWSM.HF 70; 7b, 1-8a, 1)

537. December 15, 1860. MEMORIAL: The Imperial Commissioner for Military Affairs in Anhwei Expresses Distrust of a Foreign Operated Tribute Transport.

Yüan Chia-san further memorializes: ...As to arranging to purchase rice and utilizing the Russian or American flag to protect transport to Tientsin, considering present barbarian conditions, their attitude is very proud and their hearts are even more extravagant. In all probability after we have paid them the money the situation will change and it is greatly feared there will be no way out. The need for grain within the capital is very great. Your official is not thoroughly familiar with transportation matters by sea. Some means must be found for transportation to give us firm control. Tseng Kuo-fan and others can surely manage suitably in accord with Edict and then wait upon Sacred decision.

Vermilion endorsement: Let the Grand Councillors keep this on file temporarily. (IWSM.HF 70; 18b, 4...20a, 3-10)

538. January 5, 1861. MEMORIAL: Tseng Kuo-fan Rejects Russian Military Assistance Against Rebels but Favors American Aid in a Tribute Transport Program.

Imperial Commissioner, Governor General of Liang-chiang Tseng Kuo-fan memorializes. Your official humbly acknowledges the receipt on December 7th of a confidential Court Letter from the Grand Councillors that on November 23rd they had received an Imperial Edict that in the fall of this year England and France led troops against the capital.

Acknowledging Your Majesty's holy concern for everything, which never fails to reach every detail, Your official has considered the two proposals of the Russian chief. Regarding the request to send three or four hundred barbarian soldiers to assist in the suppression of the Nanking rebels, it is noted that the Atlantic countries, England, France, and America, rely on the strength of their ships and size of their cannon to dominate the seas; the Russian capital adjoins the Atlantic and her ships and cannon and her skills are comparable to theirs. Only recently coming to China by sea, these barbarians have never had any enmity toward China so their request to use gunboats to help suppress the Long-haired Rebels has no ulterior scheme. In the K'ang-hsi period (1662-1723) in the attack on T'ai-wan, the use of Dutch sailing vessels to assist is an example of China's employment of barbarian ships.

But the Yangtze is more than 2000 li long. In the upper reaches, An-ch'ing, Wu-hu, and such places there are the marines of Yang Ts'ai-fu and P'eng Yü-lin and in the lower reaches, Yang-chou, Chen-chiang, etc., the marines of Wu Ch'uan-mei and Li Te-liu. At present Your official is building more warships at Changsha and Wu-ch'eng [present Wuhsien or Soochow, near Shanghai] for use next year in the Huai-Yang sector.

Thus the deficiency in the government forces in Anhwei and Kiangsu is on land rather than on the water. The violence of the Nanking Long haired Rebels is also on land rather than on the water. Under present circumstances our infantry cannot advance on Nanking. If the Russian barbarian warships came up from the seaport, we still could not effect a pincer movement. So we must ask that Imperial orders be issued to the Princes and Ministers to transmit word to the said barbarian chief, commending the sincerity of his desire to conform but delaying the time for him to mobilize. After the infantry has recaptured the various Yangtze districts, have the ministers in charge of troops arrange with the said chief to send ships to assist in the fighting. This will ensure our independence and also suffice to please him. France has also made this request and can also be commended and allowed to come to our assistance in order to show we are friendly and without suspicion, delaying the time for mobilization to make clear that we are not being rescued in a crisis.

In the past, outside barbarians have helped China, and after the victory there are always many unreasonable demands and then we are not in a position to satisfy them or else further controversy is developed. It would seem better to make an agreement in advance stipulating so many warships, so much rental, so many barbarian soldiers per ship, so many provisions per month, and so much expense for all munitions, item by item. In the future when assistance is given, it should be handled entirely by the Shanghai arsenals, avoiding possible wrangling and blocking causes for trouble.

As to the suggestion that American merchants buy up grain for shipment to Tientsin, in the various districts of Chekiang and Kiangsu much of the country is devastated and next year's new transport can under the circumstances hardly be handled. The American merchants' and Canton merchants' willingness to buy up Formosan and foreign rice and send it to Tientsin and Ta-ku by sea is really a veritable godsend. Since the Russian chief made this request it would seem that it could be acceded. Except for the rice bought up by the Canton merchants, which they must handle themselves, there being no need of flying the Russian or American flag, for all the rice bought up and shipped to Tientsin by American merchants, Imperial Orders are requested ordering Hsüeh Huan at Shanghai to make clear to the said merchants the fact that we require the Canton merchants' price to be secured. Since the American merchants are subject to the control of the American chief, we are confident that there will be no defaulting. Under the circumstances, it would seem that other than this there is no good plan. It is humbly asked that the Sacred Intelligence investigate and carry it out.

Now, Your official ventures to suggest the way to manage barbarians is to understand barbarian temperament. Of all western

barbarians, the English are the most crafty, the French next; the
Russians are stronger than either the English or the French and are
always struggling with the English barbarians, who are afraid of them.
The Americans are of pure-minded and honest disposition and long
recognized as respectful and compliant toward China. In 1839, when
the English barbarians precipitated the crisis over opium and her
warships went up the Canton River, the American chief[5] reported to
Assistant Military Governor Yang Fang that he was willing to act as
mediator and that the English chief, Elliot had promised in writing
that all he would ask for was trade and would not demand anything
else. Thus he did not even demand the price of the opium [i.e. payment for the opium destroyed by Commissioner Lin]. Yang Fang
memorialized this but did not dare sponsor the proposal alone.
When the government forces burned the foreign factories and accidentally injured several American barbarians, the (mediation proposal) was forgotten and so the barbarian trouble flared up immediately.

In 1853 the rebels occupied Nanking and it was reported that the
American chief proffered his good offices at the headquarters of
Hsiang Jung and asked to use a gunboat to assist in the suppression.
It is not known whether Hsiang Jung memorialized this or not. When
the English and French barbarians attacked the capital of Kwangtung,
the American chief never assisted the rebels. Last year when Tientsin repulsed the barbarian ships, the American chief took the initiative in going to Peking to exchange ratifications, nor did he object to
anything. Thus, while the American barbarians have always been
sincerely loyal to China, they have never been in close alliance with
the English and French barbarians. This has become apparent.

This time, as the Russian barbarians say that American merchants are willing to buy up rice, it would seem that if instructions
were given Hsüeh Huan to make a personal arrangement with the
American chief he could handle it suitably. Probably by secretly
blocking the Russian barbarians' overtures to China and preventing
them from winning over the American barbarians' hearts, the American barbarians could be made to realize that China is not the least
suspicious of them and might even turn around completely and draw
nearer to us, one cannot tell.

Although negotiations are completed for the present, how can
China neglect preparation a single day? Since the (Yellow) River
has changed its course,[6] how can ocean transport be interrupted a

5 This apparently refers to Commodore Lawrence Kearny, U. S. N.

6 In 1853, the course of the Yellow River changed from the Huai channel flowing into the Yellow Sea, to the northern channel flowing into the Gulf of
Chihli.

single year? If it is possible to arrange these two matters suitably, even though we temporarily rely on barbarian strength to assist in suppression and to save transportation to gain temporary relief, in the future we can acquire the barbarians' knowledge to cast cannon and build ships for ourselves, so we can still hope for permanent advantage. For whatever these petty stupid fears are worth they are brought together and reported. (IWSM.HF 71; 9b, 9-12a, 8)

539. January 5, 1861. EDICT: Accepts Tseng's Advice to Refuse Russian Military Aid and Orders Further Study of American Proposal to Assist in Tribute Transport.

Edict to the Grand Councillors. Previously was received a memorial of I-hsin Prince Kung and others on their reception of the (Russian) barbarians and exchange of ratifications. It said that the (Russian) chief personally told them that as the Long-haired Rebels were acting perversely in Chiang-nan, he was willing to send barbarian troops to assist in their suppression. As next year's southern tribute transport to Peking might be obstructed, the Shanghai American and Canton merchants were willing to collect Formosan and foreign rice and ship it to Tientsin. Orders were immediately issued for Tseng Kuo-fan, Hsüeh Huan, and Yüan Chia-san to confer wholeheartedly and memorialize suitable proposals. Subsequently memorials in reply were received from Yüan Chia-san and Hsüeh Huan respectively. Each reported fully his own views.

Today Tseng Kuo-fan memorializes that the marauding of the Nanking Long-haired rebels and the deficiency of the Anhwei-Kiangsu government troops are both on land rather than on sea. At this time the infantry cannot assault Nanking, so to have the Russian barbarian gunboats proceed from the seaport would still not effect a pincer and he is impelled to ask that word be sent the said chief commending the sincerity of his support but delaying the time of utilization. After the infantry has recovered Soochow and Ch'ang-chou and places in Anhwei and Chekiang, have the officials in charge of troops arrange with the said chief to send ships to assist in the campaign. This would be enough independence for us and also suffice to please him. The French chief's request can also be commended and accorded but an agreement should be made with him beforehand stipulating the number of gunboats and the outlay. In the future when there is military assistance everything should be paid from the Shanghai arsenal in order to avoid disputes.

In general, this is little different from what Hsüeh Huan memorialized. As soon as ratifications were exchanged, the various countries offered military assistance and rice transport intending to make overtures to China. Yüan Chia-san says that in the past barbarian assistance has done harm rather than good. While this is sound reasoning, to oppose him too strenuously would make the said chief suspicious. If we take advantage of circumstances and keep the strings in our hands it will not be without advantage in military affairs and tribute transport.

That which Tseng Kuo-fan memorializes, to wait until the government forces have the land sector under control and then arrange for their cooperation on the water, seems fairly practicable but whether or not the necessary expenditures can be agreed upon in advance, order I-hsin Prince Kung and the others to investigate thoroughly, deliberate and memorialize.

As to the request to assist in transporting southern tribute, Tseng Kuo-fan asks that Hsüeh Huan be instructed to make it clear at Shanghai that the Canton merchants are to give security for the amount but that we will trust the American merchants to manage for themselves. But Hsüeh Huan memorializes that Kuei-liang and others have already agreed at Shanghai that no rice and other grain can be shipped abroad but they do allow barbarian merchants to transport it from one port to another, still paying the export duty, so it seems according to this they can be allowed to ship to Tientsin for official purchase. American merchants buying up Formosan and foreign rice to ship to Tientsin, Hsüeh Huan fears, will become a pretext for their taking over the tribute transport of grain.

This view is also correct but it is also feared that in official purchase there are the evils of extortion and speculation. Whether either merchant transport or merchant purchase is practicable or is of any advantage to the granaries, also order I-hsin (Prince Kung) and the others to consider minutely. When all regulations have been agreed upon, confer and arrange with the said country.

The memorials of Tseng Kuo-fan, Yüan Chia-san, and Hsüeh Huan are all ordered copied and sent out for perusal. (IWSM.HF 71; 12a, 9-13b, 3)

540. January 24, 1861. MEMORIAL: Prince Kung Reviews Foreign Policy and Opposes Foreign (Russian) Aid against the Rebels but Favors Greater Reliance on America and Greater Use of Foreign Armaments.

Imperial Commissioner Prince Kung, Grand Secretary Kuei-liang, and Senior Vice-president of the Board of Revenue Wen-hsiang memorialize. Your officials beg to state that on January seventh they received a Confidential Edict and also copies of the four memorials of Tseng Kuo-fan, Yüan Chia-san, and Hsüeh Huan with Imperial Instructions for Your officials to evaluate them carefully.

Looking up with respect at Your Majesty's concern for southern affairs, His evaluation of the light and the heavy neglects no available resource. After reading it on bended knee with indescribable

respect, Your officials find from their memorials that Yüan Chia-
san's discussion, in matters of advantage and disadvantages, is very
lucid. Truly as Sacred Edict says, it is proper reasoning. Tseng
Kuo-fan considers the exigencies of military affairs and the way of
controlling outside barbarians, determined according to the time,
and (his memorial) is really carefully prepared. While Hsüeh
Huan's idea is to overthrow the lair of the Long-haired rebels, advancing both by water and land to effect a quick victory, in general
he differs little from Tseng Kuo-fan.

Your officials previously memorialized that as the Nien (-fei)
and Long-haired (Taiping) rebels were at large and government
troops were insufficient to exterminate them, they hoped to use
barbarian strength as it had been used in the past. Ostensibly, it
was a method of quelling the rebels, while secretly it was a scheme
to block collusion. But having respectfully received the Imperial
Edict as well as the said ministers' original memorials, they have
conferred intently for several days. At present the Chiang-nan government force is still unable to attack Nanking, so to have barbarian
ships sail up not only could not effect a capture, but it is also feared
if they are in contact with the rebels too long, they will join up with
the rebels, as Hsüeh Huan apprehends, and start another rebellion.
So it is still more essential to be prepared. As for the said governor's suggestion to have barbarian troops advance on Nanking by
water, not only could disturbances be expected in the country traversed, but there would be many difficulties in meeting the demands.
Since the exchange of ratifications in Peking, the barbarian soldiers
in Tientsin still have not all withdrawn south. How could we send all
the Peking crack troops south and incite people's ridicule? The proposal need not be discussed.

In their humble opinion, while all barbarians are insatiably
avaricious by nature, Russian barbarians are inscrutable and French
barbarians are crafty. As for this offer of assisting in suppressing
rebellion, although not encouraged by China, once consent is given
they are sure to demand written communications; not stopping with
communications they will request an Imperial Edict; not satisfied
with Edicts they will request an Audience. Even before we get any
benefit they will start making demands. Once they incur expenses
they will present their bills and the countryside will feel their oppressive exactions. Before the rebels are pacified the source of
supplies will have been exhausted; before a city is recovered oppression will have become heavy. To refuse them will be impossible
under the circumstances; to accede to them will be even more cala-
mitous. If their strength is insufficient to overcome the rebels, we
shall be depleting our supplies supporting useless barbarian troops
--surely enough to make the rebels laugh. If the (rebel) capital is
recaptured they will expect to occupy it and if we send troops to

garrison it, the government troops having disposed of the rebels will quarrel with the barbarians. Before the Central China rebels are suppressed, border [i.e. foreign] troubles will arise. If we secretly tolerate them, these barbarians will seek to win popularity with petty loyalty and petty faith, so men's hearts will gradually be lost with no means of recall.

Previously the Russian barbarians encroached on our borders without open warfare and up to now it has been impossible to expel them. If on the pretext of suppressing rebels they take territory in the southern provinces, then north and south sectors will be gnawed into separately and how can we bear to think of it? Considering everything, it transpires that the gain is slight and the loss great, but it is still hoped that it still may be possible to do something.

Consequently when the English Thomas Wade came to the office for an interview, (Your officials) employed sincerity and justice and a display of confidence in order to bring out his natural goodness. After talking with him all day long, the said chief finally spoke frankly, saying that the suppression of the rebellion is primarily a matter for China to handle. If she borrows the assistance of others, what have they to gain without the occupation of territory? Not only would France and Russia be unwilling to relinquish the capital after it was captured, but even if England took it he would not venture to say that she would not claim it for herself, citing the said barbarians' conquest of India as an example. Although the said chief's statement was not necessarily uttered in sincerity, what Your officials fear is already apparent.

Previously, when the French chief Meritens came, Your officials also discussed the matter with him. When the crux of the matter was reached his expressions were shifty; it seemed as if his idea was openly to help the government forces put down the rebellion and at the same time keep an eye on the winner.

Yüan Chia-san, relying on reason, makes a forthright report and his views are correct, while Tseng Kuo-fan asks to wait until Soochow, Ch'ang-chou and various districts of Anhwei and Chekiang have been recovered and then make a joint attack on Nanking. Examining this idea it appears that he himself has forebodings of trouble because our strength is inadequate and therefore he first encourages them in order to dispel their doubts. But if the various districts are all recovered and the prestige of the army is greatly improved, why borrow barbarian troops? It would seem his idea cannot be called practicable.

In military affairs, Your officials are not completely versed. Hence in previous memorials they were apprehensive of consequences and asked that Orders be given Tseng Kuo-fan and others to consider them. Now they have made a thorough investigation and selected the good to follow, namely: if we employ barbarians to suppress the rebels, the consequent evils will be legion; while we should not use them to suppress the rebels, as it is feared that they would ally with the rebels, means must be found to ensnare them, entice them with petty gain. As the avariciousness of the French barbarians is greatest, in case it can be arranged to purchase munitions and ships to give them some profit to look forward to, then we can hope to take them in.

Thus they are impelled to request that an Edict be issued to Tseng Kuo-fan and Hsüeh Huan, with the military strength now available, to devise means to attack; that they cannot covet immediate petty gains and incur endless consequences. As to the Shanghai barbarians, in case they repeat their request, commend them just enough to placate them; if any warships sail into the interior, stop them in accordance with the treaty. If the said barbarians coming to Peking bring up this matter again, Your officials will subdue their hearts with reason in order to block their schemes.

They humbly read in the Edict, "if opposed unduly, it is feared the said chief will be suspicious and apprehensive." They note that previously the Russian chief brought up this matter and Your officials explained that the ministers in charge of troops on the various fronts led several hundred thousand soldiers and so could sweep (the rebels) away one after the other, so at present there was still no need for assistance. The said chief could not think of anything to say. In case he makes this request again they will still commend him adroitly. If the said chief figures there is nothing to be done, he must needs submit and not be brought to develop more misgivings.

As to the matter of taking over the southern tribute transport, Tseng Kuo-fan requests that Hsüeh Huan at Shanghai be Imperially instructed to make clear to them that the Canton merchants give security for a fixed price, while the American merchants will be allowed to manage for themselves. Hsüeh Huan stated in his memorial that he feared once the matter was started, in the future on the pretext that the tribute grain must be transported by them, annual extortion for purchase money would be made and if their wishes were not accorded they would prevent the southern tribute grain from coming North. It would be better, in accordance with commercial regulations, to let barbarian merchants transport it to Tientsin themselves and then we buy it officially at the current price, without the necessity of advancing money for purchase. Your officials find his proposal is true preparation against calamity and in conformity with their own views. As these barbarians are by nature wholly avaricious, if there is a report of buying up rice, word is sure to get around and it would seem unnecessary to establish conditions. In the future a proclamation can be issued by the Shanghai Imperial Commissioner calling for merchants for Tientsin transport, without distinguishing Chinese or barbarian merchants, all undertaking the transportation to pay duties according to the tariff schedule and (the rice) to be bought officially.

In this way, there will be no opportunity for the barbarians to specu-
late; the rice will be taken at the current price, fairly determined.
Nor will there be any extortion. It would seem that the lever would
be with us, not controlled by the barbarians, nor would there be the
need of making an agreement in advance with the barbarians to give
rise to ideas of coercion.

Tseng Kuo-fan makes the statement that as the American barbarians are pure-minded and honest in disposition and have always been
loyal to China and are not allied to England and France, we should
secretly prevent the Russian barbarians from winning over the hearts
of the American barbarians; that by not arousing the least bit of suspicion it may be possible to draw them near to us in good faith.

It is noted that in the Tao-kuang period, when the English barbarians opposed authority in Kwangtung, the said barbarians and the
French both respectfully obeyed Imperial Edict and did not dare illegally sell opium. In 1842 the English barbarians exchanged ratifications at Nanking, and these barbarians finally, in 1844, asked
for like treatment. In 1853 these barbarians asked to use gunboats
to assist in the assault on Nanking and Governor Yang Wen-ting reported accordingly. Later, as Hsiang Jung considered it impracticable,
it was not accepted. Thus the American barbarians' attitude toward
China is not the same as England's or France's, and the problem is
how to control them to make them exploitable by us. They are impelled to ask for a Confidential Edict for Tseng Kuo-fan and Hsüeh
Huan to handle the situation so to captivate them that they will be
grateful and draw near to us, rather than be won over by the Russian
barbarians. If means are found to control them, the benefit will not
be inconsiderable.

Tseng Kuo-fan also says in his memorial that in the future to acquire barbarian knowledge in casting cannon and building ships will be
of permanent advantage. Your officials have resolved to deliberate
and act accordingly. They find that during the K'ang-hsi (1662-1723)
period, in quelling the San-fan (rebellion)[7] Europeans [Lit. Western
Ocean men] were employed to make munitions and their strength relied on.[8] At present, although barbarian affairs are not comparable
with past ones, the French barbarians are entirely willing to sell
munitions as well as to send craftsmen to instruct in manufacture
and if we engaged several barbarian craftsmen to manufacture at
Shanghai for use in the rebel campaign, it would be practicable under
the circumstances. (Your officials) are impelled to ask for Imperial

---

7 The San-fan Rebellion, led by Wu San-kuei, Keng Ching-chung, and Shang Chih-
hsin, covered the period from 1674 to 1681, at the beginning of the Manchu
dynasty.

8 This is a reference to the Jesuit scholars in Peking in the late Ming and
early Ch'ing dynasties.

Instructions to Tseng Kuo-fan and Hsüeh Huan to deliberate and act. Although at present there is not time enough to build warships, perhaps copying their models or chartering their ships to make up our deficiency in warships would still be advantageous. Hence Your officials' request to tempt them with petty profits to bind their hearts and, at the same time, get something useful for the bandit campaign. Might not the said governor general and governor be Confidentially Instructed to deliberate and try this out? If they can be of use in the campaign, have Hsüeh Huan collect funds from the customs receipts of the various ports and take action immediately.... (IWSM.HF 72; 3a, 5-7b, 4)

541. February 9, 1861. MEMORIAL: Hsüeh Huan Reports Continued Progress at Shanghai in Clearing Up the Loss of the Ratified American Treaty.

       Imperial Commissioner, Governor of Kiangsu Hsüeh Huan memorializes. Your official received a confidential Court Letter from the Grand Councillors that on December 2, 1860, they received an Imperial Edict acknowledging the receipt of a memorial of I-hsin (Prince Kung) and others regarding the Russian and American treaties exchanged in 1858. They note that as the American credentials and the original text of the treaty and tariff schedule have been lost, it is necessary, just as with Russia, forthwith to recognize the current printed text as official and that it is most essential to explain beforehand to the American chief in order to prevent future dispute.

       It is learned from Acting Su-Sung-T'ai Tao-t'ai Wu Hsü's inquiry that the American chief, John Ward, has returned home,[9] so Your official immediately prepared an official letter of clarification apprising John Ward fully of the communication sent him by the Imperial Commissioners and has ordered Wu Hsü to deliver it to the American consul, Smith,[10] for transmission to his country, and to have the said chief reply as evidence of good faith.

       Vermilion endorsement: Noted. (IWSM.HF 72; 37a, 8-37b, 7)

542. April 3, 1861. MEMORIAL: Hsüeh Huan Reports Admiral Stribling's Reassurance Regarding the Lost Treaty and Accepts his Offer to have a Copy Sent to China.

       Imperial Commissioner, Governor of Kiangsu Hsüeh Huan memorializes. It is humbly noted that since the American credentials and original treaties and tariff schedules were destroyed or lost at Hai-tien, in the future when there are matters of intercourse it will be necessary to regard the printed text as authoritative. Last year Your

---

9   Ward resigned and returned to the United States in December, 1860. He was succeeded by Anson Burlingame.
10   W. L. G. Smith was United States consul at Shanghai from March 30, 1858.

official respectfully received an Imperial Edict to notify the American envoy, John Ward, explaining to him in advance. Since John Ward had returned home, he ordered the Su-Sung-T'ai tao-t'ai to deliver his communication to the American consul for transmittal. Previously Your official appended this to a memorial as well as a copy of the communication, receiving the Vermilion endorsement: Noted.

Now is received from Su-Sung-T'ai Tao-t'ai Wu Hsü, who in turn received it from the American consul, a communication from the Ameri-American envoy, [C. K.] Stribling, under the titles of Admiral and Acting Minister Plenipotentiary, saying that as John Ward is on leave and is not in China, he has been delegated to act. He received Your official's letter and notes that the printed edition has been circulated in China and abroad and even though the original be destroyed, there is no difficulty. Moreover, if subsequently the two countries have any questions regarding the provisions of the treaties or tariff schedules, there is an original copy retained by the said envoy and if we want to see it, a clear copy will be made and sent.

Your official notes that as what Stribling says is quite reasonable, he immediately sent him a communication to have him make a copy and send it. When it comes, he will send it to the Board of Rites, to transmit to the Tsungli T'ung-shang Yamen [i.e. the new Foreign Office] for examination.

Vermilion endorsement: Noted. (IWSM.HF 75; 8b, 1-9a, 5)

543. June 3, 1861. MEMORIAL: Ch'ang-sha Governor General Kuan-wen Reports a Friendly Tour of Inspection and Visit with U. S. Admiral Stribling at Hankow.

Imperial Commissioner, Grand Secretary, Governor General of Hu-kwang Kuan-wen memorializes. ...There is also received a report from the prefect of Hanyang, Liu Ch'i-hsien, that on May 11 two American gunboats, one large and one small, came to Hankow. He found that it was the said country's Admiral Stribling and interpreter McCartee[11] coming to Hankow to investigate and arrange matters of trade. They proposed to leave a consul, Williams,[12] to reside at the Hankow Ch'ung-chi Factory. They further proposed securing a site and building a residence. At present they have not brought any goods here.

Your slave immediately had the said prefect, Liu Ch'i-hsien, and others take due charge.

On the 13th the said Admiral Stribling, accompanied by fourteen civil and military officers, entered the city and came to Your slave's

---

11 Dr. D. B. McCartee, Presbyterian medical missionary, was stationed for many years at Ningpo.

12 O. D. Williams held an appointment as acting consul at Hankow, May 11, 1861, from Flag Officer C. K. Stribling, U. S. N., who was temporarily in charge of the American legation at Shanghai. Griffin, op. cit., p. 308n.

yamen for an interview. The said interpreter, McCartee, understands the native dialect and his expressions were compliant, so they were received with courtesy and everybody was pleased. Also Stribling and the others then announced their forthcoming trip to Yüeh-chou and Tung-t'ing Lake, saying that all foreign countries knew Tung-t'ing to be a famous place of the empire and they were going there for sight-seeing and had no other motive. They would proceed on the 15th, with one steamer.

Your slave hastily sent full instructions to the prefects of Yüeh-chou, Chang-sha, and Ch'ang-te respectively, explaining that when the American ship arrived to treat it courteously, for all merchants to proceed with their business calmly, as there was no need for alarm nor should any trouble be started.

On the afternoon of the 17th, then, the said steamer returned to Hankow. They propose to select three sites in the outskirts of Hankow, below the English location, to construct warehouses. The price of the land will be discussed by the foreign merchant with the land-lord personally and there is to be a fair transaction and mutual good faith. The prefect of Hanyang, meanwhile, will place on file the contract containing the measurements of this land and construction will not be started until the purchase has been completed with the payment of the money. Between 3 and 5, on the afternoon of the 20th, the said two American steamers started downstream to return to Shanghai.

Vermilion endorsement: Noted. (IWSM.HF 78; 3a, 7...4a, 1-4b, 8)

544. June 6, 1861. MEMORIAL: Prince Kung Reports the Receipt of a Copy of the American Treaty to Replace the Lost Original in the Government Archives at Peking.

Prince Kung and others further memorialize. As the original text of the American treaty and convention exchanged in 1858 was destroyed last autumn by fire, it was memorialized and word sent to the governor of Kiangsu to transmit word for the consul of that country to have another copy presented for the files. Now is received from the said governor a copy of the said treaty, submitted with a letter and on the twenty-sixth of last month sent to Your officials' yamen from the Board of Rites. Besides comparing the treaty and convention carefully with the printed text now retained and the copy kept at the office of the Grand Council and sending it to the Board of Rites for filing, it is duly reported via this supplement.

Vermilion endorsement: Noted. (IWSM.HF 78; 11b, 5-12a, 1)

GLOSSARY OF CHINESE PERSONAL NAMES
WITH BIOGRAPHICAL NOTES

GLOSSARY OF CHINESE PERSONAL NAMES
WITH BIOGRAPHICAL NOTES

Key to Biographical References and Abbreviations

CSK   Ch'ing Shih Kao 清史稿

CSLC   Ch'ing Shih Lieh Chuan 清史列傳

CHLC   Kuo Ch'ao Ch'i Hsien Lei Cheng 國朝耆獻類徵

JM   Chung Kuo Jen Ming Ta Tz'ŭ Tien 中國人名大辭典

SJCL   Kuo Ch'ao Shih Jen Cheng Lüeh 國朝詩人徵略

PCCP   Pei Chuan Chi Pu 碑傳集補

HPCC   Hsü Pei Chuan Chi 續碑傳集

MS   Ch'in Ting Ming Shih 欽定明史

CFHCC   Ta Ch'ing Chi Fu Hsien Che Chuan 大清畿輔先哲傳

ECCP   Eminent Chinese of the Ch'ing Period, A. W. Hummel,
         ed., 2 vols., Washington, 1943-44.

All materials for which no reference is given are derived from
the text of the documents herein translated. References in parenthesis and beginning with (33.   .   ) are to the Index to Thirty-
three Collections of Ch'ing Dynasty Biographies, Harvard-
Yenching Institute Sinological Index Series, No. 9, Peiping, December, 1932, and are included to indicate biographical references not used in these notes. Only materials actually used are
cited in the biographical notes.

GLOSSARY OF CHINESE PERSONAL NAMES
WITH BIOGRAPHICAL NOTES

A-ching-a 阿精阿, Manchu general-in-chief (Tartar General) in command of the Canton garrison in 1841.

CHANG Ch'i-yüan 張起鶴, substantive Tientsin tao-t'ai in 1854, was regarded as experienced in dealing with foreigners because of his participation in the negotiations with the British in 1850. He was not called upon in the negotiations with Bowring and McLane because he was occupied with military duties at the time.

CHANG Chen-hsiung 張振熊,, second captain in the military forces at Tientsin in 1858, was used as a messenger to the foreign ships anchored at Ta-ku.

CHANG Chin-wen 張錦文, one of several Tientsin gentry and merchants called upon in 1858 to raise subscriptions and lead local militia against British and French invasion.

CHANG Ch'un 張春, was brigade general in command of government troops at Feng-huang-kang, near Hu-men (Bocca Tigris), below Canton, in 1841.

CHANG Ch'ung-k'o 張崇恪, department magistrate at Canton in 1854, was ordered by Governor General Yeh Ming-ch'en to meet Bourboulon's interpreters.

CHANG Fei 張芾 (d. 1862), native of Ching-yang-hsien, Shensi, was a chin-shih of 1835 and Hanlin academician. From the time of his appointment as governor of Kiangsi in 1852, he was active in fighting the Taiping Rebels and distinguished himself in the defense of Chen-chiang (Chinkiang) and Nan-chang. In 1854, he was impeached for misuse of government funds but continued in active command. In 1861 he was ordered to organize local militia in his native province, Shensi, against the Mohammedan Rebels and was killed in battle the following year. (33.259.1) CSLC 49.7a.

CHANG Kuo-liang 張國樑 (d. May, 1860, age 38 sui), a native of either Kao-yao or Hua-hsien, Kwangtung, started out as a bandit chief but surrendered in 1849, and used his energies for the Imperialist cause. He became assistant commander to the Manchu general, Ho-ch'un, when the latter succeeded General Hsiang Jung in 1856. Professor Teng Ssu-yü in his biography of him in Eminent Chinese of the Ch'ing Period, says: "Chang Kuo-liang was one of the most valiant generals of the imperial troops. He was responsible for most of Hsiang Jung's victories, performed most of the duties belonging to Ho-ch'un and contributed much to the Great Camp of Kiangnan by harassing the Taipings for eight years (1853-60). After his death, the so-called Great Camp was dispersed and Kiangsu and Chekiang and part of Fukien were devastated by the Taipings." (33.256.3) ECCP 1.294.

CHANG Ming-feng 張鳴鳳 was acting district magistrate of Hsi-lin-hsien, Kwangsi, in 1856, at the time of the murder of the French missionary, Abbé Chapdelaine.

CHANG P'an-lung 張攀龍 was a petty officer employed as a deputy by Niu Chien in the negotiations with Pottinger at Nanking in 1842. A lieutenant colonel in 1853, he negotiated with various foreigners at Shanghai in the matter of chartering warships to use against the Taipings.

CHANG Ping-to 張東鐸 was the brevet colonel, expectant lieutenant colonel of the Central Army, major of the Hsüan-hua (Chihli, Hopei) Brigade deputized by Heng Fu to escort Ward and his party from Pei-t'ang to Peking and back in 1859.

CHANG Shun 張順 was the chief runner of the P'an-yü-hsien (Canton) yamen who carried out the arrest of the Chinese crew of the famous lorcha Arrow, October 11, 1854.

CHANG Tien-yüan 張殿元 was provisional commander-in-chief of Chihli (Hopei) in 1854. He had experience in dealing with the British at Tientsin in 1850, but was not called upon for the negotiations with Bowring and McLane in 1854, because he was occupied with military duties.

CHANG T'ing-hsüeh 張庭學, native of Ningpo, Hanlin bachelor, expectant magistrate, was operating a foreign goods store on Yang-ching-pin, Shanghai, in 1854, and was regarded as a "specialist" on foreign affairs. Recommended by Huang Tsung-han, he was deputized by Governor Chi-erh-hang-a to negotiate with the foreign consuls for cooperation in the defense of Shanghai against the rebels.

CHANG Yü 張裕, was assistant district magistrate of Hsiang-shan (now Chung-shan)-hsien, Kwangtung, residing at Macao in 1842.

CHANG Yü-liang 張玉良 (d. 1861), native of Pa-hsien, Szechwan, was regarded as one of the outstanding generals of China in 1860. He rose from the ranks, became provincial commander-in-chief of Chekiang, and eventually succeeded Ho-ch'un and Chang Kuo-liang when they were killed in 1860. Chang Yü-liang led the imperial armies against the Taipings at Hangchow and was killed in the assault. (33.254.2) CSK 408.7a.

CH'ANG Ch'i 長啓, expectant prefect at Tientsin, was drafted by Governor General T'an T'ing-hsiang to assist in transport, registering merchant ships, and building barracks preparatory to meeting foreign invasion in 1858.

CH'ANG Shan-pao 常善保, as lieutenant colonel under the generalship of Te-hsing-a (one of Prince Seng-ko-lin-ch'in's commanders), participated in the resistance to the British and French at Pei-t'ang, August 3, 1860.

CHAO Ch'ang-ling 趙長齡, one-time prefect of Chao-ch'ing, Kwangtung, expectant ministerial secretary, was regarded as an "expert" on barbarian affairs and worked closely with Ch'i-ying in Canton in 1843. When the latter was en route to meet Cushing in 1844, he met Chao Ch'ang-ling at Nan-hsiung, Kwangtung, and promptly drafted him to assist in negotiating the American treaty.

CHAO Te-ch'e 趙德轍, first as acting tao-t'ai of Su-Sung-T'ai, later as acting governor of Kiangsu, participated in the negotiations in Shanghai in 1856 to adjust the Shanghai back customs with American consuls Murphy and Fish and Commissioner Peter Parker.

Chen-lin 振麟, a Manchu, expectant tao-t'ai at Tientsin, was drafted by Governor General T'an T'ing-hsiang to assist in transport, registering merchant ships, and repairing barracks in 1858, to resist foreign invasion.

CH'EN A-lin 陳阿林, secondary rebel leader around Shanghai in 1854, disguised himself as a barbarian and took refuge in the International Settlement. It was believed by the imperialists that he sought foreign support for the rebel cause and asked for a foreign vessel in which to flee.

CH'EN Chao-lin 陳兆麟, native of Kwangtung, was magistrate of T'ang-hsien, Chihli (Hopei) and director of the Fukien-Kwangtung Guildhall in Tientsin in 1858. He was recognized by Governor General T'an T'ing-hsiang as an "expert" on barbarian affairs and charged with raising trainbands to resist foreign invasion. Ch'en was also expected to check on his Cantonese and Fukienese compatriots in Tientsin, whose loyalty was somewhat suspect.

CH'EN Chih-kang 陳志剛, was a Canton garrison officer who assisted Ch'i-ying in his negotiations in 1843, but was not available in 1844.

CH'EN Hung-i 陳鴻翊, Shansi circuit censor, memorialized in 1859 on the need for strengthening the defenses of Pei-t'ang to prevent an attack on Ta-ku from the rear.

CH'EN I-chih 陳宜之, was the district magistrate at Canton (P'an-yü-hsien), who, under orders from Governor General Yeh Ming-ch'en, met Bourboulon's interpreters in 1854.

CH'EN Pai-ling 陳百齡, as garrison officer at Canton in 1843, assisted Ch'i-ying in negotiations with the British. Later, as chiliarch of the Hung-hu (Hundan) regiment, Ch'i-ying recalled that he was "thoroughly familiar with the barbarian temper" and drafted him to investigate the foreign (British) strength on the Kiangsu seaboard and Chu-shan. In 1844, Ch'i-ying regretted that Ch'en Pai-ling was not available to help with the Cushing negotiations.

CH'EN Te-li 陳德利, a Cantonese, was one of four hundred and seventy-five coolies aboard an English ship bound for California in 1852. When the ship passed near the Liu-ch'iu Islands the coolies mutinied and escaped ashore but were eventually brought back to Canton on another English ship for trial.

CH'EN T'ing-fang 陳廷芳, acting garrison commander, Shantung, reported three foreign ships off Miao Island, P'eng-lai-hsien, October 14, 1854.

CH'EN Ying-yün 陳應運, brigade general of Kwangtung Nan-ao (Namoa) garrison in 1857-1858.

CHENG Ch'eng-kung 鄭成功 (1624-1662), is better known in Western literature as Koxinga, the famous pirate and Ming loyalist who expelled the Dutch from Formosa (T'ai-wan) in 1661, and set up a Ming administration there. After his death, in 1662, Formosa remained Ming Chinese until 1683, when Koxinga's grandson finally submitted to the Manchus. (33.389.3) ECCP 1.108.

CHENG K'uei-shih 鄭魁士 (d. 1872), native of Hsüan-hua, Chihli (Hopei), military commander famed for his personal bravery and brilliant tactics, was promoted from the ranks. Beginning in 1850, he served under General Hsiang Jung and defeated the Taipings at Changsha. There is no record in his biography of being degraded in 1853, but he had the rank of colonel at the time under Hsiang Jung. He accompanied Shanghai Tao-t'ai Wu Chien-chang to visit the various consulates in Shanghai at that time, seeking foreign gunboats to use against the Taipings on the Yangtze River. By 1855, he was provincial commander-in-chief of Anhwei, and in 1858 was Tartar General of Chekiang, carrying out a series of campaigns against the Nien-fei. In 1866, he was appointed Tartar General of Chihli. (33.389.3) CSLC 51.17a.

Ch'eng-ch'i 成琦, a Manchu, accompanied Prince Kung to Kuang-hua Temple to meet the Russian envoy, Ignatieff, November 19, 1860.

CH'ENG Jen-chieh 程仁傑, acting magistrate of I-chou, Chihli, was delegated by Governor General of Chihli Kuei-liang to confer with Bowring and McLane on their arrival at Ta-ku in 1854.

CH'ENG Yü-ts'ai 程禹采 (d. 1858), native of Hsin-chien, Kiangsi, chin-shih of 1811, was appointed governor of Kiangsu in 1841, but was reduced to the 3rd grade in 1842, because of his failure to keep the British warships out of the Yangtze River. In 1843, he was appointed governor of Kwangtung. He cooperated with Ch'i Kung in developing a military colonization program for the defense of Hu-men (Bocca Tigris) and participated in the negotiation of the supplementary trade treaty with Great Britain (1843). In 1844, he carried on an extensive and evasive correspondence with Caleb Cushing until the arrival of Ch'iying. In 1853, he was exiled to Sinkiang for his failure to defend against the Taipings. He returned from exile in June, 1857, and died the following year. (33.284.3) CSLC 42.34a.

CH'EN K'o-ming 陳克明, first captain of Ta-ku garrison in 1854, was sent out to meet Medhurst and Parker, interpreters for Bowring and McLane respectively, on their arrival October 16th.

Chi-erh-hang-a 吉爾杭阿 (d. 1856) was a Manchu general of the Bordered Yellow Banner. He came into prominence in 1853, when General Hsiang Jung ordered him to expel the rebels occupying Shanghai. He was promoted to financial commissioner of Kiangsu in February, 1854, and became governor in July, in which capacity he sought the assistance and cooperation of the Western powers in Shanghai. Through negotiations with Bourboulon, Chi-erh-hang-a first turned France away from support of the rebels, then secured French and American cooperation in building a stockade to keep the rebels out of the International Settlement, and finally secured French aid in expelling the rebels from Shanghai. This was effected February 17, 1855. Chi-erh-hang-a was then appointed aide to General Hsiang Jung and ordered to recover Chen-chiang (Chinkiang), where he was defeated and killed in battle. (33.160.3) ECCP 1.118.

CH'I Kung 祁墳 (1777-1844), a Chinese, native of Kao-p'ing, Shansi, chin-shih of 1796, succeeded the Manchu, Ch'i-shan, as governor general of Liang-kuang, February 26, 1841, when the latter was removed for secret dealings with the British and the loss of Hu-men (Bocca Tigris) to them. In 1842 Ch'i Kung was also degraded. He later memorialized proposing a military colonization program and use of local milita for the future defense of Hu-men, but was not restored to his post, apparently sharing with Ch'i-shan the opprobrium of yielding to the British.   (33.236.2) ECCP 1.128; CSLC 37.41b.

Ch'i-ming-pao 奇明保 (d. 1843), Manchu of the Wu-cha-la clan, member of the Plain White Banner, served in various military posts in Jehol, Manchuria, and Sinkiang until 1839, when he was appointed Tartar General at Hangchow. Here he was faced with the British the following year. After the British took Ch'a-pu and Ting-hai, he took up the defense of Hangchow. He was summoned to Peking in 1842, retired on account of old age, and was succeeded in his post by Ch'i-ying. He died the following year.   (33.171.1) CHLC 322.30a.

Ch'i shan 琦善 (d. 1854), member of the Borjigit clan and of the Manchu Plain Yellow Banner, inherited the title of marquis on the death of his father in 1823. In contemporary Western works he is referred to as Kishen. In 1840, as governor general of Chihli, he conciliated instead of resisting the British squadron when it threatened Ta-ku and Tientsin, conveyed Lord Palmerston's letter to the emperor, received the British emissaries in special tents in front of the Ta-ku Forts, and negotiated their return to Canton. As reward for his success, he was appointed Imperial Commissioner to succeed Lin Tse-hsü at Canton. After the British had demonstrated their prowess, he concluded the Convention of Chuenpi (Ch'üan-pi), ceding Hong Kong, promising six million dollars indemnity, granting the privilege of direct official relations, and the reopening of trade at Canton (January 20, 1841). I-liang, governor of Kwangtung, reported the terms to Peking and the emperor, convinced that Ch'i-shan had made a deal with the British, condemned him and stripped him of rank, office, and fortune. Hu-men (Bocca Tigris) fell to the British soon after. On March 12th Ch'i-shan was escorted from Canton in chains. After the war, he was reinstated and as Imperial Commissioner to Tibet ordered the French missionaries, Huc and Gabet, back to China. In 1849, he was made governor general of Shensi and Kansu, but was impeached in 1851 for harsh treatment of the native and Mohammedan tribes, and banished the following year to Kirin. He was soon recalled, however, to fight the Taipings in central China and continued in active military duty until his death in 1854. In later years, he is frequently cited in Chinese documents as the horrible example of an official who appeased foreigners and sold China short.   (33.329.3) ECCP 1.126.

CH'I Shen 齊愼 (1774-1844), Chinese general, was a native of Hsin-yeh, Honan. He entered the imperial army from the local militia and fought in various civil wars until 1840, when he was appointed assistant military governor of Kwangtung and confronted the British. First satationed at Fo-shan (Fatshan), he was transferred to Canton and early in 1841, along with I-shan, was degraded. The following year he was restored as assistant military governor of Hupeh and was again faced with British warships, this time in the Yangtze. When Chen-chiang (Chinkiang) fell, he was again degraded. In 1844, he was appointed Tartar General of Szechwan but died en route to his post. (33. 99. 3) CSLC 39. 17b.

Ch'i-ying 耆英 (d. 1858), known in contemporary Western writings as Kiying, official and diplomat, member of the Manchu Plan Blue Banner and imperial clansman, was the most prominent single person in Chinese foreign relations down to 1850. His negotiations with Caleb Cushing in 1844, and his tragic death in 1858, are fully told in the documents translated in this work. Prior to this he had already concluded the Treaty of Nanking with Great Britain, August 29, 1842, and on the death of I-li-pu, Ch'i-ying was sent to Canton, where he exchanged ratifications and concluded the supplementary Treaty of the Bogue, October 8, 1843. He was by this time the recognized authority in China on foreign relations and so, when Cushing arrived at Macao and threatened to proceed to Peking, Ch'i-ying, now governor general of Liang-chiang, was again made Imperial Commissioner and sent to Canton to stop him. The result was the Treaty of Wang-hsia (Wanghia), July 3, 1844. Subsequently, Ch'i-ying signed treaties with France and Sweden-Norway, 1844 and 1847 respectively. From 1842 to 1850, Ch'i-ying was virtual foreign minister of China and enjoyed the full confidence of emperor and court. He was recalled to Peking in 1848, and on the death of the Tao-kuang emperor in 1850 lost his support. On November 30, 1850, he was denounced by the new emperor for having "oppressed the people to please the foreigners" and degraded. He never recovered officially, as a new "war party" was in power at court. His official humiliation and suicide followed in 1858. His early success appears to have been attributable to his ability to deal with the foreigners realistically and report romantically to the court, i.e., to make the emperor believe that the British and Americans were misguided children whom he was humoring. His failure resulted from the opposition of an uncompromising party at court under the Hsien-feng emperor and China's gradual realization of the consequences of the treaties he concluded in 1842-1844. (33. 203. 2) ECCP 1. 130.

CHIA Chao-lin 賈兆霖, gentry of Tientsin, was called upon by Governor General of Chihli T'an T'ing-hsiang in 1858, to recruit militia and raise subscriptions for defense against foreign invasion.

CHIANG Kuo-lin 江國霖, financial commissioner (vice-governor) of Kwangtung in 1856, associated with Tartar General Mu-k'o-te-na and Governor Po-kuei in memorials from Canton after Governor General Yeh Ming-ch'en was seized by the British. When Po-kuei was ordered to act as Imperial Commissioner and governor general of Liang-kuang,

Chiang Kuo-lin assumed the duties of governor during British occupation of Canton.

CH'IAO Pang-che 喬邦哲 was the provisional sub-prefect in charge of coastal defense at Ta-ku who reported the arrival of foreign ships outside the bar of the Lan River, October 15, 1854, and went aboard ship the following day for a preliminary interview with Medhurst and Parker.

CH'IEN Hsin-ho 錢炘和, having met the British in 1850 at Tientsin (i.e., H. M. S. Reynard, dispatched by Bonham to deliver Lord Palmerston's letter, June, 1850, which was contemptuously rejected by Imperial Edict of July 4, 1850), was regarded as an expert on foreign affairs. As Tientsin tao-t'ai, in 1856, he negotiated with Medhurst and Parker before the commissioners met Bowring and McLane. In 1858, as financial commissioner of Chihli (Hopei), he was summoned to assist in negotiations when the foreign envoys appeared at Ta-ku. He took an active part in the negotiations both before and after hostilities and his name appears on all memorials up to the arrival of Kuei-liang and Hua-sha-na. He is also mentioned later so it is apparent that his advice was still sought by the imperial commissioners.

CH'IEN Yen-kao 錢燕詰, magistrate of Yung-an (Wingon, Kwangtung)-hsien, was delegated by Governor Ch'eng Yü-ts'ai to confer with Consul Forbes and Peter Parker in March, 1844, and ascertain Cushing's motives in coming to China.

CHIN Wan-ch'üan 金萬全 was interpreter for the French warship which came to Wu-sung (Woosung), outside Shanghai, seeking permission to go up the Yangtze to make contact with Pottinger and mediate between Britain and China, August, 1842.

CHIN Shih-k'uei 金士奎, prominent citizen of Ting-hai sub-prefecture, reported to the Governor of Chekiang, January 27, 1843, on the activities of the British on Chu-shan (Chusan) Island.. He complained that the English treated the people harshly and "regarded the gentry as yamen runners and took good people for outlaws."

CHIN Ying-lin 金應麟, native of Ch'ien-t'ang, Chekiang, was a chin-shih of the Tao-kuang period. In 1842, as sub-director of the Grand Court of Revision, he memorialized on the strength of Western fleets and the necessity of building a strong Chinese navy, recommending, however, not Western types of ships but various native models drawn from Chinese history. He is, nevertheless, a forerunner of the later 19th century reformers. He published his collection of poems and essays under the title of Ch'ih Hua T'ang Shih Wen Chi (豸華堂詩文集). JM 613.2.

Ch'ing-ch'i 慶祺, Manchu military officer, was stationed at Fengtien (Mukden) in 1858.

Ch'ing-ch'un 清醇, Manchu official, was customs superintendent at Shanhaikwan, Chihli (Hopei), in 1858.

Ch'ing-ming 慶銘, Manchu official, was Director of the Board of Punishments in 1859. As he had been associated, anonymously, with Imperial Commissioners Kuei-liang and Hua-sha-na in Shanghai in the negotiations for modification of the Treaties of Tientsin, he was retained to assist in the exchange of ratifications with Ward at Pei-t'ang, August 16, 1859.

Ch'ing-tuan 慶端, Manchu official, was governor general of Min-Che (Fukien, Chekiang) in 1860.

Ch'ing-yün 慶昀, Manchu general of the Plain White Banner, Hsi-t'a-la clan, held various commands in Ninghsia during the Hsien-feng period. He was called to take over the duties of military lieutenant governor of Chahar when Hsi-ling-a was ordered to the defense of Shanhaikwan in April, 1858. JM 1500.4.

CH'IU Jui-hsiang 邱瑞祥, second captain in General Hsi-ling-a's command, served as officer messenger between the American ship and Chinese headquarters in the Tientsin area, August, 1860.

CH'IU Yün-t'ing 邱雲亭, native of Nan-hai, Kwangtung and a practicing Catholic, opened a medicine store in Tientsin in 1858. He was arrested on suspicion and his crucifix, books, and papers seized. The local officials found that "Bishop Meng of Shanghai had ordered him to go out and do good, distribute medicine, and heal the sick, and that he did not proselyte or deceive." He was sent to Pao-ting for trial; the governor general memorialized; and the emperor made a personal endorsement ordering thorough questioning for evidence of sedition, but under no circumstances, torture or death.

CH'IU Yung-an 邱永安, sergeant in the Nanking city garrison battalion, was ordered by Ch'i-ying, because he was "thoroughly familiar with the barbarian temper," to investigate the foreign (British) situation on the Kiangsu seaboard and Chu-shan (Chusan) Island in 1843.

Cho-ming-a 卓明阿, Manchu officer, senior bodyguard under General Te-hsing-a, participated in the defense of Pei-t'ang against the assault of the British and French forces, August 3, 1860.

CHOU Ch'i-pin 周起濱, was judicial commissioner (vice-governor)

of Kwangtung in 1858.   When the British took Canton and arrested
Governor General Yeh Ming-ch'en, he continued to serve under British
occupation.

Chu-k'o-tu-erh-p'a-mu 珠克都爾帕木, Mongol officer, commandant of the Solid Blue Banner at Chahar, Inner Mongolia, was selected
by General Hsi-ling-a to lead his forces, five hundred cavalrymen, to
defend Shanhaikwan against British-French attack in 1858.

Ch'üan-ch'ing 全慶, Manchu of the Plain White Banner, member of
the Yeh-he-na clan, was a chin-shih in the Tao-kuang period.   His
highest official rank was T'i Jen Ko Grand Secretary and in 1859, when
Ward came to Peking, he was President of the Board of War.   JM 233.2.

Ch'un-pao 春保, a Manchu, expectant tao-t'ai at Pao-ting, Chihli
(Hopei) in April, 1858, was ordered by Governor General T'an T'ing-
hsiang to proceed to Pei-t'ang to assist in defense arrangements against
foreign invasion.

Ch'ung-en 崇恩, Manchu governor of Shantung in 1854, reported three
foreign ships passing the Shanghai coast, October 14th and was ordered
to defend Teng-chou and other strategic positions against possible
British, French, American attack.

Ch'ung-hou 崇厚 (1826-1893), Manchu Bordered Yellow Bannerman,
member of the Wan-yen clan, assisted Prince Seng in coastal defense
against the British and French in 1858, but got his real start for a distinguished career in diplomacy when, as brevet salt controller, tao-t'ai
of Ch'ing-ho, Chihli (Hopei) in 1859, he was selected to escort Ward
from Pei-t'ang to Peking and back.   From 1860-1870 he served as
superintendent of trade for the three ports of Tientsin, Chefoo, and
Newchwang, with residence in Tientsin.   In this capacity he drew up
trade regulations and signed treaties with Denmark, Holland, Spain,
Belgium, Italy and Austria.   He was still in office when the Tientsin
Massacre occurred in 1870, and was later selected to go to France to
apologize on behalf of the Chinese government, thus becoming the first
Chinese envoy to the West.   He visited Paris, London, and New York.
On his return he was appointed senior vice-president of the Board of
War and served concurrently in the Tsungli Yamen.   In 1878-1879 he
was sent on a mission to St. Petersburg, where he signed the Treaty
of Livadia, which was renounced by China in 1880 and for which Ch'ung-
hou was impeached.   He was sentenced to imprisonment awaiting decapitation.   Foreign diplomats in Peking protested, Queen Victoria
reportedly sent a personal plea to the Empress Dowager, and Ch'ung-
hou was released.   He was allowed to present felicitations at court in
1884, but lived in obscurity thereafter until his death. (33.116.2) ECCP

1.209.

Ch'ung-lun 崇綸 (1792-1875), Chinese Plain White Bannerman, originally had the Chinese surname Hsü 許. As former Ch'ang-lu salt controller he was ordered to report to Governor General of Chihli Kuei-liang and take over the negotiations with England and the United States which he had begun. He reached Ta-ku on October 31, 1854 and met Bowring and McLane. He received and examined their précis, agreed to a few minor changes in the treaties, and rather summarily ordered them back to Canton. His negotiations were approved by the court and regarded as a diplomatic victory. In the Hsien-feng period, Ch'ung-lun reached the official rank of president of the Board of Works. (33.116.2) ECCP 1.379; JM 901.4.

FANG Hsiung-fei 方熊飛, undergraduate at Canton in 1842, advised General I-shan and others on the corruption involved in the building of Chinese war-junks, and was presumably involved in the building of Western-type ships for China.

FEI Yin-chang 費蔭章, native of Tientsin, former tao-t'ai of P'ing-Ch'ing Ching, Kansu, who had returned in 1850, because of the death of a parent, was selected by Governor General T'an T'ing-hsiang to enlist the support of the local gentry and command local militia to resist foreign invasion.

FENG En-fu 馮恩福, corporal on coastal and river patrol off Ta-ku, sighted two Russian vessels, went out to meet them, and received a communication asking for an interview with Tientsin officials, April 13, 1858. In 1860, when the allied fleets were ranged before Pei-t'ang, Governor General Heng-fu sent him, now a lieutenant, with gifts of food to the American ship. Lieutenant Feng returned the next day with two cases of wine for Heng-fu and the information that the English and French intended to attack Pei-t'ang.

FENG Tzu-ts'ai 馮子材 (1818-1903), native of Ch'in-chou, Kwangtung, one of the soldiers of fortune produced by the Taiping Rebellion, was regarded in 1860 as one of the ablest generals in China. He served his apprenticeship under General Hsiang Jung and after the latter's death in 1860 continued exterminating rebels and winning laurels until illness forced his temporary retirement in 1881. In 1884-1885, although in his late sixties, he resumed active duty and fought gallantly against the French armies in Annam, winning a brilliant victory at Langson. He was accorded many honors, including the rank of board president, but refused active commissions after 1894, although still pressed to do so by the court. (33.226.1) ECCP 1.244.

Fu-an 富安, minor Manchu official, was associated with the acting assistant prefect in charge of coast defense, Li Huan-wen, at Shanghai in 1858.

Fu-hsing 福興, Manchu Plain White Bannerman member of the Mu-erh-ch'a clan. By 1850 he had attained the rank of brigade general of the Kao-chou, Kiangsi, garrison. When the Taipings overran Kwangtung, he fought against them and in the course of ten years campaigned through five provinces: Kwangsi, Hunan, Hupeh, Kiangsi, and Kiangsu, winning many victories. His highest post was Tartar General of Suiyuan. JM 1366.2.

Fu-k'uei 福奎, a Manchu, deputy of the governor of Kwangsi, reported in 1841 on the uselessness of the old iron cannon stored in the garrison.

Fu-lo-tun-t'ai 富勒敦泰, a Manchu, was the lieutenant general at Shanhaikwan in 1854, whose exuberant and boastful report on the defense measures he had taken received a sarcastic comment from the emperor and an edict charging him to more diligence and less noise.

HAN Ch'ing-yün 韓錦雲, Metropolitan circuit censor, memorialized in 1856 urging a stiff foreign policy and the expulsion of the British from Canton by a combination of trade stoppage, popular boycott, and an aroused gentry and populace. He typifies the scholar-official at his impractical worst.

Heng-ch'ang 恆昌, tao-t'ai of Hsing-Ch'üan-Yung, Fukien, had an interview with the British consul, Alcock, at Amoy on November 4, 1845.

Heng-ch'i 恆祺 (1802?-1867), Manchu Plain White Bannerman, collateral relative of the Imperial House (Gioro) of the I-erh-ken clan. He was appointed superintendent of customs (Hoppo) at Canton in 1854. When Yeh Ming-ch'en was seized by the British in 1858, Heng-ch'i memorialized strongly recommending Governor Po-kuei to succeed him. In 1860 he was called to Peking and after the British and French occupied the capital and burned the Summer Palace, became one of the principal advisers to Prince Kung and negotiated on his behalf with the British. In 1861 he became assistant director of the Tsungli Yamen and in 1862 junior vice-president of the Office of Colonial Dependencies. (33.326.1) ECCP 1.381; CSLC 47.35b.

Heng-fu 恆福 (d. 1862), Mongol Bordered Yellow Bannerman, member of the E-lo-te-t'e clan, served in various posts and won victories over the Nien-fei rebels in 1859. He was rewarded with the post of governor general of Chihli (Hopei) and in 1860, was confronted with the foreign powers. While Prince General Seng-ko-lin-ch'in handled the military

phase, Heng-fu was ordered to negotiate for the good offices of Russia
and the United States and to try to appease England and France, offering exchange of ratifications in Peking following the precedent of the
United States of 1859. After the hostilities were over, he memorialized
on the collection of duties at the newly opened port of Shanhaikwan and
was appointed imperial commissioner to set up the Customs House. He
retired in 1861 and died the following year. (33.326.1) ECCP 1.429;
CSLC 48.18a.

HO Ching 何璟, Chinese scholar-official, native of Hsiang-shan
(Chung-shan), Kwangtung, was a chin-shih of the Tao-kuang period;
coming from the vicinity of Macao, he regarded himself as an authority
on the opium question and memorialized eight times during the first
Anglo-Chinese war, 1839-1842. As circuit censor of Kiangnan (Kiangsu and Anhwei) in 1858, he memorialized twice on the Canton question,
urging the utilization of the gentry and people to expel the British and
the punishment of all the provincial officials, as well as Yeh Ming-
ch'en, for negligence of duty. He was later governor general of Min-
Che (Fukien and Chekiang), became involved with the French in 1878,
and was degraded because of his failure to stop them. JM 296.1

Ho-ch'un 和春 (d. 1860), Manchu Plain Yellow Bannerman, was a
member of the He-she-li clan. As a minor officer he followed Hsiang
Jung to Kwangsi in 1851, came rapidly to the top and by 1854, was
Tartar General of Chiang-nan (Kiangnan). In 1858, when consulted by
Governor General Ho Kuei-ch'ing of Liang-chiang, he expressed approval of adopting Western munitions and of utilizing Western aid in
suppressing the Taipings. On Hsiang Jung's death in 1860, he succeeded
him as imperial commissioner charged with the suppression of the Taiping Rebellion. He was apparently a figurehead and most of the actual
generalship was carried out by his Chinese second-in-command Chang
Kuo-liang. Ho-ch'un was wounded at Ch'ang-chou, Kiangsu, in May,
1860, and died soon afterwards. (33.286.3) ECCP 1.293; CSLC 43.45b.

HO Kuei-ch'ing 何桂清 (1816-1862), native of Kuan-ming, Yunnan,
was a chin-shih of 1835, and Hanlin academician. He served as governor
of Chekiang, 1854-1857, and governor general of Liang-chiang, 1857-1860.
He was active in fighting the Taipings and became more and more involved in the foreign affairs of Shanghai. In 1858 he was made imperial
commissioner to negotiate trade regulations, along with Kuei-liang and
others, with the Western powers, and emerged as one of the statesmen
of the period. His memorials show a realistic understanding of "barbarian affairs" and his policy involved (1) rejection of the court plan to
repudiate the treaties, (2) recognition of the fallacy of trying to play one
Western power off against another, (3) advocacy of the purchase of
Western arms and ships, adopting Western training and organization,

and employment of Western aid in suppressing the Taipings. He was
opposed by the court party and in the end was officially proved to be a
coward. Miss Tu Lien-che in <u>Eminent Chinese of the Ch'ing Period,</u>
gives the official version: "In 1860, anticipating an overwhelming attack
by the Taiping army, he was seen leaving the threatened city of Ch'ang-
chou (Kiangsu) to his fate. When the people tried to stop him--begging
him to help defend that city--his guards shot their way out of the town
and killed several citizens. He was tried and executed (in Peking) in
1862, despite the efforts of many to save him." (33.380.1) ECCP 2.
620; CSLC 49.11a.

Hsi-en 禧恩 (1784-1852), Imperial Clansman, was son of Ch'un-yung
Prince Kung and descendent of Dorgon, He served as minister of the
imperial household intermittently for nearly thirty years and was several times degraded because of efforts toward reform and economy. In
1842 he was made Tartar General and ordered to defend the Manchurian
ports against possible British attack and in 1844, when Cushing was
reported en route to China, was warned against possible attack by the
United States. In 1852, he was made director general of the State
Historiographer's Office and general of the Plain White Banner, but died
by the end of the year.   (33.235.3) ECCP 2.933; CSLC 41.21a.

HSI K'uan 席寬 was a Shanghai merchant whose aid was sought, 1858,
by <u>Tao-t'ai</u> Wu Hsü to persuade the foreign envoys to exchange ratifications in Shanghai and possibly agree to some modification of the Tientsin treaties.

Hsi-la-pen 西拉本, minor Manchu official, acting grain intendant at
Canton in 1842, accompanied Kwangtung Commander-in-chief of Marine
Forces (Admiral) Wu Chien-hsün aboard one of the two American war-
ships anchored at Whampoa as guests of Commodore Kearny, U.S.N.

Hsi-la-pu 西拉布, Manchu officer stationed at Fengtien (Mukden) in
1858, was warned against possible foreign attack.

Hsi-ling-a 西凌阿 (d. 1866), Manchu Plain White Bannerman, member
of the Kuo-erh-pei clan, had an active and varied military career fighting
the Taiping rebels and Nien-fei. In 1858, he was appointed garrison
commander at Shanhaikwan, for the defense of which he made elaborate
preparations against possible attack by the British and French. He
retired due to ill-health in 1862, but was later appointed lieutenant
general of the Plain Blue Banner. (33.41.2) CSK 423.3b.

HSIANG Jung 向榮 (d. 1856), most prominent Imperialist general in
the early period of the Taiping Rebellion, was a native of Ta-ning,
Szechwan, but made his residence at Ku-yüan, Kansu. He began his

career in the local garrison and was a sergeant in 1813. By 1847, he
was provincial commander-in-chief of Szechwan and in 1850 was appointed to Hunan. The Taiping Rebellion broke out in July and he was
sent to Kwangsi to suppress it, but the movement spread. He collaborated with the imperial commissioners sent out from Peking and shared
their degradation when they also failed to stop it. In 1853, he lost Wuchang to the Taipings but through persistent fighting recovered it a
month later. When the Taipings took Nanking and set up their capital
there, he established the Great Camp at Kiangnan as permanent headquarters. In 1856, the rebels, through a strategem inflicted a smash-
ing defeat on the Great Camp. Taiping accounts say that Hsiang Jung
committed suicide but official histories say he "died of disappointment,
vexation, and illness." He was succeeded by Ho-ch'un and Chang Kuo-
liang. (33.48.3) ECCP 1.298.

HSIAO Chen 蕭槙, Tientsin gentry, was enlisted to take up subscriptions and raise militia to defend the area against the British and French
in 1858.

HSIEH Ch'i-ch'ing 謝起慶, deputy employed by Prince Seng and
Governor General Heng-fu to communicate with Ward at Pei-t'ang in
1860.

HSIEH Mu-chih 謝牧之, sub-prefect at Macao in 1844, reported the
arrival of the French mission.

Hsien-ling 咸齡, Manchu official, was made officer of the guards of
the fourth rank in 1842, and assigned to Ch'i-ying when the latter was
sent to Hang-chou, Chekiang, as acting Tartar General to replace
Ch'i-ming-pao. The following year, Hsien-ling participated in the
negotiation of the supplementary treaty of the Bogue with Britain in
Kwangtung.

HSIUNG I-pen 熊一本, brevet tao-t'ai, was prefect at T'ai-wan
(T'ai-nan), Formosa, in 1842.

HSÜ Chao 徐兆, was interpreter aboard an American merchant ship
which came to Ningpo, November 27, 1842, seeking to trade.

HSÜ Chi-yü 徐繼畬 (1795-1873), official and early geographer of
the West, was a native of Wu-t'ai, Shansi, chin-shih of 1826, and Hanlin academician. He was appointed financial commissioner of Fukien
in 1843, and in 1845, was ordered to arrange a residence area for
foreigners at Foochow. In 1846, he became governor of Fukien and
supervisor of foreign trade. He was denounced in 1851, for being too
friendly with foreigners. He was restored to rank but the old charges

were renewed and he finally retired. When the Taipings moved north, he organized local militia to resist them. In 1865, he was recalled to Peking and appointed to the Tsungli Yamen, from which he retired on account of ill-health in 1869. While in Fukien, Hsü Chi-yü met the American missionary David Abeel, who gave him a world atlas and started his interest in Western geography. Five years' study resulted in the <u>Ying Huan Chih Lüeh</u> (瀛環志略) or "World Geography," 10 chüan, printed in 1850, reprinted in 1866 by the Tsungli Yamen, and twice reprinted in Japan (1859, 1861). This was the second important Chinese work on Western geography, the first being Wei Yüan's <u>Hai Kuo T'u Chih</u> of 1844. Hsü Chi-yü also published several works on Chinese geography. (33.295.2) ECCP 1.309.

HSÜ Kuang-chin 徐廣縉 (d. c. 1858, age 73 <u>sui</u>), native of Lu-i, Honan, <u>chin-shih</u> of 1820, and Hanlin academician, was a prominent exponent of the policy of hostility and non-cooperation with foreigners made famous by his successor, Yeh Ming-ch'en. Hsü Kuang-chin was appointed governor of Kwangtung in 1846. February 3, 1848, Ch'i-ying, who was chiefly responsible for the "era of good feeling," was recalled, and Hsü became acting imperial commissioner and governor general. He temporized the issue of British entrance to the city of Canton and encouraged the gentry and populace to resist, making it impossible to carry out Ch'i-ying's promise to open the city in 1849. This "defeat" of the British was commended by the emperor as "the greatest diplomatic success in ten years." Hsü was awarded the hereditary title of viscount of the first grade and the double-eyed peacock feather. In October 1848, Hsü received U.S. Commissioner John W. Davis, outside the city walls, in a warehouse, but refused to see Peter Parker, 1850-1852. After 1850, Hsü Kuang-chin was fully occupied with the Taiping Rebellion and foreign affairs were taken over by Yeh Ming-ch'en, governor of Kwangtung. Hsü was ordered to Kwangsi in 1852, and Yeh succeeded him as imperial commissioner and governor general. Hsü became imperial commissioner and governor general of Liang-hu but in this capacity suffered a series of defeats at the hands of the Taipings. He was degraded and sentenced to imprisonment awaiting decapitation. In 1853 he was recalled to meet the Taiping invasion of Honan. He fought bravely and was restored to rank. In 1858, he was ordered to Anhwei but two months later was stricken by paralysis and died. (33.292.3) ECCP 1.319.

HSÜ Nai-chao 許乃釗, native of Ch'ien-t'ang, Chekiang, <u>chin-shih</u> of the Tao-kuang period, was governor of Kiangsu in 1854, when McLane sought treaty revision. Hsü avoided meeting him, although the governor general, I-liang, did meet McLane at K'un-shan. July 7, 1854, Hsü Nai-chao was removed from office for his failure to recapture Shanghai or to cope with the foreigners. He was charged with cowardice and incompetence

and criticized for relying too heavily on the ex-hong merchant, Wu
Chien-chang, then tao-t'ai at Shanghai, and supporting his pro-foreign
commercial policy. Hsü was recalled however, and in 1858, was still
identified with Ho-ch'un and Chang Kuo-liang in military affairs in the
Yangtze valley. He ultimately retired on account of ill health.
JM 1028.2.

HSÜ Wen-shen 許文深, expectant assistant sub-prefect, assistant
magistrate of Nan-hai, Kwangtung, was for years in charge of communications with barbarians for the Canton government and had served as
deputy magistrate of the sub-district of Chiu-lung (Kowloon), across
from Hong Kong. Being generally recognized and trusted by Hong Kong
officials and merchants, he was employed by Governor General Yeh
Ming-ch'en as major domo to handle his meeting with British and French
military officers representing Lord Elgin and Baron Gros, aboard ship
at the Pai-ho-t'an anchorage, opposite the Canton Bund, December 12,
1857.

HSÜ Yu-jen 徐有壬 (1800-1860), native of Wan-p'ing, Chihli (Hopei),
chin-shih of 1020, was a mathematician and published nine books in the
field. In 1859, he was governor of Kiangsu and cooperated with Governor General Ho Kuei-ch'ing in trying to alienate the French from the
British after their return from Ta-ku and when Ward had exchanged
ratifications at Pei-t'ang. However, he played no great part in foreign
affairs. He was killed in battle when Soochow fell, June 1, 1860. (33.
293.2) ECCP 1.479; CSLC 43.24b.

HSÜEH Huan 薛煥 (1815-1880), native of Hsing-wen, Szechwan, was
a chu-jen of the Tao-kuang period. He became tao-t'ai of Su-Sung-T'ai
(Shanghai) in 1857, organized volunteers to expel the rebels from the city,
and made many contacts with Chinese and foreign merchants and with the
foreign consuls. He was virtually in charge of foreign affairs in Shanghai from 1857 to 1863. In 1858, he escorted U.S. consul Freeman, along
with the British and French consuls, to Soochow for an interview with the
governor. In October, 1858, he was made judicial commissioner (vice-
governor) and assisted in setting up the tariff schedule. He opposed the
"Secret Plan" of the emperor and court to repudiate the treaties of
Tientsin and offer the foreigners "free trade" in exchange and, when the
commissioners arrived from Peking, persuaded them not to present it
to the foreign envoys. Despite the emperor's exasperation with the commissioners for listening to his advice, he recognized Hsüeh Huan's grasp
of foreign affairs and made the personal comment that if the foreigners
insisted on residence in Peking "Hsüeh Huan must be kept in the capital
as permanent director." When negotiations broke down in Shanghai, he
was sent to Tientsin and later to Peking to assist in dealing with the
foreigners. Later in 1860, he was made imperial commissioner in

charge of commercial affairs of the five ports with the rank of governor
and temporary authority of governor general of Liang-chiang. He remained in Shanghai and his memorials reveal a solid business sense,
statesmanship, and diplomacy such as few Chinese officials possessed
in this period. He had Ch'i-ying's knack of reporting to the throne in
terms that made a complete reversal of traditional policy palatable to the
the emperor and court. He advocated adoption of foreign arms, manufacture, trade methods and urged reform of China's state papers in dealing with foreigners. In 1862 he was promoted to vice-president of the
Board of Works and minister in the Tsungli Yamen. In 1876, he was
sent to Yunnan to investigate the Margary murder. He retired the
following year on account of ill health. (33.124.3) ECCP 2.744; JM
1670.1.

Hua-sha-na 花沙納 (1806 – 1859), chin-shih of 1832 and Hanlin academician, was a Mongol Plain Yellow Bannerman. In 1851, he memorialized
advocating the issue of paper money to be made of silk fibre with two
official seals in denominations of one to fifty taels and backed by silver.
In 1854, he was made chief historiographer to compile the annals of the
Tao-kuang period (1820-1851). In 1858, Hua-sha-na was chosen as one
of the emperor's commissioners to negotiate with the envoys of Great
Britain, France, Russia, and the United States, June 2-27, 1858, and
signed the four treaties of Tientsin. In September, he was sent with the
other commissioners to Shanghai, nominally to negotiate commercial
sections of the treaties, actually to attempt to revoke the Tientsin
treaties entirely in exchange for "free trade" for the foreign powers, in
accordance with the "Secret Plan" hatched at court. (33.139.3) ECCP
1.428; CSLC 41.30b.

HUA Shang-lin 花上林, was one of the Tientsin gentry whose support
was enlisted in 1858, to defend the area against foreign invasion by
raising subscriptions and training militia.

HUANG Chung-yü 黃仲畬, a Cantonese, brevet first-class sub-prefect,
expectant district magistrate, was regarded as an expert on handling
foreigners and was fully trusted by Kuei-liang. He was sought in 1858, to
assist the imperial commissioners at Shanghai but was reported to be in
Kwangtung "wearing the button and sash of the fifth rank and conducting
separate negotiations." He returned to Shanghai, January 1, 1859, and
was immediately employed to persuade the envoys not to go to Peking and
even mentioned by the emperor as a possible savior of the situation.

HUANG En-t'ung 黃恩彤 (1800-1882), chin-shih of 1826, was a native
of Ning-yang, Shantung. In 1840 he was appointed judicial commissioner
of Kiangsu and assisted Ch'i-ying in his negotiations with the British. In
1843, he was made financial commissioner of Kwangtung and accompanied

Ch'i-ying to Canton where he became his right-hand man, assisting in the negotiations with Cushing at Wang-hsia in 1844. In 1845 Huang En-t'ung was appointed governor of Kwangtung and memorialized on the velvet glove technique of handling foreigners. He was removed from office in 1846. In 1858, he was recalled from retirement to assist in the negotiations at Tientsin but arrived only after the treaties were signed. This may have saved him from sharing the fate of Ch'i-ying. He returned to his retirement in Shantung. (33.166.3) ECCP 1.132; CSK 377.4a.

HUANG Hui-lien 黃惠廉, a Cantonese, was brought to Tientsin by the British forces in 1858, and remained after the hostilities. He was regarded as an authority on foreign affairs and advised Prince Seng-ko-lin-ch'in on the Western practice of demanding indemnity of the party which asked for terms. He apparently spoke English fluently, and in 1859 was ordered to fraternize with the two British prisoners, one of whom was thought to be an American but was actually a Canadian, taken at the battle of Ta-ku, in the hope of utilizing the prisoners to get the British and French to ask the Chinese for terms.

HUANG Shen-wu 黃慎五, one of the gentry of Tientsin invited by the provincial authorities to raise subscriptions and train militia against foreign invasion in 1858.

HUANG Tsung-han 黃宗漢 (d. 1864), native of Chin-chiang, Fukien, chin-shih of 1835, and Hanlin academician, was appointed judicial commissioner of Chekiang in 1848, and later became governor. In this capacity, he fought with General Hsiang Jung against the Taipings and received several commendations. In 1854 he was made governor general of Szechwan but retired two years later on account of illness. When he returned to Peking he was appointed to the Grand Council. January 27, 1858, he was appointed imperial commissioner in charge of barbarian affairs and governor general of Liang-kuang, to succeed Yeh Ming-ch'en, who was taken prisoner by the British when they captured Canton. Huang Tsung-han refused to meet the foreign envoys at or near Shanghai, en route to his post, and took up his residence at Hui-chou, until the British evacuated the provincial capital. In 1859 he was again made governor general of Szechwan but was impeached in 1862 and removed from office. (33.165.2) ECCP 1.283; CSLC 48.1a.

HUNG Chih-kao 洪志高, provisional colonel in immediate command of the garrison at Ta-ku in 1854, reported the arrival of foreign ships off the bar, October 15.

I-ching 奕經 (d. 1853), imperial clansman, great grandson of Kao-

tsung, emperor of the Ch'ien-lung period, passed the examination for
the sons of princes in 1816, was given the rank of noble of imperial
lineage of the tenth degree, and was made an imperial bodyguard. In
March, 1841, he was made associate grand secretary, replacing I-li-
pu, who had just been degraded for failing to attack the British forces
at Ting-hai. October 18, 1841, I-ching was made commander of
imperial forces in Chekiang, with Wen-wei as his assistant. A favorite
of the emperor and a scholar of the Manchu written language, I-ching
was hopelessly unqualified as a general and was no match for the
British. After the humiliating Treaty of Nanking, August, 1842, he
was brought to Peking in chains and imprisoned in the Imperial Clan
Court. He was pardoned and later served in Yarkand and Ili. He was
recalled in 1853, to oppose the Taipings and died of malaria during the
seige of Hsü-chou, Kiangsu. (33.97.2) ECCP 1.377.

I-hsin Prince Kung 奕訢恭親王 (1833-1898), half-brother and boyhood companion of Emperor Wen-tsung of the Hsien-feng era, became in
1850, prince of the first degree and two years later was given a palace
of his own in Peking. In 1853, he was made Grand Councillor and the
following year made lieutenant general of a Banner and presiding controller of the Imperial Clan Court. In 1855, he was reprimanded by the
emperor for negligence in observance of mourning ceremonies for his
mother, deprived of all posts, and ordered to resume his studies in the
Palace School for Princes. He was, however, gradually restored to
power. In 1858, he criticized severely the Tientsin treaties signed by
his father-in-law, Kuei-liang, and in 1859 headed the commission which
tried and punished Ch'i-ying. When the allies, England and France,
threatened Peking in 1860, Prince Kung was ordered to make peace with
them. When the allies occupied the city and burned the Summer Palace,
he fled to Marco Polo Bridge. He returned to Peking in October and
signed the Convention of Peking with Lord Elgin, and later, treaties with
France and Russia. At his suggestion, January 20, 1861, the Tsungli
Yamen was set up to handle China's foreign relations. He continued in
charge of it and later set up the T'ung-wen Kuan to train young Chinese
and Manchus for the foreign service. In 1862, he became prince
counselor to the co-regent empress dowagers, with full charge of the
Tsungli Yamen, Grand Council, the minor emperor's education, and
the Russian-trained Peking Field Force. His powers were too great to
last in a jealous court and in 1865, he was deprived of everything. He
was later restored and continued his duties in the Tsungli Yamen but
his position was insecure and, particularly after 1875, his authority
declined. He was recalled by the crisis of the war with Japan, 1894-
1895, but was unable to do much more than sanction the Treaty of
Shimonoseki. He spent his last years in his palace and garden, now
a part of Yenching University campus, west of Peiping. As principal
figure in China's foreign relations for twenty-seven years 1861-1884,

he represented a policy of conciliation in the face of superior Western force. (33.97.2) ECCP 1.380.

I-liang 怡良 (1791-1867), Manchu of the Plain Red Banner, was a member of the Gualgiya clan. After studying in the Imperial Academy and serving in various minor posts, he became governor of Kwangtung in 1838. In the anti-opium movement, he supported Governor General Lin Tse-hsü, recommended the defense of Hu-men (Bocca Tigris) and the stoppage of trade with England. After the fall of Lin Tse-hsü, he became acting governor general of Liang-kuang until the arrival of Ch'i-shan, and in 1841, served as superintendent of customs (Hoppo). He refused to subscribe to Ch'i-shan's appeasement policy and reported his secret cession of Hong Kong to the British. When Ch'i-shan was degraded, he again acted as governor general, pending the arrival of Ch'i Kung. In March and April, 1841, he favored the resumption of trade with England and was deprived of rank but continued in office. In 1842, he became imperial commissioner and governor general of Min-Che. In 1842, he retired because of violent local objection to his report on the British in Formosa (Taiwan). In 1852-1853, as governor general of Liang-chiang he was active in suppressing the Taiping Rebellion and instrumental in setting up the Chinese Maritime Customs service under foreign supervision. He met U.S. Commissioner Marshall in 1853, and McLane in 1854, both at K'un-shan, Chekiang. When the Taiping rebels blocked the transport of tribute rice via the Grand Canal, he set up the ocean transport to Tientsin. He resigned in May, 1857, on account of illness, and died at home ten years later. (33.326.1) ECCP 1.389.

I-li-pu 伊里布 (d. 1843, age 72 or 73 sui), Manchu Bordered Yellow Bannerman and imperial clansman, was a chin-shih of 1801, but waited four years for appointment to the Imperial Academy. He served in scattered posts with merit and distinction and was finally sent to Nanking as governor general of Kiangsu, Kiangsi, and Anhwei, in 1840. The Opium War was in progress and the British had occupied the island of Chu-shan (Chusan), so I-li-pu was made imperial commissioner to investigate Ting-hai and defend the coast opposite. He was ordered to attack the British but reported that his troops were inadequate. The emperor was incensed and ordered I-li-pu back to Nanking, deprived him of rank, but retained him in his duties. In May, 1841, he was called to Peking for trial, and on July 31st sentenced to banishment. He was pardoned, however, sent back to Chekiang, and became one of the three signers of the Treaty of Nanking with Pottinger. He went from Nanking to Canton to negotiate the supplementary treaty but died there March 5, 1843. He advocated a friendly policy toward the Americans, as a means of "curbing" the British, was regarded as cordial and polite by Pottinger, but is branded as a traitor by Chinese historians. (33. 380. 3) ECCP 1. 387.

I-shan 奕山 (d. 1878), imperial clansman of the fourth grade, had an active early career in military and colonization work on the Ili frontier. When the British took two forts below Canton in 1841, I-shan was made "Rebel-quelling General" to expel them. By the time he arrived on the scene, April 14, the British had reduced the Bogue (Hu-men) forts and occupied Hong Kong. He led his troops against them but quickly discovered their superiority and agreed to a truce. He made false reports to the throne that the British had been forced to withdraw from the Canton area and had sued for peace, on the basis of which the emperor ordered Chinese troops withdrawn from the eastern seaboard, leaving it open to British attack. In June, 1842, I-shan was degraded but continued in command until replaced by I-li-pu. I-shan was tried and imprisoned in the Imperial Clan Court to await execution. He was released the following year and resumed duty in the Northwest. He negotiated the Treaty of Kuldja with Russia. In 1854 he was recalled to Peking and two years later made military governor of Heilungkiang. Here he signed the Treaty of Aigun (1858) with Muraviev, only a few days prior to the capture of the Ta-ku forts by the Allies, resulting in another treaty with Russia (Poutiatine). I-shan was denounced for his treaty, which due to his ignorance of geography surrendered a large area of Chinese territory to Russia, was recalled to Peking, and reduced in rank. The rest of his life was occupied with comparatively unimportant posts. (33. 97. 1) ECCP 1. 391.

I T'ang 易棠 (d. 1863), native of Shan-hua, Hunan, chin-shih of 1829, as Canton prefect accompanied Governor General Hsü Kuang-chin to the interview with U.S. Commissioner Davis held at the Jen-chin Factory (warehouse) across the river from the Canton Bund, October 8, 1848. Later he served in various posts and 1854-1860, as governor general of Shansi and Kansu, was prominent in suppressing the Mohammedan Rebellion. His last post was the governorship of Hunan. (33. 187. 3) CSLC 48. 22a.

I-tsung Prince Tun 奕誴惇親王 (1831-1889), fifth son of Emperor Hsüan-tsung of the Tao-kuang era, was six days younger than his half-brother, the Emperor Wen-tsung of the Hsien-feng era. He originally inherited the rank of prince of the second degree, was reduced in 1855, to the third degree, but raised to the first degree or ch'in-wang in 1860. In 1858, he served on the Imperial Clan commission headed by Prince Kung to try Ch'i-ying. After 1886, he was exempted from all services at court and retired, presumably to his villa, Ch'ing-hua Yüan, which in 1911 became the campus of Tsing Hua College, now a national university. (33. 97. 1) ECCP 1. 393.

JEN Lien-sheng 任連升, lieutenant of Ta-ku, served as officer messenger for Governor General Heng-fu to the American steamer after hostilities in July, 1859, and served as general factotum in conducting Ward and his party from Pei-t'ang to Peking and back. He was still on hand in 1860, as acting second captain.

Jen-shou 仁壽, a Manchu, senior assistant controller of the Imperial Clan Court in 1858, was ordered to carry out the imperial decree for Ch'i-ying's official suicide.

Jui-pin 瑞璸, a Manchu, governor of Fukien in 1860, memorialized on the harbors of Formosa (Taiwan) and, later, on the arrival at Amoy of an American ship carrying troops from Hong Kong, May 18, 1860.

JUAN Yüan 阮元 (1764-1849), antiquarian, scholar, bibliophile, and official, was a native of I-cheng, Yangchow prefecture, Kiangsu, chin-shih of 1789, and bachelor in the Hanlin Academy. He wrote or edited numerous works on art, calligraphy, inscriptions, classics, poetry, and local history and assisted many other scholars with their publications. Wherever he served as an official, he established academies and libraries for the encouragement of scholarship, but he was also an able and active administrator and in Chekiang, for instance, carried on a vigorous campaign against piracy. From 1817-1826, he was governor general of Liang-kuang, which brought him in contact with foreigners. Juan Yüan maintained a policy of strict control of the British, effected by stoppage of trade, and advocated friendship with the United States as a means of curbing British monopoly and of avoiding a united foreign front against China. In 1835, he was recalled to Peking to serve as associate grand secretary. He retired in 1838, was granted special honors on his eightieth birthday, in 1843, and was given the title of grand tutor on the sixtieth anniversary of his becoming a chu-jen (master). The depth of his scholarship, the breadth of his interests, and the volume of his publications, combine to make him the greatest scholar of his day. Unlike the usual official, he was never impeached and his prestige and judgment were never questioned. (33.334.1) ECCP 1.399.

Kiying, See Ch'i-ying

K'o-hsing-e 克興額, Manchu Plain White Bannerman, member of the Wo-le clan, participated with success in the campaigns against the Taipings in Hupeh and Chihli. In 1860, he was summoned to lead cavalry and government troops under Prince Seng-ko-lin-ch'in at Ta-ku and arrived at the defenses August 3rd. His highest rank was major general of the Manchu Bordered Yellow Banner. JM 304.2.

KUAN T'ien-p'ei 關天培 (d. 1841), native of Shan-yang, Kiangsu, became commander-in-chief of the Marine Forces of Kwangtung in 1834, and assisted in preparing the defenses of Hu-men (Bocca Tigris). In 1838 he backed up Governor General Lin Tse-hsü's demand for the British to surrender 20, 283 chests of opium. He was killed in the battle of San-men-k'ou, below Canton, March 18-19, 1841, due to inefficiency and treason on the part of his command. General Kuan was degraded for his loss of the fort to the British but was rewarded posthumously by imperial command for a temple to be erected in his honor, his mother to receive a government pension, and his son to be given government office. (33. 83. 3) CSLC 39. 31b.

Kuan-wen 官文 (1798-1871), Chinese Plain White Bannerman, first Earl Kuo-wei, originally had the Chinese surname of Wang (王); his family belonged to the Imperial Household division, serving the emperor as bondservants. Kuan-wen was taken into the Imperial Bodyguard and after several promotions, was made Chinese lieutenant general of the Canton garrison, 1841-1847. During the Taiping invasion of central China, he was stationed at Ching-chou, Hupeh, and in 1854 became Tartar General. He collaborated with Tseng Kuo-fan and in 1855 was made governor general of Hunan and Hupeh to command troops north of the Yangtze, and eventually succeeded in driving the rebels from the Hankow area. In 1858 Kuan-wen was made associate grand secretary and three years later, full grand secretary. In 1864, when Tseng Kuo-fan was made marquis, he was given the hereditary rank of earl of the first class with the designation, Kuo-wei. In addition, his branch of the family was exempted from bondage and raised to membership of the Manchu Plain White Banner, though he himself was a Chinese Bannerman. In 1866 he was convicted of corruption and removed from his governor generalship. The following year he was recalled to Peking, made grand secretary, and later appointed governor general of Chihli, retiring in 1869. (33. 111. 3) ECCP 1. 426.

Kuei-liang 桂良 (1785-1862), Manchu Plain Red Bannerman, member of the Gualgiya clan, had completed an active official career by 1845, when, already past sixty sui, the emperor remarked his impaired health. A second career in foreign affairs, however, was still ahead of him. In 1854, when Bowring and McLane came to Ta-ku, Kuei-liang was ordered to refuse to see them and sent subordinates to turn them back to the South. In 1858, he was co-negotiator, with Hua-sha-na, of the four Tientsin treaties with Britain, France, Russia, and the United States (Reed) respectively. He was later sent to Shanghai to negotiate the tariff schedule and secretly instructed to offer the foreigners "free trade" with China if they would forego the four most obnoxious terms of the treaties, including residence at Peking. In Shanghai, Kuei-liang became convinced that this "Secret Plan" was impracticable but tried, unsuccessfully, to get ratifications exchanged in Shanghai and forestall

the visits to Peking. He also warned the envoys that Ta-ku was fortified and that any attempt to force entrance would be resisted. In 1859,
after the British and French had been repulsed at Ta-ku, Kuei-liang
met U. S. Commissioner Ward and arranged his visit to Peking and
exchange of ratifications at Pei-t'ang. In 1860, when the Allies re-
appeared at Pei-t'ang, Kuei-liang was again sent to negotiate but the
British and French challenged his and other commissioners' credentials
and proceeded to Peking. The later negotiations were entrusted to a
commission headed by his son-in-law, Prince Kung, of which Kuei-
liang was an active member and which signed the treaties with England
and France. When the Tsungli Yamen was set up in January, 1861,
Kuei-liang was made a member, again under Prince Kung, and later
was made grand councillor. At Kuei-liang's death, he was canonized
and his name celebrated in the Temple of Eminent Statesmen. (33. 309.
3) ECCP 1. 428.

K'un-shou 崑壽, Chinese Plain White Bannerman, originally surnamed Li (李), became Tartar General of Canton and was later
stationed at Hangchow, Chekiang. When the British captured Canton
in 1858, he was made commander-in-chief of land forces and ordered
to recover the city. JM 902. 1.

KUNG Mu-chiu 宮慕久, Chinese minor official, was appointed Su-
Sung-T'ai (Shanghai) tao-t'ai May 31, 1843, to succeed Yen I-ao, who
was removed for opening Shanghai to trade without authorization.

KUO Chi-ch'ang 郭繼昌 (d. 1841), native of Cheng-ting, Chihli, was
a professional soldier and served in various campaigns in Kansu, Szechwan, Sinkiang, and Shansi with the usual promotions. In 1837, he
was made Tartar General of Kwangtung and when the Opium War broke
out, he was made commander-in-chief of land forces, originally
stationed at Hui-chou, but came to Canton in February, 1841. He was
ordered back by the governor general to defend Hui-chou. (33. 234. 2)
CSK 374. 5a.

Kuo-jui 國瑞, Manchu colonel in the Imperial Army, was transferred
to the Tientsin area in 1858, and was a regimental commander at Pei-
t'ang in 1860.

KUO Sung-t'ao 郭嵩燾, second-class compiler, attached to Prince
Seng-ko-lin-ch'in's headquarters in 1859, participated in the hostilities
and also met U. S. Commissioner Ward at Pei-t'ang, July 8th. He
was selected by the prince to carry the report to Peking and recommended for an audience. He was received by the emperor on July 23rd,
to give an eye-witness account of the victory.

LAI En-chüeh 賴恩爵, Chinese officer, was commander of naval forces of Kwangtung at the time of Cushing's arrival at Macao in 1844.

LAI Hsin-yang 賴信楊, Chinese officer, was acting commander-in-chief of sea forces in Fukien in 1858.

LAN Wei-wen 藍蔚雯, Chinese local official, was Su-Sung-T'ai (Shanghai) tao-t'ai in 1854, succeeding the notorious Wu Chien-chang; he had extensive dealings with U.S. Commissioner McLane.

LAO Ch'ung-kuang 勞崇光 (1802-1867), native of Shan-hua, Hunan, chin-shih of 1832, and Hanlin academician, after various local posts, served under General Hsiang Jung in suppressing the Taipings and became acting governor of Kwangsi. In 1851, he was granted the rank of first class official by imperial favor, and continued in fighting the rebels. In 1859, he became governor of Kwangtung, acting governor general of Liang-kuang. In 1861, he was made Canton customs superintendent and two years later, governor general of Yunnan and Kweichow. (33.179.1; ECCP 1.502) CSLC 48.36a.

Li-hsiang 立祥, Manchu officer, first captain in the Imperial Army, acting colonel of Shan-yang (Shanhaikwan),Hopei, in 1854.

LI Hsiao-ts'un 李小村, Chinese "traitor" served in the administration of Canton under British occupation, 1857-1858. The Chinese official description of Li Shao-tsun was that he was without ability but of a sinister nature, that he wore "devil" clothes and a "devil" hat, stayed in the governor's compound, and knew everything that went on. He appears to have been a protégé of Harry Parkes.

LI Hsü-pin 李續賓 (d. 1858, age 41 sui), native of Hsiang-hsiang, Hunan, was cited as one of the half-dozen able generals in China in 1858, who had risen from the people rather than being selected by examination. Li Hsü-pin was a pupil of Lo Tse-nan and when his teacher organized a militia unit called the "Hunan Braves," fought with him against the Taipings. He was famous for his archery, his powerful physique, and his personal heroism. When his teacher and commander was killed in battle in 1856, Li Hsü-pin took over the command and led the "Braves" to many victories in Kiangsi and Hupeh, including the recovery of Wuchang, and was regarded by Tseng Kuo-fan as the real hero of the famous "Hunan Braves." He was killed in battle along with many of his "Braves," in Anhwei and his son was made hereditary baron of the second class. (33.156.2) ECCP 1.463.

LI Jo-chu 李若珠, Chinese general, was cited as one of the able officers in the Yangtze Valley area in 1860.

LI Ming-t'ai 李明太, leader of a group of twelve Chinese arrested aboard the lorcha <u>Arrow</u>, October 8, 1856, at Canton at the order of Governor General <u>Yeh Ming-ch'en</u>. The lorcha was owned by Thomas Kennedy of Hong Kong but Yeh claimed that Li Ming-t'ai was a notorious Chinese pirate and that the <u>lorcha</u> was actually Chinese owned. Cf., Morse, <u>Int. Rel. of the Chinese Empire</u> 1.422.

LI Te-lin 李德麟, native of Shun-te, Kwangtung, was a senior licentiate and poet. In 1860-1861, he commanded the marine forces in the lower reaches of the Yangtze. His collected poems were published under the title, <u>Ko Shan Ts'ao T'ang Chi</u> (柯山草堂集), SJCL 14.26a.

LIANG Chang-chü 梁章鉅 (1836-1849), native of Ch'ang-lo, Fukien, <u>chin-shih</u> of 1802, bachelor of the Hanlin Academy, was descended from a long line of scholars and devoted his life to classical studies. This, however, did not interfere with his long and distinguished career in provincial administration. As governor of Kwangsi, 1836-1841, during the Opium War, he sent troops and cannon, wooden rafts and large stakes, to Canton and fortified Kwangsi against possible attack by the British. Late in 1842, he returned to Kiangsu as governor and soon after became governor general of Liang-chiang, where he was again called upon to defend his territory against the British. He retired in 1842, to his home in Fukien and spent the rest of his life in quiet scholarship. His publications number seventy titles, including commentaries on the classics and ancient books, collections of essays and poems, bibliographical and literary notes, memoirs, and geneological and historical studies. (Cf., G.E. Gaskill, "A Chinese Official's Experiences During the First Opium War," <u>American Historical Review</u> 39.82-86) ECCP 1.499.

LIANG Chien-fu 梁建富, Chinese pirate, one of the twelve arrested at the order of Governor General Yeh Ming-ch'en on board the British-owned lorcha <u>Arrow</u>, October 8, 1856, at Canton.

LIANG Chih 梁植, Chinese merchant, probably Cantonese, "expert" on foreign affairs in Shanghai in 1858, was sought by the officials to "manage" the foreigners.

LIANG Feng-chi 梁逢吉, Tientsin gentry, was utilized by Governor General T'an T'ing-hsiang in 1858, to raise subscriptions and train militia against foreign invasion.

LIANG Jen 梁仁, Chinese "traitor," was set up by the British to control Ningpo in 1858, in place of the legitimate local official.

LIANG Pao-ch'ang 梁寶常, governor of one of the coastal provinces,

1842-1844, probably Chekiang; later, 1846, he was governor general of Min-Che.

LIEN Chao-lun 廉兆綸, superintendent of government granaries in Peking in 1859, memorialized on precautions necessary in allowing U.S. Commissioner Ward to visit the capital.

LIN Fu-sheng 林福盛, Chinese local official, sub-prefect outside Canton, organized militia to assist in expelling the British from the provincial capital in 1858.

Lin-k'uei 麟魁 (d. 1862), Manchu Bordered White Bannerman, member of the So-cho-lo clan, was a chin-shih of 1823, and Hanlin academician. In 1846, as prefect at Ningpo, he had some contact with the British. As president of the Board of Punishments he was one of those charged with carrying out the vermilion edict ordering Ch'i-ying's official suicide, June 29, 1858. He was made director of the Historiographical Commission in 1861, and the next year, president of the Board of War. (33.217.3) CSLC 46.39a.

LIN Pa 林八, Cantonese rebel and religious leader, promoted the Taiping cause and made converts to the Society of God in Ling-yün-hsien, Kwangsi, in 1855-1856.

LIN Shou-t'u 林壽圖 (1822-1898), native of Fukien, chin-shih of 1845, was a scholar-official and friend of the poet, Hsieh Chang-t'ing. He served as financial commissioner of Shensi and was active in putting down the Mohammedan Rebellion. As Shantung circuit censor in 1860, he memorialized on the necessity of continued military defense against the Western powers after the victory of Prince Seng-ko-lin-ch'in in 1859. In 1876, he was again made financial commissioner of Shensi but retired after six months to his native province to lecture and write. When the French threatened the Fukien coast (1878) he was ordered to organize the local militia to oppose them. (33.306.3); ECCP 1.306; PCCP 17.24a.

LIN Tse-hsü 林則徐 (1785-1850), native of Hou-kuan, Fukien, chin-shih of 1811, and bachelor in the Hanlin Academy, is one of the half-dozen Chinese of the nineteenth century best known in the West. As judicial commissioner of Kiangsu, 1823-1824, his judgment of cases was so just and humane that people called him "Lin, Clear as the Heavens." By 1837 he had gained a national reputation as a vigorous, able, constructive administrator. In 1838 he first memorialized on the opium question and carried out a vigorous program for curing addicts and stopping the traffic in Hunan and Hupeh. He was called to Peking and after nineteen audiences with the emperor, was made

imperial commissioner with full powers to examine the problem and
eradicate the evil at Canton. His forthright program of stopping the
opium trade, confiscating and destroying 20,283 chests of British
opium, and punishing both addicts and dealers, led to the Opium War
with England. When the war went badly for China and the British
fleet threatened Tientsin, Lin Tse-hsü was blamed and on September
28, 1840, was dismissed from office and ordered to Peking. After a
year's postponement, he was banished to Chinese Turkestan. He
remained in Ili three years, working part of the time on colonization
projects under the governor. In 1845, he was ordered back to Peking
and was later appointed to various provincial posts. He retired in
1849, to Fukien, was recalled to service against the Taipings, and
died at Ch'ao-chou, Kwangtung, en route to his new posts. Temples
were erected to his honor and a monument set up for him at Hu-men
(Bocca Tigris). A huge mural in the auditorium of the Whampoa
Military Academy commemorates his burning the opium, June 3, 1838,
and in 1929 this day was designated Opium Prohibition Day by the
National Government. Besides his anti-opium activities, Lin Tse-hsü
was a pioneer in introducing Western geography and Western weapons
and methods of warfare into China. In Canton, he employed a staff to
translate Western materials into Chinese and he encouraged Wei Yüan's
Hai Kuo T'u Chih. Many of his memorials have been published. (33.
308.1) ECCP 1.511.

Ling-ch'un 齡椿; Manchu official, salt controller at Canton in 1858;
when the British occupied the city, he was ordered to Fo-shan (Fatshan),
ten miles southwest of Canton, to organize local militia and take
defense measures against further invasion.

LING Fang 陵芳, Chinese officer, lieutenant colonel in the Canton
garrison, was reported to have met the British on the city wall,
October 29, 1856, and hurled them back.

LIU Ch'i-hsien 劉齊銜, prefect of Hanyang, Hupeh, in 1861, reported to Governor General Kuan-wen the arrival at Hankow of two
American gunboats.

LIU Hung-ao 劉鴻翔, native of Wei-hsien, Shantung, chin-shih of
the Chia-ch'ing period, 1796-1821, as governor of Fukien in 1844,
was warned of the possible arrival of Cushing, en route to Peking.
JM 1489.3.

LIU K'ai-yü 劉開域, provisional prefect of Kuang-hou-fu (Canton)
in 1844, was delegated by Governor General Ch'eng Yü-ts'ai to confer
with U.S. Consul Forbes on the unexpected arrival of Cushing at Macao.

LIU Li-ch'uan 劉麗川 , native of Hsiang-shan (now Chung-shan),
Kwangtung, rebel leader of the Small Sword Society, an offshoot of the
Taipings which occupied Shanghai from September, 1853, to February,
1855, was in collusion with Shanghai tao-t'ai Wu Chien-chang. Liu-
Li-ch'uan was for a time interpreter for Western merchants and gained
popularity in Shanghai as a physician treating the poor without charge.
ECCP 1.118.

LIU Yün-k'o 劉韻珂 (d. 1853), native of Wen-hsiang, Shantung, took
highest honors in the chin-shih examinations in 1814; as governor of
Chekiang, 1840-1843, he suffered from the British occupation and at
the end of hostilities reported the first American merchant ship to visit
Ting-hai and Amoy in 1842. In 1843, he became governor general of
Ming-Che and set up with the British consul the Amoy residential
quarter at Kulangsu. In 1845 he memorialized on Christianity, maintaining that the Chinese government had the wrong attitude toward it,
that it was not bad in itself but only that certain rebels had taken advantage of it to cause trouble. He urged that China make this position
clear to the foreign missionaries so that the Christian Church could be
put on a religious rather than a political basis. (33.365.2) CSLC 48.28a.

LIU Yung-kuei 劉永桂, corporal in the Tientsin garrison employed to
carry messages to the foreign ships arriving at Ta-ku, April, 13, 1858.

LO Ping-chang 駱秉章 (1793-1867), native of Hua-hsien, Kwangtung,
chin-shih of 1832, and Hanlin academician, as governor of Hunan, 1850-
1860, actively supported Tseng Kuo-fan in his campaigns to suppress the
Taipings. As a Cantonese, he regarded himself as an expert on Western
naval warfare and armament and criticized Yeh Ming-ch'en for not
understanding the Cantonese people. He was in close touch with Canton
and memorialized letters received from there giving an entirely different
version from the official one. In 1860 Lo Ping-chang was transferred to
Szechwan and died at his post. (33.335.3) ECCP 1.537.

Lo-shan 樂善 (d. 1860), Mongol Plain White Bannerman, member of
the I-lo-t'e clan, was a professional soldier and fought against the
Mohammedans and the Nien-fei in the Northwest. In 1859 he was
Tartar General of Chihli (Hopei) and shared honors with Prince Seng-
ko-lin-ch'in for defeating the British and French. When the Allies
came back the next year and landed at Pei-t'ang, Lo-shan was second
in command and was killed in the assault. (33.178.2) CSLC 44.43a.

LO Tse-nan 羅澤南 (1808-1856), native of Hsiang-hsiang, Hunan, was
a militia leader and a driving force in the Hunan army which was largely
responsible for the suppression of the Taiping Rebellion. He was not a
professional soldier but a teacher who turned his pupils and his farmer

neighbors into an army which soon became famous for its fighting
ability and was an indispensable part of Tseng Kuo-fan's force. Lo
Tse-nan was wounded in battle and died in the barracks, eight months
before Wuchang was recovered and Taiping resistance broken. (33.190.
2) ECCP 1.540.

LO Tun-yen 羅惇衍, Cantonese, former board vice-president on
leave in Kwangtung in 1858, was ordered by edict to enlist militia
and lead his fellow countrymen to expel the British from Canton.

LOU Hao 婁浩, minor Chinese official, was provisional assistant
prefect in charge of coastal defense of Foochow, Fukien, in 1854.

LÜ Ch'üan-sun 呂佺孫 (d. 1857), native of Wu-chin, Kiangsu, chin-
shih of 1836, and Hanlin academician, became governor of Fukien in
1854. When the Taipings threatened, he was advised, on the generally
accepted theory that "the rich give their money; the poor give their
strength" to raise subscriptions and arm the local militia. He opposed
this, arguing that the Fukienese were a rough and lawless lot and it
would be dangerous to arm them. Surprisingly enough, this heterodox
view was accepted by the emperor. In 1855, he arranged for the
establishment of the American residential area in Foochow. He was
an able administrator and had a good prose style; his memorials are
regarded as classics. HPCC 25.15a.

LU Tse-ch'ang 鹿澤長, minor Chinese official, was tao-t'ai of Ning-
Shao-T'ai, Chekiang, and reported an American merchant vessel at
Ningpo, November 27, 1842.

LUNG Ju-yüan 龍汝元 (d. 1859), colonel of the Ta-ku Brigade, was
assigned to the defense of the forts on the south bank against the British
and French and was killed in the action of June 25th.

Lung-wen 隆文 (d. 1841), Manchu general, chin-shih of 1808, was
made assistant commander under I-shan at Canton in 1841. He reached
Canton April 14, suffered defeat from the British May 21, and agreed to
the truce withdrawing Chinese forces sixty miles from Canton and paying Britain an indemnity of six million dollars.   (33.335.3) ECCP 1.391.

LUNG Yüan-hsi 龍元僖, Cantonese, director of the Court of Sacrificial Worship in retirement in Kwangtung in 1858, was directed by
edict to organize local militia to assist in expelling the British from
Canton.

MA Tien-chia 馬殿甲 (d. 1849), native of Teng-chou, Honan, chin-
shih of 1811, had an active military career, particularly against the

Mohammedan rebels in Suiyuan. He was made brigade general of Nan-Shao-Lien, Kwangtung, in 1838, and in that capacity accompanied Admiral Wu Chien-hsün on board Commodore Kearny's flagship in the summer of 1842. He was ordered to Peking in 1845 and later served as Tartar General of Kwangsi. (33.83.2) CHLC 326.30a.

MA Tzu-nung 馬子農 (d. 1856), native of Canton, was a Taiping rebel according to official reports, who came to Chien-k'o village, Hsi-lin-hsien, Kwangsi, in 1856, "aroused the people with weird tales, collected crowds to worship, and also ravished women and plundered stockaded towns." He was arrested, confessed his affiliation with the rebels and was executed. He is either confused or falsely identified with the martyred Catholic priest, the Abbé Chapdelaine, who was known in China as Father Ma.

MEI Ch'i-shao 梅啓照, Chinese official, second class secretary of the Board of Civil Office, brought the ratified American treaty from Peking to Pei-t'ang for exchange with U.S. Commissioner Ward, August 16, 1859.

Mien-hsün 綿勳, Manchu prince, senior director of the Imperial Clan Court, carried the Vermilion edict to the death chamber ordering the official suicide of Ch'i-ying, June 29, 1858.

Mien-yü Prince Hui 綿愉惠親王 (1814-1865), fifth son of the Chia-ch'ing emperor, 1796-1821, and brother of the Tao-kuang emperor, 1821-1851, had an active career. In 1853, he was appointed commander-in-chief of all the forces protecting Peking and Tientsin against the Tai-pings but left the real command to his chief assistant, Prince Seng-ko-lin-ch'in. In 1855 he retired to his studio and garden. As Prince and Minister of Reserve Forces he was one of the three original memorialists charging Ch'i-ying with cowardice, lack of ability, repudiation of imperial favor, and betrayal of his country, June 15, 1858. Prince Hui was also punished for having previously recommended Ch'i-ying's restoration to office. (33.326.2) ECCP 2.968.

Ming-an 明安, Manchu officer, senior bodyguard assisting General Te-hsing-a in the encounter with the British and French at Pei-t'ang, August 3, 1860.

Ming-shan 明善 (d. 1874), Chinese Plain Yellow Bannerman, originally surnamed T'ung, (董), served as Canton superintendent of customs (Hoppo). As director of the Imperial Armory, he was one of the four imperial commissioners sent to Shanghai in 1858 to draw up the tariff supplement to the Tientsin treaties but secretly ordered to secure the abrogation of the treaties in exchange for free trade. Ming-shan later

became president of the Board of Works and lieutenant general of his
Banner.   (33. 371. 1) CSLC 47. 38a.

Mu-chang-a 穆彰阿 (1782-1856), Manchu Bordered Blue Bannerman,
chin-shih of 1805, and Hanlin academician, after 1820 gradually came
into great power at court, serving as minister of the Imperial Household,
president of the Censorate and minister of the Court of Colonial Affairs.
In 1828, he became grand councillor, soon assumed leadership, and in
1837 became chief of the Council or virtual premier of China.   In the
Opium War period he became the leader of the party favoring negotiation
and compromise and chief supporter at court of Ch'i-ying's policies.
He secured the approval of the Treaty of Nanking and of the Treaty of
Wanghia (Wang-hsia) negotiated with Cushing in 1844.   The new Hsien-
feng emperor, Wen-tsung, condemned Mu-chang-a and deprived him of
all office in an edict of December 1, 1851.   His eminent service saved
him from punishment but he never served again. (33. 283. 2) ECCP 1. 582.

Mu-k'o-te-na 穆克德訥, Manchu officer, Canton Tartar General in
1858, lost the city to the British but the blame was placed on Governor
General Yeh Ming-ch'en because the latter refused to discuss the defense
of the city with the Tartar General or the governor, Po-kuei, both of
whom continued in office during the British occupation of Canton.

Mu-yin 穆蔭 (d. 1871), Manchu Plain White Bannerman, member of
the T'o-ho-lo clan, served in various posts, almost always at court and
as grand councillor in 1858, was a member of the commission appointed
by the emperor to try Ch'i-ying.   In 1860 he was made imperial commissioner to negotiate with the British and French at T'ung-chou and
prevent their proceeding to Peking.   Failing this, he arrested the
British interpreter, Harry S. Parkes, and his party, and precipitated
the attack on Peking and the destruction of the Summer Palace.   In
1861, after the death of the Hsien-feng emperor, Mu-yin was degraded,
deprived of position, and exiled to Sinkiang, where he died. (33. 283. 1;
ECCP 2. 668) CSLC 47. 33b.

Na-erh-ching-e 訥爾經額 (d. 1857), Manchu Plain White Bannerman, member of the Fei-mo clan, was a Manchu ("translation") chin-
shih of 1803.   He had some contact with foreign affairs when, as
governor of Shantung in 1832, he prohibited British ships from the
coast.   In 1841, he was made governor general of Chihli, stationed at
Tientsin, specially charged with defense against the British fleet.
When it was turned back to the South, without fighting, he was rewarded
by the emperor.   He was regarded as a naval expert and plans for
building Western-type warships and steamers were referred to him in
1842.   He failed in 1853, however, to stop the Taipings, was sentenced
to death, pardoned, and exiled to Mongolia.   He was released in 1856,

and died the following year.   (33. 342. 3) CSLC 40. 26a.

Na-mu-chi-lo-to-erh-chi 那木濟勒多爾濟, commandant of the
Mongol Bordered Blue Banner at Chahar in 1858, was ordered to lead
his cavalry to assist in the defense of Shanhaikwan, Chihli (Hopei),
against possible British-French attack.

NI A-p'ei 倪阿培, notorious Chinese "traitor" who impressed
Chinese laborers for the "coolie trade," was arrested and executed
by Chinese authorities in 1859.

NING Li-t'i 寗立悌, minor Chinese official at Canton, accompanied
Governor General Ch'i-ying at an interview with U.S. Commissioner
Everett, held in a warehouse outside the Canton city wall, October 27,
1846.

NIU Chien 牛鑑 (d. 1858), native of Wu-wei, Kansu, chin-shih of
1814, was known as "New Tajin" in contemporary English accounts. He
became governor general of Liang-chiang in 1841 and plead for cessation of hostilities and conciliation, although the British characterized
him as sullen, resentful, and a member of the "war party." He cooperated with Ch'i-ying and signed the Treaty of Nanking with Pottinger,
August 29, 1842. For his failure to resist, Niu Chien was degraded and
sentenced to death. He was later pardoned and continued in public office
until his death.   (33. 4. 1; ECCP 1. 131) CSLC 48. 15b.

OU T'ien-min 歐天民, expectant tao-t'ai in Fukien, was sent to
Formosa (Taiwan) in 1860, by the governor general of Min-Che and
governor of Fukien to set up the customs house on the opening of Formosa to Western trade.

Ou-yang Ch'üan 歐陽泉, Canton gentry, along with the military, met
the British when they came over the city wall, October 29, 1856, and
"hurled them back. "

P'AN Cheng-wei 潘正煒 (1791-1850), native of Fukien but born and
reared in Canton, hong merchant and pioneer in Western shipbuilding
in China, used his formal name as hong merchant, P'an Shao-kuang
(潘紹光). He inherited the T'ung-wen Hong (同文行), and changed
the name to T'ung-fu Hong (同孚行). Assuming his place in the Co-
hong in 1821, he was the third in succession to be known to foreigners
as Puan Khe-qua (P'an-ch'i Kuan 潘啓官). His fortune is reported
to have reached twenty million Spanish dollars and he maintained a
luxurious garden and estate called T'ing-fan Lou (聽帆樓). His
interest in foreign ships, shipbuilding, and munitions was continued
by his successor, P'an Shih-ch'eng.   ECCP 2. 605.

P'AN Shih-ch'eng 潘仕成, native of Fukien but born and reared in
Canton, heir of a hong merchant fortune, minor official, and pioneer
in Westernization of China, was given the chu-jen degree in 1832 by
Emperor Hsüan-tsung, in return for his contribution for the relief of
famine sufferers in Chihli. His business connections made him well
known and trusted by foreigners generally, and he was particularly
friendly with Americans. He was regarded as an authority on foreign
affairs and was a trusted advisor to Ch'i-ying, assisting him in all the
negotiations with Cushing leading to the signing of the Treaty of Wanghia
(Wang-hsia) in 1844. At his own expense and with Ch'i-ying's encouragement, he undertook to build a naval squadron for the South
China Seas, built a foreign style battleship at a cost of 19,000 taels,
bought foreign cannon, experimented in steam navigation, and hired
American artisans to build torpedoes. From 1848 to 1858 he was salt
controller for Kwangtung. In 1858 he assisted Kuei-liang in setting up
the new tariff regulations for the Tientsin treaties. He maintained a
huge residence and garden in Canton famous for its luxurious archi-
tecture and rich collection of books, paintings, and calligraphy. ECCP
2.606.

P'AN Shih-jung 潘世榮, prominent and wealthy Cantonese, presumably
a relative of the hong merchant P'an Cheng-wei and the official P'an
Shih-ch'eng, built a small steamship in 1842, and launched it on the
river. The steam engine was reported to be too complicated for native
artisans and it was recommended that foreign workmen from Macao be
secured before the venture could be expected to succeed.

P'AN Tsu-yin 潘祖蔭 (1830-1890), official and scholar, was born
and reared in Peking but was a native of Soochow, Kiangsu. He was a
chin-shih of 1852, and as expositor in the Hanlin Academy in 1858 he
memorialized condemning the conciliatory policy of Ch'i-ying and Ch'i-
shan and the stupidity of Yeh Ming-ch'en. The only one who had the
right idea in dealing with foreigners was Lin Tse-hsü and the only
solution was war, especially the opposition of an aroused and militant
people. P'an Tsu-yin served in many posts in the Peking administration
and in 1880-1881 took part in the negotiations with Russia over the Ili
boundary. In 1882 he became grand councillor but had to retire to
mourn his father. He returned in 1885 and continued in office until
his death. He was a collector of books and bronzes, and catalogs of
his collections have been published. (33.208.1) ECCP 2.608.

Pao-chün 寶鋆 (d. 1891), Manchu Bordered White Bannerman, member
of the So-cho-lo clan, was a chin-shih of 1838 and Hanlin academician.
In 1860 he was one of a group under Prince Kung which acted on foreign
affairs and which later became the Tsungli Yamen. In 1871 he was made
director of the Historiographical Board. In 1884 the Empress Dowager

removed him from the Grand Council and he lived in retirement until
his death. (33.11.3) CSLC 52.29b.

P'ENG Yü-lin 彭玉麟 (1816-1890), one of the four outstanding
leaders of the Hunan Braves, was a native of Heng-yang, Hunan, although born and reared in Anhwei. His father died when he was young
and although he obtained a hsiu-ts'ai degree he remained obscure until
he joined Tseng Kuo-fan's new river patrol in 1853, of which he soon
became associate commander. He had a brilliant career in the suppression of the Taipings, his flotilla dominating the Yangtze and cooperating with Tseng Kuo-fan's land forces, until the final capture of
Nanking in 1864. P'eng Yü-lin consistently refused rewards for his
services and in nearly twenty years of naval service never acquired
any property. His retirement was proud and austere. In 1872 he was
recalled to reorganize the demoralized navy, which he did with vigor,
still declining political offices urged upon him. In 1881, old and ill,
he was called upon to participate in the war and negotiations with
France and was not allowed finally to retire until 1889. He is a model
of official integrity and incorruptibility. (33.297.2) ECCP 2.617.

P'ENG Yün-chang 彭蘊章 (1792-1862), native of Ch'ang-chou,
Kansu, finally became a chin-shih in 1835, at the age of 44 sui, having
failed the metropolitan examinations seven times. He had purchased a
position as secretary in the Grand Secretariat as early as 1827, and
after he got his degree, was promoted rapidly, becoming grand councillor,
president of the Board of Works, and grand secretary. As grand councillor, he served on the commission headed by Prince Kung, set up to try
Ch'i-ying in June, 1858. In foreign policy P'eng Yün-chang opposed the
reactionary war party and was forced to retire in 1860 because of his
insistent recommendation of Ho Kuei-ch'ing. He was reinstated but
never regained power. (33.298.1) ECCP 2.620.

Pi-ch'ang 壁昌 (d. 1854), Mongol Bordered Yellow Bannerman,
member of the E-lo-t'e clan, had an active military career, mostly
in the northwest frontier areas, until 1843, when he was made provisional governor general of Liang-chiang. Here he was active in
coastal defense and on May 31, 1843 memorialized on the inauguration
of foreign trade at Shanghai. In 1847 he was recalled to Peking for
audience and retired due to ill health. In 1853, when the Taipings
turned northward, he was made commander-in-chief in defense of the
metropolitan area, but died the following year. (33.185.3) CSK 374.
11b.

PI Ch'eng-chao 畢承昭, minor Chinese official, secretary to Wang
Yu-ling, governor of Chekiang in 1858.

PIEN Pao-shu 卞寶書, prefect of Ts'ang-chou, Chihli (Hopei) in 1856-1858, went aboard the British and American ships at Ta-ku in 1856, and was enlisted to prepare defenses in 1858.

Po-chün 柏葰 (d. 1859), Mongol Plain Blue Bannerman, member of the Pa-lu-t'e clan, was a chin-shih of 1826. As a grand councillor in 1858, he served on the commission headed by Prince Kung to try Ch'i-ying. He served as chief examiner of the Peking (Shun-t'ien) provincial examination and, at the request of a servant, substituted the paper of a successful candidate for that of a failure. He was convicted of fraud and, at the insistence of Su-shun, punished by decapitation, March 17, 1859. (33.305.3) ECCP 2.666; CSLC 40.42a.

Po-kuei 柏貴 (d. 1859), Mongol Plain Yellow Bannerman, member of the E-che-t'e clan, chu-jen of 1819, served as secretary in the Historiographical Board and worked on the compilation of the Shih Lu. He then served in the provinces, starting as magistrate. As provisional salt controller, he accompanied the other provincial authorities to meet U. S. Commissioner Davis, October 8, 1848, at Canton. In 1856, when Governor General Yeh Ming-ch'en was taken captive by the British, he was governor of Kwangtung. He served under the British during occupation and was appointed acting Imperial commissioner and governor general until the arrival of Yeh's successor. After the Canton episode, he was active in fighting the Taipings in Kwangtung. (33.305.3) CSLC 43.29a.

Po-to-hung-wu 博多宏武, Mongol local official, first-class sub-prefect of Kuang-p'ing-fu, Chihli (Hopei), was deputized to meet U.S. Commissioner Ward and make preliminary arrangements at Pei-t'ang, July 8, 1859, preparatory to proceeding to Peking.

Pu-erh-ho-te 布爾和德, Mongol officer, member of the Imperial Bodyguard in Seng-ko-lin-ch'in's command, turned over fifteen prisoners taken from the British and French, August 14, 1860, "including ten Kwangsi Long-haired (Taiping) Rebels."

Seng-ko-lin-ch'in 僧格林沁 (d. 1865), a Mongol, Prince of Korchin (Inner Mongolia), was a member of the Borjigit clan. In 1853 he turned the Taipings back from Tientsin and later pursued and annihilated them, blocking their ambition to take over Peking and overthrow the Manchus. When the British and French occupied the Ta-ku forts in 1858, Prince Seng was dispatched to T'ung-chou to keep them from Peking. When they withdrew, he reenforced the Ta-ku forts and in 1859 succeeded in repelling the Allied fleet with heavy losses. He became the hero of the nation but in 1860 was defeated at Pa-li-ch'iao by the British and French, who proceeded to Peking and burned the Summer Palace. Seng-ko-lin-ch'in was deprived of rank and titles but was retained to defend Peking from bandits. After peace was restored, he was sent to Shantung to oppose the Nien-fei (bandits), and in 1862 his princedom of the first degree was restored to him. He was killed in bandit warfare in Shantung in 1865. (33.383.1) ECCP 2.632.

Seng-ko-t'a-erh 僧格塔爾, a Mongol, commandant of the Mongol Solid Red Banner at Chahar, was ordered to lead his cavalry to defend Shanhaikwan, Chihli (Hopei) against possible foreign invasion in 1858.

SHEN Pao-i 沈保頤, a Cantonese, expectant prefect in charge of the Fo-shan (Fatshan), Kwangtung, trainband headquarters, leading popular resistance to the British occupation of Canton in 1858.

SHEN Ping-yüan 沈炳垣 (d. 1857), native of Hai-yen, Chekiang, chin-shih of 1845 and Hanlin academician, was grain intendant and sub-prefect at Wu-sung (Woosung), outside Shanghai, when the first foreign ships arrived to trade. He later became chief examiner at Nanning, Kwangsi, in 1857, when the Taipings surrounded the city. Shen Ping-yüan persuaded the populace to stand firm and after three days' fighting turned the rebels back. He was later surrounded in Wu-chou but this time was captured and taken to the Taiping camp. They tried to persuade him to go over to their side and when he persisted in refusing, killed him. (33.214.1) CSK 405.6b.

SHEN Ti-hui 沈棣輝 (d. 1856), native of Kuei-an, Chekiang, purchased a political post without going through the examination system. By 1852 he was prefect of Lien-chou, Kwangtung and became active in leading militia and suppressing rebel bands of the various off-shoots of the Taipings. He was promoted to judicial commissioner (vice-governor) and was utilized by Yeh Ming-ch'en to raise subscriptions and train militia, in which capacity he was charged with fraud and in-effeciency. In 1856 he was transferred to the post of financial commissioner of Kweichow but died en route. (33.213.2) CSK 440.1a.

Sheng-pao 勝保 (d. 1863), Manchu Bordered White Bannerman, member of the Su-wan-kua-erh-chüeh clan, was a chü-jen of 1840. He rose to the rank of general and was made imperial commissioner in 1853, but he failed to stop the advance of the Taipings northward to threaten Peking. The court became alarmed and Sheng-pao was degraded two ranks and exiled to Sinkiang. He was recalled and had an active career fighting the Nien-fei in Honan and Anhwei. By 1858-1860 he had risen to second-in-command to Seng-ko-lin-ch'in, but was characterized as "firm but boastful, determined but mean-natured and perhaps unsuited" to succeed Prince Seng, should the latter fall in battle. He was later sent to Shensi on a military mission but was convicted of corruption, sentenced to death, commuted to suicide. (33. 354.1) ECCP 1.508; JM 1136.2.

SHIH Jung-ch'un 史榮椿 (d. 1859), native of Shun-t'ien (Peking), Chihli (Hopei), followed a military career and achieved fame under generals Sai-shang-a and I-ching in campaigns against the Taipings. He later became a trusted general of Prince Seng-ko-lin-ch'in. In 1855 he was entrusted with the defense of the metropolitan area and in 1859 was made provincial commander-in-chief or Tartar General of Chihli. When the Allies attempted to storm the Ta-ku forts, he was in command of the central fort on the south bank. During the engagement on June 25, 1859, the small boat from which he was directing the defense was sunk by British naval gunfire and he was killed. (33.14.3) CSK 410.11a.

SHU Kung-shou 舒恭受, acting prefect of Ningpo, reported the arrival of the first U.S. ship to trade, November 27, 1842.

Shu-t'ung-e 舒通額 (d. 1865), Manchu Bordered White Bannerman, member of the Su-li clan, joined the command of general Te-hsing-a in 1853, and was promoted rapidly. As captain in the latter's command, he led his Mongol cavalry against the British outside Pei-t'ang, August 3, 1860. The following years he fought against the Nien-fei in Shantung, winning many battles and being promoted to lieutenant general. In 1865 he was encircled by the rebels at Lo-cheng and was killed in battle. (33.388.3) CSK 410.8b.

Shuang-hsi 雙禧, Manchu deputy lieutenant general, was in the Canton garrison in 1857-1858.

Shuang-jui 雙銳, Manchu brigade general in command of the Tientsin garrison in 1854, memorialized the arrival of Bowring and McLane at Ta-ku.

Shuang-ling 雙齡, Manchu deputy lieutenant general, was in the Canton garrison in 1857-1858.

Su-chang-a 蘇彰阿, Manchu court official and department director, conducted the Russian Orthodox archmandrite from Peking to Tientsin, June 18, 1858.

Su-la 蘇拉, Manchu court official, secretary in the Board of Rites, was ordered to convey the documents relating to foreign affairs, including treaties, from Hai-tien, near the Summer Palace, to Peking, October 6, 1860, when the British and French attacked, but was caught with his task half done and many state papers were lost.

Su-shun 肅順 (1815-1861), imperial clansman, Manchu Bordered Blue Bannerman, served in various high court posts, became president of the Censorate in 1857, and later the same year transferred to the Court of Colonial Affairs. In this capacity he memorialized, June 26, 1858, urging the summary execution of Ch'i-ying. From 1859 to a few days before his death, he was president of the Board of Revenue and gradually dominated the court and government. In 1860 he conducted the emperor to Jehol when the Allies took Peking and, on the conclusion of the Convention of Peking, was one of the four adjutant generals who took over the reins of government. When Emperor Wentsung (Hsien-feng) died, August 22, 1861, he helped form a co-regency and continued in power until he was finally overthrown November 1, 1861. A week later, November 8th, he was beheaded at the public execution ground. (33.70.1) ECCP 2.666.

SU T'ing-k'uei 蘇廷魁, Cantonese gentry, was delegated to treat with the British consul after the English troops breached the walls and burned the governor general's yamen at Canton, October 30, 1856.

SU Ya-ch'eng 蘇亞成, a Cantonese, claimed by Chinese officials to be the real owner of the lorcha Arrow, actually owned by Thomas Kennedy, Britisher of Hong Kong, was involved in the arrest of October 8, 1856, which touched off the so-called "Arrow War."

SUN Chih 孫治, poet and official, native of Ch'ien-t'ang, Szechwan; a licentiate, he was distinguished for his calligraphy, had a knack for forcasting weather, and was a specialist on the Book of Changes. His collected works were published under the title of Chien An Chi (鑒菴 集). As Tientsin tao-t'ai, he was the first Chinese official ordered to get in contact with U.S. Commissioner Ward after the hostilities at Taku, June 25, 1859. (33.276.2) CSLC 70.10b.

SUN Shan-pao 孫善寶 (d. 1853), native of Tsining, Shantung, chü-jen of 1807, was the eldest son of the scholar-official Sun Tu-t'ing. He served as governor of Kiangsu from 1843-1845, and did much to reconstruct the coastal districts after the ravages of the Opium War. On May 21, 1843, as acting governor general of Liang-chiang, he memorialized on the arrival of American ships at Woosung (Shanghai) to trade, before the new regulations were effective. ECCP 2.685.

SUN Tien-kuang 孫殿光, second captain of the left battalion, was with the Ting-hai garrison on Chusan (Chu-shan) Island in 1844, during British occupation.

Ta-hung-a 達洪阿 (d. 1854), a Manchu, as brevet provincial general-in-chief and brigadier general of Formosa (T'ai-wan) reported falsely on

the circumstances of the two British ships, <u>Nerbudda</u> and <u>Ann</u>, wrecked
on Formosa, was exposed by I-liang, and imprisoned, April-August,
1842. He was later released and served as deputy lieutenant general of
Kwangsi. He was subsequently active in resisting the Taipings in Chihli
(Hopei) and was killed in battle. (33.46.1) ECCP 1.390; JM 1338.3.

Ta-nien 達年, Manchu officer, participated in the defense program of
Tientsin in 1854. Promoted to colonel, familiar with the area through
years of service there, he was made acting brigade general in 1858, to
take charge of the defense of Ta-ku bar.

Ta-san 達三, Manchu officer, lieutenant colonel in the Hupeh garrison force, was ordered to Kwangtung in 1841, to assist in the defense
of Canton against the British.

T'a-ch'ing-an 塔清安, Manchu captain, imperially commissioned to
take charge of defeated and transferred troops, was ordered to assume
command of the forces defending Shanhaikwan in 1854, against possible
foreign attack.

T'AN T'ing-hsiang 譚廷襄 (d. 1870), <u>chin-shih</u> of 1833, native of
Shan-yin, Chekiang, prefect of the metropolitan prefecture since 1854,
assumed the duties of governor general of Chihli (Hopei) in 1858, when
Kuei-liang was called to Peking and promoted to grand secretary. He
carried on the preliminary negotiations with Reed and the other envoys
but was removed from office for failure to keep the British and French
from destroying the Ta-ku forts and proceeding to Tientsin. Later he
became governor of Shantung and in the T'ung-chih period rose to the
presidency of the Board of Punishments. (33.244.2) ECCP 428; JM
1756.1.

Te-hsiang 德祥, Manchu official, assistant department director, expert on Russian affairs, was used as officer messenger and major domo
in negotiations with Ignatieff in 1860, but was somewhat suspect because
he was too intimate with the Russians.

Te-hsing-a 德興阿 (d. 1867), Manchu general and Plain Yellow Bannerman, was a leader in the anti-Taiping campaigns out of the Great Camp
of Kiangpei and in 1856 succeeded to its command with the rank of lieutenant general and imperial commissioner. After many victories, he
was defeated by the Taipings at Pukow in September, 1858. He was deprived of rank, impeached by Ho-ch'un, and recalled to Peking. He was
gradually restored to rank and served under General Prince Seng-ko-lin-
ch'in. In 1866 he was made counselor of military affairs of Tarbagatai,
Sinkiang, and deputy lieutenant general of the Chinese Plain Red Banner.
(33.288.2) ECCP 2.711.

Te-leng-e 德楞額, Manchu general, was stationed in Shantung in 1859, to guard against rebel incursions.

T'e-k'o-shen 特克慎, commandant of the Mongol Bordered Blue Banner in Chahar, was ordered to lead his cavalry forces to Shanhai-kwan in 1858, to defend it against possible British-French attack.

Teng Ch'i-yüan 鄧啟元, Chinese officer, first captain in General Prince Seng-ko-lin-ch'in's headquarters in 1860, was officer messenger to the Russians anchored at Pei-t'ang before hostilities began.

Teng Ya-hsiu 鄧亞修, Cantonese rebel, member of one of the Taiping religious sects, was active in proselyting and stirring up trouble in Hsi-lin-hsien, Kwangsi, in 1856.

Ting-an 定安, Manchu officer, captain in General Prince Seng-ko-lin-ch'in's command, reported an oral communication from the British-French camp delivered under flag of truce, August 4, 1860, after hostilities had begun the day before.

Ting-fu 定福, Manchu officer, was in command of the garrison at Shanhaikwan, Chihli (Hopei) in 1858.

T'o-lun-pu 托倫布, Mongol officer, senior bodyguard under General Te-hsing-a who led Mongol and government troops against the British and French outside Pei-t'ang, August 3, 1860.

T'o-ming-a 托明阿 (d. 1865), Plain Red Bannerman, Manchu general-in-chief, succeeded Ch'i-shan in command of the Great Camp of Kiangpei in August, 1854, and in this capacity was ordered to block passage of the Yangtze River to foreign ships but to avoid conflict if possible. In 1856 he was deprived of rank for allowing K'ua-chou, Kiangsu, to fall to the Taipings and went home on the plea of ill health. Te-hsing-a succeeded to his command. T'o-ming-a was restored to senior bodyguard of the first rank, May 21, 1858, and ordered to proceed posthaste to Tientsin to cooperate with T'an T'ing-hsiang in handling barbarian affairs. He participated in the preliminary negotiations with Elgin, Gros, Reed and Poutiatine until the appointment of Kuei-liang and Hua-sha-na, at the end being transferred to Yang-tsun in the hope of preventing the Allies from pushing up the river above Tientsin.   (33. 324. 2) ECCP 2. 711.

Tsai-yüan Prince I 載垣怡親王 (d. 1861), had the confidence of Emperor Wen-tsung of the Hsien-feng period and played an important role at court. He advised the emperor on the demands of the British, French, American, and Russian envoys at Tientsin in 1858, and later served on the commission to try Ch'i-ying. In 1860 he investigated the

fighting at Ta-ku and reported the capture of fifteen allied prisoners,
August 14th. He began negotiations with Parkes, September 14th, but
on the 18th broke them off and ordered the arrest of Parkes and his
party, bringing on the retaliatory measures of the allies. When the
British and French took Peking and burned the Summer Palace, he
followed the emperor to Jehol. During the coup d'état of 1861, after
the death of his patron, Emperor Wen-tsung, he was punished by being
ordered to commit suicide. ECCP 2.924.

TS'AI Chen-wu 蔡振武, Cantonese resident of Shanghai, promoted by
purchase to tao-t'ai, was reported by memorial as being thoroughly
familiar with barbarian affairs. He was ordered by edict of September
24, 1858 to be sent to Peking and formally presented to the Board of
Civil Office for appointment to assist in the negotiations at Shanghai,
following up the Tientsin treaties.

TS'AI Ying-tou 蔡映斗, acting prefect of Soochow (Su-chou), Kiangsu,
was deputized to have a preliminary meeting with the English, American,
and French consuls aboard ship outside Soochow, February, 1858.

TS'AO Lien-ch'eng 曹聯城, acting magistrate of Lin-yü (Shanhaikwan),
Chihli (Hopei), in 1854, was ordered to cooperate with the military in
defense against possible foreign attack.

TS'AO Ta-shou 曹大綬, expectant department magistrate at Pei-t'ang,
was deputized on July 8, 1859 to make preliminary explanations to U.S.
Commissioner Ward, particularly that he could not use his sedan chair
but would have to ride horseback or in a cart.

TSENG Kuo-fan 曾國藩 (1811-1872), statesman, general, and scholar,
first Marquis I-yung (毅勇侯), native of Hsiang-hsiang, Hunan, is
probably the best-known and most respected Chinese of the nineteenth
century. Of poor peasant family, he was educated by his grandfather,
earned his chin-chih in 1838, and became Hanlin academician. He
served in various Peking posts until 1852, when the emperor ordered
him to recruit and drill militia in his native Hunan province against the
rising Taiping threat. His Hunan army became famous as the "Hunan
Braves," which with patient drill and good leadership was recognized as
the best disciplined and most effective fighting force in the field. He
organized an "inland navy" of gunboats to operate in the rivers, adopted
many Western techniques and some Western equipment, and became a
pioneer in modernizing China's military forces, but consistently refused
the aid of foreigners. After the Taiping Rebellion was finally broken in
1864, he continued at Nanking as governor general of Liang-chiang to
carry out reconstruction work. The following year he was called to
Shantung to take over the command of General Prince Seng-ko-lin-ch'in.

He was responsible for the first iron works in Shanghai, later the Kiangnan Arsenal. In 1867 he became grand secretary and the following year governor general of Chihli (Hopei). In 1871 he supported Yung Wing's (Jung Hung's) educational mission to the United States. Tseng Kuo-fan compiled or wrote some thirty-seven works and his letters to his family are still masterpieces of literary style, valued for their judgment and moral content. He is probably the best modern justification of the Confucian scholar-gentleman political theory and of the examination system. (33.193.2) ECCP 2.751.

Ts'un-hsing 存興, Manchu nobleman, Gioro or collateral relative of the Imperial House, financial commissioner (vice-governor) of Kiangsu in 1843, assisted Ch'i-ying in his dealings with Pottinger following the signing of the Treaty of Nanking.

TU Han 杜翰 (d. 1866), Chinese statesman, native of Pin-chow, Shantung, chin-shih of 1844, and Hanlin academician, served from 1854-1858, as senior vice-president of the Board of Works. As grand councillor in 1858, he was a member of the commission headed by Prince Kung to try Ch'i-ying. In 1860 he accompanied the emperor to Jehol and was one of the eight regents appointed to look after his son. He opposed, with Su-shun, the attempt of the two empresses to become supreme regents in 1861, and was sentenced to exile but never went. Mr. Fang Chao-ying says, in Eminent Chinese of the Ch'ing Period: "With him ended the power of one of the most influential families in China in the nineteenth century." (33.309.2) ECCP 2.779.

TUAN Ch'eng-shih 段承實, brevet director of the fifth grade, second secretary of the Board of Punishments, was a member of the Imperial Commission sent to Shanghai in September, 1858, to negotiate a commercial convention supplementary to the Tientsin treaties. He, with Ming-shan, was probably one of the authors of the ill-fated "secret plan" to secure abrogation of the treaties in exchange for "free trade" to China.

Tuan-hua Prince Cheng 端華鄭親王 (d. 1861), half-brother of the powerful minister, Su-shun, was one of the courtiers present at the death-bed of Emperor Hsüan-tsung (Tao-kuang) in 1850, enjoined to serve the new emperor, Wen-tsung (Hsien-feng), which he did loyally throughout the eleven years of his reign. Prince Cheng was one of the two original memorialists, June 15, 1858, charging Ch'i-ying with "cowardice and lack of ability, repudiation of imperial favor, and betrayal of his country." ECCP 2.666.

TUNG Pu-yün 董步雲, minor Chinese official, was deputized by Governor of Shantung Wen-yü to determine if there were any American ships at Chefoo (Yen-t'ai) in 1860, and if so, to try and enlist American good

offices to persuade England and France to follow Ward's example in ex-
exchanging ratifications peacefully at Pei-t'ang in 1859.

Tung-shun 東純, Manchu officer, was Tartar General of Foochow
(Fu-chou), Fukien, in 1860.

T'ung-lin 銅麟, a Manchu, expectant sub-prefect at Canton, was regarded by Ch'i-ying as one of the few "thoroughly conversant with barbarian affairs" and capable of advising him in the negotiation of the
Treaty of Wanghia (Wang-hsia) with Cushing in 1844. T'ung-lin was
also one of the entourage of Ch'i-ying at his meeting with U.S. Commissioner Everett in a warehouse outside the city walls of Canton,
October 27, 1846.

T'UNG Pu-nien 仝卜年, sub-prefect at T'ai-wan (T'ai-nan), Formosa,
was employed by the brigade general of Formosa to interrogate a foreign
"prisoner" (shipwrecked sailor) on barbarian affairs in 1842.

WANG Ch'eng-en 王承恩 (d. 1644), palace eunuch during the last
reign of the Ming dynasty, 1628-1644, ultimately reached the position
of secretary in the Board of Rites. His official biography makes no
mention of his "burning five barbarian ships." In 1644, when Li Tzu-
ch'eng rebelled and the Ming dynasty was overthrown, Wang Ch'eng-en
defended the capital to the last and when the emperor hanged himself,
Wang also committed suicide. He was given posthumous recognition
as a loyal martyr both by the loyalist Ming prince and by the Ch'ing
dynasty. MS 305.33b.

WANG Chia-hsi 王家熙, Tientsin gentry, was enlisted to raise subscriptions and train militia against foreign invasion in 1858.

WANG Ch'ing-yün 王慶雲 (1798-1862), official and scholar, native of
Min-hsien (Foochow), Fukien, chin-shih of 1829 and Hanlin academician,
was the author of a concise financial history of the Ch'ing empire. Appointed governor of Shensi in 1853, he was active in defense against the
Taipings and was involved in a French Catholic missionary case in 1854.
The following year he was transferred to Shansi and two years later became governor of Szechwan. In 1859 he was appointed governor general
of Liang-kuang (Canton), but resigned on account of ill health and retired
to his villa in Shansi. (33.30.2) ECCP 2.813.

WANG Hsin 王鑫, Chinese general in the Taiping Rebellion period
(1850-1864), is cited as an example of a man of ability rising from the
ranks rather than through the examination system.

WANG I-te 王懿德 (d. 1861), native of Hsiang-fu, Honan, chin-shih of

1823, became governor of Fukien in 1851, and was active in opposing the Taipings and also local rebels on Formosa. As governor general of Min-Che, he memorialized, February 12, 1855, on Commodore Perry's visits to the Liu-ch'iu (Loochoo, Ryukyu) Island of Okinawa. He also memorialized on the establishment of a foreign residential area in Foochow. (33.35.3) CSLC 42.10b.

WANG Lan-kuang 王蘭廣, acting prefect of Chiao-ho, Chihli (Hopei), who had previously held office in Tientsin, was selected by the governor general in 1858 to cooperate in raising subscriptions and training local militia against foreign invasion.

WANG Mao-yin 王茂蔭 (d. 1865), native of Hsi-hsien (Hweichow), Anhwei, chin-shih of 1832, was an economist and an able minister. He advised the emperor on the use of paper money and coinage and was regarded as a forthright and courageous censor. He was thoroughly alarmed by the appearance of the Allied forces at Tientsin in 1858, and as a senior vice-president of the Board of War memorialized, July 9, recommending Wei Yüan's Hai Kuo T'u Chih (Geography of Foreign Nations) as required reading for all officials dealing with the West and urging a mobilization of all talents to meet the crisis created by the demands of the Western envoys. Wang Mao-yin retired later the same year. (33.26.3) CSK 428.1a.

WANG P'ei-hsien 王丕顯, acting sub-prefect of Ting-hai (on Chu-shan Island) in 1843, reported every fifth day to Governor General of Liang-chiang Ch'i-ying on the activities of foreign ships and noted American ships in port by the end of 1842.

WANG Tao-ch'ung 王道崇, Chinese "traitor," native of Chia-ying, Kuangtung, was the "running dog" of Harry Parkes at Canton in 1858. Wang could read and write English and wore "devil" clothes and a "devil" hat, and in the official view of the time, "until Wang and Parkes are disposed of, Kwangtung will never have a quiet day."

WANG Tseng-ch'ien 王增謙, grain intendant ordinarily stationed at Canton, moved to Fo-shan (Fatshan) when the British occupied the provincial capital, 1857-1858. Being outside the occupied zone, Wang Tseng-ch'ien was ordered to take over the militia to prevent local bandits from causing trouble.

WANG Yu-ling 王有齡 (d. 1861), native of Hou-kuan, Fukien, became a collegian in the National Academy but obtained his first post by purchase. After serving as magistrate in Ningpo, Ting-hai, and Hangchow, he was promoted in 1858 to judicial commissioner of Chekiang and the following year became governor. He was active in the campaigns to suppress the

Taipings and was killed during the Taiping siege of Hangchow, which he was defending. (33.32.1-2) CSLC 43.21a.

WANG Yü-lung 王裕隆, Yangtze boatman, had his "sand" boat seized by the French, August 13, 1842, for passage to Nanking.

WANG Jung-chi 王榕吉, magistrate of the independent department of Ting-chou, Chihli (Hopei), in 1858, was called upon to raise subscriptions and train militia against foreign invasion.

WEI Tso-pang 衛佐邦, native of Po-lo, Hui-chou-fu, Kwangtung, as lieutenant colonel led troops and militia outside Canton in 1856 and was expected to fight it out with the British in mid-November. He was successful against the Taipings and finally became brigade general of Yang-chiang, Kiangsu. JM 1603.1.

Wen-ch'ien 文謙, Manchu Bordered Yellow Bannerman, as Ch'ang-lu salt controller in 1854 carried on the preliminary negotiations at Tientsin with Medhurst and Parker before Ch'ung-lun and Kuei-liang arrived to take up negotiations with Bowring and McLane. When the Taipings threatened the North, Wen-ch'ien was placed in command of the forces defending Tientsin and for his success was made financial commissioner of Chihli. He later became brigade general of Ma-lan (Yung-p'ing-fu), Chihli (Hopei). JM 57.3.

Wen-hsiang 文祥 (1818-1876), Manchu Plain Red Bannerman, member of the Gualgiya clan of Mukden, chin-shih of 1845, first distinguished himself for his poise and common sense amid general panic when the Taipings threatened Peking in 1853-1854. He served in various Peking posts and, when the emperor fled to Jehol in 1860, remained behind to negotiate with the British and French. When the occupation terminated, he memorialized recommending the formation of the Tsungli Yamen (Foreign Office) and the T'ung-wen Kuan (Foreign Language School), and in 1861 became a member of the former under Prince Kung. He also sponsored a training school in Western gunnery for bannermen and later led these riflemen successfully in the field. In 1872 he was made grand secretary, although illness prevented him from active duty the rest of his life. As a pioneer in China's modernization, he initiated the Burlingame Mission to Western countries. He was highly esteemed by both foreigners and Chinese for his straightforwardness and honesty. His modest and truthful autobiography is still good reading. (33.98.3) ECCP 2.853.

Wen-feng 文豐 (d. 1860), Chinese Plain Yellow Bannerman, original Chinese surname Tung (董), was Canton customs superintendent in 1842, in which capacity he sponsored, with the approval of the court, the building and purchase of China's first Western warships. He later assisted Ch'i-ying in negotiating the commercial supplement (Treaty of the Bogue) to the Nanking treaty with Great Britain. In 1860, when the emperor fled before the British and French, Wen-feng was ordered to remain behind to defend the Summer Palace. When the allies sacked and burned it, he drowned himself in the artificial lake of the imperial garden. (33.98.2) CSK 499.3b.

Wen-ko 文格, Manchu official, financial commissioner of Hunan in 1858, reported the loss of the great seals of the governor general of Liang-kuang, salt controller, and imperial commissioner to the British when they occupied Canton.

Wen-wei 文蔚 (d. 1855), Manchu Plain Blue Bannerman, chin-shih of 1820, was made assistant commander under I-ching, October 18, 1841, when the emperor determined to resist the British in Chekiang. The imperial forces were hopelessly defeated in every encounter, and after the signing of the Treaty of Nanking Wen-wei was sentenced to imprisonment awaiting execution. He was taken to Peking in chains but was eventually pardoned. (33.98.2) ECCP 1.377.

Wen-yü 文煜 (d. 1884), Manchu Plain Blue Bannerman, member of the Fei-mo clan, served in various posts in Peking and the provinces. In 1854, when Imperial Commissioner Ch'i-shan died, he took over the command and campaigned actively against the Taipings in Kiangsu. As acting governor general of Chihli (Hopei), in 1859 he was ordered to handle "conciliation" to balance the military policy of Prince General Seng-ko-lin-ch'in. In this capacity he met U.S. Commissioner Ward and arranged for his visit to Peking and exchange of ratifications at Pei-t'ang. Soon afterwards he was transferred to Shantung as governor and was ordered to use his influence with Ward to get the British to return to Shanghai from Chefoo (Yen-t'ai). When the Allies sailed North he was degraded. He was restored the following year and served as governor general of Chihli, of Min-Che, and in 1874 memorialized on the defense of Formosa (T'ai-wan) against the Japanese. In 1877 he was recalled to Peking and spent the rest of his life in office there. (33.98.3) CSLC 52.27b.

WU Chien-chang 吳健章, merchant, official, "expert" in barbarian affairs, and particular friend of Americans in China, is identified by Sir Thomas Wade as "Samqua," hong merchant of the T'ung-shun hong, founded in Canton in 1832. Wu Chien-chang obtained his chin-shih and membership in the Hanlin Academy by purchase and became acting Shanghai intendant, officially tao-t'ai of Su-Sung-T'ai, in 1843, but did not become active in foreign affairs until 1848, and assumed full control as customs superintendent in 1851. He dealt with the consuls and was regarded as an authority on all matters concerning trade. When the Triad rebels and Small Sword Society took Shanghai in 1853, Wu Chien-chang was given asylum by American friends; during the rebel occupation, customs collections were taken over by the British and American consuls and only restored to Wu Chien-chang on February 9, 1854. He was still unable to set up his Customs House in Shanghai and the foreign inspectorate, later the Imperial Maritime Customs service, gradually evolved. July 11, 1854, Wu Chien-chang was impeached for being in partnership withtthe American firm of Russell and Company and for selling supplies to the rebels. He was found guilty and sentenced to deportation, but pleas of friends and a heavy contribution to the Imperial War Chest got him off. He continued to be consulted on commercial matters and in 1858 was still active as expectant tao-t'ai. ECCP 2.865.

WU Chien-hsün 吴健勳, native of Pao-ting, Chihli (Hopei), was the filial son of the Chinese general Wu Chang. As local "admiral" in charge of maritime forces, he visited Commodore Kearny's flagship at Whampoa in the summer of 1842. Wu Chien-hsün fought in the campaigns against the Taiping Rebels in Shantung and Kiangnan and was recommended for military office by Prince General Seng-ko-lin-ch'in but preferred to give all credit to his father. In 1860, when the British and French invaded Peking, he was again called into service to defend the capital but still refused official appointment. After he returned to his home in Pao-ting he again organized the local militia against the Nien-fei. In 1878 he gave all his property to charity and retained his reputation for unselfish, unrewarded service until his death. (33.5.2) CFHCC 27.33a.

WU Ch'üan 吴泉, linguist, i.e., Chinese Customs House interpreter, was in Canton in 1858.

WU Ch'üan-mei 吴全美 (d. 1884), native of Shun-te, Kwangtung, rose from the ranks and fought against local uprisings on Hainan Island. Later he joined the river flotilla organized by General Tseng Kuo-fan against the Taiping Rebels and in 1861 was in command of naval forces in the lower reaches of the Yangtze. In 1864 he was made commander-in-chief of naval forces in Fukien and later in Kwangtung. In 1883, when the French fleet attacked Hainan Island, he was ordered to its defense but died early in the campaign. (33.52.1) CSLC 60.13a.

WU Ch'ung-yüeh 伍崇曜 (1810-1863), hong merchant, official and patron of the arts, was originally from Fukien but was the third generation in Canton. He was the fifth son of Wu Ping-chien and was the third hong merchant known to foreigners as Houqua, head of the I-ho Company (怡和行), called in contemporary literature Ewo Hong. Wu Ch'ung-yüeh and his father were the wealthiest of the hong merchants and were both particular friends and patrons of the American merchants. Wu Ch'ung-yüeh obtained his <u>hsiu-ts'ai</u> degree at the age of thirteen (<u>sui</u>) and his <u>chü-jen</u> degree in 1831, as a result of a contribution of 30,000 taels by his father to flood control. In the next sixteen years he competed four times in the metropolitan examinations but never obtained his <u>chin-shih</u>. In 1833 he entered the Co-hong and in 1843 inherited his father's immense fortune. He contributed (or was bled) heavily to the Canton government war chest and in 1856-1858 frequently negotiated with Lord Elgin and Harry Parkes. His policy was always one of conciliation and literally "peace at any price," which he willingly paid out of his own pocket. He was rewarded with the red coral button of the second class and the rank of financial commissioner (vice-governor). He patronized scholars and authors and built a fabulous garden in Canton with a rich library, from which he published numerous collectanea. ECCP 2.867.

Wu-erh-kun-t'ai 烏爾棍泰 (d. 1858), Manchu Bordered Yellow Bannerman, member of the Shu-mu-tu clan, had a rather superficial military career in the Taiping period, defending Peking at T'ung-chou. In 1858, as sub-chancellor of the Grand Secretariat, he was ordered to assist T'an T'ing-hsiang in the preliminary negotiations at Tientsin, performed his duties perfunctorily, and died soon after. (33.48.1) CSLC 44.13a.

WU Hsü 吳煦, prefect of Chia-ting-hsien (Shanghai), Kiangsu, was ordered to negotiate with the foreign consuls in Shanghai in 1854, relative to the building of a stockade against the rebel insurgents.

WU I-hsi 巫宜楔, tao-t'ai of Su-Sung-T'ai (Shanghai), reported a French warship at Woosung, July 31, 1842.

Wu-lo-hung-e 烏勒洪額, Mongol military officer at Tientsin in 1858, was ordered to defend the port against the British and French.

WU Ping-chien 伍秉鑑 (1769-1843), Canton hong merchant and pioneer in the introduction of Western ships into China, was known to foreigners as Houqua (Hao Kuan 浩官). A native of Canton, his ancestors originally came from Fukien and he inherited I-ho (Ewo 怡和) Hong. He was the most prosperous foreign trader in the first half of the nineteenth century, with a fortune estimated in 1834 at twenty-six million dollars (Spanish). In 1843 he and another hong merchant purchased one American and one French ship, to serve as models for Chinese shipbuilding. ECCP 2.877.

WU T'ing-hsien 吳廷獻, Cantonese degraded official on probation, regarded by Ch'i-ying as thoroughly conversant with barbarian conditions, was called upon to assist in the negotiations with Caleb Cushing in 1844.

WU T'ing-tung 吳廷棟 (1793-1873), native of Huo-shan, Anhwei, historian and scholar of Neo-Confucianism, was made acting judicial commissioner of Chihli (Hopei) in 1854, when Kuei-liang was ordered to negotiate with the foreign envoys. He was later made full com- missioner and served in the same capacity in Shantung until called back to Peking, where he eventually became junior secretary in the Board of Punishments. (33.31.1-2) ECCP 1.237; CSK 397.4a.

WU Ya-jen 吳亞認, Cantonese sailor, testified to the Chinese offi- cials in the case of the seizure of the lorcha <u>Arrow</u>, October 8, 1856.

WU Yüan-yu 吳元猷, Chinese general, commander-in-chief of sea forces in Kiangnan in 1858, was ordered to defend the seacoast against the British when Canton fell into their hands.

YANG Chiu-wan 楊九畹, <u>tao-t'ai</u> of Nan-Shao-Lien, Kwangtung, in 1841, was in charge of government troops being transferred from neighboring provinces to Canton but was ordered to detain new trans- fers until further development.

YANG Chü-yüan 楊鉅源, acting prefect of Ningpo, in the absence of the circuit officials, had an interview with U.S. Commodore James Biddle, June 30, 1846.

YANG Ch'un-hua, see YANG Yüeh.

YANG Fang (1) 楊芳 (1770-1846), general, first Marquis Kuo-yung, was a native of Sung-t'ao, Kweichow. He had a long and checkered military career fighting bandits and quelling insurrections before 1841, when he was sent to Kwangtung as assistant commander under I-shan, to fight the British. He memorialized on U.S. Consul Delano's behalf requesting the resumption of British trade at Canton. The court rejected this and urged him to concentrate on defeating and ex- pelling the British forces. All his efforts at Canton ended in failure and after the British warships left Canton in June, he pleaded illness and returned to his post in Hunan. He retired in 1843 and died three years later. (33.313.1) ECCP 2.884.

YANG Fang (2) 楊坊, Shanghai merchant, closely identified with foreigners and regarded as an expert in dealing with the local British, French, and American consuls. In 1854 he was deputized to deal with the foreigners regarding the construction of a stockade around the settlement to block the rebels. In 1859 he was again utilized by the Shanghai <u>tao-t'ai</u> to try to dissuade the foreigners from going to Peking.

In 1860 he was expectant <u>tao-t'ai</u>.

YANG Ts'ai-fu, see YANG Yüeh-pin.

YANG Ts'ung-lung 楊從龍, expectant prefect, resident of Canton, probably a merchant, prepared an unofficial account of developments in Canton from 1854 to 1857, which was memorialized by Governor General Huang Tsung-lun, en route to Canton.

YANG Wen-ting 楊文定 (d. 1857), native of Ting-yüan, Anhwei, <u>chin-shih</u> of 1833, was made governor of Kiangsu in 1851, and in that capacity inaugurated the ocean transport of tribute grain when the Taipings cut the inland route. In 1853 he also served as provisional governor general. He was active in opposing the Taiping rebels and was impeached when they captured Kiukiang. When Nanking fell, he was sentenced to death, later commuted to six years imprisonment and exile. He died before the sentence was served. (33. 312. 2) CSLC 43. 41b.

YANG Yüeh 楊越, original name Ch'un-hua (春華), filial son and loyal official, was a native of Shan-yin, Chekiang. In 1859, as independent department magistrate of Soochow, Kiangsu, he was sent to Shanghai to make preliminary arrangements for the imperial commissioners, Kuei-liang et al, to meet the foreign envoys. (33. 311. 3) CSK 504. 7a.

YANG Yüeh-pin 楊岳斌 (1822-1895), original name Ts'ai-fu (載福), native of Shan-hua, Hunan, was one of the famed group of Hunan leaders brought into prominence by Tseng Kuo-fan. He was closely identified with P'eng Yü-lin in the command of Marquis Tseng's gunboat flotilla from 1854, which was a large factor in the ultimate defeat of the Taipings in 1863, and the capture of Nanking in 1864. In 1860-1861 Yang Yüeh-pin was in command of the fleet in the upper reaches of the Yangtze. When the Taipings were finally put down, he was rewarded with the title of Junior Guardian of the Heir Apparent, an hereditary rank, and a post as governor general. (33. 314. 1) ECCP 2. 619.

YAO Hsü 姚煦, Tientsin district magistrate in 1860, was deputized to carry on routine affairs with the Russian mission but he was distrusted by the court because he was too "intimate with the Russians."

YAO Ying 姚瑩 (1785-1853), native of Tung-cheng, Anhwei, <u>chin-shih</u> of 1808, was the son of the famous classical scholar, Yao Nai. He served as magistrate in Fukien, was promoted to brevet provincial judge and sent to T'ai-wan (Formosa) as <u>tao-t'ai</u>. During the Opium War, he and the governor of Fukien, Ta-hung-a, memorialized that they had blocked an attempted invasion of the island, capturing British soldiers and destroying British ships. He was commended for this, but when it transpired that the British ships had encountered storms and been wrecked on the coast, he was tried and imprisoned. He was later restored to office and served under Sai-shang-a in the suppression of the Taipings. He was a scholar and left many volumes of poetry and essays. (33.303.2) ECCP 1.239; CSLC 73.9b.

YEH Ming-ch'en 葉名琛 (1807-1859), notorious governor general of Liang-kuang, known in contemporary English accounts as Viceroy Yeh, was a native of Han-yang, Hupeh, chin-shih of 1835, and a Hanlin academician. Sent to Kwangtung as financial commissioner in 1847, he became governor the following year and later governor general. By the Chinese government he was respected for his vigorous campaigns against the Taipings and his stern dealings with the foreigners, although the court was quick to repudiate him when he failed. By Britains and Americans he was regarded as obstinate, uncommunicative and committed to a policy of non-fulfillment of treaties. He was responsible for the arrest of the lorcha Arrow, October 8, 1856, and the burning of the foreign factories in December. The British stormed Canton, October 29, 1857, and the following January 5th, Yeh Ming-ch'en was captured and imprisoned aboard HMS Inflexible. He was later taken to Calcutta, India, where he remained until his death. His remains were returned to China and buried at Han-yang. Miss Tu Lien-che, his biographer, in Eminent Chinese of the Ch'ing Period, characterizes him: "Brutalized by the harsh treatment he had meted out to rebellious natives of Kwangtung, he came to believe that Westerners might be brought to terms, if not by force, at least by arrogance, obstruction, and interminable delay. He had little conception of the gravity of the international problems involved, and took little pains to learn." A contemporary Canton ditty caricatured him: "He would not fight, he would not make peace, and he would not take steps for defense. He would not die, he would not surrender, and he would not flee. In his pretense at being a minister and a governor, there was none like him in antiquity and there is hardly his equal today." (33.132.3) ECCP 2.904.

YEH Yung-yüan 葉永元, prefect of Foochow in charge of trade in 1856, was ordered to prevent U.S. Commissioner Peter Parker from proceeding to Soochow.

YEN I-ao 顏以燠, acting tao-t'ai of Su-Sung-T'ai (Shanghai), reported the arrival of an English steamer in the Whangpoo (Huang-p'u) River, April 20, 1843, and an interview with the officers of the said ship the following day at his yamen.

YEN Kuo-jeng 嚴國礽, sub-district magistrate at Chefoo (Yen-t'ai),

Shantung, in 1860, tried unsuccessfully to arrange an interview between the French general, Montaubon, and Governor Wen-yü's deputy,
Tung Pu-yün.

YEN Tuan-shu 晏端書 (d. 1882), native of I-cheng, Kiangsu, chin-
shih of 1838, and Hanlin academician, was appointed magistrate in
Chekiang in 1847, and served in various offices in that province for
fifteen years. In 1855, as controller of ocean tribute transport, he was
sent to Shanghai to make a secret investigation of the charges against
the one-time Shanghai tao-t'ai, Wu Chien-chang. Later the same year,
he was made judicial commissioner, called to Peking for an imperial
audience, promoted to governor, and specially charged with the defense
of the province against the Taipings. In 1862 he was made governor of
Kwangtung, acting governor general, and ordered to collect likin to
support military operations. He retired in 1863, to observe the
mourning period for the death of his mother and never returned to public
public office. (33.187.2) CSLC 55.5b.

Ying-lung 英隆, Manchu military governor of Mukden, was specially
charged by edict of October 19, 1854, to make adequate military defense
of the Manchurian coast against possible foreign attack.

Ying-yü 英毓, Manchu tao-t'ai of Tientsin 1858, responsible for the
defense of the port against the Allies. When the latter arrived, April
18, 1858, he took charge of the preliminary negotiations with them.

YU P'o 尤渤 (d. 1852), native of Wu-wei, Kansu, rose from the ranks
and was commanding general of Chiang-nan in 1842, collaborating with
Ch'i-ying and Niu Chien in the treaty settlement with Great Britain in
1842. (33.12.2) CSLC 44.37b.

Yu-feng 有鳳, Manchu provisional governor general of Min-Che
(Fukien-Chekiang), memorialized, February 26, 1854, in the case of
an English coolie ship marooned on the Liu-ch'iu Islands.

Yü-ch'eng 裕誠 (d. 1858), Manchu, Bordered Yellow Bannerman,
member of the Tung-chia clan, had a routine career in court office,
largely in the imperial household and in some military posts. As grand
secretary in 1858, the foreign envoys addressed their correspondence to
him but he was not allowed to reply. He was not a member of the Grand
Council which might have assumed responsibility for foreign affairs.
(33.250.3) CSLC 40.14b.

Yü-ch'ien 裕謙 (1793-1841), known as Yü-t'ai (裕泰) until 1826,
when he was obliged to change his name because his official superior
had the same name, was a Mongol Bordered Yellow Bannerman,

member of the Borjigit clan, <u>chin-shih</u> of 1817, and Hanlin academician.
He was made judicial commissioner of Kiangsu in 1834, and later
governor. In the period of the Opium War, he favored a strong military
policy against the British and scorned the conciliatory policy of Ch'i-
shan and Ch'i-ying. In 1841 he was made imperial commissioner charged
with the attack on the British at Tinghai, but arrived after the British had
evacuated, which he interpreted as proof of their weakness. March 21,
he memorialized on the efficacy of using "barbarians to curb barbarians,"
particularly Americans against British. At Tinghai, he tortured several
British captives to death and executed native collaborationists. He was
promoted to governor general to succeed I-li-pu. When Tinghai was
again threatened he was rushed back to defend it but lost it again to the
British. When Chinkiang was about to fall, he attempted to commit
suicide by drowning but was rescued. He was carried away in defeat
and died the following day, reportedly from swallowing opium. (33.250.
3) ECCP 2.939.

Yü-ch'ing 毓清, Manchu official, was appointed Canton superintendent
of customs in 1859, succeeding Heng-ch'i at the time of the inauguration
of the foreign managed Chinese Maritime Customs service on the Shanghai model.

YÜ En-heng 余恩鑅, minor Chinese official, deputy of Acting Governor General of Liang-kuang Lao Ch'ung-kuang in 1859, reported a
foreigner named Sullivan (?) in league with Chinese smugglers at Swatow.

Yü-jui 裕瑞 (d. 1866), Manchu Bordered Blue Bannerman, member
of the Tung-chia clan, had a professional military career. As Manchu
lieutenant general of Canton in 1843, he memorialized the death of I-li-
pu on March 4th. He twice acted as commanding general of Kwangtung.
After the Opium War he was made Tartar General of Fukien, transferred to Chengtu. After serving as governor general of Min-Che and
Szechwan, he was degraded in 1854, but was gradually restored until he
reached the rank of vice-president of the Court of Colonial Affairs in
1859. (33.250.3) CSLC 50.33b.

Yü-k'un 豫堃, Manchu official, was Canton superintendent of customs
(Hoppo) prior to 1841.

YÜ Pao-shun 余保純, acting prefect of Canton in 1841, interviewed
U.S. Consul Delano regarding the possibility of reopening Canton to
British traders.

YÜ Ssu-i 俞思益, district magistrate of Ling-shui (southeast coast of
Hainan Island), Kwangtung, was delegated to inaugurate the new Customs
House at Swatow in 1860.

Yü-to 裕鐸, Manchu official, acting financial commissioner of Fukien in 1860, formerly <u>tao-t'ai</u> of T'ai-wan (Formosa), reported on ports of the island suitable for foreign trade.

YÜAN Chia-san 袁甲三 (1806-1863), native of Hsiang-cheng, Honan, <u>chin-shih</u> of 1835, gained a reputation as a forthright and farsighted official. From 1853 he was active in organizing Chinese forces in Anhwei against the Taipings. In 1859 he was made imperial commissioner for military affairs in Anhwei and memorialized, December 15, 1860, on the advisability of using American and Russian aid. He fought desperately to recover his province from the Taipings and died in the field. His nephew (by adoption) was Yüan Shih-k'ai. (33.161.2) ECCP 2.949.

YÜAN Hsi-tsu 袁希祖 (1809-1861), native of Han-yang, Hupeh, <u>chin-shih</u> of 1847 and Hanlin academician, was acting junior vice-president of the Board of Revenue, sub-chancellor of the Grand Secretariat in 1860, when he memorialized on Chinese foreign policy. He belonged to the "war party," and when Harry Parkes and his party were captured, he urged that they be killed in order to intimidate and defy the British. (33.428.5b) CSLC 41.43a.

YÜN Shih-lin 惲世臨 (1815-1871), native of Yang-hu, Kiangsu, <u>chin-shih</u> of 1845, and Hanlin academician, established a reputation as an honest administrator. He was appointed Shansi circuit censor and memorialized, June 12, 1858, on the barbarian menace and the necessity of keeping them out of Peking by military force. Later, as magistrate of Changsha, he assisted Tseng Kuo-fan in raising military supplies. He eventually became governor of Hunan but was removed for raising the tax on salt. (33.325.1) PCCP 27.7b.

GLOSSARY OF FOREIGN NAMES WITH CHINESE
EQUIVALENTS AND TRANSLITERATIONS

GLOSSARY OF FOREIGN NAMES WITH CHINESE
EQUIVALENTS AND TRANSLITERATIONS

A-li-kuo, see Alcock.

A-t'u-t'u-li, see Ottoman Turks.

AFRICA 非亞.

ALCOCK 亞刺國, 阿刺國, Rutherford B. (1809-1897) was the first
regularly appointed British consul at Amoy, 1845.

AMERICA 咪唎堅, 咪國, 美國, 亞墨理駕, 美理駕, 亞美理加,
亞國, 大雅美理賀.

AMERICAN BARBARIANS 咪夷.

AMERIGO 亞墨理哥, Vespucius, the discoverer of America.

ARMSTRONG 俺師大郎, Commodore James, U. S. N., commanded
the Asiatic Squadron in 1856.

ATLANTIC OCEAN 壓瀾的海, 大西洋.

AUSTRIA 雙鷹國.

BALL (?) 伯理, an unidentified American who applied in 1842 for
employment in astronomy and mathematics at the Chinese court.

BALLUSECK 巴氏, aide-de-camp to Ignatieff.

BARNES 巴爾那斯, David 達匪特, one of a party of four American adventurers who landed in Korea and were transferred via Peking
to Shanghai in 1855.

BELGIUM 甚波立國.

BENGAL 嗑咖啦.

BETTLEHEIM 帕憶吟, Reverend B. J., was an English Protestant
missionary on Okinawa, 1846-1854.

BIDDLE 嗶咡, Commodore James, U. S. N., was in command of the
Asiatic squadron in 1845-1846.

763

BOMBAY 望邁.

BONHAM 哎嗡, Sir Samuel George (d. 1863), was British superintendent of trade and governor of Hong Kong, 1848-1854.

BOURBOULON 咘爾咘隆, 普布倫, Alphonse de (b. 1809), was
French minister to China, 1851-1859.

BOWRING 咆吟, Sir John (1792-1872), was British superintendent of
trade and governor of Hong Kong, 1854-1859.

BRAILEY 巴拉里, Edward A. 頟都瓦爾特, one of a party of
four American adventurers who landed in Korea and were transferred
via Peking to Shanghai in 1855.

BRIDGMAN 嘿咟哎, Reverend Elijah C. (1801-1861), was an
American Board missionary to China and Chinese secretary to Cushing,
1844.

BRUCE 嗜嚕斯, Frederick William Adolphus (1814-1867), brother
of Lord Elgin, was envoy to China in 1859 and again in 1861-1865.

BUCHANAN 布駕南, James 雅各, President of the United States,
1857-1861.

BURMA 緬甸.

CAMBODIA (?) 噆啵哎國.

CASS 駕士, Lewis 呂士, Secretary of State in 1858.

CÉCILLE 吐嗯喇, 則濟勒, 嘝哂嗊, Captain, commanding the
French warship Érigone at Macao in 1841-1842.

CHALLAYÉ 吵喱, Charles Alexandre, attaché of the French consulate at Manila, was made consul at Canton in 1840.

CHAPDELAINE 馬神父, Auguste, martyred abbé of the Missions
Etrangères, 1856.

Che-erh, see Childs.

Che-shih-mo-ko-shen 擇時莫格甚, transliteration of the name of
an unidentified British prisoner of war at Ta-ku in 1859.

Chen-sheng-i, see Jancigny.

Chen-shih-erh, see Jancigny.

Cheng-t'ung-ling, see president.

Chi-li-pu, see Gribble.

Chia-ni, see Kearny.

Chia-shih, Lü-shih, see Cass, Lewis.

Chiang-shih-p'o (inverted order), see Powers.

CHILDS, John 者爾 , captain of the American ship, <u>Two Brothers</u>, off Korea in 1855.

Chin-chih-erh, see Jones.

Chin-neng-hsiang, see Griswold.

Ch'in-chen-hsi, see Jenkins.

Ching, see King.

CONTADES 宮達嘰 , French secretary of legation at Shanghai in 1858.

CUSHING 顧嘰 , Caleb (1800-1879), the first United States minister to China, 1844.

DAVIS 嘰哗呀 , Sir John Francis (1795-1890), succeeded Sir Henry Pottinger as British envoy to China, 1842.

DAVIS 德嘰吐 , John W., the second American commissioner to China, 1848-1850.

DELANO 哆喇哪, 哆喇哪 , Edward, of the American firm of Russell and Company, 1841-1846, and United States merchant consul at Canton in 1841.

DENHAM 顛林 , F. A., captain of the English brig <u>Ann</u> wrecked on Formosa, March 11, 1842.

DENMARK 連國, 黃郝, 丹麻爾國, 花旗國 .

DuPONT 杜磐 , Captain S. F., U. S. N., commanded the steam frigate <u>Minnesota</u> in 1860.

E-erh-chin, see Elgin.

ÉDAN 吖噆, M. B., chancellor in the French consulate at Shanghai in 1851.

ELGIN 頤爾唫, Lord, Earl of Elgin and Kincardine, was British high commissioner and plenipotentiary, 1857-1858, and again in 1860.

ELLIOT 義律, Captain Charles, British superintendent of trade at Canton, was active in China, 1834-1842.

ENGLAND 唤國, 英國, 唤咭唎.

ENGLISH BARBARIANS 唤夷.

EUROPE 歐羅巴.

Évariste, see Huc.

EVERETT 噦嘩喋, Alexander H. (d. 1847), first American commissioner to China.

Fei-ya, see Africa.

Fei-erh-wen, see Freeman.

FISH 咹嗯, Dr. M. W., was acting vice consul for the United States at Shanghai, 1856.

"Flowery-flag" Country, see United States, Denmark.

Fo-lan-hsi, see France.

Fo-lang-chi, see France, Franks.

FORBES 福吐, Paul S., United States consul at Canton in 1843.

FORTH-ROUEN 陸英, Alexandre, French representative in China in 1849.

FRANCE 佛郎機, 咈蘭哂, 咈蘭哂.

FRANKS 佛郎機.

FREEMAN 費爾吹, A. L., acting United States vice-consul at Shanghai, 1858.

Fu-shih, see Forbes.

Fu-ssu-tsan 嗌吅饡 , transliteration of the name of an unidentified foreign merchant at Canton in 1858.

GABET 噶嗶 , Lazarist priest arrived in Canton in 1846 from Tibet.

GRIBBLE 記哩哺 , Henry, officiated as acting British consul at Amoy in 1845.

GRISWOLD 金能享 , J. Alsop, United States consul at Shanghai, 1848-1851.

GROS 噶嚕勞士 , 葛爾巴倫 , 噶囉 , Baron, Jean Baptiste Louis (b. 1793), French high commissioner to China, 1857-1860.

GULLY 肐哩 , R., passenger on the English brig Ann, wrecked on Formosa, March 11, 1842.

GUTZLAFF 郭士立 , Karl F. A. (1803-1851), British German-born missionary, was attached to Sir Hugh Gough's staff in 1842.

Ho, see Hope.

Ho-chung-kuo, see United States.

Ho-lan-kuo, see Holland.

Ho-sheng-kuo, see United States.

HOLLAND 荷蘭國 , 賀蘭 .

HOPE 赫 , Sir James (1808-1881), British naval commander in 1859; he did not reach the rank of admiral until 1870.

Hsi-li-wei-shih-lin 喜喇喊士林 , transliteration of the name of an unidentified foreign merchant at Foochow in 1855.

Hsi-ma-mi-ko-li, see Seymour, Sir Michael.

Hsiao-lü-sung, see Philippines.

Hsieh-hsi-erh, see Cécille.

HUC (ÉVARISTE) 喲唎額窪哩斯塔 , Lazarist priest arrived in Canton in 1846 from Tibet.

Hua-ch'i-kuo, see United States, Denmark.

Hua-ling-chia-li 吡吟咖唎, transliteration of the name of an unidentified Catholic priest in China, 1850-1851.

Hua-sheng-tun, see Washington.

Hua-yüeh-han, see Ward.

Huang-ho, see Denmark.

I-hua-yeh, see Everett.

I-ko-na-t'i-yeh-fu, see Ignatieff.

I-li-ta 咿哩吡, transliteration of the name of an unidentified French
Catholic priest in Macao in 1841-1842.

I-lü, see Elliot.

I-na-hsüeh, see Ignatieff.

I-ta-li-ya, see Italy.

I-tan, see Édan.

IGNATIEFF 喝呦嚶, 伊格那揑業福, Nicholas, succeeded
Count Poutiatine as Russian envoy to China.

INDIA 港脚, 五印.

ITALY 意大里亞.

JANCIGNY 嗊哱嚼, 嗊蟩噫, Colonel A. de, French agent in
China, 1841-1842.

Jen-lei-ssu 壬雷斯, transliteration of the name of an unidentified
American officer who aided the Chinese in the manufacture of explosives
at Canton in 1842.

JENKINS 秦鎮西, F. H. B., acting American vice-consul at
Shanghai, served as interpreter with Ward in 1858.

JESUS 耶蘇.

JONES 金執爾, Caleb, United States consul at Foochow from 1854.

Jui-kuo, see Sweden.

Kang-hsi, see India.

KELSEY 克勒塞, Melville 減勒匪勒, one of a party of four American adventurers who landed in Korea and were transferred via Peking to Shanghai in 1855.

KEARNY 咖呢, Commodore Lawrence, U. S. N. (1789-1868), in command of the Asiatic Squadron, 1840-1842.

KING 喀喨, 喨, Edward, United States vice-consul, acting for P. W. Snow at Canton in 1843.

KLESKOWSKY 哥士耆, 顧嗯, Count Michel Alexandre (1818-1885), native of Galicia, a naturalized French citizen attached to the French legation as interpreter in 1854.

Ko-erh-pa-lun, see Gros, Baron.

Ko-lo, see Gros.

Ko-li, see Gully.

Ko-mo-lao-shih, see Gros.

Ko-pi, see Gabet.

Ko-shih-ch'i, see Kleskowsky.

K'o-ching, see King.

K'o-lo-sai, Mieh-lo-fei-lo, see Kelsey, Melville.

K'o-tan-chin-erh, see O'Donnell.

Ku-sheng, see Cushing.

Ku-ssu, see Kleskowsky.

Kung-ta-te, see Contades.

K'ung-ch'üan-te-fu-pien-fei-mo 吼吠噂哺噼嘍嚜, transliteration of the name of an unidentified foreigner in Shanghai in 1858.

Kuo-shih-li, see Gutzlaff.

La-ch'i-ni, see Lagrené.

La-e-erh 嘞呃爾, transliteration of the name of an unidentified French naval officer in China in 1855.

La-o-ni, see Lagrené.

La-ti-meng-tung, see Ratti-Menton.

LAGRENÉ 喇吃呢, 㖠嘢呃, Thomas de, French envoy to China in 1844.

LAY 李太郭, George Tradescant (d. 1845), first British consul at Foochow.

LAY 李太國, 哮嗉喎, Horatio Nelson, son of George Tradescant Lay, was active in China from 1849 to 1864.

Li-mei 哮嗨, transliteration of the name of an unidentified foreign translator in Shanghai in 1858.

Li-t'ai-kuo, see Lay, George Tradescant and Horatio Nelson.

Lieh-t'o, see Reed.

Lieh-wei-lien, see Reed.

Lien-kuo, see Denmark.

Lo-ch'i-chen 羅啟楨, transliteration of the name of an unidentified Catholic priest in China in 1848.

Lo-po-sun, see Robinson.

Lo-pu-t'an, see Thom, Robert.

Lü-sung, see Luzon, also Spain.

Lu-ying, see Forth-Rouen.

Luzon (Philippines) 呂宋.

Ma-hui, see Murphy.

Ma-la-hua, see opium.

Ma-li-sun, see Morrison.

Ma-sha-li, see Marshall.

Ma-shen-fu, see Chapdelaine.

Ma-ssu-t'e-erh, T'o-mo-ssu, see McQuire, Thomas.

MADIERA (?) 彌爹喇.

Mao-er-tun, see Moreton.

MARQUES 梅德爾 , secretary in the French legation in 1859.

MARSHALL 馬沙利 , Humphrey, third American commissioner to China, 1852-1854.

MARTIN 丁韙良 , William Alexander Parsons (1827-1916), American missionary, sinologist, and Chinese secretary to Ward in 1859.

McCARTEE 麥嘉諦 , Dr. D. B., Presbyterian medical missionary stationed at Ningpo.

McQUIRE 馬斯特爾 , Thomas 托默斯 , one of a party of four American adventurers who landed in Korea and were transferred via Peking to Shanghai in 1855.

McLANE 麥連 , Robert M. 勒畢唵 , fourth American commissioner to China, 1853-1854.

MEADOWS, Thomas Taylor 密迪樂 , British interpreter in China.

MEDHURST 麥華陀 , Walter Henry (1796-1857), English missionary and sinologist in China.

Mei-erh-teng, see Méritens.

Mei-kuo, see America.

Mei-li-chia, see America.

Mei-te-erh, see Marques.

Meng-chia-la, see Bengal.

Meng-te 嗑噦, transliteration of the name of an unidentified Catholic priest in China in 1851.

Meng-tou-pan, see Montaubon.

MÉRITENS 梅爾登, member of the French legation at Shanghai in 1859.

MEXICO 墨息哥.

Mi-i, see American barbarians.

Mi-kuo, see America.

Mi-li-chien, see America.

Mi-ti-lo, see Meadows.

Mien-hsün, see Wilson.

Mien-tien, see Burma.

Min-t'i-ni 嗷嚕呢, transliteration of the name of an unidentified French consular official at Shanghai in 1858.

Ming-ch'ang 明常, transliteration of the name of an unidentified Russian interpreter in China, 1858-1860.

Mo-chia-ti, see McCartee.

Mo-hsi-ko, see Mexico.

Mo-hua-t'o, see Medhurst.

Mo-li 摩利, transliteration of an unidentified place name.

Mo-lien, Lo-pi-yen, see McLane, Robert M.

Montaubon 孟斗班, General Cousin de, Comte de Palikao, in command of French forces in China in 1860, under Baron Gros.

MORETON 冒耳亂, G. H., replaced Bettleheim as English Protestant missionary on Okinawa in 1854.

MORRISON 嗎嚕遜, Reverend Robert (1782-1834), English Protestant missionary to China, served as interpreter and Chinese secretary for the East India Company and the British government.

Mu-li-fei-yüeh-fu, see Muraviev.

MURAVIEV 木哩斐岳幅 , Count Amurski, Russian governor of Eastern Siberia in 1860-1861.

MURPHY 馬輝, Robert C., United States consul at Shanghai, 1853-1857.

Nan-huai-jen, see Verbiest.

NEWMAN 怒文, F., seacunnie (steersman or quartermaster) on the English brig Ann, wrecked on Formosa, March 11, 1842.

Ni-chi-li-li 呢嗟哩唎, transliteration of the name of an unidentified Catholic priest in China, 1850-1851.

Nu-wen, see Newman.

O'DONNELL 啊呀嗏嚹, unidentified American naval officer in China with Cushing in 1844.

O-li-fan, see Oliphant.

O-lo-ssu, see Russia.

OLIPHANT 俄裡範, Laurence (b. 1859), secretary to Lord Elgin.

OPIUM (MALWA) 嗎喇嘩, 鴉片.

OTTOMAN TURKS 阿土突利.

Ou-lo-pa, see Europe.

Ou-lo-ssu, see Russia.

Pa-chia, see Parker (Commodore and Dr. Peter).

Pa-erh-na-ssu, Ta-fei-t'e, see Barnes, David.

Pa-hsia-li, see Parkes, Harry.

Pa-la-li, E-tu-wa-erh-t'e, see Brailey, Edward A.

Pa-la-ti 巴拉第, transliteration of the name of an unidentified Russian ecclesiastic in Peking in 1858.

Pa-shih, see Balluseck.

Pa-t'u 巴圖, transliteration of the name of an unidentified Russian interpreter at Ta-ku in 1860.

PACIFIC OCEAN 太平洋.

Pao-ha-tan, see Powhatan.

Pao-ling, see Bowring.

PARKER 吧嚀, Commodore Foxhall A., U. S. N., commanding the East India Squadron in 1844.

PARKER 吧嚀, 咱嚀, Dr. Peter 褌德 (1804-1888), American medical missionary in China and later United States commissioner to China.

PARKES, Harry 吧嘎嘈 (1828-1885), Chinese linguist and British civil servant in China, 1844-1865.

PARTRIDGE 撤力撤, D., third officer on the English brig Ann, wrecked on Formosa, March 11, 1842.

Pei-chih-wen, see Bridgman.

PERU 鼻盧.

PHILIPPINES 小呂宋.

Pi-erh, see Biddle.

Pi-lu, see Peru.

Pi-tieh-la, see Madiera.

P'ieh-li-p'ieh, see Partridge.

Po-chia, Pei-te, see Parker, Peter.

Po-li, see Ball.

Po-li-hsi-t'ien-te, see president.

Po-na 波吶, transliteration of the name of an unidentified American ship captain at Ningpo in 1842.

Po-te-ling, see Bettleheim.

PORTUGAL 大西洋.

POTTINGER 噗鼎喳, Sir Henry, succeeded Captain Elliot in command of British forces in China and negotiated the Treaty of Nanking in 1842.

POUTIATINE 普提雅廷. Count Euphemius, Russian envoy to China, 1858.

POWERS, John 蔣什坡, Canadian ("American") prisoner of war taken by the Chinese from the British forces at Ta-ku, 1859.

POWHATAN 寶哈旦, United States warship which brought Ward to China in 1859.

PRESIDENT 正統領, 伯理璽天德.

PRUSSIA 單鷹國.

Pu-chia-nan, Ya-ko, see Buchanan, James.

Pu-erh pu lung, see Bourboulon.

P'u-lu-ssu, see Bruce.

P'u-pu-lun, see Bourboulon.

P'u-t'i-ya-t'ing, see Poutiatine.

P'u-ting-ch'a, see Pottinger.

RATTI-MENTON 啦哋嚎咚, Count de, succeeded Challayé as French consul in China.

REED 唎嘟嘛, 唎𠸄, William B., United States minister to China, 1857-1858.

ROBINSON 囉啪遜, British consul at Shanghai in 1858.

RUSSIA 俄羅斯, 鄂羅斯.

Sa-na-t'e, see Senate.

SCHALL 湯若望, Jean Adam, von Bell (1591-1666), German Jesuit

missionary in China.

SENATE 薩納特 , Russian state council.

SEYMOUR, Sir Michael 呞嗎嚛咚哩 (1802-1887), in command of British naval forces in China, 1855-1864.

Sha-li, see Challayé.

Sha-li-yün 沙黎雲 , transliteration of the name of an unidentified foreigner at Swatow in 1858; cf., Su-li-wan.

She-fei (inverted order), see Fish.

Shen-pi-li-kuo, see Cambodia.

Shen-po-li-kuo, see Belgium.

Shih-mi-wei, see Smith.

Shih-mi-wei-liang, see Smith.

Shih-ssu-li, see Cécille.

Shih-ta-chih, see Sturgis.

Shih-ta-ling, see Sterling.

Shih-t'ing-po-erh 嗖廷啪呪 , transliteration of the name of an unidentified American consular official in Shanghai in 1858, possibly W. L. G. Smith.

Shuang-ying-kuo, see Austria.

Shui-kuo, see Sweden.

SMITH 士覓威良 , 士覓威 , W. L. G., United States consul at Shanghai, 1858-1859.

SPAIN 大呂宋 , 呂宋 .

STRIBLING 司百齡 , C. K., Flag Officer, U. S. N., acting United States minister in 1860.

Ssu-pai-ling, see Stribling.

STERLING 吐叮吟, unidentified British naval officer on the China coast in 1843, probably in charge of coastal surveys, and subsequently mentioned in 1854.

STURGIS 吐嗹唅, R. S., American merchant, member of Russell and Company, in Canton in 1857.

Su-li-wan 穌里完, transliteration of the name of an unidentified Englishman at Swatow in 1859; cf., Sha-li-yün.

SWEDEN 嚧國, 瑞國.

Ta, see Tattnall.

Ta-hsi-yang, see Atlantic Ocean, Portugal.

Ta-lü-sung, see Spain.

Ta-ya-mei-li-chia, see America.

Ta-ti-nu, see Tattnall.

T'ai-chen-hsi, see Jenkins.

T'ai-p'ing-yang, see Pacific Ocean.

Tan-ma-erh-kuo, see Denmark.

Tan-ying-kuo, see Prussia.

T'ang-jo-wang, see Schall.

TATTNALL 達, 達底孥, Commodore Jōsiah, U. S. N., in command of the Asiatic Squadron in 1859.

Te-i-shih 德巳士, transliteration of the name of an unidentified British officer at Ningpo in 1843, apparently engaged in coastal survey work.

Te-pi-shih, see Davis, John Francis.

Te-wei-shih, see Davis, John W.

THOM, Robert 羅布坦 (1807-1846), interpreter and student of Chinese, British consul at Ningpo and attached to Sir Hugh Gough's staff in 1842.

Ti-hsi-shih 的赊士, transliteration of an unidentified place name used to locate the United States, which "lies to the west of Ti-hsi-shih."

Tien-lin, see Denham.

Tien-tien-ti 喋嗔的, transliteration of the name of an unidentified foreign merchant in Canton in 1858.

Ting-wei-liang, see Martin.

To-la-na, see Delano.

To-li-na, see Delano.

Tse-chi-lo, see Cécille.

Tu-p'an, see DuPont.

T'u-shih, 土士, transliteration of the name of an unidentified Danish ship captain, who visited Ting-hai in 1846.

T'u-ta-chih, see Sturgis.

UNITED STATES (Flowery Flag Country) 花旗國, 合眾國, 合省國.

VERBIEST 南懷仁, Ferdinand (1623-1688), Belgian Jesuit missionary in China.

WADE, Thomas 威妥瑪 (1818-1895), British vice consul at Shanghai in 1854.

Wang-mai, see Bombay.

WARD, John 華約翰, United States minister to China, 1859-1861.

WASHINGTON 嘩盛頓.

WEBSTER 喊咟吐唯, Daniel Fletcher (1818-1862), son of Secretary of State Daniel Webster, was one of Cushing's secretaries in China in 1844.

Wei-li-pa 喊喱吧, transliteration of an unidentified British title.

Wei-liang-shih, see Williams, O. D.

Wei-lien-shih, see Williams, S. Wells.

Wei-po-shih-wei, see Webster.

Wei-shih-pi 未氏碧, transliteration of the name of an unidentified British officer at Ningpo in 1843, apparently engaged in coastal survey work.

Wei-t'o-ma, see Wade, Thomas.

Wen-han, see Bonham.

WILLIAMS 韋良士, O. D., acting United States consul at Hankow, 1861.

WILLIAMS 衛廉士, S. Wells (1812-1884), American missionary, sinologist, and Chinese secretary to Ward, 1859-1861.

WILSON 勉詢, E., seacunnie (steersman or quartermaster) on the English brig Ann wrecked on Formosa, March 11, 1842.

WOLCOTT 烏兇吉, Henry 軒理 G. 知, was United States vice-consul at Ningpo in 1844.

Wu-erh-chi, Han-li Chih, see Wolcott, Henry G.

Wu-yin, see India.

Ya-lan-ti-h'ai, see Atlantic Ocean.

Ya-kuo, see America.

Ya-li-kuo, see Alcock.

Ya-mei-li-chia, see America.

Ya-mo-li-chia, see America.

Ya-mo-li-ko, see Amerigo.

Ya-p'ien, see opium.

Ya-shui-ming 雅水明, transliteration of the name of an unidentified Catholic priest in China in 1855.

Yeh-su, see Jesus.

Yen-shih-ta-lang, see Armstrong.

Ying-chi-li, see England.

Ying-i, see English barbarians.

Ying-kuo, see England.

Yü-che 吒嘘, transliteration of the name of an unidentified French Catholic priest in Macao in 1841-1842.

Yüeh-tse-e-wa-li-ssu-t'a, see Huc (Évariste).

GLOSSARY OF GEOGRAPHICAL NAMES
WITH DESCRIPTIVE NOTES

An-ch'ing 安慶 , p. o. spelling Anking, Anhwei, important inland port city, 150 miles up the Yangtze from Nanking, one-time capital of Anhwei province, is now in Huai-ning-hsien.

Ch'a-p'u 乍浦 , P'ing-hu-hsien, Chekiang, small port midway between Shanghai and Hangchow, was a port of call for European ships in the Yüan dynasty and is mentioned by Marco Polo. It became a walled city during the Ming. It has a good natural harbor but was gradually superseded by Shanghai during the 19th century.

Chang-chia-k'ou 張家口 , or Kalgan, Chang-pei-hsien, formerly in Chihli province, now in Chahar, lies just outside the Great Wall, some one hundred miles northwest of Peiping.

Chang-Ch'üan 漳泉 , Fukien, i. e., Chang-chou and Ch'üan-chou prefectures (p. o. spellings, Changchowfu and Chuanchowfu), on the eastern seaboard of Fukien. Chang-chou is some fifteen miles inland from the treaty port of Amoy.

Chang-hua 彰化 , Formosa, Japanese spelling, Shoka, is a district on the west coast of the island, directly opposite Amoy, in T'ai-wan prefecture.

Ch'ang-chou 常州 , p. o. spelling Changchowfu, prefectural city on the Grand Canal, is midway between Chinkiang and Soochow. It is now called Wu-chin (武進), p. o. spelling, Wutsin.

Ch'ang-sha 長沙 , p. o. spelling Changsha, provincial capital of Hunan, is a treaty port on the Hsiang River (p. o. spelling, Siang Kiang), now on the Canton-Hankow railway line.

Ch'ang-shan 常山 , Chekiang, hsien city in the extreme western part of the province, is noted for the manufacture of paper.

Ch'ang-te 常德 , Hunan, p. o. spelling Changteh, prefectural city on the Yüan River and west of Tungting Lake, is a river and canal junction and the communications hub of eight provinces. It lies about 100 miles northwest of Changsha.

Chao-pao Shan 招寶山 , Chekiang, small hill half a mile northeast of Chen-hai (Chinhai), which in turn is fifteen miles northeast of Ningpo and constitutes the fort protecting the entrance to the port. Chao-pao Shan derives its name "Gather Treasure Hill" from the fact that tribute ships anchored there with their treasure destined for the emperor of China.

Ch'ao-chou 潮州 , Kwangtung, prefectural city, twenty miles north and inland from the treaty port of Swatow.

Chen-chiang 鎮江 , Kiangsu, p.o. spelling Chinkiang, prefectural city on the Yangtze about fifty miles below Nanking, at the point where the Grand Canal crosses the Yangtze River, is a strategic and commercial city, now on the rail line between Nanking and Shanghai.

Chen-hai 鎮海 , Chekiang, p.o. spelling Chinhai, fort at the mouth of the Yangtze River some fifteen miles northeast of Ningpo.

Ch'en-ts'un 陳村 , p.o. spelling Chongtsun, on local maps, Chanchuen, Kwangtung, is a small village in Shun-te-hsien, ten miles southwest of Whampoa.

Ch'eng-t'ou-ku 蟶頭沽 , Hopei, village north of Pei-t'ang.

Cheng-tzu-chuang 涅子莊 , Hopei, village in the vicinity of Ta-ku.

Chi-hsin-t'an 雞心灘 , Hopei, sand or mud bank outside Ta-ku bar at the entrance to Tientsin.

Ch'i-k'ou 祁口 , Hopei, p.o. spelling Chikow, port at mouth of Shih-pai River some forty miles south of Ta-ku, was a battalion (ying 營) garrison post during the Ch'ing dynasty.

Chia-ting 嘉定 , p.o. spelling Kiatinghsien, Kiangsu, district city fifteen miles northeast of Shanghai, ten miles west of Woosung.

Chia-ying-chou 嘉應州 , p.o. spelling Kaying, Kwangtung, department city in the extreme northeastern part of the province, some eighty miles northeast of Swatow, now in Mei-hsien.

Chiang-ning 江寧 , Kiangsu, alternate name for Nanking.

Chiang-p'u 江浦 , p.o. spelling Kiangpu, Kiangsu, district city across the Yangtze River from Nanking.

Chiao-ho 交河 , p.o. spelling Kiaoho, Chihli (Hopei), district city one hundred miles southwest of Tientsin, is west of the Grand Canal and now on the Tientsin-Pukow railway line.

Chiao-shan 焦山 , Kiangsu, island and fortress in the Yangtze River, some three miles east of Chinkiang, is a strategic point in the river approach to Nanking.

Chien-k'o 尖客, Kwangsi, village in Hsi-lin-hsin, is located in the extreme western part of the province, two hundred miles northwest of Nanning and more than six hundred miles interior from Canton.

Chien-sha-tsui 尖沙嘴 , Kwangtung, cove opposite Hong Kong, now in Kowloon territory.

Chin-chou 金州, p.o. spelling Kinchow, Manchuria, district city on the tip of the Liaotung peninusla across a narrow strait from Dairen, is now on the South Manchurian railway line.

Chin-i 鄞邑 , Chekiang, southeast of Ningpo, is the present Chin-hsien.

Ch'in-chou 欽州, Kwangtung, present Ling-shan-hsien at the extreme southwest tip of the province, is northwest of the French leasehold of Kwangchow Wan and directly north of the port of Pakhoi.

Ch'in-huang-tao 秦皇島 , p.o. spelling Chinwangtao, Hopei, Lin-yü-hsien. seaport just inside the Great Wall near Shanhaikwan, is on the present Peking-Mukden railway line, some one hundred seventy-five miles north and east of Tientsin.

Ching-hai 靜海, p.o. spelling Tsinghaihsien, Hopei, district city twenty-five miles south and east of Tientsin, is now on the Tientsin-Pukow railway line.

Ching-k'ou 京口 , Kiangsu, another name for Chen-chiang (Chinkiang), is downstream some fifty miles from Nanking.

Ch'ing-chiang 清江 , (1) Kiangsi, district city in Linkiang prefecture, south of Nanchang; (2) vicinity of Hsü-chou (Suchow) on the Shantung-Kiangsu border, near the intersection of the Grand Canal and the Yellow River.

Ch'ing-ho 清河 , Hopei, district city in the present Ta-ming prefecture, is located in the extreme southern tip of Hopei.

Ch'ing-hsien 青縣 , p.o. spelling Tsinghsien, Hopei, district city fifty miles south of Tientsin.

Ch'ing-yüan 清遠 , Kwangtung, district in Kuang-chou, i.e., Canton, prefecture.

Chiu-chou 九州, Kwangtung, spelled Chichau on local maps, is an anchorage in a group of islands of the same name located in the mouth of the Canton or Pearl River about midway between Macao and Hong Kong.

Ch'iung-chou 瓊州, p.o. spelling Kiungchow, Kwangtung, is the prefectural city on Hainan Island, off the southeast coast of China but administratively a part of Kwangtung province. Ch'iung-chou, the largest city and port on the island, is on the north coast, facing Kwangchow Wan.

Chou-chih 盩厔, p.o. spelling Chowchih, district city on the Wei River some forty miles west of Sian, the provincial capital, is located in south central Shensi.

Chou-shan 舟山, p.o. spelling Chusan, Ting-hai-hsien, Chekiang, about one hundred miles south of Shanghai and directly east of Hangchow, is the largest of a group of strategically important islands, occupied by England during the Opium War and evacuated after the Treaty of Nanking in 1842.

Chu-shan-men 竹山門, Chekiang, is an unidentified village in the vicinity of Tinghai on Chusan Island.

Ch'ü-chou 衢州, p.o. spelling Chuchowfu, prefectural city in west central Chekiang, is on the Ch'ü River.

Ch'üan-chou 泉州, p.o. spelling Chwanchowfu, Fukien, is a port and former prefectural city, one hundred miles north of Amoy.

Ch'uan-sha 川沙, p.o. spelling Chwansha, is a sub-prefectural (t'ing) city, ten miles east of Shanghai in Kiangsu province.

Ch'ui-shan 圌山 Barrier, Kiangsu, an important defense position up-river from Chinkiang, is located at a narrow rapids in the Yangtze River.

Chün-liang-ch'eng 軍糧城, Hopei, is located in the southwestern part of Ning-ho-hsien near Pei-t'ang; originally a military grain storehouse in the Yüan (Mongol) dynasty, in Ch'ing times it was made a military colony.

Ch'ung-an 崇安, district city in Chien-ning prefecture (Kienningfu), is located in the northern tip of Fukien province.

Ch'ung-ming 崇明, p.o. spelling Tsungming, is a district city on a large delta-like island of the same name in the mouth of the Yangtze River, north of Woosung and Shanghai.

Feng-huang-kang 鳳凰岡, probably refers to Feng-huang-hsien on the Liaotung Peninsula, Manchuria, where Manchu Banner troops were trained.

Fo-shan 佛山, p.o. spelling Fatshan, sub-prefectural (t'ing) city, ten miles southwest of Canton, is now on the Canton-Samshui railway line.

Fu-shan 福山, Shantung, is a district city eight miles west of Chefoo, Tengchow prefecture.

Hai-chu-ssu 海珠寺, Kwangtung, a small island in the Canton or Pearl River, opposite the Canton Bund, was originally a Chinese fort and temple, now a public park of Canton, connected by bridge to the Bund. In early Western books, it is referred to as "Dutch Folly."

Hai-tion 海淀, Hupei, village four miles west of Peiping (Peking) and site of Yenching University, was formerly the barracks of the Manchu Banner forces, near the old Summer Palace.

Han-yang 漢陽, Hupeh, prefectural city, is the western-most of the "Three Han" cities, Hanyang, Hankow, and Wuchang, located at the junction of the Yangtze and Han Rivers. This is now the center of China's heavy industries.

Hang-ch'eng 杭城, another name for Hangchow, capital and treaty port of Chekiang.

Heng-tang 橫檔, Kwangtung, is a mountainous island in the Canton River estuary, southeast of Hu-men (Bocca Tigris), which formerly was the site of a river fort and anchorage.

Ho-chien 河間, p.o. spelling Hokienfu, former prefectural, now a hsien city, is located some sixty miles southwest of Tientsin.

Ho-chou 和州, Anhwei, former department (chou), now a hsien city, is located forty-five miles up the Yangtze from Nanking.

Ho-nan 河南 Island, local spelling, Honam, Kwangtung, lies in the Pearl River opposite the Canton Bund and Customs House. It is now a suburb of Canton City and the site of Lingnan University.

Hsi-ku 西固 , Kwangtung, island fort in the Canton or Pearl River between Whampoa and Canton.

Hsi-lin 西林, p.o. spelling Silin, district city in the extreme west tip of Kwangsi.

Hsiang-ho 香河 , p.o. spelling Sianghohsien, district city twenty miles southwest of Tungchow, thirty-five miles east and south of Peiping (Peking) in Hopei.

Hsiang-shan 香山, now Chung-shan, Kwangtung, district adjoining Macao, is the birthplace of Dr. Sun Yat-sen and renamed in his honor.

Hsin-an 新安, p.o. spelling Sinan, Kwangtung, a small town on the east shore of the Canton or Pearl River estuary between Hong Kong and Canton and opposite Lintin Island, is now just outside British New Territory and connected by a branch railway line with Kowloon.

Hsin-ch'eng 新城, p.o. spelling Sincheng, Hopei, district city formerly in Paoting prefecture, is located to the east of the Peiping-Pukow railway line some fifty miles south of Peiping (Peking).

Hsin-ho 新河, small village in Ning-ho-hsien, Hopei, north of Taku and south of Pei-t'ang in the Tientsin area.

Hsing-Ch'üan-Yung 興泉永 , former circuit (tao) in southern Fukien, comprising Hsing-hua 興化 prefecture, Ch'üan-chou 泉州 prefecture, and Yung-ch'un 永春 department; it included the treaty port of Amoy within its boundaries.

Hsü-chou 徐州 , p.o. spellings Suchow and Suchowfu, former prefectural city in northern Kiangsu near the Shantung border, near the junction of the Grand Canal and the Yellow River, is now on the Peiping-Pukow railway line as well as the east-west or Lung-Hai line.

Hsüan-hua 宣化, p.o. spelling Swanhwafu, Hopei, former prefectural, now district, city about one hundred seventy-five miles northwest of Peiping and twenty miles southeast of Kalgan, is now located located on the Peiping-Suiyuan railway line.

Hu-chou 湖州, p.o. spelling Huchowfu, former prefectural, now district, city, just south of Tai Lake in the extreme northern part of Chekiang, forty-five miles north of Hangchow.

Hu-lang 虎狼, Chekiang, unidentified river barrier, is located to the east of Ningpo.

Hu-men 虎門, variously referred to in Western writings as Bocca Tigris, the Bogue, Tiger Gate, and Fumen, is a fort at the mouth of the Canton or Pearl River, Kwangtung, midway between Canton, Macao, and Hong Kong. Hu-men was a point of controversy throughout the Sino-British struggle, 1839-1842, and the site of the signing of the supplementary treaty with England in 1843.

Hu-wei 滬尾 is an anchorage in T'ai-pei, Japanese spelling, Taihoku, northern city and port, as well as administrative capital of Formosa (Taiwan).

Huai-Yang 淮揚, former circuit (tao) comprising Huai-an 淮安 and Yang-chou 揚州 prefectures, thirteen hsien in Kiangsu province, north of Nanking.

Huan-hao 環壕, unidentified fort in the vicinity of Ta-ku, Hopei.

Huang-p'u 黃浦, spelled Whampoa in Western accounts, is the port of Canton, nine miles down-river from the city, in P'an-yü-hsien, Kwangtung.

Huang-p'u-wei 黃浦尾, unidentified anchorage in the Canton or Pearl River, Kwangtung, probably in the vicinity of Whampoa.

Hui-Ch'ao-Chia 惠潮嘉, former circuit (tao) comprising Hui-chou 惠州 -fu, Ch'ao-chou 潮州 -fu, Chia-ying 嘉應 -chou, and Fo-kang 佛岡 -t'ing, in eastern Kwangtung, included the treaty port of Swatow within its jurisdiction.

Hui-chou 惠州, p.o. spelling Waichow, prefectural city seventy-five miles east of Canton, Kwangtung, was in the former Hui-Ch'ao-Chia circuit.

Hung Hu 洪湖, lake in southern Hupeh province, just north of Tung-ting Lake in northern Hunan.

Hung-tan-ch'uan 紅單船, unidentified place on the Yangtze River associated with Nanking and Chinkiang.

Jen-hua 仁化, p.o. spelling Yanfa, is a district city in Shao-chou (Shiuchow) prefecture, Ling-Nan circuit, in the extreme northern part of Kwangtung.

Jung-ch'eng 榮成, district city on the eastern tip of Shantung peninsula, is about fifteen miles east of Wei-hai-wei.

K'ai-chou 開州 , department (chou) city in the southern panhandle of Hopei, some three hundred miles south of Peiping.

Kalgan, see Chang-chia-k'ou.

Kao-sha-ling 高沙嶺 , unidentified place in the Tientsin-Ta-ku area, Hopei.

Kiakhta 恰克圖 , Chinese spelling, Ho-k'o-t'u, formerly a part of Outer Mongolia, now in the U.S.S.R. on the Mongolian frontier, is located south of Lake Baikal, seventy-five miles north of Urga. After Kiakhta was ceded to Russia in 1792, Chinese merchants established Mai-mai-ch'eng on the south side of the frontier to carry on trade with Russia.

Ko-ku 葛沽 , army camp (ying 營) was located twenty-four miles southeast of Tientsin, Hopei.

Ku-lang-hsü 鼓浪嶼 , p.o. spelling Kulangsu, Fukien, is a small island forming one side of the inner harbor of Amoy; the British consulate was established here in 1844, and Kulangsu later became the foreign residential quarter for Amoy.

K'u-lun 庫倫 , Urga, capital city of Outer Mongolia, some five hundred miles northwest of Peiping.

Kuang-feng 廣豐 , district city in the extreme eastern tip of Kiangsi, some one hundred sixty miles east of Nanchang.

Kuang-p'ing-fu 廣平府 , prefectural city in the southern panhandle of Hopei, two hundred fifty miles south of Peiping, now lies to the east of the Peiping-Pukow railway line.

Kuei-chiang 龜江 , unidentified river fort in the Canton-Whampoa area, Kwangtung.

Kuei-hua 歸化 , generally known as Kuei-hua-ch'eng, is a sub-prefectural city in northwest Shansi, one hundred miles north and west of Ta-t'ung.

Kua-chou 瓜州 , Yangchow prefecture, Kiangsu, is located just across the Yangtze River from Chinkiang.

K'un-shan 崑山 , district city in Kiangsu province, forty miles west of Shanghai, is now on the railway line between Shanghai and Nanking.

Lao-chün-t'ang 老居堂 , hostel in Peiping where Ward stayed in 1859, is located on the Hutung of the same name paralleling Ch'ao-yang Men Street and just inside the eastern city gate, Ch'ao-yang Men. It is in the eastern so-called Tartar City, outside the Forbidden City.

Li-ching 利津 , p.o. spelling Litsinghsien, district city in northern Shantung province, is on the north channel of the Yellow River near its mouth on the Gulf of Chihli.

Lieh-te 獵得 , unidentified place in Kwangtung province, is probably in the general Canton area.

Lin-yü 臨楡 , an alternate name for Shanhaikwan, Yung-p'ing prefecture, Hopei, where the Great Wall comes down to the sea near the Hopei-Liaoning border.

Ling-shui 陵水 , district city, Kiungchow prefecture, Kwangtung, is located on the southeast coast of the island of Hainan, off the southeast coast of China.

Ling-yün 凌雲 , district city, Szecheng prefecture, is located in western Kwangsi.

Liu-ch'iu 琉球 , Western spelling, Loochoo, Japanese spelling, Ryukyu, is an island chain across the East China Sea from Chekiang province, the principal island of which is Okinawa.

Liu-ho 六合 , p.o. spelling Luho, district city in Kiangning prefecture, Kiangsu, is located across the Yangtze River, twenty miles north of Nanking.

Lü-chü-ho 驢駒河 , unidentified place in Hopei, apparently in the Tientsin and Ta-ku area.

Lu-erh-men 鹿耳門 , harbor entrance near Anping, is located ten miles west of the district city of Tai-wan (Tainan, under the Japanese), on the southwest coast of Formosa.

Lu-t'ai 蘆臺 , garrison town ten miles south of Ningho district city, Hopei, is located about twenty-five miles east of Tientsin and is now on the Peiping-Mukden railway line.

Lu-tzu-kang 鹿仔港 , Chang-hua-hsien, is located in the north-western part of the island of Formosa.

Ma-chia-k'ou 馬家口 , unidentified cove or river entrance south of

Tientsin, Hopei.

Ma-yung 麻涌, unidentified anchorage in the Pearl River below Canton, Kwangtung.

Mei-ling 梅嶺, mountain range and pass on the Kwangtung-Kiangsi border.

Meng-chia 艋舺, local spelling Banka; ssu in San-shui-t'ing, northern Formosa, is located near T'ai-pei (Japanese spelling, Taihoku).

Mi-yün 密雲, district city on the Pei River, fifty miles north of T'ung-chou, just inside the Great Wall, in Hopei.

Miao Islands 廟島, P'eng-lai-hsien 蓬萊縣, island group in the Chihli Strait, is located between Teng-chou-fu, Shantung, and Port Arthur.

Nan-ao 南澳, commonly spelled Namoa, Ch'ao-chou-fu, Kwangtung, is an island off the coast of Kwangtung just east of Swatow.

Nan-hai 南海, Cantonese spelling Namhoi, hsien in Kwangtung, constitutes, with P'an-yü-hsien, the city of Canton.

Nan-hsiung-chou 南雄州, p. o. spelling Namyung, former department, now district, city in the extreme northern part of Kwangtung, sixty miles northeast of Shiuchow and one hundred seventy miles north of Canton.

Nan-Shao-Lien 南韶連, circuit (tao) comprising northern Kwangtung province, is made up of three prefectures, Nan-hsiung (Namyung), Shao-chou (Shiuchow), and Lien-p'ing.

Nan-t'ai 南臺, mountain three miles south of Foochow, Fukien, is used as an alternate or literary name for Foochow; the largest of three suburbs of Foochow and the one in which the foreign residential quarter is located.

Ning-ho 寧河, district city in Hopei, is located forty-five miles northeast of Tientsin and eighty miles southeast of Peiping.

Ning-Shao-T'ai 寧紹台, circuit (tao) comprising Ning-po 寧波 -fu, Shao-hsing 紹興 -fu, and T'ai-chou 台州 -fu, includes the central Fukien coast, the treaty port of Ningpo, and the Chusan archipelago.

Niu-chuang 牛莊, p. o. spelling Newchwang, port in Fengtien province,

Manchuria, is located at the head of the Gulf of Liaotung, northeast of Chinwangtao and north of Dairen and Port Arthur. It is now known as Yingkow.

Pa-ch'ung-shan 八重山 , unidentified island in the Liu-ch'iu or Ryukyu Island chain.

Pa-li-ch'a 八里岔 , port or anchorage in T'an-shui-t'ing, in northern Formosa, is located near modern T'ai-pei (Japanese spelling, Taihoku).

Pai-ho-t'an 白鶴潭 , anchorage in the Canton (Pearl) River, opposite Canton, Kwangtung, is located in the back reach or Macao Passage, facing Honam Island. In Western works it is frequently translated White Goose Tything; the local spelling is Pakhoktung.

P'an-yü 番禺 -hsien, Kwangtung; with Nan-hai-hsien forms the pre-fectural city of Canton.

Pao-shan 寶山 , district city in Kiangsu, is located five or six miles northwest of Woosung, some fifteen miles north of Shanghai.

Pao-ting 保定, capital city of Hopei, eighty miles south of Peiping, is now on the Peiping-Pukow railway line.

Pei-t'ang 北塘 , Ning-ho-hsien, Hopei, is a port at the mouth of the Pei-t'ang River, ten miles north of Ta-ku and thirty-five miles east of Tientsin.

Pei-ts'ang 北倉 , garrison town in Hopei, is located on the Pei River, six miles north of Tientsin.

P'ing-Ch'ing-Ching 平慶涇 , former circuit (tao) comprising P'ing-liang 平凉 -fu, Ch'ing-yang 慶陽 -fu, Ching 涇 independent pre-fecture, Hua-p'ing-ch'uan 花平川 independent sub-prefecture, and Ku-yüan 固原 independent department, is located in eastern Kansu province.

P'u-k'ou 浦口 , p.o. spelling Pukow, district city in Kiangsu province, directly across the Yangtze River from Nanking, is now the terminus of the Tientsin-Pukow railway line.

P'u-ssu 浦司 , unidentified place near Tinghai, on Chusan Island.

San-ch'a-ho 三岔河, unidentified anchorage near Ta-ku, Hopei.

San-chiang-k'ou 三江口 , unidentified anchorage in the vicinity of

Ningpo, Chekiang.

Shao-chih-k'ou 稍直口 , unidentified place in the Tientsin-Ta-ku-area, Hopei.

San-ch'ü 三衢, alternate name for Ch'ü-chou 衢州 , is located in western Chekiang.

San-mao-ke 三茅閣 Bridge, unidentified place in the city of Shanghai.

San-shui 三水 , p.o. spelling Samshui, district city twenty-five miles west of Canton, is now on the Canton-Hankow railway line.

Sang-tao 桑島 , island off the north coast of Shantung, is located fifteen miles west of Tengchowfu.

Sha-chiao-t'ou 沙角頭 , island opposite Hu-men (Bocca Tigris), at the mouth of the Canton or Pearl River, Kwangtung, formerly had a fort, which was destroyed by the British during the first Opium War.

Sha-t'ou 沙頭, also called Sha-shan-t'ou 沙汕頭 , both of which are alternate names for Shan-t'ou 汕頭 or Swatow, Kwangtung treaty port.

Shan-hai-kuan 山海關 , p.o. spelling Shanhaikwan, Lin-yü-hsien, Hopei, barrier town of great importance, is located at the point where the Great Wall comes down to the sea and separates China proper from Manchuria.

Shang-tu 商都 , district city in Chahar, seventy-five miles northwest of Kalgan and one hundred sixty miles northwest of Peiping, is the Xanadu of Coleridge's "Kublai Khan."

Shang-yüan 上元 , former district city, now called Chiang-ning (Kiangning)-hsien, Kiangsu, is up the Yangtze River from Nanking.

Shan-Yung 山永, literary designation for Shanhaikwan and the surrounding area, is a combination of the names Shan-hai-kuan and Yung-p'ing-fu 永平府 , in eastern Hopei.

Shao-chou 韶州 , p.o. spelling Shiuchow, former prefectural, now a district, city in northern Kwangtung, is located on the North River, one hundred forty miles north of Canton.

Shen-ching 深井 , P'an-yü-hsien, Kwangtung, an anchorage in the back reach or Macao Passage of the Pearl or Canton River, is located opposite the city of Canton.

Shih-hsiao 十漖, Woosung estuary, is located on Ch'ung-ming (Tsungming) Island, near Shanghai, Kiangsu.

Shih-pa-t'o 十八托, apparently mistakenly written for 石臼坨, an island in the Gulf of Chihli, about sixty-five miles east Tientsin.

Shih-ho-k'ou 石河口, inlet three miles southwest of Lin-yü-hsien (Shanhaikwan), where the Shih River empties into the sea, was the site of a Ch'ing dynasty coast defense fort.

Shuang-kang 雙港, garrison town southeast of Tientsin, Hopei, is located on the west bank of the Pei 北, or Hai 海 River.

Shun-t'ien 順天, former prefecture in Hopei, comprising twenty hsien, had its administrative headquarters in Peiping.

So-lun 索倫, area comprising the southeastern part of Hulun (Hailar)-hsien, in the extreme western part of Heilungkiang, Manchuria; it borders Chita, U.S.S.R., and lies four hundred miles northwest of Harbin.

Su-Ch'ang 蘇常, former circuit (tao) comprising Su-chou (Soochow) 蘇州 and Ch'ang-chou 常州 prefectures, is located west of and included Shanghai, Kiangsu.

Su-chou 蘇州, p.o. spelling Soochow, former prefectural city, fifty miles east of Shanghai, Kiangsu, is the terminal city of the Grand Canal.

Su-Sung-T'ai 蘇松太, former circuit (tao), comprising Su-chou (Soochow), Sung-chiang (Sungkiang 松江), and T'ai-tsang 太倉, made up eastern Kiangsu province; the tao-t'ai of this circuit was popularly called the "Shanghai tao-t'ai" or "Shanghai intendant."

Sung-chiang 松江, p.o. spelling Sungkiangfu, former prefectural city in southeastern Kiangsu, is located thirty miles southwest of Shanghai.

Ta-hao-t'ou 大蠔頭, unidentified anchorage in the Canton or Pearl River, Kwangtung, lies below Canton.

Ta-huang-chiao 大黃窖, P'an-yü-hsien, Kwangtung, is a small island in the Macao Passage or back reach of the Pearl or Canton River and is located southeast of Canton, south of Honan (Honam) Island.

Ta-kou 打狗 , unidentified bridge over one of the creeks in the city of Shanghai.

Ta-ku 大沽 , p.o. spelling Taku, Hopei port, thirty-five miles southeast of Tientsin, is located on the Gulf of Chihli.

Ta-li 大瀝 , village in Nan-hai-hsien, Kwangtung, is located three miles northwest of Canton.

Ta-shan 大山 , village in Wu-li-hsien, is located on the extreme north tip of Shantung, seventy miles south of Ta-ku.

T'a-pa 他八 , also spelled Naha or Napha, port city of Okinawa, Liu-ch'iu Islands, serves as the port of Shuri, castle and former capital city.

Tan-t'u 丹徒 , district city, Chen-chiang (Chinkiang) prefecture, Kiangsu, is located at the point where the Grand Canal intersects the Yangtze River.

Tan-yang 丹陽 , district city, Chen-chiang (Chinkiang) prefecture, Kiangsu, is located twenty-five miles south of Chen-chiang on the Grand Canal, now on the Shanghai-Nanking railway line.

T'an-shui 淡水 , p.o. spelling Tamsui, district city and port at the mouth of the river, ten miles northeast of T'ai-pei (Japanese spelling, Taihoku), capital city of Formosa (Taiwan), on the northern tip of the island.

Tang-t'u 當塗 , district city in T'ai-p'ing prefecture in east central Anhwei, some fifty miles up the Yangtze River from Nanking, is the site of the T'ai-p'ing Iron Mines.

T'ang-erh-ku 唐兒沽 , another name for T'ang-ku, fort across the Pei River and just north of Ta-ku, Tientsin prefecture, Hopei, is located between Ta-ku and Pei-t'ang.

T'ang-hsien 唐縣 , district city, Paoting prefecture, Hopei, is located fifteen miles southwest of Paoting-fu.

Tao-t'ou 道頭 , township (ssu) in Ting-hai-hsien, Chusan Island, Chekiang, off the coast from Ningpo, forms an island in Ting-hai harbor of considerable strategic importance.

Teng-chou 登州 , prefectural (fu) city on the northern tip of Shantung, is located fifty miles northeast of Chefoo, on the Gulf of Chihli.

T'ien-hou-kung 天后宮, unidentified place in the vicinity of Ting-hai on Chusan Island, Chekiang, opposite Ningpo.

Tien-po 電白, p.o. spelling Tinpak, district city, Kao-chou-fu, Kwangtung, is located on the coast, fifty miles east of the former French leasehold, Kwang-chow-wan, some two hundred miles south-east of Hong Kong.

Tien-yüan 淀園, another name for Hai-tien, garrison town four miles northwest of Peiping, Hopei, adjoining the old Summer Palace, is the present site of Yenching University.

Ting-chou 定州, former independent departmental city, now a district city, Hopei, is located fifty miles southwest of Paoting-fu, one hundred sixty miles southwest of Peiping, and is now on the Peiping-Hankow railway line.

Ting-hai 定海, former sub-prefectural (t'ing), now district, city on Chusan Island, Chekiang, is located off the coast from Ningpo.

Ts'ao-Shan 曹單, literary contraction of Ts'ao-hsien and Shan-hsien, Tsaochow prefecture, is located in the extreme southwestern part of Shantung, adjoining Honan.

Ts'ang-chou 滄州, former prefectural (fu), now district, city, Hopei, is located some sixty miles south of Tientsin and is now on the Peiping-Pukow railway line.

Tu-shih-k'ou 獨石口, former sub-prefectural (t'ing), now district, city, Chahar, occupies a narrow pass in the Great Wall, about a hundred miles north of Peiping.

Tung-an 東安, unidentified fort in the Canton or Pearl River below Canton.

Tung-chiang 東港, is the "East Harbor" of Western accounts, on Chusan Island, Chekiang, opposite Ningpo.

Tung-kuan 東莞, district city, Kwangtung, lies midway between Canton and Hong Kong, near Sheklung, and is now on the Canton-Kowloon railway line.

Tung-tien 東淀, an anchorage in the Pei River estuary, is in the vicinity of Ta-ku, Hopei.

Tung-ting 東定, unidentified fort on the Canton or Pearl River,

Kwangtung.

Tung-t'ing-Lake 洞庭湖 , a large fresh-water lake, south of the Yangtze River in northeastern Hunan, just north of Changsha.

T'ung-chou 通州 , district city and former circuit (tao) in Hopei, comprising T'ung-chou, Tsun-hua 遵化 -chou and Yung-p'ing 永平 - fu; the city is now called T'ung-hsien and lies ten miles east of Peiping; it was the terminus of the canal for bringing tribute into Peiping and is now connected by rail to the city.

T'ung-Yung 通永 , literary abbreviation of T'ung-chou 通州 and Yung-ch'ing 永清 , used to designate the location of a brigade garrison (chen) between Peiping and Tientsin, Hopei; was formerly under the command of a brigade general or chen-t'ai.

Urga, see K'u-lun.

Wan-miao 灣廟 , unidentified place in the vicinity of Ting-hai, Chusan Island, Chekiang, is located opposite Ningpo.

Wang-chia-chuang 王家莊, unidentified village in the vicinity of Ta-ku and Tientsin, Hopei.

Wang-hsia 望廈 , spelled Wanghia and Wanghiya in contemporary American documents, is a village in Chung-shan (formerly Hsiang-shan and known locally as Heung-shan) hsien, south of Canton and adjoining Macao, separated from the latter only by a narrow neck of land and the Barrier Gate.

Wen-chou 溫州, former prefectural (fu) city, comprising also the district (hsien) city of Yung-chia, is a treaty port on the southeast coast of Chekiang province.

Wen-teng 文登 , district city in Teng-chou prefecture, Shantung, is located on the eastern tip of the peninsula, forty miles south of Wei-hai-wei.

Wu-ch'eng 吳城 , district seat of Wu-hsien, which with Ch'ang-chou-hsien and Yüan-ho-hsien forms the former prefectural city of Soochow, Kiangsu, fifty miles west of Shanghai.

Wu-Ch'eng-Yung-Ku 武城永固 , literary abbreviation for the Peiping-Tientsin-Taku area in Hopei, comprising Wu-ch'ing 武清 -hsien, Ch'eng-an 成安 -hsien, Yung-ch'ing 永清 -hsien, and Ku-an 固安 -hsien.

Wu-chiang 吳江, district city, Soochow prefecture, Kiangsu, is located twelve miles south of Soochow on the west shore of Lake Tai.

Wu-chow 梧州, former prefectural (fu) city, also district city of Ts'ang-wu-hsien, is located on the eastern border of Kwangsi, immediately adjoining Kwangtung; Wu-chou is one hundred fifty miles up the West River from Canton.

Wu-hu 蕪湖, district city in the former T'ai-p'ing prefecture, Anhwei, was one of the Yangtze River treaty ports, located seventy-five miles southwest of Nanking.

Wu-sung 吳淞, p.o. spelling Woosung, is located in the southeastern part of Pao-shan-hsien, Kiangsu, at the point where the Huang-p'u (Whampoo) and the Wu-sung rivers empty into the Yangtze estuary. This is the river entrance ten miles north of Shanghai and a most important commercial site.

Wu-yung 烏涌, wasteland in the eastern part of P'an-yü-hsien (Canton), Kwangtung, on the north shore of the Pearl or Canton River, was the site of a river fort and is now on the Canton-Kowloon railway line.

Yang-ching-pin 洋涇濱, commonly spelled Yang-king-pang in Western works, is a creek traversing the city of Shanghai; when the foreign settlements developed, this creek separated French Town from the International Settlement.

Yang-chou 揚州, former prefectural (fu), now district (hsien), city in southeastern Kiangsu, is located across the Yangtze River and ten miles north of Chinkiang.

Yang-ts'un 楊村, former brigade (chen) garrison town in Wu-ch'ing-hsien, Hopei, located fifty-five miles south of Peiping, twenty-five miles north of Tientsin, is now on the Peiping-Tientsin railway line.

Yen-t'ai 烟臺, used in Western writings interchangeably with Chefoo, which strictly belongs to another village, but Yen-t'ai is the Chinese name of the place known as Chefoo by foreigners. Yen-t'ai is a treaty port in Fu-shan-hsien, in the former Teng-chou prefecture, Shantung province, and is located on the north coast of the peninsula midway between Tengchowfu and Wei-hai-wei.

Yüeh-chou 岳州, p.o. spelling Yochow or Yoyang, is a former prefectural (fu), now a district (hsien),city in Hunan, located at the northeast outlet of Tung-t'ing Lake and now on the Canton-Hankow railway line, midway between Hankow and Changsha.

Yung-an 永安 , p.o. spelling Wingon, district city in Hui-chou (Wai-chow) prefecture, Kwangtung, is located some sixty-five miles north-east of Waichow City.

Yung-chen 永鎮 , unidentified garrison town for a brigade in the vicinity of Tientsin, probably in Yung-ch'ing 永清 hsien, Hopei.

BIBLIOGRAPHY

BIBLIOGRAPHY

I. DOCUMENTS AND MANUSCRIPTS

British and Foreign State Papers, London, v. 23-50.

Covering the period 1834-1860.

Chang Ku Ts'ung Pien 掌故叢編 (Collected Historical Documents), published monthly by the Department of Historical Research, Wen Hsien Kuan 文獻館, Palace Museum, Peiping, 1938; continued as *Wen Hsien Ts'ung Pien,* q. v.

Documents selected from the national archives and published without regard for chronology or subject matter, with index.

Chin Tai Chung Kuo Wai Chiao Shih Tzu Liao Chi Yao 近代中國外交史資料輯要 (Source Book of Important Documents Relating to the Modern Diplomatic History of China), compiled with preface by Chiang T'ing-fu 蔣廷黻 (T. F. Tsiang), 2 v., Shanghai, 1931,1934.

Selection of important documents, mostly from the IWSM, but containing some not in that compendious collection.

China Archives, Peiping Legation, National Archives, Washington, D.C., 1844-1861, 20 v.

Peiping Legation archives with complete copies of correspondence with the State Department, local materials, and, after 1848, the Chinese versions of all correspondence, which were not forwarded to Washington after that date.

China Despatches, Department of State, National Archives, Washington, D. C., v. 1-7, 1843-1853.

Complete correspondence of Cushing, Everett, Davis, Marshall, Parker, and McLane in original manuscript.

China Instructions, Department of State, National Archives, Washington, D. C., v. 1-2, 1843-1860.

Instructions, Cushing through Ward, in manuscript books, bound.

China Letters Received, Department of State, National Archives, Washington, D.C., 1841-1861.

Index and abridged texts of letters received by the State Department, listed chronologically in annual volumes.

Ch'ing Tai Ch'ou Pan I Wu Shih Mo 清代籌辦夷務始末 (The Management of Barbarian Affairs of the Ch'ing Dynasty from Beginning to End), Peiping, Palace Museum, 1930, 80v. Cited as IWSM.

Photolithograph edition of the original manuscript copy, 60 *chüan* for the later Tao-kuang period, 1841-1850, and 80 *chüan* for the Hsien-feng period, 1851-1861.

Ch'ing Tai Wai Chiao Shih Liao 清代外交史料(Historical Materials Concerning Foreign Relations in the Ch'ing Period), Palace Museum, Peiping, 1932-1933.

Includes four volumes on the Tao-kuang period, 1821-1850.

Clyde, Paul Hibbert, *United States Policy Toward China: Diplomatic and Public Documents, 1839-1939,* Durham, North Carolina, 1940.

Selected documents from American state papers.

Everett, Alexander Hill, *A. H. Everett Papers, Private, 1841-1857,* Massachusetts Historical Society, Boston, 16 cases.

Manuscript personal papers, one case of which deals with his China mission.

IWSM, see *Ch'ing Tai Ch'ou Pan I Wu Shih Mo.*

Miller, Hunter, ed., *Treaties and Other International Acts of the United States of America,* 8 v., Washington, 1934-1948.

Volume 4 contains the Cushing Treaty (1844) with full notes on the negotiations; there is the same coverage of the Treaty of Tientsin (1858).

Reed, William B., *Private Diary, July 5, 1857-April 13, 1858,* MS, 2 v., Library of Congress, Washington, D. C., Manuscript Division.

Personal journal of events and reactions addressed to his wife; paucity of political or diplomatic material.

Richardson, J. D., *Messages and Papers of the Presidents,* v. 4, Washington, D. C., 1896-1898.

President Tyler's message to Congress proposing a treaty with China, December 30, 1842.

Shih Liao Hsün K'an 史料旬刊(Historical Material Published Every Ten Days), edited by Chiang T'ing-fu 蔣廷黻 (T. F. Tsiang), Palace Museum, Peiping, 1930-1931, 4 v.

Contains some secret memorials of Ch'i-ying not included in the IWSM.

Tso Shun-sheng 左舜生, *Chung Kuo Chin Pai Nien Shih Tzu Liao Hsü Pien* 中國近百年史資料續編 (Sources for the Last Hundred Years of Chinese History), Shanghai, 1933.

Unofficial compilation adding some materials to the standard collections.

U. S. Congress, 26:1, *House Journal,* Washington, D. C., p. 781.

Memorial of Boston and Salem merchants on the matter of negotiating a treaty with China, 1840.

U. S. Congress, 26:1, *House Executive Document* 119, Washington, D. C.

Correspondence relating to extraterritorial jurisdiction before 1844.

U. S. Congress, 26:2, *House Executive Document* 71, Washington, D. C.

Collection of documents dealing with China up to 1841.

U. S. Congress, 27:3, *House Report* 93, Washington, D. C., p. 1-3.

Proposal for a mission to negotiate a treaty with China, 1843.

U. S. Congress, 28:2, *Senate Document* 58, Washington, D. C., p. 1-14.

Cushing's submission of the Treaty of Wang-hsia to the Senate, with comments.

U. S. Congress, 28:2, *Senate Document* 138, Washington, D. C.

Instructions to Cushing.

U. S. Congress, 29:1, *Senate Document* 139, Washington, D. C., p. 1-47.

Kearny papers, 1842-1843, printed in 1846.

U. S. Congress, 31:1, *Senate Executive Document* 72, Washington, D. C., p. 1-20.

Davis' regulations in pursuance of the Act of August 11, 1848, setting up consular courts in China.

U. S. Congress, 33:1, *House Executive Document* 123, Washington, D. C., p. 1-368.

Marshall's correspondence, 1853-1854.

U. S. Congress, 35:2, *Senate Executive Document* 22, Washington, D. C., p. 1-1052.

McLane correspondence, p. 1-500; Parker correspondence, p. 301-1052.

U. S. Congress, 36:1, *Senate Executive Document* 30, Washington, D. C., p. 1-589.

Reed and Ward correspondence.

Wen Hsien Ts'ung Pien 文獻叢編 (Collectanea from the Historical Records Office), published monthly by the Historical Records Office, Wen Hsien Kuan 文獻館, 1930-1937, 37 v.

Continuation of *Chang Ku Ts'ung Pien*, q. v.

II. CONTEMPORARY NON-DOCUMENTARY MATERIALS, INCLUDING CONTEMPORARY PERIODICALS

Alcock, Sir Rutherford, "Chinese Statesmen and State Papers," *Frazer's Magazine* 83 (New Series 3, 1871), 328-342, 503-514, 613-628.

Contemporary account based on personal acquaintance with Chinese officials, mostly of the period after 1860.

Bazancourt, Le Baron de, *Les expéditions de Chine et de Cochin-Chine*, 2 v., Paris, 1861.

Good account of the military campaigns of 1858, 1859, and 1860.

Bridgman, E. C., "Translation of the Chinese Text of the Treaty of Wanghia," *Chinese Repository* 15 (1845), 30-40.

Chinese text translated back into English for comparison with the original English version.

Callery, Joseph Marie, *Journal des operations diplomatiques de la légation française en Chine*, Macao, 1845.

Translator-secretary for the Lagrené mission in 1844, Callery was formerly with the Missions Etrangères and later wrote favorably on the Taiping rebels.

-----, *Correspondence diplomatiques chinoise relative aux negotiations du traité de Whampoa: conclu entre la France et la Chine le 24 Octobre 1844*, Paris, 1879.

Correspondence between Lagrené and Ch'i-ying reproduced in Chinese and French, covering the period August 22, 1844 to January 7, 1846.

Chinese Repository, 1832-1851, Canton, Macao, Victoria.

Miscellaneous but invaluable collection of contemporary materials edited by the American missionaries, E. C. Bridgman and S. Wells Williams.

Clark, Mr. J. C., of N. Y., *Speech on the Bill Appropriating Forty Thousand Dollars to Enable the President to Establish Commercial Relations between the United States and China*. Delivered in the House of Representatives, February 22, 1843. Pamphlet in Widener Library, Harvard.

Good evidence that the issue in Congress was domestic politics rather than diplomacy.

Cooke, George Wingrove, *China: Being "The Times" Special Correspondence From China in the Years 1857-58*, London, 1858.

Vicious and unsympathetic dissection of Commissioner Yeh Ming-ch'en as a mandarin in captivity.

Courcy, René de, "L'insurrection chinois: son origine et ses progrés," *Revue des deux mondes* 34 (1861), 5-35, 312-360.

Discredits Issachar Roberts' claims as Taiping mentor; generally sympathetic toward the rebels.

Davis, John Francis, *The Chinese: A General Description of the Empire of China and its Inhabitants*, 2 v., London, 1836; 2nd ed. entitled *China: A General Description of that Empire and its Inhabitants; with the History of Foreign Intercourse down to the Events which Produced the Dissolution of 1857*, 2 v., London, 1857.

Best general account of China in English until the appearance of Williams' *Middle Kingdom*.

-----, *Sketches of China*, 2 v., London, 1841.

Personal accounts of travels in China and observations on the Amherst mission and early stages of the first Opium War by the later baronet and governor of Hong Kong.

-----, *China During the War and Since the Peace*, 2 v., London, 1852.

Valuable descriptions of the Chinese officials of the period; utilizes Chinese documents captured during the war and translated by Gutzlaff.

De Bow's Review, New Orleans (incomplete in Widener Library), 1846-1864.

Journal devoted primarily to business and commerce.

Democratic Review, New York, January-December, 1852.

Journal reflecting the opinions of trade regarding international affairs of the period.

"Embassies to the Court of Peking, Indicating the Way They Came, the Period of Time, and the Number of Persons Composing Them," translated by a Chinese from the *Ta Ch'ing Hui Tien,* ch. 31, *Chinese Repository* 14 (1845), 153-156.

Early translation from the standard work, *Institutes of the Ch'ing Dynasty;* superseded by later translations by Pauthier, Rockhill, *et al.*

Ellis, Henry, *Journal of the Proceedings of the Late Embassy to China,* London, 1817.

Account of Amherst mission to Peking in 1816.

Forbes, Robert Bennet, *Remarks on China and the China Trade,* Boston, 1844.

Reflects American businessmen's opposition to the opium trade; written after the Cushing mission left for China but before news of the Treaty of Wang-hsia reached America.

-----, *Personal Reminiscences,* Boston, 1882.

Personal tribute to Chinese merchants, particularly Houqua; warm admiration for Chinese in general.

Ford, Worthington Chauncy, ed., "Address by John Quincy Adams, 1841, on the Opium War, communicated for the President," Massachusetts Historical Society, *Proceedings* 43 (1909-1910), 295-325.

Text of Adams' famous aid-to-Britain speech which the Society refused to publish in 1841.

Fortune, Robert, *Tea Districts of China and India,* London, 1852.

-----, *Tea Countries of China,* 2 v., London, 1853.

Descriptions of the Chinese interior by an early plant explorer who, on the basis of these travels, introduced tea culture into India and Ceylon.

Gros, Baron J. B. L., *Négotiations entre la France et la Chine en 1860,* Paris, 1864.

Account of negotiations along with Lord Elgin, of an experienced French diplomat in a new field.

Gutzlaff, Charles, *The Life of Taou-Kwang, Late Emperor of China: With Memoirs of the Court of Peking: Including a Sketch of the Principal Events in the History of the Chinese Empire During the Last Fifty Years,* London, 1852. German translation of same, Leipzig, 1852.

Contemporary account of the period 1821-1851 by a Protestant missionary able to use the Chinese materials available at that time.

Hart, Sir Robert, "These From the Land of Sinim," in *Essays on the Chinese Question,* London, 1901.

Personal reminiscences of the famous Inspector General of the customs service; the Chinese officials described are mostly of the period after 1860, with a few valuable exceptions.

Herald, New York, September 28, 1852.

Article on Humphrey Marshall, attacking his appointment as commissioner to China.

Hsia Hsieh 夏燮 (Pen-name Chiang Shang Chien Sou 江上蹇叟 "The Old Cripple on the River"), *Chung Hsi Chi Shih* 中西紀事 (An Account of China and the West), original preface dated 1850; second preface, 1859; date of publication about 1868, 24 *chüan,* 6 v.

Contemporary Chinese work of little other than curious interest; the author is vigorously anti-foreign.

Hunt's Merchants' Magazine or The Merchants' Magazine and Commercial Review, ed.
Freeman Hunt, 1839-1870, New York.

Business journal of interest largely because of the interest of the editor, Freeman
Hunt, in foreign trade and in extending American trade.

Hunt, Freeman, *Lives of American Merchants,* New York, 1856, 2 v.

Contains biographies of Thomas Handasyd Perkins, Samuel Appleton, and Major Samuel Shaw.

Hunter, William C., *The 'Fan Kwae' at Canton Before Treaty Days, 1825-1844,* 3rd Ed.,
Shanghai, 1938 (1st ed., 1882; 2nd ed., 1911).

Interesting account by one of the more sensitive of the Old China Hands; Hunter was with
Russell and Company at Canton, 1829-1842.

-----,*Bits of Old China,* 2nd ed., 1911.

Contains an interesting description of P'an Shih-ch'eng's estate at P'an-t'ang, near
Canton.

Lavolée, Charles Hubert, *La Chine contemporaine,* Paris, 1860.

Contemporary account of events to 1859, by a young Frenchman who came out to China with
Lagrené in 1844.

-----, *France et Chine: traité de Whampoa, 1844, correspondance diplomatique de M.
de Lagrené; expédition de 1860 contre la Chine,* Paris, 1900.

Supplements Callery and adds new material on the 1860 events.

Liang T'ing-nan 梁廷枏 , *I Fen Chi Wen* 夷氛記聞(Contemporary Account of the
Barbarian Trouble), preface dated 1874; National University ed., Peiping, 1937.

Cantonese bibliophile, protégé of Juan Yüan, who, besides this book, wrote descriptions
of Christianity, of London, and of the United States; he was regarded as a literary
authority on foreign countries.

Littell, Robert S., "Sir Henry Pottinger in China," *Living Age* 4 (1845), 387-389.

Account of Pottinger's reception by the merchants and manufacturers of Liverpool and
Manchester.

Loring, Charles G., *Memoir of the Hon. William Sturgis* (prepared agreeably to a
resolution of the Massachusetts Historical Society), Boston, 1864.

Mainly concerned with the Indian Northwest trade but with reference to China.

Lucy, Armand, *Souvenirs de voyage: Lettres intimes sur la campagne de Chine en 1860,*
Marseilles, 1861.

Personal observations by a minor officer on the expedition of 1860; suspected the
Americans and Russians of aiding the Chinese against the British and French.

Martin, Robert Montgomery, *China: Political, Commercial, and Social; in an official
report to Her Majesty's Government,* 2 v., London, 1847.

Special pleading by the treasurer of Hong Kong; bitterly opposed to Pottinger.

Martin, W. A. P., *A Cycle of Cathay or China, South and North with Personal Reminiscences,* 2nd ed., New York, 1897.

Valuable commentary on affairs of 1858-1859 by a scholarly American missionary and participant.

-----, *Awakening of China,* New York, 1907.

Written in retrospect; not so useful as the *Cycle of Cathay* for the early period.

McLane, Governor Robert E., *Reminiscences, 1827-1897,* privately printed, 1903.

Memoirs of a busy life with a very brief account of his China mission.

M'Ghee, The Rev. R. J. L., *How We Got to Pekin: A Narrative of the Campaign of 1860,* London, 1863.

Account of the campaign by a patriotic and vindictive Irish army chaplain.

Moges, Le Marquis de, *Souvenirs d'une ambassade en Chine et au Japon en 1857 et 1858,* Paris, 1860.

Personal account by a member of the staff of Baron Gros.

Montauban, General Cousin de, Comte de Palikao, *Souvenirs,* Paris, 1932.

Papers of the commander-in-chief of the French forces in 1860, published by his grandson.

Mutrécy, Charles de, *Journal de la campagne de Chine, 1859-1860-1861,* 2 v., Paris, 1862.

Best account of the French military expeditions to China by a member of General Montauban's staff.

Neumann, Karl Friederich, *Ostasiatische Geschichte vom ersten chinesischen Krieg bis zu den Vertragen in Peking (1840-1860),* Leipsig, 1861.

Observations of a young German professor who traveled in China and was dazzled by the opium barons of the China ports.

New York *Herald,* see *Herald.*

Nye, Gideon, Jr., *Peking the Goal--the Sole Hope of Peace, Comprising an Inquiry into the Origin of the Pretension of Universal Supremacy by China and into the Causes of the First War: With Incidents of the Imprisonment and the First Campaign of Canton, 1841,* Canton, 1873.

-----, *Rationale of the China Question,* Macao, 1857.

-----, *The Memorable Year of the War with China; the Mutiny in India; the Opening up of the Resources of Siam; the Projected Movement upon Indo-China; and the Monetary Crisis in Europe and America:--Being a Record of Periodical Reflections and Comments Elicited by the Course of Events in the East, with Incidental Notices of Political and Geographical Topics of the Period; and Including a Sketch of the Collapse of Mr. High Commissioner Yeh,* Macao, 1858.

-----, *The Gage of the Two Civilizations: Shall Christendom Waver? Being an Inquiry into the Causes of the Rupture of the English and French Treaties of Tientsin; and Comprising a General View of Our Relations with China: with Notices of Japan, Siam, and Cochin China*, Macao, 1860.

Contemporary effusions by a contentious American merchant with pro-British views.

Oliphant, Laurence, *Narrative of the Earl of Elgin's Mission to China and Japan in the Years 1857, '58, '59*, New York, 1860.

Authentic account by Lord Elgin's private secretary.

P'an I-fu, see Wang Hsien-ch'ien.

Pauthier, M. C., *Memoire secret addressé a L'Empereur Hien-foung, actuellement regnant par un lettré chinois sur la conduite à suivre avec les puissances européennes* (Reprinted from the *Revue de l'Orient*), Paris, 1860.

Translation of a memorial by Yin Tchao-young (Yin Chao-yung 殷兆鏞) protesting against the signing of the Tientsin treaties.

Reed, William B., "The China Question," *North American Review* 40 (1860), 125-180.

Popular presentation of events of 1858, of only limited background value.

Scarth, John, *Twelve Years in China: The People, the Rebels, and the Mandarins, by a British Resident*, London, 1860.

Unofficial account by an English businessman resident in China, 1847-1859; deplores high-handed methods of British diplomacy; favors cultivation of Chinese good will.

Seward, William F., *Works*, ed. George E. Baker, 3 v., New York, 1853.

Public and political papers.

Sirr, Henry Charles, *China and the Chinese: their Religion, Character, Customs, and Manufactures: the Evils arising from the Opium Trade: with a Glance at Our Religious, Moral, Political, and Commercial Intercourse with the Country*, 2 v., London, 1849.

By a British resident, violently opposed to the opium trade; valuable judgments of Parker, Roberts, and other Americans.

Staunton, Sir George, *Authentic Account of an Embassy from the King of Great Britain to the Emperor of China, etc.*, 3 v., London, 1797.

Official account by the secretary of the Macartney mission.

Stevens, G. B., and Marwick, W. F., *Life and Letters of Peter Parker*, Boston and Chicago, 1896.

Largely made up of Parker's diary and correspondence.

Timkowski, George (Egor Fedorovitch Timkovski), *Travels of the Russian Mission through Mongolia to China, and Residence in Peking, in the Years 1820-1821*, 2 v., London, 1827.

Records residence in Peking but no audience or contact with the court.

Train, Geo. Francis, *An American Merchant in Europe, Asia, and Australia: A series of letters from Java, Singapore, China, Bengal, Egypt, the Holy Land, the Crimea and its battle grounds, England, Melbourne, Sydney, etc.*, New York, 1857.

Breezy comments by a young Bostonian businessman, mostly on trade but occasionally touching on diplomatic affairs.

Trescot, William Henry, *A Few Thoughts on the Foreign Policy of the United States*, Charleston, 1849.

Forceful early presentation of the policy of Anglo-American cooperation in foreign affairs; advocates an alliance.

Tung Hua Lu, see Wang Hsien-ch'ien.

United States Democratic Review, New York, 1856-1858.

Successor to the *United States Review*.

United States Magazine and Democratic Review, Washington, 1837-1851.

Magazine of trade and politics.

United States Review, New York, 1852-1855.

Successor to the *Democratic Review*.

Varin, Paul, *Expedition de Chine*, Paris, 1862.

Second-rate account of the Arrow War and military expeditions through 1860.

Wang Hsien-ch'ien 王先謙 and P'an I-fu 潘頤福 , *Shih I Ch'ao Tung Hua Lu* 十一朝東華錄, Ts'un Ku Chai 存古齋 ed., Peking, 1911.

Digest of edicts and other court enactments with some summaries of incoming memorials, arranged chronologically by months.

Wei Yüan 魏 源 , *Sheng Wu Chi* 聖武記 (Military Operations of the Present Dynasty), Ssu Pu Pei Yao 四部備要 ed., Shanghai; original preface dated 1842, second preface dated 1846.

Military history and theory of the Tao-kuang period by the scholarly collaborator of Lin Tse-hsü.

-----, *Chinese Account of the Opium War (Being essentially a translation of the last two chapters of Sheng Wu-ki, or "Military Operations of the Present Dynasty")*, tr. by E. H. Parker, Shanghai, 1888.

Not included in the foregoing edition of Wei Yüan's *Sheng Wu Chi*.

Wetmore, W. S., *Recollections of Life in the Far East*, Shanghai, 1894.

Reminiscences of life in Shanghai and Japan by an American businessman; contains a description of the "Battle of Muddy Flat" (Shanghai), in which he participated.

Williams, Frederick Wells, *Life and Letters of Samuel Wells Williams, Ll. D.: Missionary, Diplomatist, Sinologue*, New York and London, 1889.

Incorporates many of the writings of Williams; not as illuminating as his "Journal."

Williams, Frederick Wells, ed., "Journal of S. Wells Williams. Reed and Ward Missions," *Journal of the North China Branch of the Royal Asiatic Society* 42 (1911), 3-232.

By far the best account of the American negotiations, 1858-1859, by the saintly missionary-interpreter.

Williams, S. Wells, "Narrative of the American Embassy to Peking, in July 1859," *Journal of the North China Branch of the Royal Asiatic Society* 1 (1859), 315-349.

Paper read before the Society in Shanghai, which, under the fire of British criticism, is more of an apology than a narrative; glosses all controversial matters.

III. SECONDARY MATERIALS, INCLUDING ARTICLES IN RECENT PERIODICALS

(Abbreviated titles used in listing the periodicals cited below: *American Historical Review*, AHR; *Chinese Social and Political Science Review*, CSPSR; *Harvard Journal of Asiatic Studies*, HJAS; *Journal of the American Oriental Society*, JAOS; *Journal of Modern History*, JMH; *Pacific Historical Review*, PHR; *T'oung Pao*, TP.);

Bau, Mingchien Joshua, *The Foreign Relations of China: A History and a Survey,* New York and Chicago, 1821.

Early period to 1860 treated briefly; based entirely on Western materials.

-----, *The Open Door Doctrine in Relation to China,* New York, 1823.

Follows American tradition on Kearny episode; deals chiefly with the Hay period.

Biggerstaff, Knight, "The Official Chinese Attitude Toward the Burlingame Mission," AHR 41 (1936), 682-702.

-----, "Some Notes on the *Tung-hua Lu* 東華錄 and the *Shih-lu* 實錄," HJAS 4 (1939), 101-115.

Callahan, James Morton, *American Relations in the Pacific and the Far East, 1784-1900,* Baltimore, 1901.

Accepts all the popular errors and originates some new ones.

Chang Yü-chüan, "The Organization of the *Waichiaopu,*" CSPSR 1 (1916), 21-39.

Chen Ching-jen, "Opium and Anglo-Chinese Relations," CSPSR 19 (1935), 386-437.

Ch'en, Gideon, *Lin Tse Hsü: Pioneer Promoter of the Adoption of Western Means of Maritime Defense in China,* Peiping, 1934.

Provocative treatment of a new field; rev. by John C. Ferguson, *T'ien Hsia Monthly* 7 (1938), 310-313; T. F. Tsiang, CSPSR 19 (1936), 564-565.

Ch'en Huai 陳懷, *Ch'ing Shih Yao Lüeh* 清史要略 (Outline of Ch'ing Dynasty History), Peking, National University Press, 1920; 1925.

Carefully reasoned treatment of China's foreign relations, utilizing Chinese un-official materials; slight reference to the United States.

Ch'en Huai, *Chung Kuo Chin Pai Nien Shih Yao* 中國近百年史要 (Essentials of Chinese History for the Last Hundred Years), Shanghai, 1930.

Begins period with the Opium War; foreign affairs appear to follow Western materials almost exclusively.

Ch'en Kung-lu 陳恭祿, "Ssu Kuo T'ien Ching T'iao Yüeh Chih Ching Kuo" 四國天津條約之經過 (The Making of the Tientsin Treaties, 1854-1860), *Chin Ling Hsüeh Pao* 金陵學報 (Nanking Journal) 1 (1931), 407-422.

Chiang Kung-sheng 蔣恭晟, *Chung Mei Kuan Hsi Chi Yao* 中美關係記要 (Digest of Sino-American Relations), Shanghai, 1930.

General survey of Chinese-American relations from the point of view of a modern, nationalist Chinese; based on secondary Chinese and Western materials.

Chiang T'ing-fu, see Tsiang, T. F.

Ch'ing Shih Kao 清史稿 (Draft History of the Ch'ing), 134 v., Peiping, 1928.

Traditional and authorized (although unaccepted) history of the Manchu dynasty; contains a section on foreign relations, the 4th *chüan* of which deals with the United States. See review by T. F. Tsiang.

Ch'iu, Alfred K'ai-ming, "Chinese Historical Documents of the Ch'ing Dynasty, 1644-1911," PHR 1 (1932), 324-336.

Cordier, Henri, "Les marchands honistes de Canton," TP 3 (1902), 281-315.

-----, "La France et l'Angleterre en Indo-Chine et en Chine sous le Premier Empire," TP 4 (1903), 201-227.

-----, *Histoire des relations de la Chine avec les puissances occidentales, 1860-1890,* 3 v., Paris, 1901.

Standard, authoritative work by a distinguished French sinologist.

-----, *Conférence sur les relations de la Chine avec l'Europe,* Rouen, 1901.

Resumé of Chinese foreign relations.

-----, *Les douanes Imperiales maritimes chinoises,* Paris, 1902.

Traditional account of the formation of the customs inspectorate in 1854, according a large measure of credit to Robert M. McLane.

-----, *L'Expédition de Chine de 1857-58: histoire diplomatique: notes et documents,* Paris, 1905.

Careful, discriminating use of French correspondence.

-----, *Mélanges américaines,* Paris, 1913.

General account of Americans and French in Canton in the 18th century; describes the voyage of the *Empress of China* and friendly relations with France.

-----, *Histoire générale de la Chine; et de ses relations avec les pays étrangers,* 3 v., Paris, 1920.

Standard and remarkably condensed account.

Costin, W. C., *Great Britain and China,* 1833-1860, Oxford, 1937.

Valuable recent work summarizing a vast store of British official and private manuscript material.

Courcy, (René), Marquis de, *L'Empire du Milieu: Description géographiques, précis historique, institutions sociales, réligieuses, politiques, notions sur les sciences, les arts, l'industrie, et le commerce,* Paris, 1867.

Balanced, trustworthy, although strongly pro-missionary, account by the French chargé d'affaires at Macao and perennial secretary to French missions.

Cranston, Earl, "Shanghai in the Taiping Period," PHR 5 (1936), 146-160.

-----, *American Missionary Outlook in China, 1830-1860,* Harvard University thesis, MS, 1934.

Summary of a great volume of missionary printed and manuscript materials, inadequately digested.

Dennett, Tyler, "How Old is American Policy in the Far East," *Pacific Review* 2 (1921), 463-474.

-----, "Seward's Far Eastern Policy," AHR 28 (1922), 45-62.

-----, *Americans in Eastern Asia: A Critical Study of the Policy of the United States with reference to China, Japan, and Korea in the 19th Century,* New York, 1922.

Valuable but out-of-date and out-of-print synthesis of State Department materials marked by strong preconceived opinions.

Danton, George H., *The Culture Contacts of the United States and China: The Earliest Sino-American Contacts, 1784-1844,* New York, 1931.

Preliminary survey of a promised and promising project.

-----, *The Chinese People: New Problems and Old Backgrounds,* Boston, 1938.

Popular presentation of serious and valuable material.

Duniway, Clyde Augustus, "Daniel Webster," *American Secretaries of State and Their Diplomacy,* New York, 1928; (First term) 5. 3-64; (Second term) 6. 71-113.

American background of an important period in Sino-American relations.

Einstein, Lewis, "Lewis Cass," *American Secretaries of State and Their Diplomacy,* New York, 1928, 6. 297-375.

Goes behind Cass to the real Secretary of State, Buchanan.

Fairbank, John King, "The Legalization of the Opium Trade Before the Treaties of 1858," CSPSR 17 (1933), 215-263.

-----, "Foreign Consular Administration of the Chinese Customs: The Provisional System at Shanghai 1853-54," CSPSR 18 (1934), 1-50; 18 (1935), 455-504; 19 (1935), 65-124.

Fairbank, John King, "The Creation of the Foreign Inspectorate of Customs at
Shanghai," CSPSR 19 (1936), 469-514; 20 (1936), 42-100.

-----, "The Definition of the Foreign Inspectors' Status, 1845-55: A Chapter in
the Early History of the Inspectorate of Customs at Shanghai," *Nankai Social
Science Review* 19 (1936), 125-163.

-----, "The Mechanics of Imperialism in China," *Amerasia* 1 (1937), 295-300.

-----, "The Manchu Appeasement Policy of 1843," JAOS 59 (1939), 469-484.

-----, "Chinese Diplomacy and the Treaty of Nanking, 1843," JMH 7 (1940), 1-30.

-----, and S. Y. Teng, "On Types and Uses of Ch'ing Documents," HJAS 5 (1940),
1-71.

-----, and S. Y. Teng, "On the Transmission of Ch'ing Documents," HJAS 4 (1939),
12-46.

Foster, John W., *American Diplomacy in the Orient,* Boston and New York, 1903.
Good general account; perpetuates several Kearny and Cushing legends.

-----, *The Practice of Diplomacy: As Illustrated in the Foreign Relations of the
United States,* Boston and New York, 1906.
Valuable work from first-hand experience and information.

Fredet, Jean, see Maybon, Ch. B.

Fuess, C. M., *Life of Caleb Cushing,* 2 v., New York, 1923.
High-powered biography, exploiting many hitherto inaccessible Cushing-family papers in
a very unacademic way.

Gaskill, Gussie Ester, "A Chinese Official's Experiences during the First
Opium War," AHR 39 (1933), 82-86.

Griffin, Eldon, *Clippers and Consuls: American Consular and Commercial Relations
with Eastern Asia, 1845-1860,* Ann Arbor, 1938.
Competent digest of a great volume of consular materials; valuable for reference.

Griswold, A. Whitney, *The Far Eastern Policy of the United States,* New York, 1938.
Re-examination of American 20th century policies dealing only casually with earlier
periods.

Gulik, R. H. van, "Kakkaron 隔鞾論: A Japanese Echo of the Opium War," *Monumenta Serica* 4 (1940), 478-545.

Haenisch, Erich, "Das Ts'ing-shi-kao und die sonstige Chinesische Literatur sur
Geschichte der letsten 300 Jahre," *Asia Major* 6 (1930), 403-444.

Hornbeck, Stanley Kuhl, "The Most Favored Nation Clause in Commercial Treaties,"
University of Wisconsin *Bulletin* 6 (1910), 327-447.

Hornbeck, Stanley Kuhl, "Count Caleb Cushing," *New England Quarterly* 1 (1928), 80-82.

Hsiao I-shan 蕭一山, *Ch'ing Tai T'ung Shih* 清代通史 (General History of the Ch'ing Period), Shanghai, v. 1, 1927; v. 2, 1928; v. 3, in two parts, 1931.

Most ambitious attempt thus far of a general Manchu history along modern lines, in contrast to the traditional *Ch'ing Shih Kao*, by a competent scholar; beyond the early period it consists largely of tables and charts for reference.

Hsieh Pao-chao, *The Government of China 1644-1911*, Baltimore, 1925.

Valuable general work summarizing parts of the *Ta Ch'ing Hui Tien*, Kuang-hsü ed.; lacks index and exact references.

Huang Hung-shou 黃鴻壽, *Ch'ing Shih Chi Shih Pen Mo* 清史紀事本末 (Complete Topical History of the Ch'ing Dynasty), Shanghai, Chung Hua Book Company ed., 1925, 80 *chüan*, 8 v.

Good traditional history with account of early European trade and missions in *chüan* 15; opium war and peace, *chüan* 44; and Anglo-French expedition to Peking, *chüan* 46.

Hummel, Arthur W., *The Autobiography of a Chinese Historian*, Leiden, 1931.

Excellent background of Chinese scholarly and literary life of the Ch'ing dynasty.

Johnson, E. R., *History of the Domestic and Foreign Commerce of the United States*, New York, 1915, 2 v.

Standard work with useful statistical tables and summaries.

Johnson, Willis Fletcher, *America's Foreign Relations*, New York, 1916, 2 v.

Contains chapters on the Far East with good but uncritical summaries of the important phases.

Kearny, Thomas, "The Tsiang Documents. Elipoo, Ke-ying, Pottinger and Kearny and the Most Favored Nation and Open Door Policy in China in 1842-1844: An American Viewpoint," CSPSR 16 (1932), 75-104; with "Note in Reply," by T. F. Tsiang, *ibid.*, 105-109.

-----, "Commodore Lawrence Kearny and the Open Door and Most-Favored-Nation Policy in China in 1842 to 1843," New Jersey Historical Society *Proceedings* 50 (1936), 162-190.

-----, "Commodore Kearny and the opening of China to Foreign Trade," *T'ien Hsia Monthly* 3 (1936), 323-329.

Kubota Bunzo 窪田文三, *Shina Gaikō Tsūshi* 支那外交通史 (General History of Chinese Foreign Relations), Tokyo, 1928.

Undistinguished work based largely on secondary Western materials.

Kuo, Ping-chia (Kuo Pin-chia 郭斌佳), "Canton and Salem: The Impact of Chinese Culture upon New England Life During the Post-Revolutionary Era," *New England Quarterly* 3 (1930), 420-442.

Kuo, Ping-chia, "Caleb Cushing and the Treaty of Wanghia, 1844," JMH 5 (1933), 34-54.

-----, "Hsien Feng Ch'ao Chung Kuo Wai Chiao Kai Kuan" 咸豐朝中國外交概觀 (Survey of China's Foreign Relations During the Reign of Hsien-feng), *Kuo Li Wu Han Ta Hsüeh, She Hui K'o Hsüeh Chi K'an* 國立武漢大學社會科學季刊 (Quarterly Journal of Social Science, The National Wuhan University) 5 (1935), 81-126.

-----, *A Critical Study of the First Anglo-Chinese War: With Documents,* Shanghai, 1935.

Originally a Harvard Ph.D. thesis, including transcriptions of three important documents from IWSM on American relations.

Latané, John Holladay, and Wainhouse, David W., *A History of American Foreign Policy,* 2nd rev., New York, 1940.

New revision of a standard and reliable book of the better textbook sort.

Latourette, Kenneth Scott, "The History of Early Relations between the United States and China, 1784-1844," *Transactions of the Connecticut Academy of Arts and Sciences* 22 (1917), 1-209.

-----, "Voyages of American Ships to China, 1784-1844," *ibid.,* 28 (1927), 237-271.

Learned, Henry Barrett, "William Learned Marcy," *American Secretaries of State and Their Diplomacy,* New York, 1928, 6. 145-294.

Covers American background for McLane and Parker periods.

Leavenworth, Charles Samuel, *The Arrow War with China,* London, 1901.

Apologetic account by an undiscriminating professor at Nanyang College, Shanghai.

Lin, T. C., "The Amur Frontier Question Between China and Russia, 1850-1860," PHR 3 (1934), 1-27.

-----, "Manchuria Trade and Tribute in the Ming Dynasty: A Study of Chinese Theories and Methods of Control Over Border Peoples," *Nankai Social and Economic Quarterly* 9 (1937), 855-892.

Littell, John B., "Missionaries and Politics in China--the Taiping Rebellion," *Political Science Quarterly* 43 (1928), 566-599.

Liu Yen 劉彥, *Chung Kuo Chin Shih Wai Chiao Shih* 中國近世外交史 (History of the Foreign Relations of Contemporary China), Shanghai, 3rd ed. rev., 1921.

Early general work based on secondary materials and dealing with American affairs only casually.

Lubbock, Basil, *The China Clippers,* Glasgow, 1914.

-----, *The Opium Clippers,* Boston, 1933.

Two popular works by a great enthusiast for the sailing ship days; often salty and occasionally informative.

Ma, Wen Hwan, *American Policy Toward China; As Revealed in the Debates of Congress,* Shanghai, (circa 1932).

Summary of parts of the *Congressional Record,* but not as interesting or informative as the original.

Macgowan, Rev. J., *Imperial History of China: Being a History of the Empire as Compiled by Chinese Historians,* Shanghai, 1906.

Belies its title but does contain some interesting contemporary materials.

MacNair, H. F., "Some Aspects of China's Foreign Relations in Long Retrospect," CSPSR 22 (1939), 346-362.

Mao, Yee-hang, *Relations politiques et économiques entre la Chine et les puissances de 1842 à 1860,* Lyon, 1923.

Doctoral thesis at the University of Paris, listing among his sources documents from the archives of the minister of foreign affairs at Peking, but showing little evidence of them in the text.

Mason, Mary Gertrude, *Western Concepts of China and the Chinese, 1840-1876,* New York, 1939.

Extensive use of periodical and other Western materials.

Maspero, Henri, "Chine et Asie Centrale," *Histoire et historiens depuis cinquante ans,* Paris, 1927-1928, 2, 517-599.

Maybon, Ch. B. and Fredet, Jean, *Histoire de la concession française de Shanghai,* Paris, 1929.

Monumental work beginning with 1847.

Moore, John Bassett, *The Principles of American Diplomacy,* New York and London, 1918.

Standard work by recognized authority in the field.

Morse, Hosea Ballow, *The Gilds of China: With an Account of the Gild Merchant or Co-hong of Canton,* London, 1909.

Valuable account of the working of the Co-hong at Canton and comparison with the Steelyard of London.

-----, *The Trade and Administration of China,* 3rd rev. ed., London, 1920.

Admirable, concise summary of the Chinese government under the Manchus.

-----, *Chronciles of the East India Company Trading to China, 1635-1834,* 5 v., Oxford, 1926-1929.

Excellent digest of the materials in the archives of the East India Company.

Oikawa Giuemon 及川儀右衛門, *Sankō Tōyō Shi* 参考東洋史 (Manual of Far Eastern History), Tokyo, 1928.

Chronological outline with index by a professor at Hiroshima Normal College.

Other Merchants and Sea Captains of Old Boston, State Street Trust Company, Boston, 1919.

Good reference for background of Boston merchants trading to China.

Overdijkink, G. W., *Lin Tse-hsü: een Biographische Schets,* Leiden, 1938.

Parallels and relies rather heavily on Gideon Chen's biography; well written and documented.

Owen, David Edward, *British Opium Policy in China and India,* New Haven, 1934.

Comprehensive work on an interesting and controversial subject; finds opium trade vital to Britain until the 1850's.

Pan, Stephen C. Y., "The First Treaty Between the United States and China," CSPSR 21 (1937), 155-189.

-----, "Study of American Diplomacy in China," CSPSR 22 (1938), 10-27.

Paullin, C. O., *Diplomatic Negotiations of American Naval Officers,* Baltimore, 1912.

Extensive but uncritical use of the archives of the Navy Department.

-----, "Early Voyages of American Naval Vessels to the Orient," United States Naval Institute *Proceedings* 36. 429-462; 707-734; 1073-1099, 37. 239-275, 307-417.

Contains some important materials not included in his *Diplomatic Negotiations of American Naval Officers,* although most of it is the same.

Pauthier, G., *Histoire des relations politiques de la Chine avec les puissances occidentales depuis les temps les plus anciens jusqu'à nos jours, suivé du cérémonial observé à la cour de Pe-king pour la reception des ambassadeurs,* Paris, 1859.

Early scholarly effort based on the author's own translation of sections of the *Ta Ch'ing Hui Tien,* q. v.

Peake, Cyrus H., "Documents Available for Research on the Modern History of China," AHR 38 (1932), 61-70.

-----, "A Comparison of the Various Editions of the *Ch'ing Shih Kao* 清史稿," TP 35 (1939), 354-363.

Phen, V. S., "The Most Favored Nation Clause in China's Treaties," CSPSR 8 (1924), 157-171.

Pritchard, E. H., "The Struggle for Control of the China Trade During the Eighteenth Century," PHR 3 (1934), 280-296.

-----, *The Crucial Years of Early Anglo-Chinese Relations, 1750-1800,* Research Studies of the State College of Washington, Pullman, Washington, 1936.

Thoroughly scholarly work, the bulk of which was submitted as a doctoral thesis at Oxford; excellent bibliography.

Rockhill, W. W., "Diplomatic Missions to the Court of China. The Kowtow Question," AHR 2 (1897), 627-643.

Rossiter, William S., "The First American Imperialist," *North American Review* 182 (1906), 239-254.

Russell, Francis, *A Short History of the East India Company; Exhibiting the State of their Affairs, Abroad and at Home, Political and Commercial. . .* 2nd ed., London, 1793.
Interesting early account with remarks on the beginnings of American trade in competition with the English East India Company at Canton.

Saito Ryoei 齊藤良衛, *Kinsei Tōyō Gaikō Shi Josetsu* 近世東洋外交序説 (Introduction to the History of Modern Far Eastern Foreign Relations), Tokyo, 1927.
Includes six chapters on the early years of China's intercourse with the West.

Setser, Vernon G., "Did Americans Originate the Conditional Most Favored Nation Clause?" JMH 5 (1933), 319-323.

Shen Wei-tai, *China's Foreign Policy, 1839-1860,* Columbia University Ph. D. thesis, New York, 1932.
Makes use of T. F. Tsiang's work but apparently very little independent use of Chinese materials.

Snyder, Richard C., "The Most-Favored-Nation Clause and Recent Trade Practices," *Political Science Quarterly* 40 (1940), 77-97.

Stearns, Foster, "Edward Everett," *American Secretaries of State and Their Diplomacy,* New York, 1928, 6. 117-141.
Fills in a five-month gap between Webster and Marcy.

Stearns, Worthy Putnam, "The Foreign Trade of the United States from 1820-1840," University of Chicago *Journal of Political Economy* 8 (1900), 452-490.

Swisher, Earl, "The Character of American Trade with China, 1844-1860," *University of Colorado Studies,* Series C (*Studies in the Social Sciences,* v. 1, No. 2), Boulder, 1941.

-----, "Commodore Perry's Imperialism in Relation to America's Present-day Position in the Pacific," PHR 16 (1947), 30-40.

-----, "Extraterritoriality and the *Wabash* Case," *American Journal of International Law* 45 (1951), 564-571.

-----, "The Adventure of Four Americans in Korea and Peking in 1855," PHR 21 (1952), 237-242.

Tai, En-sai, *Treaty Ports in China: A Study in Diplomacy,* New York, 1918.
Deals with the first five treaty ports and the treaties of 1858-1860.

T'ang Ch'ing-tseng 唐慶增, *Chung Mei Wai Chiao Shih* 中美外交史 (History of Sino-American Relations), Shanghai, 1928.
General account of early period, but the emphasis is on the period after 1900.

Teng, S. Y., see Fairbank, John King.

Tsiang, T. F. (Chiang T'ing-fu 蔣廷黻), "P'ing Ch'ing Shih Kao Pang Chiao Chih"
評清史稿邦交志 (Critique of the Foreign Relations Monograph of the Draft
Ch'ing History), Pei P'ing Pei Hai T'u Shu Kuan Yüeh K'an 北平北海圖書館
月刊 (Bulletin of the Metropolitan Library) 2 (1929), 479-492; 3 (1929), 49-54.

-----, "China After the Victory of Taku, June 25, 1859," AHR 35 (1929), 79-84.

-----, "China, England, and Russia in 1860," Cambridge Historical Journal 3 (1929),
115-121.

-----, "Origins of the Tsungli-Yamen," CSPSR 15 (1931), 92-97.

-----, "The Extension of Equal Commercial Privileges to Other Nations than the
British after the Treaty of Nanking," CSPSR 15 (1931), 422-444.

-----, "The Secret Plan of 1858," CSPSR 15 (1931), 92-97.

-----, "New Light on Chinese Diplomacy, 1836-49," JMH 3 (1931), 578-591.

-----, "Difficulties of Reconstruction After the Treaty of Nanking," CSPSR 16
(1932), 317-327.

-----, "The Government and the Co-Hong of Canton, 1839," CSPSR 15 (1932), 602-607.

Vattel, E. de, The Law of Nations, or the Principles of Natural Law, Applied to the
Conduct and to the Affairs of Nations and Sovereigns, 1758, tr. by Joseph Chitty,
Philadelphia, 1865; tr. by Charles G. Fenwick, Washington, 1916.
Early classic, parts of which were translated into Chinese by Peter Parker for Lin Tse-hsü.

Vinacke, Harold Monk, Modern Constitutional Development in China, Princeton, 1920.

Wainhouse, David W., see Latané.

Wheaton, Henry, Elements of International Law, 1st ed. London, 1836; 3rd. Philadelphia, 1846; W. B. Lawrence ed. Boston, 1863.
Standard work of the period, parts of which were translated into Chinese by W.A.P. Martin.

Williams, S. Wells, The Middle Kingdom, A Survey of the Geography, Government,
Literature, Social Life, Arts and History of the Chinese Empire, 2 v., 1st ed.
London, 1848; rev. ed. London, 1883.

19th century classic which has never been entirely superseded; contains valuable contemporary material in the second volume.

Wilson, Andrew, England's Policy in China, Hong Kong, 1860.

One of the more philosophical and critical of the English commentators on the 19th century
scene; tries to appreciate the Chinese position.

Wu, Chih-fang, Chinese Government and Politics, Shanghai, 1935.

Primarily on the period since 1911, with an inaccurate and inadequate survey of Manchu
government; strong bias of the modern Chinese revolutionary student.

Wu Chün-ju 吳君如, *Chin Shih Chung Kuo Wai Chiao Shih* 近世中國外交史 (China's Foreign Relations in the Modern Period), Shanghai 1932.

Modern nationalistic treatment of unequal treaties and imperialism, based largely on Morse.

Wu Hung-chu, "China's Attitude Towards Foreign Nations Historically Considered," CSPSR 10 (1926), 13-45.

Yano Jinichi 矢野仁一, *Kindai Shina Ron* 近代支那論 (Essays on Contemporary China), Kyoto, 1923.

Japanese criticism of China for failure to develop a strong national state, with two chapters on the position of the United States *vis-à-vis* China and Japan.

-----, *Kindai Shina Shi* 近代支那史 (Recent Chinese History), Kyoto, 1926.

Deals with internal history of the Ch'ing dynasty, 1644-1912.

-----, *Kinsei Shina Gaikō Shi* 近世支那外交史 (History of Modern Chinese Foreign Relations), Kyoto, 1930.

Standard work by a man regarded in Japan as an authority on China.

IV. REFERENCE WORKS

Bemis, Samuel Flagg and Griffin, Grace Gardner, *Guide to the Diplomatic History of the United States, 1775-1921,* Washington, 1935.

Generally useful but naturally inadequate in this specialized field; chapter 17 is on the Far East to 1922.

Brunnert, H. S., and Hagelstrom, V. V., *Present Day Political Organization of China,* rev. by N. Th. Kolessoff; tr. by A. Beltchenko and E. E. Moran, Shanghai, 1912

Used together with Mayers for the translation of all Chinese official titles.

CFHCC, see *Ta Ch'ing Chi Fu Hsien Che Chuan.*

CHLC, see *Kuo Ch'ao Ch'i Hsien Lei Cheng.*

CSLC, see *Ch'ing Shih Lieh Chuan.*

Cheng Hao-sheng 鄭鶴聲, *Chin Tai Chung Hsi Shih Jih Tui Chao Piao* 近代中西史日對照表 (Day-by-day Concordance of Modern Chinese-Western Chronology), Shanghai, 1936.

Used for all transfers of Chinese lunar and cyclical dates into the Western calendar and chronology; an extremely useful and convenient handbook, entirely superseding Père Hoang's concordance for the modern period.

Ch'ing Shih Lieh Chuan 清史列傳 (Biographies of Ch'ing History), 80 v., Shanghai, 1928.

Closely, although not exactly, parallels the biographical section of *Ch'ing Shih Kao,* but is fuller in detail and more readable in style.

Chung Hsing Chiang Shuai Lieh Chuan 中興將帥列傳 (Biographies of Commanders of the Revival Period), ed. Chu K'ung-chang 朱孔彰, 30 chüan, 4 v., Shanghai.

Covers period around the middle of the nineteenth century.

Chung Kuo Jen Ming Ta Tz'u Tien 中國人名大辭典 (Cyclopaedia of Chinese Biographical Names), Shanghai, 7th ed., 1930.

Handy biographical dictionary for quick reference and identification; inadequate for anything else, although occasionally some official is listed here who is not found in the standard collections.

Chung Kuo Ku Chin Ti Ming Ta Tz'u Tien 中國古今地名大辭典 (Chinese Historical Dictionary of Geographical Names), Shanghai, 1931 ed.

Usually adequate, with the aid of a modern atlas, for the identification of place names used in the official documents.

Cordier, Henri, *Bibliotheca Sinica: Dictionaire bibliographique des ouvrages relatifs à l'Empire Chinois,* 5 v., 2nd ed., Paris, 1922.

Indispensable, standard reference work.

Fang, Chao-ying, see Tu Lien-che.

HCSL, see *Kuo Ch'ao Hsien Cheng Shih Lüeh.*

HPCC, see Hsü Pei Chuan Chi.

Hagelstrom, V. V., see Brunnert, H. S.

Hasse, Adelaide R., *Index to United States Documents Relating to Foreign Affairs, 1828-1861,* Washington, 1914-1921.

Indispensable guide to this period before the beginning of the annual volumes on foreign relations in 1861.

Hoang, P., *Concordance des chronologies néomeniques, chinoise et européene, in Varietés sinologiques* No. 29, Shanghai, 1910.

Standard concordance, now supplanted for the modern period by Cheng Hao-sheng's convenient tables, but still useful for pre-modern references.

Hsü Pei Chuan Chi 續碑傳集 (Continuation of Biographies from Stone Tablets), ed. Miao Ch'üan-sun 繆荃孫 , 86 *chüan,* 24 v.

Continuation of biographical notices from inscriptions through 1908.

Hummel, Arthur W., (ed.), *Eminent Chinese of the Ch'ing Period* Washington, 1943-1944, 2 v.

Standard and invaluable work on biographies of Chinese and Manchus of this period, 1644-1912, written by competent modern scholars; fully documented and indexed.

Kuo Ch'ao Ch'i Hsien Lei Cheng 國朝耆獻類徵 (Ch'ing Dynasty Biographies Systematically Arranged), 1st series, ed. Li Huan 李桓 , 732 *chüan,* 300 v., Hsiang-yin, Hunan, 1890.

Biographies of Manchu and Chinese officials and scholars compiled at imperial order.

Kuo Ch'ao Hsien Cheng Shih Lüeh 國朝先正事略 (Brief Accounts of Ch'ing Dynasty Worthies), ed. Li Yüan-tu 李元度 , 60 *chüan,* 32 v., Shanghai.

Mayers, William Frederick, *The Chinese Government: A Manual of Chinese Titles, Categorically Arranged and Explained, With an Appendix,* Shanghai, 1878; 2nd ed., Shanghai, 1897.

An old work, largely displaced by Brunnert and Hagelstrom, but still useful for the earlier part of the 19th century.

PCC, see *Pei Chuan Chi.*

Pei Chuan Chi 碑傳集 (Collected Biographies from Stone Tablets), ed. Ch'ien I-chi 錢儀吉, 160 *chüan,* 60 v., 1893.

Ch'ing biographies through the Chia-ch'ing era (1821); brief notices, but valuable for finding birth and death dates.

Pei Chuan Chi Pu 碑傳集補 (Supplement to Biographies from Stone Tablets), ed. Min Erh-ch'ang 閔爾昌, 61 *chüan,* Peiping, 1931.

Supplement to the two other collections of inscriptions, published by the Harvard-Yenching Institute.

Pfister, Louis, *Notices biographiques et bibliographiques sur les Jesuites de l'ancienne mission de Chine, 1552-1772,* in *Variétés sinologiques,* No. 59, Shanghai, 1932.

Valuable reference work, used for references to early Jesuit missionaries in China.

TCKFL, see *Ts'ung Cheng Kuan Fa Lu.*

Ta Ch'ing Chi Fu Hsien Che Chuan (Fu Lieh Nü Chuan) 大清畿輔先哲傳 (附烈女傳) (Ch'ing Dynasty Biographies of Palace Officials, with an Appendix of Women's Biographies), ed. Hsü Shih Ch'ang 徐世昌, 40 + 6 *chüan,* 22 v., Tientsin.

Ta Ch'ing Hui Tien 大清會典 (Collected Institutes of the Ch'ing), 1899 ed., 36 v.

Compendious encyclopaedia of Ch'ing dynasty government, summarized in Mayers and in Brunnert and Hagelstrom.

Ting Wen-chiang 丁文江, *Chung Kuo Fen Sheng Hsin T'u* 中國分省新圖 (New Chinese Atlas by Provinces), Shanghai, 1936.

Small, indexed atlas, usually adequate for ordinary place names with the use of an historical geographical dictionary (necessary because of the frequent changing of place names in China).

Ts'ung Cheng Kuan Fa Lu 從政觀法錄 (Record of Ministers and Administrators), ed. Chu Fang-tseng 朱方增, 30 *chüan,* 6 v., 1884.

Tu Lien-che 杜連喆 and Fang Chao-ying 房兆楹, *San Shih San Chung Ch'ing Tai Chuan Chi Tsung Ho Yin Te* 三十三種清代傳記綜合引得 (Index to Thirty-three Collections of Ch'ing Dynasty Biographies), *Harvard-Yenching Institute Sinological Index Series,* No. 9, Peiping, 1932.

Finger-tip guide to all the principal biographical collections of the Ch'ing dynasty.

INDEX

INDEX

3, 687-8, 698, 700.

Triad Rebels, 21-2.

tribute rice, transport of, 404,
406, 408, 448, 467, 496, 540,
609, 612, 625-6, 630, 685-7,
689, 691-3, 696.

Ts'ai Chen-wu, 34, 520.

Ts'ai Hsiang-ch'ing, 201-2.

Ts'ai Lien-ch'eng, 258.

Ts'ai Ying-tou, 377.

Ts'ai-yüan Prince I, 472, 490,
492-3, 559, 678.

Ts'ang-chou, 407, 433.

Ts'ao-shan, 606.

Ts'ao Ta-shou, 586, 592, 595,
598, 621.

Tseng Kuo-fan, 53-4, 512, 549,
686-7, 689, 692-8.

Tsiang, T. F., 102, 516, 594, 650.

tsou, see memorial.

Ts'un-hsing, 116.

tsung-tu, 3, 13.

Tsungli Yamen, 1, 12-3, 17, 23-
4, 27, 37, 41, 53, 649-650, 699.

Tu Han, 492-3.

T'u-liang, 439.

T'u-shih, 185-6, 234.

Tuan Ch'eng-shih, 515-7, 519-
520, 524, 526, 530-1, 539, 543,
545, 548, 553, 557, 565, 573.

Tuan-hua Prince Cheng, 490, 492-
3.

Tun, Prince, see I-tsung Prince
Tun.

Tung braves, 399.

Tung-chiao-ch'ang, 400.

Tung-chih-men, 566.

Tung-hsiao, 300.

Tung-kuan, 373, 376.

Tung Pu-yün, 665, 679.

Tung-shun, 645.

Tung-tien, 667.

Tung-ting fort, 327.

Tung-t'ing Lake, 700.

T'ung-chou, 235, 237, 239, 254,
478, 487, 491-3, 498-9, 501-3,

509, 559-560, 588, 594, 596,
598, 681.

T'ung-lin, 33, 155, 186, 189.

T'ung Pu-nien, 97.

T'ung-shun Hong, 21.

T'ung-wen Hong, 38.

T'ung-Yung circuit, 407, 582, 603.

Turban Bandits, see Nien-fei.

Turks, Ottoman, 598.

Two Brothers, whaler, 308.

Tyler, President, 17, 39, 173,
176.

Urga, 383, 683-4, 686.

Verbiest, Ferdinand, 98, 135, 457.

Vermilion endorsement, see chu-p'i.

viceroy, see tsung-tu.

Viceroy Yeh, see Yeh Ming-ch'en.

Wade, Thomas, 7, 10, 50, 207,
218-9, 220, 222, 242-3, 336, 344,
374, 489, 498, 502, 517, 577, 695.

Wan-li period, 182.

Wang Ch'eng-en, 370.

Wang Chia-chin, 202.

Wang-chia-chuang, 473.

Wang Chia-hsi, 407.

Wang Ch'ing-yün, 278.

Wang-hai-lou, 474, 501-2.

Wang Hiya, see Wang-hsia.

Wang-hsia, treaty of, 2, 4-5, 25,
48, 131, 159; analyses of, 160-4,
166-170; exchange of ratifications
of, 179, 184, 192; 197, 205, 216,
222, 241, 250-1, 270, 281, 311,
315-6, 318, 449, 451, 533, 641.

Wang Hsin, 511.

Wang I-te, 287, 296-7, 299, 311,
317-320, 324, 328, 366, 397.

Wang Lan-kuang, 419.

Wang Mao-yin, 37, 417, 428, 509.

Wang P'i-hsien, 112, 114.

Wang Tao-ch'ung, 375, 377.

Wang Ting, 25-7.

Wang Tseng-ch'ien, 361, 469.